Sardinian and Aegean Chronology
Towards the Resolution of Relative and Absolute
Dating in the Mediterranean

*Proceedings of the International Colloquium
'Sardinian Stratigraphy and Mediterranean Chronology',
Tufts University, Medford, Massachusetts, March 17–19, 1995*

Edited by

Miriam S. Balmuth and Robert H. Tykot

Studies in Sardinian Archaeology V

Oxbow Books

1998

Published by
Oxbow Books, ParkEnd Place, Oxford OX1 1HN

© Oxbow Books and the individual authors, 1998

ISBN 1 900188 82 1

This book is available direct from

Oxbow Books, Park End Place, Oxford OX1 1HN
(Phone: 01865–241249; Fax: 01865–794449)

and

The David Brown Book Company
PO Box 511, Oakville, CT 06779, USA
(Phone: 860–945–9329; Fax: 860–945–9468)

or from our website

www.oxbowbooks.com

Printed in Great Britain at
The Short Run Press
Exeter

Contents

1. Introduction, *Miriam S. Balmuth & Robert H. Tykot* 1

CHRONOLOGY & CHRONOMETRY
2. Radiocarbon Dating and Sardinian Archaeology: A View from an Editor's Desk, *Renee Kra* 5
3. Some Cautionary Points on the Use of Radiocarbon Dates, *David H. Trump* 11
4. Sardinia and Dendrochronology: Any Potential? *Peter I. Kuniholm* 13
5. Dating Sardinian Archaeological Obsidian, *Christopher Stevenson & J.Grace Ellis* 17
6. Unacceptable Anomalies or Incorrect Use of Radiocarbon Dating in Sardinia? *Santo Tinè* 25
7. Mediterranean Chronology in Crisis, *Peter James, Nikos Kokkinos & I.J. Thorpe* 29

PRE-NEOLITHIC
8. Paleolithic Sardinians: Paleontological Evidence and Methods, *Paul Y. Sondaar* 45
9. Premier Peuplement Holocène et Néolithique de l'Île de Corse, *François de Lanfranchi* 53
10. Preliminary Results on the Exploitation of Animal Resources
    in Corsica During the Preneolithic, *Jean-Denis Vigne* 57

NEOLITHIC
11. Stratigrafie ed altri elementi di cronologia della Sardegna preistorica e protostorica, *Ercole Contu* 63
12. Articolazione e cronologia del Neolitico Antico, *Giuseppa Tanda* 77
13. Obsidian Usage at the Filiestru Cave, Sardinia: Choices and Functions
    in the Early and Middle Neolithic Periods, *Linda Hurcombe & Patricia Phillips* 93
14. L'oléastre et le lentisque, plantes oléagineuses sauvages dans l'économie néolithique
    en Corse et en Sardaigne, *François de Lanfranchi & Bui Thi Mai* 103

CHRONOLOGICAL CONTRIBUTIONS FROM ARCHITECTURE & SCULPTURE
15. Le statuette di 'Dea Madre' nei contesti prenuragici: Alcune considerazioni, *Angela Antona* 111
16. Cronologia dell'arte delle *domus de janas*, *Giuseppa Tanda* 121
17. Aspetti del megalitismo nel territorio di M. Acuto (Sassari). Considerazioni preliminari, *Paola Basoli* 141
18. Nota geologica su Punta Isteddi (Buddusò – Sassari), *Carlo Alberto Artizzu* 159
19. Muraglie megalitiche e recinti nella Sardegna prenuragica, *Alberto Moravetti* 161
20. Nuovi elementi di datazione dell'Età del Bronzo Antico e Medio:
    Lo scavo del Nuraghe Talei di Sorgono e della tomba di giganti Sa Pattada di Macomer,
    Maria Ausilia Fadda 179
21. Cronologia relativa del paramento murario dei vani interni di alcuni complessi nuragici.
    Osservazioni preliminari, *Anna Grazia Russu* 195
22. Datazione e significato della scultura in pietra e dei bronzetti figurati
    della Sardegna nuragica, *Ercole Contu* 203

CHALCOLITHIC: DEVELOPMENTAL CHANGES AS CHRONOLOGICAL CRITERIA

23. Nuovi dati materiali per una definizione dell'Eneolitico Antico in Sardegna, *Luisanna Usai* 217

24. La tipologia come strumento per lo studio di alcuni problemi dell'Età del Rame in Sardegna, *Maria Grazia Melis* 235

25. Considerazioni sulle sequenze culturali e cronologiche tra l'Eneolitico e l'epoca Nuragica, *Giovanni Ugas* 251

26. Una fase Ozieri dell'Età del Rame nella Tomba I di Janna Ventosa (Nuoro), *Alba Foschi Nieddu* 273

AEGEAN CHRONOLOGY & SARDINIA

27. Introductory Remarks, *Lucia Vagnetti* 285

28. A Catalog of Aegean Finds in Sardinia, *Licia Re* 287

29. The Chronology of the Aegean Late Bronze Age: Unanswered Questions, *Philip Betancourt* 391

30. Aegean and Sardinian Chronology: Radiocarbon, Calibration, and Thera, *Sturt W. Manning* 297

31. The Absolute Chronology of Late Helladic IIIA2, *Malcolm H. Wiener* 309

32. The Late Cypriot White Slip I-Ware as an Obstacle of the High Aegean Chronology, *Manfred Bietak* 321

33. Aegean Late Bronze 1–2 Absolute Chronology: Some New Contributions, *Peter Warren* 323

SARDINIA IN THE MEDITERRANEAN

34. Introduction, *Fulvia Lo Schiavo* 333

35. Remarks on the Presence of Nuragic Pottery on Lipari, *Maria Luisa Ferrarese Ceruti* 335

36. The Sardinian Pottery from the Late Bronze Age Site of Kommos in Crete: Description, Chemical and Petrographic Analysis, and Historical Context, *L. Vance Watrous, Peter M. Day & Richard E. Jones* 337

37. Protocolonizzazione fenicia in Sardegna, *Piero Bartoloni* 341

38. Phoenicians in Sardinia: Tyrians or Sidonians? *Brian Peckham* 347

39. Sardinian Pottery from Carthage, *Magna Køllund* 355

40. The Nuraghe and Village of Sant'Imbenia, Alghero (Sassari), *Susanna Bafico* 359

41. Bearing Greek Gifts: Euboean Pottery on Sardinia, *Sarah P. Morris* 361

42. From Macedonia to Sardinia: Problems of Iron Age Aegean Chronology and Assumptions of Greek Maritime Primacy, *John K. Papadopoulos* 363

ROMAN AND AFTER

43. Problemi di cronologia ceramica nella Sardegna romana, *Carlo Tronchetti* 371

44. The Chronological and Cultural Definition of Nuragic VII, AD 456–1015, *Gary Webster & Maud Webster* 383

CONCLUDING REMARKS

45. Sardinia and the Mediterranean: Remarks on Data and Interpretation, *Patricia Phillips* 397

IN MEMORIAM

46. On Behalf of the Archaeology of Sardinia. Maria Luisa Ferrarese Ceruti, 1928–1993, *Fulvia Lo Schiavo* 399

1. Introduction

Miriam S. Balmuth and Robert H. Tykot

An international colloquium devoted to the chronology of the ancient Mediterranean was convened at Tufts University, in Medford, Massachusetts on March 17, 1995 with the stated purpose of demonstrating the current status of laboratory dating techniques; observing the stratigraphic record at excavated sites in Sardinia; finding typological correlations with extra-insular sites in the Mediterranean; and creating an interplay among the three. The ultimate goal was to discuss and define, and to move toward the resolution of the chronological problems of Sardinian archaeology. With the increasing number of excavations on the island, and the growth of the ability to date contexts, the time had come to begin establishing a precise and absolute chronology. A first step in this direction was the compilation, calibration and preliminary interpretation of radiocarbon dates from Sardinia and Corsica (Tykot 1994), which was reprised as a poster at the colloquium.

The proceedings of this book are the product of the 17th colloquium held at Tufts University since 1979 on the subject of Sardinian archaeology. We have designated this volume *Studies in Sardinian Archaeology V* after its four antecedents: *Studies in Sardinian Archaeology* (Balmuth & Rowland eds., University of Michigan Press, 1984); *Studies in Sardinian Archaeology, Vol. II: Sardinia in the Mediterranean* (Balmuth ed., University of Michigan Press, 1986); *Studies in Sardinian Archaeology III: Nuragic Sardinia and the Mycenaean World* (Balmuth ed., British Archaeological Reports, 1987); and *Sardinia in the Mediterranean: A Footprint in the Sea. Studies in Sardinian Archaeology Presented to Miriam S. Balmuth* (Tykot & Andrews eds., Sheffield Academic Press, 1992).

For this colloquium, each session was designed, and speakers chosen, to provide chapters for a coherent publication. The subject matter is so dynamic, however, that publication was delayed by the need to change or add to some of the papers after they had been submitted. Some relevant communications that were not given at the colloquium were volunteered and accepted, among them the most recent catalogue of Aegean finds in Sardinia. A few presentations from the colloquium were not submitted for publication, but were significant enough to be cited in some of the individual papers and comments in this volume.

Like the ancient Mediterranean itself, the list of contributors is multicultural, and their contributions multidisciplinary. That all were not in total agreement was shown by the spectrum of opinions expressed. Variations in the orthography reflect the same individuality in the Sardinian language as in the participants: Maiore and Majore refer to the same site, and so do Cuccuru s'Arriu, Cuccuru Is Arrius, and Cuccuru Arrius; beyond Sardinia, Cypriot=Cypriote, and C14 and ^{14}C are used by different authors to mean the same thing. With such an extensive list of chapters, homogenization is justified only in cases of potential misunderstanding.

Chronology & Chronometry

The method most widely used for dating is radiocarbon analysis. Its applications, and their results, however, have provoked some expressions of dissatisfaction. In assessing its proper use, Kra emphasizes that the correctness of a particular radiocarbon age must be discussed between the dating laboratory and the excavator, using supporting evidence. A major conclusion is that many more new samples must be dated. "We must harvest dates if we expect to obtain a good crop yield." And these must focus not only on ceramic associations of cultural levels, but also on environments, paleoclimates and their roles in cultural change. Not only must charcoal be dated, but, when available, a whole range of plant, bone, food remains and marine-related samples must also be dated. Now that

---

Miriam S. Balmuth, Department of Classics & Archaeology, Tufts University, Medford, Massachusetts 02155, USA; Robert H. Tykot, Department of Anthropology, University of South Florida, Tampa, Florida 33620, USA

^{14}C dating technology approaches the 21st century, so too must the tools of the field archaeologist.

James, Kokkinos & Thorpe document misuses of the technique which result in false dates. Trump and Tinè illustrate some archaeological and chronological dilemmas from their own work. Ugas finds uncalibrated dates more accurate than those that have been calibrated. According to Phillips, calibrated radiocarbon dates may not be sufficiently precise for short periods like the Chalcolithic, maintaining that the variation in chronological schemes for Chalcolithic pottery styles and associated structures (villages, tombs, the Monte d'Accoddi temple) is partly due to the broad spread of calibrated dates.

New possibilities raised by dendrochronology within the Mediterranean (Kuniholm) offer a chance to establish an independent time-scale and see whether apparent environmental and social change in Sardinia is coeval with the Thera eruption. A wistful hope kept being expressed that the use of dendrochronology to compute dating would clarify situations of doubt. Obsidian hydration dating techniques also continue to be refined (Stevenson & Ellis), and in the case of Sardinia where obsidian is present at most archaeological sites, can be used not only as a complement to radiocarbon dating, but also as a means to date sites where bone and charcoal are absent.

Pre-nuragic Sardinia

Attempts to determine the earliest human presence on the island have concentrated on the excavation at the Corbeddu cave in Oliena. The excavator (Sondaar) has concluded that his finds there include the oldest human fossil so far on Sardinia (or any Mediterranean island), and that it demonstrates the presence of humans in the Paleolithic of the island. Settlement in the Mesolithic was not as uncommon on Corsica, where six sites are now known (de Lanfranchi). Archaeozoological analysis indicates that these early settlers subsisted on small mammals and birds, coastal fishing, and to a lesser extent by gathering shellfish (Vigne).

Contu provides a master synthesis of Sardinian stratigraphic sequences and the bases of Sardinian chronology, while Tanda provides some justification for three phases of the Early Neolithic. Obvious changes in ceramic styles define the various Neolithic periods, but chronological changes in lithic exploitation, technology and use are also becoming apparent (Hurcombe & Phillips). In addition to the domesticated animals and plants introduced to Sardinia and Corsica in the Neolithic, wild plants were also exploited in an organized manner, judging from the oil or resin extracting installation identified at Scaffa Piana in Corsica (Lanfranchi & Mai).

'Beyond the Laboratory' was the name of the session at the colloquium in which relative chronologies were shown and discussed, for the most part by local Sardinian archaeologists. Definitions of sequence are the building blocks of chronology, providing relative dates, and are essential even where ^{14}C ages are available (Phillips). They concentrate for the most part on changing styles in the Chalcolithic period, such as of ceramics and other artifacts (Usai) and their architectural contexts (Ugas; Foschi Nieddu); engraved superimposed bull protomes in hypogea (Tanda); building styles (Fadda; Moravetti); masonry (Russu); and the effect of megaliths on hypogeum design (Basoli). The evidence from figurines is discussed by Antona for the Neolithic ('*Dea Madre*') and by Contu for the Nuragic period (*bronzetti*). Typology as a chronological tool is discussed in an extracolloquial contribution (Melis).

Aegean Chronology & Sardinia

The most recent map and catalogue of sites in which Aegean material was found on Sardinia has been included to allow the growing number of sites and their positions on the island to be shown graphically (Re). A chronology of the Aegean Bronze Age was sought to aid in dating the contexts of the Aegean material found on the island. In turn, the speakers approached Aegean chronology by seeking its own extra-insular synchronisms: the eruption of Thera, and the Aegean-style wall painting in Egypt at Tel el-Dab^{c}a. After the colloquium, the excavator of Tel el-Dab^{c}a requested and received agreement to submit a communication for purposes of clarification, describing his own current work and dates (Bietak). Betancourt's statement that disagreement between specialists is caused by the ambiguous nature of the correlations that survive, anticipates the conflicting dates for the eruption: 17th century (Betancourt; Manning) or 16th century (Warren; Bietak). Betancourt continues that most of the correlations are so imprecise that they could accommodate either an early or a late chronology. What began as an informal conversation among participants during meals at the colloquium ended as a note in *Nature* (vol. 381, 27 June 1996, 780–783). The finds of Sardinian pottery at Kommos in Crete (Watrous) are presently recognized as the earliest Sardinian ceramics found outside the island, and the first from the Bronze Age in the Aegean.

Sardinia in the Mediterranean

Appropriately, Fulvia Lo Schiavo presided at a Round Table at which aspects of her specialty, Sardinia's place in the Mediterranean, were discussed. The purpose of the Round Table was to try to establish synchronisms with datable contexts outside of the island. This attempt not only succeeded in enlarging the known presence of Sardinian material in the Mediterranean from Kommos in Crete to Carthage, but also in extending its temporal range. The areas treated included the islands of the Tyrrhenian Sea: Corsica (Lanfranchi) and Sicily (Tusa) with the Aeolian islands (Ferrarese Ceruti); the Iberian peninsula (Gilman); the Aegean Sea and the eastern Aegean: Cyprus (Karageorghis) and Crete (Watrous); and North Africa: Carthage (Køllund). Two previously published extracolloquial contributions were added to this session: Ferrarese Ceruti on Sardinian finds on Lipari, and Bafico on finds from Sant'Imbenia, the nuraghe at which Phoenician, Greek, and Nuragic material were found in a context interpreted as a Phoenician emporium dating at least to the early eighth century.

Documentation of the mix of Euboean and Phoenician pottery with Nuragic at a Nuragic site sets the stage for the spectrum of interpretations on the interrelationship between Greek and Phoenician, both in the Bronze Age, when they are referred to as Mycenaean and Levantine, and in the Iron Age. Divergent opinions ranging from doubt of Greek maritime primacy, forcefully stated (Morris; Papadopoulos), to an evenly handled discussion of a more complex relationship (Peckham), to firm assertion of symbiosis between Phoenicians and Greeks from the Bronze Age onward (Bartoloni) represent another example of a controversy for which Sardinia is in a position eventually to point to a solution. At the same time, it illustrates how the same incomplete data are interpreted in different ways. The identification of sites with Mycenaean material as subsequent major Phoenician cities (Bartoloni; Vagnetti) reinforces the island's ability to reflect precolonization activity in the West Mediterranean, with evolving reconsiderations based on changing information.

Certain archaeological sites in the Mediterranean have acted as catalysts for interpretation of Greek/Phoenician involvement by virtue of the mix of material found: Al Mina and Ialysos, for example. Now such sites in Sardinia as Sant'Imbenia (see Bafico) and Tharros (see Re; Vagnetti) have become catalysts, not only because of the material found there, but because the whole package that includes material, site, and subsequent developments, offers insights into the evolution of new interpretations. Both Morris and Papadopoulos see the Phoenician material at Sant'Imbenia and actual Phoenician settlement at Sulcis as compelling evidence rather than as ceramic hints of Phoenician involvement. Phoenician carriers would also account for the growing quantities of Greek pottery at Carthage as well as the Sardinian pottery now found both in Carthage and in Crete.

Denying Phoenicians one single ethnicity, Peckham illuminates the separate identities among Tyrians and Sidonians in western Mediterranean settlements. He further defines the mix of nationalities in the description of the tomb in which Nuragic pottery was found buried on Crete at Khaniale Tekke: in what has been understood as the family tomb of a resident alien, whose work resembles North Syrian products and is especially like that found at Tell Halaf. He and his family were probably the offspring of Sidonians who had moved at some earlier time into North Syria. It was characteristic of the Sidonians to settle and assimilate: the oriental traditions of this goldsmith,

who had married into a Cretan family, were maintained for some time by his children, but gradually were adapted to local styles and taste. It was in this same tomb, but with a later burial, that a Sardinian *askos*, impressed with concentric circles of the kind found on the sherds in Carthage, was buried with its Sardinian owner or with a Sidonian traveller from Crete, one of the itinerant craftsmen who frequented the western island.

Some possibilities of the identification of Sardinia with *šrdn* as related to a tribe of "Sea Peoples" were briefly discussed (Cross; Mazar; James). Like oxhide ingots, this is another subject that involves Sardinia on which entire colloquia can be and are held. This is not to trivialize the profound importance of the metal trade to Sardinian archaeology of which new information was added by Ceruti and Watrous, but to concede the limits imposed by time and space.

Roman and After

Tronchetti points out regional diversity in Roman pottery in Sardinia; the problem of production; local imitation of imported styles; and the dates of arrival and period of use of imported pottery. The Websters propose Nuragic VII as an Early Medieval phase of Nuragic chronology beyond Punic and Roman, lasting until the Arab invasion and the end of Byzantine rule in 1015 AD.

Ceramic Fossils

While radiocarbon and other dating techniques are being perfected to increase their accuracy in dating, pottery, likened to fossils by Fadda and Tronchetti, still remains the universal medium for interpetation of place as well as time in all phases after the Paleolithic; yet the weaknesses of this practice are constantly pointed out. The problems are especially expressed by Phillips, Wiener, Papadopoulos, Tronchetti and the Websters.

Pottery is not the ideal cross-dating medium in the Chalcolithic because ceramic shapes and decoration may vary according to raw material or skill of the potter, or more importantly the affiliations of each local group, trade requirements, ritual requirements and so on (Phillips).

Wiener's enumeration of factors that affect the absolute dates assignable to imported Aegean pottery of a particular ceramic phase can be applied to other times and places as well: the length of time between creation and deposition in the archaeological record; the extent of time over which the pottery type(s) in question were produced, and the links between the ceramic phase and absolute dates derived from a historical chronology or by scientific means. Padopoulos and the Websters both point to the vulnerability of the notion of a rigidly linear development of style. The claim that "Euboean pottery does not necessarily equal Euboean presence, nor does that pottery have to be carried by a Euboean" (Papadopoulos) further emphasizes the fragility of the use of pottery as a material witness. Tronchetti deals with more datable material in Roman pottery in Sardinia, long overlooked, that still presents problems of regional diversity; local imitation of imported styles; and the dates of arrival and period of use of imported pottery. Local imitations of pottery styles, especially frequent in Sardinia, confound even more; do they imply presence of the originals or makers of the originals or memory of the originals?

Conclusions?

The colloquium with the ambitious title, Sardinian Stratigraphy and Mediterranean Chronology, was planned to begin seeking results by combining stratified contexts and extrainsular synchronisms with the newest scientific testing techniques. The wealth of information, insights, and hypotheses that emerged, however, have prompted continuing research and writing. Conclusions are not yet appropriate for such a vital, dynamic subject. Rather than conclusions, we list new developments as they have emerged from this colloquium: the appearance of the oldest human fossil so far on Sardinia; a responsible way to date by radiocarbon on Sardinia; the fact that radiocarbon and other dating methods are always being improved; a confirmation once more of Sardinia's place in Bronze Age Mediterranean long distance trade; the earliest find off the island of Sardinian ceramic material (Kommos); the extension of area in which Sardinian material is found (Carthage); the extension of time for the duration of Nuragic cultures; Sardinia as a catalyst in the interpretation of Mediterranean uncertainties; Sardinia as a reflection of activity elsewhere in the Mediterranan (the Ialysos effect); the narrowing of the knowledge gap for the crucial transition from Late Bronze Age long-distance trade to Iron Age colonial activity; the recognition of changes in interpretation prompted by changes in material or ideas; and the hazards of overdependence on ceramics for chronological determinations.

Acknowledgments

The international colloquium on which this volume is based would not have been possible without the generous support of the Samuel H. Kress Foundation, the Wenner-Gren Foundation, the Institute for Aegean Prehistory, Tufts University, and a number of private donors. The publication of this volume was supported by an additional grant from the Institute for Aegean Prehistory.

In Memoriam

In a touching tribute to Maria Luisa Ferrarese Ceruti, whose presence at this colloquium would have added lively discussions, Fulvia Lo Schiavo points out the range in the work of this scholar, whose professional career in a sense paralleled the development of archaeology in Sardinia; her death is a loss to the profession. The statement that archaeological work should not be measured by its timelessness but rather by its ability to stimulate more research and to accomodate changes that time may bring, once more emphasizes the dynamic, fast-moving quality of archaeology, especially in Sardinia.

2. Radiocarbon Dating and Sardinian Archaeology: A View from an Editor's Desk

Renee S. Kra

Introduction

Over the years, I have proofread thousands of papers and date lists for the journal *Radiocarbon*. Had I been blessed with a photographic memory, I would probably now be a "guru" of ^{14}C dating, and people would come from around the world to ask me, "Do you remember when...?" But I have no such extraterrestrial powers. However, what I bring you, as a non-expert in Sardinian archaeology and as a non-scientist working in the field, are a few observations that I have made over the years on the development and advancement of the technique of ^{14}C dating, especially as it relates to Sardinian archaeology.

With little over 100 radiocarbon dates generated as a result of archaeological excavations in Sardinia, one may consider ^{14}C dating in Sardinia at the threshold of its potential contribution. Investigations in Sardinian prehistory and history have revealed a long and complex record of human settlement and interaction, from the Paleolithic to the present (Balmuth 1992; Balmuth and Rowland 1984). Tracking this record has led to unique and remarkable findings. It has also led to problems in establishing a firm chronology and understanding of the processes of human development and change in this island environment, where resources must have always been limited and competition for these resources fierce.

Sardinia presents an excellent opportunity for intensive ^{14}C investigations because of its rich archaeological treasures most of which fit well within limits of ^{14}C dating as well as within the boundaries of the dendrochronologically based calibration curves. ^{14}C dating can help solve some of the open questions of Sardinian archaeology, but only when applied with caution and interpreted with supporting evidence from other, interdisciplinary studies.

Corbeddu Cave

For over a decade, an international and interdisciplinary team have been investigating Corbeddu Cave (Klein Hofmeijer *et al.* 1987; 1989). Their findings and ^{14}C results of >30 samples address a combination of issues unique to Sardinian archaeology. Not only are answers beginning to emerge, but the investigations are also illustrating the multiple possibilities of interdisciplinary research.

Corbeddu Cave is one of the best ^{14}C-dated sequences in Sardinia. More samples were dated from these excavations than any other on the island. More than 30 samples were dated using accelerator mass spectrometry (AMS), the most technologically advanced ^{14}C dating method, which enables the dating of milligram-sized samples, and at a greater speed than conventionally dated samples. We have both facilities at The University of Arizona. AMS dating is truly revolutionary for many fields, as it allows the researcher to date samples that could not be dated previously. For the science-based archaeologist, such samples might include, among many other materials, grains, seeds and organic residues, such as bone fragments and food remains, for example from ceramic vessels.

At Corbeddu Cave, a benchmark date, UtC-300: 8750 ± 140 (*ca.* 8000–7500 cal BC) (Klein Hofmeijer *et al.* 1987) was generated from human bone and at the time documented the earliest evidence for human occupation on Sardinia. Also found in Corbeddu Cave was a sparse lithic assemblage and a rich bone tool industry consisting of the island species *Prolagus sardus*, *Megaloceros cazioti* and *Cynotherium sardous* (Klein Hofmeijer *et al.* 1989). The implications are that the human residents of the cave not only hunted the three endemic mammals for food, but also used the leftovers. Further, it seems most of the stone tools were fashioned from limestone, the

---

Renee S. Kra, Department of Geosciences, The University of Arizona, Tucson, Arizona 85721 USA

structural material of the cave. This would seem to be a highly efficient subsistence strategy. However, both these assemblages (the oldest lithic date at *ca.* 14,600 BP and the worked bone dates as old as 25,000 BP) predate the human bone date (to *ca.* 25,000 BP). The question then was, "Was *Homo sapiens* on Sardinia during the Paleolithic?" Some strong new evidence seems to confirm this (Sondaar *et al.* 1995; this volume), but I believe that we need to date bone samples directly, and then we need to find and date more samples, especially of human fossil bone.

Excavations at Corbeddu Cave reveal two major issues in Sardinian archaeology: 1) the arrival of the first humans; and 2) shifting endemic faunal populations and faunal extinctions. To trace the arrival of the first humans on Sardinia, one must first look at the sea-level history of the Mediterranean (Cherry 1992). By studying oxygen isotope ratios in pelagic fossils, van Andel and Shackleton (1982) and Shackleton, van Andel and Runnels (1984) report that the western Mediterranean was at its lowest level at *ca.* 18,000 years ago, at the last glacial maximum. This would have been an optimal time for humans (and animals) to cross the sea at its shortest distance between the mainland and the island (Corsica and Sardinia were attached at this time). In a recent study (Edwards *et al.* 1993), paired ^{14}C and ^{230}Th ages were determined on fossil corals to estimate rates of sea-level rise. These authors found a great reduction of melting because of cooler conditions during the Younger Dryas (*ca.* 13,000 to 11,000 BP). It was not until *ca.* 6000 BP that sea level rose again to its approximately present level, leaving a possibly longer migration period than originally estimated.

Besides the obvious loss of coastal sites and archaeological evidence of human fossil remains, rising sea levels and changing climate could also have critically limited the resource base of endemic faunal species (Kirch 1986). Such paleogeographic speculations have been made for Greece in the area of Franchthi Cave (van Andel & Shackleton 1982). Klein Hofmeijer and Sondaar (1992) presented corroborating evidence for Sardinia in noting that the Early Pleistocene fauna was typically endemic, with small and short-legged species of elephant, hippopotami and deer. No human fossil remains were associated. By the Middle Pleistocene, this fauna shifted drastically to the normal-sized deer, canid and pika, which seemingly attributes sudden extinction of the original population to environmental factors, and which contrasts markedly to the animal population of Crete, where Simmons and Wigand (1994) found Early Holocene evidence for human-related extinction.

Data gathered from ^{14}C dating deep-sea sediments in the Eastern Mediterranean (Fontugne *et al.* 1994), as well as stratigraphic and geomorphologic sequences (Goldberg 1994), palynologic data (Baruch 1994) and faunal analyses of the Near East (Tchernov 1994) combine to draw a paleoenvironmental picture much needed in comprehensive archaeological investigations everywhere.

The findings at Corbeddu Cave represent several recurring themes in ^{14}C dating, the first of which is bone dating. Bone is a very complex material whose composition changes drastically when the living organism dies, interacting with the elements of its burial environment. Three processes greatly affect bone composition after death: 1) degradation of its protein content; 2) length of burial time; and 3) contamination from its environment. The amount of collagen (the best material to date because it does not exchange carbon during diagenesis) remaining in the fossil bone is also critical for dating. Many sophisticated pretreatment strategies exist by which the dater can purify and extract the essential material to produce a reliable date, but ^{14}C dating of bone is a delicate balance requiring much experience, good science, costly and elaborate chemical treatment and well-preserved samples (Hedges 1992; Taylor 1987). From *Aetokremnos*, Cyprus, with an extinct endemic population of pygmy hippopotami, Simmons and Wigand (1994) analyzed 31 ^{14}C determinations on bone, shell and charcoal, using weighted averages, paired dates and ^{13}C corrections, to date this Eastern Mediterranean site to the Early Holocene and to help corroborate a 400-year marine reservoir effect for the area. To allow for the fact that ocean water is 400 years older than land in most places, one must factor in the marine reservoir effect in dating shell, aquatic plants or bone from an animal whose diet had been marine-based (aquatic plants, fish, shellfish) (A.J.T. Jull, personal communication).

Important to the interpretation of any ^{14}C dates are the context of the sample, in this case a limestone or karstic system, its geomorphologic and sedimentary processes and its climate history. One of the dangers involved in dating sediment samples is that their humic fraction can easily migrate up or down in the sediment with groundwater, reflecting the age of other organic matter in the profile (Simmons & Wigand 1994). In preparing the sample for dating, the humic fraction must be removed. Bioturbation is another factor that must be considered in interpreting ^{14}C dates of stratigraphic samples. Corbeddu Cave offers an example: UtC-22: 8040 ± 180 BP was later rejected when another charcoal sample from the same level dated to 6690 ± 80 (UtC-1251), and researchers realized that the charcoal must have been moved up to a younger level by worms (Klein Hofmeijer & Sondaar 1992).

Grotta del Guano

Grotta del Guano, also a karst limestone cave, yielded three ^{14}C dates, one of which (a duplicate charcoal sample) was reported in *Radiocarbon* (Alessio *et al.* 1971: R-609: 4830 ± 50 and R-609*a* : 4900 ± 50): because caution should still be used in accepting these at face value. Another factor to be considered here is the length of time between the sampling and the dating. This sample was collected in 1961, submitted in 1968 and dated somewhere between 1968 and 1971, when it was published. Under the best circumstances, storage of a sample for *ca.* 10 years is not an optimal condition for reliable dating.

Grotta Filiestru

The Bonu Ighinu Valley holds a cluster of well-dated sites: Grotta Filiestru, Su Tintirriolu and Nuraghe Noeddos. One date, BM-2139: 7530 ± 80 (Burleigh, Ambers and Matthews 1984), was determined on bone collagen of *P. sardus* from Grotta Filiestru. The discovery of the oldest human fossil remains, dating to 8750 ± 140 BP (Klein Hofmeier *et al.* 1987), and the survival of *P. sardus* until the 18th century (Clutton-Brock 1981) point to the unlikely association of pika extinction and the arrival of humans on the island.

Second, in 1990, Bowman, Ambers and Leese discovered that the British Museum had made a laboratory error in all samples dated between 1980 and 1984, which led to a revision of the date (BM-2139R) to 7760 ± 130, and a *ca.* 200-year difference. The consistent laboratory error was revealed after the results of an intercomparison of radiocarbon measurements (ISG 1982) were published. The British Museum's dates were, on average, 200 years younger than all the other laboratories. The error lay in the fact that modern reference samples were kept in the counter for long periods without reweighing to account for evaporation losses. In revising the results of 470 samples, the laboratory added ± 60 years to the uncertainty figures of the measurements.

This incident caused quite a stir among the radiocarbon community. Interestingly enough, the time was ripe for soul-searching; the Glasgow group (two ^{14}C laboratories and a statistician) had already initiated their intercomparison program, an internal and external quality control/ assurance study that is still ongoing as the Third International Radiocarbon Intercomparison (TIRI), in conjunction with the International Atomic Energy Agency (IAEA) (Scott, Long & Kra 1990; Scott *et al.* 1992). Thus, for the archaeologist in search of a high-precision laboratory, one would do well to investigate its quality before committing one's precious samples.

An active contributor to this quality assurance exercise, Roy Switsur (1990a) of Cambridge measured a reliable suite of dates on charcoal samples submitted by David Trump from Grotta Filiestru (Switsur 1990b). Sample selection avoided the danger of mixing of samples between layers and sufficient pretreatment destroyed limestone and humic substances. Table 2.1 presents the ^{14}C dates in descending chronological order with the 1986 (Stuiver & Kra) and 1993 (Stuiver, Long & Kra) dendrochronologically based calibration curves. Note that the first four dates were calibrated before the 1986 calibration curves were made available, when 1950 (before present) was simply subtracted from the raw date. This did not take into account atmospheric variations of ^{14}C concentration. The calibration curves allow the user to measure ^{14}C dates against "known-age" tree rings. From sample Q-3024 on, Trump (1990) used the 1986 curves and Tykot (1994) used the 1993 curves. A *ca.* 1000-yr difference between calibrated and uncalibrated dates can be noted for Q-3020 to -3023, which demonstrates the importance of using the calibration curves. The rest of the calibrations compare very well. Note that the highest probabilities are within parentheses.

Seeds of *Triticum monococcum, T. diococcum* and *Pisum* spp. were also identified at Grotta Filiestru (Switsur and Trump 1983). Had these been AMS-dated, information may have been gained on the food procurement activities and dietary habits of the cave inhabitants.

Grotta di Sa 'Ucca de Su Tintirriolu

A ritual cave site in the Bonu Ighinu region, Su Tintirriolu yielded charcoal samples, submitted by Trump in 1971

Sample no. (Q-)	^{14}C age (yr BP)	Switsur & Trump (1983); Trump (1990) cal BC	Tykot (1994) cal BC
3020	6710 ± 75	4760 ± 75*	5693 (5587) 5444
3021	6615 ± 75	4665 ± 75	5607 (5561, 5557, 5522) 5350
3022	6515 ± 65	4565 ± 65	5570 (5437) 5290
3023	6470 ± 65	4520 ± 65	5521 (5430, 5394, 5386) 5269
3024	6120 ± 55	5095–4855†	5218 (5051) 4870
3025	5900 ± 50	4895–4730	4906 (4783) 4629
3026	5625 ± 65	4570–4360	4592 (4461) 4343
3027	5250 ± 60	4220–4000	4233 (4038, 4015, 4006) 3957
3028	4950 ± 50	3900–3695	3907 (3709) 3643
3029	4430 ± 50	3300–2930	3333 (3075, 3067, 3040) 2915
3030	3805 ± 40	2335–2145	2396 (2270, 2268, 2202) 2049
3031	3440 ± 40	1875–1695	1876 (1740) 1630

* In the next four dates, the year 1950 was subtracted from the raw dates (Switsur and Trump 1983).
† The remaining eight dates were calibrated using Stuiver and Kra (1986).

Table 2.1. ^{14}C Dates and Calibrated Ages for Grotta Filiestru

and reported by the Rome laboratory in 1978 (Alessio et al. 1978). The results indicated a long occupational sequence from the Late Neolithic to Roman times. Present at the site were also human skeletons, animal bone remains, freshwater and marine mollusk shells, and food refuse, which all would make excellent ^{14}C samples. Again, future research should include analyses of other suitable organic materials, if only to act as paired samples to support the dates on charcoal.

Monte d'Accoddi

The six AMS ^{14}C dates from the Monte d'Accoddi sanctuary site span the middle 4th millennium to the late 3rd millennium BC. The first result, UZ-2475 (Tykot 1994), was dated by the Zürich laboratory, whose lab code designation is really ETH. Confusion could be avoided if official laboratory acronyms, published each year by *Radiocarbon*, were used. Although associated with sub-Ozieri ceramics, samples UtC-1465 through -1468 seem too old and may represent the "old wood" factor (Kuijt & Bar-Yosef 1994), whereby wood from a previous occupation is used for new construction.

Su Foxi 'e S'Abba

Three samples from Su Foxi 'e S'Abba hypogean nuragic temple/cave dated by the Rome laboratory (Alessio et al. 1978) were internally consistent. The oldest of the three by *ca.* 250 years, R-1074, a well-preserved fragment of a wooden vessel, seems entirely justified, because either it had been in use for *ca.* 250 years, or it was made out of 250-year-old wood.

Nuraghi

One of the cluster of sites from the Bonu Ighinu valley (Trump 1990), Nuraghe Noeddos has yielded seven ^{14}C dates (Switsur 1990a), with ages ranging from *ca.* 2500 to 1400 cal BC (Tykot 1994). Built of crude volcanic ash masonry, Noeddos is probably an early example of simple single-tower construction, whose dates reveal an earlier-than-estimated development of the nuraghe (*ca.* 1500 ± 500 BC; Trump 1990).

Wood from a beam in the wall of Nuraghe Barumini (K-151: 3420 ± 200) (Tauber 1960) represents an interesting problem occurring in the early years of ^{14}C dating. This sample had been dated previously with the solid carbon technique in which the contemporary standard used was wood growing near Copenhagen from 1951–1953. This was before the ^{14}C community became aware of depletion of ^{14}C levels in the atmosphere due to fossil-fuel combustion since the Industrial Revolution. This is called the Suess Effect (Suess 1955). Further, it was also found that atmospheric concentrations of ^{14}C varied geographically. Thus, 200 years was added to the original result to correct for the discrepancy; the 200-year uncertainty figure makes this result unreliable, however.

Sporadic single dates have been published (in English), for example, for Nuraghe Albucciu (Gif-242), Nuraghe Brunku Madugui (Gif-243) (Delibrias, Guillier & Labeyrie 1966) and Grotta ASI (R-492) (Alessio et al. 1970: 607). Speleologists carried out this excavation; the description is exceedingly dramatic: "… a votive place, probably an hypogean nuragic temple for magic religious rites; sole discovery of this kind made intact in Sardinia." The artifactual assemblage here was indeed interesting: "More than 1800 small pottery vases destined as votive offerings were arranged in 3 heaps near an imposing stalagmite used as an altar on ledge of which were laid a variety of used metal Nuragic objects, largely of copper, also destined as votive offerings."

Less spectacular, but important and interesting, nonetheless, are a series of dates from Ortu Comidu (P-2788, P-2399 to -2402) (Meulengracht, McGovern & Lawn 1981; Fishman, Forbes & Lawn 1977) on charcoal samples from a nuragic complex in which both Nuragic and Punic materials were present, illustrating the increasing complexity of the social and economic structure of Sardinian society. The age of sample R-916: 790 ± 50 (Alessio et al. 1976) from Su Crucifissu Mannu, charcoal from a tomb in a domus de janas hypogean necropolis, does not agree with its provenience, and is thought to have been mixed with more recent charcoal from above when it was washed downhill with percolating water. This result is an example of sample mixing and misassociation discussed above.

At this writing, Robert Tykot sent me three new dates from Nuraghe Santa Barbara (Bauladu), apparently the first ^{14}C dates for this site. I hope that this is only the beginning of a large dating program, because the astounding number of domesticated animal remains would shed a great deal of light on the stock-raising practices of Iron Age Sardinia. Even with the faunal assemblage largely dominated by domesticated animals, it is reassuring to observe the presence of *Prolagus sardus*. In analyzing and dating bone samples from this site, it is important to treat with equal importance the remains of wild game, including birds and fish, that were also found here (Gallin & Fonzo 1992).

Concluding Remarks

In assessing the existing ^{14}C dates produced as part of archaeological investigations in Sardinia, I have centered my discussion on some problems and pitfalls of the procedure as well as the interpretions of its results. The determinations were discussed, for the most part, in chronological order, selected for their illustrative value. My examples were gathered from the pages of Sardinian archaeological literature, which, in itself, can be considered a case of sampling bias, as I have missed so much of the data because of my ignorance of the Italian language. In this vein, I apologize for misconceptions based on lack of understanding of the full data.

Many of the problems of Sardinian archaeology were not discussed here today, or touched on briefly, for example: the origins, development and functions of megalithic monuments and nuraghi; the development of metallurgy; the transition from hunting and foraging to pastoralism, agriculture and animal domestication; trade relations; and boundaries, durations and floruits of cultural periods and phases. Much of the fault lies in the fact that so few samples have been dated, especially for later periods of Sardinian prehistory. On the other hand, the interdisciplinary investigations at Corbeddu Cave are revealing exciting insights into the peopling of Sardinia and the evolution of its mammalian population.

A major conclusion is that many more new samples must be dated. We must harvest dates if we expect to obtain a good crop yield. And these must focus not only on ceramic associations of cultural levels, but also on environments, paleoclimates and their roles in cultural change. Not only must charcoal be dated, but, when available, a whole range of plant, bone, food remains and marine-related samples must also be dated. Now that ^{14}C-dating technology approaches the 21st century, so too must the tools of the field archaeologist.

I am sure all archaeologists would agree that their problems may have only begun when their ^{14}C results have been obtained. Interpreting ^{14}C results is just as crucial as dating the sample itself. Some of the considerations that must be addressed in interpreting a date are: 1) provenience; 2) stratigraphy; 3) geology or geomorphology of the site; 4) associated finds; 5) possible disturbances, such as reversed stratigraphy, bioturbation, percolation; 6) marine reservoir effect; 7) old wood effect; 8) calibration; and 9) paleoenvironmental, paleogeographic and paleoclimatic data.

I have also talked about some of the challenges facing producers of ^{14}C dates: 1) sampling bias; 2) sample contamination, especially for bone samples; 3) pretreatment methods; laboratory precision; 4) quality control/assurance; and 5) standardization of laboratory procedures. Recommendations for future research obviously include all of the above. Realistic objectives would have to comprise the keywords: interdisciplinarity; paleoenvironment; and more dates.

Acknowledgments

I greatly appreciate helpful discussions with Tim Jull as well as with Warren Beck and George Burr of the NSF-Arizona AMS Facility. Were it not for Miriam Balmuth's nurturing support and Robert Tykot's comprehensive work and continuing help with the ^{14}C dates of Sardinia, this presentation would not have been possible. I cannot thank Miriam enough for giving me this opportunity to explore a new world.

References

Alessio, M., Allegri, L., Bella, F., Improta, S., Belluomini, G., Calderoni, G., Cortesi, C., Manfra, L. & Turi, B. 1978. University of Rome carbon-14 dates XVI. *Radiocarbon* 20: 79–104.

Alessio, M., Bella, F., Improta, S., Belluomini, G., Calderoni, G., Cortesi, C. & Turi, B. 1976. University of Rome carbon-14 dates XIV. *Radiocarbon* 18: 321–349.

Alessio, M., Bella, F., Improta, S., Belluomini, G., Cortesi, C. & Turi, B. 1970. University of Rome carbon-14 dates VIII. *Radiocarbon* 12: 599–616.

Alessio, M., Bella, F., Improta, S., Belluomini, G., Cortesi, C. & Turi, B. 1971. University of Rome carbon-14 dates IX. *Radiocarbon* 13: 395–411.

Balmuth, M.S. 1992. Archaeology in Sardinia. *American Journal of Archaeology* 96: 663–697.

Balmuth, M.S. & Rowland, R.J., Jr. (eds.) 1984. *Studies in Sardinian Archaeology*. The University of Michigan Press, Ann Arbor.

Baruch, U. 1994. The Late Quaternary pollen record of the Near East. In Bar-Yosef, O. & Kra, R.S., (eds.), *Late Quaternary Chronology and Paleoclimates of the Eastern Mediterranean*, 103–119. Radiocarbon, Tucson, Arizona.

Bowman, S.G.E, Ambers, J.C. & Leese, M.N. 1990. Re-evaluation of British Museum radiocarbon dates issued between 1980 and 1984. *Radiocarbon* 32: 59–79.

Burleigh, R., Ambers, J. & Matthews, K. 1984. British Museum natural radiocarbon measurements XVII. *Radiocarbon* 26: 59–74.

Cherry, J. 1992. Palaeolithic Sardinians? Some questions of evidence and method. In Tykot, R.H. & Andrews, T.K. (eds.), *Sardinia in the Mediterranean: A Footprint in the Sea. Studies in Sardinian Archaeology Presented to Miriam S. Balmuth*. Monographs in Mediterranean Archaeology 3: 28–39. Sheffield Academic Press, Sheffield.

Clutton-Brock, J. 1981. *Domesticated Animals From Early Times*. University of Texas Press, Austin; British Museum (Natural History).

Delibrias, G., Guillier, M.T. & Labeyrie, J. 1966. GIF natural radiocarbon measurements II. *Radiocarbon* 8: 74–95.

Edwards, R.L., Beck, J.W., Burr, G.S., Donahue, D.J., Chappell, J.M.A., Bloom, A.L., Druffel, E.R.M & Taylor, F.W. 1993. A large drop in atmospheric $^{14}C/^{12}C$ and reduced melting in the Younger Dryas, documented with ^{230}Th ages of corals. *Science* 260: 962–968.

Fishman, B., Forbes, H. & Lawn, B. 1977. Unversity of Pennsylvania radiocarbon dates XIX. *Radiocarbon* 19: 188–228.

Fontugne, M., Arnold, M., Labeyrie, L., Paterne, M., Calvert, S.E. & Duplessy, J.-C. 1994. Paleoenvironment, sapropel chronology and Nile River discharge during the last 20,000 years as indicated by deep-sea sediment records in the Eastern Mediterranean. In Bar-Yosef, O. & Kra, R.S. (eds.), *Late Quaternary Chronology and Paleoclimates of the Eastern Mediterranean*, 75–88. Radiocarbon, Tucson, Arizona.

Gallin, L.J. & Fonzo, O. 1992. Vertebrate faunal remains at the Nuragic village of Santa Barbara, Bauladu (OR). In Tykot, R.H. & Andrews, T.K. (eds.), *Sardinia in the Mediterranean: A Footprint in the Sea. Studies in Sardinian Archaeology Presented to Miriam S. Balmuth*. Monographs in Mediterranean Archaeology 3: 28–39. Sheffield Academic Press, Sheffield.

Goldberg, P. 1994. Interpreting Late Quaternary continental

sequences in Israel. In Bar-Yosef, O. & Kra, R.S. (eds.), *Late Quaternary Chronology and Paleoclimates of the Eastern Mediterranean,* 89–102. Radiocarbon, Tucson, Arizona.

Hedges, R.E.M. 1992. Sample treatment strategies in radiocarbon dating. In Taylor, R.E., Long, A. & Kra, R.S. (eds.), *Radiocarbon After Four Decades: An Interdisciplinary Perspective,* 165–183. Springer-Verlag, New York.

International Study Group (ISG). 1982. An inter-laboratory comparison of radiocarbon measurements in tree-rings. *Nature* 298: 619–623.

Kirch, P.V. 1986. Introduction: The archaeology of island societies. In Kirch, P.V. (ed.), *Island Societies. Archaeological Approaches to Evolution and Transformation,* 1–5. Cambridge University Press, Cambridge.

Klein Hofmeijer, G., Alderliesten, C., van der Borg, K., Houston, C.M., de Jong, A.F.M., Martini, F., Sanges, M., Sondaar, P.Y. & de Visser, J.A. 1989. Dating of the Upper Pleistocene lithic industry of Sardinia. *Radiocarbon* 31: 986–991.

Klein Hofmeijer, G. & Sondaar, P.Y. 1992. Pleistocene humans in the island environment of Sardinia. In Tykot, R.H. & Andrews, T.K. (eds.), *Sardinia in the Mediterranean: A Footprint in the Sea. Studies in Sardinian Archaeology Presented to Miriam S. Balmuth.* Monographs in Mediterranean Archaeology 3: 49–56. Sheffield Academic Press, Sheffield.

Klein Hofmeijer, G., Sondaar, P.Y., Alderliesten, C., van der Borg, K. & de Jong, A.F.M. 1987. Indications of Pleistocene man on Sardinia. *Nuclear Instruments and Methods in Physics Research* B29: 166–168.

Kuijt, I. & Bar-Yosef, O. 1994. Radiocarbon chronology for the Levantine Neolithic: Observations and data. In Bar-Yosef, O. & Kra, R.S. (eds.), *Late Quaternary Chronology and Paleoclimates of the Eastern Mediterranean,* 227–245. Radiocarbon, Tucson, Arizona.

Meulengracht, A., McGovern, P. & Lawn, B. 1981. University of Pennsylvania radiocarbon dates XXI. *Radiocarbon* 23: 227–240.

Scott, E.M., Cook, G.T., Harkness, D.D., Miller, B.F. & Baxter, M.S. 1992. Further analysis of the International Intercomparison Study (ICS). *Radiocarbon* 34: 520–527.

Scott, E.M., Long, A. & Kra, R.S. (eds.) 1990. Proceedings of the International Workshop on Intercomparison of Radiocarbon Laboratories. *Radiocarbon* 32: 253–397.

Shackleton, J.C., van Andel, T.H. & Runnels, C.N. 1984. Coastal paleogeography of the central and western Mediterranean during the last 125,000 years and its archaeological implications. *Journal of Field Archaeology* 11: 307–314.

Simmons, A.H. & Wigand, P.E. 1994. Assessing the radiocarbon determinations from Akrotiri *Aetokremnos,* Cyprus. In Bar-Yosef, O. & Kra, R.S. (eds.), *Late Quaternary Chronology and Paleoclimates of the Eastern Mediterranean,* 247–264. Radiocarbon, Tucson, Arizona.

Sondaar P.Y., Elburg R., Klein Hofmeijer G., Martini F., Sanges M., Spaan A. & Visser H. de. 1995. The human colonization of Sardinia: a Late-Pleistocene human fossil from Corbeddu Cave. *ComptesRendus de l'Académie des Sciences Paris* 320, serie IIa: 145–150.

Stuiver, M. & Kra, R. (eds.) 1986. Calibration Issue. *Radiocarbon* 28, 2B: 805–1030.

Stuiver, M., Long, A. & Kra, R.S. (eds.) 1993. Calibration 1993. *Radiocarbon* 35: 1–244.

Suess, H.E. 1955. Radiocarbon concentration in modern wood. *Science* 122: 415–417.

Switsur, V.R. 1990a. Appendix I. Radiocarbon ages and dates in Sardinian prehistory. In Trump, D.H., *Nuraghe Noeddos and the Bonu Ighinu Valley. Excavation and Survey in Sardinia,* 54–59. Oxbow Books, Oxford.

Switsur, V.R. 1990b. A consideration of some basic ideas for quality assurance in radiocarbon dating. In Scott, E.M., Long, A. & Kra, R.S. (eds.) 1990. Proceedings of the International Workshop on Intercomparison of Radiocarbon Laboratories. *Radiocarbon* 32: 341–346.

Switsur, V.R. & Trump, D.H. 1983. A radiocarbon chronology for the early prehistory of Sardinia. In Mook, W.G. & Waterbolk, H.T. (eds.), *Proceedings of the First International Symposium, ^{14}C and Archaeology, Groningen 1981. PACT* 8: 453–464. Strasbourg.

Tauber, H. 1960. Copenhagen natural radiocarbon measurements III, corrections to radio-carbon dates made with the solid carbon technique. *American Journal of Science Radiocarbon Supplement* 2: 5–11.

Taylor, R.E. 1987. *Radiocarbon Dating: An Archaeological Perspective.* Academic Press, Orlando, Florida.

Tchernov, E. 1994. New comments on the biostratigraphy of the Middle and Upper Pleistocene of the Southern Levant. In Bar-Yosef, O. & Kra, R.S. (eds.), *Late Quaternary Chronology and Paleoclimates of the Eastern Mediterranean,* 333–350. Radiocarbon, Tucson, Arizona.

Trump, D.H. 1990. *Nuraghe Noeddos and the Bonu Ighinu Valley. Excavation and Survey in Sardinia.* Oxbow Books, Oxford.

Tykot, R.H. 1994. Radiocarbon dating and absolute chronology in Sardinia and Corsica. In Skeates, R. & Whitehouse, R. (eds.), *Radiocarbon Dating and Italian Prehistory,* 115–145. Archaeological Monographs of the British School at Rome, London.

Tykot, R.H. & Andrews, T.K. (eds.), 1992. *Sardinia in the Mediterranean: A Footprint in the Sea. Studies in Sardinian Archaeology Presented to Miriam S. Balmuth.* Monographs in Mediterranean Archaeology 3. Sheffield Academic Press, Sheffield.

van Andel, T.H. & Shackleton, J.C. 1982. Late Paleolithic and Mesolithic coastlines of Greece and the Aegean. *Journal of Field Archaeology* 9: 445–454.

3. Some Cautionary Points on the Use of Radiocarbon Dates

David H. Trump

Those professionals who work with radiocarbon frequently, and rightly, warn of the snags – those things which can go wrong between the recovery of a sample for dating and the application of the result to the archaeological record. These fall into four main groups, namely the sampling procedure, the results of contamination with older or younger organic material, laboratory errors, and misunderstanding of the statistics underlying the quoted figures, both in the original processing and even more in the calibration of the results. These have often, but never too often, been spelled out, as by Manning in this volume. There is no need for me to repeat them.

Three more mistakes commonly appear in the archaeological interpretation of the results, and, if they cannot be eliminated entirely, can and should be constantly borne in mind by all archaeologists.

Firstly, even if all other pitfalls have been avoided, there is always the chance, however remote, of a completely 'rogue' date. 5% of dates fall outside the 2-sigma bracket often quoted. As a result, much increased by all the other possibilities of error, one has always to some extent to 'pick and choose' with radiocarbon dates, to place more reliance on some results than on others.

The major protection against errors here lies in multiple determinations from single contexts or, useful but rather less effective, in series of dates in known, usually stratigraphically determined, order. In both, any wildly discrepant date will stand out, and though this may only be a statistical anomaly, reasons for its unacceptability should be sought. In theory, if there were such reasons they should have been noticed before the sample was submitted and indeed, if found, that sample should have been rejected at that early stage. Unfortunately that is not always possible.

We are still left with the statistical outlier. Indeed, to make matters worse there is still the remote chance, however unlikely, that the one apparent 'rogue', whether in a supposedly contemporary group or in a successive run, is correct and the consistent group wrong.

This does not, however, mean that we are free to accept the accuracy of dates which agree with our preconceptions, and to reject those which run counter to them, much as we might like to. We must bear in mind what we are doing and why, and judge the validity of each date as fairly as possible against its archaeological context and any other relevant dates, from whatever source.

Let me quote two Sardinian examples. At Sa Ucca de Su Tintirriolu (Mara, SS), in 1972 (Loria & Trump 1978) the stratigraphy showed in successively higher levels Bonu Ighinu (here recognized for the first time), Ozieri, a little Monte Claro and a thin surface scatter of Roman. Samples from the first two were submitted, analyzed, and produced fully consistent and acceptable results. One from the third, R-885, yielded a date of 1890±50 BP. This had to be rejected as being impossibly late, since it suggested that Monte Claro extended down to the Christian era. The explanation must surely lie in the sample having infiltrated from the Roman surface. The excavator, myself, must accept the blame for misattributing it.

At the Grotta di Gonogosula (Oliena, NU), the Dottoressa E. Castaldi found carbon which yielded dates of 4900±60 and 4830±50BP. In the late 1960s, the Ozieri material with which they were associated was assumed to date to the second half of the 3rd millennium BC, making R-609 and R-609a some seven centuries too early. Instead of suppressing them, which she may well have been sorely tempted to do, she published them with her reservations (Alessio *et al.* 1971). This was the perfectly proper thing to do, and was fully vindicated when results from the Su Tintirriolu samples R-879, R-883a and R-884a came out (Loria & Trump 1978). Five results in such close agreement could hardly be wrong, and there have been others since. The apparent 'rogue' dates were no such thing. Instead it was the radiocarbon which was right and the archaeologists who were badly wrong.

Here is a good illustration both of the importance of multiple samples and of the use of radiocarbon as an

David H. Trump, 87 De Freville Avenue, Cambridge CB4 1HP, England, UK

independent check on archaeologically derived chronologies. However, the remarkable consistency of these dates is probably more apparent than real. Manning (this volume) points out that a plateau in the radiocarbon calibration curve occurs at just this time, so that samples from a range of dates yield misleadingly similar results.

Secondly, one can fall into circularity of argument with radiocarbon dates. If the context yielding the sample has poor or undiagnostic cultural associations, it may be attributed to one or another phase on the basis of the date obtained rather than vice versa. Circularity comes in if the date is then quoted for the cultural phase it has itself suggested. At the Grotta Filiestru (Mara, SS), a sequence of twelve dates all fell in the right stratigraphic order. Eleven of them had unimpeachable cultural associations. Q-3026 was associated with pottery which had one or two quite strong hints of Bonnanaro B, angled handles (*anse a gomito*) in particular, but nothing absolutely diagnostic. It certainly came in the right point in the sequence, and was published as a date for Bonnanaro (Trump 1990). I am reasonably confident that that attribution is correct, but would have to admit that my grounds for this confidence are weak.

At the Nuraghe Noeddos a few years later, I took a wiser course. Samples from huts preceding the archaic monotorre nuraghe were analyzed to give dates of 4030 ± 50 to 3480 ± 70 BP (Q-3069, Q-3167: Trump 1990), which fell comfortably within the Monte Claro range. Associated pottery had an occasional red surface and evolved tripod legs, but lacked completely the characteristic broad parallel groove decoration which was present at Su Tintirriolu only 3.5 km distant. Although tempted to publish these dates as Monte Claro, I thought it better not to prejudge them. Instead the material was called Noeddos I and II (the former without, the latter with, '*tegame*' platters) to prevent the dates being used unjustifiably for Monte Claro in the stricter sense. This has, of course, substantially reduced their value to this one site, at least until comparable material turns up elsewhere, but better minor and reliable value than major but unreliable.

The solution to this problem lies not in further radiocarbon determinations, which in this case would not help, but in additional archaeological material from the context in question, or at the very least from comparable contexts.

Thirdly, and in a sense a counter argument to the one that samples should be chosen to answer particular problems, they can rarely date precise events, even if this is really what we want of them. If we seek to know when a given culture or phase started - the introduction of the first neolithic to an area for example - we obtain a carbon date to fix it. But if the point at issue is not the beginning but the end of a phase, as with the well-known example of the collapse of the Tarxien-culture temples in Malta, the carbon date obtained might well be used to fix that. A pause for consideration will immediately show that a single date cannot possibly apply to both beginning and end of a phase at the same time. Indeed it is most unlikely to 'date' either. All it gives us (and again, of course, only if it is unaffected by the various collection, contamination, analysis or statistical problems) is a point somewhere within the duration of that phase.

Once again, as in our first case, the best protection against this problem must lie in multiple samples. The more we have, the likelier it is that the first and last will approximate ever more closely to that beginning and end, though they may well never actually reach them. What we have are only *termini ante* and *post quos*, not dates for precise events.

With these additional difficulties, the argument for the abandonment of radiocarbon as a dating method because of its uncertainties, which is still occasionally heard, might seem to be further strengthened. That is far from my aim. The more clearly we understand the limitations of radiocarbon, which it must be admitted are certainly there, and make due allowance for them, the better we can rely upon their results. If we reject them, we are left with only archaeologically derived dates, and their reliability is appreciably worse. It would be nothing short of arrogance to insist otherwise, as the example of the dating of Ozieri instanced above shows immediately. We cannot work without radiocarbon, but we must make every effort to use it fairly and honestly.

References

Alessio, M., Bella, F., Improta, S., Belluomini, G., Cortesi, C. & Turi, B. 1971. University of Rome Carbon-14 Dates IX. *Radiocarbon* 13: 395–411.

Loria, R. & Trump, D. 1978. Le scoperte a 'Sa 'Ucca de Su Tintirriolu' e il neolitico sardo. *Monumenti Antichi* serie misc. II.2. Accademia Nazionale dei Lincei, Roma.

Trump, D. 1990. *Nuraghe Noeddos and the Bonu Ighinu Valley.* Oxbow, Oxford.

4. Sardinia and Dendrochronology: Any Potential?

Peter Ian Kuniholm

As I reported (with regret) at the Tufts Colloquium, we have as yet no wood or charcoal from Sardinia, although the eastern half of the Mediterranean is well covered by tree-ring chronologies for the last several thousand years (Fig. 4.1). After the colloquium, one sample was sent to me by Gary and Maud Webster but it proved to have too few rings for crossdating. That does not mean we should not try to start building a tree-ring chronology for the island. At first we can try to compare Sardinian wood with material from the mainland. We should also look north to Corsica and south to Sicily and see what comparisons may be made among the three islands. Eventually we may have enough material for a Sardinian tree-ring sequence that stands by itself.

Readers of this paper who work in Sardinia can help us develop chronologies by collecting samples from the

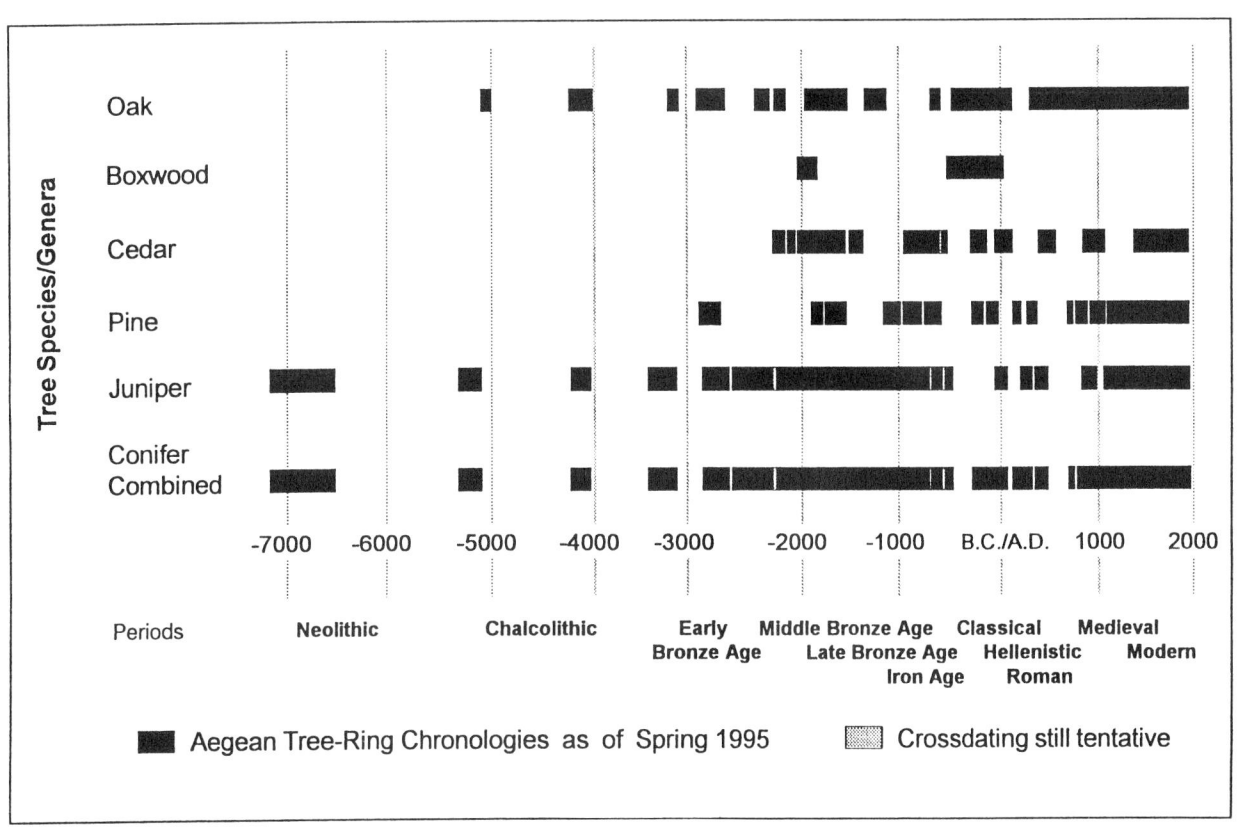

Fig. 4.1. Schematic summary of 22 years' work on building tree-ring chronologies for the Aegean and neighboring regions.

Peter Ian Kuniholm, Department of the History of Art & Archaeology, Cornell University, Ithaca, New York 14853–3201 USA

Sardinian forests (the foresters will be glad to help), and archaeological wood or charcoal from all periods. Even if no immediate crossdating with external sites is apparent it may be possible to work out relative dates within Sardinia itself. As the following how-to-collect-charcoal Appendix explains, the longer the ring-sequence the better. We prefer to work with specimens which have more than 100 rings preserved. 200 rings or more are even better. Single samples are to be avoided as are those which come from contexts that are either insignificant or not secure.

We know that tree-ring chronologies from parts of the Italian mainland match profiles from further east. For example, an 833-year chronology of *Pinus leukodermis* from Mt. Pollino in Calabria (Serre-Bachet 1985) fits splendidly with forests in both Greece and Turkey (Kuniholm 1995; Kuniholm *et al.* 1992). Now, what about Sardinia?

References

Kuniholm, P.I. 1995. Dendrochronology. In P.J. McGovern *et al.*, Science in archaeology: a review. *American Journal of Archaeology* 99: 79–142.

Kuniholm, P.I., C.B. Griggs, S.L. Tarter & Kuniholm, H.E. 1992. A 513-year Buxus chronology for the Roman ship at Comacchio (Ferrara). *Bollettino di Archeologia* 16–18: 291–299. Ministero per i beni Culturali e Ambientali, Rome.

Serre-Bachet, F. 1985. Une chronologie pluriséculaire du Sud de L'Italie. *Dendrochronologia* 3: 45–66.

Appendice: Metodi per raccogliere legno archeologico per un'analisi dendrocronologica

Il laboratorio di Dendrocronologia Egea della Cornell University analizza materiali lignei e carbonizzati provenienti da siti archeologici delle regioni egee, balcaniche, del Mediterraneo orientale e del Levante. Questi limiti geografici riflettono la nostra attuale capacità di applicare il metodo di analisi dendrocronologica a materiale ligneo ben conservato e a carbone in questa area. Non è ancora certo se il nostro campo d'azione si amplierà verso est in Mesopotamia o verso nord nella Crimea e nel Caucaso. Per quanto riguarda gli scavi eseguiti in Turchia, sono in nostro possesso campioni rappresentanti la maggior parte dei periodi storici e preistorici sino al Neolitico. La cronologia rilevata sino ad ora (Maggio 1995) copre 6.500 anni (vedi susseguenti grafici per la distribuzione cronologica della quercia e delle conifere).

Cosa si intende per campione significativo?

In genere ogni campione di quercia, pino, abete, abete rosso, ginepro o cedro che abbiano 50 o più anelli possono essere datati se già esiste una sicura cronologia per quel periodo. I migliori campioni, comunque, hanno 100 o più anelli. Non è la *dimensione* del campione che è importante, ma il *numero degli anelli* (Figg. 4.2–4.3). Per esempio abbiamo tronchi carbonizzati usati per fondazione provenienti dalla Turchia (Kültepe e Acemhöyük) della Media Età del Bronzo, tronchi del diametro di cm. 40 con un numero di anelli variabile da 250 a 430; dai medesimi siti abbiamo altri campioni che sono datati anche se hanno un diametro di cm. 4 e 150 anelli. Nel caso in cui l'archeologo incontri difficoltà nel contare gli anelli durante lo scavo, è necessario conservare il materiale ligneo che verrà poi analizzato sul sito stesso o in laboratorio secondo le indicazioni date più avanti. Si può misurare sia il legno carbonizzato che quello non carbonizzato (il legno bruciato ha il vantaggio di non marcire). Per migliori risultati bisogna avere più reperti possibili. É evidente che non in ogni scavo si trova legno ben conservato, perciò quando si è così fortunati da trovare legno o carbone noi cerchiamo di avere campioni da ogni tronco disponibile.

Come raccogliere un campione:

1. Per tronchi non carbonizzati in buone condizioni, avvolgere più volte intorno al tronco una corda *al momento dello scavo* e tagliare una sezione. Rinforzare la corda avvolgendola con del nastro adesivo da imballaggio oppure con stoffa. Etichettare con precisione e chiarezza indicando la posizione e la provenienza del reperto come si suole fare con ogni reperto archeologico. Per un tronco in buone condizioni, dovrebbe essere sufficiente la corda; per campioni tarlati o erosi bisognerebbe usare più corde o nastro adesivo per mantenere il campione intatto, soprattutto se la sezione è stata prelevata dal terreno. Bisogna sottolineare che per ogni anello perso, un anno è perso.

2. Per campioni carbonizzati totalmente o in parte, la corda è il materiale migliore per avvolgerli e tenerli compatti. Ogni pezzo di carbone rinvenuto deve essere legato con la corda in modo da formare una sorta di "guscio" protettivo intorno al reperto, altrimenti questo può frantumarsi e quindi perdere anelli. Il campione deve riportare chiaramente su un'etichetta il luogo di provenienza e può essere poi impacchettato. (Qualora il campione debba essere spedito al laboratorio della

Cornell University, per assicurare una maggior protezione al reperto, è consigliabile usare ulteriore imbottitura oppure cotone). Spesso interi tronchi carbonizzati sono preservati nelle fondamenta di edifici. In questo caso è necessario mettere in luce la parte terminale del tronco, avvolgere più volte la circonferenza con della corda e tagliarne una sezione (se è totalmente carbonizzato l'operazione è piuttosto facile). Una persona dovrebbe tenere la sezione appena rimossa ed un'altra dovrebbe avvolgere con la corda l'intero campione che è necessario riporre subito in una borsa di plastica sigillata e lontana dal sole.

3. Per campioni situati in acqua è molto importante evitare di rimuoverli e non farli seccare. Dopo aver tagliato la sezione dal tronco o trave, bisogna metterla immediatamente in una borsa di plastica (preferibilmente ermetica), quindi marcarla con una penna indelebile e se possibile tenerla in un luogo fresco.

4. Vi sono siti con ritrovamenti lignei, talora anche ricchi, come il Tumulo di Mida a Gordion, nei quali l'archeologo preferisce non rimuovere una sezione da un tronco o da una trave. In questi casi possiamo procedere con il carotaggio che rimuove dal tronco un campione cilindrico del diametro di mm. 9 (che poi rimpiazziamo con riempitivo) lasciando un segno non visibile nel legno. Per questo servizio bisogna prendere accordi con noi.

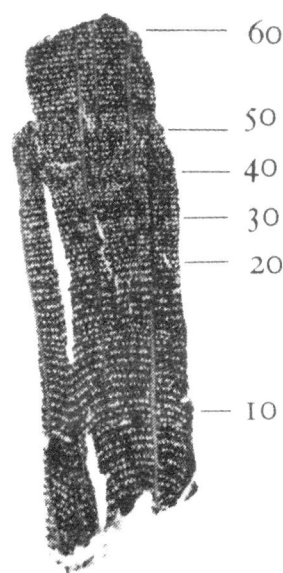

Fig. 4.2 Campione di Demircihöyük con 63 anelli (buona probabilità di datazione).

Come spedire i campioni

I campioni devono essere inviati a: Prof. Peter Ian Kuniholm, Aegean Dendrochronology Project, Department of the History of Art & Archaeology, B-48 Goldwin Smith Hall, Cornell University, Ithaca, New York 14853–3201 USA. Telefono del laboratorio: 001–607–255–8650; fax: 001–607–255–1454.

I campioni devono essere avvolti in cotone o in qualche altro tipo di involucro protettivo come fogli di plastica con bolle d'aria per evitare danni durante la spedizione. É possibile inoltre per la nostre equipe raccogliere i campioni in loco, previo accordo, durante le nostre campagne estive.

NOTA: Ricordate di etichettare tutti i campioni nel modo più esauriente possibile così da permetterci di identificare con precisione il luogo del ritrovamento. Sarebbe consigliabile allegare una pianta dell'edificio che indichi i luoghi da dove sono stati prelevati i campioni.

Fig. 4.3 Campione di Demircihöyük con 12 anelli (nessuna possibilità di datazione).

5. Dating Sardinian Archaeological Obsidian

Christopher M. Stevenson & J. Grace Ellis

Introduction

Despite the widespread occurrence of obsidian within the Mediterranean region the use of the obsidian hydration dating method (OHD) has received only passing attention. Instead, archaeological research has focused on the trace element characterization of geological sources and artifacts within the context of developing models of exchange and production systems (Renfrew *et al.* 1965; Cann and Renfrew 1964; Dixon 1976; Torrence 1981; 1984; Tykot 1995; 1996; 1997).

Recent application of OHD within the Mediterranean region began with The Pennsylvania State University archaeological field school in 1981, then under the direction of Joseph W. Michels and Gary S. Webster. In 1982, Michels developed the first laboratory hydration rate for the Monte Arci obsidian source (Michels 1982) which was later revised in 1985. This hydration rate has been applied to obsidians excavated by Webster and Michels from Nuragic sites in Borore (Michels *et al.* 1984; Michels 1987) and by Dyson *et al.* (1990) in their study of open-air habitations and *nuraghi* in the territories of Bauladu, Paulilatino, and Fordongianus.

This early work on Sardinian obsidian was based upon two assumptions which were characteristic of research at the time: 1) obsidian sources are homogeneous with respect to chemical composition, and 2) trace element or major oxide uniformity within an obsidian source or flow implies that a single hydration rate may be applicable to archaeological materials obtained from that location. Within the last ten years both of these assumptions have been critically examined.

Characterization of obsidian sources in a variety of localities has indicated that sources are frequently complex entities characterized by multiple flows which are different in trace or minor element chemistry (Ericson & Glascock 1992; Hughes 1994; Shackley 1995). Recent work by Tykot (1991; 1992; 1995; 1997) has demonstrated that this situation applies to the Monte Arci source as well, where differences in trace element concentrations can be used to characterize five distinct source groups. In addition, it has also been shown that obsidian flows are not homogeneous with respect to water content, the rate controlling factor (Stevenson *et al.* 1993), and that a range of hydration rates may be required for material obtained from a single obsidian flow or source. In light of these discoveries, we apply the new methodological developments to the Sardinian area and suggest how OHD may be best utilized as a dating method.

Recent Developments in Obsidian Hydration Dating

In order to use OHD as a chronometric dating method two procedures must be successfully completed:

1. Estimation of the hydration constants based upon compositional factors that affect the rate of molecular water diffusion into obsidian;
2. Adjustment of the hydration rate to reflect the ambient conditions of site soil temperature and relative humidity.

Hydration rate determination

The development of obsidian hydration rates has been a fundamental issue for users of the method. Conventional methods of hydration rate definition for specific obsidian sources have included the correlation of hydration rim widths with associated radiocarbon dates and by high temperature induced hydration on geological samples. The latter approach has been extensively investigated using a variety of reaction media and temperature settings

(Ambrose 1976; Ericson 1981; Friedman & Long 1976; Michels et al. 1983; Stevenson & McCurry 1990; Stevenson & Scheetz 1989; Stevenson et al. 1989). In these experimental designs, fresh obsidian surfaces were exposed to either a liquid or vapor atmosphere within an open or sealed reaction vessel maintained at temperatures between 100°C and 250°C. The hydration rims formed at high temperature were measured and used to calculate the hydration rate constants (A, E). These constants were used to estimate archaeological hydration rates at ambient conditions with the Arrhenius equation:

$$K = A^{Exp\ E/RT} \qquad (1)$$

where K = archaeological hydration rate; A = source specific rate constant; E = activation energy; R = universal gas constant; and T = temperature.

The dependence of hydration rate on obsidian chemical composition has been addressed through theoretical considerations (Ericson 1981) and by correlation of high temperature hydration rates with glass chemical constituents (Friedman & Long 1976). Recent work by Mazer et al. (1991), Stevenson et al. (1993; 1998) has shown a strong dependence between the structural water content (OH) of the glass with the 100% relative humidity hydration rate at high temperature (A) and the activation energy (E) (Fig. 5.1). With this calibration established, it is now possible to estimate archaeological hydration rates for individual artifacts from the concentration of OH contained within the glass.

In order to develop a hydration rate calibration the structural water content is precisely determined on transparent obsidian sections using the infrared spectroscopy protocol of Newman et al. (1986). However, the application of the calibration to archaeological obsidians was significantly hindered by the lack of infrared transparency in many obsidians. A method to avoid this limitation was proposed by Ambrose & Stevenson (1994) who developed an additional calibration by demonstrating a mathematical relationship between total water content and density. High density obsidians will have low quantities of structural water and hydrate slowly while low density glasses will have higher water concentrations and faster hydration rates (Fig. 5.2). With this relationship precisely established, water values, and thus hydration rates, for virtually all archaeological obsidians can be non-destructively estimated. Artifacts with mineral or vesicle inclusions can also be measured for density provided that corrections are made for the different density inclusions in the obsidian (Ericson 1981: 59).

Soil temperature and relative humidity

Determinations of soil temperature and relative humidity are required for the depth at which the artifacts are found. These values are used to adjust the high temperature experimental rate (Friedman et al. 1994) to reflect the environmental history of the location at which the artifacts

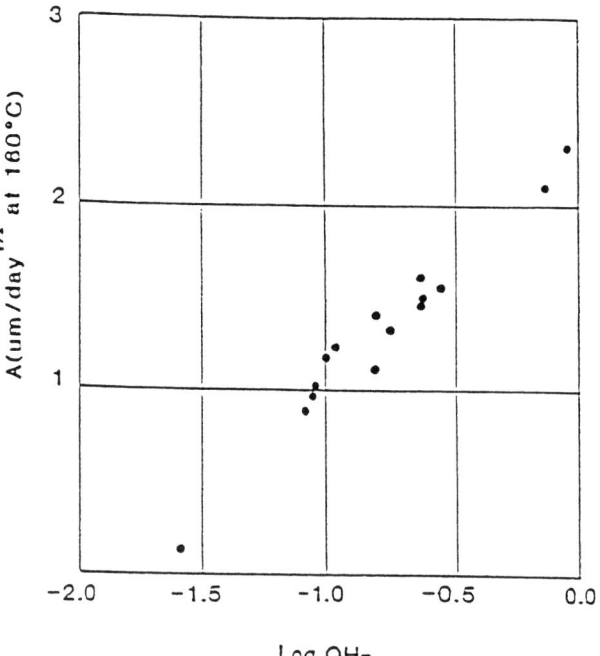

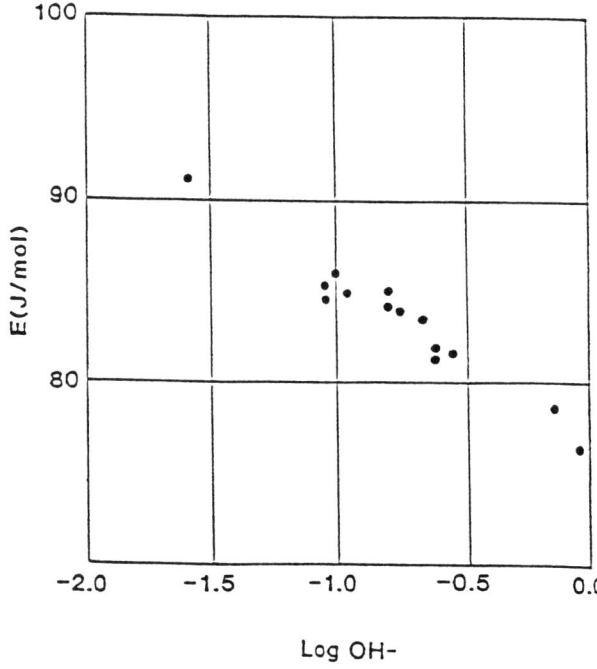

Fig. 5.1. The relationships between the obsidian water content and the high temperature hydration rate constants.

have been deposited. In this procedure it is assumed that the artifacts have been within a stable context since their entrance into the archaeological record.

Soil temperature data are currently being collected by Gary Webster and Maud Webster at Duos Nuraghes. Temperature monitors designed by Trembour et al. (1988) have been buried at depths ranging from 10 cm to 100 cm and will provide a temperature and relative humidity value by depth for this location. In the current study, we assume

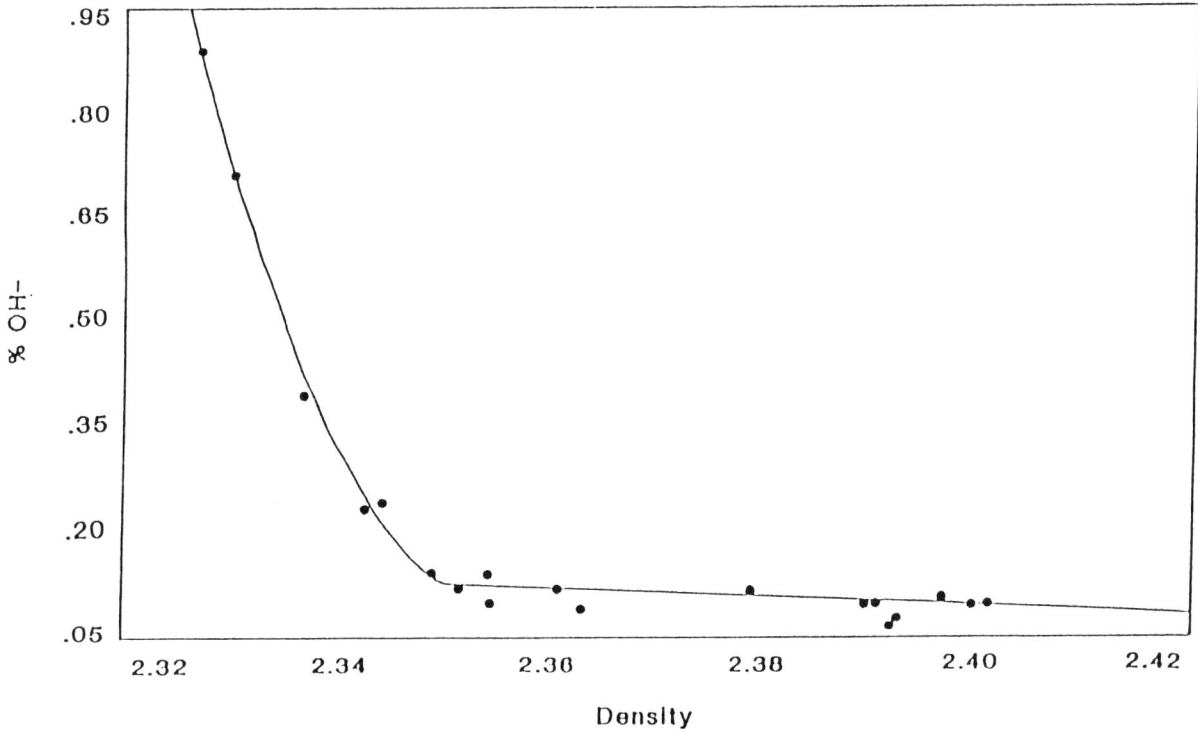

Fig. 5.2. The relationship between obsidian density and the initial water content of unhydrated obsidian.

that the relative humidity of the soil is 100% at depths of 25 cm and greater. An effective hydration temperature of 19.3 °C has been calculated from air temperature data using Lee's (1969) temperature integration equation.

Dating Obsidian from the Monte Arci Geological Source

Hydration rate estimation

In the application of the developments discussed above we would like to address three fundamental questions. First, what range of hydration rates apply to each of the Monte Arci obsidian geochemical types? Second, do archaeological obsidians possess the same range of hydration rates as exhibited by the geological flows? Third, can the archaeological hydration rates produce chronometric dates for proveniences which are in agreement with age assessments implied by other cultural material from the same context?

The trace element characterization of Mediterranean artifacts by Hallam *et al.* (1976) was the first to recognize that three chemically distinct types of Sardinian obsidian (SA, SB, SC) were present but only the provenience of type SA could be determined as coming from a locality near Uras. Recent field survey and chemical analysis by Tykot (1991; 1992; 1995; 1997) has spatially defined the distribution of all three geochemical source groups and subdivided types SB and SC into 2 subgroups each (SB1, SB2, SC1, SC2).

Twenty geological samples from each of the three main obsidian geochemical source groups were obtained for hydration rate determination through the estimation of intrinsic water content. All of the samples were opaque to visible in infrared light at a thickness of 1 mm therefore precluding the use of direct measurement of structural water by infrared spectroscopy (Newman *et al.* 1986). As a result of this situation the intrinsic water was estimated from the glass density (Ambrose & Stevenson 1994). Density values were determined using a Mettler AC/100 analytical balance and density kit (Appendix A). Water was used as the measuring medium and Pervitro was added as a surficant to prevent the adhesion of air bubbles. Three samples were eliminated from the SB sample and 4 samples from the SC sample because of perlitic inclusions or other observable flaws which would result in skewed density values. The estimated error of each density determination is 0.001 gm/cm^3.

Figure 5.3 shows the range of density values for the SA, SB, and SC obsidians. All of the specimens studied have high densities (>2.35 gm/cm^3) in comparison to the known range for obsidian (2.31–2.41 gm/cm^3). This indicates that the glasses contain relatively small amounts of intrinsic water and that the hydration rates will be relatively slow. However, each obsidian geochemical type has a range of density values that is significantly greater than the measurement error associated with the method

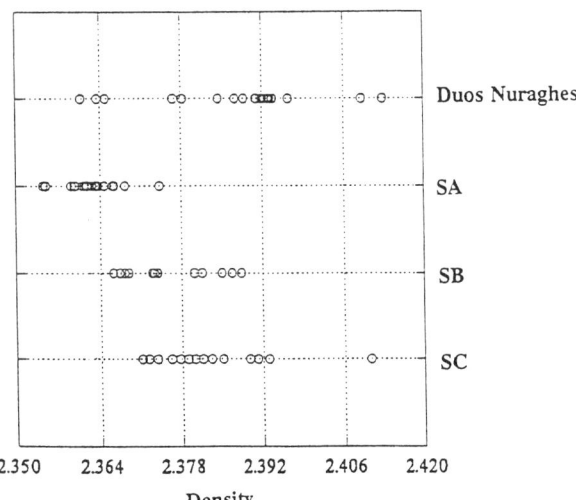

Fig. 5.3. Obsidian density values for the Monte Arci obsidian flows (SA, SB, SC) and archaeological specimens from Duos Nuraghes, Sardinia, Italy

of determination. In comparison to each other, the glass types also have different density ranges with SA having the most restricted range and SC the largest. The archaeological specimens exhibit almost the same range as the geological samples. It is interesting to note that many of the archaeological specimens have a density range greater than the SA obsidian indicating that the people at Duos Nuraghes were obtaining much of their obsidian from the SB and SC source locations.

Table 5.1 converts the density values to hydration rate ranges at an arbitrarily selected temperature of 20°C. It can be seen from an inspection of the values that the range of hydration rates for Sardinian obsidians may range between 3.4 and 6.1 um²/1000 years depending upon the amount of water contained within the sample. This hydration rate range brackets the hydration rate of 4.5 um²/1000 years proposed by Michels (1982, revised 1985). With this increased resolution in hydration rate determination it should be possible to enhance the application of OHD to archaeological situations.

Hydration Dating of Duos Nuraghes

In order to evaluate the ability of this dating method to provide absolute age determinations samples from contexts of known age were obtained. Twenty-five specimens from Duos Nuraghes, a habitation complex occupied from approximately 1800 BC to AD 1000 (Webster 1985; 1988a; 1988b; Teglund & Webster 1992) were dated (Table 5.2). The estimated age ranges for each of the dated contexts were determined by the Websters based upon stratigraphic, architectural, and ceramic evidence.

A comparison of the obsidian ages with the estimated context ages (Table 5.3) shows an amazing lack of correspondence between the two data sets. Only the AD 1301 and the 484 BC obsidian dates were considered acceptable. Nearly all of the remaining specimens are either significantly earlier or later than the estimated age. No single transformation of the hydration rate, such as an adjustment in the effective hydration temperature, could improve the correspondence between the two data sets. It is interesting to note that nine of the samples are at least 1000 years too early for their contexts, and six samples date well before the proposed occupation of the site.

The data presented above suggests that two processes have in this case limited the ability of OHD to provide useful chronological information. The presence of numerous dates much earlier than the initial occupation of the site suggests that obsidian obtained from early contexts was imported to the site. These early materials may have been obtained from refuse deposits at other sites or from the actual quarry locality. Here, the byproducts of material evaluation and initial reduction created at an early time were later re-utilized. In addition, the lack of convergence between the two data sets indicates that once discarded the obsidian has probably been redistributed in fill material moved during structure renovation and rebuilding over the course of site occupation.

Summary

The ability to estimate the hydration rate for individual artifacts based upon intrinsic water content has the potential to increase the resolution of OHD through the production of accurate age determinations. The variability of structural water, and its effect on hydration rate, within a geological flow or source can be taken into account by a measurement of the glass density. As a result, assumptions concerning source compositional uniformity and the representative nature of single hydration rates no longer need to be made. Working under the new methodological procedures is potentially very useful since it holds the promise of dating many contexts at a lesser cost, thereby increasing our temporal resolution with which we can track changes in social systems over time.

Source	Density Range (gm/cm³)	A (um²/day @ 160°C)	E (Joles/mol)	20°C Rate (um²/1000 years)
SA	2.3546–2.3744	1.29–1.15	84867–85310	6.10–5.11
SB	2.3629–2.3882	1.23–1.04	85047–85652	5.69–4.44
SC	2.3637–2.4105	1.22–0.86	85064–86277	5.64–3.37

Table 5.1. Monte Arci Obsidian Density Ranges and Hydration Rate Constants

Lab No.	Provenience	Density	Rim	Rate	AD/(BC)	SD*
DL-95-120	U4, TR.10, L.2	2.3635	1.83	5.16	1301	73
DL-95-121	U4, TR.11, L.4	2.3920	4.56	3.88	(3414)	238
DL-95-122	U1, TR.20, L.4	2.3932	3.19	3.82	(711)	169
DL-95-123	U1, TR.34, FEA.100	2.3934	3.21	3.82	(751)	171
DL-95-124	U1, TR.34, FEA.100	2.3917	–	3.89	–	–
DL-95-125	U1, TR.38, FEA.1	2.4127	–	2.98	–	–
DL-95-126	U1, TR.38, FEA.1(A)	2.3966	4.27	3.68	(3011)	235
DL-95-127	U1, TR.38, FEA.1(B)	2.3872	4.47	4.09	(2937)	221
DL-95-128	U1, TR.38, FEA.1(C)	–	4.4	–	–	–
DL-95-129	U1, TR.42, L.8	2.3917	3.25	3.89	(765)	170
DL-95-130	U1, TR.47, L.8	2.3842	3.21	4.22	(490)	154
DL-95-131	U1, TR.48, L.3	2.3909	3.25	3.92	(741)	168
DL-95-132	U1, TR.48, L.4	2.3930	4.47	3.83	(3263)	236
DL-95-133	U1, TR.54, L.2(A)	2.3608	3.16	5.28	60	121
DL-95-134	U1, TR.54, L.2(B)	2.3925	3.89	3.85	(1976)	204
DL-95-135	U1, TR.54, L.3(A)	2.4091	4.17	3.14	(3593)	269
DL-95-136	U1, TR.54, L.3(B)	2.3782	3.88	4.49	(1402)	175
DL-95-137	U1, TR.54, L.6	2.3921	3.07	3.87	(484)	161
DL-95-138	U1, TR.55, L.3(A)	2.3650	3.88	5.09	(1007)	154
DL-95-139	U1, TR.55, L.3(B)	2.3767	3.5	4.56	(737)	156
DL-95-140	U1, TR.57, L.2	–	–	–	–	–
DL-95-141	U1, TR.57, L.3	2.3888	4.06	4.02	(2153)	205
DL-95-142	U1, TR.55 & 57, L.3	2.3939	4.26	3.79	(2834)	227
DL-95-143	U1, FEA.101	2.3910	3.16	3.92	(597)	164
DL-95-144	U1, FEA.100	2.3909	2.9	3.93	(193)	150

* SD = Standard Deviation

Table 5.2. Obsidian Hydration Dates for Duos Nuraghes, Sardinia

Provenience	Obsidian Hydration Ages	Stratigraphic Age
Tower B	AD 1301	Post Roman Period (after AD 600)
	3414 BC	Punic Period (500 BC–238 BC)
Hut 3, E. Village (Interior deposit)	193 BC	Late Bronze Age (1300–900 BC)
	490 BC	
	490 BC	
	597 BC	
	711 BC	
	751 BC	
	3263 BC	
Hut 3, E. Village (Exterior deposit)	765 BC	Middle Bronze Age–Late Bronze Age (1500 BC– 1300/900 BC)
Hut 5, E. Village	2937 BC	Late Bronze Age (1000 BC)
	3011 BC	
Vano 8, Room 8 (E. Village)	AD 60	Punic Period (after 500 BC)
	1976 BC	
	1402 BC	
	3593 BC	
	484 BC	Iron Age (900 BC–500 BC)
Vano 6, Room 6	737 BC	Punic Period (after 500 BC)
	1007 BC	
	2153 BC	
	2834 BC	

Table 5.3. A Comparison of Stratigraphic Age Estimates for Duos Nuraghe

However, our initial application of OHD to contexts of known age at Duos Nuraghes has demonstrated the presence of intervening processes which have altered the original depositional context of the artifact and thereby its usefulness as a temporal marker. Therefore, in sites with complex depositional and recycling histories a series of evaluative decisions must be made in the field and in the laboratory. For each datable context the formation processes and type of depositional event will need to be carefully assessed. It may be the case that an adequate context interpretation cannot be completed in intricate sites such as Duos Nuraghes and that the application of OHD will be more useful in less complex archaeological deposits.

Acknowledgments

We would like to thank Robert H. Tykot, University of South Florida, for providing us with geological samples from the Monte Arci obsidian flows. In addition, archaeological samples from Duos Nuraghes were kindly provided by Gary Webster and Maud Webster, The Pennsylvania State University. Without these contributions this work would not have been possible.

References

Ambrose, W. 1976. Intrinsic hydration rate dating of obsidian. In R.E. Taylor (ed.), *Advances in Obsidian Glass Studies*, 81-105. Noyes Press, Park Ridge, New Jersey.

Ambrose, W. & Stevenson, C. 1994. *Estimation of hydration rates from obsidian density measurements*. Manuscript on file, Diffusion Laboratory, Columbus, Ohio.

Cann, J.R. & Renfrew, C. 1964. The characterization of obsidian and its application to the Mediterranean region. *Proceedings of the Prehistoric Society* 30: 111-131.

Dixon, J.E. 1976. Obsidian characterization studies in the Mediterranean and Near East. In R.E. Taylor (ed.), *Advances in Obsidian Glass Studies*, 288-333. Noyes Press, Park Ridge, New Jersey.

Dyson, S., Gallin, L., Klimciewicz, M., Rowland, R. & Stevenson, C. 1990. Notes on some obsidian hydration dates in Sardinia. *Quaderni della Soprintendenza Archeologica di Cagliari e Oristano* 7: 25-42.

Ericson, J. 1981. *Exchange and Production Systems in California Prehistory: The Results of Hydration Dating and Chemical Characterization of Obsidian Sources*. BAR International Series 110. British Archaeological Reports, Oxford.

Ericson, J.E. & Glascock, M.D. 1992. Chemical characterization of obsidian flows and domes of the Coso volcanic field, China Lake, California (Abstract). In *Abstracts*, 28th International Symposium on Archaeometry, 23-27 March, Los Angeles, California.

Friedman, I. & Long, W. 1976. Hydration rate of obsidian. *Science* 159: 347-352.

Friedman, I, Smith, F. & Smith, G. 1994. Is obsidian dating affected by relative humidity? *Quaternary Research* 41: 185-190.

Hallam, B.R., Warren, S.E. & Renfrew, A.C. 1976. Obsidian in the western Mediterranean: characterization by neutron activation analysis and optical emission spectroscopy. *Proceedings of the Prehistoric Society* 42: 85-110.

Hughes, R. 1994. Intrasource separation of artifact quality obsidians from the Casa Diablo area, California. *Journal of Archaeological Science* 21: 263-271.

Lee, R. 1969. Chemical temperature integration. *Journal of Applied Meteorology* 8: 423-430.

Mazer, J., Stevenson, C., Ebert, W. & Bates, J. 1991. The experimental hydration of obsidian as a function of relative humidity and temperature. *American Antiquity* 56: 504-513.

Michels, J. 1982. Hydration rate constants for Monte Arci obsidian, Sardinia, Italy. *MOHLAB Technical Report* No. 15. 1188 Smithfield Street, State College, PA 16801.

Michels, J. 1987. Obsidian hydration dating and a proposed chronological scheme for the Marghine region. In Michels, J.W. & Webster, G. (eds.), *Studies in Nuragic Archaeology*. BAR International Series 373: 119-126. British Archaeological Reports, Oxford.

Michels, J., Tsong, I.S.T. & Smith, G. 1983. Experimentally derived hydration rates in obsidian dating. *Archaeometry* 25: 107-117.

Michels, J., E. Atzeni, Tsong, I.S.T. & Smith, G. 1984. Obsidian hydration dating in Sardinia. In Balmuth, M.S. & Rowland, R.J. (eds.), *Studies in Sardinian Archaeology*, 83-114. University of Michigan Press, Ann Arbor.

Newman, S., Stolper, E. & Epstein, S. 1986. Measurement of water in rhyolitic glasses: calibration of an infrared spectroscopic technique. *American Mineralogist* 71: 1527-154.

Renfrew, C., Cann, J. & Dixon, J. 1965. Obsidian in the Aegean. *Annual of the British School of Archaeology at Athens* 60: 225-247.

Shackley, S. 1995. Intersource and intrasource geochemical variability in two newly discovered archaeological obsidian sources in the southern Great Basin. *Journal of California and Great Basin Anthropology* 16: 119-129.

Stevenson, C., Knaus, E., Mazer, J. & Bates, J.K. 1993. Homogeneity of water content in obsidian from the Coso volcanic field: implications for obsidian hydration dating. *Geoarchaeology* 8: 371-384.

Stevenson, C. & McCurry, M. 1990. Chemical characterization and hydration rate development for New Mexican obsidian sources. *Geoarchaeology* 5: 149-170.

Stevenson, C., Mazer, J. & Scheetz, B. 1998. Laboratory obsidian hydration rates: theory, method, and application. In Shackley, S. (ed.), *Method and Theory in Archaeological Obsidian Studies*. Advances in Archaeological and Museum Science. Plenum, New York.

Stevenson, C. & Scheetz, B. 1989. Induced hydration rate development of obsidians from the Coso volcanic field: a comparison of experimental procedures. *Current Directions in California Obsidian Studies* 48: 23-30. Contributions of the University of California Archaeological Research Facility, Berkeley.

Stevenson, C., Carpenter, J. & Scheetz, B. 1989. Recent advances in the experimental determination and application of obsidian hydration rates. *Archaeometry* 31: 193-206.

Teglund, M. & Webster, G. 1992. Report of the excavations at Duos Nuraghes, Borore (NU) 1992. *Old World Archaeology Newsletter* 16(2): 19-23.

Torrence, R. 1981. *Obsidian in the Aegean: Towards a Methodology for the Study of Prehistoric Exchange*. Ph.D. dissertation, University of New Mexico, Albuquerque, New Mexico.

Torrence, R. 1984. Monopoly or direct access? Industrial organization at the Melos obsidian quarries. In Ericson, J.E. & Purdy, B.A. (eds.), *Prehistoric Quarries and Lithic Production*, 49-64. Cambridge University Press, New York.

Trembour, F., Smith, F. & Friedman, I. 1988. Diffusion cells for integrating temperature and humidity over long periods of time. In Sayre, E.V., Vandiver, P.B., Druzik, J. & Stevenson, C.

(eds.), *Materials Issues in Art and Archaeology*. Materials Research Society Symposium Proceedings 123: 245–252. Materials Research Society, Pittsburgh.

Tykot, R.H. 1991. Survey and analysis of the Monte Arci (Sardinia) obsidian sources. *Old World Archaeology Newsletter* 14(2–3): 23–27.

Tykot, R.H. 1992. The sources and distribution of Sardinian obsidian. In Tykot, R.H. & Andrews, T.K. (eds.), *Sardinia in the Mediterranean: A Footprint in the Sea. Studies in Sardinian Archaeology Presented to Miriam S. Balmuth*. Monographs in Mediterranean Archaeology 3: 57–70. Sheffield Academic Press, Sheffield.

Tykot, R.H. 1995. *Prehistoric Trade in the Western Mediterranean: The Sources and Distribution of Sardinian Obsidian*. Ph.D. dissertation, Department of Anthropology, Harvard University. University Microfilms, Ann Arbor.

Tykot, R.H. 1996. Obsidian procurement and distribution in the central and western Mediterranean. *Journal of Mediterranean Archaeology* 9: 39–82.

Tykot, R.H. 1997. Characterization of the Monte Arci (Sardinia) obsidian sources. *Journal of Archaeological Science* 24: 467–479.

Webster, G.S. 1985. Field report of excavations at Duos Nuraghes and San Giorgio in Borore, Sardinia 1985. *Old World Archaeology Newsletter* 9(3): 14–18.

Webster, G.S. 1988a. Duos Nuraghes: Preliminary results of the first three seasons of excavation. *Journal of Field Archaeology* 15: 465–472.

Webster, G.S. 1988b. Excavations at Duos Nuraghes 1985, 1987, 1988. *Old World Archaeology Newsletter* 12(3): 17–21.

Appendix A. Density Measurements for Monte Arci Obsidian Sources

Sample No.	Source	Density	Sample No.	Source	Density
554	SA	2.3550	734	SB1	2.3813
555	SA	2.3614	735	SB1	2.3847
556	SA	2.3647	736	SB1	2.3865
557	SA	2.3633	737	SB1	2.3882
558	SA	2.3546	756	SB2	2.3594*
559	SA	2.3631	757	SB2	2.3707
560	SA	2.3611	759	SB2	2.3608*
561	SA	2.3636	760	SB2	2.3629
562	SA	2.3633	761	SB2	2.3663
563	SA	2.3592	936	SC	2.3713
564	SA	2.3598	946	SC	2.3848
565	SA	2.3618	947	SC	2.3615
566	SA	2.3662	948	SC	2.3739
567	SA	2.3744	951	SC	2.3828
568	SA	2.3597	952	SC	2.3789
569	SA	2.3685	953	SC	2.3724
570	SA	2.3611	954	SC	2.3762
571	SA	2.3626	967	SC	2.3896
572	SA	2.3665	968	SC	2.3637
573	SA	2.3617	969	SC	2.3535*
714	SB1	2.3731	974	SC	2.3813
722	SB1	2.3735	976	SC	2.3910
723	SB1	2.3731	977	SC	2.3930
724	SB1	2.3634*	978	SC	2.3645*
725	SB1	2.3732	979	SC	2.3800
726	SB1	2.3675	980	SC	2.4105
729	SB1	2.3800	981	SC	*

Note: Starred (*) samples contained visual flaws such as perlitic inclusions or cortex surfaces that affected (lowered) the density value. These samples were eliminated from analysis.

6. Unacceptable anomalies or incorrect use of radiocarbon dating in Sardinia?

Santo Tinè

It would be far too simple just to point to the unacceptable radiocarbon dating provided by C14 for the area we are dealing with and declare the method unreliable on this basis alone. As has been stated many times, minimal attention should be paid to single or isolated dates and those which are simply deviations from a logical series should be ignored altogether. I am therefore going to deal with only a few of these series, all apparently in logical sequence. I would also like to emphasize that I am referring to uncalibrated dating, expressed in years before Christ (using the conventional English term "BC"). This is not because I prefer them, merely that I realize many people still use them. In any case, my conclusions should not differ in terms of relative sequence compared with calibrated dating.

I am going to start with the dating relating to the Sardinian culture of the Ozieri. A total of seven datings place this between 3300 and 2800 uncal BC. In almost every case, these are samples taken stratigraphically, starting with those from the Guano Cave (Castaldi 1972), the Su Tintirriolu Cave (Loria & Trump 1978) and the Filiestru Cave (Trump 1983). The reliability of the "stratigraphic base" obviously still remains open to question. This may alter and, as we know, frequently does, depending on the technical skills of the operator, the latter's mental preparation and therefore more or less preconceived ideas of the sequence of historical events. To this we may also add the degree of faith the operator places in radiocarbon dating results. Stratigraphy should therefore not be accepted at face value, but rather subjected to intense self-criticism, casting aside the powerful temptation to consider one's own stratigraphy "more stratified than everyone else's".

This is an old quip of mine (Tinè 1985–87) and it is still valid, although no one listens. Stratigraphic excavation continues, over smaller and smaller areas, which eliminates the chance of noticing redeposition caused by elements as close as 10 cm from the testing area. Samples are collected, radiocarbon tests made by various laboratories and, with "scientific honesty", the results are published for posterity. There is always going to be someone waiting for that particular date to confirm their own theory and invalidate everyone else's! Is this the way science is going? The only result will be to place in doubt sequences confirmed by time, "due comparison" and long-settled disputes.

Without going as far as considering stratigraphy an exception rather than a rule, as my experience induces me to do, I feel its possibly uncertain nature must be taken into account. The temptation to give a "literal" interpretation to the strata should also be avoided, since factors completely unrelated to the actual sequence of historical events to be reconstructed may have contributed to their formation.

It is this belief which guided me through *Dieci anni di nuovi scavi a Monte d'Accoddi* (Tinè & Traverso 1992) and discouraged me from analyzing samples of carbon to obtain dates which would have been as useless as they were damaging, before I was sure of the mechanism of strata formation and the sequence of architectonic phases which occurred in the area.

We only took the first carbon sample when I thought I had discovered a moment which definitely preceded construction of Santuario I, comprising several buried structures full of pebbles and carbon, onto which the Great Menhir had collapsed (or been deliberately pushed). This was sent to the laboratory at the University of Zurich. The date obtained (2490 uncal BC [ETH-2475: 4440 ± 85 BP]) was incredibly late if, as we have reason to believe, the sample refers to the Ozieri culture (even its final stage). A reason can be found for everything, so I had considered the possibility that the sample sent to Zurich had been contaminated in some way. The stratum containing it was almost reached by excavations during

Santo Tinè, Istituto di Scienze Archeologiche e Storia dell'Arte Antica, Università degli Studi di Genoa, Via Balbi, 4, 16126 Genova, Italia

the 1950s and had perhaps been altered by the vegetation which has grown there over the last forty years.

I was also encouraged in this by the conviction of many Sardinian archaeological colleagues, all firm believers in C14, who refused to accept that the Culture of the Ozieri could have continued to such a late date. On the basis of radiocarbon dating obtained, almost all Sardinian scholars or those working in Sardinia are firmly convinced that the Ozieri culture represents the most recent Neolithic period of the island in its entirety and that it cannot go far into the 4th millennium BC (again in uncalibrated chronology).

This is despite the presence here (though rare) of metal (Lo Schiavo 1989), the widespread use of hypogea for collective burials and the presence of marble idols, which are clearly of the Cycladic type or at least an unmistakable local imitation of the originals imported from those islands (which would be even more significant in chronological terms). I cannot agree with A. Antona's attempt (this volume) to place all Sardinian idols in an evolutionary sequence in order to demonstrate total autochthonism. This is once again based only on radiocarbon dating. Tykot apparently does not disagree with this theory, which suggests the possibility that the direction of the influences which led to production of these idols may be reversed, given that "well-known Cycladic types were produced mainly in the EC II periods" (Tykot 1994: 125). In other words, only well into the third millennium BC.

I therefore reluctantly abandoned this late date for the Ozieri from Monte d'Accoddi, which had seemed to support my belief that the Ozieri culture belonged for the most part to the Aeneolithic period and therefore developed mostly during the 3rd millennium BC. I only recently learned, from a note by R. Tykot to "Radiocarbon dating and absolute chronology in Sardinia and Corsica" (Tykot 1994: 138, n. 2), that he accepts this date, since, with calibration, it would place the end of the Ozieri period at 3360–2890 BC. This was the date we had generally accepted after dating (uncalibrated!) from the Grotta del Guano.

Tykot is less willing to accept (as post-Ozieri) a series of another four dates collected subsequently on Monte d'Accoddi, all referring to the period when Santuario I (the so-called "Red Temple") was used. These four dates, which fall between 3,020 and 2,860 uncal BC (UtC-1465, 4870 ± 50 BP; UtC-1466, 4810 ± 80 BP; UtC-1467, 4970 ± 100 BP; UtC-1468, 4920 ± 50 BP), were provided by the Laboratory of Utrecht and are certainly attributable to a post-Ozieri cultural facies. This facies has been variously called Sub-Ozieri, Filigosa or, as F. Lo Schiavo prefers, "painted Ozieri".

In any case, it should be noted that this is a phase in which the typical decoration of the classical Ozieri period had disappeared. The vases are usually ridged, with a shiny black, whitish or pink surface; there are often traces of black painted lines on the pink examples. It was when this appeared that construction began on Monte d'Accoddi of Santuario I, on top of the former Classical Ozieri village and its megalithic sanctuary, represented by the Great Menhir and the nearby Table of Sacrifice. The above four dates, which more or less coincide with those we know for the end of the Ozieri period, are basically accepted by my Sardinian colleagues and by me, but not by Tykot. If calibrated, they would fall 700 years before (3,750–3,630 BC) and therefore in what he considers the moment of maximum splendor of the entire classical Ozieri period. Tykot considers reliable the one date I considered dubious, while he suggests these early dates may be due to a possible "reuse of wood from the underlying Ozieri village", dates which most of us (including myself, with some reservations) believed reliable.

I continue to believe that Sardinia participated in the events and cultural evolution which took place in the countries of the Eastern Mediterranean during the Bronze Age. I therefore find it hard to imagine Sardinia as the focal point of Mediterranean civilization, until such time as the elements supporting this are based on radiocarbon dating alone. I might change my mind when, along with the dating, I am provided with a convincing explanation of the process which led to spreading of civilization in the opposite direction to the one which common sense and large quantities of data have suggested up to now.

But this is not all! An Ozieri village has been discovered underneath the oldest of the sanctuaries on Monte d'Accoddi, together with yet another village underneath this. Polished, light-colored pottery has been found here, with no decoration and with characteristic shapes completely different from those of the Ozieri (Tinè & Traverso 1992: table XXXIIIb). Fragments with pointillé decoration which appear to be associated with these also exist, possibly evidence of the existence of an even older village closer to the Bonu Ighinu facies, although this facies has yet to be confirmed at Monte d'Accoddi. It has been surmised that the village underneath developed autonomously in a facies between the Bonu Ighinu and the Ozieri. For this new facies of Sardinian prehistory, G. Ugas and V. Santoni have proposed the name "San Ciriaco". Evidence of it is found throughout the island, from Monte d'Accoddi in the Sassari area to Cuccuru S'Arriu in the Oristano area (Santoni et al. 1982) and Decimoputzu in the Cagliari area (Ugas 1990). Given the typical spindle-shaped handles found at Cuccuru S'Arriu, the most immediate comparisons with this pottery have been seen (and this is fundamental in my opinion) in the Diana-Bellavista-Skorba style, which characterized the final Neolithic period on the Italian mainland, Sicily and Malta.

In Sardinia, the San Ciriaco/Diana-Bellavista facies therefore appears to predate the Ozieri period and follow the Bonu Ighinu period. We do not have radiocarbon dating for the San Ciriaco horizon yet, but given its stratigraphic position, we may expect dates somewhere between the end of the Bonu Ighinu (3,730 uncal BC) and the start of the Ozieri (3,300 uncal BC), according to Tykot (1994).

We must ask ourselves whether this chronology is

acceptable for San Ciriaco, when radiocarbon dating for the corresponding facies on the Italian mainland, Sicily and Malta are after 3,225 uncal BC (Cardini 1957; Bernabò Brea & Cavalier 1980; Trump 1966).

Besides anything else, how is it possible to accept the idea that these last dates for the Diana/San Ciriaco facies in Sardinia almost coincide with those (3,300–2,800 BC) which are now attributed to the completely different Ozieri culture in Sardinia?

At this point, the unshakeable supporters of C14 will bring up standard deviation, the famous "±" or "σ" of calibration (possibly two), in order to give the largest possible space of time within which to place datings. For the period in question, taking a single σ into account, there is a 66% probability that the date falls within a time period of two centuries; with 2σ, there is a 95% probability that it falls within a period of approximately 500 years. Use of such wide periods will obviously be of little help in accurate chronological seriation of the facies in question. This takes us back in time to the old argument between those in favor of "raising" and those in favoring of "lowering", when in fact, both positions, without definite outside references, were equally tenable. I refuse to proceed in this direction, where everything is possible and reconcilable with one's own personal vision of events. I prefer to remain anchored to the sequence of cultures found using stratigraphy and supported by stylistic comparison (obviously within a reasonable geographical area). I will only accept absolute dates provided by C14 as indicative when they do not blatantly contradict the information already obtained using the above methods. I therefore refuse to change the sequence already consolidated simply because radiocarbon analysis has come up with a different picture.

In conclusion, and in answer to those who, on the basis of the vaguest chronological indications supplied by C14, propose a model which either completely reverses the direction of civilization or supports the idea of improbable autochthonous and autonomous civilizations, I have decided to remain with the few who fondly recall the old "*ex Oriente lux*" model. I shall wait patiently, refusing to be influenced by the fashionable theories of the moment (I noticed a few signs of doubt during the conference on which this volume is based, particularly from the "scientists", who as such are "less holy than the Pope", unlike my illustrious archaeological colleagues).

References

Bernabò Brea, L. & Cavalier, M. 1980. *Meligunis Lipara IV. L'acropoli di Lipari nella preistoria*. Palermo.

Cardini, L. 1970. Praia a Mare, Relazione degli scavi 1957–1970 dell'IIPU. *Bullettino di Paletnologia Italiana* 79: 31–54.

Castaldi, E. 1972. La datazione con il C-14 della Grotta del Guano o Gonagosula (Oliena-Nuoro). Considerazioni sulla cultura di Ozieri. *Archivio per l'Antropologia e la Etnologia* 102: 233–275.

Loria, D. & Trump, D.H. 1978. Le scoperte a "Sa 'Ucca de su Tintirriolu" e il neolitico sardo. *Monumenti Antichi* II(2)49. Accademia Nazionale dei Lincei, Rome.

Lo Schiavo, F. 1989. Le origini della metallurgia ed il problema della metallurgia nella cultura di Ozieri. In Campus, L.D. (a cura di), *La Cultura di Ozieri. Problematiche e nuove acquisizioni. Atti del I convegno di studio (Ozieri, gennaio 1986-aprile 1987)*: 279–292. Il Torchietto, Ozieri.

Santoni, V., Atzeni, E., Forresu, R., Giorgetti, S., Mongiu, M., Sebis, S., Siddu, A. & Tore, G. 1982. Cabras, Cuccuru S'Arriu. Nota preliminare di scavo (1978, 1979, 1980). *Rivista di Studi Fenici* 10(1): 103–127.

Tinè, S. & Traverso, A. 1992. *Monte d'Accoddi. 10 anni di nuovi scavi*. Genova.

Trump, D.H. 1966. *Skorba*. Society of Antiquarians of London Research Report 22. Oxford.

Tykot, R.H. 1994. Radiocarbon dating and absolute chronology in Sardinia and Corsica. In Skeates, R. & Whitehouse, R.D. (eds.), *Radiocarbon Dating and Italian Prehistory*. Accordia Specialist Studies on Italy 3: 115–145. Accordia Research Centre, University of London.

Ugas, G. 1990. *La tomba dei guerrieri di Decimoputzu*. Norax 1. Edizioni della Torre, Cagliari.

7. Mediterranean Chronology in Crisis

Peter James, Nikos Kokkinos and I. J. Thorpe

In 1990 E. Lipiński referred to a growing 'crisis' in West Semitic epigraphy. The focus of his discussion was the Nora Fragment from Sardinia, the 'crisis' springing from the serious divergence of opinion among palaeographers regarding its date – the 9th century BC according to Lipiński, but the 11th according to Cross. As Lipiński rightly stressed, the controversy over the Nora Fragment should be seen in the broader context of numerous related epigraphic tangles from the same time range. The inscribed bowl found at Tekke in Crete has created similar difficulties. Its date, originally published as c. 900 BC, was raised by Cross (1986: 125–126, n.12) to the 11th century. As it was found with Attic Late Protogeometric vessels (generally dated to the late 10th century BC), Cross suggested that PG chronology should be raised as a whole. At Tell Fakhariyah in northern Mesopotamia we have the disturbing anomaly of an Aramaic inscription, dated by most palaeographers to the 11th century (see James *et al.* 1991a: 276–277), on the statue of an official dated by Assyriologists to the mid-9th century (Millard 1993).[1] There also remains the classic puzzle of the origins of the Greek alphabet: the forms of the 8th-century Greek letters seem to resemble most closely those of the Proto-Canaanite alphabet of three centuries earlier (James *et al.* 1987: 24–25; 1991a: 81–85).

There is a strange whiff of unreality to these problems. Our approach is that there is no need to take sides regarding whether the script of the Nora Fragment belongs to the 11th or 9th centuries: *both sides may be partly right*. Instead, the debate should be widened even further, taking into account many similar tensions in Mediterranean archaeology across the same centuries. These suggest that it is *chronology*, rather than palaeography, that is in crisis. A solution to the dilemma seems to lie in shortening the overall chronological framework for the Late Bronze and Early Iron Age in the Old World, which is still ultimately dependent on the accepted chronology for Egypt. This approach may be controversial, but we are pleased to note that the proposals we made, initially in a monograph in 1987 and then in expanded book form in 1991, are attracting increasing support from new research and discoveries.

Archaeologists working in the Central Mediterranean and Aegean may not be fully aware of the critical stage which the arguments over the dating of Palestinian stratigraphy – central to the epigraphic puzzles – have now reached. W. Dever (1990: 127) remarked: 'How can we know *anything* with certainty about the past (in this case, ancient Palestine and Israel), if we cannot even date the major phases of historical and cultural development within a margin of a century or less?' Indeed – and the problem is worse than Dever imagines. For example, with regard to Edom, southern Jordan, we now find two polarized schools of thought: one (Bienkowski 1992a; 1992b) insisting that the earliest Iron Age settlements date no earlier than the end of the 9th century, the other (Finkelstein 1992a; 1992b) placing them as early as the 12th-11th century, on the basis of parallels with Israelite pottery.

Rethinking of the conventional chronology for the Israelite Iron Age has been prompted by the recent discovery of a 9th-century Aramaean stele at Tel Dan (Biran & Naveh 1993). Fragments of the inscription were re-used in Stratum III (mid-9th to early 8th century) according to the excavator Biran, but Chapman's analysis (1993–94) has argued that it was actually re-used in a gateway belonging to Stratum IV. Given this, Chapman (1994: 4) notes:

> ... it would necessitate a reconsideration of the dating of the ceramic assemblage of that stratum from 1050–950 BC (Stratum IVB), 950–883 BC (Stratum IVA), with the initial date being lowered to at least 883 BC for whichever of these phases

---

Peter James, c/o Artellus, 30 Dorset House, Gloucester Place, London NW1 5AD, England; Nikos Kokkinos, Institute of Archaeology, University College London, 31–34 Gordon Square, London WC1H 0PY, England; I. J. Thorpe, Department of Archaeology, King Alfred's College Winchester, Winchester SO22 4NR, England

marks the construction of the gate containing the inscription. Should such a chronological revision be required at Dan, it would also be required at all other sites which have been placed in the same archaeological horizon on the basis of their ceramic assemblages.

Palaeographic and historical analysis (e.g. Lemaire 1994; cf. Halpern 1994), evidently confirmed by the discovery of new fragments (Biran & Naveh 1995), has now shown that the stele actually dates from c. 800 BC, meaning that Chapman's *terminus post quem* for the construction of the Level IV gateway should be reduced even more.

Further waves are certain to be created by the find of a late PG 'bowl krater' at Tel Hadar in northern Israel (Kopcke forthcoming; cf. Waldbaum 1994: 57). It came from a sealed context in a level which the excavators believe was destroyed 'sometime in the 11th century' (Kochavi 1993: 551), yet according to the accepted PG chronology such vessels should date to c. 900 BC or later. The find has been welcomed by those who wish to raise the dates of Aegean 'Dark Age' chronology (see Morris, this volume), placing the beginning of Protogeometric at ca. 1100 or even earlier. The fallouts of such a revision would be extraordinary. The start of Early Geometric would have to be raised to c. 1000 BC. Long ago Desborough (1957: 218) warned of the consequences when a similar attempt was made to raise Aegean dates by strict adherence to a 'high' chronology based on Palestine (via Cyprus). While, we might, with Morris, question the existence of Submycenaean as a separate phase, the massive lengthening of the Early and Middle Geometric phases entailed is as unacceptable now as it was in Desborough's time – even more so given that Morris, echoing our criticisms of the Near Eastern 'fixed points' for Greek chronology, is happy to *lower* the dates for the Late Geometric. The extension of the Geometric to over three centuries (from its present two) will only attenuate further the limited material available for the interpretation of Greek 'Dark Age' culture. It seems clear that the vast majority of Aegean and Cypriot archaeologists will reject these proposals. The alternative solution is, of course, to lower the dates for Israelite archaeology.

Light on these interminable 11th-9th century controversies can be shed by proceeding from the known to the unknown, working backwards from the more securely dated archaeological sequences of the late 8th to early 7th centuries. In particular, continuing work in Phoenicia, Cyprus and Carthage over the last twenty years has sharply focussed a 'Cypro-Phoenician' pottery horizon which is firmly dated and can be used as a control over the dating of related, earlier, periods.

The Cypro-Phoenician Horizon

Though limited, the excavation of Tyre by Bikai in 1973–74 provided an Iron Age ceramic sequence – confirmed since by other excavations, notably at Sarepta – which is of vital importance for Mediterranean chronology. The discovery of an inscribed Egyptian urn of the late 25th or 26th Dynasty in the closing stage of Stratum III, sets the end of this stratum no earlier than 725 BC, or possibly later, according to Bikai (1987: 69; cf. 1978a: 68; 1978b: 47; 1981: 33; James *et al.* 1991a: 108).[2] The absolute date for the close of Stratum III is corroborated by the discovery of associated pottery of the Cypro-Archaic I period (Bikai 1978b: 47), initially dated by Gjerstad to 700–600 BC, and revised by Karageorghis to 750–600 BC (see James *et al.* 1991a: 152–153). The chronology of Cypro-Archaic I is itself fixed by synchronisms with approximately secure evidence from Greece (Late Geometric), by influences from safely dated Assyrian material and, again, by finds of Egyptian origin. For example, many scarabs of the precisely-dated 26th Dynasty (664–525 BC), found on the floor of the Period 4 sanctuary at Ayia Irini together with Cypriot Period IV wares, unquestionably set the middle of Archaic I (i.e. CAIA to CAIB) around 650 BC (see James *et al.* 1991a: 367, n. 37). Further corroboration comes from Carthage, where the earliest local pottery is associated with material akin to Tyre III–II (Bikai 1978: 54–55). Lancel's current summary of the archaeological evidence (1995: 25–34, 43, 67–70; cf. Køllund in this volume) shows without doubt that the earliest trace of habitation (tombs, *tophet* and domestic settlements) date to the late 8th/early 7th centuries: firm limits are set by the presence of a substantial amount of Greek pottery, and large numbers of Egyptian amulets and scarabs.[3]

As a result, many characteristic shapes and forms of later Phoenician ceramics – such as the Crisp-Ware storage jars and the Fine Ware plates – can thus now be confidently placed within relatively narrow time margins and used as a chronological index for sites from the East to the West Mediterranean. For example, Tyrian storage jars (so-called 'Torpedo jars'), *should* help to date archaeological strata in Israel. However, Geva (1982) questioned their Phoenician origin solely on the grounds that they appear earlier in Israel, notably in the 9th-century Stratum VII at Hazor. Bikai (1985) firmly objected to this early date and defended the Phoenician origin of these jars, which are found in great numbers at Tyre III in a pottery manufacturing area of the second half of the 8th century BC. The logical thing to do, clearly, would be to lower the chronology of Hazor VII and associated levels at other sites.

The same tension between Cypro-Phoenician and Israelite chronologies lies behind the conflict over the dating of Black-on-Red Ware. Using the firm dates for the second phase of Black-on-Red in the Cypriot Period IV (750/700–600 BC), Gjerstad – on the basis of a statistical method involving numerous sites on the island – set the beginning of the first phase of Black-on-Red no earlier than 850 BC. Naturally, the occurrence of Black-on-Red I in Palestinian contexts dated by local chronology to the 11th-10th centuries created pandemonium. The well-known debate between Gjerstad and Albright/Van Beek, raging since the 1940s, has never been resolved (James *et al.* 1987: 53–57; 1991a: 155–161). As Sörensen (1993: 18) remarked in response to our work: 'Some of the finds from Palestine appear indeed to match the finds from Cyprus to perfection, and a discrepancy of several centuries is disturbing.' The problem is highlighted by the conclusions of the excavators of Tel Mevorakh and Tel Qiri in Israel: the 'solution' at Tel Mevorakh was to introduce a four-century hiatus into the site's chronology, and at Tel Qiri to reject the dates offered by Cyprus. Recently, at Tel Dor, Gilboa (1989: 211, n. 14) simply chose to temporarily exclude Black-on-Red finds from publication, concentrating on what she classified as earlier pottery of Cypriot Geometric origin:

> We have not included in this list the Cypriot Black-on-Red vessels: their occurrence outside Cyprus seems to represent a different phenomenon [*sic*]. Their initial appearance, moreover, both on Cyprus and the mainland, is later than that of the other decorated Cypro-Geometric groups. The non-Cypriot Black-on-Red vessels [*sic*] do not concern us here [*sic*].[4]

Even if one takes the extraordinary step of ignoring the Black-on-Red finds, the other Cypriot material from Tel Dor raises many questions. Gilboa published three 'early' Cypro-Geometric fragments from Phase 9 (dated by local pottery to 1050–980 BC): a White Painted I amphoriskos, a White Painted bowl, and a Bichrome bowl. Yet it seems certain that the bowls (both of which she describes as 'advanced') are much closer to White Painted II types rather than to I. This would date them not earlier than c. 900 BC, and almost a century later than the closing date of Phase 9. One can see why, therefore, the Philistine sherds uncovered in the same context could not 'be ascribed with confidence to Phase 9' (Gilboa 1989: 205). It was precisely the occurrence of Cypro-Geometric pottery together with 'Philistine Ware' in Palestinian sites which sparked off the chronological argument between Van Beek and Gjerstad.

The Black-on-Red Ware controversy embroils the long-standing debate over the chronology of the Israelite capital of Samaria. Kenyon assigned the construction of the site to the time of King Omri (888–877 BC) – known from the Old Testament as the founder of Samaria – and, as the earliest pottery includes early Black-on-Red, her dates were broadly consistent with Gjerstad's. Wright, however, insisted that Samaria Pottery Periods 1 and 2 should date to the 10th century (and precede the Omride palace), a view which attracted increasing support among American and Israeli archaeologists. The Kenyon-Wright controversy has been simmering since the 1950s (James *et al.* 1991a: 183–185), and was recently the centre-piece of a major debate as to whether the archaeological levels in Israel deemed to be 'Solomonic' (10th century) are really 'Ahabic' (9th century BC), or vice versa (see especially Stager 1990; Wightman 1990). Tappy, after a detailed analysis of the finds from Samaria, has now plumped for a 'high' chronology, dating Pottery Period 1 in the 11th century. In doing so, he (1992: 131–132) accused Kenyon of blindly following Cypro-Phoenician 'low' dating. Tappy's mentor Stager (1990: 103) had already pinned the problem down well:

> ... A surprise number of types (of pottery from Samaria Periods I and II) ... has its most impressive parallels from Megiddo Strata VII–VI, Taanach Strata IA, IB, IIA, and Tell Qasile Strata XI–X, *where those types overlap with Philistine painted pottery, which cannot be dated much later than ca. 1000 B.C.*

The question is: on what basis has 'Philistine' pottery been dated so accurately? The answer, of course, is the hitherto generally accepted Egyptian chronology (via Mycenaean pottery styles, serving as a prototype to Philistine). But as this can now legitimately be thrown into doubt, the alternative is clear: in assessing Samaria, the Cypro-Phoenician low dating should be preferred.

Indeed, even Kenyon's much debated low dates for Samaria seem to be too high (James *et al.* 1991a: 187, tab. 8:2; see also now Forsberg 1995: 49–50). For example, it is clear that the so-called 'Samaria Bowls B', of the kind known from Tyre V–IV as Fine Ware plates (Class 2.1), begin in Pottery Period 3 (Crowfoot *et al.* 1957: 157; Tappy 1992: 159, *contra* Bikai 1978b: 52–53). This type is dated at Tyre c. 800/760–750/740 at the earliest (Bikai 1978b: 52; cf. 1981: 33–34; 1987: 69). Yet, Pottery Period 3 was dated by Kenyon to the time of King Jehu (842–816 BC), and Tappy has allocated the earliest Fine Ware bowl, on stratigraphic grounds, to the reign of Omri (888–877 BC) – impossible in view of Bikai's dates for Tyre.

The tension between Israelite and Cypro-Phoenician chronologies has now come to a head at Rosh Zayit in Galilee. Gal (1992a: 184) decided to date the destruction of this short-lived site to the middle of the 9th century, on the basis of an entirely hypothetical connection with the campaign of the Assyrian king Shalmaneser III in 841 BC. Fudging some of his local pottery, which according to Palestinian typology would date to the 10th century, but to the late 9th according to Phoenician (Gal 1992a: 175), he went on to analyse the Cypriot imports, claiming, not uncharacteristically, that Cypriot dating is too low. Indeed, Black-on-Red I does not begin before 850 BC, and some of the examples Gal illustrates (fig. 5, nos. 9–12) may well belong to the Black-on-Red II phase, conventionally dated no earlier than 750 BC!

Gal's conclusion is that there is a need to revise a large part of Tyrian chronology *upwards*. But he is confused regarding the real consequences that Cypro-Phoenician dating has for Palestinian archaeology. While raising the dates for Tyre XI–VI, Gal (1992a: 184; 1992b: 73–74) also lowers IV–I to post-700 BC! Such lowering might be welcome, but it has to be applied throughout in a consistent fashion – the 'Fine Ware plates' which Gal (1992a: 182, fig. 9:1; 1992b: 51, no. 2) claimed not to *postdate* the mid-9th century at Rosh Zayit, are now also claimed by him not to *predate* the 7th century at Tyre!

No amount of mental gymnastics will get Palestinian chronology out of the mess in which it presently rests. There is a clear need to perceive the situation from a broader perspective, taking in the extraordinary range of problems we have documented affecting areas as widely separated as Greece, Sicily, Libya, Nubia, Edom and ultimately Egypt itself, the source of the accepted dates for the Palestinian Iron Age.

The Egyptian Third Intermediate Period

The fragile nature of the chronology of the Egyptian 'Third Intermediate Period' (c. 1070–664 BC), which precedes the well-established era of the 26th Dynasty, cannot be overstressed. The evidence on which the 21st Dynasty has been reconstructed is particularly slender (James & Morkot forthcoming). It presently occupies 125 years of history (1070–945 BC), covering much of the problematic area under discussion, yet the full gamut of its materials has been summarised by Niwinski (1988: 37–38) in less than one page: burials of kings, high priests, and their families; a few official scenes with inscriptions; and a handful of letters and papyri. In all other respects this 125-year slice of Egyptian history is a mysterious grey area. Records for burials of the sacred Apis bulls, known from the 20th and 22nd dynasties, are completely missing for the 21st. Likewise, as Bierbrier (1975: 45) notes:

> With the advent of Dynasty XXI the copious sources of information which were available in the previous two dynasties vanish. Administrative papyri and ostraca prove practically non-existent. Votive statuary would seem to disappear almost totally. Graffiti and inscriptions decline to a few badly preserved examples... because of this dearth of material, it is not possible as in Dynasty XIX and Dynasty XX to present a coherent outline of the descent of various families and their interrelations.

Plentiful source material on private individuals, in the form of votive statues and administrative documents, reappears under the following 22nd Dynasty (Bierbrier 1975, 54). This includes two genealogies which stretch back to the 19th. These (the genealogies of the priests of Memphis and Ankhefenkhons) have given particular trouble to Egyptologists because they are *too short* to cover the 125 years required for the 21st Dynasty on the conventional chronology – so it is assumed (Kitchen 1986: 189–192; Bierbrier 1975: 51–53; see James *et al.* 1991a: 238–242) that six to seven and three to four generations respectively were accidentally omitted by the scribes drawing up the documents!

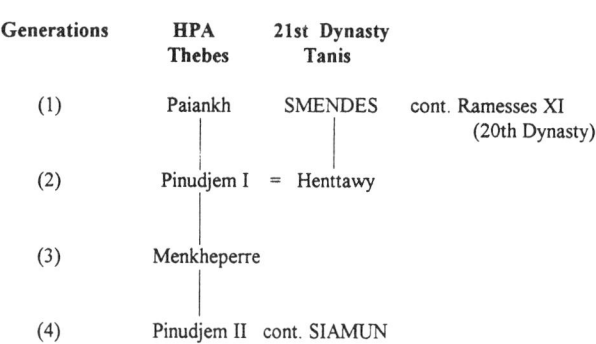

Figure 7.1. Genealogy of 21st-dynasty High Priests of Amun (HP As) at Thebes, as known from contemporary evidence. Links with the 21st-dynasty kings ruling at Tanis are shown to the right.

Such an attitude, that the primary evidence must be faulty because it does not fit the accepted model, surfaces again with respect to the royal genealogy for this Dynasty. Actually, there is *no* royal genealogy. The nearest thing we have is a sequence for the High Priests of Amun at Thebes – closely interlinked with the kings at Tanis – which provides the backbone for its internal chronology. The High Priests' genealogy, reconstructed from contemporary documents, occupies four generations (Fig. 7.1). This can be instructively compared with the reconstruction provided by Kitchen, doyen of TIP chronology (Fig. 7.2): by using a stream of entirely hypothetical links, the 21st-Dynasty kings known from the monuments are strung into a neat succession, with the result that a full five generations (i.e. approximately 125 years) are made to separate Ramesses XI, last ruler of the 20th, from Shoshenq I, first ruler of the 22nd. Yet it is known from several documents that the first generation, Paiankh and Smendes, were already mature and in office by the end of Ramesses XI's reign. At the end of the 21st, a pattern of genealogical evidence (Fig. 7.3) shows that Pharaoh Siamun (from generation 4) must actually have been of the same generation as the second ruler (Osorkon I) of the succeeding 22nd (James & Morkot forthcoming). This means that as well as an overlap of one generation between the late 20th and early 21st, there was also a substantial overlap of some two generations between the late 21st and the early 22nd. (The chronological overlapping of dynasties, ruling from different centres in Egypt, was a common phenomenon in the TIP). In short, the time when the 21st Dynasty ruled as an independent entity can be whittled down to one generation (time of Pinudjem I), say about 25 years. There is nothing to prevent its chronology being reduced by a clear century.[5]

Why, then, was the 21st Dynasty allocated 125 years in the first place? It was clearly *not* on the evidence from the monuments. The succession and regnal years of its kings actually come from the extant fragments of the hellenistic Egyptian priest Manetho. He is now scrupulously shunned as a source by Egyptologists, except, it

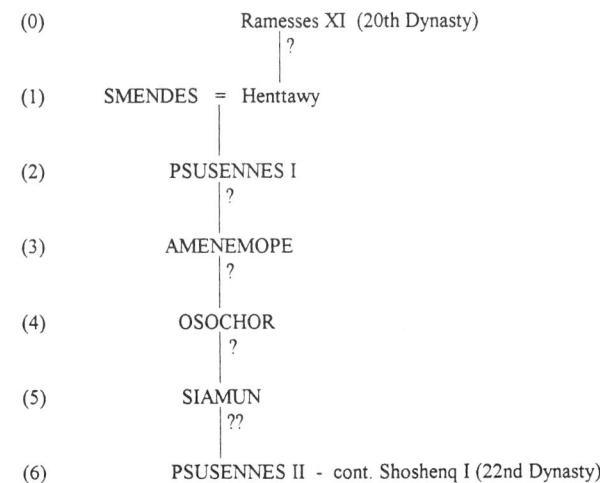

Figure 7.2. Royal 21st-dynasty genealogy from Kitchen 1986. The question marks are Kitchen's.

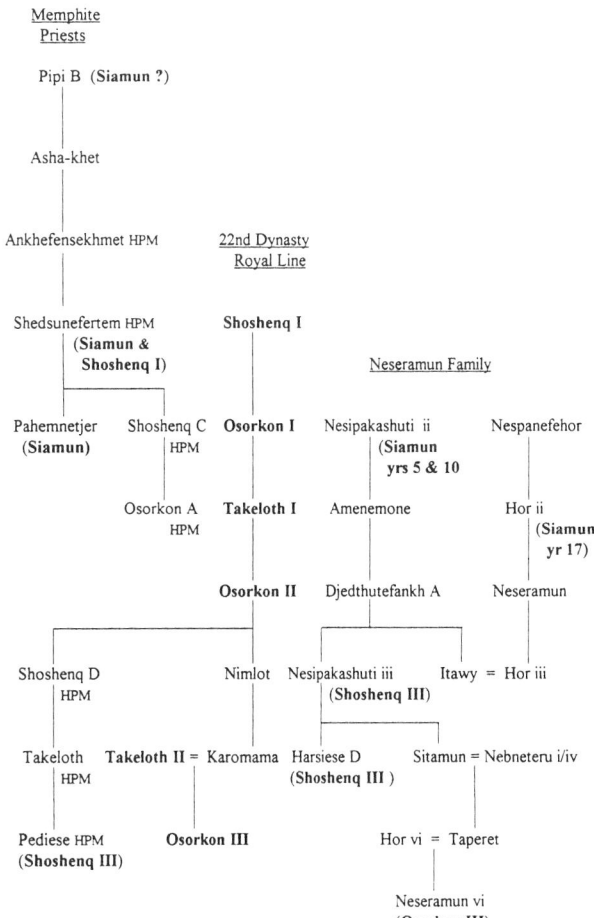

Figure 7.3. TIP genealogies showing the placement of King Siamun of the 21st Dynasty. Royal names are shown in **bold** letters. Kings known to be contemporary with individuals in the genealogies follow their names in brackets. HPM=High Priest at Memphis.

seems, when he helps to fill in grey areas. As for its absolute chronology, its beginning is set by the date, c. 1070 BC, for the end of the 20th Dynasty, which is calculated by dead reckoning forward from the 18th Dynasty. This, in turn, is placed c. 1525–1300 BC on the basis of a supposed fix provided by astronomical or Sothic dating. The theory of Sothic dating is rarely taught to Egyptologists, and hence rarely understood by them. Those that do understand it are generally more critical, even of the primary evidence on which it is based. For example Helck (1989: 40–41) has demonstrated that the 'Sothic date' which has been read into the Ebers Papyrus, supposedly fixing the beginning of the 18th Dynasty, is illusory. In the absence of the Ebers Papyrus reference, the chronology of New Kingdom Egypt is left dangling by a thread from the second major 'astronomical' point, ostensibly provided by the Illahun Papyrus of the 12th Dynasty (Middle Kingdom). Even if this document could provide a usable date,[6] it hardly provides a meaningful *terminus post quem* for the New Kingdom as the length of the 'Second Intermediate Period' (or 'Hyksos Period') is still unknown. In other words, there is no real astronomical dating for the 18th Dynasty and the New Kingdom as a whole.

Few Egyptologists today are prepared to defend the validity of Sothic chronology. In lieu of the supposed astronomical fixes, the claim is now being made that dead-reckoning *back* from the established dates of the Nubian (25th) and Saite (26th) dynasties of the early 7th century arrives at the same results (e.g. Kitchen 1991a; Kitchen 1991b: 236; cf. Bietak 1989: 91). This claim is a myth. All that has really been done is to fill a preconceived framework. The real linch-pin of TIP chronology is provided by the identification of Shoshenq I, founder of the 22nd Dynasty, with the 'King Shishak', who looted Solomon's Temple, around 925 BC on Biblical chronology. As a text at Karnak dated to Shoshenq I's 21st year records a campaign in Palestine, the beginning of his reign (and consequently the beginning of the 22nd Dynasty and end of the 'preceding' 21st) is set at 945 BC. Hughes (1990: 192) clearly realized this: 'Egyptian chronologists, without always admitting it, have commonly based their chronology of this period on the *Biblical* synchronism for Shoshenq's invasion.' Yet there is no real resemblance between the geography of Shoshenq's Palestinian campaign (largely restricted to Israel) and the biblical account of Shishak's invasion of Judah. The biblical Shishak story also contains a conspicuously Ramesside element (the Tjukten/Sukkiim troops) which seems anomalous in a 22nd-dynasty context (James *et al.* 1992: 127). The other side of the coin is that acceptance of such an early date for Shoshenq I has forced the rejection of a perfectly good synchronism between Shipitbaal of the Byblite inscriptions (whose grandfather was a contemporary of Shoshenq I) with the Shipitbaal of

Byblos mentioned in Assyrian records, c. 740 BC (Mazar 1986: 231–247; James *et al.* 1991a: 250; 1992: 233). Criticism of our case against the identification of Shishak with Shoshenq I has, apart from sheer mis-statements of fact (James *et al.* 1992: 127; James & Morkot forthcoming), amounted to simple repetition of the commonplace that the name Shoshenq makes a good philological match with 'Shishak'.

It is a frightening prospect that Cypriot and Greek archaeologists are now being asked to raise their dates by reference to a Palestinian chronology which is based on the Egyptian. This Egyptian chronology is not based on astronomical evidence, not based on genealogical or contemporary inscriptional evidence, and not based on dead-reckoning back from the known 7th century, but on faith in a single identification with a biblical character – and with that, faith in the veracity of the biblical verse in question, with no respect to source criticism. The whole of TIP chronology – and, incidentally, the dates for early Phoenician palaeography – ultimately rests on the belief that the deuteronomist, who prepared his text no earlier than the 6th century BC – possessed the correct orthography of a Pharaoh's name from some four centuries earlier (James *et al.* 1992: 127).

Because of this act of faith nothing is allowed to shift. Yet it is already clear that various students of TIP chronology have admitted, albeit individually and in a piecemeal fashion, that it needs considerable revision. For example, we proposed (James *et al.* 1991a: 230, 235) that Kitchen's date of 716 BC (ultimately based on a mistranslation) for the accession of Shabago (25th Dynasty) can be lowered to as late as 708/707 BC. A study published by Depudyt (1993) now gives the same date (with no acknowledgment), with a consequent lowering of that for Piye's invasion of Egypt (Kitchen: 728 BC) by 19 years. (We would also argue a figure of this order.) As Piye's conquest of the Egyptian Delta is the benchmark from which all earlier reigns are calculated, lowering its date by 19 years would require an equivalent reduction in all TIP dates. Add to this Aston's demonstration (1989) that there was a 20-year overlap between Takeloth II and Shoshenq III (22nd Dynasty), and Dodson's (1987) that an independent reign of 14 years for Psusennes II (21st Dynasty) should be scrapped, and we already have more than fifty years which Egyptologists – by their own admission – are prepared to remove from TIP chronology. Indeed Dodson (1992) and Ray (1992) have allowed that the New Kingdom can be lowered by some fifty years. We should be grateful for small mercies. This reduction might be well received by archaeologists of the Eastern Mediterranean who have been struggling over the last century to fit their material into an Egyptian framework. Much more dead wood, however, should be cut. As we have seen, the real length of the 21st Dynasty as an independent chronological unit may be a full century shorter than is currently supposed. Further lowering of New Kingdom chronology can be effected up to an absolute maximum (and possible optimum) of 250 years – with a consequent lowering of Eastern Mediterranean Late Bronze Age chronology of the same scale. The problematic 'Dark Ages' of Greece, Anatolia, Nubia, the Levant and other regions would largely melt away.

Central Mediterranean Chronology

Such a revision would only have beneficial results for the Central Mediterranean. The accepted scenario was summarized frankly by Colin Renfrew, in the foreword he wrote to *Centuries of Darkness*:

> It is already widely known that the chronology for early Italy, during the Iron Age period, down to and including the foundation of Rome, is a complete shambles. Swedish scholars debate with Italian scholars over dates which may differ by as much as two centuries.

We have drawn attention to the fact that these contentious two centuries may simply not have existed – they can be seen as an artefact produced by reliance on Mycenaean chronology, which is in turn based on an incorrect Egyptian chronology.

For Sicily we argued that dependence on the 13th-century dates provided by Mycenaean links for the Thapsos culture has produced an attenuated and unnecessarily long sequence of phases for the Late Bronze to Iron Age (c. 1250–650 BC). In particular we suggested that the Pantalica III ('South') phase, which currently intervenes between Cassibile (Pantalica II) and the Early Colonial (Finocchito) phases, should be scrapped as an independent period. On a number of grounds it seemed logical to see Cassibile (currently dated c. 1000–850 BC) lowered to meet the time of the earliest Greek colonies and the start of the Finocchito, c. 735 BC. This step would, at a stroke, remove some 120 years from the 'Dark Age' of Sicily. We suggested further telescoping, by the overlapping and shortening of earlier periods in the 'Dark Age' sequence – for example there seems to have been a considerable overlap between the Thapsos culture and the Pantalica I ('North') phase.

We are pleased to see that Leighton (1993) has considered the broad consequences of our model for Sicily and noted that:

> The relative sequence and stratigraphy of settlement occupation would be unaltered, and it would become even easier to believe in uninterrupted Aegean and East Mediterranean contacts with Sicily (and the West Mediterranean) from Mycenaean times until the colonial period, by closing the gap which coincides with the Greek Dark Age.

While Leighton does not agree with the overall lowering we argued for Bronze Age chronology – preferring to wait and see what happens with the Mycenaean dates –

he accepted some of the overlaps we argued in an attempt to move away from the 'chest-of-drawers' model for the Sicilian 'Dark Age'. He agreed that it is 'increasingly likely' that the Pantalica I ('North') phase did overlap with the preceding one of Thapsos. He also accepted our argument that the Cassibile culture continued until the time of the Greek colonisation in the mid to late 8th century, and in so doing provided more arguments in support of our case for scrapping Pantalica III ('South') as an independent phase. Leighton suggested that much of the Pantalica South material could be contemporary with the Finocchito/Early Colonial period (c. 735–650 BC), as some of the pottery from the Pantalica South necropolis seems to betray knowledge of early Greek colonial wares.[7] He also considers reducing the date of the Ausonian abandonment of Lipari from 900/850 BC to the mid-8th century, which would be in step with our reduction of the related Cassibile period.

The problem with Leighton's otherwise welcome approach is that, by lowering the date of the end of Cassibile (and related Ausonian) at one end of the scale and by raising the starting point of Pantalica I at the other, he is merely lengthening the 'Dark Age'. The evidence from all other areas of the Mediterranean – and from Italy itself – strongly suggests that this period should actually be shortened, by effecting a considerable lowering of the traditional dates for the Bronze Age. It would be instructive to see what would result if archaeologists of the Central Mediterranean held the dates they receive from the Aegean and further east *sub judice* and developed independent chronologies, based on local stratigraphy and fixed by ^{14}C dating.

Unfortunately, the application of radiocarbon to the problems of Central Mediterranean archaeology has yet to begin in earnest. A trickle of dates continues to accumulate, but generally in an undirected and random fashion. The attitude taken by many archaeologists working in this area towards the use of radiocarbon dates also continues to be a cause of concern, particularly their lack of awareness of the crucial importance of good quality samples. A case in point is the chronological treatment of the evidence from the recent excavations at Contrada Scirinda in southwestern Sicily. A *single* ^{14}C determination of 460 ± 90 bc (A-5446), with a supposed calibrated result of 764–679 BC (at 1σ), is used by Castellana (1993: 49) to date Phase VI of the site to the 8th century BC. This is held to support his dating of the earlier phases, which is based on associations with eastern Sicily and the Lipari islands; for example, the preceding Phase V, linked to Ausonian II, is placed in the 9th century. The result is held to contradict the lower chronology we advocated (Maniscalco & McConnell 1993: 43). Unfortunately, Castellana's interpretation is both illogical and uncritical. First, sweeping conclusions must never be drawn from a single determination. Second, even if the ^{14}C date came from a well-contexted short-lived sample, the *terminus ante quem* for Phase V would of course be 680 BC, not 'the 8th century'. Third, if the date were to be calibrated in the now preferred way, at 2σ (using the Stuiver 1993 curve), it would fall in the range 800–200 BC, allowing for a much later dating for Phase VI.

As we noted (James *et al.* 1991a: 42–47), the dating of Sardinian archaeology for the same time range remains equally uncertain. The Phoenician connection with Sardinia, which acts to tie the Early Iron Age chronology of the island to the Eastern Mediterranean, has recently been revived by examination of the pottery from the tomb of Tekke in Crete (where the controversial bronze bowl with a Phoenician inscription was found). That there were two burials in the tomb is widely accepted, although their dating is less secure and ranges between 950 and 680 BC (Boardman 1967; Coldstream 1982; Vagnetti 1989). Among the pottery is a small jug (*askos*) decorated with concentric circles and horizontal lines. This has been identified by Vagnetti (1989) as a Late Nuragic vessel, a type with an apparently long time-span in Sardinia itself, running from the Final Bronze to Early Iron Age (in Tykot's chronology 12th-8th centuries BC). Outside Sardinia, these jugs are also found on Lipari in Ausonian II levels (conventionally 12th-9th centuries BC) and in Villanovan (9th-8th centuries) contexts in Italy; Køllund (this volume) has reported three askos fragments in 7th-century levels from Carthage, which she interprets as residual pieces. Of the known exported examples only that from Kommos (Watrous in this volume) can be used to support an early date within the time-range given in Sardinia itself.

Slight though this evidence is, it may act as a corrective to the recent trend in Sardinian studies to push back the dating of Nuragic civilization. In particular, a single calibrated date (2888–1520 BC) from Brunku Madugui was used to date the *floruit* of Nuragic developments (understood as Nuragic II/Sardinian Late Bronze Age) to the mid 2nd millennium BC (e.g. Lilliu 1988: 18). More cautious opinions are beginning to prevail as further dates with much smaller standard deviations have been produced, and current feeling is that *nuraghi* begin to be constructed around 1600 BC, reaching their height of development between 1300 and 1150 BC (Ugas 1992; Tykot 1994). This is far closer to the chronology we proposed (James *et al.* 1991a: 44), with the Sardinian Late Bronze Age ending c. 1000 BC – a date which ^{14}C results would accomodate quite happily. Although there are now many more radiocarbon dates available, there are few sites with good date sequences, and even fewer where they have been fully published with an assessment of their stratigraphic integrity. Hence the broad measure of uncertainty noted by Balmuth (1993: 39), who jokingly suggested that Nuragic dates change on an almost daily basis.

This still leaves the Early Iron Age (Nuragic IV) use of *nuraghi* curiously unclear. At Serucci three ^{14}C dates come from the final use of one of the 'Chambers' making up the village (Balmuth 1992: 679–680); all are on charcoal, and when calibrated at 2σ range from 1266 to 800 BC (Tykot 1994: 132). Judging by the brief account of the context from which the samples were taken, it seems likely that this broad date range does not truly reflect the chronological spread of activity, but rather results from the use of charcoal with its well established 'old wood' effect (see below).

Even with new findings, the early stages of the Phoenician phase of Sardinian history remain extremely difficult to detect. The claims for a Phoenician presence in Sardinia towards the beginning of the first millennium BC, based on one interpretation of the Nora inscriptions and the Tekke jug, still await confirmation by stratified archaeological evidence. The earlier dates ascribed to the Iron Age *nuraghi*, and thus the bronze figurines (of possible Phoenician inspiration) they contain have been cited by Balmuth (1992: 690–691; 1993) in support of the high date for a Phoenician presence, but the dating for this material is still far from secure, as we have seen. As recent reviews by Balmuth (1992) and Negbi (1992) make it clear, there is no new, direct, evidence to support the high dates proposed for the arrival of the Phoenicians in Sardinia, only the knock-on effect of raising the overall Nuragic dates, a trend which is now in reverse.

Radiocarbon Dating of the Aegean

In *Centuries of Darkness* we advanced the theory that the end of LHIIIC in the Aegean needs to be lowered from c. 1075 to c. 900 BC (James *et al.* 1991a: 111). In his otherwise favourable reviews, Snodgrass (1991a; 1991b) stated that the currently available radiocarbon dates from the Aegean create a problem – but without quantifying. This position was taken further by Manning and Weninger (1992: 637), who claimed that the ^{14}C record actually demonstrates that our proposal is 'impossible'. Their claim, while it has been cited approvingly (e.g. Dickinson 1994: 17), is fallacious, being based on a poor understanding of the archaeological significance of the radiocarbon results.

On a general level, Manning and Weninger's approach to logical debate is very loose. Something can be deemed 'impossible' only if there is contrary evidence of absolute certainty – not through arguments based on supposed probabilities or guesswork. In discussing ^{14}C dates, they often forget what *terminus post quem* really means, a particularly acute problem when dealing with long-lived samples, as well as underestimating other problems of interpretation. Despite acknowledging some well-known caveats, they utilize any available results (some going back to the 1950s!) with little regard for source criticism. Archaeology, however, is primarily about context and association – not inventive statistics. As Jope (1986: 1060) noted when discussing the 'stringent credentials' necessary for a sound ^{14}C determination:

No amount of statistical manipulation will yield calendric dates of meaningful accuracy out of data from samples that do not meet these requirements.

Manning and Weninger collected 109 determinations, of extremely variable quality (and not always pertinent to the dating of the close of the Aegean LBA). Only ten came from short-lived material. Thus, from the outset one could argue that 90% of the figures embroiled in their presentation can be discarded. What, then, of the ten short-lived samples? Again, five (Bln-2658, P-2046, OxA-2096, 2097, 2098) are, strictly speaking, irrelevant as they belong to earlier periods. Of the remaining five (P-760, KI-1784, St-1267, St-1549, OxA-146) only two are results produced after 1980, one of which has a calibrated error of ± 169 years (OxA-146)! In a sense M & W's case rests on a single result, with a calibrated error of ± 102 years (KI-1784). The sample is a chestnut from Phase 10 of Kastanas, giving a date of 1134–930 BC as calibrated by Weninger at 1σ (and 1210–840 BC at 2σ, using the Stuiver 1993 curve). Phase 10 belongs to the beginning of the PG, conventionally dated to c. 1050 BC, on our chronology c. 900/875 BC. Evidently no verdict is possible.

It is not normal practice in the interpretation of ^{14}C dates to reach sweeping conclusions from such a poor set of data. Indeed, it is surprising that an antiquated approach of this kind could still be adopted in the 1990s. Numerous pleas for intelligent caution have been made; for example, Whittle (1990: 301), citing a paper co-written by one of the authors of *Centuries of Darkness*, predicts that 'the next radiocarbon revolution will be very closely to scrutinize the contexts, associations and compositions of samples (Kinnes & Thorpe 1986)...' Aside from the familiar problems at laboratory level, concerning individual samples (contamination; lack of pretreatment; undersize; ^{13}C normalization; environmental effects from volcanos, seas, lakes and rivers; etc), we must remember four other areas of uncertainty:

1. Interlaboratory differences, which have been been reported as being as great as '310 to 730 years' (Scott *et al.* 1990: 319);

2. The 'publishing filter' – as it might be described – is rarely discussed in print, but it is well known that a number of radiocarbon results not suiting preconceptions have never been published (e.g. Nelson *et al.* 1990: 201; Warren 1990; James *et al.* 1991a: 387, n. 137; cf. Iakovidis 1990);

3. Lack of a year-by-year calibration – the presently available curves lack the detail needed for short-lived samples and could mask significant differences in time (Mook *et al.* 1987: 147–148; Aitken 1988a: 21; Bruins & Mook 1989: 1026). Further, in calibrating radiocarbon dates, it is increasingly realized (e.g. Tykot 1994) that there is a need to use two standard deviations (95% certainty), rather than one (68%), especially with results obtained before high-precision counting was

introduced (Warren 1987: 209; cf. Aitken 1990: 107);
4. As the majority of Aegean results are from long-lived samples, the most crucial uncertainty – from the archaeological perspective – is the 'old-wood effect'. In the words of Aitken (1988b, 19):

> It is well known that long-lived samples carry a particular problem of interpretation, *viz.* what length of time elapsed between fixation of the carbon atoms in the cellulose of wood (for example) and the event being dated? For a large tree, this might be several centuries.

Several case studies involving sites with established historical dates illustrate the seriousness of the problem, for example: the medieval settlement of Starigard, N.W. Germany, where in many cases the calibrated results on wood and charcoal were 'several hundred years too old' (Willkomm 1983: 645); the Viking site of L'Anse aux Meadows, where the mean charcoal age is about 125 years greater than the short-lived and historical ages, pointing to a maximum age of 500 years for wood used at the site (Waterbolk 1971: 23); at Pompeii results from the wood samples gave calibrated age ranges between 60 and 205 years older than the burial of the site in AD 79 (Vogel *et al.* 1990: 536).

While paying lip service to the importance of the 'old wood effect', Manning and Weninger apply a correction *only* at Kastanas. But even here they gloss over the extent of the problem, by assuming 'that wood is normally about 50 years older than its context of cultural employment in the Mediterranean' – citing Vogel *et al.*, who actually used this figure as a hypothetical correction for undersized charcoal samples from North America. In fact, a correction figure deduced from Pompeii would be 132.5 ± 72.5. Cf. two charcoal results from Manning and Weninger's own listing: 1209–1043 BC (KI-1785) from the Kastanas level that produced the chestnut result of 1134–930 BC; and 862–580 BC (I-9054) from a 4th-century BC context at Nichoria.

Even allowing for the poor quality of most of the available dates, if one applies realistic 'old wood' corrections, with due consideration for archaeological context, a different picture emerges from that arrived at by Manning and Weninger and *even with* Weninger's 1σ calibrations.

No weight can be given to the evidence of sites with only one or two samples (Cape Gelidonya, Asine, Lefkandi, Midea), though different interpretations to those of Manning and Weninger could be offered. Likewise, little can be done with the 17 results from Nichoria (from Middle Helladic to Byzantine), admitted by Manning and Weninger to be 'worryingly inconsistent'. Yet they still conclude that a peak from the entire set falls in the early 1st millennium BC – 'as would be expected'. Expected by whom, from what? That trees were growing near Nichoria at this time has never been in doubt!

Turning to Mycenae, the one short-lived sample, of 'charred wheat' (OxA-146) is thought by Manning and Weninger to have limited value because of 'its solitary nature, and the large standard error of the measurement'. Three of the four LHIIIB long-lived samples were from the destruction level of the Citadel House, usually dated to c. 1200 BC: two of charcoal (P-1455; P-1456) and one from a burned beam (P-1457). They produced dates of 1298–1118 BC, 1399–1211 BC, 1256–1078 BC – combined range 1399–1078 BC. This merely gives a *terminus post quem*, from which one must subtract a figure that takes account of three time spans: (a) the further growth of the tree after that of the rings present in the samples; (b) the time that elapsed before its use (and possible later reuse) in the construction in question, and (c) the age of the building before its destruction. The Citadel House was built at the beginning of LHIIIB, conventionally c. 1335 BC. Using a notional 'old wood' correction of up-to-200 years derived from Pompeii, the destruction at Mycenae could have fallen as late as 1199–878 BC, in perfect agreement with our chronology, which ends LHIIIB c. 975 BC. This also agrees with both the fourth result (P-1454) from 'carbonized matter' (1149–961 BC) and the fifth (P-1459), described only as 'Mycenaean' but evidently from the same LHIIIB context (1278–1096 BC). For a visualisation of this archaeologically realistic approach, see Fig. 7.4.

From Pylos there are three 'Late LHIIIB' charcoal samples (P-332, 337, 341) which give a *terminus post quem* (combined range: 1498–1183 BC) slightly higher than Mycenae's. With an 'old wood' correction, the destruction could have occurred within the period 1498/1298 to 1183/983 BC – again, a lower trend than that of accepted chronology. The rest of the Pylos (mostly 'mid-LHIIIB') charcoal samples (P-326, 328, 329, 330, 340, Gro-998), have produced a massive scatter (combined range: 1868–1186 BC) not worth further consideration.

The Iron Age results from Assiros are consistent with our chronology if one allows for the 'old wood effect', while those from the Bronze Age (even lower than Mycenae's) clearly support us. Manning and Weninger (1992: 641) have considerable difficulty with the three results (BM-1431, 1432, 1433) from the earliest Bronze Age phases, and are forced to suggest that either they are wrong or the excavator's classification is too early. As for Kastanas, the 'wood correction' used by Manning and Weninger is, as mentioned above, far too small. Willkomm (1990: 177) has also made the important observation that the results from the LHIIIC to Geometric phases (conventionally c. 400 years) 'do not span more than 150 years'. An obvious explanation is that wood cut at an early period was extensively re-used. This by itself raises the question whether the kind of statistical massage ('archaeological wiggle matching') performed by Manning and Weninger to conclude that this site 'offers remarkably strong support for the conventional chronology', is really applicable to Kastanas – or indeed anywhere.

Despite the inadequacy of the available radiocarbon evidence from the Aegean in the LBA (James *et al.* 1991a:

xviii-xx, 321–325; 1991b: 231–233; 1992: 128–129), Manning and Weninger are prepared to use it in a 'probabilistic' (as they see it) statistical defence of the conventional chronology. But the fact is that ^{14}C cannot presently demonstrate the accuracy of the accepted dating framework. Setting the standard for future ^{14}C dating, we only need to quote Betancourt & Lawn (1984: 279): 'A more rigid use of evidence should insist upon at least 20–30 dates from each of the several levels at each site, all of good samples...' When something approaching even half this ideal becomes reality, then statistics can come into play, but Manning and Weninger will have to co-ordinate their interpretations since with respect to Thera the two authors (Manning 1990; Weninger 1990) have disagreed by as much as 150 years! It seems absurd to assume that greater precision can be obtained from sites where only a fraction of the number of radiocarbon tests have been performed. It is also incredible that Manning (1990: 37) himself could only shortly earlier have made the following statement:

> ... new series of high quality dates from sealed stratigraphic contexts from all the Aegean periods are required. The current corpus consists of dates from very different technical processes, and dates usually lacking carbon-13 normalization, or alkali pre-treatment! This is unacceptable .... The pressing need is therefore for Aegean radiocarbon dates with the contextual and measurement quality to match the precision of the current radiocarbon calibration curves.

At the end of their presentation, Manning and Weninger appeal to the radiocarbon record from Egypt, as presented by Weninger (1990), and to the developing dendrochronological sequence from Anatolia (see below) as evidence that all is well with Late Bronze Age chronology. The real situation with the ^{14}C dates from Egypt is that they are equivocal and almost as many dates could be cited in favour of lowering chronology as maintaining the *status quo*. Almost all of them have been performed on unsuitable material (wood, charcoal, reeds), and there are vast interlaboratory differences (particularly between the Universities of Uppsala and Pennsylvania). Weninger's study itself should be treated with the utmost caution, containing as it does numerous factual errors. (For more reliable studies, see Shaw 1985; Hassan & Robinson 1987.)

Dendrochronological Prospects

For Snodgrass (1991a; 1991b), strong evidence against our low chronology comes from the emerging dendrochronological record. Somewhat optimistically, he predicted that this would in the near future, 'perhaps within less than five years', have produced a volume of evidence sufficient to build up a new scientifically based chronology which would show that the conventional dates are sound. We are still waiting.

Snodgrass made his prediction on the basis of a preliminary report for Bronze Age Anatolia published by Kuniholm (1988: 8). This stated that the last preserved ring of charcoal from a 'Hittite palace' of Suppiluliuma I at Maşat lay 654 years before the end of the master dendrochronological sequence from Gordion, producing a date of c. 1379 BC following a notional end of c. 725 BC for the sequence. As Suppiluliuma is generally thought to have died c. 1320 BC, the result represented, in Snodgrass' view, 'a shot in the arm' for the conventional chronology. A subsequent report (Kuniholm 1990: 4) adjusted this figure to 635 years, and as new radiocarbon dates were available for the master sequence, gave a date of 1392 ± 37 for Maşat. The context was also said to contain Mycenaean LHIIIB pottery.

As we stressed in reply to Snodgrass (James *et al.* 1992: 128), such a result, far from giving a date for the building's construction, merely gives a date for the death of the last tree-ring preserved, not even the felling of the trees involved. (Note that there was no bark present on the samples.) Further, the information about the timber's context makes no sense in terms of the site as it is published (Özgüç 1978: 52–67; 1982: 76–78). There are three Hittite levels at Maşat: III, which contained a palace (time of Tudhaliya, father of Suppiluliuma); II, with new buildings (time of Suppiluliuma); and I, the final level of Hittite times (13th century BC) which contained a stirrup jar and fragments of four other Mycenaean LHIIIB vessels. Kuniholm's presentation of the timber's context as a 'palace' of 'the time of Suppiluliuma' with associated LHIIIB pottery thus seems to be a pastiche of elements from Levels I, II and III.[8] The stress laid on the Mycenaean pottery found in the context leads one to conclude that the samples came from Level I. Had they been found at a one-level site the result may have seemed significant, highlighting the serious danger inherent in uncritical use of a single dendrochronological date. Yet as the result actually predates the reign of Suppiluliuma, who built the *preceding* level (II), then it has to be accepted either that the tree was much older than the context it was employed in (there was no bark present on the sample), or that it was reused from a much earlier level.[9] In either case it cannot possibly be used to demonstrate that the conventional date for Suppiluliuma I is correct.

The misleading case of Maşat highlights three problem areas which face the application of the developing dendrochronological sequence from Anatolia. First, there is the danger of drawing premature conclusions. Second, unless full and precise details for each sample are published by the excavators, dendrochronological results are not susceptible to archaeological interpretation and are simply wasted effort. Third, one must be mindful of the extensive reuse of the precious resource of timber in the ancient world, as illustrated by two other sites. The royal tombs at Gordion (Kuniholm 1988: 8; cf. James et al. 1992: 128)

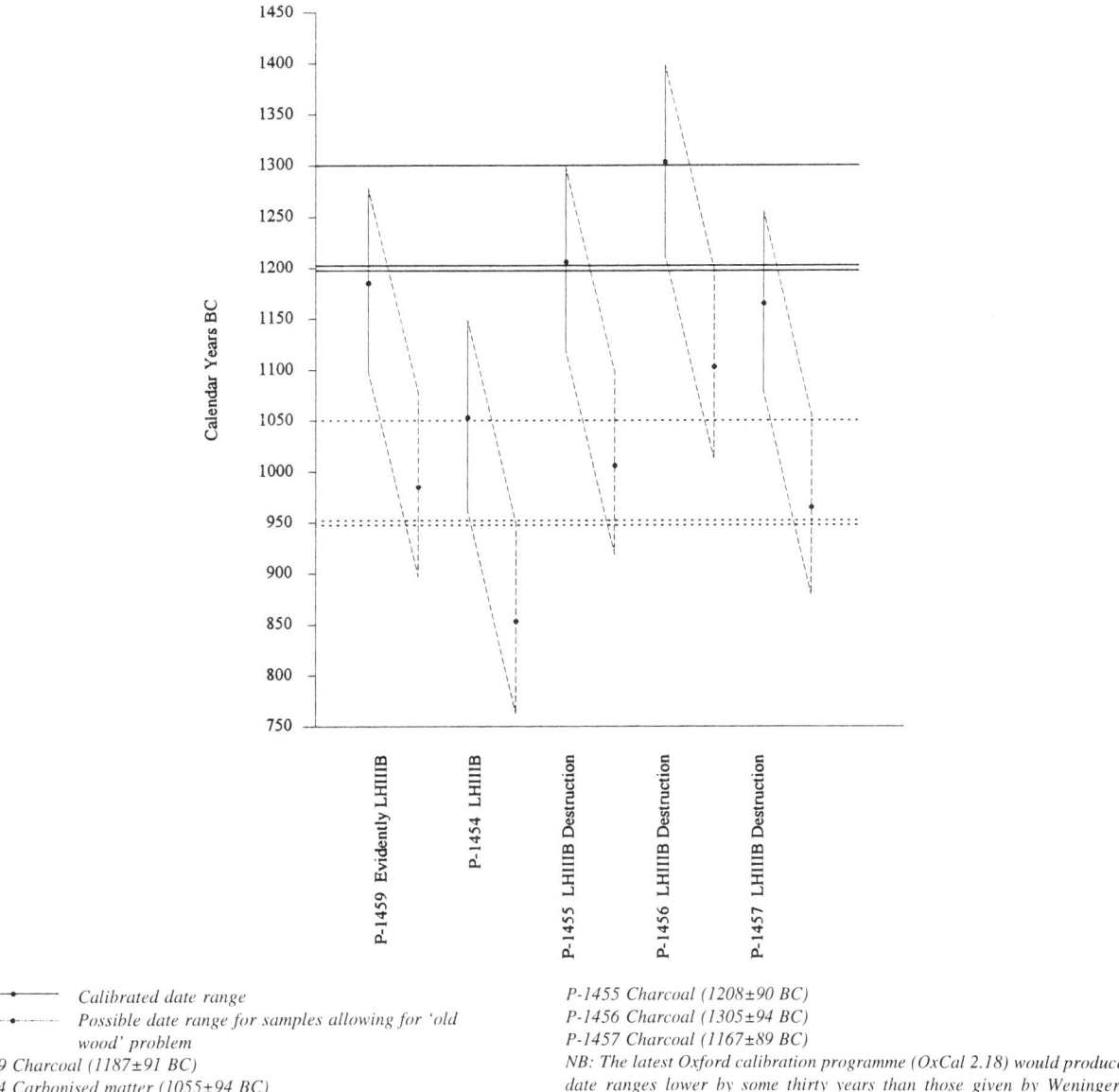

Figure 7.4. The radiocarbon dates from the Citadel House, Mycenae, plotted at one standard deviation, following Weninger's calibration. Conventional dates for the construction (1300 BC) and destruction (1200 BC) of Citadel House, together with revised dates for the construction (1050 BC) and destruction (950 BC) events are indicated.

and the Middle Bronze Age building complex at Aksaray, Açemhöyük, Northwest Trench (Kuniholm 1994: 7) have demonstrated that timber was reused on a large scale, sometimes centuries later.

From another LBA site, Tille Höyük on the Euphrates, enough detail on the context of the dendrochronological samples has been published to make discussion more worthwhile (Summers 1993). The excavation focussed on a massive Gateway, which was burned down along with the rest of the site near the end of the LBA. Charcoal samples were taken from the wooden roof which had collapsed into the passageway of the Gate. These fell into two groups, which had outer rings of 1210 ± 37 and 1140 ± 37 years respectively,[10] with the older timbers assumed to represent an earlier phase of construction in the Gateway. Kuniholm et al. (1993: 188) believe 'for subjective reasons' that there are no more than six rings missing from the latest timbers, so that their felling date would fall near 1134 ± 37 BC by cross-matching with his master sequence from Gordion. Allowing for an unknown number of years for the use of the Gateway before it was burnt, this date is uncomfortably tight for the conventional chronology of the LBA, which, in this region ends c. 1175 BC.

Understandably, Summers (1993: 38) attempted to circumvent the effects of the dendrochronological results by minimising the period of the Gateway's use. From the lack of material accumulated in the Gate passage, the degree of wear on the lime plaster of the passage floor, the fact that the walls were not re-plastered and the slight traces of occupation in the rooms attached to the Gateway, he argued that this period was fairly brief, 'perhaps no more than a few years' (Summers 1993: 14). While these factors may give the impression of a short period, to ascribe such a tight limit appears unrealistic, and depends on a series of assumptions concerning the expected level of activity which may well not be correct. The pottery associated with the destruction level was Drab Ware (Summers 1993: 47) known from other sites to belong to the LBA. Although the excavators (Blaylock 1991: 5) at one point considered reallocating the Tille Höyük Drab Ware to the early Iron Age ('perhaps 12th or 11th century'), they have retracted this suggestion and now envisage the site as a Hittite fortified centre which outlasted the fall of the Empire by anything up to one hundred years, with the Drab Ware demonstrating continuity of pottery production into the early Iron Age (Summers 1993: 47).

Finally comes the significant question of the overall calibration of Anatolian dendrochronology. Unfortunately, a *continuous* tree-ring series running back to the Bronze Age has yet to be developed, and the Gordion 'floating' sequence presently relies on ^{14}C dating to be fixed in time. The first radiocarbon tests performed gave results up to two centuries lower than those expected. Kuniholm (1977: 45–49) then considered lowering the end of the Gordion master sequence from its assumed archaeological date of c. 725 BC to c. 547/6 BC. However, such a radical revision seemed unwarranted, and a larger set of radiocarbon tests (performed at Heidelberg and still unpublished) were used to peg the end of the sequence to 757 ± 37 BC (Kuniholm 1990: 3, 6). Calibrating these results by the 1993 Stuiver curve, Manning suggested (at this conference) that the Gordion master chronology should be lowered again by 39 years, a conclusion approved by Kuniholm. This now means that the *construction* of the last phase of the Tille Höyük Gateway must be reckoned at 1101 ± 1 BC, with its use lying in the 11th century BC, surely an impossible result for the conventional chronology.

Conclusion

In conclusion, we might echo the words of our predecessor Cecil Torr (1896: 1) who exactly a hundred years ago resisted the attempts of Egyptologists to raise the dates of Mycenae and interpose a lengthy 'dark age' before the floruit of Archaic Greek civilization: 'A statement is current that the Mycenaean age in Greece can definitely be fixed at 1500 BC, or thereabouts, on the strength of evidence from Egyptian sources.' A 'statement' now seems to be current that radiocarbon dating and dendrochronology demonstrate that the conventional chronology for the Mycenaean and Late Bronze Age world is correct. Far from it, we submit that a significant lowering of LBA chronology is not only compatible with the available ^{14}C evidence – when assessed critically – but is also beginning to receive support from dendrochronology. After a century of further excavation and study, the weakness of the traditional Egyptian chronology highlighted by Torr is still apparent. We believe that we have shown that a radically lower model (again with the proviso of a maximum of 250 years) for Egyptian chronology is desirable, given the multiple tensions and conflicts that exist in Iron Age Mediterranean archaeology. In particular the current impasse between Cypriot/Greek and Israeli dating systems *must* be resolved, and the only logical solution seems to be a general compression of the Early Iron Age. We can only appeal to specialists in Sardinian archaeology to take the dates they have received in the past from the Aegean and Eastern Mediterranean worlds *cum grano salis*.

Acknowledgments

Our thanks to Dr. Robert Morkot for collaboration on Egyptological matters, and to Geoff Couling (King Alfred's College, Winchester) and Richard Dean for help with the figures.

Notes

1. Cross (1993: 541, n. 23) states, that 'The Tell Fekheriyeh inscription either dates to the 11th century (and the names of the dynasts repeat in the 9th century), or is from the second half of the 9th century and is a stunning piece of archaizing.' Yet one must ask why archaic forms were used and what they were copied from. Can any parallels for such archaising be made for comparable political inscriptions from this period/region?
2. The initial Egyptological diagnosis of this urn by de Meulenaere had actually pointed to a date *not earlier* than 700 BC (in Bikai 1978a: 84; cf. James *et al.* 1991a: 361, n. 41), and Bikai (1987: 69) later considered the suggestion by Anderson that some elements of Tyre III–II seem to recall the 7th-century. Interestingly, Gal (1992b: 73–74) argues a post-700 date for all strata from IV to I at Tyre.
3. Nothing, it should be noted, has been found to contradict the low chronology for Carthage which we advocated (James *et al.* 1991a: 53–54).
4. There are many problems with this statement. First, what does a 'different phenomenon' mean other than a serious archaeological inconsistency? Second, although the application of Neutron Activation Analysis has produced varying results, which tend to suggest that perhaps some of the Black-on-Red Ware may have been copied on Palestinian soil (James *et al.* 1991a: 155–156), there is no evidence over a number of sites for assigning any specific type of presumed *non*-Cypriot Black-on-Red Ware to any specific chronological horizon. Therefore, it is a mystery why Black-on-Red vessels do not concern Gilboa in her discussion of Phase 9 at Dor, dated between 1050 and c. 980 BC (Gilboa 1989: 205), when Black-on-Red vessels are commonly included in the publications of '11th-10th century' sites in Israel (e.g. see James *et al.* 1991a: 67, n. 45).
5. When attacked by Kitchen (1991a) on this point we challenged him to prove that the 21st and 22nd Dynasties did not overlap by reference to primary evidence alone (James & Morkot 1991), as Kitchen had referred to it as the 'single point which must suffice' to destroy our model. As we subsequently noted (James 1991) Kitchen's reply turned to different matters entirely.
6. For a damning critique, see Rose 1994, which shows that the

conventional placements of the document (19th and early 18th centuries BC) provide a very poor match with the lunar data it also contains. See also Read (1970), curiously overlooked by Rose, who showed that the Illahun lunar data finds a perfect match in the year 1549 BC. Taken literally, this would necessitate a reduction of Middle Kingdom Egyptian chronology by some 250 years! (James *et al.* 1991a: 228–229.)

7. Maniscalco & McConnell (1993: 45) admit that 'the Cassibile and Pantalica South material cultures have yet to be distinguished stratigraphically', yet objected to our suggested change in Pantalica South's chronological status: 'If Pantalica South were eliminated as a chronologically distinct phase, the Pantalica South material culture would have to be mixed with some other group – where does one put it'? Leighton (1993) seems to have answered their question.

8. Elsewhere the same dendrochronological result was vaguely reported as coming from 'Levels I & II' (Kuniholm 1989: 96). Matters are further confused by the statement that the timber came from a 'room...from the time of Suppiluliumas I with imported Late Helladic IIIA pottery' (Kuniholm 1992: 383). Only LHIIIB pottery was reported in the original excavations (Özgüç 1978: 66; 1982: 102–103), though an LHIIIA2 stirrup jar was subsequently excavated from Level II in the lower city (see conveniently Bloedlow 1988: 41, n. 150), which would be more consistent with the date for Suppiluliuma, but can have no connection with the wood samples taken from the 'palace' on the acropolis. In conversation (at this conference) Kuniholm admits that the original data for the context of the dendrochronology samples from Maşat is probably irretrievable and that the date should be discounted as historically meaningful.

9. Indeed, Kuniholm 'seems to remember that wood allegedly from Level II postdates wood allegedly from Level I' – pers. comm. 12/12/91.

10. Further, it should be remembered that the Tille results are matched to the sequence by statistical analysis. Kuniholm's data show that an alternative fit for the later group falling at 981 ± 37 BC (in Manning's revision 942 ± 1 BC) is actually the *best* in terms of the T-score normal for dendrochronological correlation. Our thanks to Bob Porter for drawing our attention to this important point.

Postscript

Two developments since this paper was written need to be noted. First, the 39-year reduction of the Anatolian Bronze-Iron Age dendrochonological sequence, discussed by Manning and Kuniholm at this conference, has now been published – see P.I. Kuniholm, B. Kromer, S.W. Manning, M. Newton, C.E. Latini & M.J. Bruce: 'Anatolian tree rings and the absolute chronology of the eastern Mediterranean, 2220–718 BC', *Nature* 381 (1996): 7807–83. Second, in 'The archaeology of the United Monarchy: an alternative view' (*Levant* 28: 1996: 177–187), Israel Finkelstein has outlined a radical revision of the Iron Age in Palestine which argues a lowering of Iron II ('10th-century') levels to the 9th-century, similar to that proposed by the authors although attempting to work within the conventional chronology.

Bibliography

Aitken, M.J. 1988a. The Thera eruption: continuing discussion of the dating. I. Resumé of dating. *Archaeometry* 30: 165–169.

Aitken, M.J. 1988b. The Minoan eruption of Thera, Santorini: a re-assessment of the radiocarbon dates. In Jones, R.E. & Catling, H.W. (eds.), *New Aspects of Archaeological Science in Greece*. Fitch Laboratory Occasional Paper 3: 19–24. British School at Athens, Athens.

Aitken, M.J. 1990. *Science-based Dating in Archaeology*. Longman, London.

Aston, D.A. 1989. Takeloth II – a king of the 'twenty-third dynasty'? *Journal of Egyptian Archaeology* 75: 139–153.

Aston, D.A. 1993. Review of 'Centuries of Darkness'. *Discussions in Egyptology* 27: 101–104.

Balmuth, M.S. 1992. Archaeology in Sardinia. *American Journal of Archaeology* 96: 663–697.

Balmuth, M.S. 1993. Sardinia. In Leonard, A. (ed.), *A Review of Peter James et al. Centuries of Darkness... A workshop held at the 93rd Annual Meeting of the Archaeological Institute of America, Chicago, Illinois, USA, December 1991*. Colloquenda Mediterranea A/2: 39–41. Loid Publishing, Bradford.

Betancourt, P.P. & Lawn, B. 1984. The Cyclades and radiocarbon chronology. In MacGillivray, J.A. & Barber, R.L.N. (eds.), *The Prehistoric Cyclades,* 277–295. Department of Classical Archaeology, University of Edinburgh, Edinburgh.

Bienkowski, P. 1992a. The beginning of the Iron Age in Edom: a reply to Finkelstein. *Levant* 24: 167–169.

Bienkowski, P. 1992b. The date of sedentary occupation in Edom: evidence from Umm el-Biyara, Tawilan and Buseirah. In Bienkowski, P. (ed.), *Early Edom and Moab: the Beginning of the Iron Age in Southern Jordan*. Sheffield Archaeological Monographs 7: 99–112. J.R. Collis Publications, Sheffield.

Bierbrier, M. 1975. *The Late New Kingdom in Egypt (c. 1300–664 B.C.): A Genealogical and Chronological Investigation*. Aris & Phillips, Warminster.

Bietak, M. 1989. The Middle Bronze Age of the Levant: a new approach to relative and absolute chronology. In Aström, P. (ed.), *High, Middle or Low? Acts of an International Colloquium on Absolute Chronology Held at the University of Gothenburg 1987*, Vol. 3: 78–120. Paul Aströms Förlag, Gothenburg.

Bikai, P.M. 1978a. *The Pottery of Tyre*. Aris & Phillips, Warminster.

Bikai, P.M. 1978b. The Late Phoenician pottery complex and chronology. *Bulletin of the American Schools of Oriental Research* 229: 47–56.

Bikai, P.M. 1981. The Phoenician imports. In Karageorghis, V. (ed.), *Kition IV: The Non-Cypriot Pottery,* 27–35. Department of Antiquities, Cyprus, Nicosia.

Bikai, P.M. 1985. Observations on archaeological evidence for the trade between Israel and Tyre. *Bulletin of the American Schools of Oriental Research* 258: 71–72.

Bikai, P.M. 1987. *The Phoenician Pottery of Cyprus*. A.G. Leventis Foundation, Nicosia.

Biran, A. & Naveh, J. 1993. An Aramaic stele fragment from Tel Dan. *Israel Exploration Journal* 43: 81–98.

Biran, A. & Naveh, J. 1995. The Tel Dan inscription: a new fragment. *Israel Exploration Journal* 45: 1–18.

Blaylock, S.R. 1991. Tille Höyük excavation. *Anatolian Studies* 41: 4–7.

Bloedlow, E.F. 1988. The Trojan War and Late Helladic IIIC. *Prähistorische Zeitschrift* 63: 23–52.

Boardman, J. 1967. The Khaniale Tekke Tombs, II. *Annual of the British School at Athens* 62: 57–75.

Bruins, H.J. & Mook, W.G. 1989. The need for a calibrated radiocarbon chronology of Near Eastern archaeology. *Radiocarbon* 31: 1019–29.

Castellana, G. 1993. New data for the culture-sequence and chronology of Central-Western Sicily. In Leonard, A. (ed.), *A Review of Peter James et al. Centuries of Darkness... A workshop held at the 93rd Annual Meeting of the Archaeological Institute of America, Chicago, Illinois, USA, December*

1991. Colloquenda Mediterranea A/2: 48-50. Loid Publishing, Bradford.

Chapman, R. 1993-94. The Dan stele and the chronology of Levantine Iron Age stratigraphy. *Bulletin of the Anglo-Israel Archaeological Society* 13: 23-29.

Chapman, R. 1994. Dan, Damascus and the House of David: an update on the David inscription. *Minerva* 5(4): 3-4.

Coldstream, N. 1982. Greeks and Phoenicians in the Aegean. In Niemeyer, H.G. (ed.), *Phönizier im Westen,* 261-272. Deutsches Archäologisches Institut Madrider Beiträge Band 8. Madrid.

Cross, F.M. 1986. Phoenicians in the West: the early epigraphic evidence. In Balmuth, M.S. (ed.), *Studies in Sardinian Archaeology. Volume II: Sardinia in the Mediterranean,* 116-130. University of Michigan Press, Ann Arbor.

Cross, F.M. 1993. Newly discovered arrowheads of the 11th Century B.C.E. In Biran, A. & Aviram, J. (eds.), *Biblical Archaeology Today, 1990: Proceedings of the Second International Congress on Biblical Archaeology Jerusalem, June-July 1990,* 533-542. Israel Exploration Society, Jerusalem.

Crowfoot, J.W., Crowfoot, G.M. & Kenyon, K.M. 1957. *Samaria Sebaste III. The Objects from Samaria.* Palestine Exploration Fund, London.

Depuydt, L. 1993. The date of Piye's Egyptian campaign and the chronology of the twenty-fifth dynasty. *Journal of Egyptian Archaeology* 79: 269-274.

Desborough, V.R. d'A. 1957. A group of vases from Amathus. *Journal of Hellenic Studies* 77: 212-219.

Dever, W.G. 1990. Of myths and methods. *Bulletin of the American Schools of Oriental Research* 277/8: 121-130.

Dickinson, O. 1994. *The Aegean Bronze Age.* Cambridge University Press, Cambridge.

Dodson, A. 1987. Psusennes II. *Revue d'Égyptologie* 38: 49-54.

Dodson, A. 1992. Review of 'Centuries of Darkness'. *Palestine Exploration Quarterly* 124: 71-72.

Finkelstein, I. 1992a. Edom in the Iron I. *Levant* 24: 159-166.

Finkelstein, I. 1992b. Stratigraphy, pottery and parallels: a reply to Bienkowski. *Levant* 24: 171-172.

Forsberg, S. 1995. *Near Eastern Destruction Datings as Sources for Greek and Near Eastern Iron Age Chronology. Archaeological and Historical Studies. The cases of Samaria (722 B.C.) and Tarsus (696 B.C.).* Boreas 19. Uppsala University, Uppsala.

Gal, Z. 1992a. urbat Rosh Zayit and the early Phoenician pottery. *Levant* 24: 173-186.

Gal, Z. 1992b. *Lower Galilee During the Iron Age.* Eisenbrauns, Winona Lake, Ind.

Geva, S. 1982. Archaeological evidence for the trade between Israel and Tyre? *Bulletin of the American Schools of Oriental Research* 248: 69-72.

Gilboa, A. 1989. New finds at Tel Dor and the beginning of Cypro-Geometric pottery import to Palestine. *Israel Exploration Journal* 39: 204-218.

Halpern, B. 1994. The stela from Dan: epigraphic and historical considerations. *Bulletin of the American Schools of Oriental Research* 296: 63-80.

Hassan, F.A. & Robinson, S.W. 1987. High-precision radiocarbon chronology of ancient Egypt, and comparisons with Nubia, Palestine and Mesopotamia. *Antiquity* 61: 119-135.

Helck, W. 1989. Discussion. In Aström, P. (ed.), *High, Middle or Low? Acts of an International Colloquium on Absolute Chronology Held at the University of Gothenburg 1987,* Vol. 3: 40-48. Paul Aströms Förlag, Gothenburg.

Hughes, J. 1990. *Secrets of the Times: Myth and History in Biblical Chronology.* Journal for the Study of the Old Testament Supplement Series 66. Sheffield Academic Press, Sheffield.

Iakovidis, S. 1990. Discussion. In Hardy, D.A. & Renfrew, A.C. (eds), *Thera and the Aegean World III. Vol. 3: Chronology,* 240. The Thera Foundation, London.

James, P.J. 1991. Centuries of Darkness [letter]. *Times Literary Supplement* July 12: 13.

James, P.J. & Morkot, R. 1991. Centuries of Darkness [letter]. *Times Literary Supplement* June 7: 15.

James, P.J. & Morkot, R. forthcoming. Egyptology in isolation: a response to David Aston [1993].

James, P.J., Thorpe, I.J., Kokkinos, N. & Frankish, J. 1987. *Bronze to Iron Age Chronology in the Old World: Time for a Reassessment?* Studies in Ancient Chronology I. Institute of Archaeology, London.

James, P.J., Thorpe, I.J., Kokkinos, N., Morkot, R., Frankish, J. 1991a. *Centuries of Darkness: A Challenge to the Conventional Chronology of Old World Archaeology.* Jonathan Cape, London.

James, P.J., Thorpe, I.J., Kokkinos, N., Morkot, R., Frankish, J. 1991b. Centuries of Darkness: context, methodology and implications. *Cambridge Archaeological Journal* 1: 228-235.

James, P.J., Thorpe, I.J., Kokkinos, N., Morkot, R., Frankish, J. 1992. Centuries of Darkness: a reply to critics. *Cambridge Archaeological Journal* 2: 127-130.

Jope, E.M. 1986. Sample credentials for high-precision ^{14}C dating. *Radiocarbon* 28: 1060-1064.

Kinnes, I. & Thorpe, I.J. 1986. Radiocarbon dating: use and abuse. *Antiquity* 20: 221-223.

Kitchen, K.A. 1986. *The Third Intermediate Period in Egypt (1100-650 B.C.).* 2nd edition. Aris & Phillips, Warminster.

Kitchen, K.A. 1991a. Blind dating [review of 'Centuries of Darkness']. *Times Literary Supplement* May 17: 21.

Kitchen, K.A. 1991b. Egyptian chronology: problem or solution? *Cambridge Archaeological Journal* 1: 235-239.

Kochavi, M. 1993. Hadar, Tel. In Stern, E. (ed.), *The New Encyclopedia of Archaeological Excavations in the Holy Land,* vol. 2: 551-552. Israel Exploration Society, Jerusalem.

Kopcke, G. forthcoming. A Greek Protogeometric bowl krater from Tel Hadar. *Eretz Israel.*

Kuniholm, P.I. 1977. *Dendrochronology at Gordion and on the Anatolian Plateau.* Ph.D. dissertation, Department of Anthropology and Archaeology, University of Pennsylvania. University Microfilms, Ann Arbor.

Kuniholm, P.I. 1988. Dendrochronology and radiocarbon dates for Gordion and other Phrygian sites. *Source: Notes in the History of Art* 7(3-4): 6-8.

Kuniholm, P.I. 1989. Aegean dendrochronology project: 1988-1989 results. *Arkeometri Sonuçlari Toplantisi* 5: 87-96.

Kuniholm, P.I. 1990. Aegean dendrochronology project: December 1990 progress report. Department of the History of Art, Cornell University, Ithaca, N.Y. (circular).

Kuniholm, P.I. 1994. Aegean dendrochronology project: December 1994 progress report. Department of the History of Art, Cornell University, Ithaca, N.Y. (circular).

Kuniholm, P.I., Tarter, S.L., Newton, M.W. & Griggs, C.B. 1992. Dendrochronological investigations at Porsuk/Ulukisla, Turkey, preliminary report, 1987-1989. *Syria* 69: 379-389.

Kuniholm, P.I., Tarter, S.L. & Griggs, C.B. 1993. Appendix 2: Dendrochronological Report. In Summers, G.D., *Tille Höyük 4: The Late Bronze Age and the Iron Age Transition,* 179-90. British Institute of Archaeology at Ankara, London.

Lancel, S. 1995. *Carthage: A History.* Blackwell, Oxford.

Leighton, R. 1993. Sicily during the centuries of darkness. *Cambridge Archaeological Journal* 3: 271-276.

Lemaire, A. 1994. Epigraphie palestinienne: nouveaux documents I. Fragment de stèle araméenne de Tell Dan (IXe s. av. J.- C.). *Henoch* 16: 87-93.

Lilliu, G. 1988. *La civiltà dei Sardi dal Paleolitico all'età dei nuraghi.* 3rd edition. Nuova ERI, Torino.

Lipiński, E. 1990. Epigraphy in crisis. *Biblical Archaeology Review* 16,4 (Jul/Aug): 42-44.

Maniscalco, L. & McConnell, B.E. 1993. Sicily, the Lipari Islands and Malta. In Leonard, A. (ed.), *A Review of Peter James et al. Centuries of Darkness... A workshop held at the 93rd Annual Meeting of the Archaeological Institute of America, Chicago, Illinois, USA, December 1991.* Colloquenda Mediterranea A/2: 43–47. Loid Publishing, Bradford.

Manning, S.W. 1990. The eruption of Thera: date and implications. In Hardy, D.A. & Renfrew, A.C. (eds.), *Thera and the Aegean World III. Vol. 3: Chronology,* 29–40. The Thera Foundation, London.

Manning, S.W. & Weninger, B. 1992. A light in the dark: archaeological wiggle matching and the absolute chronology of the Aegean Late Bronze Age. *Antiquity* 66: 636–663.

Mazar, B. 1986. *The Early Biblical Period* (ed. Ahituv, S. & Levine, B.A.). Israel Exploration Society, Jerusalem.

Millard, A.R. 1993. The Tell Fekheriyeh inscriptions. In Biran, A. & Aviram, J. (eds.), *Biblical Archaeology Today, 1990: Proceedings of the Second International Congress on Biblical Archaeology Jerusalem, June-July 1990,* 518–524. Israel Exploration Society, Jerusalem.

Mook, W.G., Hasper, H. & van der Plicht, J. 1987. Background and procedures of ^{14}C calibration. In Aurenche, O. *et al.* (eds.), *Chronologies du Proche Orient/Chronologies in the Near East. Relative Chronologies and Absolute Chronology 16,000–4,000 BP.* BAR International Series 379: 145–150. British Archaeological Reports, Oxford.

Negbi, O. 1992. Early Phoenician presence in the Mediterranean islands: a reappraisal. *American Journal of Archaeology* 96: 599–615.

Nelson, D.E., Vogel, J.S. & Southon, J.R. 1990. Another suite of confusing radiocarbon dates for the destruction of Akrotiri. In Hardy, D.A. & Renfrew, A.C. (eds.), *Thera and the Aegean World III. Vol. 3: Chronology,* 197–206. The Thera Foundation, London.

Niwinski, A. 1988. *21st Dynasty Coffins from Thebes.* P. von Zabern, Mainz.

Özgüç, T. 1978. *Maşat Höyük: Excavations at Maşat Höyük and Investigations in its Vicinity.* Türk Tarih Kurumu, Ankara.

Özgüç, T. 1982. *Maşat Höyük II: A Hittite Centre Northeast of Bogazköy.* Türk Tarih Kurumu, Ankara.

Ray, J. 1992. Review of 'Centuries of Darkness'. *Journal of Hellenic Studies* 112: 213–214.

Reade, J.G. 1970. Early eighteenth dynasty chronology. *Journal of Near Eastern Studies* 29: 1–11.

Rose, L. 1994. The astronomical evidence for dating the end of the Middle Kingdom of ancient Egypt to the early second millennium: a reassessment. *Journal of Near Eastern Studies* 53: 237–261.

Scott, E.N., Baxter, M.S., Harkness, D.D., Aitchison, T.C. & Cook, G.T. 1990. Radiocarbon: present and future perspectives on quality assurance. *Antiquity* 64: 319–322.

Shaw, I.M.E. 1985. Egyptian chronology and the Irish Oak Calibration. *Journal of Near Eastern Studies* 44: 295–317.

Snodgrass, A. 1991a. Collapses of civilization [review of 'Centuries of Darkness']. *London Review of Books* July 25: 18–19.

Snodgrass, A. 1991b. The Aegean Angle. *Cambridge Archaeological Journal* 1: 246–247.

Sörenson, L.W. 1993. Cyprus. In Leonard, A. (ed.), *A Review of Peter James et al. Centuries of Darkness... A workshop held at the 93rd Annual Meeting of the Archaeological Institute of America, Chicago, Illinois, USA, December 1991.* Colloquenda Mediterranea A/2: 17–19. Loid Publishing, Bradford.

Stager, L.E. 1990. Shemer's Estate. *Bulletin of the American Schools of Oriental Research* 277/8: 93–107.

Summers, G.D. 1993. *Tille Höyük 4: The Late Bronze Age and the Iron Age Transition.* British Institute of Archaeology at Ankara, London.

Tappy, R.E. 1992. *The Archaeology of Israelite Samaria. Volume I: Early Iron Through the Ninth Century BCE.* Scholars Press, Atlanta.

Torr, C. 1896. *Memphis and Mycenae.* Cambridge University Press, Cambridge.

Tykot, R.H. 1994. Radiocarbon dating and absolute chronology in Sardinia and Corsica. In Skeates, R. & Whitehouse, R. (eds.), *Radiocarbon Dating and Italian Prehistory.* Archaeological Monographs of the British School at Rome 8: 115–145. Accordia Research Centre, London.

Ugas, G. 1992. Considerazioni sullo sviluppo dell'architettura e della società nuragica. In Tykot, R.H. & Andrews, T.K. (eds.), *Sardinia in the Mediterranean: A Footprint in the Sea. Studies in Sardinian Archaeology Presented to Miriam S. Balmuth.* Monographs in Mediterranean Archaeology 3: 221–234. Sheffield Academic Press, Sheffield.

Vagnetti, L. 1989. A Sardinian askos from Crete. *Annual of the British School at Athens* 84: 355–60.

Vogel, J.S., Cornell, W., Nelson, D.E. & Southon, J.R. 1990. Vesuvius/Avellino, one possible source of seventeenth century BC climatic disturbances. *Nature* 344: 534–537.

Waldbaum, J.C. 1994. Early Greek contacts with the Southern Levant, ca. 1000–600 B.C.: the eastern perspective. *Bulletin of the American Schools of Oriental Research* 293: 53–66.

Warren, P.M. 1987. Absolute dating of the Aegean Late Bronze Age. *Archaeometry* 29: 205–211.

Warren, P.M. 1990. Discussion. In Hardy, D.A. & Renfrew, A.C. (eds.), *Thera and the Aegean World III. Vol. 3: Chronology,* 206. The Thera Foundation, London.

Waterbolk, H.T. 1971. Working with radiocarbon dates. *Proceedings of the Prehistoric Society* 37(2): 15–33.

Weninger, B. 1990. Theoretical radiocarbon discrepancies. In Hardy, D.A. & Renfrew, A.C. (eds), *Thera and the Aegean World III. Vol. 3: Chronology,* 216–231. The Thera Foundation, London.

Whittle, A. 1990. Radiocarbon dating of the Linear Pottery culture: the contribution of cereal and bone samples. *Antiquity* 64: 297–302.

Wightman, G.J. 1990. The myth of Solomon. *Bulletin of the American Schools of Oriental Research* 277/8: 5–22.

Willkomm, H. 1983. The reliability of archaeologic interpretation of ^{14}C dates. *Radiocarbon* 25: 645–646.

Willkomm, H. 1990. Systematic differences between radiocarbon and archaeological ages. *PACT* 29: 173–181.

8. Paleolithic Sardinians: Paleontological Evidence and Methods

Paul Y. Sondaar

Introduction

Overseas dispersal is mostly considered a relatively recent event in human history. In this view *Homo sapiens* was the first to cross sea barriers. *Homo sapiens* should have reached the island continent Australia about 50,000 years ago. Allen (1991), Bellwood (1985), and Bartstra *et al.* (1991) place the colonization of the islands of Southeast Asia in the same time interval. The arrival of humans on the Mediterranean islands is thought to be a later event. In the Late Pleistocene there were occasional visits on some islands (Cherry 1992), but colonization was thought to have been a Holocene event.

This view, however, is no longer tenable. Martini (1992) and Bini *et al.* (1993) describe artifacts *in situ* from Middle Pleistocene sediments at Sa Coa de sa Multa, near Perfugas on Sardinia. At this site, three different horizons with artifacts can be distinguished. This is hard evidence for a Middle Pleistocene presence of humans on the island of Sardinia. Recently, a human phalange was found in Upper Pleistocene deposits of Corbeddu Cave, which is hard evidence for human presence at about 20,000 BP on Sardinia (Sondaar *et al.* 1995).

On the island of Flores (Indonesia) a lithic industry was found *in situ*, associated with fossils of the Middle Pleistocene *Stegodon trigonocephalus* (Maringer & Verhoeven 1970). Though the age of the *Stegodon* was mostly accepted, its association with stone artifacts was doubted or not quoted (Bartstra *et al.* 1991). Recently, these finds were confirmed (Sondaar *et al.* 1994; Morwood 1995), and dated approximately 700,000 BP. This implies that it was not *Homo sapiens* who was the first to cross the sea barrier, but *Homo erectus* instead.

Just as in the case of Flores, where the hard evidence of an early colonization was doubted or not quoted for 25 years without any sound scientific argument, Cherry (1992) questioned the evidence and methodology presented by Sondaar (1987), Sondaar *et al.* (1991), Klein Hofmeijer & Sondaar (1992), and Martini (1992) without quoting them properly.

The statement of Cherry (1992: 36) that "A 300,000-year history for *Homo sardus* is too large a claim to swallow without documentation beyond a reasonable doubt" tells us something about how Cherry evaluates new claims by not discussing the evidence properly. To create the new specific name *sardus*, a nomen nudem in the genus *Homo,* demonstrates little respect for the rules of nomenclature.

Not only human fossils and stone artifacts but also paleontological evidence may be indicative of human presence on islands. On the islands of Flores and Sardinia a dramatic faunal turnover occurred in the Middle Pleistocene. Sondaar (1987) relates these dramatic faunal turnovers to the arrival of human hunters on the islands. The arrival of this predator had an impact on the island environment and caused extinctions among the endemic island species: the dwarf *Stegodon* and the giant tortoise on Flores, and a dwarf pig and monkey on Sardinia.

Another aspect is the taphonomy to recognize human involvement in the site formation processes. An example is provided by Corbeddu Cave (Oliena, Sardinia). During the Oliena conference of 1988, some of the systematic damage and aberrant wear of the *Megaloceros* teeth was discussed. There was general agreement that natural agents, like geological transport or trampling, could not explain this damage or wear of the teeth. The alternative was a *premortem* origin, due to aberrant chewing of stones by the deer. This alternative was refuted as paleobiologically impossible by the paleontologists among the delegates, but was supported by some archaeologists. They wanted hard evidence for a *post mortem* agent for the damage. If this could be demonstrated, then human activity might not be excluded. Since 1988 much laboratory work has been carried out, and we were happy that we could

---

Paul Y. Sondaar, Institut d'Estudis Avançats de les Illes Balears (CSIC-UIB), Ctra de Valldemossa km 7,5, 07071, Palma de Mallorca

report the first results in the Festschrift dedicated to Miriam Balmuth (Klein Hofmeijer & Sondaar 1992; 1993). It was possible to refit the broken cusps to the teeth in the mandible. The relatively small distance between these mandibles and their broken off molar fragments can only have a *post mortem* origin, and thus points to human activities. The other explanation, namely that the deer ate stones in the cave and died immediately afterwards is extremely unlikely. Klein Hofmeijer (1997) describes in detail the taphonomy of Hall 2. His well founded conclusion is that humans played an important role in the site formation processes.

In the discussion on the early colonization of islands little attention has been paid to paleontological events in relation to the arrival of humans on islands. The purpose of this contribution will be to discuss some aspects of it.

Paleogeography and Faunal Evolution

It is evident that the fauna on islands largely depend on which animals could reach the islands and at what time. For land mammals the most obvious obstacle is water, like channels, straits or wider seas. Simpson (1965) and Dermitzakis & Sondaar (1979) pointed out the dispersal routes of land mammals and their relation to faunal compositions. They distinguished the following routes:

1. A corridor route, in which faunal interchange from one region to another is possible;
2. A filter dispersal route, where spread is probable for some animals but definitely improbable for others;
3. A sweepstakes route, in which spread is impossible for most species, and very improbable for a number of other species, but occurs accidentally;
4. The pendel route, which can be easily crossed by some mammals, while it is an insurmountable barrier for others.

An example of the corridor is a broad land connection; a filter route may consist of a land bridge, while the sweepstake route may be caused by a wider sea.

The faunal evolution of a region depends highly on the possible dispersal routes. If there is a corridor, the fauna will not differ essentially from other parts of the continent. But if an island becomes populated by sweepstakes dispersal, very few taxa will reach the island, and if this colonization is successful then an endemic fauna will evolve with very few taxa (unbalanced). Examples already mentioned are known from the Pleistocene Mediterranean islands and the Indonesian Archipelago.

The other way around can also be observed. It is possible to find such unbalanced endemic faunas with a few taxa on the present mainland. The only conclusion that can be drawn from this fact is that such areas of the mainland must once have been an island in the remote past. An example is provided by the Gargano Peninsula in Italy, which was an island in the Miocene/Pliocene (Freudenthal 1978).

In the Pleistocene, Java was connected several times with the mainland of Asia. The present day fauna of Java is balanced and continental. But the Early Pleistocene Satir fauna (Sondaar 1984) is clearly unbalanced, endemic, and has a low diversity in taxa. Only a giant tortoise, *Mastodon*, deer and a hippo are known from this fauna. Recent discoveries of a pygmy *Stegodon* from Sambungmacan in Central Java even suggest that during Early Pleistocene times Java was made up of more than one island, as pygmy stegodonts are not known from the Satir fauna (Aziz & van den Bergh 1995).

If we analyze the fossil fauna, it is possible to draw certain conclusions concerning the paleogeography:

1. If we find fossils that indicate a balanced fauna similar to the mainland, and we find this fauna on an island, then this implies that the present island must have been connected by means of a corridor with the mainland in the past. The Miocene, balanced mainland faunas on the islands of Samos, Rhodes, Crete, etc. are clear examples. These islands were connected to the mainland in the Miocene. The Upper Pleistocene mainland fauna of Sicily indicates a connection of the present island with the mainland in that period.
2. A somewhat impoverished, balanced fauna can have several explanations, such as a restricted environment, a disconnected landmass, or a dispersal route which is possible for most animals, while for others it forms an insurmountable obstacle (filter bridge). This is the case with the late Early Pleistocene Trinil H.K. fauna (de Vos *et al.* 1982).
3. An unbalanced endemic fauna points to the conclusion that there was a broader sea barrier, crossed only occasionally by some animals through swimming or drifting on natural islets. If we find such a fauna on the present mainland, it indicates that that specific part of the mainland must have been an island in the past.

The Effect of Isolation

The effect of insularity on mammal evolution is approached by considering endemic fossil mammals of islands in the Mediterranean and the Indonesian Archipelago. In general, the same mammals will arrive on the islands by sweepstakes dispersal. Among the large mammals this includes the elephants, hippopotamids, deer and pigs, since these mammals are well-known for their good swimming and floating capacities.

Dispersal of the Mammals

If we look at the way of life of elephants, deer and hippos, then we see that they are all excellent swimmers, especially the elephants, who love bathing. There are plenty of reports of elephants swimming in the open sea near Ceylon. The trunk can be considered an excellent snorkel device. Deer flee to the water if they are in danger, and there are plenty of reports of swimming deer. The swimming capability of hippos is sufficiently well-known; there are reports of hippos swimming from the mainland of Africa to the island of Zanzibar, a distance of about 25 miles. In other words, elephants, deer and hippos swim very well even in the open sea, and it is not really surprising that these were the first large mammals to arrive on the islands.

Another character which enhances their potential to arrive safely on an island is their digestive system. Bacteria in the intestines of these herbivores abundantly produce gases, which give them a high floating capacity. This means that they could manage large sea distances by a combination of drifting and swimming. If the island happened to be close to the coast, they could return to the mainland. It is well-known that elephants visit islands close to the coast of India and Ceylon in order to gather food and return the same day, thus remaining in contact with the parent population (Johnson 1978). However, in certain cases, due to strong currents or in stress situations, animals might go further from the coast, and if they reached an island from which it was impossible to return, they had to settle there. Migration to islands might also have been triggered by behavior. In danger deer flee into the water. Overpopulation in the parental herds of hippos and elephants might be another case. Small mammals like rodents and insectivores may have come to the islands on natural rafts.

For a successful colonization the founder population must not be too small. In that respect, the large carnivores, which have a solitary way of life, consequently have a very small chance of becoming successful island colonizers. Moreover, they do not have the floating capacities of deer, elephants and hippos. For these reasons they are not able to cover the same large distances in the sea. Probably many of the Pleistocene islands were colonized in this way, and the immigrants became isolated from the mainland population and were compelled to live in a completely different environment in which large carnivores were lacking.

The fossils we have found on the islands show us which effect this insularity has had on subsequent mammal evolution. To some extent, we can compare this sequence of events to what happens in laboratory experiments. In a laboratory we repeat experiments, compare the results, and arrive at a conclusion. The island fossils can be regarded as the results of natural experiments. Similar ancestors came to different islands which had the same natural environment. The evolutionary changes these mammals underwent follow parallel patterns on different islands restricted within their geological age and geography. This can be explained as an adaptational process to an island environment lacking large carnivores (Sondaar 1977).

Size

The most striking change the larger mammals underwent on the islands was diminution in size. The Pleistocene dwarf elephants of Cyprus, Crete and Sicily had the size of a pig (Ambrosetti 1968; Bate 1906). On the mainland, elephants and hippos did not have natural enemies, because of their larger size. On the Pleistocene islands, where there were no large predators in the fauna, size lost its significance. Small size has several advantages, such as less food needed daily, a greater mobility and a reduction of the territorial area.

There is a relation between the size of the mammal and the size of the island. Cherry (1992) points to a decrease in size of *Prolagus* in the post-glacial period. He relates this observation to hunting activities of man. The large size of *Prolagus* of the Pleistocene is an argument that humans were not present. Cherry does not mention the provenience of the *Prolagus*. In the Pleistocene, Sardinia and Corsica were connected, and in the post-glacial period Sardinia and Corsica became separated by higher sea levels. In the post-glacial period, the *Prolagus* of the larger island, Sardinia, is significantly larger than the *Prolagus* of the much smaller Corsica. A relation between the size of the island and the size of *Prolagus* is more likely than that the smaller size of *Prolagus* on Corsica is due to human predation. On Miocene Gargano on the other hand, predation pressure of giant owls is related to the gigantism of rodents (Freudenthal 1978).

Low Gear Locomotion

In smaller mammals one would expect slender limb bones, but finds the opposite. The limbs are heavily built, and the lower part of the leg is shortened. This is especially clear in the endemic island ruminants. This character is just as common in the island mammals as is the diminution in size. An extreme example of this is the bovid *Myotragus* from the Balearic islands. The proportions of this small bovid could be best compared with those of very large bovids such as bison. On the islands, speed lost its significance because there were no big carnivores. The extremely short metapodials and phalanges resulted in feet of a solid construction, which is advantageous for low speed locomotion in a variety of mountainous environments. The changes that occurred in the island mammals can be explained as an adaptation to the island environment. They follow parallel patterns not bound to geography nor time. The dwarf elephants, hippos and ruminants with low gear locomotion were independent products of an evolution occurring in similar environments on different islands.

Giants and Birds

In the case where islands are not too far away from the mainland, the small mammals will face the same predators as on the mainland. Birds of prey and small rodents can hide easily. However, generally speaking, the endemic island rodents are larger than their mainland ancestors, and in some cases, they show gigantism. An explanation for this gigantism is more complex than the dwarfism in large mammals.

Giant rats are known from the islands of Southeast Asia, like the Philippines, Sulawesi and the smaller Sunda islands. Some species are not yet extinct. An interesting case is that of the giant rodents from the Miocene island of Gargano (Italy). In the stratigraphically younger deposits giant murids and hamsters are found (Freudenthal 1978). There were also endemic owls (Ballmann 1973) and, ironically, also in the younger deposits there are giant owls. It is supposed that the evolution of giant owls is related to their prey, "the giant rodents."

Giant tortoises might be another possible element of an island fauna. The Galapagos Islands provide such an example. In the past, giant tortoises were living on the Balearic islands and the islands of Southeast Asia, like Sulawesi and the smaller Sunda islands, though it remains uncertain whether this gigantism in island tortoises evolved on the islands or was inherited from giant mainland ancestors. The only natural enemy of giant tortoises are humans, and their extinction on islands is usually related to the arrival of humans. As such they are good indicators for the presence of man.

Human Presence and Faunal Evolution on Islands

Arrival by Corridor or Filter Route

The effect of Pleistocene humans on island environments is obscured by the fact that often human groups came not alone, but together with other mainland mammals. The first question to answer is how humans reached the island, by sea or over land? In the latter case the island was not an island anymore but became part of the mainland. Such a land connection between the mainland and the island can easily be detected. In this case we will find a mainland fauna, including humans, on the former island. This faunal turnover is dramatic. Good examples of such are Sicily in the Upper Pleistocene and Java in the Lower Pleistocene. In both cases, the unbalanced island fauna without large carnivores was replaced by a mainland fauna and the endemic island forms became extinct: for Sicily the dwarf elephant and hippo, for Java the Satir fauna with a *Mastodon*, hippo, deer and a giant tortoise (Sondaar 1984; 1987). It may be clear that the slow moving dwarfs with low gear locomotion had no chance to survive when the mainland predators entered their biotope. It may also be clear that it is difficult to judge which part humans played in the final extinction of the island endemics, perhaps with one exception, the *Geochelone* from Lower Pleistocene Java. Giant tortoises do not have many natural enemies besides humans.

Arrival by Sweepstakes Dispersal

Once an endemic island fauna is established, then it does not change much through time. A striking example is the five million year faunal history of the Balearic islands. The fauna was not affected by global climatological changes in that time interval. On the mainland, in contrast, we find dramatic changes such as extinctions and evolution of new taxa during that period. The arrival of humans on the Balearic islands approximately 8000 BP did change the fauna and flora, just as on the other Mediterranean islands (Sondaar *et al.* 1995).

Islands with Paleolithic humans outside the Mediterranean are Flores, Timor, Sulawesi and the Philippines. On those islands giant rats were present, and still are. Even now, they are eaten by the people on these islands, and they must also have been an important source of food for humans in the past. Arrival of humans by sweepstakes dispersal means the arrival of a predator on the island, and may have caused the extinction of the island megafauna. On Flores we find an endemic island fauna comprising a dwarf *Stegodon* and a giant tortoise (*Geochelone*). In a stratigraphic higher level in the same profile a *Stegodon* of mainland proportions is found. With this same *Stegodon trigonocephalus*, a giant rat (*Hooijeromys*) and a lithic industry are found (Maringer & Verhoeven 1970). This fauna is Middle Pleistocene in age (Sondaar 1987; 1989; Sondaar *et al.* 1994).

The following scenario may be constructed. In the Middle Pleistocene humans arrived on Flores. The dwarf *Stegodon* and the giant tortoise were easy prey and became extinct. The giant rats could survive by their high reproduction rate. These rats were at the same time a major source of protein for Paleolithic humans.

The extinction of the dwarf proboscideans and giant tortoises of Sulawesi and Timor may be explained in a similar way. In Timor, lack of stratigraphic control of the fossil bearing localities makes it impossible to verify this supposition. On Sulawesi, however, we find a similar faunal turnover as on Flores, namely an older, Late Pliocene to Early Pleistocene fauna with a giant tortoise and two pygmy proboscideans, *E. celebensis* and *S. sompoensis*. This fauna is replaced by a Middle Pleistocene to Upper Pleistocene fauna lacking tortoises and pygmy proboscideans, but instead containing two large sized proboscideans, *Stegodon* sp. B and an *Elephas* species (van den Bergh *et al.* 1992; 1994). Though no artifacts have been found so far in association with the younger faunal unit on Sulawesi, the arrival of humans might have had something to do with this pattern analogous to Flores.

The move of humans into the insular environment of Sardinia might have taken place in the early part of the Middle Pleistocene. A dramatic faunal change can be noted at that age. Many endemics became extinct like the dwarf pig, *Nesogoral* and probably *Maccaca majori* (Sondaar *et al.* 1984). The younger insular fauna with *Cynotherium*,

Megaloceros cazioti, Rhagamys, Tyrrhenicola and probably *Homo* replaced this fauna.

The lithic industry found in northern Sardinia (Arca *et al.* 1982) is evidence for a Middle Pleistocene human presence on the island, and the extinction of many elements of the *Nesogoral* fauna might have been caused by the hunting activities of humans. The presence of humans gave rise to the development of an unbalanced island fauna with a character different from that of other Mediterranean islands. The deer has mainland size and proportion.

The question is who were these humans? Human fossils were found in Corbeddu Cave (Oliena): a temporal, a maxilla (without teeth) and a proximal part of an ulna. The specimens show some distinct characters, which may set them apart from contemporary mainland populations (Spoor & Sondaar 1986).

In order to obtain more information about the chronostratigraphy of Corbeddu Cave, a new pit was excavated in 1993 on the location of the boring. The depth of this pit is 645.5 cm with respect to our reference point, and we counted 53 distinct levels. It is still uncertain if we have reached the bottom of the red clay deposits or not; further excavations will shed light on this discussion. From a depth of 4 meters on, deer fossils decrease in quantity, and the 2 meters above the bottom of the new pit are characterized by the dominance of *Prolagus sardus*. In almost all levels charcoal was found. The proximal part of a first human phalanx was discovered in a layer situated at a depth of 343 cm with respect to the reference point. This level lies a few centimeters beneath the lowest level excavated until now in the main excavation pit. The level in which the human fossil was found shows pollen spectra corresponding to a high glacial period. This information, in combination with extrapolations based on the carbon dates obtained on material from both excavation pits, points to an age of approximately 20,000 BP for the human phalanx. This means that this fossil is the oldest human fossil found so far on Sardinia and it demonstrates the presence of humans in the Paleolithic of this island. It is therefore of great importance in the discussion of the earliest human occupation of Sardinia (Sondaar *et al.* 1995).

Other arguments for an isolated endemic human population are provided by the artifacts. The Upper Pleistocene bone and lithic artifacts found in Corbeddu Cave, dated 16,000–10,000 BP, are unique. These characteristics do not suggest that the artifacts were left by sporadic visits, as put forward by Cherry (1984), but are evidence for a permanent colonization of the island. It can be argued that these cultures were very well adapted to the Pleistocene island environment of Sardinia with deer and ochotonids. This changed when Neolithic humans settled on the island. They had, as farmers, a completely different living strategy. Neolithic humans caused the downfall of the Paleolithic island hunter of Sardinia.

Survivals and Local Evolution

The arrival of humans, sometimes together with members of a contemporary mainland fauna, caused drastic changes in the local endemic fauna. The survivors are mainly the smaller mammals, like rodents and insectivores. In the *Tyrrhenicola* fauna, *Rhagamys* and *Prolagus* are represented by different species than in the older *Nesogoral* fauna. On the islands of Flores, Timor and Sulawesi it was the giant rats which did survive.

Within the *Tyrrhenicola* fauna only small evolutionary changes can be observed. The evolutionary change from one species into the other must have been a fast process, and might be considered an adaptative response to the drastic change in the environment. The mainland mammals, which arrived on the island, changed also; *Tyrrhenicola* is different from its ancestor *Allophaiomys* from the mainland. Again the evolutionary change must have been fast. Within the *Tyrrhenicola* there is little variation in this monospectic genus. The ancestor of *Cynotherium* was probably *Canis etruscus* and the ancestor of *Megaloceros cazioti* might have been a *Megaceros verticornis*-like deer (Malatesta 1970; Caloi & Malatesta 1974). Human fossils are found together with the *Tyrrhenicola* fauna.

So far no human fossils have been found on the island of Flores. The *Stegodon*, which arrived on the island with *Homo erectus*, shows only small morphological changes if compared with its ancestor from the mainland. Human presence on a Pleistocene island has its impact on the local faunal evolution. The fauna will stay impoverished and endemic, but dwarfism and low gear locomotion will not evolve.

Conclusions

The following may be concluded:

1) If a corridor or filter route comes into existence between the island and the mainland, humans will migrate to the former island together with its accompanying fauna. The local endemic island fauna will be replaced by the mainland fauna. It is possible, however, that some endemic, mostly small mammals will survive (examples are Early Pleistocene Java and Upper Pleistocene Sicily).

2) Sweepstakes dispersal of humans to an island will result in a dramatic faunal turnover. In the fossil record this is characterized by the extinction of endemic megafaunal elements, and the arrival of a few mainland species which do not evolve further. This dramatic faunal turnover can be dated at approximately 700,000 BP on both Flores (paleomagnetism) and Sardinia (paleontological evidence). The smaller mammals may survive, and will show some evolutionary changes just after the human arrival. Once settled on the island,

the fauna will evolve differently from islands without humans. Dwarfism and low gear locomotion will not evolve (Sardinia, Flores, possibly Sulawesi and the Philippines).

3) Islands with unbalanced faunas are only suitable for permanent colonization by Pleistocene humans if exploitation of the natural resources on the island can support a viable human population over a longer period of time, without exhaustion of the resources. On islands with endemic and unbalanced fauna, with a low diversity, the presence of a mammal large enough in size, with a high rate of reproduction, seems to be essential for the permanent settlement of a hunter-gatherer population. Examples for this are the ochotonid *Prolagus* from Sardinia/Corsica and the giant rats from the islands of Southeast Asia.

4) The dramatic Middle Pleistocene faunal turnover on Sardinia, together with the fact that the deer in the younger fauna show mainland proportions, points to the presence in this fauna of a large predator. The human hunter is a plausible candidate. This supposition is corroborated by the finds of Middle Pleistocene stone artifacts near Perfugas.

References

Allen, H. 1991. Stegodonts and the dating of stone tool assemblages in islands of S.E. Asia. *Asian Perspectives* 30: 243–660.

Ambrosetti, P. 1968. The Pleistocene dwarf elephants of Spinagallo (Siracuse, Southeastern Sicily). *Geologica Romana* 7: 277–398.

Arca M., Martini F., Pitzalis G., Tuveri C. & Ulzega A. 1982. *Paleolitica dell'Anglona (Sardegna Settentrionale). Richerche 1979–1980.* Quaderni 12. Sassari.

Aziz, F. & van den Bergh, G.D. 1995. A dwarf Stegodon from Sambungmacan (Central Java, Indonesia). *Proc. Kon. Nederl. Akad. Wetensch.* 93: 229–241.

Ballmann, P. 1973. Fossile Vogel aus dem Neogen der Halbinsel Gargano (Italien). *Scripta Geologica* 17: 1–75.

Bartstra, G.J, Keates, S.G., Basoeki, B. & Kallupa, B. 1991. On the dispersion of *Homo sapiens* in eastern Indonesia. *Current Anthropology* 32: 317–321.

Bate, D.M.A. 1906. The pygmy hippopotamus of Cyprus. *Geology Magazine*.

Bellwood, D. 1985. *Prehistory of the Indo-Malaysian Archipelago.* Academic Press.

Bergh, G.D. van den; Aziz, F., Sondaar, P.Y. & Hussain, S.T. 1992. Taxonomy, stratigraphy and paleozoogeography of Plio-Pleistocene proboscideans from the Indonesian Islands. *Publication of the Geological Research and Development Centre Bandung, Paleontology Series* 7: 28–58.

Bergh, G.D. van den, Aziz, F., Sondaar, P.Y. & Vos J. de. 1994. The first Stegodon fossils from Central Sulawesi and a new advanced Elephas species from South Sulawesi. *Publication of the Geological Research and Development Centre Bandung, Paleontology Series* 17: 22–39.

Bini, C., Martini, F., Pitzalis, G. & Ulzega, A. 1993. Sa Coa de Sa Multa e Sa Pedrosa Pantallinu: due 'Paleosuperfici' clactoniane in Sardegna. *Atti della XXX Riunione Scientifica, "Paleosuperfici del Pleistocene e del primo Olicene in Italia, Processi di Formazione e Interpretazione," Venosa ed Isernia, 26–29 ottobre 1991*, 179–197. Istituto Italiano di Preistoria e Protostoria, Firenze.

Caloi, L. & Malatesta, A. 1974. Il cervo Pleistocenico di Sardegna. Studi di Paletnologia, Paleoantropologia, Paleontologia e Geologia del Quaternario. *Memorie dell'Istituto Italiano di Paleontologia Umana* 2: 163–247.

Cherry, J.F. 1984. The initial colonization of the West Mediterranean islands in the light of island biography and paleogeography. In Waldren, W.H., Chapman, R., Lewthwaite, J. & Kennard, R.-C. (eds.), *The Deya Conference of Prehistory: Early Settlement in the Western Mediterranean Islands and the Peripheral Areas.* BAR International Series 229: 7–23. British Archaeological Reports, Oxford.

Cherry, J.F. 1992. Paleolithic Sardinians? In Tykot, R.H. & Andrews, T.K. (eds.), *Sardinia in the Mediterranean: A Footprint in the Sea. Studies in Sardinian Archaeology Presented to Miriam S. Balmuth.* Monographs in Mediterranean Archaeology 3: 28–39. Sheffield Academic Press, Sheffield.

Dermitzakis, M.D. & Sondaar, P.Y. 1979. The importance of fossil mammals in reconstructing paleogeography with special reference to the Pleistocene Aegean Archipelago. *Annales Geologique des Pays Hellenique* 29: 808–840.

Freudenthal, M. 1978. Zoogdierfauna's van het Miocene eiland Gargano, Itali'. *Mededelingen van de Werkgroep voor Tertiaire en Kwartaire Geologie* 15: 19–34.

Johnson, D.L. 1978. The origin of island mammoths and the Quaternary land bridge history of the northern Channel Islands, California. *Quaternary Research* 10: 204–25.

Klein Hofmeijer, G.J.M. 1997. *Late Pleistocene Deer Fossils from Corbeddu Cave (Implications for Human Colonization of the Island of Sardinia).* BAR International Series 663. British Archaeological Reports, Oxford.

Klein Hofmeijer, G. & Sondaar, P.Y. 1992. Pleistocene humans in the island environment of Sardinia. In Tykot, R.H. & Andrews, T.K. (eds.), *Sardinia in the Mediterranean: A Footprint in the Sea. Studies in Sardinian Archaeology Presented to Miriam S. Balmuth.* Monographs in Mediterranean Archaeology 3: 49–56. Sheffield Academic Press, Sheffield.

Klein Hofmeijer, G. & Sondaar, P.Y. 1993. The upper Paleolithic taphonomy in Corbeddu cave (Oliena, Sardinia): post-mortem damage of the lower dentition of Megaloceros caziotti. *Atti della XXX Riunione Scientifica, "Paleosuperfici del Pleistocene e del primo Olicene in Italia, Processi di Formazione e Interpretazione," Venosa ed Isernia, 26–29 ottobre 1991*, 277–288. Istituto Italiano di Preistoria e Protostoria, Firenze.

Leinders, J.J.M., Aziz, F., Sondaar P.Y. & De Vos, J. 1985. The age of the hominid-bearing deposits of Java: state of the art. *Geologie en mijnbouw* 64: 164–73.

Malatesta, A. 1970. *Cynotherium sardous Studiati.* An extinct Canid from the Pleistocene of Sardinia. *Memorie dell'Istituto Italiano di Paleontologia Umana* n.s. 1: 1–72.

Maringer, J. & Verhoeven, Th. 1970. Die Steinartefakte aus der Stegodon-Fossilschicht von Mengeruda auf Flores, Indonesien. *Anthropos* 65: 229–247.

Martini, F. 1992. Early human settlements in Sardinia: the Palaeolithic industries. In Tykot, R.H. & Andrews, T.K. (eds.), *Sardinia in the Mediterranean: A Footprint in the Sea. Studies in Sardinian Archaeology Presented to Miriam S. Balmuth.* Monographs in Mediterranean Archaeology 3: 40–48. Sheffield Academic Press, Sheffield.

Morwood, M.J. 1995. A preliminary report on stone material from Mata Menge, West Central Flores, Indonesia. International report for Dr. Aziz, G.R.D.C., 1–7.

Simpson, G.G. 1965. *The Geography of Evolution.* Philadelphia and New York, Chiltonbooks.

Sondaar, P.Y. 1977. Insularity and its effect on mammal evolution. In Hecht, M.N., Goody, P.L. & Hecht, B.M., *Major patterns in*

Vertebrate evolution, 671–707. Plenum, New York.

Sondaar, P.Y. 1984. Faunal evolution and the mammalian biostratigraphy of Java. *Courier Forschungsinstitut Senckenberg* 69: 219–235.

Sondaar, P.Y. 1987. Pleistocene mammals and extinctions of islands endemics. *Memoires de la Societe Geologique de France* n.s. 150: 159–165.

Sondaar, P.Y. 1989. Did man reach Australia via the giant rat and dingo route? *Bulletin of the Geological Research and Development Centre*. Bandung.

Sondaar, P.Y., Elburg, R., Klein Hofmeijer, G., Martini, F., Sanges, M., Spaan, A. & Visser, H. de. 1995. The human colonization of Sardinia: a Late-Pleistocene human fossil from Corbeddu Cave. *ComptesRendus de l'Académie des Sciences Paris* 320, serie IIa: 145–150.

Sondaar, P.Y., Martini F., Ulzega A, and Klein Hofmeijer G. 1991. L'homme Pleistocéne en Sardaigne. *L'Anthropologie* 181–200.

Sondaar, P.Y., Sanges, M., Kotsakis, T., Esu, D. & De Boer, P.L. 1984. First report on a Paleolithic culture in Sardinia. In Waldren, W.H., Chapman, R., Lewthwaite, J. & Kennard, R.-C. (eds.), *The Deya Conference of Prehistory: Early Settlement in the Western Mediterranean Islands and the Peripheral Areas*. BAR International Series 229: 29–47. British Archaeological Reports, Oxford.

Sondaar, P.Y., Sanges, M., Kotsakis, T. & De Boer, P.L. 1986. The Pleistocene deer hunter of Sardinia. *Geobios* 19: 17–25.

Sondaar, P.Y., Bergh, G.D. van den, Mubroto, B., Aziz, F., Vos, J. de & Batu, U.L. 1994. Middle Pleistocene faunal turnover and colonization of Flores (Indonesia) by Homo erectus. *ComptesRendus de l'Académie des Sciences Paris* 319, serie II: 1255–1262.

Sondaar, P.Y, Mcminn, M., Segui, B. & Alcover, J.A. 1995. Paleontological interest of karstic deposits from the Gymnesic and Pityusic islands. ENDINS 20. Mon. Soc. Hist. Nat. Balears 3: 155–171.

Spoor, F. & Sondaar, P.Y. 1986. Human fossils from the endemic island fauna from Sardinia. *Journal of Human Evolution* 15: 399–408.

Vos, J. de, Sartono, S., Hardja-Sasmita, S. & Sondaar, P.Y. 1982. The fauna from Trinil, type locality of Homo erectus: a reinterpretation. *Geologie en Mijnbouw* 61: 207–211.

9. Premier Peuplement Holocène et Néolithique de l'Île de Corse

François de Lanfranchi

En 1966 fut découverte en Corse, dans l'abri sous roche de Curacchiaghju (Lanfranchi 1967), une couche sous-jacente à celle du Néolithique ancien. Les structures, le mobilier et la position chronologique de ce niveau, apportaient les preuves archéologiques qu'une première fréquentation de l'abri fut réalisée lors de la phase climatique du Boréal. Nous avons donné à cette culture le nom de *Prénéolithique*. Il s'agissait, bien entendu, d'un terme d'attente qui comportait implicitement deux notions principales.

D'abord, nous souhaitions marquer l'antériorité de cette culture par rapport à celle du Néolithique ancien. Le fait est bien attesté par une première mesure d'âge radiométrique réalisée lors du sondage de 1966 et une seconde à l'occasion de l'élargissement du chantier de fouilles en 1967: 8560 ± 170 BP (Gif 795: calibrées 7967–7106 av. J.-C.); 8300 ± 130 BP (Gif 1963: calibrées: 7546–7007 av. J.-C.). Toutes nos mesures d'âge ont été calibrées, à notre demande, par J. Evin, et réalisées à partir des courbes de Stuiver *et al.* (Stuiver & Pearson 1993; Pearson & Stuiver 1993; Pearson *et al.* 1993).

Il fallait ensuite indiquer que ce premier peuplement holocène de la Corse n'offre aucune solution de continuité avec un hypothétique peuplement pléistocène. Le groupe humain s'est installé sur le substrat rocheux de cet abri sous auvent, après avoir aménagé sommairement le site, en confectionnant notamment des rigoles (évacuation de l'eau?). L'économie foncièrement prédatrice était fondée sur la collecte de nourriture et sur la chasse. L'outillage lithique du groupe était réalisé avec des roches locales comme le quartz et la rhyolite. Il s'agissait donc d'une industrie tirée d'éclats. L'absence de céramique constituait un marqueur négatif de l'équipement matériel de ce groupe.

D'où venaient ces premiers habitants de l'intérieur de l'île?

Pour répondre à cette interrogation, nous avons étendu nos recherches à la zone côtière et plus particulièrement à celle de Bonifacio (Fig. 9.1). Les raisons en sont très simple. L'archéologie qui se pratiquait dans les années soixante, n'utilisait qu'accessoirement les données anthropologiques, paléozoologiques et économiques. Notre conception tendait à offrir à ces travaux une place privilégiée plutôt que celle d'études annexes qu'on leur attribuait. La zone calcaire de Bonifacio, nous semblait convenir au mode de recherche que nous souhaitions conduire. Pour avoir suivi le précepte de l'abbé Breuil suivant lequel "On ne trouve que ce que l'on cherche", nous avons découvert en 1966 l'abri d'Araguina-Sennola que nous avons sondé cette même année en collaboration avec J. Liégeois. Durant l'été, nous avons commencé avec M.C. Weiss, l'étude de cet abri sous roche. Dix années allaient être consacrées à cette recherche. Nous avons mis au jour (Lanfranchi & Weiss 1973) une couche se rapportant à une occupation prénéolithique du site. Elle se trouvait à la base du dépôt archéologique et comprenait une sépulture en parfait état de conservation (Lanfranchi & Weiss 1973). Les mesures d'âge radiométriques étaient sensiblement semblables à celles de Curacchiaghju (8520 ± 150 BP: Gif 2705; calibrées 7923–7105 av. J.-C.).

La sépulture permit une étude anthropologique (Duday 1975) et une approche des rites funéraires (Lanfranchi & Weiss 1977). Les restes de repas (os, coquillages et arêtes de poissons) donnèrent une tout autre dimension à la définition du Prénéolithique de Corse (Lanfranchi & Weiss 1977).

Récemment, nous avons découvert puis fouillé les sites de Longone (Lanfranchi 1993) et de Monte Leone (Lanfranchi 1991). Dans ce dernier, nous avons reconnu une occupation prénéolithique hypothèse qui fut confirmée par une mesure d'âge radiométrique réalisée à partir d'un os: 8225 ± 80 BP (ETH8–305; calibrées 7425–7043 av. J.-C.).

Comme nous avons la responsabilité d'un grand chantier de fouilles dans le village néolithique de Presa-Tusiu, nous avons demandé à J.-D. Vigne de bien vouloir

François de Lanfranchi, Centre d'Etudes et de Recherches Archéologiques en Alta Rocca (CERAAR), 20170 Levie, Corse, France

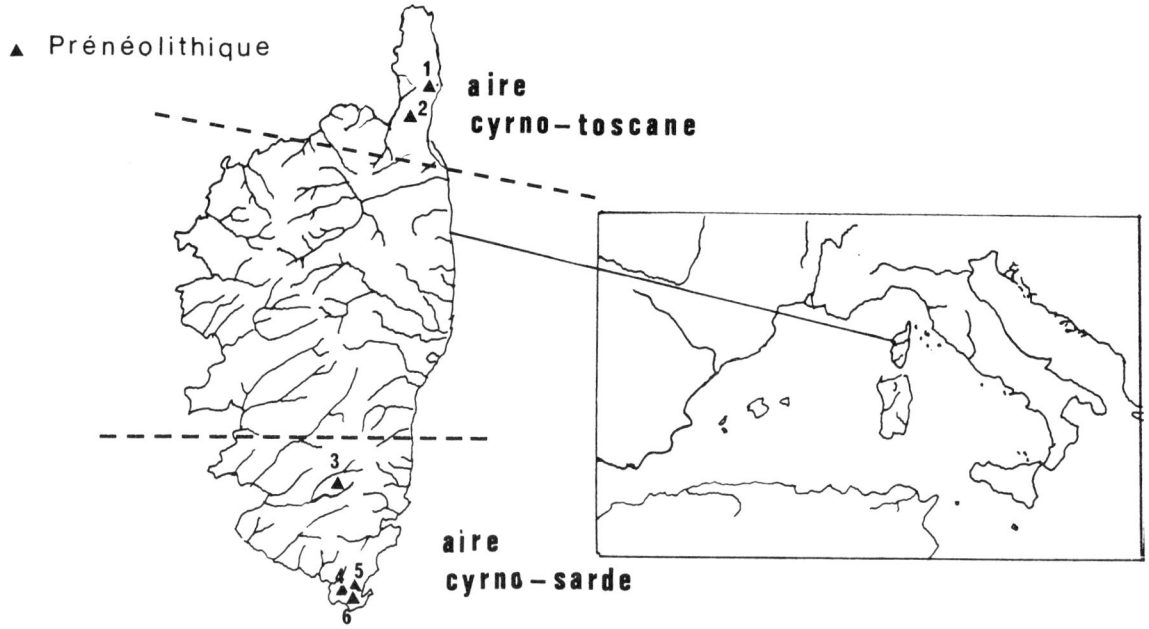

Fig. 9.1. Sites prénéolithiques de Corse.
1 - Pietracorbara; 2 - Strette; 3 - Curacchiaghju; 4 - Araguina-Sennola; 5 - Monte Leone; 6 - Longone.

assurer la direction du chantier de fouille de Monte Leone en 1995. Nous avons ainsi réuni les conditions pour réaliser une fouille collective.

Depuis nos propres travaux sur le premier peuplement de l'île, de nouvelles découvertes sont signalées en Haute Corse par J. Magdeleine (1983–1984). Comme en Corse méridionale, un peuplement prénéolithique a précédé celui du Néolithique. Dans les deux sites mentionnés, les mesures d'âge radiométriques sont les suivantes:

Strette II   Ly 2837   9140 ± 300 BP   calibrées 9015–7538 av. J.-C.
Pietracorbara   LGQ 507   7840 ± 310 BP   calibrées 7439–6073 av. J.-C.
Pietracorbara   LGQ 508   6920 ± 300 BP   calibrées 6341–5255 av. J.-C.

Les récents progrès réalisés en Toscane (Grifoni Cremonesi & Tozzi 1994), par exemple, invitent à voir dans notre Prénéolithique un Mésolithique de type italique. Dans une phase avancée du Mésolithique, soit à la fin du Boréal et au début de l'Atlantique, le complexe tardenoïde se substitue au complexe Sauveterrien. L'économie est fondée sur la chasse aux petits mammifères et aux oiseaux. Les aires préférentielles sont alors les rives des lacs et des mares, les zones côtières et surtout l'étage montagneux que l'on commence à exploiter. En Toscane, il se produit un sensible dépeuplement de la vallée de l'Arno en faveur des aires appennines. En Corse, l'équipement lithique serait à corréler avec celui de l'Epigravettien final et du Sauveterrien de l'Italie (Tozzi 1995).

A cette similitude culturelle s'ajoute pour la Corse une même tendance qu'en Italie, à savoir que dans une phase avancée du Boréal, les Prénéolithique implantés sur le territoire de l'actuel Bonifacio, ont prospecté l'intérieur de l'île, plus précisément les territoires de l'Alta Rocca. Relevons, toutefois, qu'à la différence de la Toscane où les vallées se dépeuplent, celles de Corse témoignent d'un certain développement.

Ainsi, la loi naturelle qui consiste à exploiter les ressources de la *piaghja* et de la montagne naît au Prénéolithique. Elle se perpétuera jusque dans les années cinquante et marquera les fondements de l'économie agro-sylvo-pastorale de la Corse. Les relations *piaghja*-montagne s'affirment au Néolithique. L'étude de cette période ainsi que celle des phénomènes de néolithisation de l'île passe par celle de l'identification des groupes humains et de leurs zones d'influence. Actuellement nous pouvons en distinguer trois.

La première est l'aire méridionale avec ses *piaghji* qui vont de Bonifacio à Solenzara et ses montagnes qui couvrent l'Alta Rocca. C'est le modèle qui a été réalisé par les Prénéolithiques (Fig. 9.2). La seconde, centrale, est constituée par les versants orientaux et occidentaux de l'étage mésoméditerranéen inférieur, à partir desquels les paysans-éleveurs vont accéder à la zone montagneuse centrale. L'aire ainsi définie va de Vizzavona à Vivario et du Manganello à Vezzani. C'est la Zone centrale. La troisième qui constitue le modèle septentrional comprend les *piaghji* du Nebbiu et de la Balagne et les montagnes du Niolu.

L'étage mésoméditerranéen inférieur (*piaghja*) apparaît comme une zone préférentielle choisie par les groupes porteurs d'une culture néolithique (Fig. 9.3). L'été venu, les zones montagneuses méridionale, centrale et septentrionale, reçoivent les éleveurs des régions basses. Il s'agit donc d'un habitat temporaire pour les bergers, et permanent pour les paysans. Ainsi apparurent lentement, au fil du temps, des communautés montagnardes qui continuèrent à entretenir des relations

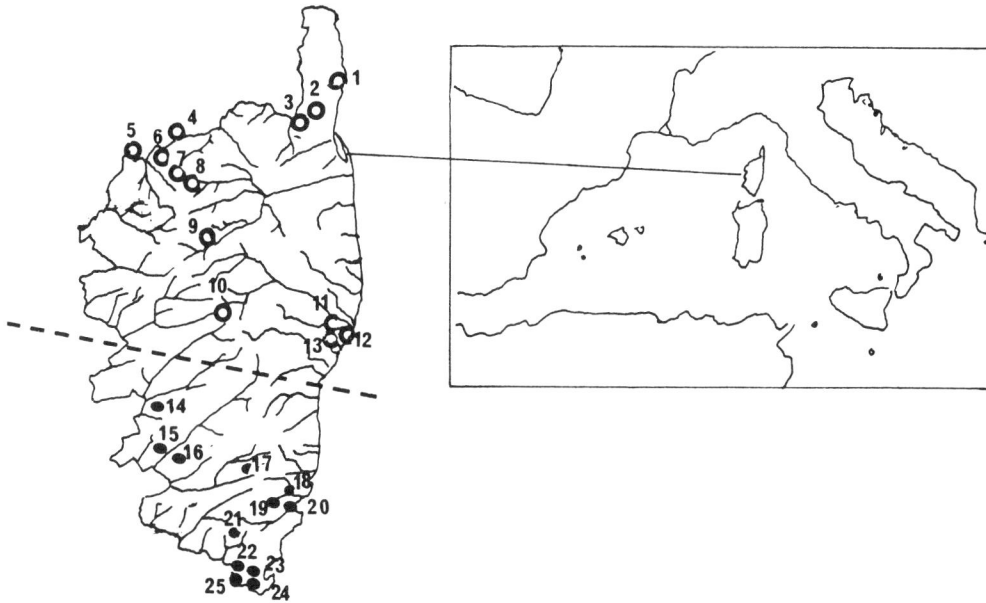

Fig. 9.2. Sites néolithiques de Corse.
1 - Pietracorbara; 2 - Strette; 3 - Grotta Scritta de St Florent; 4 - A Petra; 5 - A Revellata; 6 - Monte Ortu; 7 - Porte Vecchie Corsu; 8 - Carcu; 9 - Abri Albertini; 10 - Grotte Southwell (Vizzavone); 11 - Terrina I; 12 - Casabianda I; 13 - Casabianda II; 14 - Petrosella; 15 - Basi; 16 - Filitosa abri D'; 17 - Curacchiaghju; 18 - Ortale; 19 - San Ciprianu; 20 - Foce; 21 - Bufua (Figari); 22 - Araguina-Sennola; 23 - Monte Leone; 24 - Longone; 25 - Abri du Goulet.

avec celles des *piaghji*. Au Néolithique post-cardial, on verra par exemple se développer dans les zones montagneuses, les premiers villages, preuve d'une réelle sédentarisation des groupes.

Dans le domaine des influences externes, les deux aires qui avaient été perçues au Prénéolithique s'affirment encore plus nettement. Il s'agit de l'aire cyrno-toscane et de l'aire cyrno-sarde dont nous avons déjà parlé.

La néolithisation de l'île se réalise à partir du modèle prénéolithique entre l'étage mésoméditerranéen inférieur du pays de Bonifacio et l'étage mésoméditerranéen supérieur de l'Alta Rocca. Il s'agit en somme de l'élargissement d'un écosystème marin par l'adjonction de biotopes divers: forêts, lacs, fleuves, etc.

La néolithisation de la Corse se fonde sur la mise en place d'un système pastoral fondé sur la transhumance, mais également sur la technique de l'errance quotidienne du troupeau d'ovins ou de caprins (Lanfranchi, 1994). Elle a également comme moteur une agriculture qui se développe au fil des ans pour devenir prépondérante à la fin du premier néolithique de la Corse. Les paysans néolithiques exploitent les potentialités de la montagne et celles de la *piaghja*: la première offrant des récoltes tardives, alors que la seconde est l'espace de la précocité. Les céréales ont par exemple une double origine. Les unes proviennent d'une culture de montagne; les autres, de la *piaghja*. La bi-polarisation de l'économie de production néolithique est l'une des caractéristiques de la Corse. La "montagne dans la mer" (Ratzel) façonne son économie primitive en fonction d'un certain déterminisme géographique.

Bibliographie

Duday, H. 1975. *Le squelette du sujet féminin de la sépulture prénéolithique de Bonifacio (Corse).* Etude anthropologique, Essai d'interprétation palethnographique, Cahiers d'Anthropologie, Mémoire 24.

Grifoni Cremonesi, R. & Tozzi, C. 1994. Gli insediamenti dal Paleolitico all'età del Bronzo. In *La Pianura di Pisa e i rilievi contermini. La natura e la storia,* 153–182. Provincia di Pisa, Roma.

Lanfranchi, F. de. 1967. La grotte sépulcrale de Curacchiaghju (Levie, Corse). *Bulletin de la Société Préhistorique Française* 64: 587–612.

Lanfranchi, F. de. 1972. *Le peuplement des hauts bassins du Rizzanese et de l'Ortolo, des origines à l'arrivée des Romains.* Thèse Universitaire, Faculté des Lettres de Toulouse.

Lanfranchi, F. de. 1991. Monte Leone (Bonifacio). *Bilan Scientifique, Service Régional de l'Archéologie,* 21–22.

Lanfranchi, F. de. 1993. Le Néolithique ancien méditerranéen. *Corsica Antica* 1: 2–8.

Lanfranchi, F. de. 1994. Pastoralisme et paysannerie à l'aube de l'Age du Bronze. In Biagi, P. & Nandris, J. (eds.), *Highland Zone Exploitation in Southern Europe.* Monografie di "Natura Bresciana" 20: 272–295. Museo Civico di scienze naturali di Brescia, Brescia.

Lanfranchi, F. de & Weiss, M.C. 1973. *La civilisation des Corses, Les origines.* Ed. Cyrnos et Méditerranée, Ajaccio.

Lanfranchi, F. de & Weiss, M.C. 1977. *Araguina-Sennola, dix années de fouilles préhistoriques à Bonifacio.* Archéologia Corsa, Etudes et Mémoires 2: 1–167.

Magdeleine, J. 1983–84. Les premières occupations de l'abri de Strette. *Archéologia Corsa* 8–9: 30–50.

Pearson, G.W., Becker, B. & Qua, F. 1993. High-precision 14C measurement of German and Irish oaks to show the natural 14C variations from 7890 to 5000 BC. *Radiocarbon* 35: 93–104.

Pearson, G.W. & Stuiver, M. 1993. High-precision bidecadal

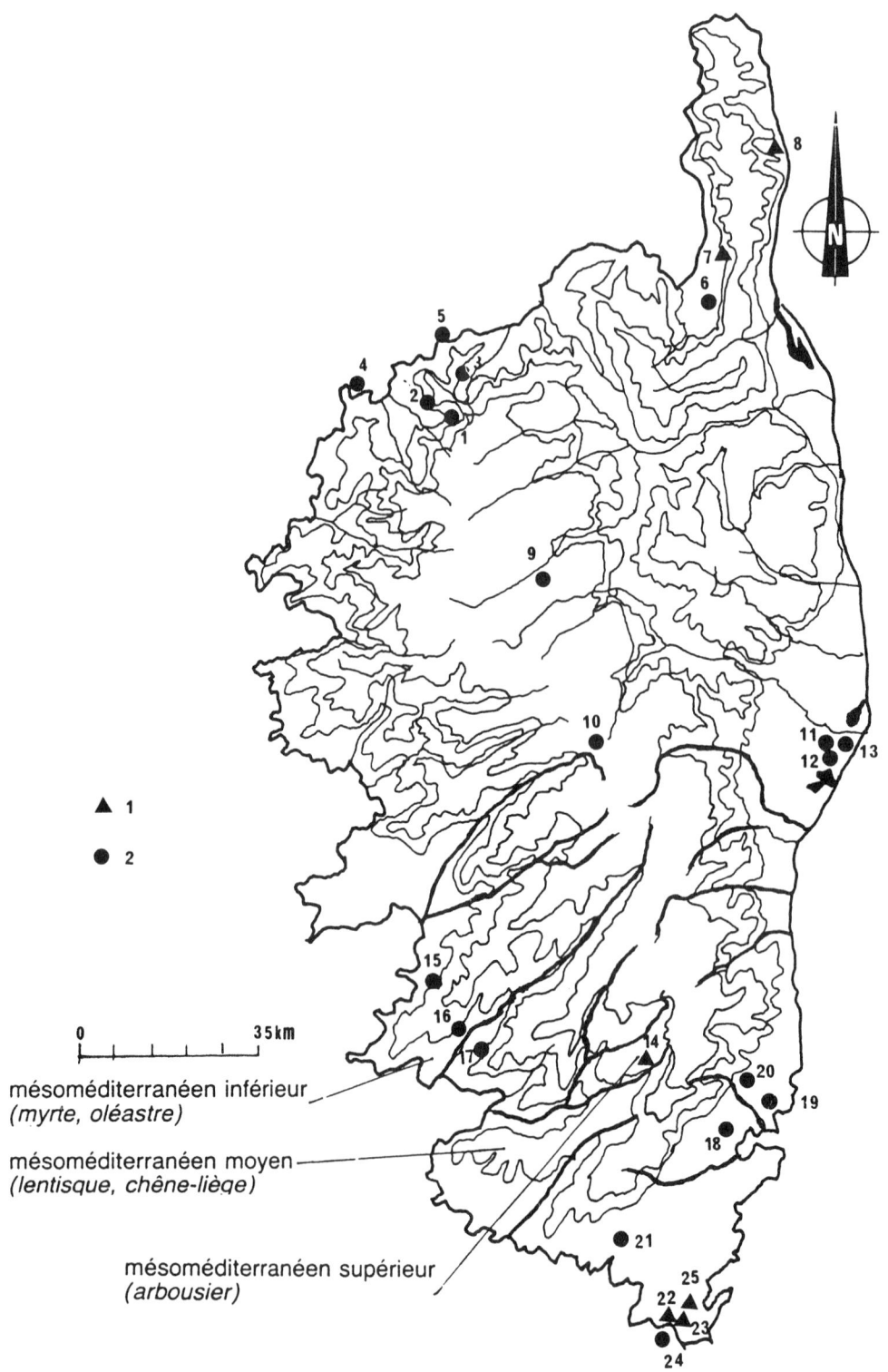

Fig. 9.3. Carte de répartition des sites prénéolithiques (représentés par un triangle) et néolithiques (cercle).

calibration of the radiocarbon time scale 500–2500 BC. *Radiocarbon* 35: 25–33.

Stuiver, M. & Pearson, G.W. 1993. High-precision bidecadal calibration of the radiocarbon time scale, AD 1950–500 BC and 2500–6000 BC. *Radiocarbon* 35: 1–23.

Tozzi, C. 1995. Rapports entre Corse et littoral tyrrhénien péninsulaire durant la Préhistoire (Paléo-mésolithique, Néolithique. In *Ouvrage collectif* en cours de parution aux Ed. Albiana.

Vigne, J.-D. 1992. Rapport annuel de fouille sur le site de Monte Leone, campagne de 1992 (Monte Leone Bonifacio Corse). *Bilan Scientifique, Service régional de l'archéologie.*

Vigne, J.-D. 1988. *Les Mammifères Post-Glaciaires de Corse, Etude archéozoologique*. Gallia Préhistoire supplément 26. CNRS, Paris.

10. Preliminary Results on the Exploitation of Animal Resources in Corsica During the Preneolithic

Jean-Denis Vigne

By the new territories and by the edible plant and animal resources that they provided, the Mediterranean islands form "an essential part of the wider patterns of change in post-Pleistocene subsistence regimes throughout the Near East, the Mediterranean and Europe" (Cherry 1990: 202). In addition, their utilization and colonization by Late Paleolithic or Mesolithic people offer very consistent data about the relationships between humans and the sea during the Preneolithic periods. At last, the abilities of the Mesolithic people for adaptation to different kinds of environments can be richly documented by the Mediterranean islands, whose very long isolation produced pristine environments for the Mesolithic colonizers.

Corsica is one of the less poorly documented Mediterranean islands for the Preneolithic colonization contemporaneous with the Mesolithic. This note, which has partly been given to the conference "Man and Sea in the Mesolithic" at Kalundborg (Denmark, 1993), consists of a first tentative synthesis of the evidence for animal exploitation during the Preneolithic in Corsica (9000–7000 BP), based on the preliminary archaeozoological study of three new sites (Vigne & Desse-Berset 1995).

The General Framework

Corsica has been isolated from the mainland for a very long time. Even during the largest sea regressions of the last Glacial, it remained isolated from the mainland (but linked to Sardinia). The sea level, which was -120 m during the glacial maximum (ca. 18,000 BP), rose very rapidly (~ 1 m/century) up to -35 m around 8000 cal BC, then more slowly (~ 0.6 m/c.) since it was around -7 m ca. 4000 BC. When Mesolithic cultures emerged in Italy, most of the rise had occurred, present continental shelves were partly in place and the coastlines were more similar to the present ones than to the pleniglacial ones (Shackleton *et al.* 1984; van Andel 1989; 1990). At this time Corsica was probably already separated by sea from Sardinia.

Palynological data suggest that during the 'Boreal Phase' the vegetation of Corsica was dominated by deciduous oak and *Erica arborea* forests, which was replaced during the 'Sub-Boreal' by human induced maquis and *Quercus ilex* forests (Reille 1992).

Being isolated for several hundred millennia, Corsica (and Sardinia) developed an endemic and taxonomically impoverished terrestrial fauna. As for large mammals, Late Pleistocene deposits indicate the presence of a small megacerine deer (*Megaloceros cazioti*) and of a canid of fox-like size (*Cynotherium sardous*) (Sondaar 1987; Vigne 1990; 1992a; Vigne *et al.* 1997). In addition, the Corsico-Sardinian massif contained populations of several small mammal species: an ochotonid lagomorph (*Prolagus sardus*), the size of a big rat; a large field mouse (*Rhagamys orthodon*); a large vole (*Tyrrhenicola henseli*); and a large soricid insectivore (*Episoriculus similis-corsicanus*) (Vigne 1990). As with birds and frogs, their populations should have been dense, particularly in low-vegetation areas (Vigne & Valladas 1996) and may have provided attractive food resources for human groups.

Middle Paleolithic frequentation sites in Sardinia (Arca *et al.* 1982), and perhaps in Corsica (Bonifay 1994), indicate that seafaring was actually within the capabilities of Paleolithic people. However, as emphasized earlier (Vigne 1989: 41; see also Cherry 1990), it is necessary to establish a clear-cut difference between occasional visits and the actual *colonization* ('occupation' of Cherry 1990: 198) of islands, the latter being identifiable by relevant archaeological criteria such as human graves, evidence of occupation throughout the yearly cycle, exclusive utilization of local biological and mineral resources, etc. So far, such evidence has not been collected for the Paleolithic on the Corsico-Sardinian massif.

Jean-Denis Vigne, CNRS (URA 1415), Muséum national d'Histoire naturelle, Laboratoire d'Anatomie comparée, 55, rue de Buffon, F-75005 Paris, France

On Corsica, three sites have provided evidence of Preneolithic occupations: Curacchiaghiu (layer 7: Lanfranchi 1967; 1974), Araguina-Sennola (layer XVIII: Lanfranchi et al. 1973; Lanfranchi & Weiss 1977) and Strette II (layers XXIV and XXII: Magdeleine 1985; Magdeleine & Ottaviani 1986). Radiocarbon dating (Table 10.1) defines a period from ca. 8000 to 7500 BC. These three sites have only been excavated over a very limited area (two to four square meters). Pottery is absent as well as domestic mammals. Artifactual material is always composed of idiosyncratic lithics made from local quartz and rhyolite, without the imported obsidian which marks the beginning of the Early Neolithic. Animal remains (Magdeleine & Ottaviani 1986; Vigne 1988) consist mainly of shellfish, fish, birds and small endemic mammals dominated by *Prolagus sardus* (Vigne 1988). Large game is absent, and probably became extinct just before this period. In addition, layer XVIII of Araguina-Sennola provided the grave of an individual female, whose anthropological study demonstrated that she was severely physically handicapped for several years before her death. The burial features are the same as those known on the mainland during the final Paleolithic and Mesolithic, and completely different from those used in Corsica during the Neolithic (Duday 1975). All these data suggest permanent hunter-gatherer human groups on Corsica during the 9th millennium BP. Chronological data clearly antedate the first appearance of the Neolithic in Italy and the Western Mediterranean, which seems to exclude Neolithic hunter-gatherer groups. But the very atypical lithic material involves a cautious attribution to a poorly defined Preneolithic.

Recent Discoveries and General Characteristics of Preneolithic Corsican Sites

Three new Preneolithic sites have been recently discovered in Corsica (Fig. 10.1). The first is situated in the northern part of the island (*Cap Corse*). In the *abri 2* of Pietracorbara, J. Magdeleine (1991; 1995) discovered a 1.5 m thick stratigraphy, the deepest cultural layer of which (layer 9) produced a Preneolithic grave (Bouville 1995). The skeleton's pelvis and posterior limbs had been amputated, probably at the time of the burial, and it was accompanied by crude lithics made of local rocks. Just on top of layer 9, layer 8 provided charcoal, crude artifacts, shellfish, fish and numerous small mammal bones (Vigne 1995). The two radiocarbon dates (Table 10.1) are not very consistent internally, nor with the stratigraphy, but seem to indicate a recent Preneolithic phase between the 7th and the 6th millennia cal BC.

The two other sites are in the very southern part of the island, on the *commune de Bonifacio*, very close to Araguina-Sennola. Longone is situated 650 m south of Araguina-Sennola, in an adjacent small valley. It is an

Lab No.	Provenance	Date BP	Date cal BC
Strette II (Barbaggio, Haute-Corse)			
Ly 2867	Layer XXIV	9080 ± 300	8989 (8081) 7501
Araguina-Sennola (Bonifacio, Corse-du-Sud)			
Gif 2705	Layer XVIII (charcoal)	8520 ± 150	7923 (7535) 7254
Curacchiaghiu (Lévie, Corse-du-Sud)			
Gif 797	Layer 7 (charcoal)	8560 ± 170	7967 (7543) 7254
Gif 1963	Layer 7 (charcoal)	8300 ± 180	7591 (7111) 6758
Monte Leone (Bonifacio, Corse-du-Sud)			
ETH-8305	Layer 2	8225 ± 80	(biased δ^{13}C)
AA-18108	Layer 2a	8050 ± 60	6697 (7030) 7098
AA-18109	Layer 2b	8965 ± 70	8021 (7892) 8095
AA-18110	Layer 3	8335 ± 70	7505 (7422) 7233
AA-18111	Layer 4	9750 ± 175	9279 (9018) 8465
AA-18112	Layer 5	8415 ± 65	7546 (7452) 7294
Pietracorbara (Haute-Corse)			
LGQ 507	Layer 8	7840 ± 310	7496 (6607) 6013
LGQ 508	Layer 9	6920 ± 300	6373 (5733) 5263

Table 10.1: Radiocarbon dates from Corsican Preneolithic sites

open-air site just in front of a small calcareous cliff and beside an abundant spring. The long Neolithic stratigraphy (Lanfranchi 1987) starts with a sterile layer (5a1-2), itself covering a sandy layer (5a3) which lies on the bedrock. No archaeological remains have been discovered in layer 5a3, but sieving (1 mm mesh size) of a sample of sediment (15 liters) yielded some charcoal fragments and a few animal remains, some of the latter bearing clear marks of having been eaten by humans (see below). This layer has not been radiocarbon dated, but it is certainly older than 6320 ± 140 BP (LGQ 617; Lanfranchi, unpublished data), which is the oldest radiocarbon date obtained for the Early Neolithic (Epicardial) of Longone (layer 4a2). Layer 5a3 of Longone is not a real cultural one, but provides new, if fleeting, evidence of the Preneolithic presence of human beings in Southern Corsica.

One kilometer higher in the same St-Julien valley, the Monte Leone site is a very large rock shelter opening northwards. A sounding indicated that the upper two meters of the sediments are practically lacking any evidence at all for a human presence, except a terminal Late Neolithic grave (Lanfranchi 1995). But the deepest explored layer (layer 5) was subjected to preliminary excavation during 1992 over a very limited area (1 m²). Half of a 50 cm thick complex deposit has been excavated. Excavation and systematic sieving (at 1 mm mesh for 284 liters of sediments) produced thousands of small vertebrate bones (fish and mammals), a few sea-shells and less than 20 quartz and rhyolite lithics. Radiocarbon dating on *Prolagus* bones gave 8225 ± 80 BP (ETH-8305), but this dating is not acceptable because of a biased ^{13}C ratio. Extensive excavations conducted on 20 m² during 1995 have yielded four mesolithic layers, some small graves (probably for food storage), a very rich faunal material (Vigne in press) and five good radiocarbon dates (Table 10.1) which indicate an occupation from the middle to the end of the 8th millennium cal BC (Vigne et al. in press). This is the first large Preneolithic site with domestic structures in Corsica.

The chronological position of the five Corsican Pre-

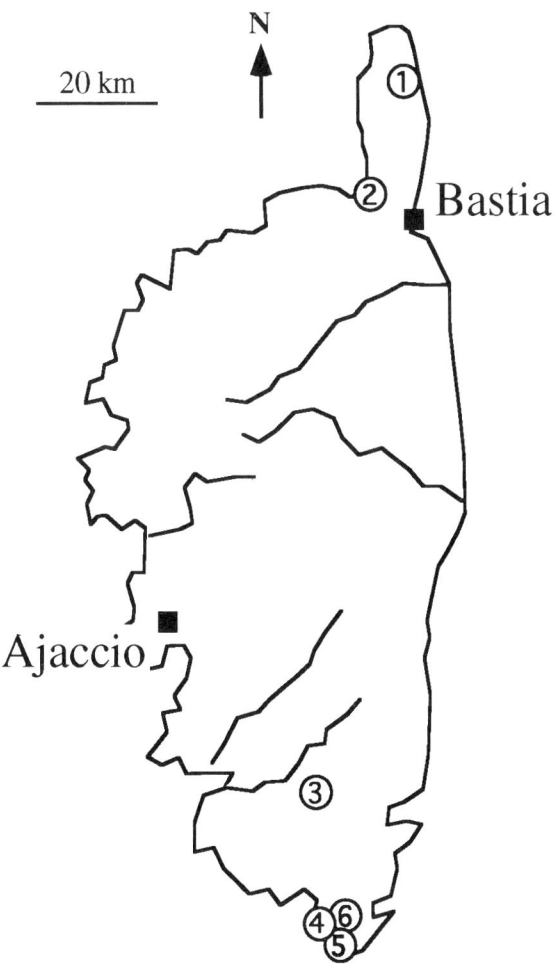

Fig. 10.1. Geographical location of the Preneolithic sites in Corsica: 1. Pietracorbara; 2. Strette; 3. Curacchiaghiu; 4. Araguina-Sennola; 5. Longone; 6. Monte Leone.

neolithic sites with radiocarbon dates covers the middle and the second half of the 9th millennium and, perhaps, the 8th millennium BP (Table 10.1; Vigne *et al.* in press). They share common characteristics: rock shelters, idiosyncratic artefacts and great amounts of small vertebrate bones. Except for Curacchiaghiu (ca. 800 m asl; 20 km from the present seashore), all of them are situated at low altitude, very near the present seashore. According to a drop of sea level of ca. -35 m during the 8th millennium, Araguina-Sennola, Longone and Pietracorbara were situated about 1.2 to 2 km from the sea-shore, Monte-Leone about 2.7 to 3.2 km and Strette at less than 4 km. That indicates that they were not real littoral sites but settlements on the coastal plain situated less than an hour's walk from the sea.

Archaeozoological Data

Layer XVIII of Araguina-Sennola provided more than 7000 animal remains (Vigne 1988), in spite of the lack of systematic water-sieving. They were mainly composed of 6552 *Prolagus* bones, more than 20% of which bear distal burn marks ('*brûlures distales*'; Vigne *et al.* 1981). Endemic rodents are represented by at least 18 individuals, some of them also bearing distal burn marks (Vigne & Marinval-Vigne 1983). Birds are very few and the only species represented are terrestrial (one sparrow and one buzzard). Shellfish are represented by a few dozen *Patella* and *Monodonta;* fish have not yet been completely studied, but they are attested by 480 bone remains, only 28 of them being skull bones. One vertebra indicates the presence of a young seal (*Monachus monachus*).

Layer 5a3 at Longone provided two sea-shells (one burnt), two *Rhagamys-Tyrrhenicola* bones (one bearing distal burn marks), seven *Prolagus* bones (three bearing distal burn marks) and seven indeterminate small vertebrate remains.

The Preneolithic layer of Monte Leone yielded tens of thousands of faunal remains. So far, only one sample (D4-VIII: 10 liters of sediment) has been exhaustively studied, and is composed of 3459 remains. Here again, *Prolagus* is the most abundant, with 3095 determinate remains, a large number of which bear distal burn marks; this number extrapolates to more than 80,000 *Prolagus* bone remains for the excavated area of only one square meter, and, basing on sampling of the whole site, to 50,000 to 150,000 individuals for the whole site, i.e. 25 to 75 tons of edible meat! In the 10 liter sample, the rodents are represented by 50 bones. Birds and shellfish are absent from this sample, but they are represented in the excavated sediments as a whole by bones of large birds (especially the great buster: Cuisin & Vigne in press) and fragments of edible sea gastropods, respectively. Fish are represented by 314 identified bones in the 10 liter sample, but they are much more numerous on the whole site. Most of them are small to very small size fish, the head of which is completely absent from the deposit, which suggests special food treatment. Large fish are scarce. New excavations also produced one seal bone and a small number of small dolphin bones.

Yet again, *Prolagus sardus* is the most abundant species in the bone remains of Pietracorbara layer 8 (3918 bones remains; Vigne 1995). Except for three fish teeth and four rodent mandibles, they are the only vertebrate remains, perhaps because of the poor sieving of sediments. In addition, 295 sea-shells (*Patella* and *Monodonta*) have been found.

Only the vertebrate remains of layers XXIV and XXII of Strette II have been studied (Vigne, unpublished data). Layer XXIV only produced 41 *Prolagus* and one fish bones; layer XXII contained 1979 *Prolagus* (MNI = 92) and 2 bird bones. More than 7% of *Prolagus* bones were burnt, but there were no clear distal burn marks. As for sea-shells, which were less than 500, Magdeleine (1985) emphasizes the diversity of species (*Mytilus, Ostrea, Patella, Cardium, Venus,* etc.).

Curacchiaghiu layer 7 did not produce any animal

Estimation of the Proportions of Animal Resources

On the basis of archaeozoological observations (distal burn marks, absence or scarcity of fish head bones, etc.), this first estimation postulates that all bones and shells at these sites represent food remains, even if a few small mammal remains may come from owl pellets. Following a method described elsewhere (Vigne 1988: 219–20; 1992b; Vigne & Desse-Berset 1995), the Weight of Edible Matters (WEM) for each zoological group has been estimated on the basis of the Minimal Numbers of Individuals (MNI) and on the Average Individual Weight of Edible Matter (AIWEM) for each species.

Figure 10.2 gives a picture of the percentages of animal species in the diets of each site. *Prolagus*, rodents, and birds, i.e. terrestrial resources, always constitute more than 78% (Monte Leone) and up to 95–98% (Araguina-Sennola, Strette and Pietracorbara). Curiously, shellfish yielded very few edible resources, as demonstrated by the Monte Leone sample, where the collection has been systematic. However, Strette II seems to have provided, if not more abundant, at least a more diversified sample of sea-shells. The abundance of fish is probably underestimated on all sites except Monte Leone, because of the very small size of most of their bones and because of the absence of systematic fine-sieving at Pietracorbara, Strette and Araguina-Sennola. This latter site however yielded rather important quantities of medium-sized fish, which suggests that, if systematic fine-sieving had been used, their abundance could have been as great as at Monte Leone.

On the basis of these remarks, it appears that (i) the diets observed in the five sites do not differ greatly from each other; (ii) the Monte Leone data probably offer the most secure picture of a Preneolithic diet, because of fine water-sieving; (iii) maritime resources did not represent more than 20 to 30% in these Preneolithic diets. This last assertion must be tempered by the possibility of seal hunting, although at present poorly documented by few bones at Araguina-Sennola and Monte Leone.

Discussion and Conclusion

Five archaeozoological samples show, in much the same way, how human beings survived on the Mediterranean islands by hunting and gathering during the 9th millennium BP, in spite of the lack of large game. They did so by hunting (or trapping) small terrestrial mammals (and birds), by coastal fishing and, to a much lesser extent, by gathering shellfish. The special characteristics of these resources, together with "more 'relaxed' conditions in a less crowded, newly settled environment" (Lewthwaite 1989: 840; Cherry 1990: 181) may explain why there are no classical Mesolithic microliths in these cultures.

Nevertheless, these five sites were situated at approximately the same distance from the Preneolithic sea-shore (1.2 to 4 km). It is thus impossible to decide if the picture of the diet that they give is a general one, or one relevant only to specialized sites all of the same kind. We cannot exclude the possibility of more significant exploitation of maritime resources at littoral settlements which may presently lie below sea level; although it is not completely confirmed by the fish bones of Araguina-Sennola, the absence of fish heads at Monte Leone suggests the existence of fishing sites on the seashore for the treatment and perhaps storage of fish. In the same perspective of specialized settlements, it cannot be excluded that settlements at higher altitude were used for collecting other food resources, although the absence of any large mammal remains in the plain sites seems to exclude hunting of large endemic game which may have had their refuge in the highlands. Since the endemic mammals of Corsica, especially *Prolagus*, lived in low vegetation rather than in forests (Vigne & Valladas 1996), the presently known Preneolithic sites of Corsica may only be specialized coastal plain settlements for small mammal hunting (or trapping). These hypotheses will be tested by the analysis of the data coming from the recent excavations at Monte Leone.

This discussion highlights the great scarcity of data about the hunter-gatherers of Corsica, which appears to be the least poorly documented Mediterranean island for this purpose. For the future, systematic surveys and very careful extensive excavations (with fine water-sieving), including underwater archaeology, are a high priority for understanding the Preneolithic *mode de vie* on the Mediterranean islands and, in this way, for making some contribution to an appreciation of the reasons why Mesolithic people deliberately went and lived on them.

References

Arca, M., Martini, F., Pitzalis, G., Tuvieri, C. & Ulzega, A. 1982. Il deposito quaternario con industria del Paleolitico inferiore di Sa Pedrosa-Pantallinu (Sassari). *Rivista di Scienze Preistoriche* 37(1–2): 31–53.

Bonifay, E. 1994. Rogliano, grotte de la Coscia. *Bilan Scientifique du Service Régional de l'Archéologie* 1994: 59. Ministère de la Culture et de la Francophonie, Paris.

Bouville, C.P. 1995. Préhistoire du Cap Corse: les abris de Torre d'Aquila, Pietracorbara (Haute-Corse) – Anthropologie. *Bulletin de la Société Préhistorique Française* 92(3): 378–380.

Cherry, J.F. 1990. The first colonization of the Mediterranean islands: a review of recent research. *Journal of Mediterranean Archaeology* 3: 145–221.

Cuisin, J. & Vigne, J.-D. In press. Note sur la présence de la grande outarde (*Otis tarda*) au 8e millénaire av. J.-C., dans la région de Bonifacio (Corse-du-Sud, France). *Géobios*.

Duday, H. 1975. *Le Squelette du Sujet Féminin de la Sépulture*

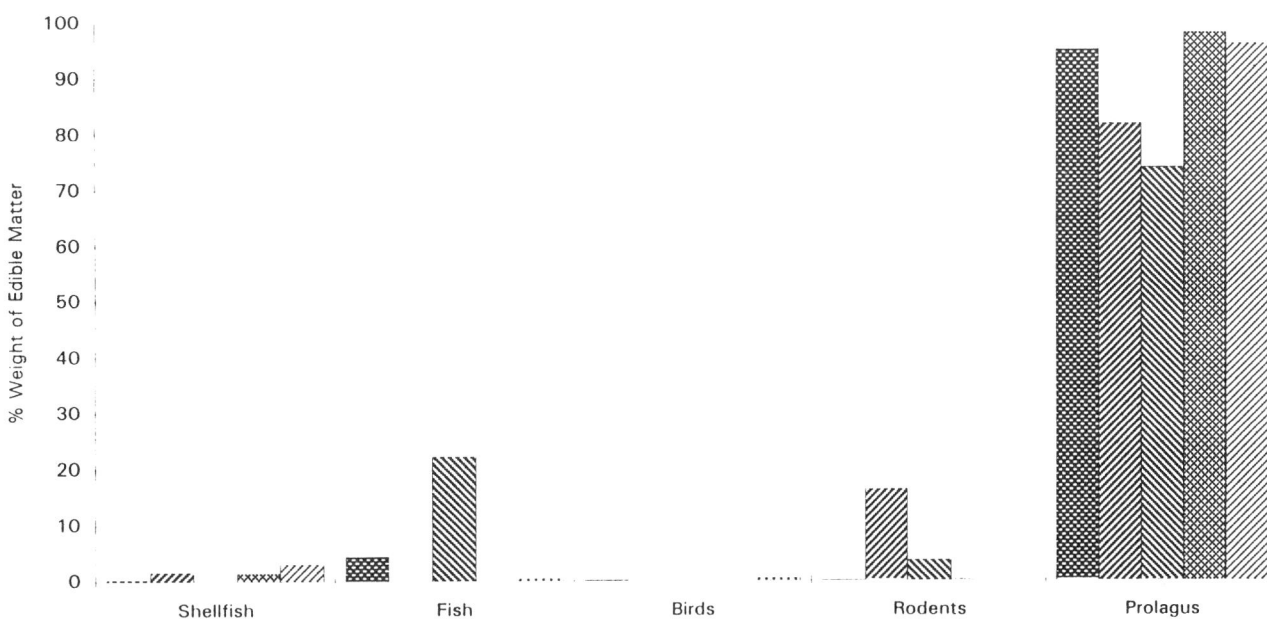

Fig. 10.2. *Proportions of weights of edible matter from sea-shells, fishes, birds, rodents and* Prolagus *in four Preneolithic sites of Corsica.*

Préneolithique de Bonifacio (Corse). Etude Anthropologique, Essai d'Interprétation Palethnographique. Cahiers d'Anthropologie, Mémoire 24. Paris.

Lanfranchi, F. de. 1967. La grotte sépulcrale de Curacchiaghiu. *Bulletin de la Société Préhistorique Française* 64: 587–612.

Lanfranchi, F. de. 1974. Le Néolithique ancien méditerranéen, faciès Curacchiaghiu, à Lévie. *Cahiers Corsica* 43: 39–48.

Lanfranchi, F. de. 1987. Le Néolithique de l'estrême sud de la Corse. *Archeologia Corsa* 10-11(1985–86): 44–54.

Lanfranchi, F. de. 1995. Sepoltura a inhumazione a Monteleone (Bonifacio). *Sardegna Antica* 7: 24–29.

Lanfranchi, F. de, Weiss, M.-C. & Duday, H. 1973. La sépulture prénéolithique de la couche XVIII de l'abri d'Araguina-Sennola. *Bulletin de la Société des Sciences Historiques et Naturelles de la Corse* 606: 7–26.

Lanfranchi, F. de & Weiss, M.-C. 1977. Araguina-Sennola, dix années de fouilles préhistoriques à Bonifacio. *Archeologia Corsa* 2: 1–167.

Lewthwaite, J.G. 1989. Balanophagy and the prehistory of Corsica: recent books. *Antiquity* 63: 838–42.

Magdeleine, J. 1985. Les premières occupations humaines de l'abri de Strette, Barbaghju. *Archeologia Corsa* 8–9 (1983–84): 30–50.

Magdeleine, J. 1991. Une deuxième sépulture pré-néolithique de Corse. *Bulletin de la Société Préhistorique Française* 88(3): 80.

Magdeleine, J. 1995. Préhistoire du Cap Corse: les abris de Torre d'Aquila, Pietracorbara (Haute-Corse). *Bulletin de la Société Préhistorique Française* 92(3): 363–377.

Magdeleine, J. & Ottaviani, J.-C. 1986. L'abri préhistorique de Strette. *Bulletin des Sciences Historiques et Naturelles de la Corse* 650: 81–90.

Reille, M. 1992. New pollen-analytical researches in Corsica: the problem of *Quercus ilex* L. and *Erica arborea* L., the origin of *Pinus halepensis* Miller forests. *New Phytologist* 122: 359–378.

Shackleton, J.C., Van Andel, T.H. & Runnels, C.N. 1984. Coastal paleogeography of the central and western Mediterranean during the last 125,000 years and its archaeological implications. *Journal of Field Archaeology* 11: 307–314.

Sondaar, P.Y. 1987. Pleistocene man and extinctions of island endemics. *Mémoire de la Société Géologique de France, Nouvelle série* 150: 159–165.

van Andel, T.H. 1989. Late Quaternary sea-sevel changes and archaeology. *Antiquity* 63: 733–745.

van Andel, T.H. 1990. Addendum to 'Late Quaternary Sea-Level Changes and Archaeology'. *Antiquity* 64: 151–152.

Vigne, J.-D. 1988. *Les Mammifères post-glaciaires de Corse, étude archéozoologique. Gallia Préhistoire* XXVIe supplément. Paris, C.N.R.S.

Vigne, J.-D. 1989. Le peuplement paléolithique des îles: le débat s'ouvre en Sardaigne. *Les Nouvelles de l'Archéologie* 34: 42–43.

Vigne, J.-D. 1990. Biogeographical history of the mammals on Corsica (and Sardinia) since the final Pleistocene. *Atti dei Convegni Lincei* 85: 369–392.

Vigne, J.-D. 1992a. Zooarchaeology and the biogeographical history of the mammals of Corsica and Sardinia since the last Ice Age. *Mammal Review* 22(2): 87–96.

Vigne, J.-D. 1992b. The meat and offal weight (MOW) method and the relative proportion of ovicaprines in some ancient meat diets of the north-western Mediterraean. *Rivista di Studi Liguri* 57(2): 21–47.

Vigne, J.-D. 1995. Préhistoire du Cap Corse: les abris de Torre d'Aquila, Pietracorbara (Haute-Corse) – La faune. *Bulletin de la Société Préhistorique Française* 92(3): 381–389.

Vigne, J.-D. In press. L'abri du Monte Leone (Bonifacio, Corse-du-Sud): vaste site prénéolithique en contexte insulaire. In *Actes Ve Congrès International UISPP, 12e commission : Epipaléolithique et Mésolithique en Europe* (Grenoble, 18–23 septembre 1995).

Vigne, J.-D., Bailon, S. & Cuisin, J. 1997. Biostratigraphy of amphibians, reptiles, birds and mammals in Corsica and the role of man in the Holocene faunal turnover. *Anthropozoologica*.

Vigne, J.-D., Bourdillat, V., André, J., Brochier, J.-E., Bui Thi Mai, Cuisin, J., David, H., Desse-Berset, N., Heinz, C., Lanfranchi, F. de, Ruas, M.-P., Thiébault, S., & Tozzi, C. In press. Nouvelles données sur le Prénéolithique corse: premiers résultats de la fouille de l'abri du Monte Leone (Bonifacio, Corse-du-Sud). In *Actes 2e Rencontres méridionales de Préhistoire récente* (Arles, 8–9 nov., 1996).

Vigne, J.-D. & Desse-Berset, N. 1995. The exploitation of animal resources in the Mediterranean islands during the Preneolithic: the example of Corsica. In Fishcer, A. (ed.), *Man and Sea in the Mesolithic: Coastal Settlement Above and Below Present Sea Level. Proceedings of the International Symposium, Kalundborg, Denmark 1993*. Oxbow Monograph 53: 309–318. Oxford, Oxbow.

Vigne, J.-D. & Marinval-Vigne, M.-C. 1983. *Méthode pour la mise en évidence de la consommmation du petit gibier*. BAR International Series 163: 239–242. Oxford, British Archaeological Reports.

Vigne, J.-D., Marinval-Vigne, M.-C., Lanfranchi, F. de & Weiss, M.-C. 1981. Consommation du "Lapin-Rat" (*Prolagus sardus* Wagner) au Néolithique ancien méditerranéen: abri d'Araguina-Sennola (Bonifacio, Corse). *Bulletin de la Société Préhistorique Française* 78(7): 222–224.

Vigne, J.-D. & Valladas, H. 1996. Small mammal fossil assemblages as indicators of environmental change in northern Corsica during the last 2500 years. *Journal of Archaeological Science* 23: 199–215.

11. Stratigrafia ed altri elementi di cronologia della Sardegna preistorica e protostorica

Ercole Contu

Le stratigrafie principali

Ritorno in questa occasione a parlare in maniera generale e specifica, dopo poco meno di vent' anni, di un argomento di cui mi occupai particolarmente nel Congresso di Preistoria e Protostoria che si tenne in Sardegna nel 1978 (Contu 1980): cioè la ricostruzione della seriazione cronologica della preistoria sarda sulla base principalmente delle stratigrafie. Ciò non significa che io o altri non ci siamo occupati occasionalmente dell'argomento dopo quella volta, ma che mi è parso necessario riprenderlo per intero, sia per aggiungervi nuove considerazioni sia per aggiornarlo con le nuove scoperte. Trascurerò invece di proposito altri elementi che, pur se ugualmente degni di considerazione, non fanno parte del mio assunto.

Per quanto riguarda le nuove scoperte, due mi paiono le più significative: quella relativa al paleolitico (in almeno due fasi, cioè antico e recente) e quella del neolitico antico in depositi stratificati (Trump 1983); anzi per il paleolitico la novità è costituita in assoluto dalla sua inaspettata presenza nell'isola (Arca *et al.* 1982; Martini 1992; Sondaar *et al.* 1984; 1991), tanto da trovare ancora, ingiustificatamente, qualche scettico (Cherry 1992).

Lo studio delle stratigrafie effettuato nel 1978 riguardava solo *undici* vere sequenze stratigrafiche, mentre in quello attuale ne presento, in tabella 1 e nella lista qui di seguito, *trenta*; ma potrebbero reperirsene anche altre quattro o cinque in più, come si specificherà meglio più avanti.

L'insieme di tutte queste stratigrafie va dal Paleolitico Inferiore, con industria clactoniana, alla fine dell'Età Nuragica: cioè include un ampio arco di tempo che va da circa il 170.000 a.C. a circa il 500 a.C. (Contu, in stampa).

Sono state prese in considerazione e sistemate in altrettante colonne verticali le seguenti stratigrafie che sono contraddistinte, innanzitutto, da due elementi principali: in alto dalla denominazione (località, Comune e Provincia) dei siti e, in sequenza ordinata progressivamente, dall'alto verso il basso nella colonna ma inversamente sul terreno, dalla individuazione delle culture sulla base dei vari "fossili guida" (ovviamente soprattutto ceramici a partire dal Neolitico) e, solitamente, dalla denominazione con la quale le stesse sono conosciute. Il fattore dei rapporti stratigrafici e di altra natura fra i resti culturali, nei singoli siti o anche in assoluto, è espresso con varie simbologie, riportate primariamente nell'apposita "legenda", e riguarda:

→ Culture in sequenza stratigrafica;
[ ] Intrusione di elementi culturali dovuta a turbamento della stratigrafia;
° Resti culturali con particolari caratteri distintivi ma non in corrispondenza stratigrafica;
+ Resti culturali in aggregazione casuale e non distinguibili stratigraficamente da quelli che li precedono immediatamente;
_/ Resti culturali associati a quelli indicati precedentemente;
** Resti culturali presenti in quantità notevole;
* Resti culturali poco rappresentati.

Per intendere rettamente, sia le tabelle stratigrafiche (Tab. 11.1) che la lista (con uguale numero d'ordine) delle localizzazioni stratigrafiche che si riporta qui di seguito, è necessario ovviamente tenere presente il quadro cronologico generale dell'archeologia della Sardegna (Tab. 11.2); quadro che è, con poche variazioni e l'aggiunta anche della cronologia del Tykot (1994), quello stesso da me proposto già qualche anno fa (Contu 1982; 1987a; 1987b; 1992; in stampa). Ma qui si privilegierà di solito, su quella assoluta/a, la cronologia relativa. La

Ercole Contu, Dipartimento di Scienze Umanistiche e dell'Antichità, Università di Sassari, Piazza Conte di Moriana 8, 07100 Sassari, Sardegna, Italia

LEGENDA   -> Culture in sequenza stratigrafica; [ ] Intrusione stratificata
    ° Distinto ma non stratigraficamente; + Inscindibile dal precedente (aggregazione casuale);
_/ Associato al precedente; ** molto rappresentato; * poco rappresentato

1	2	3	4	5	6	7	8
Preideru (Martis-SS)	G. Corbeddu (Oliena-NU)	G. Filiestru (Mara-SS)	G. M.Maiore (Thiesi-SS)	G.S.Bartolomeo- CA	Sa Ucca'e Su Tintirriolu (Mara-SS)	Altare M. d' Accoddi-SS	S. Pedru T.I (Alghero-SS)
Paleol. Inf. Clactoniano +Interg.R.W.	Paleolitico Superiore -> Cardiale ->Bonuighinu ->Bonnan.'+ C. pettine nuragica	Cardiale -> Filiestru -> Bonuighinu -> Ozieri -> M Claro + Campan.A1+ CampanA2 + Bonnanaro II	Cardiale ->Bonuighinu -> Ozieri	C.impressa? -> Ozieri -> M Claro -> CampanA +Bonnan. II	Bonuighinu -> Ozieri Campan.A2	Ozieri** -> Ozieri*+ -> Filigosa' ->Abealzu** [Ozieri] -> M. Claro+ Campan.A + Bonnanaro II + Nuragico	Ozieri ->Filigosa** -> Abealzu -> M. Claro ->CampanA ->Bonna.II** ° Nuragico

9	10	11	12	13	14	15	16
Cuccuru S' Arriu (Cabras-OR) Sa.380,382	S. Iroxi (Decimopu.-tzu-OR)	Perda Lada (Decimopu.-tzu-OR)	M.d'Accoddi (Sassari), T. II	S. Giuseppe (Padria-SS)	Padru Jossu (Sanluri-CA)	Pani Loriga (Santadi-CA)	Marinaru (Sassari)
S. Ciriaco ->? Ozieri	° S. Ciriaco Ozieri -> ° M. Claro ->Bonnan.I-a ->Bonnan.I-b	Ozieri -> Filigosa	Ozieri+ Filigosa + Abealzu + M. Claro -> Bonnan. II	Fligosa -> Abealzu	M. Claro-> Camp. A2 ->Bonnàn. I	M. Claro 2 -> Campan.	Campanif. -> Bonnàn. I

Tab. 11.1a. Stratigrafie della Sardegna preistorica e protostorica.

17	18	19	20	21	22	23	24
Bingia 'e Monti (Gonnostramatza-CA)	Nur. Duos Nuraghes (Bòrore-NU)	Nur. Noeddos (Mara-SS)	Nur. S.Pietro (Torpé-NU)	Punta Candela (Arzachena-SS)	Nur. Palmavera(Alghero)Cap. Riunioni	Nur. Antigori (Sarrok-CA)	Nur. Madonna d. Rimedio (Oristano)
Campanif. -> Bonn. II	M. Claro ?-> Br. Antico-> Br. Medio-> B. Recente-> Età d. ferro	M. Claro 2 + Bonn. II -> Bonn. III -> Nurag. Med.	fine Br. A. o inizi Br. M. _/cer.pett* pettine**	cer. nervature -> Nur. Medio	cer.pettine ->cer. geom.	Br. Med.? + Br. Recen.-> inizi Br.Fin. +Età d.Ferro	Br. Med.II-> Br. Finale

25	26	27	28	29	30
Nur. Piscu (Suelli-CA)	Nur. Albuciu (Arzac.-SS)	Nur. Lugherras-Paulilàtino-OR)	Nur.Sa Mandra 'e Sa Giua (Ossi-SS)	Nur. Su Nuraxi (Barumini- CA)	Nur. Su Molinu (Villanovafranca-CA)
Bron. Rec.-> Bron. Fin.-> Età Ferro-> Orient.Ant. e Medio	cer. pettine ->cer. geom	olle globoi. a collo -> ->cer. geom.	cer.pregeom. +bronzetto? ->cer. geom.	Bronzo M.+ Br. Rec.-> Bron.Fin.-> Età Ferro->	Bron. Rec.-> Bron. Fin.-> Età Ferro+ Punico+Rom.

Tab. 11.1b. Stratigrafie della Sardegna preistorica e protostorica.

cronologia del Tykot può servire anche ad ampliare la calibrazione delle date da me proposte, tramite l'Uranio-Torio, che prima non era possibile (Stuiver *et al.* 1993; Stuiver & Reimer 1993).

Elenco delle stratigrafie

1. Sa Pedrosa-Pantallinu (Perfugas-SS) & Preideru (Martis-SS): → Paleolitico Inferiore (Clactoniano); interglaciale Riss-Würm.
2. Grotta Corbeddu (Oliena-NU): Paleolitico Superiore → Cardiale → Bonuighinu → Bonnànaro I–III + ceramica a pettine.
3. Grotta Filiestru (Mara-SS): Ceramica impressa → Filiestru → Bonuighinu → Ozieri → M. Claro + Campaniforme A1(punti) + A2 (G.Volpe) + Bonnànaro I → Bonnànaro III
4. Grotta di Sa Korona di Monte Majore (Thiesi-SS): Cardiale → Bonuighinu → Ozieri.
5. Grotta di San Bartolomeo (Cagliari): Ceramica impressa? → Ozieri → M. Claro → Campaniforme A → Bonnànaro II.
6. Sa Ucca 'e Su Tintirriolu (Mara-SS): Bonuighinu → Ozieri + Campaniforme A2.
7. Altare di Monte d'Accoddi (Sassari): Ozieri** → Ozieri* + → Filigosa* → Abealzu** [Ozieri] → M. Claro + Campaniforme A + Bonnànaro II + Nuragico.
8. Santu Pedru (Alghero-SS), Tomba I: Ozieri → Filigosa** → Abealzu → Campaniforme A → Bonnànaro II** + Nuragico*.
9. Cùccuru S'Arriu (Cabras–OR), sacche 380 e 382: [San Ciriaco] Ozieri
10. Sant'Iroxi (Decimiputzu–OR): [San Ciriaco] Ozieri → [M. Claro?] → Bonnànaro Ia → Bonnànaro Ib
11. Perda Lada, Tomba II (Decimiputzu-OR): Ozieri → Filigosa ("Sub-Ozieri" di Ugas 1990: 21; 38, n. 42; 84–85)
12. Monte d'Accoddi, Ipogeo T. II: Ozieri + M. Claro + Filigosa + Abealzu → Bonnànaro II.
13. San Giuseppe (Padria-SS): Filigosa → Abealzu.
14. Padru Jossu (Sanluri-Ca): Monte Claro →

ETA' ↓	CULTURE	DATE		DURATA	DATE CALIBRATE R.H. Tykot 1994
		C 14, K40-Ar40	C ALIBRATE, STORICHE		
PALEOLITICO	INFERIORE (Clactoniano)	500.000/ 300.000; 250.000; 120.000	500.000? 120.000	circa 400.000	> 150.000
	MEDIO	35.000	35.000	c. 90.000	−15.000
	SUPERIORE	10.000	10.000	25.000	−11.000
MESOLITICO		6.000	6.000	4.000	−6.000?
NEOLITICO	ANTICO — CERAMICA IMPRESSA E "CARDIALE"	4.600	5.800	1.400	−5.300 −4.700
	MEDIO — BONUIGHINU	3.240	3.800	2.000	−4.000
	RECENTE — SAN MICHELE (od OZIERI)	2.360	2.900	900	−3.200?
ENEOLITICO	FILIGOSA / ABEALZU / M. CLARO / CAMPANIFORME / B(=I° Bonnan.)	2.300 2.130 2.200 2.100 2.000 1.650 1.600	2.850 2.400 2.630 2.550 2.350 2.000 1.800	Filigosa 500 / Abealzu 220 / M. Claro 350 / Camp. 850: 500(A)+ 350(B)	−2700? −2.200? −1900

Tab. 11.2a. Quadro cronologico della Sardegna preistorica e protostorica (a destra le datazioni calibrate del Tykot).

ETA' DEL BRONZO		B(=I°Bonnan.) B O N N- II° A N A- Nuraghi sempl. III° RO C I V I L T A'	1.650 1.600 1.500	2.000 1.800 1.600	BONNAN. I°,II°,III° 700	--2200? --1900 --1600
	N U R	Nuraghi semplici e complessi;.tombe megal.; ceram. a pettine; importaz.i micenee	1.300 1.200	1.500 1.200	NU- RA- GI- CO	--1300 --1150
		Stessi nuraghi e tombe; capanne circolari semplici; pozzi sacri; bronzi vari;cer. pregeom.	850	850	1.400 o	--850
ETA' DEL FERRO	A G I	Nuraghi; tombe mono- some e a "tafone"; pozzi sacri; capanne a settori; statuaria e bronzetti figurati; ceramica geom. a cerchiel. e spina pesce; askoi, brocche pir.; bronzi vari	750	750	1.000	--730
CIV. U R B A N A	C A	ORIENTALIZ- ZANTE: decoraz. a falsa cordic.,cerch., lambda e dipinta; askoi, bronzi askoi ecc. ceram. tardonur. rozza,anche dipinta, CIV. askoi, brocche vassoi,fiasche PUNICA	720 580 535 238 a.C.	720 580 535 238 a.C.	FENICIO- PUNICI 518/ 500 *E. Contu*	--580 --510
		ETA' ROMANA	476 d.C.	476 d.C.	ROMA 710	

Tab. 11.2b. Quadro cronologico della Sardegna preistorica e protostorica (a destra le datazioni calibrate del Tykot).

Campaniforme A2 → Campaniforme B (Bonnànaro I).
15. Pani Lóriga (Santadi-CA): Monte Claro 2 → Campaniforme A.
16. Marinaru-Sassari: Campaniforme A → Bonnànaro I.
17. Bingia 'e Monti (Gonnostramatza-OR): Campaniforme (A o B) → Bonnànaro II.
18. Nuraghe Duos Nuraghes (Bòrore-NU): Tardo Eneolitico? → Bronzo Antico → Bronzo Medio → Bronzo Recente → Età del Ferro.
19. Nuraghe Noeddos (Mara-SS): M. Claro (non decorato o "Noeddos") + Bonnànaro II → Bonnànaro III → Nuragico Medio
20. Nuraghe San Pietro (Torpè-NU): fine Bronzo Antico/inizio Bronzo Medio (vasi a fruttiera e poca ceramica a pettine) → Bronzo Medio (molta ceramica a pettine).
21. Cavità Punta Candela (Arzachena-SS): Bonnànaro III (ceramica a nervature) → Nuragico Medio.
22. Nuraghe Palmavera (Alghero-SS), Capanna d. Riunioni: ceramica a pettine → ceramica geometrica a cerchielli.
23. Nuraghe Antigori (Sarrok-CA): "Bronzo Medio" ?+ inizi "Bronzo Finale" + Miceneo III B/C (str. 9–10) → "Bronzo Finale" + Età del Ferro (str. 1–8)
24. Nuraghe Madonna del Rimedio-0ristano: Bronzo Medio II → Bronzo Finale.
25. Nuraghe Piscu (Suelli-CA), cap. 1: Bronzo recente (str.VI) → Bronzo Finale (str. IV–V) → I° Età del Ferro (str. II–III) → Orientalizzante Antico-Medio (str. I).
26. Nuraghe Albucciu (Arzachena-SS): ceramica a pettine → ceramica "geometrica".
27. Nuraghe Lugherras (Paulilatino-0R), pozzo: globoidi con collo → Ceramica "geometrica".
28. Nuraghe Sa Mandra 'e Sa Giua (Ossi-SS): ceramica "pregeometrica" (con associato (?) bronzetto di guerriero) → ceramica "geometrica".
29. Nuraghe Su Nuraxi (Barùmini-CA): Bronzo Medio + Bronzo Recente (Nuragico I inferiore) → Bronzo Finale (Nuragico I superiore) → Età del Ferro (Nuragico II).
30. Nuraghe Su Molinu (Villanovafranca-CA), vano F1: Bronzo Recente → Bronzo Finale + I° Età del Ferro + Punico + Romano.

Altre stratigrafie

Nelle tabelle e nella lista che ho esposto ho tralasciato, perchè già altrimenti meglio rappresentati o perché ne ho parlato altre volte (Contu 1980) o per altri motivi, i casi seguenti:

1. *Su Crucifissu Mannu* (Portotorres-SS), Tomba XVI: Ozieri+ M. Claro+ Campaniforme A → Bonnànaro II (Ferrarese Ceruti 1972–74);

2. *Cavità Punta Candela* (Arzachena-SS): ceramica nuragica a nervature → ceramica nuragica comune (Contu 1980);
3. *Nuraghe Genna Maria* (Villanovaforru-OR): ceramica "pregeometrica" → ceramica "geometrica", perché non si hanno notizie sufficienti in bibliografia (Atzeni 1988; Badas 1987);
4. *Cuccuru S'Arriu* (Cabras-Oristano). Nonostante qualche non confermata e documentata notizia in proposito (Meloni 1993: 11), non si ha invece reale documentazione di natura stratigrafica del fatto che l'aspetto culturale denominato "San Ciriaco" (o "Cuccuru S'Arriu") (Santoni 1982) preceda quello "Ozieri" nelle "sacche" 380 e 382 di Cuccuru S'Arriu; benché una tale sequenza possa essere opportunamente suggerita dalla tipologia dei materiali ceramici. "San Ciriaco" fu individuato primariamente nell'omonima località di Terralba-Cagliari (Puxeddu 1975: 83, 113) ed è ritenuto coevo alla cultura di Diana (Ugas 1990: 87). All'aspetto culturale di San Ciriaco potrebbe inoltre appartenere interamente un ripostiglio o "sacca", inedito, di ceramiche (denominato "Saggio E.T.F.A.S.": nn. di scavo 1842, 1844b, 1848b, 1871 ecc.), trovato isolato a circa 200 m ad est dell'altare preistorico di Monte d'Accoddi (Sassari) nel 1953 (Contu 1984; 1992).
5. *Conca Fravià* (Ololai-Nuoro). Sette strati distinti (?) con abbondante materiale ceramico vennero in luce nel riparo sotto roccia di Conca Fravià, loc. S. Basilio-Ollolai: e vanno dal Neolitico Medio all'Età del Bronzo (Fadda 1988).
6. *Locci Santus* (San Giovanni Suergiu-Cagliari). Esterno dell'ipogeo a *domus de janas* Tomba IV: sequenza Ozieri Abealzu Monte Claro Campaniforme 2 (a linea incisa) + Bonnanaro II (Atzeni in stampa).
7. *Cronicario* (S. Antioco-Cagliari). Ceramica nuragica a "falsa cordicella" si trovò associata, nel contesto fenicio di Sulci, a ceramica fenicia arcaica a ad elementi di importazione euboica e protocorinzia (Bernardini 1992: 396; E. Usai 1990: 194, f. 8,a-b).
8. *Nuraghe Sant'Imbenia* (Alghero-Sassari). Ceramica nuragica a "cerchielli" insieme a kotyle e skyphos protocorinzi e a ceramica fenicia furono trovati al Nur. S. Imbenia di Alghero (Lo Schiavo 1986: 100, 107, ff. 147–148): VIII sec. a.C.; ma l'attribuzione cronologica non è chiara.

Denominazione e identificazione di altri aspetti culturali e cronologici

Ritengo utile e necessario chiarire alcuni problemi che riguardano l'identificazione e la stessa denominazione di vari aspetti culturali, specie quando non si conoscano elementi di natura stratigrafica ad essi correlati; e specificare meglio, anche stratigraficamente, quelli che appaiono nelle tabelle stratigrafiche.

Denominazione

Come appare chiaro dalle tabelle e dalla lista, la diversa formazione scientifica degli studiosi che hanno pubblicato o studiato i vari siti di interesse stratigrafico ha portato talora a privilegiare diverse terminologie, ma ho ritenuto utile che esse fossero per quanto possibile qui mantenute. Perciò il "fossile guida" potrà essere sia una caratteristica tecnica (p. es. ceramica a nervature) che un inquadramento cronologico generale (p. es. Età del Bronzo Finale) e così via.

Unità associative originarie

Può essere considerata stratigrafia (come nel caso dell'aspetto culturale "San Ciriaco", trattato più sopra), anche quella costituita, in un certo senso, da un solo strato o dal corredo di una tomba non collettiva, in cui un gruppo di reperti si presenta come un contesto chiuso, con caratteri distintivi unitari e reale associazione cronologica e culturale.

Un caso parzialmente analogo, ma con le tipiche implicazioni geologiche del Pleistocene, è quello del Clactoniano in giacitura primaria di Serra Preideru-Martis e di Sa Coa de Sa Multa-Perfugas (Pitzalis 1988; Martini 1992), trovato in un paleosuolo, formatosi durante l'ultimo inter glaciale e che riposa su un terrazzo attribuito al glaciale di Riss.

Su Coddu (Selargius-Cagliari)

In questa località, che presenta circa 120 "strutture" preistoriche ("sacche" o silos, pozzi, capanne, focolari ecc.), è stata rinvenuta della ceramica incisa di tipo "Ozieri" (Ugas 1989a; 1989b), più che "sub-Ozieri", come dichiarato da qualcuno (Usai 1989), associata a ceramica figulina dipinta in rosso (*red on white*), in sé comunque sempre piuttosto rara. La ceramica dipinta è associata con la ceramica a decorazione incisa tipo "Ozieri" anche nella stratigrafia di Monte d'Accoddi-Sassari (Contu 1992: 27) (Tab. 11.3), e come tale era nota anche nei casi di Monte Ollàdiri-Monastir-Cagliari e di Terramàini-Pirri-Cagliari (Ugas 1989b: 240).

Culture di Filigosa ed Abealzu

Gli scavi di Monte d'Accoddi hanno documentato, anche statisticamente, il succedersi, sia pure graduale, dell'aspetto culturale Abealzu (con vasi a fiasco) a quello Filigosa (con tazze a profilo pluriangolare) (Contu 1992b: 23–27; in stampa) (Tab. 11.4). Questi due aspetti potrebbero corrispondere a quello che, specie nel sud della Sardegna, viene spesso impropriamente chiamato "sub-Ozieri" ma che proprio nel sud non ha una reale attestazione stratigrafica, neanche nello stanziamento di Cùccuru S'Arrìu-Cabras-Oristano (Santoni 1989; 1992a), ove appare, almeno, una cosiddetta stratigrafia orizzontale, per il sovrapporsi di almeno quattro momenti insediativi (Santoni 1989: fig. 1).

Ceramiche lisce di accompagno del Vaso Campaniforme ("Begleitkeramik")

In Sardegna esse, come tutti i tipici elementi culturali del Vaso Campaniforme, si rinvengono solitamente in tombe collettive e per giunta, come le sepolture ipogeiche, molto spesso riutilizzate e sconvolte in epoche successive; perciò solo di rado si ha la prova che si tratti veramente di ceramiche di accompagno come a Santu Pedru-Alghero-Sassari, Tomba I^ (Contu 1964: 65, 108) e forse – ma qui si trattava probabilmente di una sepoltura singola – in tomba a fossa a Nuraxi Nieddu-Oristano (Atzeni 1996a). Un altro indizio o addirittura un'altra prova di *Begleitkeramik* si ha nel caso di Bingia e Monti (Gonnostramatza, Oristano) (Atzeni 1996b), dove la ceramica inornata, in specie ciotoloni tripodi (*cuenco*), appartiene ad una fase iniziale di Bonnànaro (Bonnànaro I) (Contu in stampa; 1995) chiamata, come nel caso di Padru Jossu-Sanluri-Cagliari, anche Campaniforme B (Ugas 1982).

Comunque come culture in parte contemporanee del Vaso Campaniforme (e talora da esso influenzate) sono da intendersi anche quelle di Filigosa, Abealzu, Monte Claro (Contu 1980; 1982; 1987b). Particolarmente complesso è il rapporto del Vaso Campaniforme con Bonnànaro per i numerosi e progressivi esempi di commistione fra elementi caratteristici dei due aspetti culturali nel cui insieme è possibile individuare, su base tipologica e non stratigrafica, almeno quattro fasi o cinque (se vi si comprende quella, già nuragica, di Bonnànaro III o Sa Turrìcula) (Atzeni 1996a); ma che potrebbero essere anche una decina (Contu 1996) (Tab. 11.5).

Noeddos

Non è solo un problema di denominazione quello del Nuraghe Noeddos-Mara (Trump 1990: 15), nei pressi del quale si individuò una complessa stratigrafia ed in essa, in particolare, un aspetto culturale *sui generis*, che, avendo caratteri sia di "Ozieri" che di "Monte Claro" o "Bonnànaro", fu chiamato appunto "Noeddos".

Inizio della Civiltà Nuragica

É a questo punto che si innesta il problema dell'inizio della Civiltà Nuragica, che io continuo a ritenere non possa essere anteriore alle fasi iniziali della Media Età del Bronzo (Contu 1992a), cioè al 1600 a.C. in date calibrate. Perciò considero frutto di turbamento della stratigrafia la datazione – anche se sostenuta dal ^{14}C –

Legenda

////////// : piano di posa grandi murature

▓▓▓▓▓ : fondo roccioso

: livelli non scavati

- A : ansa ad asca o gomito, tipo Bonnanaro (/a2)
- B : oggetti di rame e bronzo (vo-ve)
- B' : ansa ad asca o altri metalli (vi-vii)
- C : vaso campaniforme (/d)
- D : vaso campaniforme (go-gc)
- F : idoli cicladici a placca (r)
- G : vasi a fiasco (d)
- T : ansa aviforme, tipo Sos Laccheddos
- H : menhir
- I : decorazione a bande tratteggiate (i-ib)
- L : lastroni con fori
- M : piedi di tripode decorati (e)
- N : decorazione a segmento dentellato (n)
- O : anse a lunel (ga-gc)
- P : figure a clessidra, incise (mi²)
- R : pesi da telaio a rene
- T : lastrone trachitico
- U : asce a martello (n)
- V : vasi a solcature M. Claro (oo-op)
- W : ceramica dipinta (pe)
- X : tazze plurangolari, tipo Filigosa (Cen)
- Y : vaso in marmo con presa forata (uo)
- Z : vaso in arenaria (uo)
- $\hat{Z}$: asce piatte in pietra levigata (ri-rj)
- (...) : le indicazioni alfanumeriche tra parentesi e in corsivo della legenda si riferiscono alle voci di codice della rubrica dei materiali di M. d'Accoddi, classificati da E. Contu

numeri arabi: nella tabella le indicazioni numeriche esponenziali dopo le lettere indicano la quantità assoluta de' materiali indicati dalla lettera che precede

numeri romani ecc.: nella tabella i numeri romani indicano le trincee (p.es.: X, VIII); mentre le due lettere maiuscole sottostanti indicano i settori delle medesime; ed i numeri arabi ordinali, sui lati della tabella, indicano (dal 1° al 10°) i livelli o strati.

Tab. 11.3 - Quadro generale stratigrafico di Monte d'Accoddi-Sassari.

Livelli	X S N̂	X-N̂- III	III S N̂	IX E Ô	VII E Ô	VI E Ô	II E Ô	VIII E Ô	XI E Ô	XII A	I	XVI	XXIII (sc. TINE')	Livelli
1°	B, D, L, Z3, O2, n1	B', Z5, n1, m1									n4		A	1°
2°	F1, Z2, i3, n1, R1	n1							F9, i4, n1		F1, i1, n1, x?	O2, i1, x1	F, G, n, i	2°
3°	B, F1, O4, Z2, m2	B', i2, O1, Z1, i2, m2	n1	O1, i1				B, Z1	V1, i1, m3, U, i2, m2		O1, i1	H	n+, i+, O, W	3°
4°	R8, Z1, O3, i3, W1, m2	Z1	F1, i2, O1, Z1, i2, m2	O1, i1	F1, Z4, m2	B, Z1	F1, i2, O1, m2	F2, O3, i2, n1, U1	n1		O1, i1		n, i	4°
5°	B3, B', F2, R1, Z8, O2, i8, W7	B, Z2, O1, i6, W1	F1, i2, W1, m2	F1, R1, Z3, i3, W2, m1	B, Z1, O1, i7, n1	Z1, i2	C?, B, O1, i1,	B, F1, Z1, i2			O1, i1	m		5°
6°	B2, O1, Z1, n1, m2	B2, Z3, O1, i1, W4, Y1, x3	Z2, O1, W1, m2		F1, R2, i1	B, F1, Z1, i2	V?, F1, O1, m2	F2, O3, i2, m3			F2, O2, n7, x?	O4		6°
7°	Z2, O1, i21, n1, T, m3, P, m1	B2, Z3, O1, W1	n1		F1, D2, Z1, i3, n1, m1, x1	F1, R1, Z4, O1, i4, W2	Z1, i2, x2, m1, x1	O1, i5, m3			O1, i1		n, i	7°
8°	i2, W3	O3, i59, n2, P, m1	n1	i3	i1	i2	B, i2, n1	F1, i5, n1	V1, i1, m3, U, i2, m2		Z1, i13, n26		n+, i+, O, W	8°
9°											....			9°
10°														10°

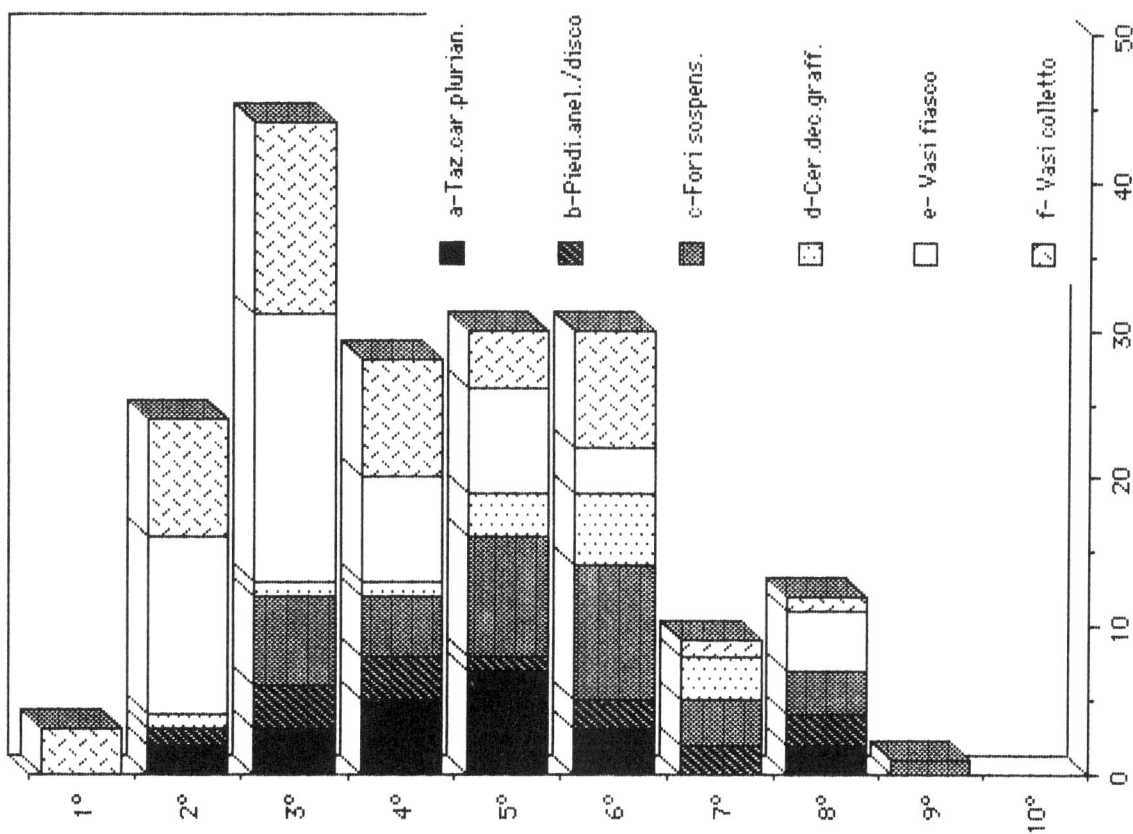

Tab. 11.4. Monte d'Accoddi-Sassari: correlazione stratigrafica fra elementi di Filigosa (a–d) e Abealzu (e–f).

Campaniforme Iniziale, 1°. Vasi campaniformi non ansati a profilo *suave* e *cuenco* apodi; decorazione a campitura puntinata o, rara, a cordicella.

Campaniforme 2°. Vasi campaniformi non ansati a profilo rigido e *cuenco* tripodi o tetrapodi; decorazione a campitura puntinata.

Campaniforme 3°. Vasi campaniformi non ansati a profilo ondulato e *cuenco* tripodi; decorazione a campitura puntinata.

Campaniforme 4°. Vasi campaniformi ansati a profilo ondulato e *cuenco* tripodi; decorazione a campitura puntinata.

Campaniforme 5°. Vasi campaniformi con ansa a gomito o a ponte, profilo suave e *cuenco* tripodi; decorazione lineare puntinata.

Campaniforme 6°. Vasi campaniformi con ansa a gomito a profilo rigido; decorazione a linee incise semplici.

Campaniforme Finale, 7° (Bonnànaro I). Vasi campaniformi con ansa a gomito a profilo rigido o ondulato e *cuenco* tripodi; assenza di decorazione Bonnànaro II-a, o Fase di Corona Moltana (S. Iroxi, 10° strato): tripodi e tazze carenate; anse a gomito assenza di decorazione.

Bonnànaro II-b, o Fase finale di Corona Moltana (S. Iroxi, 7°-5° strato). Spade e pugnali; tazze carenate; assenza di tripodi; anse a gomito; assenza di decorazione.

Bonnànaro III, o fase di Sa Turrìcula. Tegami vasi con nervature ed assenza di tripodi; anse a gomito; vasi polipodi.

Tab. 11.5. Ipotesi di evoluzione delle culture del Vaso Campaniforme e di Bonnànaro

del nuraghe a *tholos* di Duos Nuraghes (Bòrore-Nuoro), un monumento che qualcuno tende ad attribuire al Bronzo Antico o addirittura all'Eneolitico (Webster 1988; Weiss Grele 1992: 278–279). Tanto è vero che la stessa ipotesi non è ritenuta proponibile per il caso pressoché del tutto simile del Nuraghe Noèddos (Mara-Sassari) (Trump 1990) (Tab. 11.6).

Rapporto con l'architettura Micenea a tholos ed in genere ad aggetto

Nonostante qualche diverso parere in proposito (Bernardini 1985; Ugas 1992), questo rapporto non esiste perché la diffusione della Civiltà Micenea, anche se si accettassero le più alte datazioni recenti (Michael & Betancourt 1988a; 1988b), risulterebbe per gran parte posteriore al sorgere della Civiltà Nuragica (Contu 1992a) (Tab. 11.7).

Bronzi figurati

La proposta di rialzare la datazione dei bronzetti figurati di Età Nuragica, derivante dal Nuraghe Sa Mandra'e Sa Giùa-Ossi-Sassari (Ferrarese Ceruti 1985; Contu 1993), dove si ebbe una statuetta di guerriero, non ha serio fondamento: non è infatti accertata l'appartenenza del manufatto (Contu, nel presente volume) allo strato

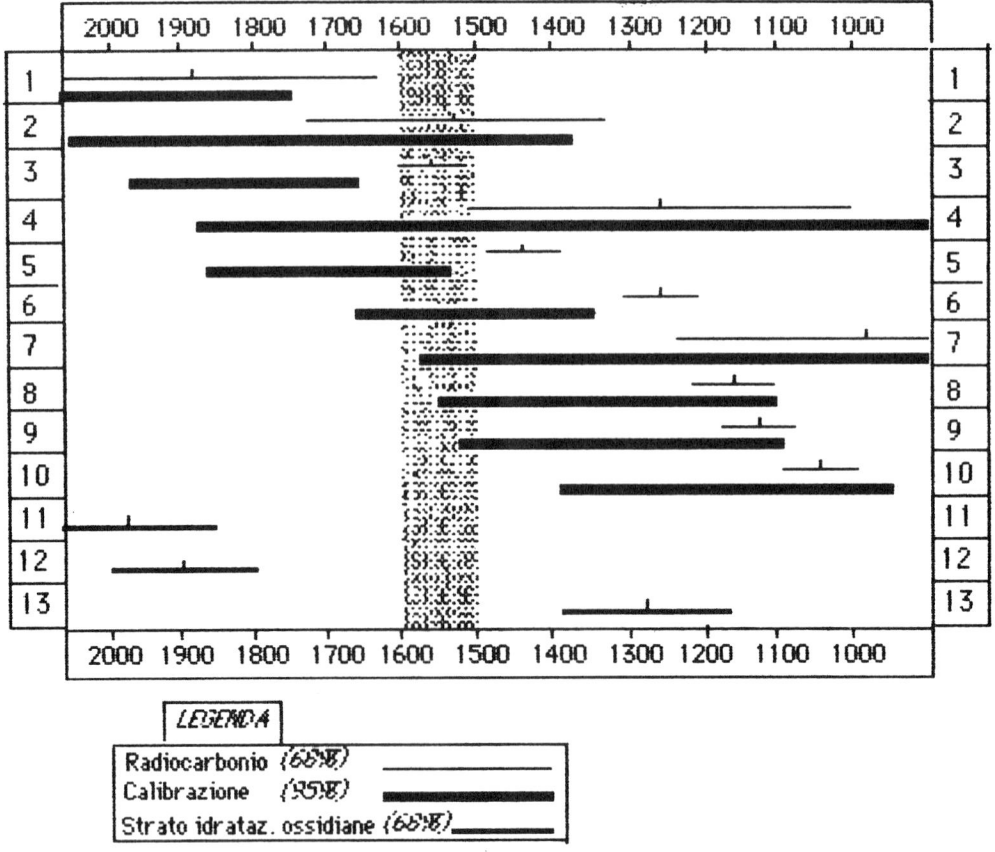

1a) 1–14774; 2210±320 (2530÷1890): 3300÷2340: Duos Nuraghes, t. A
1b) 1–15465; 1114±90 (1204÷1024): 1510÷1270: Duos Nuraghes, t. A
1c) 1–15466; 910±80 (990÷830): 1250÷930: Duos Nuraghes, t. A
1d) 1739±119: 1858÷1620: Duos Nuraghes, vill. "M.Claro" (s.i.ossid.)
1e) 1515±69: 1584÷1446: Duos Nuraghes, vill. "M.Claro" (s.i.ossid.)
1f) 1364±41: 1433÷1323: Duos Nuraghes, t. B (s.i.ossidiana)

2a) Q–3068: 1195±50: 1520+÷1310: Nur. Noeddos-Mara: Noeddos II
2b) Q–3070: 1410±50: 1860+÷1520: Noeddos III
2c) Q–3169: 1380±70: 1870+÷1450: Noeddos IV (Nur. Antico)
2e) Q–3031: 1490±40: 1880+÷1680: G. Filiestru-Mara (Sa Turric.)
2f) Q–3170: 1060±70: 1420÷1050: Nur. Sala e Serru-Mara (Medio Nura
(N.B.: +÷ = datazioni multiple)

Tab. 11.6. Grafico delle datazioni della Civiltà Nuragica nel II millennio a.C. Linea grossa: datazione ^{14}C calibrata (95%); linea di spessore medio: strato di idratazione delle ossidiane (68%); linea sottile: datazione ^{14}C (68%) non calibrata.

sottostante a quello caratterizzato da ceramiche nuragiche tipicamente "geometriche", decorate ad occhi di dado; mentre al Nuraghe di Barùmini una figura di offerente con gonnellino, trovata sotto il vano ll, è attribuibile solo al IX-VIII sec. a.C. e perciò alla fase *d* o "Nuragico I Superiore" (Lilliu & Zucca 1988: 55–57). Anzi nello stesso villaggio si ebbe anche una fibula cipriota del VII sec. a.C.

Seriazione cronologica evolutiva della Civiltà Nuragica

Sulla base principalmente degli scavi stratigrafici di Barùmini è possibile redigere uno schema – non privo di problemi – sulla seriazione evolutiva della Civiltà Nuragica (Contu in stampa), diviso in sette fasi distinte (Tab. 11.8). Altro schema, forse di tre fasi, può trarsi anche dagli scavi del Nuraghe Santu Antine di Torralba-Sassari (Bafico & Rossi 1987; 1988).

Presenze percentuali

Onde poter misurare se e quanto sia significativa cronologicamente, per esempio a Barumini (Tab. 11.9) (Lilliu 1982; Contu in stampa), la presenza percentuale di determinati materiali negli strati, è bene tenere presente che nello scavo del Nuraghe Genna Maria, e in specie delle capanne di epoca "geometrica" (Badas 1987), è stato dimostrato che tali differenze possono dipendere non da diversa cronologia ma dalla afferenza ad ambienti con funzioni differenti nell'ambito di un abitato.

Considerazioni conclusive

Di recente mi è capitato di sentir dire ad un archeologo italiano che le stratigrafie non servono a niente perché troppi possono essere i turbamenti subiti dalle medesime; e che al massimo si può accettare la "stratigrafia orizzontale", come quella che si potrebbe

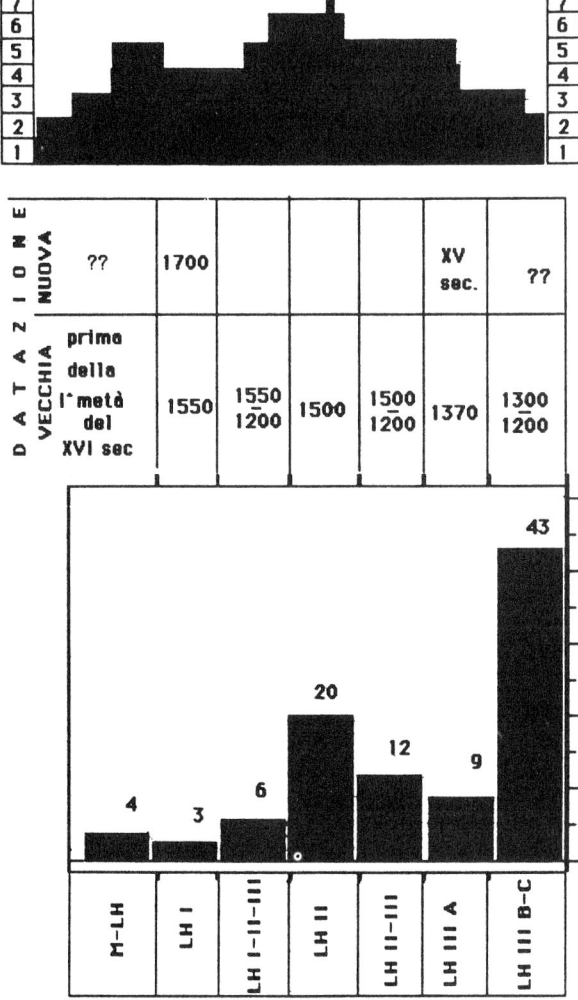

Tab. 11.7. *Raffronto fra le datazioni nuragiche calibrate del II millennio (somma dei dati della Tab. 11.6) (in alto) e quelle delle* tholoi *micenee (in basso).*

riscontrare in un esteso abitato o in una grande necropoli.

Io resto invece del parere che sono proprio le stratigrafie, se considerate con acume e prudenza, la base principale del ragionamento archeologico. Ciò vale ovviamente anche per la Sardegna e giustifica appieno il presente lavoro.

Bibliografia

Arca, M., Martini, F., Tuveri, C., Pitzalis, G. & Ulzega, A. 1982. *Paleolitico dell'Anglona (Sardegna settentrionale), Ricerche 1979–80.* Quaderni della Soprintendenza ai Beni Archeologici di Sassari e Nuoro 12. Dessì, Sassari.

Atzeni, E. 1988. Il Nuraghe Genna Maria. *L'umana avventura* 3(8): 15–24.

Atzeni, E. 1996a. La cultura del Vaso Campaniforme e la facies di Bunnànaro nel Bronzo Antico. In D. Cocchi Genick (a cura di), *L'antica età del bronzo in Italia. Atti del Congressi di Viareggio, 9–12 Gennaio 1995*, 19–20. Octavo, Firenze.

Atzeni, E. 1996b. La sepoltura campaniforme di Bingia e Monti (Gonnostramatza, Oristano). In D. Cocchi Genick (a cura di), *L'antica età del bronzo in Italia. Atti del Congressi di Viareggio, 9–12 Gennaio 1995*, poster n. 40. Octavo, Firenze.

Atzeni, E. Iin stampa. La "cultura del vaso campaniforme" nella necropoli di Locci Santus (S. Giovanni Suergiu. In *Carbonia e il Sulcis. Archeologia e Territorio.*

Badas, U. 1987. Genna Maria-Villanovaforru (Cagliari). I vani 10–18. Nuovi apporti allo studio delle abitazioni della Corte Centrale. In *Atti del III° Convegno di studi, "Un millennio di relazioni fra la Sardegna ed i Paesi del Mediterraneo, Selargius-Cagliari, 27–30 novembre 1986: La Sardegna nel Mediterraneo tra il secondo e il primo millennio a.C.*, 133–146. Stef, Cagliari.

Bafico, S. & Rossi, G. 1987. Una proposta di attribuzione cronologica per le ceramiche decorate del cortile del Nuraghe Santu Antine di Torralba (SS). In *Atti del III° Convegno di studi, "Un millennio di relazioni fra la Sardegna ed i Paesi del Mediterraneo," Selargius-Cagliari, 27–30 novembre 1986*, 41–53. Stef, Cagliari.

Bafico, S. & Rossi, G. 1988. Gli scavi e i materiali. In Moravetti, A. (a cura di), *Il Nuraghe Santu Antine nel Logudoro-Meilogu.* Carlo Delfino, Sassari.

Bernardini, P. 1985. Tholoi in Sardegna: alcune osservazioni. *Studi Etruschi* 51: 43–54.

Bernardini, P. 1992. La facies orientalizzante in Sardegna: problemi di individuazione e di metodologia. In Tykot, R.H. & Andrews, T.K. (eds.), *Sardinia in the Mediteranean: A Fooprint in the Sea. Studies in Sardinian Archaeology Presented to Miriam S. Balmuth.* Monographs in Mediterranean Archaeology 3: 396–

Tab. 11.8. *Seriazione cronologica evolutiva della Civiltà Nuragica.*

Bronzo Medio I, XVI-fine XV sec. Fase Sa Turricula, vasi a tesa interna, vasi a nervature: Nuraghe Santu Antine (Torralba-SS); nuraghe complesso Accas-Gésico (NU); Su Muru Mannu-Tharros.

Bronzo Medio II, XIV-inizi XIII sec. Tegami, ceramica a pettine: nuraghe complesso Madonna del Rimedio I (Oristano); bastione del Nuraghe Santu Antine (Torralba-SS); Nuraghe La Prisciona (Arzachena-SS).

Bronzo Recente, inizi XIII-fine XII sec. Ceramica varia tornita o no, ceramica grigia e micenea III B/C: Nuraghe Antigori, str. 9–10. Vasi ad orlo ingrossato piano: villaggio di S. Gemiliano (Sestu-CA) e di Monte Ollàdiri (Monastir-CA), tomba di giganti di Is Concas (Quartucciu-CA).

Bronzo Finale, XII-IX (o fine del XII-metà del IX) sec. Vasi askoidi; anse a gomito rovescio; anse a piccola maniglia, tazze carenate, vasi ad orlo ingrossato; decorazione a stralucido, ventosa plastica: nuraghe complesso Madonna del Rimedio II (Oristano). Ceramica pregeometrica (con associato bronzetto figurato di guerriero?): Nuraghe Sa Mandra 'e Sa Giua (Ossi-SS). Lipari: Ausonio II.

Età del Ferro, metà IX – fine o primi decenni VIII sec. Ceramica geometrica a spina-pesce (vano F del villaggio di S'Urbale [Teti-NU]), a spina-pesce e cerchielli, stralucido, vasi askoidi, brocche piriformi con falso beccuccio; grandi tegami-vassoio, lucerne a piattello, lucerne a barchetta con protome animalesca, pintadere decorate. Fibula dell'Italia Meridionale con arco serpeggiante (capanne del Nuraghe Genna Maria [Villanovaforru-CA], pozzo del Nuraghe La Prisciona [Arzachena-SS]; 4° strato del vano F di Nuraghe Antigori).

Orientalizzante, fine VIII-VII sec. Decorazioni geometriche complesse, cerchielli, occhi di dado, lambda, falsa cordicella; decorazione dipinta e plastica, anche figurata; vasi askoidi (pozzo e capanne di S. Anastasìa [Sàrdara-CA]); askoi con decorazione complessa, fiasche scanalate discoidi, tazze con ansa sull'orlo Monte Ollàdiri (Monastìr-CA).

Età Arcaica, VI sec. Ceramica tardo-nuragica rozza, crateri con anse a rocchetto ed anse a ponte (Nuraghe Su Igante [Uri-SS]), presentatoi, askoi, brocche.

Non del tutto corrispondente alla suddivisione della Tab. 11.8, ma più ricco di particolari, specie su base percentuale, è il quadro delle tipologie ceramiche del "Nuragico I inferiore", del "Nuragico I superiore" e del "Nuragico II" di Barùmini: periodi da sistemarsi, nel quadro generale, fra l'Età del Bronzo Finale, l'Età del Ferro e l'Orientalizzante e corrispondenti, al Nuraghe Su Nuraxi di Barùmini, il primo soprattutto al deposito votivo antecedente il villaggio, il secondo alle capanne circolari contemporanee dell'antemurale e del paramento esterno del bastione e calcolato sul 23,3% (cioè 14 su 60) degli spazi abitativi (corrispondenti ai nn. 97, 103, 112, 135–137, 144, 150, 152, 177, 182–184, 189) ed il terzo calcolato sul 17,33% (cioè 26 su 150) delle capanne o dei vani posteriori alla distruzione del nuraghe (vani 1–2, 4, 6–7, 95–98, 100, 103, 106, 108–109, 111–115, 117, 120, 135, 137) e su 1500 pezzi. È bene anche tenere presente che vari materiali provengono anche da strati diversi di spazi uguali.

Tipologia ceramica (superfici e impasti)
Per i tre periodi si sono contati almeno tre tipi di ceramica con diversa presenza percentuale (ma non sempre chiaramente disdinguibili fra loro):

A. Impasto nero o grigio compatto a grana fine ben depurato, superfici degli stessi toni e lucidate a spatola: il 60% nel Nuragico I Superiore ed il 22,15% nel Nuragico II;
B. Impasto nerocarbonioso o strisciato con zona interna nera, meno compatto e talvolta friabile, superfici giallo ocra (passante al giallo bruno, rosso arancio), lucidate a spatola che rende consistente e brillante l'engobbio: 28% nel Nuragico I Superiore ed il 71,18% nel Nuragico II. In questo tipo è da includersi anche la ceramica del Nuragico I inferiore, che presenta impasto compatto prevalentemente scuro, con superficie per lo più bruna, spesso lisciata, per il 17% lucidata a stecca ed il 5, 71% a stralucido di aspetto metallico, per il 20% ingubbiata di rosso;
C. Impasto nocciola o rossastro compatto con inclusi medio e microgranulari, superfici nocciola rosato e talvolta bruno, lucidate con spatola: 12% nel Nuragico I Superiore ed il 6,67% nel Nuragico II.

Quanto alle forme esse sono all'incirca una ventina in entrambi i periodi; ma alcune, come le brocche piriformi con falso colatoio (in sé e per sé piuttosto rare), le ciotole troncoconiche, i fornelli fittili e i lisciatoi fittili, si hanno solo nel primo periodo, mentre il vaso a cestello ovale e il vasetto clindrico sembrano caratterizzare il secondo. In quest'ultimo periodo si riducono notevolmente le tazze carenate e nelle brocche a becco si allarga il collo e si preferisce la ceramica di tipo B.

Forme dei vasi fittili
Nello stesso ordine che si è seguito per i tipi ceramici, si hanno circa venti forme dei vasi, percentualmente distribuite come segue:

I. olle globoidi e ovoidi ad orlo ingrossato: 17,80% (16,38% nel Nuragico II: in un caso falsa cordicella e circoletti su olla ad orlo semplice); il 17,14% nel Nuragico I Inferiore
II. olle a colletto di varia altezza, verticale o inclinato in fuori o in dentro: 18,72% (talora con decorazione di linee incise e punti impressi a bastoncello) (17,71% nel Nuragico II; tre vasi a colletto di ceramica tipo B sono dipinti a fasce, in un caso festonate)
III. tazze-ciotole carenate, talvolta a carena smussata (pseudocarenate) con spalla insellata o rigida, verticale od obliqua all'interno o all'esterno: 35,36% (talvolta con decorazione di file multiple di andamento contrapposto di spina di pesce sulla parete e sul fondo) (8,22% nel Nuragico II); il 57,14% nel Nuragico I Inferiore
IV. ciotole emisferiche: 10,64% (7,58% nel Nuragico II); ciotole emisferiche e troncoconiche – vedi qui di seguito – si avevano anche nel Nuragico I Inferiore (28,54%), talora con beccuccio di versamento
V. ciotole troncoconiche: 6,03%
VI. tegami-piatti troncoconici: 5,27% (4,42% nel Nuragico II)
VII. conche: 2,00% (più frequenti nel Nuragico II)
VIII. bollitoi: 0,45% (3,29% nel Nuragico II)
IX. coperchi di bollitoi: 0,50%
X. ziri (o giare):1,00% (1,72%'nel Nuragico II)
XI. calefattoi o fornelli: 0,23%; anche nel Nuragico I Inferiore
XII. lisciatoi fittili: 0,23%
XIII. brocche a becco (o vasi askoidi): 9,84% (di solito di ceramica tipo A, pure anche di tipo B ma di maggiori dimensioni e forme più sciatte. Hanno corpo globoide, piriforme e ad anatrella) (7,15% nel Nuragico II, di solito di tipo B e della forma a largo collo; con decorazione a falsa cordicella ed occhi di dado, linee orizzontali e zig-zag)
XIV. brocche piriformi, con falso colatoio: 0,23% (dai vani 36, 135, 289)
XV. lampade a piattello e a cucchiaio: 2,30% (2,19% nel Nuragico II con ceramica B e decorazione a falsa cordicella ed occhi di dado)
XVI. coppe a fruttiera, talora con incisioni di spina di pesce (1,08% nel Nuragico II); anche nel Nuragico I Inferiore
XVII. vasi per distillazione: senza % (uguale numero % nel Nuragico II)
XVIII. vaso a cestello ovale: nel Nuragico II, quantità con ceramica di tipo B
XIX. minuscolo vaso cilindrico: nel Nuragico II

Tab. 11.9. Presenze percentuali di manufatti ceramici nelle varie fasi del Nuraghe su Nuraxi di Barùmini.

409. Sheffield Academic Press, Sheffield.

Cherry, J.F. 1992. Palaeolithic Sardinians? Some questions of evidence and method. In Tykot, R.H. & Andrews, T.K. (eds.), *Sardinia in the Mediteranean: A Fooprint in the Sea. Studies in Sardinian Archaeology Presented to Miriam S. Balmuth.* Monographs in Mediterranean Archaeology 3: 28–39. Sheffield Academic Press, Sheffield.

Contu, E. 1958. Argomenti di cronologia a proposito delle tombe a poliandro di Ena 'e Muros (Ossi-Sassari) e Motrox 'e Bois (Usellus-Cagliari). *Studi Sardi* 14–15: 129–196.

Contu, E. 1964. La Tomba dei Vasi Tetrapodi in località Santu Pedru (Alghero-Sassari). *Monumenti Antichi dei Lincei* 57: 3–201.

Contu, E. 1980. La Sardegna Preistorica e Protostorica. Aspetti e problemi. In *Atti della XXII Riunione Scientifica dell'Istituto Italiano di Preistoria e Protostoria, "Sardegna Centro-settentrionale," 21–27 ottobre 1978*, 13–43. Istituto Italiano di Preistoria e Protostoria, Firenze.

Contu, E. 1982. Alcuni problemi cronologici della preistoria sarda nel contesto mediterraneo. *Archivio Storico Sardo* 33: 91–102.

Contu, E. 1984. Monte d'Accoddi-Sassari. Problematiche di studio e di ricerca di un singolare monumento preistorico. In Waldren, W.H., Chapman, R.W., Lewthwaite, J.G. & Kennard, R.-C. (eds.), *The Deya Conference of Prehistory: Early Settlement in the Western Mediterranean Islands and their Peripheral Areas.* BAR International Series 229: 591–608. British Archaeological Reports, Oxford.

Contu, E. 1987a. Cronologia della Sardegna preistorica e protostorica. In Brigaglia, M. (a cura di), *Sardegna.* Vol. 3: 405–410.

Contu, E. 1987b. Problematica ed inquadramento culturale. In Atzeni, E., Contu, E., & Ferrarese Ceruti, M.L. La Sardegna del Rame nell'Italia insulare: la Sardegna, *Atti del Congresso Internazionale, "L'Età del Rame in Europa," Viareggio, 15–18 ottobre 1987*. Rassegna di Archeologia 7: 441–448.

Contu, E. 1992a. L'inizio dell'Età Nuragica. In *Atti del III° Convegno di studi, "Un millennio di relazioni fra la Sardegna ed i Paesi del Mediterraneo," Selargius-Cagliari, 27–30 novembre 1987: La Sardegna tra il Bronzo Medio e Recente (XVI-XIII sec. a.C.)*, 13–40. Edizioni Della Torre, Cagliari.

Contu, E. 1992b. Nuove anticipazioni sui dati stratigrafici di Monte d'Accoddi. Scavi 1952-1958. In *Monte d'Accoddi. 10 anni di nuovi scavi*, 21–36. Istituto Italiano di Archeologia Sperimentale, Soprintendenza Archeologica di Sassari e Nuoro, Genova.

Contu, E. 1993. Statues en pierres et petits bronzes figurés de la Sardaigne de l'âge Nouragique. In *L'Arte des Peuples Italiques. 3000 a 300 avant J.C*. Genève, Musée Rath, 6 nov. 1993-13 febbr. 1994, Paris, Mona Bismarck Foundation, Ier mar- 30 avril 1994, catalogo della mostra, "Hellas et Roma", Electa Napoli, 52–57. Articolo tradotto dall'italiano e pubblicato anche col titolo originale italiano, nella copia italiana del catalogo: Scultura in pietra e bronzetti figurati della Sardegna Nuragica, *L'arte dei Popoli Italici dal 3000 al 300 a.C.*, 51–58.

Contu, E. 1995. La Sardegna nell'antica età del bronzo. Problematica e inquadramento culturale. In Cocchi Genick, D. (a cura di), *L'antica età del bronzo in Italia. Atti del Congresso di Viareggio, 9–12 Gennaio 1995*, 17–19. Octavo, Firenze.

Contu, E. In stampa. *La Sardegna preistorica e nuragica*. Chiarella, Sassari.

Fadda, M.A. 1988. Lo strato eneolitico del riparo di S. Basilio-Ollolai (Nuoro). *Rassegna di Archeologia* 7: 535.

Ferrarese Ceruti, M.L. 1972–74. La Tomba XVI di Su Crucifissu Mannu e la Cultura di Bonnànaro. *Bulletino di Paletnologia Italiana* 81: 113–210.

Ferrarese Ceruti, M.L. 1985. Un bronzetto nuragico da Ossi (Sassari). In *Studi in onore di G. Lilliu per il suo settantesimo compleanno*, 51–59. Cagliari.

Ferrarese Ceruti, M.L. 1991. Creta e Sardegna. Una nota. In *La transizione dal Miceneo all'Alto Arcaismo. Dal palazzo alla città in età post-micenea*, 587–591. Monografie scientifiche Serie Scienze Umane e sociali, Roma, CNR.

Lilliu, G. 1982. *La Civiltà Nuragica*. Carlo Delfino, Sassari.

Lilliu, G. & Zucca, R. 1988. *Su Nuraxi di Barumini*. Sardegna Archeologica, Guide e Itinerari 9. Carlo Delfino, Sassari.

Lo Schiavo, F. 1986. L'Età dei nuraghi. In *Il Museo Sanna a Sassari*. Banco di Sardegna, Pizzi, Cinisello Balsamo, Milano.

Lo Schiavo, F., Fadda, M.A. & Boninu, A. 1988. Nuoro. In *L'Antiquarium Arborense e i civici musei archeologici della Sardegna*. Banco di Sardegna, Cinisello Balsamo, Milano.

Martini, F. 1992. Early human setlements in Sardinia. In Tykot, R.H. & Andrews, T.K. (eds.), *Sardinia in the Mediterranean: A Fooprint in the Sea. Studies in Sardinian Archaeology Presented to Miriam S. Balmuth*. Monographs in Mediterranean Archaeology 3: 40–48. Sheffield Academic Press, Sheffield.

Meloni, L. 1993. Le ceramiche Bonu Ighinu e San Ciriaco di "Puisteris" (Mogoro) nella collezione Puxeddu. *Quaderni della Soprintendenza Archeologica di Cagliari e Oristano* 10: 5–16.

Michael, H.N. & Betancourt, P.P. 1988a. Dating of the Aegean Late Bronze Age with Radiocarbon, II. Further Arguments for an early date. *Archaeometry* 30: 169–175.

Michael, H.N. & Betancourt, P.P. 1988b. Dating of the Aegean Late Bronze Age with Radiocarbon, IV. Addendum. *Archaeometry* 30: 180–182.

Michels, J. & Webster, G. (eds.) 1987. *Studies in Nuragic Archaeology: Village Excavations at Nuraghe Urpes and Nuraghe Toscono in West-Central Sardinia*. BAR International Series 373. British Archaeological Reports, Oxford.

Pitzalis, G. 1988. Perfugas. In *L'Antiquarium Arborense e i civici musei archeologici della Sardegna*, 55–66. Banco di Sardegna, Sassari-Milano.

Santoni, V., Atzeni, E., Forresu, R., Giorgetti, S., Mongiu, M., Sebis, S., Siddu, A. & Tore, G. 1982. Cabras, Cuccuru S'Arriu. Nota preliminare di scavo (1978,1979, 1980). *Rivista di Studi Fenici* 10: 103–110.

Santoni, V. 1989. Cuccuru S'Arriu – Cabras. Il sito di cultura San Michele di Ozieri. Dati preliminari. In Campus, L.D. (a cura di), *La Cultura di Ozieri. Problematiche e nuove acquisizioni*, 239–244. Ozieri. Il Torchietto.

Santoni, V. 1992a. Cuccuru S'Arriu (Cabras). L'Orizzonte Eneolitico Sub-Ozieri. In Tykot, R.H. & Andrews, T.K. (eds.), *Sardinia in the Mediterranean: A Fooprint in the Sea. Studies in Sardinian Archaeology Presented to Miriam S. Balmuth*. Monographs in Mediterranean Archaeology 3: 157–175. Sheffield Academic Press, Sheffield.

Santoni, V. 1992b. Nuraghe Piscu di Suelli: documenti e materiali del Bronzo Medio-Recente. In *Atti del III° Convegno di studi, "Un millennio di relazioni fra la Sardegna ed i Paesi del Mediterraneo," Selargius-Cagliari, 27–30 novembre 1987: La Sardegna tra il Bronzo Medio e Recente (XVI-XIII sec. a.C.)*, 167–186. Edizioni Della Torre, Cagliari.

Santoni, V. & Sebis, S. 1984. Il complesso nuragico di "Madonna del Rimedio" (Oristano). *Nuovo Bullettino Archeologico Sardo* 1: 97–114.

Sondaar, P.Y., De Boer, P.L., Sanges, M. Kostsakis, T. & Esu, D. 1984. First report on a paleolithic culture in Sardinia. In Waldren, W.H., Chapman, R., Lewthwaite, J. & Kennard, R.-C. (eds.), *The Deya Conference of Prehistory: Early Settlement in the Western Mediterranean Islands and their Peripheral Areas*. BAR International Series 229: 29–47. British Archaeological Reports, Oxford.

Sondaar, P.Y., Martini, F., Ulzega, A. & Klein Hofmeijer, G. 1991. L'homme pléistocene en Sardaigne. *L'Anthropologie* (Paris) 95: 181–200.

Stuiver, M., Long, A. & Kra, R. 1993. Calibration 1993. *Radiocarbon* 35(1).

Stuiver, M. & Reimer, P.J. 1993. Extended ^{14}C data base and revised Calib 3.0 ^{14}C age calibration program. *Radiocarbon* 35: 215–230.

Switsur, V.R. 1990. Appendix I. Radiocarbon ages and dates in Sardinia prehistory. In Trump, D.H., *Nuraghe Noeddos and the Bonu Ighinu Valley. Excavations and Survey in Sardinia*. Oxbow Books, Oxford.

Switsur, V.R. & Trump, D.H. 1983. A radiocarbon chronology for the early prehistory of Sardinia. In Mook, W.G. & Waterbolk, H.T. (eds.), *Proceedings of the First International Symposium, ^{14}C and Archaeology*, Groningen 1981. PACT 8: 453–464. Strasbourg.

Trump, D.H. 1990. *Nuraghe Noeddos and the Bonu Ighinu Valley. Excavations and Survey in Sardinia*. Oxbow Books, Oxford.

Tykot, R.H. 1994. Radiocarbon dating and absolute chronology in Sardinia and Corsica. In Skeates, R. & Whitehouse, R.D. (eds.), *Radiocarbon Dating and Italian Prehistory*. Accordia Specialist Studies on Italy 3: 115–145. Accordia Research Centre, University of London.

Ugas, G. 1982. Testimonianze dell'età prenuragica. In *Ricerche archeologiche nel territorio di Sanluri. Mostra grafica e fotografica, Sanluri, 16–22 giugno, 1982*, 9–11. Tipografia Concu, Sanluri-Cagliari.

Ugas, G., Lai, G & Usai, L. 1989a. L'insediamento prenuragico di Su Coddu (Selargius-Cagliari). Notizia preliminare sulle campagne di scavo 1981–1984. *Nuovo Bullettino Archeologico Sardo* 2: 7–40.

Ugas, G. 1989b. Premessa e brevi cenni sulla ceramica dipinta neolitica e protocalcolitica sarda. In Ugas, G., Usai, L., Nuvoli, M.P., Lai, G. & Marras, M.G., Nuovi dati sull'insediamento di Su Coddu-Selargius. In Campus, L.D. (a cura di), *La Cultura di Ozieri. Problematiche e nuove acquisizioni*, 239–244. Il Torchietto, Ozieri.

Ugas, G. 1990. *La Tomba dei Guerrieri di Decimoputzu*. Norax 1. Edizioni Della Torre, Cagliari.

Ugas, G. 1992. Considerazioni sullo sviluppo dell'architettura e della società nuragica. In Tykot, R.H. & Andrews, T.K. (eds.), *Sardinia in the Mediterranean: A Footprint in the Sea. Studies in Sardinian Archaeology Presented to Miriam S. Balmuth*. Monographs in Mediterranean Archaeology 3: 221–234. Sheffield Accademic Press, Sheffield.

Usai, E. 1990. S. Antioco. Area del Cronicario. Ceramica preistorica dall'area del Cronicario. *Studi Fenici* 18(1).

Usai, L. 1989. La struttura 27. In Ugas, G., Usai, L., Nuvoli, M.P., Lai, G. & Marras, M.G., Nuovi dati sull'insediamento di Su Coddu – Selargius. In Campus, L.D. (a cura di), *La Cultura di Ozieri. Problematiche e nuove acquisizioni*, 245–251. Il Torchietto, Ozieri.

Webster, G.S. 1988. Duos Nuraghes: preliminary results of the first three seasons of excavations. *Journal of Field Archaeology* 15: 465–472.

Weiss Grele, A. 1992. A temporal analysis of the ceramic industry at Duos Nuraghes: a step toward chronology. In Tykot, R.H. & Andrews, T.K. (eds.), *Sardinia in the Mediterranean: A Footprint in the Sea. Studies in Sardinian Archaeology Presented to Miriam S. Balmuth*. Monographs in Mediterranean Archaeology 3: 271–286. Sheffield Accademic Press, Sheffield.

12. Articolazione e cronologia del Neolitico Antico

Giuseppa Tanda

I siti che hanno restituito tracce materiali del Neolitico antico sono trenta, per lo più concentrati nella regione occidentale dell'Isola (Fig. 12.1); il 57% di essi è costituito da grotte o ripari ed il 43% da stazioni all'aperto (Tanda 1995[1]: 17–19; 1995[2]: 17–29: ivi bibliografia precedente). In sette siti (77%: Grotta Verde, Riparo di Cala Corsara, Monte d'Accoddi, Grotta Filiestru, Grotta Monte Maiore, Grotta Corbeddu, Riparo di Su Carroppu) sono stati eseguiti scavi (Tanda 1980; Ferrarese Ceruti & Pitzalis 1987; Tanda 1977; Trump 1983; Foschi Nieddu 1981; 1987; Foschi 1991; Sanges 1987; Atzeni 1987); in tre di essi (23%: Ripari di Su Carroppu e di Cala Corsara, altare di Monte d'Accoddi) sono state osservate tracce, antiche e moderne, di sconvolgimenti o di riutilizzazioni. Pertanto, i contesti culturali utili per l'argomento di questa relazione, allo stato attuale, sono soprattutto quattro: Grotta Filiestru (Mara), Grotta Sa Korona o Monte Maiore (Thiesi) e Grotta Corbeddu-Oliena, ai quali si aggiunge, a causa della significatività dei suoi materiali, il complesso materiale di Grotta Verde-Alghero, recuperato dal Gruppo Speleologico Algherese (Tanda 1980) ed arricchito, sia pure con pochi dati, dagli scavi (Lo Schiavo 1987).

Le informazioni disponibili finora edite, nel loro complesso, non sono numerose: non tutti gli scavi, infatti, sono stati interamente pubblicati. Tuttavia tali informazioni, rielaborate e adeguatamente interpretate, all'interno del quadro mediterraneo di riferimento, consentono di costruire un'ipotesi cronologica articolata ed attendibile, allo stato attuale, sull'articolazione del Neolitico Antico della Sardegna. Lo studio toccherà brevemente due punti: l'articolazione culturale e la cronologia.

L'articolazione culturale

Il riesame approfondito dei dati e dei lavori editi consente oggi di ritenere ancora valida la suddivisione in tre fasi ipotizzata, con qualche variante, in vari luoghi e da differenti studiosi: dalla Tanda (1983; 1988; 1990), dall'Atzeni (1987) e dalla Foschi (1981; 1987; 1991).

Il Neolitico antico I o Fase I è attestato (spesso da materiali scarsi e sporadici) in dodici località certe ed in undici probabili (Fig. 12.2). Le tipologie vascolari caratteristiche della fase sono riassunte nelle Figg. 12.3–12.6: olle, ciotole carenate, tegami, vasi a corpo globulare schiacciato e collo non distinto, e vasi a corpo globulare. Particolarmente interessanti appaiono i vasi ad orlo ondulato e le scodelle con presa sopra o sull'orlo (Fig. 12.4). Nel grafico si possono apprezzare i valori in percentuale delle forme vascolari di Grotta Filiestru ed in particolare delle olle e delle ciotole (Fig. 12.6), che sono prevalenti su tutti gli altri tipi. Frequenti sono le anse a maniglia, decorate o non decorate, tra le quali si individua una ricca tipologia (anse orizzontali, volte all'insù, sull'orlo o sopra l'orlo) (Fig. 12.7). Sono presenti anche le bugne forate o non forate. La ceramica non decorata (82%) a Filiestru (trincea D) prevale su quella decorata (7%), su quella ingubbiata rossa (8,2%) e su quella cordonata (2,2%). La decorazione sembra interessare l'intera superficie del vaso. La tecnica decorativa prevalente è quella ad impressione cardiale. I motivi più frequenti sono la banda verticale e quella orizzontale; seguono il triangolo campito delimitato da una banda angolare non decorata; la banda a zig-zag (Fig. 12.8). In alcuni casi triangoli e bande coesistono nello stesso vaso.

L'industria litica, per lo più in ossidiana per il 71% ma anche in selce per il 29% vede la prevalenza dei geometrici (64%, n. 40, quasi assenti a Filiestru) sugli altri tipi come i bulini, i grattatoi, le punte a dorso, le punte, le lame-raschiatoio, i raschiatoi, i denticolati (Depalmas 1995: 3–10). All'analisi tipometrica (Fig. 12.9) gli strumenti analizzati mostrano una tendenza al microlitismo (56%) intorno ai valori di 1 e 2,5 cm; 29%

Giuseppa Tanda, Dipartimento di Studi Classici ed Antichità, Università di Sassari, Piazza Conte di Moriana 8, 07100 Sassari, Sardegna, Italia

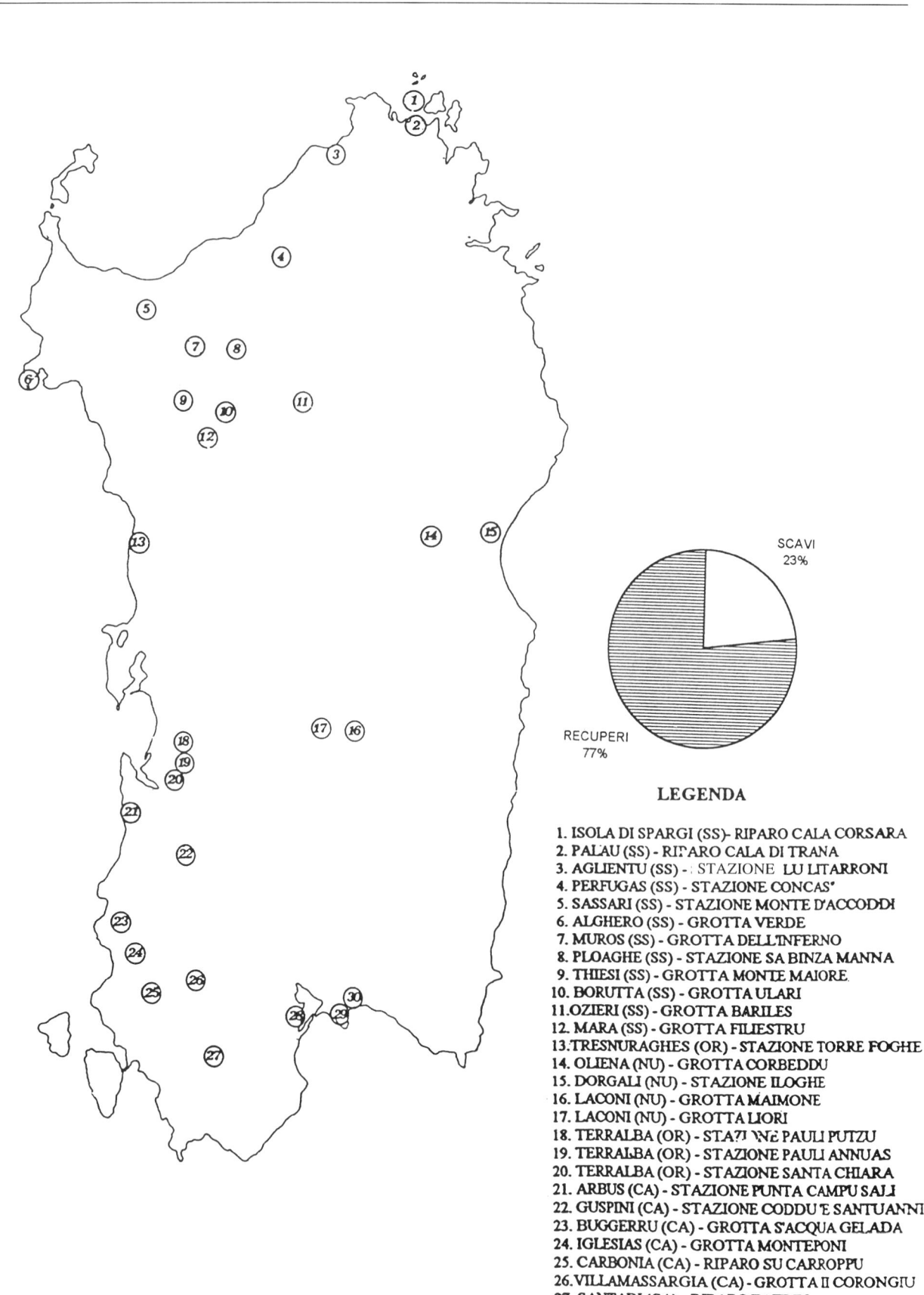

Fig. 12.1. Carta di distribuzione dei siti.

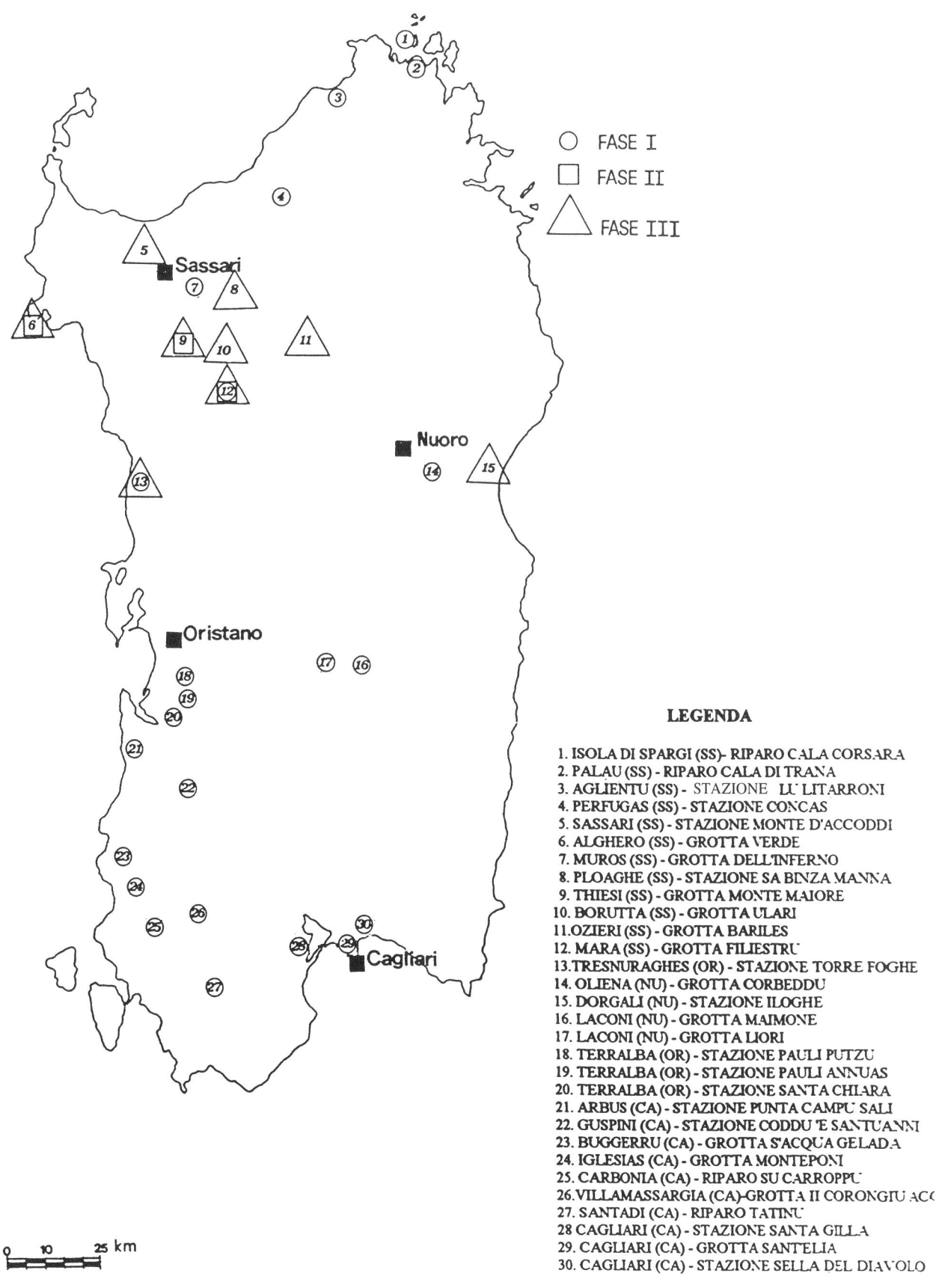

Fig. 12.2. Diffusione delle tre fasi di articolazione del Neolitico antico.

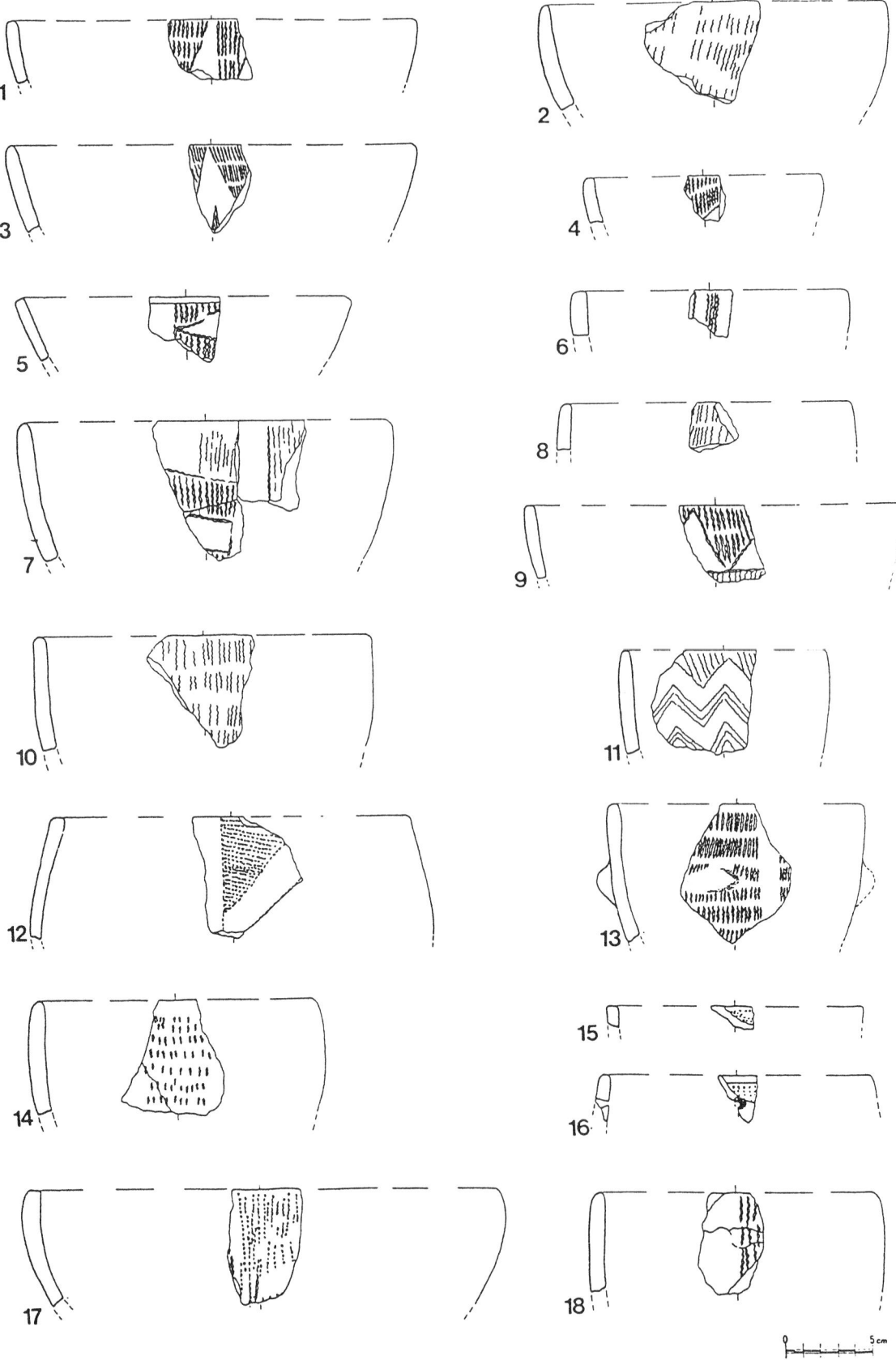

Fig. 12.3. Fase I. Ciotole decorate.

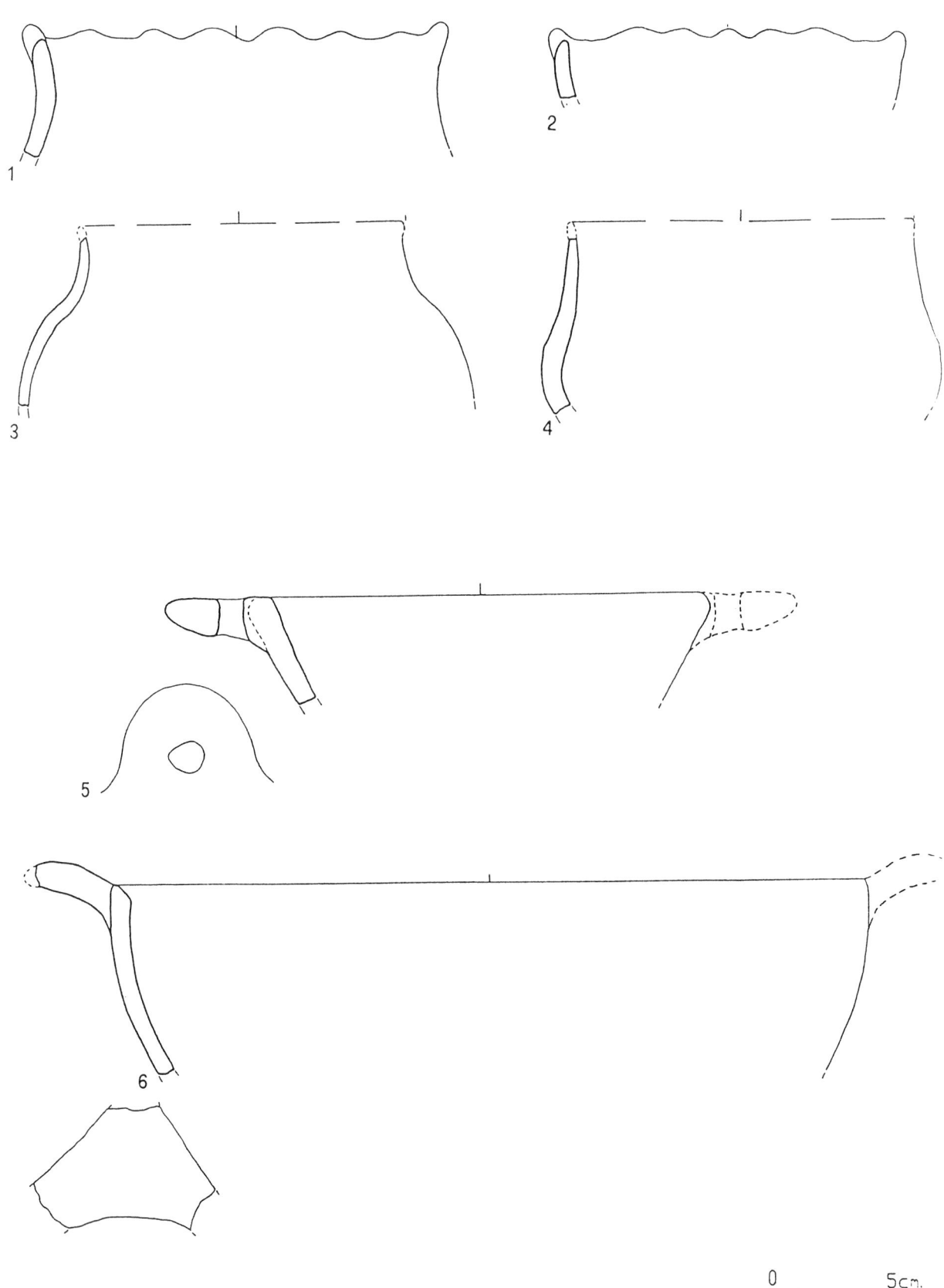

Fig. 12.4. Fase I. Ceramica non decorata. Olle ad orlo ondulato (1–2), olle a corpo globulare (3–4) e a presa sull'orlo (5) o sopra l'orlo (6).

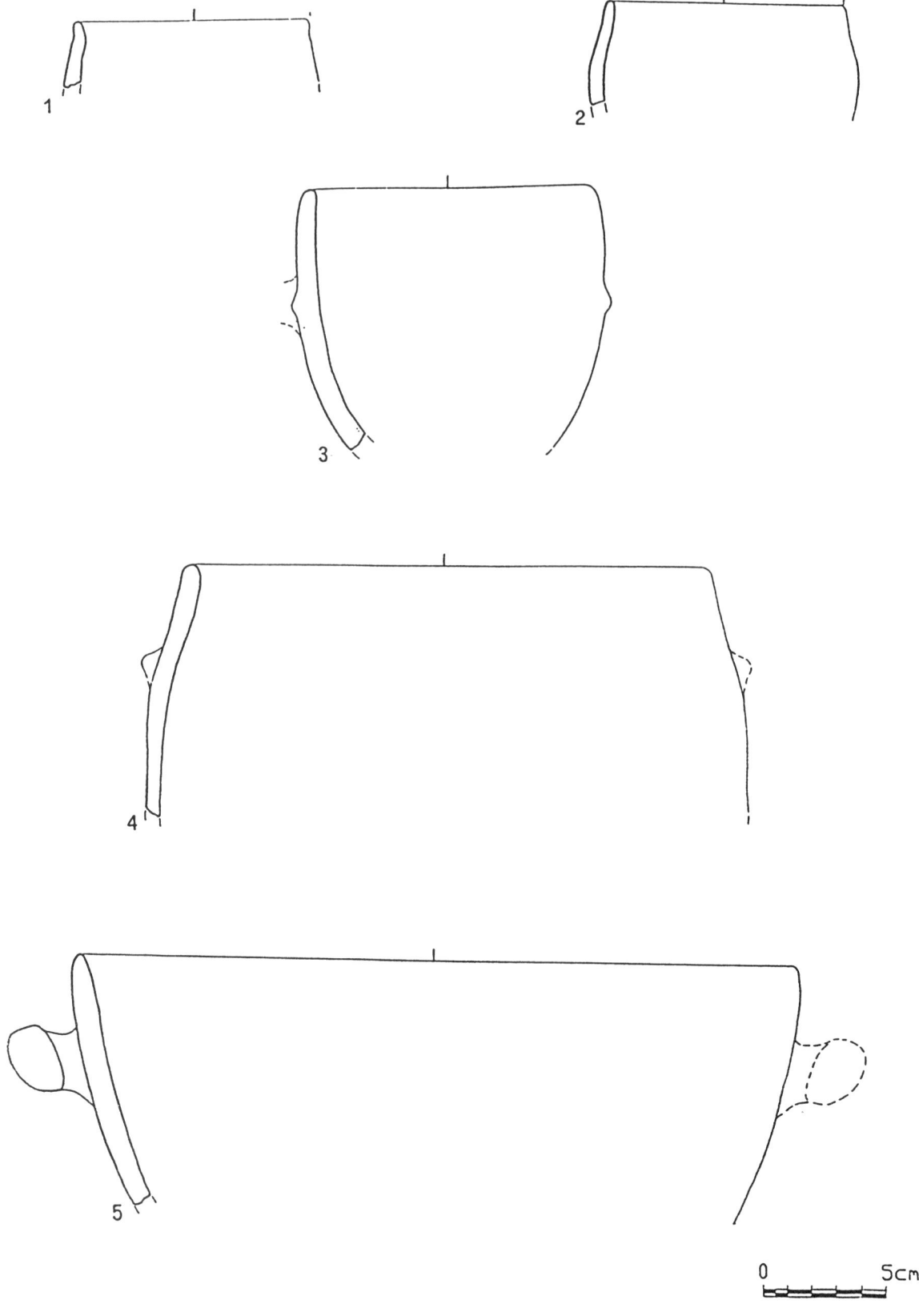

Fig. 12.5. Fase I. Ceramica non decorata: olle.

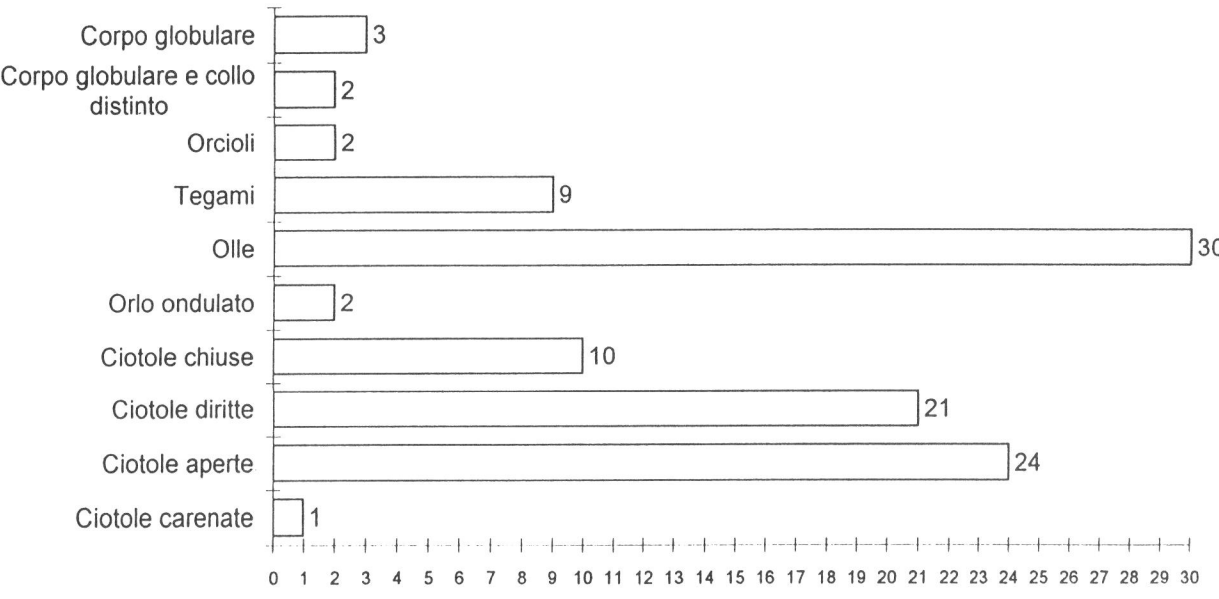

Fig. 12.6. Fase I. Elaborazione dei dati di tipologia vascolare (Grotta Filiestru).

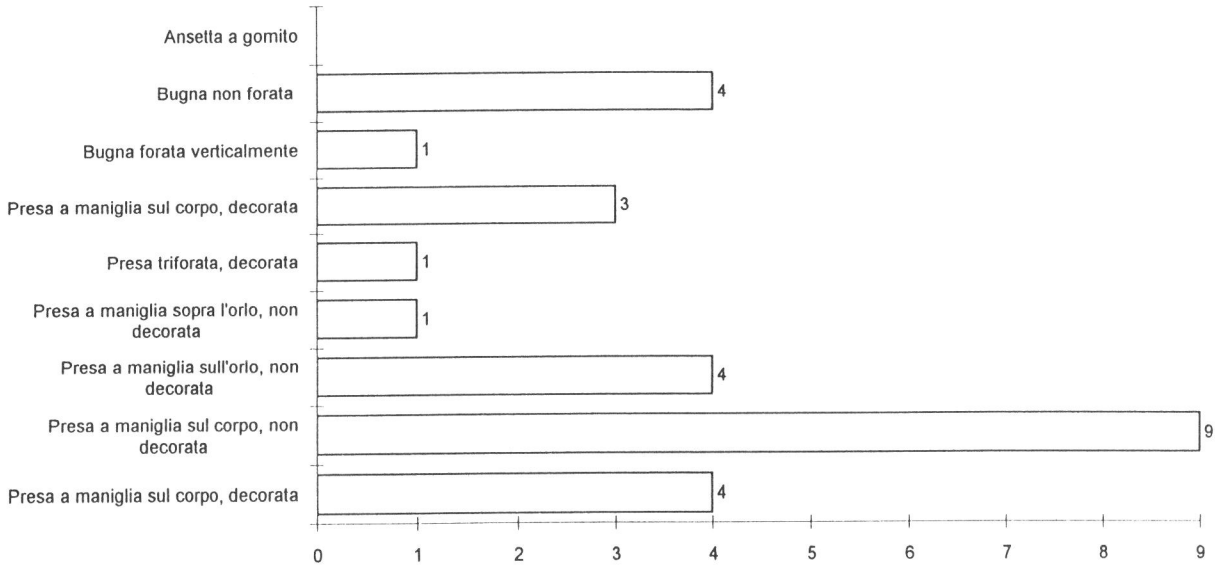

Fig. 12.7. Fase I. Tipologia delle anse e delle prese.

tra 2,5 e 5 cm; 11% tra 5 e 9 cm; un esemplare al di sopra dei 10 cm. Rari appaiono gli elementi in pietra levigata: un pendaglio di scisto ovale, con una estremità appuntita, decorato su entrambe le facce da sette o tre fori non pervi da Filiestru; levigatoi ed un affilatoio in calcare siliceo da Cala Corsara.

L'economia documentata rivela situazioni di notevole rilievo. Sono praticati la raccolta di molluschi eduli (Cala Corsara, Grotta Corbeddu), la pesca (pesci e crostacei), l'allevamento (con prevalenza degli ovicaprini sui bovini, con una buona percentuale di suini), l'agricoltura (scarsamente indiziata) (Trump 1983: 79–81; Levine 1983: 111–131). Il quadro economico di questa fase suggerisce la presenza di un manto forestale ampio e poco intaccato dal disboscamento indispensabile per l'agricoltura (alto valore percentuale della presenza dei suini); la conseguente scarsa pratica dell'agricoltura; il carattere secondario dell'allevamento del bue, che acquisterà maggiore rilevanza nella fase III (Fig. 12.10). Il contesto materiale, soprattutto la ceramica, rivela stringenti analogie con la Corsica, ad esempio Basi (5750 ± 150), Abri du Goulet, Strette, Aleria ecc. (Camps 1988: 53–64; de Lanfranchi 1993: 2–9), con la Toscana, a Pienza (Calvi Rezia 1987: 285–299) e con la Grotta dell'Uzzo a Palermo (5960 ± 70 a.C.: Costantini *et al.* 1987: 397- 405, fig. 3).

Queste affinità da un lato definiscono un'area regionale di manifestazione della ceramica cardiale, una sorta di

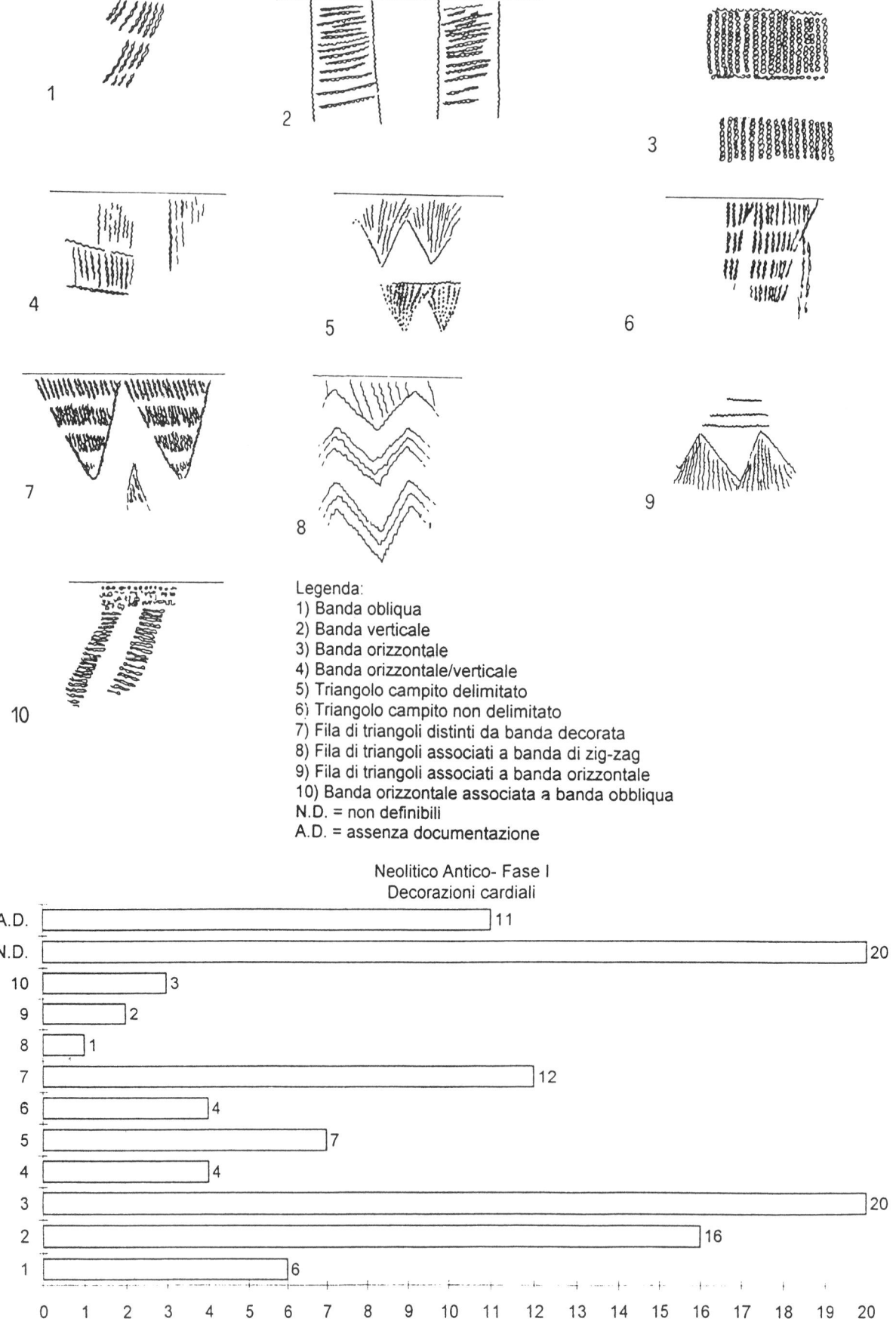

Fig. 12.8. Fase I. Tipologia decorativa.

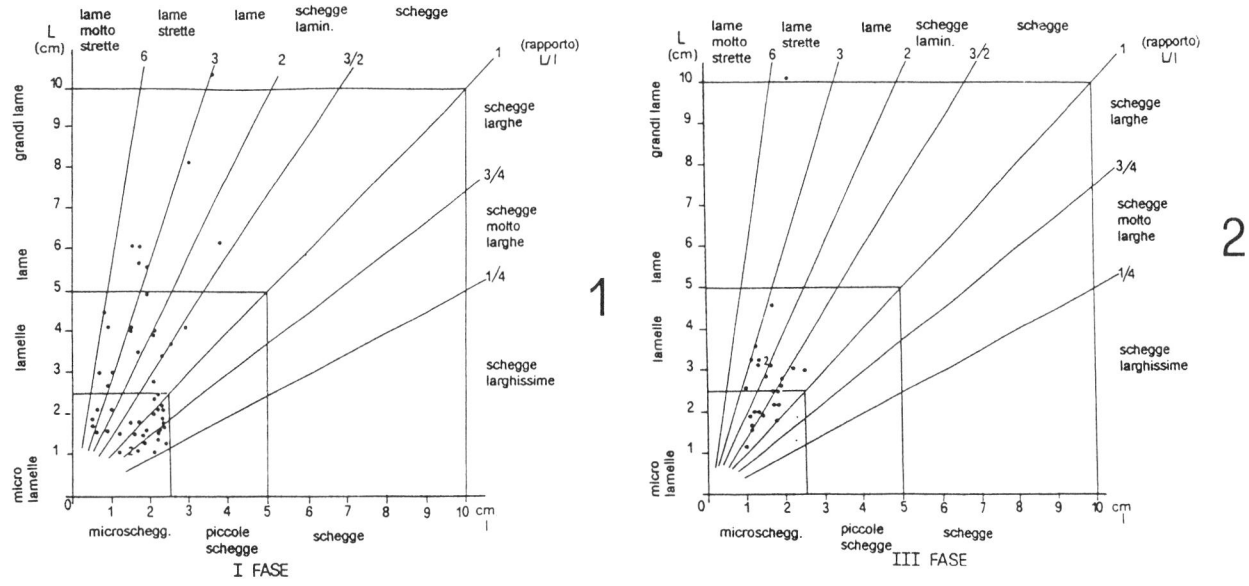

Fig. 12.9. Analisi tipometrica del materiale litico delle fasi I e III.

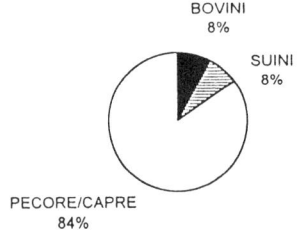

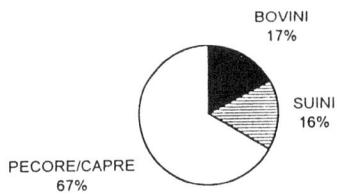

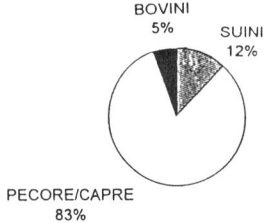

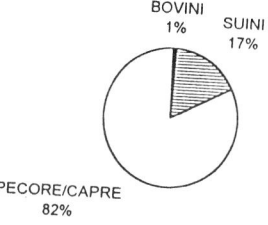

Fig. 12.10. Fasi I e III. Elaborazione dei dati sull'allevamento.

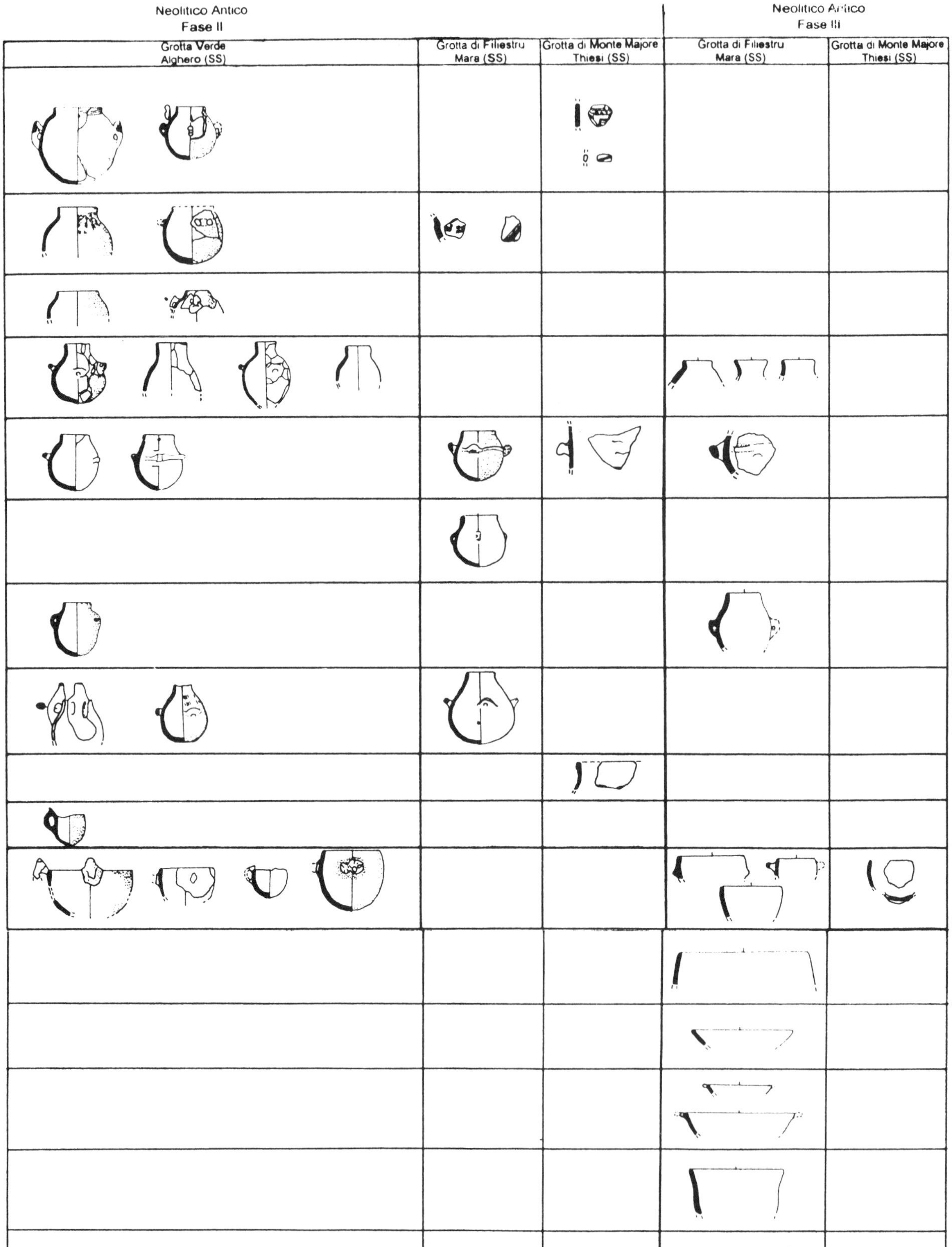

Fig. 12.11. Fasi II e III. Tipologia vascolare.

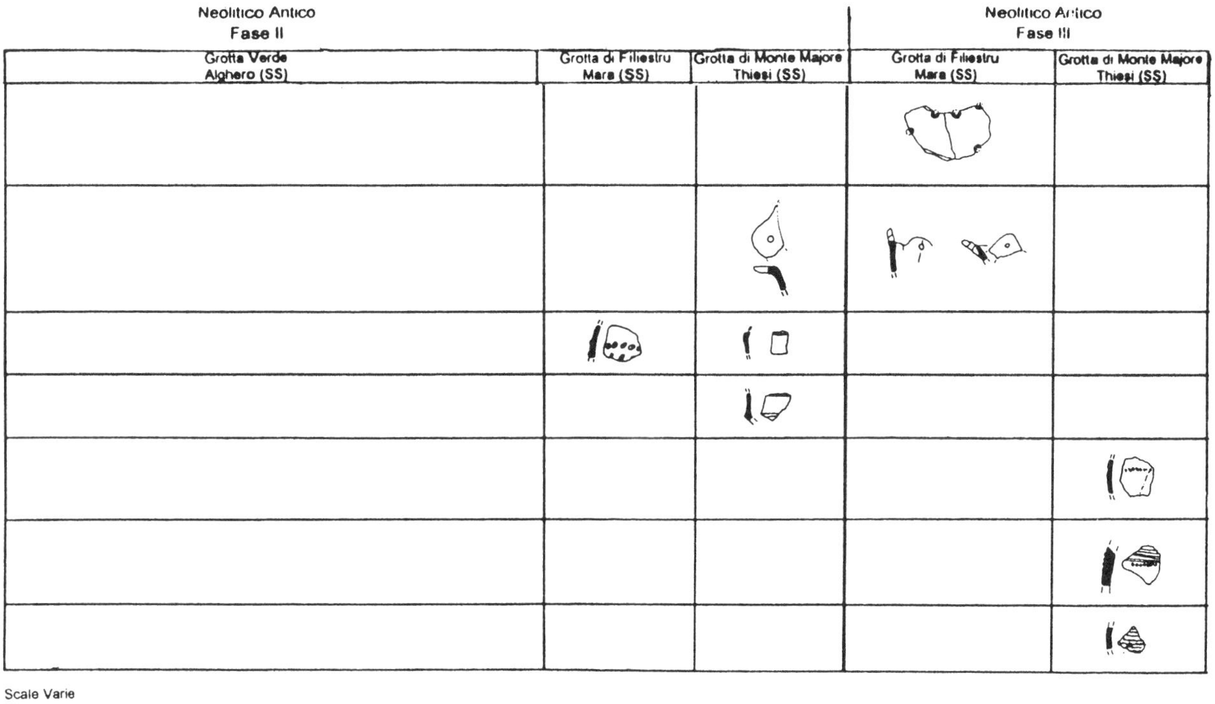

Fig. 12.11. Fasi II e III. Tipologia vascolare (cont.).

"provincia tirrenica del cardiale"; dall'altro suggeriscono la probabile zona di provenienza della nuova fauna, attestata negli strati del Neolitico antico di Grotta Corbeddu: la Toscana attraverso la Corsica. L'area tirrenica sembra quindi assumere la fisionomia di un'area genetica nella quale i gruppi umani preneolitici, interagendo tra di loro, avviarono e portarono a compimento, com'è presumibile, il passaggio dal Mesolitico (e/o Preneolitico corso) al Neolitico. È ragionevole supporre che una certa incidenza, in questo processo di formazione dell'economia produttiva, abbia avuto lo scambio dell'ossidiana e della selce.

Il Neolitico antico II (Figg. 12.1–12.2, 12.11) compare a Grotta Verde, a Filiestru (trincea D, tagli 1–3 dello strato 7, taglio 5 dello strato 6) e Monte Maiore (tagli 4–6 dello strato 3). È caratterizzato dalla coesistenza, nella tecnica ad impressione, dell'uso della decorazione cardiale e strumentale. Quest'ultima compare per la prima volta in Sardegna ed utilizza lo strumento a pettine, il punzone e la stecca.

Il repertorio vascolare, assai ricco e vario, comprende: ciotole a parete curvilinea (Grotta Verde e Monte Maiore); ciotole troncoconiche ad orlo rientrante (Monte Maiore); ciotole carenate (Monte Maiore); vasi globulari a collo distinto o no, a bocca larga o stretta (Grotta Verde); vaso ovoide a collo cilindrico (Monte Maiore); bicchieri; cucchiai; mestoli. Le anse sono a gomito, talvolta apicate e antropomorfe; a maniglia orizzontale, triplici o quadruplici; sopraelevate sull'orlo; a tesa; numerose sono le bugne.

La decorazione, assai sobria, è impostata sull'orlo, al di sotto di esso, in una fascia ristretta, sul labbro e sull'ansa. Sul labbro piatto il motivo è costituito da una fila di tacche trasversali ai margini. I motivi sotto l'orlo sono per lo più costituiti da linee orizzontali raggruppate a formare fasce orizzontali oppure oblique. Sull'ansa, per lo più interamente decorata, talvolta (Grotta Verde) la decorazione realizza figure antropomorfe (Fig. 12.12). Compaiono (a Filiestru con percentuale più alta) l'ingubbiatura rossa ed i cordoni plastici lisci; a Monte Maiore grumi di ocra; a Filiestru ocra rossa in una olla e pigmento carbonioso nero in due olle.

L'industria litica è poco nota. Da Monte Maiore provengono un'accettina, frammenti di macine, due macinelli, un *croissant* e numerose schegge di selce e di ossidiana. Anche l'industria ossea è presente, ma solo a Monte Maiore, con punzoni e stecche. Purtroppo non ci è consentito di fare alcuna precisazione sull'economia di questa fase poichè gli abbondanti elementi in possesso (Monte Maiore) non sono stati ancora studiati. D'altra parte non si è ancora proceduto ad un riesame dei dati di Filiestru (brillantemente studiati, ma con riferimento a sole due fasi, dalla Levine, 1983), necessario dopo l'individuazione della fase intermedia o fase II.

Il quadro di riferimento mediterraneo in questa Fase si è allargato: la coesistenza della tecnica ad impressione cardiale con quella strumentale è accertata a Filitosa, in Corsica (Atzeni 1966: 169–192). Le forme di Grotta Verde (Tanda 1980: 72–80) richiamano però il Midi (Courtin 1974: cfr. Tanda 1980: 76; Binder & Courtin 1987: 491–499), la Toscana (Grotta Lattaia e Grotta dell'Orso di Sarteano: Grifoni Cremonesi 1967; 1969; Cocchi Genick 1993: fig. 39) e soprattutto la Penisola Iberica, con la Cova de l'Or (Marti Oliver & Cabanelles 1987: figg. 57–

58, fot. nn. 55–56; Marti Oliver & Hernandez Perez 1988: figg. 11, 13–14; Bernabeu 1988: 131, fig. 34; 1989: 11sgg.), la Cueva de la Sarsa (Bernabeu 1988: 136sgg., fig. 34; 1989: 11sgg.), Cueva de Los Murcielagos (Munoz & Vicent 1973; Lopez 1988: 214–218, fig. 71), e la Cova Fosca (Olaria 1988: 101sgg., fig. 23). I bordi ondulati di Grotta Filiestru e di Grotta Monte Maiore trovano analogie nei materiali della Cueva de la Dehesilla, in Spagna (Acosta Martinez 1987: fig. 2,6; Lopez 1988: 212- 213). L'area d'influenza o di frequentazione intensa si è quindi ampliata, e sembra coincidere con l'area di scambio dell'ossidiana sarda (Fig. 12.13).

Il Neolitico antico III, attestato in otto località (Figg. 12.1–12.2) è contraddistinto dalla quasi totale scomparsa della decorazione cardiale e dalla notevole carenza di decorazioni plastiche o incise o impresse strumentali o ingubbiate in rosso (a Filiestru risulta solo il 10% di ceramiche decorate; il restante 90% è costituito da ceramiche non decorate (Fig. 12.14). Nella vasaria si distinguono: vasi a collo distinto, breve o alto, troncoconico aperto; vasi ovoidi a collo cilindrico; ciotole troncoconiche a parete curvilinea, ad orlo rientrante; ciotole carenate; olle, tra cui le olle cilindriche; tazze a parete curvilinea; piatti; tegami anche con ansa a tesa, forata o no; vasi a tulipano; vasi con orlo ondulato (Monte Maiore); cucchiai; e un peso da telaio dalla forma non determinabile.

Tra le anse si osservano: anse a maniglia orizzontale, talvolta associate a cordoni; bugne e anse verticali, più numerose che nella Fasi precedenti. Decorazioni particolari sono presenti a Monte Maiore, nei tagli superiori rimaneggiati della trincea B, attribuibili, presumibilmente, ai tagli di contatto con lo strato di cultura Bonuighinu (Neolitico Medio) asportato (Foschi Nieddu 1981).

L'industria litica è nota per una macina ed un macinello recanti entrambi tracce di ocra rossa (Filiestru) e per ventisette strumenti realizzati per il 70% in selce e per il restante 30% in ossidiana, per lo più opaca, con due soli elementi o di ossidiana traslucida (Depalmas, in Tanda 1992: 80 sgg., n. 36, figg. 10–13; Depalmas 1995: 6–9, figg. 6–8). Prevalgono anche in questa fase i geometrici (77,7%), tra i quali la classe più frequente è quella dei segmenti. Presenti le punte a dorso (3,7%), i foliati (7,44%), le punte (7,4%), i raschiatoi (3,7%). Il numero dei tipi è quindi più ridotto rispetto alle altre Fasi. All'analisi tipometrica (Fig. 12.9) risulta una dominanza delle schegge (33,3%) e delle schegge laminari (33,3%), seguite dalle lame (26%) e dalle lame strette (7,4%). Rispetto alle Fasi precedenti in questa Fase sembra verificarsi una maggiore concentrazione dei manufatti di piccole dimensioni (2,5–5 cm). In questa fase sono anche documentati gli anelloni litici nei tipi noti (Tanda 1977). L'industria ossea è attestata solo da un punzone da Monte Maiore.

I dati faunistici di Filiestru (pur con qualche cautela per le ragioni più sopra esposte) testimoniano un allevamento ancora prevalente degli ovicaprini (83%), un decremento dei suini (12%), un incremento dei bovini

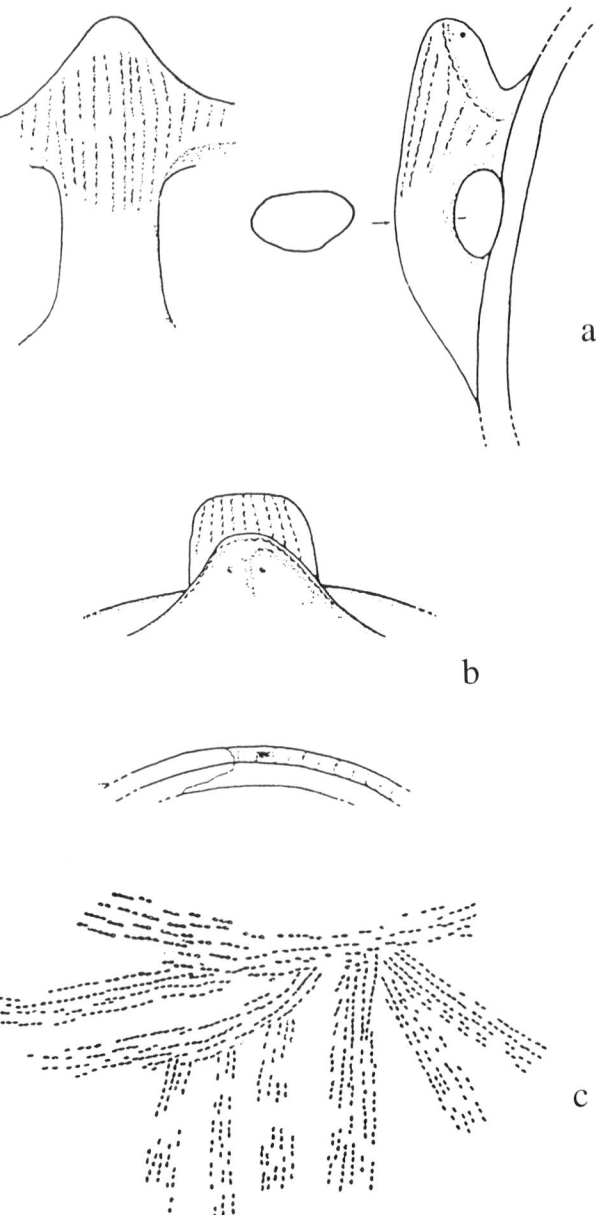

Fig. 12.12. Fase II. Motivi decorativi cardiali (a–b) e a pettine (c).

(5%) (Fig. 12.10). La diminuzione dei suini indicherebbe una riduzione dei boschi; il disboscamento potrebbe essere messo in relazione con l'incremento dell'agricoltura, accertata dalla presenza delle macine e dei macinelli. Quanto al quadro di riferimento la diffusione degli anelloni litici amplia il quadro dei rapporti con la Penisola Italiana e con il resto dell'Europa Occidentale.

Cronologia e quadro Mediterraneo di riferimento

Nella Fig. 12.15 sono riassunte le datazioni C14 finora edite (non calibrate), correlate con quelle di confronto. In proposito si osserva come l'alta datazione C14 di

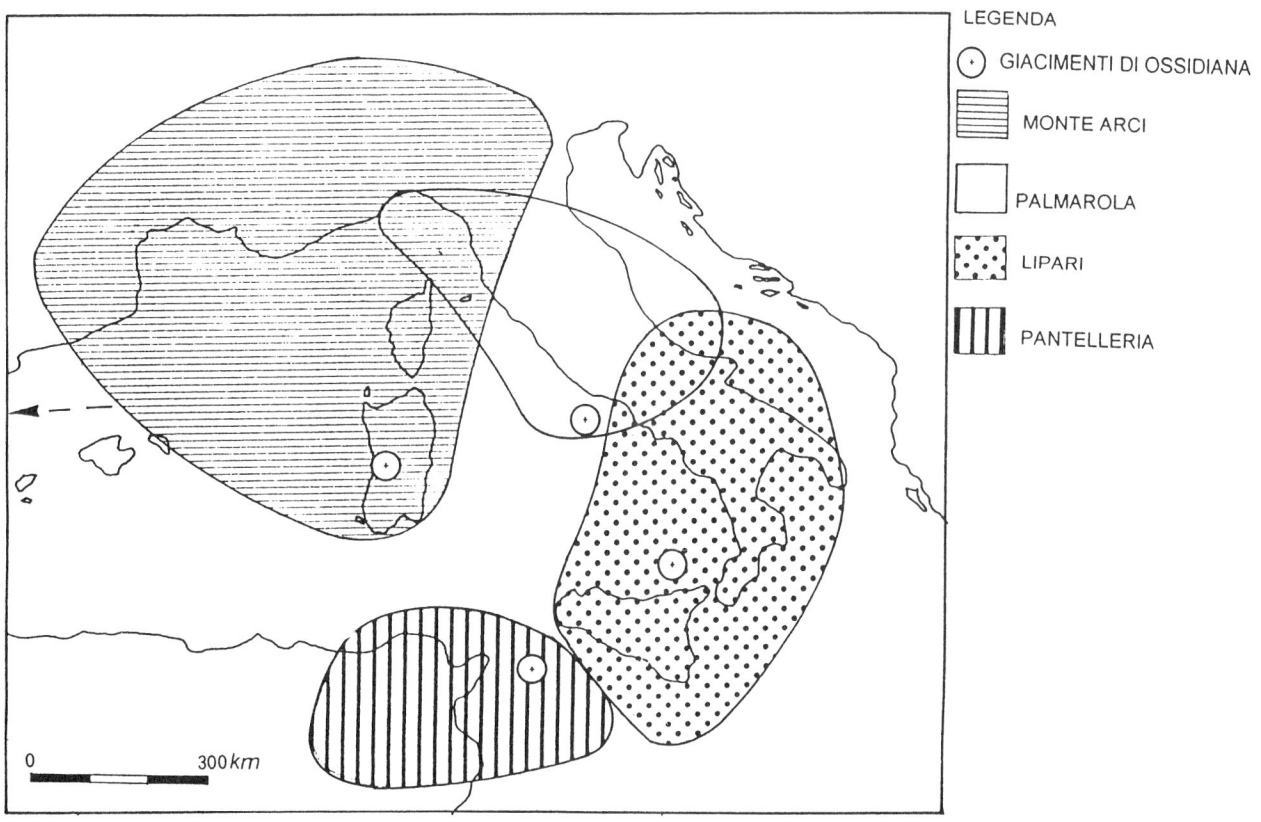

Fig. 12.13. Circuiti commerciali dell'ossidiana nel Mediterraneo occidentale.

Grotta Corbeddu (6273 ± 180 a.C.) e, per contro, la scarsità dei reperti (dei quali peraltro non è stata prodotta alcuna illustrazione grafica o fotografica) destano forti perplessità. Pertanto per il momento essa non viene presa in considerazione. Per quel che concerne il complesso degli altri materiali della I Fase (Filiestru, Su Carroppu, Terralba ecc.), le analogie rilevate con contesti extrainsulari datati C14 (Basi e Casabianda in Corsica, Grotta dell'Uzzo in Sicilia) consentono di attribuire almeno alla metà del VI millennio questa Fase, con sviluppo nella prima metà del V. Il VI millennio è peraltro suggerito dalla misura dello strato di idratazione dell'ossidiana di campioni di Su Carroppu, 5548 a.C. È un Neolitico con chiare connotazioni regionali, come si è già affermato, ma che non è estraneo a tematiche comuni al cardiale mediterraneo (tecnica di decorazione ecc.).

Con la Fase II l'apparizione di vasi a corpo globulare con o senza collo distinto (Grotta Verde) e le analogie con l'area catalana, con il Midi, ancora con la Toscana allargano l'area di confronto verso il Bacino Occidentale del Mediterraneo. Purtroppo non risultano datazioni tra la più bassa di Filiestru, fase cardiale (4520 ± 65 a.C.), e la più alta della Fase III la cosiddetta Cultura di Filiestru (4170 ± 55 a.C.). Le datazioni di alcuni contesti paletnologici di confronto, come Araguina XVII e Cova de l'Or forniscono indicazioni per collocare questa Fase in una fascia cronologica posta nei primi tre secoli della II metà del V millennio a.C. (4500–4200 a.C.).

Con la Fase III e con l'apparizione degli anelloni litici l'area si amplia ancora fino a comprendere anche l'Italia centro-settentrionale. I rapporti non sembrano estendersi al resto dell'Italia. A Monte Maiore compaiono, però, anche nuovi elementi (decorazione ad incisione e file di punti impressi, pittura a bande orizzontali): sono dati che preannunciano il passaggio dal Neolitico antico al Neolitico medio. Sulla III Fase risultano acquisite due sole datazioni C14 da Filiestru, 4170 ± 55 a.C. e 3950 ± 50 a.C., che pongono negli ultimi due secoli del V e nel primo del IV lo sviluppo di questa fase.

È ragionevole supporre che questo progressivo dilatarsi dell'area dei rapporti culturali sia il riflesso del progressivo sviluppo degli scambi di materie prime essenziali come la selce ma soprattutto l'ossidiana. Non è chiaro però se tale riflesso possa essere interpretato come un fenomeno di influenza, esercitata con esiti chiaramente apprezzabili nelle analogie materiali oppure come fenomeno di convergenza. In sintesi, tenendo conto delle datazioni radiometriche acquisite, dei dati stratigrafici e delle analogie culturali riscontrate si ipotizzano le seguenti fasi cronologiche (sempre datazione non calibrate):

Neolitico antico I (Corbeddu, Su Carroppu, Filiestru 7 ecc.): VI millennio-I metà del V millennio a.C. (6000–4500 a.C.);

Neolitico antico II (Grotta Verde; Filiestru D7 tagli 1–3,

Fig. 12.14. Fase III. Ceramica non decorata: ciotole (nn. 1–5), olle (nn. 7–13).

Grotta Filiestru	Riparo Su Carroppu	Grotta Corbeddu	Grotta dell'Uzzo	Basi	Riparo di Araguina Sennola	Casabianda	Curacchiaghiu	Cova Fosca	Cova del'Or	Cueva Los Murcielagos	Cueva Dehesilla	
	5548	6273±180	5960±70	5750±150			5650±180 ? 5360±170 ? 5350±160 ?	5690±100 5260±70 5150±70			5720±400 5170±200 5090±170	**Fase** **I**
4760±75 4665±75 4585±65 4520±65		4882±80 4676±90			4700±140	4720±150			4770±380 4680±290 4560±160			
					4480±140				4315±75			**Fase** **II**
4170±55 3950±50									4030±260	4240±130 4220±130 4200± 45 4150±130 4030±130 4010±130 3980±130	3970±160	**Fase** **III**

Fig. 12.15. Ipotesi di cronologia delle tre Fasi.

D6 taglio 5; Monte Maiore strato 3, tagli 3–6): primi tre secoli della II metà del V millennio a.C. (4500–4200 a.C.);

Neolitico antico III (Filiestru 6; Monte Maiore strato 3, tagli 1–2): ultimi due secoli-primo secolo della I metà del IV millennio a.C. (4200–3900 a.C.).

Autori dei disegni

Figg. 12.1–12.8, 12.10–12.12, 12.14–12.17: geom. Giampiero Sechi; Fig. 12.9: dr.ssa Anna Depalmas; Fig. 12.13: C. Cubeddu.

Bibliografia

Acosta Martinez, P. 1987. El Neolitíco antiguo en el Suroeste español. La Cueva de la Dehesilla (Cadiz). In *Premières comunautés paysannes en Méditerranée occidentale. Actes du Colloque International du C.N.R.S. (Montpellier, 26–29 avril 1983)*, 653–659. Paris.

Atzeni, E. 1966. L'Abri sous roche D' du village préhistorique de Filitosa (Sollacaro, Corse). *Congrès Préhistorique de France*, 18.me session, 169–189. Ajaccio.

Atzeni, E. 1972. Su Carroppu (Carbonia-Sirri). Notiziario. *Rivista di Scienze Preistoriche* 27(2): 478–479.

Atzeni, E. 1975. Nuovi idoli della Sardegna prenuragica (nota preliminare). *Studi Sardi* 23(1973–74): 3–51.

Atzeni, E. 1987. Il Neolitico della Sardegna. *Atti della XXVI Riunione Scientifica "Il Neolitico in Italia," Firenze 7–10 novembre 1985*, 381–400. Istituto Italiano di Preistoria e Protostoria, Firenze.

Atzeni, E. 1992. Reperti neolitici dall'Oristanese. In *Sardinia Antiqua. Studi in onore di Piero Meloni in occasione del suo settantesimo compleanno*, 35–62. Cagliari.

Bernabeu, J. 1988. El Neolitíco en las comarcas meridionales del Pais Valenciano. In Lopez, P. (a cura di), *El Neolitíco in España*, 131–166. Madrid.

Bernabeu Auban, J. 1989. *La tradicion cultural de las ceramicas impresas en la zona oriental de la Peninsula iberica*. Valencia.

Binder, D. & Courtin, J. 1987. Nouvelles vues sur les processus de Néolithisation dans le sud-Est de la France. Un pas avant, deux pas en arrière. In Guilaine, J., Courtin, J., Roudil, J.-L. & Vernet, J.-L. (eds.), *Premières comunautés paysannes en Méditerranée occidentale. Actes du Colloque International du C.N.R.S. (Montpellier, 26–29 avril 1983)*, 491–499. C.N.R.S., Paris.

Camps, G. 1988. *Préhistoire d'une Ile. Les origines de la Corse*. Errance, Paris.

Calvi Rezia, G. 1987. Livelli a ceramica impressa nel gradone del Bronzo di Pienza. In *Atti della XXVI Riunione Scientifica, "Il Neolitico in Italia," Firenze 7–10 novembre 1985*, 603–610. Istituto Italiano di Preistoria e Protostoria, Firenze.

Cocchi Genick, D. 1993. *Manuale di Preistoria, II, Neolitico*. Viareggio.

Costantini, L., Piperno, M. & Tusa, S. 1987. La Néolithisation de la Sicile occidentale d'après les résultats des fouilles à la Grotte de l'Uzzo (Trapani). In Guilaine, J., Courtin, J., Roudil, J.-L. & Vernet, J.-L. (eds.), *Premières comunautés paysannes en Méditerranée occidentale. Actes du Colloque International du C.N.R.S. (Montpellier, 26–29 avril 1983)*, 397–405. C.N.R.S., Paris.

Courtin, J. 1974. *Le Néolithique de la Provence*. Mémoires de la Société Préhistorique Française 11. Paris.

Depalmas, A. 1995. L'industria litica del Neolitico Antico in Sardegna. In *Interreg. Préhistoire Corse-Sardaigne* 2: 3–10. Istituto di Antichità, Arte e Discipline Etnodemologiche della Facoltà di Lettere e Filosofia dell'Università di Sassari.

Ferrarese Ceruti, M.L. & Pitzalis, G. 1987. Il tafone di Cala Corsara nell'Isola di Spargi (La Maddalena-Sassari). In *Atti della XXVI Riunione Scientifica, "Il Neolitico in Italia," Firenze, 7–10 novembre 1985*, 871–886. Istituto Italiano di Preistoria e Protostoria, Firenze.

Foschi, A. 1991. Il Neolitico Antico e Medio. *Sardegna Archeo-*

logica, Roma, S. Michele 4 dicembre 1990–4 gennaio 1991. Roma.

Foschi Nieddu, A. 1981. Il Neolitico Antico della Grotta Sa Korona di Monte Majore (Thiesi, Sassari). Nota preliminare. In Montjardin, R. (ed.), *Le Néolithique Ancien Méditerranéen. Actes du Colloque Internationale de Préhistoire, Montpellier 1981,* 339–346. Fédération Archéologique de l'Hérault, Sète.

Foschi Nieddu, A. 1987. La Grotta Sa Korona di Monte Majore (Thiesi, Sassari). Primi risultati dello scavo 1980. In *Atti della XXVI Riunione Scientifica, "Il Neolitico in Italia," Firenze, 7–10 novembre 1985,* 859–870. Istituto Italiano di Preistoria e Protostoria, Firenze.

Grifoni Cremonesi, R. 1967. La Grotta dell'Orso di Sarteano. Il Neolitico. *Origini* 1: 53–115.

Grifoni Cremonesi, R. 1969. I materiali preistorici della Toscana esistenti al Museo archeologico di Perugia. *Atti della Società Toscana di Scienze Naturali, Memorie* Ser. A 76: 151–194.

Lanfranchi, F. de. 1993. Le Néolithique ancien méditerranéenne de la Corse. *Corsica Antica* 1: 2–9.

Levine, M. 1983. La fauna di Filiestru (trincea D). In Trump, D., *La grotta di Filiestru a Bonuighinu, Mara (SS).* Quaderni 13. Dessì, Sassari.

Lewthwaite, J. 1987. Three steps to leaven: applicazione del modello di disponibilità al Neolitico italiano. In *Atti della XXVI Riunione Scientifica, "Il Neolitico in Italia," Firenze, 7–10 novembre 1985,* 89–102. Istituto Italiano di Preistoria e Protostoria, Firenze.

Lilliu, G. 1988. *La civiltà dei Sardi dal Paleolitico all'Età dei nuraghi.* ERI, Torino.

Lopez, P. 1988. El Neolítico andaluz. In Lopez, P. (a cura di), *El Neolítico in España,* 195–220. Madrid.

Lopez, P. 1988. El Neolítico en Cataluña. In Lopez, P. (a cura di), *El Neolítico en España,* 65–100. Madrid.

Lo Schiavo, F. 1976. Grotta di Monte Maiore (Thiesi, Sassari). *Nuove Testimonianze Archeologiche della Sardegna Centro-Settentrionale. Sassari-Museo Nazionale "G.A. Sanna," 18 luglio-24 Ottobre 1976,* 15–25. Dessì, Sassari.

Lo Schiavo, F. 1987. Grotta Verde 1979: un contributo sul Neolitico antico della Sardegna. In *Atti della XXVI Riunione Scientifica, "Il Neolitico in Italia," Firenze, 7–10 novembre 1985,* 845–858. Istituto Italiano di Preistoria e Protostoria, Firenze.

Loria, R., & Trump, D. 1978. Le scoperte a Sa Ucca de su Tintirriolu e il Neolitico sardo. *Monumenti antichi dei Lincei,* Serie Miscellanea II-2. Roma.

Marti Oliver, B. & Cabanilles, J.J. 1987. *El Neolitíc Valencia. Els primers agricultors i ramaders.* Valencia.

Marti Oliver, B. & Hernandez Perez, M.S. 1988. *El Neolitíc Valencia. Art rupestre i cultura material.* Valencia.

Munoz, A. & Vicent, A. 1973. *Segunda campaña de excavaciónes en la cueva de los Murcielagos, Zuheros (Cordoba), 1969.* Excavaciones arqueologicas en España 66. Madrid.

Munoz Amilibia, A. 1987. Problemas metodologícos del Neolítico en el sudeste de España. In Guilaine, J., Courtin, J., Roudil, J.-L. & Vernet, J.-L. (eds.), *Premières comunautés paysannes en Méditerranée occidentale. Actes du Colloque International du C.N.R.S. (Montpellier, 26–29 avril 1983),* 627–632. C.N.R.S., Paris.

Olaria, C. 1988. El Neolítico en las comarcas castellonenses. In Lopez, P. (a cura di), *El Neolítico in España,* 101–130. Madrid.

Rezia Calvi, G. 1972. I resti dell'insediamento neolitico di Pienza. *Atti del XIV Riunione Scientifica,* 285–299. Istituto Italiano di Preistoria e Protostoria, Firenze.

Sanges, M. 1987. Gli strati del Neolitico Antico e Medio nella Grotta Corbeddu di Oliena (Nuoro). Nota preliminare. In *Atti della XXVI Riunione Scientifica "Il Neolitico in Italia," Firenze, 7–10 novembre 1985,* 825–830. Istituto Italiano di Preistoria e Protostoria, Firenze.

Tanda, G. 1977. Gli anelloni litici italiani. *Preistoria Alpina* 13: 11–155.

Tanda, G. 1980. Il Neolitico antico e medio della Grotta Verde, Alghero. In *Atti della XXII Riunione Scientifica nella Sardegna centro-settentrionale, 21–27 ottobre 1978,* 45–94. Istituto Italiano di Preistoria e Protostoria, Firenze.

Tanda, G. 1983. Le culture preistoriche. In *La Provincia di Sassari-I Secoli e la Storia,* 11–12. Milano.

Tanda G. 1987. Nouveaux éléments pou une définition culturelles des materiaux de la Grotta Verde (Alghero, Sassari, Sardaigne). In Guilaine, J., Courtin, J., Roudil, J.-L. & Vernet, J.-L. (eds.), *Premières comunautés paysannes en Méditerranée occidentale. Actes du Colloque International du C.N.R.S. (Montpellier, 26-29 avril 1983),* 425–431. C.N.R.S., Paris.

Tanda, G. 1988. A proposito delle figurine a clessidra di Tisiennari, Bortigiadas. In *Studi in onore di Piero Meloni.* Sassari.

Tanda, G. (a cura di). 1990. *Ottana. Archeologia e Territorio.* Nuoro.

Tanda, G. 1992. La tomba n. 2 di Sas Arzolas de goi a Nughedu S. Vittoria (Oristano). *Sardinia antiqua. Studi in onore di Piero Meloni in occasione del suo settantesimo compleanno,* 75–95. Cagliari.

Tanda, G. 1995. *Interreg. Préhistoire Corse-Sardaigne,* 1–2. Istituto di Antichità, Arte e Discipline Etnodemologiche della Facoltà di Lettere e Filosofia dell'Università di Sassari.

Tusa, S. 1987. Il neolitico della Sicilia. In *Atti della XXVI Riunione Scientifica, "Il Neolitico in Italia," Firenze, 7–10 novembre 1985,* 361–380. Istituto Italiano di Preistoria e Protostoria, Firenze.

Trump, D. 1983. *La grotta di Filiestru a Bonuighinu, Mara (SS).* Quaderni 13. Dessì, Sassari.

13. Obsidian Usage at the Filiestru Cave, Sardinia: Choices and Functions in the Early and Middle Neolithic Periods

Linda Hurcombe and Patricia Phillips

Introduction

Obsidian, a conchoidally fracturing glass, was widely used during the Neolithic period in the west Mediterranean. Artifacts from one of the source areas, Monte Arci in central Sardinia, have been identified from as far away as northern Italy and southern France (Hallam *et al.* 1976; Williams Thorpe *et al.* 1979; 1984; Tykot 1996). Less attention has been paid to the role of Sardinian obsidian nearer to the geological source. The material studied in this report is a first step towards filling this gap. In particular, attention has focused on the function of obsidian at a settlement site. Function is used here in its broadest sense to cover both utilitarian or pragmatic roles and the social purpose or significance of the material. Throughout the study function has been assumed to be the major factor affecting all cultural choices related to the selection, procurement, manufacture, modification and discard of lithic material in the Early and Middle Neolithic periods.

The authors made a series of predictions about possible changes in artifact choice and function over time in the two periods. Firstly, there would be a change in the preferred type of obsidian, from the SC (Perdas Urias) and SB (probably Santa Maria Zuarbara) obsidian exported during the earlier time period to Corsica, to use of best quality SA (Conca Cannas) raw material exported to northern Italy and southern France during the period covered by Bonu Ighinu and Ozieri in Sardinia. Secondly, because these latter exports frequently consisted of blades and blade cores, and because of a general increase in agriculture and harvesting tools in the western Mediterranean in the Middle Neolithic, there would also be an increase in standardization and a greater proportion of blades to flakes over time.

The artifacts studied in this report were excavated from Early Neolithic and Middle Neolithic levels of the Filiestru cave, commune of Bonu Ighinu, in northwestern Sardinia by David Trump and Renato Loria (Trump 1983) (see Fig. 13.1). The lithic assemblages from the excavations were first examined by the authors in the Sassari Museum in 1983. We also visited two of the obsidian sources on the western slopes of Monte Arci, some 75 km to the south of Filiestru cave, and the Perfugas flint source in northeast Sardinia. One of us (LH) examined all the obsidian artifacts from Filiestru under a low-power microscope, and made a brief assessment of the assemblage's suitability for wear analysis. The Soprintendenza all'Antichità, Sassari, thereafter granted permission for obsidian pieces to be taken to the University of Sheffield on loan. The 448 artifacts of the Sheffield assemblage were investigated using novel classification systems, to investigate the technology and the pressure upon raw material supplies. The flakes, broken or segmented blades and irregular fragments at our disposal were exactly the group of material which would show the pressures of availability and use, and allow us to assess trends or identify changes. A sample of 75 artifacts from the two levels were chosen for functional study via microwear analysis. We have woven the information on raw material, technology and function together to examine the question of cultural choice. The data from the two approaches have shed new light on the role of obsidian near its source.

The site is discussed first followed by the methodology adopted, the results, and our conclusions.

The Filiestru Site and Lithic Assemblages

The Filiestru cave has a wide entrance and is adjacent to a perennial spring. The location, the hearths, and the ceramic, lithic and bone assemblages recovered by the excavators all led them to suggest that this was a residential site during at least part of its prehistoric occupation.

Three trenches B, C and D were dug across the central

Linda Hurcombe, Department of Archaeology, University of Exeter, EX4 4RJ, UK; Patricia Phillips, Department of Archaeology and Prehistory, University of Sheffield, S10 2TN, UK

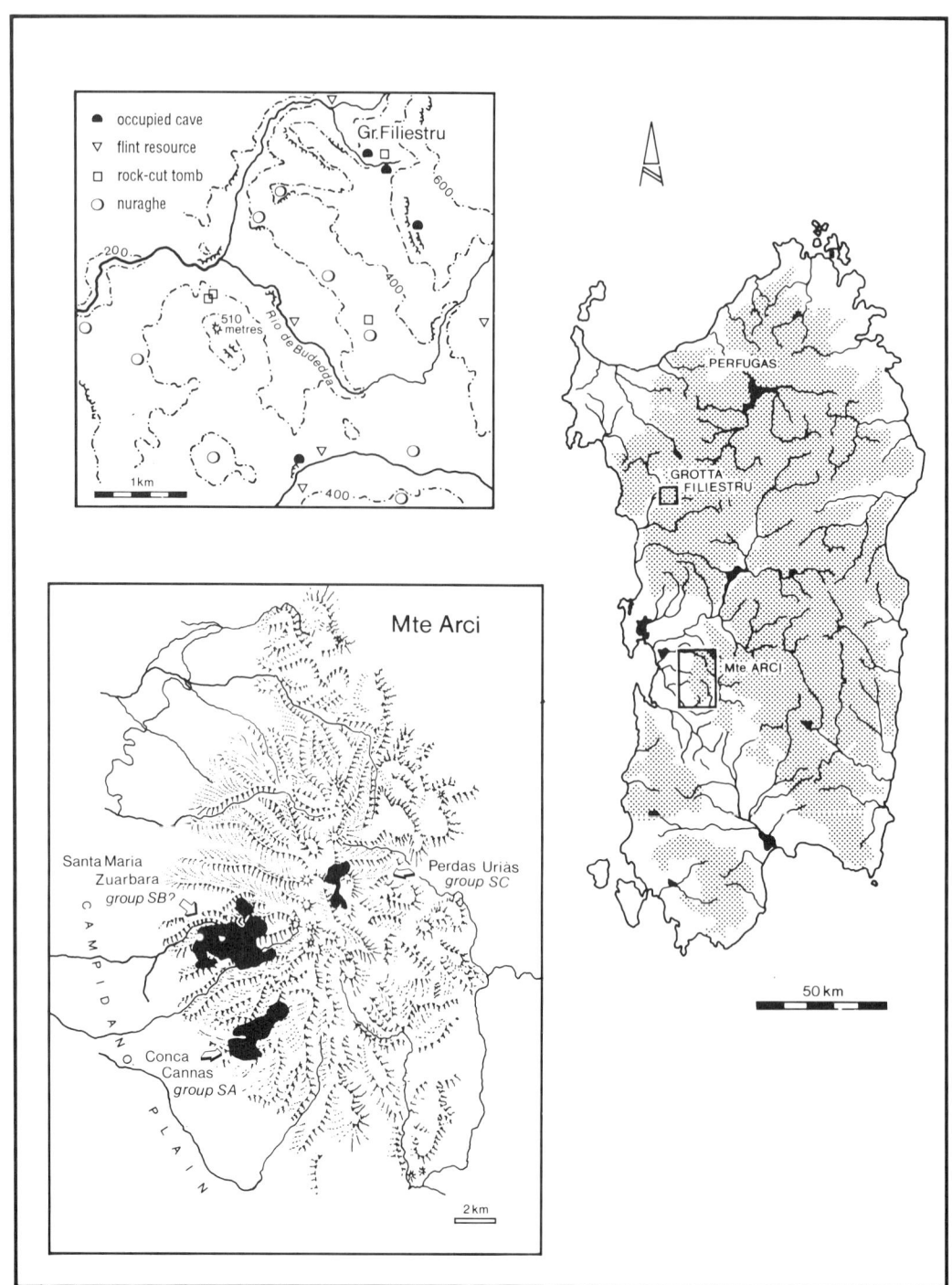

Fig. 13.1. The location of Grotta Filiestru, the Monte Arci obsidian sources and other lithic resources (after Trump 1983: fig. 1; Mackey & Warren 1983).

part of the cave, with B and D being carried down to bedrock (Trump 1983: figs. 2, 4 and 5). The three-meter deep stratigraphy consisted of a Cardial Early Neolithic, with four radiocarbon ages of 4760 ± 75 to 4520 ± 65 uncal BC; a subsequent Early Neolithic or Filiestru level, with two radiocarbon ages of 4170 ± 55 and 3950 ± 50 uncal BC; a Middle Neolithic or Bonu Ighinu level, dated 3675 ± 65 uncal BC; and a Copper Age or Ozieri level, dated 3300 ± 60 and 3000 ± 50 uncal BC (Trump 1983: table 9).

The obsidian brought back to Sheffield comes from Trench D. This is the largest trench, 3 x 4 m², straddling access to the gallery from the front of the cave. It lies under a shelving roof, and the archaeological deposits were built up on a rock floor sloping down towards the rear gallery; according to the profile in Trump 1983: fig.

5, this part of the cave would have sloped steeply during the Filiestru Early Neolithic occupation, becoming more horizontal during the Middle Neolithic occupation. This might have affected how the area was used in the two periods, and the material deposited. However, although our studies in the Sassari Museum archives included a check on the technology and raw material of lithic finds from trench B, there are no marked differences in overall composition between the relevant levels in trenches B and D, or between the earlier and later levels in either of the stratigraphic units. Trench D material was chosen because of the more numerous lithic artifacts and good stratigraphic sequence. The artifacts in the Sheffield assemblage consist of approximately half the obsidian artifacts in each of the two levels 6 and 5 in Trench D. As the material had been excavated in levels and spits, but not given individual numbers, the present authors have simply given each artifact a number within the division of level and spit. For example D5+3.10 indicates trench D, level 5, spit 3 and artifact number 10.

Other chipped stone materials, jasper and flint, occur in abundance in the Early and Middle Neolithic levels at Filiestru cave, and offer the opportunity for complementary functional studies in the future. In the Sassari museum we noted the large sizes and irregular knapping of cores and flakes in the jasper, and the length and precision of the best flint blades. Together with other flint types, these raw materials offered a variety of textures, edges and shapes for different usages. As regards raw material, Trump (1983) has divided up the non-obsidian chipped stone by color, and states that most of the flint types outcrop in the Bonu Ighinu basin or nearby (Trump 1983: fig. 8; 76–79). Only two flint types, golden-red and striped brown, may have been imported, though he does not say from where. Figure 13.1 shows the site of Filiestru with the local, Perfugas and Monte Arci lithic source areas indicated.

According to table 12 of the Filiestru report (Trump 1983), level 5 contains a total of 1169 pieces of chipped and ground stone, and level 6 a total of 945 pieces. In the Sassari Museum archives the authors counted a minimum of 580 pieces of obsidian from level 5, and 288 pieces of obsidian from level 6. The percentage of obsidian compared with other lithic materials would thus be respectively, 49% in the Bonu Ighinu level, and 30% in the Filiestru level. These figures are higher than those plotted in table 6 of the same report (Trump 1983), in which a maximum of 30% of obsidian is identified for any of the spits in the two levels. However, our figures support Trump's assertion that obsidian usage increased from the Early to the Middle Neolithic.

Trump subdivides the obsidian found at Filiestru into two types, translucent and non-translucent. Three Monte Arci sources have been characterized by Mackey & Warren (1983). These authors describe Conca Cannas material as translucent and glassy, with a perfect conchoidal fracture, found in lumps up to 40 cm in diameter, 'of very high quality'; Santa Maria Zuarbara obsidian as opaque and glassy, containing small white spherules, with flow banding and bubble tracks, generally occurring in smaller lumps; and Perdas Urias raw material as opaque and matte, with a sub-conchoidal fracture and marked flow banding, occurring as large angular fragments. Since our work was completed, further research on the Monte Arci sources by Tykot (1995; 1997) has produced more detailed knowledge of the individual sources and subsources, and their physical and chemical characteristics.

The Sheffield sample was classified according to the criteria of Mackey & Warren (1983). Determinations are macroscopic, and subject to laboratory checking. To date only four Filiestru artifacts have been analyzed by neutron activation, all from the Ozieri levels (Mackey & Warren 1983: table 3). However, other authorities have found such macroscopic separation of obsidian source materials useful as a first step (e.g. Ammerman *et al.* 1990; Tykot 1995; 1996).

As indicated above, obsidian is only one variety of lithic material used at the site and it is worth stating its advantages and weaknesses in comparison to jasper and flint as these properties will affect both the technology and function of obsidian. Obsidian flakes are easily detached, and the material has good conchoidal fracture. Flakes and spherules in the matrix can cause slightly irregular flaking, even in the Conca Cannas raw material, but for the most part obsidian flakes easily and in predictable ways. It makes a good material for blades and pressure-flaking. The glassy conchoidal fracture gives obsidian an exceptionally keen edge but one that will damage easily on casual treatment, or in use on hard materials or with forceful actions. Used in experiments the material is very good for cutting meat, hide, and plants, and for any work where fine detail is required (Hurcombe 1992a: chap. 4). The edge does not retain its sharpness for very long on hard materials making it less suitable for working bone, antler, or wood. Hence, obsidian could be expected to be used on softer materials if efficiency of performing the task is a factor in the cultural choices of which lithic types are used for a particular purpose.

The Sheffield Sample: Hypotheses and Results

A number of hypotheses derived from the numerous analytical programmes of exotic obsidian finds in the western Mediterranean (e.g. Hallam *et al.* 1976; Williams Thorpe *et al.* 1979; 1984) were tested. These studies have shown that during the Filiestru Early Neolithic period Sardinian obsidian was being transported mainly to Corsica and to the Ligurian coast (Phillips 1986; 1992). The majority of pieces from these foreign assemblages which have been analyzed come from the SC (Perdas Urias) and SB (probably Santa Maria Zuarbara) sources (e.g. Williams Thorpe *et al.* 1979). During the Bonu Ighinu Middle Neolithic period Sardinian obsidian was widely distributed in the western Mediterranean, with most pieces analyzed coming from the SA (Conca Cannas) raw material (e.g. Williams Thorpe *et al.* 1984). If the pattern of usage of raw materials within Sardinia followed the external pattern, one might expect the Level 6 raw material to consist primarily of Perdas Urias (PU) and Santa Maria Zuarbara (SMZ) raw materials. These are the poorer materials for knapping as they occur in smaller sizes (SMZ) and poorer quality (PU), and so there should be an emphasis on flakes rather than blades, and on flakes of a wide range of sizes. More pieces, and more erratically sized pieces, should remain from the manufacturing stages.

Secondly, the Level 5 raw material should consist primarily of Conca Cannas raw material. With agriculture becoming more generalized, and blades and blade cores in this raw material being exported, the obsidian may have come into the Filiestru cave as prepared cores. A more standardized and more blade-based assemblage could be expected. Fewer and smaller-sized pieces should remain from the manufacturing stages. In terms of the total lithic assemblage, the greater exchange activity might bring in good quality, more exotic flint, for instance from the Perfugas area of northeast Sardinia.

Thirdly, functional hypotheses can also be made. Blanks formed from nodules of different sizes and shapes may lead to differently shaped pieces being used for the same purpose. Morphological or edge types may correlate with a specific function. As obsidian sources were among the most distant of the raw material locations, pressures on the raw material might lead to extensive use of simple flakes, and the use of blades and blade segments to maximize cutting edge per unit of material. The range of uses for obsidian may be restricted to softer use-materials as other materials from the site would perform tasks on harder materials more efficiently. Based on comparable analyzes of European material (Ammerman *et al.* 1988; Hurcombe 1986; 1992a: chap. 7; Perlès & Vaughan 1983) the more blade-like industry expected in the Middle Neolithic might be restricted to use on plant materials.

The Obsidian Sample

The material brought back to England for functional study was biased in three respects. Firstly, obsidian was only one of several lithic materials in use at the site (see above). As a sharp but brittle material in comparison to the other lithic types, it may have had a specialized series of uses. Secondly, no special finds were allowed out of Italy. This meant that whole retouched obsidian blades and other formal tool types are largely absent from the sample. Thirdly, as the chief purpose of the research was functional analysis, pieces that were on initial examination, unused, were not included in the sample, e.g. cores and decortication flakes. The objects which are the usual focus of attention in a lithic report were absent. Instead, the sample

	Level 6	Level 5
cores	9	15
flakes	127	243
blades	12	20
projectile points	1	3
scrapers	2	5
borers/piercers	2	5
knives/denticulates		4
Totals	153	295

Table 13.1. The typological composition of the Sheffield assemblage.

was biased overall in favor of the blades, flakes and fragments that make up the bulk of most lithic assemblages yet often have the least attention paid to them; one author has linked these to women's work (Gero 1991). Table 13.1 shows the typological composition of the sample.

It was necessary to select a subsample for microwear analysis because the combination of cleaning, drawing, microscopic examination and photography can take several hours or more per tool. As we wished to look at the use, or otherwise, of simple unretouched flakes in both levels a grab sample was selected of twenty pieces from the first spit of each level, irrespective of the type of artifact and whether it seemed to be used or not. A further sample of 35 pieces with retouch/edge damage or other features of particular note formed sample B. The latter was by no means an exhaustive list.

All the pieces brought back to Britain were studied in detail. Our approach was to use a novel classification system (see Table 13.2) in tandem with microwear analysis to look at the range of uses and pressure of use on this range of material. If obsidian needs to be used efficiently, there are many tasks which the unretouched flakes can fulfill and the use-duration may suggest greater tool use-life. We were concerned not so much with knowing that an artifact was a blade or a flake, as describing it as a broken, usable, secondary worked or exhausted blade or flake. The flake or blade shape depends upon technology which is itself a cultural choice but our classification system allowed more direct information on the systemic phase of the tool when it entered the archaeological record (Schiffer 1972). Our classification system looked at the phases of tool production through to discard and the categories of lithic evidence that could be expected for the different phases and strategies (Table 13.2). The system was devised to cover all lithic evidence and is based on the work of Zvelebil *et al.* (1984) but as already mentioned, our sample was biased.

This study identified the phase of production, edge characteristics and location of possible use-wear, and probable raw material type of each artifact. Table 13.3 shows the numbers and percentages of tools in three broad phases; phase of initial manufacture, potentially usable phase, and no longer usable phase. The majority of finds

Systemic Phases	Behavior Strategies	Lithic Evidence
Initial Manufacture	Preparation	1. nodules out of geological context
		2. raw material testing waste
		3. decortication flakes
		4. core trimming flakes
		5. failed cores
	Finishing	6. partly finished/broken as making
		7. rough-outs
		8. evidence of heat treatment
	For Future Tool	9. usable core
	Unretouched Artifacts	10. usable flakes
		11. usable blades
Potentially Usable	Retouched Artifacts	12. retouched flakes
		13. retouched blades
		14. formal tool types + numbers
	Hafted Tools	15. squared (retouched) blades
		16. signs of hafting wear
		17. facets and retouch to facilitate hafting
	Extended Use	18. resharpening flakes
		19. stubby tools
		20. unmodified re-used tools
		21. modified re-used tools
	Exhausted	22. tools/blades/flakes
No Longer Usable		23. cores/wedges
	Broken	24. tools/blades/flakes
		25. cores

Table 13.2. The classification system used to identify systemic phases and behavior strategies from lithic evidence.

	Level 6	Level 5
Manufacturing stages	67 (44%)	99 (33%)
Usable stages	72 (47%)	156 (53%)
Worn-out stages	14 (8%)	42 (14%)
Totals	153	295

Table 13.3. The systemic phases of artifacts making up the Sheffield Assemblage (as classified using Table 13.2)

	Level 6			Level 5		
length in mm	mean	sd	n	mean	sd	n
complete flakes and blades *usable phases 10–13,15*	34.63	8.22	61	32.03	8.50	104
complete flakes *manufacturing phases 3,4*	29.06	10.80	50	24.50	6.52	67
weight in mg	mean	sd	n	mean	sd	n
complete flakes and blades *usable phases 10–13,15*	412.6	333.7	61	324.8	276.7	104
complete flakes *manufacturing phases 3,4*	368	569.4	61	241.6	201.1	67

Table 13.4. The metric characteristics of complete flakes and blades in the Sheffield Assemblage.

in order to assess the potentially usable pieces within the assemblage. It was also designed to indicate whether a particular weight, size, or edge shape was being selected for a specific task. The study of edge characteristics enables the most useful artifacts to be identified. The edge shape in plan view and the edge shape in side view have respectively 6 and 5 possible states or attributes. Since straight or sinuous edges are the most advantageous for cutting or sawing (Hurcombe 1992a: chap. 4) the artifacts with 1/1,1/2 and 2/1 states offer the best potential for results in use-wear analysis. Based on our personal experience in experimental tool use we recognized that uneven edges do not perform cutting tasks as efficiently as straight ones, and because the pressure of the tool action is unevenly applied more edge damage occurs and the irregular-edged tools do not last as long as the straight edged tools. This problem is particularly noticeable on brittle obsidian edges, which are easily damaged. The edge shape may matter less in scraping motions. We thus had some ideas related to tool efficiency which could be tested using these descriptive techniques.

Tables 13.3 and 13.4 show that the technological choices made in the Early and Middle Neolithic at Filiestru broadly follow the predictions made in the introductory section. In Level 6 there is a higher percentage of pieces, and more erratically sized pieces, remaining from the manufacturing stages than in Level 5. There are few blades. Flakes and blades vary in length and weight, particularly flakes from the manufacturing stages. The cores are wedge-like and appear to have been struck using the anvil technique.

In level 5, proportionately fewer pieces remain from the manufacturing stages, and those that do are overall shorter and less heavy than similar pieces in level 6. There are a larger percentage of broken flakes than in level 6. Usable flakes and blades vary in length and weight, but are overall smaller and slightly more standardized than in level 6. The expected increase in blade cores does not occur, although previous blade removals appear on the back of core trimming flakes. Only one of the cores is a blade core, but the others are more regular in shape than the examples in level 6. The anvil technique is still in use.

There are high standard deviations for length and

fell into sub-phases D and J, that is, they comprised core trimming flakes and usable flakes. The category of core trimming flakes covered all those irregular flakes which could have been removed to tidy up a core or an edge; they were very varied in shape and we had some difficulty in assessing the difference between these two categories. The definition of a flake from manufacturing as usable or simply a by-product of the manufacturing process was difficult because it is a subjective decision. As our results were to show, the concept of a usable flake in prehistory need not match our own perception of usability.

In addition to the systemic phase classification, all the material was measured and weighed (Table 13.4). The edges were classified for their shape in plan and side view

weight of complete flakes and blades in the different systemic phases in both levels 5 and 6, but knapping appears marginally more standardized in level 5. This level also contains broken flakes and blades (there are hardly any in the earlier level), and includes the only apparently hafted pieces. It is possible that flake and blade snapping occurred due to an increase in artifact hafting.

As noted below, the wear analysis identified wear traces on some of the pieces classified under manufacturing stages. If our categories are erring in this way, an even higher percentage of usable material exists among the Sheffield sample than originally imagined. In particular, the sub-conchoidally fracturing Perdas Urias material may have been misidentified to the manufacturing stage, while its unmodified primary and secondary flakes were in fact utilized.

The technological changes occur despite our predictions regarding raw material usage not being entirely fulfilled. All three raw material sources were used in both periods (Table 13.5). A greater overall number of artifacts occur in Santa Maria Zuarbara obsidian in level 6, partly fulfilling one prediction. In level 5 the three raw materials are evenly represented overall, with rather more usable artifacts occurring in the Santa Maria Zuarbara raw material, and more of the manufacturing by-products in the Perdas Urias raw material. Conca Cannas artifacts mainly occur in the usable and worn-out categories.

It was also predicted that in the Middle Neolithic period the Conca Cannas raw material would include blades and blade cores, following the 'export' tendency. There are fewer blades and blade cores than anticipated, though with most cortical flakes and cores being left behind in Sassari it is difficult to be dogmatic about the latter. The apparently limited numbers of Conca Cannas cores and blades may have several possible explanations, including biases due to prehistoric activities and discard behavior; cores and blades moving out of the site in exchanges; or a small quantity of cores and blades entering the site. In support of the last explanation there is the simultaneous reduction in the supply of high quality red-yellow flint (probably from the Perfugas area of northeast Sardinia). This raw material makes up 15% of chipped stone in the early levels, reducing to 5% in the middle of the stratigraphy, according to Trump (1983: 79). Was it more of an exchange good in the Early Neolithic, when the main dispersal of obsidian was overland as far as the straits of Bonifacio, thence to Corsica and Liguria? And did the Middle Neolithic dispersal of Conca Cannas obsidian bypass the Filiestru cave and develop along different, probably maritime, routes?

The Microwear Study

The wear analysis undertaken offered a rare opportunity to discover the pragmatic functional information of use-

	Level 6				Level 5			
	M	U	W		M	U	W	
Conca Cannas	13	17	5	(N=35)	27	45	14	(N=86)
Perdas Urias	17	11	4	(N=32)	41	42	15	(N=98)
Santa Maria Zuarbara	34	42	4	(N=80)	18	53	8	(N=79)
Unassigned	4		2	(N=6)	13	14	5	(N=32)

Table 13.5. Raw material characteristics of the Sheffield Assemblage showing the ratio of manufacturing, usable and worn-out pieces with their totals.

action and use-material and to offer some indication of use-time. We also wished to look at groups of pieces with a similar function according to the wear traces to see if there were obvious groups according to macroscopic features. Hence, our study offered a reversal of the normal procedure of using morphology to indicate function.

The method of obtaining the pragmatic functional information for obsidian tools uses the technique described by Hurcombe (1992a). All functional interpretations were based on this study. It is a technique which has to be used carefully as some post-depositional and cultural effects can affect the survival and clarity of wear traces. The Grotta Filiestru material was suitable for this study as most pieces showed little evidence of post-depositional chemical or physical change. The preservation of the wear traces was good and use-related residues were found (Hurcombe 1992b). It is not known if the residues on the Grotta Filiestru material are typical, or if the stable cave environment provided exceptional conditions as so few comparable microwear analyses of obsidian exist. However, the survival of residues has been noted on flint tools (Anderson 1980; Mansur-Franchomme 1983) and on other obsidian pieces (Hurcombe 1986; 1992a).

For this study each piece examined was drawn and the location of wear and other features marked on it according to a key. The features of the polish (surface smoothing at 250X), striations, attrition and residues were noted systematically on a recording form using 18 variables and coded descriptions. Photographs of interesting aspects were taken as necessary. In order to examine patterns, this primary data was transformed into categories of used/unused, use-material type, use-action, use-duration and number of used edges using the experimental framework and interpretive steps outlined in Hurcombe (1992a). Full details and drawings are included in Phillips & Hurcombe (1990).

The functional interpretations are indicated by Table 13.6 which shows the combination of use-action and use-material for the two levels. The numbers of artifacts involved are too small to draw firm conclusions but differences can be usefully highlighted. In particular, obsidian is used for more transverse motion functions in the earlier period and for more plant or hard use-material functions in the later period (where these two interpretations account for 20% of the assemblage). The earlier

	Level 6		Level 5	
Use-materials				
Projectiles	1	3%	2	5%
Flesh/Butchery	5	14%	5	13%
Flesh/Hide	6	17%	5	13%
Hide	5	14%	3	8%
Plants/Hide	3	9%	4	10%
Plants	1	3%	4	10%
Multiple	3	9%	1	3%
Not Identified	5	14%	7	18%
Soft	4	11%	2	5%
Soft/Resilient	2	6%	3	8%
Hard	0	0%	4	10%
Use-actions				
Parallel	22	63%	31	78%
Transverse	11	31%	3	8%
Pierce	0	0%	2	5%
Other	2	6%	4	10%

Table 13.6. Summary of the use-action and use-material interpretations for the microwear sample from levels 5 and 6 expressed as numbers and percentages

period sees more multiple function tools. Hence there is a suggestion that the later period sees obsidian being used for a greater range of functions but in a more individually specialized way. This point is explored below in relation to the morphology of the artifacts.

One further point should be made from this table. Obsidian can show distinctive 'gramineae', 'wood' and 'bone/antler' wear traces (Hurcombe 1992a: 52–57) but the table shows that these were mostly absent; the plant wear traces observed were not of the type caused by working siliceous species such as gramineae and there is only one artifact which shows bone/antler wear and this is found on just one area of one of the multiple use-material tools. As obsidian gives a very sharp but brittle edge this is not surprising. The other lithic materials found at the site may have been fulfilling the harder functional requirements and the flint and jasper will certainly give more robust edges than the obsidian. These functional results have more interesting implications if the types of activities are considered in relation to the rate of formation of distinctive wear traces. This has been explored in more detail elsewhere (Hurcombe 1992b) but essentially there are two points to make. Firstly, the specific use-material identifications mostly relate to animal (or fish) carcass activities. Projectiles may also be added to this group. Secondly, experiments have shown the soft use-materials such as flesh and fresh hide cause little wear and so distinctive wear traces form only after a long period of time. Compared to more quickly forming wear traces from harder materials these soft materials are likely to be under-represented in the microwear identification of use-materials. Thus the use-material identification categories of 'unknown', 'soft' and 'soft/resilient' are likely to contain some wear from materials such as flesh and fresh hide. In reality, therefore, the 43% of the assemblage known to be associated with carcass-related functions is a minimum figure with only 12% (Plants + Hard use-material categories) of the assemblage known NOT to be related to these activities. This emphasis on a restricted range of functions is more pronounced in the earlier levels where 49% are associated with carcass activities and only 3% are known NOT to be.

It would seem that obsidian has been particularly used for such activities. The animal bones from the site were analyzed by Levine (in Trump 1983). She found dense collections of bone in the older layers of trench D connected with the intensive preparation of food. As a 1 cm mesh was used small animals should be represented but the majority of the bones were sheep. The obsidian tools may therefore be part of the carcass processing activities that may have been a principal function of the site. The utilitarian, economic and social reasons for this functional preference will be explored below, but first the functional data will be used to examine choices in the morphology of the working edge and in the overall shape and technology of the pieces that have been culturally selected for use.

A major surprise in the functional analysis was that most of the pieces in the grab sample (A) appeared to be used. Seventy-five pieces were examined for wear traces, and of these 65 were used, 8 were possibly used, and only 2 were not used. The pieces selected for export to Britain had left out decortication flakes and most cores, but even so this is a surprising figure. Many of those flakes found to be used had been categorized among the manufacturing by-products as core trimming flakes. These were irregular in shape and had uneven edges caused by hinge fractures and other knapping problems. Many also showed no obvious signs of wear to the naked eye. This suggests that either there is a great deal of pressure on the use of the obsidian, or that use is very casual and informal; even 'unsuitable' shapes are used because there is little specialization (?) or formation of conceptual tool categories. However, the third possibility is not so much a reflection of these cultural choices as a comment on our own misconceptions. Perhaps this kind of level of use is normal behavior and our archaeological studies favoring typology have unduly emphasized the stylistically recognizable end point at the expense of the irregular flakes. Terms such as 'debris' and 'waste flakes' may be archaeological terms with no validity in prehistoric societies. The high 'used pieces' totals are thus difficult to interpret fairly without more functional studies to show whether these figures are culturally abnormal or standard.

Wear analysis offers a rare chance to explore such issues. Further surprises were almost inevitable given the paucity of information on function, especially on obsidian tools where only a few functional studies have been carried out (Ammerman *et al.* 1988; Hurcombe 1986; 1992b; Perlès & Vaughan 1983). Starting with the function of a tool, we looked back in a reversal of the normal order, at edge shape, tool morphology and procurement to see whether the functional groups bore any relation to the morphological, technological, or source groups by which these objects are usually classified. The pieces were grouped by their level in the cave and by the typological variations they showed. Some of these groupings are illustrated in Hurcombe (1993: figs. 8–9).

It is clear that the function of parallel use-actions on flesh, butchery and hide does not equate with a single morphological or technological shape. Instead, there were two groups, blades and the larger broader pieces which have been called knives (Hurcombe 1992b). The length (average 520 mm) and weight (average 106 g) appear to be important for this knife group, and their edge characteristics show either a straight or sinuous edge in plan view and a straight, sinuous or concave shape in side view. In slight contrast, the blades have an average length of 302 mm and an average weight of 158 g. They too have straight or sinuous edges in plan view and straight, sinuous or concave shapes in side view. It could be argued that the blades are more efficient in terms of cutting edge per unit weight, but the overall weight and shape of the knives may have made them handle better than the blades during use. However, as both types may have been hafted (e.g. the proximal end of artifact 5+5.2 could be shaped to facilitate hafting), it would be difficult to assess their relative merits without allowing for the weight and shape of a handle.

There is a difference between the two layers; the earlier level 6 has more irregularly shaped knives and only two blades in the carcass-related functional category. Level 5 has more blades and the knives from this level have finer shapes. However, since the blades with this function all come from the top spit of level 5 little emphasis can be placed on this. It is worth noting that the shapes of the other pieces used with a parallel motion on these materials do not fit into the blade or knife morphological groups. Some could be deliberately or accidentally broken blades but there are also very irregular pieces and these come from the earlier level.

If attention is focused on the usable edge shape rather than the overall shape of the tool, then a more obvious pattern can be discerned. The shape of the edge in plan and side view was recorded as straight, sinuous, concave or convex. Roughly half of the edges used in parallel use-actions have a straight edge in side view. The artifacts from the later levels are more likely to have a straight edge in plan view as well. This could suggest greater knapping skills and control over edge shape and also reflects the trend towards more blades. For transverse use-actions the edges are predominantly straight in side view and sinuous in plan view.

For the same material range, but with use-actions of piercing, and transverse motions the artifacts have some carefully shaped pieces but other, very irregular shapes are used (e.g. 6+1.62). It was a surprise to note wear traces on such pieces and the possibility that they were the broken fragments of a more regularly-shaped used piece was always borne in mind (e.g. 6+3.11), but this could not be substantiated from the wear traces in at least some cases (e.g. 6+2.62).

Hafting was evident on tool 6+1.12 from the distribution of wear residues over half the surface and the hafting substance was applied hot judging by the heat-crazing of parts of the surface. Further studies of the residue composition may lead to more specific information. In other cases there was an abrupt end to the wear traces which could signify hafting, e.g. 6+2.12.

The artifacts used with a parallel motion on plants indicate that the small blade category was also being used on plants as well as flesh/hide, and that two of the pieces (5+1.15 and 5+6.19) have retouch or snap fractures suggesting squaring of the ends to make blade elements for hafts. The single piece from the lower level is not an obvious type as it is too small to be included with the other blade group described previously.

Use intensity can be indicated by the number of edges used on one tool, and from the longevity of tool use. The latter can only be estimated broadly, and it should be borne in mind that the softer materials and the weaker use-actions cause much less polish and wear than do harder materials or forceful actions. Hence, even within the broad indications of time as short, medium and long there is still a bias against the weaker and softer functions being recognized. Table 13.7 compares the number of used edges and the use-duration for each layer and sample type. The later levels and selected sample B group show longer use-times. The number of used edges does not differ greatly for the two periods but sample B does show more tools with three used edges.

Residues

Obsidian's naturally bright smooth surface makes residues show up clearly on this use-material. Residues from the use-material were observed on experimental tools and some survived extensive cleaning procedures. The Grotta Filiestru material has a number of interesting residues which may make the material of international importance. Residues akin to epidermal cells have been found on many of the tools (Hurcombe 1992a; 1992b). Some are associated with used edges, others concentrate on the bulb and dorsal ridges of a tool where one could expect fingers and thumb to rest during use. Hence some of these residues could be from the use-material, but others may be from the prehistoric user's hand. Obviously this data could be of great importance. Further verification and tests are being undertaken for these residues. Despite excellent surface preservation, it has not yet proved possible to extract DNA. A range of residue techniques may be more successful.

Taken altogether the morphological range for each functional group seems to indicate more irregular pieces

	Sample A		Sample B	
	(grab)		(chosen)	
Levels	6	5	6	5
Use Duration Estimates				
Short	4%	0%	4%	21%
Short to Medium	24%	21%	33%	14%
Medium	24%	21%	33%	14%
Medium to Long	17%	42%	17%	38%
Long	10%	17%	13%	14%

Table 13.7. Comparisons of the use-duration estimates by sample type and by level, expressed as percentages.

being used in the earlier period, whilst greater shaping and speciality seems to be indicated for the later levels. One morphological group, the knives, do relate to a particular function, but other types serve similar functions. The knives may have a cultural significance beyond their pragmatic wear evidence. For example, they could be personal items and/or kept for specific occasions. The nodule shape is affecting the shape and characteristics of some tools (e.g. the Perdas Urias knife 6+1.11 has cortex remaining). The increase in blades in the later level may reflect a more efficient use of the raw material. The later levels indicate more shaping to make an obsidian tool.

Conclusions

Our hypotheses about obsidian acquisition, technology and use by the inhabitants of Grotta Filiestru in the Early and Middle Neolithic have been shown to be partly accurate. The main discrepancy was in the predicted change to use of Conca Cannas obsidian, which did not occur. The study specifically suggested the following:

1. The macroscopic study demonstrates that overall obsidian usage increased from the Early to the Middle Neolithic. There was a technological improvement and standardization in knapping obsidian over time, with an increasing trend towards more blade production, and greater control over edge shape. This was combined with a more intensive use of individual pieces and possibly greater use of hafting.
2. The microwear study has emphasized the use of unretouched straight edges, particularly edges straight in both plan and side views in the later period. A new type of "knife" on a broad flake has been identified, with perhaps more irregular specimens in the earlier period and more standardized ones in the later.
3. The survival of excellent residues from this site has been demonstrated. Residues may allow future identification of function to be much more specific but if the residues are shown to be of human origin, and if biological techniques can be applied to examine genetic material, a wealth of extra information is possible.
4. The range of functions represented in the lithic assemblage was restricted. In particular there was no bone/antler and scant evidence for wood. The plant wear traces found were few and by far the most significant use seems to be for meat and hide cutting. Compared to other raw materials obsidian is brittle but very sharp, hence its properties were used to best advantage even relatively close to an obsidian source. This begs the question of even more restricted usage further away from source.
5. As regards obsidian raw material, the pattern of usage of the three Monte Arci source materials varies slightly over time, but does not mimic the 'export' trend of emphasis upon Conca Cannas (SA) raw material in the Middle Neolithic period.

Acknowledgments

We are grateful to Dr. Fulvia Lo Schiavo, the Soprintendente alle Antichità at Sassari, Sardinia, for permission to export the material, and for facilities in Sassari; Dr. David Trump for permission to use material from his excavations and for allowing us to reproduce his (1984) figure 1.2; SERC who funded LH's research in Sardinia and the initial microwear technique via a Ph.D. grant and PP's visit to Sardinia (European Short visit Grant GRC 54005T); the Department of Archaeology and Prehistory, Sheffield for microscope and laboratory facilities; and the Department of History and Archaeology, Exeter University for funding the time on a scanning electron microscope. Sue Rouillard (Exeter University) and Sue Clements (Sheffield University) aided the production of this article and produced the figure. We also wish to thank Professor Miriam S. Balmuth and Dr. Robert H. Tykot for inviting us to present the results of this work at the 1995 Tufts University Colloquium on Sardinian Stratigraphy and Mediterranean Chronology.

References

Ammerman, A., Shaffer, G.D. and Hartmann, N. 1988. A neolithic household at Piana di Curinga, Italy. *Journal of Field Archaeology* 15: 121–140.

Ammerman, A., Cesana, A., Polglase, C., Terrani, M. 1990. Neutron activation analysis of obsidian from two neolithic sites in Italy. *Journal of Archaeological Science* 17: 209–220.

Anderson, P.C. 1980. A testimony of prehistoric tasks: diagnostic residues on stone tool working edges. *World Archaeology* 12: 181–194.

Gero, J. 1991. Genderlithics: women's roles in stone tool production. In Gero, J.M & Conkey, M.W. (eds.), *Engendering Archaeology. Women and Prehistory*, 163–193. Cambridge (Massachusetts), Blackwell.

Hallam, B.R., Warren, S.E., Renfrew, C. 1976. Obsidian in the western Mediterranean: characterisation by neutron activation analysis and optical emission spectroscopy. *Proceedings of the Prehistoric Society* 42: 85–110.

Hurcombe, L. 1986. Residue studies on obsidian tools. In Owen, L.R. & Unrath, G. (eds.), *Technical Aspects of Microwear Studies on Stone Tools (Tübingen). Early Man News* I & II (9-11): 83-90.

Hurcombe, L. 1992a. *Use Wear Analysis and Obsidian: Theory, Experiments and Results.* Sheffield Archaeological Monographs 4. Sheffield, Sheffield Academic Press.

Hurcombe, L. 1992b. L'analyse des traces d'usure sur l'obsidienne. *L'Anthropologie* 96: 179-185.

Hurcombe, L. 1992c. The function of Sardinian obsidian artefacts. In Tykot, R.H. & Andrews, T.K. (eds.), *Sardinia in the Mediterranean: A Footprint in the Sea. Studies in Sardinian Archaeology Presented to Miriam S. Balmuth.* Monographs in Mediterranean Archaeology 3: 83-97. Sheffield, Sheffield Academic Press.

Hurcombe, L. 1993. The restricted function of Neolithic obsidian tools at grotta Filiestru, Sardinia. In Anderson, P., Beyries, S., Otte, M. & Plisson, H. (eds.) *Traces et Fonction: Les Gestes Retrouvés.* Colloque International de Liège. Edition ERAUL 50: 87-96. Centre de Recherches Archéologiques du CNRS, Etudes et Recherches Archéologique de L'Université de Liège.

Hurcombe, L. 1994. From functional interpretation to cultural choices in tool use. In Ashton, N. & David, A. (eds.), *Lithic Studies: Looking Backwards – Looking Forwards,* 145-155. Occasional Paper of the Lithic Studies Society.

Levine, M. 1983. La Fauna di Filiestru (Trincea D). In Trump, D.H., *La Grotta di Filiestru a Bonu Ighinu, Mara (SS),* 109-131. Quaderni 13. Sassari.

Mackey, M.P. & Warren, S.E. 1983. The identification of obsidian sources in the Monte Arci region of Sardinia. In Aspinall, A. & Warren, S.E. (eds.), *Proceedings of the 22nd Symposium on Archaeometry,* 420-431. Bradford.

Mansur-Franchomme, M.E. 1983. Scanning electron microscopy of dry hide working tools: the role of abrasives and humidity in microwear polish formation. *Journal of Archaeological Science* 10: 223-230.

Perlès, C. & Vaughan, P. 1983. Pièces lustrées, travail des plantes et moissons à Franchthi (Grèce) (Xeme-IVeme millenaires B.C. In *Traces d'Utilisation sur les outils néolithiques du Proche-Orient.* Travaux de la Maison de l'Orient 5: 209-224.

Phillips, P. 1986. Sardinian obsidian and neolithic exchange in the west Mediterranean. In Balmuth, M.S. (ed.), *Studies in Sardinian Archaeology, Volume II: Sardinia in the Mediterranean,* 203-209. Ann Arbor, University of Michigan Press.

Phillips, P. 1992. Western Mediterranean obsidian distribution and the European Neolithic. In Tykot, R.H. & Andrews, T.K. (eds.), *Sardinia in the Mediterranean: A Footprint in the Sea. Studies in Sardinian Archaeology Presented to Miriam S. Balmuth.* Monographs in Mediterranean Archaeology 3: 71-82. Sheffield, Sheffield Academic Press.

Phillips, P. & Hurcombe, L. 1990. *Archive Report on the obsidian flaked material from levels 5 and 6, Grotta Filiestru (Mara, Sardinia): A macroscopic and microscopic analysis.* Unpublished archive report, Sassari, Sardinia.

Schiffer, M. 1972. Archaeological context and systemic context. *American Antiquity* 37: 156-165.

Trump, D.H. 1982. The Grotta Filiestru, Bonu Ighinu, Mara (Sassari). *Le Néolithique Ancien Méditerranéen.* Archeologie en Languedoc, numero special 1982: 333-338.

Trump, D.H. 1983. *La Grotta di Filiestru a Bonu Ighinu, Mara (SS).* Quaderni 13. Sassari.

Trump, D. 1984. The Bonu Ighinu project and the Sardinian Neolithic. In Balmuth, M.S. & Rowland, R.J. Jr. (eds.), *Studies in Sardinian Archaeology,* 1-22. Ann Arbor, University of Michigan Press.

Tykot, R.H. 1995. *Prehistoric Trade in the Western Mediterranean: The Sources and Distribution of Sardinian Obsidian.* Ph.D. Dissertation, Department of Anthropology, Harvard University. Ann Arbor, University Microfilms.

Tykot, R.H. 1996. Obsidian procurement and distribution in the central and western Mediterranean. *Journal of Mediterranean Archaeology* 9: 39-82.

Tykot, R.H. 1997. Characterization of the Monte Arci (Sardinia) obsidian sources. *Journal of Archaeological Science* 24: 467-479.

Williams Thorpe, O., Warren, S.E. & Barfeld, L.H. 1979. The sources and distribution of archaeological obsidian in Northern Italy. *Preistoria Alpina* 15: 73-92.

Williams Thorpe, O., Warren, S.E. & Courtin, J. 1984. The distribution and sources of archaeological obsidian from Southern France. *Journal of Archaeological Science* 11: 135-146.

Zvelebil, M., Hurcombe, L., Henson, D. & Edmonds, M., 1984. Behavioural variables and the generation of lithic scatters. Unpublished paper delivered at the Theoretical Archaeology Group Conference, Cambridge, 1984.

14. L'oléastre et le lentisque, plantes oléagineuses sauvages dans l'économie Néolithique en Corse et en Sardaigne

François de Lanfranchi and Bui Thi Mai

Les études sur l'alimentation de l'homme durant le Néolithique sont d'autant plus complexes que les documents archéologiques sont généralement fort rares ou très imprécis. Les vestiges ne fournissent évidemment pas toutes les informations que le fouilleur attend. Pour pallier cette lacune, les Préhistoriens font appel à l'ethnologie qui peut, dans certains cas, aider à comprendre des structures difficiles à interpréter.

C'est ainsi que nos travaux sur la paysannerie traditionnelle de l'ensemble cyrno-sarde, nous ont permis de recueillir des informations inédites sur des techniques aujourd'hui disparues, mais pas encore oubliées. Ces données ethnologiques permettent de faire une nouvelle lecture des témoins, ce qui nous amène, ici, à en proposer une autre interprétation.

L'histoire de l'Holocène, période post-glaciaire dont l'origine se situe autour de 10 000 ans environ avant J.-C., se divise en deux grands moments: le premier concerne les hommes collecteurs de nourriture; le second, celui des populations productrices. Pour des périodes de la Préhistoire récente, cette partition est relativement théorique, dans la mesure où une économie n'est jamais entièrement productrice; à cette époque, le prédateur est peu ou prou producteur, et inversement.

Pour illustrer ce propos, nous rapporterons un exemple de survivance assez exceptionnelle, concernant une technique archaïque faisant partie de l'économie traditionnelle de la Corse et de la Sardaigne. Il s'agit de la cueillette de deux plantes sauvages, le lentisque (*Pistacia lentiscus*) et l'oleastre (*Olea europaea* var. *sylvestris*) dont les paysans tiraient, jusque dans les années cinquante, une huile végétale à partir des fruits.

Pistacia lentiscus est une espèce sauvage, jamais domestiquée dont les fruits renfermant une huile grasse servaient à l'alimentation, l'éclairage et à la fabrication du savon. Par entaillement de l'écorce, on extrait une résine appelée "mastic de Chio" qui est encore employée pour parfumer les produits alimentaires. Son usage se retrouve également dans l'industrie des vernis. Cette plante présente aussi des propriétés médicinales. Bonnier et Doin (1934) rapportent qu'elle soigne les maux de dents et d'oreille, la goutte et les rhumatismes.

Par incision du tronc de la variété *Chia* D.C., on provoque une sécrétion s'écoulant en larmes jaunes pâles et brillantes, de quelques millimètres de diamètre, qui durcissent à l'air. Ces larmes se ramollissent par mastication et dégagent une odeur balsamique de saveur térébentinée. Ce "mastic" qui renferme 1 à 3% de pinène, est surtout constitué par une résine correspondant à un ester triterpénique (masticodiénique, oléanolique). Selon Paris et Moyse (1981), ce produit est à la fois un topique cutané et un antiseptique.

Le mastic en larmes est également employé, en Tunisie, comme masticatoire parfumé; il sert d'autre part à préparer par distillation, une boisson aromatique: le *mastic vrai*, fait à partir de 9% d'anis et 12% de mastic en larme. Cette préparation diffère du *raki* qui ne contient pas de mastic (Jacob de Cordomoy 1911).

Olea europaea est un arbuste qui produit des fruits de petite taille. Les variétés cultivées fournissent des fruits plus gros (condiments bien connus) dont on extrait une huile à usages alimentaires et industriels. Son bois est un bon combustible fournissant un charbon de très bonne qualité. L'écorce de l'arbre a des propriétés fébrifuges et antiscrofuleuse (Bonnier & Doin 1934). Cet arbre sauvage, probablement originaire de Syrie et d'Anatolie (côte méridionale de l'Asie mineure), est cependant connu par ses pollens en France dès avant 7300 BP, en particulier dans l'étang de Berre (Triat-Laval 1982).

Le lentisque et l'oléastre, se développent dans une zone située entre 0 et 400/600m, selon qu'il croissent à l'ubac (*umbria*) 400 m ou à l'adret (*suliu*) 600 m. Les botanistes considèrent que ces végétaux font partie de l'*Oleo-Ceratonion*, association qui comprend l'olivier sauvage,

---

François de Lanfranchi, Centre d'Etudes et de Recherches Archéologiques en Alta Rocca (CERAAR), 20170 Levie, Corse, France; Bui Thi Mai, Laboratoire de Palynologie, CNRS CRA, Sophia-Antipolis, 06560 Valbonne, France

le caroubier et le lentisque. Cette formation se développe dans l'étage thermoméditerranéen et mésoméditerranéen inférieur, auquel nous donnons le nom de *piaghja*.

Avant de développer notre relation, rappelons que, depuis les origines du peuplement de l'île de Corse, se sont établies des relations privilégiées entre la piaghja et la montagne. Si l'on observe une carte de la Corse méridionale (Lanfranchi, ce volume, fig. 9.3) on verra, par exemple, que les groupes humains prénéolithiques, implantés dans l'aire bonifacienne, ont, très tôt exploré puis occupé le pianu de Levie. Les groupes du Néolithique ancien poinçonné, dont les habitats se situent dans la zone géographique allant de Bonifacio à Porti Vechju, se sont également développés dans la région de Levie, à Curacchiaghju. A l'Age du Bronze, la répartition des tours mégalithiques n'a de sens que si l'on tient compte des grandes voies de transhumance. Ainsi, jusqu'en 1950, au moment où s'éteint la paysannerie traditionnelle, chaque village de l'Alta Rocca est en relation avec une aire particulière de la *piaghja*. Aullène et Monacia d'Aullène; Zirubia et Pianottoli-Caldarello; Quenza et Porti Vechju; Serra et Sorbollano avec la *piaghja* de Sotta; Zonza et Santa Lucia di Porti Vechju; San Gavinu di Carbini et Lecci-Araghju; Levie et Carbini en relation avec Figari. Si l'on oublie cette loi naturelle *piaghja*-montagne, on ne peut comprendre ni l'histoire, ni l'économie, ni le peuplement. La connaissance de la zonation et des étages botaniques est un cadre qu'il faut rappeler avant toute étude sur la Corse.

En 1994, nous avons recueilli en Gallura (province septentrionale de la Sardaigne), des informations relatives à l'utilisation de ces deux espèces végétales sauvages. Les habitants du village de San Teodoro, situé sur la côte nord orientale de Sardaigne, au sud d'Olbia, utilisaient il n'y a pas bien longtemps, les baies du Lentisque (*listincu*) pour en extraire une huile destinée surtout à la préparation des beignets (*fritelli*), du savon en temps de guerre, mais aussi pour l'éclairage comme combustible dans les petites lampes à main. Une habitante de ce village a bien voulu nous décrire le processus de fabrication d'huile à partir des fruits du lentisque par extraction à l'eau chaude. Elle nous indiqua d'ailleurs que ce procédé était également appliqué aux fruits de l'oléastre.

Cueillette

La cueillette se fait en décembre, lorsque les baies noires du pistachier sont mûres. La cueilleuse porte en sautoir un large panier plat fabriqué par tissage de fibres végétales en jonc et en raphia. Il a une forme circulaire, et mesure 0,70 m de diamètre. L'opératrice le glisse sous les branches du lentisque qu'elle emprisonne entre ses deux mains qu'elle frotte l'une contre l'autre. Les fruits se détachent ainsi de la branche par l'effet de friction: "*bisogno a fregare le mano*", puis ils tombent dans le large panier qui porte le nom de "*culiri*", récipient fabriqué par tissage de fibres végétales en jonc et en raphia. La récolte terminée, on procède au "nettoyage" des fruits. Pour ce faire, on les plonge dans un bac rempli d'eau: les baies gâtées remontent à la surface pendant que les saines tombent au fond.

Technique d'extraction

Par l'eau bouillante

Pour extraire l'huile, le produit de la récolte est bouilli, puis les baies sont mises dans un sac de jute (*u cestinu*) posé dans une sorte de bac en bois (*u palmentu*). Un homme, nu pieds, piétine le sac et son contenu. Durant cette opération, on verse par trois fois de l'eau chaude sur le sac. Malgré les précautions prises, il arrive que le liquide bouillant tombe par mégarde sur les pieds de l'opérateur. Inutile de dire les réactions.

Quand la pâte atteint la contexture voulue[1] on la place dans un récipient en cuivre, non sans avoir ajouté de l'eau chaude. Le chaudron est posé ensuite sur un trépied, de sorte que son ouverture soit inclinée vers le sol. Un feu doux est entretenu sur un seul côté du foyer. L'huile qui remonte à la surface est recueillie à l'aide d'une cuiller puis versée dans un récipient contenant de l'eau chaude. Ces informations confirment celles recueillies en Corse par Casanova (1968).

Avec la presse à torsion

Une autre technique ancienne était également employée par les habitants de Sardaigne et de Corse pour extraire l'huile d'olive: il s'agit de la presse à torsion (Casanova 1966; 1968; 1974). La première étape qui va de la cueillette à l'obtention de la pâte (détritage) ne change pas. Le sac d'olives était placé dans une auge en bois (*palmentu*), semblable à celle utilisée pour fouler le raisin lors des vendanges.

Un homme se chargeait alors d'écraser les fruits (*calcicati*) par piétinement. Par contre, lors de la phase correspondant à l'extraction de l'huile, la pâte était mise dans un autre sac en laine de brebis ou en cordelettes de poils de chèvre (*sacco di lana* ou *sacco di pelo di pecora*) long de 2 m environ et large de 0,60 m, et d'une contenance de 30 litres. Cette poche comporte des ourlets aux extrémités, destinés à recevoir deux rondins de bois (*i torcini*).

L'huile de première pression s'écoulait dans le *palmentu* puis se déversait dans un récipient disposé à cet effet. Lorsque le piétinement ne permettait plus l'extraction de l'huile, on procédait alors à la torsion du sac. Pour ce faire, deux personnes tournaient les bâtons en sens inverse. De temps à autre, on jetait de l'eau chaude afin d'activer l'évacuation de l'huile. Cette dernière remontait à la surface du récipient collecteur puis était recueillie à l'aide d'un instrument plat.

La persistance, en Corse, de ce mode d'extraction de l'huile d'olive par torsion, est attestée jusqu'au lendemain de la première guerre mondiale (Casanova 1968). Cette technique archaïque qui a subsisté fort tard dans le Cortenais et la Haute Balagne, nous fait constater la similitude des procédés utilisés en Corse et en Sardaigne.

Le lieu de la récolte (*a piaghja*), et la saison (*l'hiver*) durant laquelle s'effectue le ramassage et la transformation des fruits du lentisque sauvage ou de l'olivastre, montrent que la production d'huile à partir d'espèces végétales non domestiquées est limitée à la zone de la *piaghja*, et qu'elle s'effectue en hiver.

L'approvisionnement en huile des groupes humains demeurant à la montagne n'a donc pu se faire qu'à partir de relations avec la *piaghja*. Ou bien ils y descendent pour produire leur huile, ou pour s'approvisionner dans les étages thermoméditerranéen et mésoméditerranéen inférieur (ou *piaghja*). On a pu remarquer qu'à diverses époques pré- et historiques, les bergers, par exemple qui constituent une partie du groupe humain montagnard descendent à la *piaghja* où ils y passent environ huit mois, le reste de l'année étant réservée à la montagne. Jusqu'en 1950 environ, la loi économique naturelle fondée sur la complémentarité *piaghja*-montagne, est une des caractéristiques fondamentales de l'économie corse.[2]

A la *piaghja*, paysans et éleveurs, propriétaires ou non, protégeaient donc une végétation spontanée, source du précieux liquide. Dans sa thèse *Pâtres et paysans de Sardaigne,* Le Lannou (1941) précise que les deux caractères fondamenraux de la couverture végétale de la Sardaigne étaient la médiocrité de la forêt et l'exubérance du maquis et que ce dernier faisait effectivement l'objet d'une attention toute particulière. Cette prise de conscience du milieu, d'ordre socio-économique, révèle ainsi la solidarité qui unissait les habitants de la Gallura.

Les enquêtes ethnographiques et les analyses historiques réalisées dans une région où subsistent ces archaïsmes sont une aubaine pour les chercheurs en sciences humaines. Elles permettent de constater le fonctionnement de machines rurales préindustrielles encore en usage jusqu'aux années 1910–1920. On ajoutera, de surcroît, aux deux méthodes familiales évoquées plus haut, une troisième, artisanale, mettant en oeuvre un pressoir à arbre. Celui-ci comporte dans sa forme la plus élémentaire, un levier à l'extrémité duquel est suspendue une grosse pierre (Casanova 1968). En Haute Corse, à Bisinchi, par exemple, la poutre (a pertica), à l'extrémité de laquelle était fixée la pierre, mesurait 3,20 m de long.

La simplicité, pour ne pas dire l'archaïsme de ces deux techniques, fait penser qu'elles pourraient bien remonter à la Préhistoire. Elles nous invitent, de la sorte, à reconsidérer les données archéologiques obtenues dans l'abri de Scaffa-Piana par Magdeleine et Ottaviani (1983).

Cet abri, long de 70 m et large de 15, est creusé dans la falaise de calcaire miocène de la commune de Poggio-d'Oletta, dans la région de Saint-Florent, au nord ouest de la Corse. La fouille a permis de mettre en évidence plus d'une vingtaine de couches (de XX à XXIII) dont les plus anciennes attribuées au Néolithique moyen, retiendront notre attention (Fig. 14.1–14.3). Trois datations ont été effectuées dans ces niveaux (Delibrias *et al.* 1982: 186):

couche XXI MC-2056 5320 ± 100 cal 4352–3953 av. J.-C.
couche XXI MC-2054 5330 ± 100 cal 4355–3957 av. J.-C.
couche XXII MC-2057 5360 ± 100 cal 4435–3969 av. J.-C.

Ces couches présentées par les auteurs de la fouille comme étant situées dans l'étage XXI/XXII, peuvent être considérées comme appartenant à la même unité stratigraphique.

Les témoins archéologiques retrouvés dans ces niveaux comprennent des piquets de bois, deux amoncellements de pierres en forme de couronne et abritant des vanneries, un troisième ensemble comprenant un panier bien conservé. Ce vestige de forme sphérique de 0,80 m de diamètre, est surmonté d'un col cylindrique de 0,50 m de diamètre à l'ouverture. Par ailleurs, il a été retrouvé une cordelette en poil de chèvre (*funi*), une accumulation de charbons (foyer), une concentration de cendres, et, surtout, des noyaux d'oléastres dont la quantité n'est malheureusement pas indiquée.

Les auteurs ont estimé qu'il s'agissait d'un aménagement destiné à la conservation de graines et de vivres (silo), cependant le petit nombre de meules, de molettes, de lames, de lamelles, ne semble pas confirmer l'hypothèse d'une agriculture prépondérante. Ces structures ont attiré l'attention d'autres préhistoriens. Toutefois, la forme bizarre de ces vanneries n'a pas donné lieu à des explications convaincantes (Camps 1988).

Si l'on se réfère aux données ethnologiques exposées plus haut, il est possible de proposer une interprétation différente pour justifier la présence de ces témoins et émettre l'hypothèse qu'il s'agit d'un lieu où les néolithiques ont extrait de l'huile à partir des fruits de l'oléastre.

En effet, la présence de noyaux d'oléastres constitue un des éléments déterminants de l'enquête. Des noyaux ont été trouvés dans d'autres abris de même époque comme celui de Cucuruzzu par exemple (Marinval, comm. orale). L'existence effective de noyaux d'oléastres dans les sites préhistoriques résulte très vraisemblablement d'un apport volontaire sous forme de fruits mûrs. Retrouvés en grand nombre, il pourraient éventuellement correspondre aux rejets après pressage et constituer ainsi des témoins probables de l'extraction d'huile dans l'abri.

En revanche, il n'est guère possible de s'appuyer aussi sereinement sur les pollens dont la présence peut dépendre d'une action naturelle (transport éolien) ou d'une action anthropique (par exemple le transport dans l'habitat de branches en fleurs) (Bui Thi Mai 1988; 1993; Renault-Miskovsky 1972). Les pollens d'*Olea* et de *Pistacia* ont été signalés dans les sites de A Petra, Monte Lazzu, Cucuruzzu, Ciutulaghja et Araguina-Sennola. Leurs

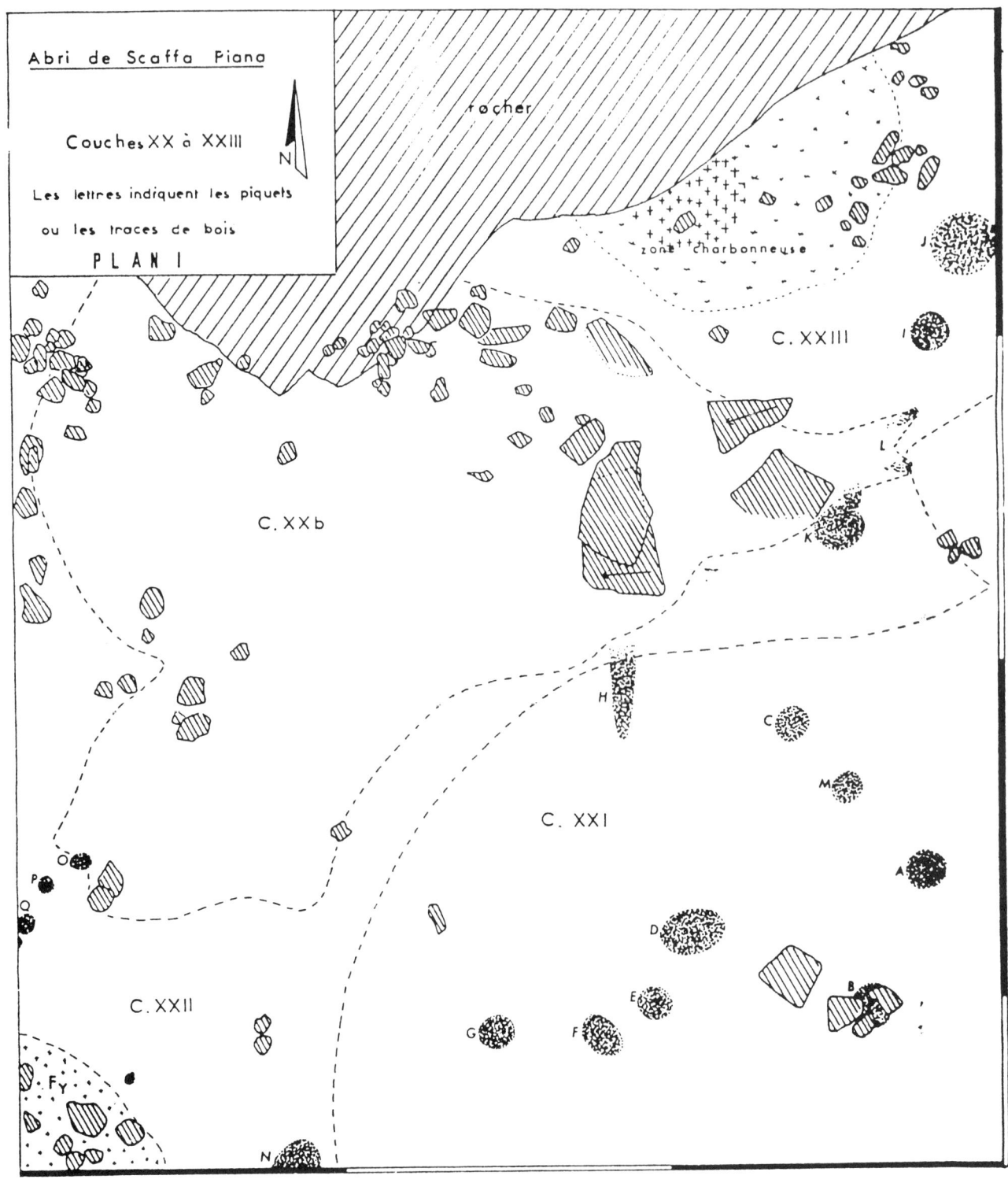

Fig. 14.1. Plan de l'abri de Scaffa Piana (Dessin J. Magdeleine).

fréquences sont généralement faibles (1% environ), exception faite du site de Monte Lazzu (ech.11) où *Olea* atteint 2,5% et de l'Araguina-Sennola (VI-J2) où la fréquence de *Pistacia* atteint 4,6%. Cette dernière valeur est cependant comparable à celles communément observées dans les analyses des marais côtiers de la Corse sud-orientale où *Pistacia* atteint, au Sub-Atlantique, des taux qui s'étendent de 3 à près de 9% (Reille 1984).

Les vanneries découvertes dans ce site, ressemblent fortement aux scourtins d'alfa tressé utilisés dans les pressoirs à pression de Corse et de Sardaigne (Fig. 14.4). Elles pourraient correspondre, sans difficulté, aux *cestini*

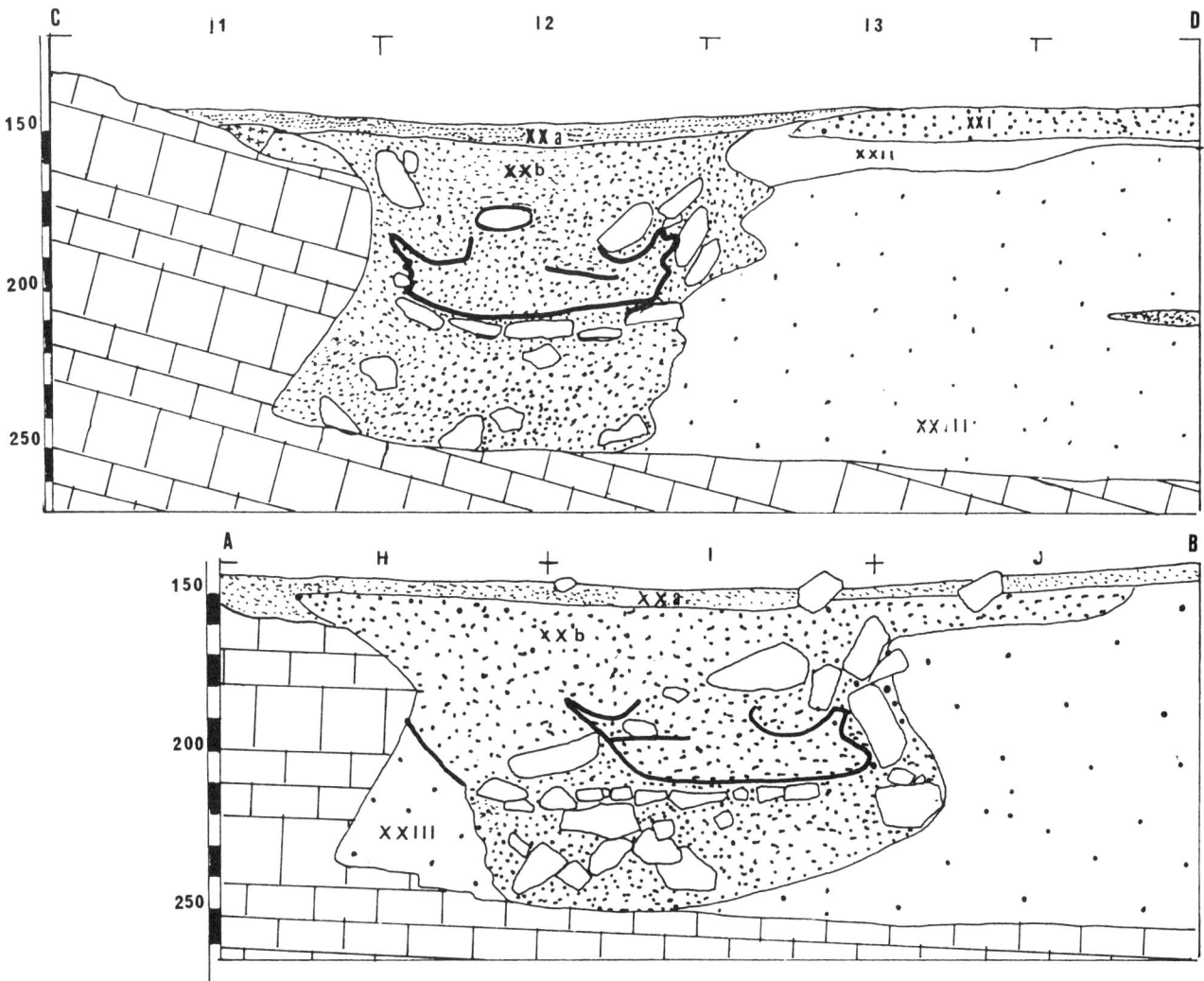

Fig. 14.2. Sections de l'abri de Scaffa Piana (dessin J. Magdeleine).

décrits par l'habitante de San Teodoro, et que l'on nomme *sacculeddu* en Corse méridionale, et *zimbinu* dans le Cortenais.

L'accumulation de charbons près de la paroi rocheuse de l'abri semble bien être une structure de chauffe dont l'une des fonctions pouvait se rapporter à la production d'eau chaude destinée à activer l'extraction de l'huile.

Quant aux fragments de cordelette en poils de chèvre, ils évoquent les fils de trame d'un autre type de récipient (sac à torsion?) dans lequel on aurait mis des olives écrasées. Il peut tout aussi bien avoir pu servir à attacher la pierre fixée à la poutre de la presse. On peut ainsi penser que l'extraction de l'huile par cette technique pouvait être en usage en Corse dès le Néolithique évolué, longtemps avant l'apparition des oliviers cultivés. L'hypothèse peut paraître bien hardie car, dans l'état actuel de nos connaissances, l'origine des procédés d'extraction de l'huile est située au Chalcolithique dans la région syro-phénicienne (Amouretti 1991).

Les pieux de 9 à 13 cm de diamètre et les piquets de 5 à 8 cm semblent avoir eu une double fonction. D'après les alignements de ces témoins (Fig. 14.1), on voit que les uns (J,I,K,F et A,B,C,D,E,M) peuvent être considérés comme les composantes d'une clôture ou d'une partie d'enclos; les autres, que nous désignerons par les lettres Z et Y, pourraient être les éléments constitutifs d'un système qui n'est pas sans évoquer une presse à huile. Dans ce cas, la poutre horizontale ou *pertica* aurait pris appui sur les pieux verticaux. On observera d'ailleurs que la ligne imaginaire qui relie les deux pieux Z et Y passe exactement au-dessus des deux structures en pierre qui enferment les vanneries. Cette interprétation qui s'impose à nous peut surprendre car elle suppose que des presses à huile fonctionnaient en Corse, au Néolithique évolué. Des outils ou des systèmes particuliers auraient donc été installés dans une partie de l'habitat, bien séparée par une palissade en bois du reste de l'abri. Dans l'autre partie de l'habitation, la présence des bêtes est attestée par l'existence d'excréments (crottes) de moutons ou de chèvres. Les auteurs de la fouille en déduisent d'ailleurs que les Néolithiques de l'endroit étaient également des pasteurs.

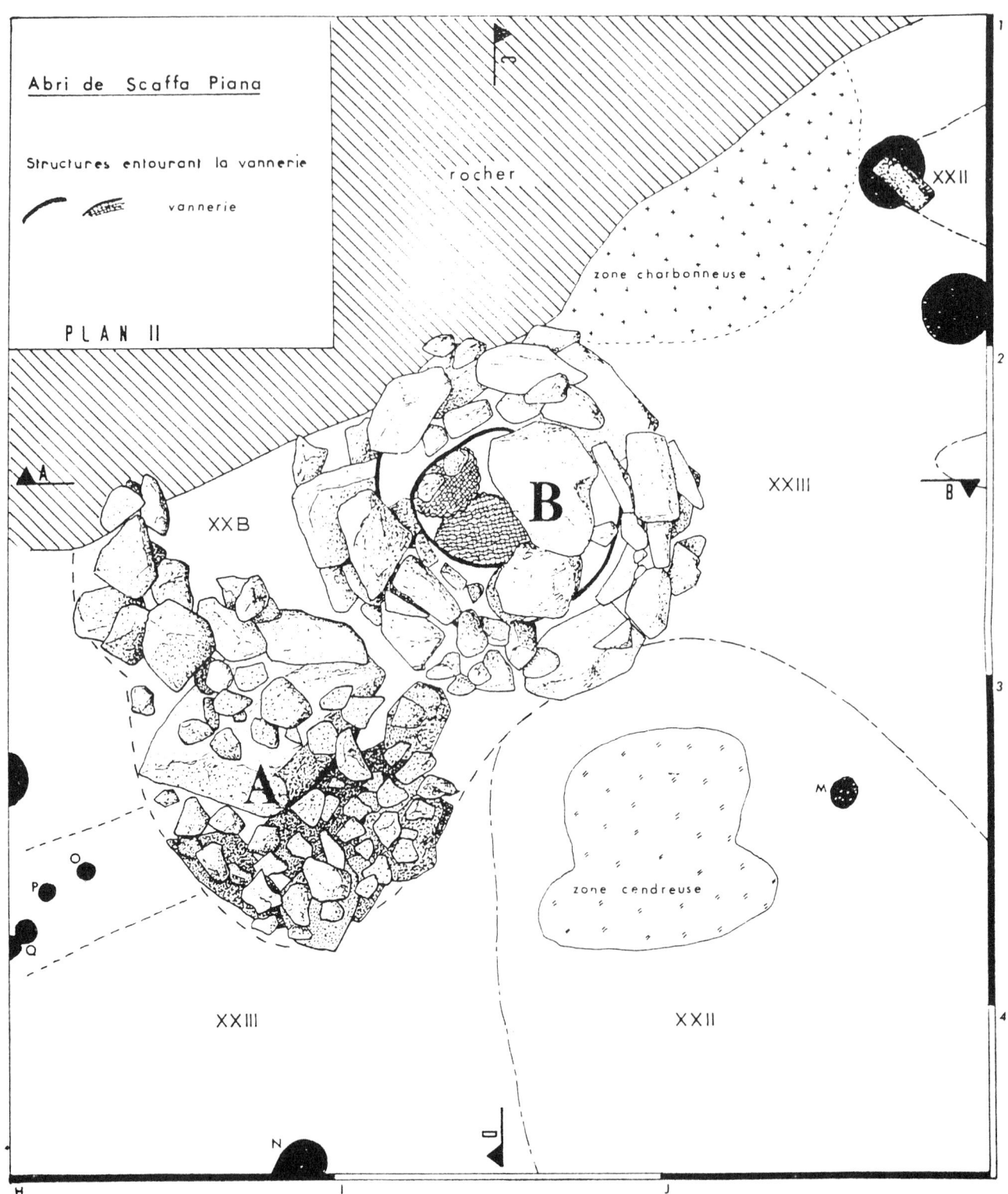

Fig. 14.3. Planimétrie de l'abri avec les structures et la vannerie (dessin J. Magdeleine).

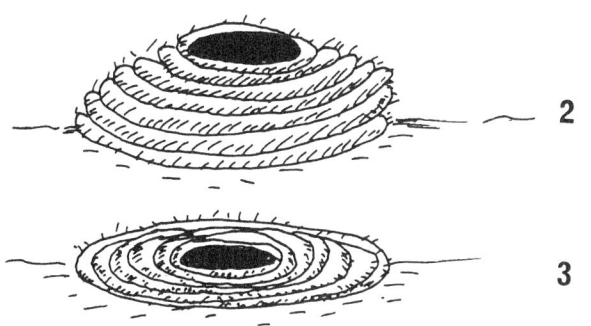

Fig. 14.4. La presse à pression de la Corse rurale traditionnelle. 1-Restitution graphique de la presse; 2- Le scourtin plein; 3-Le scourtin vide.

Les grosses pierres trouvées dans des structures en pierre sèche, ne sont pas sans évoquer les poids que l'on attachait à l'extrémité de la poutre horizontale et qui maintenait la pression. Elles peuvent avoir été l'un des éléments d'une presse à arbre.

La production de l'huile est donc fortement suggérée par les structures mises en évidence dans la couche du Néolithique évolué de Scaffa Piana. La procédure qui mène de la récolte des fruits à l'obtention du précieux liquide, comporte au moins cinq stades opératoires: la cueillette, le nettoyage, le foulage, le pressage et la conservation de l'huile. "Foulage et torsion tiennent au moins autant de l'outil que de la machine proprement dite" (Casanova 1974). Effectivement, le bois, les fibres végétales ou animales, les roches, sont des matières premières abondantes et que l'on peut se procurer facilement. Quant aux outils obtenus, ils restent à l'état brut, comme le bois (poutre) et les roches (poids), ou prennent la forme d'un outil élaboré (panier, sac, récipient pour contenir l'huile).

Vers la fin du premier Néolithique en Corse, qu'il s'agisse du Cardial ou du Poinçonné, une évolution généralisée s'observe dans les domaines de la production. En ce qui concerne l'agriculture et l'élevage, par exemple, l'obtention de sous-produits apparaît mieux structurée dans toute la Corse. On dispose d'informations nombreuses et variées sur les chaînes opératoires relatives aux productions aussi diverses que les céréales, les fruits, le lait, par exemple. La présente étude ne nous permet évidemment pas de nous attarder sur ces divers domaines de la recherche. Par contre, nous pouvons le faire pour l'huile.

A Scaffa Piana, nous pouvons être en présence d'une production d'huile de type *"familial"*, voire *"artisanal "*. Le savoir, la maîtrise des techniques, l'élaboration de produits alimentaires à partir de végétaux, sont autant de facteurs qui marquent l'évolution du Néolithique vers 5300 BP. Ce dernier que l'on nomme Néolithique moyen, est caractérisé par un grand nombre de changements qui attestent une évolution marquant les époques post-cardiales. On constate en effet une évolution qui va de l'habitat isolé des Cardials à l'habitat groupé des Présiens, de l'économie à dominante pastorale à l'explosion de l'agriculture, de l'utilisation de produits naturels à leur consommation sous la forme de produits alimentaires.

Ce Néolithique évolué (par rapport au premier Néolithique) semble bien être apparu, en Corse, très précocement comme l'indiquent les mesures d'âge radiométriques obtenues à Monte Leone et à Presa-Tusiu. Pour le premier site: 5855 ± 95 BP (Ly 6099: calibrée 4934–4470 av. J.-C.); pour le second: 6210 ± 80 BP (Rom 428: calibrée 5285–5937 av. J.-C.). Les calibrations ont été réalisées à notre demande par J.Evin qui a utilisé les courbes de Stuiver *et al.* (Stuiver & Pearson 1993; Pearson & Stuiver 1993; Pearson *et al.* 1993). Celles de Scaffa Piana, beaucoup plus récentes (5320, 5330 et 5360 BP) que celles des sites de la Corse méridionale, seraient plutôt contemporaines du Basien qui, rappelons-le, est une phase évoluée du Présien.

La corrélation de tous les témoins retrouvés dans l'abri de Scaffa Piana semble bien indiquer que les hommes du Néolithique ont procédé à l'extraction de l'huile à partir de fruits de l'olivier sauvage, qu'il s'agisse du procédé par torsion ou par pression ou tout simplement par la seule action de l'eau chaude. Jusqu'à présent, les informations situaient les plus anciens pressoirs à torsion à l'Ancien Empire Egyptien (XXVIIe-XXIIe siècles avant J.-C.). En Corse, cette technique serait bien plus ancienne puisqu'elle se situerait dès le Néolithique moyen. Les données ethnologiques (Fig. 14.4) et archéologiques (Fig. 14.1 à 14.3), montrent à la fois la grande ancienneté de l'extraction de l'huile végétale à partir des oléacées et des lentisques et la persistance jusqu'à nos jours d'une technique primitive. Les recherches préhistoriques devront donc s'attacher à trouver ces témoins discrets que sont les noyaux d'olivier sauvage et du lentisque, d'en effectuer le dénombrement (rejets éventuels) et établir le plus précisément possible la corrélation spatiale et chronologique entre ces vestiges et le mobilier qui les accompagne. Par ailleurs il faudra sans doute élargir les recherches à l'extérieur de l'abri, dans une zone assez vaste, car l'étude des pressoirs traditionnels montre que les déchets sont portés assez loin (une cinquantaine de mètres) de la zone d'activité. Les paysans de Sardaigne nous ont d'ailleurs montré les lieux où ils rejetaient les restes de la pression des fruits du pistachier; leur dépotoir se situe en effet à une centaine de mètres environ de la maison. Les renseignements ainsi recueillis contribueront à accroître nos connaissances sur les activités traditionnelles des populations préhistoriques cyrno-sardes.

Notes

1. Cette opération qui se nomme le détritage, est considérée comme entièrement achevée, lorsqu'il n'adhère plus un seul morceau de chair sur le noyau.
2. Une telle information éclaire l'interprétation que l'on peut proposer pour expliquer les modalités de l'occupation d'un site archéologique. Il est indispensable, pour cela, de connaître quelques lois naturelles qui régissent les mouvements des groupes humains, avec des déplacements de la montagne à la *piaghja*. Ce qui était valable il y a quelques décennies, peut avoir été de règle durant la Préhistoire.

Bibliographie

Amouretti, M.-C. 1986. *Le pain et l'huile dans la Grèce antique: de l'araire au moulin*. Annales Littéraires de l'Université de Besançon 328. Belles Lettres, Paris.

Amouretti, M.-C. 1991. Variations historiques des chaînes opératoires de transformation des produits agricoles méditerranéens: l'olivier et la vigne. *Techniques et Cultures* 17–18: 245–272.

Bois, D. 1927–37. *Les plantes alimentaires chez tous les peuples et à travers les âges*. t. III: Plantes à épices, aromates et condiments. Lechevallier éd., Paris.

Bonnier, G. & Douin, R. 1934. *Flore complète illustrée en couleur de France, Suisse et Belgique*. XII tomes, Librairie générale de l'Enseignement, Paris.

Bui Thi Mai. 1988. Quelques aspects de la flore néolithique révélés par l'analyse pollinique de deux sites archéologiques de Balagne (La Pietra et Carcu). In Weiss, M.C. (sous la direction de), *Les temps anciens du peuplement de la Corse: La Balagne*, 97–108. Université de Corse.

Bui Thi Mai. 1993. L'abri sous roche n°1 du casteddu de Cucuruzzu (Levie), Apports de la palynologie. *Corsica Antica* 2: 11–15.

Camps, G. 1988. *Préhistoire d'une île*. Ed. Errance, Collection des Hespérides.

Casanova, A. 1966. Notes sur les pressoirs préindustriels de Corse. *Corse Historique* 21–22.

Casanova, A. 1968. Typologie et diffusion des pressoirs préindustriels dans les communes rurales de Corse. *Corse Historique* 31–32.

Casanova, A. 1968. L'aire de diffusion en Corse, au début du XIXe siècle, du type le plus archaïque de pressoir, le pressoir à torsion. *Arts et Traditions Populaires* juillet-décembre: 237–257.

Casanova, A. 1974. Technologies et communautés rurales en Corse à la fin du XVIIIe siècle: Aspects de la prédominance des machines élémentaires. *Etudes Corses* 3: 83–121.

Casanova, A. 1990. *Paysans et machines à la fin du XVIIIe siècle: essai d'ethnologie historique*. Annales Littéraires de l'Université de Besançon 415. Les Belles Lettres, Paris.

Jacob De Cordomoy, H. 1911. *Les plantes à gommes et à résines*. Encyclopédie scientifique. Doin éd., Paris.

Le Lannou, M. 1941. *Pâtres et paysans de la Sardaigne*. Turs, Arnault et Cie, Maîtres imprimeurs.

Leroi-Gourhan, A. 1945 et 1973. *Milieu et techniques*. Sciences d'aujourd'hui. Albin Michel, Paris.

Magdeleine, J. & Ottaviani, J.-C. 1983. Découverte de vanneries datées du Néolithique moyen dans un abri de Saint-Florent en Corse. *Bulletin de la Société Préhistorique Française* 80: 24–32.

Paris, R.R. & Moyse, H. 1981. *Matière médicale*. t.II. Masson éd.

Pearson, G.W., Becker, B. & Qua, F. 1993. High-precision 14C measurement of German and Irish oaks to show the natural 14C variations from 7890 to 5000 BC. *Radiocarbon* 35: 93–104.

Pearson, G.W. & Stuiver, M. 1993. High-precision bidecadal calibration of the radiocarbon time scale 500–2500 BC. *Radiocarbon* 35: 25–33.

Reille, M. 1981. Origine de la végétation actuelle de la Corse sud-orientale: analyse pollinique de cinq marais côtiers. *Pollens et Spores* 26: 43–60.

Renault-Miskovsky, J. 1972. *Contribution à la climatologie du Midi méditerranéen pendant la dernière glaciation et le Post-Glaciaire d'après l'étude palynologique du remplissage des grottes et abris-sous-roches*. Thèse de Doctorat es Sciences Naturelles, Paris VI.

Stuiver, M. & Pearson, G.W. 1993. High-precision bidecadal calibration of the radiocarbon time scale, AD 1950–500 BC and 2500–6000 BC. *Radiocarbon* 35: 1–23.

Triat-Aval, H. 1982. Pollen-analyse des sédiments quaternaires récents du pourtour de l'éyang de Berre. *Ecologia-Mediterranea* 8: 97–115.

Van Zeist, W. 1981. Aperçu sur la diffusion des végétaux cultivés dans la région méditerranéenne. *Actes du colloque organise a l'Institut de botanique de Montpellier les 9 et 10 avril 1980 par la Fondation Louis Emberger: la mise en place, l'evolution et la caracterisation de la flore et de la vegetation circummediterraneennes*, 129–145. Naturalia Monspeliensia, Institut de Botanique, Montpellier.

15. Le statuette di 'Dea Madre' nei contesti prenuragici: alcune considerazioni

Angela Antona

La conoscenza delle statuette femminili della Sardegna prenuragica si è arricchita, con gli studi degli ultimi venti anni, grazie al rinvenimento di un numero notevole di esemplari (circa 140), riconducibili a tipi e stili diversi. La scarsità dei dati relativi ai contesti di rinvenimento e la conseguente difficoltà per un'attribuzione culturale delle statuette mi indussero, alla fine degli anni '70, ad un tentativo di analisi della morfologia dei singoli esemplari, considerati nei loro elementi costitutivi e rappresentativi (Antona 1980).

Tale studio consentì di isolare alcuni dati caratterizzanti, in considerazione della resa complessiva della figura e del grado di sintesi raggiunto nell'espressione artistica. Sulla base dei risultati ottenuti, fu proposto uno schema tipologico, che ribadiva le tre classi principali evidenziate dal Lilliu e dall'Atzeni (Lilliu 1965: 25, 138 sgg.; Atzeni 1976) e ne puntualizzava, al loro interno, le varianti. Nell'ambito di tale tipologia, parve di poter cogliere una seriazione evolutiva che lasciava presumere l'appartenenza dei singoli tipi ad episodi culturali differenziati.

Il proseguire e l'evolversi degli studi, nonché le scoperte degli anni recenti, hanno aggiunto ulteriori esemplari a quelli noti, ma purtroppo pochissimi sono stati rinvenuti in contesti culturali certi. Sulla base dello schema tipologico allora proposto, si è qui operata una verifica del medesimo alla luce dei recenti ritrovamenti, per accertarne o meno la sua validità (Figg. 15.1–15.2).

Tipo "volumetrico ellissoidale" o "volumetrico naturalistico"

Per quanto concerne il tipo "volumetrico ellissoidale" o "volumetrico naturalistico", i rinvenimenti di Cuccuru S'Arriu hanno arricchito il repertorio e ne hanno suggerito l'attribuzione alla cultura di Bonu Ighinu (Atzeni 1989: 34 sgg.). Dal punto di vista stilistico, va confermata l'omogeneità riconosciuta nel tipo, caratterizzato dalla tendenza a condensare le masse corporee in volumi compatti, compenetrati armonicamente fra di loro, così da risultare racchiusi all'interno di una elegantissima linea ellittica.

Come è noto, il rinvenimento delle statuette di Cuccuru S'Arriu si riferisce a contesti tombali contraddistinti dalla deposizione singola degli inumati in ipogei monocellulari a forno, con pozzetto d'accesso (Santoni 1982a; 1982b; 1995).

Il corredo che accompagnava i defunti, deposti in posizione rannicchiata su un lastricato di pietra scistosa, ricoperto di ocra rossa, è rappresentato da vasi in fine ceramica monocroma, fra i quali vanno annoverate le ormai note ciotole emisferiche carenate e a colletto svasato o rientrante, la ciotola cipolliforme con brevissimo colletto distinto, la tazza troncoconica monoansata (Santoni 1982a; 1982b); forme molto vicine a quelle di Bonu Ighinu, ma prive dell'ornamentazione a tacche e punti impressi che caratterizzavano i noti repertori di Sa 'Ucca de Su Tintirriolu. Vanno inoltre ricordate le punte di zagaglia in osso, i microliti geometrici, i piccoli vaghi di collana a rotellina in pietra dura. In attesa che l'edizione integrale dei giacimenti di Cuccuru S'Arriu definisca un'eventuale articolazione della cultura in argomento, l'attribuzione a questa delle statuette naturalistiche non può che essere generica.

Alla luce delle più recenti datazioni calibrate, si deve constatare la lunga durata di questa cultura, che avrebbe un'estensione di duemila anni (5800–3800) secondo la cronologia di Contu (in questo volume), di settecento anni (4700–4000) secondo quella di Tykot (1994: 122); un percorso che, sia in un caso che nell'altro, lascia spazio alle logiche evoluzioni a cui va soggetta una cultura vitale lungo il suo arco di sviluppo.

Sulla base di questo presupposto, possono farsi alcune osservazioni in merito agli ormai noti elementi che

Angela Antona, Soprintendenza ai Beni Archeologici per le Provincie di Sassari e Nuoro, Piazza S. Agostino 2, Sassari 07100, Sardegna, Italia

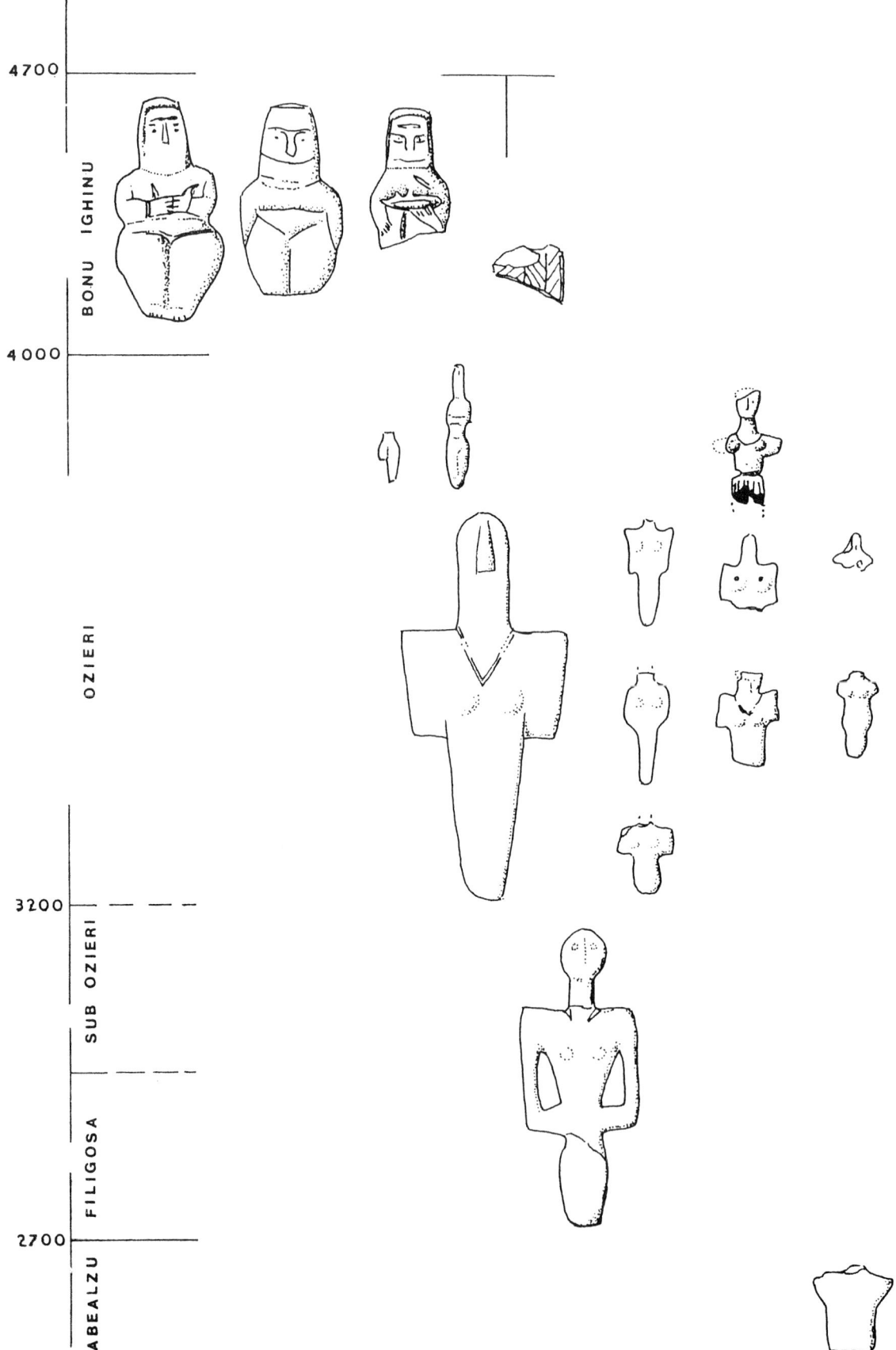

Fig. 15.1. Schema tipologico e cronologico delle statuette. Disegno di Gianpietro Dore.

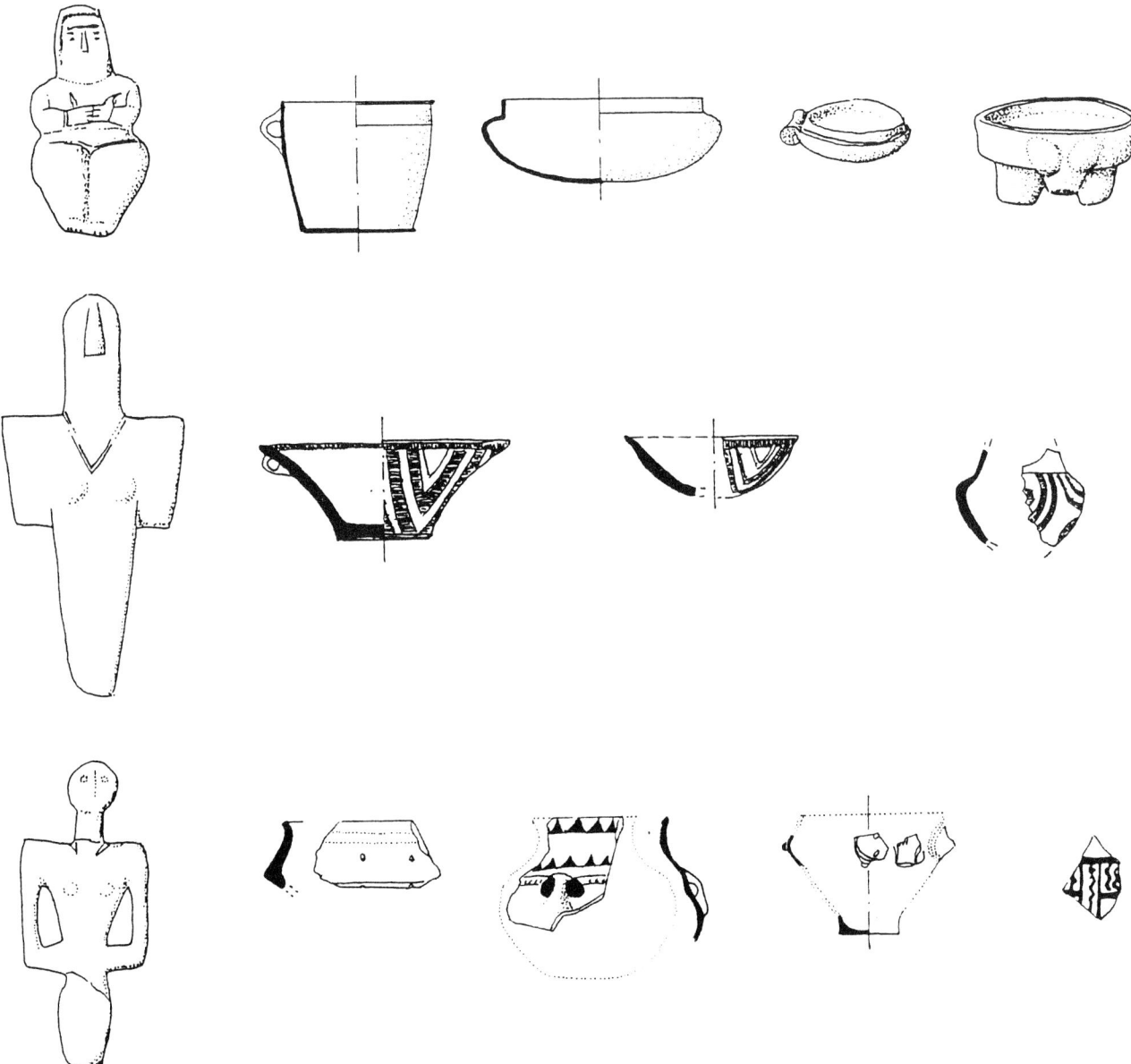

Fig. 15.2. Esempi di statuette e ceramiche dai contesti culturali di Bonu Ighinu, Ozieri, e Filigosa-Abealzu. Disegno di Gianpietro Dore.

risultano innovativi rispetto ai contesti, fino ad ora conosciuti, di Bonu Ighinu. Il primo di essi è costituito dalla comparsa delle grotticelle artificiali ipogeiche, il tipo tombale che avrà pieno sviluppo ed evoluzione nell'ambito della cultura di Ozieri (Lilliu 1988: 81 sgg.).

Fino alla scoperta del deposito archeologico di Cuccuru S'Arriu, l'unico contesto funerario noto di cultura Bonu Ighinu era costituito da un pozzo della Grotta Rifugio di Oliena, dove i morti risultavano gettati alla rinfusa, insieme ai loro corredi composti da recipienti fittili, strumenti di ossidiana e selce, elementi di adorno in pietra levigata, conchiglie ed osso (Biagi 1980: 96 sgg.).

A fronte di una simile pratica, che pone interessanti interrogativi anche da un punto di vista meramente paletnologico, l'aspetto funerario di Cuccuru S'Arriu risulta decisamente sorprendente e complesso, documentando contemporaneamente l'uso dell'ipogeo artificiale e della tomba a fossa. Nessun elemento di carattere materiale chiarisce i problemi derivanti dalla loro coesistenza, nè aiuta a precisare l'eventuale anteriorità di un tipo rispetto all'altro. Ad essi è comune l'uso del seppellimento singolo primario, con la giacitura degli inumati in posizione contratta. Comuni sono anche alcuni elementi dei corredi, quali i piccoli vaghi di collana in pietra dura, le punte di zagaglia in osso, i microliti geometrici.

Esclusiva degli ipogei, per quanto noto fino ad oggi, è invece la presenza delle statuette e quella dell'ocra rossa, elementi entrambi particolarmente qualificanti, che lasciano spazio all'ipotesi di distinzioni nell'ambito sociale, ma che potrebbero anche suggerire il carattere innovativo dell'ipogeo rispetto alla tomba terragna.

Un altro elemento di nuova affermazione nei contesti noti della cultura di Bonu Ighinu è ravvisabile proprio nella comparsa del tipo di rappresentazione volumetrica della Dea Madre, riflesso di una linea di gusto artistico molto diversa da quella individuata da Trump nello "strato Bonu Ighinu puro" di Sa 'Ucca de Su Tintirriolu (Loria & Trump 1978: 128, fig. 10,3; tav. IX,2). Il frammento di statuetta qui rinvenuto, infatti, era caratterizzato dallo stile geometrico delle sue linee di contorno; in esso si era ritenuto di ravvisare il diretto antecedente del geometrismo proprio delle successive rappresentazioni "a placca intera" (Antona 1980: 134). A dare forza a questa ipotesi, si è aggiunto di recente un altro esemplare di stile geometrico, in terracotta, rinvenuto in un riparo sotto roccia a San Basilio di Ollolai (Nuoro), associato a frammenti ceramici con decorazione a tacche sull'orlo e sulla carena, secondo le sintassi più tipiche della cultura di Bonu Ighinu (Fadda 1991: 12, fig. 2).

Il terzo elemento di innovazione si riscontra nella scarsa o nulla decorazione dei recipienti, le cui forme si discostano di poco da quelle conosciute nelle grotte di Sa 'Ucca de Su Tintirriolu, dell'Inferno, del Bagno Penale, contraddistinte da note di particolare raffinatezza nell'ornamentazione.

Da più parti è stato giustamente proposto di riconoscere, in questo mutamento, il riflesso di modifiche sostanziali della cultura, corrispondenti a tempi evoluti, riferibili probabilmente ad un momento non lontano dalle prime manifestazioni Ozieri (Santoni 1982a; Ugas 1990: 89 sgg.; Ferrarese Ceruti 1992: 74), e particolarmente ricco di stimoli culturali derivanti dai numerosi contatti favoriti dal commercio dell'ossidiana, più volte evidenziati.

In questa ipotesi, non sarebbero casuali i confronti dell'orizzonte culturale in questione con contesti nei quali il prezioso materiale sardo è presente in quantità ben evidente. Ci si riferisce, in particolare, a quello chasseano della Francia Meridionale e a quello "Basien" della Corsica, che le più recenti datazioni calibrate pongono oggi fra il 4300 ed il 3800 (Tykot 1994: 122), in sufficiente coerenza, dunque, con una facies matura di Bonu Ighinu (Atzeni 1985: 27).

Se si dovessero avere ulteriori conferme a questa datazione, risulterebbe superato il divario cronologico che scoraggiava i confronti dei noti vasi corsi a fondo emisferico (de Lanfranchi & Weiss 1974: fig. 24), caratterizzati da anse ad appendici cilindriche e decorazione a punti impressi, con vasi sardi simili, quali quelli provenienti dalle grotte dell'Inferno di Muros (Loria & Trump 1978: fig. 6) e Rifugio di Oliena (Biagi 1980), di cultura Bonu Ighinu. La caratteristica del fondo emisferico richiama anche i vasi provenienti dalla grotta del Bagno Penale di Cagliari (Atzeni 1978: fig. 18:8).

Nella stessa ipotesi, dunque, non sarebbero certamente casuali neppure le similitudini che la statuetta corsa di Campu Fiorellu (de Lanfranchi & Weiss 1973: 144) trova nel tipo naturalistico sardo, soprattutto per la peculiare resa della figura in compatte volumetrie dal contorno complessivo ellissoidale, sulle quali le parti caratterizzanti del corpo sono accentuate da profondi solchi ed il copricapo ricadente sulle spalle è reso con delicati segni grafici.

Purtroppo non si conosce il contesto di rinvenimento dell'esemplare in questione, che continua a rimanere unico. Alcune statuette, di tipo ancora indefinito, sono state ritrovate negli ultimi anni (De Lanfranchi & Weiss 1994: 48), ma non si hanno ancora notizie relative alle loro caratteristiche, nè ai contesti di rinvenimento.

La povertà numerica delle piccole sculture si riscontra anche nella regione Nord-orientale della Sardegna, da dove proviene un solo esemplare, rappresentato dalla nota "dea" di Olbia; la sua presenza risultava fino ad oggi anomala, poichè non erano note manifestazioni culturali del Neolitico Medio. Ma è recentissima, e fino a questo momento inedita, la notizia dell'individuazione, nel suddetto territorio, di un deposito archeologico riferibile alla cultura di Bonu Ighinu; il rinvenimento, ancora in fase di accertamenti, riguarda alcuni tafoni, il tipo di cavità naturale propria del granito. I frammenti raccolti sono pertinenti a vasi decorati a file di puntini impressi, singole o doppie, che richiamano gli esemplari appena citati (Fig. 15.3).

Un altro richiamo di carattere stilistico concerne alcuni dei noti vasi in pietra, dei quali si conoscono ormai numerosi esemplari (Atzeni 1978: 17 sgg.). Fra di essi appaiono particolarmente significativi i due da Bingia 'Eccia di Dolianova (Lo Schiavo 1986: 41, fig. 51). L'ansa zoomorfa del vaso tetrapode, nonchè gli effetti di raffinata lavorazione che contraddistinguono entrambi gli oggetti, fanno registrare una notevole affinità di gusto rispetto alla produzione delle statuette di tipo naturalistico.

Per l'ansa a rocchetto pieno della ciotolina, il confronto più vicino è stato sempre indicato nella coppetta di steatite della necropoli di Li Muri di Arzachena. Anse dello stesso tipo sono state rivenute nell'Oristanese, in ambito c. d. San Ciriaco (Ugas 1990: 92; Ferrarese Ceruti 1995: 102–103).

Va ora segnalato che durante un recente esame della ciotolina di Dolianova, si è notata, sulla parte esterna del fondo, la presenza di alcuni minutissimi vaghi di collana a rotellina, in pietra dura nera (clorite o aragonite), di tipo simile a quello rinvenuto nella Grotta Rifugio di Oliena, di certa pertinenza Bonu Ighinu (Biagi 1980), e nelle tombe di Cuccuru S'Arriu. I piccoli vaghi sono rimasti inglobati in una incrostazione di ocra rossa, probabilmente determinata dall'originaria giacitura del vaso (Fig. 15.4). Purtroppo, le poche notizie che si hanno in merito si limitano a farne registrare la provenienza da un ipogeo artificiale, senza nessun dato utile a precisarne il tipo.

Ai fini di una valutazione del contesto cultuale, nel quale potrebbero ravvisarsi ulteriori aspetti comuni nelle pratiche sepolcrali degli ipogei e dei circoli megalitici, è da ricordare la presenza di ocra rossa anche all'interno delle ciste funerarie di Li Muri e di La Macciunitta di Arzachena, dove gli oggetti rinvenuti erano impregnati di tale materia colorante (Puglisi & Castaldi 1965: 65).

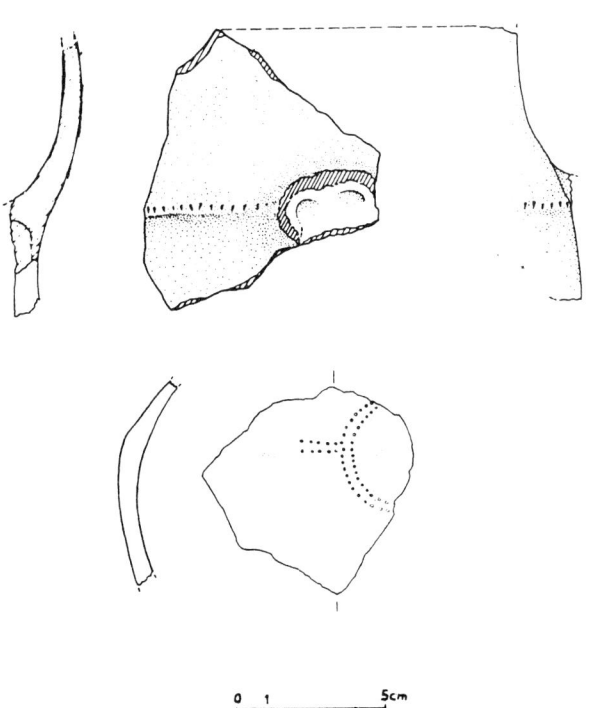

Fig. 15.3. Porto Rotondo (Olbia, SS): frammenti ceramici di cultura Bonu Ighinu. Disegno di G. Sedda.

Alla luce delle osservazioni sopra esposte, potrebbe essere non insensato proporre, almeno per i suddetti vasi di stile così consono a quello delle statuette naturalistiche, l'ambito cronologico-culturale di queste ultime, senza escludere, ovviamente, il continuare della produzione anche nella successiva cultura di Ozieri.

Tipo "a placca intera"

Alle forme volumetriche espresse nelle statuette di Bonu Ighinu si sostituiscono, con la cultura di Ozieri, le eleganti fogge geometriche slanciate di quelle classificate nel tipo "a placca intera". Il loro ambito culturale era stato suggerito dal rinvenimento, nella grotta di Sa 'Ucca de Su Tintirriolu, di diversi esemplari in terracotta, di certa pertinenza stratigrafica Ozieri. L'esame stilistico aveva fatto constatare che le linee di gusto, ispirate rispettivamente all'organicità (espressa nelle forme volumetriche delle statuette obese) e al geometrismo (suggerito dal frammento di statuetta prima citato dello strato Bonu Ighinu di Su Tintirriolu, probabilmente provenienti da esperienze culturali inizialmente autonome, sembravano fondersi in un unico modello rappresentativo.

Parve inoltre di poter indicare nelle note statuette di Monte Meana di Santadi (Atzeni 1975: tav. 2) il momento di incontro delle due tendenze stilistiche suddette, impressione che continua a permanere insieme alla carenza di dati che non consentono di indicare con

Fig. 15.4. Vasetti in pietra calcarea da Dolianova-CA (A); particolare del fondo della ciotolina con l'ocra e i vaghi di collana (B).

certezza la loro appartenenza. Benchè in via ipotetica, si potrebbe pensare all'ambito culturale di San Ciriaco – Cuccuru S'Arriu.

Il frammento in marmo grigio simile agli esemplari di Monte Meana, ma più slanciato nelle forme, rinvenuto nell'ipogeo XXIII di Anghelu Ruju (Antona 1980: 125; fig. 25), dal quale provengono solo pochi frammenti di cultura Ozieri (Taramelli 1909), potrebbe testimoniare la continuazione del tipo di rappresentazione anche in questo ambito.

Nuove conferme si sono evidenziate, intanto, per l'attribuzione alla piena cultura di S. Michele del tipo definito "a placca intera", sia nelle forme rigidamente geometriche degli esemplari in pietra che in quelle più morbide e talvolta più naturalistiche della variante in terracotta (Antona 1980: 129–135).

Una conferma in tal senso è rappresentata da una statuetta fittile da Cuccuru S'Arriu (Santoni 1989: 176 sgg.; fig. 6). La sintesi delle braccia in due moncherini rettangolari, l'appiattimento del busto, il volume quadrangolare della testa, col volto distinto dal collo e con il rilievo del naso a pilastrino, la definizione del disegno a V sul petto (Antona 1980: 129, n. 39), infine le linee rigide e spigolose del volume del bacino, consentono di inquadrare l'esemplare nel tipo in questione.

Ma va posta in evidenza la particolarità dei dettagli dell'abbigliamento, in particolare la meticolosa rappresentazione della gonna che, oltre a richiamare la statuetta in terracotta da Conca Illonis (Atzeni 1978: tav. XXVI), si riconnette alle notissime figurine femminili a spalle apicate, che decorano i vasi di cultura Ozieri della grotta di Su Tintirriolu e di Monte d'Accoddi e a quella con gonna a campana incisa sul frammento ceramico da Serrugiu (Cuglieri, OR) (Loria 1971; 1978: fig. 241; Demartis 1992).

Per quanto concerne la più diffusa varietà in marmo o calcite del tipo "a placca intera", determinante risulta il rinvenimento, nella struttura 27 dell'insediamento di Su Coddu, di una statuetta in marmo, in "stretta associazione" con ceramiche caratterizzate da una grande varietà di forme, riccamente ornate secondo le sintassi decorative più peculiari della cultura di Ozieri (Usai 1989: 246, fig. 2).

Un altro esemplare che denuncia l'inequivocabile appartenenza a questa cultura del tipo "a placca intera" è quello rinvenuto nella tomba VIII della necropoli a *domus de janas* di Puttu Codinu (Villanova Monteleone, SS) (Demartis 1991: figg. 36–37).

Rispetto alle statuette note della stessa classe, questo esemplare mostra alcune novità: la testa, generalmente compresa in un unico volume cilindrico che compendia anche il collo, è qui distinta e modellata in forma subtriangolare. Anche il viso è distinto dal collo, similmente alla statuetta fittile sopra descritta, ed ha gli occhi segnati da due cavità circolari; infine la nuca è smussata in una linea obliqua e accentuata da una leggera convessità. La ricerca veristica espressa in questi particolari, evidente anche nell'esemplare in terracotta anzidetto, prelude a quella ancora più marcata delle statuette "a placca traforata", facendo così riconoscere un ulteriore anello di congiunzione fra i due tipi distinti, ma strettamente concatenati.

L' attribuzione della statuetta di Villanova alla piena cultura di Ozieri si accorda anche con le caratteristiche dell'ipogeo che lo ha restituito. Questo, infatti, ha subito un'imponente ristrutturazione in un momento apogeico della cultura in argomento, nella quale sono inquadrabili anche i pochi frammenti ceramici rinvenuti. Con tale intervento, le pareti della tomba sono state arricchite dei motivi architettonici e delle rappresentazioni taurine a bassorilievo, secondo le sintassi che gli studi relativi a queste manifestazioni riferiscono, appunto, alla cultura di Ozieri (Tanda 1977).

Gli esempi appena citati rendono dunque non accettabile la recente proposta dell'attribuzione della comparsa del tipo in questione alla *facies* Sub-Ozieri (Santoni 1992a; Tykot 1994: 123); piuttosto non va esclusa la possibilità che le due espressioni, almeno per un certo periodo, possano aver convissuto sincronicamente, fino alla totale decadenza delle forme rigide e compatte delle statuette di tipo Senorbì, maturate ed espresse in quelle geometriche, ma più organiche della "placca traforata".

Tipo "a placca traforata"

Resta infine da esaminare quest'ultimo tipo, che nella seriazione evolutiva prospettata, veniva proposto come espressione di una fase molto evoluta della cultura di Ozieri, per continuare nel quadro allora poco chiaro di quelle di Filigosa e Abealzu (Antona 1980: 135–138).

Il rinvenimento delle statuette in contesti confusi e incerti, privi di associazioni (l'unica eccezione era costituita dall'anomala presenza dell'esemplare da Ponte Secco-SS, in un corredo funerario campaniforme), avevano consentito appena di constatare l'assenza del tipo in esame in situazioni che fossero caratterizzate dall'esclusiva presenza di materiali Ozieri. Al contrario, si era notata nei corredi tombali, seppure sconvolti, la costante frequenza di forme ceramiche a profilo carenato, lisce o prive di decorazione, abitualmente riferite ad ambito culturale Filigosa.

Ulteriori esemplari si sono aggiunti negli ultimi anni, rinvenuti nelle *domus de janas* di Ponte Secco (Sassari) e Su Crucifissu Mannu (Ferrarese Ceruti 1989: figg. 2 e 5), Littoslongos (Ossi, SS) (Moravetti 1989: fig. 4, tav. 1) e Serra Crabiles (Sennori, SS) (Foschi 1984: fig. 10). Non si è in grado di valutare il ritrovamento di quest'ultima località poiché i pochissimi frammenti pubblicati non ne consentono un'interpretazione che vada oltre una generica attribuzione alla cultura di Ozieri.

Relativamente alle situazioni prive di stratigrafia dei primi due siti citati, alla luce delle conoscenze recenti, i materiali pubblicati fanno registrare la presenza di forme ceramiche a profilo rigido, inornate, che sarebbero classificabili nella *facies* "Sub-Ozieri" o "Ozieri dipinto", recentemente evidenziata (Ugas 1989; Santoni 1992).

Sembra pertanto ancora plausibile l'attribuzione delle statuette in questione al quadro cronologico e culturale del Neolitico finale e dell'Eneolitico iniziale, quest'ultimo compreso, secondo le datazioni calibrate, entro il 2.700 a.C. (Tykot 1994).

Un'ultima considerazione riguarda i rapporti fra le statuette sarde e quelle egee, queste ultime da sempre indicate come prototipi dei quali gli esemplari sardi hanno spesso assunto valore di copia, tanto da essere enfaticamente detti "idoli cicladici". Al contrario, i confronti fra i diversi tipi continuano a far evidenziare tratti di similitudine, che pare di dover ricondurre solo al fatto formale della rappresentazione sintetica, più che all'imitazione pedissequa, quale spesso è stata proposta.

Tanto più questa considerazione appare valida, quanto più si continua a voler cogliere motivi di analogia fra espressioni artistiche improntate ad una ricerca di forme sintetiche, quale si coglie nelle statuette sarde e manifestazioni vicine all'astrazione (Antona 1980: 136, n. 63, ivi bibl.), quali quelle dell'idolo cicladico "a violino", tipo "Grotta-Pelos", cui più di frequente si fa riferimento per la "placca intera".

L'impostazione strutturale degli esemplari "a placca traforata" è stata invece accostata spesso a "prototipi Keros-Siros" (Castaldi 1991: 236–237), con i quali le statuette sarde condividono il gusto per la rappresentazione geometrica, ma non l'esigenza della minuziosa e realistica definizione dei tratti somatici, se non quella essenziale dell'indicazione delle mammelle.

Nelle somiglianze formali sembrerebbe di dover riconoscere piuttosto che la prova inconfutabile di "importazioni" in Sardegna di prototipi egei (peraltro finora mai rinvenuti), o di "copie" dei medesimi, l'esito di produzioni autoctone accomunate da una linea di gusto che predilige le forme geometriche. Le differenze concettuali insite nelle rispettive produzioni plastiche sono il segno della loro originalità.

È stato inoltre rilevato che i frequenti sfasamenti cronologici, riscontrabili fra le culture di appartenenza dei rispettivi tipi generalmente messi a confronto, fanno spesso constatare la maggiore arcaicità degli esemplari sardi rispetto a quelli egei chiamati in causa (Trump 1983: 138–139), almeno per l'inizio della produzione.

Le affinità più volte evidenziate tra materiali delle due aree (Lilliu 1988: 90 sgg.; ivi bibl.), a partire dal Neolitico medio, peraltro riscontrate non fra intere classi di oggetti, ma fra singoli elementi all'interno di queste ultime, e, per di più, in prodotti di particolare raffinatezza ed elevato valore artiginale, continuano a far persistere in molti l'esistenza di contatti dei quali non sono tuttavia chiari nè l'entità, nè i vettori.[1]

Ringraziamenti

Desidero ringraziare la Dott.ssa Fulvia Lo Schiavo e il Dott. Ermanno Arslan per avermi consentito lo studio delle statuette in questione. Sono inoltre riconoscente al Dott. Gian Mario Demartis, al quale si deve l'osservazione dei piccoli vaghi della coppetta di Dolianova.

Appendice

Una nuova statuetta è entrata, di recente, a far parte delle Civiche Raccolte Archeologiche e Numismatiche di Milano (Inv. A. 985.05.01). Si tratta di un esemplare "a placca traforata", realizzato in marmo bianco (Fig. 15.5).

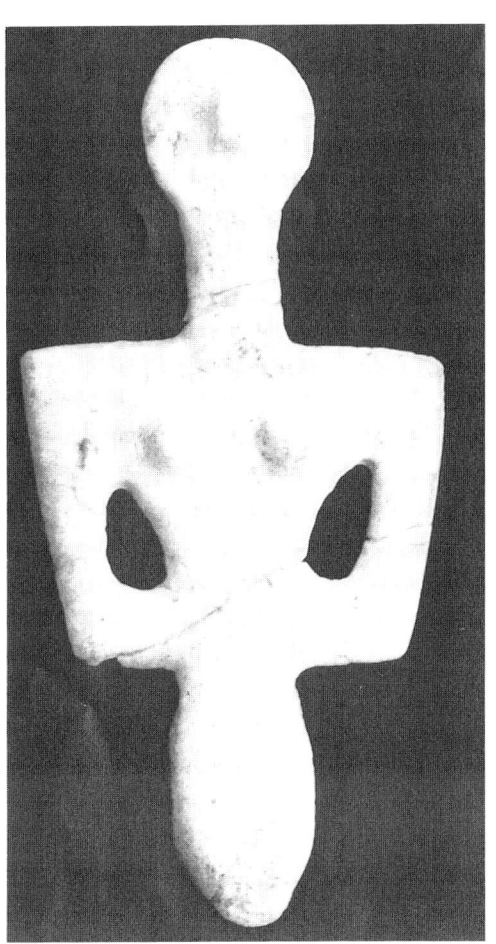

Fig. 15.5. Civiche Raccolte Archeologiche e Numismatiche di Milano: statuetta a placca traforata, da località ignota.

La sua altezza è di cm 14,8, la larghezza alle spalle cm 7,4, lo spessore massimo cm 1,3. La testa, a dischetto piatto, sviluppata su uno slanciato collo di sezione trasversale ellissoidale, presenta sul volto un pronunciato naso aquilino, che si diparte al di sotto della brevissima fronte e si sviluppa per tre quarti della lunghezza del volto.

Nella tipica placca trapezoidale, delimitata dalle larghe spalle rettilinee (cm 7,4) e dalle braccia piegate a squadra sulla vita, è ritagliato il busto triangolare, sul quale sono rappresentati i seni di forma troncoconica. Posteriormente, è presente un solco trasversale, quasi ad indicare una separazione di tipo organico fra le spalle ed il resto del busto. La parte inferiore del corpo è sintetizzata in un piccolo volume ovoidale, anteriormente piatto, posteriormente rigonfio.

La statuetta non si discosta, dunque, dalle caratteristiche canoniche del tipo cui appartiene, del quale si continua a confermare la notevole omogeneità formale. Anche la particolarità del solco sopra descritto richiama elementi simili rappresentati in altri esemplari, risultato di un probabile intento di creare un effetto per così dire naturalistico. Nella nota statuetta della tomba II di Monte d'Accoddi (Tanda 1976: tav. VIII) ad esempio, una scanalatura presente sulla schiena indica lo sviluppo della colonna vertebrale. Lo stesso elemento è espresso anche in un'altra statuetta dalla stessa necropoli (Tanda 1976: tav. IX, n. 187); su di essa è segnata anche una solcatura mediana che attraversa longitudinalmente il busto, segnando fra i due seni ben modellati, il solco sternale e prolungandosi ancora fino alla vita.

In un esemplare da Porto Ferro, invece, una decorazione a piccole tacche in rilievo, con effetto di banda tratteggiata, segue la larghezza delle spalle e le braccia fino ai gomiti. Tale elemento, che sembrerebbe riferirsi a particolari dell'abbigliamento, richiama anche la campitura delle spalle e delle braccia di alcune figurine incise su un frammento ceramico da Sa 'Ucca de Su Tintirriolu (Loria 1978: fig. 26:6), di cultura Ozieri. Quest'ultimo riferimento è stato talvolta chiamato in causa per attribuire alla stessa cultura l'intera produzione delle statuette traforate (cfr. da ultimo Moravetti 1989: 91).

Per quanto concerne la piccola scultura di Milano, non si conosce alcun dato relativo al rinvenimento, nè al luogo di provenienza. Resta, pertanto, affidato al solo esame stilistico la sua attribuzione al quadro culturale del Neolitico finale – Eneolitico iniziale, di cui si è detto più sopra.

Nota

1. Nelle more della pubblicazione dei presenti Atti, un interessantissimo e ben documentato studio (Usai 1996), ricco di un notevole apparato bibliografico, ha posto in discussione i rapporti fra culture sarde ed egee. Il divario cronologico che emerge dall'analisi e dal confronto di date radiocarboniche convenzionali della Sardegna e dell'Egeo, insieme alle diversità di carattere formale e strutturale che caratterizzano i fenomeni culturali delle due aree, portano ineluttabilmente l'Autore ad escludere gli stretti rapporti di relazione sostenuti dalla dottrina tradizionale (di parere opposto, Santoni 1997). Dalla revisione e confutazione delle teorie diffusionistiche e soprattutto della stretta connessione fra le culture egee e quelle sarde neolitiche, scaturisce il riconoscimento della capacità di sviluppi innovativi autonomi di queste ultime. Le diverse tendenze artistiche compositive, poste in evidenza come fatti autoctoni nella marcata fisionomia culturale della Sardegna del Neolitico medio e recente (Antona 1980: 126, 134 sgg., 138), certamente arricchita degli impulsi derivanti dai rapporti transmarini, connessi al commercio dell'ossidiana e della selce, appaiono consone ad una simile ipotesi.

Bibliografia

Antona Ruju, A. 1980. Appunti per una seriazione evolutiva delle statuette femminili della Sardegna prenuragica. In *Atti della XXII Riunione Scientifica dell'Istituto Italiano di Preistoria e Prostoria, 'Sardegna Centro-Settentrionale', 21–27 ottobre 1978*, 115–139. Istituto Italiano di Preistoria e Protostoria, Firenze.

Antona, A. 1995. Porto Rotondo (Olbia). *Bollettino di Archeologia*.

Atzeni, E. 1976. Nuovi idoli della Sardegna prenuragica. *Studi Sardi* 22: 1–51.

Atzeni, E. 1978. La Dea Madre nelle culture prenuragiche. *Studi Sardi* 24: 1–69.

Atzeni, E. 1985. Tombe eneolitiche nel Cagliaritano. In *Studi in onore di Giovanni Lilliu per il suo settantesimo compleanno*, 11–49. Annali della Facoltà di Lettere, Cagliari.

Atzeni, E. & Santoni, V. 1989. L'Età Prenuragica. Il Neolitico. L'Eneolitico. In *Il Museo Archeologico Nazionale di Cagliari*, 31–42. Banco di Sardegna, Sassari.

Biagi, P. 1980. Caverna sepolcrale della cultura di Bonuighinu. Nota preliminare. In *Atti della XXII Riunione Scientifica dell'Istituto Italiano di Preistoria e Prostoria, 'Sardegna Centro-Settentrionale', 21–27 ottobre 1978*, 95 sgg. Istituto Italiano di Preistoria e Protostoria, Firenze.

Castaldi, E. 1991. "Idoletti sardi" quale prova di contatti Est-Ovest. *Origini* 15: 231–239.

Demartis, G.M. 1991. *La necropoli di Puttu Codinu*. Sardegna Archeologica, Guide e Itinerari 13. Carlo Delfino, Sassari.

Demartis, G. M. 1992. Un frammento fittile con figurette umane danzanti da Monte Forte. *Nuovo Bullettino Archeologico Sardo* 4:7–15.

Fadda, M.A. 1991. *Il Museo speleo-archeologico di Nuoro*. Sardegna Archeologica, Guide e Itinerari 17. Carlo Delfino, Sassari.

Ferrarese Ceruti, M.L. 1989. La necropoli di Su Crucifissu Mannu – Porto Torres e di Ponte Secco – Sassari. In Campus, L.D. (a cura di), *La Cultura di Ozieri. Problematiche e nuove acquisizioni*, 37–47. Il Torchietto, Ozieri.

Ferrarese Ceruti, M.L. 1992. Statuine di Dea Madre da Torralba e Ozieri (Sassari). In *Sardigna Antiqua. Studi in onore di Pietro Meloni*, 63 -74. Cagliari.

Ferrarese Ceruti, M.L. 1995. Nuovi elementi dalla grotta funeraria di Tanì (Carbonia). In Santoni, V. (a cura di), *Carbonia e il Sulcis. Archeologia e territorio*, 97–115. S'Alvure, Oristano.

Foschi, A. 1984. I risultati degli scavi 1981 nella necropoli prenuragica di Serra Crabiles, Sennori (Sassari). In Waldren, W.H., Chapman, R.W., Lewthwaite, J.G. & Kennard, R.-C. (eds.), *The Deya Conference of Prehistory: Early Settlement in the Western Mediterranean Islands and their Periferal Areas*. BAR International Series 229: 533–541. British Archaeological Reports, Oxford.

Graziosi P. 1976. *L'arte preistorica in Italia*. Firenze.

Lanfranchi, F. de & Weiss, M.C. 1973. *La civilisation des Corses. Les origines*. Ajaccio.

Lanfranchi, F. de & Weiss, M.C. 1994. *Arts et Croyances. Pratiques funéraires et symboliques des populations préhistoriques corses*. Ajaccio.

Lilliu, G. 1965. *La civiltà dei Sardi. Dal Neolitico all'età dei nuraghi*. E.R.I., Torino.

Lilliu, G. 1988. *La civiltà dei Sardi. Dal Paleolitico all'età dei nuraghi*. Terza edizione. E.R.I., Torino.

Lo Schiavo, F. 1986. La Preistoria. In *Il Museo Sanna in Sassari*, 19–62. Banco di Sardegna, Sassari.

Lo Schiavo, F. & Antona, A. 1989. Oredda – Sassari. La domus delle doppie spirali. In Campus, L.D. (a cura di), *La Cultura di Ozieri. Problematiche e nuove acquisizioni*, 49–74. Il Torchietto, Ozieri.

Loria, R. 1971. Figurette schematiche femminili nella ceramica eneolitica della Sardegna. *Rivista di Scienze Preistoriche* 26: 179–202.

Loria, R. & Trump, D.H. 1978. Le scoperte a "Sa 'Ucca de Su Tintirriolu" e il Neolitico Sardo. *Monumenti Antichi Lincei*, serie Miscellanea, 2.

Moravetti, A. 1989. La tomba ipogeica di Littoslongos – Ossi. In Campus, L.D. (a cura di), *La Cultura di Ozieri. Problematiche e nuove acquisizioni*, 83–102. Il Torchietto, Ozieri.

Puglisi, S.M. & Castaldi, E. 1965. Aspetti dell'accantonamento culturale nella Gallura preistorica e protostorica. *Studi Sardi* 19: 59–148.

Renfrew, C. 1972. *The Emergence of Civilisation. The Cyclades and the Aegean in the Third Millenium B.C*. Methuen, London.

Santoni, V. 1982a. Cabras-Cuccuru S'Arriu. Nota preliminare di scavo (1978, 1979, 1980). *Rivista di Studi Fenici* 10: 103–110.

Santoni, V. 1982b. Il mondo del sacro in età neolitica. *Le Scienze* ottobre: 70–80.

Santoni, V. 1989. Cuccuru S'Arriu – Cabras. Il sito di cultura san Michele di Ozieri. Dati preliminari. In Campus, L.D. (a cura di), *La Cultura di Ozieri. Problematiche e nuove acquisizioni*, 169–200. Il Torchietto, Ozieri.

Santoni, V. 1992. Cuccuru S'Arriu (Cabras). L'orizzonte eneolitico sub-Ozieri. In Tykot, R.H. & Andrews, T.K. (eds.), *Sardinia in the Mediterranean. A Footprint in the Sea. Studies in Sardinian Archaeology Presented to Miriam S. Balmuth*. Monographs in Mediterranean Archaeology 3: 157–174. Sheffield Academic Press.

Santoni, V. 1995. Il sito preistorico di Cuccuru S'Arriu (Cabras, Oristano). In Moravetti, A. & Tozzi, C. (a cura di), *Sardegna. Guide Archeologiche: Preistoria e Protostoria in Italia* 2: 130–138. A.B.A.C.O., Forlì.

Santoni, V. 1997. In Santoni, V., Bacco, G., Sabatini, D., L'orizzonte Neolitico Superiore di Cuccuru s'Arriu di Cabras. Le sacche C.S.A. nn. 377/1979 e n. 2/1989. In Campus, L. (a cura di), *La Cultura di Ozieri, La Sardegna e il Mediterraneo nel IV e III Millennio a.C.*, 227–295. Il Torchietto, Ozieri.

Tanda, G. 1977. *Arte Preistorica in Sardegna*. Quaderni della Soprintendenza ai Beni Archeologici per le Provincie di Sassari e Nuoro 5. Dessì, Sassari.

Taramelli, A. 1909. Nuovi scavi nella necropoli a grotte artificiali di Anghelu Ruju. *Monumenti Antichi Lincei* 19: 397–540.

Trump, D.H. 1983. *La Grotta di Filiestru a Mara (SS)*. Quaderni della Soprintendenza ai Beni Archeologici per le Provincie di Sassari e Nuoro 13. Dessì, Sassari.

Tykot, R.H. 1994. Radiocarbon dating and absolute chronology in Sardinia and Corsica. In Skeates, R. & Whitehouse, R. (eds.), *Radiocarbon Dating and Italian Prehistory*. Archaeological Monographs of the British School at Rome 8 and Accordia Specialist Studies on Italy 3, 115–145. Accordia Research Centre, London.

Ugas, G., Lai, G. & Usai, L. 1989. L'insediamento prenuragico di su Coddu (Selargius-Cagliari). Notizia preliminare sulle campagne di scavo 1981–1984. *Nuovo Bullettino Archeologico Sardo* 2: 7–38.

Ugas, G. 1990. *La tomba dei guerrieri di Decimoputzu*. Norax 1. Edizioni Della Torre, Cagliari.

Usai, A. 1996. Considerazioni sulle relazioni tra la Sardegna e l'Egeo durante il Neolitico e il Calcolitico. *Studi Sardi* 30 (1992–93): 329–439.

Usai, L. 1989. La struttura 27. In Nuovi dati sull'insediamento di Su Coddu (Selargius). In Campus, L.D. (a cura di), *La cultura di Ozieri. Problematiche e nuove acquisizioni*, 245–247. Il Torchietto, Ozieri.

Zervos, C. 1954. *La civilisation de la Sardaigne du début de l'éneolithique à la fin de la periode nouragique*. Paris.

Zervos, C. 1957. *L'art des Cyclades du dèbut à la fin de l'âge du Bronze 2500 – 1100 avant de notre ére*. Paris.

16. Cronologia dell'arte delle *domus de janas*

Giuseppa Tanda

Gli studi e le scoperte effettuate negli ultimi cinque anni hanno reso opportuna una nuova verifica della cronologia proposta nel 1989 in occasione della XXVI Riunione Scientifica "L'arte in Italia dal Paleolitico all'Età del Bronzo" (Tanda 1992: 488, fig. 4). Il riesame è stato fatto sulle 148 *domus de janas* ornate di figurazioni scolpite, incise e dipinte al tempo conosciute. In questi ipogei i motivi scolpiti (32%) prevalgono su quelli dipinti (27%) e su quelli incisi (11%); le tecniche associate, inoltre, coesistono in un gruppo di tombe pari al 30% dell'intero numero delle *domus de janas* (Fig. 16.1).

Quanto alla tipologia morfologica delle figurazioni, riconosciuta all'interno delle tecniche di esecuzione, essa appare assai ricca e varia, come si può agevolmente constatare nelle tavole già note (Tanda 1984; 1985, figg. 4–6; 1992), relative ai motivi scolpiti ed incisi, riproposte in questa sede (Figg. 16.2–16.4). Gli elementi utili per gli obiettivi programmati da questo congresso sono di varia provenienza e, in sintesi, comprendono (Fig. 16.5):

1. Dati desunti dallo studio tipologico degli ipogei (tecnica di scavo, fenomeni di costruzione per fasi o di ristrutturazione tombale, individuazione di moduli di architettura domestica, rapporti fra ipogei e strutture architettoniche in elevazione);
2. Elementi di cronologia relativa dedotti dalle sovrapposizioni di tecniche di esecuzione e di motivi figurativi;
3. I risultati delle analisi chimico-fisiche condotti sulle patine e sui pigmenti di ventidue campioni di *domus de janas* dipinte;
4. I materiali degli scavi;
5. Le analogie individuabili tra motivi figurativi ipogeici e figurazioni materiali;
6. I confronti con l'arte figurativa europea e mediterranea occidentale in particolare.

Dati desunti dallo studio tipologico degli ipogei

L'osservazione attenta delle tracce ancora visibili lasciate dagli strumenti di esecuzione, siano essi a percussione o ad abrasione, in parte già noti, come i martelli e i picconi (strumenti a percussione) o ricostruibili come gli scalpelli e le "gradine" (strumenti ad abrasione) rende possibile la ricostruzione nelle grandi linee delle fasi di scavo e di ristrutturazione delle *domus de janas*. Purtroppo non sempre si riesce ad individuare ed apprezzare tali tracce: ciò si verifica soprattutto nelle tombe scavate nel calcare, per effetto dei naturali processi di degrado. Se a ciò si aggiunge la consuetudine, ormai accertata, dell'uso generalizzato di riutilizzare nei millenni le *domus de janas*, con la conseguente asportazione e/o mescolamento dei resti funerari (ossei umani e di corredo) e successivo accantonamento all'interno dei sepolcri, in cellette o in fosse scavate appositamente (Monte d'Accoddi, domus de janas II: Tanda 1976: 35–50) oppure nel corridoio d'ingresso o dromos, si possono recepire il livello ed il tipo di difficoltà nel definire la cronologia dell'arte ipogeica. In quest'ottica, infatti, il solo ritrovamento di materiali in *domus de janas* di per sè non è un sicuro indicatore di cronologia. L'esito positivo di studi condotti secondo un approccio tecnico può costituire, quindi, un contributo apprezzabile e significativo. A questo proposito (e per esemplificare) si ricordano la Tomba dei Vasi Tetrapodi di Alghero, la Tomba Maggiore di Ossi, la tomba di Oredda 1 a Sassari.

Nella domus di Alghero è documentata la ristrutturazione della cella principale, in seguito alla quale venne scolpito sopra il portello d'ingresso nella cella *l* un

---

Giuseppa Tanda, Dipartimento di Studi Classici ed Antichità, Università di Sassari, Piazza Conte di Moriana 8, 07100 Sassari, Sardegna, Italia

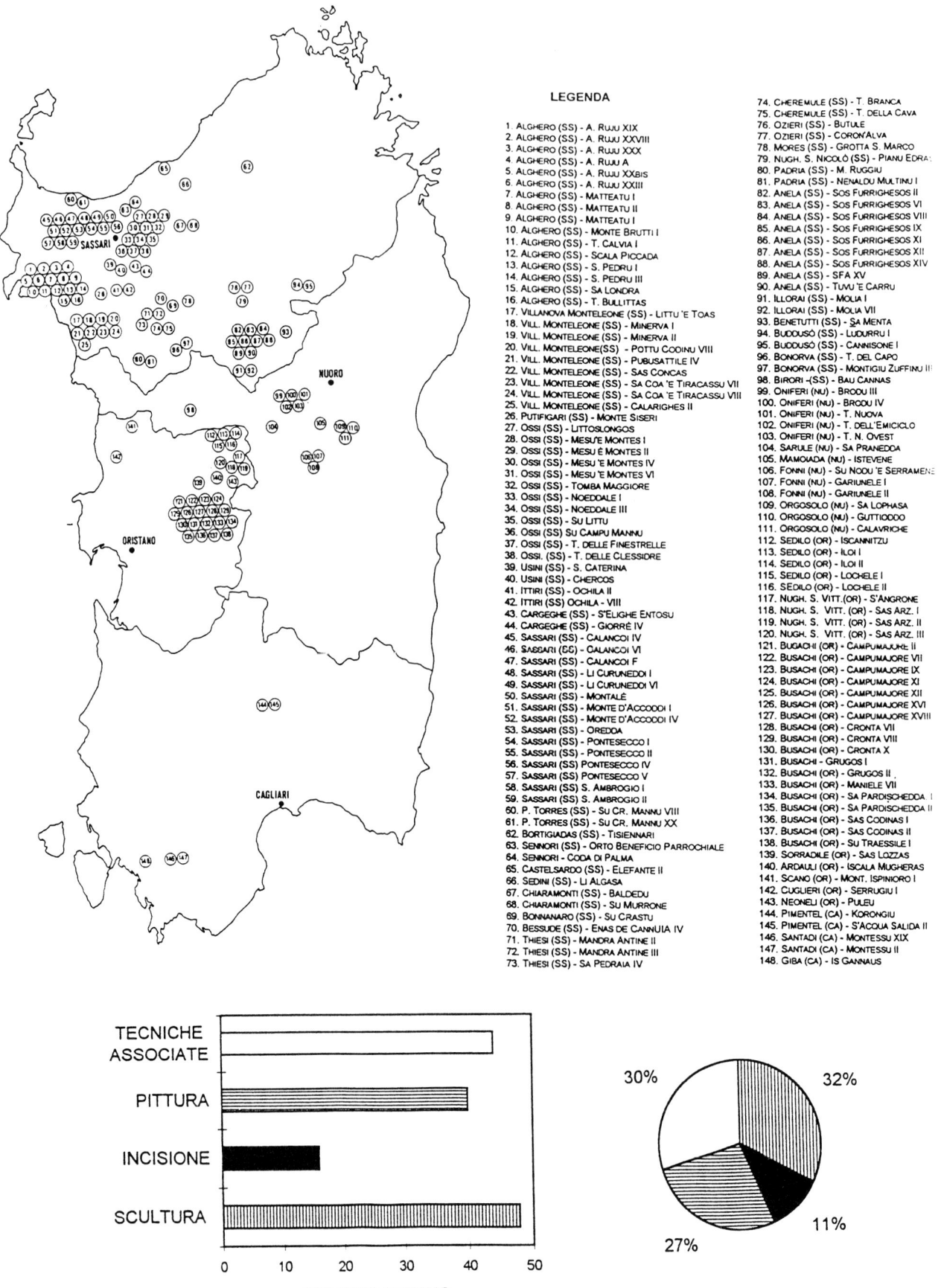

Fig. 16.1. Carta di diffusione delle domus de janas decorate. Elaborazione dei dati relativi alle tecniche decorative.

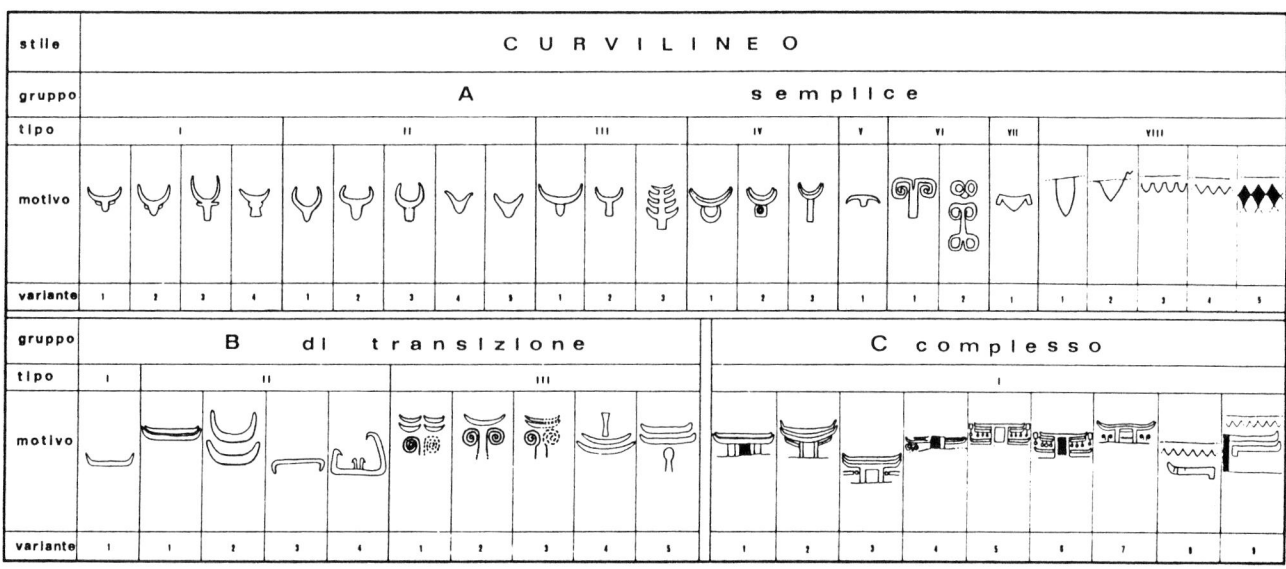

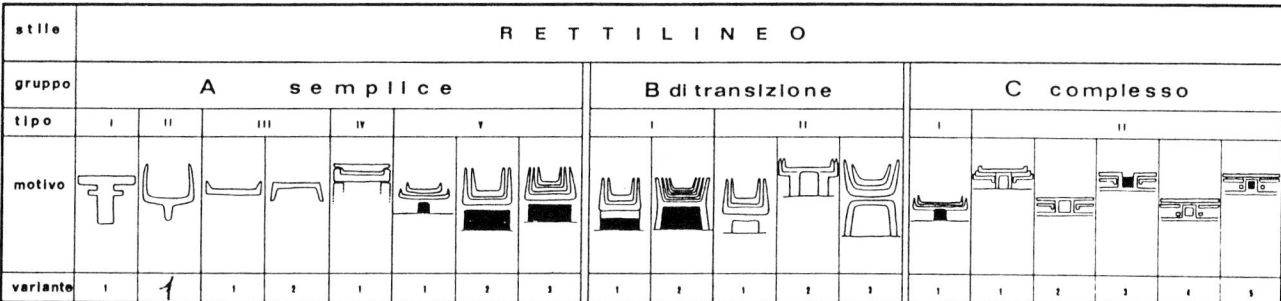

Fig. 16.2. Tipologia delle figurazioni scolpite nelle domus de janas.

duplice motivo di corna di stile rettilineo (Contu 1964: 24–25). É presumibile che tale ristrutturazione sia posteriore alla cultura di Ozieri (attestata da alcuni frammenti), contemporanea allo strato basale VI-VII b, attribuito alla cultura di Filigosa, comunque anteriore alla cultura di Bonnanaro (Bronzo Antico), cui vengono riferiti i corredi della cella *l*.

La Tomba Maggiore, a sua volta, risulta essere stata eseguita in almeno tre fasi (Fig. 16.6), di cui una, la seconda, di ristrutturazione (Tanda 1985: 78–81). Nella prima venne scavato il nucleo principale dell'ipogeo, costituito dall'anticella e dalla cella successiva, che, sulla parete fondale, mostrava una falsa porta; nella seconda vennero ristrutturati questi due ambienti, con ampliamento del secondo (del quale restarono la falsa porta ed una porzione di parete, la cui esistenza è oggi suggerita dall'unico pilastro presente), vennero istoriate le pareti ed eseguite le ale Ovest e Nord-Est; nella terza fu escavata l'ala Est (celle *s-u*). Nella tomba 1 di Oredda, d'altra parte (Tanda 1983: 264, denominata "Bancali-Sassari"; 1985, fig. 4, A VI, 2 dello stile curvilineo, pp. 24, 40–42; Antona Ruju & Lo Schiavo 1989: 49 e sgg.), è testimoniata una Fase di ristrutturazione indiziata dall'unico pilastro centrale, dall'accentuata concavità della parete istoriata e, soprattutto, dal differente grado di rifinitura della parete Sud della cella *b*.

Lo studio delle tipologie planimetriche riconosciute secondo un approccio tecnico può fornire utili indicazioni cronologiche anche quando porti all'individuazione di moduli di architettura domestica oppure quando consenta di stabilire analogie di base (sostanziali) tra ipogei e strutture architettoniche in elevazione. Il modulo architettonico costituito da un ambiente semicircolare seguito da un vano quadrangolare, individuabile negli ipogei (Fig. 16.7), è attribuibile ad un arco compreso tra la cultura Ozieri, seguendo la cronologia del Villaggio di Serra Linta a Sedilo (Fig. 16.8) (Tanda 1992: 80–83, figg. 8–13) e la cultura di Filigosa, come suggerisce la Tomba dei Vasi Tetrapodi (Contu 1964: 189–190). Un'altra analogia individuata tra gli ipogei a sviluppo longitudinale come Filigosa (Foschi 1986: 15) o Brodu IV-Oniferi (Tanda 1985: 164) e la Tomba V di Pranu Muttedddu ("puro contesto Ozieri": Atzeni 1988: Fig. 5,2), nella quale le cellette a sviluppo longitudinale sono costruite in elevazione (Fig. 16.9), pone nello stesso orizzonte cronologico (tra Ozieri e Filigosa) il motivo corniforme di Brodu IV.

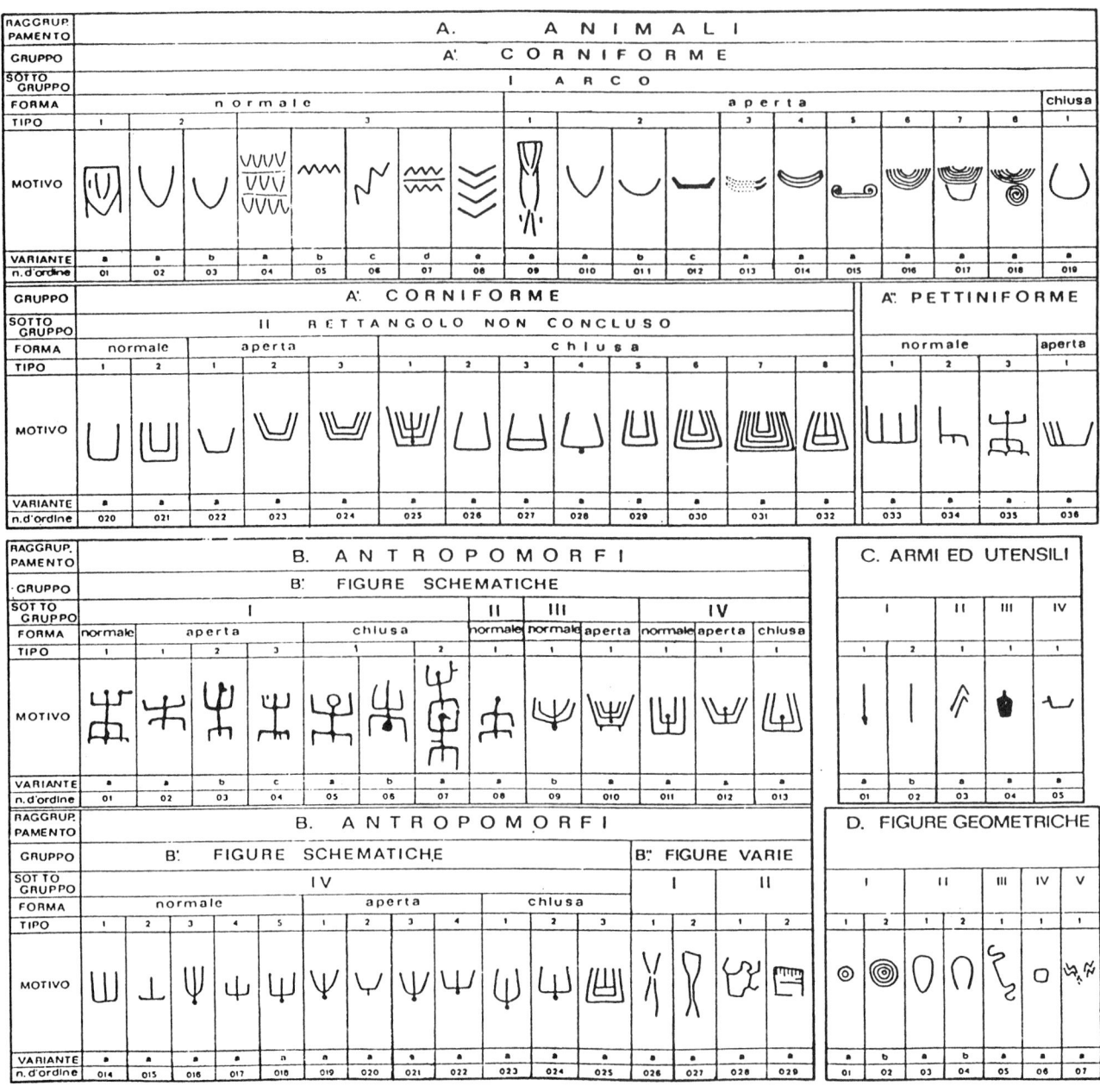

Fig. 16.3. Tipologia delle figurazioni incise "a martellina".

Elementi di cronologia relativa dedotti dalle sovrapposizioni di tecniche di esecuzione e di motivi figurativi

Una sicura cronologia relativa, in linea con il criterio di datazione relativa formulato dal Breuil per l'Arte, viene suggerita dalle sovrapposizioni di tecniche e di motivi figurativi osservata nella necropoli di Sos Furrighesos, ad Anela. Tale sequenza è documentata in dieci sovrapposizioni di motivi osservate nelle tombe VIII, IX e XI (Tanda 1984: 107 sgg.) (Fig. 16.10). I rapporti di anteriorità o recenziorità desunti sono stati estesi ai motivi che hanno la medesima sezione di solco, assunta come parametro distintivo delle fasi di istoriazione delle tombe, secondo un approccio esclusivamente tecnico. Nella tomba VIII (Fase II di Sos Furrighesos), ad esempio, il motivo centrale n. 1, costituito da una falsa porta a specchio ribassato sormontata da un duplice motivo corniforme a basso rilievo (Fig. 16.11,a), appare sottoposto ai motivi a martellina nn. 6 a-d (sezione b, semiellissoidale: Fase III; Tanda 1984: 109-110) (Fig. 16.11,b).

Altre sovrapposizioni interessanti (Fig. 16.10) sono: il motivo n. 82 (sezione d o "festonata", Fase VI) che si sovrappone al motivo n. 81, in tecnica lineare; il n. 99 (tecnica *a polissoir*, Fase VII) al n. 100 (sezione a, trapezoidale, Fase V); il motivo n. 4 (sezione a, trapezoidale, Fase V) al motivo n. 3 (sezione b,

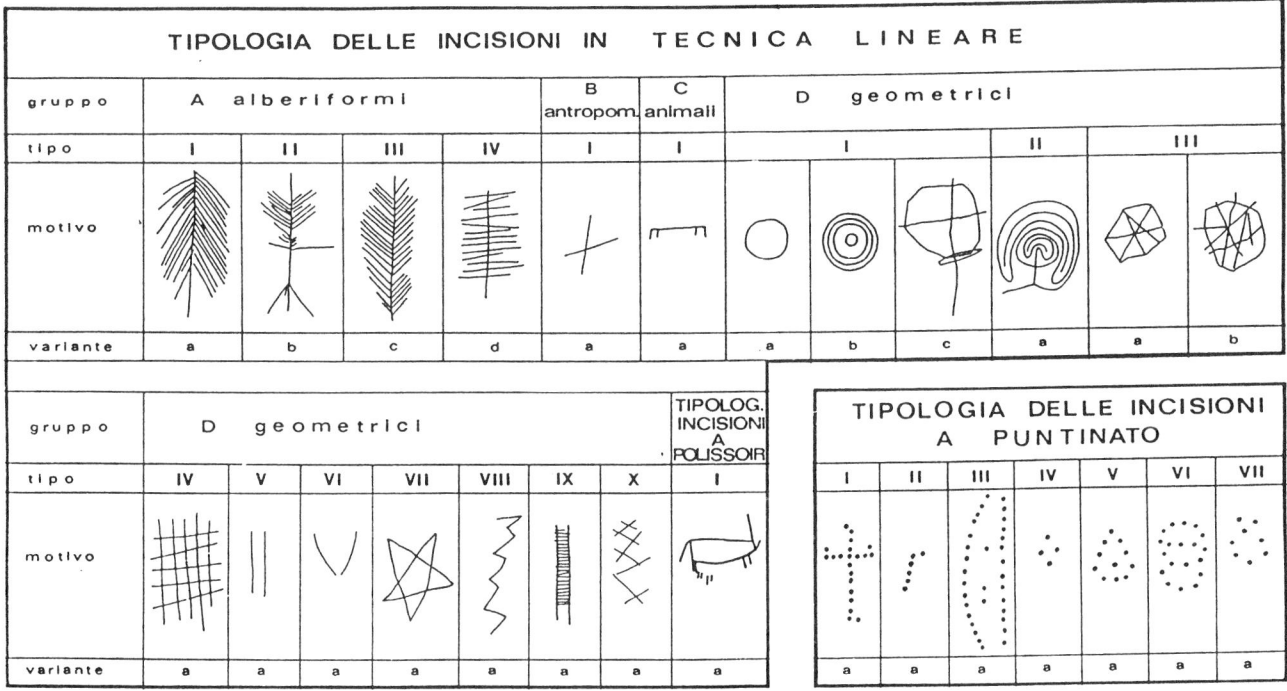

Fig. 16.4. Tipologia dei motivi incisi in tecnica lineare, "a puntinato", "a polissoir".

semiellissoidale, Fase III); il motivo n. 32 (sezione c, emisferica, Fase IV) allo stipite-lesena d'ingresso nella cella C della tomba VIII; il n. 85 (sezione d, festonata, Fase VI) al n. 86 (sezione a, trapezoidale, Fase V); il n. 24 (sezione d, festonata, Fase VI) alla falsa porta sottostante il motivo 1 (Fase II); il n. 7a (sezione b, semiellissoidale, Fase III) alla coppella n. 13.

Altre sovrapposizioni si osservano nella tomba XI (Figg. 16.12–16.14): il pigmento color rosso copre il motivo n. 135 (tecnica lineare); i motivi nn. 132 (sezione a, trapezoidale, Fase V) e 133–134 (sezione c, emisferica, Fase IV) si sovrappongono al motivo n. 135 (tecnica lineare).

Da questi elementi si deduce la seguente stratigrafia o cronologia relativa: bassorilievo, coppelle, pittura rossa, incisioni in tecnica lineare (Fase II); sezione b, semiellissoidale (Fase III); sezione c, emisferica (Fase IV); sezione a, trapezoidale (Fase V); sezione d, festonata (Fase VI); tecniche a *polissoir*, puntinato, lineare.

Appare evidente che: le incisioni a martellina sono più recenti della scultura e della pittura; alcune incisioni lineari sono molto antiche (Fase II), mentre altre, sulla base di analogie tipologiche, sono d'Età romano-altomedievale; il motivo a *polissoir* è più recente della Fase V e, per ragioni tipologiche, della Fase VI.

La sequenza cronologica di Sos Furrighesos, correlata con i risultati ottenuti negli altri settori dell'indagine, viene estesa all'intero fenomeno artistico ipogeico, come verrà puntualizzato a conclusione dell'intervento.

I risultati delle analisi chimico-fisiche condotti sulle patine e sui pigmenti di 22 campioni di *domus de janas* dipinte

Purtroppo questa parte della ricerca non è ancora conclusa. Per quel che concerne le analisi mineralogiche e spettrografiche, i risultati raggiunti sui campioni d'intonaco dipinto di Molia, tomba I (Illorai) danno informazioni interessanti ed utili per la determinazione dei pigmenti e per la ricostruzione dei metodi tecnologici di esecuzione degli intonaci e delle pitture (Cariati *et al.* 1981: 291–300). Restano irrisolti i problemi del legante utilizzato per amalgamare l'ocra rossa e della datazione, secondo le nuove metodologie, dei pigmenti stessi.

I materiali degli scavi

Sul valore dei materiali restituiti dagli scavi pesano le osservazioni fatte a proposito dell'eventualità o dell'accertato verificarsi di fenomeni di ristrutturazione architettonica e di riutilizzo delle *domus de janas*. Tracce di ristrutturazione sono state osservate da Vari Autori in almeno 16 tombe, come, ad esempio, ad Alghero, Anghelu Ruju XX bis e S. Pedru 1 (Tanda 1984: 57–59; 1985: 19, 160; 1977a: 23–24; Contu 1964: 74 sgg.), a Villanova Monteleone, Pottu Codinu VIII (Demartis 1991a: 15), a Sassari, Oredda 1 (Antona Ruju & Lo Schiavo 1989: 49–74), ad Ossi, Tomba Maggiore (Tanda 1985: 78–81) e Noeddale I, a Porto Torres, Su Crucifissu Mannu, tombe VIII e XXI (Ferrarese Ceruti 1989: 39–40), ad Illorai,

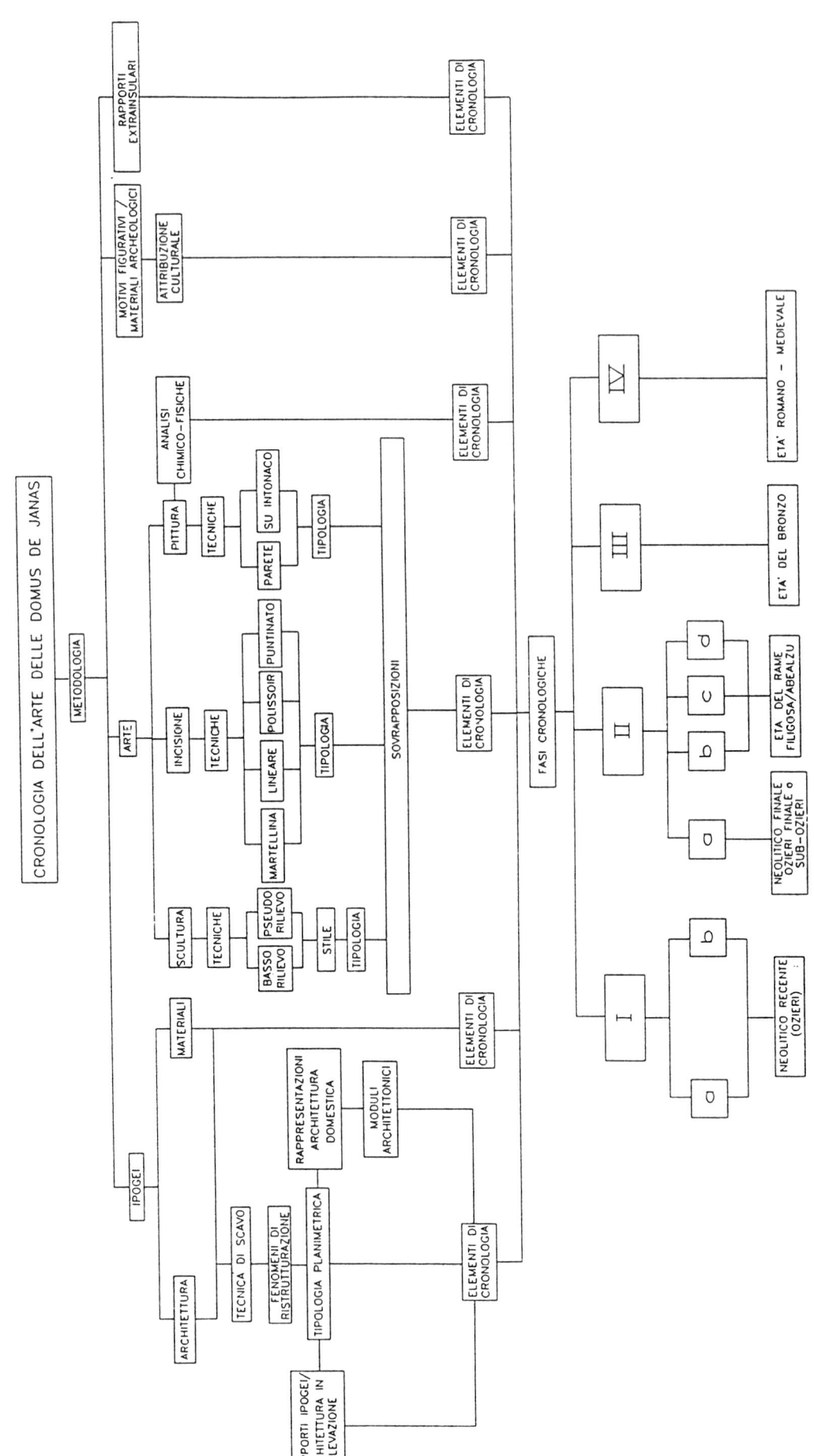

Fig. 16.5. *Percorso metodologico seguito per la formulazione dell'ipotesi di cronologia dell'arte delle domus de janas.*

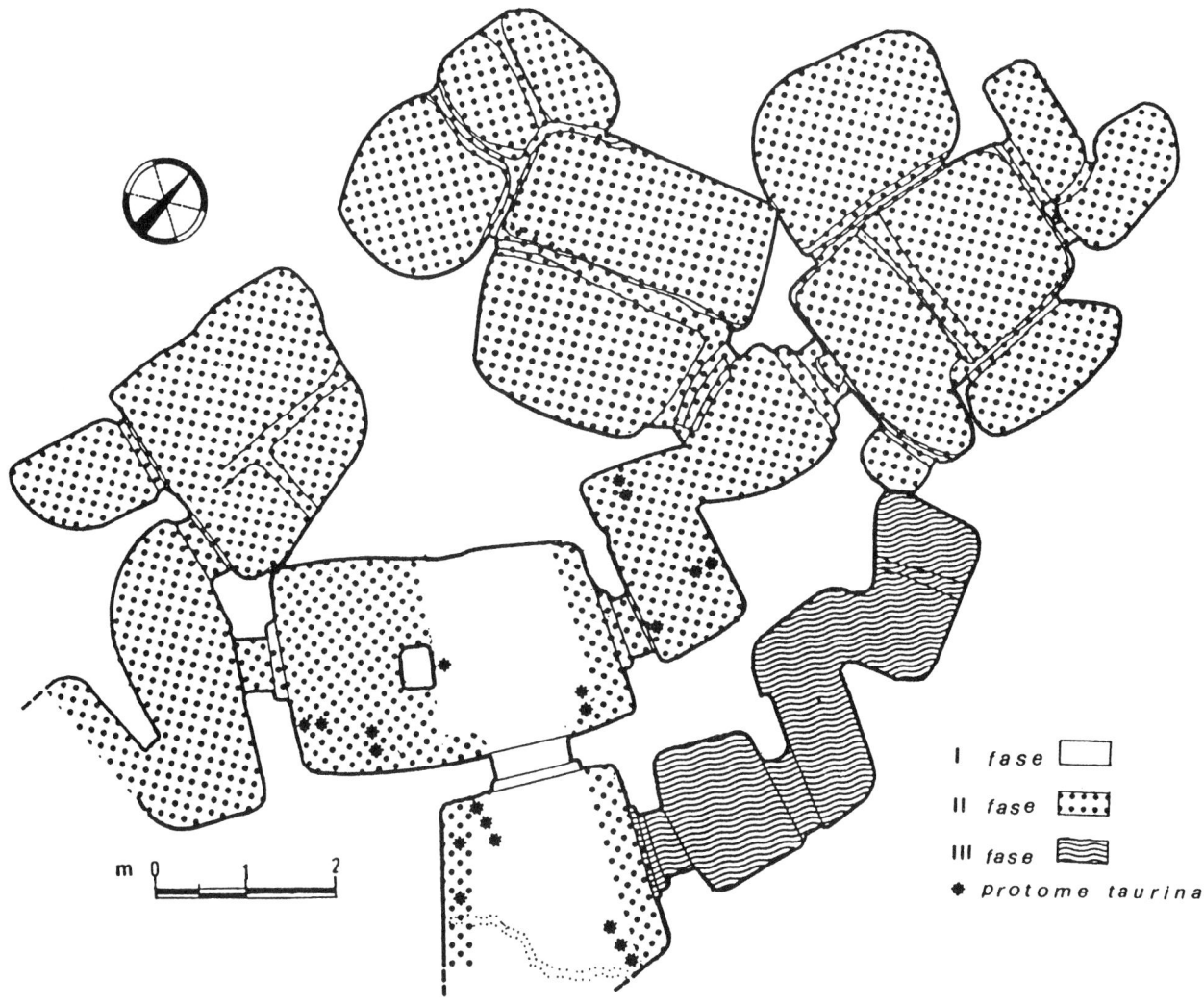

Fig. 16.6. Ipotesi di ristrutturazione della Tomba Maggiore (Ossi).

Molia 1 e 7 (Tanda 1980), a Bonorva, Tomba del Capo (Tanda 1984: 57–58), ad Oniferi, Tomba dell'Emiciclo (Contu 1965: 69 sgg.), a Sedilo, Iloi II, a Pimentel, S'Acqua Salida 1 (Usai 1984). É attualmente in corso una verifica personale sulla tecnica di scavo dell'intero gruppo di *domus de janas*, tra cui le tombe di Putifigari-Monte Siseri (Demartis 1991) ed Ossi-Littoslongos (Moravetti 1989).

Cinquantuno tombe (34%) su 149 sono state esplorate scientificamente. Sedici di esse (31,3 %), Ossi-Su Littu (Tanda 1983: 269, fig. 103,a; Ferrarese Ceruti 1992), Sassari-Li Curuneddi I e VI (Contu 1962), Pontesecco I e II (Contu 1955: 21–80), Bortigiadas-Tisiennari (Tanda 1977b), Bessude-Enas de Cannuia (Contu 1964 a: 233 sgg.), Cheremule-Tomba Branca e Tomba della Cava (Contu 1965: 69 sgg.), Ozieri-Butule (Galli 1982: 267–276) e Coron'Alva (Basoli 1989: 117 sgg., fig. 2), Bonorva-Tomba del Capo (Taramelli 1919: 842–843; 844 sgg.), Oniferi-Tomba dell'Emiciclo e Tomba Nuova Ovest (Contu 1965), Pimentel-Korongiu (Atzeni 1962:

189 sgg.) e S'Acqua Salida (Usai 1984) sono risultate prive di sedimenti antropici, evidentemente svuotate da tempo; otto (15,7%), non sono state pubblicate in maniera esaustiva (Alghero-S. Pedru III, Ossi-Tomba delle Clessidre, Porto Torres-Su Crucifissu Mannu VIII e XXI, Oniferi-Tomba Nuova, Santadi-Montessu II e XIX, Giba-Is Gannaus); le rimanenti ventisette (53%), hanno restituito materiali di varia pertinenza, come si può agevolmente constatare nella Figura 16.15 (Culture di Ozieri, di Filigosa e/o Abealzu, di Monte Claro, di Bonnanaro, del Vaso Campaniforme, della civiltà nuragica, d'età punica, romana, altomedievale, età storica recente).

Correlando i materiali con le figurazioni corniformi scolpite dello stile curvilineo e delle relative categorie distintive (semplici, di transizione e complesse) si osserva che la cultura Ozieri è presente come cultura più antica in tutti gli ipogei, fatta eccezione della tomba di Montalè (ceramica Monte Claro), di Mandra Antine III (lame e punte di freccia dell'Età del Rame) e di Mesu

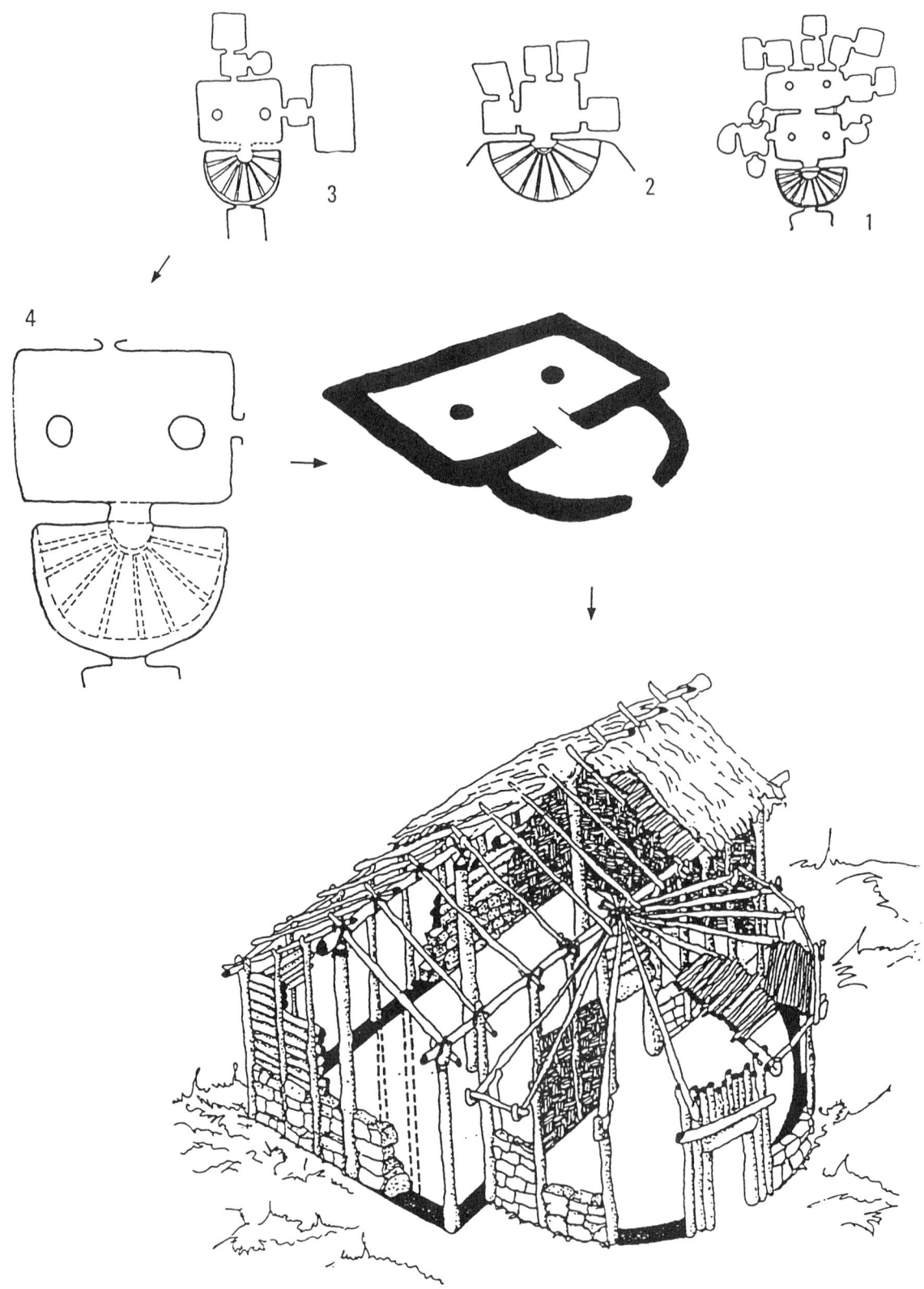

Fig. 16.7. Ipotesi di ricostruzione di un modulo abitativo del Neolitico recente-Età del Rame, utilizzando elementi architettonici rappresentati nelle domus de janas.

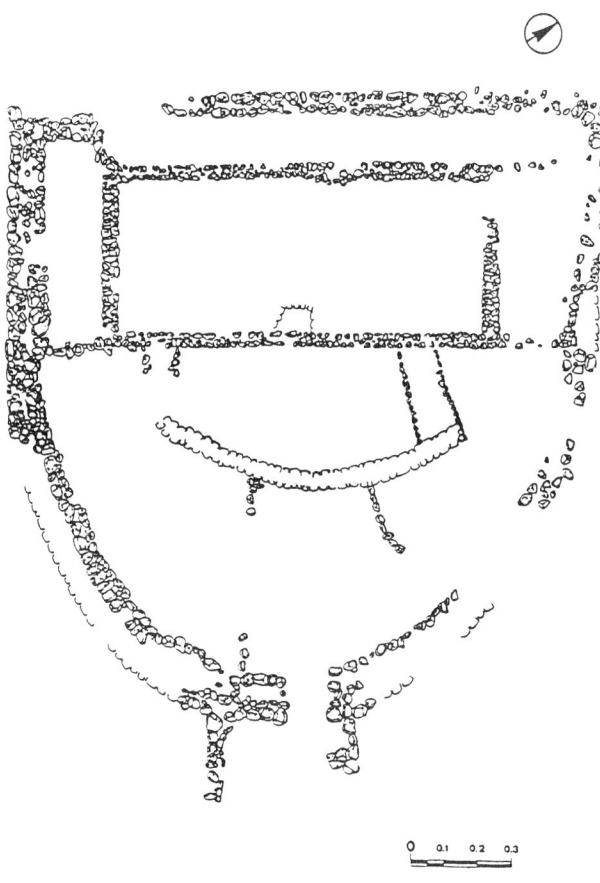

Fig. 16.8. Villaggio preistorico di Serra Linta (Sedilo). Capanna 1: uno dei moduli imitati nelle domus de janas.

'e Montes II (cultura di Filigosa). Si tenga, però, presente che la prima tomba è risultata violata. Si sottolinea, inoltre, che in alcuni ipogei decorati con figurazioni complesse sono documentate tracce sicure di ristrutturazione architettonica (tombe di Pottu Codinu VIII, di Oredda II e di Mesu 'e Montes II) oppure probabili (M. Siseri). Pertanto la cronologia dei materiali archeologici più antichi non può essere attribuita con certezza alle figurazioni scolpite, in quanto non è sicuro che queste possano essere attribute al primo e più antico impianto delle *domus de janas*, datato dalle ceramiche Ozieri.

Quanto ai motivi di stile rettilineo, immagini delle ceramiche Ozieri sono presenti sul pilastro di un ipogeo (Anghelu Ruju XX bis) in fase di ristrutturazione o di escavazione per fasi (interrotta, come si evince dall'esame di alcune celle appena iniziate e di un portello delineato), in due ipogei ristrutturati (Noeddale I e S. Pedru I) ed in una tomba di dubbia interpretazione, almeno per quel che riguarda la tecnica escavazione della grotticella, Littoslongos. In sole otto *domus de janas* dipinte (Fig. 16.16) sono presenti materiali; in cinque (SFA XII, Serrugiu II, SFA XV, Lochele 1, Molia 1) è presente la ceramica Ozieri. Soltanto una tomba, Molia 1, risulta essere costruita per fasi. Si noti, infine, che in una sola

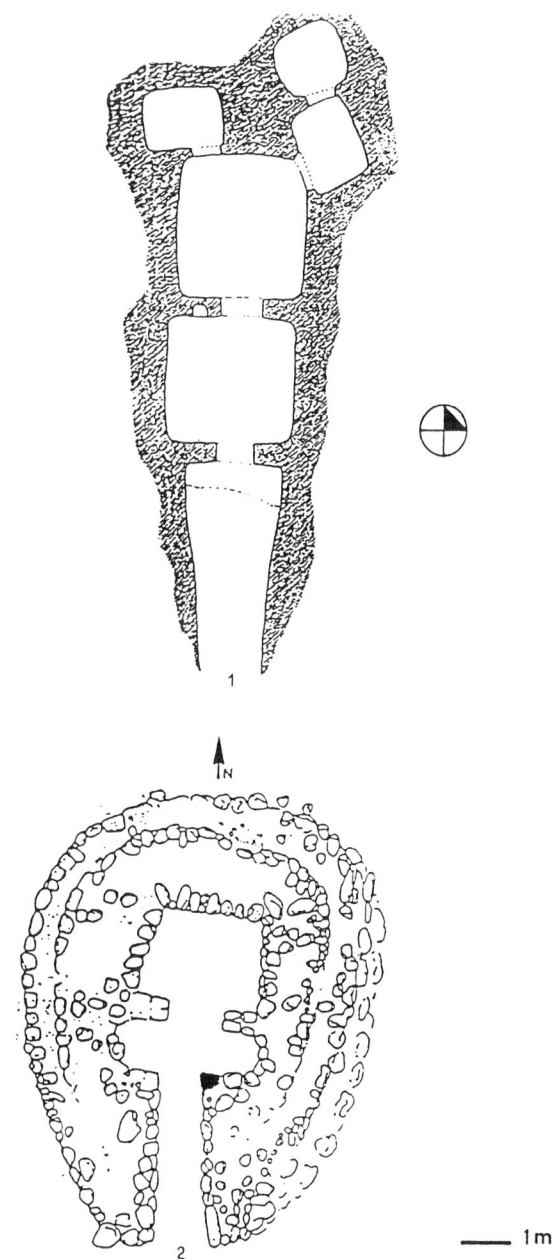

Fig. 16.9. Elementi di analogia fra ipogei a domus de janas *e tombe in elevazione: 1,* domus de janas *di Brodu IV (Oniferi); 2, Pranu Mutteddu (Goni), tomba V.*

domus de janas decorata con incisioni, peraltro di dubbia classificazione, Anghelu Ruju tomba XXIII, sono presenti materiali, tra cui ceramiche Ozieri.

Le analogie individuabili tra motivi figurativi ipogeici e figurazioni materiali

Utili elementi di cronologia provengono dalle rispondenze con decorazioni su materiali (Tanda 1983: 261 sgg., figg. 101–105; 1995a):

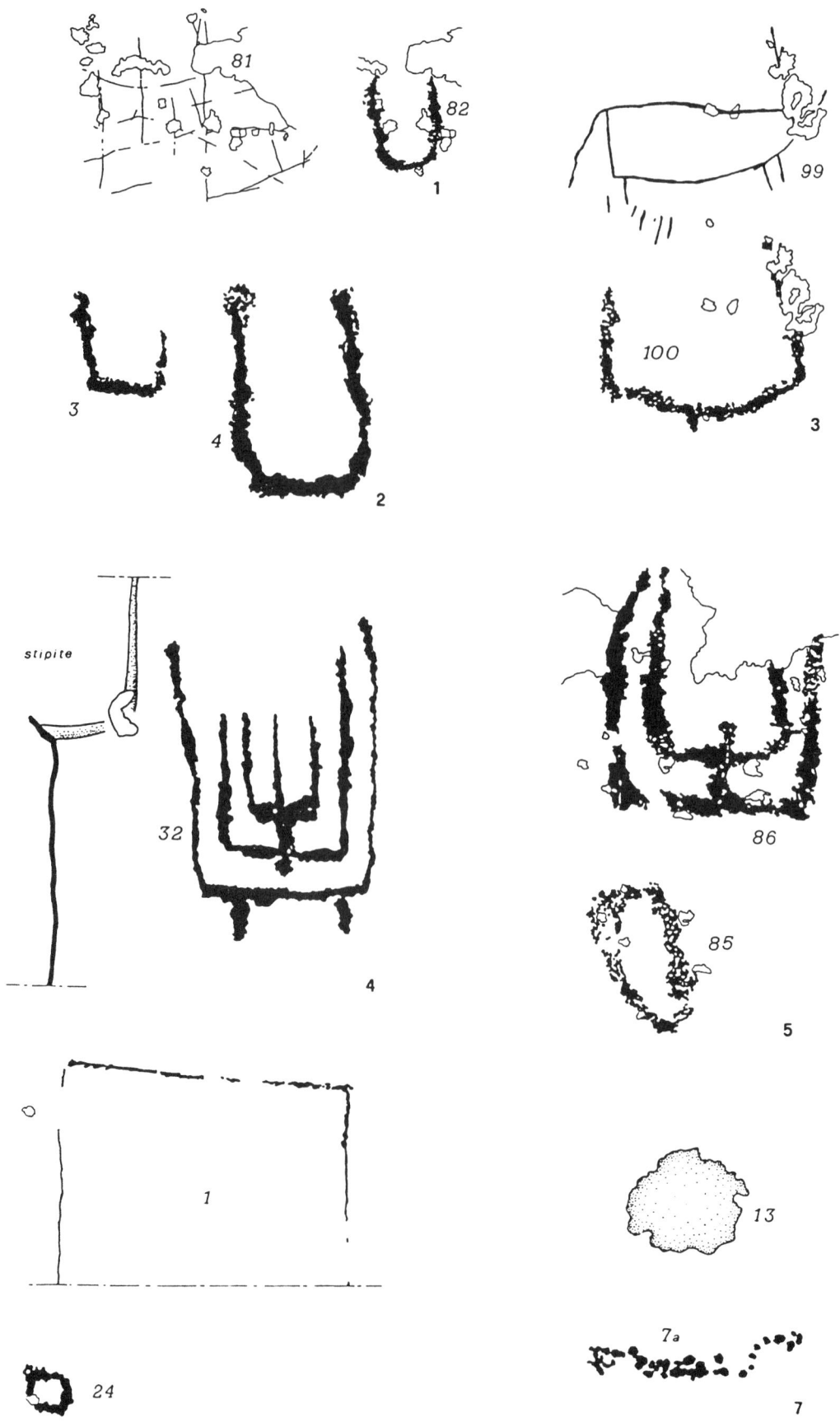

Fig. 16.10. Sovrapposizioni di motivi nelle domus de janas VIII e IX di Sos Furrighesos (Anela).

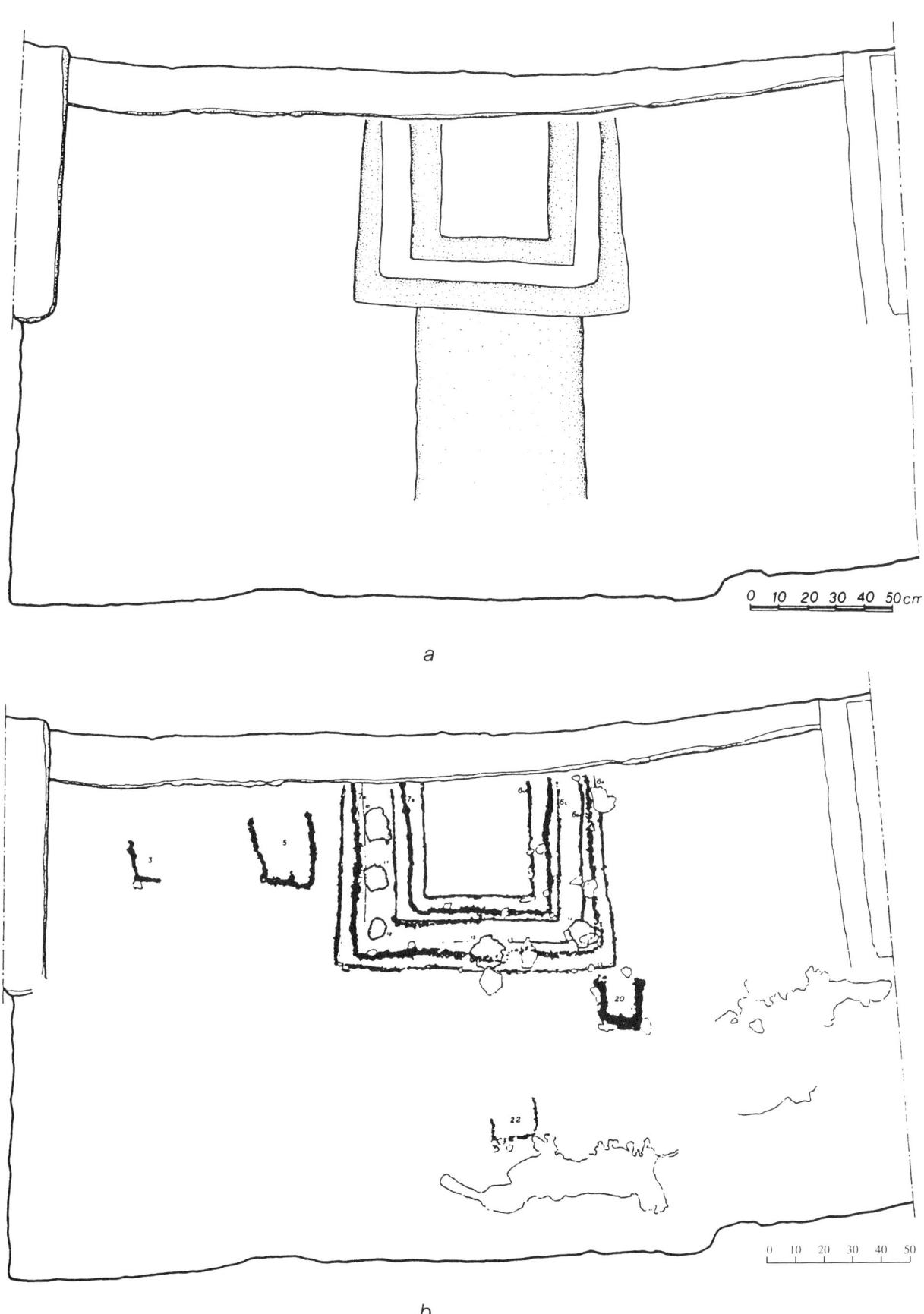

Fig. 16.11. Sos Furrighesos (Anela), tomba VIII, Fase II (a); Sos Furrighesos VIII, Fase III (b).

Fig. 16.12. Sos Furrighesos (Anela), tomba XI: sovrapposizioni. 1, motivi nn. 81–82; 2, motivi nn. 3–4; 3, motivi n. 99–100; 4, motivo n. 32; 5, motivi nn. 85–86; 6, motivi nn. 24–1; 7, motivi nn. 7–13 (scale differenti).

Fig. 16.13. Sos Furrighesos XI, le incisioni in tecnica lineare: sono coperte dal pigmento rosso e dalle incisioni "a martellina".

Fig. 16.14. Sos Furrigheos XI, le incisioni "a martellina" coprono le lineari.

DOMUS DE JANAS CON MOTIVI CORNIFORMI SCOLPITI			CULTURE									
N°	Stile	Denominazione	Ozieri	Filigosa/Abealzu	Monte Claro	Campaniforme	Bonnanaro	Nuragica	Punica	Romana	Medievale	Storica
	Stile curvilineo											
1		A. Ruiu XIX (Alghero)	●		●							
2		A. Ruiu A (Alghero)	●		●							
3		A. Ruiu XXVIII (Alghero)	●		●	●	●					
4		Montalè (Sassari)			●							
5		Tomba delle Finestrelle (Ossi)	●									
6		A. Ruiu XXX (Alghero)	●	●	●	●	●					
7		Pottu Codinu VIII (Villanova M.)	●	●								
8		Monte Siseri (Putifigari)	●								●	●
9		Oredda II (Sassari)	●									●
10		Mandra Antine III (Thiesi)		● litica							●	●
11		Mesu 'e Montes II (Ossi)		●	●		●				●	
	Stile rettilineo											
12		A. Ruiu XX bis (Alghero)	●			●						
13		Noeddale I (Ossi)	●	●	●		●					
14		Santu Pedru I (Alghero)	●	●		●	●					
15		Littoslongos (Ossi)	●	●								
DOMUS DE JANAS CON MOTIVI SPIRALIFORMI SCOLPITI												
16		Funtana Pulida (Perfugas)	●				●	●		●	●	
DOMUS DE JANAS CON MOTIVI SPIRALIFORMI INCISI												
17		A. Ruiu XVIII (Alghero)	●		●							

Fig. 16.15. I materiali restituiti dalle domus de janas *decorate da motivi scolpiti.*

DOMUS DE JANAS DIPINTE						CULTURE								
N°	parete	intonaco	colore	figura	Denominazione	Ozieri	Filigosa/Abealzu	Monte Claro	Campaniforme	Bonnanaro	Nuragica	Punica	Romana	Medievale	Storica
18	●		●		Sos Furrighesos XII	●			●						
19	●		●		Serrugiu II	●									
20	●		●		Molia 7									●	
21	●			●	Sos Furrighesos XV	●	●	●	●	●					
22	●			●	Lochele II					●				●	
23		●	●		Molia 1		●	●	●						
24		●	●		Lochele 1	●								●	
25		●	●		Iloi 2				●					●	

Fig. 16.16. Domus de janas *dipinte: materiali restituiti.*

1. La decorazione zoomorfa applicata su un frammento ceramico di Monte Maiore (Thiesi), di cultura Ozieri, analoga ai motivi scolpiti della Tomba A di Anghelu Ruju (tipo A, II, 1 di stile curvilineo) (Fig. 16.17,1–2); i motivi plastici ad arco o "a barca" che decorano ceramiche Ozieri, simili ai motivi scolpiti semplici o duplici di Anghelu Ruju XXX, Tomba delle Finestrelle, Su Murrone ecc. (stile curvilineo, B, I,1 e B-II, 1–2) (Fig. 16.17,3–4); i motivi a rettangolo non concluso dipinti, da Terramaini, Sub-Ozieri (Usai 1984; fig. 11,2), simili ai motivi semplici o duplici di S. Pedru I, ad esempio, o di Monte Minerva II o di Littoslongos (Fig. 16.17,5–7); il motivo antropomorfo "orante" inciso su un peso fittile da telaio, da Conca Illonis, di cultura Filigosa (Atzeni 1988: fig. 4,8), simile ai motivi "oranti" incisi di Tomba Branca e Sos Furrighesos XV (Tanda 1995b) (Fig. 16.17,6–7); il motivo corniforme inciso su di un'accettina-amuleto di cultura Ozieri, da Bau Porcos (Oristano), simile ai motivi scolpiti di Sa Londra (tipo A, IV, 1, stile curvilineo); il peso fittile da telaio, da Monte d'Accoddi, di probabile cultura Filigosa o Abealzu, decorato da un motivo ancoriforme acefalo, analogo ai motivi ancoriformi incisi di Pontesecco VI e Monte d'Accoddi IV (quest'ultimo scolpito) e di Sos Furrighesos VIII; i motivi ancoriformi o a candelabro,

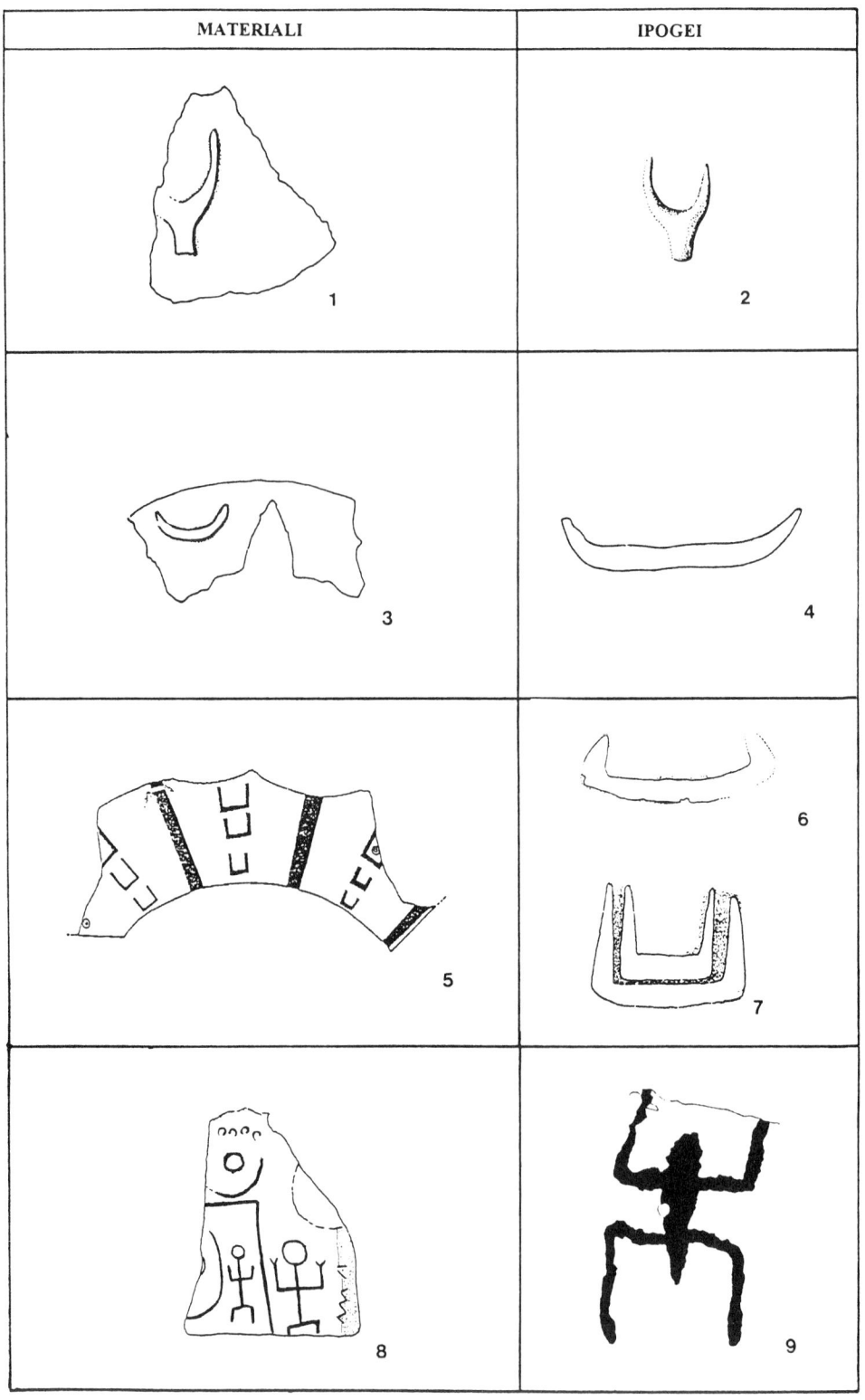

1: Monte Maiore (Thiesi); 2: Anghelu Ruiu A (Alghero); 3: Sa Ucca de Su Tintirriolu (Mara); 4: Anghelu Ruiu XXX (Alghero); 5: Terramaini (Pirri); 6: Monte Minerva II (Villanova Monteleone); 7: S. Pedru I (Alghero); 8: Conca Illonis (Cabras); 9: Sos Furrighesos XV (Anela).

Fig. 16.17. Alcuni esempi di rispondenze fra motivi figurativi dei materiali e degli ipogei a domus de janas.

scolpiti sulle statue-menhir trovate a Laconi e dintorni, del Calcolitico-Bronzo Antico (Atzeni 1988: 454–455, fig. 6,5; il motivo antropomorfo a braccia e gambe levate, scolpito sulla statua stele di Monte D'Accoddi, di cultura Filigosa (Tanda 1984: 78; Tinè 1989: tav. 19,2).

In sintesi i materiali di cultura Ozieri hanno puntuale rispondenza in figurazioni scolpite dello stile curvilineo (Tipi A e B); le ceramiche del cosiddetto Sub-Ozieri (forse sarebbe più opportuna la definizione di Ozieri finale) si confrontano con motivi dello stile rettilineo (tipi A III, 1 e V, 2 di S. Pedru 1, Minerva II e Littoslongos); le analogie con incisioni a martellina, siano esse ancoriformi o antropomorfi, provengono da materiali archeologici fittili (pesi da telaio) o litici (statue- menhir), incisi su ceramiche di cultura Filigosa o scolpiti a basso rilievo su stele della medesima cultura o su statue-menhir attribuite a! Calcolitico (Laconi ecc.).

I confronti con l'arte figurativa europea e mediterranea occidentale in particolare

Le figurazioni scolpite non sembrano trovare confronti extrainsulari storicamente ammissibili: le datazioni di tali confronti, infatti, sono troppo antiche o troppo recenti rispetto alle figurazioni sarde. Infatti motivi figurativi del Vicino Oriente, come quelli osservati a Çatal Hüyük (Mellaart 1975: 98 sgg., fig. 58) che rieccheggiano le figurazioni bovine scolpite di tipo A, I dello stile curvilineo sono molto più antiche, del VII-VI millennio a. C. (Mellaart 1972: 120–121).

D'altra parte, le "corna sacrificali" d'ambiente cretese-miceneo (Contu 1964: 78–79; 81–82), attribuite al Tardo Miceneo, che ricordano i motivi scolpiti dello stile rettilineo di tipo A, 5 e B sono certamente, allo stato attuale delle conoscenze, troppo recenti rispetto alle figurazione sarde, in quanto poste fra il 1650 ed il 1550 a.C. (LM: Betancourt 1985: 19). Ciò rende ancora più attendibile l'ipotesi di un'origine autoctona dell'arte ipogeica sarda, che trova le sue radici nel sostrato del Neolitico medio o cultura di Bonuighinu. Nella Figura 16.18 sono esemplificati alcuni precedenti figurativi eseguiti, però, su oggetti della cultura materiale, litici (Ludosu-Riola Sardo: ipotesi di attribuzione cronologica al Neolitico medio in Tanda 1983: 268) e ceramici (Puisteris-Mogoro) (Tanda 1995a).

Il vasto repertorio incisorio, invece, soprattutto le incisioni ancoriformi, antropomorfi e corniformi fanno convergere confronti significativi e storicamente attendibili verso la Penisola iberica, in primo luogo, con l'arte schematica dipinta o incisa dell'Età del Rame (Prehistoria 1986: 280–299) e verso la zona alpina centro-occidentale (Valle d'Aosta, Valcamonica e Svizzera (Tanda 1992: 489 sgg.). Altrettanto puntuali analogie (ma talvolta con cronologie assai varie), sono state osservate per i motivi dipinti di rosso a scacchiera e a fascio di zig-zag della domus IV di Pubusattile (Tanda 1992: 484–485).

Il primo motivo compare su ceramiche di varia cultura e cronologia (Masseria La Quercia, Chasseen, tipo Matera), realizzato con varie tecniche (pittura, graffito); inciso su statue-stele della Val d'Aosta e di Sion, sul masso di Borno (faccia 1) su idoli-placa iberici; dipinto nella Grotta di Porto Badisco. Il secondo è documentato, dipinto, nella stessa grotta, nella Grotta Chindiei, nel dolmen di Gohiltzsch-Merseburgo e in dolmen portoghesi; inciso in tombe megalitiche dell'Irlanda (Newgrange) e della Germania (Zuschen-Kassel) (Tanda 1992: 484–485). Questi confronti suggeriscono tre orizzonti cronologici: seconda metà del V millennio a.C., seconda metà del IV, prima metà del III. La terza ipotesi, la prima metà del III millennio a.C. appare la più attendibile.

In conclusione, i risultati degli studi effettuati secondo il percorso logico-operativo proposto all'inizio dell'intervento, si possono sintetizzare come segue. L'arte delle *domus de janas* ha origine presumibilmente nella cultura di Bonuighinu e si sviluppa soprattutto durante il Neolitico recente, con manifestazioni cospicue durante il Neolitico finale (Sub-Ozieri?) e l'età del Rame, con la cultura di Filigosa, con rare manifestazioni nell'Età del Bronzo. Compare, infine, con manifestazioni totalmente diverse in età romano-altomedievale.

Si articola, pertanto, in quattro fasi (con numerose sottofasi):

Ia. *Fase I di SFA, cultura Ozieri*: comprende motivi semplici scolpiti dello stile curvilineo (Tipi A I-II) ad es. Grugos II, Anghelu Ruju XIX e XXVIII e dello stile rettilineo (Tipo A 1–2, Anghelu Ruju XX bis); pittura rossa, incisioni lineari;

Ib. *Cultura Ozieri*: motivi semplici, tipi A III-IV , come Montalè, Tomba Maggiore-Ossi e Roccia dell'Elefante;

IIa. *Fase II di SFA, cultura Ozieri finale* (Sub-Ozieri) (ex Fase di passaggio cultura Ozieri/Filigosa, Tanda 1985): motivi scolpiti di transizione di entrambi gli stili (Tipi B, Tomba delle Finestrelle, Anghelu Ruju XXX, Brodu IV, Sos Furrighesos VIII, Littoslongos);

IIb. *Fase III di SFA, Età del Rame, cultura di Filigosa*: motivi scolpiti complessi di entrambi gli stili, incisioni corniformi;

IIc. *Fase IV di SFA, cultura di Filigosa*: motivi antropomorfi scolpiti di Pontesecco IV; incisioni antropomorfe e pettiniformi; statue menhir; motivo bitriangolare inciso di Monte Pazza;

IId. *Fase V di SFA, cultura di Filigosa*: motivi ancoriformi scolpiti di Monte d'Accoddi IV; incisioni antropomorfe ed ancoriformi;

III. *Fase VI di SFA, Età del Bronzo*: incisioni geometriche;

IV. *Fase VII di SFA, Età romano-altomedievale*: incisioni in tecnica lineare, a *polissoir*, a puntinato.

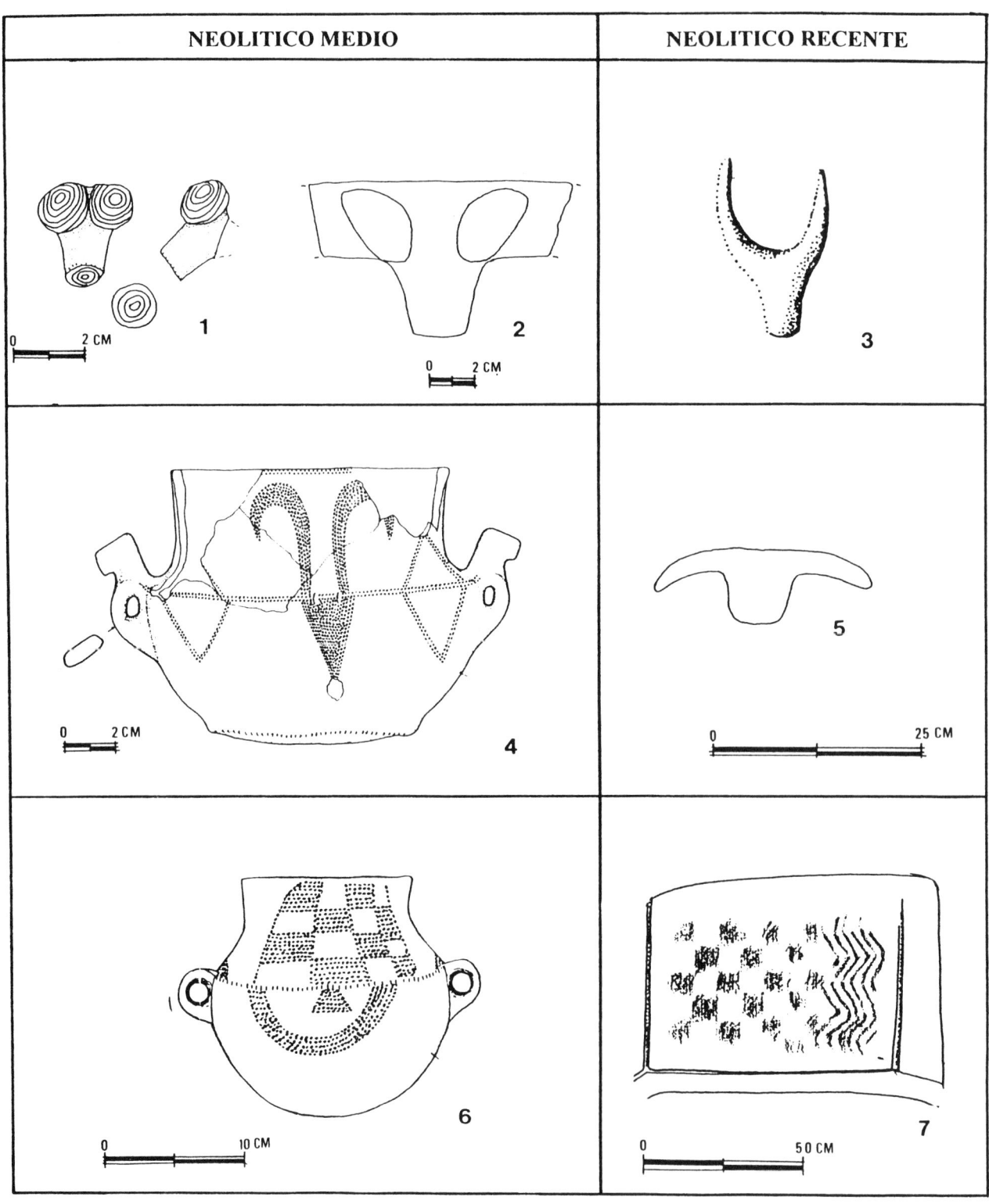

1: Puisteris (Mogoro); 2: Ludosu (Riola Sardo); 3: Anghelu Ruiu A (Alghero); 4: Grotta del Rifugio (Oliena); 5: Sas Concas (Padria); 6: Grotta del Bagno Penale (Cagliari); 7: Pubusattile IV (Villanova Monteleone).

Fig. 16.18. Origine dell'arte delle domus de janas: i precedenti figurativi.

Ringraziamenti

Gli autori dei disegni e delle fotografie sono: geom. Giampiero Sechi (Figg. 16.1–16.5, 16.17–16.18); Sig. Angelo Auzzas, da originali di Vari Autori (Figg. 16.2–16.4, 16.6–16.7); Società Archeoturistica Iloi (Fig. 16.8); Autori Vari, non identificati (Fig. 16.9); Prof. Francesco Carta (da rilievi di Giuseppa Tanda) (Figg. 16.10–16.14); Dr.ssa Giovanna Meloni (Figg. 16.15–16.16).

Bibliografia

Antona Ruju, A. & Lo Schiavo, F. 1989. Oredda-Sassari, la Domus delle Doppie Spirali. In Campus, L.D. (a cura di), *La cultura di Ozieri. Problematiche e Nuove acquisizioni. Atti del I Convegno di studio. Ozieri, gennaio 1986-aprile 1987*, 49–74. Il Torchietto, Ozieri.

Atzeni, E. 1962. I villaggi preistorici di S. Gemiliano di Sestu e Monte Olladiri di Monastir presso Cagliari e le ceramiche della "facies" di Monte Claro. *Studi Sardi* 17: 1–216.

Atzeni, E. 1988. Megalitismo e arte, in L'età del Rame in Sardegna, *Atti del Congresso Internazionale: L'Età del Rame in Europa, Viareggio 15–18 ottobre 1987*. Rassegna di Archeologia 7: 449–456. Firenze.

Basoli, P. 1989. La cultura di Ozieri nel territorio di Ozieri. Considerazioni preliminari. In Campus, L.D. (a cura di), *La cultura di Ozieri. Problematiche e Nuove acquisizioni. Atti del I Convegno di studio. Ozieri, gennaio 1986-aprile 1987*, 113–144. Il Torchietto, Ozieri.

Betancourt, P.P. 1985. *The History of Minoan Pottery*. Princeton University Press, Princeton.

Cariati, F., Piredda, G., Serri, R. & Tanda, G. 1981. Analisi chimico-mineralogiche di un campione di parete dipinta della *domus de janas* I di Molia-Illorai. *Rivista di Scienze Preistoriche* 26(1–2): 291–300.

Contu. E. 1955. Ipogei eneolitici di Pontesecco e Marinaru presso Sassari. *Studi Sardi* 12–13: 21–80.

Contu, E. 1962. Alcune osservazioni su domus de janas edite ed inedite del Sassarese. *Studi Sardi* 17: 626–635.

Contu, E. 1964. La Tomba dei Vasi Tetrapodi in località Santu Pedru (Alghero-Sassari). *Monumenti Antichi dei Lincei* 47: 3–201.

Contu, E. 1964a. Tombe preistoriche dipinte e scolpite di Thiesi e Bessude. *Rivista di Scienze Preistoriche* 19: 233–263.

Contu, E. 1965. Nuovi petroglifi schematici della Sardegna. *Bullettino di Paletnologia Italiana* 74: 69–122.

Demartis, G. 1991. La Tomba dell'Architettura dipinta. Un ipogeo neolitico di Putifigari. *Bollettino di Archeologia* 7: 1–21.

Demartis, G. 1991a. *La Necropoli di Pottu Codinu*. Sardegna Archeologica, Guide e Itinerari 13. Dessì, Sassari.

Ferrarese Ceruti, M.L. 1989. La Necropoli di Su Crucifissu Mannu-Porto Torres e di Ponte Secco-Sassari. In Campus, L.D. (a cura di), *La cultura di Ozieri. Problematiche e Nuove acquisizioni. Atti del I Convegno di studio. Ozieri, gennaio 1986-aprile 1987*, 37–47. Il Torchietto, Ozieri.

Ferrarese Ceruti, M. L. 1992. Elementi architettonici e del culto funerario nella domus de janas di Su Littu (Ossi-Sassari). In Tykot, R.H. & Andrews, T.K. (eds.), *Sardinia in the Mediterranean: A Footprint in the Sea. Studies in Sardinian Archaeology Presented to Miriam S. Balmuth*. Monographs in Mediterranean Archaeology 3: 98–104. Sheffield Academic Press, Sheffield.

Foschi Nieddu, A. 1986. *La tomba I di Filigosa (Macomer-Nuoro). Alcune considerazioni sulla cultura di Abealzu-Filigosa nel contesto eneolitico della Sardegna*. Coop. Grafica Nuorese, Nuoro.

Galli, F. 1982. La domus de janas di Butule (Ozieri-SS). *Rivista di Scienze Preistoriche* 37: 267–276.

Mellaart, J. 1972. L'Anatolia prima del 4.000 a.C. In *Storia del Mondo Antico. I. Preistoria e nascita delle civiltà in Oriente*, 117 sgg. Milano.

Mellaart, J. 1975. *The Neolithic of the Near East*. London.

Moravetti, A. 1989. La tomba ipogeica di Littoslongos-Ossi. In Campus, L.D. (a cura di), *La cultura di Ozieri. Problematiche e Nuove acquisizioni. Atti del I Convegno di studio. Ozieri, gennaio 1986-aprile 1987*, 83–102. Il Torchietto, Ozieri.

Prehistoria. 1986. Prehistoria. *Historia De España*. Madrid.

Tanda, G. 1976. Monte d'Accoddi-Sassari, tomba II. In *Nuove testimonianze archeologiche della Sardegna centro-settentrionale*, 27–35. Dessì, Sassari.

Tanda, G. 1977a. *Arte preistorica in Sardegna. Le figurazioni taurine scolpite dell'Algherese nel quadro delle rappresentazioni figurate degli ipogei sardi a domus de janas*. Quaderni della Soprintendenza ai Beni Archeologici per le Province di Sassari e Nuoro 5. Dessì, Sassari.

Tanda, G. 1977b. Le incisioni della "domu de janas" di Tisiennari-Bortigiadas. *Archivio Storico Sardo* 3: 199–211.

Tanda, G. 1980. Alcune considerazioni sul sito archeologico di Molia-Illorai (Sassari). *Quaderni Bolotanesi* 6: 63–77.

Tanda, G. 1983. Arte e religione in Sardegna. Rapporti tra i dati monumentali e gli elementi della cultura materiale (Nota preliminare). In Anati, E. (a cura di), *The Intellectual Expressions of Prehistoric Man, Art, and Religion: Acts of the Valcamonica Symposium '79*, 261–279. Edizioni del Centro Camuno di Studi Preistorica, Brescia.

Tanda, G. 1984. *Arte e Religione della Sardegna preistorica nella necropoli di Sos Furrighesos-Anela*. Chiarella, Sassari.

Tanda, G. 1985. *L'arte delle domus de janas nelle immagini di Ingeborg Mangold*. Chiarella, Sassari.

Tanda, G. 1992. L'arte del Neolitico e dell'Età del Rame in Sardegna: Nuovi studi e recenti acquisizioni. In *Atti della XXVIII Riunione Scientifica dell'Istituto Italiano di Preistoria e Protostoria, "L'arte in Italia dal paleolitico all'età del bronzo", 20–22 novembre 1989, Firenze*, 479–493. Istituto Italiano di Preistoria e Protostoria, Firenze.

Tanda, G. 1995a. Arte, Simbologia, Religione. In *Atti del Congresso Internazionale "L'ipogeismo nel Mediterraneo. Origini, sviluppo, quadri culturali," Sassari-Oristano, 23–28 maggio 1994*. Sassari.

Tanda, G. 1995b. La tomba XV di Sos Furrighesos, Anela (SS). In *Atti del Congresso Internazionale "L'ipogeismo nel Mediterraneo. Origini, sviluppo, quadri culturali," Sassari-Oristano, 23–28 maggio 1994*. Sassari.

Taramelli, A. 1919. Fortezze, recinti fonti sacre e necropoli preromane nell'agro di Bonorva (SS). *Monumenti Antichi dei Lincei* 25: 765–900.

Tinè, S. 1989. Monte d'Accoddi e la cultura di Ozieri. In Campus, L.D. (a cura di), *La cultura di Ozieri. Problematiche e Nuove acquisizioni. Atti del I Convegno di studio. Ozieri, gennaio 1986-aprile 1987*, 19–25. Il Torchietto, Ozieri.

Usai, E. 1984. Pimentel. Loc. S'Acqua Salida e Corongiu. In *I Sardi. La Sardegna dal Paleolitico all'Età romana*, 124–129. Electa, Milano.

17. Aspetti del megalitismo nel territorio di Monte Acuto (Sassari). Considerazioni preliminari

Paola Basoli

Il territorio di Monte Acuto, che ricalca nelle linee generali l'area occupata da una curatoria del Medioevo (Meloni 1992: 9), è oggi una circoscrizione amministrativa della Sardegna, la VI Comunità Montana, suddivisa in undici comuni con centro ad Ozieri (Fig. 17.1). Si tratta di un territorio di Kmq 1496.91 che comprende l'area granitica della catena del Limbara, la pianura solcata dal Coghinas e dai suoi affluenti, gli altopiani granitici di Buddusò e Alà dei Sardi, i massicci calcarei di Ozieri e Mores, l'altopiano basaltico di Ardara, l'altopiano trachitico di Monte Sassu (Basoli 1985; Basoli-Foschi 1991). È altresì nota l'esistenza di giacimenti minerari sul cui sfruttamento nell'antichità sono tuttora in corso ricerche (Lo Schiavo 1988; Lo Schiavo *et al.* 1990).

Gli studi finora effettuati hanno evidenziato l'esistenza di significativi monumenti megalitici, costituiti da dolmens, menhirs, circoli e muraglie, concentrati per lo più nelle aree granitiche di Berchidda e Buddusò con esempi monumentali, apparentemente isolati, a Mores e ad Ozieri (Basoli 1984a; 1985). Se deboli sono le tracce di abitati, notevoli sono i resti di complessi sepolcrali. La lettura dei monumenti non è sempre agevole a causa della conformazione delle rocce granitiche, degli spietramenti e delle giustapposizioni nelle epoche successive. É in corso di elaborazione il corpus di tutti i monumenti individuati. Un rapido sguardo alla cartina del territorio individua il sito di questi monumenti (Fig. 17.1).

Ozieri

I resti megalitici si trovano in zone elevate, concentrati verso il confine con Chiaramonti e Ittireddu. In alcuni casi sono in un'area in cui si aprono una grotta o ipogei, in altri casi in una zona interessata da un forte ipogeismo senza peraltro giustapporsi a questo, in un caso infine isolati.

1. Borroiles (Fig. 17.1,1). Oltre ai resti di menhirs piramidali citati dall'Amadu, residuano ortostati ormai fuori contesto di quello che doveva essere un dolmen (Amadu 1978: 291ss.; Basoli 1985: 37; 1991–92: 778).
2. Luzzanas (Fig. 17.1,2). Riparo sotto-roccia con antropomorfi itifallici dipinti in ocra in cui sono evidenti i legami con la religione megalitica (Basoli 1992a: 495–506, fig.1; Atzeni 1979–80: passim).
3. Montiju Coronas (Fig. 17.1,3 e 17.2). I resti del dolmen sono situati su un'altura trachitica a quota 220 m. (Amadu 1978: 419). Il monumento orientato est-ovest è a pianta rettangolare con pareti laterali costituite da due ortostati e quella di fondo da una sola pietra ed è coperto da un solo lastrone. Altri quattro ortostati, appartenenti alla stessa struttura, giacciono ormai fuori contesto. Il monumento sembra continuare in direzione Nord con un'*allée* di cui si seguono le strutture laterali per metri 9,80. Numerosi lastroni sono ormai fuori contesto. Sul lato orientale dell'*allée* si seguono due allineamenti: uno di m. 2,70 e un altro di m. 9 di massi di grande pezzatura interrati, forse riferibili a muri di contenimento (Basoli 1984a: 37). I materiali ceramici e litici, rinvenuti dall'Amadu, sono illustrati nelle Figure 17.3–17.4.
4. Punta S'Arroccu (Fig. 17.1,4). Muraglia megalitica con due varchi a Nord e ad Ovest che per quaranta metri recinge una parte dell'altopiano di Su Sassu che domina la pianura di Chilivani (Basoli 1984a: 39; 1985: 37–39).
5. M. Silvari (Fig. 17.1,5). Menhir tronco-piramidale su un'altura con resti di muraglia megalitica (Basoli 1985: 37–38).
6. Grotta di San Michele (Fig. 17.1,6). Situata nell'abitato di Ozieri, l'imboccatura di questa grotta, oggi distrutta, era chiusa da due menhirs di pietra granitica andati dispersi (Taramelli 1915: 124).
7. Conca Nicolitta (Fig. 17.1,7 e Pl. 1). Un megalito giace a breve distanza da un ipogeo e da un'area

---

Paola Basoli, Soprintendenza Archeologica di Sassari e Nuoro, Piazza S. Agostino, 2, Sassari, 07100 Sardegna, Italia
References to Pl. refer to the section of colour plates.

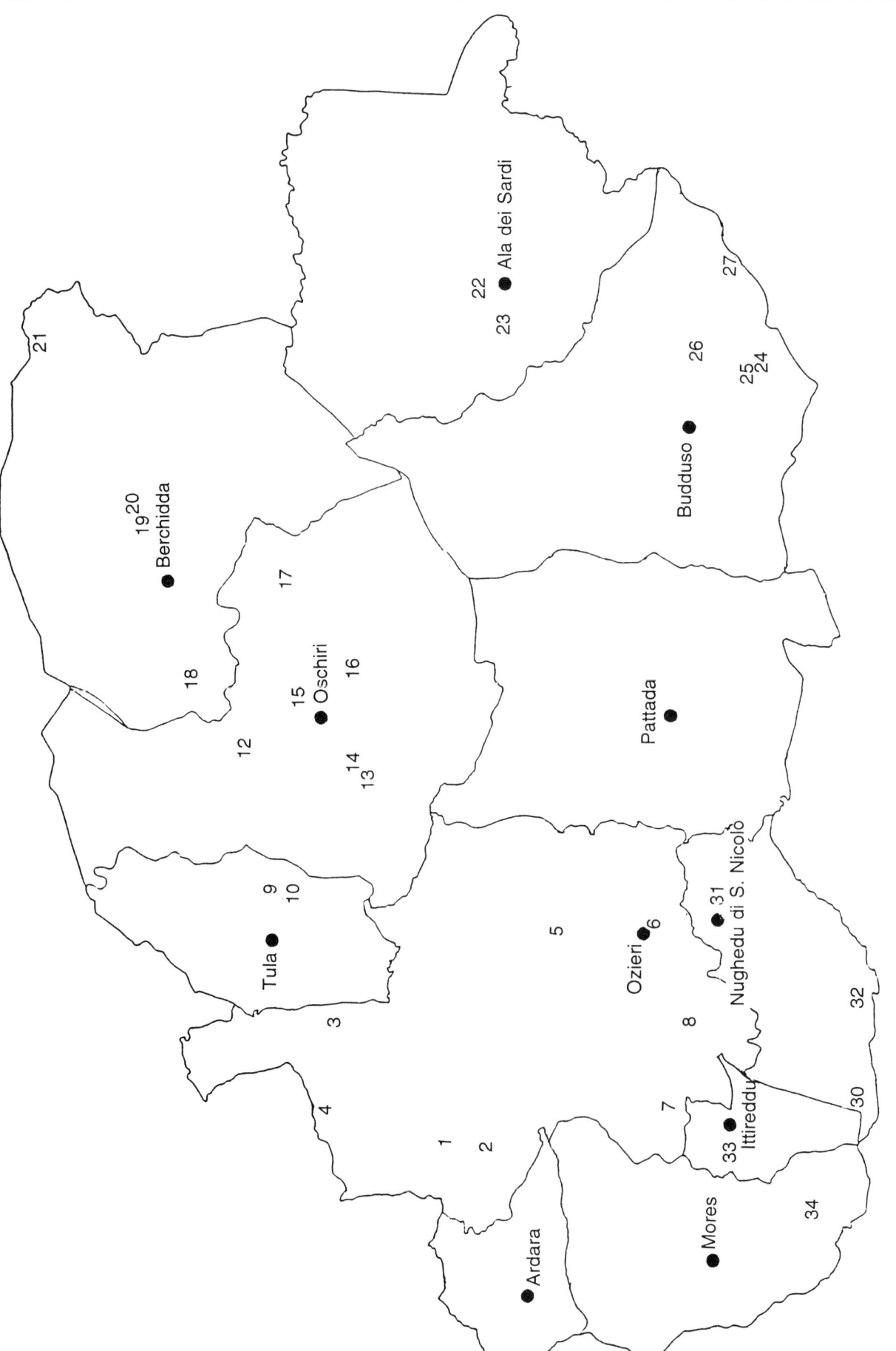

Fig. 17.1. Il territorio di Berchidda – Monte Acuto: siti megalitici.

sepolcrale nuragica in cui è presente una tomba di giganti a struttura megalitica che sembra tradire un'origine dolmenica (Basoli 1985: 37).
8. Tres Coronas (Fig. 17.1,8). I menhirs in trachite citati dal Lilliu (1957: 92–93 n. 7, 48 fig. 4) non sono attualmente più individuabili. Nel sito sono presenti due ipogei (Basoli 1985: 37).

Tula

In questo territorio il megalitismo, situato sempre in posizione dominante, si sovrappone all'ipogeismo o si integra con quest'ultimo.
1. Mandra Manna (Fig. 17.1,9 e Pl. 2–4). La muraglia megalitica recinge un pianoro che termina con un dirupo su cui si apre l'ingresso ad un ipogeo. Residuano fino a quattro filari con paramento di grossi massi di trachite con scheggioni di ammorsamento e faccia a vista appiattita. Tra i due paramenti è un riempimento di pietrame minuto. All'esterno di questa muraglia si addossa un dolmen di tipo semplice con un ortostato parallelepipedo quadrangolare e l'altro informe che definiscono una pianta rettangolare. All'interno della muraglia si delinea un circolo irregolare di pietre di cui residuano fino a due filari, entro cui sono una stele a contorno sub-rettangolare tra due menhirs sub-triangolari rovesciati. Il monumento ha un varco a luce rettangolare di quattro filari per lato, piattabandato con quattro lastroni.
2. Coloras (Fig. 17.1,10 e Pl. 5). L'ipogeo bicellulare presenta un circolo megalitico antistante l'ingresso.

Oschiri

In questo territorio il megalitismo si trova in zone più o meno elevate, concentrato verso il confine con Berchidda. Si integra e si sovrappone all'ipogeismo. Si conserva traccia di persistenza sacrale dei luoghi megalitici fino ad epoca storica.

1. Mandras (Fig. 17.1,11). Numerosi tafoni chiusi da muretti e piccoli anfratti chiusi da pietre hanno restituito materiale preistorico non altrimenti precisabile (Basoli 1984b: 398). Vi sono inoltre due menhirs a contorno sub-triangolare di cui uno reca numerose coppelle. Nei pressi sono alcuni ipogei.
2. Pedredu (Fig. 17.1,12). Su un pianoro che domina un'estesa necropoli ipogeica sono i resti di un circolo megalitico sconvolto da lavori agricoli.
3. Berre (Fig. 17.1,13). Sono noti una necropoli dolmenica, due menhirs e numerosi tafoni chiusi da muretti. Il sito è stato interessato da lavori di spietramento.
4. Furrighesu (Fig. 17.1,14 e Pl. 6). L'ipogeo, aperto a vista sul piano di campagna, presenta una lavorazione ad esedra della facciata, segnata da due piccoli menhirs, e tracce di un circolo megalitico ormai in dissesto. Anche i lati del monumento, soprattutto il sinistro, mostrano segni di adattamento a struttura epigeica di tipo dolmenico.
5. Santo Stefano (Fig. 17.1,15 e Pl. 7–8). Procedendo dalla chiesa verso la necropoli ipogeica sono evidenti rocce a nicchie ed a coppelle e un dolmen che sfrutta la roccia naturale per le pareti laterali su cui è stata rovesciata la lastra di copertura; a sinistra del monumento giace un menhir. Precede la concentrazione di ipogei una roccia isolata in cui si apre un portello subquadrato scorniciato e sopraelevato rispetto al piano di calpestio che introduce in una celletta ad uovo. Il portello è inquadrato in un ampio incavo superiormente convesso con una cornice aggettante, quasi un portale simile agli ipogei con fronte a stele (Basoli 1993: 26ss.).
6. Monte Cuccu (Fig. 17.1,16; Pl. 9–10). Le pendici del monte, alla cui base è una necropoli ipogeica, presentano caratteristiche rocce a nicchie e coppelle e anfratti chiusi da pietre. Alla sommità sono piccoli dolmens semplici con pareti costituite da filari di scheggioni di granito sormontati da un lastrone di copertura e due menhirs aniconici rovesciati. La muraglia megalitica è stata sconvolta da lavori di spietramento.
7. Malghesi (Fig. 17.1,17; Pl. 11–12). In posizione dominante una estesa necropoli ipogeica, sono i resti di un dolmen ormai in dissesto e un menhir rovesciato.

Berchidda

Il fenomeno megalitico, che privilegia luoghi elevati, è profondamente legato alle caratteristiche del territorio con rocce granitiche ricche di anfratti. Le estese necropoli, che occupano i crinali e le aree pedemontane, conservano deboli tracce di ipogeismo che si trasforma e si integra alle strutture megalitiche. La localizzazione dei siti megalitici è sulle direttrici che conducono all'alta Gallura. È caratteristica la persistenza sacrale dei luoghi in epoca storica.

1. Monte Acuto (Fig. 17.1,18; Figg. 17.5–17.7; Pl. 13–16). La montagna è stata frequentata in età preistorica, nuragica ed infine medioevale, come documenta la presenza di resti del castello giudicale. Residuano parti di una muraglia megalitica di difficile attribuzione culturale. Sono presenti inoltre tafoni, se ne contano almeno cinque, chiusi da muretti a secco e articolati in più anfratti; un dolmen che sfrutta la roccia granitica per i lati sormontati da un lastrone; numerose rocce con incavi e coppelle; un menhir e un dolmen. Quest'ultimo monumento sepolcrale, orientato a sud-ovest, ha pianta rettangolare. A sinistra dell'ingresso si addossa un muro di circa tre filari e nei pressi giace un menhir aniconico; l'area antistante subcircolare è

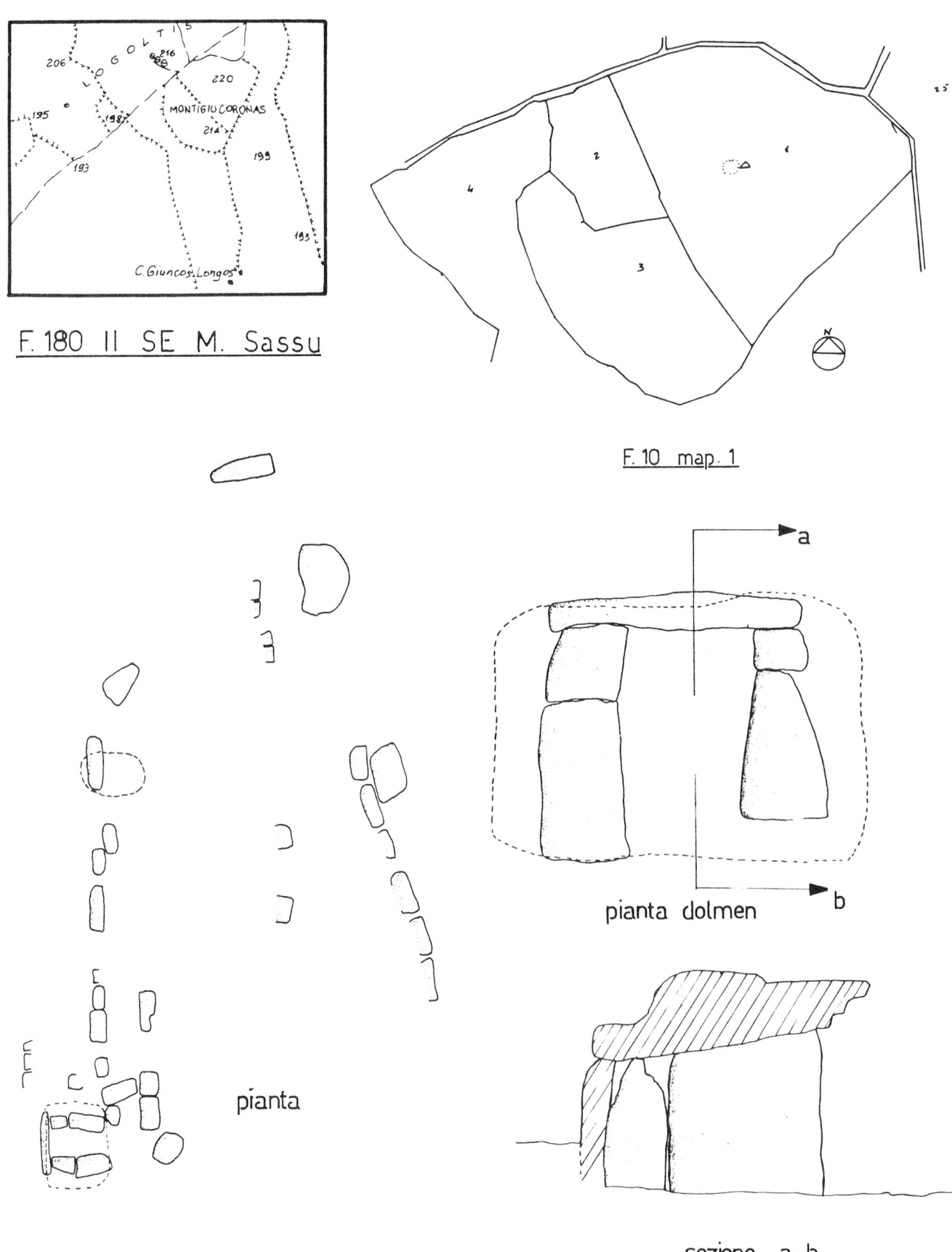

Fig. 17.2. Ozieri – Montiju Coronas. Corografia, planimetria catastale, pianta della tomba ad allée (scala circa 1:185), pianta e sezione del dolmen. Rilievi e disegni di L. Murgia.

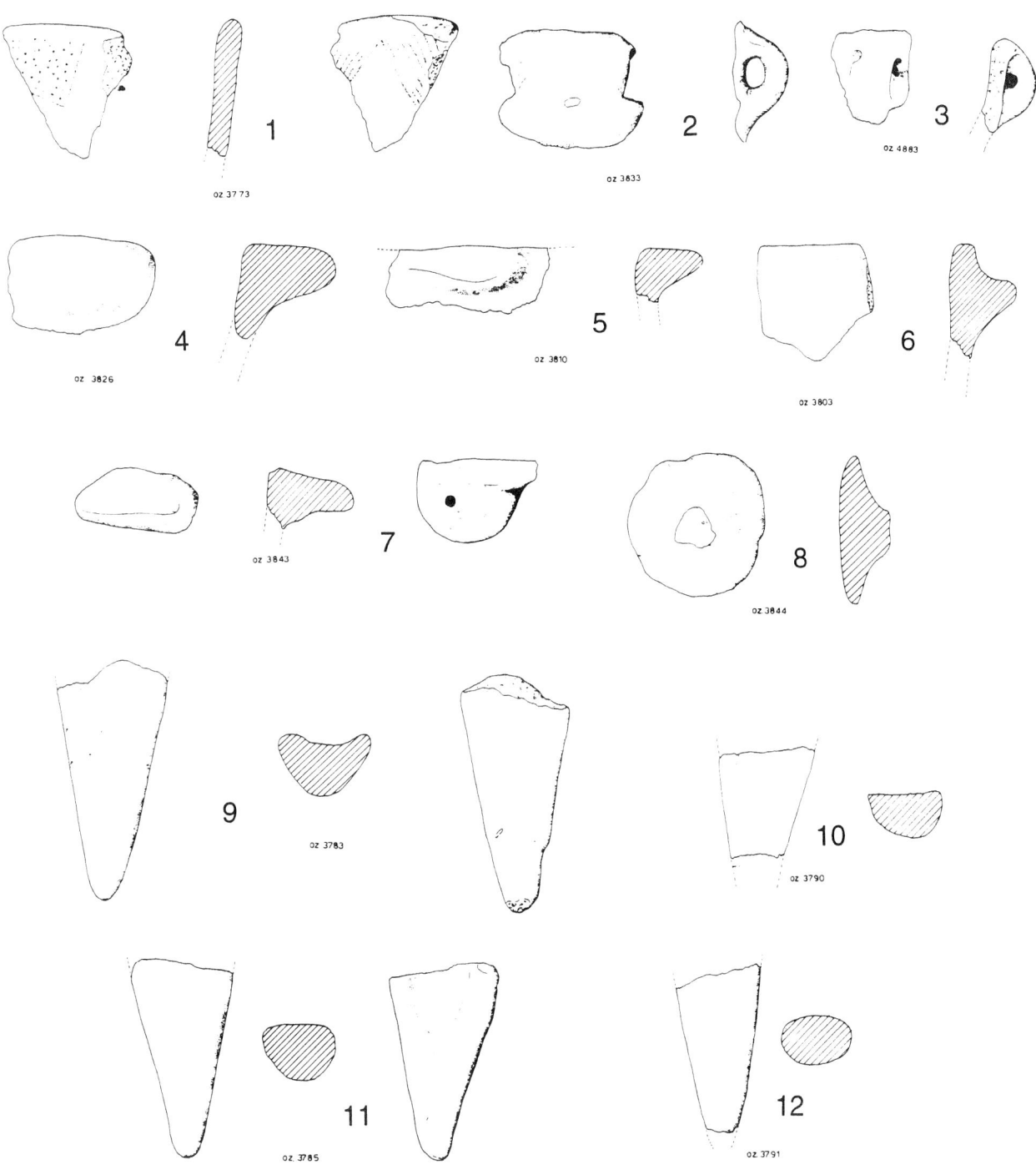

Fig. 17.3. Ozieri – Montiju Coronas. Materiali ceramici. Scala circo 1:2.

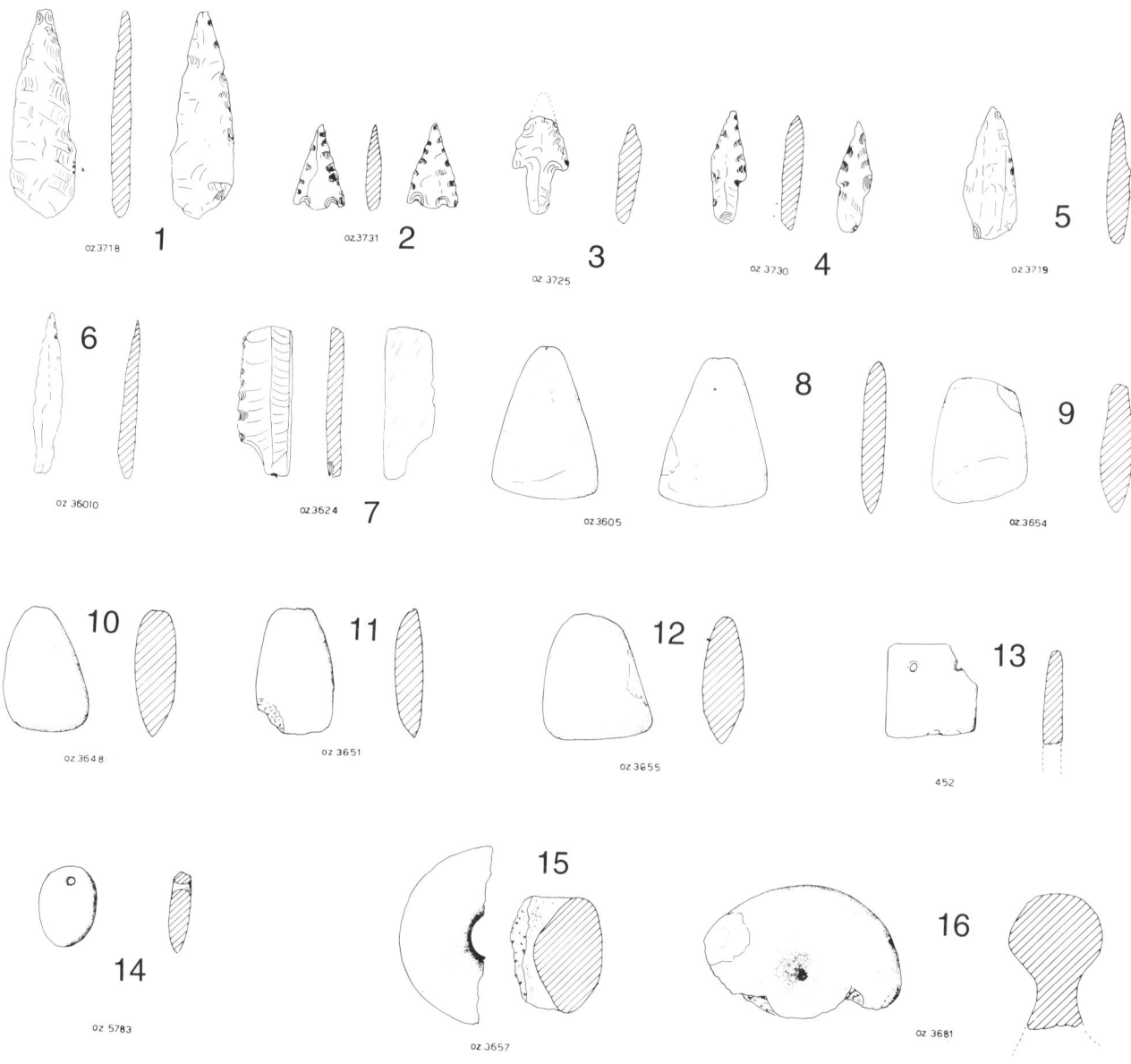

Fig. 17.4. Ozieri – Montiju Coronas. Materiali litici. Scala circo 1:2.

delimitata sul ciglione da un muro e in parte da rocce. La camera è delimitata lateralmente da due rocce con pareti lisciate. Quella destra presenta all'estremità distale in alto una bella coppella. La parete di fondo è costruita con pietre di grande pezzatura: se ne contano cinque. La copertura è costituita da due lastroni: su quello interno sono incavate otto coppelle. Il dolmen è sovrastato da una singolare roccia con un'apertura a forma di finestra, visibile da ogni luogo, che fa presumere indicasse l'ubicazione del monumento e del menhir. La valenza sacra del luogo rimane fino ad età tardo antica, come documenta il masso granitico con superficie appiattita molto erosa (m. 2,80 x 2,55 misure massime) che presenta incisioni a reticolo molto irregolari e profonde. I grafemi incisi trovano confronto con quelli individuati nella tomba IX della necropoli ipogeica di Sos Furrighesos di Anela datati in età altomedioevale (Tanda 1984: 6). I materiali ceramici e litici rinvenuti nel dolmen sono illustrati nelle Fig. 17.6–17.7.

2. Santa Caterina – Abialzos (Fig. 17.1,19 e Figure 17.6–17.7; Pl. 17–22). Sulle pendici del monte sono i dolmens di Sa Contrizzola e, presso la chiesa, quello di Santa Caterina. Il primo è stato sconvolto da lavori agricoli, il secondo è a pianta rettangolare con un ortostato che costituisce la parete di fondo e due che delimitano i lati della camera, sormontati da un lastrone pentagonale. Il crinale conserva notevoli resti megalitici preceduti da una muraglia gravemente compromessa da spietramenti. All'interno di questa struttura si trovano un ipogeo monocellulare, scavato in un roccione isolato sulla cui parete esterna sono

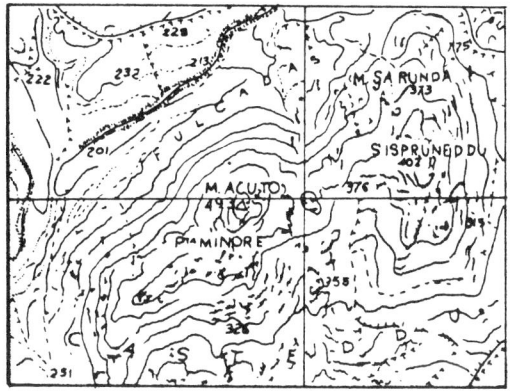

F. 181 III S.E. Berchidda
Lat. 40° 46' 40"
Long. 3° 20' 11"

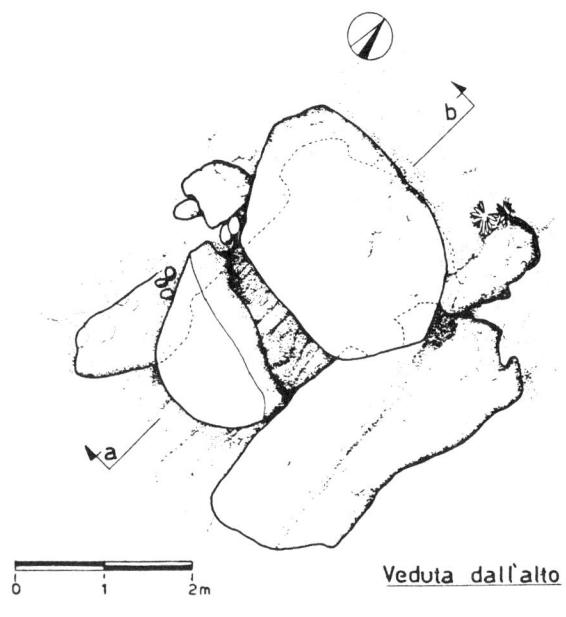

Veduta dall'alto

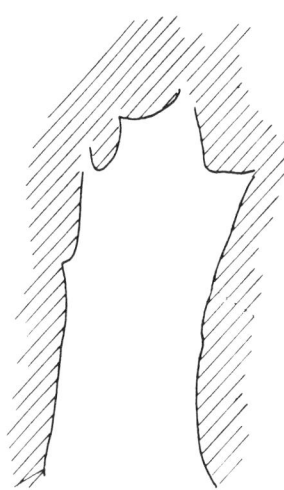

Pianta interno

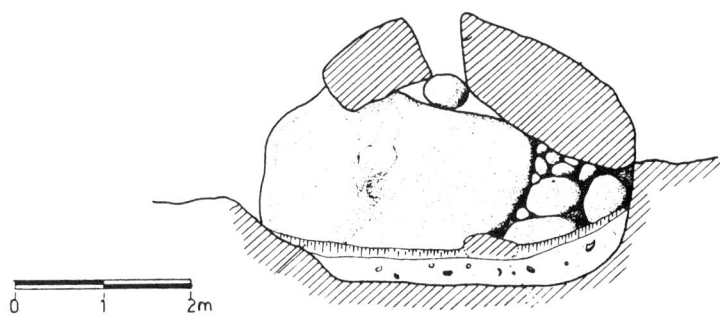

Sezione a-b

Fig. 17.5. Berchidda – Monte Acuto. Corografia, veduta dall'alto, pianta interno e sezione del dolmen. Rilievi e disegni di G. Fenu. Pianta e sezione circo 1:83.

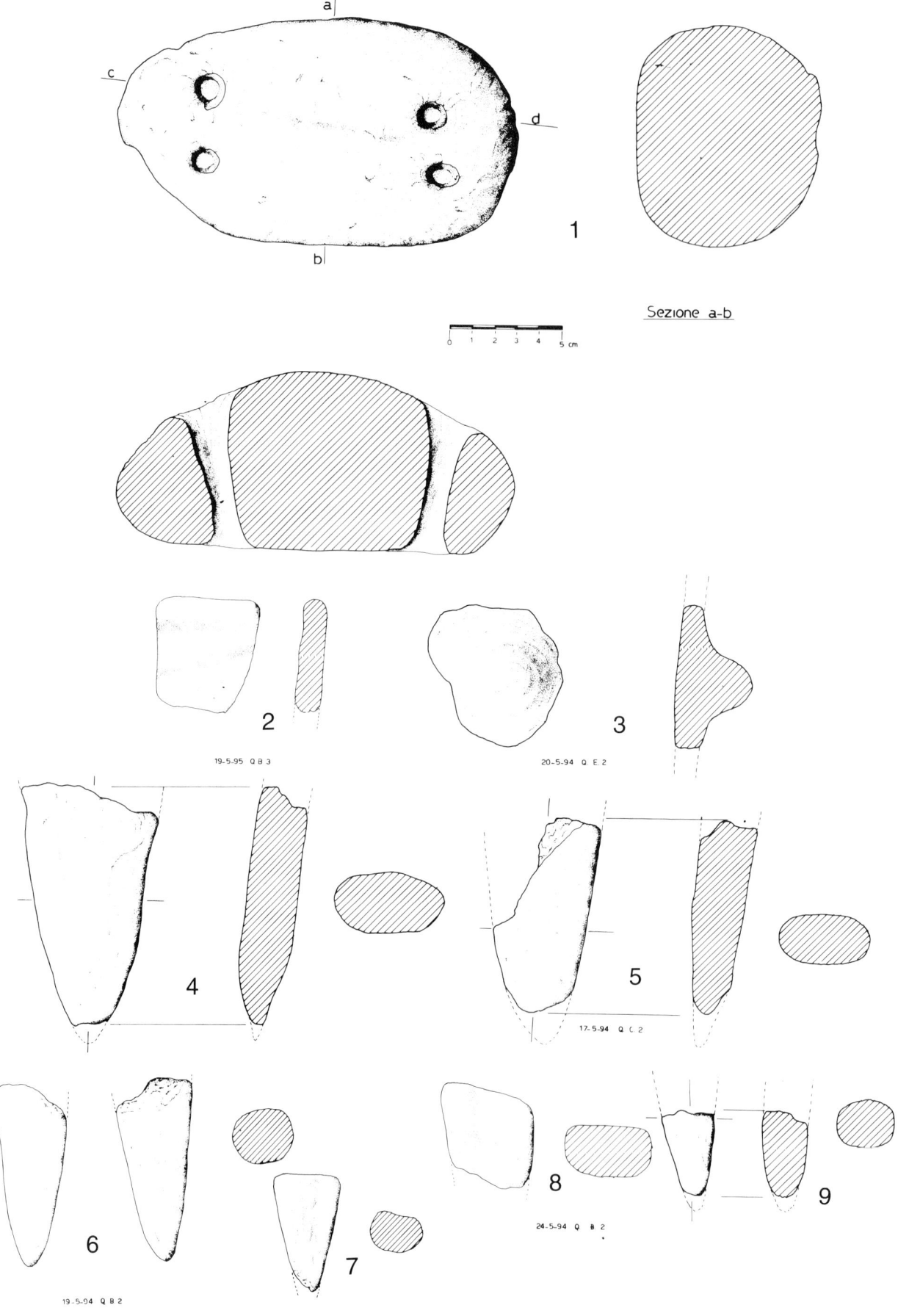

Fig. 17.6. Dolmen di Berchidda – Monte Acuto. Materiali ceramici. Scala circa 1:2.5.

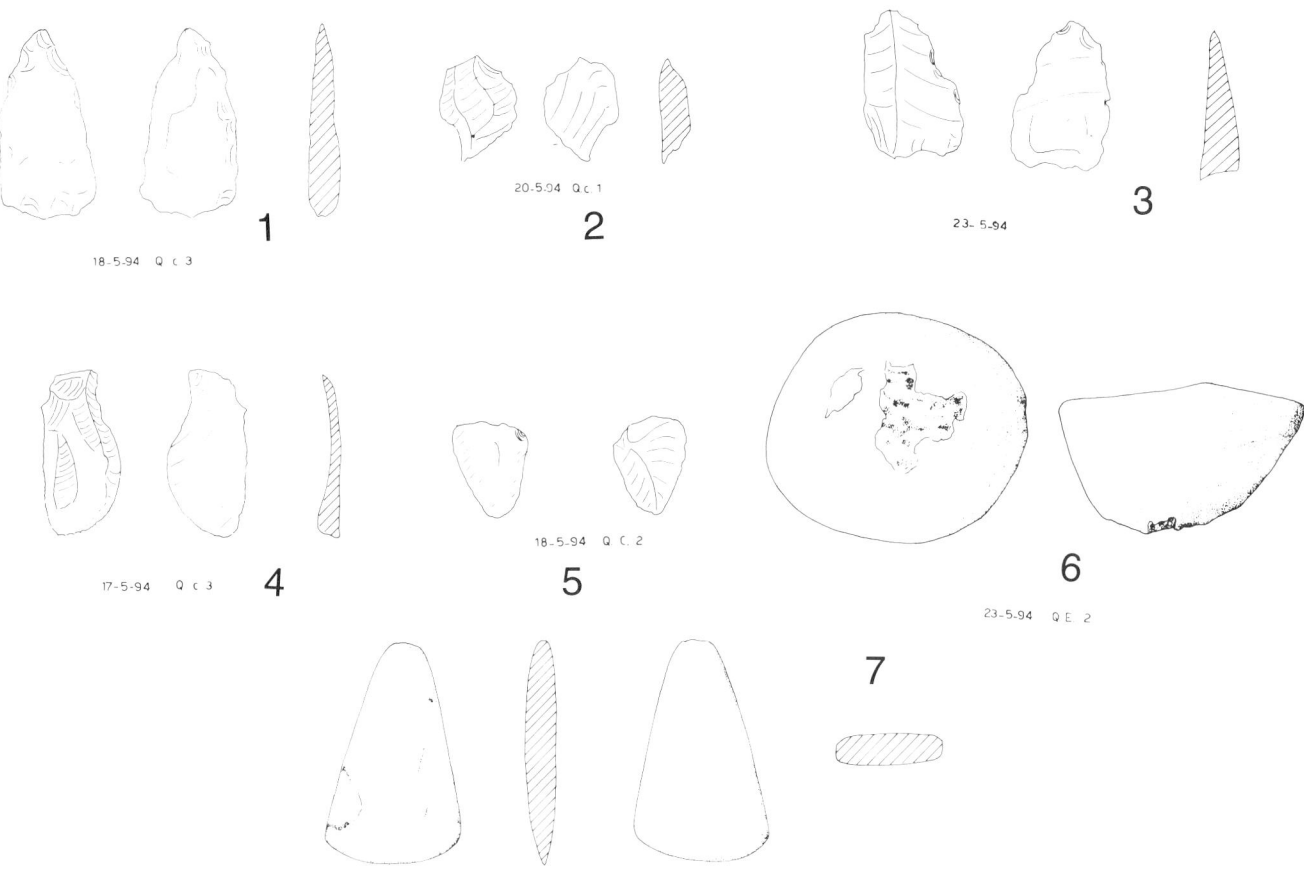

Fig. 17.7. Dolmen di Berchidda – Monte Acuto. Materiali litici. Scala 1:2.

numerose coppelle e nicchiette, mentre nella parte opposta, sulla punta è stata scavata una coppella. Procedendo verso la cresta montana, un menhir piramidale con base distinta sub-parallelepipeda (alt. 2,12 m.) giace rovesciato. Alla sommità si staglia un dolmen monumentale a lunga pianta rettangolare con pareti di fondo e laterali ricavate nella roccia e sormontate da un grande lastrone con coppelle e nicchie, seguito da scheggioni di granito che completano la copertura. Lungo il costone roccioso si individuano un anfratto sormontato da scheggioni di granito; una roccia a coppelle, nicchiette, un ipogeo monocellulare degradato, un dolmen a pianta rettangolare delimitato da due ortostati e scheggioni laterali e sormontato da un lastrone poligonale di copertura. Un altro dolmen ha le pareti laterali di roccia integrata con scheggioni di granito. Un muro megalitico in dissesto costruito con pietre di media pezzatura recinge un pianoro dove si seguono strutture a fil di suolo e una cista litica, che sovrastano il dolmen monumentale e i monumenti sopra descritti. Numerosi sono inoltre i tafoni con nicchie e coppelle e almeno un altro dolmen con copertura di rozzi scheggioni alcuni dei quali recano delle coppelle. Singolare un dolmen a pianta rettangolare con lastrone di copertura a doppio spiovente. Alla base del versante opposto si staglia un menhir con coppella e un dolmen che sfrutta la roccia per le pareti laterali sormontate da un lastrone.

3. Sant'Andrea – Mesu Serra (Fig. 17.1,20; Pl. 23–25). Sul versante di fronte ad Abialzos, nell'area pedemontana presso la chiesa di Sant'Andrea sono i due dolmens omonimi. Il primo è costituito da due grossi massi di granito, uno per lato, appiattiti all'interno e uno simile da sua fondo, integrati da scheggioni di granito. Il monumento è sormontato da un lastrone di copertura rozzamente circolare, lavorato nella parte superiore e appiattito in quella interna. Intorno sono le tracce del peristalite. Del secondo dolmen, a pianta rettangolare, residuano una pietra di fondo, una della parete destra appiattita all'interno e un'altra di quella sinistra. La lastra di copertura spezzata è stata riutilizzata in un vicino muro a secco. Sul crinale, del versante opposto a questo, è situato il dolmen di Mesu Serra, a pianta rettangolare, delimitato da due ortostati laterali lavorati sulla parete interna. La parete di fondo è costituita da un lastrone irregolare o una roccia

lavorata all'interno, integrata da scheggioni di granito. Un lastrone giace davanti al monumento; altri, forse di copertura, si trovano presso il lato destro, il sinistro e in corrispondenza del fondo. Residua in posto un lastrone subrettangolare di copertura, spaccato in senso longitudinale. Intorno sono tafoni con coppelle incavate sul soffitto. In una roccia isolata a poca distanza dal dolmen è stata scavata una nicchia, forse per offerte, che ha restituito materiale ceramico indeterminabile e che doveva forse indicare la presenza del monumento sepolcrale e quindi la valenza cultuale del sito. Circa cento metri più a nord, in un'area recintata ad est da un muro megalitico, di cui residuano almeno tre filari, si trova un allineamento di almeno sei menhirs aniconici e un dolmen a pianta rettangolare privo di lastra di copertura con roccia adattata ad ortostato sinistro, ortostato di fondo e pietre a filari sul lato destro. Nei pressi si trovano un ampio tafone chiuso da un muretto a secco con pareti a coppelle; anfratti a coppelle e due nicchioni sormontati da una punta con coppelle.

4. Nulvara (Fig. 17.1,21 e Pl. 26–29). Presso la chiesa di San Salvatore di Nulvara sono i resti del dolmen di Sa Cheja, a pianta rettangolare costituita da un paio di filari, mentre il lastrone di copertura pentagonale è rovesciato a lato. Segue quindi un'area rocciosa in cui si aprono numerosi tafoni. Su una roccia isolata a circa un metro dal piano di calpestio è stata scavata una nicchia emisferica con portello rettangolare con angoli arrotondati e lati appiattiti. Sul lato opposto si apre un tafone. Più avanti è un circolo megalitico con almeno tre steli. Segue quindi un ipogeo circondato da un muro con un corridoio d'ingresso delimitato da lastroni infissi a coltello. Ancora nell'area è un dolmen che sfrutta la roccia naturale; un menhir protoantropomorfo ed uno antropomorfo con segno dell'orifizio del glande nella parte superiore; un lastrone subcircolare fuori contesto; resti di una muraglia megalitica che recingeva il sito.

Alà dei Sardi

Il megalitismo si situa in una zona di altopiano granitico e in particolare ai piedi del monte che domina il paese.

1. Dolivichima (Fig. 17.1,22). Dei due dolmens presenti nella località il meglio conservato ha la camera rettangolare costituita da due filari di pietre visibili, sormontati da un unico lastrone rettangolare (Baltolu 1973: 94 fig. 13 e tav. XIII,1–3; Santoni 1973: 29–30 n. 27–28).
2. Malacarruca (Fig. 17.1,23). La sepoltura, racchiusa da un cordone ellittico a grossi blocchi poligonali di granito, si compone di un vano anteriore a cassetta coperto da un'unica lastra e da una lunga galleria posteriore ricoperta da lastre. Un portellino, compreso fra due blocchi-stipiti sormontati da architrave, mette in comunicazione i due vani (Baltolu 1973: 68–75).

Buddusò

Il megalitismo in quest'area privilegia zone dell'altopiano granitico nettamente diverse da quelle in cui si aprono gli ipogei che sono assai numerosi. Compaiono tuttavia negli ipogei di Ludurru, Pedru Ischintu e Oltulò i segni della religione megalitica (Baltolu 1973: 44ss.; Basoli 1991: 37). Tali segni si ritrovano in località Ludurru nei salti di Buddusò, lungo le vie della transumanza verso Olbia.

1. Monimentos (Fig. 17.1,24). Il dolmen semplice subcircolare si trova vicino ad un altro monumento simile crollato e ad un menhir protoantropomorfo (Taramelli 1919: 127–132; Basoli 1984b: 398).
2. Sa Janna de su Laccu (Fig. 17.1,25; Pl. 30). Coffre rettangolare costituito da tre lastroni laterali ed uno di copertura di granito, orientato a sud con resti del muro che doveva sorreggere il tumulo (Taramelli 1931: 10, n. 13; Lilliu 1988: 607; Sanciu 1982: 331ss.).
3. Elcomis (Fig. 17.1,26). Dolmen a pianta rettangolare con cinta ellittica destinata a reggere il tumulo di copertura della cassa (Lilliu 1988: 195ss.).
4. Orunitta (Fig. 17.1,27). Della necropoli residuano un dolmen e tracce di altri tre. Il monumento è a pianta rettangolare con pareti ricavate nella roccia granitica, sormontate da lastrone di copertura irregolare. Nei pressi giace un menhir aniconico (altezza 2,40 m.) (Basoli 1991: 40). Altri dolmens citati dal Lilliu e dal Santoni in territorio di Buddusò non sono finora stati ritrovati (Lilliu 1957: 68; Santoni 1973: 30–31).
5. Padru (Fig. 17.1,28). Una necropoli dolmenica, costituita da oltre una decina di monumenti sepolcrali con vano tombale a filari sormontato da lastra di copertura, si trova presso le chiese medioevali di Santu Miali e Santu Larentu.
6. Punta Isteddi (Fig. 17.1,29; Pl. 31–32). Nei salti di Buddusò, frazione di Ludurru in località Sa Pedra bianca, in una zona obbligata di passaggio di transumanza, si apre un riparo sottoroccia nel granito che presenta innumerevoli protuberanze di forma irregolare subcircolare e subellittica, variamente articolate, circondate da una linea di contorno verdastra marcata. Si tratta di formazioni rocciose denominate migmatiti a cui sono state aggiunte dalla mano dell'uomo le linee di contorno. Di questo si parlerà più diffusamente nella scheda geologica allegata.

Nughedu San Nicolò

Il megalitismo si situa in zone elevate nettamente distinte dalle numerose aree caratterizzate dalla presenza dell'ipogeismo. Solo in località S'Istria il dolmen semplice si integra con la necropoli ipogeica che reca i segni della religione megalitica.

1. Punta Sordanu (Fig. 17.1,30; Pl. 33–37). Su un altopiano in località Su Pedrighinosu, una muraglia megalitica a doppio paramento con pietrame minuto all'interno, di cui si conservano fino a tre filari per una lunghezza di circa 60 m., recinge il dirupo e delimita una necropoli dolmenica. Un dolmen, inserito in un muro a secco, ha pianta rettangolare con ortostati laterali integrati da scheggioni di granito e sormontati da un monolito sub-triangolare con vertice in corrispondenza del fondo. La faccia a vista dell'apertura è appiattita. A circa tre metri dal monumento giace un menhir aniconico (altezza 1,20 m. circa) che ha la punta arrotondata e i lati divergenti che nella parte inferiore convergono verso la base rozzamente sbozzata. Un altro megalito simile a questo è rovesciato nelle vicinanze. Dei dolmens a nord e a est di quello già descritto si individuano i lastroni di copertura. In particolare quello ad ovest ha il lato sinistro costituito dalla roccia naturale integrata da pietre che formano gli altri lati sui quali poggia il lastrone di copertura. Questo si inarca nella parte superiore dell'ingresso e presenta sulla fronte una coppella al centro ed una coppellina sulla destra di chi guarda. Un altro dolmen a sud del primo descritto ha pianta rettangolare. Il lato destro è costituito da tre lastroni coperti da una lastra rettangolare e da uno all'esterno; il lato sinistro presenta due pietre con rincalzi e quello di fondo una.
2. Su Crabu Figu (Fig. 17.1,31; Pl. 38). Uno scheggione di granito a contorno rozzamente rettangolare costituisce la lastra di copertura di un dolmen semplice. I sostegni sono crollati e il lastrone poggia attualmente sulla roccia e su una pietra. Nei pressi giace un menhir aniconico. Sono inoltre numerose le rocce con nicchie e coppelle presenti nell'area. C'è anche un tafone chiuso da un muretto.
3. S'Istria (Fig. 17.1,32; Pl. 39). A mezza costa dell'altura che sovrasta la fertile vallata solcata dal rio Iscias de Trigu si individua il rozzo lastrone sub-ovale di un dolmen di tipo semplice, a pianta rettangolare contornata da pietre. Questo sembra appoggiarsi nella parte terminale ad un muro di contenimento che si individua per almeno due filari ed è rincalzato nel lato sinistro scosceso da grosse pietre. Sul lastrone, coperto di muschio, si riconoscono almeno due piccole coppelle senza ordine. In alto sul costone di tufo trachitico si aprono gli ipogei omonimi e quelli vicini di Pianu Edras, che recano i segni della religione megalitica (Basoli 1992a: 157). L'altura è a breve distanza dalla necropoli ipogeica di Sos Furrighesos, al confine tra i territori di Nughedu San Nicolò e di Anela, nota per le importanti raffigurazioni di arte preistorica (Tanda 1984).

Ittireddu

1. Lavrudu (Fig. 17.1,33). Menhir (Galli 1983: 24).

Mores

1. Sa Coveccada (Fig. 17.1,34). Su un altopiano trachitico che domina un'estesa necropoli ipogeica, è situato il dolmen monumentale con lastrone frontale con portellino, nicchia esterna e nicchia-stipo interna. Nei pressi giace il menhir aniconico (Atzeni 1966a: 129–151).

L'ambiente

Il Lilliu, tracciando il panorama in cui si manifesta il fenomeno megalitico, parla di rapporto ecologico che si viene ad instaurare fra il monumento e l'ambiente in cui questo si inserisce (Lilliu 1968: 90). Questo aspetto si evidenzia in modo mirabile nel territorio di Berchidda, in cui si trovano le ultime propaggini della catena montuosa del Limbara e della Gallura, i cui aspetti archeologici sono stati intuiti ed evidenziati dal Puglisi (1941–42; Puglisi & Castaldi 1966) e dal Lilliu (1950) e i cui rapporti con l'area corsa sono stati puntualizzati ancora da quest'ultimo studioso (Lilliu 1966: 67; 1968a: 32). La roccia granitica modellata e frantumata dagli agenti atmosferici si presta a costituire la facile materia prima per dar vita a ripari naturali, a tafoni sepolcrali chiusi da muretti, a forme architettoniche miste naturali e costruite, a costruzioni subaeree, a segni quali coppelle e nicchiette che a stento tradiscono l'impronta lasciata dalla mano dell'uomo.

Sono proprio questi luoghi elevati che recano il segno degli elementi scatenati dalla natura, che devono aver colpito l'immaginario di queste genti sì da indurle a farne la dimora sacro-sepolcrale delle loro memorie. Non è un caso che miti e leggende siano rimaste nell'immaginario collettivo delle attuali popolazioni. La roccia forata che sovrasta il dolmen di Monte Acuto, quasi a segnalarne l'ubicazione, è ancora oggi denominata Sa inestra (la finestra). Ancora oggi questi ambienti suscitano nel visitatore profonde suggestioni e un'atmosfera di sacralità.

Le aree megalitiche – scarsamente circoscritte e isolate, più frequentemente vaste e complesse – occupano cime montane, circondate da muraglie in cui si snodano percorsi forse rituali, segnati da nicchie e megaliti anche in allineamento. È questa la situazione di Monte Acuto, con il dolmen che non doveva essere accessibile da alcun luogo, circondato com'era nell'area antistante da muri e da rocce che formavano uno spiazzo rozzamente circolare. Forse la roccia forata di cui si è detto sopra doveva giocare un ruolo particolare nell'ambito di un rituale, attualmente non più ricostruibile. Un percorso si snodava poi verso l'alto segnato da tafoni, utilizzati come sepolture, e da megaliti.

Ancora più vaste e complesse da definire sono le aree megalitiche contigue di S. Caterina-Abialzos e di S. Andrea-Mesu Serra che si articolano verso le creste montane e dominano un antico sentiero che conduce a Nulvara e quindi in Gallura. Nell'area di S. Salvatore di Nulvara è presente anche l'ipogeismo con forme contratte e degradate, circoscritto com'è ad una nicchia ben lavorata che si integra con un tafone e ad un ipogeo di fattura rozza con un corridoio dolmenico che sembra costituire un forte elemento di sostrato, profondamente radicato nella sfera cultuale.

L'articolazione delle aree megalitiche verso l'alto si individua in agro di Ozieri sulla montagna che sovrasta Bisarcio (Borroiles–Luzzanas) e a Monte Silvari; ad Oschiri a Berre e a Monte Cuccu; ad Alà sul monte che sovrasta il paese (Malacarruca e Dolivichima); a Nughedu San Nicolò sulla cima di Punta Sordanu; a Su Crabu Figu e a S'Istria. Ampie visuali su zone scoscese e dirupate configurano inoltre quegli spazi delimitati dalle muraglie megalitiche di Punta S'Arroccu (Ozieri), di Tanca Manna (Tula) e di Punta Sordanu (Nughedu San Nicolò) nonché i ripari istoriati di Luzzanas (Ozieri) e di Punta Isteddì (Buddusò). Non sfuggono i legami di queste aree megalitiche con habitat pastorali ed antiche vie di transumanza quali sono state ampiamente sottolineate per la Sardegna dal Lilliu (1981: 66; 1988: 188) e dall'Atzeni (1982: 17ss.).

In questo territorio è evidente la presenza di siti megalitici presso antichi sentieri in località Borroiles-Luzzanas in agro di Ozieri; Mandras-Pedredu-Monte Acuto in agro di Oschiri e di Berchidda; S. Caterina-Abialzos, S.Andrea-Mesu Serra, S. Salvatore-Nulvara in agro di Berchidda; S'Istria in agro di Nughedu S. Nicolò; Monimentos-Sa Janna de su Laccu in agro di Buddusò; Punta Isteddì e Padru nei Salti di Buddusò. Tali percorsi, ancora presenti nella memoria delle locali popolazioni pastorali, conservano consistenti tracce (miliari e ponti) dell'utilizzo in età romana (P. Meloni 1975: 70, 274ss.; Belli 1988: 376ss.; G. Meloni 1988: 16ss.; 1994: 21 n. 15, 28 n. 29). L'esistenza di uno stretto nesso culturale tra ambiente pastorale e megalitismo sembra peraltro trovare conferma nella raffigurazione di una protome di ariete, scolpita nell'ipogeo con corridoio dolmenico di Perfugas (Lo Schiavo 1982).

I monumenti

Pur devastati dall'ingiuria del tempo, depredati, riutilizzati e manomessi dalle opere di spietramento, i monumenti megalitici sono ben documentati in questo territorio con forme diverse riconducibili a tipologie insulari ed extrainsulari. Tra questi sono assai frequenti i dolmens di tipo semplice, ubicati sovente lungo le pendici di alture ma anche sulle cime. Presentano una struttura a pianta generalmente rettangolare con sostegni ad ortostati integrati con pietrame più piccolo oppure sono perimetrati interamente da pietre o in parte costituiti dalla roccia naturale. Sono sormontati da lastroni generalmente rettangolari o sub-ovali (S'Istria a Nughedu S. Nicolò e S. Andrea a Berchidda).

Il dolmen di Monimentos a Buddusò è l'unico a pianta circolare con lastrone di copertura circolare. Il vicino dolmen di Sa Janna de Su Luccu, per la perfetta positura delle strutture portanti e della copertura, costituisce un vero e proprio cassone litico, unico finora in tutto il territorio. Ad Abialzos (Berchidda) un dolmen a pianta rettangolare infossato ha un lastrone di copertura a doppio spiovente.

Questi monumenti megalitici più o meno interrati sono talvolta inseriti in muri che fungono da sostegno delle strutture portanti e da contenimento del terreno in pendenza (S'Istria). Talvolta sono circondati da peristalite per sostenere il tumulo e da menhirs peritafici. Isolati o in necropoli questi dolmens si trovano sia in aree caratterizzate dalla presenza solamente di resti megalitici oppure convivono con l'ipogeismo. In queste ultime situazioni gli ipogei sembrano recepire influenze che si manifestano nell'adozione di particolari elementi simbolici (coppelle e nicchie esterne) ma anche di particolari architettonici, come ad esempio la lavorazione dei lati esterni dell'ipogeo di Furrighesu ad Oschiri, presso il complesso megalitico di Berre, che lo fanno somigliare ad un dolmen. L'area di diffusione comprende i territori di Tula, Oschiri, Berchidda, Alà, Buddusò e Nughedu in una zona che fa da cerniera fra la Gallura e l'interno della Sardegna.

Esiste poi una categoria di dolmens che per le dimensioni possono essere considerati monumentali; su tutti spicca per compiutezza e originalità Sa Coveccada di Mores che sovrasta con la sua imponenza una estesa necropoli ipogeica. Ancora maestoso, a giudicare dai resti rovesciati sul terreno doveva essere quello di Borroiles (Ozieri), non distante dal riparo istonato di Luzzanas e ancora quello di Malghesi (Oschiri) ormai in dissesto che sovrastava l'omonima necropoli ipogeica. A questi va aggiunto il dolmen di Montiju Coronas (Ozieri) che presenta una struttura complessa in cui alla imponente struttura dolmenica si associa un corridoio con lastroni di copertura che la precede. Il monumento, apparentemente isolato, si trova in un ambiente in cui non sono presenti necropoli ipogeiche.

È già stato sottolineato come le strutture megalitiche siano ovunque fortemente legate all'ambiente naturale particolarmente nelle aree granitiche di questo territorio. Si tratta di monumenti i cui lati sono ricavati nella roccia opportunamente adattata a costituire una pianta rettangolare e su cui poggia un lastrone più o meno naturale. Tra essi si individuano tipologie di modeste dimensioni, ma anche forme monumentali e articolate. Al primo tipo possono essere ricondotti esemplari individuati a S. Stefano (Oschiri), a Monte Acuto e ad Abialzos (Berchidda), ad Orunitta (Buddusò). Questi sembrerebbero costituire una sorta di dolmens naturali, assimilabili al tipo semplice, in cui convergono forse antiche tradizioni nella escavazione della roccia naturale e sovrapposizione della tecnica megalitica nell'uso della copertura cui ovviamente non può essere estranea la particolare conformazione della roccia granitica che si presta a particolari lavorazioni.

Un confortante confronto è rappresentato dal dolmen di Arbu I a pianta rettangolare di Birori, dove peraltro sono presenti per lo più monumenti megalitici a pianta sub-circolare (Moravetti 1985). Questo genere di monumenti è situato nel nostro territorio in ambienti estranei all'ipogeismo o comunque è localizzato in aree distanti da questo. A questa tipologia monumentale possono essere ascritte le sepolture di Monte Acuto e di Abialzos. Quest'ultimo presenta un grande lastrone di copertura nella parte iniziale, seguito da scheggioni di granito nella parte restante del monumento.

Anche qui, al trattamento interno delle pareti rocciose si unisce l'uso della copertura monolitica che nel monumento di Abialzos si integra con lastroni più piccoli, tipici dei corridoi che accompagnano ad esempio il dolmen di Montiju Coronas (Ozieri). D'altra parte i contesti nei quali sono inseriti questi dolmens con strutture naturali non lasciano dubbi che ci troviamo in aree megalitiche. Rientrano nell'utilizzo da parte dell'uomo dell'ambiente naturale in questa area gli anfratti (tafoni) chiusi da pietre che formano muretti e le cavità sigillate da scheggioni di granito presenti a Mandras, Berre, Monte Cuccu (Oschiri), Monte Acuto, Abialzos, S. Caterina e Mesu Serra (Berchidda). Sono presenti inoltre in tali aree anche anfratti sulla cui parete opposta si aprono nicchie ben lavorate con tecnica ipogeica (Su balcone a Nulvara –Berchidda; Pedredu–Oschiri).

Vi sono poi ipogei che si uniscono a strutture dolmeniche, così il corridoio rettangolare ad ortostati che precede l'ipogeo S. Salvatore di Nulvara; così la domus di Coloras (Tula) con un circolo antistante l'ingresso, così la domus di Furrighesu (Oschiri) che mostra gli adattamenti esterni già citati, nonché parte di un cerchio di pietre che forse chiudeva l'area davanti all'ingresso, come a Campu Marinu I (Dorgali), nel cui sito era anche un dolmen ora scomparso, e che ha restituito un frammento di tazza carenata (Manunza 1995: 43 fig. 50, 65 n. 13, 66; Fadda 1980: 55.14).

Funzione peritafica rivestono i menhirs di questo territorio in quanto situati presso i monumenti sepolcrali generalmente singoli, e raramente disposti in raggruppamento (Abialzos) ed in allineamento (Mesu Serra). Si tratta di megaliti aniconici a contorno sub-triangolare, anche se non mancano quelli a pilastro angolare, sub-ellittico, conico o piramidale. Un menhir conico da Abialzos con coppella si trova in raggruppamento con altri megaliti non altrimenti definibili. Un menhir piramidale, sempre da Abialzos ha la base distinta sub-circolare. Un megalito di S. Salvatore di Nulvara presenta il segno dell'orifizio del glande che lo fa assomigliare ad un fallo come il betilo in loc.

S'Abbaia di Silanus (Lilliu 1957: 52 fig. 17,3).

Le muraglie megalitiche, di cui si è già accennata la tecnica costruttiva, sono finora in numero di tre in questo territorio. Di queste almeno due, quelle di Tula e di Nughedu, sono in relazione ad un'area sacro-sepolcrale le cui caratteristiche andranno meglio precisate con uno scavo. Tutte trovano confronti per la tecnica costruttiva con la muraglia di Monte Baranta di Olmedo (Contu 1962: 640–641; Moravetti 1979a: 334; 1981: 282ss.). Altri confronti possono essere instaurati con le strutture megalitiche di Monte Ossoni (Castelsardo) (Moravetti 1979b: 332ss.) e di Biriai (Oliena) (Castaldi 1979: 231–242; 1981: 153–221; 1984a: 567–584; 1984c: 119–153; 1985: 29–54). Più labili sono le tracce, tutte da verificare con uno scavo archeologico, di muri di contenimento che terrazzano alture o recingono aree sacre, note a Biriai (Castaldi 1981: 154, 163).

I simboli

La coppella è certamente un simbolo ricorrente nelle aree megalitiche. Si ritrova nel terzo superiore del menhir di Abialzos in raggruppamento con altri menhirs aniconici in una sorta di accoppiamento rituale e culturale già ipotizzato per situazioni simili. Sulla funzione simbolica del menhir ha disquisito ampiamente il Lilliu analizzando i riscontri insulari ed extrainsulari (Lilliu 1981: 73ss.).

Particolarmente interessante è una roccia che introduce ad Abialzos, la cui punta è segnata da una coppella mentre sulla faccia opposta numerose coppelle sovrastano una nicchia che si apre nella parte inferiore, chiusa ancora in parte da scheggioni di granito. Il Lilliu cita un menhir barbaricino forato con coppelle a cui attribuisce un significato di megalito femminile in cui si sentitizzano i concetti di nutrice e fattrice (Lilliu 1981: 74). Tale concetto è forse da estendere a questa roccia profondamente pregnante di motivi simbolici.

La coppella si ritrova nel lastrone di copertura del dolmen semplice di S'Istria. Sulla fronte del lastrone di copertura di uno dei dolmens di Punta Sordanu a Nughedu le coppelle sono due, disposte in modo asimmetrico. Uno solo di questi simboli si ritrova sulla parete destra del dolmen di Monte Acuto, mentre numerosi si stagliano nella parte più interna della copertura. In questo caso i segni del rituale sono indicati all'interno del monumento.

Importanti confronti per la presenza del motivo a coppella sono la grotta del Bue marino di Dorgali e la domus V di Pontesecco di Sassari. Nel primo esempio la coppella compare sulla parete all'interno della grotta in relazione ad antropomorfi itifallici incisi in atteggiamento di oranti e a due grafemi costituiti da due cerchi con una piccola coppella al centro. La Lo Schiavo assimila i grafemi e la coppella alla raffigurazione del disco solare (Lo Schiavo 1980: 43; 1986: 12). Ancora nella *domus* V di Pontesecco abbiamo l'associazione fra coppella e capovolto, considerato un simbolo antropomorfo funerario e attribuito alla cultura di Filigosa-Abealzu (Atzeni 1980: 37ss.; 1988: 454; Tanda 1984: II,121; 1988: 541ss.; Ferrarese Ceruti 1989: 40; 1992: 14; Tiné 1992: vii ss.). Forse il significato della coppella sulla parete del dolmen di Monte Acuto e gli incavi nella parete più interna del lastrone di copertura vanno ricercati in simbologie cosmiche (luna e stelle?) legate alla fine della vita e all'oscuro mondo ultraterreno che si alternano ai simboli solari nell'eterno divenire. Un importante riscontro interpretativo del capovolto è stato individuato dall'Atzeni nell'ambito dell'arte schematica iberica che compare in dolmens e ripari (Atzeni 1979–80: 39, n. 30–31).

Le coppelle si trovano soprattutto a segnare rocce, forse in relazione ad un rituale di cui ci sfugge il significato. Particolarmente significative sono le rocce con questi simboli presenti nel sito di Santo Stefano ad Oschiri. Sono espressioni di quel tipo di culto all'aperto di cui parla il Lilliu a proposito delle rocce a nicchie e coppelle presenti in Italia e all'estero, a cui la Sardegna sembrava essere estranea (Lilliu 1981: 80–82).

Alla stessa concezione rituale vanno forse ascritte quelle nicchie naturali che introducono a siti sepolcrali megalitici presenti, come si è visto sopra, a Mesu Serra e ad Abialzos. È interessante sottolineare che una nicchietta si trova a lato del lastrone frontale del dolmen di Sa Coveccada di Mores (Atzeni 1966a).

Sono inoltre da citare quelle nicchie – tafoni di cui si è parlato per S. Salvatore di Nulvara e Pedredu e quelle nicchie esterne presenti a Santo Stefano, a Monte Cuccu, a Malghesi e a S'Istria.

In relazione a queste pratiche cultuali e rituali va letto il riparo istoriato di Luzzanas per cui si rimanda alla citazione bibliografica e il cui nesso con il megalitismo è evidente in Sardegna e fuori dell'isola. Allo stesso ambito culturale va riferito, pur con le cautele dovute ad una incompleta investigazione dell'area, il riparo sotto-roccia, segnalato di recente nei Salti di Buddusò, nella frazione di Ludurru.

Il sito denominato Punta Isteddì, Su Monte di sa Femina, Sa Pedra Bianca, Sa Pedra Longa è situato lungo una via naturale di transumanza che da Buddusò conduce tuttora i pastori verso il mare. Il riparo presenta formazioni granitiche in rilievo (migmatiti), circondate da una larga solcatura verdastra che non appartiene alla formazione naturale come si evince dalla nota geologica di C. A. Artizzu (in questo volume, p. 159). I motivi figurativi non trovano precisi riscontri ma solo generiche analogie che potrebbero forse assimilarle a coppelle in positivo. L'immaginario collettivo, sotteso ai toponimi del sito, suggerisce particolari riferimenti alla religione megalitica e in particolare Isteddì ricorda simbologie cosmiche, ipotizzate per dolmens, menhirs e statue-stele (Lilliu 1981: 78).

Un ultimo riferimento va fatto alla forma del monumento dolmenico spesso interpretato come tipo di abitazione (Lilliu 1988: 196). Porta forse un contributo a questa ipotesi la presenza di quella singolare lastra di copertura del dolmen di Abialzos, che sembra potersi collegare ad un tetto a doppio spiovente di un tipo di casa rettangolare che ci proponiamo di ricercare sul terreno.

La toponomastica di alcuni siti megalitici del Monte Acuto riporta continui riferimenti a S. Michele, Santa Caterina, S. Andrea, S. Stefano che indicano la continuità di culto dei luoghi in epoca cristiana dove sono edificate chiese. La storiografia tardo-antica ricorda quanto fosse radicato nelle popolazioni della Sardegna il culto megalitico (Lilliu 1981: 127ss.). In particolare i santi citati sono assai venerati nel momento bizantino a cui forse dobbiamo ricondurre l'impegno di cristianizzare i luoghi del paganesimo. D'altra parte l'uomo bizantino sentiva molto profondamente l'impegno nella lotta contro il demonio che riteneva insediato nei luoghi sacri al paganesimo (Cavallo 1992: 387ss.). In questo momento storico va forse inserito l'altare rupestre di Santo Stefano di Oschiri che si inquadra in una profonda tradizione megalitica radicata nel sito (Basoli 1993: 26–29). Allo stesso ambito culturale può forse essere ascritta la pietra scritta che alla base di Monte Acuto, presso l'antico sentiero, segna il percorso verso l'altura.

Inquadramento culturale

I siti megalitici del Monte Acuto sono stati spesso interessati da lavori di spietramento che hanno sconvolto i luoghi sì da rendere quanto mai difficile la lettura dei monumenti ad una semplice ricognizione di superficie. I dolmens più appariscenti hanno rappresentato nel corso degli anni un patrimonio sepolcrale da riutilizzare oppure sono stati del tutto depredati del deposito culturale. Gli unici elementi in nostro possesso per procedere ad un tentativo di inquadramento culturale sono costituiti dalle tipologie monumentali e da resti di cultura materiale, spesso poco significativi frutto di raccolte superficiali (dolmen di Montiju Coronas-Ozieri) o di scavo di un deposito interessato da un riutilizzo in età medioevale (dolmen di Monte Acuto-Berchidda). L'analisi fin qui condotta evidenzia una notevole diversificazione tipologica dei monumenti dolmenici che potrebbe essere in relazione ad influssi diversi in un'area caratterizzata dalla presenza di una pianura fertile solcata da corsi d'acqua e da vie naturali di comunicazione con la costa, come si è visto sopra; ad influssi temporalmente differenti e ad interazioni originali col sostrato autoctono che potrebbero aver dato origine a particolari localismi.

Tracciando questa strada, Maria Luisa Ferrarese Ceruti aveva individuato un filone culturale caratterizzato da dolmens a pianta rettangolare che dal Midi della Francia e dalla Penisola Iberica attraverso la Corsica avrebbe favorito il sorgere dei monumenti della Gallura, di Sa Coveccada di Mores e Dolivichima di Ala dei Sardi, presenti nel nostro territorio, nonché del dolmen di Monte Longu di Dorgali (Ferrarese Ceruti 1980b: 68). Si vanno inoltre precisando le collocazioni culturali dei complessi ipogeico-megalitici, per i quali l'Atzeni riconosce influssi occidentali e cambiamenti culturali collegabili a mutate ideologie influenzate dagli inizi della metallurgia a partire dalla Cultura di Ozieri (Atzeni 1989: 201ss.; 1992: 49ss.).

In particolare le strutture che integrano gli ipogei, compiutamente analizzate dalla Ferrarese Ceruti con particolare riferimento alle domus di Canudedda e Mariughia di Dorgali, vengono ormai attribuite a momenti di Cultura Ozieri sulla scorta dei dati di scavo (Ferrarese Ceruti 1980a: 57–65; Lo Schiavo 1982; Foschi Nieddu 1985; 1989; Atzeni 1989). La *domus* con ortostati a semicerchio davanti all'ingresso trova confronto con quella di Campu Marinu I o Valverde o Lussorgia di Dorgali, da cui proviene una tazza carenata (Fadda 1980: 55, n. 14; Manunza 1995: 43), che per le caratteristiche tipologiche sembra poter essere inquadrata genericamente nel Calcolitico. Le nicchie esterne presenti nei complessi ipogeico-megalitici, anche in forme naturali, hanno un parallelo nel Dorgalese dove presso il dolmen di Sos Dorroles una piccola apertura ha restituito alcuni frammenti di ciotoline e vasetti a cestello tipici della cultura di Ozieri (Manunza 1995: 70, 86ss., 89ss.).

Forti tradizioni ipogeiche si riscontrano in quei monumenti megalitici che presentano le pareti adattate nella roccia naturale come si evidenziano nel territorio di Berchidda, di Buddusò ma anche nel Marghine (Arbu 1). La struttura di Corte Noa (Laconi) costituisce un elemento di parziale confronto in quanto le pareti rocciose sono integrate dagli ortostati. La presenza del lastrone forato con la classica *porte de four* costituisce un elemento di raffronto alla lastra forata di Mores. I materiali conducono ad un inquadramento culturale Ozieri-Filigosa, ma sopratutto Abealzu (Atzeni 1988: 526ss.).

Particolarmente interessante per quanto riguarda la presenza nel nostro territorio di strutture miste naturali e artificiali che si configurano come gallerie integrate con lastre e tafoni chiusi da muretti sono le notazioni di J. Zammit circa il rinvenimento nell'Aude, nella parte occidentale della Linguadoca, di strutture simili utilizzate come sepolture nel Calcolitico. Lo stesso autore cita simili usanze funerarie attestate nella cultura di Fontbouisse (Zammit 1990–91: 151ss.).

Un esempio significativo è costituito dal dolmen di Monte Acuto (Berchidda), interessato da un intervento di scavo nell'area antistante e nella camera del monumento (Tav. 17.7). Il deposito terroso scuro, attraversato dalle radici degli alberi, ha evidenziato due livelli di cui quello superficiale con materiali preistorici e medioevali e l'altro con esclusiva ceramica preistorica, caratterizzata dalla presenza di un peso di grandi dimensioni, piedi di tripode e sopratutto due frammenti di ceramica decorata a scanalature attribuibili alla cultura di Monte Claro (Fig. 17.6, 1, 4–9, 2). Un'accentina in pietra nera proviene dall'area esterna al dolmen (Fig. 17.7).

La pietra forata che sovrasta il dolmen, denominata "Sa inestra" (la finestra), si può forse confrontare con i massi forati ed altri segni culturali e rituali e megaliti disseminati fra l'abitato Ozieri di Genna Sorti e le aree cimiteriali ipogeiche di Funtanassu, Padrillonis e Brentoni di Villa Sant'Antonio (Oristano) (Atzeni 1992: 49).

Più significativi taluni materiali provenienti dall'area del dolmen di Montiju Coronas (Ozieri) che presenta un corridoio laterale di chiaro influsso occidentale del Midi (Fig. 17.2).

All'orizzonte campaniforme può essere avvicinato il frammento forse di vaso a campana, decorato con motivo angolare campito da punteggio all'esterno e con triangoli campivi da linee all'interno (Fig. 17.3,1), che trova confronti in motivi decorativi presenti nella stazione di Quarciola in Toscana i cui materiali rientrano nell'ambito campaniforme dell'area centrale europea (Vigliardi 1988: 380ss., fig. 20, n. 2, n.5).

Rapporti tra la Sardegna e la Toscana, in relazione forse a traffici diretti o mediati dai gruppi beaker verso le colline metallifere, sono stati individuati per la presenza nel Grossetano (grotta del Fontino) di vasi molto simili alla ceramica a coppelle Abealzu-Filigosa in un contesto con vasi campaniformi e pugnali di rame che si confrontano con materiali coevi della Sardegna (Vigliardi 1980: 269; Foschi Nieddu 1986: 133ss.). In particolare il materiale fittile del Fontino graviterebbe nell'area campaniforme del Mediterraneo occidentale (Vigliardi 1988: 383).

Allo stesso orizzonte può essere attribuito il frammento di *brassard* (Fig. 17.4,13) che può essere confrontato con quello rinvenuto nel dolmen di Motorra di Dorgali in associazioni a materiali ceramici di cultura St. Vérédème (Lilliu 1966: 81; Ferrarese Ceruti 1980a: 64, tav. XVIII,13).

Il pendaglio ellittico forato in pietra (Fig. 17.4,14), trova confronto in un ornamento di collana in arenaria da Cuccuru Is Arrius presente nella collezione Falchi di Oristano, che la Depalmas confronta con materiali della Corsica e del Midi della Francia (Depalmas 1989: 129, n. 34, tav. XIX,1).

Più generica l'attribuzione dei piedi di tripode (Fig. 17.3, 9–12) a causa della framentarietà, per alcuni dei quali più chiaramente riconducibili ai tipi a sezione concavo convessa si può individuare una matrice Abealzu Filigosa, presenti in ambiti megalitici e/o ipogei in contesti riferibili a questa cultura. In ambito megalitico sono presenti a Sa Korona di Villagreca (Atzeni 1966b: 122–123, 125 fig. 12E), nel dolmen di Motorra (Dorgali) (Lilliu 1968a: 83), nel santuario di Monte d'Accoddi (Sassari) (Contu 1953: 201; Tinè 1992: 161; Tinè *et al.* 1989: 27, 31 tav. 3), nel villaggio di Cabula Muntones (Sassari) (Basoli 1988: 534; 1989: 15–31ss., 36). In contesto ipogeico riferibile alla cultura suddetta questo tipo di piedi di tripode è noto nella tomba I di Filigosa (Foschi Nieddu 1986: 64) e nella tomba A di Serra Cannigas (Villagreca) (Atzeni 1985: 14, 19 fig. 4,8 e 20,8). Sono inoltre noti nell'abitato di Terramaini di Pirri (Usai 1987: 177, 193 fig. 2,1–4, fig.3,1–2, fig. 4,2–3, 182).

Il piccolo coperchio in argilla rosata molto depurata con resti di presa (Fig. 17.3,8) non trova finora precisi confronti fra quelli noti in ambito Abealzu Filigosa e Monte Claro.

La cuspide a foglia (Fig. 17.4,1) sembra potersi confrontare con il pugnaletto di tipo "remedelliano" di Pranu Mutteddu di Goni (Atzeni 1979–80: 60,2; Atzeni & Cocco 1989: 201, 212 fig. 4.1). Particolarmente interessante è la notazione della Cocco sui confronti dell'esemplare dal dolmen di Bois de Mar e delle varianti rinvenute nella Francia meridionale.

Una grande lama a ritocco foliato – confrontata con i pugnali della necropoli di Remedello nel Bresciano e proveniente dal sepolcreto eneolitico di Covoloni del Broion (Colli Berici) – è del tutto simile alla nostra (Bianchin Citton & Guerreschi 1988: 621,8).

La tipologia delle armature di freccia (Fig. 17.4, 2–7) e delle accette litiche (Fig. 17.4, 8–12) non consente di individuare confronti con elementi caratteristici neolitici o eneolitici, forse anche in relazione a caratteristiche tecniche elaborate localmente. Gli oggetti in pietra levigata con foro pervio (Fig. 17.4,15) e impervio (Fig. 17.4,16) possono essere assimilati alle teste di mazza sferoidi e discoidi, note in contesti megalitici a Li Muri (Puglisi 1941–42: 131), a Monte d'Accoddi (Museo G.A. Sanna– Sassari), a Su Cungiau de Marcu di Decimoputzu (Ferrarese Ceruti 1974: 268), a S. Michele di Fonni (Lilliu 1981: 103) e a Goni (Atzeni & Cocco 1989: 201, 211, fig. 4,7). Si ritrovano altresì fra i materiali della cultura di Monte Claro, che presenta significativi complessi megalitici (Lilliu & Ferrarese Ceruti 1960: 82, n. 50 e fig. 23,11, tav. XXXIV,1; Contu 1988: 448; Basoli & Foschi Nieddu 1993: 71). L'Atzeni individua rapporti in ambiti del Mediterraneo centrale ed orientale (Atzeni & Cocco 1989: 201). Sull'utilizzo delle teste di mazza si rimanda alle considerazioni della Castaldi che sembra interpretarle come insegne di comando (Castaldi 1985: 36).

L'oggetto con foro impervio si potrebbe forse confrontare con le *galets à cupules*, presenti in contesti calcolitici di antica metallurgia nel Midi della Francia (Ambert 1990–91: 52 fig.1, 53 fig. 2). Occorre rilevare che nell'area antistante il dolmen di Montiju Coronas sono stati rinvenuti resti di fusione.

I menhirs citati rientrano generalmente nella tipologia dei megaliti aniconici rinvenuti in contesti di cultura di Ozieri a Goni (Atzeni 1989) a Monte d'Accoddi (Tinè 1992: XXss.), a S.Michele di Fonni (Lilliu 1981) a Cabula Muntones (SS), in contesto Abealzu Filigosa (Basoli 1989).

Le muraglie megalitiche del Monte Acuto presentano una struttura a doppio paramento a filari inframmezzato da pietrame minuto che può essere confrontata con il tipo 8 di muraglia individuato in base alle analisi di questo tipo di strutture presenti nei siti di Teyran (Hérault) e datate al calcolitico (G.B. Arnal *et al.* 1990–1991: 139 fig. 7,8). I confronti tipologici sono con strutture attribuite alla cultura di Monte Claro in cui sono presenti elementi campaniformi (vedi sopra). A. Moravetti in particolare per Monte Baranta confronta le strutture del villaggio con quelle dei siti francesi di cultura Fontbouisse di cui sono noti i paralleli con la cultura di Monte Claro (Moravetti 1981: 288). In particolare la muraglia di Tula è associata ad un circolo con menhirs come Monte Baranta di Olmedo (Moravetti 1981; 1988: 528ss.). Il circolo di Tula che ha all'interno tre menhirs, sembra potersi confrontare con il recinto di Terrier à Avrilé (Vandée) di contesto campaniforme in cui sono presenti armature ad alette e peduncolo e frammenti ceramici con impressione di solcature (Benéteau *et al.* 1992: 268, 271, 277–278 e fig. 22). Andranno meglio precisate le relazioni fra la muraglia megalitica di Punta Sordanu di Nughedu con l'area sepolcrale e i dolmens semplici ed i menhirs.

Per il riparo sotto-roccia di Luzzanas di Ozieri con gli antropomorfi dipinti, in cui è evidente il riferimento all'Occidente e in particolare all'arte schematica iberica con confronti in Corsica nelle grotta Scritta di Olmeta du Cap e nel riparo sotto roccia con esempi di pittura di Monte Bego attribuito al calcolitico (Burroni & Mezzena 1988: 428), è stata proposta l'attribuzione a fasi finali della cultura di Ozieri (Basoli 1992a: 502–504).

Gli elementi fin qui esposti in queste considerazioni preliminari evidenziano un quadro estremamente composto e frammentario con monumenti diversificati che sembrano essere articolati in relazione ad influssi diversi anche temporalmente e ad interazioni col sostrato autoctono che sembrano aver dato origine a particolari localismi. Si riconoscono tuttavia connotazioni e manifestazioni del megalitismo che presentano particolari somiglianze. Se per il dolmen di Sa Coveccada sono stati individuati accanto a marcati influssi occidentali anche confronti con l'Oriente, di cui potrebbero costituire parallelo quegli elementi di cultura materiale di Li Muri e forse l'architettura dell'altare-ziqqurat di Monte d'Accoddi, molto precisa e puntuale nel megalitismo di questo territorio sembra essere la matrice occidentale, principalmente iberica, giunta attraverso l'arco Eracleo, le Baleari e la Corsica lungo le rotte segnate dalla ricerca dei metalli. In questo quadro composto si inseriscono anche i contatti con le culture eneolitiche dell'Italia settentrionale e centrale di cui si è detto sopra. Più complessi da analizzare con i dati attualmente a disposizione i rapporti con le concentrazioni megalitiche della Gallura e qualle dell'interno dell'Isola, anche se non mancano elementi per individuare labili influssi di queste aree sul megalitismo di questo territorio che costituisce una zona di cerniera fra gli ambiti citati.

Ringraziamenti

I disegni sono di Giandomenico Fenu e le foto di Giovanni Porcu a cui va un sentito ringraziamento. Si ringraziano inoltre Mario Muredda, Leonardo Murgia, dell'ufficio operativo di Ozieri e gli ispettori onorari Salvatore Cuccu, Sebastiano Fenu e Tommaso Tuccone.

Bibliografia

Amadu, F. 1978. *Ozieri e il suo territorio dal Neolitico all'Età romana.* Ozieri.

Ambert, P. 1990–91. L'émergence de la Métallurgie Chalcolithique dans le Midi de la France. In *Le Chalcolithique en Languedoc. Ses relations extra-regionales*, 51–58. Saint-Mathieu de Tréviers.

Arnal, G.B. *et al.* 1990–1991. Propos sur l'évolution de l'architecture préhistorique des sites de Teyran (Hérault). In *Le Chalcolithique en Languadoc. Ses relations extra-regionales*, 133–139. Saint Matheu de Tréviers.

Atzeni, E. 1966a. Il dolmen di "Sa Coveccada" di Mores e la tomba di giganti di "Sa domu 'e S'orcu" di Quartucciu. *Studi Sardi* 20: 129–151.

Atzeni, E. 1966b. Il "nuraghe" sa Korona di Villagreca. *Atti del XIII Congresso di Storia dell'Architettura*, 119–124. Roma.

Atzeni, E. 1985. Tombe eneolitiche nel Cagliaritano. In *Studi in onore di Giovanni Lilliu per il suo settantesimo compleanno*, 11–49. Cagliari.

Atzeni, E. 1988. Megalitismo e Arte. *Rassegna di Archeologia* 7: 449–456.

Atzeni, E. 1992. Reperti neolitici dallo Oristanese. In *Sardinia Antiqua. Studi in onore di Piero Meloni*, 35–62. Cagliari.

Atzeni, E. & Cocco, D. 1989. Note sulla necropoli di Pranu Mutteddu – Goni. In Campus, L.D. (a cura di), *La Cultura di Ozieri: problematiche e nuove acquisizioni*, 201–209. Il Torchietto, Ozieri.

Baltolu, A. 1973. Alcuni monumenti inediti dell'altopiano di Buddusò e di Alà dei Sardi. *Studi Sardi* 22 (1971–72): 38–98, in particolare 68–75.

Belli, E. 1988. La viabilità Romana nel Logudoro-Meilogu. In *Il nuraghe S. Antine nel Logudoro-Meilogu*, 331–395. Sassari.

Basoli, P. 1984a. Il megalitismo. In *Il Monte Acuto*. Ozieri.

Basoli, P. 1984b. Buddusò (Sassari) – Loc. Pedru Ischintu. Loc. Oltulò. Loc. Monimentos. Oschiri (Sassari). Loc. Mandras, Notiziario. *Rivista di Scienze Preistoriche* 32: 398.

Basoli, P. 1985. Il megalitismo. In *Il Museo Civico Archeologico Ozieri*, 37–40. Il Torchietto, Ozieri.

Basoli, P. 1988. Il villaggio di Cabula Muntones (Sassari). *Rassegna di Archeologia* 7: 534.

Basoli, P. 1989. L'età prenuragica e nuragica. In *Sassari: le origini*, 11–48. Edizioni Gallizzi, Sassari.

Basoli, P. 1991. Buddusò dalla preistoria all'età romana. In *Buddusò: il territorio, l'economia, la memoria*, 29–52. Sassari.

Basoli, P. 1991–92. La stele di Luzzanas. In *"L'Età del Bronzo in Italia nei secoli dal XVI al XIV a.C.", Viareggio 26–30 ottobre 1989.* Rassegna di Archeologia 10: 778–779.

Basoli, P. 1992a. Scavi e scoperte. *Bollettino di Archeologia* 13–15 (gennaio-giugno): 157, 239ss.

Basoli, P. 1992b. Dipinti preistorici nel riparo di Luzzanas (Ozieri, Sassari). Tecniche di rilevamento, esame iconografico ed inquadramento culturale. In *Atti della XXVIII Riunione Scientifica dell'Istituto Italiano di Preistoria e Protostoria*, 495–506. Firenze.

Basoli, P. 1993. Oschiri: l'altare di S. Stefano, testimonianza della tradizione greco-bizantina. *Il Monte Acuto* 1: 26–29.

Basoli, P. & Foschi, A. 1991. Il sistema insediativo nuragico nel Monte Acuto: analisi preliminare dei fattori geomorfologici e socio-economici. In Frizell, B. Santillo (ed.), *Arte Militare e Architettura Nuragica. Proceedings of the First International Colloquium on Nuragic Architecture at the Swedish Institute in Rome, 7–9 December 1989*, 23–40. Stockholm.

Basoli, P. & Foschi Nieddu, A. 1993. Alcune annotazioni riguardo ai rapporti tra le Culture di Rinaldone e quella di Abealzu – Filigosa. In *La Cultura di Rinaldone. Ricerche e scavi*, 69–74. Milano.

Bénéteau, G. *et al.* 1992. L'enclos campaniforme à monolithes des Terriers à Avrilé (Vendée). *Gallia Prèhistoire* 3–4: 259–288.

Bianchin Citton, E. & Guerreschi, A. 1988. Il sepolcreto eneolitico della grottina dei Covoloni del Broion (Colli Berici). *Rassegna Archeologica* 7: 620–621.

Burroni, D. & Mezzena, F. 1988. Megalitismo ed arte rupestre in Italia settentrionale durante l'Eneolitico. *Rassegna di Archeologia* 7: 422–434 e 437–439.

Castaldi, E. 1979. Biriai (Oliena, Nuoro):il villaggio di cultura Monte Claro. *Rivista di Scienze Preistoriche* 34(1–2): 231–242.

Castaldi, E. 1981. Villaggio con santuario a Biriai (Oliena-Nuoro). *Rivista di Scienze Preistoriche* 36(1–2): 153–221.

Castaldi, E. 1984a. Cultura calcolitica di Monte Claro nel sito di Biriai (Oliena, Nuoro, Sardegna). In Waldren, W., Chapman, R. & Lewthwaite, J. (eds.), *Early Settlement in the Western Mediterranean Islands and Their Peripheral Areas.* BAR International Series 229: 567–584. British Archaeological Reports, Oxford.

Castaldi, E. 1984b. La necropoli di Li Muri. In *Arzachena*, 29–35. Sassari.

Castaldi, E. 1984c. L'architettura di Biriai (Oliena,Nuoro). *Rivista di Scienze Preistoriche* 39: 119–153.

Castaldi, E. 1985. Biriai e le fortezze prenuragiche: per una valutazione socio-culturale. *Studi Urbinati* B3, anno 58: 29–54. Università degli Studi di Urbino.

Cavallo, G. (a cura di). 1992. *L'uomo bizantino.* Editori Laterza.

Contu, E. 1953. Costruzione megalitica in località Monte d'Accoddi (Sassari). *Rivista di Scienze Preistoriche* 8: 199–202.

Contu, E. 1962. Il nuraghe Monte Baranta in località "Su Casteddu" o "Pala Reale" (Olmedo, Sassari). *Studi Sardi* 17(1959–61): 640–641.

Depalmas, A. 1989. Cuccuru Is Arrius (Cabras – OR) e Isca Maiori (Riola Sardo – OR) nella collezione Falchi di Oristano. *Antichità Sarde* 2: 95–144. Sassari.

Fadda, M.A. 1980. Domus de Janas: aspetti di architettura ipogeica. In *Dorgali. Documenti archeologici*, 47–55. Sassari.

Ferrarese Ceruti, M.L. 1974. Su Cungiau de Marcu. *Rivista di Scienze Preistoriche* 29(1): 268.

Ferrarese Ceruti, M.L. 1980a. Le domus de janas di Maringhia e Canudedda e il dolmen di Motorra. In *Dorgali. Documenti archeologici*, 57–65. Sassari.

Ferrarese Ceruti, M.L. 1980b. Il dolmen di Monte Longu. In *Dorgali. Documenti archeologici*, 67–69. Sassari.

Ferrarese Ceruti, M.L. 1989. Le necropoli di Su Crucifissu Mannu – PortoTorres e di Ponte Secco – Sassari. In Campus, L.D. (a cura di), *La cultura di Ozieri: problematiche e nuove acquisizioni*, 37–47. Il Torchietto, Ozieri.

Ferrarese Ceruti, M.L. 1992. Le necropoli a domus de janas nel territorio di Monte d'Accoddi. In *Monte d'Accoddi. 10 anni di nuovi scavi*, 10–20. Genova.

Foschi Nieddu, A. 1985. La tomba di Janna Ventosa (Nuoro). In *10 anni di attività nel territorio della provincia di Nuoro, 1975–1985*, 35. Nuoro.

Foschi Nieddu, A. 1989. Documenti di Cultura Ozieri provenienti dalla grotta di Sa Corona di Monte Majore – Thiesi e dalla necropoli di Janna Ventosa – Nuoro. In Campus, L.D. (a cura di), *La cultura di Ozieri. Problematiche e nuove acquisizioni*, 145–152. Il Torchietto, Ozieri.

Galli, F. 1983. *Archeologia del territorio: il Comune di Ittireddu (Sassari).* Quaderni 14. Dessì, Sassari.

Lilliu, G. 1950. Scoperte e scavi fattisi in Sardegna durante gli anni 1948-1949. *Studi Sardi* 9: 394-561.

Lilliu, G. 1957. Religione della Sardegna prenuragica. *Bullettino di Paletnologia Italiana* 15(1966): 7-96.

Lilliu, G. 1966. Sviluppo e prospettive dell'archeologia. *Studi Sardi* 19: 3-35.

Lilliu, G. 1968. Il dolmen di Motorra (Dorgali – NU). *Studi Sardi* 20(1966-67): 74-128.

Lilliu, G. 1968a. Rapporti tra la cultura "torreana" e gli aspetti pre e protonuragici della Sardegna. *Studi Sardi* 20(1966-67): 3-47.

Lilliu, G. 1981. *Monumenti antichi barbaricini*. Quaderni 10. Dessì, Sassari.

Lilliu, G. 1988. *La Civiltà dei Sardi dal Paleolitico all'Età dei nuraghi*. ERI, Torino.

Lilliu, G. & Ferrarese Ceruti, M.L. 1960. La "facies" nuragica di Monte Claro (Sepolcri di Monte Claro e Sa Duchessa e villaggi di Enna Pruna e Su Guventu – Mogoro). *Studi Sardi* 16: 3-266.

Lo Schiavo, F. 1980. La grotta del Bue Marino a Calagonone. In *Dorgali. Documenti archeologici*, 39-45. Sassari.

Lo Schiavo, F. 1982. La domus dell'Ariete (Perfugas – Sassari). *Rivista di Studi Preistoriche* 37: 135-186.

Lo Schiavo, F. 1985. Figure antropomorfe nella grotta del Bue marino (Dorgali – Nuoro). In *10 anni di attività nel territorio della provincia di Nuoro, 1975-1985*, 12-13. Nuoro.

Lo Schiavo, F. 1988. Il ripostiglio di Chilivani, Ozieri (Sassari). *Quaderni della Soprintendenza Archeologica per le Province di Cagliari e Oristano* 5: 77-90.

Lo Schiavo, F. 1992. Una matrice di fusione dal Monte Acuto (Berchidda-Sassari). In *Sardinia Antiqua. Studi in onore di Piero Meloni*, 153-163. Cagliari.

Lo Schiavo, F., Maddin, R., Merkel, J., Muhly, J.D. & Stech, T. 1990. *Analisi metallurgiche e statistiche sui lingotti di rame della Sardegna*. Quaderni 17. Il Torchietto, Ozieri.

Manunza, M.R. 1995. *Dorgali: monumenti antichi*. Oristano.

Meloni, G. 1988. *Mediterraneo e Sardegna nel Basso Medioevo*. Pisa.

Meloni, G. 1992. *Tula e il suo territorio nel Medioevo. Insediamento rurale nella Sardegna settentrionale*. Pisa.

Meloni, G. 1994. *Il castello di Monte Acuto – Berchidda*. Berchidda.

Meloni, G. & Modde, P. 1993. Il Monte Acuto. *Archivio Storico Sardo* 37: 89-124.

Meloni, P. 1975. *La Sardegna romana*. Sassari.

Meloni, P. 1991. *La Sardegna romana*. Sassari.

Moravetti, A. 1979a. Monte Baranta (Olmedo, prov. di Sassari). *Rivista di Scienze Preistoriche* 34(1-2): 334.

Moravetti, A. 1979b. Monte Ossoni (Castelsardo prov. di Sassari). *Rivista di Scienze Preistoriche* 34(1-2): 332 s.

Moravetti, A. 1981. Nota agli scavi del complesso megalitico di Monte Baranta (Olmedo – Sassari). *Rivista di Scienze Preistoriche* 36(1-2): 281-290.

Moravetti, A. 1985. *Il patrimonio archeologico del Comune di Birori*. Cagliari.

Moravetti, A. 1988. La cultura di Monte Claro nella Sardegna Settentrionale. *Rassegna di Archeologia* 7: 528-529.

Puglisi, S.M. 1941-42. Villaggi sotto-roccia e sepolcri megalitici della Gallura. *Bullettino di Paletnologia Italiana* 5-6: 123-141.

Puglisi, S.M. & Castaldi, E. 1966. Aspetti dello accantonamento culturale nella Gallura preistorica e protostorica. *Studi Sardi* 29: 59-148.

Santoni, V. 1973. Il dolmen di Sculacacca (Oniferi – Nuoro). *Studi Sardi* 22(1971-72): 3-37.

Sanciu, A. 1982. Buddusò – Sa Janna de su Laccu e Monte Colvos. *Rivista di Scienze Preistoriche* 37: 331-332.

Tanda, G. 1984. *Arte e religione della Sardegna preistorica nella necropoli di Sos Furrighesos*. Vol. I-II. Sassari.

Tanda, G. 1985. *L'arte delle domus de janas*. Sassari.

Tanda, G. 1988. L'arte dell'età del rame in Sardegna. *Rassegna di Archeologia* 7: 541-543.

Taramelli, A. 1915. Ozieri – Grotta sepolcrale e votiva di S. Michele ai Cappuccini. *Notizie degli Scavi* 12: 124-136.

Taramelli, A. 1931. *Foglio 194 Ozieri*. Firenze.

Tinè, S. 1992. Dati di scavo 1979-1987. In *Monte d'Accoddi. 10 anni di nuovi scavi*, iv-xvi. Genova.

Tinè, S. & Bafico, S. 1989. Monte d'Accoddi e la Cultura di Ozieri. In Campus, L.D. (a cura di), *La Cultura di Ozieri. Problematiche e nuove acquisizioni*, 14-35. Il Torchietto, Ozieri.

Usai, L. 1987. Il villaggio di età eneolitica di Terramaini presso Pirri (Cagliari). In *Atti del IV Convegno nazionale di preistoria e protostoria, Pescia 8-9 dicembre 1984*. Preistoria d'Italia IV: 175-197.

Vigliardi, A. 1980. Rapporti fra la Sardegna e la Toscana nell'eneolitico finale primo bronzo: la grotta del Fontino nel Grossetano. In *Atti della XXII Riunione Scientifica dell'Istituto Italiano di Preistoria e Protostoria, Firenze 1980*, 247-588. Firenze.

Vigliardi, A. 1988. Il vaso campaniforme nell'Italia centrale. *Rassegna di Archeologia* 7: 378-387 e 395.

Zammit, J. 1990-91. Les sépoltures chalcolithiques du département de l'Aude. Nouvelles découvertes, approche synthétique. In *Le Chalcolithique en Languedoc. Ses relations extra-regionales*, 149-156. Saint-Mathieu de Tréviers.

18. Nota geologica su Punta Isteddi (Buddusò – Sassari)

Carlo Alberto Artizzu

Le migmatiti o rocce miste sono costituite parzialmente da materiale granitico e parzialmente da residui di rocce preesistenti, intimamente mescolati. Queste rocce si sono formate probabilmente in regioni profonde della crosta terrestre, contemporaneamente a deformazioni orogeniche, per iniezione di magma e cristallizzazione sotto pressione orientata, ovvero per metasomatismo delle rocce preesistenti ad opera di emanazioni gassose provenienti da regioni più profonde. Il metamorfismo termico ad opera di magmi granitici fluidi è evidenziata dalle zone marginali dei piccoli ammassi, dove si riscontrano strutture microgranulari dovute a raffreddamento rapido. Dove la fusione o anatessi differenziale è più intensa si forma un magma di anatessi, cioè una massa mobile costituita da una mescolanza di fuso sialico prevalente e di cristalli femici non disciolti.

Ancora oggi le opinioni sulle origini delle migmatiti non sono concordi, anche perché la questione si allaccia strettamente al problema della genesi del granito. In conclusione l'aureola che si trova intorno agli ammassi è dovuta, come precedentemente detto, a raffreddamento rapido del magma, ma non si esclude che sia stata ripresa dalla mano dell'uomo.

Plate 1. Ozieri – Conca Nicolita: menhir

Plate 2. Tula – Mandra Manna: muraglia megalitica.

Plate 3. Tula – Mandra Manna: circolo con menhirs.

Plate 4. Tula – Mandra Manna: menhirs rovesciati.

Plate 5. Tula – Coloras: ipogeo con resti del circolo megalitico.

Plate 6. Oschiri – Furrighesu: ipogeo con circolo.

Plates 1–6: see chapter 17, Paola Basoli, pp. 141–158

Pls. 1–39 are from chapter 17, Paola Basoli, *Aspetti del megalitismo nel territorio di Monte Acuto (Sassari). Considerazioni preliminari*; **Pl. 40** is from chapter 20, Maria Ausilia Fadda, *Nuovi elementi di datazione dell'Età del Bronzo Medio: Lo scavo del Nuraghe Talei di Sorgono e della tomba di giganti Sa Pattada di Macomer*; **Pls. 41–46** are from chapter 21, Anna Grazia Russu, *Cronologia relativa del paramento murario dei vani interni di alcuni complessi nuragici. Osservazioni preliminari*; **Pls. 47–55** are from chapter 43, Carlo Tronchetti, *Problemi di cronologia ceramica nella Sardegna romana*.

Plate 7. Oschiri – Santo Stefano: nicchia.

Plate 8. Oschiri – Santo Stefano: roccia con coppelle.

Plate 9. Oschiri – Monte Cuccu: resti di dolmen.

Plate 10. Oschiri – Monte Cuccu: menhirs.

Plate 11. Oschiri – Malghesi: resti di dolmen.

Plate 12. Oschiri – Malghesi: menhir.

Plates 7–12: see chapter 17, Paola Basoli, pp. 141–158

Plate 13. Berchidda – Monte Acuto: area antistante il dolmen.

Plate 14. Berchidda – Monte Acuto: coppella sulla parete interna del dolmen.

Plate 15. Berchidda – Monte Acuto: roccia forata (Sa Inestra).

Plate 16. Berchidda – Monte Acuto: roccia scritta.

Plate 17. Berchidda – Santa Caterina: dolmen.

Plate 18. Berchidda – Abialzos: roccia con nicchia e coppelle.

Plate 19. Berchidda – Abialzos: menhir.

Plates 13–19: see chapter 17, Paola Basoli, pp. 141–158

Plate 20. Berchidda – Abialzos: dolmen.

Plate 21. Berchidda – Abialzos: dolmen con lastra a doppio spiovente.

Plate 22. Berchidda – Abialzos: menhir con coppella.

Plate 23. Berchidda – S. Andrea: dolmen.

Plate 24. Berchidda – Mesu Serra: dolmen.

Plate 25. Berchidda – Mesu Serra: menhirs.

Plate 26. Berchidda – S. Salvatore di Nulvara: dolmen di Sa Cheja.

Plates 20–26: see chapter 17, Paola Basoli, pp. 141–158

Plate 27. Berchidda – S. Salvatore di Nulvara: nicchia-tafone di Su Balcone.

Plate 28. Berchidda – S. Salvatore di Nulvara: circolo.

Plate 29. Berchidda – S. Salvatore di Nulvara: ipogeo con corridoio dolmenico.

Plate 30. Buddusò – Sa Janna de su Laccu: dolmen.

Plate 31. Buddusò – Punta Isteddi: riparo istoriato.

Plate 32. Buddusò – Punta Isteddi: particolare.

Plate 33. Nughedu S. Nicolò – Punta Sordanu: muraglia.

Plate 34. Nughedu S. Nicolò – Punta Sordanu: dolmen.

Plates 27–34: see chapter 17, Paola Basoli, pp. 141–158

Plate 35. Nughedu S. Nicolò – Punta Sordanu: dolmen.

Plate 37. Nughedu S. Nicolò – Punta Sordanu: dolmen.

Plate 36. Nughedu S. Nicolò – Punta Sordanu: dolmen con particolare delle coppelle.

Plate 38. Nughedu S. Nicolò – Su Crabu Figu: dolmen.

Plate 39. Nughedu S. Nicolò – S'Istria: dolmen.

Plate 40. Nuraghe Talei (Sorgono). Nuraghe e villaggio.

Plates 35–39: see chapter 17, Paola Basoli, pp. 141–158. Plate 40: see chapter 20, Maria Ausilia Fadda, p. 184

Plate 41. Sa Domu 'e S'Orku (Sarroch). Interno mastio.

Plate 42. Orolo (Bortigali). Interno mastio: nicchia centrale.

Plate 43. S. Barbara (Macomer). Torre C: interno camera.

Plate 44. Lugherras (Paulilatino). Interno camera del primo piano.

Plate 45. Losa (Abbasanta). Mastio: tholos.

Plate 46. S. Antine (Torralba). Torre C: feritoie.

Plates 41–46: see chapter 21, Anna Grazia Russu, pp. 195–201

Plate 47. Urna in rozza terracotta (II sec. d.C.)

Plate 48. Brocca in ceramica comune (III sec. d.C.)

Plate 50. Brocche in ceramica fiammata e coppetta in ceramica comune da Sant'Antioco (Cagliari) (III–IV sec. d.C.)

Plate 49. Corredo della tomba 152 di Sant' Antioco (Cagliari), con brocchette in ceramica comune (fine II – III sec. d.C.)

Plate 51. Brocchette in ceramica fiammata ed in ceramica comune da Sant'Antioco (Cagliari) (III sec. d.C.)

Plate 53. US 270 del Cronicario di Sant'Antioco (Cagliari) (fine I – primi decenni del II sec. d.C.): patera F 2286 in ceramica a vernice nera a pasta grigia; boccalino a pareti sottili; piatto in sigillata italica.

Plate 54. US 270 del Cronicario di Sant'Antioco (Cagliari) (fine I – primi decenni del II sec. d.C.): pentole e zuppiera con versatoio.

Plate 52. Boccalino a pareti sottili di fabbrica locale sarda (seconda metà del II sec. d.C.)

Plate 55. US 270 del Cronicario di Sant'Antioco (Cagliari) (fine I – primi decenni del II sec. d.C.): tegami.

Plates 47–55: see chapter 43, Carlo Tronchetti, pp. 371–381

19. Muraglie megalitiche e recinti nella Sardegna Prenuragica

Alberto Moravetti

Agli inizi degli anni '80 gli scavi di Monte Ossoni (Moravetti 1979) e di Monte Baranta (Moravetti 1981) nella Sardegna nord-occidentale, consentirono una più corretta attribuzione culturale e cronologica di una classe monumentale – le muraglie megalitiche – fino ad allora poco nota e genericamente riferita all'età nuragica.

A Monte Ossoni (Figg. 19.1–19.3) una muraglia in opera poliedrica (lungh. m 60) delimita per circa un terzo del suo perimetro il breve pianoro terminale di una altura tronco-conica, proprio nell'unico tratto non difeso dallo strapiombo. Nell'area compresa fra la muraglia e il margine scosceso dell'altura (mq 1.636,60 di superficie) sono intuibili tracce di strutture antiche, mentre all'esterno della stessa muraglia i mezzi meccanici hanno sconvolto e distrutto parte dell'abitato lasciando sul terreno pietrame e frammenti ceramici in prevalenza della Cultura di Monte Claro, anche se non mancano fittili della Cultura di Bonnanaro ed altri riferibili ad età

Fig. 19.1. Monte Ossoni, Castelsardo: veduta aerea.

Alberto Moravetti, Dipartimento di Storia, Università di Sassari, Piazza Conte di Moriana 8, 07100 Sassari, Sardegna, Italia

Fig. 19.2. Monte Ossoni, Castelsardo: veduta aerea con particolare della muraglia megolitica.

storica, ad indicare l'intensa frequentazione del sito nel tempo.

Il sistema fortificato di Monte Baranta (Figg. 19.4–19.9), più complesso ed articolato del precedente, è ugualmente situato sull'estremità di un altopiano e risulta costituito da un recinto-torre aperto e da una poderosa muraglia che racchiude un gruppo di capanne rettangolari pluricellulari, separandole dall'area sacra esterna, segnata da menhir e da un circolo megalitico. Il recinto-torre, di forma semiellittica (m 20,65 di corda; m 15,30 di saetta; mq 380,80 di superficie), è stato costruito sul ciglio dell'altura e presenta il lato rettilineo ad Est, totalmente sprovvisto di muratura perché difeso naturalmente dalla roccia precipite. Due ingressi piattabandati introducono all'interno di un ampio cortile a cielo aperto (m 12,60 di corda; m 9,75 di freccia; superficie, mq 191,30) ove una rudimentale scala, ricavata nei filari a vista della parete sudorientale, svolgendosi a cielo aperto conduce alla sommità del muro e più precisamente ad una sorta di cammino di ronda. La parete esterna della costruzione è data da grandi blocchi poligonali sovrapposti in modo irregolare e connessi con grosse zeppe di rincalzo, mentre all'interno i massi risultano di minori dimensioni e sono messi in opera a file orizzontali abbastanza regolari. Lo spessore murario, a due paramenti (esterno ed interno) riempiti da pietrame minuto, è compreso fra m 4,14 e m 6,50, mentre l'altezza residua, non troppo lontana da quella originaria, è di m 3,45.

Il rapporto massa-spazio di questa costruzione risulta nettamente a favore dello spessore murario (mq 189,50) rispetto agli ambienti coperti (corridoi), mentre è vicino a quello a cielo aperto (cortile) (mq 191,30). É probabile che la scala e lo stesso cammino di ronda fossero in funzione di probabili strutture lignee impiantate nello spessore murario, il quale proprio in quel tratto raggiunge la massima dimensione. D'altra parte, soltanto l'esistenza di strutture lignee consente di giustificare lo spessore veramente eccessivo del muro, poco adatto da solo alla difesa di una costruzione che proprio a tal fine era stata concepita così grandiosa e in posizione strategica privilegiata. É anche possibile che una tettoia di pali e frasche abbia interessato, almeno in parte, le pareti del cortile.

Ad un centinaio di metri a nord-ovest dal recinto-torre, ma in posizione lievemente più elevata, un breve pianoro (mq 3.308) risulta delimitato per due terzi da un modesto dislivello e per il resto, nella parte più aperta ed indifesa, da una muraglia megalitica (lungh. m 97) tagliata nell'estremità settentrionale da un ingresso seguito da corridoio piattabandato. La tecnica costruttiva, a doppio paramento, è la stessa del recinto-torre, anche se l'opera muraria, a grandi lastroni sovrapposti, appare più "megalitica": si conserva per una altezza massima di m 3,00 ed una minima di m 1,48, mentre lo spessore medio risulta di m 3,75 e quello massimo, in prossimità dell'ingresso, è di circa 5 metri. Appena superato il corridoio d'ingresso, nella parte destra della muraglia, è visibile una scala a cielo aperto del tutto analoga a quella

Fig. 19.3. Monte Ossoni, Castelsardo: pianta e sezione.

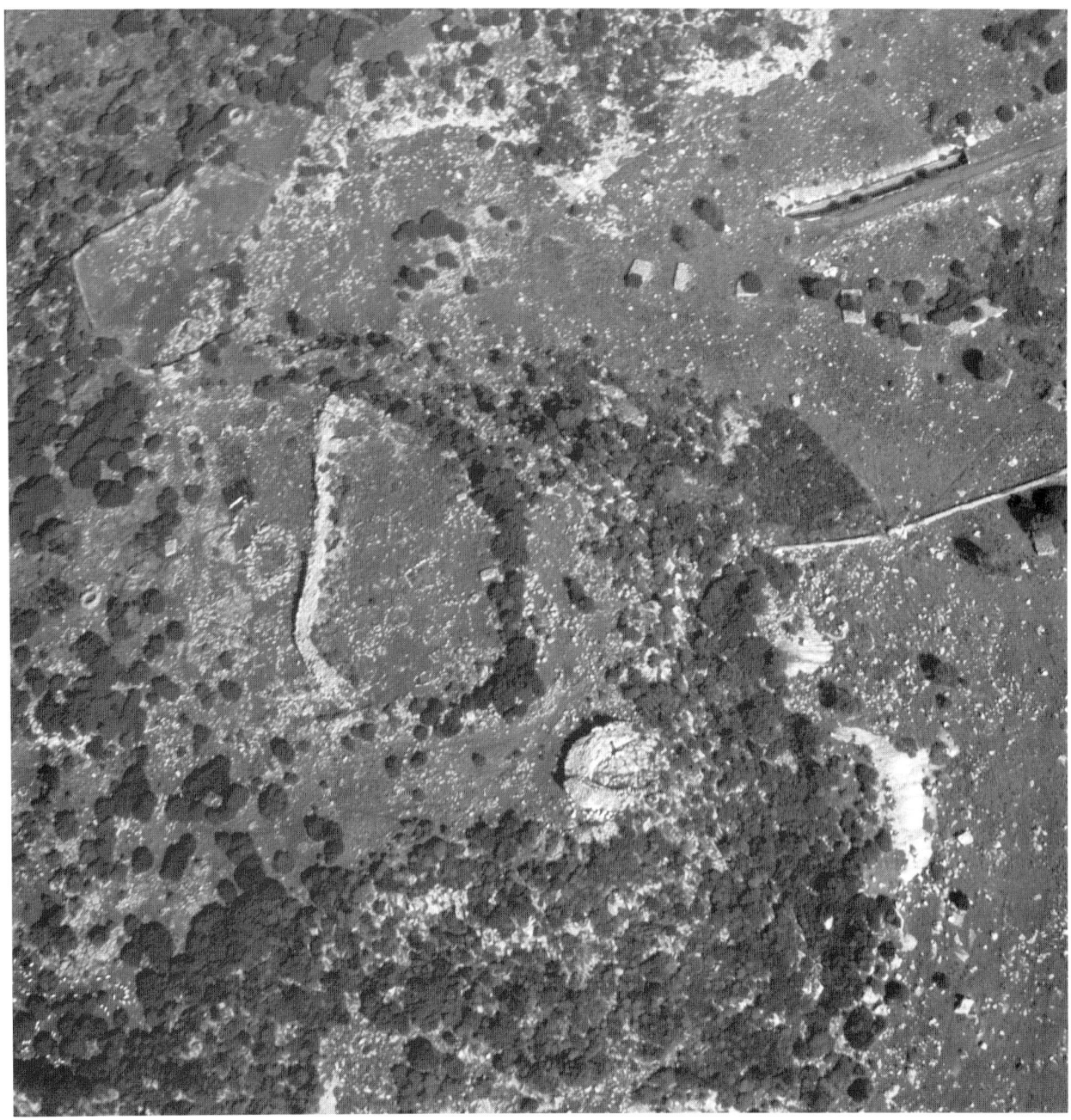

Fig. 19.4. Monte Baranta, Olmedo: veduta aerea del complesso megalitico.

del recinto-torre. All'interno di questa muraglia sono rilevabili, ora soltanto nel profilo di base, alcune capanne quadrangolari, mentre all'esterno, quasi al centro e a ridosso della stessa muraglia, un circolo sacro (mq 108,10) con menhir, costituito da una trentina di grandi lastroni spezzati e rovesciati ed ancora oltre, verso il centro dell'altopiano, da tracce di un più vasto abitato non pienamente leggibile sul terreno a causa della fitta vegetazione arbustiva che lo nasconde: in superficie si raccolgono fittili di Cultura Monte Claro.

In entrambi i siti si avverte un senso di insicurezza ed una esigenza di difesa che si esprime con un dispositivo topografico comune che prevede la scelta di un luogo alto, su estremità di pianori che si affacciano a strapiombo su vallate, ove l'area d'insediamento appare definita dal margine scosceso dell'altura e quindi dalla muraglia che si colloca a sbarramento del lato più debole e aperto dell'altura. L'istanza difensiva non è suggerita soltanto dalla scelta dell'altura ma risulta evidente con la volontà di integrare difese naturali con poderose strutture megalitiche. I dati di scavo hanno poi indicato nella cultura eneolitica di Monte Claro il momento della costruzione di queste due muraglie, ed anche del recinto-torre di Monte Baranta (Moravetti 1981).

Fig. 19.5. Monte Baranta, Olmedo: veduta aerea con particolare del recinto-torre.

Fig. 19.6. Monte Baranta, Olmedo: planimetria generale del complesso megalitico.

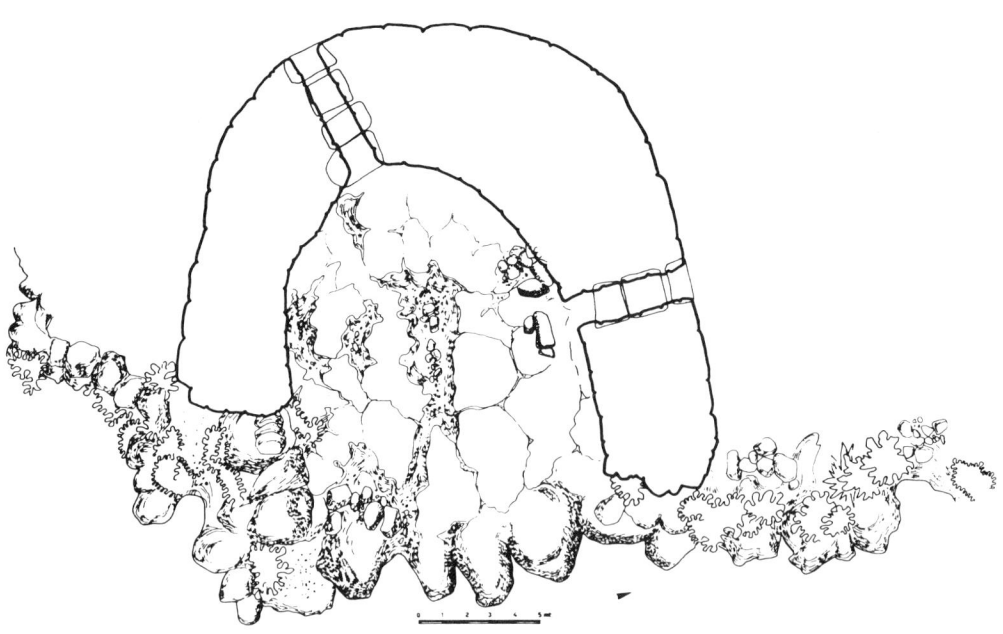

Fig. 19.7. Monte Baranta, Olmedo: planimetria del recinto-torre.

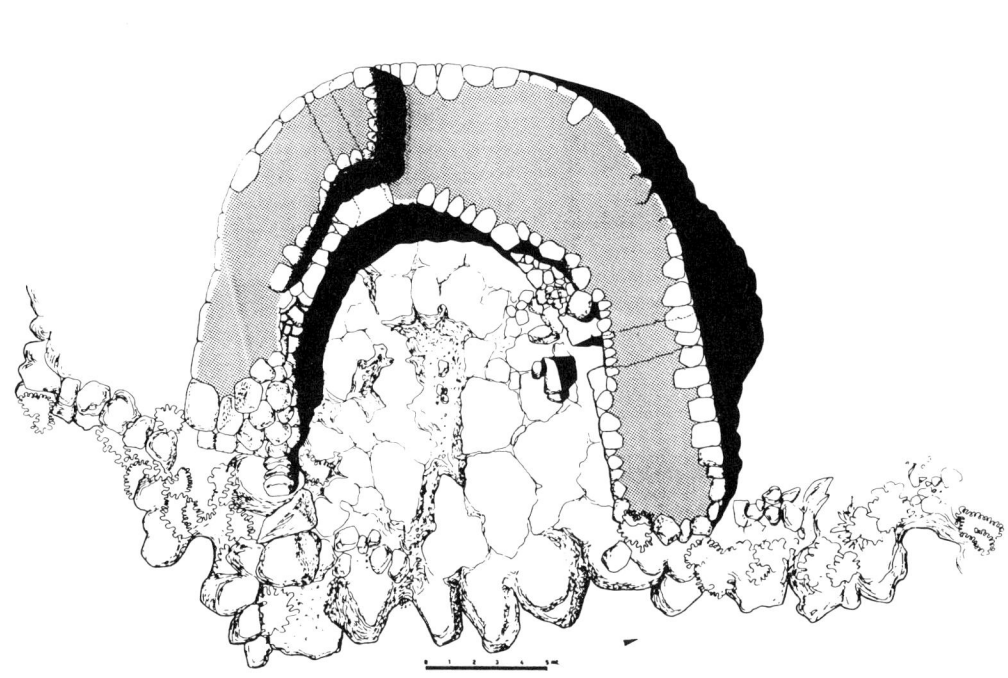

Fig. 19.8. Monte Baranta, Olmedo: planimetria del recinto-torre allo svettamento.

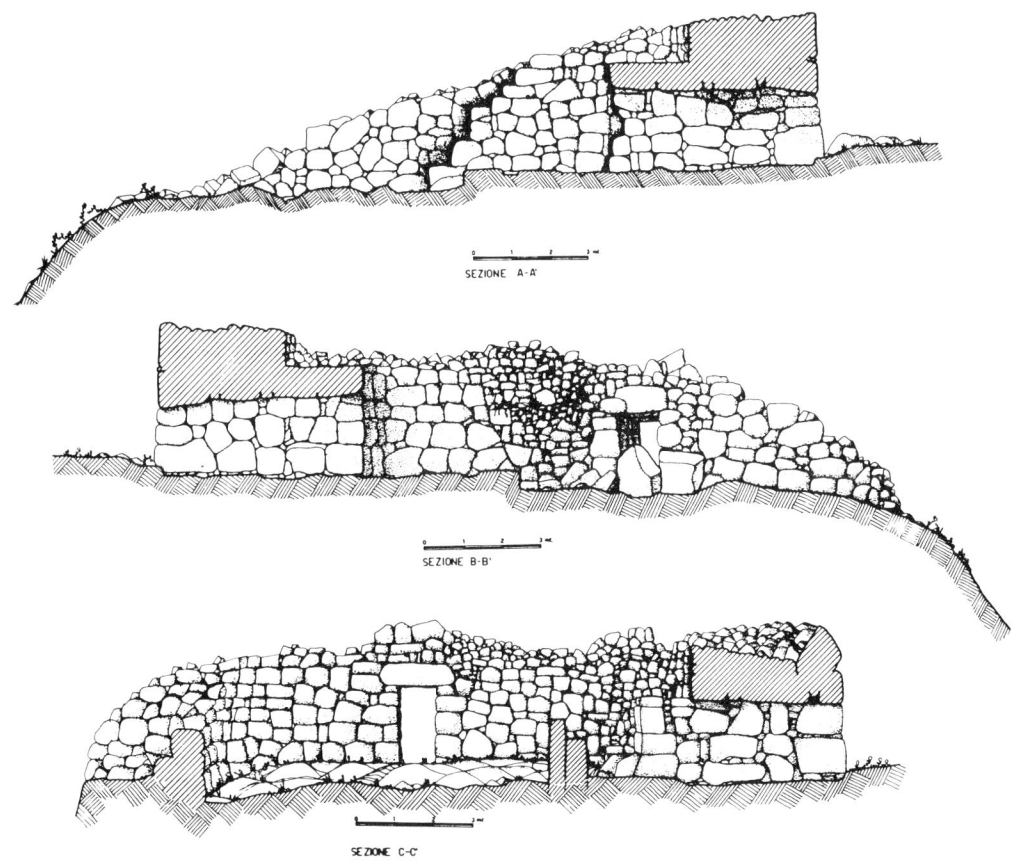

Fig. 19.9. Monte Baranta, Olmedo: sezioni del recinto-torre.

Pur in assenza di dati di scavo, per stringenti affinità costruttive e per una uguale concezione insediativa, è stata attribuita alla stessa cultura di Monte Claro la fortificazione di Punta s'Arroccu-Chiaramonti (Moravetti 1981), una muraglia lunga circa 120 metri e munita di due ingressi piattabandati dallo svolgimento irregolare determinato dal piano roccioso, a chiudere un'area vagamente semicircolare (mq 922 di superficie) con le estremità tangenti il profilo scosceso dell'altopiano (Fig. 19.10). Il lato rettilineo, difeso dal taglio verticale della roccia, è totalmente privo di murature – come a Monte Ossoni e Monte Baranta – mentre nell'area racchiusa dalla muraglia sono visibili tracce di murature non pienamente definibili senza un intervento di scavo. La tecnica costruttiva è quella a due paramenti con intercapedine riempita di pietrame; lo spessore medio è di m 2,30, mentre quello massimo, in corrispondenza dei due ingressi, risulta di m 4,52 e m 2,70.

In questi anni, sulla base dei dati emersi a Monte Ossoni e Monte Baranta, sono state "reinterpretate" strutture megalitiche già note (Contu 1981; Moravetti 1981) e vi è la tendenza, non sempre giustificata, di attribuire alla Cultura di Monte Claro tutte le muraglie megalitiche che si vanno scoprendo nell'Isola, ribaltando in tal modo quanto avveniva in passato quando, al contrario, tutte le muraglie erano riferite ad età nuragica!

In attesa che nuovi e mirati interventi di scavo su muraglie diversamente disposte sul terreno rispetto a quelle sopra esaminate ne chiariscano il ruolo, la funzione e l'inquadramento cronologico, occorre quindi individuare un modello insediativo, una tipologia architettonica ed una tecnica costruttiva che insieme ci consentano in qualche modo di formulare delle ipotesi fondate sugli esigui elementi culturali disponibili che al momento provengono da Monte Ossoni e da Monte Baranta.

Fra le muraglie che più di altre sembrano rispondere ai requisiti topografici ed architettonici sopra indicati sono da segnalare quelle di Pedra Oddetta (Macomer-Nuoro) (Manca Demurtas & Demurtas 1992), Crastu (Soddì-Oristano) (Manca Demurtas & Demurtas 1992), s'Albaredda (Tresnuraghes-Oristano) (Moravetti 1994) e Frenegarzu (Bortigali-Nuoro), mentre per altre ancora permangono riserve che inducono ad una maggiore prudenza.

S'Albaredda è una muraglia megalitica che si dispone in senso longitudinale, per una lunghezza di circa 200 metri, sul breve altopiano trachitico di Sa Sea segnato a valle dal Riu Mannu, a delimitare un'area di almeno un ettaro all'interno della quale si intuisce la presenza di strutture abitative. L'opera muraria dello spessore medio di circa 3 metri e con una altezza massima residua di 2/

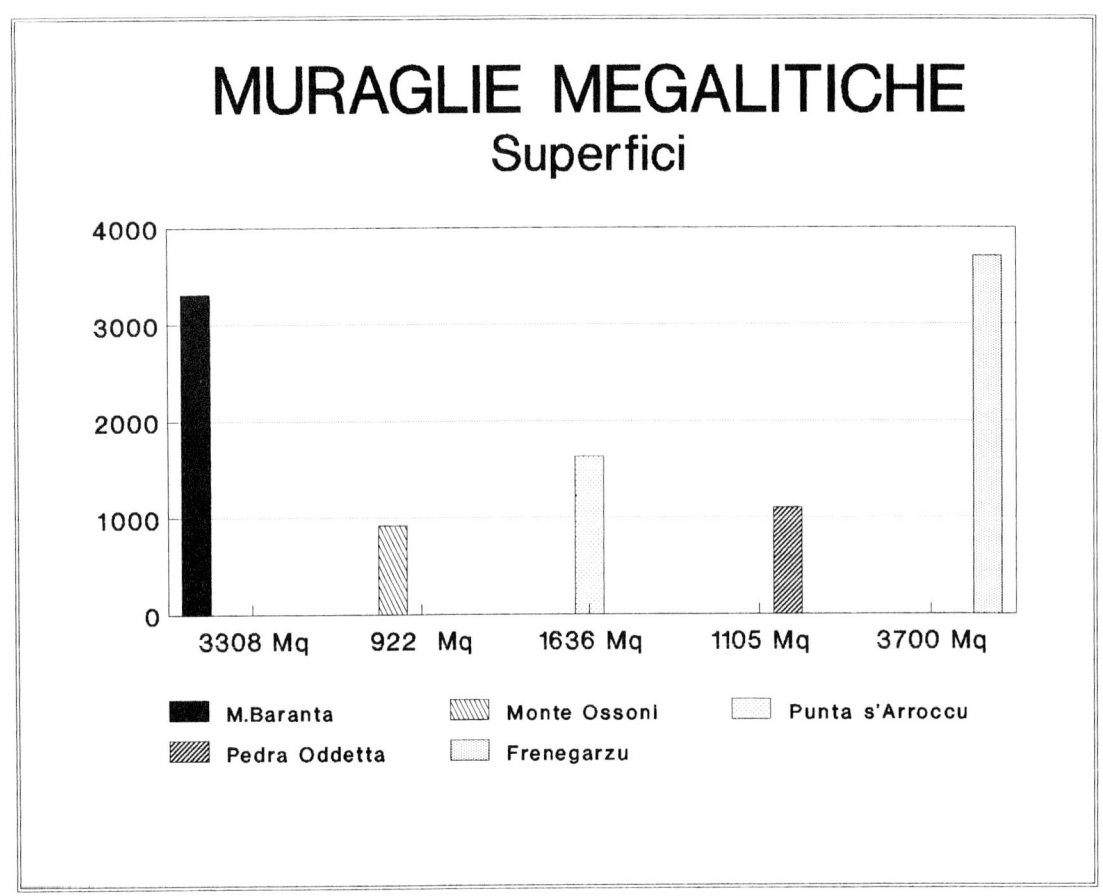

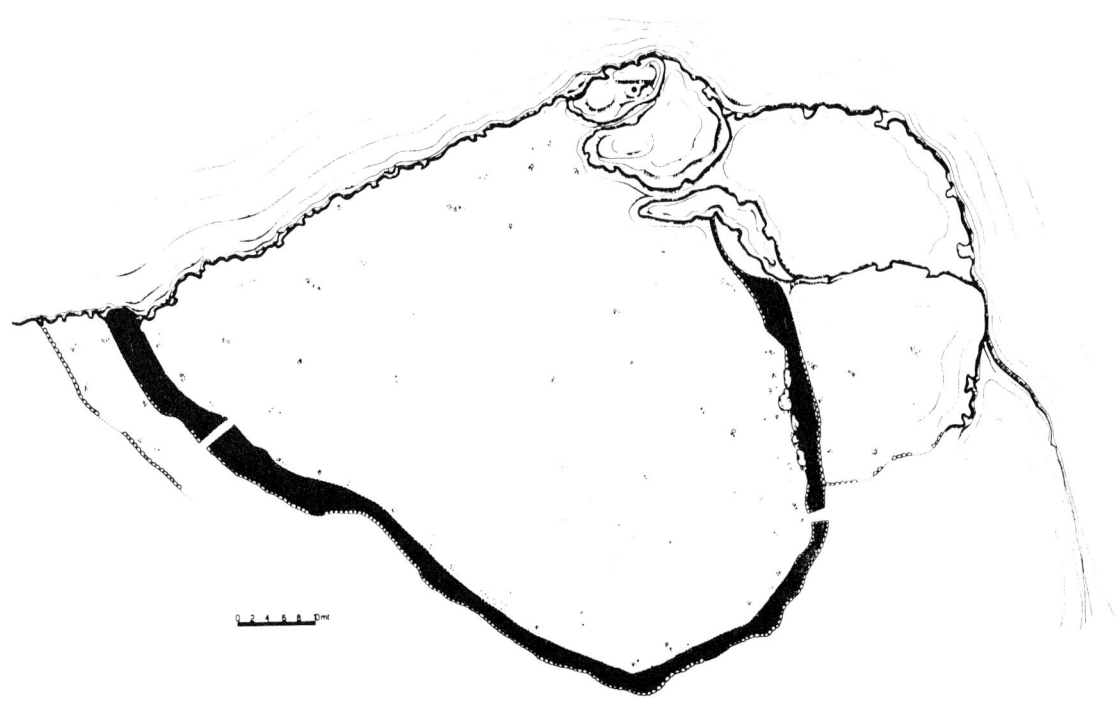

Fig. 19.10. Punta s'Arroccu, Chiaramonti: planimetria generale della muraglia megalitica.

3 metri, assai rovinata a causa di estesi crolli e vegetazione arbustiva che la ricopre in parte, risulta a doppio paramento come a Monte Baranta, Punta s'Arroccu, etc., vale a dire con parete esterna costituita da grandi lastroni sovrapposti e quella interna invece formata da pietre di minori dimensioni disposte a filari; l'intercapedine è riempita da pietrame minuto.

Il complesso fortificato di Crastu (Fig. 19.11) occupa l'estremità di uno sperone basaltico dell'altopiano di Abbasanta, delimitato da due solchi vallivi attraversati dal Riu Siddo e Riu Messe Cappai. Un'area abitativa con strutture di forma quadrangolare e circolare è compresa fra la muraglia megalitica e il margine scosceso dell'altopiano. La muraglia megalitica di Crastu si

Fig. 19.11. Crastu, Soddì-Oristano: planimetria generale della muraglia megalitica.

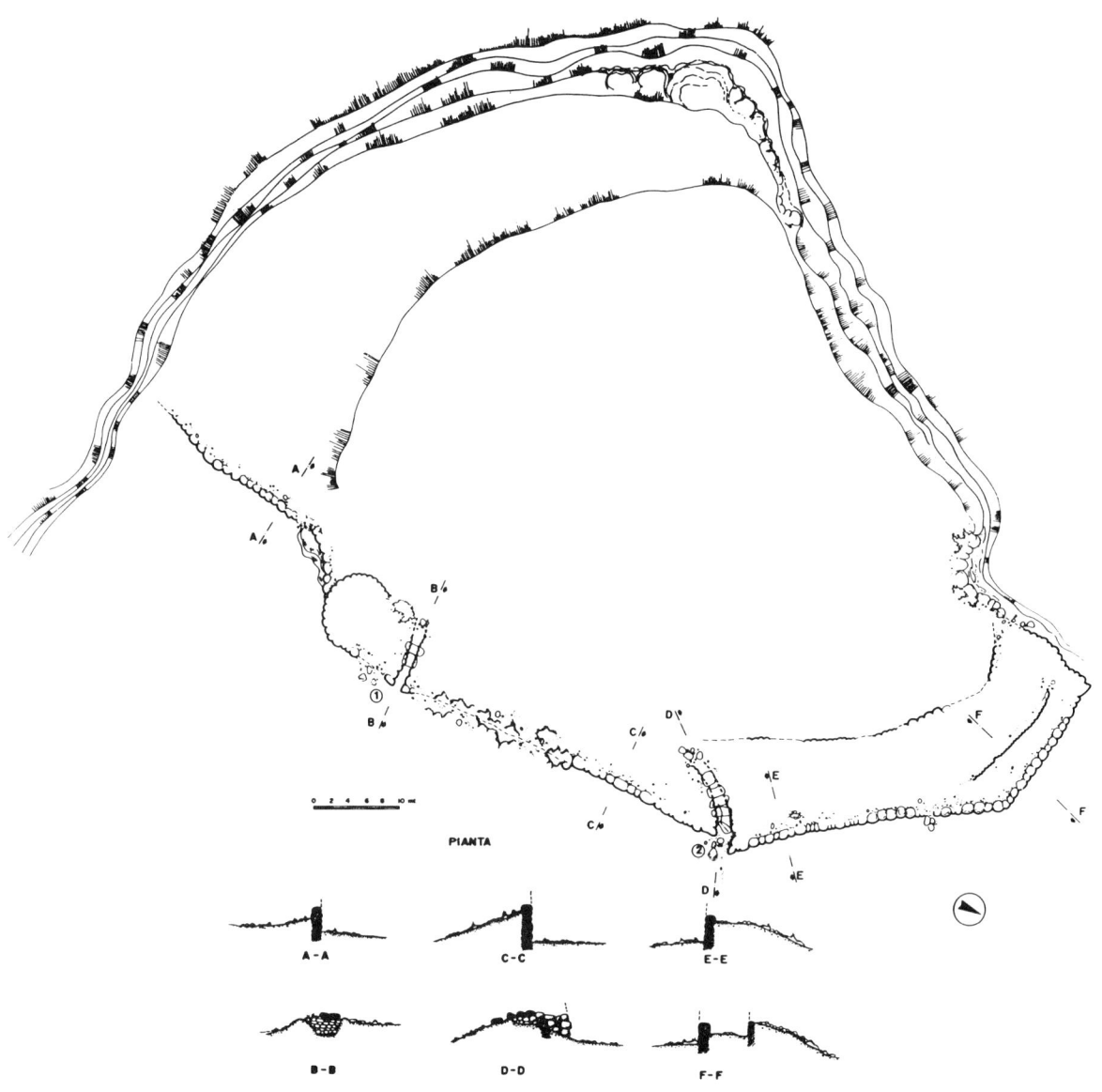

Fig. 19.12. Pedra Oddetta, Macomer: planimetria generale della muraglia megalitica.

sviluppa con tracciato irregolare da Nord a Sud per una lunghezza di 135 metri, con uno spessore di circa 2 metri ed una altezza massima residua di m 3,50. A Nord, dopo un tratto iniziale di una quindicina di metri, il profilo interno della muraglia presenta una struttura semicircolare che sporge per una lunghezza di m 7,00 con una larghezza massima di m 10 ed una altezza residua di m 4,20. A m 81,40 da questa singolare torre semicircolare, la muraglia presenta un struttura rettangolare, questa volta sporgente all'esterno, lunga m 18,50, larga m 7,50 e alta m 1,50/3,00. Le due strutture sporgenti, quasi a torre, sono state interpretate come piattaforme piene, prive di ambienti, e per questo ancora poco comprensibili almeno per quanto riguarda la loro funzione (Manca Demurtas & Demurtas 1992). La tecnica costruttiva è data da blocchi di grandi dimensioni messi in opera con poche zeppe di rincalzo.

La muraglia di Pedra Oddetta è posta a circa 500 metri sullo sperone trachitico che guarda la valle del Riu s'Adde, a controllo della via naturale che dall'altopiano di Campeda discende verso la piana di Macomer (Fig. 19.12). Si estende per circa 160 metri, da nord-ovest a sud-est, con svolgimento irregolare a racchiudere per circa 2/5 un'area (mq 1.103 di superficie) che nel lato sprovvisto di muratura è difesa naturalmente dallo strapiombo. La struttura muraria di questa fortificazione appare piuttosto singolare ed ancora da definire, soprattutto nel profilo interno: infatti la sua larghezza sembra data da distinti spessori, quasi dei piani terrazzati a normalizzare il dislivello del terreno. La parete esterna di questa muraglia è costituita da pietre di grandi dimensioni disposte a filari irregolari, mentre non è precisabile, come si è detto, la tecnica costruttiva della parete interna che ancora non emerge con chiarezza dal pietrame di crollo. Fra i crolli sono visibili 2 o 3 ingressi

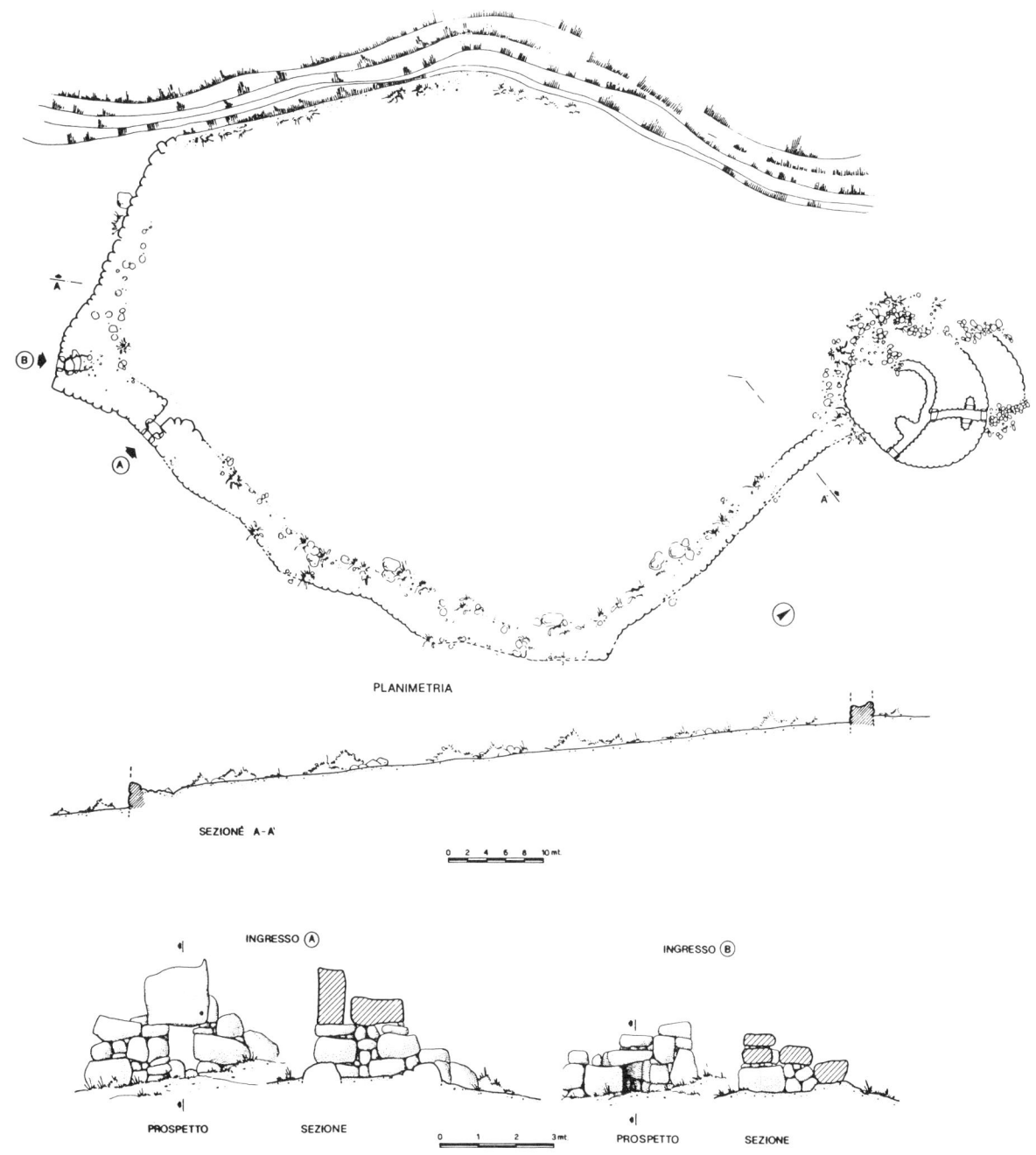

Fig. 19.13. Su Frenegarzu, Bortigali: planimetria generale della muraglia megalitica con protonuraghe.

che introducevano in altrettanti corridoi piattabandati, ora in gran parte ingombri di crollo, mentre il profilo della muratura presenta una struttura circolare del diametro di circa 10 metri, appena sporgente verso l'esterno e per la maggior parte contenuta nello spessore murario verso l'interno.

La muraglia di Frenegarzu (Fig. 19.13) si dispone per una lunghezza di 133 metri, sui tre lati di un'area vagamente poligonale che mostra un lieve dislivello da Est a Ovest (da m 336 a m 229 s.l.m.), ove il quarto lato (m 88 di lunghezza) è costituito dal margine di una modesta scarpata (circa 25 metri) che guarda il Rio Murtazzolu. A Nord, la muraglia si raccorda ad un protonuraghe dallo stesso nome – costruito, forse, in tempi più recenti – mentre nel tratto compreso fra questo monumento e la scarpata, a NNO, la folta vegetazione arbustiva e le macerie non consentono di accertare la presenza o meno di muratura.

All'interno della muraglia, che occupa una superficie di 3700 mq, si accede attraverso due ingressi (ma è probabile che fossero almeno tre), uno a SSE ed il secondo a SSO. A SSE, una porta di luce rettangolare (alt. m 1,40; largh. 0,70), con architrave (lungh. m 1,70; alt. m 1,65; spess. 0,70), introduce in un lungo corridoio (lungh. m

4,60; largh. m 2,00; alt. m 1,30), ora coperto a piattabanda. L'ingresso SSO risulta invece meno conservato e presenta un corridoio valutabile m 3,00 lunghezza e m 1,20 di larghezza.

L'opera muraria di Frenegarzu è data da grandi blocchi di basalto, appena sbozzati e disposti a file irregolari. Lo spessore, a parte quello registrato in prossimità degli ingressi sopra descritti, è compreso tra m 2,40/2,00, mentre l'altezza massima residua risulta di m 2,45 da m 2,40/2,00.

Oltre alle muraglie che si vanno scoprendo sempre più numerose nell'Isola, soprattutto nelle parte centro-settentrionale, ora anche il singolare recinto-torre di Monte Baranta ha trovato uno stringente e finora isolato confronto in un edificio megalitico situato in località Fraicata, nel territorio di Bortigiadas (Fig. 19.14). Segnalato come 'tempietto dedicato alle acque' (Maxia 1991: 72–73, fig. 29, tav. XXXII), e rivisitato più correttamente da P. Melis (1995–96: 44 ss.), l'edificio si trova sulla sponda settentrionale del fiume Coghinas, dal quale dista attualmente circa 8/10 metri, con un dislivello di 10/11 metri fra la linea dell'acqua e l'ingresso. Si tratta di una struttura a "U" con un prospetto rettilineo (lungh. m 16,25) lievemente rientrante (saetta m 0,85), le cui estremità piegano ad angolo retto verso il fiume con pareti fra di loro parallele e normali alla linea di prospetto. La parete laterale sinistra si conserva in tutta la sua lunghezza (m 10,35; spess. m 2,60/2,20), mentre quella contrapposta risulta in gran parte crollata e ricoperta dalla fitta vegetazione arbustiva. Lo spessore della parete frontale è di m 4,00/4,10, mentre l'altezza massima residua si misura a Nord, sull'ingresso, con m 3,00 su 5 filari. L'opera muraria a doppio paramento è costituita da pietre di medie e grandi dimensioni disposte a filari con numerose zeppe di rincalzo. L'accesso all'edificio avviene a Nord per un ingresso a luce rettangolare (largh. m 0,94; alt. m 1,50), architravato, che introduce in un corridoio (lungh. m 4,00; sup. mq 3,95), a sezione quadrangolare e coperto da lastroni trasversali, che tende a restringersi verso il fondo (largh. 0,94/0,82). Il cortile, di forma quadrangolare ma con spigoli arrotondati, risulta privo di muratura sul lato che guarda verso il fiume ed era certamente a cielo aperto date le sue dimensioni (m 12,00 x 6,43; sup. mq 73,52). Appena varcato il corridoio che introduce nel cortile, nella parete sinistra si apre una nicchia vagamente rettangolare (prof. m 2,25; largh. 0,90/0,75; alt. m 0,55 s.r.; sup. mq 2,04), con ingresso architravato e copertura tabulare. A ridosso della stessa parete una scala a vista costituita da almeno sette gradini conduce alla sommità dell'edificio, ad una sorta di cammino di ronda del tutto simile a quello presente a Monte Baranta.

Anche a Sa Fraicata il rapporto spazio-massa muraria risulta a vantaggio dello spessore (mq 106,42) sia nei confronti degli spazi coperti (mq 5,99) – corridoio e nicchia – che del cortile a cielo aperto (mq 73,52). Come ipotizzato per il recinto-torre di Monte Baranta anche a Sa Fraicata si può pensare a delle strutture lignee sia all'interno del cortile che nello spessore murario. Tuttavia, in attesa che una indagine stratigrafica possa fornire elementi utili per un puntuale inquadramento culturale e cronologico, questo interessante monumento di Bortigiadas può essere attribuito alla Cultura di Monte Claro, agli stessi tempi quindi del recinto-torre di Monte Baranta con il quale presenta forti e significative analogie.

Fra le muraglie sopra descritte, quelle di Monte Ossoni, Monte Baranta, s'Albarredda e Punta s'Arroccu si limitano a racchiudere uno spazio più o meno ampio all'interno del quale – ma anche all'esterno – sono presenti strutture abitative. Sono muraglie di tipo semplice con la sola funzione di integrare una difesa naturale e delimitare e difendere un'area nella quale potevano trovare rifugio uomini ed animali, e dove si suppone si svolgesse la vita di una piccola comunità. Gli unici spazi coperti – i corridoi – sono elementi legati esclusivamente al passaggio: non sono previsti ambienti d'uso, sia per la vita che per immagazzinare derrate o altro. A Pedra Oddetta e a Crastu rimane intatto il dispositivo topografico ed il modello insediativo, ma si avverte, pur con i limiti dovuti ad un rilevamento effettuato su estese macerie di crollo che ne hanno reso difficile la lettura – non consentendo fra l'altro di individuare eventuali fasi edilizie cronologicamente distinte – una qualche evoluzione architettonica per la presenza di un corpo murario nel loro tracciato, una torre o comunque una struttura non ancora determinata che potrebbero tuttavia contenere dei vani coperti.

Sulla base degli elementi finora acquisiti si potrebbero dividere le muraglie in esame in due varietà tipologiche: quelle semplici (A) e quelle complesse (B), intendendo per quest'ultima varietà la presenza di una qualche struttura nel profilo murario. Si tratta, ovviamente, di una suddivisione semplicistica e quanto mai preliminare, dal momento che prende in considerazione soltanto strutture difensive che rispondono a quei requisiti riscontrati a Monte Ossoni e a Monte Baranta, i soli complessi fortificati che possono offrire elementi di cronologia, ed esclude invece le molte muraglie che non presentano queste stesse caratteristiche e che non disponendo di dati di scavo, anche indiretti, risultano di difficile inquadramento culturale.

Nei recinti-torre di Monte Baranta e Sa Fraicata si riproduce in tono minore lo stesso dispositivo topografico delle muraglie, nel senso che la superficie racchiusa è di gran lunga inferiore, ma con lo stesso concetto di racchiudere uno spazio parzialmente difeso dallo strapiombo naturale. Ma come nelle muraglie anche in questi edifici i vani coperti sono funzionali solo agli spostamenti (corridoi), oppure, come a Sa Fraicata, si dispone di una nicchia che può essere utile per custodire derrate od altro ma non è certo funzionale alla vita. Anche per questi due recinti-torre, in via del tutto ipotetica data l'esiguità della campionatura, si può proporre un tipo semplice (A) ed uno più complesso (B) per la presenza della nicchia che in qualche modo articola la massa

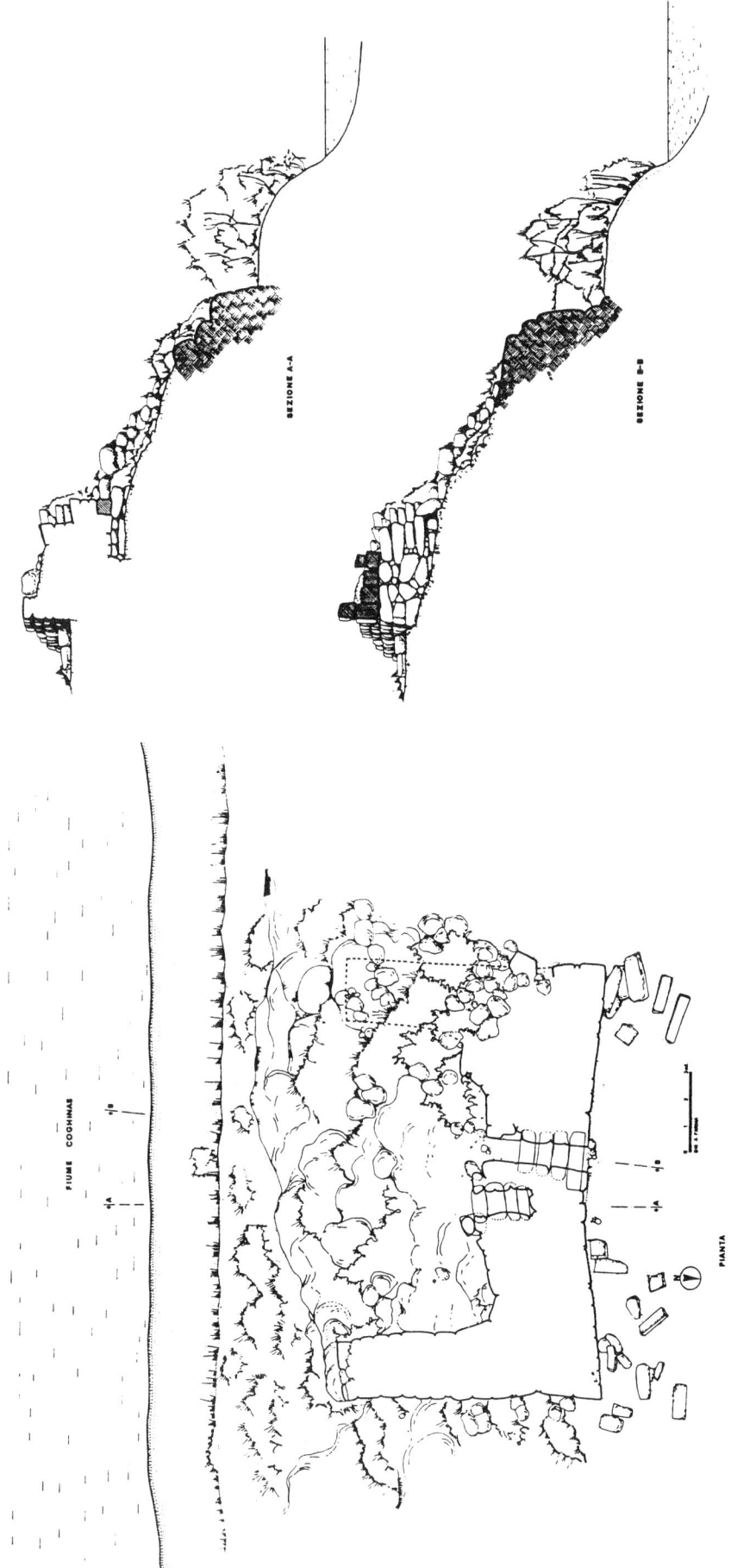

Fig. 19.14. Sa Fraicata, Bortigiadas: planimetria e sezioni del recinto-torre.

muraria. A differenza di quanto avveniva per le muraglie, nei recinti-torre non sembra esservi spazio sufficiente per contenere uomini ed animali, ma soltanto uomini con le loro attività.

Fra i monumenti megalitici riferiti più di recente alla cultura di Monte Claro (Contu 1981; Moravetti 1981) vi sono anche le c.d. 'muras' di Bonorva (Fig. 19.15), interpretate in passato come *castra* della tarda età nuragica (Lilliu 1966). Si tratta come è noto di almeno otto recinti di grandi dimensioni e di varia forma (circolari, ellitici e poligonali), sparsi in un territorio non molto ampio – raggio di circa 2 km – e posti fra loro ad una distanza massima di 1900 metri ed una minima di poche decine di metri. Questi recinti di Bonorva sono molto vasti, sia quelli tondeggianti (da m 96 x 90 a 46 x 27), con una media di m 68,50 x 52,50 che quelli a pianta trapezoidale (m 70,50 x 66,50 x 56,00 x 40,00; m 75,00 x 36,00 x 54,00 x 42,00), e negli esempi meglio conservati residuano per una altezza di m 2,00/2,30, con uno spessore compreso fra m 3,00 e m 2,20. L'opera muraria risulta a doppio paramento, mentre l'ingresso, ove ancora rilevabile, è a luce rettangolare con stipiti monolitici-ortostatici, sovrastati da un poderoso architrave. L'andito retrostante presenta ortostati per pareti e lastroni disposti a piattabanda per copertura.

All'interno dei recinti non si è trovata traccia, almeno in apparenza, di strutture abitative, anche se occorre tenere presente che nessuna di queste strutture è stata interessata da indagini stratigrafiche. Indubbiamente l'opera muraria a doppio paramento, lo spessore murario e lo stile architettonico a trilite impiegato per i corridoi sono segno di arcaicità e sono elementi di significativo confronto con muraglie e recinti-torre, anche se da questi si discostano per la differente impostazione sul terreno.

D'altra parte, se le affinità costruttive con le muraglie e i recinti-torre suggeriscono anche per questi monumenti di Bonorva una generica attribuzione alla cultura di Monte Claro, questa non sembra contraddetta dalla diversa disposizione topografica. Infatti in terreni pianeggianti, come nel caso delle *muras*, in assenza di quelle caratteristiche geomorfologiche che favorivano l'insorgere delle muraglie (pianori con pareti scoscese), lo spazio insediativo dei recinti, che nelle muraglie era delimitato dalla stessa muraglia e dal margine precipite dell'altura, doveva per necessità essere interamente chiuso dalla muratura. In questi recinti di Bonorva l'area racchiusa dalle murature è considerevole ed è in genere superiore a quella delimitata dalle muraglie: 5.760 mq (Baddadolzu) e 2.180 mq (S'Eligheddu) nei recinti interamente conservati, e 2.850 mq (Mura Cariasas), 1.360 mq (Mura Cariasas 2), 2.140 mq (Tilìpera) e 3.440 mq (Aeddo) in quelli che conservano solo parzialmente il loro tracciato murario. Si tratta di una superficie sufficiente ad accogliere strutture, uomini ed animali, proprio come ipotizzato per le muraglie.

Vi è semmai, sempre che l'attribuzione alla Cultura di Monte Claro trovi conforto in sondaggi di scavo che occorrerà promuovere quanto prima, una diversa concezione dell'uso del territorio rispetto alle muraglie. Infatti, mentre le muraglie che abbiamo esaminate sembrano isolate e autonome, ciascuna con un suo territorio di pertinenza per le risorse della vita, in queste *muras* di Bonorva, così vicine le une alle altre, sembra invece di cogliere una sorta di 'sistema' insediativo che prevede una occupazione intensiva del territorio con recinti che potevano avere funzione differenziata (per animali, per gruppi familiari estesi, etc.), sempre che non si tratti di costruzioni che si sono andate aggiungendo nel tempo.

Si contano ormai a decine i recinti di grandi dimensioni che si vanno scoprendo nell'Isola – soprattutto nella Sardegna settentrionale ed in particolare nella Gallura – ma tutti ancora da verificare sia per quanto riguarda la loro funzione che la loro attribuzione culturale e cronologica. Il recinto di Santa Vittoria di Esterzili-Nuoro (Contu 1981: 12, fig. 115; Ortu 1993: 25; Moravetti 1993: 206), di forma ellittica e con tre ingressi, a differenza delle *muras* di Bonorva sopra citate non sembra presentare alcun carattere difensivo data la modestia delle murature che invece si prestano a delimitare un ampio spazio (mq 1174) destinato, soprattutto, ad accogliere e custodire gli animali (Fig. 19.16).

Queste muraglie – e gli stessi recinti, se l'attribuzione all'Età del Rame venisse confermata da indagini stratigrafiche – costituiscono una significativa testimonianza del frantumarsi dell'assetto socio-economico che aveva caratterizzato la precedente fase neolitica della Sardegna, nella quale, almeno finora, non sono state documentate strutture difensive (muraglie, fossati, terrapieni) o scelte insediative d'altura che adombrino in qualche modo una esigenza di difesa, presente invece, negli stessi tempi, in altre aree del Mediterraneo (Passard 1980: 37–114).

Questa rottura con il passato e lo stato di conflittualità che sembra investire anche la Sardegna nell'Età del Rame sono attestati fin dai primi esempi dell'Eneolitico con la cultura di Filigosa, alla quale sono stati riferiti la fortificazione (?) di San Giuseppe di Padria (Santoni 1976; Lilliu 1982) e le numerose statue-menhir "armate" che sempre più numerose si vanno ritrovando soprattutto nella Sardegna centrale (Atzeni 1982; 1994; Moravetti 1984).

Se per il muro di Padria gli elementi disponibili risultano ancora troppo scarsi per una più precisa definizione della stessa struttura, le statue-menhir sono indicative di gruppi umani gerarchizzati nei quali il ceto dominante appare costituito da guerrieri che con queste statue armate possono perpetuare il loro *status* anche dopo la morte in una sorta di culto degli antenati.

Ma è solo con la successiva cultura di Monte Claro che sembra diffondersi, almeno nelle Sardegna settentrionale, la ricerca di siti insediativi d'altura con difese naturali integrate da possenti muraglie megalitiche.

Questa esigenza di difesa e questo stato di conflittualità

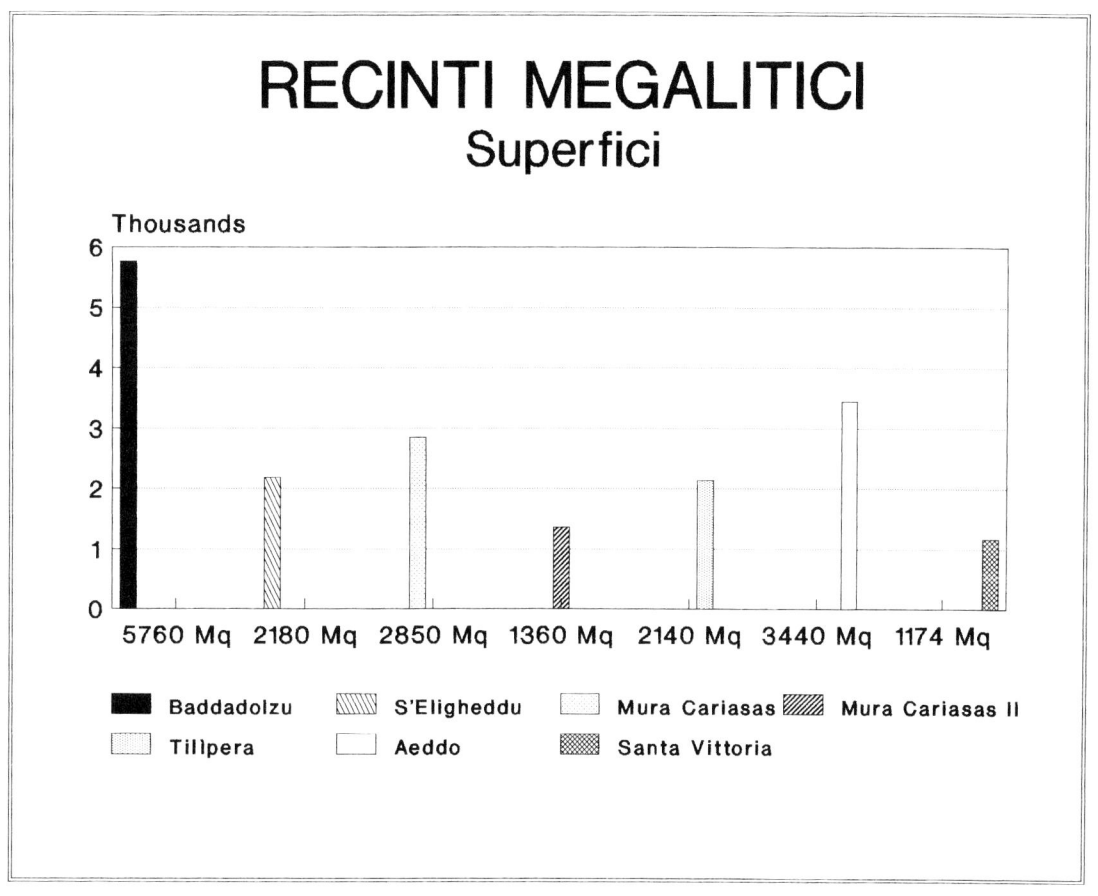

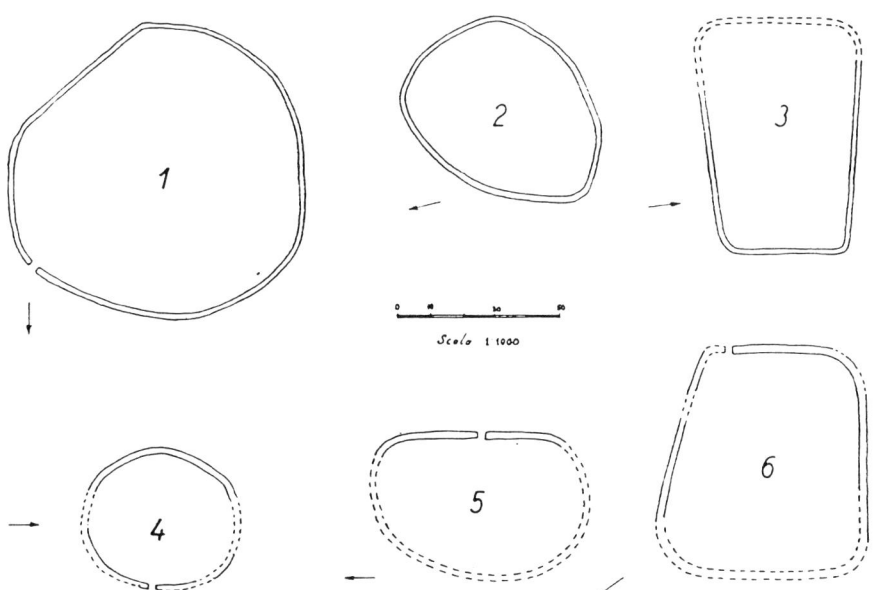

Fig. 19.15. Recinti di Bonorva: 1. Baddadolzu; 2. S'Eligheddu; 3. Mura Cariasas 1; 4. Mura Cariasas 2; 5. Tilìpera; 6. Aeddo.

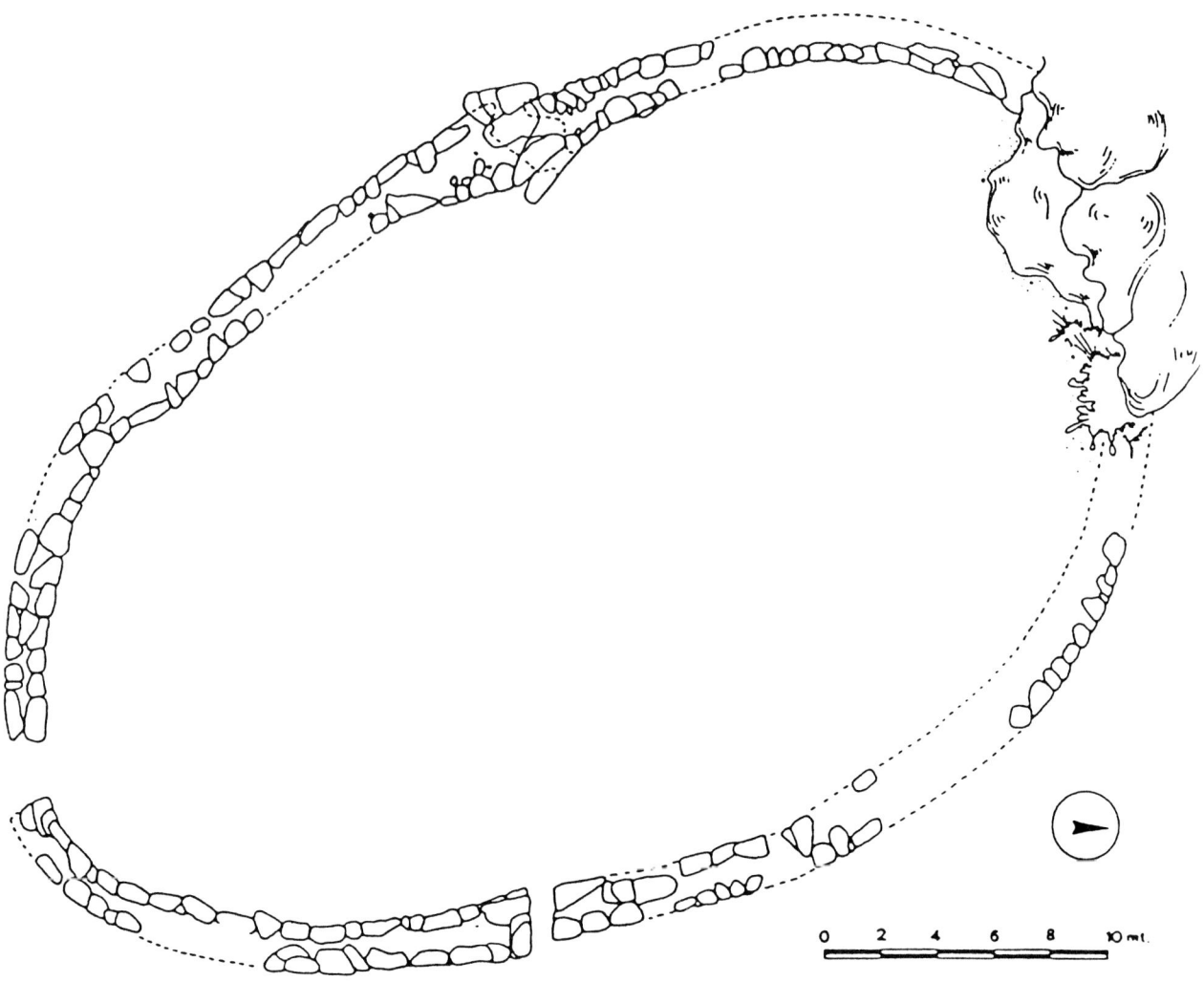

Fig. 19.16. Monte Santa Vittoria, Esterzili: planimetria del recinto.

trovano riscontro in altre parti del Mediterraneo (Camps-Fabrer *et al.* 1984; D'Anna & Gutherz 1989), ed in particolare nella penisola iberica e nella Francia ove strutture megalitiche similari sono presenti a Zambujal (Schubart & Sangmeister 1987: 16ss.), Los Millares (Almagro Basch & Arribas Palau 1963: 475ss.), Lebous (Arnal 1973; Gutherz & Jallot 1989), Vauvenargue (D'Anna 1989), Les Lauzières (D'Anna *et al.* 1989), per segnalare soltanto alcune di quelle più note.

Bibliografia

Almagro Basch, M. & Arribas Palau, A. 1963. *El Poblado y la Necrópolis Megalíticos de Los Millares (Santa Fe de Mondújar, Almería)*. Bibliotheca Praehistorica Hispana 3. Madrid.

Arnal, J. 1973. Le Lebous. *Gallia Prehistoire* 16: 131–193.

Atzeni, E. 1982. Menhirs antropomorfi e statue-menhirs della Sardegna. *Annali del Museo Civico U. Formentini della Spezia* 1979-80: 9–64. La Spezia.

Atzeni, E. 1994. La statue a antropomorfa sarda. In *La statuaria antropomorfa in Europa dal Neolitico alla romanizzazione*, 193–213. Istituto Internazionale di Studi Liguri.

Camps-Fabrer, H. *et al.* 1984. Le aenceints du Néolithique à l'age du Bronze dans le Sud-Est de la France. In Waldren, W.H., Chapman, R., Lewthwaite, J. & Kennard, R.-C. (eds.), *The Deya Conference of Prehistory: Early Settlement in the Western Mediterranean Islands and the Peripheral Areas*. BAR International Series 229: 339–366. British Archaeological Reports, Oxford.

Contu, E. 1981. L'architettura nuragica. In *Ichnussa. La Sardegna dalle origini all'età classica*, 5–175. Libri Scheiwiller, Milano.

D'Anna, A. 1989. L'habitat perché néolithique final de la Citadelle (Vauvenargues, Bouches du Rhone). In D'Anna, A. & Gutherz, X. (ed.), *Enceints, habitats ceinturés, sites perchés du Neolithique au Bronze Ancien dans le Sud de la France et les régions voisines*. Mémoire de la Société Languedocienne de Préhistoire 2: 209–224. Montpellier.

D'Anna, A., Courtin, J., Coutel, R. & Muller, A. 1989. Habitats perchés et enceints du Neolitique final et Calcolithique dans le Luberon central (Vaucluse). In D'Anna, A. & Gutherz, X. (ed.), *Enceints, habitats ceinturés, sites perchés du Neolithique au Bronze Ancien dans le Sud de la France et les régions voisines*.

Mémoire de la Sociéte Languedocienne de Préhistoire 2: 165–193. Montpellier.

D'Anna, A. & Gutherz, X. (a cura di). 1989. *Enceints, habitats ceinturés, sites perchés du Neolithique au Bronze Ancien dans le Sud de la France et les régions voisines*. Mémoire de la Sociéte Languedocienne de Préhistoire 2. Montpellier.

Gutherz, X. & Jallot, L. 1989. Les habitats chalcolitique ceinturés de l'Hérault oriental. In D'Anna, A. & Gutherz, X. (ed.), *Enceints, habitats ceinturés, sites perchés du Neolithique au Bronze Ancien dans le Sud de la France et les régions voisines*. Mémoire de la Sociéte Languedocienne de Préhistoire 2: 111–126. Montpellier.

Lilliu, G. 1966. Architettura nuragica. In *Atti del XIII Congresso di Storia dell'Architettura (Sardegna), Cagliari 6–12 aprile 1963*, 3–77. Roma.

Lilliu, G. 1982. Stato delle ricerche di archeologia preistorica in Sardegna nell'ultimo decennio. In Stato attuale della ricerca storica in Sardegna. *Archivio Storico Sardo* 33: 35–36.

Manca Demurtas, L. & Demurtas, S. 1992. Il complesso fortificato di Crastu-Soddi (Oristano). In *Le Chalcolitique en Languedoc (20/22 settembre 1990)*, 315–321. Archéologie en Languedoc no. special 1990–91.

Maxia, M. 1991. *Un tesoro riscoperto*. Editrice Archivio Fotografico Sardo, Nuoro.

Melis, P. 1995–96. Bortigiadas. Storia archeologica. In *Almanacco gallurese*, 43–47. Chiarella, Sassari.

Moravetti, A. 1979. Notiziario. *Rivista di Scienze Preistoriche* 34: 332–334.

Moravetti, A. 1981. Nota agli scavi del complesso megalitico di Monte Baranta (Olmedo-Sassari). *Rivista di Scienze Preistoriche* 36: 281–290.

Moravetti, A. 1984. Statue-menhir in una tomba di giganti del Marghine. *Nuovo Bullettino Archeologico Sardo* 1: 41–67.

Moravetti, A. 1993. Gli insediamenti antichi. In *Montagne di Sardegna*, 161–212. Carlo Delfino, Sassari.

Moravetti, A. 1994. Dalla Preistoria all'età Fenicio-Punica. In *Planargia*, 94–103. Cagliari.

Ortu, G. 1993. *Testimonianze archeologiche di Esterzili e del suo territorio*, 19–26. Sassari.

Passard, F. 1980. L'habitat au Néolithique et début de l'age du Bronze en Franche Comté. *Gallia Prehistoire* 23: 37ss.

Schubart, H. & Sangmeister, E. 1987. *Zambujal. O Povoado fortificado de idade do Cobre*. Camera Municipal Torres Vedras.

20. Nuovi elementi di datazione dell'Età del Bronzo Medio: Lo scavo del Nuraghe Talei di Sorgono e della tomba di giganti Sa Pattada di Macomer

Maria Ausilia Fadda

L'articolazione delle varie fasi dell'età del bronzo della Sardegna è ancora argomento di discussione. Le cronologie attualmente in uso in mancanza di elementi chiari, si basano sostanzialmente sulla presenza di alcuni tipi ceramici assunti come fossili guida per la determinazione di particolari momenti culturali. Le proposte di cronologia e le diverse definizioni si moltiplicano soprattutto nei momenti di passaggio dal Bronzo Antico al Bronzo Medio quando la rassicurante produzione di manufatti, per la sua inconfondibile tipologia lascia il posto a nuovi materiali fittili che si rinvengono in associazioni stratigrafiche diverse.

Lo scavo dell'abitato di Sa Turricola (Muros) diede modo a Maria Luisa Ferrarese Ceruti di introdurre per la prima volta la distinzione di due fasi della cultura di Bonnanaro interpretando la più recente fase B come l'espressione più arcaica del periodo nuragico (Ferrarese Ceruti 1978). Il passaggio dal Bronzo Antico al Bronzo Medio è segnato soprattutto dalla presenza della forma del tegame e da un'evidente ritorno al decorativismo sia esso di tipo plastico o ottenuto con una punteggiatura impressa a crudo, oppure con uno strumento a pettine. La produzione dei vasi decorati trova la massima espressione nelle olle biconiche a tesa interna con fori passanti ornati da motivi metopali, a scacchiera, a zig zag e triangoli campiti da una punteggiatura fitta o rada. Altra forma di decorazione impressa a pettine è presente, con numerosi schemi decorativi, nel fondo e nelle pareti interne dei tegami, soprattutto nel territorio centro settentrionale della Sardegna. Quest'ultima produzione ceramica viene concordemente collocata nelle varie proposte di cronologia nelle fasi finali del Bronzo Medio, mentre i vasi con decorazione metopale ne occupano le fasi iniziali (Ferrarese Ceruti & Lo Schiavo 1991–92: 130–132).

Lo scavo di una tomba di giganti sita in agro di Macomer ha i piedi del piccolo tacco, dove poggia il Nuraghe Sa Pattada e a breve distanza dal complesso delle tombe di Tamuli, che hanno restituito resti ceramici con decorazioni metopale, ripropone il problema della differente datazione di manufatti, che talvolta si rinvengono in associazione stratigrafica. La tomba di giganti Sa Pattada (Fig. 20.1) (Fadda 1992:168) conserva una camera rettangolare (lungh. metri 5,70 largh. metri 1,15 sul fondo, 1 metri 1,10 nella parte anteriore). Della muratura della camera si conserva un unico filare incompleto di blocchi basaltici ben lavorati nella faccia a vista e allineati fino ad un'altezza di metri 0,75. La tomba, conserva parte del tumulo composto da pietrisco e terra, tenuto da un peristalite che nella parte posteriore forma una parete absidata. La lunghezza complessiva della camera con il tumulo è di metri 10,60. L'esedra ha una corda di metri 3,20 conserva sul lato destro parte del muro a sacco, mentre sul lato sinistro, la parte superiore del muro è stata danneggiata durante l'apertura di un sentiero che conduce ad un ovile che sorge a poche decine di metri dalla tomba.

Lo scavo ha evidenziato, al centro dell'esedra e coassiale all'ingresso, una conca circolare scavata intenzionalmente sul piano della roccia basaltica e delimitata da pietre di piccole dimensioni collocate come rincalzo. La fossetta che originariamente risultava al di sotto della stele e della quale non è stata ritrovata traccia, conteneva sei oggetti di basalto bolloso e di pietra pomice, di forma troncoconica a sezione piano convessa di diverse dimensioni (Fig. 20.2). La particolare cura nella lavorazione delle superfici di questi oggetti di difficile definizione e soprattutto il fatto che intenzionalmente fossero collocati tutti all'interno della fossetta, ne denuncia l'uso rituale, da interpretare come un probabile rito di fondazione finora sconosciuto. Lo scavo della camera, che era completamente piena di pietrame e terra di riporto, è risultata saccheggiata in antico ed è priva di testimonianze nuragiche. Due piccoli frammenti di ceramica campana potrebbero indicare una successiva

---

Maria Ausilia Fadda, Soprintendenza ai Beni Archeologici per le Provincie di Sassari e Nuoro, Ufficio Operative di Nuoro, Via Ballero 30, 08100 Nuoro Sardegna, Italia
References to Pl. refer to the section of colour plates.

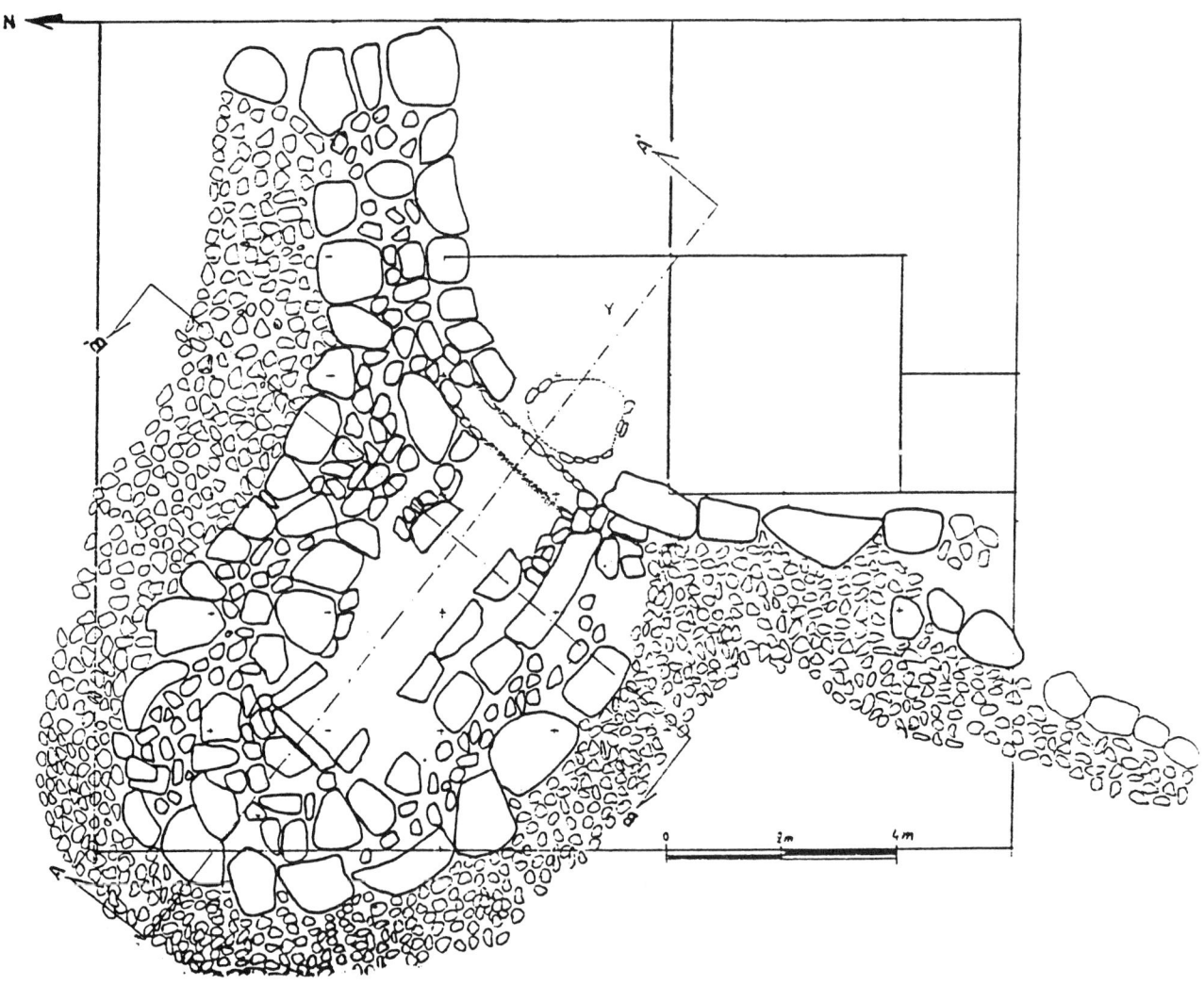

Fig. 20.1. Sa Pattada. La tomba di giganti, planimetria.

utilizzazione del monumento funerario in epoca romana.

In corrispondenza dell'esedra, ove il terreno non aveva subito manomissioni, sono stati esplorati quattro quadrati che contenevano abbondanti materiale fittili. La concentrazione dei resti fittili è stata documentata alla base dei blocchi che delimitavano l'esedra ed aderenti alle zeppe di rincalzo delle stesse pietre. I quadranti "b" e soprattutto il quadrante "8" corrispondente al centro dell'esedra, hanno restituito numerosi frammenti di vasi biconici a tesa interna con diverse decorazioni impresse sulle pareti esterne (Fig. 20.3). I motivi decorativi ripropongono quelli già noti delle tombe di Tamuli, vicinissime alla tomba in esame (Lilliu 1982: 44–49, figg. 41–42), Su Cuaddu de Nixias (Lunamatrona), Goronna (Paulilatino), nel l'ipogeo 3 di Sa Figu di Ittiri, nei nuraghi: Bruncu Madugui (Gesturi), Domu Beccia (Uras) (Lilliu 1963: 191) all'esterno del nuraghe Orgiddas (Samassi), a Pisciu 'e S' Ortu (San Sperate), Pisciu 'e S'Acqua (Monastir), Monte Olladiri (Monastir) (Ugas 1982: 7–20) e nella tomba di giganti di Palatu (Birori) (Moravetti 1985: 92, figg. 19–20).

In associazione ai vasi biconici c'erano diversi frammenti di olle decorate da costolature sul collo (Fig. 20.4,1 e Fig. 20.5) e da linee irregolari graffite disposte in senso verticale sul collo (Fig. 20.4,2). Le ciotole con decorazione plastica o graffite hanno pareti lisciate a traslucido e sono di colore grigio molto scuro.

Gli altri materiali in associazione erano alcuni frammenti di tegame con presa a lingua in prossimità del fondo (Fig. 20.5,5), e altri con decorazione a pettine impresso con motivo geometrico sulla superficie interna ottenuto con la stessa tecnica usata per decorare i vasi biconici (Fig. 20.6). Questa associazione di vasi biconici a tesa interna con decorazione metopale con tegami potrebbe significare una maggiore durata dell'uso di vasi biconici che nelle fasi più evolute del Bronzo Medio convivevano con i tegami decorati a pettine. Questa interpretazione però non potrebbe essere estesa al territorio della Sardegna Centro Meridionale dove è nota la scarsissima presenza di tegami decorati a pettine. Nel territorio nuorese sono diversi casi di associazione della ceramica a pettine con altri manufatti collocati in fasi

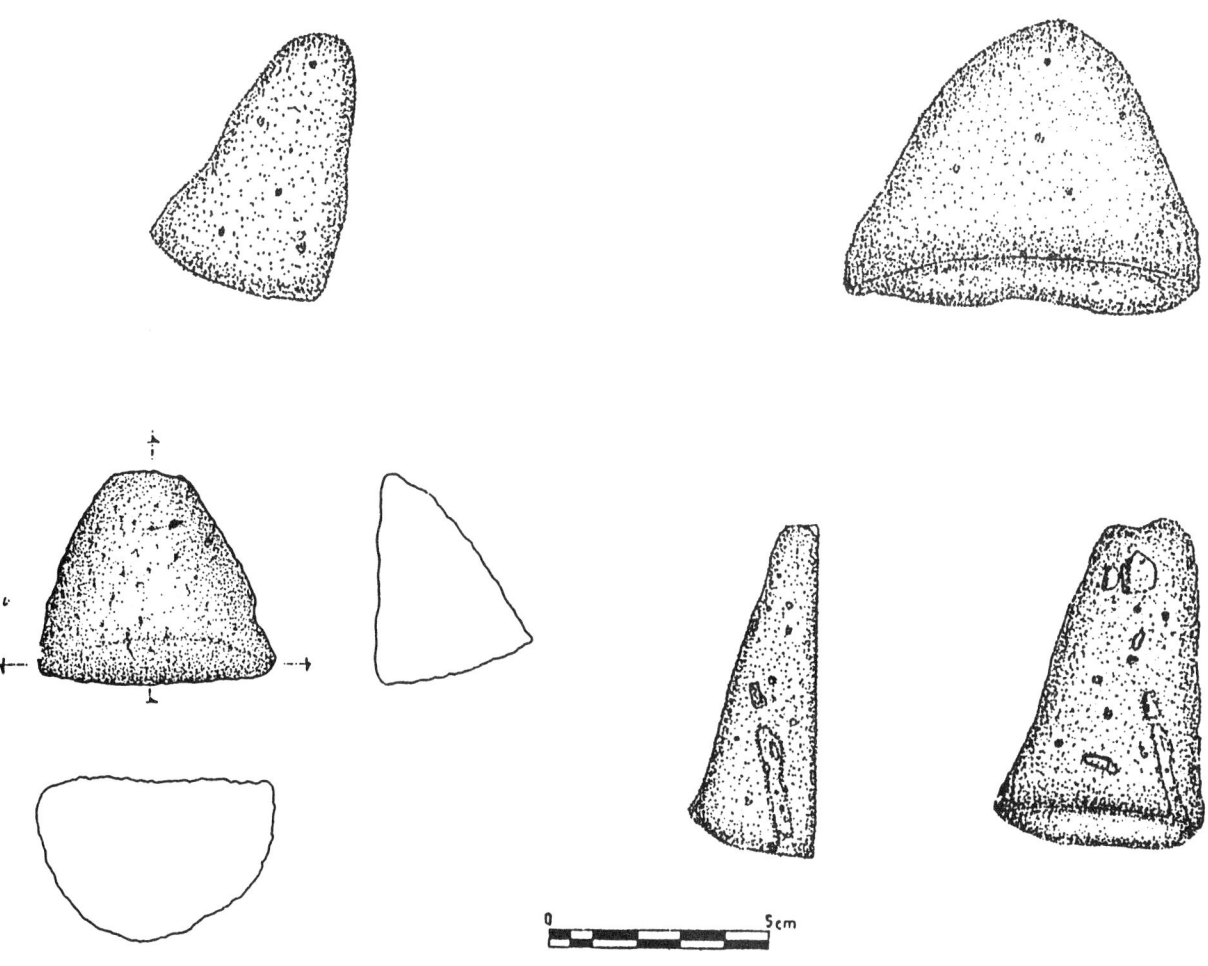

Fig. 20.2. Sa Pattada. Elementi litici.

più arcaiche dell'età del Bronzo Medio. Si citano come esempio il nuraghe Monte Idda (Posada), dove tegami inornati o decorati a pettine convivevano con vasi decorati con costolature sul collo e con vasetti a peducci (Fadda 1984: fig. 10) di tradizione Bonnanaro. Nell'esedra della tomba di giganti di Genna Troculu (Villagrande Strisaili) la ceramica decorata a pettine giaceva con tre anse asciformi con appendici lunate ed un frammento di ciotola del campaniforme attardato, frutto di rielaborazione locale, ed infine con diversi tegami inornati ed olle di grandi dimensioni (Mazzella 1992: 172).

Macomer "Sa Pattada"

1. Vaso biconico con orlo a tesa frammentario, decorazione a metope ottenuta con grossi punti impressi, disposti in modo irregolare. Spalla segnata da profonde linee perpendicolari che partono dall'innesto della tesa e finiscono sul filo della carena. Le scanalature terminano con piccole bugne e impostate lungo la carena. Impasto con inclusi di piccole dimensioni. Superfici lisciate a stecca di color bruno rossiccio all'esterno non uniforme, color bruno all'interno.
Diametro alla bocca cm. 42; altexxa cm. 18; spessore cm. 1 quadrante delta.

2. Vaso biconico ansato frammentario, privo di orlo. Spalla con decorazione a metope campite da piccoli punti impressi a pettine che si alternano con spazi inornati fino alla carena. Le metope sono inserite fra profonde linee impresse tra orlo e carena. Ansa a nastro a ponte impostato tra la carena e la parete inferiore. Impaso ricco di inclusi di diverse dimensioni. Superfici appena lisciate color bruno rossiccio non uniforme all'esterno, grigio all'interno. Diametro alla carena cmm. 48,9; larghezza cm. 19,5; spessore cm. 1,15 quadrante delta.

3. Vaso con orlo a tesa frammentario, spalla decorata da irregolari linee di grossi punti impressi a pettine che avviano sotto l'orlo, una probabile decorazione

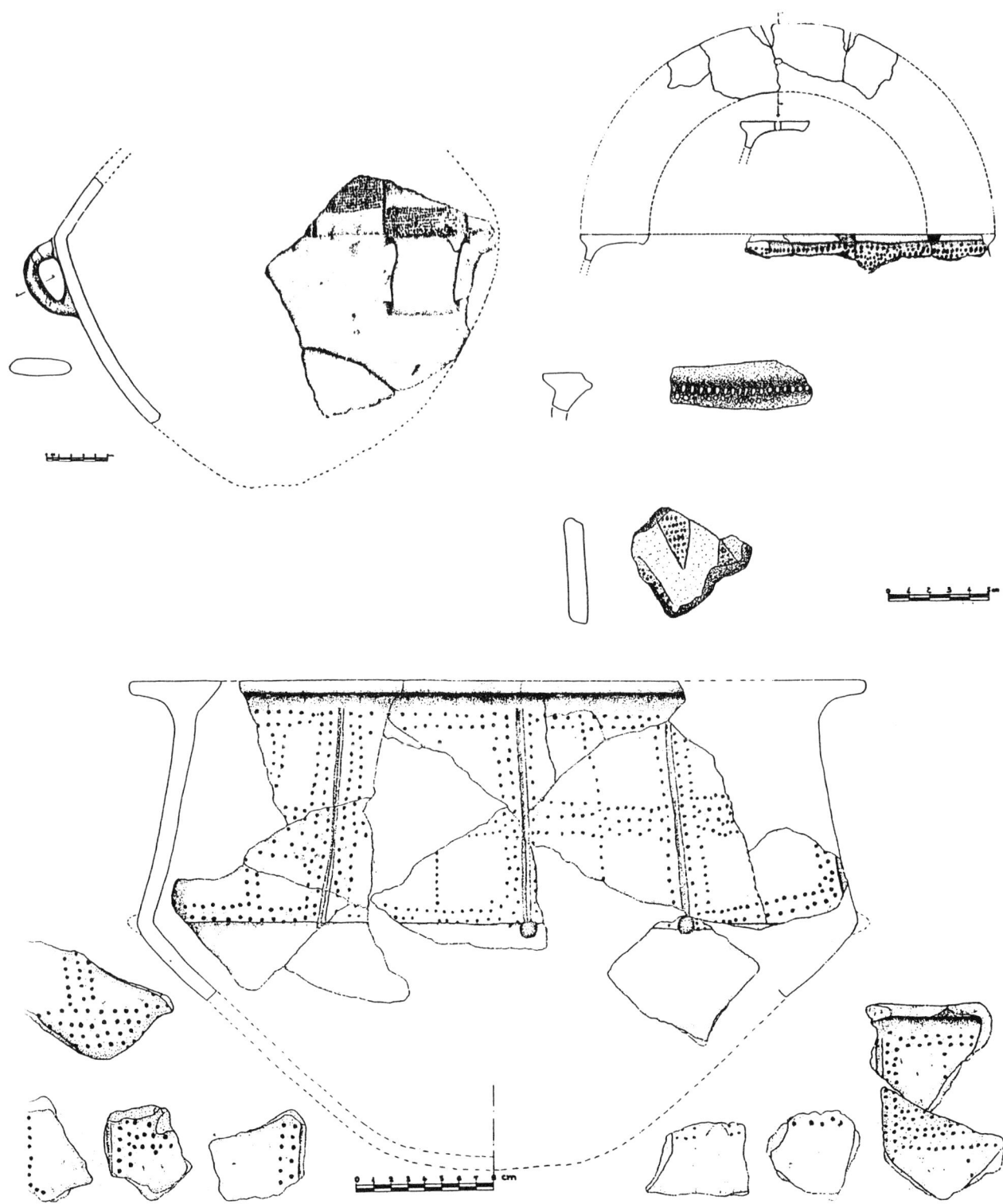

Fig. 20.3. Sa Pattada. Vaso biconico e frammenti di vasi biconici con decorazione metopale.

metopale. Impasto ricco di inclusi. Superfici lisciate color bruno rossiccio, non uniforme all'esterno, grigio scuro all'interno.
Diametro cm. 40; larghezza tesa cm. 6,5; lunghezza cm. 24.
4. Tegame frammentario. Fondo piatto con decorazioni a pettine impresso che forma un motivo a metope comprese fra linee concentriche di irregolari punti impressi. Impasto ricco di inclusi. Superfici appena lisciate, di color bruno non uniforme.
Lunghezza cm. 15,6; spessore cm. 1,6.
5. Vaso con orlo a tesa frammentario. Decorazione a

metope campite da fitti punti impressi disposti in modo irregolare, che partono dalla base all'orlo estroflesso della parete esterna. Impasto ricco di inclusi basaltici e calcarei. Superfici lisciate color bruno con zone di colore rossiccio e grigio all'esterno, color grigio all'interno.
Diametro cm. 28,4; lunghezza cm. 10,4; spessore cm. 0,6.
6. Probabile lisciatoio di basalto bolloso integro, di forma conica a sezione piano concava. Superfici lavorate. Altezza cm. 6 x 8.
7. Probabile lisciatoio di basalto bolloso, integro, di forma conica a sezione piano concava. Superfici lavorate ed erose.
Altezza cm. 7,5 x 5,5.
8. Idem.
Altezza cm. 7 x 4,5.
9. Idem.
Altezza cm. 7 x 5,5.
10. Idem.
Altezza cm. 5 x 5.
11. Idem.
Altezza cm. 4,5 x 5.

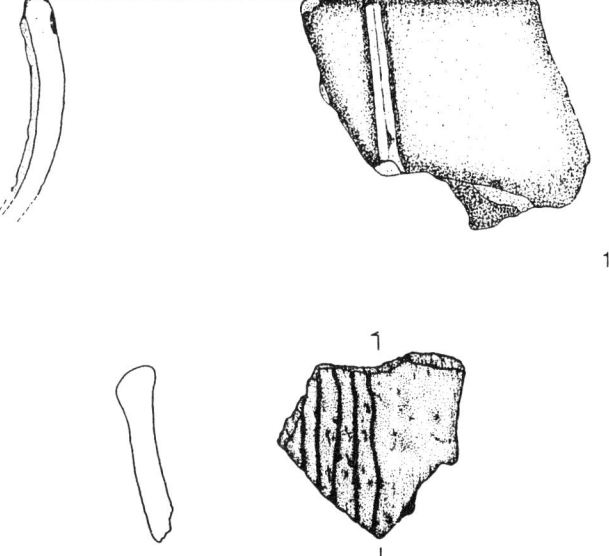

Fig. 20.4. Sa Pattada. Frammenti fittili con decorazione plastica (1) e graffita (2).

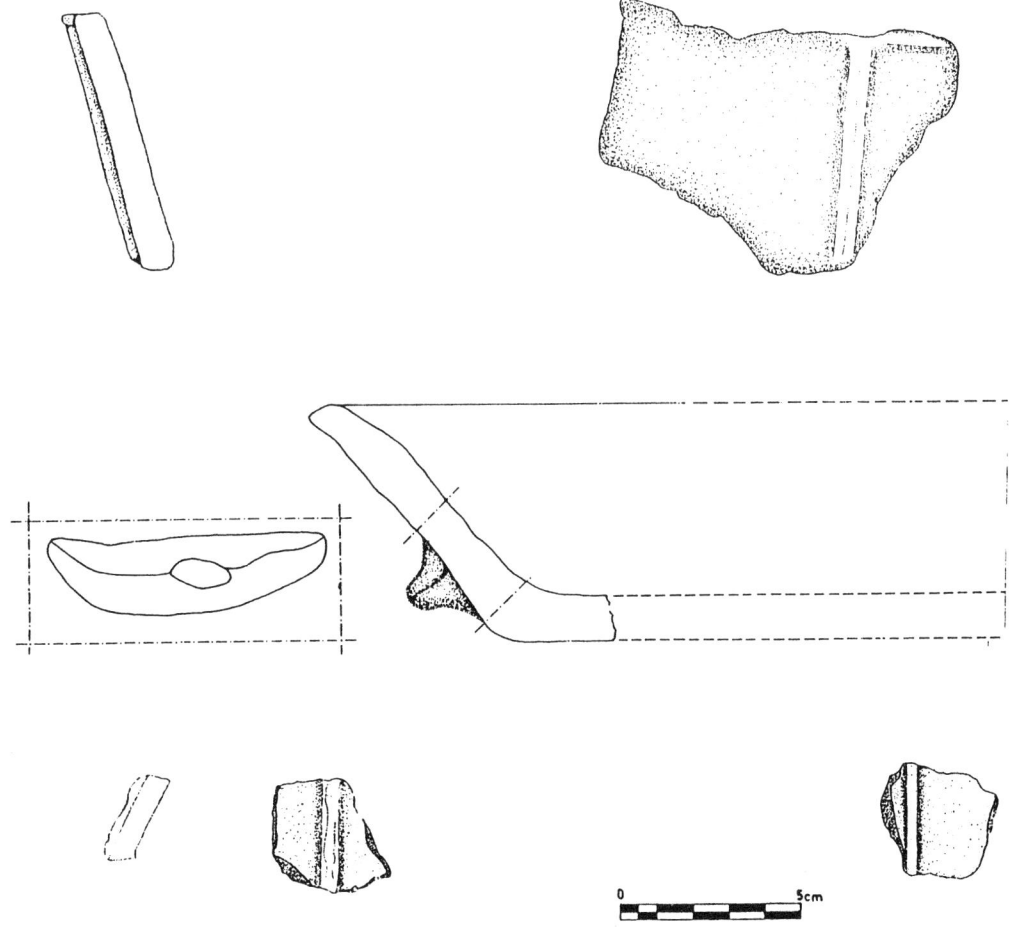

Fig. 20.5. Sa Pattada. Frammenti di vasi con decorazione plastica; frammento di tegame (centro).

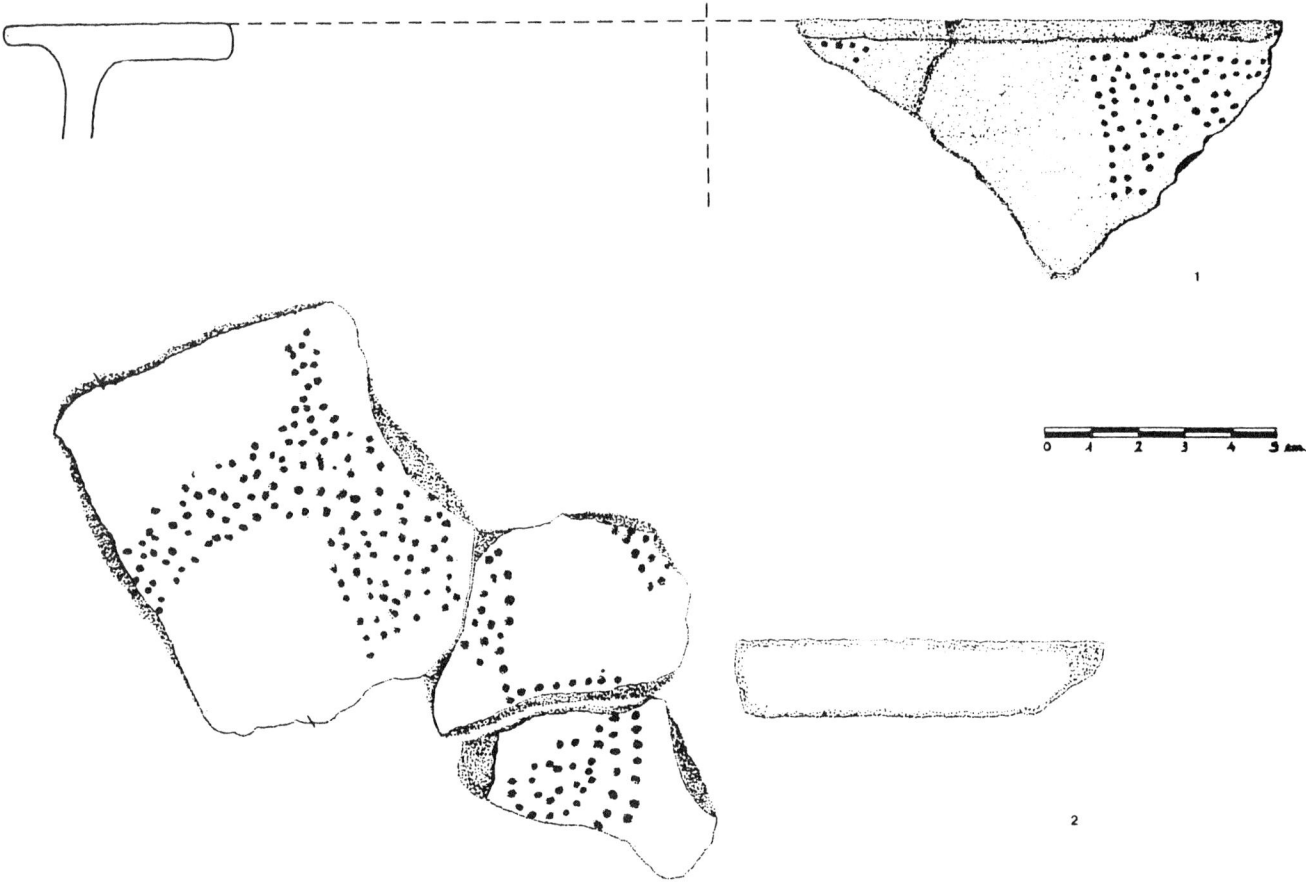

Fig. 20.6. Sa Pattada. 1. Frammento di vaso con orlo a tesa con decorazione metopale. 2. Frammento di tegame con decorazione a pettine.

12. Frammenti non ricomponibili di vaso, probabilmente biconico con decorazioni a fascie irregolari di punti impressi a pettine disposti a bande curvilinee dall'orlo alla spalla. Superfici lisciate a stecca, color bruno chiaro. Impasto ricco di piccoli inclusi color grigio scuro.
   Altezza cm. 9 x 9; spessore cm. 1.
   Altezza cm. 5,5 x 8,7.
   Altezza cm. 8,6,5.
   Altezza cm. 5,5 x 5,5.
   Altezza cm. 8,4.
   Altezza cm. 9 x 7,5.

Scavi ancora in corso di tombe di giganti nel territorio ogliastrino, di prossima pubblicazione, ripropongono l'associazione di vasi biconici con decorazione metopale e tegami decorati a pettine. Altri elementi di datazione vengono dallo scavo condotto nel nuraghe Talei. L'esplorazione del monumento è stata resa possibile da un progetto finanzian la valorizzazione di nuraghi: Bardacolo, Calamaera, Crebos, Arrubiu, Talalù, Terriscana e Talei, tutti gravitanti sul complesso del Santuario campestre di San Mauro. Nel progetto rientra anche l'area di Bidu 'e Concas, con un insediamento prenuragico che conserva un notevole concentrazione di megaliti. Il nuraghe Talei (Pl. 40 e Fig. 20.7) edificato alla sommità di un modesto rilievo collinare, direttamente sull'affioramento granitico, a circa 495 metri s.l.m., sorge a breve distanza dal complesso di San Mauro dominando con la sua mole il sottostante tracciato della SS 388. Mentre i versanti est e sud del rilievo, alla cui base scorre un torrentello attualmente a regime perenne, mostrano un profilo piuttosto accidentato con repentini scarti di quota, il versante ovest e nord-ovest, utilizzato a pascolo, digrada in modo non traumatico, con una lieve pendenza est-ovest, verso il sottostante fondovalle; qui, quasi alla base del pendio, 100 metri circa a sud-ovest del nuraghe, sono visibili i resti di una tomba di giganti in cattivo stato di conservazione.

Il nuraghe, del tipo cosiddetto "a corridoio", non organizzato cioè sul modulo canonico a camera circolare, presenta un pianta ellissoidale con sezione maggiore SW-NE, caratterizzata dall'articolazione degli spazi interni in un lungo corridoio a sviluppo irregolare, appena curvilineo, con copertura a piattabanda (a solaio piano) comunicante verso S-SE con la camera vera e propria a pianta ogivale e copertura originaria (attualmente crollata) a falsa volta, nella struttura cosiddetta a "schiena d'asino". Due ingressi architravati senza finestrello di scarico, a luce rettangolare l'uno e sub-trapezoidale l'altro, si aprono rispettivamente in corrispondenza dei lati "brevi" NE-SW. Poco oltre la soglia dell'ingresso nord una rampa di

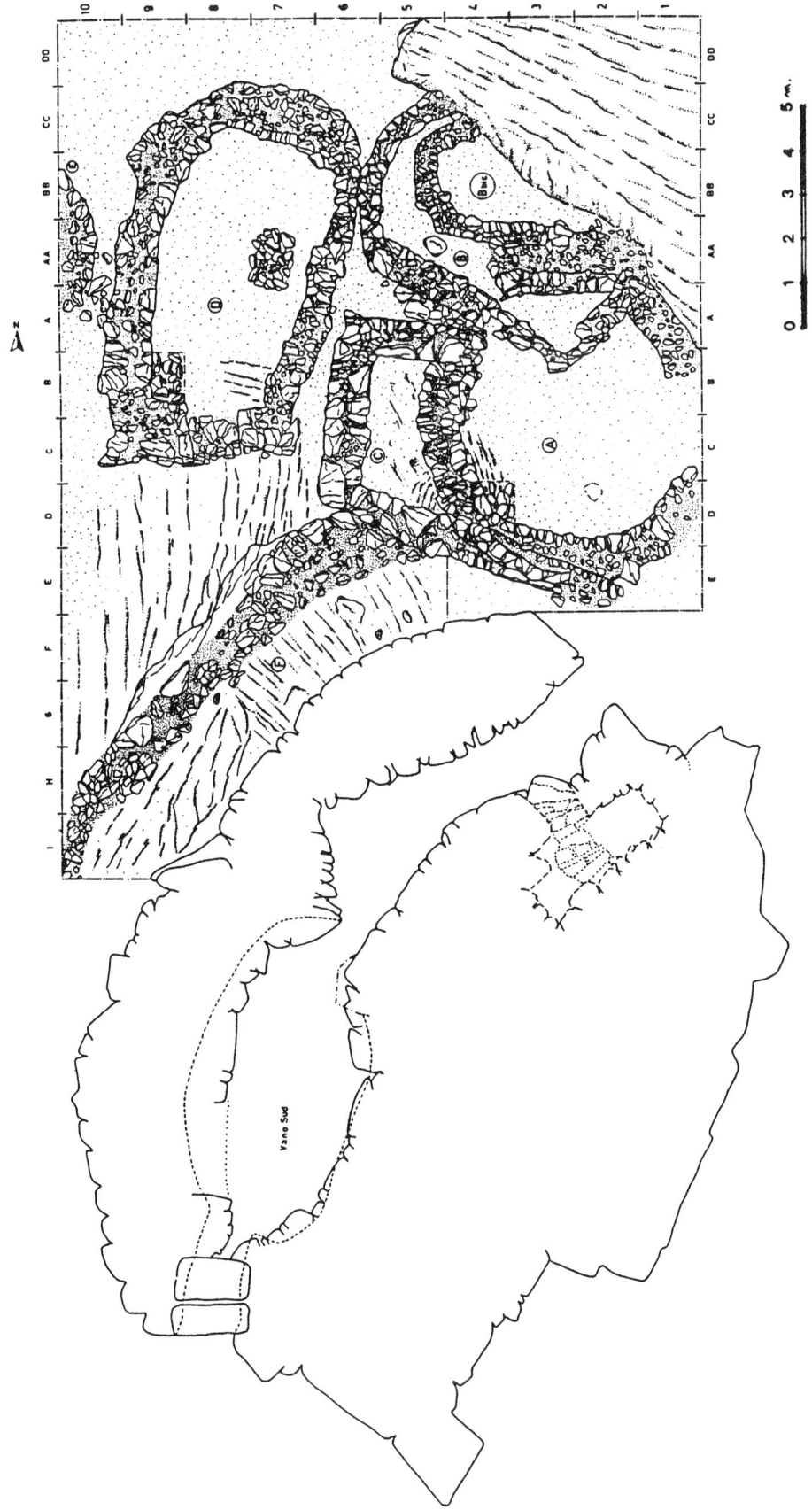

Fig. 20.7. Nuraghe Talei (Sorgono). Planimetria.

dodici gradini, sul lato est del corridoio, immette al terrazzo sommitale attualmente non raggiungibile attraverso l'accesso originario, ostruito dal crollo di parte della copertura; due nicchie contrapposte sono presenti all'estremità superiore della rampa. Il nuraghe, come detto, è stato edificato direttamente su di uno sperone granitico, le strutture murarie e la planimetria complessiva del monumento sono state di conseguenza adattate al profilo irregolare e fortemente accidentato dell'affioramento roccioso di cui, peraltro, inglobano ampie porzioni in particolare sui lati E-S. Le cortine murarie, realizzate in rozza opera poligonale, mostrano l'impiego esclusivo di conci in granito di dimensioni spesso davvero cospicue, disposti lungo filari piuttosto irregolari con l'impiego assai frequente di zeppe. Una cura maggiore, con conci talora squadrati, allettati lungo filari più regolari, sembra aver presieduto alla realizzazione del lato N-NE, a sviluppo pressoché rettilineo in cui si apre uno degli ingressi. L'intervento di scavo, da prima mirato all'indagine della camera e del corridoio del nuraghe, ha successivamente interessato la fascia esterna limitrofa al monumento nel tentativo di individuare la presenza eventuale di un'area insediativa connessa al nuraghe medesimo. Parallelamente si è proceduto ad un intervento parziale di consolidamento e di restauro del tratto sommitale delle cortine murarie mediante la costruzione del muro a sacco e la rimessa in opera di alcuni conci di crollo recuperati alla base delle strutture.

Un primo intervento di scavo condotto nel 1982 nella parte superiore e nel primo tratto del corridoio di ingresso restituì pochi frammenti ceramici di olle con grosse pastiglie plastiche, tegami troncoconici e frammenti di spiana con impressione di canestro.

L'indagine condotta in corrispondenza della camera, al di sotto del potente deposito di crollo prodotto dal disfacimento della copertura e della porzione sommitale degli alzati, ha evidenziato, fino all'affioramento della roccia madre posto in luce sull'intera superficie dell'ambiente, una stratificazione di vespai realizzati in pietre di dimensioni varie, alternati a livelli di battuti argillosi. Tra le opere di livellamento, resa indispensabile dall'andamento fortemente obliquo NE-SW dello sperone granitico su cui il monumento è impostato garantiva una soddisfacente orizzontalità del piano d'uso e uno sfruttamento adeguato dell'intero spazio interno individuato dai muri perimetrali del vano. Le strutture murarie, evidenziate fino al piano di posa, risultano impostate direttamente sulle creste dell'affioramento granitico, alle cui asperità e irregolarità i filari di base sono stati adattati con cura. Una situazione sostanzialmente analoga è emersa dallo scavo del corridoio dove, eccezion fatta per l'assenza di un significativo deposito di crollo dovuta ad una assai migliore conservazione delle strutture, è stata posta in luce una stratigrafia parallela e raccordabile a quella del vano attiguo.

I dati ricavati dagli abbondanti resti di cultura materiale e recuperati (materiale ceramico con grande frequenza di porzioni di piatti e tegami, pestelli e macine litiche), sembrerebbero poter far rifinire l'impianto del nuraghe ad un momento di passaggio fra l'Antica e la Media età del Bronzo. Di notevole interesse appare la situazione emersa dallo scavo eseguito all'esterno, nella zona antistante l'ingresso nord del nuraghe, dove in una fascia in leggera pendenza E-W è stata individuata e riportata alla luce parte di un'area insediativa di cui, al momento, non è noto lo sviluppo planimetrico complessivo. Delle cinque capanne a tutt'oggi poste in luce, quattro ("A","B","C","D") sono state indagate compiutamente, mentre nella quinta ("E") è stato evidenziato un breve tratto curvilineo del muro perimetrale. Un ulteriore struttura muraria ("Struttura F") piuttosto mal conservata ad andamento apparentemente concentrico a quello del tratto W-NW della cortina del nuraghe e di funzione ancora non chiara, è stata esplorata a ridosso del monumento per un tratto di circa 11,50 metri. Le capanne, distribuite a piccoli scarti di quota, a seguire il profilo naturale del pendio, mostrano l'adozione di due distinti moduli planimetrici: a pianta rettangolare absidata di dimensioni e orientamento vari, le capanne "B", "D", presumibilmente "C" e forse "E"; la capanna "D", maggiore delle altre, mostra una lunghezza complessiva di metri 8,90 per una larghezza max di metri 4,90 e a semplice pianta circolare (capanna "A", diametro esterno di metri 7,50 circa).

La capanna "A", a pianta circolare, si sovrappone in modo evidente alle capanne a pianta rettangolare absidata "C" e "B", inglobandone tratti delle strutture murarie all'interno del proprio muro a sacco perimetrale, attestando in tal modo la presenza di almeno due fasi ben distinte nella vita dell'insediamento. Degli alzati, eseguiti in muratura a secco, si conserva spesso soltanto il filare di posa, impostato a volte direttamente sull'affioramento della roccia madre granitica; il cattivo stato di conservazione delle strutture ha permesso di individuare con buona sicurezza soltanto l'ingresso della capanna "D", localizzato in corrispondenza del lato breve rettilineo sud.

Lo scavo, probabilmente in ragione della situazione poco conservativa, non ha evidenziato la presenza di focolari e di articolazioni interne degli ambienti; un solo lembo di battuto, per altro assai esiguo, è stato posto in luce all'interno della capanna "A". La copertura delle capanne, infine, doveva essere realizzata mediante una trama di elementi lignei, impermeabilizzata con uno strato di argilla, come testimonia il recupero di numerosi frammenti di "intonaco", recanti in negativo le impronte della struttura lignea.

Gli abbondantissimi resti ceramici recuperati sembrano richiamare sostanzialmente il quadro cronologico delineato per il nuraghe, documentando una compresenza di elementi tipologici riferibili a olle con rifei a listello interno, spiane) riconducibili ad un'orizzonte appena recensione (inizi della Media età del Bronzo). Il rinvenimento di numerosi pestelli e macine litiche e di elementi di falcetti in ossidiana attestano infine l'importanza dell'agricoltura nella sfera delle attività economiche del sito, nonostante vada peraltro registrata l'assenza dei tipici recipienti di grandi dimensioni, destinati allo stoccaggio e alla conservazione delle scorte alimentari.

Lo scavo del vano interno del nuraghe e delle capanne dell'abitato hanno restituito abbondanti materiali ceramici. La percentuale più alta dei frammenti si rispedisce a tegami troncoconici con pareti molto inclinate (Fig. 20.8,7) di diverse dimensioni. Gli orli piatti ed obliqui sono rozzamente ribattuti all'esterno e lisciati da irregolari colpi di stecca. Nei fondi piatti, distinti e non, sono visibili le impronte vegetali impresse durante l'asciugatura su un piano di paglia. Alcuni tegami conservano l'ansa impostata tra orlo e fondo, oppure un cordone plastico appiattito disposto in senso verticale sulla parete (Fig. 20.8,10). Gli impasti poco depurati rendono le superfici irregolari e ruvide evidenziate da una cattiva cottura. Alcuni frammenti di spiana con impronte di canestro, hanno gli stessi impasti dei tegami (Fig. 20.9,2). Un'altra classe ceramica presente al Talei è costituita dalle olle di forma aperta decorata da grosse bugne mammellate o piatte (Fig. 20.9,5–6–7; Fig. 20.10,6–7) e da nervature "a naso" che partendo dall'orlo si sviluppano assottigliandosi verso la spalla (Fig. 20.11,13–14–15–17). Fra i vasi a corpo globulare sono presenti alcuni vasi a bollitoio con colletto e listello interno (Fig. 20.10,2–3 e Fig. 20.11,1), con i contenitori a corpo globulare giacevano alcuni bicchieri troncoconici (Fig. 20.11,4), anse a nastro con appendice asciforme (Fig. 20.12,2–3), ciotole con presine rettangolari (Fig. 20.13,3–7–8), ciotole carenate di forma aperta e diverse fusaiole troncocilindriche (Fig. 20.11,8–9–10–11–12).

Il complessivo quadro dei manufatti è stato prodotto in un unico momento culturale che trova la sua collocazione nella prima fase del Bronzo Medio (1900–1600 a.C. Tykot o 1700–1600 a.C. Peroni) che caratterizzata da evidenti relazioni formali con il Bronzo Antico. Nel vano a pianta circolare chiaramente sovrapposto alle precedenti strutture a pianta rettangolare, con una parete curva sul fondo, la produzione ceramica continua a mantenere le stesse forme, ma si registra un sensibile aumento in percentuale delle tazze carenate e delle olle di forma aperta. Questo graduale cambiamento, considerato con l'adozione di moduli architettonici diversi a determinato il passaggio ad una fase più recente, ma sempre all'interno dell'età del Bronzo Medio. In tutti gli ambienti del nuraghe e dell'abitato è assente la produzione ceramica con decorazione impressa, anche quella a pettine, che in molti contesti barbaricini si rinviene in associazione con molti tipi di manufatti presenti nel Talei. Il dato più rilevante è costituito dai materiali rinvenuti negli strati all'interno del nuraghe corridoio e all'interno delle capanne rettangolari, risalenti all'impianto più antico dall'abitato e contemporanee al nuraghe Talei, sorto in un periodo compreso tra la fase iniziale del Bronzo Medio II e prima fase del Bronzo Medio III.

Sulla base degli elementi di cultura materiale provenienti dallo scavo della tomba di giganti di Sa Pattada (Macomer) e dallo scavo del nuraghe e del villaggio Talei (Sorgono) risulta più chiaro il fatto che le varie possibilità di associazioni di tipi ceramici, non si manifestano in modo univoco nel territorio e quindi non sembrano ancora possibili schematizzazioni cronologiche rigide soprattutto per la Media età del Bronzo.

Bibliografia

Fadda, M.A. 1992. Tomba di giganti in località Sa Pattada. *Bollettino di Archeologia* 13–15.

Fadda, M.A. 1984. Il nuraghe Monte Idda e la ceramica a pettine in Sardegna. In Waldren, W.H., Chapman, R., Lewthwaite, J. & Kennard, R.-C. (eds.), *The Deya Conference of Prehistory. Early Settlement in the Western mediterranean Islands and their Peripheral Areas.* BAR International Series 229: 671–702. British Archaeological Reports, Oxford.

Ferrarese Ceruti, M.L. 1978. *Sisaia: una sepoltura in grotta della Cultura di Bonnanaro.* Quaderni della Soprintendenza ai Beni Archeologici per le Provincie di Sassari e Nuoro 6. Dessì, Sassari.

Ferrarese Ceruti, M.L. & Lo Schiavo, F. 1991. L'età del Bronzo in Italia nei secoli dal XVI al XIV a.C. *Rassegna di Archeologia* 10.

Lilliu, G. 1963. *La civiltà dei Sardi dal neolitico all'età dei nuraghi.* ERI, Torino.

Lilliu, G. 1982. *La civiltà nuragica.* Carlo Delfino, Sassari.

Mazzella, N. 1992. La tomba dei giganti di Genna Troculu (Villagrande Strisaili). *Bollettino di Archeologia* 13–15.

Moravetti, A. 1985. La tomba di giganti di Palatu (Birori). *Nuovo Bullettino Archeologico Sardo* 1(1984): 69–96.

Ugas, G. 1982. La tomba megalitica di San Cosimo (Gonnosfanadiga). *Archeologia Sarda* 2(1981): 7–30.

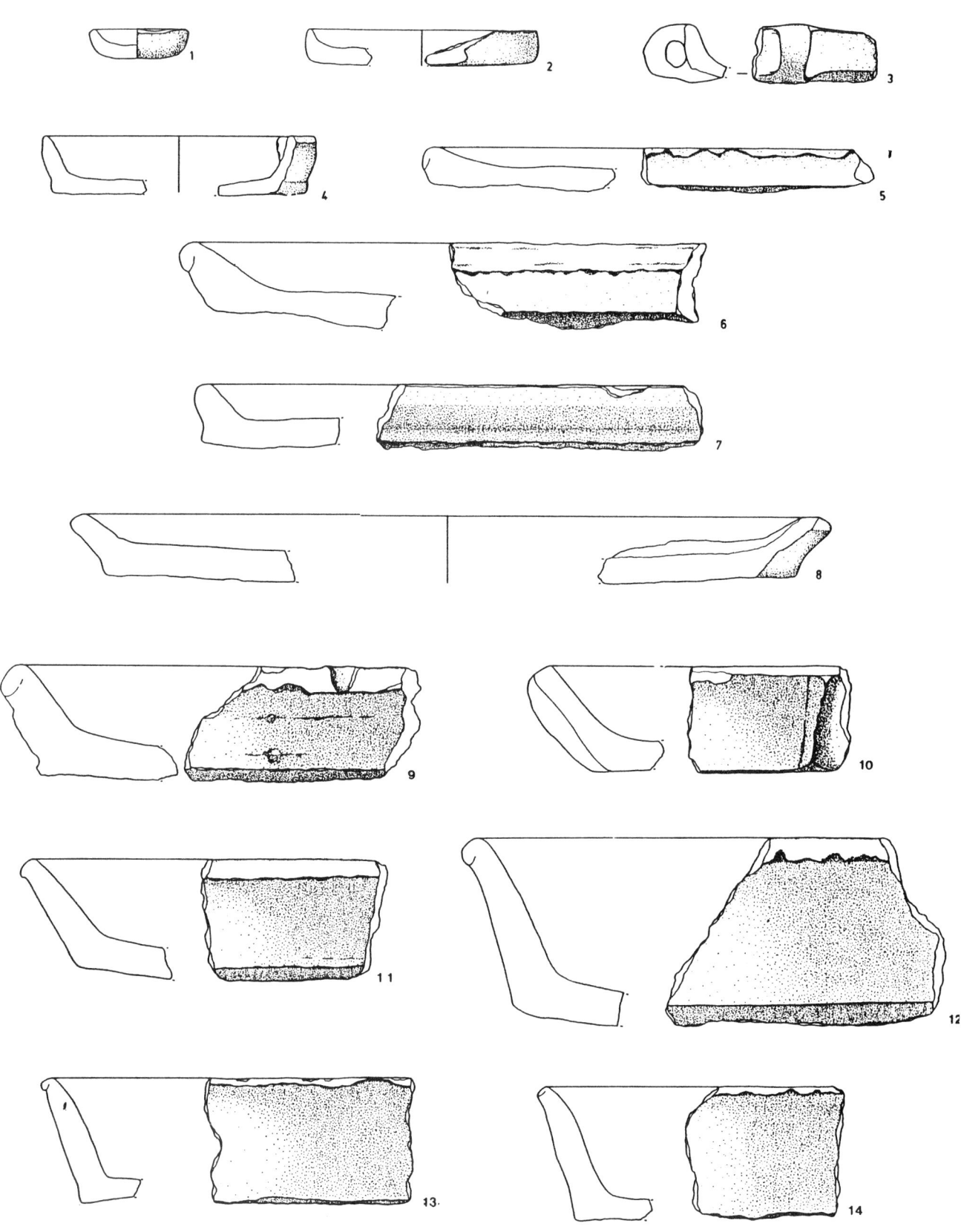

Fig. 20.8. Nuraghe Talei (Sorgono). Tegami.

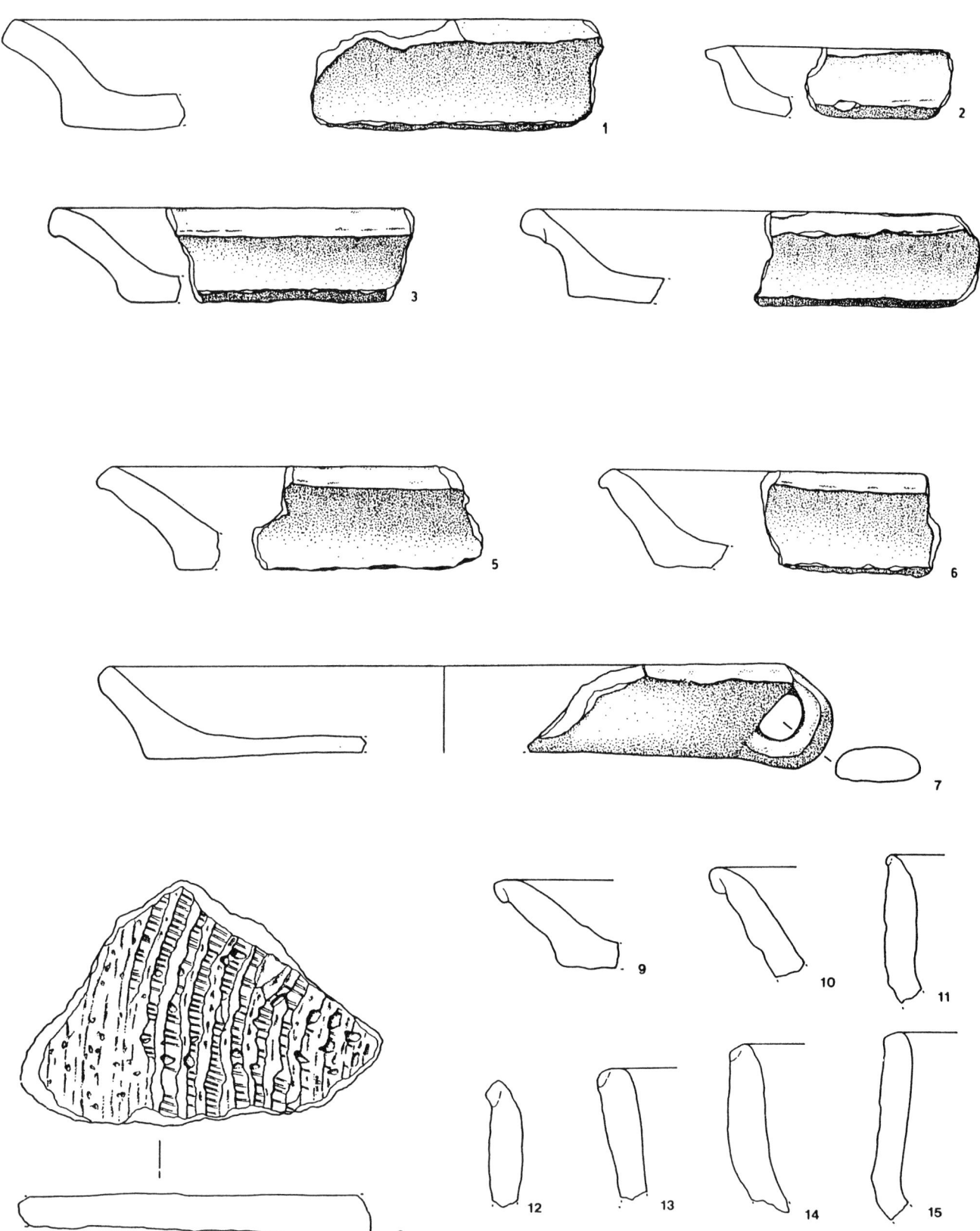

Fig. 20.9. Nuraghe Talei (Sorgono). Tegami.

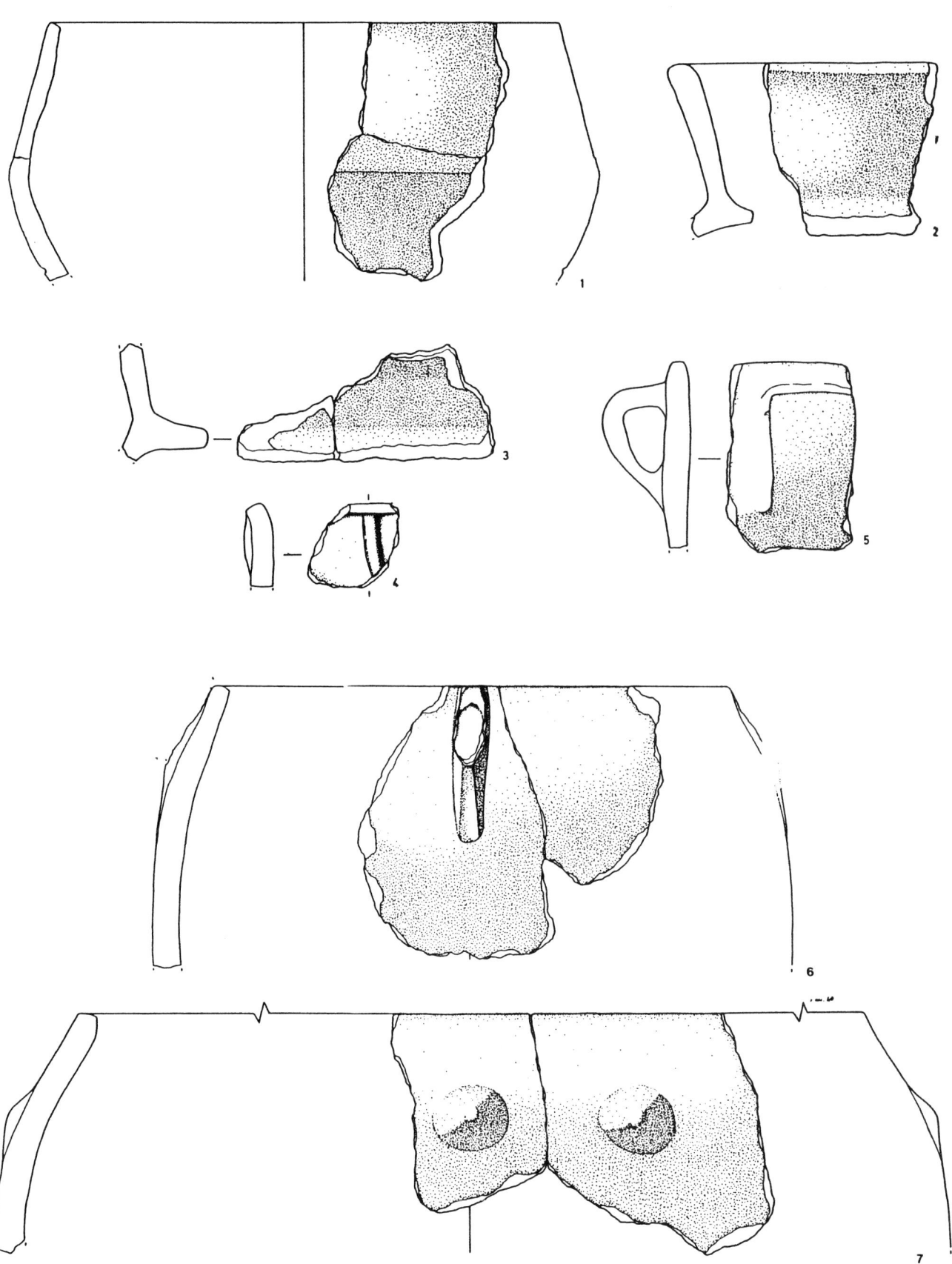

Fig. 20.10. Nuraghe Talei (Sorgono). Olle con decorazioni plastica.

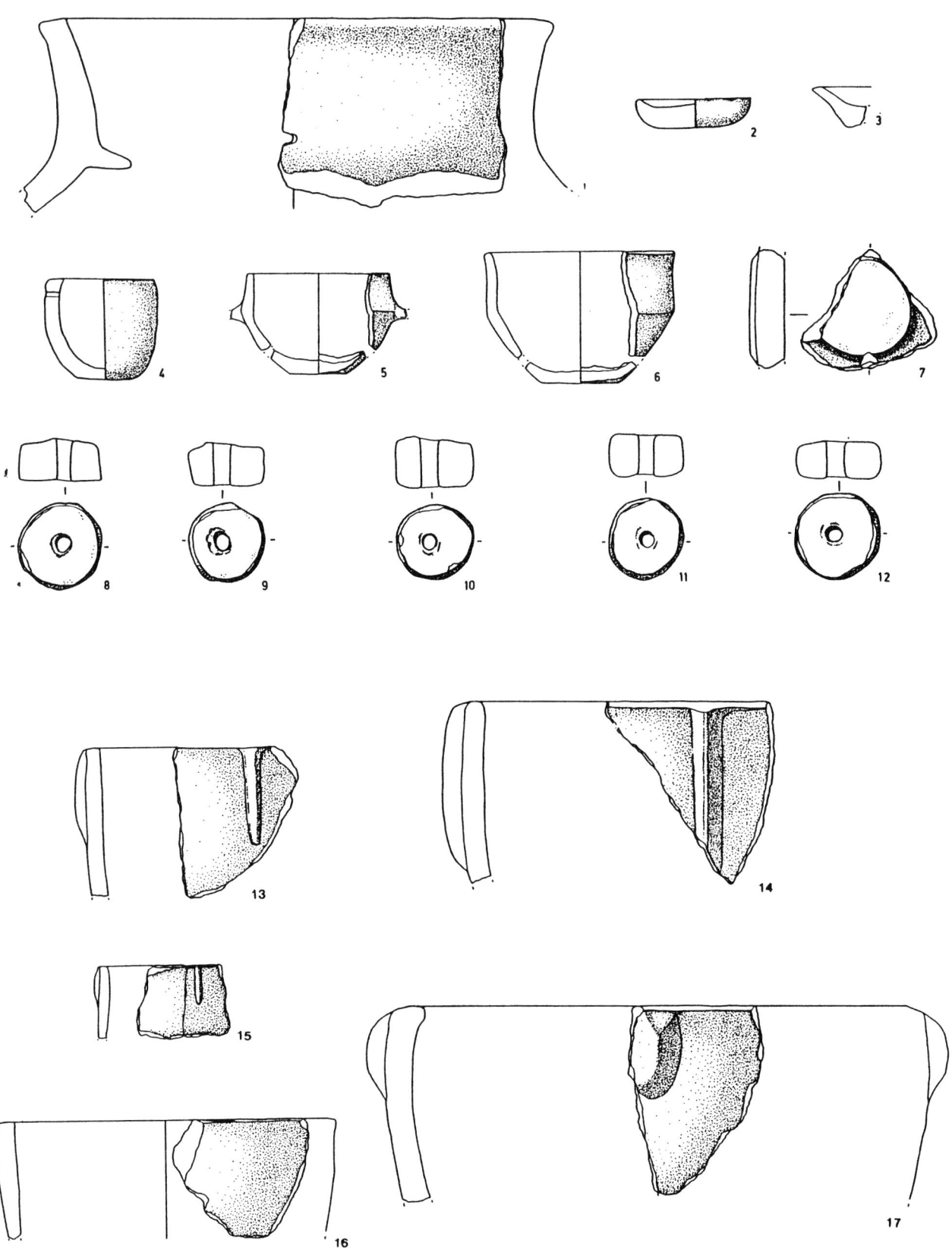

Fig. 20.11. Nuraghe Talei (Sorgono). Vasi con decorazioni plastica.

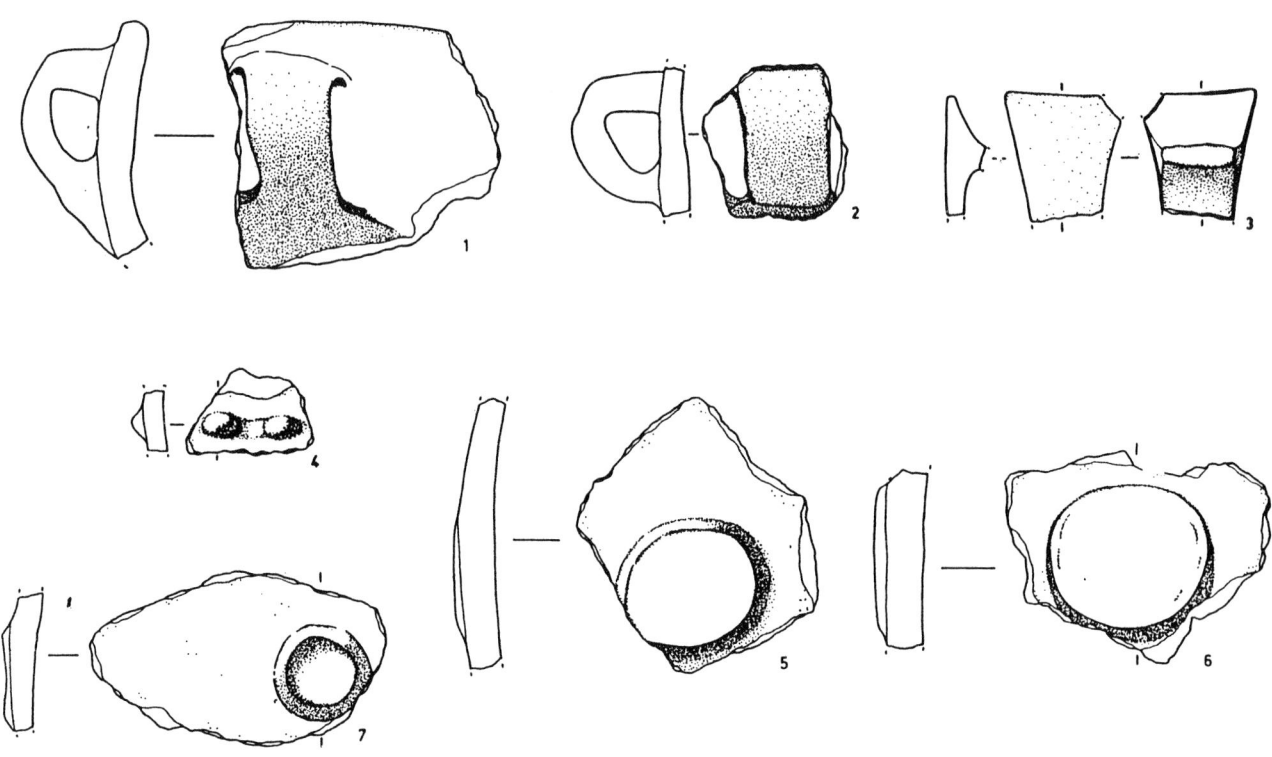

Fig. 20.12. Nuraghe Talei (Sorgono). Anse.

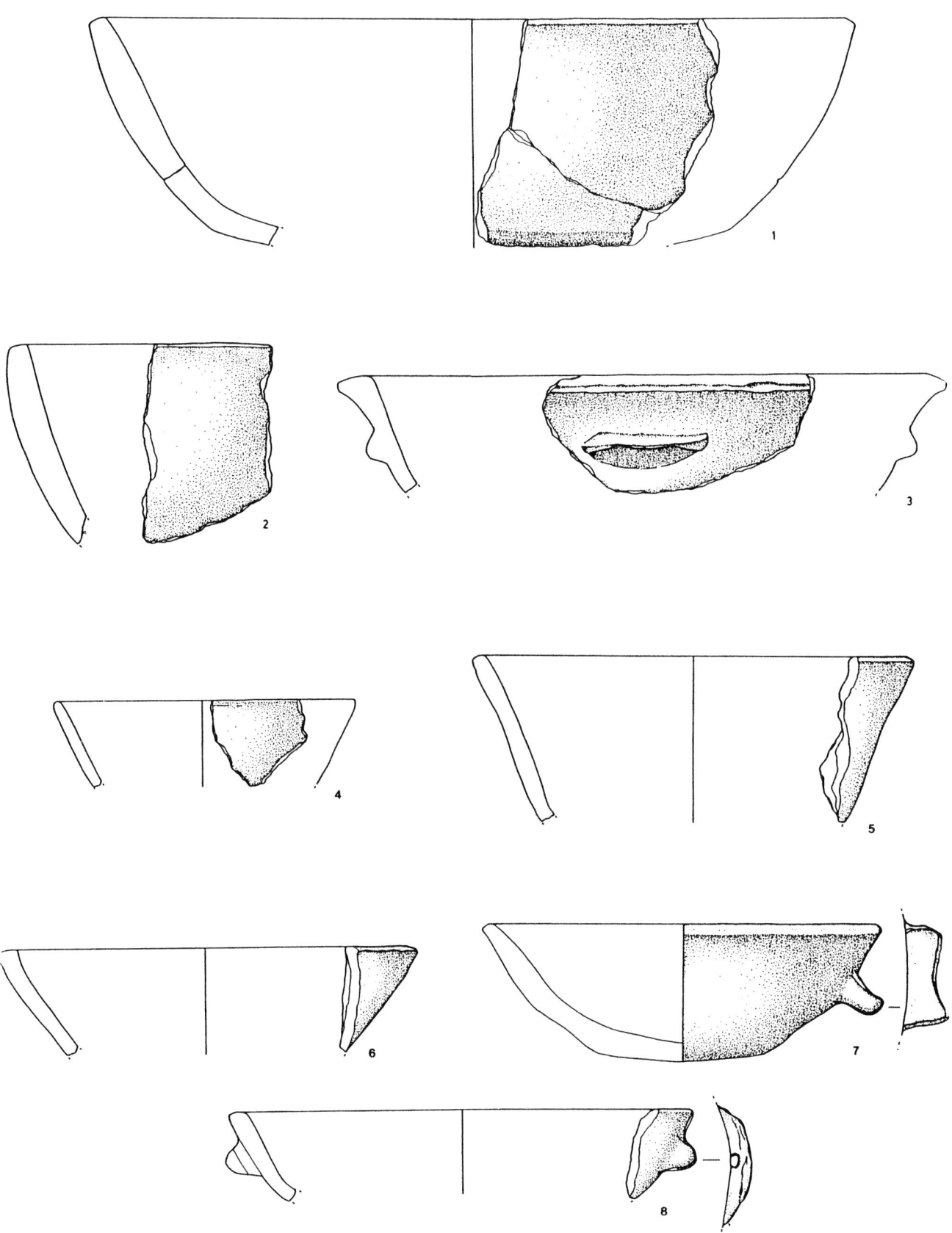

Fig. 20.13. Nuraghe Talei (Sorgono). Frammenti di ciotole.

21. Cronologia relativa del paramento murario dei vani interni di alcuni complessi nuragici

Anna Grazia Russu

Introduzione

Benché la tessitura del paramento murario dei nuraghi si sia dimostrata un argomento notevolmente interessante anche ai fini dello studio dell'evoluzione dell'architettura nuragica, essa non era stato finora oggetto di una specifica ricerca che è, invece, lo scopo di quello che si esporrà nelle pagine seguenti. Lo studio, condotto sull'esame autoptico dei siti, è basato prevalentemente sul confronto, all'interno di un complesso nuragico, fra la muratura dei vani interni del mastio e quelli delle torri aggiunte. Ma non tutti i monumenti complessi sono sopravvissuti integri alle azioni distruttrici del tempo e dell'uomo. In genere, i soli dati accessibili sono quelli della camera del primo piano.[1]

L'analisi è limitata, per ora, ad una campionatura di monumenti in discreto stato di conservazione, ubicati in diverse regioni dell'Isola: Sa Domu 'e S'Orku-Sarroch (Cagliari), Órolo-Bortigali (Nuoro), S. Barbara-Macomér (Nuoro), Duos Nuraghes-Borore (Nuoro), Lugherras-Paulilatino (Oristano), Losa-Abbasanta (Oristano), S. Antine-Torralba (Sassari) e S. Sabina-Silanus (Nuoro).

Obiettivi

Argomento specifico del lavoro è la disposizione dei blocchi nelle superfici di contatto di cui la parete è costituita, per approfondire quanto si evince da osservazioni generiche. Gli elementi noti e comunemente riportati da vari Autori sull'argomento sono i seguenti. I blocchi, in generale, furono messi in opera senza preparazione; la rifinitura, se c'è stata, fu quella finale della superficie esterna. Le facce di contatto, superiormente, inferiormente o lateralmente, non collimano, creando così degli interstizi che vengono colmati, per regolarizzare le superfici di contatto, con zeppe di rincalzo. Solo in taluni casi i blocchi sono disposti a filari.

In prossimità delle luci di ingresso o di nicchie le irregolarità diminuiscono. Le superfici di contatto di rado sono regolarissime, per cui anche in questa porzione di muro si ricorre all'uso di zeppe. Solitamente, nelle regioni murarie lontane dal completamento della copertura delle nicchie, lo sviluppo del paramento murario avviene secondo un registro diverso: la parete mostra, infatti, effetti di avvitamento elicoidale nella disposizione dei conci che costituiscono la cosidetta *tholos*.

Studio dei monumenti

Il nuraghe Sa Domu 'e S'Orku di Sarroch (Taramelli 1926: 115–140; Lilliu 1962: 74–76, figg. 2.1; 3, *1*, cartina B, 108; Ferrarese Ceruti 1982; Sequi 1985: 60) (Fig. 21.1,a) è stato edificato in due diversi momenti: prima il mastio (torre A, diam. 5.00 m), ed in seguito, appoggiata ad esso, la torre aggiunta (torre C diam. 4.40 m). Entrambi gli edifici sono stati costruiti con massi porfirici di varia forma, in generale non lavorati, posti in opera in una muratura d'accumulo, priva di qualsiasi ordinamento (Pl. 41). In prossimità dell' ingresso, comunque, i blocchi mostrano una maggiore cura nella lavorazione e nella disposizione in piani di posa più o meno regolari.

Il complesso di Órolo di Bortigali (Foschi Nieddu 1990: 119; Sequi 1985: 46) (Fig. 21.1, b) è costituito da un mastio cui sono state affiancate, rispettivamente a destra ed a sinistra, due torri secondarie. La camera del piano terra del mastio (diam. interno 4.65 m) è caratterizzata da superfici di contatto pressoché orizzontali di blocchi di basalto allungati. Come si è visto a Sarroch, anche nel caso in esame, in prossimità dell'ingresso e delle nicchie, in generale, quindi, dove è necessario risparmiare un'apertura, i blocchi tendono

---

Anna Grazia Russu, Via Giovanni Prati, 15, 07100 Sassari, Sardegna, Italia
References to Pl. refer to the section of colour plates.

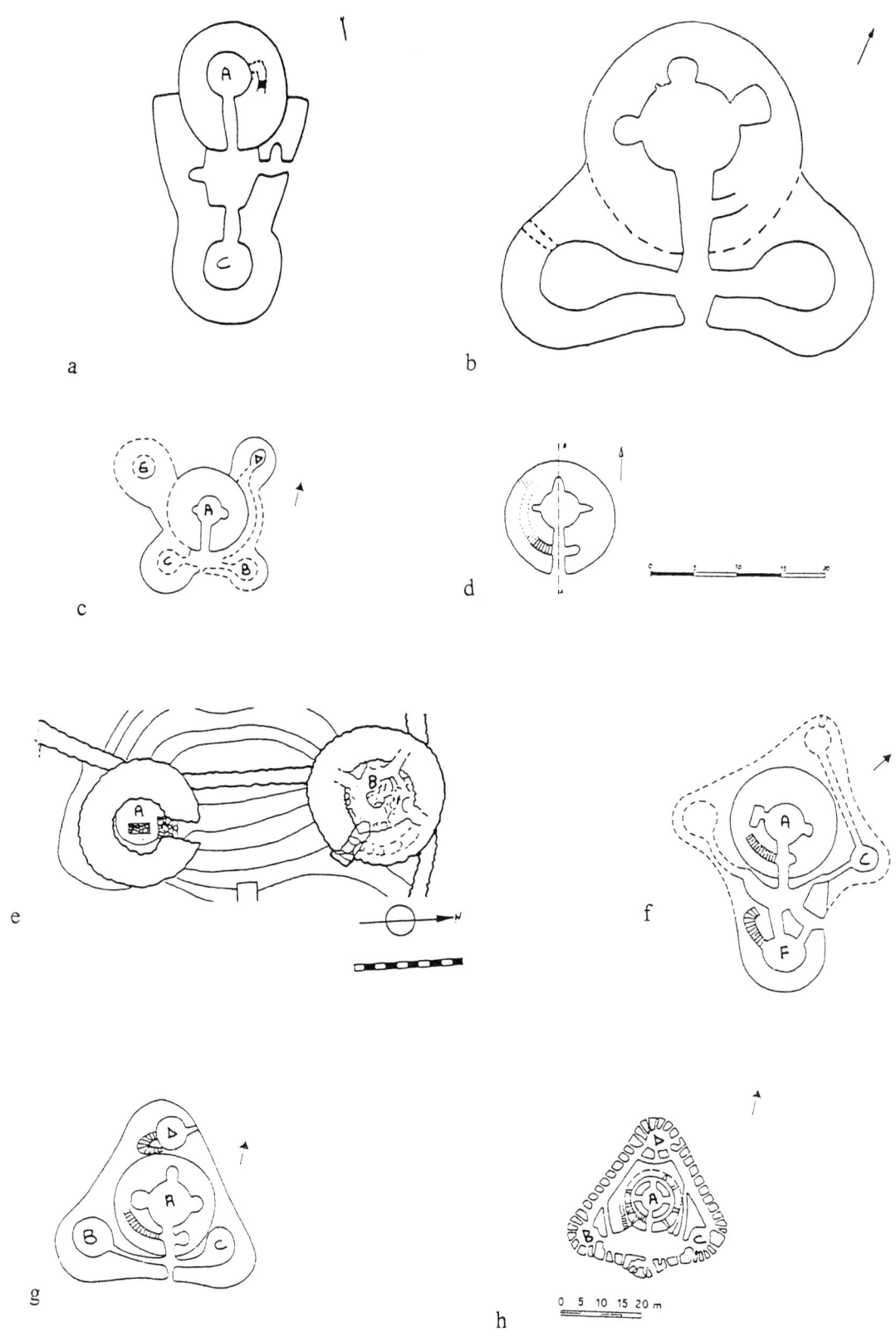

Fig. 21.1. Sa Domu 'e S'Orku-Sarroch (a); Orolo-Bortigali (b); Santa Barbara-Macomer (c); Santa Sabina-Silanus (d); Duos Nuraghes-Borore (e); Lugherras-Paulilatino (f); Losa-Abbasanta (g); Sant'Antine-Torralba (h).

sempre ad una maggiore regolarità, legata prevalentemente a motivi di ordine statico (Pl. 42). La muratura della camera, dall'attuale piano di calpestio fino a 150 cm ca, non risulta essere una superficie continua, a causa della presenza di tre nicchie, disposte secondo il solito schema a pianta cruciforme. Nei piani di posa della muratura degli stipiti di queste e della porzione di muro che le separa, abbondante è l'uso di zeppe, per aumentare le superfici di contatto. Mediante una scala d'andito si accede, con non poca fatica, alla camera del primo piano.[2] Le pareti della camera sono realizzate con superfici di contatto orizzontali che si intrecciano con linee oblique. Fatta eccezione per il nuraghe S. Antine, in nessuno degli altri monumenti oggetto del presente articolo sono state rinvenute nicchie nella camera del primo piano. Queste, nel sito in esame, sono due, a destra ed a sinistra rispetto all'ingresso. Il vano prende luce da una finestra, in prossimità della quale si trovano altre due aperture di modeste dimensioni[3]; nel pavimento di ciascuna di queste si apre un silo. Lo schema costruttivo della camera è simile a quello del corrispondente spazio abitativo al piano terra. I piani di posa dei blocchi prevalentemente rettangolari tendono all'orizzontale. Non essendo stati oggetto di un lavoro di preparazione, però, i blocchi non collimano nei giunti e nei letti, per cui, con lo scopo di ottenere una superficie di contatto estesa, notevole è l'uso di zeppe. Costante è l'intento di rendere le superfici di contatto regolari in prossimità delle aperture, siano queste le due nicchie più grandi, le due più piccole oppure la finestra. Specialmente nella piccola nicchia in prossimità della finestra è possibile osservare che i blocchi si addentrano profondamente nello spessore della muratura.

Nella torre a sinistra del mastio (diam. interno 3,65; 5 m), le pareti dell'unica camera sono costituite da superfici di contatto pressoché orizzontali: gli interstizi sono colmati da un numero rilevante di zeppe.

Il vano della torre a destra (diam. interno 3.65; 4.50 m), invece, nella parte inferiore, presenta un paramento murario decisamente irregolare, indice di pessime maestranze o di una impellente necessità di costruzione dell'elemento turrito.

Nel nuraghe S. Barbara di Macomér (Contu 1981: 34, tav. II, i; Lilliu 1962: 113–115, fig. 9, *1*, tav. LV, cartina B, 29; Moravetti 1990: 49–113; Sequi 1985: 65) (Fig. 21.1, c) è stato possibile cogliere indicazioni di carattere cronologico. Il Mastio viene datato ai primi secoli del Bronzo Medio (XVI–XIII sec. a.C.); le torri B e C, pur appartenenti alla stessa fase, sono state edificate in tempi più recenti.

La camera del piano terra del mastio (diam. interno 5.05; 5.80 m) è costituita da blocchi poligonali collegati secondo superfici di contatto variamente orientate. I numerosi interstizi fra i giunti ed i letti sono regolarizzati da un abbondante uso di zeppe. Anche in tale caso, le parti inferiori delle pareti non creano una superficie continua, in quanto a destra ed a sinistra dell'ingresso si aprono due nicchie. Di fronte a questo si nota una rientranza che, probabilmente, nell'intenzione dei costruttori, doveva costituire una terza nicchia. È interessante notare ancora una volta come, in prossimità delle due nicchie e dell'ingresso, la disposizione dei blocchi si faccia più regolare.

Usciti dalla camera, a sinistra, si segue la scala, le cui pareti permettono una lettura orizzontale che individua superfici di contatto orizzontali, ed una verticale che permette di individuare allineamenti obliqui. La scala conduce all'ambiente del primo piano (diam. interno 3.50 m) che ha dimensioni ridotte rispetto al corrispondente vano sottostante, e presenta le pareti costituite da blocchi di medie dimensioni disposti su superfici di contatto pressoché orizzontali. Si nota un abbondante uso di zeppe per regolarizzare gli spazi fra giunti e superfici di contatto. È ipotizzabile la presenza di un secondo piano, come testimoniano due corsi di muratura superstiti nell'attuale parte terminale del monumento.

Il vano della torre B (diam. interno 3.30 m) ha pareti costituite sempre da blocchi di medie dimensioni che non seguono una disposizione regolare: leggibili sono, però, gli allineamenti in direzione obliqua (Pl. 43). Le fratture all'appoggio al contatto dei blocchi evidenziano come il materiale impiegato sia scadente: conseguenza di cio è, chiaramente, una pessima muratura.

La torre C (diam. interno 4.25; 4.15 m), a sinistra rispetto al mastio, presenta nel vano un paramento costituito da superfici di contatto decisamente irregolari, scandite da blocchi di medie dimensioni e varia morfologia, rozzamente lavorati (Pl. 43). Questo determina la presenza di numerosi interstizi, regolarizzati con zeppe.

Come esempio di struttura monotorre è senza dubbio degno di nota il *nuraghe S. Sabina di Silanus* (Fadda 1990: 123–124; Lilliu 1962: 76–77, tav. X, cartina B, 31, fig. 2, *3*; 1988: 496; figg. 181; 182, *3*; 197, *10*; Sequi 1985: 70) (Fig. 21.1, d), la cui costruzione viene datata al Bronzo Medio-Bronzo Recente (XIV–XI sec. a.C.).

Mediante un ingresso a luce trapezoidale, dopo un breve corridoio interrotto a destra da una nicchia d'andito ed a sinistra dal vano scala, si accede alla camera (diam. interno 4.15 m). Lo schema costruttivo della medesima è simile a quello dei monumenti già visti. Le pareti hanno un doppio registro costruttivo: dall'attuale piano di calpestio fino a 252 cm ca, ossia fino alla copertura superiore delle nicchie, i letti di posa sono pressoché orizzontali, e su di essi giacciono blocchi di pezzatura simile ma non ben rifiniti. Gli interstizi che si individuano fra gli stessi sono colmati da zeppe. Completata la porzione di muro interessata da aperture, le pareti si sviluppavano secondo uno schema che conferisce effetti di avvitamento elicoidale. Da un'altezza di 250 cm ca fino alla cosidetta *tholos,* una serie di linee oblique converge verso l'apice della medesima. I letti di posa sono più regolari in prossimità dell'ingresso.

Al nuraghe Duos Nuraghes di Borore (Webster 1988a; 1988b: 465–472; 1990: 258–259, fig. 5) (Fig. 21.1, e), la torre A (diam. interno 4.15 m), che è la più antica, presenta una camera priva di nicchie. In questo vano la posa in opera dei blocchi, assolutamente privi di preparazione, ha dato come risultato una muratura d'accumulo.

Essendo ancora in corso lo scavo della torre B, non è possibile avere una visione completa dell'elevato. E' chiaro, comunque sin d'ora, che a delimitare lo spazio abitativo sono delle pareti con letti pressoché orizzontali. Ad un'analisi più approfondita, però, la muratura risulta priva di uno schema fisso. Nella porzione di parete a sinistra dell'ingresso (Fig. 21.2, a), i primi letti sono, nel complesso regolari e su di essi si appoggiano due blocchi posti in pila ("a sorella"). Il terzo ed il quarto piano di posa non seguono lo stesso ordine: ad un primo blocco, disposto come base per il piano di posa successivo, con in vista il lato con maggiore lunghezza, segue un secondo che mostra quello con lunghezza minore. Il blocco in questione, inoltre, ha la forma di un trapezio rovesciato, perciò, con la base minore che giace più in basso del contesto dei blocchi. Da segnalare è anche la parete a destra dell'ingresso (Fig. 21.2, b), nella porzione di muro compresa fra il primo ed il quarto letto, i quali, nel complesso possono essere definiti pressoché orizzontali. Fa eccezione il terzo letto di posa: in esso un blocco giace trasversalmente, andando a poggiare con l'estremità destra sul blocco sottostante.

Il nuraghe quadrilobato Lugherras di Paulilatino (Taramelli 1910: coll. 153–234; Contu 1981: 34, tav. II, f; Lilliu 1962: 105–108, figg. 8, *5*, 10, *1*, cartina B, 61; 1988: 178, 328, 364, 387, 435, 471, 584, 591, 615, figg. 3, *48*; 9, *2*; tav. 76, *a*; Sequi 1985: 29) (Fig. 21.1, f), conserva il mastio e due delle torri secondarie, a NE ed a SE, rispettivamente C ed F.

Il mastio consta del piano terra e di parte del primo piano. Il piano terra presenta una camera (diam. interno 4.80; 5 m) in cui si aprono due nicchie, rispettivamente a destra ed a sinistra dell'ingresso.[4] Le pareti del vano sono costituite da blocchi di basalto che costituiscono un bellissimo paramento estremamente curato, con superfici di contatto dei blocchi molto studiate e con una sottomurazione interstiziale in cui il rincalzo dei blocchi è ottenuto con pietre di pezzatura molto differenziata a seconda delle necessità, con effetti di chiusura completa.

I blocchi, inoltre, pur privi di lavorazione, sono stati disposti in modo tale da offrire all'esterno la superficie naturale più regolare. È fondamentale sottolineare come la parvenza di regolarità, a volte, sia data dalla progressione costruttiva che procede per livelli successivi, senza curare, però, un' idea di orizzontalità e di filare, estranea alla concezione stessa di queste murature ciclopiche. Le dimensioni dei blocchi si riducono, per motivi di ordine ergonomico e visibilistico, man mano che la muratura tende verso la parte alta della cosiddetta *tholos*, in cui si rilevano i consueti effetti di linee oblique, indizio di accuratezza costruttiva. In prossimità delle aperture, come al solito, le superfici di contatto si regolarizzano. Una scala a destra dell'ingresso conduce

Fig. 21.2. Duos Nuraghes, Torre B. Porzione di parete a sinistra dell'ingresso (a); porzione di parete a destra dell'ingresso (b).

al primo piano. La spalla di questa è costituita da blocchi che giacciono su superfici di contatto orizzontali. Nello spazio abitativo del primo piano (diam. interno 2.80 m) la muratura è costituita da superfici di contatto pressoché orizzontali, su cui poggiano blocchi appena sbozzati. Gli interstizi sono regolarizzati mediante l'uso di zeppe (Pl. 44). Gli stessi interstizi sono più larghi rispetto a quelli visti al piano inferiore a causa della degradazione dei blocchi.

Il vano della torre C (diam. interno 3.50; 4.45 m), a NE, serve come attuale accesso al monumento. Le sue pareti sono costituite da superfici di contatto pressoché orizzontali di blocchi con varia morfologia. Gli interstizi fra questi sono regolarizzati da zeppe. Notevole è il numero di fratture dovute a cedimento fondale, ossia alla base della muratura, a sua volta causato dallo schiacciamento. Un ordito simile a quello della Torre C si ripete nella torre F (diam. interno 4.95; 3.20 m), SE, ove la disposizione per filari, sia pure irregolari, è accentuata.

Il nuraghe Losa di Abbasanta (Contu 1981: 34, tav. II, d; Lilliu 1962: 130–132, figg. 3, *4*, 8, *4*, 11, tavv. XXIX–XXXVIII, cartina B, 57; 1985: 141–143; 1988: 178, 328, 362, 381, 435, 436, 473, 487, 496, 505, 507, 509, 510, 513, 521, 524, 584, 587, 591, 621, 625; figg. 184, *4*; 193; 197, *12*; tav. 85; Santoni 1994: 5–64, tavv. I–XXXIV; Sequi 1985: 28–29) (Fig. 21.1, g), che è di tipo trilobato, conserva il mastio e le torri aggiunte. Le fasi culturali riconosciute nel complesso sono quattro: a) Bronzo Medio II (fine XV – inizio XIII); b) Bronzo recente; c) Bronzo finale – Prima Età del Ferro; d) Orientalizzante antico.

Il monumento, edificato con blocchi di basalto, a differenza dei precedenti nuraghi, costituisce un unico blocco costruttivo, in cui, mediante l'addizione del bastione, le varie componenti architettoniche sono state fuse. Non è, perciò, possibile studiare il paramento esterno delle medesime, ma tale problema non riguarda il presente lavoro.

La camera del piano terra del mastio (diam. interno 4.80; 5 m) presenta le pareti costituite da superfici di contatto pressoché orizzontali: i numerosi interstizi in essi presenti sono colmati da zeppe. Come al solito nel vano si aprono tre nicchie i cui stipiti sono ottenuti mediante una maggiore cura nella disposizione dei blocchi sulle superfici di contatto. Quanto è stato detto vale anche per l'ingresso. Nella porzione di parete che si sviluppa oltre le aperture, l'elevato procede per linee oblique che hanno il fuoco nella cosidetta *tholos* (Pl. 45).

Usciti dalla cella, a sinistra si apre il vano scala, il cui paramento murario è costituito da blocchi disposti su piani di posa orizzontali. La camera del primo piano (diam. interno 2.80 m) presenta un elevato completamente diverso da quello visto nel corrispondente spazio abitativo al piano terra. Non esiste, infatti, soprattutto nelle parti basali, una scansione in letti di posa. Notevole è l'uso di zeppe anche multiple per regolarizzare gli interstizi fra i blocchi di varie dimensioni, indizio certo di scarsa abilità costruttiva.

Il vano della torre C, a destra dell'ingresso, presenta le pareti realizzate con cura maggiore rispetto a quelle della camera al piano terra del mastio. Questo, però, non significa che manchino le zeppe di rincalzo.

La camera della torre B (diam. interno 4 m ca), a sinistra dell'ingresso, invece, ha le pareti costituite da superfici di contatto pressoché orizzontali: nella parte basale delle pareti sembrerebbe che i blocchi fossero stati disposti senza un ordine apparente. Di più facile lettura sono, senza dubbio, le linee oblique della parte superiore. In ogni caso, abbondante è l'uso di zeppe.

La cella della torre D (diam. 3.50 m) che costituisce la punta del trilobo, agibile tramite una postierla (per motivi di sicurezza una catena impedisce di entrare) mostra le pareti costituite da superfici di appoggio pressoché piane ed orizzontali con blocchi che tendono al rettangolare. La mancata opera di rifinitura di questi impose la necessità di riempire i numerosi interstizi con zeppe.

Il *nuraghe S. Antine di Torralba* (Contu 1981: 34, tav. II, g; 1988; Lilliu 1988: 178, 362, 364, 379, 423, 435, 493, 395, 496, 500, 502, 505, 507, 510, 511, 516, 545, 561, 585, 587, 592, 615, 621, 626; figg. 184, 5; 190, 2; 194; 195; tavv. 87, 88; Basoli 1990: 105, 106; Moravetti 1988: 45–60; Sequi 1985: 71) (Fig. 21.1, h), trilobato come il precedente, presenta il mastio, a tre piani, di cui solo due interamente conservati, e tre torri secondarie collegate da corridoi. I ritrovamenti ceramici individuano due fasi costruttive: il Mastio viene datato fra il XVI ed il XIII sec. a.C., mentre il Bastione fra il XIII ed il X sec. a.C.

La camera del piano terra (diam. interno 5.40 m) nel mastio offre una novità rispetto a quanto visto finora. In essa si aprono quelle che altrove sono nicchie ma che qui risultano passaggi al corridoio che corre intorno alla camera. Al di sopra dell'ingresso si apre un ripostiglio. Il paramento murario è costituito da blocchi di basalto disposti su superfici di contatto orizzontali. Gli interstizi sono colmati da zeppe e malta di fango. Al di sopra delle coperture delle tre aperture, i cui stipiti sono stati realizzati con cura maggiore, ha inizio lo sviluppo elicoidale della muratura che culmina nella bella cosidetta *tholos*. Una situazione simile si presenta anche nella camera del primo piano (diam. m 4.80), su cui si aprono due nicchie ripostiglio. La scala che collega i due ambienti ha le pareti costituite da superfici di contatto orizzontali in cui si leggono, come al solito, anche linee oblique.

I vani delle torri del trilobo (Torre A diam. 5.40 m; Torre B diam. 5.80 m; Torre D diam. 5.70 m) sono state edificate con la stessa tecnica. I blocchi di basalto giacciono su superfici di contatto pressoché orizzontali e gli interstizi sono regolarizzati da un abbondante uso di zeppe. Si segnala, inoltre, la presenza di numerose feritoie nel paramento murario delle celle (Pl. 46).

Valutazioni

L'unico complesso che non presenta nicchie è il nuraghe Sa Domu 'e S'Orku, che è anche l'unico ad avere lo stesso schema costruttivo all'interno dei due elementi turriti. I nuraghi Órolo, S. Barbara, Lugherras, Losa e S. Antine, pur avendo in comune nel mastio e nelle torri aggiunte le superfici di contatto pressoché orizzontali, le zeppe, in alcuni casi frammiste alla malta, nelle camere delle torri più antiche presentano una cura maggiore nell'esecuzione. Regola, questa, che si può cogliere anche nel nuraghe monotorre di S. Sabina. Il rapporto si capovolge solo nel complesso di Duos Nuraghes, in cui è possibile cogliere una maggiore maestria e complessità di costruzione nella torre B.

Le nicchie degli otto monumenti sono state realizzate con filari aggettanti, con progressiva riduzione della luce.

Si desidera mettere, quindi, in evidenza la costante delle pareti delle scale d'andito: dove presenti, hanno le pareti costituite da superfici di contatto orizzontali che si intrecciano con linee oblique. Ridotto, rispetto ai vani, è, invece, l'uso di zeppe di rincalzo. Solo a Sa Domu 'e S'Orku si trova la scala di camera. In tutti i monumenti più sopra esaminati le zeppe sono coerenti con il litotipo utilizzato per tutto il monumento.⁵

Conclusioni

L'esame delle pareti dei monumenti ha condotto alla individuazione di alcune caratteristiche chiave ai fini della ricerca sulla cui presenza o assenza è possibile istituire confronti puntuali rispetto all'insieme dei campioni in studio ed alla loro, sia pur sommaria cronologia relativa.

Le caratteristiche da citare sono di due ordini: il primo, relativo ai materiali impiegati, comprende: scelta della pezzatura; preparazione dei blocchi; rifinitura superficiale; il secondo, relativo all'ordinamento dei blocchi, comprende muratura d'accumulo; muratura ciclopica; muratura a letti di posa pressoché orizzontali; muratura a filari.

Il monumento degno di nota per l'evidenza architettonica è senza dubbio il S. Antine. I blocchi inseriti nelle pareti del mastio e in quelle delle torri del trilobo sono stati oggetto di preparazione. La *tholos* del mastio del medesimo nuraghe è stata ottenuta quasi con filari aggettanti.

Il nuraghe Lugherras presenta una muratura ciclopica per la quale è stata operata una scelta dei blocchi per la posa in opera. Gli interstizi sono molto stretti e regolarizzati con zeppe adeguatamente inserite.

La muratura d'accumulo si trova nei complessi di Duos Nuraghes, nella torre A, e di Sa Domu 'e S'Orku.

I nuraghi Losa, S. Sabina, S. Barbara e Órolo offrono un apparecchio murario scandito da due diverse caratteristiche: i blocchi che costituiscono la base della *tholos* hanno subito una lavorazione sommaria, seppur successiva ad una precedente scelta, mentre quelli che nello sviluppo dei letti costituiscono la copertura vera e propria sono stati selezionati con maggiore attenzione. Indice di un simile fatto è la diminuzione della quantità di zeppe nel contesto murario.

Dal punto di vista della tipologia i nuraghi S. Antine e Lugherras sono differenti, pur condividendo lo stesso litotipo. La presenza di una muratura scandita prima da superfici di contatto pressoché orizzontali e poi da filari pressoché regolari nel primo monumento parrebbe rivendicare una certa recenziorità rispetto all'omogeneo contesto murario ciclopico del secondo. L'ipotesi, però, per il momento non trova conforto di dati archeologici che possano permettere una comparazione culturale e, perciò, oggettiva.

Peraltro la maggiore o minore semplicità di apparecchio di una muratura rispetto ad altre, pur essendo un elemento importante di valutazione generale, non è di per sé sufficiente ad indicare una maggiore antichità: infatti, devono essere tenuti in conto, tra gli altri, alcuni fondamentali elementi quali le caratteristiche del materiale impiegato per la costruzione e, specificamente, la sua lavorabilità.

Il nuraghe Sa Domu 'e S'Orku, per esempio, non può essere ritenuto più antico di quello di S. Antine a causa della maggiore semplicità di apparecchio che lo caratterizza, ma è necessario anche considerare che il primo monumento è stato costruito in porfido, un materiale molto duro e di difficile lavorazione, mentre il secondo è stato edificato con il basalto, la cui maggiore lavorabilità consente un apparecchio più preciso e più serrato.

Osservando e rapportando, nell'ambito di uno stesso complesso, la camera del mastio e quella delle torri aggiunte, realizzate con lo stesso litotipo, si è colta una maggiore attenzione nella realizzazione del paramento murario delle celle delle torri principali. Questo non significa necessariamente che le maestranze avessero col tempo modificato le capacità costruttive. Anzi, l'acquisizione della padronanza delle tecniche consentiva di realizzare strutture durevoli ed idonee alle funzioni per le quali erano state edificate, pur senza ricorrere necessariamente agli accorgimenti costruttivi più elaborati noti. In taluni casi si potrebbe anche avanzare l'ipotesi che le diverse parti di un unico complesso fossero concepite per usi differenziati.

Riduzione di dimensioni dei blocchi usati, lavorazione meno accurata ed apparecchio meno elaborato si rilevano nel tempio nord del complesso megalitico preistorico di Gigantija (prima metà del IV millennio a.C.) più tardo ma di poco del tempio sud, nucleo iniziale dello stesso complesso (Tampone 1987: 5).

Nelle strutture murarie dei monumenti micenei vennero utilizzate strutture ciclopiche accanto ad altre, tipologicamente più evolute: esempio sono le due coperture a *tholos* di Médeon (Pelon 1976: 337, n. 4).

La regolarità della muratura in prossimità delle luci, colta negli otto monumenti in esame, può lasciar adito all'ipotesi, per la quale non è possibile trovare una conferma avvalorata da fonti dirette o indirette, della presenza nell'ambito della manodopera qualificata di maestranze diverse, specializzate ed impiegate per le porzioni murarie interessate da aperture.

A prescindere dalla suddetta considerazione di ordine tecnico, vanno evidenziate le motivazioni di carattere economico (Antona 1995: 50) che possono consentire la costruzione di strutture più o meno poderose, caratterizzate da una maggiore o minore cura nell'esecuzione. Conseguenza di benessere economico è, ad esempio, la disponibilità di forza lavoro qualificata, che condiziona l'impiego consistente o il risparmio di mano d'opera e di tempo.

Note

1. È il caso, ad esempio, del nuraghe Nuraddeo di Suni, al quale,

allo stato attuale, si può accedere solo dalla camera del primo piano, attraverso la finestra, arrampicandosi sulla muratura esterna del mastio.

2. Allo stato attuale l'accesso migliore è senza dubbio la finestra del primo piano, cui si arriva facilmente arrampicandosi sul bastione; sono imminenti, però, lavori di scavo e di riapertura degli accessi e di consolidamento della breccia esterna del mastio. Nella fase preparatoria di questi lavori sono stati scoperti i vani ricavati nella muratura.

3. Le due nicchie si sviluppano per un'altezza di 250 cm, quella di sinistra, e 258 cm, quella di destra, le due aperture più piccole, invece, hanno un'altezza di 90 cm, quella a destra della finestra, e di 97 cm, quella a sinistra della medesima.

4. Da segnalare l'ulteriore sviluppo di questa all'interno della muratura, in cui si piega a gomito. Seppur non inclusi in questo articolo, i nuraghi Nastasi di Tertenia ed Arrubiu di Orroli presentano la stessa peculiarità in corrispondenza dell'omologa nicchia.

5. Altri monumenti oggetto dello studio e non citati in questa sede, ad esempio i nuraghi Nastasi di Tertenia (Nuoro) in porfido e Santu Millanu di Nurallao (Nuoro) in marna calcarea, hanno le zeppe in basalto (Murru 1990: 24).

Ringraziamenti

L'attuale ricerca è stata resa possibile da una borsa di studio della Fondazione Banco di Sardegna. Responsabile scientifico è il Prof. Ercole Contu, Professore di Antichità Sarde e Direttore dell'Istituto di Antichità, Arte e Discipline Etnodemologiche della Facoltà di Lettere e Filosofia dell'Università degli Studi di Sassari. Sull'argomento si veda anche la tesi di laurea della Dr.ssa M. R. Piras, *Tessitura architettonica del paramento murario dei nuraghi della Sardegna*, Università di Sassari, Facoltà di Magistero, Corso di Laurea in Materie Letterarie, Anno Accademico 1988–89, che ringrazio per la disponibilità. Un sincero ringraziamento va alla Dr.ssa Fulvia Lo Schiavo, alla Dott.ssa Angela Antona ed al Prof. Gennaro Tampone per i loro preziosi consigli e suggerimenti. Desidero ancora ricordare con gratitudine l'aiuto ricevuto dal Dr. Franco Campus e dalla Dr.ssa Marina Pizzonia per il nuraghe Sa Domu 'e S'Orku, da Pietro Luigi Uras per il nuraghe Órolo, da Alessandro Vozzo per il nuraghe Santa Barbara, dal Prof. Gary Webster e dalla Dr.ssa Maud Teglund per il complesso di Duos Nuraghes, da Tonino Atzori, Massimo Muscas e Francesco Oppo della Società Archeologica di Paulilatino per il nuraghe Lugherras. Le foto sono dell'autore, la Figura 2 del Geom. Massimo Meloni, che ringrazio con fraterno affetto.

Bibliografia

Antona, A. 1995. In Antona, A. & D'Oriano, R., Il territorio dalla Preistoria al Medioevo. In *Tempio e il suo volto*, 50. Sassari.

Basoli, P. 1990. Nuraghe S. Antine-Torralba (SS). In *Archeologia e terrritorio*, catalogo dell'omonima mostra allestita a Sassari dal 16 Giugno al 15 Luglio 1990, 105–106. Milano.

Contu, E. 1981. L'architettura nuragica. In *Ichnussa: La Sardegna dalle origini all'età classica*, 5–175. Scheiwiller, Milano.

Contu, E. 1988. *Il nuraghe S. Antine di Torralba*. Sardegna Archeologica: Guide e Itinerari 6. Carlo Delfino, Sassari.

Fadda, M.A. 1990. Nuraghe Santa Sabina-Silanus (NU). In *Archeologia e terrritorio*, catalogo dell'omonima mostra allestita a Sassari dal 16 Giugno al 15 Luglio 1990, 123–124. Milano.

Ferrarese Ceruti, M.L. 1982. Il complesso nuragico di Antigori (Sarroch, Cagliari). In *Magna Grecia e Mondo Miceneo, Nuovi Documenti. XXII Convegno di Studi sulla Magna Grecia (Taranto 4–11 ottobre 1982)*, 167–176. Napoli.

Foschi Nieddu, A. 1990. Nuraghe Órolo-Bortigali (NU). In *Archeologia e terrritorio*, catalogo dell'omonima mostra allestita a Sassari dal 16 Giugno al 15 Luglio 1990, 119. Milano.

Lilliu, G. 1962. *I Nuraghi. Torri preistoriche della Sardegna*. La Zattera, Roma.

Lilliu, G. 1985. Abbasanta (Oristano). Loc. Nuraghe Losa. In *I Sardi. La Sardegna dal Paleolitico all'Età romana*, 141–143. Jaca Book, Milano.

Lilliu, G. 1988. *La civiltà dei Sardi dal Paleolitico all'età dei nuraghi*. ERI, Torino.

Moravetti, A. 1988. Il nuraghe S. Antine di Torralba. Architettura. In Moravetti, A. (a cura di), *Il nuraghe S. Antine nel Logudoro-Meilogu*, 45–60. Carlo Delfino, Sassari.

Moravetti, A. 1990. Nota preliminare agli scavi del nuraghe S. Barbara di Macomer. *Nuovo Bollettino Archeologico Sardo* 3(1986): 49–113.

Murru, G. 1990. Proposta di indagine sui materiali da costruzione dei monumenti archeologici. *Geologia Tecnica* 1990: 23–28.

Pelon, O. 1976. *Tholoi, tumuli et cercles funéraires. Recherches sur les monuments funéraires de plan circulaire dans l'Égée de l'Âge du Bronze (IIIe et IIe millenaire a. J.C.)*. Bibliotèque des Écoles Françaises d'Athène et Rome 29. Parigi.

Piras, M.R. 1988–89. *Tessitura architettonica del paramento murario dei nuraghi della Sardegna*. Università di Sassari, Facoltà di Magistero, Corso di Laurea in Materie Letterarie, Anno Accademico 1988–89 (Tesi di Laurea).

Santoni, V. 1994. L'architettura e la produzione materiale nuragica. In *Il nuraghe Losa di Abbasanta. 1.* Quaderni della Soprintendenza Archeologica per le Provincie di Cagliari e Oristano 10 (1993) supplemento: 5–110. STEF, Cagliari.

Sequi, M. 1985. *Nuraghi. Manuale per Conoscere 90 Grandi Torri Megalitiche della Sardegna*. Oristano.

Tampone, G. 1987. Nuove ipotesi sull'architettura del tempio megalitico di Gigantija a Gozo. *Bollettino degli Ingegneri* 3: 3–21.

Taramelli, A. 1910. Il nuraghe Lugherras di Paulilatino. *Monumenti Antichi dei Lincei* 20: coll. 153–234.

Taramelli, A. 1926. Scavi nel nuraghe Sa Domu 'e S'Orku di Sarrok. *Monumenti Antichi dei Lincei* 31: coll. 405–456.

Webster, G.S. 1988a. Excavations at Duos Nuraghes in Sardinia 1985, 1987, 1988. *Old World Archaeology Newsletter* 12(3): 17–21.

Webster, G.S. 1988b. Duos Nuraghes: Preliminary Results of the First Three Seasons of Excavation. *Journal of Field Archaology* 15: 465–472.

Webster, G.S. 1990. Borore (Nuoro). Loc. Duos Nuraghes. *Bollettino di Archeologia* 1–2: 258–259.

22. Datazione e significato della scultura in pietra e dei bronzetti figurati della Sardegna Nuragica

Ercole Contu

Premessa

Oltre all'architettura, l'elemento più significativo, che permette un ampio discorso sulla Civiltà Nuragica della Sardegna è costituito indubbiamente dalla scultura in bronzo e in pietra, che occupa solo la parte finale di questo periodo, corrispondente almeno all'Età del Ferro; ma che potrebbe essere cominciata prima e finita dopo. Nella scultura in bronzo si tratta di statuine che erano offerte in dono alle divinità; nell'altro caso ci troviamo invece di fronte a grandi statue a tutto tondo in pietra arenaria gessosa, che erano erette soprattutto presso il monumento funerario di Monti Prama-Cabras-Oristano, ma ritrovate anche vicino a qualche pozzo sacro e altrove.

Mentre le grandi statue in pietra potevano, nelle figure antropomorfe raggiungere, senza la base, i m 3 di altezza, i bronzi – molto varii nel soggetto – erano invece di modeste e talora minuscole proporzioni (altezza massima ed eccezionale circa 40 cm., minima, con una capretta, cm 2,5); forse perché ognuno di questi rappresentava un'offerta individuale o familiare, entro una società, rimasta al livello di villaggio, che non conosceva disuguaglianze sociali molto marcate né parallelamente notevole accumulo di ricchezze nelle mani di un singolo o di un ristretto gruppo di persone costituenti un'aristocrazia privilegiata. Per cui le realizzazioni grandi o grandiose, come il nuraghe, il pozzo, la capanna delle riunioni federali e la tomba, erano o potevano essere tali solo perché erano beni comunitari. Quindi doveva essere una società in cui ognuno dei capi, pur godendo di qualche particolare privilegio, era rimasto un *primus inter pares* (Contu 1993). Qualcosa del genere perciò a quello che, oltre un millennio prima, pare accertato – sulla base della documentazione scritta (che è qualcosa di più dell'interpretazione archeologica dei dati di scavo) – per la Siria ad Ebla (Pettinato 1985: 149, 152).

Non ci nascondiamo comunque che altri validi studiosi sono per la Civiltà Nuragica (pur riconoscendo il livello evolutivo di "villaggio") di parere opposto: e parlano per essa sia di schiavi che di "prìncipi" o *aristoi* (Bernardini 1982; Lilliu 1985: 195–196; 1986: 80), oltreché di sacerdoti e sacerdotesse o matriarche. Mai anche senza si ha rappresentazione di "umili lavoratori", se con lo stesso *ex voto* essi dimostrano di avere doni da offrire (Tronchetti 1988: 79).

Ben diversa era invece l'organizzazione sociale di una civiltà "urbana" come quella fenicio-punica, costituita veramente da aristocrazia, plebe e servitù (Barreca 1986b: 91).

Sia le statue in pietra che i bronzetti raffigurano uomini (nel ruolo che ad essi attribuisce la società o nel rapporto diretto che essi stabiliscono con la divinità), animali, cose. I bronzetti mostrano anche esseri fantastici o, meglio, iperantropici che meglio si specificheranno più avanti.

Mentre le statue in pietra sono circa una trentina (di cui 25 esemplari provenienti da Monti Prama), le figurine di bronzo (in continuo accrescimento per nuove scoperte, come quelle di Nuraghe Nurdòle in regione Loghélis-Oràni-Nuoro e di Su Tempiesu-Orùne-Nuoro) (Fadda & Madau 1991; Fadda & Lo Schiavo 1992; Fadda 1988; 1991a) sono circa 600 e si rinvennero e si rinvengono ancora in ogni parte dell'Isola, particolarmente nelle regioni più interne. Questi bronzetti figurati, oltre che dai pozzi sacri, vengono talvolta dalle tombe, dalle abitazioni, dagli stessi nuraghi e persino dai ripostigli dei santuari o dei ramai; nel quale ultimo caso erano destinati ad essere rifusi, ma particolari circostanze, a noi ignote, impedirono che che ciò avvenisse.

I soggetti e loro supposti riferimenti al mondo classico

Nonostante la presenza di numerose donne, animali e

cose varie, nèi bronzi il soggetto più comune sono i soldati o comunque gli uomini armati, e per lo più essi sono presentati in posizione frontale ed eretta e riguardano sostanzialmente tutte le specialità di un esercito piuttosto perfezionato e complesso e forse anche i gradi particolari entro di esso.

Di nessun altro esercito dell'antichità sappiamo, anche nei particolari, attraverso l'arte figurata, quanto possiamo conoscere di quello nuragico.

Da notarsi è la presenza dei frombolieri (Lilliu 1966: 204, nn. 8, 107, 108; 1985: n. 176), data la grande fama che una popolazione della Sardegna, i Bàlari, ebbe nell'antichità per la perizia nell'uso della fionda (Floro 1, 43, 5; Diod. 5, 18, 3; Strabo 3, 5, 1).

Una statua di pugilatore aveva, come l'analogo bronzetto di Cala Gonòne-Dorgali-Nuoro, l'avambraccio destro ricoperto da una guaina di pelle o tessuto e dal suo pugno sporgeva come un guantone la temibile protuberanza di una manopola di cuoio e metallo.

Fra gli offerenti, che sono anch'essi talora dei guerrieri, si hanno anche uomini e donne comuni. Le offerte sono costituite dal montone portato sulle spalle o da un muflone; oppure da altri animali o cose, tenuti in mano o su un vassoio, di rado sulla testa: quali un porcellino, una colomba, una focaccia, ciambelle, pezzi di carne, un mazzo di pelli disseccate, grano, una ciotola o un vaso. Un malato guarito (ma in parte mutilato ad un piede) offre, come avviene negli attuali santuari cristiani, la sua gruccia o anche un pane (Lilliu 1966: nn. 62, 179; 1985: 212, fig. 214).

Un altro offerente, eccezionalmente nudo, che solleva la destra in segno di saluto e con la sinistra offre un gallo o una colomba (Santa Teresa di Gallura-Sassari), è stato interpretato da qualcuno come elemento di raccordo con la piccola e grande plastica di tipo ellenico e persino con lo spirito e il significato di essa (D'Oriano 1986). Qualcosa del genere si ha infatti in Grecia nelle raffigurazioni della "tomba delle Arpie" a Xanthos o in un bronzetto di Argo e in altri ancora. Ma, continuando ad esemplificare ancora, vorremmo anche aggiungervi soprattutto il bronzetto col Minotauro del Louvre (Bianchi Bandinelli & Paribeni 1976: f. 18), che è datato agli inizi del VII sec. a.C.

Nudi sono anche un bronzetto maschile, con le mani protese in avanti in preghiera, dal Nuraghe Nurdòle-Orani-Nuoro (Fadda 1991a: f. 29), e un altro del Nuraghe Cummossariu-Furtei-Cagliari (Lilliu 1966: n. 184).

La stessa nudità maschile (che, più che "eroica", come spesso si usa dire, è per noi da definirsi "rituale", in quanto frutto dello stretto rapporto dell'offerente con la divinità invocata) è in un bronzetto armato di lancia da Antas-Fluminimaggiore-Cagliari, nel quale qualcuno ha voluto riconoscere un dio cacciatore e guerriero fenicio-punico, oppure nuragico, poi passato al pantheon semitico, cioè *Sid Addir Baby* (o *Babay*); prima o poi divenuto *Sardus Pater* (Ugas 1987a; Zucca 1989); e di cui potrebbe aversi anche la corrispondenza con *Iolaus pater*, estensibile anche alla identificazine con Iolao-Herakles ecc. (Breglia Pulci Delia 1981: 75, 83, 84). É forse solo un soldato con corona orientale di piume e non il dio Sardus o il suo predecessore Sid o altri ancora anche quello rappresentato in un bronzetto da Decimoputzu-Cagliari.

Un'altra figurina maschile, armata di lancia come l'esemplare di Antas ma interamente vestito, porta al guinzaglio un muflone (pozzo sacro di Serra Nièdda-Sorso-Sassari) (Rovina 1986; Zucca 1989).

Il mondo greco verrebbe richiamato anche in un bronzetto frammentario, di incerta provenienza e conservato al Museo Nazionale G. A. Sanna di Sassari, che ha sulla spalla una sacca con tre "zucche": qualora esso rappresentasse, non un semplice contadino o un soldato addetto ai rifornimenti, ma una personalità divina di natura agricola come Aristeo (Nicosia 1985: 426), che dona il latte, il vino e il miele agli uomini e che, secondo varie fonti, avrebbe colonizzato la Sardegna.

Altre sfumature di significato di contenuto erotico-orgiastico, a nostro parere del tutto umano, sembra comunque di poter cogliere in un suonatore di triplice flauto da Ittiri-Sassari, che alla assoluta nudità aggiunge una drastica evidenza itifallica (presente anche nel suddetto bronzetto di Furtei).

Qui vien di trattare degli armatissimi guerrieri con quattro occhi e quattro braccia di Abiti-Teti-Nuoro. Oltre alle solite spiegazioni mitologiche, quale quella che li identificava con Kronos (Pais 1984: 68), o di tipo mitologico, ma al femminile (le misteriose *bitie* assassine con quattro occhi, citate da Plinio, *nat. hist.*, VII, 16, 18, e Solino I, 101), altre se ne hanno di natura metafisica o ad essa collegate. Il Lilliu (1985: 214, 223) ha infatti ritenuto di dover riconoscere in questi esseri iperantropici di Abini persino qualcosa di divino o demoniaco e perciò stesso facente parte dei misteri del soprannaturale nuragico. Altrettanto dicasi del toro androcefalo da Su Casteddu di Santi Lisei-Nule-Sassari (Lilliu 1985: 214), a voler tacere per essi tutti e in specie per il toro androcefalo, dei richiami sia cipriotti che mesopotamici (Bossert 1951: figg. 121–123, 124, 125). Nei guerrieri con quattro occhi e quattro braccia il modellato del viso e in particolare gli occhi e il mento sono stati confrontati con statuine di bronzo cipriote, siriache e soprattutto del Luristan (Lilliu 1966: 198). All'interpretazione come personagi divini, noi contrapponiamo invece quella che, tramite la "magia del doppio", l'offerente volesse chiedere alla divinità una straordinaria forza guerresca o, meglio ancora, ringraziarla per averla ottenuta.

Per altro una figura guerresca in tutto simile, ma senza attributi iperantropiti, è ugualmente presente in un bronzetto da Padria (Lilliu 1985: f. 199).

Non molto diverso come significato dal guerriero con quattro occhi – nonostante la presenza di un elmo a pennacchio, che ha riscontri in manici a forma di Sirena (*Assurattachen*) di calderoni, etruschi e di tipologia orientale (Urartu, nell'ex-Armenia sovietica) (Pallottino

1957; 1958: 91; Giuliano 1960: 980; Akurgal 1966; Roncalli 1986: 565) – a noi pare il toro androcefalo: ove si chiederebbe appunto la forza, il coraggio e la fecondità del toro (Contu 1986; 1993). E c'è ugualmente da notare che l'elmo, con pennacchio ricadente sulla fronte, si ritrova in altre normalissime figure di guerrieri.

Al Nuraghe Nurdòle-Orani un altro quadrupede androcefalo pare che venga sottomesso, in segno di vittoria, da un offerente (Fadda 1991a).

Che infine, almeno nel primo caso, sia stato scelto proprio il toro non fa meraviglia né deve far pensare ad una zoolatria (Zervos 1954), sia perché lo stesso concetto è espresso di sovente negli stessi elmi cornuti dei guerrieri, sia perché anche nella civiltà prenuragica è il simbolo del toro quello che esprime comunemente l'elemento maschile delle forze generative della natura, sia infine perché il toro, o più genericamente il bue, è l'animale più comunemente rappresentato, oltre alle figure umane, fra i piccoli bronzi sardi di questo periodo. I buoi, anzi – a documento di una civiltà che era non solo pastorale ma anche, sia pur secondariamente, agricola – sono in diversi casi rappresentati anche aggiogati.

E con i bovini (presenti eccezionalmente anche nella scultura in pietra a Santa Vittoria di Serri-Nuoro) è rappresentata con estrema vivezza pressoché tutta la fauna sarda del tempo (che è in gran parte anche quella attuale), sia quella domestica, sia quella selvaggia: i cervi, i daini, i mufloni, le capre, i cinghiali, i maiali (compresa una scrofa gravida), la volpe, il cane, le colombe, sole o in coppia, ed altri volatili, nonché diversi piccoli animali.

Mentre lo stile "geometrico-volumetrico" potrebbe richiamare concetti che modernamente chiamiamo "espressionistici", quello "libero-popolaresco" può realizzarsi anche in raffigurazioni, diciamo così, "impressionistiche". Come esempi di entrambi i casi citiamo delle rappresentazioni zoomorfe: al primo caso appartiene il muflone "stante" del Camposanto di Olmedo-Sassari; mentre fanno parte del secondo, il cane "in punta" e la volpe "in agguato" di Santa Vittoria-Serri-Nuoro. Testa piccola cilindroide con enormi corna ricurve e lungo corpo cilindrico, segnato da marcate striature parallele verticali, stilizzazione del vello, nel primo (alt. cm 8); essenzialità e vivacità di forme, che suggeriscono la tensione che immediatamente precede il moto, negli altri due (alt. cm 4,5 e 3,5) (Lilliu 1966: nn. 223, 238, 239).

Talvolta l'offerente cavalca un bue ma non manca la figura di un arciere acrobata che lancia le frecce stando in piedi sulla groppa di un cavallo, rappresentato in modo rudimentale.

Per noi, quella che per molti è "La Madre dell'Ucciso" (Sa Domu 'e S'Orcu-Urzulei-Nuoro) o una Divinità Materna, cioè una specie di Pietà michelangiolesca con un uomo in grembo, una Madonna nuragica (Lilliu 1985: 214; Lo Schiavo 1994: 79; Ugas & Paderi 1990), è solo una madre che ringrazia la divinità perché il figlio, che era andato in guerra, è tornato salvo, anche se ferito.

Per cui le immagini classiche che potrebbero richiamarsi appartengono a mondi e civiltà spiritualmente e socialmente (e spesso anche cronologicamente) differenti.

Perciò la divinità, sola o meglio in coppia, o le vaghe entità divine, alle quali, come ex-voto, erano dedicate le sculture nuragiche, appaiono perennemente senza volto. Tale coppia divina è raffigurata solo da bétili maschili o femminili (indicati, questi, dalle mammelle), come quelli conico-convessi della Tomba I di Tamùli a Macomèr-Nuoro; e, nella stessa forma betilica, sembra che siano stati riprodotti persino in un minuscolo bronzetto da Abìni-Teti.

Anzi la principale o unica manifestazione religiosa era forse costituita, come si vedrà ancora più avanti, solo dal culto degli antenati. Il che sembrerebbe concordare anche con le notizie delle fonti classiche sugli antichi abitatori della Sardegna (Lilliu 1988: 563; Contu in stampa).

Non contrastano con questo quadro generale, di una religiosità semplice ed elementare, le "magie di caccia": per la caccia infatti (e forse anche per i riti del sacrificio cruento) si avevano anche simboli specifici, come le doppie protomi di cervo o di muflone e persino di bue, infilate in lunghe spade votive.

Anzi in un caso, ad Abìni, un guerriero-cacciatore armato d'arco si erge tra le due protomi.

Talora il cervo è uno solo e la spada votiva lo trapassa (Monti Arcòsu-Uta-Cagliari). Certo non è possibile pensare che si riferisse alla caccia – ma poteva ricordare il sacrificio cruento – il bue da lavoro, con una colomba posata sulla cervice, anch'esso sospeso su una spada (Santa Vittoria di Serri).

Misterioso, ma anch'esso con ogni probabilità una "magia di caccia", è il singolare oggetto di Pàdria-Sassari, costituito da tre spade e una specie di stendardo quadrangolare in cui si aprono due sportelli. Gli angoli superiori di questo "stendardo" sono terminati da protomi cervine e nel mezzo del lato superiore è infilata una lama di pugnale.

Meritano particolare menzione fra gli oggetti votivi di bronzo due modellini di nuraghi complessi (ma ve ne sono anche in pietra e di varia grandezza), del tipo cosiddetto tetralobato, con cinque torri (Ittireddu ed Olmedo-Sassari). Forse si intendeva ringraziare per delle fortezze conquistate o perché le divinità avevano prestato il loro aiuto nella difesa.

Ma l'arte che così bene si manifesta nelle vere e proprie piccole sculture di bronzo a tutto tondo, interessa anche oggetti eleganti di uso comune di uguale materia, come else di spade, anse di vasi, un candelabro, dei bottoni conici ecc. Degni di nota sono in particolare un'elsa di spada da Albini-Teti con figura di guerriero in rilievo e qualche manico raffinato di specchio, a treccia di stile orientalizzante (Pallottino 1963a: 752, 753; 1963b: 236), con figura di colomba o di lucertola o di ranocchio o di leone; nonché, nello stesso stile, uno scrigno a forma di carretto votivo con quattro ruote piene, ornato da teste di ariete (dal Nuraghe Lunghénia-òschiri – Sassari) (Tanda 1982).

Diversi studiosi, quindi – sulla base di mode grecocentriche superate, ogni tanto riaffioranti sia per l'arte figurata che per l'architettura (Bernardini 1983; Ugas 1987b: 92) ed altro ancora! –, ritengono, come abbiamo detto, che, per analogia col mondo greco e fenicio, si possano individuare nelle piccole figure antropomorfe delle divinità e persino quella specifica dell'eroe eponimo *Sardus*. Mentre noi siamo del parere che proprio non sarebbe possibile, tanto nei bronzetti quanto nella statuaria in pietra, riconoscere – nel loro insieme o prevalentemente o per chiari elementi distintivi stilistici o attributi formali – delle immagini di divinità (e quindi degli "idoli", come si diceva nell'Ottocento): dal che deriva che, se tutti non lo sono o lo sarebbero, come si è visto, sostanzialmente in pochi, nessuno lo è veramente (Contu 1986; 1993; in stampa). D'altronde pensare che tutti siano degli idoli, cioè delle figure divine, corrispenderebbe a voler attribuire ai Nuragici un *pantheon* più ampio addirittura di quello greco!

Ebbene bisogna dire che, nemmeno forzando per quanto si vuole le cose si otterrebbero – sulla base dei princìpi e delle considerazioni per cui i bronzetti siano la rappresentazione di divinità ed in particolare di quelle del *pantheon* ellenico o anche fenicio-punico – altri risultati analoghi a quei pochi evidenziati dagli studiosi che si fanno sedurre imprudentemente dalle interpretazioni di tipo greco classico.

Per dare solo qualche esempio fra i molti possibili – mi si conceda il tono scherzoso! –, non è rappresentato Ares nei guerrieri in panoplia o una specie di Afrotite fanciulla in una bambina nuda; così come nel bronzetto che offre una gruccia non potrebbe essere riconosciuto, al posto di un offerente miracolato, il claudicante Efesto; in quello che offre una focaccia o un porcellino o in genere delle primizie, non è certo presente uno sconosciuto assistente di Demetra-Cerere; né, in in quelli che portano sulle spalle un ariete, Hermes *Kriophoros*, né, in quello che offre una pelle, un assistente di Artemide cacciatrice o lo stesso Eracle; e tanto meno una ninfa nella donna con brocca sul capo, né Priapo o Dioniso o Pan o un altro satiro del suo corteggio infine in quello itifallico che suona il triplice flauto. Eppure è avvenuto a qualcuno di citare Ares o Marte per il bronzetto sardo di Cavalupo (Lilliu 1966: 211). Comunque una specie di Astarte-Demetra-Cerere era indubbiamente oggetto di culto agrario "propiziatorio" in certi nuraghi; ma in età punico-romana (C. Lilliu 1988).

Chi pensa ad un'interpretazione come idolo, quando trasforma una donna col figlio in braccio (piccolo o adulto che sia) in una divinità, è costretto anche a dare significato di benedizione ad un gesto che in altri numerosissimi bronzetti è solo di saluto o di adorazione (Ugas & Paderi 1990: 479).

Insomma non si può individuare, come si è fatto per L'Etruria del VII sec. a.C. (Torelli 1986: 171–173), anche per la Sardegna "l'arrivo del mito greco" e la sua progressiva assimilazione.

Nessun risultato più positivo si ricaverebbe da un'indagine che cercasse di individuare se, nei bronzi nuragici, una maggiore grandezza o una più marcata accuratezza di esecuzione o uno specifico stile siano conseguenza della realizzazione di supposte immagini di divinità o di entità ad esse in qualche modo collegate.

I bronzetti e la statuaria rappresentano perciò – in stili e schemi originali e con la massima caratterizzazione possibile – l'offerente o l'offerta o l'uno e l'altro insieme e non delle figure divine o divinizzate; per cui la presenza di queste opere anche nelle tombe, oltre che nei templi ed in altri luoghi sacri, potrebbe tutt'al più confermare invece solo un culto degli antenati. Col che non cotrasterebbe neanche la figura di Sardus Pater-Sid Baby, per lo stesso attributo di *pater* (Ferron 1973; Zucca 1989); così come non vi contrasta la tarda notizia di Solino I: 61 (Perra 1993: 38, 39), riferita al mitico Iolao, ove è detto che gli Iolensi *sepulcro eius templum addiderunt*.

Fra gli oggetti di culto un posto a sè spetta alle lampade, in forma navicelle di bronzo con prora ornata di protome animalesca (Contu 1981; 1993; Filigheddu 1994). Si tratta di circa 110 esemplari, che ci illuminano moltissimo sull'attività marinara dei Nuragici e, soprattutto attraverso il rinvenimento anche fuori dall'isola (una decina in Etruria; e una di recente in Calabria: Spadea 1996), ci suggeriscono notevoli elementi di cronologia, di cui si tratterà meglio più avanti.

Queste navicelle votive documentano in primo luogo la cantieristica marinaresca a cui si ispirano.

Oltre che in bronzo tali lampade a forma di navicella erano di terracotta, ed avevano protome variamente animalesca, compresa quella di uccello (Ugas 1989a; 1989–90: 556–560; Ugas & Paderi 1990). Numerose, queste lampade fittili, erano nella cella sacra del Nuraghe Su Mulinu di Villanovafranca-Cagliari.

Interesse notevolissimo presenta perciò il fatto che una nave nuragica con testa di uccello a prora appaia rappresentata su un vaso miceneo del XII sec. (Mic. III c), proveniente dall'isola di Skyros nell'Egeo. Ma la somiglianza maggiore si ha con le imbarcazioni fenicie di un rilievo di Korshabad, dove è presente sia l'albero con la coffa che la protome zoomorfa (Filigheddu 1994).

Della grande familiarità dei Nuragici col mare è prova il fatto che nessun altro popolo dell'antichità (neanche i Fenici e i Greci) ci ha lasciato un numero ed una varietà minimamente comparabile di modellini di imbarcazione.

Ma le navicelle votive (specie quelle di bronzo) uniscono alle immagini del reali anche altri elementi semplicemente rituali, il cui significato riesce spesso difficile interpretare. Infatti su di esse si hanno figure di buoi aggiogati – in un caso accompagnati anche dall'uomo che deve guidarli – ed altri animali. Più comunemente si hanno una o più colombe (o anatrelle? o gabbiani?) variamente distribuite sulle murate o in cima all'albero maestro (a rappresentare forse il "piccione nocchiero", che, lasciato libero durante la navigazione, serviva a ritrovare presto la terra ferma); in qualche caso alle colombe si accompagnano anche dei cani. In due esemplari interessantissimi di navicella votiva gli animali sono veramente molti e vari. In particolare in quello proveniente dalla Tomba del Duce a Vetulonia se ne hanno ventuno, fra domestici e selvatici; per cui ben gli si addice la denominazione di "Arca di Noè", anche se il significato può essere molto diverso.

Forse quello della navicella votiva era un modo ritenuto particolarmente valido per chiedere alle divinità ricchezza di armenti e di caccia, e animali da lavoro per rendere più fertili i campi: una specie di cornucopia nuragica.

Un posto a sé fra le barchette occupa quella che mostra all'interno una figura antropoide scimmiesca accovacciata.

Lo stile

Sullo stile dei piccoli bronzi e della statuaria resta da chiarire meglio con quali espressioni formali si realizzano i concetti più sopra espressi e come essi possano inquadrarsi nelle manifestazioni dell'arte mediterranea ed euro-asiatica di questo tempo, cioè fra circa il IX ed il VI sec. a.C.: ma forse solo i bronzi inizierebbero nel IX e più tardi la statuaria in pietra, se questa fosse derivata da quelli.

Intanto si deve constatare, soprattutto ma non esclusivamente nelle figure umane di bronzo, che di stili, benché contemporanei, se ne possono riconoscere almeno due, che si influenzarono anche reciprocamente: l'uno che tende a rappresentare delle figure auliche, ieratiche in forme allungate, rigide, severe, volumetriche e geometrizzanti (che è lo stile p. es. del capotribù di Monti Arcosu-Uta-Cagliari) e l'altro che mostra forme sciolte e per dir così popolaresche (come certi offerenti seminudi o l'uomo che cavalca il bue, dal Nuraghe Orku di Nulvi – Sassari). Il primo stile è documentato in varie zone della Sardegna mentre l'altro si ha soprattutto nella Barbàgia e nell'Ogliàstra.

Il primo fa presumere un'influenza della tecnica rigida della scultura in legno ed è anche l'unico documentato nella grande statuaria in pietra; il secondo invece deve aver subìto l'influenza della semplice modellazione in creta (di cui non manca qualche rozzo esempio anche a tutto tondo) o anche, molto meglio, della stessa duttile cera che era tecnicamente alla base della successiva fusione in bronzo (tecnica della "cera persa").

Inoltre i soggetti rappresentati nello stile "geometrico-volumetrico" sono quelli che sembrano riflettere maggiormente lo spirito della tradizione, incarnato da quella parte della popolazione che ne era custode, in quanto aveva maggiori compiti di responsabilità civile, religiosa e militare, pur in una società, come si è detto,

dove le differenze di classe sociale non dovevano essere molto marcate; mentre lo stile sciolto e popolaresco era quello, più spontaneo, della gente comune ed era frutto, diremmo, di un istinto elementare di creare forme plastiche. Nel primo prevale il senso del sacro ed il distacco dal contingente, espresso entro l' astrazione razionale "geometrica"; nel secondo il sacro si fonde col reale, umanizzandosi, al di fuori di precisi schemi e cogliendo il senso umile della vita di tutti i giorni; ma anche nell'astrazione l'umano continua a vibrare e nel popolaresco il sacro non perde il suo senso profondo. Ed è proprio la capacità di una tale sintesi che permette di individuare, sia nei bronzetti che nelle statue in pietra, un vero e notevole valore artistico (Contu 1993).

C'è inoltre da notare che, anche se è vero che i bronzetti più grandi si hanno fra quelli di stile "geometrico"-volumetrico, è altrettanto vero che gli stessi soggetti di capi o di guerrieri (o di supposte "divinità materne" o "sacerdotesse" o "matriarche", che noi respingiamo) e così via, e con non diversa accuratezza, sono presenti anche in bronzetti relativamente piccoli. Quindi la grandezza ed anche la cura nell'esecuzione, non sono direttamente proporzionali alla posizione sociale o meglio alla classe della persona rappresentata. Altrettanto si dica del fatto che la rappresentazione antropomorfa includa un vestiario o un'armatura estremamente semplici o piuttosto complessi. Insomma da tutto ciò e dalla struttura delle abitazioni e delle tombe (sia a poliandro che monosome) e dal modesto corredo di entrambe non si ricava, come si è detto, l'immagine di una società divisa in classi.

Nei bronzetti, degno di particolare esame è il rendimento dei tratti fisionomici: in essi il mutare del rendimento del capo e del viso, il cui insieme, partendo da un aspetto "geometrico-volumetrico" cilindroide, può passare in altre opere ad una semplice sferetta con fori, potrebbe suggerire anche un tale processo evolutivo; ma qualcosa sarà da attribuirsi anche all'estro individuale e alle diverse capacità dell'artigiano-artista. Entro quest'arco evolutivo (posto che esso fosse accertato) bisognerebbe sistemare anche le statuine in cui i tratti del viso sono di tipo particolarmente espressionistico, come p.es. "Barbetta" di Vallermosa-Cagliari, l'offerente con focaccia da Nuoro (Lilliu 1985: 212–213, ff. 215–216, 233) e la figurina maschile maschile dal profilo "negroide" del Nuraghe Santa Lulla-Orani-Nuoro (Fadda 1991a: 35, f. 21). In altri esempi gli stessi tratti sono racchiusi entro un ovale piuttosto naturalistico (Lilliu 1985: f. 186).

Vario è nei bronzetti anche il rendimento degli occhi: dai globetti cerchiati, alle pastiglie o alle cavità circolari, all'ovale plastico, al rettangolo inciso o in rilievo ecc.).

Ma dove collocare, entro l'evoluzione dello stile "geometrico-volumetrico", i tre splendidi bronzetti (S'Arriddeli-Terralba-Oristano e Uta-Cagliari) le cui lunghe e profonde cavità orbitali vuote dovevano essere ravvivate, secondo un antico uso medio-orientale (ma che ha esempi anche in Grecia ed Etruria), dalla pasta vitrea (Lilliu 1985: f. 219; Ortiz 1993: ff. 176–177)?

Quanto a i due stili principali e al resto che ad essi si accompagna, ciò non significa evidentemente (e qualcosa si è su ciò già accennato) che essi non si inquadrino entro gusti e tendenze che non furono solo della Sardegna, anche se quello della Sardegna è uno degli esempi principali e di più ricca documentazione. Per altro i confronti, quand'anche validi, che queste opere suggeriscono possono essere vari ma riguardano solo dei particolari e mai l'insieme, per cui il prodotto artistico non perde né la sua sostanziale originalità né la sua validità assoluta; neppure in alcuni casi di fattura senz'altro scadente.

Infatti nei bronzetti lo stile aulico volumetrico-"geometrico" sembrerebbe richiamare per diversi particolari – come p. es. il rendimento del volto umano – l'arte del del lontano Luristan (Iran), nelle forme in cui si espresse e si diffuse dalla fine del II millennio all'VIII sec. a.C.; mentre elementi orientalizzanti dell'VIII sec., del non meno lontano Urartu sono stati riconosciuti in certi motivi araldici di figure umane che stanno su un animale e – come si è accennato – in qualche particolare copricapo a pennacchio; presente, questo, anche in Etruria e ritenuto di uguale provenienza. Pertanto è stato ipotizzato che tali influssi possano essere pervenuti in qualche modo alle nostre regioni tramite il Nord della Siria, attraverso il porto di Al Mina (che era emporio Greco-euboico: Pallottino 1963a: 751; Boardman 1990; Ridgway & Ridgway 1992: 356, 357) e gli scali di Cipro e Creta (Pallottino 1958: 91). E da Cipro possono essere venuti suggerimenti per la lavorazione dei bronzi comuni e di quelli figurati, come la tecnica della "cera persa" (Macnamara 1985: 51–71; Lo Schiavo 1994: 89; Atzeni *et al.* 1992).

Parimenti qualche figura di toro dal Nuraghe Pizzinnu di Posada-Nuoro (Contu 1982: t. XII, b) (trovato insieme a figure di guerrieri di stile "geometrico-volumetrico") richiama al "Geometrico" greco.

Tali elementi comunque si ritrovano solo nel primo gruppo di bronzetti, mentre in quello di stile popolaresco gli elementi che si colgono sono in prevalenza, come si vedrà meglio più avanti, di tipologia o provenienza squisitamente mediterranea e più precisamente siro-fenicio-ciprioti, anche se portano ad esiti stilistici diversi.

Ma, frammista ai monumenti e, in modo non molto chiaro, ai bronzetti nuragici può riscontrarsi anche la significativa presenza di qualcosa che è solo fenicio, come p. es. le quattro figurine in bronzo di divinità del santuario nuragico di Santa Cristina-Paulilàtino-Oristano (XI-VIII sec. a.C.) o il piccolo leone gradiente del Nuraghe Nurdòle (Fadda 1991a: f. 34; Fadda & Madau 1991) o l'orante nudo con braccio al petto e ai fianchi della stessa località (Fadda 1991a: f. 28) o infine l'orante da Olmedo-Sassari ; il quale ultimo potrebbe meglio richiamarsi alla plastica arcaica greca o vulcente tirrenica (Gras 1981; Tore 1983; Nicosia 1985: 473). Esso avanza nell'incedere la gamba sinistra, con una ponderazione di origine egizio-greca arcaica, sconosciuta all'arte nuragica (che, ove la figura sia ferma, si presenta con l'eccezione di qualche arciere che tende l'arco, in visione costantemente frontale), ma analoga a quella della figura maschile di "demone" egittizzante, in un altorilievo della tomba ipogeica punica di Is Pilluncheddas a Sulci-Cagliari (Barreca 1986a).

Pur tenendo presente che l'arte fenicia entra solo di riflesso in quella nuragica (Lilliu 1985: 229), così che un itinerario dello stile e dei soggetti dei bronzetti dal fenico al nuragico "non risulta convincente" (Bernardini 1992: 403), di provenienza fenicio-punica potrebbe essere, anche se non necessariamente, specie in certi bronzetti più semplici di stile popolaresco, qualche stilismo concernente sia la ponderazione delle braccia che il rendimento appiattito del corpo, o certi particolari del capo e del viso; così come alcuni particolari, in vero molto elementari, del vestiario, come perizomi e qualche tipo di cappello. Il confronto non si estende invece al più tipico e complesso abbigliamento nuragico, per altro riccamente documentato, sia nelle figure maschili che in quelle femminili. Negli uomini armati, se si tolgono soprattutto i grembiuli-corazza di tipo siriaco con borchie (Lilliu 1966: nn. 24, 25, 103), rari e per solito generici sono invece gli elementi di richiamo al Mediterraneo orientale.

Per le figurazioni zoomorfe c'è da osservare che la minuscola figura di leone dello specchio nuragico da Tharros, compare su un manico traforato e a treccina "orientalizzante". Tutti elementi che potevano provenire sia dall'Etruria che direttamente da Cipro. Tanto è vero che una fibula di tipo cipriota a gomito con nodulo forato, della seconda metà dell'VIII-inizi VII o VI sec. (Tore 1981: 289; Zucca 1988: 134), fu rinvenuta, assieme a ceramica decorata a cerchielli, presso il Nuraghe di Barùmini-Cagliari, vano 135; e sempre a Cipro richiamano tipi e stile dei tripodi bronzei e dei calderoni e bacili nuragici (Lilliu 1973; 1985: 239; Ferrarese Ceruti *et al.* 1987). Un'altra fibula di consimile tipo viene dal Nuraghe Nurdòle-Orani-Nuoro (Lo Schiavo 1992).

Per quanto riguarda l'elemento "geometrico" del primo stile dei bronzetti nuragici, come nell'esempio citato del toro (ben indicato dal sesso) realizzato in lamina ripiegata del Nuraghe Pizzinu di Posada e in un altro ancora (Lilliu 1966: n. 215), qualche notevole raffronto (anche se non completo), geograficamente più vicino di quelli già indicati, è possibile, per la resa sottile e schematica (in vero piuttosto eccezionale) del corpo dei quadrupedi, con alcune rare ed essenziali manifestazioni plastiche del "Geometrico" in Grecia (Schweitzer 1969; Zimmermann 1989; Byrne 1991): p. es., tralasciando appunto la ceramica dipinta, con il bronzetto di cavallo "geometrico" dei Musei di Stato di Berlino e col centauro Titano che lotta con Zeus del Metropolitan Museum di New York (Bianchi Bandinelli & Paribeni 1976: ff. 14, 15); ai quali si possono solo aggiungere alcune altre figure bronzee di cavalli di una collezione privata svizzera (Ortiz 1993).

Ma – si noti bene – solo in Sardegna il "Geometrico",

partendo da premesse in gran parte analoghe, sviluppa una vera grande statuaria: e questa risulta anche esteticamente valida. Anzi lo stesso termine di "geometrico" solo in parte può corrispondere a quello in uso per la Grecia e va inteso genericamente come indicazione di uno stile, più propriamente sardo-nuragico, che nel rendimento della figura segue una schematizzazione geometrica che non ottunde ma esalta l'essenza del reale.

A ciò bisogna aggiungere alcuni generici raffronti con l'Etruria ove i concetti di "geometrico" ed "orientalizzante" sembrano integrarsi. Ciò è dovuto alla relativa vicinanza fra le due regioni ed ai commerci fra le due sponde del Tirreno o a scambi di esperienze fra botteghe sarde ed etrusche. Ma neanche in questa sponda orientale del Tirreno – in cui l'artista, tra la fine VII-inizi del VI sec. a.C., nella "palese rudimentalità dei mezzi espressivi", si mostra "agile e privo di inibizioni" ma fa ricorso all'"improvvisazione" senza creare una tradizione (Roncalli 1986: 561, 590–593) – gli accostamenti tentati con la plastica nuragica (Bonfante 1986) mostrano una giustificazione sostanziale.

Si consideri inoltre che, quando a qualcuno (Bernardini 1992: 393, 403) è sembrato di riconoscere nella stessa plastica il gusto dell' "esagerato" e del "barocco" tipici dell' Orientalizzante – come nella ricerca dei particolari dell'armatura nella grande statuaria di Monti Prama e in alcuni bronzetti, p. es., di Padria o di Abini e nella veste dello stesso toro androcefalo da Nule (Lilliu 1985: figg. 201, 206, 225, 228) –, tale espressione artistico-artigianale non ha mero carattere ornamentale, come appunto nell'Orientalizzante, ma riproduce elementi specifici del reale. Perciò si tratta di ben altro che di "calligrafismo orientalizzante mediato dall'ambiente artigianale etrusco" (Bernardini 1992: 406).

Per altro si è già visto che anche parlare per la sola grande scultura nuragica, stavolta nei riguardi della Grecia, di "elaborazione dei moduli stilistici e formali della plastica dedalica" (Bernardini 1992: 406) non ha senso né cronologicamente né stilisticamente. Si tratta infatti di confronti generici e non di reali "*comparanda*" (Sismondo Ridgway 1986). Ne consegue che non ci riesce di trovare neanche nella plastica minore nuragica – i bronzetti – il "sapore ionico" che si è creduto di riconoscervi (Bernardini 1985: 150); pur con qualche voce genericamente discorde (Tronchetti 1988: 116–119). Mentre la B. Sismondo Ridgway (1986: 61–72), che ha studiato a fondo questi confronti nei riguardi della Grecia e del Mediterraneo in generale, deve spassionatamente riconoscere che non ha trovato corrispondenze significative (Sismondo Ridgway 1986: 61, 63, 69: *there are no true parallels*; Ridgway & Ridgway 1992a: 360).

La cronologia

Il problema della cronologia assoluta dei bronzi figurati nuragici, che vengono quasi solo dai depositi di lunga durata dei santuari, è complicato dall'assenza quasi totale nell'Isola di corredi individuali unitari o di altri contesti "chiusi" che possano servire da preciso riferimento (Lo Schiavo 1994: 79, 81). Per cui esiste, astrattamente parlando, la possibilità che la produzione dei bronzetti abbia avuto inizio prima del IX sec a.C. (cioè nell'Età del Bronzo Recente e Finale) ma non si ha di ciò prova sicura (Macnamara 1985: 60–61), nonostante la particolare insistenza di alcuni studiosi a proposito dei rinvenimenti relativi alla fonte nuragica di Su Tempiesu ad Orune-Nuoro (Fadda & Lo Schiavo 1992; Ridgway & Ridgway 1992b: 9–15; 1995).

Che poi, se tale Età del Bronzo Finale (Peroni 1980; D'Agostino 1979) corrispondesse in cronologia assoluta alla fine del XII-inizi del IX sec. (Santoni 1994: 35) o al 1150–900 (Lo Schiavo 1984) o alla fine del XII-metà del IX sec. come noi supponiamo (Contu in press e in questo volume), confortati (1150–850) da dati cronologici calibrati (Tykot 1994a: 129) – mentre l'Età del Ferro andrebbe dalla metà del IX alla fine o ai primi decenni dell'VIII, e l'Orientalizante subito dopo –, potrebbe trattarsi davvero di problemi di poco conto: in quanto una netta cesura cronologica fra questi due momenti non sarebbe né ragionevole né possibile.

Più significativa, per suggerire l'Età del bronzo Finale (Lo Schiavo 1981a: 10), avrebbe potuto essere l'associazione di un vago d'ambra a botticella trapezoidale, tipo "Allumiere", nella rara tomba monosoma con un bronzetto di stile popolaresco di Antas-Fluminimaggiore-Cagliari; anche se lo scopritore non esclude neanche l'Età del Ferro (Ugas 1987a; Zucca 1989) e la datazione così (e per altri elementi associati) non supererebbe o supererebbe di poco l'VIII sec. É problematico anche il suddetto caso del Nuraghe Sa Mandra'e Sa Giùa-Ossi-Sassari (Ferrarese Ceruti 1985; Lo Schiavo *et al.* 1987: 180; Contu 1993), ove un bronzetto di tipo geometrico-volumetrico viene da un'incerta giacitura e non da quella anteriore alla metà del IX sec., caratterizzata dall'assenza della ceramica nuragiche tipicamente "geometrica", decorata ad occhi di dado. Nè, come si è accennato, maggior certezza di data anteriore al 900 a.C. si può ricavare dalla fonte di Su Tempiesu-Orune, dove, assieme ai bronzetti, sono presenti fibule di produzione locale dell'VIII sec a.C. (Ridgway & Ridgway 1992b; 1995: 8).

Al Nuraghe di Barùmini, come abbiamo detto in questo volume trattando delle stratigrafie della Sardegna, una figura di offerente con gonnellino, trovata sotto il vano ll, è attribuibile solo al IX-VIII sec. a.C. (Lilliu & Zucca 1988: 55–57).

I rinvenimenti di bronzetti sardi in Etruria consentono un inquadramento cronologico più significativo dei semplici accostamenti stilistici; cioè più di quanto non ce lo permettano, anche per le ragioni suesposte, le vaghe associazioni stratigrafiche riscontrate nella Sardegna stessa.

Fra i ritrovamenti nuragici in Etruria, il più interessante, a questo proposito, perché di più alta cronologia, è costituito da un bronzetto sardo di stile "geometrico-volumetrico" della tomba vulcente di Cavalupo, che viene datata alla seconda metà o alla fine del IX sec. o alla metà o poco prima della metà dell'VIII sec. a.C. (Contu in stampa; Lo Schiavo 1994: 81). Segue a questo il caso delle barchette sarde trovate a Vetulonia nel Circolo delle tre Navicelle, ove l'associazione con materiali protocorinzi permette di stabilire una data intorno al 650–630 a.C. (James 1992); così come per un altro esemplare di Falda della Guardiola a Populonia. Mentre la bella barchetta ad "Arca di Noè" della Tomba del Duce può essere più tarda di alcuni decenni, dentro lo stesso VII secolo.

Fra l'VIII e il VII secolo possono datarsi tanto le altre due barchette di Vetulonia, che i modellini di sgabello e pisside della tomba di Cavalupo, nonché i bottoni conici della necropoli arcaica di Populonia e la "faretrina" votiva di Falda della Guardiola. Al suddetto periodo sono attribuiti i consimili modesti bronzetti trovati in tombe fenicie di Tharros e Nora. Mentre sembrano più antichi (seconda metà del IX sec.) i modelli in bronzo di cesti ed i bottoni nuragici con decorazione plastica trovati a Sant'Antonio-Pontecagnano-Salerno (Lo Schiavo 1994).

Infine si ha in Etruria, frutto forse più di una lunga tesaurizzazione che di una persistenza funzionale e stilistica, la navicella del santuario greco di Hera a Gravisca-Tarquinia, che viene da un contesto datato al VI sec. a.C.

Un'altra barchetta, quella trovata in Calabria nel santuario di Hera Lacinia a Capo Colonna-Crotone (Lo Schiavo 1994: 79; Giannattasio 1992: 106; Spadea 1996: 56), viene datata dai materiali associati al VII sec. a.C.

Ancor più significativo per un rialzo della cronologia potrebbe essere il considerare le datazioni della Penisola Italiana come *terminus ante quem* (Ridgway & Ridgway 1995: 8). Ma la data più alta resta quella dei reperti nuragici di Pontecagnano.

Degno di particolare interesse é anche il ritrovamento di due bronzetti, strettamente legati alla plastica nuragica ma già animati da soggetto e spirito diversi, nello stanziamento punico di Monte Siràì-Carbònia-Cagliari, in strati del VII–VI sec. a.C. (Tronchetti 1988: 33). A questi bronzi infine può corrispondere in parte come cronologia (VII sec. a.C.) il rinvenimento di una navicella nuragica di bronzo, con ceramiche fenico-puniche e tardo-nuragiche ed un vaso di bronzo e argento, riutilizzato, con imposta del manico a palmetta, al Nuraghe Su Igante di Uri-Sassari (Nicosia 1985; Tore 1981; Contu in stampa); se l'estrema semplicità della barchetta, ove manca qualunque richiamo all'Orientalizzante e l'assenza della classica ceramica nuragica non facessero propendere invece per una datazione al sec. VI a.C. (Contu 1974: 149).

Conservato infine come tesoro o talismano o frutto di molto più tarda produzione è da intendersi un pugnaletto con elsa gammata, del genere di quelli portati a tracolla dai bronzi figurati, trovato con monete puniche del IV-III sec. a.C., ad Aritzo-Nuoro.

Concludendo, la produzione dei bronzi sardi figurati si può ragionevolmente datare circa fra l'VIII ed il VI sec. a.C.; non escludendo anche il IX e non trascurando la possibilità che sia durata, per oggetti miniaturistici di minore importanza, con funzione amuletica, anche in secoli successivi (cioè almeno sino al IV nelle zone montane della Sardegna di meno intensa punicizzazione). Per cui si avrebbe una durata di almeno circa 250 anni (Lilliu 1985: 238–9): e si tratterebbe di una persistenza stilistica che fa discutere (Gras 1980; 1985: 137–139), sia perché troppo lunga sia perché non si riesce, almeno per ora, a individuare all'interno di questo ampio lasso di tempo (se si tolgono, ma non bastano, i bronzetti sardo-punici di Monte Sirai-Carbonia-Cagliari) delle scansioni cronologico-stilistiche. Sebbene dei tentativi molto articolati in tal senso siano stati realizzati (molto acutamente ma pur senza reali dati di fatto), in analogia o in dipendenza dallo svolgimento dell'arte greca, a partire dallo stile dedalico sino a giungere a quello ellenistico (Bernardini 1985), i risultati conseguiti non ci paiono soddisfacenti. Tanto che non resta che arrendersi alla constatazione di una lunga durata di forme stilistiche (anche apparentemente differenti) e di soggetti che, per citare un esempio molto lontano, ricorda quel che è ben noto per certi periodi della Civiltà Egizia (Donadoni 1960: 268).

E in particolare sull'argomento c'è da notare che grossi problemi di cronologia sorgerebbero, se addirittura si potesse riconoscere nell'arte figurata nuragica di stile sciolto e popolaresco un tardo periodo evolutivo che permettesse richiami a moduli, significati e tempi come quelli rappresentati dai confronti con certa plastica votiva fittile punico-romana di Bithia (Ferron & Aubet 1974; Bernardini 1985: 159–162). Questi reperti sono infatti da datarsi ad epoca ellenistica e da porsi non prima del III sec. a.C.: il che sarebbe in contrasto con l'alta cronologia (non prima dell'VIII sec.: Ugas 1987a) del bronzetto di guerriero o cacciatore nudo, armato di lancia, di analogo stile "sciolto o libero e popolaresco", trovato ad Antas (nudità rituale – solo una calottina sul capo – con evidenza del sesso, testa a palla, occhi a globetto, bocca aperta, orecchie ampie e inorganiche) (Zucca 1989: 27–31).

A ciò si aggiunga che, entro lo stesso stile "popolaresco", non può scostarsi dall'VIII-VII sec. a.C. il bronzetto, già citato, del Nuraghe Santa Lulla-Orani-Nuoro (Fadda 1991a: 35, f. 21) che presenta delle stilizzazioni ad occhi di dado di seni ed ombelico, derivate dai motivi decorativi di ceramiche "geometriche" e orientalizzanti nuragiche (Santoni 1990; 1991: 1223, 1242). Tali motivi pervennero alla Sardegna dal Villanoviano peninsulare, dove sono invece fra le decorazioni più comuni di armi e strumenti di bronzo (Contu in stampa). Ma qualche richiamo più preciso si ha nella nota figura plastica, rituale o decorativa, antropomorfa di S. Anastasia-Sàrdara-Cagliari, attribuibile almeno al VII sec. a.C. (Bernardini 1992:

317); oltre che all'Orientalizzante Antico, che viene datato alla fine del'VIII sec. (Ugas 1985: 41, 42, 49).

Al Nuraghe Palmavera è stato ritrovato anche il punzone con cui venivano stampigliate nella ceramica queste decorazioni "geometriche" (Moravetti 1992); già presenti anche, nell'Antica Età del Bronzo Finale, nelle Alpi francesi settentrionali (Bocquet & Lesbascle 1983: 97).

Perciò l'accostamento – che noi respingiamo – con le predette manifestazioni di plastica ellenistica di Bithia e stato reso possibile solo dal fatto che in entrambi si tratta di arte spontanea, legata appunto, al di fuori di tempi e circostanze, ad un istinto plastico elementare.

Per altro, nonostante la presenza a Monti Prama di un sigillo scaraboide "pseudo-Hiksos", in osso o avorio, del VII sec. a.C. (Tronchetti 1986: 47), frutto forse di una più tarda sepoltura, il confronto stilistico col bronzetto di Cavalupo, che è del IX o anche dell'VIII sec., e, per quel che può valere, con quello di Ossi, oltre a molte altre considerazioni sin qui fatte, permettono di sostenere che anche la grande statuaria in pietra ebbe inizio, se non nel IX, almeno nell'VIII sec. a.C. (Lilliu 1982: 200, 204).

Sorprende comunque di constatare – ma qualcosa indubbiamente ci sfugge – che tutte queste figure di armati in bronzo e in pietra compaiano quando la civiltà delle grandi torri di difesa aveva finito o stava per finire il suo slancio architettonico, visto che sono ormai molti gli indizi e le prove che non pochi nuraghi cessarono la loro funzione di difesa già nel IX sec. (Lilliu 1985: 194).

Come questione cronologica di carattere generale, c'è da osservare che le datazioni proposte dagli studiosi per la plastica figurata nuragica seguono principalmente due distinti filoni: uno che si riferisce a Cipro e suggerisce – specie su basi tecniche e caratteri ornamentali, ma anche, nonostante ragionevoli dubbi, non solo cronologici (Sismondo Rigway 1986: 63), sul solito bronzetto con elmo cornuto da Enkomi, del XII se. a.C. (Dikaios 1962) – delle datazioni piuttosto alte al Bronzo Recente o Finale; ed uno, che ha per oggetto la Grecia Continentale e (non volendo togliere all'arte ellenica il suo primato cronologico e qualitativo) propone di ricercare in essa ogni più diverso elemento di somiglianza che possa suggerire una datazione che non vada oltre il VII sec. (prima metà del VII o anteriormente alla fine del VII: Tronchetti 1978: 589; 1981: 527) e, ovunque risulti possibile, suggerisca quella del VI o giunga addirittura a due o tre secoli più tardi (Bernardini 1985).

A questo secondo filone si riallaccia il tentativo di spiegare non solo la protostoria della Sardegna con la mitologia greca (come i Greci stessi avevano fatto senza reali intenti storici e non solo per la Sardegna) ma le stesse figurazioni umane della plastica nuragica con le figure mitologiche divine della tradizione greca (Ugas 1980: 33; 1981; 1987a; 1989a). E credere alla mitologia è un po' come credere alle favole, visto che, come affermano storici che pure hanno tentato la massima seria valutazione possibile di tali dati, molte antiche narrazioni, di cui si hanno anche "versioni notevolmente discordi",

sono "scaturite dall'esigenza di giustificare nomi, miti e racconti" o politiche coloniali (Mastino 1980: 261, 266; Bondì 1975). Le stesse fonti che, mito o non mito, parlano di una colonizzazione greca della Sardegna, tutta da dimostrare (Tronchetti 1988: 114–119, 122, 128), ignorando invece quasi del tutto – con l'eccezione di Età Augustea di Diodoro Siculo, V, 35 – la reale colonizzazione fenicia della nostra isola.

Il confronto col bronzetto cipriota di Enkomi – che può comunque avere qualche richiamo in Sardegna in ambito sardo-fenicio (Macnamara 1985: 54–55) – è altrettanto deviante della supposta corrispondenza fra Nuragici e Shardana, uno dei "Popoli del Mare" rappresentati in Egitto, intorno al XIII sec. a.C., in scene di guerra marittima, a Medinet Habu (guerrieri con elmi cornuti o piumati e scudi rotondi). Ma "se è vero che c'è qualche rassomiglianza, questo sarebbe un argomento che collegherebbe anche con i ritrovamenti del Vicino Oriente e dell'Egeo; ma tali ritrovamenti suggeriscono datazioni al IX e VIII sec. a.C., come per i bronzetti nuragici" (Stary 1991: 138). Tutt'al più si tratterebbe, per gli Shardana, di popoli orientali facenti parte della colonizzazione fenicia, giunti in Sardegna più o meno "fra il 1100 e l'800 a.C." (Tykot 1994b: 75).

Ma anche in questo ultimo caso si tratta, a nostro parere, di considerazioni non sufficientemente fondate: infatti questa interpretazione, che pure trova tanti sostenitori e detrattori (Sandars 1985; Garbini 1988; Tykot 1994b; P. James, A. Mazar e V. Karageorghis in questo colloquio), è basata solo su una assonanza di nomi (gli Shardana rispetto ai Sardoi), che ignora discrepanze cronologiche e culturali.

In un certo senso più giustificato sarebbe il ricorso alla mitologia greca, frutto della splendida fantasia mitogenetica dei Greci (Tykot 1994b: 59, n. 4): non per nulla la cultura di ognuno di noi affonda le sue radici nel mondo classico.

A turbare ancor più il quadro, già di per sé confuso, di questi confronti casuali e parziali, bisogna aggiungere che chi li propone tende a ignorare che la quasi totalità di essi può essere effetto di semplici fenomeni di "convergenza" (Childe 1960: 45, 49).

Inoltre le concezioni ideali, culturali e religiose nuragiche, così come l'economia e, quindi, la stessa organizzazione civile e militare, erano di origine e tradizione pre- e protostorica locale; per cui quella nuragica fu una stupenda produzione artistica e artigianale originale che, in anticipo e in eccellenza rispetto ad altre del Mediterraneo (come appunto quella greca e quella etrusca; e non parliamo di quella, estremamente frusta, formale e ripetitiva, fenicio-punica), lasciò splendida e ricchissima traccia di sé prima di scomparire per sempre in seguito agli eventi storici che tutti noi conosciamo.

Bronzetti e statuaria in pietra

Si discute se siano stati i bronzetti a precedere la statuaria

(Bernardini 1985: 140, 141; Bernardini & Tronchetti 1990) o viceversa (Lilliu 1985: 192); ma il problema, a nostro avviso, è legato alla possibile e quasi certa presenza della scultura in legno (come gli *xoana* dei Greci) (Bermond Montanari *et al.* 1961: 533, 534), anche se essa è documentata sinora in Sardegna solo per la Civiltà Fenicio-punica (Nicosia 1985: 471, 472; Madau 1994; Contu in stampa).

Le figure umane armate sono nella statuaria in pietra le più comuni e a Monti Prama fra queste primeggia soprattutto (17 su 25 esemplari), con caratteristiche costantemente simili, quella del pugilatore che si protegge il capo con uno scudo leggero. Ad essa segue una figura di arciere, con diverse varianti. Tutte queste statue trovano perfetta corrispondenza, come si è accennato, sia nell'armamento di offesa e di difesa, che nello stesso abbigliamento e nello stile, nelle piccole rappresentazioni in bronzo p. es. di Abìni-Teti e di Cala Gonòne-Dorgàli-Nuoro, e comunque entro lo stile "geometrico"-volumetrico; anche se il più accurato rendimento stilistico che caratterizza la grande statuaria non si ritrova e non sarebbe stato possibile nelle piccole dimensioni dei bronzi: dove invece, ed è ovvio che sia così, prevale sul particolare l'unità stilistica della figura nel suo insieme. Ma anche il particolare alfine si recupera nella accurata resa grafica di elementi specifici dell'armamento e del vestiario. Bronzetti e statue trattano comunque la figura per grandi masse lisce, che presentano strutture ferme e lineari.

Infine la presenza, sia pure non abbondante, di colore rosso-"mordente", noi crediamo, più che rosso funerario (Sismondo Ridgway 1986: 68) – nelle statue di Monti Prama ci garantisce inoltre che le medesime erano (come in Grecia e altrove: p. es. il Guerriero di Capestrano) in genere dipinte in vari colori.

Non ha uguali in tutto il Mediterraneo la perfetta sintesi di plastica formale "geometrica" e rendimento del particolare che si riscontra, fra le sculture in pietra, nell'esempio, pieno di tensione, della mano elegantemente guantata e munita di salvabraccio che regge l' arco o, in quello, di una mano che regge lo scudo. Ma il guanto lascia scoperte le dita e, con manifestazione intenzionale ed efficacissima di uno stilismo geometrico che con rara potenza espressiva trascende il dato reale, la prima falange del pollice è ripiegata ad angolo retto sulle altre dita che, allineate ed uniformi, si stringono all'oggetto da sostenere. Per cui si capirà perfettamente il significato quasi "cubistico" che abbiamo inteso dare, nell'accezione della plastica nuragica, alla parola "geometrico" (Crispolti 1958: 163).

Notiamo quindi che entro il chiuso ovale del viso, dal mento squadrato, si erge, profondamente scavata, la colonna obliqua del naso, su cui si innesta il taglio netto delle arcate sopracciliari. Analogamente ai bronzetti di Abìni e Cavalupo, nei quali gli occhi sono resi con due globetti cerchiati, si hanno nelle statue due cerchi concentrici incisi, su un fondo piano pressoché parallelo al naso e che continua sulle guance. Sempre nella statuaria, appena accennata da un semplice taglio orizzontale doveva essere la bocca, che non si è conservata intatta in nessuno degli esemplari rinvenuti. Le orecchie hanno forma di mezzo disco leggermente depresso nel centro e su di esse si appoggiano le trecce di capelli che scendono verticalmente sino al petto.

Nella figura sobria e severa di bovino in calcare di Santa Vittoria di Serri vediamo che l'occhio è reso nello stilismo "geometrico" di un cerchio con un punto al centro.

A quali confronti extrainsulari si presta tutto ciò, pur con le riserve precedentemente espresse? Ben pochi, a dire il vero, e non molto significativi cronologicamente, oltre che stilisticamente (lo stile da solo può talora, come si è detto, essere ingannevole). I confronti più sorprendenti (ma cronologicamente più tardivi: VI sec.) si hanno nell'Italia meridionale: stele daunie (De Juliis 1988) e guerriero di Capestrano (Landolfi 1988). Ma si tratta di opere più rigide e fredde, oltre che più semplici ed elementari. Nelle stele addirittura l'unica parte plastica è la testa.

Il rendimento "geometrico" degli occhi con doppi cerchi che includono un punto si ha sia nelle stele maschili che in quelle femminili. Queste opere, che erano state già datate all'VIII e VII sec. a.C., ora si tende piuttosto ad attribuirele al VI (Siponto-Foggia). In una testa in pietra di guerriero con elmo da Numana-Ancona e, con poche differenze, nel più famoso Guerriero da Capestrano-L'Aquila, attribuiti ugualmente al VI secolo, è presente invece nel rendimento dell'occhio qualcosa di simile – ma realizzato col compasso, come i rari esempi greci di Olimpia e Corfù (Sismondo Ridgway 1986: 66, 67) – al globetto cerchiato di diversi bronzi di Abìni e dello stesso bronzo di Cavalupo; i quali ultimi abbiamo messo, anche per questo particolare, in diretta relazione con le statue di Monti Prama. Considerata la sicura alta datazione del bronzo di Cavalupo, la cosa non è priva di significato, specie se la si ricollega anche al fatto che lo stilismo a globetto cerchiato era presente nei bronzi del Luristan – oltre che in una statua in pietra, pressoché inedita da Gordion (Young s.d.: 6) –, con i quali altri riscontri presentano i nostri bronzetti dello stile "geometrico".

Se, come abbiamo affermato e pare indubbio, le sculture antropomorfe o zoomorfe in pietra di Monti Prama e di Santa Vittoria di Serri ed una buona parte degli stessi bronzetti rientrano in una produzione unitaria originale di stile "geometrico", è utile ricordare – anche se si tratta di altra cosa – che in Grecia e zone contermini il Protogeometrico è datato da circa il 1025 al 900 ed il Geometrico dal 900 al 700 a.C.; per cui l'arte "geometrica" della Sardegna dovrebbe svilupparsi, in tutto o almeno in parte, in contemporanea col Geometrico Medio II-Tardo II (James 1992: 92–115), che occupa l'intero VIII sec. E questo inquadramento cronologico e stilistico sarebbe stato accettato, noi crediamo, da tutti se non fosse stato in contrasto con il ritrovamento avvenuto, come si è detto, in una delle tombe del cosiddetto *heroon* di Monti Prama, assieme ad altri materiali di importazione, del sigillo scaraboide databile appunto al VII sec. a.C.

A parte la considerazione che, se anche questa data si adattasse alla nostre statue, non segnerebbe obbligatoriamente l'inizio dello stile: infatti sarebbero soprattutto i confronti stilistici con i bronzetti a far risultare preferibile una attribuzione all'VIII sec. Infatti non è stato lo stile ma questo corredo funerario di accompagno ad avvalorare l'accostamento con la rigidezza di forme dell'arcaismo greco. Mentre, per la propensione greco-centrica di alcuni studiosi, sarebbe troppo sconvolgente che le statue nuragiche dovessero risultare più antiche dei "modelli" ellenici messi a confronto.

Se inoltre dell'arte nuragica almeno i bronzetti (e non la statuaria in pietra) potessero attribuirsi, anche se parzialmente, a prima della metà del IX sec., osserviamo che essi corrisponderebbero per questa parte al Geometrico Antico I: 900–850 a.C.

Tutto ciò non rende davvero molto significativi neppure gli accostamenti, che pure sono stati tentati, con la struttura degli ossuari di Chiusi della seconda metà del VII sec., sormontati da teste fittili di tipologia non greca ma chiaramente etrusca e con occhi a mandorla notevolmente naturalistici.

Quanto ai confronti con la scultura in pietra o ceramica della Penisola Italiana, si tratta di elementi di modesta portata, considerati per altro anch'essi non sempre paralleli ma comunque indipendenti (almeno per ragioni cronologiche!) rispetto sia all'espansione del "geometrico" ellenico che alla successiva arte "dedalica" (Bernardini 1985: 141, 142) o "arcaica" che dir si voglia.

Anzi anche in terra ellenica il "Geometrico" fu, al suo inizio, un fenomeno estremamente modesto, anche se da esso nascerà poi quello spirito di ordine ed organicità che sarà sotteso alle straordinarie manifestazioni dell'arte greca nei secoli successivi: infatti nella stessa Grecia è presente soprattutto nella ceramica e in un numero piuttosto ridotto di bronzetti (Schweitzer 1969; Byrne 1991); tanto che nessuna vera scultura in pietra vi si avrà fino al manifestarsi dell'arte "dedalica" della metà del VII sec.

Dai piccoli bronzi figurati e dalla statuaria della Sardegna emergono perciò, in tutta la gamma delle loro espressioni e in forme artistiche originali, la società, il gusto, l'animo e la semplice e profonda religiosità delle genti nuragiche, che non raggiunsero mai il livello di civiltà "urbana". Una tale creazione artistica si manifestò, come abbiamo cercato di dimostrare, indipendentemente prima e meglio che altrove; e scomparve col progressivo affermarsi nell'Isola di una civiltà straniera ed urbana: quella fenicio-punica.

Bibliografia

Akurgal, E. 1966. Urartu, Centri. *Enciclopedia Univ. dell'Arte* 14: coll. 531–540.

Atzeni, C., L. Massidda, U. Sanna & P. Virdis. 1992. Some metallurgical remarks on the Sardinian bronzetti. In Tykot, R.H. & Andrews, T.K. (eds.), *Sardinia in the Mediterranean: A Footprint in the Sea. Studies in Sardinian Archaeology Presented to Miriam S. Balmuth*. Monographs in Mediterranean Archaeology 3: 347–354. Sheffield Accademic Press, Sheffield.

Barnett, R.D. 1956. Oriental Influences on Archaic Greece. In *The Aegean and Near East. Studies Presented to Hetty Goldman*. Locust Valley, N.Y.

Barreca, F. 1986a. *La Civiltà Fenicio-punica in Sardegna*. Delfino, Sassari.

Barreca, F. 1986b. La Sardegna e i Fenici. In *Ichnussa. La Sardegna dalle origini all'epoca classica*, 2° ediz., 349–417. Scheiwiller-Garzanti, Milano.

Bermond Montanari, G., L. Vlad Borrelli, G. Grana. 1961. Legno. *Enc. Arte Antica Classica ed Orientale* 4: 530–537.

Bernardini, P. 1982. Le aristocrazie nuragiche nell'VIII e VII sec. a.C. Proposte di lettura. *La Parola del Passato* 203: 81–101.

Bernardini, P. 1983. Tholoi in Sardegna: alcune osservazioni. *Studi Etruschi* 51: 43–54.

Bernardini, P. 1985. Osservazioni sulla bronzistica figurata sarda. *Nuovo Bullettino Archeologico Sardo* 2: 119–166.

Bernardini, P. 1992. La facies orientalizzante in Sardegna: problemi di individuazione e di metodologia. In Tykot, R.H. & Andrews, T.K. (eds.), *Sardinia in the Mediterranean: A Footprint in the Sea. Studies in Sardinian Archaeology Presented to Miriam S. Balmuth*. Monographs in Mediterranean Archaeology 3: 396–409. Sheffield Accademic Press, Sheffield.

Bernardini, P. & C. Tronchetti. 1990a. La Sardegna, gli Etruschi e i Greci. In *La Civiltà nuragica*, 264–282. Electa Editrice, Milano.

Bernardini, P. & C. Tronchetti. 1990b. L'effigie. In *La Civiltà nuragica*, 211–228. Electa Editrice, Milano.

Bianchi Bandinelli, R. 1960. Greca, Arte. *Enc. Arte Antica Classica ed Orientale* 3: 1005–1055.

Bianchi Bandinelli, R. & Paribeni, E.. 1976. *L'arte dell'antichità classica. Grecia*.

Bisi, A.M. 1977. L'apport phenicien aux bronzes nouragiques de Sardaigne. *Latomus* 36.

Bisi, A.M. 1978. Elements anatoliens dans les bronzes nouragiques de Sardaigne. In *Proceedings of the Xth International Congress of Classical Archaeology, Ankara, 1978*, 349–359.

Boardman, J. 1990. Al Mina and History. *Oxford Journal of Archaeology* 9: 169–190.

Bocquet, A. & M.-C. Lesbascle. 1983. Metallurgia e relazioni culturali nell'Età del Bronzo finale delle Alpi del Nord Francesi. In M. Rossi (ed.), *Antropologia Alpina*. Torino. [traduzion dal francese a cura di A. Gattiglia. Titolo originale: *Les dépôts de bronzes dans les Alpes Françaises du Nord et la Chronologie du Bronze final. Les rapports entre les Alpes du Nord et l'Itaie au Bronze final*. In italiano sono riuniti due articoli distinti e di date diverse, con ampliamenti: A. Bocquet & M.-C. Lesbascle, Les dépôts de bronzes dans les Alpes Françaises du Nord et la Chronologie du Bronze final, *IXe Congrès de l'U.I.S.P.P., Colloque XXVI, Les Âges del Metaux dans les Alpes, Nice 13–18 dic. 1976*; A. Bocquet, Les rapports entre les Alpes du Nord et l'Italie au Bronze final, *Bulletin de la Société Préhistorique Française* 78(1981): 144–153.]

Bondì, S.F. 1975. Osservazioni sulle fonti classiche per la colonizzazione della Sardegna. *Saggi fenici* 1: 49–66.

Bonfante, L. 1986. The Etruscan connections. In M.S. Balmuth (ed.), *Studies in Sardinian Archaeology II: Sardinia in the Mediterranean*, 73–84. University of Michigan Press, Ann Arbor.

Bossert, H. 1951. *Altsyrien*. Tubinga.

Breglia Pulci Delia, L. 1981. La Sardegna arcaica tra tradizioni euboiche ed attiche. In Nouvelle contribution à l'étude de la societé et de la colonisation eubéennes. *Cahier du Centre J. Berard* 6: 61–95. Ist. Franç. de Naple, Napoli.

Burkert, W. 1992. *The Orientalizing Revolution*. Cambridge.

Byrne, M. 1991. *The Greek Geometric warrior figurine. Interpretation and origin*. Archaeologia Transatlantica X. Université Catholique de Louvain, Louvain-la Neuve and Brown University, Providence, Rhode Island.

Camporeale, G. 1993. Dal villanoviano all'orientalizzante. In *L'arte dèi Popoli Italici dal 3000 al 300 a.C.*, 33–35. Electa, Napoli.

Childe, V.G. 1960. *I frammenti del passato. Archeologia della preistoria*. Milano.

Coldstream, J.N. 1968. *Greek Geometric Pottery: A Survey of Ten Local Styles and Their Chronology*. Methuen, London.

Coldstream, J.N. 1977. *Geometric Greece*. London.

Contu, E. 1974. La Sardegna dell'Età Nuragica. In *Popoli e Civiltà dell'Italia Antica* 3: 141–203. Biblioteca di Storia Patria, Roma.

Contu, E. 1981. Considerazioni sulle barchette votive di Eta Nuragica. In P. Brandis (a cura di), *Atti del Primo Convegno Internazionale di Studi Geografico-Storici, Sassari il 7–9 aprile 1978. La Sardegna nel Mediterraneo. 1. Gli aspetti geografici*, 9. Gallizzi, Sassari.

Contu, E. 1982. In E. Contu & M.L. Frongia, *Il nuovo Museo Nazionale G. A. Sanna di Sassari*. Itinerai dei Musei e Monumenti d'Italia, Ministero per i Beni Culturali e Ambientali, 2° ediz.

Contu, E. 1987. Conclusioni. In *La Sardegna nel Mediterraneo tra il secondo e il primo millennio av.C. Atti del II° Convegno di studi "Un millennio di relazioni fra la Sardegna ed i Paesi del Mediterraneo," Selargius-Cagliari, 27–30 novembre 1986*, 558–559. Stef, Cagliari.

Contu, E. 1993. Scultura in pietra e bronzetti figurati della Sardegna Nuragica. In *L'arte dei Popoli Italici dal 3000 al 300 a.C.*, 51–58. Electa, Napoli.

Contu, E. In press. *La Sardegna preistorica e nuragica*. Chiarella, Sassari.

Crispolti, E. 1958. Cubismo e futurismo. *Enc. Univ. Arte* 4: coll. 163–173.

D'Agostino. 1979. Il periodo del Bronzo Finale in Italia. In *Atti della XXI Riunione scientifica in memoria di F. Rittatore Vonwiller*. Istituto Italiano di Preistoria e Protostoria, Firenze.

D'Oriano, R. 1986. Un bronzetto di offerente da Santa Teresa di Gallura. Nuove considerazioni. *Studi Etruschi* 2: 61–65.

De Juliis, E.M. 1988. L'origine delle genti iapige e la civiltà dei Dauni. In *Italia. Omni terrarum alumna*, 593–652. Scheiwiller, Milano.

Dikaios, P. 1962. The Bronze Statue of Horned God from Enkomi. *Archäologischer Anzeiger*: 1–40.

Donadoni, S. 1960. Egiziana, Arte. *Enc. Arte A.C. O.* 3: 255–282.

Fadda, M.A. 1988. *La fonte sacra di Su Tempiesu*. Guide e Itinerari 8. Delfino, Sassari.

Fadda, M.A. 1991a. Nurdole. Un tempio nuragico in Barbagia. Punto d'incontro del Mediterraneo. *Rivista di Studi Fenici* 19(1): 108–120.

Fadda, M.A. 1991b. *Il Museo speleo-archeologico di Nuoro*. Guide e Itinerari 17. Delfino, Sassari.

Fadda, M.A. & F. Lo Schiavo. 1992. *Su Tempiesu di Orune. Fonte sacra nuragica*. Quaderni della Soprintendenza ai Beni Archeologici delle Provincie di Sassari e Nuoro 18. Il Torchietto, Ozieri.

Fadda, M.A. & M. Madau. 1991. Scavi a Nurdole (NU). *Rivista di Studi Fenici* 19(1): 108–129.

Ferrarese Ceruti, M.L. 1985. Un bronzetto nuragico da Ossi (Sassari). In *Studi in onore di G. Lilliu per il suo settantesimo compleanno*, 51–59. Cagliari.

Ferron, J. & M. E. Aubet. 1974. *Orants de Carthage*. Paris.

Filigheddu, P. 1994. Navicelle bronzee della Sardegna nuragica: prime annotazioni per uno studio delle attitudini e funzionalità nautiche. *Nuovo Bullettino Archeologico Sardo* 4(1987–1992): 65–116.

Garbini, G. 1988. Popoli del Mare, Tarsis e Filistei, E. Acquaro, L. Godart, F. Mazza & D. Musti (a cura di), *Momenti precoloniali del Mediterraneo antico. Questioni di Metodo – Aree di Indagine – Evidenze a Confronto*, 235–242. Roma.

Gehrig, U.L. 1964. *Die geometrischen Bronzen vom Heraion von Samos*.

Giannattasio, B.M. 1992. Nora I. I Serdaioi a Nora? Un'ipotesi. *Quaderni della Soprintendenza Archeologica per le Provincie di Cagliari e Oristano* 9: 105–111.

Giuliano, A. 1960. Gordion. *Enc. Arte Antica Classica ed Orientale* 3: 978–980.

Gras, M. 1980. Sardische Bronzen in Etrurien. In *Kunst und Kultur Sardiniens*. Karlsruhe.

Gras, M. 1981. Bronzetto arcaico da Olmedo. In M. Gras & G. Tore, *Bronzetti arcaici della Nurra*. Quaderni della Soprintendenza ai Beni Archeologici delle Provincie di Sassari e Nuoro 9. Dessì, Sassari.

Gras, M. 1985. *Trafics tyrréniens arcaïques*. École Fraçase de Rome, Roma.

Hmayakian, S.G. 1995. Urartu – Vermächtnisse einer Hochkultur. In *Armenien, 500 Jahre. Kunst und Kultur*, 49–54. Wasmuth, Tubingen.

Homann-Wedeking, E. 1960a. Geometrica, Arte. *Enciclopedia dell'Arte Antica, Classica e Orientale* 3: 813–832.

James, P. 1991. *Centuries of Darkness. A Challenge to the Conventional Chronology of Old World Archaeology*. London.

La Rosa, V. 1968. *Bronzetti indigeni della Sicilia*.

Landolfi, M. 1988. I Piceni. In *Italia. Omni terrarum alumna*, 313–374. Scheiwiller, Milano.

Lilliu, C. 1988. Un culto di Età Punico-Romana al Nuraghe Genna Maria di Villanovaforru. *Quaderni della Soprintendenza Archeologica per le Provincie di Cagliari e Oristano* 5: 109–128.

Lilliu, G. 1966. *Sculture della Sardegna nuragica*. La Zattera, Cagliari.

Lilliu, G. 1973. Tripode bronzeo di tradizione cipriota dalla Grotta Pirosu-Su Benatzu di Santadi (Cagliari). In *Estudios dedicados al Prof. dr. Luis Pericot*, 283–313. Barcelona.

Lilliu, G. 1982. *La Civiltà Nuragica*. Delfino, Sassari.

Lilliu, G. 1985. Bronzetti e statuaria nella Civiltà Nuragica. In *Ichnussa. La Sardegna dalle origini all'epoca classica*, 2° ediz., 178–251. Scheiwiller-Garzanti, Milano.

Lilliu, G. 1986. Società ed economia nei centri nuragici. In *Atti del I° Convegno di studi "Un millennio di relazioni fra la Sardegna ed i Paesi del Mediterraneo," Selargius-Cagliari, 1985*, 77–87. Stef, Cagliari.

Lilliu, G. 1988. *La civiltà dei Sardi dal Paleolitico all'Età dei Nuraghi*. Nuova ERI, Torino.

Lo Schiavo, F. 1978. Le fibule della Sardegna. *Studi Etruschi* 46: 25–46.

Lo Schiavo, F. 1981a. Ambra in Sardegna. In *Studi in onore di Ferrante Rittatore Vonwiller*. Como.

Lo Schiavo, F. 1981b. Osservazioni sul problema dei rapporti fra Sardegna ed Etruria. In *L'Etruria mineraria, Atti del XII Convegno di Studi Etruschi e Italici, Firenze – Populonia – Piombino, 16–20 giugno 1979*, 299–314. Firenze.

Lo Schiavo, F. 1984. Appunti sull'evoluzione culturale della Sardegna nell'età dei metalli. *Nuovo Bullettino Archeologico Sardo* 1: 21–40.

Lo Schiavo, F. 1990. La Sardegna nuragica e il mondo mediterraneo. In *La Civiltà nuragica*, 238–263. Electa Editrice, Milano.

Lo Schiavo, F. 1992. Un'altra Fibula 'Cipriota' dalla Sardegna. In Tykot, R.H. & Andrews, T.K. (eds.), *Sardinia in the Mediterranean: A Footprint in the Sea. Studies in Sardinian*

Archaeology Presented to Miriam S. Balmuth. Monographs in Mediterranean Archaeology 3: 296–303. Sheffield Accademic Press, Sheffield.

Lo Schiavo, F. 1994. Bronzi nuragici nelle tombe della Prima Età del Ferro di Pontecagnano. In *La presenza etrusca nella Campania meridionale, Atti delle giornate di Studio, Salerno-Pontecagnano, 16–18 novembre 1990*, 61–82. Olski, Firenze.

Lo Schiavo, F. E. Macnamara & L. Vagnetti. 1985. Late Cypriot imports to Italy and their influence on local bronzework. *Papers of the British School at Rome*.

Lo Schiavo, F., T. Stech, R. Maddin & J.D. Muhly. 1987. Nuragic metallurgy in Sardinia: second preliminary report. In Balmuth, M.S. (ed.), *Studies in Sardinian Achaeology III: Nuragic Sardinia and the Mycenean World*. BAR International Series 387: 179–187. British Archaeological Reports, Oxford.

Lucidi, M. T. 1961. Luristan, Arte del. *Enciclopedia dell'Arte Antica, Classica e Orientale* 4: 733–739.

Matthiae Scandone, G. 1989. Egitto e Sardegna, contatti fra culture, Sardò. *Atlante della Sardegna Fenicia e Punica* 3. Sassari.

Macnamara, E. 1985. Figurines. In F. Lo Schiavo, E. Macnamara & L. Vagnetti, Late Cypriot Imports to Italy and their Influence on local Bronzework. *Papers of the British School at Rome* 53: 51–71.

Macnamara, E. 1985a. Tripod-stands. In F. Lo Schiavo, E. Macnamara & L. Vagnetti, Late Cypriot Imports to Italy and their Influence on local Bronzework. *Papers of the British School at Rome* 53: 35–42, 62–71.

Madau, M. 1994. Xoana lignei e idoli fenici. *Quaderni della Soprintendenza Archeologica per le Provincie di Cagliari e Oristano* 10(1993): 69–80.

Mastino, A. 1980. La voce degli antichi. In *NUR. La misteriosa civiltà dei Sardi*, 231–274, 318. Cariplo, Milano.

Mastino, A. 1994. La Sardegna nelle fonti classiche. *Rivista di Storia Italiana* 22–23(1992–93): 239–256.

Maxwell, K.R. 1956. Urartian Bronzes in Etruscan Tombs. *Iraq* 18(2): 150–167.

Moravetti, A. 1992. *Il complesso nuragico di Palmavera*. Guide e Itinerari 20. Delfino, Sancasciano, Firenze.

Nicosia, F. 1985. La Sardegna nel mondo classico. In *Ichnussa. La Sardegna dalle origini all'epoca classica*, 2^ ediz., 419–476. Scheiwiller-Garzanti, Milano.

Ortiz, G. 1993. *Kollektsiia Gzorgza Ortisa. Grevnosti ot Ura go Vizantii – The George Ortiz Collection. Antiquities from Ur to Byzantium*. Catalogo delle mostre al The State Hermitage Museum, St. Petersburg, 17-February-11 April 1993, e al The State Pushkin Museum of Fine Arts, Moskow, 6 May-27 June 1993. Benteli-Werd Publishers, Berne. Testo in russo ed inglese (bronzetti nuragici: nn. 175–181; bronzetti del geometrico greco nn. 76–78, 80).

Pais, E. 1984. *Bullettino Archeologico Sardo* 1.

Pallottino, M. 1957. Etruria e Urartu. *Archeologia Classica* 9(1): 89–96.

Pallottino, M. 1963a. Orientalizzante. Arte. *Enciclopedia dell'Arte Antica, Classica e Orientale* 5: 749–760.

Pallottino, M. 1963b. Orientalizzante. *Enciclopedia dell'Arte Antica, Classica e Orientale* 10: 223–237.

Peroni, R. (a cura di). 1980. *Il Bronzo Finale in Italia*. Bari.

Perra, M. (a cura di). 1993. *La Sardegna nelle fonti classiche dal VI sec. a.C. al VI sec. d. C.* Opera di compilazione comprendente la ricerca e il riordino cronologico di tutte le antiche testimonnianze letterarie latine e greche riguardanti la Sardegna, con testo italiano a fronte. S'Alvure, Oristano.

Pettinato, G. 1985. *Ebla. Nuovi orizzonti della storia*. Milano.

Piotrovsky, B.B. 1969. *The Ancient Civilization of Urartu. An archaeological Adventure*. New York

Ridgway, D. 1986. Sardinia and the first western Greeks. In Balmuth, M.S. (ed.), *Studies in Sardinian Archaeology, vol. II: Sardinia in the Mediterranean*. University of Michigan Press, Ann Arbor.

Ridgway, D. 1994. In G.R. Tsetskladze & F. De Angelis (eds.), *The Archaeology of Greek Colonisation*, 35–37. Oxford.

Ridgway, D. & Serra Ridgway, F. 1992a. Sardinia and history. In Tykot, R.H. & Andrews, T.K. (eds.), *Sardinia in the Mediterranean: A Footprint in the Sea. Studies in Sardinian Archaeology Presented to Miriam S. Balmuth*. Monographs in Mediterranean Archaeology 3: 355–363. Sheffield Academic Press.

Ridgway, D. & Serra Ridgway, F. 1992b. Presentazione. In M.A. Fadda & F. Lo Schiavo, *Su Tempiesu di Orune. Fonte sacra nuragica*. Quaderni della Soprintendenza ai Beni Archeologici delle Provincie di Sassari e Nuoro 18. Il Torchietto, Ozieri.

Ridgway, D. & Serra Ridgway, F. 1995. Su Tempiesu and the Ceri effect: two Nuragic notes. *Acta Hyperborea* 5.

Roncalli, F. 1986. L'arte. In *Rasenna. Storia della civiltà degli Etruschi*, 531–676. Scheiwiller, Milano.

Rovina, D. 1986. Il santuario nuragico di Serra Niedda (Sorso). *Nuovo Bullettino Archeologico Sardo* 3: 37–47, figg. 6–9.

Sandars, N.K. 1985. *The Sea Peoples. Warriors of the Ancient Mediterranean*. London.

Sanna, M. 1982. Navicelle nuragiche e navigatori. Un'ipotesi di ricerca. *Sardigna Antiga* 1: 18–19.

Santoni, V. 1980. Il segno del potere. In *Nur. La misteriosa civiltà dei Sardi*, 141–188. Cariplo, Milano.

Santoni, V. 1990. Nuraghe Piscu. L'Orientalizzante antico e medio, Suelli (Cagliari). *Bollettino di Archeologia* 3: 145–48.

Santoni, V. 1991. Suelli (Cagliari). Nota preliminare sull'Orientalizzante Antico-Medio della capanna n° 1 del nuraghe Piscu. In *Atti del II Congresso Internazionale di Studi Fenici e Punici, Roma 9–14 novembre 1987*, vol. 3: 1233–1244. Roma.

Santoni, V. 1994. L'architettura e la produzione materiale nuragica. In *Il nuraghe Losa di Abbasanta. I*. Quaderni della Soprintendenza Archeologica per le Provincie di Cagliari e Oristano 10 (1993), supplemento.

Schweitzer, B. 1969. *Die geometric Kunst Griechlands*. Köln, 2^ediz.

Schweitzer, W. Fuchs. 1958. Geometrico. *Enciclopedia U. Arte* 5: 684–709.

Sismondo Ridgway, B. 1986. Mediterranean comparanda for the statues from Monte Prama. In Balmuth, M.S. (ed.), *Studies in Sardinian Archaeology, vol. II: Sardinia in the Mediterranean World*, 61–71. University of Michigan Press, Ann Arbor.

Spadea, R. 1996. Il santuario di Hera; I doni alla dea; Materiali votivi dell'edificio B. In R. Spadea (a cura di), *Il Tesoro di Hera. Scoperte nel santuario di Hera Lacinia a Capo Colonna di Crotone*, mostra al Museo Barracco, Roma, 28 marzo-30 giugno 1996, 43, 48, 56–58. Milano.

Stary, P.F. 1991. Arms and armour of the nuragic warrior-statuettes and their relations to the contemporary armament in the Mediterranean and Europe. In B. Santillo Flizell (ed.), *Colloquio Internazionale Arte Militare e architettura Nuragica, Roma 7–9 Dicembre 1989*, 119–142. Uppsala.

Strøm, I. 1971. *Problems Concerning the Origin and Early Development of the Etruscan Orientalizing Style*. Odense.

Tanda, G. 1987. Il carro in età nuragica. In *Atti del II° Convegno di studi "Un millennio di relazioni fra la Sardegna ed i Paesi del Mediterraneo", Selargius-Cagliari*, 63–80. Selargius.

Thimme, J. 1980. Kunst. In *Kunst und Kultur Sardiniens vom Neoliticum bis zum Enden der Nuraghenzeit*, 109–120. Verlag C. F. Müller, Karlsruhe.

Tore, G. 1981. Elementi sulle relazioni commerciali della Sardegna nella prima età del ferro. In *I° Convegno internazionale di studi geografico-storici, La Sardegna nel mondo mediterraneo, Sassari, 7–9 aprile 1978*, 256–295.

Tore, G. 1983. I bronzi figurati fenicio-punici in Sardegna. In *Atti del I Congresso Internazionale di Studi Fenici e Punici*, II: 449–461. C. N. R., Roma.

Tore, G. 1992. La Sardegna fenicio-punica: aspetti e problemi. In *La Preistoria de les illes de la Mediterrània occidental*. X Jornades d'Estudis Historics Locals 367–368, nn. 35–36. Palma de Mallorca

Torelli, M. 1986. La religione. In *Rasenna. Storia della civiltà degli Etruschi*, 157–237. Scheiwiller, Milano.

Tronchetti, C. 1978. Monti Prama (Com. di Cabras-OR). *Studi Etruschi* 46: 571–590.

Tronchetti, C. 1985. I Greci e la Sardegna. *Dialoghi di Archeologia* 17–34.

Tronchetti, C. 1986. Nuragic statuary from Monte Prama. In Balmuth, M.S. (ed.), *Studies in Sardinian Archaeology, vol. II: Sardinia in the Mediterranean*, 41–60. University of Michigan Press, Ann Arbor.

Tronchetti, C. 1988. *I Sardi. Traffici, relazioni, ideologie della Sardegna arcaica*. Milano.

Turchi, D. 1982. Statuaria nuragica in Barbagia. *Sardigna Antiga* 1: 19.

Tykot, R.H. 1994a. Radiocarbon dating and absolute chronology in Sardinia and Corsica. In Skeates, R. & Whitehouse, R. (eds.), *Radiocarbon Dating and Italian Prehistory*. Accordia Specialist Studies on Italy 3: 115–145. Accordia Research Centre, University of London, and Archaeological Monographs of the British School at Rome 8, British School at Rome, London.

Tykot, R.H. 1994b. Sea Peoples in Etruria? Italian contacts with the Eastern Mediterranean in the Late Bronze Age. *Etruscan Studies. Journal of the Etruscan Foundation* 1: 59–83.

Ugas, G. 1980. Altare modellato su castello nuragico di tipo trilobato con figura in rilievo dal Sinis di Cabras (Oristano). *Archeologia Sarda* 7–32.

Ugas, G. 1981. A proposito dei rapporti fra i Lidi, gli Etruschi e i Sardi nuragici. *Archeologia Sarda* 77–88.

Ugas, G. 1985. La produzione materiale nuragica. Note sull'apporto etrusco e greco. In *Società e cultura in Sardegna nei periodi orientalizzante ed Arcaico (fine VIII sec. a.C. – 480 a.C.). Rapporti fra Sardegna, Fenici, Etruschi e Greci. Atti del I° Convegno di studi "Un millennio di relazioni fra la Sardegna ed i Paesi del Mediterraneo," Selargius-Cagliari, 29–30 nov. -1 dic. 1985*, 41–.

Ugas, G. 1987a. Le tombe a pozzetto T1-T3. In G. Ugas & G. Lucia, Primi scavi nel sepolcreto nuragico di Antas. *Atti del II° Convegno di studi "Un millennio di relazioni fra la Sardegna ed i Paesi del Mediterraneo"*, Selargius-Cagliari, 255–261.

Ugas, G. 1987b. Un nuovo contributo per lo studio della tholos in Sardegna. La fortezza di Su Mulinu-Villanovafranca. In Balmuth, M.S. (ed.), *Studies in Sardinian Arcaeology III. Nuragic Sardinia and the Mycenaean World*. BAR International Series 387: 77–128. British Archaeological Reports, Oxford.

Ugas, G. 1989a. Il sacello del vano E della fortezza di Su Mulinu-Villanovafranca (CA). In *Prétirage per il Convegno Anathema, Università La Sapienza di Roma 15–18.VI.1989*. In stampa.

Ugas, G. 1989b. Il mondo religioso nuragico. In *La Civiltà nuragica*, 196–210. Electa Editrice, Milano.

Ugas, G. 1989–90. Il sacello del vano E nella fortezza nuragica di Su Mulinu-Villanovafranca (CA). In *Atti del Convegno internazionale ANATHEMA: Regime delle offerte e vita dei santuari nel Mediterraneo antico, 15–18 giugno 1989. Scienze dell'Ant. Storia. Archeologia. Antropologia*, 3–4: 556–560, f. 9. Università "La Sapienza", Roma.

Ugas, G. & Paderi, M.C. 1990. Persistenze rituali in età punica e romana nel sacello nuragico del vano e della fortezza di Su Mulinu – Villanovafranca (Cagliari). In Mastino, A. (a cura di), *L'Africa romana 7°, I, Atti del VII convegno di studio, Sassari, 15–17 dicembre 1989*, 475–486.

Vandenabeele, F. & Laffiner, R. (eds.).1994. *Cypriote Stone Sculpture. Proceedings of the Second International Conference of Cypriote Studies, Brussels-Liège, 17–19 May, 1993*. Brussels-Liège.

Von Bissin, F.W. 1928. Die sardinischen Bronzen. *Mittheilungen des Deutschen Archaeologischen Instituts* 43.

Young, R.S. s.d.. *Gordion. Aux fouilles et au Musée*. Ankara, Societé d'Ankara pour la Promotion du Tourisme, des Antiquitées e des Musées.

Zervos, Ch. 1954. *La civilsation de la Sardaigne du début de l'énéolithique à la fin de la période nouragique*. Cahiers d'Art, Paris.

Zimmermann, J.-L. 1989. *Les chevaux de bronze dans l'art geometrique grec*.

Zucca, R. 1988. Itinerario. In G. Lilliu & R. Zucca, *Su Nuraxi di Barumini*. Guide e Itinerari 9: 83–143. Delfino ed., Roma.

Zucca, R. 1989. *Il tempio di Antas*. Guide e Itinerari 11. Delfino ed., Roma.

23. Nuovi dati materiali per una definizione dell'Eneolitico Antico in Sardegna

Luisanna Usai

Come è noto con l'avvento dei primi metalli si verifica di fatto in Sardegna il lento e graduale dissolvimento della cultura di Ozieri che caratterizza il Neolitico Recente in tutta l'isola. Pur non escludendo, specie in alcune aree geograficamente più conservative, il prolungarsi dell'eperienza Ozieri in tempi del Calcolitico, i dati acquisiti in anni recenti, in particolare nella Sardegna meridionale, consentono di affermare che alla produzione dei primi oggetti in rame e in argento si accompagna un graduale cambiamento nella produzione fittile, in quella collegata alla lavorazione della pietra ma anche nelle strutture abitative e, verosimilmente, nell'impostazione planimetrica degli ipogei scavati ex novo (Santoni 1989: 53–54).

Come si sa, non tutti gli studiosi hanno raggiunto un accordo su quali fasi culturali, cronologicamente ben distinte, si possano individuare nell'ambito dell'Eneolitico Antico della Sardegna. E. Contu (1988a: 441–443) ha già da tempo proposto e ribadito anche in sede di convegno una seriazione delle culture di Filigosa e Abealzu alle quali, peraltro, si sovrapporrebbero in parte quelle di Monte Claro e del vaso Campaniforme. Una distinzione tra gli esiti finali della fase Ozieri e le successive culture o facies di Abealzu e Filigosa è in E. Atzeni (1990: 30–31).

Chi scrive è tra coloro che ritiene si possano identificare nel primo Calcolitico tre fasi ben distinte denominate Sub-Ozieri, Filigosa e Abealzu susseguitesi in linea di massima nell'ordine qui proposto pur tenendo presenti le possibili differenziazioni legate a fattori geografici ed ambientali con la conseguente persistenza di un aspetto culturale rispetto agli altri. Tale successione culturale è già stata proposta da V. Santoni (1991: 34–35) ma con scansioni cronologiche che avanzano nel pieno Eneolitico. Per un'articolazione in tre fasi è anche F. Lo Schiavo (1992: 120) che propende per una distinzione, anche nella Sardegna Settentrionale, tra il Sub-Ozieri o, secondo la Sua proposta, "Ozieri dipinto" e la cultura di Filigosa, in contrasto con chi (Tinè 1992: 116) vedrebbe i due termini intercambiabili o comunque indicativi di uno stesso ambito culturale.

Per altro verso c'è chi continua a considerare gli aspetti Abealzu e Filigosa come pertinenti ad una stessa cultura (Foschi Nieddu 1986: 130, cultura di Abealzu-Filigosa), talvolta invertendo i termini (Moravetti 1992: 198, cultura di Filigosa-Abealzu).

Notevoli contributi al problema dell'ambito cronologico di queste tre culture (Contu 1988a: 441–442; Tykot 1994: 124–125) derivano dalle recenti datazioni assolute fornite dal sito di Monte d'Accoddi. La serie di datazioni non calibrate di Monte d'Accoddi pongono, infatti, le due fasi del santuario riferibili rispettivamente alla cultura di Sub-Ozieri o Filigosa (ma direi meglio e Filigosa, come vedremo in seguito) e a quella di Abealzu tra il 2.900 e il 2550 (Tinè 1992: 116). Le datazioni sono particolarmente significative per la fase più antica Sub-Ozieri e/o Filigosa, in quanto ben quattro di esse si collocano intorno al 2.900 mentre la datazione al 2590 ± 90 a.C. della II fase del santuario non esclude una persistenza della cultura di Abealzu nella seconda metà del III millennio (Tinè 1992: 115–116).

L'ambito cronologico dei tre aspetti culturali (Sub-Ozieri, Filigosa e Abealzu), sulla base soprattutto delle recenti datazioni assolute di Monte d'Accoddi ma anche di alcuni confronti già da tempo proposti con contesti extrainsulari, in particolare per la fase Sub-Ozieri con contesti siciliani (Usai 1987: 183–184; Santoni 1991: 26–27), può essere quindi stabilito tra il 2900 e 2.500 a.C. circa. A ciò non ostano, tra l'altro, le datazioni conosciute per la precedente cultura di San Michele (Trump 1983: tab. 9; Tykot 1994: 123).

Se non sembrano esserci dubbi sulla differenziazione cronologica più che geografica tra le tre fasi è certamente più difficile allo stato attuale delle conoscenze, ancora

---

Luisanna Usai, Soprintendenza Archeologica per le Provincie di Cagliari e Oristano, Piazza Indipendenza, 7, Cagliari, 09124 Sardegna, Italia

troppo parziali e lacunose, asserire che si tratti di tre distinte culture in senso stretto o piuttosto di un graduale e parziale cambiamento.

La differenziazione tra le tre fasi culturali proposte si coglie, soprattutto, nell'ambito della produzione ceramica e quindi su questa soffermerò la mia attenzione con particolare riguardo agli aspetti Sub-Ozieri e Filigosa, considerato che alcuni studiosi tendono a ritenerli facies locali di una stessa cultura. Propongo qui delle tavole riassuntive delle forme più diffuse dei tre aspetti culturali (Figg. 23.1–23.3) desunte dai quadri materiali noti già da tempo o di più recente acquisizione.

Per quanto riguarda la facies Sub-Ozieri (Fig. 23.1) i siti di prioritario interesse permangono quelli già noti, almeno parzialmente, di Pirri-Terramaini (Cagliari) (Usai 1987), Su Coddu (Selargius) (Ugas et al. 1989; Ugas et al. 1989a), Cuccuru S'Arriu (Cabras) (Santoni et al. 1982: 109–111; Santoni 1991) nonchè di Is Arridelis (Uta) (Sanna 1989). A questi si è di recente aggiunto il contesto della tomba II di Perda Lada (Decimoputzu) (Ugas 1990: 21) che consente di intravedere anche l'aspetto funerario della cultura. Esaminando le forme più documentate nel villaggio di Pirri-Terramaini e negli altri siti citati si può notare, come ho già avuto modo di sottolineare (Usai 1987: 185), e come hanno evidenziato diversi studiosi (Atzeni 1990: 31; Ugas 1989a: 14–15), la scomparsa pressochè totale, oltre che della decorazione, di alcune forme caratteristiche della cultura Ozieri quali la pisside, il vaso a cestello, la spiana nonchè la presenza diffusa di altre fogge quali il tegamone biansato, l'olletta monoansata, le forme carenate con perforazioni verticali. Ma appare soprattutto caratteristica la presenza sia a Pirri-Terramaini (Usai 1987: figg. 11, 14, 15) che a Su Coddu di Selargius (Usai 1989: figg. 13–14; Lai 1989: fig. 2) della ceramica depurata con sobri motivi dipinti o del tutto inornata. Mi pare anzi che sia proprio la presenza o meno di ceramica dipinta l'elemento di maggiore distinzione tra la fase Sub-Ozieri e quella Filigosa, mancando al momento per quest'ultima cultura, qualsiasi attestazione di ceramica figulina a pasta chiara. Non rientrano infatti in questa categoria i fittili con ingubbiatura bianco-rosa della tomba I di Filigosa (Foschi Nieddu 1986: 28–32) per i quali si deve pensare, date anche le forme documentate, ad una produzione più recente piuttosto che ad una imitazione più povera e mal riuscita delle ceramiche a pasta chiara.

La presenza di ceramica dipinta nel sito di Monte d'Accoddi (Bafico & Rossi 1989) sembrerebbe quindi attestare anche nell'area del santuario una fase Sub-Ozieri distinta da quella Filigosa, secondo una seriazione cronologica già proposta da F. Lo Schiavo (1992: 122).

Per quanto riguarda gli aspetti culturali di Filigosa (Fig. 23.2) e Abealzu (Fig. 23.3), come ha più volte sottolineato E. Contu (1988a: 443–447), si coglie bene la differenziazione tra una fase (Filigosa) in cui prevalgono le forme con carena spigolosa, fondi a tacco, vasi chiusi a colletto anche di piccole dimensioni, semplici decorazioni graffite, o con piccoli punti impressi o a coppelle e una (Abealzu) caratterizzata principalmente da vasi a fiasco e a colletto solitamente con due o un'ansa a cui si può contrapporre una coppia di bozze mammillari.

Di certo nell'ambito della produzione ceramica, esaminando contesti ben caratteristici e non soggetti ad infiltrazioni successive, si coglie meglio la differenziazione tra gli aspetti Filigosa e Abealzu che non quelli tra Sub-Ozieri e Filigosa. Le ultime due facies, infatti, mostrano diversi elementi simili quali le perforazioni alla carena, i fondi a tacco, le tazze carenate a profilo molto angoloso, la decorazione impressa a file di piccoli punti o a grana di riso. Le stesse superfici spesso ben levigate e lucide conservano in entrambi gli aspetti culturali echi della precedente tradizione Ozieri.

Agli aspetti già da tempo noti di Filigosa, in particolare dalla tomba dei vasi tetrapodi di S. Pedru (Contu 1966: 52–55; tavv. XV e XVI) e dalla tomba 1 del sito eponimo (Foschi Nieddu 1986), si sono aggiunti quelli recenti di sepolture del cagliaritano edite da E. Atzeni (Atzeni 1985: 11–36) e di ipogei venuti in luce nella regione del Sulcis.

Oltre alla tomba 12 di Cannas di Sotto di Carbonia (Cocco & Usai 1988c; Santoni 1988b: 218–219; Santoni & Usai 1995), e alla tomba IV di Locci Santus (San Giovanni Suergiu) (Atzeni 1995: 120, 124, fig. 10) hanno fornito recentemente dati di estremo interesse alcune sepolture nella necropoli a *domus de janas* in località Cungiau Su Tuttui o Sa Tutta in territorio di Piscinas, nella Sardegna sud-occidentale. A questi si vanno aggiungendo i dati di indagini in corso nella necropoli a domus de janas di Marchiana, in territorio di Villaperuccio. In quest'ultima località tra i materiali raccolti nei depositi rimossi da scavatori abusivi e nei lembi residui sono documentati frammenti fittili chiaramente pertinenti all'orizzonte Filigosa, oltre ad abbondanti materiali di cultura Monte Claro e Bonnanaro.

Ho già avuto occasione di presentare al Convegno sull'ipogeismo in Sardegna del 1994 parte del corredo della tomba 2 della necropoli di Piscinas (Usai, in stampa). In questa sede si presentano le forme più significative della stessa tomba 2 e della tomba 9. Il quadro formale in parte si riallaccia a quello di contesti già noti ma arricchisce notevolmente la tipologia delle forme vascolari, sottolineando nel contempo il distacco dalla precedente esperienza Sub-Ozieri e dalla successiva Abealzu.

Della necropoli ipogeica di Piscinas si conosceva già da tempo (Frau & Monticolo 1990: 32) una ampia tomba con una serie di coppelle presso l'angolo ovest dell'anticella. In anni recenti (1990 e 1994) sono state scavate integralmente due tombe (la n. 2 e la n. 9) e parte del deposito del corridoio della grande tomba prima richiamata (la n. 1). Sono state, inoltre, scavate diverse tombe a fossa di età tardo-romana, ricavate nello stesso pendio roccioso degli ipogei prenuragici.

Tutta l'area, peraltro, è ricca di emergenze archeologiche. Oltre che dalle tombe ipogeiche, l'età

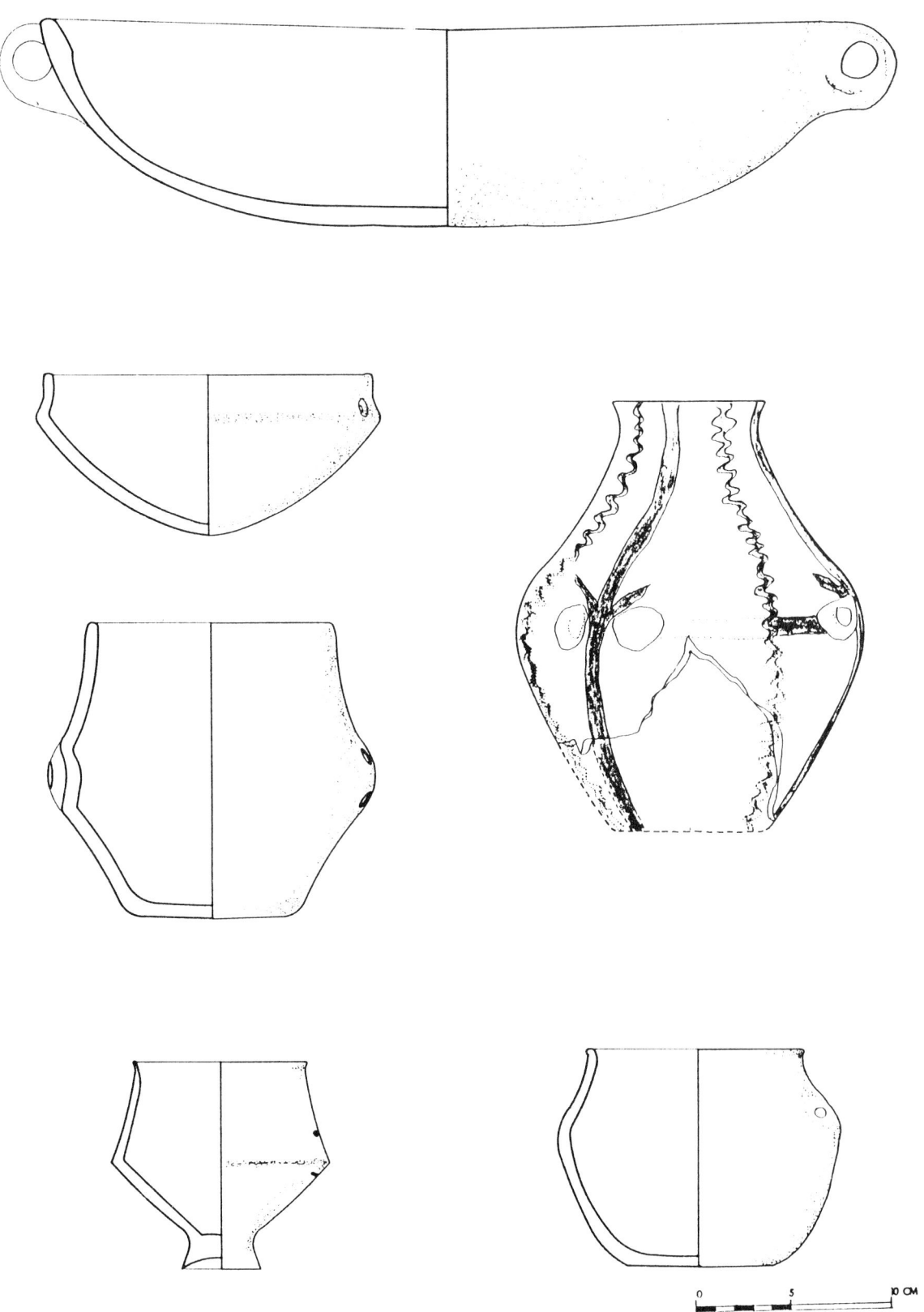

Fig. 23.1. Forme vascolari di facies Sub-Ozieri (elaborazione grafica Arch. Giancarlo Bernardo).

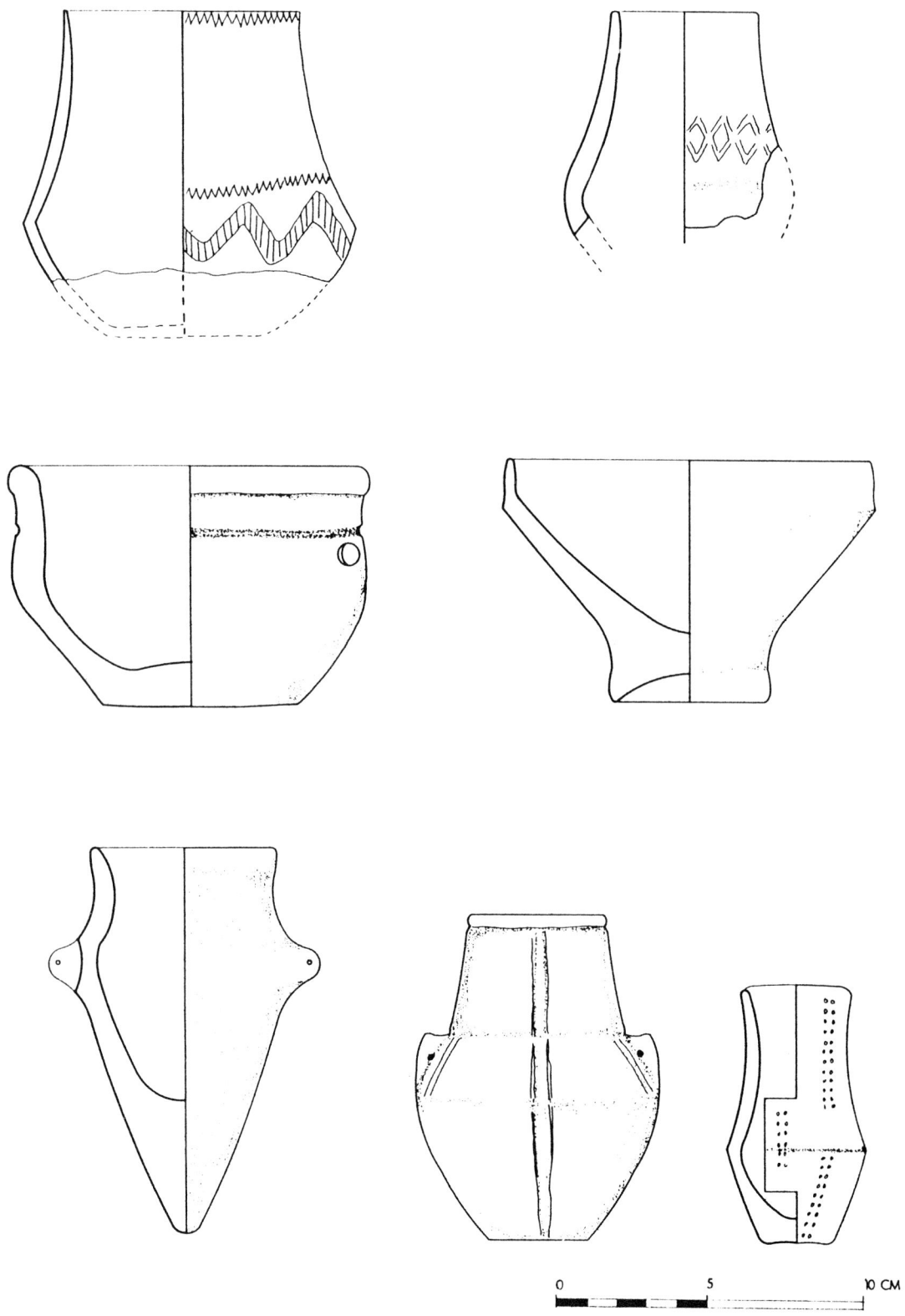

Fig. 23.2. Forme vascolari di facies Filigosa (elaborazione grafica Arch. Giancarlo Bernardo).

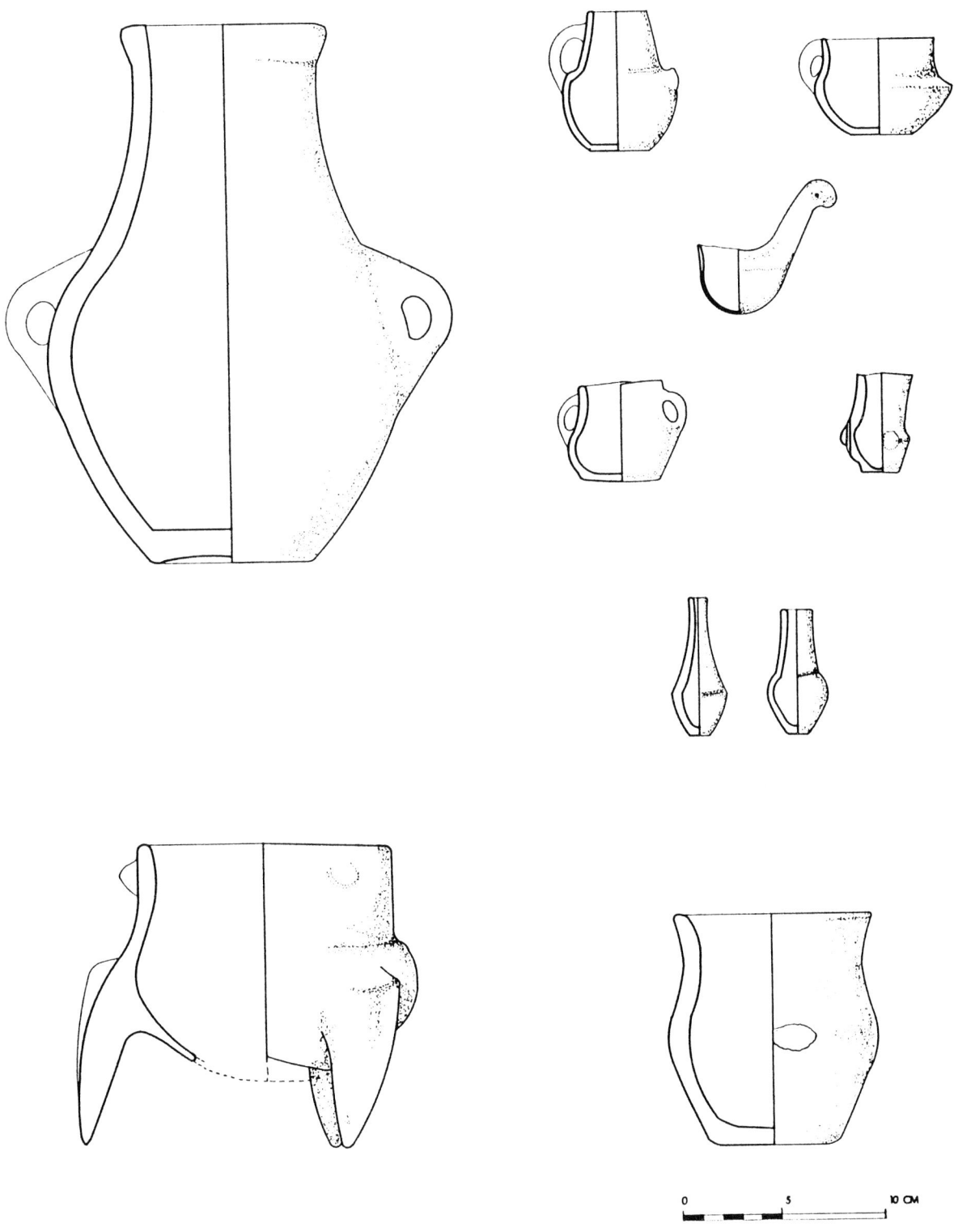

Fig. 23.3. Forme vascolari di facies Abealzu (elaborazione grafica Arch. Giancarlo Bernardo).

prenuragica è documentata da un insediamento di cultura Monte Claro, mentre l'occupazione del sito in età nuragica è attestata da un nuraghe, con il relativo villaggio, e da ben tre tombe di giganti. Almeno una di queste ultime è del tipo con stele a dentelli, poichè un frammento di tale stele è stato rinvenuto nei pressi della domu n. 1.

Gli inumati della tomba 2 con i relativi corredi sono stati deposti in due ambienti distinti, uno interno con motivi incisi sulle pareti e uno esterno che presenta un'integrazione delle pareti con lastre infisse a coltello (Usai, in stampa). I contesti dei due ambienti (Figg. 23.4–23.6) sono da riferire alla stessa cultura anche se può esserci un leggero divario cronologico nella realizzazione e utilizzazione dei due spazi sepolcrali. Come si vede, nella ceramica accanto ai piccoli vasi "a tulipa" (Figg. 23.4,4 e 23.4,6; Fig. 23.5, A e B) si trovano tazze carenate con perforazione verticale (Fig. 23.4,1), vasetti con collo più o meno distinto e con carena in genere arrotondata (Fig. 23.4,3 e 23.4,5), semplici tazze ad orlo rientrante (Fig. 23.4,2).

Nella tomba 2 le ceramiche si accompagnano ad una grande quantità di oggetti in metallo (argento e rame) (Fig. 23.5, C e D) a indicare una già notevole padronanza della nuova tecnica di produzione. L'abbondanza di oggetti in metallo rispetto ad altri contesti noti può spiegarsi con la localizzazione geografica del sito in un'area, il Sulcis, ricca di risorse minerarie poichè sembra difficile pensare ad un'importazione dall'esterno data la varietà e quantità di reperti (Usai, in stampa). Sono ben documentati, in particolare, gli oggetti d'ornamento in argento: si tratta di una serie di anelli a semplice fascia ma più frequentemente a spirale e di alcuni bracciali a sottile filo avvolto anch'esso a spirale. Gli anelli (Fig. 23.5, C) trovano precisi riscontri in altri contesti sepolcrali della Sardegna e più precisamente a Serra Cannigas di Villagreca (Atzeni 1985: fig. 7, tavv. IV e V), a Corte Noa di Laconi (Atzeni 1988b: 527) ed a S. Caterina di Pittinuri di Cuglieri (Cocco & Usai 1988a: fig. 14), mentre appaiono al momento privi di riscontri i sottili braccialetti. Tra i numerosi elementi in rame compaiono due accette piatte, diversi anelli e bracciali, un paio di pugnali frammentari e una serie di punte (?) a lama foliacea lunga e stretta e piccolo codolo a base arrotondata (Fig. 23.5, D). Le particolari caratteristiche e l'assoluta mancanza di confronti interni rende difficile capire al momento l'uso e la funzione di questi piccoli oggetti (pratica o rituale?). In altra sede (Usai in stampa) ho già proposto, anche se solo come ipotesi, un possibile confronto con i pendenti "en languette" del Midi francese (Costantini 1990–91: figg. 2 e 7) del tutto simili per forma e dimensioni ma provvisti di foro per la sospensione.

Per altro verso si registra in tutti i corredi di Piscinas finora emersi la pressochè totale assenza di industria litica in ossidiana mentre nella tomba 2 sono numerosissimi i vaghi di collana (Fig. 23.6). Oltre a quattro elementi in argento (Fig. 23.6, 3–6) sono stati rinvenuti 170 vaghi in pietra di varie forme ma tutti più o meno riconducibili ai tipi illustrati ai numeri 2, 7–27 di Figura 23.6. Gli elementi in pietra richiamano quelli documentati in numerosi contesti eneolitici della Toscana (Cocchi Genick 1989: 168–186; figg. 73 e 74), oltre agli analoghi esemplari in osso di Serra Cannigas di Villagreca (Atzeni 1985: tav. VI).

Il contesto vascolare della piccola tomba ipogeica n. 9 (Figg. 23.7–23.8) è solo in parte simile a quello illustrato in precedenza. Accanto alle forme a colletto (Fig. 23.7,2) e a "tulipa" (Fig. 23.7,3 e 23.7,4) compaiono numerose le fogge aperte a calotta sferica (Fig. 23.8, 2–6), spesso con orlo nettamente ingrossato e appiattito superiormente. Queste ultime potrebbero rappresentare la fase più tarda della cultura se, come sembra, trovano confronto con le forme documentate nel livello superiore del villaggio fortificato di San Giuseppe di Padria (Santoni 1976: 36; 1988a: 123).

Lo stesso aspetto delle superfici dei vasi della tomba 9, in genere ruvido e opaco e non lucido, con segni chiari di steccatura come nei vasi della tomba 2, potrebbe indicare una loro recenziorità.

Tra i vasi della tomba 9 appaiono numerosi frammenti pertinenti ad una o più forme del tipo illustrato al n. 1 di Figura 23.8. La foggia richiama i tegamoni biansati, documentati in numerosi contesti, ma conosciuti in forma quasi integra a Pirri-Terramaini (Usai 1987: fig. 4,1) e, con lievi varianti, a S'Arrideli di Uta (Sanna 1989: fig. 2), in contesti cioè di fase Sub-Ozieri. Identico è il trattamento della superficie interna, ben lisciata, e di quella esterna resa intenzionalmente ruvida. Negli esemplari di Piscinas sembrano, però, mancare totalmente le anse.

Confronti significativi possono essere istituiti tra alcuni fittili della già citata tomba IV di Locci Santus (Atzeni 1995: fig. 10, 18 e 21) e forme del tutto analoghe della tomba 9 (Fig. 23.8,2 e Fig. 23.7,2). Altri confronti precisi per i contesti funerari di Piscinas possono essere trovati soprattutto nelle poche sepolture sulcitane conosciute.

Significativa appare, in particolare l'ampia diffusione dei piccoli vasi "a tulipa" con orlo leggermente svasato e sbiecato all'interno, bassa carena più o meno arrotondata, muniti talvolta di piccole anse a tunnel talmente atrofizzate da sembrare semplici coppie di coppelle. Oltre che nelle due tombe di Piscinas (Fig. 23.4,4 e 23.4,6; Fig. 23.5, A e B; Fig. 23.7,3 e 23.7,4; Usai, in stampa) la forma si ritrova a Cannas di Sotto di Carbonia (Cocco & Usai 1988c; Santoni 1988b: fig. 2; Santoni & Usai 1995), Montessu di Villaperuccio (Atzeni 1987: fig. 10) e Pani Loriga di Santadi (Atzeni 1987: 42). Sagome analoghe si ritrovano su alcuni tripodi del villaggio di Fenosu in territorio di Palmas Arborea (Lugliè 1989: fig. 9). Per una tazza carenata della tomba 2 (Fig. 23.4,1) il confronto più stringente è con una forma del contesto Sub-Ozieri del villaggio di Cuccuru Ambudu di Serramanna (Frau 1991: fig. 19,4) anche se i fondi incavati e le perforazioni verticali alla carena sono molto comuni, oltre che a Cuccuru Ambudu (Frau 1991: fig. 27, 2–7) nella tomba

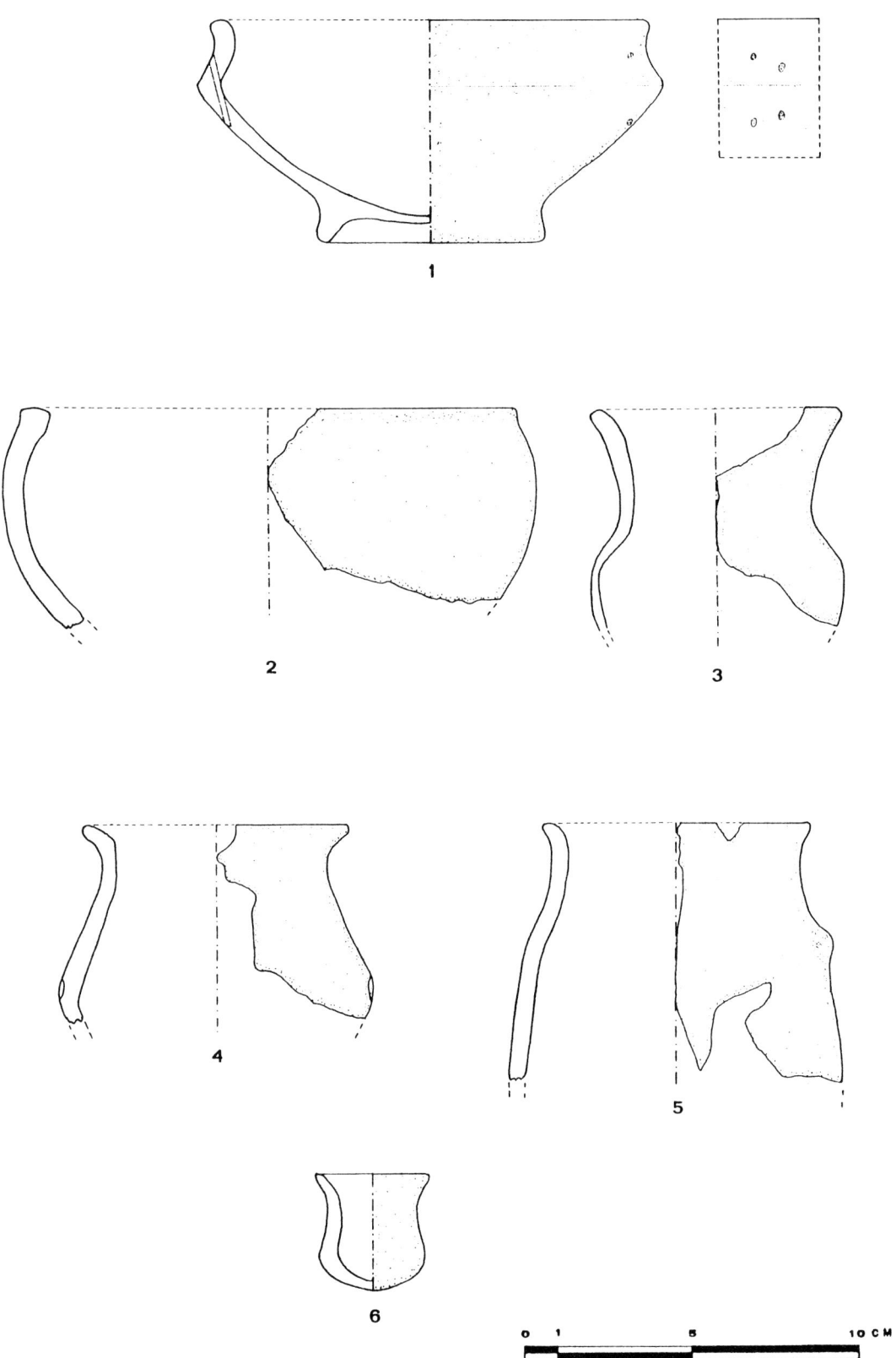

Fig. 23.4. Piscinas. Necropoli a domus de janas "Cungiau Sa Tutta". Forme vascolari della tomba 2 (disegni Eliseo Lai).

Fig. 23.5. Piscinas. Necropoli a domus de janas "Cungiau Sa Tutta". Vasi miniaturistici (A e B), monili in argento C) ed elementi in rame (D) della tomba 2 (fot. Soprintendenza Archeologica di Cagliari e Oristano).

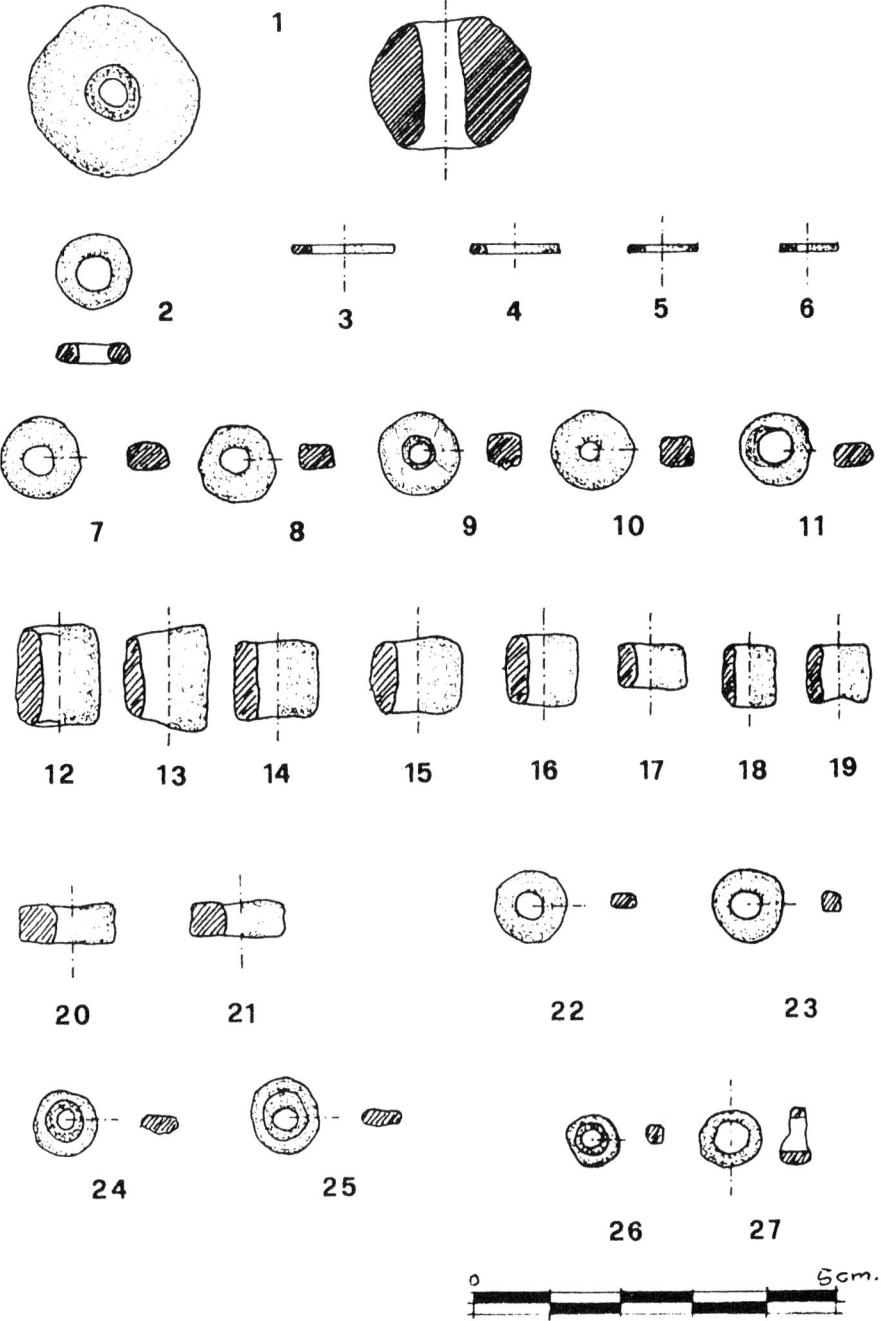

Fig. 23.6. Piscinas. Necropoli a domus de janas "Cungiau Sa Tutta". Fusaiola o vago in terracotta (1) ed elementi di collana in argento (3–6) e in pietra (2, 7–27) della tomba 2 (disegni Geom. Franco Mereu).

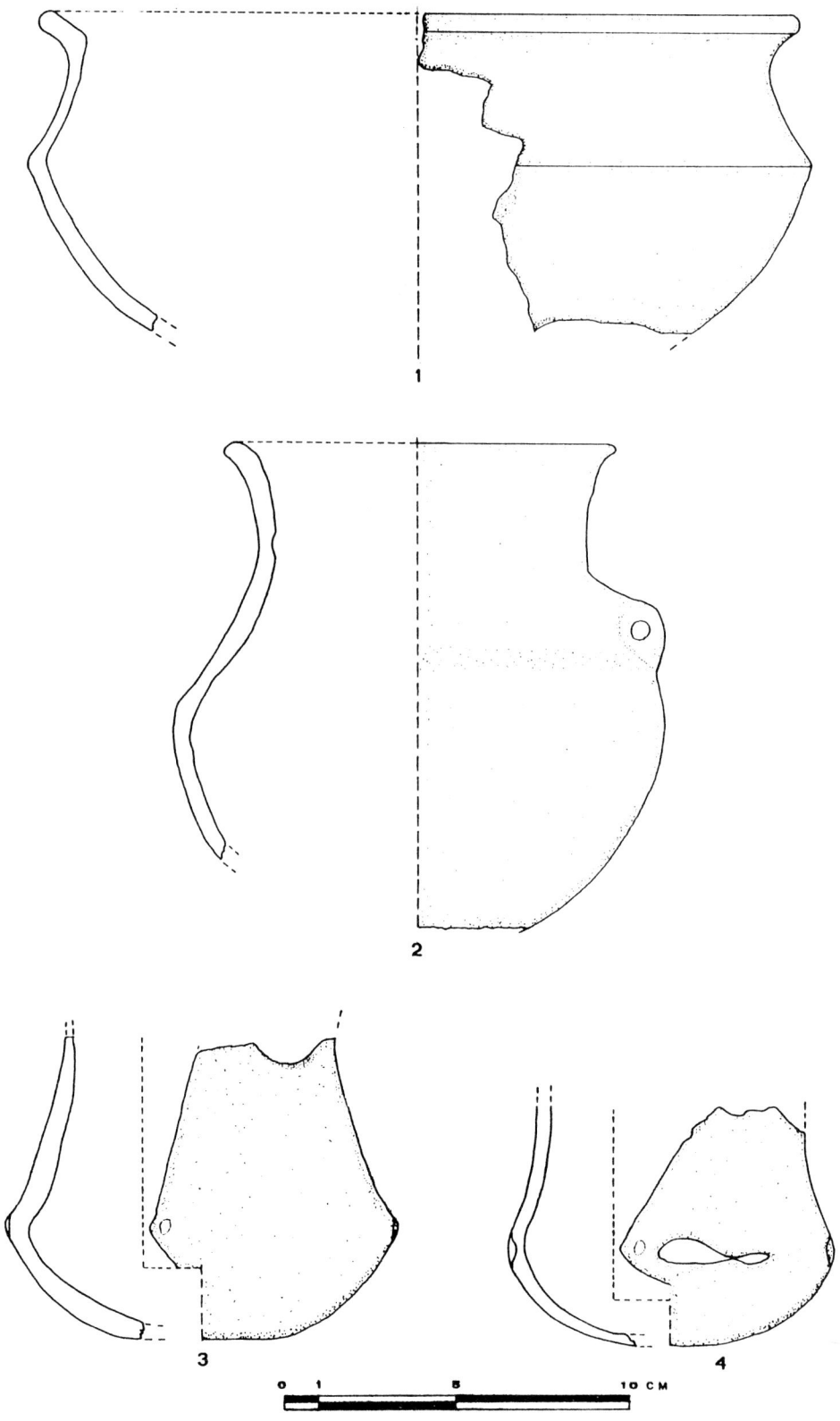

Fig. 23.7. Piscinas. Necropoli a domus de janas "Cungiau Sa Tutta". Forme vascolari della tomba 9 (disegni Eliseo Lai).

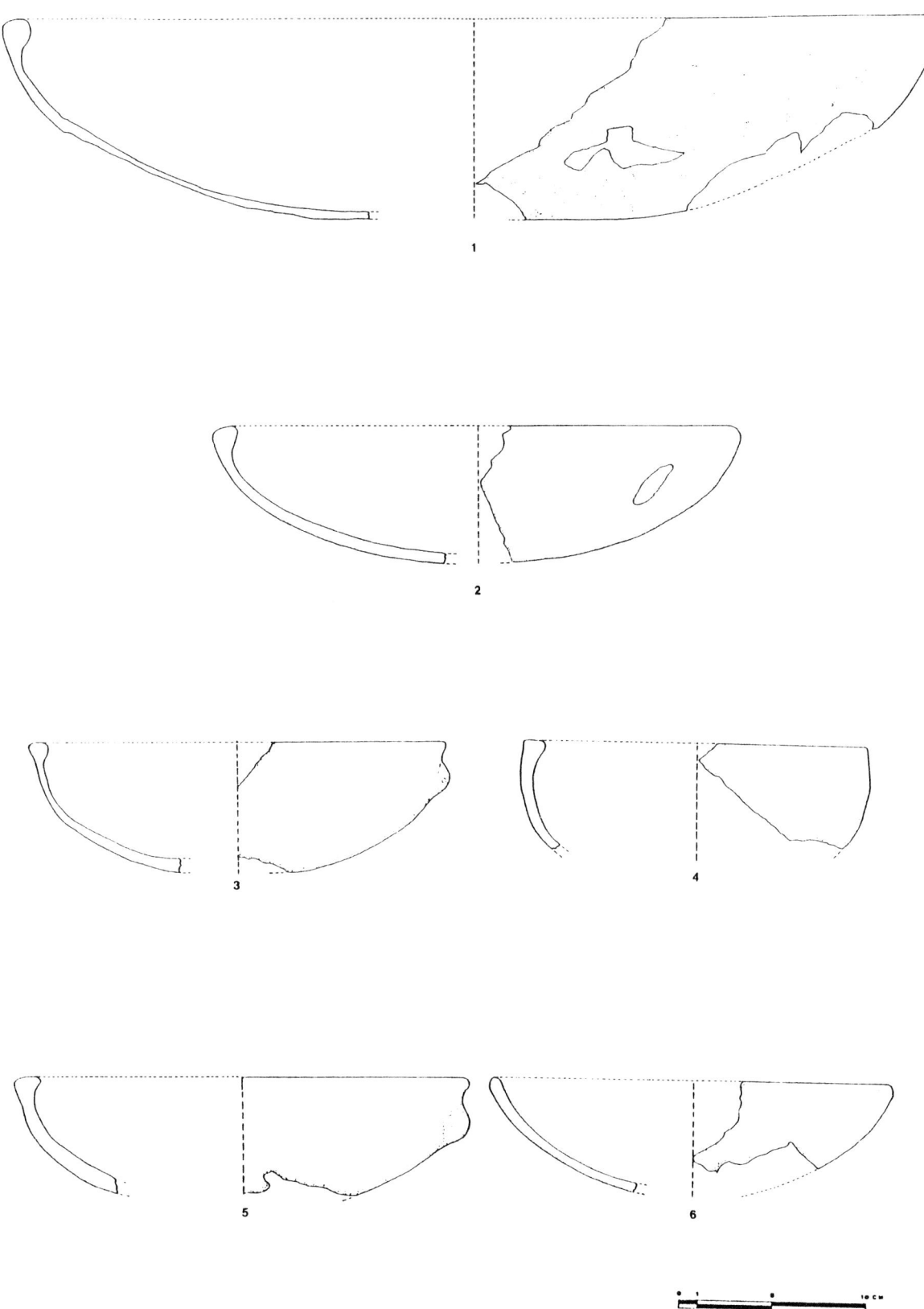

Fig. 23.8. Piscinas. Necropoli a domus de janas "Cungiau Sa Tutta". Forme vascolari della tomba 9 (disegni Eliseo Lai).

di S. Pedru di Alghero (Contu 1966: tavv. XII, XVIII e XIX). Confronti per alcune forme possono anche essere istituiti con i materiali della tomba I di Filigosa dove, oltre alle coppie di perforazioni alla carena (Foschi Nieddu 1986: tav. 18 A, 1-2) come a Figura 23.4,1, compaiono vasetti dei tipi illustrati ai numeri 3 e 5 della stessa tavola (Foschi Nieddu 1986: tav. 36). Più generici appaiono i confronti con i reperti più antichi di S. Caterina di Pittinurri (Cocco & Usai 1988a: figg. 8, 9 e 11; Cocco & Usai 1988b) dove, tra l'altro, è documentata la decorazione graffita, totalmente assente al momento a Piscinas e, sembrerebbe, in tutta l'area sulcitana.

Sulla base dei confronti, oltre che dai caratteri dei materiali, non sembra dubbia la pertinenza dei contesti di Piscinas alla cultura di Filigosa. Ai quadri formali già noti della cultura si aggiungono, però, come già detto, elementi nuovi che ho presentato solo in parte e che verranno quanto prima editi in maniera completa.

Dalle tombe del Sulcis finora conosciute, ma direi anche da quelle del Cagliaritano, in particolare la tomba A di Serra Cannigas (Atzeni 1985: 14-35) che pure presenta caratteri un po' particolari forse di transizione alla fase seguente, sembra emergere un quadro culturale Filigosa leggermente variato rispetto a quello noto nel centro (S. Caterina di Pittinurri, Filigosa di Macomer) e nel nord della Sardegna (S. Pedru di Alghero). Sembra trattarsi, ma bisogna certamente attendere maggiori dati, di facies locali caratterizzate da alcune differenze nell'ambito della produzione ceramica, in particolare la presenza o l'assenza di decorazione graffita, così come avverrà nella successiva cultura di Monte Claro.

Purtroppo sulle poche ossa conservatesi all'interno delle tombe 2 e 9 non è stato possibile, nonostante diversi tentativi, ottenere alcuna datazione al C14. Ciò a causa del sovrapporsi nell'area delle tombe preistoriche delle già citate sepolture di tarda età romana imperiale che hanno in parte intaccato e sconvolto le precedenti deposizioni.

Non è stato, per il momento, possibile individuare sequenze stratigrafiche nell'ambito della necropoli poiché le tombe 2 e 9 sono state utilizzate in un unico ambito culturale. Qualche indizio di una successione Filigosa-Monte Claro si coglie solo nella tomba 1 dove nel corridoio una congerie di frammenti Monte Claro sembra sovrapporsi a uno straterello con resti Filigosa ma la situazione è molto confusa e compromessa dalla lunga frequentazione successiva dell'area e lo scavo non è stato ancora ultimato.

Per completare il quadro delle nuove acquisizioni presento, infine, un altro contesto inedito rinvenuto in località Mind'e Gureu, in territorio di Gesturi. L'insieme vascolare (Figg. 23.9-23.10), rinvenuto fortuitamente ma chiaramente pertinente ad una sepoltura della quale permane anche un cranio, rientra appieno nella cultura Abealzu. Le forme sono tutte di dimensioni piuttosto ridotte ma con pareti spesse. Come si vede (Fig. 23.9,1 e 23.9,4; Fig. 23.10,5 e 23.10,6) sono ben documentate le

caratteristiche anse opposte a piccola bugna conica che richiamano i contesti noti del Sassarese, in particolare quelli di Molimentos di Benetutti (Ferrarese Ceruti 1967: fig. 24), Sos Laccheddos di Osilo (Basoli 1989: fig. 30) e Filigosa di Macomer. Appare significativa la presenza in quest'ultimo contesto di vasi (Foschi Nieddu 1986: tav. 13,3 e tav. 33b, 3) del tutto simili a quelli di Gesturi (Fig. 23.10,2 e 23.10,5) a confermare il succedersi delle due fasi culturali di Filigosa e Abealzu anche nel contesto sepolcrale di Macomer. Confronti possono anche essere istituiti con i corredi funerari delle tombe megalitiche di Corte Noa e Masone Perdu nel vicino territorio di Laconi (Atzeni 1988b: 526–527) mentre più generiche appaiono le somiglianze con i materiali di Serra Cannigas di Villagreca (Atzeni 1985: figg. 4-5, tav. II) e delle deposizioni più recenti della domu di S. Caterina di Pittinuri (Cocco & Usai 1988a: figg. 6-7).

Riassumendo quanto detto in precedenza e tentando, anche grazie ai nuovi dati materiali acquisiti, di dare, sulla base di quanto proposto già dai diversi studiosi, una successione culturale dei contesti più significativi, pur riconoscendo che la situazione è troppo complessa e ancora non sufficientemente nota per consentire quadri culturali strettamente definiti e completi, si propone il seguente schema preliminare.

Fase Sub-Ozieri

Caratterizzata, come già detto, nell'ambito del repertorio fittile dalla scomparsa quasi totale della decorazione e dalla presenza di ceramica figulina in argilla chiara liscia o con motivi sovradipinti, documenta un utilizzo dei primi e più semplici oggetti in metallo (Ugas 1993: 23). I contesti più caratteristici sono quelli di Pirri-Terramaini (Cagliari) (Usai 1987), Su Coddu (Selargius) (Ugas et al. 1989; Ugas et al. 1989a), Cuccuru Ambudu (Serramanna) (Frau 1991: 103–106), la sacca 4 di Is Arridelis di Uta (Sanna 1989: figg. 4-5) ai quali si affiancano o più verosimilmente precedono i contesti di Cuccuru S'Arriu di Cabras (Santoni 1991) e della sacca n. 3 di Is Aridelis di Uta (Sanna 1989: figg. 1-2), che appaiono più legati alla precedente cultura Ozieri, e forse lo stanziamento dell'area del Cronicario di Sant'Antioco (Usai 1990: 111–114). Sarei propensa a collocare nella fase più antica del Sub-Ozieri anche il contesto della capanna 160 di Monte Olladiri di Monastir (Ugas 1989: 240–243) nel quale ai frammenti con decorazione dipinta del tipi di Terramaini e di Su Coddu si accompagnano fittili con decorazioni del tipo documentati a Is Arridelis e a Cuccuru S'Arriu, come ha già avuto modo di sottolineare V. Santoni (1991: 26).

La differenziazione con le precedenti esperienze si coglie in ambito di villaggio anche nella stesura planimetrica degli spazi abitativi, in particolare a Su Coddu di Selargius (Ugas 1989a: 7-20). A questa fase si potrebbe collegare la realizzazione del primo santuario di Monte d'Accoddi mentre è difficile individuare una

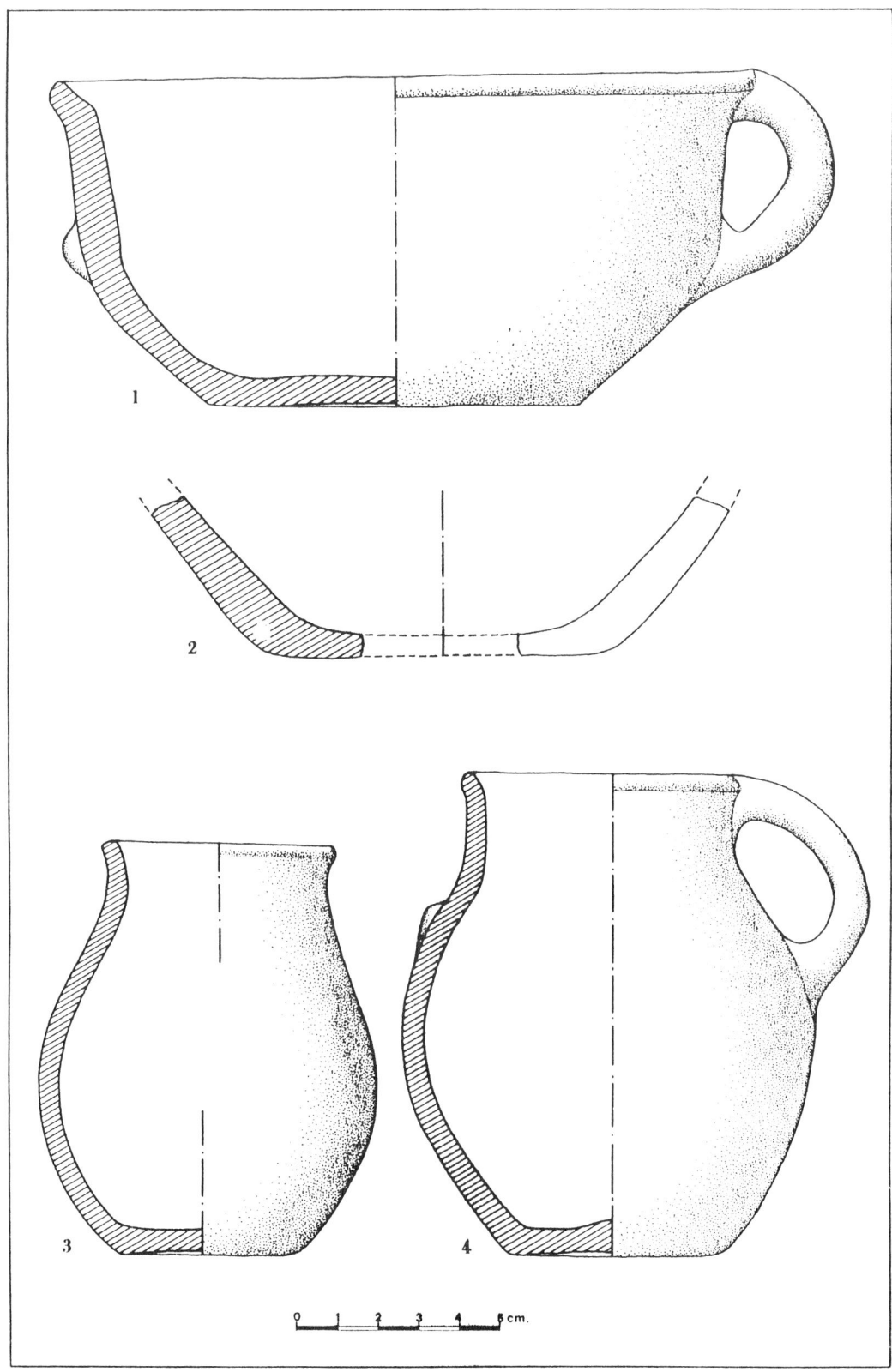

Fig. 23.9. Gesturi. Loc. Mind'e Gureu. Forme vascolari da contesto sepolcrale (disegni Valentino Tuveri).

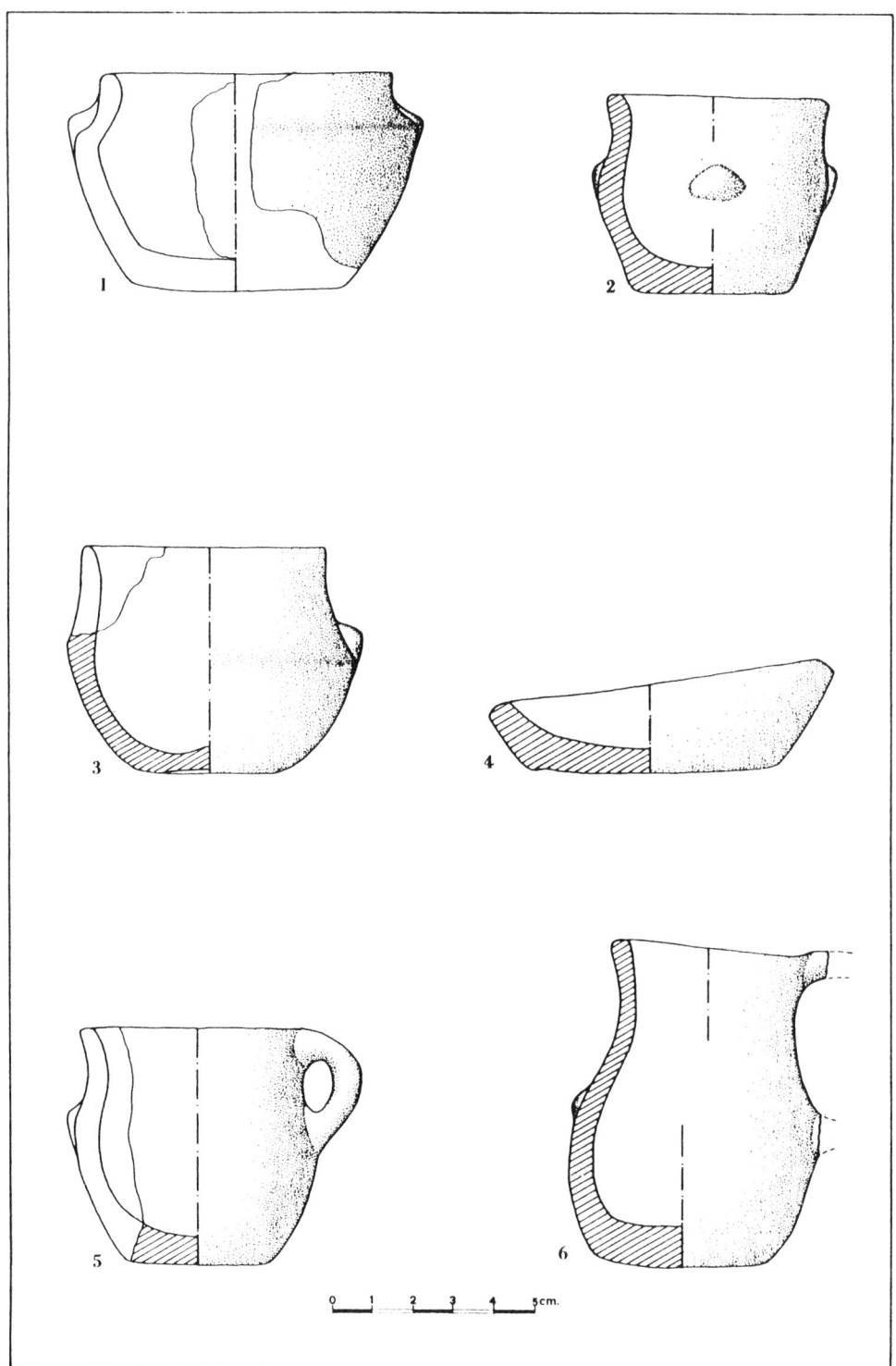

Fig. 23.10. Gesturi. Loc. Mind'e Gureu. Forme vascolari da contesto sepolcrale (disegni Valentino Tuveri).

precisa tipologia sepolcrale per questo ambito culturale dato che l'unico corredo noto, quello di Perda Lada di Decimoputzu, è stato rinvenuto in un sepolcro realizzato nella precedente cultura Ozieri (Ugas 1990: 21).

Fase Filigosa

Caratterizzata nella Sardegna centro-settentrionale da ceramica graffita come a Santu Pedru di Alghero (Contu 1966), Filigosa di Macomer (Foschi Nieddu 1986), S. Caterina di Pittinuri (Cocco & Usai 1988a; 1988b), mostra nella parte meridionale dell'isola fittili con semplici decorazioni a linee incise documentati a Serra Cannigas di Villagreca (Atzeni 1985: tav. I, fig. 3), Cannas di Sotto di Carbonia (Santoni & Usai 1995) o del tutto lisci con vasi a "tulipa" (Montessu di Villaperuccio: Atzeni 1987: fig. 10; Cungiau Sa Tutta di Piscinas; Cannas di Sotto di Carbonia: Santoni & Usai 1995), tazze o scodelle carenate o a porzione di sfera con orlo ingrossato (Cungiau Sa Tutta di Piscinas; Locci Santus di San Giovanni Suergiu: Atzeni 1995: fig. 10).

Nell'ambito dell'industria litica scheggiata, in questa fase ma già anche in quella precedente, si assiste ad un impoverimento della litotecnica. Infatti, pur continuando la produzione di punte di freccia in ossidiana e, in misura molto minoritaria, in selce, queste appaiono in genere di dimensioni minori rispetto agli esemplari precedenti di ambito Ozieri e non si accompagnano di solito agli altri utensili comuni nei contesti del Neolitico Recente in Sardegna, come si nota in particolare a S. Caterina di Pittinuri (Cocco & Usai 1988a: fig. 12; 1988b: 523) e a Serra Cannigas di Villagreca (Atzeni 1985: fig. 7, 1–10).

Si constata una presenza consistente di oggetti in rame e argento che fanno presupporre un'attività metallurgica locale, fornita già di buone capacità tecniche (Ugas 1993: 26).

Sembrano essere caratteristiche di questa fase, oltre alle varie espressioni di arte schematica e del megalitismo (Tanda 1988; Atzeni 1988a), le tombe con fossetta o coppelle nell'anticella come a suo tempo ipotizzato da V. Santoni (1976: 26–27) e come sembrano documentare la tomba di S. Caterina di Pittinuri (Cocco & Usai 1988a: 15), la tomba I di Filigosa (Macomer) (Foschi Nieddu 1986: 14) e la tomba 1 di Piscinas che non hanno restituito materiali di cultura Ozieri.

Per quanto riguarda gli abitati propenderei a riferire alla fase in esame il contesto di Fenosu di Palmas Arborea (Lugliè 1989; 1995: 72–73; figg. 2–5), nonchè il villaggio fortificato di Padria (Santoni 1988a: 121–123).

Fase Abealzu

Alle caratteristiche della ceramica già sottolineate precedentemente si accompagnano per il momento pochi altri tratti peculiari a causa delle limitate conoscenze. Va sottolineato per altro il rinvenimento in sepolture di oggetti in rame e argento (Corte Noa di Laconi: Atzeni 1988b: 527) e l'attestazione di asce a martello in pietra levigata (Contu 1988a: fig. 2, 11; Basoli 1989: fig. 30), oltre a piccole punte di freccia in ossidiana (Atzeni 1988b: 527).

In ambito abitativo sono significative le strutture con muri rettilinei in rozze pietre ed ambienti multipli documentate a Monte d'Accoddi (Contu 1988a: 445–446; 1988b: 536–537).

A questa ricostruzione possono fare da supporto i confronti con la Sicilia dove alla sostanziale unità territoriale del neolitico, caratterizzato dalla cultura di Diana, si sostituisce a partire dall'Eneolitico antico un'ampia distinzione in facies locali in parte contemporanee, in parte successive con zone di incontro tra diversi aspetti (Tusa 1992: 237–240). Per altro verso sembra che proprio in Sicilia si possano trovare i maggiori confronti per le ceramiche della fase Sub-Ozieri in particolare ma anche, seppure meno consistenti, per la fase Filigosa. I maggiori riscontri si hanno nell'ambito della ceramica dipinta negli stili del Conzo e Conca d'Oro e nelle forme di ollette o piccoli vasi a colletto documentati in quest'ultima cultura ma anche nella facies di S. Cono-Piano Notaro (Tusa 1992: 241–273). Le recenti datazioni di Monte d'Accoddi, che per la cultura di Sub-Ozieri e/o Filigosa si collocano tutte attorno al 2.900–2.800 a.C., ben si accordano, peraltro, con quelle ipotizzate per il più antico Eneolitico siciliano (Tinè 1992: 116–117; Tusa 1992: 230–231).

A ben guardare gli stessi vasi a fiasco di ambito Abealzu richiamano per la forma slanciata più fogge siciliane della Conca d'Oro (Tusa 1992: fig. 17,6) che non forme eneolitiche di Rinaldone (Negroni Catacchio 1988: fig. 12), a confermare rapporti tra le due isole per tutto l'Eneolitico, forse da collegare all'espansione della tecnica metallurgica dall'Oriente.

Bibliografia

Atzeni, E. 1985. Tombe eneolitiche nel Cagliaritano. In *Studi in onore di Giovanni Lilliu per il suo settantesimo compleanno*, 11–49. Cagliari.

Atzeni, E. 1987. *La preistoria del Sulcis-Iglesiente*. Cagliari.

Atzeni, E. 1988a. Megalitismo e arte. In Atzeni, E., Contu, E. & Ferrarese Ceruti, M.L., L'età del rame nell'Italia insulare: la Sardegna. *Atti del Congresso Internazionale "L'Età del Rame in Europa," Viareggio, 15–18 ottobre 1987*. Rassegna di Archeologia 7: 449–465.

Atzeni, E. 1988b. Tombe megalitiche di Laconi (Nuoro). *Atti del Congresso Internazionale "L'Età del Rame in Europa", Viareggio, 15–18 ottobre 1987*. Rassegna di Archeologia 7: 526–527.

Atzeni, E. 1990. Le premesse: il mondo prenuragico. In *La civiltà nuragica*, 9–34. Electa, Milano.

Atzeni, E. 1995. La "cultura del vaso campaniforme" nella necropoli di Locci-Santus (S. Giovanni Suergiu). In V. Santoni (a cura di), *Carbonia e il Sulcis. Archeologia e territorio*, 117–143. Editrice S'Alvure, Oristano.

Bafico, S. & Rossi, G. 1989. Le ceramiche del Saggio XXIII di Monte d'Accoddi. In Tinè, S., Bafico, S., Rossi, G. & Mannoni, T., *Monte d'Accoddi e la cultura di Ozieri*. In Campus, L.D. (a cura di), *La cultura di Ozieri. Problematiche e nuove acquisizioni. Atti del I convegno di studi (Ozieri, gennaio 1986-aprile 1987)*, 27–29. Il Torchietto, Ozieri.

Basoli, P. 1989. L'età prenuragica e l'età nuragica. In *Sassari le origini*, 15–48. Edizioni Gallizzi, Sassari.

Cocchi Genick, D. 1989. Analisi dei materiali. In Cocchi Genick, D. & Grifoni Cremonesi, R., *L'età del rame in Toscana*, 97–211. Viareggio.

Cocco, D. & Usai, L. 1988a. Un monumento preistorico nel territorio di Cornus. In *Ampsicora e il territorio di Cornus. Atti del II Convegno sull'archeologia romana e altomedievale nell'Oristanese (Cuglieri - 22 dicembre 1985)*, 13–24. Editrice Scorpione, Taranto.

Cocco, D. & Usai, L. 1988b. Tomba ipogeica di facies "Abealzu-Filigosa". *Atti del Congresso Internazionale "L'Età del Rame in Europa", Viareggio, 15–18 ottobre 1987*. Rassegna di Archeologia 7: 522–523.

Cocco, D. & Usai, L. 1988c. Necropoli ipogeica in località Cannas di Sotto (Carbonia-CA). In *Museo Villa Sulcis*, 31–33. Cagliari.

Contu, E. 1966. La tomba dei vasi tetrapodi in loc. Santu Pedru (Alghero-SS). *Monumenti Antichi dei Lincei 47*. Accademia Nazionale dei Lincei, Roma.

Contu, E. 1988a. Problematica ed inquadramento culturale. In Atzeni, E., Contu, E. & Ferrarese Ceruti, M.L., L'età del rame nell'Italia insulare: la Sardegna. *Atti del Congresso Internazionale "L'Età del Rame in Europa," Viareggio, 15–18 ottobre 1987*. Rassegna di Archeologia 7: 441–448.

Contu, E. 1988b. Monte d'Accoddi (Sassari). *Atti del Congresso Internazionale "L'Età del Rame in Europa," Viareggio, 15–18 ottobre 1987*. Rassegna di Archeologia 7: 536–537.

Costantini G. 1990–91. Les productions métalliques du groupe des Treilles et leur répartition dans le Midi de la France. In *Le Chalcolithique en Languedoc. Archéologie en Languedoc. Colloque International Hommage au D'Jean Arnal*, 59–66.

Ferrarese Ceruti, M.L. 1967. Domus de janas in località Molimentos (Benetutti-Sassari). *Bullettino di Paletnologia Italiana*, 69–135.

Foschi Nieddu, A. 1986. *La tomba I di Filigosa (Macomer-Nuoro)*. Coop. Grafica Nuorese, Nuoro.

Frau, M. 1991. Caratteristiche culturali ed elementi inediti dal villaggio preistorico di Cuccuru Ambudu (Serramanna-Cagliari). *Studi Sardi* 29 (1990–1991): 95–161.

Frau, M. & Monticolo, R. 1990. *Sulcis. Guida Archeologica*. Editrice Arte e Natura, Firenze.

Lai, G. 1989. Struttura 43. In Ugas, G., Usai, L., Nuvoli, M.P., Lai, G. & Marras, M.G., Nuovi dati sull'insediamento di Su Coddu. In Campus, L.D. (a cura di), *La cultura di Ozieri. Problematiche e nuove acquisizioni. Atti del I convegno di studio. Ozieri, gennaio 1986-aprile 1987*, 261–267. Il Torchietto, Ozieri.

Lo Schiavo, F. 1992. Monte d'Accoddi: una riflessione. In Tinè, S. & Traverso, A. (eds.), *Monte d'Accoddi: 10 anni di nuovi scavi*, 118–123. Istituto Italiano di Archeologia Sperimentale, Genova.

Lugliè, C. 1989. Ceramiche eneolitiche dall'insediamento di Fenosu-Palmas Arborea (Oristano). *Studi Sardi* 28 (1988–89): 73–100.

Lugliè, C. 1995. Forme ceramiche della prima età dei metalli c della cultura di Monte Claro nell'Oristanese. In *La ceramica racconta la storia*, 71–99. Editrice S'Alvure, Oristano.

Moravetti, A. 1992. La Tomba II della necropoli ipogeica di S. Pedru (Alghero-Sassari). In *Sardinia Antiqua*, 97–122. Edizioni Della Torre, Cagliari.

Negroni Catacchio, N. 1988. La cultura di Rinaldone. In Cazzella, A., Cocchi Genick, D., Del Lucchese, A., Grifoni Cremonesi, R., Maggi, R., Moscoloni, M., Negroni Catacchio, N., Radi, G., Sarti, L. & Vigliardi, A., L'età del rame nell'Italia centrale, *Atti del Congresso Internazionale "L'Età del Rame in Europa," Viareggio, 15–18 ottobre 1987*. Rassegna di Archeologia 7: 348–362.

Sanna, R. 1989. Il villaggio di Is Arridelis - Uta. In Campus, L.D. (a cura di), *La cultura di Ozieri. Problematiche e nuove acquisizioni. Atti del I convegno di studio. Ozieri, gennaio 1986-aprile 1987*, 231–238. Il Torchietto, Ozieri.

Santoni, V. 1976. Nota preliminare sulla tipologia delle grotticelle funerarie in Sardegna. *Archivio Storico Sardo* 30: 3–49.

Santoni, V., Atzeni, E., Forresu, R., Giorgetti, S., Mongiu, M.A., Sebis, S., Siddu, A. & Tore, G. 1982. Cabras, Cuccuru S'Arriu. Nota preliminare di scavo (1978, 1979, 1980). *Rivista di Studi Fenici* 10: 103–127.

Santoni, V. 1988a. I materiali pre-protostorici. In Galli, F., Santoni, V. & Tore, G., Padria. Lilliu, G. (ed.), *L'Antiquarium arborense e i civici musei archeologici della Sardegna*, 118–123. Amilcare Pizzi Editore, Milano.

Santoni, V. 1988b. Il repertorio preistorico e protostorico. In Santoni, V., Bartoloni, P. & Bondì, S.F., Carbonia. In Lilliu, G. (ed.), *L'Antiquarium arborense e i civici musei archeologici della Sardegna*, 215–220. Amilcare Pizzi Editore, Milano.

Santoni, V. 1989. L'Eneolitico. In Atzeni, E. & Santoni, V., L'età prenuragica. Il Neolitico. L'Eneolitico. Santoni, V. (ed.), *Il museo archeologico nazionale di Cagliari*, 51–56. Amilcare Pizzi Editore, Milano.

Santoni, V. 1991. Cabras - Cuccuru S'Arriu. L'orizzonte Eneolitico Sub-Ozieri. *Quaderni della Soprintendenza Archeologica per le Provincie di Cagliari e Oristano* 8: 15–47.

Santoni, V. & Usai, L. 1995. Domus de janas in località Cannas di Sotto (Carbonia). In Santoni, V. (a cura di), *Sulcis. Archeologia e territorio*, 51–82. Edizioni S'Alvure, Oristano.

Tanda, G. 1988. L'arte dell'età del Rame in Sardegna. *Atti del Congresso Internazionale "L'Età del Rame in Europa," Viareggio, 15–18 ottobre 1987*. Rassegna di Archeologia 7: 541–543.

Tinè, S. 1992. La cronologia assoluta di Monte d'Accoddi. In Tinè, S. & Traverso, A. (eds.), *Monte d'Accoddi: 10 anni di nuovi scavi*, 115–117. Istituto Italiano di Archeologia Sperimentale, Genova.

Trump, D.H. 1983. *La Grotta di Filiestru a Mara (SS)*. Quaderni della Soprintendenza ai Beni Archeologici per le Province di Sassari e Nuoro 13. Dessì, Sassari.

Tusa, S. 1992. *La Sicilia nella preistoria*. Sellerio, Palermo.

Tykot, R.H. 1994. Radiocarbon dating and absolute chronology in Sardinia and Corsica. In Skeates, R. & Whitehouse, R. (eds.), *Radiocarbon Dating and Italian Prehistory*, 115–145. Archaeological Monographs of the British School at Rome 8 and Accordia Specialist Studies on Italy 3. Accordia Research Centre, London.

Ugas, G. 1989. Premessa e brevi cenni sulla ceramica dipinta neolitica e protocalcolitica sarda. In Ugas, G., Usai, L., Nuvoli, M.P., Lai, G. & Marras, M.G., Nuovi dati sull'insediamento di Su Coddu. In Campus, L.D. (a cura di), *La cultura di Ozieri. Problematiche e nuove acquisizioni. Atti del I convegno di studio. Ozieri, gennaio 1986-aprile 1987*, 239–243. Il Torchietto, Ozieri.

Ugas, G. 1989a. Caratteristiche generali dell'insediamento. In Ugas, G., Lai, G. & Usai, L., L'insediamento prenuragico di Su Coddu (Selargius-CA). Notizia preliminare sulle campagne di scavo 1981-1984. *Nuovo Bullettino Archeologico Sardo* 2: 7–20.

Ugas, G. 1990. *La tomba dei guerrieri di Decimoputzu*. Norax 1. Edizioni Della Torre, Cagliari.

Ugas, G. 1993. La metallurgia del piombo, dell'argento e dell'oro nella Sardegna prenuragica e nuragica. In Kirova, T.K. (ed.), *L'uomo e le miniere in Sardegna*, 24–35. Edizioni Della Torre, Cagliari.

Ugas, G., Usai, L., Nuvoli, M.P., Lai, G. & Marras, M.G. 1989. Nuovi dati sull'insediamento di Su Coddu. In Campus, L.D. (a cura di), *La cultura di Ozieri. Problematiche e nuove acquisizioni. Atti del I convegno di studio. Ozieri, gennaio 1986-aprile 1987*, 239–278. Il Torchietto, Ozieri.

Ugas, G., Lai, G. & Usai, L. 1989a. L'insediamento prenuragico di Su Coddu (Selargius-CA). Notizia preliminare sulle campagne di scavo 1981–1984. *Nuovo Bullettino Archeologico Sardo* 2: 7–40.

Usai, L. 1987. Il villaggio di età eneolitica di Terramaini presso Pirri (Cagliari). In *Atti del IV Convegno Nazionale di Preistoria e Protostoria, Pescia 8–9 dicembre 1984*, 175–196. Pescia.

Usai, L. 1989. Il gruppo delle capanne 16 e il pozzo 16 F. In Ugas, G., Lai, G. & Usai, L., L'insediamento prenuragico di Su Coddu (Selargius-CA). Notizia preliminare sulle campagne di scavo 1981–1984. *Nuovo Bullettino Archeologico Sardo* 2: 30–36.

Usai, L. 1990. La ceramica preistorica dell'area del Cronicario. *Rivista di Studi Fenici* 18: 103–123.

Usai, L., in stampa. La tomba n. 2 di "Cungiau Su Tuttui" in territorio di Piscinas (Cagliari). Nota preliminare. In *Atti del Congresso Internazionale "L'ipogeismo nel Mediterraneo. Origini, Sviluppo, Quadri Culturali (Sassari-Oristano - 23–28 maggio 1994)*.

24. La tipologia come strumento per lo studio di alcuni problemi dell'Età del Rame in Sardegna

Maria Grazia Melis

L'avvento dell'età del Rame in Sardegna, pur apportando fondamentali innovazioni nell'economia e nella società prenuragiche, non sembra aver dato origine a mutamenti repentini ma a graduali trasformazioni apparentemente senza soluzione di continuità. L'uso del metallo, le cui prime esperienze s'individuano in seno alla cultura di Ozieri, acquista una graduale importanza senza sostituirsi all'industria su pietra, che conserva un ruolo importante; tuttavia è la ceramica che consente di seguire il lento evolversi delle "culture" sul *philum* dell'Ozieri.

Oggetto del presente lavoro è uno studio sistematico della produzione fittile relativa alle fasi definite nella letteratura archeologica Sub-Ozieri, Filigosa e Abealzu, che ereditano alcuni elementi della cultura di Ozieri, modificando il repertorio sia nelle forme sia nelle tematiche decorative. Il metodo utilizzato è lo studio tipologico dei materiali editi e di alcuni elementi inediti, articolato in sei fasi:

- Raccolta bibliografica;
- Documentazione grafica;
- Tipologia;
- Analisi statistica dei dati quantitativi e qualitativi;
- Elaborazione di una tabella di associazione tra siti di rinvenimento e tipi ceramici;
- Confronti e cronologia.

Si presenteranno in questa sede i risultati dell'analisi tipologica e la tabella di associazione.

Introduzione

La storia degli studi in questo campo è scandita dagli importanti scavi e ricerche succedutisi nel corso dei decenni; a questi lavori si farà un breve accenno allo scopo di approfondire l'evoluzione della materia e i diversi orientamenti che tuttora distinguono i vari autori. Dopo i primi importanti ritrovamenti a Cagliari (grotte di San Bartolomeo, Sant'Elia) e nel Sassarese (Anghelu Ruju-Alghero e San Michele-Ozieri) numerose indagini arricchirono il quadro dell'orizzonte San Michele, attribuito inizialmente all'Eneolitico. Le prime datazioni al C14 e l'importante stratigrafia della grotta di Sa Ucca de su Tintirriolu-Mara consentirono una migliore definizione cronologica ed un'attribuzione al Neolitico Recente, opinione, quest'ultima non condivisa da qualche autore, ancora sostenitore dell'inquadramento nell'ambito dell'età del Rame (Santoni 1982: 109–110; 1992; Tinè *et al.* 1992: 31–32). Quanto alle fasi successive sono note le differenti posizioni relative al Filigosa e all'Abealzu (Contu 1965: 103, n. 23; Ferrarese Ceruti 1967: 130–132; Lilliu 1967: 90), da alcuni studiosi ritenuti elementi di una stessa cultura, da altri due culture distinte. Quest'ultima ipotesi era basata sulla presenza delle forme carenate e della ceramica graffita nel Filigosa e sulla prevalenza dei vasi a fiasco nell'Abealzu. In tempi più recenti il quadro si è notevolmente arricchito grazie ai ritrovamenti (tra i più importanti) dei contesti di Terramaini-Pirri (Usai 1987a) e Su Coddu-Selargius (Ugas *et al.* 1989a; 1989b), che hanno evidenziato la presenza di un nuovo aspetto definito "Sub-Ozieri", caratterizzato dal persistere delle forme ceramiche Ozieri quasi del tutto prive di decorazione e da un'incipiente metallurgia. In questo campo si registrano delle novità sia nel campo delle sintassi decorative, sia nella forte incidenza dell'uso della tecnica della pittura.

I materiali

I reperti esaminati, circa 1300, sono in prevalenza editi e provengono da scavi, indagini di superficie, recuperi in seguito a scavi clandestini, ritrovamenti nel corso della realizzazione di opere pubbliche, collezioni private. Tra i materiali inediti rivestono un grande interesse quelli

---

Maria Grazia Melis, Dipartimento di Scienze Umanistiche e dell'Antichità, Università di Sassari, Piazza Conte di Moriana 8, 07100 Sassari, Sardegna, Italia

rinvenuti nella capanna p-s, o *capanna dello stregone*, del santuario di Monte d'Accoddi presso Sassari (Contu 1984; 1992), appartenenti ad un contesto unitario intatto attribuito alla seconda fase del santuario. A questi si aggiungono alcuni manufatti inediti provenienti dagli scavi di Loria e Trump nella grotta di Sa Ucca de Su Tintirriolu-Mara (Loria & Trump 1978) che si discostano sia dall'Ozieri classico sia dal Monte Claro, relativi alle trincee F2, I4, M2, C, B2, L2, M2. Sono inoltre stati inseriti nel lavoro alcuni vasetti miniaturistici appartenenti alla collezione Pischedda e conservati presso l'Antiquarium Arborense di Oristano, qualche frammento rinvenuto nel corso dello scavo della tomba n 32 di Iloi-Sedilo (Melis 1994), una ciotola carenata rinvenuta nell'insediamento di Su Cungiau de is Fundamentas-Simaxis (Melis 1985–1986: 10; tav. XII,b,c). Quest'ultima fu messa in luce casualmente nel centro abitato di Simaxis, a qualche centinaio di metri dall'area di raccolta dei reperti noti, alla profondità di circa tre metri. È dunque riferibile ad una struttura ipogeica o semi-ipogeica.

Metodologia

La consistente quantità di dati pubblicata negli ultimi decenni ha arricchito notevolmente il panorama dell'Età del Rame, ampliando le problematiche, chiarendo alcuni aspetti e ponendo nuovi interrogativi. La difficoltà principale alla comprensione dei fenomeni relativi alle fasi successive alla cultura di Ozieri è l'assenza di stratigrafie complete, articolate ed accompagnate da datazioni assolute; a tale problema s'affianca quello della pubblicazione solo parziale di molti contesti, che ostacola lo studio complessivo degli eventi culturali. A ciò si aggiunge inoltre la discordanza a livello terminologico oltre che concettuale tra i vari studiosi e tra le diverse scuole di pensiero. Da qui è sorta l'esigenza di uniformare i dati e riordinarli su base tipologica, allo scopo di rendere più comprensibile la sequenza culturale delle prime fasi dell'Eneolitico.

Lo strumento utilizzato ai fini del presente lavoro è l'analisi tipologica, seguita dall'analisi combinatoria dei dati, il cui risultato è una tabella di associazione, che evidenzia l'evoluzione culturale degli aspetti in esame. Allo scopo di contribuire al raggiungimento di un linguaggio comune agli studi archeologici, la terminologia adottata, che tiene conto sia degli aspetti funzionali che di quelli morfologici, si rifà a quella spesso utilizzata nella protostoria della penisola italiana e più volte chiarita e meglio definita dal Peroni (1985: 81–87; 1994: 102–133).

L'analisi tipologica è stata portata avanti secondo il principio dell'individuazione del tipo come insieme di caratteri che si presenta in diversi manufatti e non in altri, ma senza trascurare che nell'Eneolitico la produzione ceramica non avveniva su scala industriale e che il livello di standardizzazione delle forme doveva essere molto basso. Ciò ha suggerito di privilegiare la visione d'insieme del manufatto in relazione alla funzionalità ed al modello ipotetico.

I materiali sono stati ordinati a partire dalle forme basse e semplici verso quelle più profonde ed articolate, utilizzando nella maggior parte dei casi forme intere o delle quali sia ricostruibile il diametro, o che presentano elementi significativi tali da permettere l'identificazione di un tipo.

La tabella alla Fig. 24.1 evidenzia l'associazione tra i tipi ceramici, relativi sia alla morfologia, sia alla sintassi ed alla tecnica decorativa (prima ed ultima riga), ed i siti di rinvenimento (prima colonna). Non appaiono i tipi rinvenuti in un solo sito ed i siti che hanno restituito un solo tipo, in quanto non utilizzabili per le associazioni in una tabella di questo genere. Un'eccezione è rappresentata da alcuni tipi presenti esclusivamente nella capanna p-s di Monte d'Accoddi, inseriti in tabella per l'importanza che rivestono. Sono inoltre esclusi dalla tabella gli *unica* e le varianti.

Il vantaggio di una simile rappresentazione, in condizioni ottimali, è la possibilità di individuare una successione di fasi culturali e momenti di transizione, che consentano di recepire la complessa articolazione di un dato periodo. Un limite a questo tipo di analisi è dato dalla differente distribuzione dei dati disponibili, dalla rarità di indicazioni stratigrafiche e dalla presenza di contesti editi solo parzialmente. Nel caso specifico inoltre esiste una differenza tra i siti Sub-Ozieri, di carattere quasi esclusivamente abitativo e localizzati prevalentemente nel Sud dell'isola, e quelli Filigosa e Abealzu, di carattere quasi esclusivamente funerario e localizzati prevalentemente nel Nord. Questo aspetto porterebbe a non escludere che le differenze tra il Sub-Ozieri, il Filigosa e l'Abealzu possano essere di tipo geografico e/o funzionale. Ma a questo proposito sono importanti, a sostegno dell'ipotesi di una differenza cronologica piuttosto che geografica o funzionale, i ritrovamenti della tomba n. 32 di Iloi, che si ricollegano al Sub-Ozieri di Su Coddu-Selargius, Terramaini-Pirri e Cronicario-S. Antioco (Usai 1990) e provengono da un contesto non abitativo ma funerario e da una zona geografica ben distinta da quella dei suddetti villaggi.

Va infine sottolineato che un simile genere di analisi non può costituire l'unico approccio di studio, ma deve essere affiancato da indagini differenziate che contribuiscano a chiarire i caratteri dei fenomeni esaminati. Nel caso specifico infatti la tipologia dei reperti ceramici appartiene ad una più vasta ricerca, caratterizzata dallo studio delle altre categorie di manufatti, su pietra, osso e metallo, dall'analisi architettonica, territoriale, dei rituali funerari, dal confronto con le coeve manifestazioni culturali extra-insulari.

La tabella di associazione e la sequenza culturale

L'analisi combinatoria ha portato all'individuazione nella

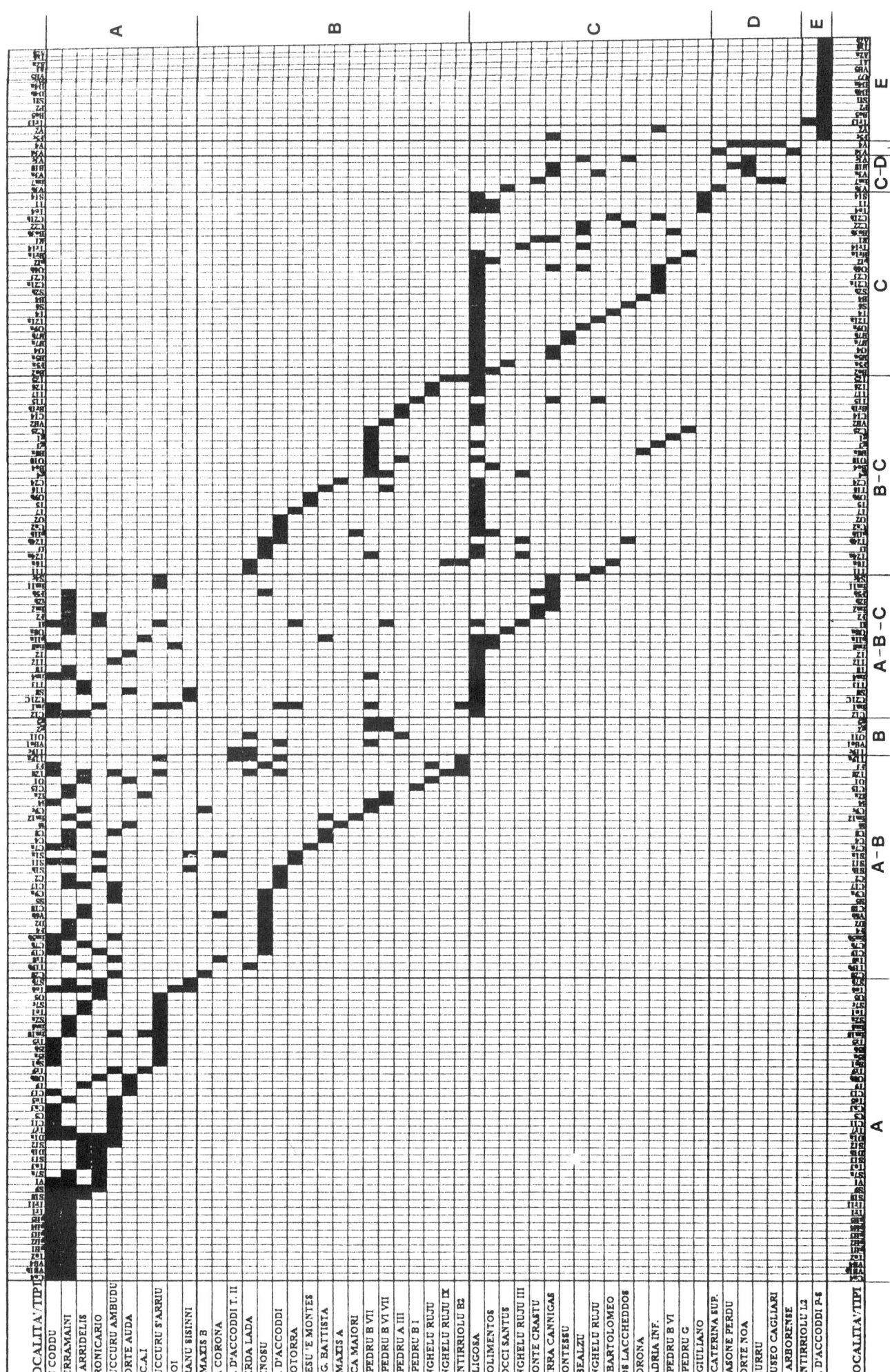

Fig. 24.1. Tabella di associazione tra i tipi ceramici ed i siti di rinvenimento dei materiali.

tabella di gruppi di tipi e di siti che figurano in modo esclusivo o in associazione con altri (Fig. 24.1). Partendo dall'alto e da sinistra si riconosce un gruppo di tipi (A) associato esclusivamente a determinati siti, quindi un secondo gruppo presente nei primi siti ma anche in altri (A–B). Pochi tipi sono riferibili in maniera esclusiva al secondo gruppo di siti (B). I tipi del gruppo A–B–C si ritrovano nei siti A, B e C; nel gruppo C–D sono assenti i primi siti, una serie di tipi è presente solo nei siti C, segue ancora un gruppo di tipi comune ai siti C e D (C–D), quindi due soli tipi presenti in alcuni siti del gruppo D, altri due tipi individuati sia nei siti C che in quelli E (C–E), ed infine una serie di tipi caratteristici dei siti E.

Dalla lettura della tabella emergono alcuni aspetti di notevole interesse, che in parte confermano ipotesi già formulate da alcuni autori, in parte evidenziano delle novità.

Si distinguono chiaramente i due poli estremi, costituiti in alto a sinistra dai tipi e dai siti definiti Sub-Ozieri, in basso a destra dai tipi presenti nella capanna p-s di Monte d'Accoddi e nella grotta di Sa Ucca de Su Tintirriolu, trincea L, strato 2. Nel primo caso è ampiamente documentato un insieme di tipi presenti in un gruppo di siti in maniera esclusiva. Ciò avvalora l'ipotesi della presenza di una fase successiva all'Ozieri e distinta dalle manifestazioni successive. Il secondo caso, più problematico, pone degli interrogativi nuovi riguardo agli ultimi sviluppi culturali sul filone della cultura di Ozieri. I materiali di Monte d'Accoddi infatti, pur presentando delle associazioni con il gruppo C, in maggioranza se ne discostano, proponendosi come insieme ben distinto.

Emerge distintamente un'evoluzione molto graduale, senza cambiamenti repentini, senza cesure, di una tradizione che si evolve, si modifica ma conserva a lungo molti caratteri. Ciò conferma la considerazione che il Contu fece riguardo all'evoluzione lenta del Filigosa nell'Abealzu a Monte d'Accoddi (Contu 1992: 24). È dunque difficile identificare delle vere e proprie fasi, anche in considerazione del fatto che la presenza di uno stesso tipo in due siti diversi può sancirne la contemporaneità, ma può anche indicare che il tipo ebbe lunga durata, eventualità che si verifica in special modo per le forme più semplici e per quelle più funzionali. Ciò nonostante tali associazioni consentono di seguire con maggiore chiarezza lo sviluppo della produzione ceramica del periodo.

Gruppo A (Fig. 24.2)

È costituito da tipi presenti in 10 località, di cui 8 nella provincia di Cagliari (Su Coddu-Selargius, Terramaini-Pirri, Is Arridelis-Uta, Cronicario-S. Antioco, Cuccuru Ambudu-Serramanna, Corte Auda-Senorbì, grotta A.C.A.I-Carbonia, Pranu Sisinni-Sardara), 2 in quella di Oristano (Cuccuru s'Arriu-Cabras e Iloi-Sedilo). Si tratta generalmente di ritrovamenti in abitato, fatta eccezione per quelli di Iloi, che provengono da una *domus de janas*. I tipi individuati si riferiscono alle seguenti forme funzionali: spiane, tegami, scodelle troncoconiche, a calotta di sfera ed emisferiche, ciotole e tazze carenate, tripodi, vasi carenati, biconici, a collo, olle e dolii (Fig. 24.6,1). Le spiane sono presenti in maniera esclusiva, notevole incidenza hanno i tripodi, i tegami (12,2%), le scodelle a calotta emisferiche e troncoconiche (9,7%). Tra queste ultime figurano anche i vasi a cestello, che nella classificazione seguita si inquadrano nella forma funzionale *scodella*, nella categoria *troncoconica* e nella famiglia tipologica *a parete concava*. Nell'ambito delle ciotole carenate sono rappresentati il 7,3% dei tipi, mentre sono meno diffuse le tazze carenate (2,4%). Anche i vasi carenati, i vasi biconici, le olle e i dolii sono presenti ciascuna classe con una percentuale del 4,9%, mentre i vasi a collo sono rari (2,4%). I bicchieri sono attestati in due varianti da Is Arridelis e Cuccuru s'Arriu ed in un *unicum* da Is Arridelis i vasetti a bottiglia si riconoscono in due *unica* da Terramaini e Is Arridelis. Tra la ceramica non vascolare appaiono i pesi da telaio reniformi di Terramaini che costituiscono un tipo, alcune varianti da Su Coddu ed alcuni pesi con fila di forellini da Su Coddu, Terramaini e Cuccuru s'Arriu dai caratteri non omogenei. Nel campo degli elementi decorativi sono esclusivi di questo gruppo i tipi realizzati con la tecnica della pittura e sono ben attestate anche l'incisione e l'impressione. La decorazione graffita appare sporadicamente.

Gruppo A–B (Fig. 24.3,1–11)

Una serie di tipi è attestato nei siti del gruppo A ma anche in un altro insieme, il quale a sua volta presenta delle associazioni con i gruppi successivi. Esso è caratterizzato da una riduzione dei siti della provincia di Cagliari, da una presenza sporadica nel Nuorese ed una marcata frequenza di siti dell'Oristanese (36%; Campu 'e Cresia-Simaxis, Fenosu-Palmas Arborea, S. Giovanni Battista-Nurachi, Su Cungiau de is Fundamentas-Simaxis, Isca Maiori-Riola Sardo) e del Sassarese (43%; Monte d'Accoddi tomba 2-Sassari, Monte d'Accoddi-Sassari, Mesu 'e Montes-Ossi, S. Pedru-Alghero, Anghelu Ruju-Alghero, Sa Ucca de Su Tintirriolu-Mara). Va sottolineato che alcune località, in cui la differenza di strato, o di ambiente o di settore si è dimostrata significativa, compaiono più volte nella tabella ed occupano posizioni spesso differenti. È il caso della *domus de janas* di S. Pedru in cui gli strati I, VI-VII e VII dell'anticella b ed il III del *dromos* a appartengono al gruppo B, mentre lo strato VI dell'anticella b ed alcuni materiali della cella g si inseriscono nel gruppo C. Una distinzione è stata operata anche per i materiali della capanna p-s di Monte d'Accoddi che si inquadrano nel gruppo E e si discostano da materiali provenienti da altre zone, inseriti nel gruppo B. Tra i materiali della necropoli di Anghelu Ruju, distinti per tomba, appartengono al gruppo di siti B quelli della tomba IX ed alcuni pubblicati senza l'indicazione precisa della provenienza. Anche nel

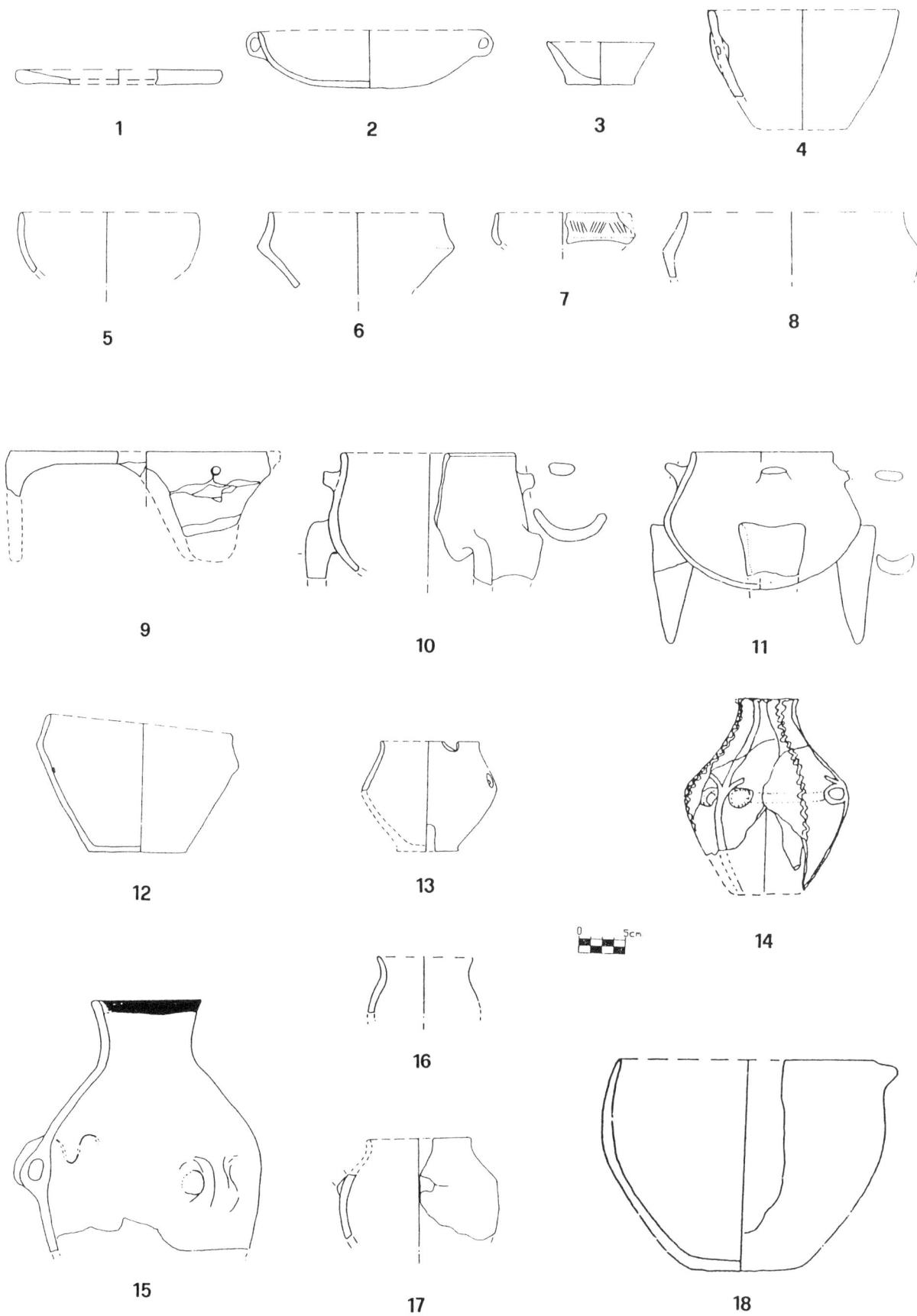

Fig. 24.2. Tavola tipologica: gruppo A

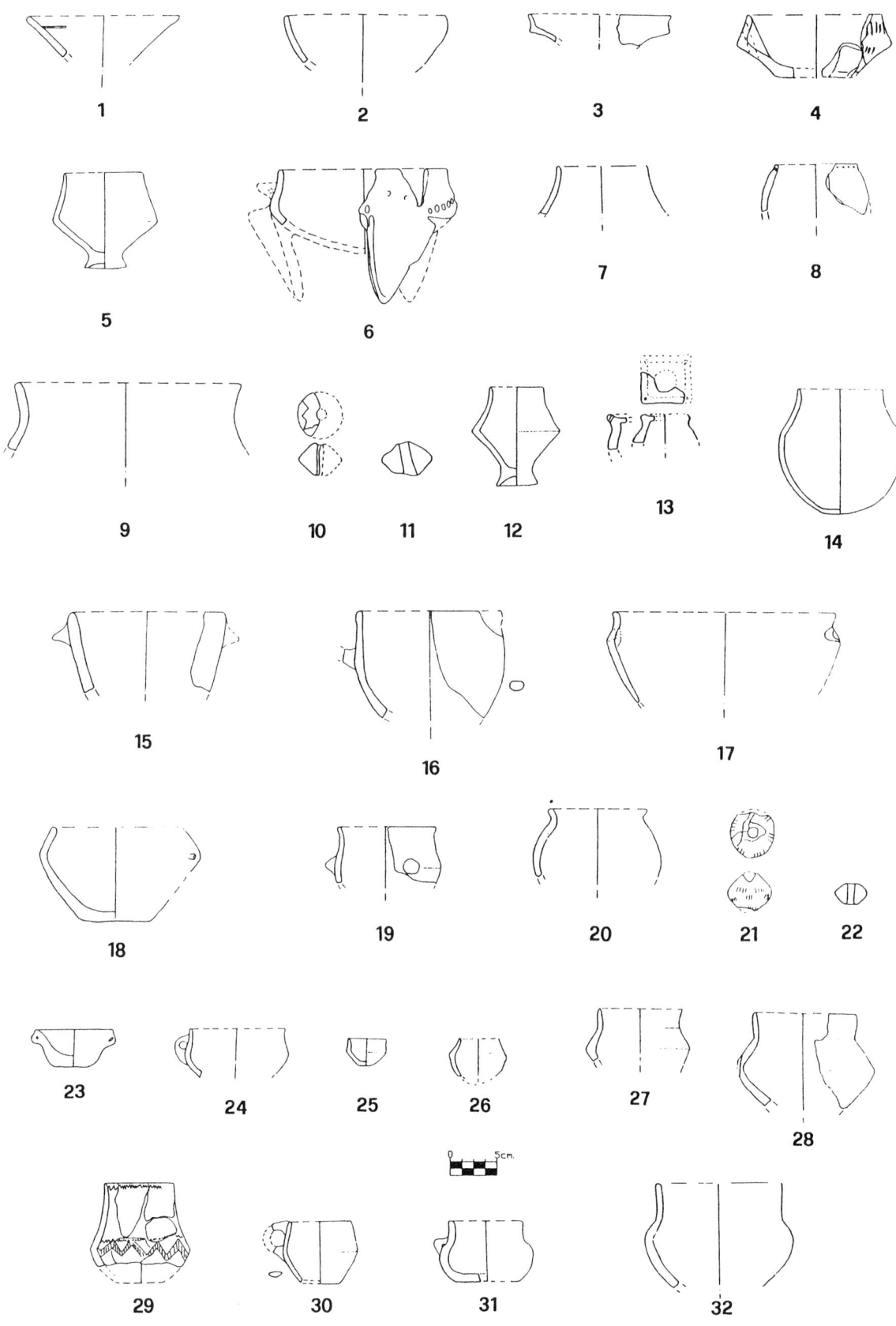

Fig. 24.3. Tavola tipologica: gruppi A–B (1–11), B (12–14), A–B–C (15–22), B–C (23–32)

contesto della grotta di Sa Ucca de Su Tintirriolu è significativa la differenza tra i tipi individuati nelle trincee B e M, strato 2, inseriti nel gruppo di siti B ed un tipo proveniente dalla trincea L, strato 2, inserito nel gruppo E. Non sono state riscontrate differenze significative in altri casi come le capanne di Terramaini, Su Coddu, Is Arridelis e Filigosa i cui materiali sono stati accorpati.

Le forme funzionali rappresentate nel gruppo di tipi A–B sono scodelle troncoconiche, a calotta di sfera ed emisferiche, ciotole e tazze carenate, tripodi, olle, dolii e fusaiole; tra le tecniche figurano l'incisione e l'impressione (Fig. 24.6,2). Tra le peculiarità emerge una minore varietà tipologica (31 tipi contro i 48 del gruppo A), l'assenza di alcune forme, spiane, tegami, vasi carenati e biconici e della tecnica della pittura. Sono inoltre presenti le brocche in un *unicum* da Isca Maiori, le pissidi in due *unica* da Cuccuru s'Arriu e Monte d'Accoddi ed i vasi biconici in una variante da Fenosu. È evidente (Fig. 24.6,2) la marcata incidenza delle ciotole carenate (40%) rispetto alle altre forme, tra le quali sono ben attestate le scodelle troncoconiche e le tazze carenate (il 10 % ciascuna).

Gruppo B (Fig. 24.3,12–14)

Sono pochissimi gli elementi riconducibili in modo esclusivo ai siti B (Fig. 24.6,3): tazze carenate, vasetti a bottiglia ed olle. Appaiono i primi tipi di decorazione a graffito, preceduti da manifestazioni isolate nell'ambito del gruppo A.

Gruppo A–B–C (Fig. 24.3,15–22)

Comprende i siti dei gruppi A e B, ai quali si aggiungono alcuni del gruppo C (Filigosa-Macomer, Molimentos-Benetutti, Locci Santus-S. Giovanni Suergiu, Anghelu Ruju tomba III-Alghero, Monte Crastu-Serrenti, Serra Cannigas-Villagreca, Abealzu-Sassari). È costituito da 19 tipi, dei quali 16 sono relativi alle forme funzionali e 3 alle tecniche decorative (Fig. 24.6,4). Si conoscono scodelle troncoconiche, ciotole carenate, tazze cilindriche e carenate, olle e fusaiole. È da sottolineare la maggiore incidenza delle tazze carenate sulle ciotole carenate, che capovolge la proporzione riscontrata nei gruppi A ed A–B, nei quali erano più frequenti le seconde rispetto alle prime. Tra le tecniche decorative ha un notevole sviluppo l'impressione, è attestata l'incisione ed appare la decorazione plastica.

Gruppo B–C (Fig. 24.3,23–32)

Scompaiono in questo gruppo i siti A ed alcuni del gruppo B (Campu 'e Cresia-Simaxis, Sa Corona-Villagreca, Monte d'Accoddi, tomba 2-Sassari). Sono presenti quasi tutti i siti del gruppo C (Filigosa-Macomer, Molimentos-Benetutti, Locci Santus-S. Giovanni Suergiu, Anghelu Ruju tomba III-Alghero, Monte Crastu-Serrenti, Serra Cannigas-Villagreca, Montessu-Villaperuccio, Abealzu-Sassari, Anghelu Ruju tomba XVII, S: Bartolomeo-Cagliari, Sos Laccheddos-Osilo, Corona Moltana-Bonnanaro, S. Giuseppe strato inferiore-Padria, S. Pedru cella B strato VI e cella g-Alghero). Si registra un'uguale distribuzione numerica di siti nella provincia di Sassari ed in quella di Cagliari (45%), mentre un solo sito si trova in provincia di Nuoro e nessuno in provincia di Oristano. I tipi rappresentati (Fig. 24.7,1) sono relativi a ciotole e tazze carenate, bicchieri, boccali, brocche, vasi carenati e biconici, olle. Anche in questo caso, come nel gruppo precedente rivestono notevole rilievo le tazze carenate (41%), seguite dalle ciotole carenate e dalle olle con la stessa frequenza (11%). È da sottolineare inoltre la maggiore frequenza dei vasi di dimensioni piccole e miniaturistiche. Nel campo delle tecniche decorative riveste una notevole importanza il graffito e sono attestate in uguale misura l'incisione e la decorazione plastica.

Gruppo C (Fig. 24.4,1–21)

Dalla tabella risulta che una serie di tipi appare esclusivamente nei siti del gruppo C (Filigosa-Macomer, Molimentos-Benetutti, Locci Santus-S. Giovanni Suergiu, Anghelu Ruju tomba III-Alghero, Monte Crastu-Serrenti, Serra Cannigas-Villagreca, Montessu-Villaperuccio, Abealzu-Sassari, Anghelu Ruju tomba XVII, S: Bartolomeo-Cagliari, Sos Laccheddos-Sassari, Corona Moltana-Bonnanaro, S. Giuseppe strato inferiore-Padria, S. Pedru cella B strato VI e cella g-Alghero, S. Giuliano-Alghero). Quanto alle forme si rileva una notevole frequenza delle ciotole e delle tazze carenate (Fig. 24.7,2), con una prevalenza delle prime sulle seconde (rispettivamente il 16% e il 12%). Un'altra caratteristica del gruppo è la notevole diffusione dei bicchieri (16%) che non ha risconti nei gruppi precedenti né in quelli successivi. Sono abbastanza diffuse anche le olle (12%) ed i boccali (8%). Rari i tripodi, le brocche, i tegami e le fusaiole. Anche in questo caso si registra un accentuato miniaturismo, con forme che imitano quelle a scala normale. Tra i vasi di dimensioni ridotte sono da segnalare i due *rytà* (Fig. 24.4,20), provenienti da Serra Cannigas-Villagreca e Monte Crastu-Serrenti (Atzeni 1985: figg. 1,1; 3,3). Da Sos Laccheddos infine provengono un tipo ed una variante di attingitoio.

Gruppi C–D (Fig. 24.4,22–25), D (Fig. 24.4,26–27), E (Fig. 24.4,28–29)

Una serie di siti (S. Caterina-Pittinuri livello superiore, Masone Perdu-Laconi, Corte Noa-Laconi, Seurru-Sestu, località sconosciuta in provincia di Cagliari) ha in comune con i siti C alcuni tipi (C–D), mentre solo due tipi li caratterizzano in modo esclusivo. I tipi in comune

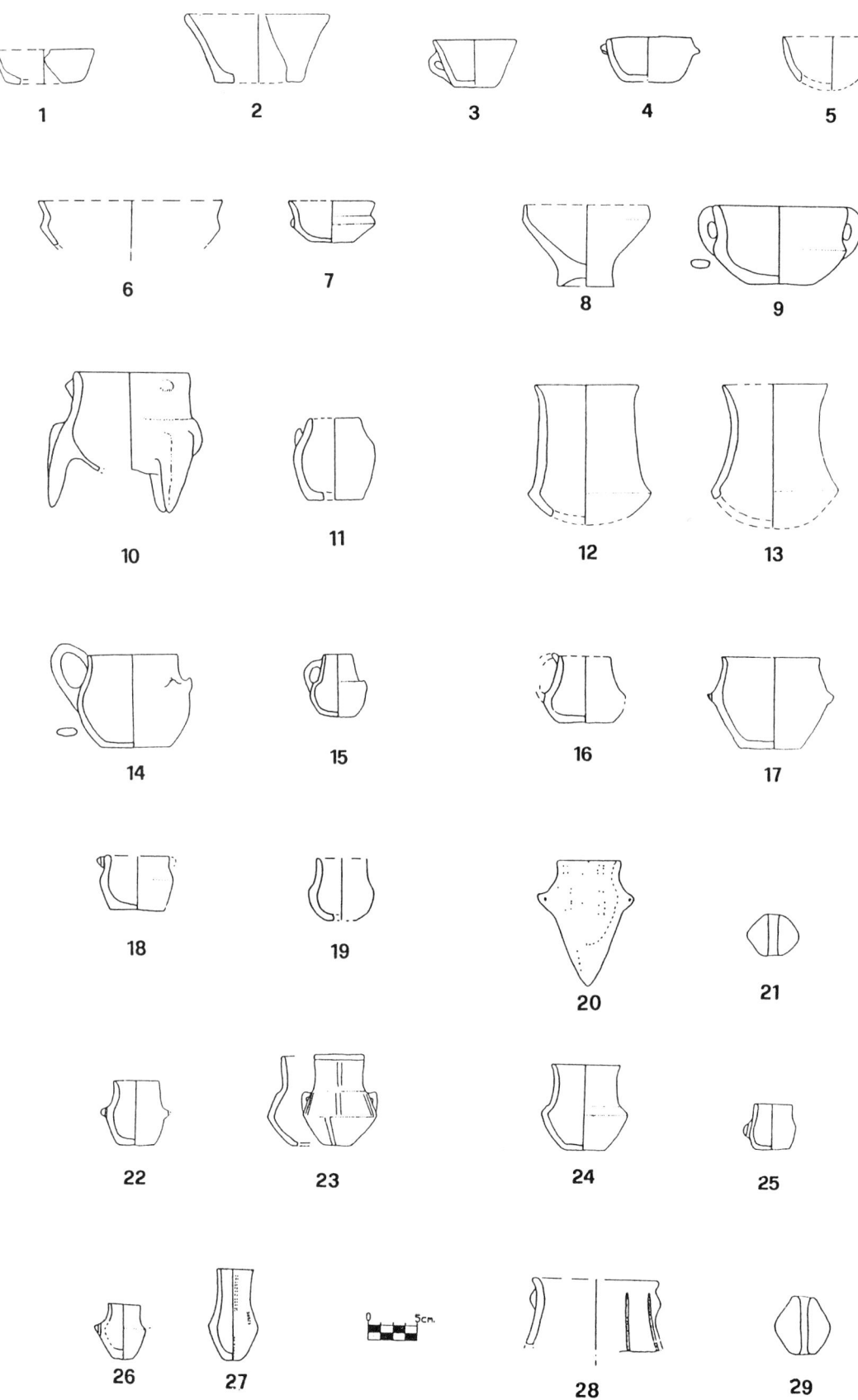

Fig. 24.4. Tavola tipologica: gruppi C (1–21), C–D (22–25), D (26–27), C–E (28–29)

sono bicchieri, vasi a collo e tipi di decorazione ad impressione; quelli esclusivi sono relativi a vasi a collo (Fig. 24.7,3–4). Un tipo di vaso a collo ed uno di fusaiola infine sono comuni ai gruppi C ed E (Fig. 24.7,5). È di notevole interesse il frammento alla Fig. 24.4,29, proveniente dalla capanna p-s di Monte d'Accoddi, per la decorazione a leggere scanalature verticali che suggeriscono i contatti con la cultura di Monte Claro. Si registra ancora una volta un'apprezzabile frequenza di vasi miniaturistici.

Gruppo E (Fig. 24.5)

I tipi del gruppo E sono attestati unicamente nella capanna p-s di Monte d'Accoddi, fatta eccezione per un tipo di tripode presente anche nella trincea L strato 2 della grotta di Sa Ucca de Su Tintirriolu-Mara. Si tratta in maggioranza di grossi contenitori per derrate, dolii, anfore, vasi biconici (Fig. 24.7,6). Tra i vasi di dimensioni medie figurano i boccali, che manifestano alcune analogie con quelli dei gruppi precedenti. Da sottolineare la sopravvivenza della forma del vaso a cestello, di tradizione Ozieri, in un *unicum*.

La rappresentazione della Fig. 24.8 sembra dunque rispecchiare una situazione di graduale sviluppo dai contesti presumibilmente più antichi (A) verso quelli più recenti (E). I tipi ed i siti A, pur in assenza di datazioni assolute, possono considerarsi come i più antichi, in quanto ancora piùttosto vicini alle tematiche dell'Ozieri. Inoltre essi sono caratterizzati da un'attività metallurgica ancora alle prime esperienze, mentre nei gruppi successivi è ben sviluppata. I caratteri uniformi dei tipi ceramici, dei contesti di provenienza, le peculiarità come la presenza esclusiva della tecnica della pittura e, tra le forme, delle spiane, le differenze nelle frequenze di alcune forme funzionali rispetto agli altri gruppi, suggeriscono l'identificazione di una fase a sé stante. I tipi A–B costituiscono il *trait d'union* con i momenti successivi e sono presenti sia nei gruppi A che in quelli B. Si può ipotizzare che si tratti di tipi di lunga durata, utilizzati nella "fase" A ed anche in tempi successivi, oppure che identifichino un momento di transizione, contraddistinto dagli aspetti più recenti di A e da quelli più antichi di B. Quest'ultimo gruppo d'altronde si caratterizza più per le associazioni con altri gruppi che per i suoi elementi distintivi. I siti B infatti hanno dei caratteri in comune sia con A che con C. Anche in questo caso si può supporre che si tratti di siti di lunga durata, o che presentino caratteri di transizione.

È verosimile ritenere che i tipi A–B–C siano di lunga durata; essi sono caratterizzati sia da forme semplici come le scodelle troncoconiche o le fusaiole che perdurano nel tempo senza variazioni di rilievo, sia le ciotole e le tazze carenate, che costituiscono una forma di tradizione Ozieri tra le più diffuse.

A partire dal gruppo B–C si registra un mutamento, costituito dall'assenza dei tipi e dei siti A, sostituiti dai siti C. Si intravede una cesura che divide la prima serie di gruppi dalla seconda e segna forse il passaggio ad una fase di transizione B–C e ad una fase C. Più difficile è l'interpretazione dei gruppi C–D e D, in quanto contraddistinti da scarsi elementi, mentre il gruppo C–E è costituito presumibilmente da tipi di lunga durata. Quanto al gruppo E, costituito, quasi esclusivamente dai materiali della capanna p-s di Monte d'Accoddi, non va trascurato che i dati provengono da una sola capanna, che potrebbe aver fornito solo alcuni aspetti del momento che rappresenta; ad esempio la presenza di grossi contenitori in un vano della capanna suggerisce la destinazione dell'ambiente a magazzino per la conservazione di derrate.

I dati finora esposti possono essere riassunti nello schema che segue:

gruppi	1° ipotesi	2° ipotesi	3° ipotesi
A	Fase I	Fase Ia	---
A–B, B	Fase di transizione	Fase Ib	Tipi di lunga durata
A–B–C	Tipi di lunga durata	---	---
B–C	Fase di transizione	Fase IIa	Tipi di lunga durata
C	Fase II	Fase IIb	---
C–D, D	Fase di transizione	Fase IIIa	Tipi di lunga durata
C–E	Tipi di lunga durata	---	---
E	Fase III	Fase IIIb	---

I grafici alla Fig. 24.9 indicano le frequenze delle forme ceramiche e delle tecniche decorative nel corso dei diversi momenti individuati, evidenziando gli elementi di continuità e di differenza; va sottolineato ancora una volta che i dati si riferiscono alla presenza di tipi, con esclusione delle varianti e delle forme isolate e non presentano il quadro completo delle fasi in esame. Le forme semplici (spiane, piatti, tegami, scodelle) sono molto diffuse nei primi gruppi ed appaiono solo sporadicamente dopo la "fase" C. Anche le ciotole e le tazze carenate vanno in disuso dopo il momento C, con un picco di frequenza per le prime nel gruppo A–B, per le seconde nel gruppo B–C. I tripodi, molto diffusi nei gruppi A ed A–B, si ritrovano in un tipo del gruppo C e nel gruppo E. Bicchieri, boccali, brocche ed anfore mostrano invece un andamento inverso, non essendo attestati prima del gruppo B–C. I vasi a collo, rari nei gruppi A ed A–B, assenti in quelli B, A–B–C, B–C e C, sono frequenti a partire dal gruppo C–D. Le olle sono una forma utilizzata in quasi tutte le fasi, mentre i dolii sono frequenti nei gruppi più antichi ed in quelli più recenti. Fusaiole e pesi da telaio appaiono anche in forme isolate in tutti i gruppi; le sfere d'argilla, interpretabili come porzioni di argilla da modellare, sono attestate esclusivamente nella capanna dello stregone di Monte d'Accoddi.

Nel campo delle tecniche e delle tematiche decorative si è osservata una contrazione dopo il gruppo B–C, fatta eccezione per la decorazione plastica, che si diffonde in tempi più recenti rispetto alle altre tecniche ed è

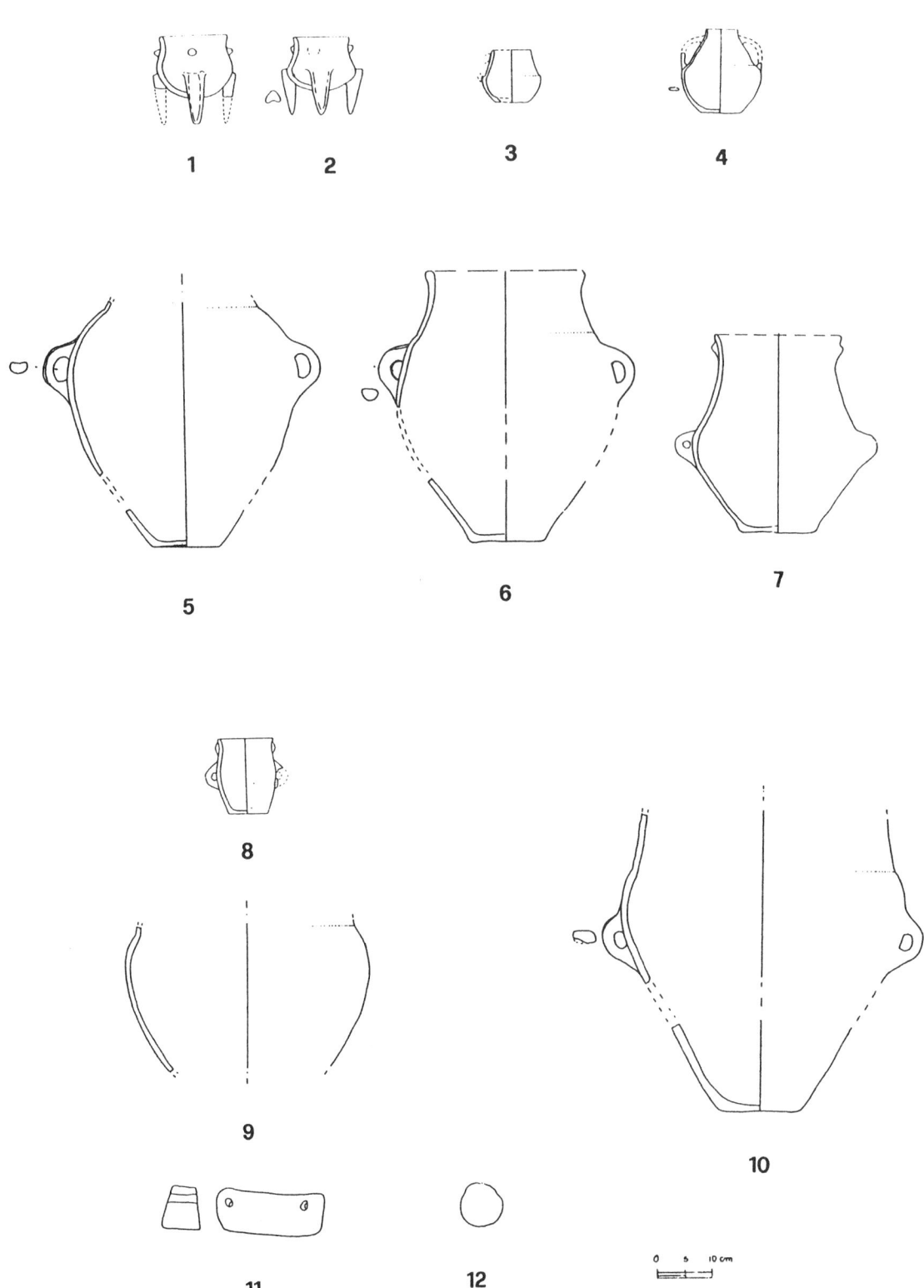

Fig. 24.5. Tavola tipologica: gruppo E

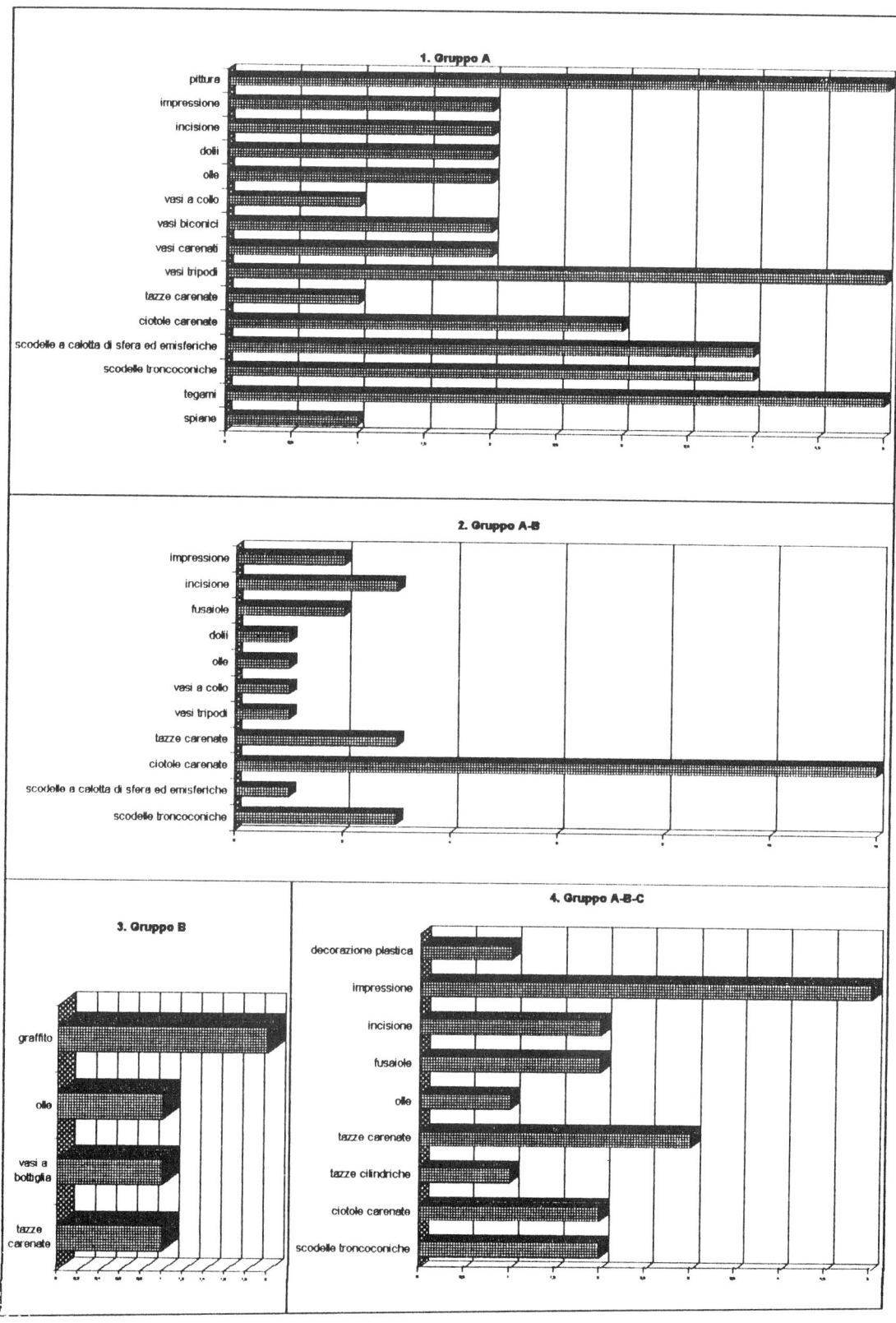

Fig. 24.6. Diagrammi della distribuzione dei tipi ceramici nei gruppi A (1), A–B (2), B (3), A–B–C (4)

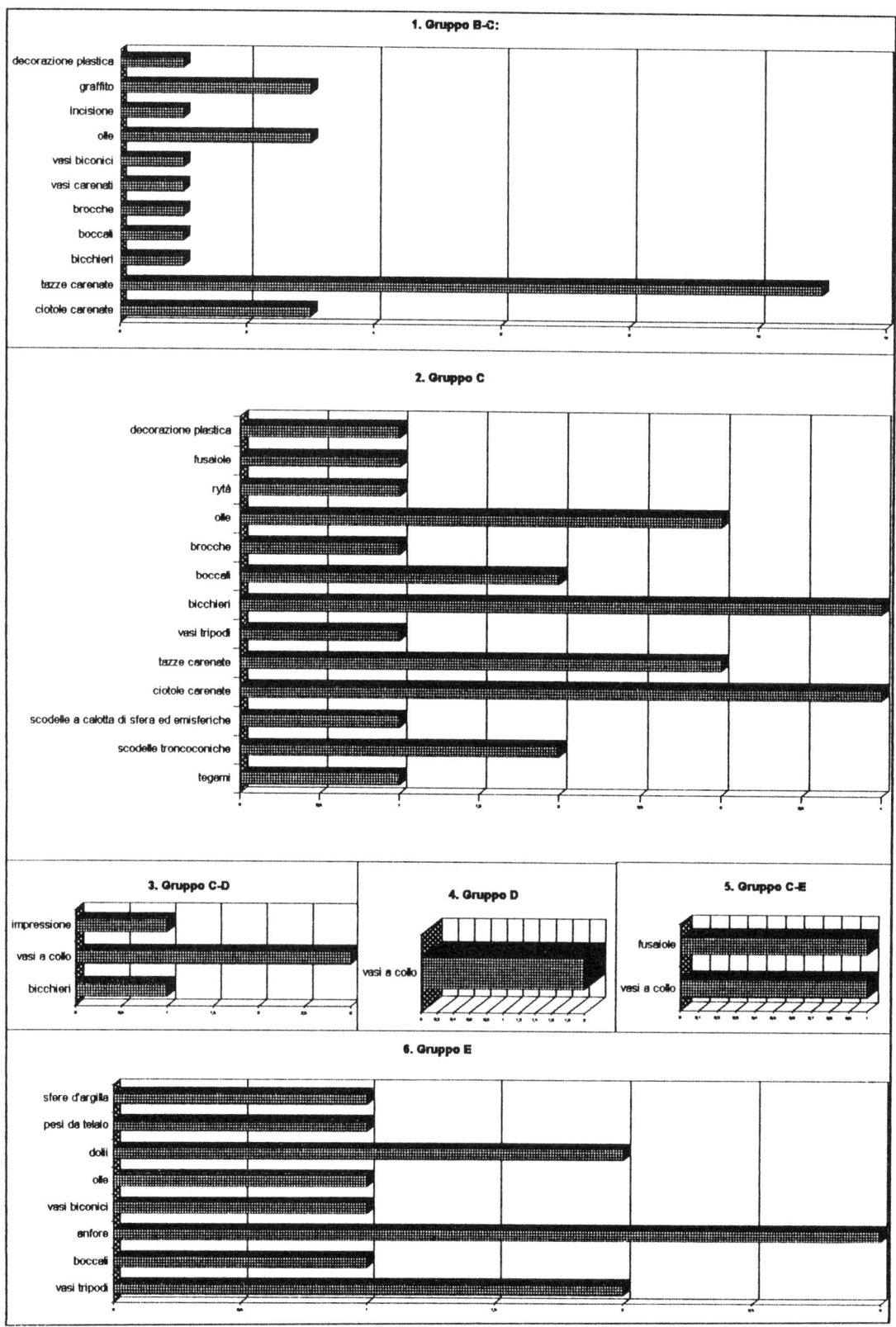

Fig. 24.7. Diagrammi della distribuzione dei tipi ceramici nei gruppi B–C (1), C (2), C–D (3), D (4), C–E (5), E (6)

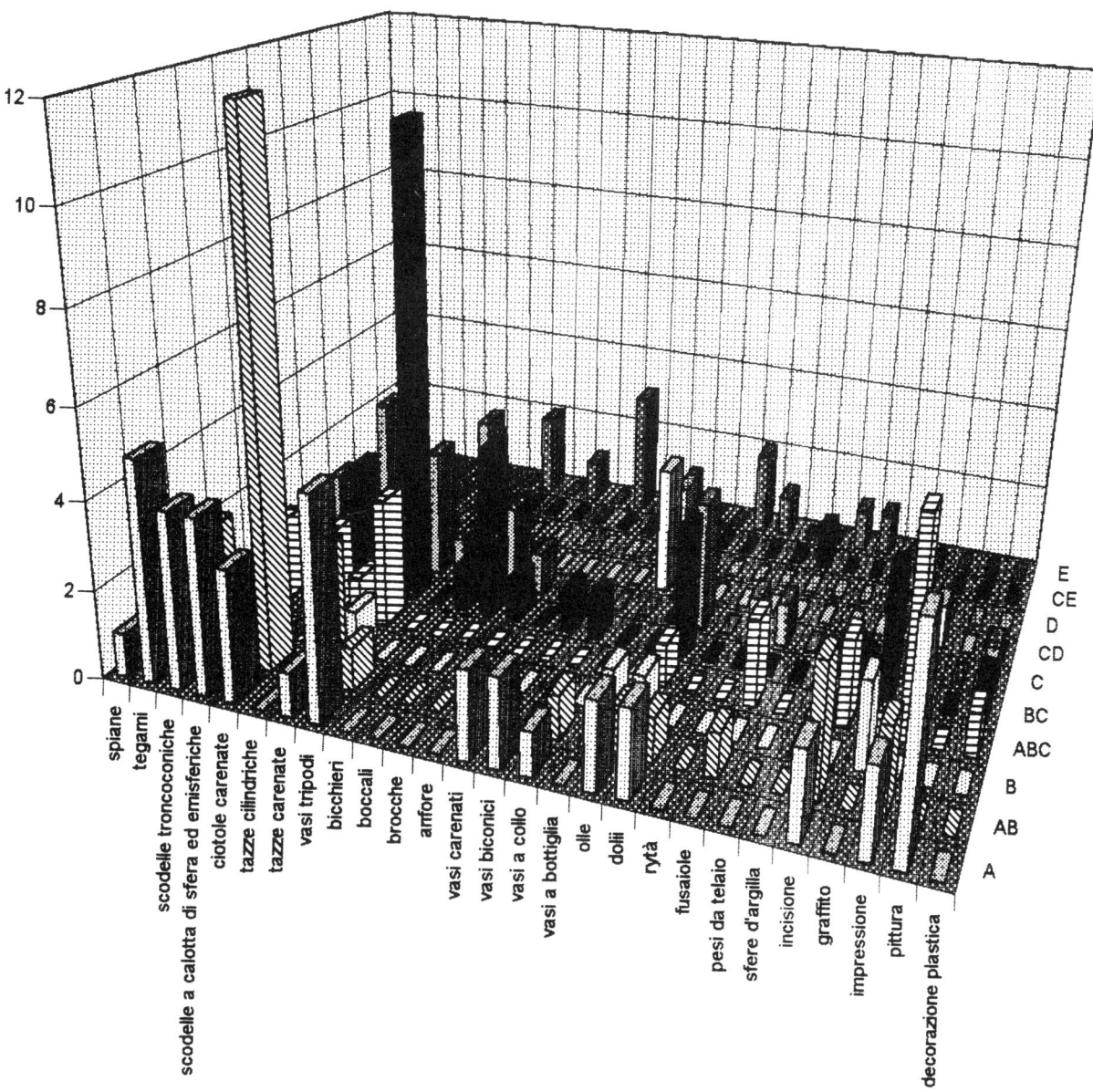

Fig. 24.8. Diagramma riassuntivo della distribuzione dei tipi ceramici

attestata anche nel gruppo C. La pittura appare esclusivamente nella fase A, l'impressione e l'incisione sono presenti sporadicamente anche nel gruppo E.

Considerazioni conclusive

Allo stato attuale dello studio, in attesa di acquisire ulteriori elementi dall'approfondimento degli altri aspetti della ricerca, in riferimento alla terminologia tradizionale utilizzata per definire gli aspetti culturali in esame si possono fare le seguenti osservazioni: la "fase" A si identificherebbe con il Sub-Ozieri, che si manifesta chiaramente come momento distinto dal successivo Filigosa; il gruppo A–B potrebbe essere considerato una fase di transizione tra il Sub-Ozieri ed il Filigosa (ma non compaiono materiali dal sito eponimo); il Filigosa sembra articolarsi in due sottofasi attraverso i gruppi B–C e C. A partire dal momento B–C la fase Sub-Ozieri dei grandi villaggi di Terramaini e Su Coddu si esaurisce, forse in seguito all'apparire della cultura di Monte Claro, la cui presenza sembra sortire effetti diversi in altre zone, in cui pare invece influenzare ma non sostituire il Filigosa (tomba I di Filigosa-Macomer). Pur tenendo conto della povertà di dati relativi ai momenti più recenti, considerati i mutamenti nella diffusione delle forme ceramiche dopo il gruppo C, si può far corrispondere i gruppi C–D, D ed E all'aspetto che viene definito Abealzu, caratterizzato da presenza di vasi a collo e assenza di ciotole e tazze carenate, del quale alcuni elementi sono anticipati nella precedente fase C (i boccaletti con bugne contrapposte all'ansa). Sembra di poter intuire inoltre la possibilità di un'articolazione all'interno dell'Abealzu, in considerazione delle differenze tra i suddetti gruppi, ma

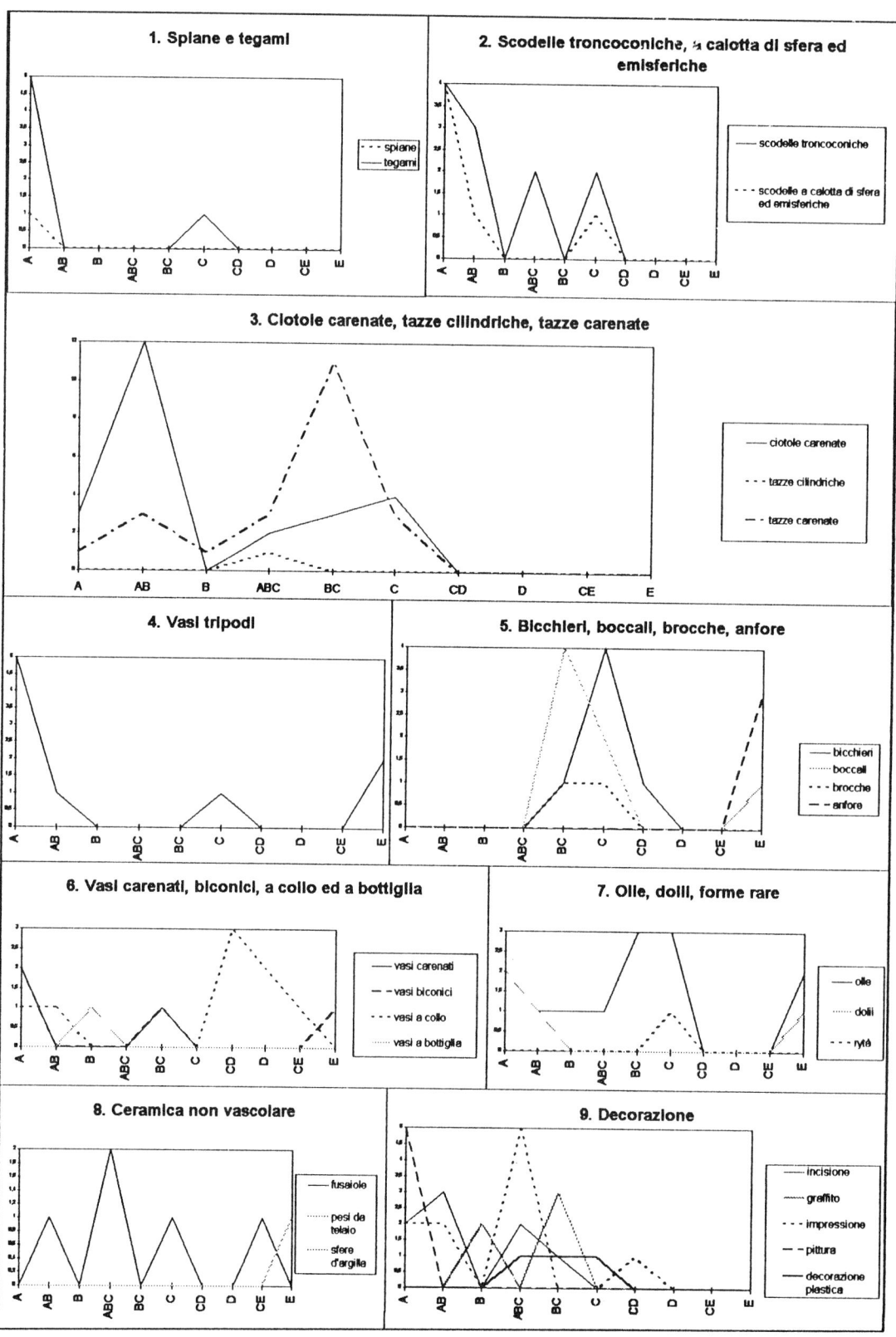

Fig. 24.9. Diagrammi dell'evoluzione delle frequenze delle forme funzionali relative ai tipi individuati

l'esiguità dei dati a disposizione non consente ulteriori approfondimenti.

Nella tabella che segue si presenta l'ipotesi di corrispondenza tra i gruppi individuati e gli aspetti culturali tradizionalmente conosciuti:

Gruppi	Aspetti culturali
A	Sub-Ozieri
A–B, B	Sub-Ozieri-Filigosa
B–C	Filigosa I
C	Filigosa II
C–D, D	Filigosa-Abealzu
E	Abealzu

Il metodo utilizzato nel presente studio, adottato per la prima volta in Sardegna, ha permesso di individuare un'articolazione complessa degli aspetti culturali sviluppatisi in seguito alla cultura di Ozieri e di apprezzare la lenta evoluzione dai momenti più antichi a quelli più recenti caratterizzati dalla persistenza di alcuni tipi e da innovazioni parziali, ma ha consentito anche di isolare gruppi o forse fasi che in virtù delle associazioni di tipi ceramici si distinguono dagli aspetti successivi e da quelli precedenti. L'approfondimento dell'indagine attraverso lo sviluppo dei diversi aspetti della ricerca e l'acquisizione di nuovi elementi consentirà di completare il quadro delineatosi e di chiarificare i problemi non ancora risolti.

Ringraziamenti

Desidero ringraziare il prof. Ercole Contu per i consigli preziosi e per avermi proposto di presentare l'argomento in questa sede. Un ringraziamento particolare anche alla prof.ssa Miriam S. Balmuth per aver accettato il lavoro nell'ambito del presente colloquio internazionale. Al prof. Ercole Contu, autore degli scavi a Monte d'Accoddi, sono grata per avermi generosamente autorizzata ad effettuare lo studio dei materiali della capanna p-s di Monte d'Accoddi.

I disegni alle Figg. 2–5 sono rielaborazioni grafiche realizzate dal geom. Giampiero Sechi e dalla scrivente su originali dei vari autori. I tipi rappresentati sono i più significativi di ciascun gruppo.

Bibliografia

Atzeni, E. 1962. The cave of San Bartolomeo, Sardinia. *Antiquity* 36: 184–189.

Atzeni, E. 1966. Il "nuraghe" Sa Corona di Villagreca. *Atti del XIII Congresso di Storia dell'Architettura, 1–2, Cagliari, 1963, Roma, 1966*, 119–124.

Atzeni, E. 1985. Tombe eneolitiche nel Cagliaritano. In *Studi in onore di Giovanni Lilliu per il suo settantesimo compleanno*, 11–49. Cagliari.

Atzeni, E. 1987. La preistoria del Sulcis-Iglesiente. In *Iglesias. Storia Società*, 7–57. Iglesias.

Cocco, D. & Usai, L. 1988. Un monumento preistorico nel territorio di Cornus, Ampsicora e il territorio di Cornus. *Atti del II Convegno sull'archeologia romana e altomedievale nell'Oristanese (Cuglieri, 22 dicembre 1985)*, 13–18. Taranto.

Contu, E. 1964. La tomba dei vasi tetrapodi in località Santu Pedru (Alghero-Sassari). *Monumenti Antichi dei Lincei* 57: 3–201.

Contu, E. 1980. La Sardegna preistorica e protostorica – Aspetti e problemi. *Atti della XXII Riunione Scientifica dell'Istituto Italiano di Preistoria e Protostoria*, 13–39. Istituto Italiano di Preistoria e Protostoria, Firenze.

Contu, E. 1984. Monte d'Accoddi-Sassari. Problematiche di studio e ricerca di un singolare monumento preistorico. In Waldren, W.H., Chapman, R., Lewthwaite, J. & Kennard, R.C.(eds.), *The Deya Conference of Prehistory: Early Settlement in the Western Mediterranean Islands and their Peripheral Areas*. BAR International Series 229: 591–608. British Archaeological Reports, Oxford.

Contu, E. 1992. Nuove anticipazioni sui dati stratigrafici di Monte d'Accoddi. Scavi 1952–1958. In *Monte d'Accoddi, 10 anni di nuovi scavi*, 21–36. Genova.

Depalmas, A. 1989. Il materiale preistorico di Isca Maiori nella collezione Falchi di Oristano. *Studi Sardi* 28(1988–1989): 37–59.

Ferrarese Ceruti, M.L. 1963. Vasetti inediti dal Cagliaritano e dall'Iglesiente. *Rivista di Scienze Preistoriche* 28: 191–208.

Ferrarese Ceruti, M.L. 1967. Domus de janas in località Molimentos (Benetutti-Sassari). *Bullettino di Paletnologia Italiana* 18: 69–135.

Foschi Nieddu, A. 1986. *La tomba I di Filigosa (Macomer – Nuoro). Alcune considerazioni sulla cultura di Abealzu-Filigosa nel contesto eneolitico della Sardegna*. Nuoro.

Frau, M. 1991. Caratteristiche culturali ed elementi inediti del villaggio preistorico di Cuccuru Ambudu (Serramanna-Cagliari). *Studi Sardi* 29 (1990–91): 95–161.

Lilliu, G. 1967. *La civiltà dei Sardi dal Neolitico all'età dei nuraghi*. ERI, Torino.

Lilliu, G. 1988. *La civiltà dei Sardi dal Paleolitico all'età dei nuraghi*. ERI, Torino.

Loria, R. & Trump, D.H. 1978. Le scoperte a "Sa Ucca de su Tintirriolu" e il Neolitico sardo. *Monumenti Antichi dei Lincei* II (ser. misc.) 49(2): 115–253.

Luglie', C. 1989. Ceramiche eneolitiche dall'insediamento di Fenosu-Palmas Arborea (Oristano). *Studi Sardi* 28(1988–1989): 73–100.

Manunza, M.R. 1991. La tomba III di Anghelu Ruju-Alghero (Sassari). *Quaderni della Soprintendenza Archeologica per le Provincie di Cagliari e Oristano* 7(1990): 43–61.

Melis, M.G. 1985–1986. *Gli insediamenti preistorici di "Su Cungiau de is Fundamentas" e di "Campu 'e Cresia" presso Simaxis (Oristano)*. Tesi di laurea, Anno Accademico 1985–1986. Università degli Studi di Cagliari.

Melis, M.G. 1992. Materiali preistorici dall'insediamento di Cuccuru Ambudu-Serramanna. *Quaderni della Soprintendenza Archeologica per le Provincie di Cagliari e Oristano* 8(1991): 49–67.

Melis, M.G. 1994. La tomba n. 3 di Iloi – Sedilo (OR). *Congresso Internazionale L'ipogeismo nel Mediterraneo. Origini, sviluppo, quadri culturali, Sassari – Oristano, 23–28 maggio 1994*.

Peroni, R. 1985. Spunti terminologici. In *Studi di Paletnologia in onore di Salvatore M. Puglisi*, 81–90. Roma.

Peroni, R. 1994. *Introduzione alla protostoria italiana*. Roma-Bari.

Sanna, R. 1989. Il villaggio di Is Arridelis-Uta. In Campus, L.D. (a cura di), *La cultura di Ozieri. Problematiche e nuove acquisizioni. Atti del I Convegno di Studio (Ozieri, gennaio 1986 – Aprile 1987)*, 231–238. Il Torchietto, Ozieri.

Santoni, V. 1976. Nota preliminare sulla tipologia delle grotticelle artificiali funerarie della Sardegna, *Archivio Storico Sardo*, 30: 3–49.

Santoni, V. 1982. Cabras – Cuccuru s'Arriu. Nota preliminare di scavo (1978, 1979, 1980). *Rivista di Studi Fenici* 10(1): 103–127.

Santoni, V. 1992. Cabras – Cuccuru s'Arriu. L'orizzonte eneolitico Sub-Ozieri. *Quaderni della Soprintendenza per le Provincie di Cagliari e Oristano* 8(1991): 15–47.

Tanda, G. 1976. Monte d'Accoddi, tomba II. In *Nuove testimonianze archeologiche nella Sardegna centro settentrionale, Sassari, 18 luglio-24 ottobre 1976*, 35–50. Dessì, Sassari.

Taramelli, A. 1904. Alghero – Scavi nella necropoli preistorica a grotticelle artificiali di "Anghelu Ruju". *Notizie dagli Scavi* 29(8): 301–351.

Taramelli, A. 1909. Nuovi scavi nella necropoli preistorica a grotte artificiali di Anghelu Ruju. *Monumenti Antichi dei Lincei* 19: 397–540.

Tinè, S. & Traverso, A. 1992. Relazione preliminare, con la collaborazione di Giannitrapani, E., Giomi, F., Lokosek, I., Tinè, V. & Traversone, B. In *Monte d'Accoddi, 10 anni di nuovi scavi*, I-XLIII. Genova.

Ugas, G. 1985. Elementi culturali prenuragici e nuragici da San Giovanni Battista. In *Nurachi. Storia di un'ecclesia*, 21–26. Oristano.

Ugas, G. 1990. *La tomba dei guerrieri di Decimoputzu*. Norax 1. Edizioni Della Torre, Cagliari.

Ugas, G., Lai, G. & Usai, L. 1989a. L'insediamento prenuragico di Su Coddu (Selargius-Ca). Notizia preliminare sulle campagne di scavo 1981-1984. *Nuovo Bullettino Archeologico Sardo* 2(1985): 7–40.

Ugas, G., Usai, L., Nuvoli, M.P., Lai, G. & Marras, M.G. 1989b. Nuovi dati sull'insediamento di Su Coddu-Selargius. In Campus, L.D. (a cura di), *La cultura di Ozieri. Problematiche e nuove acquisizioni. Atti del I Convegno di Studio (Ozieri, gennaio 1986 – Aprile 1987)*, 239–278. Il Torchietto, Ozieri.

Usai, L. 1987a. Il villaggio di età eneolitica di Terramaini presso Pirri (Cagliari). In *Preistoria d'Italia alla luce delle ultime scoperte. Atti del IV Convegno Nazionale di Preistoria e Protostoria, Pescia (8-9 dicembre 1984)*, 175–192. Pescia.

Usai, L. 1987b. Tracce di insediamenti dalla preistoria al Medio Evo in località Corte Auda di Senorbì (Sardegna). *Studi per l'Ecologia del Quaternario* 8(1986): 147–167.

Usai, L. 1989. Il villaggio prenuragico di Pranu Sisinni (Sardara). *Quaderni della Soprintendenza Archeologica per le Provincie di Cagliari e Oristano* 5(1988): 21–33.

Usai, L. 1990. La ceramica preistorica dell'area del Cronicario. *Rivista di Studi Fenici* 18(1): 103–123.

25. Considerazioni sulle sequenze culturali e cronologiche tra l'Eneolitico e l'epoca nuragica

Giovanni Ugas

Datazioni al C14 con o senza correttivi dendrocronologici?

Mentre nell'ultimo quindicennio si è registrato un sostanziale accordo fra gli archeologi sulle sequenze stratigrafiche e sulla collocazione in cronologia relativa delle *facies* culturali pre-protostoriche sarde, diversamente sono stati espressi pareri anche piuttosto discordanti sulle cronologie assolute, essendosi essi divisi sulle datazioni al C14, ora preferendole non calibrate, ora confidando sui correttivi dendrocronologici.

Ma più che dalla scelta tra due metodi di datazione che definiscono sistemi cronologici paralleli e riducibili l'uno all'altro, entrambi teoricamente accettabili, sono dell'avviso che le diversità di vedute scaturiscano piuttosto dal gran numero di datazioni radiometriche connesse con situazioni contestuali non pienamente definite. L'accertamento della omogeneità del contesto è prioritario poiché quasi sempre sono culturalmente neutri i campioni che si impiegano per le analisi: carboni, legni, ossa, conchiglie e ossidiana atipica. Va aggiunto che, per datare gli edifici, talora vengono presi in considerazione campioni prelevati non già da strati di fondazione e di prima frequentazione, ma da depositi formatisi in tempi di riuso, se non anche dalla superficie.

Nel complesso, nonostante che un numero consistente di datazioni radiometriche debba essere valutato con molta attenzione, specie in campo nuragico, i dati non calibrati del C14 appaiono coerenti con le sequenze delle culture protosarde e con le affini espressioni culturali extrainsulari. Per contro, le correzioni dendro-cronologiche determinano spesso stati di interferenza e sovrapposizione tra le bande cronologiche delle diverse *facies* preistoriche, dilatando in modo così ampio la rosa delle potenziali datazioni da rendere sovente impossibile la loro attribuzione ad uno specifico aspetto culturale, che generalmente non è di lunga durata. Pertanto, in questo lavoro si farà ancora ricorso ai dati radiometrici non calibrati (*half life* 5730 ± 40), nell'attesa che vengano superate le difficoltà qui evidenziate e le altre su cui si era già pronunciato, tra gli altri, il Müller Karpe (1974).

Dal tramonto del Neolitico al Bronzo Antico

Il tema delle sequenze cronologiche e stratigrafiche delle antiche culture della Sardegna, al centro del convegno della Tufts University, è da tanti anni oggetto di ricerche da parte di Giovanni Lilliu (1982; 1988), Ercole Contu (1992a) ed Enrico Atzeni (1981; 1989). Questo mio contributo, che si volge in modo specifico alla Civiltà nuragica, inizia con un richiamo alle premesse culturali eneolitiche che hanno visto radicarsi il primo megalitismo, nell'ambito del più ampio percorso delle tappe preistoriche e storico-antiche della Sardegna (Tab. 25.1).

Le ricerche più recenti inducono a considerare la data del 3200 a.C. come un limite finale non solo per il Neolitico elladico, cicladico e minoico (Treuil *et al.* 1989: 112), ma anche per le *facies* culturali di Bellavista (Cardini 1970: 31–59; Lo Porto 1972: 357–372; Geniola 1987; 1987a; Fedele 1987), di Diana (Bernabò Brea & Cavalier 1960: 47–54; Tiné 1965: 134–145; 1975: 99ss.; Tusa 1983: 174; Cazzella & Moscoloni 1992: 279–289) e di San Ciriaco-Cuccuru Is Arrius (Ugas 1990: 87–92).

Il Neolitico dell'Italia meridionale e insulare volge al tramonto in sincronia con la fine degli orizzonti culturali mediterranei affini: Grey e Red Skorba (Evans 1971: 36–39; 208–212; Trump 1967: 24); Larissa e Orchomenos (Bernabò Brea 1961: 54; cfr. Schachermeyer 1976: 63, tav. 16); El Amrat (Vandier 1952: 368–370); Basien recente (Weiss & de Lanfranchi 1976).

Se, come pare, le prime esperienze metallurgiche per l'ambito peninsulare e insulare italiano vanno attribuite alla cultura di Diana (Bernabò Brea & Cavalier 1981:

678), si sarebbero già manifestate preliminarmente nel tardo Neolitico le più importanti espressioni proprie del Calcolitico centro-meridionale italiano, di Sicilia e di Sardegna: l'ipogeismo, a partire dai sepolcri di Arnesano-Lecce (Lo Porto 1972) e Cuccuru Is Arrius (Santoni 1982); il megalitismo, documentato inizialmente dalle tombe a circolo sarde e corse tipo Li Muri e Portovecchio le quali hanno restituito entrambe coppe in steatite con anse a rocchetto (Ugas 1992: 92; Weiss & de Lanfranchi 1976: 437–441); forme di religiosità espresse dalle statuette antropomorfe di Dea Madre e da simboli di divinità therimorfe e astrali, proprie di popolazioni agricole e pastorali; infine, la stessa metallurgia.

L'arco cronologico della *facies* di San Ciriaco può ben essere compreso all'incirca tra il 3400 e il 3200 a.C. (Ugas 1990), come implica la precoce presenza di elementi tipo Diana in contesti medio-peninsulari assegnati al Neolitico Medio (Radi 1986–87; Cazzella & Moscoloni 1992: 242–245). Ben si raccorderebbero all'orizzonte in questione, e non già a quello di Bonuighinu o di *facies* Ozieri, le datazioni di due livelli di Filiestru al 3399 ± 60 a.C. e al 3234 ± 50 a.C. (Trump 1983).

Per la Cultura di Ozieri si propone il segmento cronologico 3200–2850/2800 a.C., tenendo presenti sia il complesso delle datazioni al C14, sia gli estremi compresi tra il 3140 ± 50 a.C. di Sa Ucca de Su Tintirriolu (Loria & Trump 1978) e 2850 ± 50 a.c. di Grotta del Guano (Castaldi 1972; 1980), oltre che 2880 ± 80 a.C. di Filiestru (Trump 1983: 85). Alla stessa conclusione portano le datazioni e le affinità di complessi e contesti culturali extrainsulari europei e mediterranei: Zebbug (Evans 1971; Loria & Trump 1978: 24; Lilliu 1988: 280); San Cono (Bernabò Brea 1961: 72–73; Tusa 1983: 206–208, 229–230); Lagozza (Barfield 1972; Guerreschi 1965); Peu Richard I (Joussaume 1976: 355–356, fig. 2b); El Gerzeh in Egitto (Vandier 1952: 230–272), che conclude il periodo predinastico intorno al 3100 ± 150 a.C. (Gardiner 1971: 392); Minoico antico I e Cicladico antico I (Treuil 1983; Treuil *et al.* 1989; Schachermeyer 1976).

Sul piano cronologico occorre tenere in considerazione anche le datazioni dei contesti peninsulari che presentano affinità con la cultura ozierese come Mulino di Sant'Antonio (3120 ± 70 a.C.), Rivoli Pozzetto (3125 ± 45 a.C.), Praia a Mare (Cardini 1970), della 3ª fase della Bocca quadrata (Bagolini 1987: 193) e in genere quelli legati all'aspetto di Lagozza, i cui estremi sono compresi tra il 3125 ± 45 e il 2844 ± 90 a.C. (Loria & Trump 1978: 203, n. 238).

La cultura di Ozieri dunque si inquadra nella stessa temperie delle più antiche manifestazioni calcolitiche del Mezzogiorno italiano ed egeo-cretesi ma, nonostante le comprensibili perplessità di Santo Tinè (1992a: 117), poiché la sua industria è fondata sostanzialmente su strumenti litici, essa può ben essere ancora definita neolitica al pari della *facies* di Lagozza e delle fasi tarde di Cortaillod e Chassey (Lilliu 1988: 91–92).

Non si conoscono riferimenti cronologici al C14 per le *facies* Sub-Ozieri, a ceramica subfigulina dipinta in rosso o in bruno (Ugas *et al.* 1985: 14–20; L. Usai 1987) e di Filigosa (Contu 1965; 1988; 1992a; Foschi 1980: 289–303), con predominante vasellame grigio-nerastro "metallico". Entrambe appaiono oramai in diverse sequenze stratigrafiche dopo la cultura di Ozieri, ma mentre la prima nell'insediamento di Su Coddu (strutt. 14) (Ugas *et al.* 1985: 22) dichiara palesemente la propria derivazione dalla matrice ozierese, la seconda nello stesso insediamento di Selargius (strutt. 51), oltre che nella tomba eponima di Filigosa di Macomer e nella sepoltura di Perda Lada (Ugas 1990: 21, tavv. XL, XLIX; 1992b: 43) ha perso gran parte delle caratteristiche formali e tecniche della stessa. Certo è che la ben ridotta quantità d'ossidiana e la già consistente affermazione della metallurgia (Atzeni 1981: XL; Ugas *et al.* 1985: 13; Lilliu 1988: 113, 124–125; Lo Schiavo 1989; Ugas 1993a: 25) tolgono ogni dubbio riguardo alla collocazione nell'Età del Rame, a differenza della cultura di San Michele, di questi due orizzonti culturali.

Tanto le analogie riscontrate tra forme fittili e schemi decorativi Sub-Ozieri e di Serraferlicchio (Ugas *et al.* 1985) quanto le affinità formali e tecnologiche tra materiali degli orizzonti Sub-Ozieri-Filigosa e manufatti di tradizione lagozziana, documentati a Panighina di Bertinoro (Farolfi 1976), Paterno (Cremonesi 1976), Attigio di Fabriano, strato 6 (Lollini 1965), Leone di Agnano, Tana della Mussina, a Lagozza stessa (Cazzella & Moscoloni 1992: 435, 438), inducono a prospettare per le *facies* culturali Sub-Ozieri e Filigosa uno sviluppo intorno al 2850/2800–2700 a.C. e al 2700–2600 a.C., considerate le datazioni al C14 di Paterno al 2850 ± 90 a.C. oltre che di Attigio di Fabriano e Lagozza rispettivamente intorno al 2700 e al 2630 a.C.

Nell'ambito dell'edilizia monumentale, oltre il già citato tempio di Monte d'Accoddi, vanno ricordati i sepolcri ipogeici a pianta rettangolare preceduta da lungo *dromos* che ricalcano lo schema dell'edificio di Monte d'Accoddi (Ugas, in stampa c).

Gli ipogei a lungo *dromos* trovano un riscontro puntuale nella regione parigina della Seine-Oise-Marne in eccezionale contestualità con raffigurazioni petroglifiche della dea madre e di armi (Bailloud 1974: 35, 37,6,9), che richiamano sia le statue-stele sarcidanesi (Atzeni 1994: 206), sia i petroglifi di Moseddu, Is Concas e della tomba della Cava (Contu 1965a). Non sappiamo, però, se le rappresentazioni figurate siano coeve con la realizzazione degli ipogei, che continuano ad essere utilizzati e forse ancora scavati nei tempi di Abealzu. Ora infatti sono documentate nell'anticella sepolcrale offerte rituali successive allè deposizioni (Cocco & Usai 1988) che appaiono ben in sintonia con le raffigurazioni dei defunti-eroi, delle armi e degli oranti delle statue-stele e degli ipogei e pertanto da porsi in relazione con culti eroici.

La specificità della Cultura di Abealzu (Atzeni 1985; Lilliu 1988; Contu 1988: 445–46; 1992a) appare sempre

Palaeolithic		-----	Lower?
		RIO ALTANA-CODROVULOS	450000? BC
		-----	Middle?
		-----	Upper?
		GROTTA CORBEDDU A	15000–11000
Mesolithic		GROTTA CORBEDDU B	11000–6000
Neolithic	Early I	SU CARROPPU	?6000–4700
	Early II	GROTTA VERDE-FILIESTRU	4700–4300
	Early III	FILIESTRU II	4300–3800
	Middle	BONU IGHINU	3800–3400
	Late	SAN CIRIACO	3400–3200
Neol. Final/ Eneol. Initial		OZIERI	3200–2850
Eneolithic (Copper Age)	Early	SUB-OZIERI/FILIGOSA	2850–2600
	Middle	ABEALZU	2600–2400
	Late	MONTE CLARO	2400–2100
	Final	BEAKER A (A1-A2)	2100–1900
Bronze Age	Early I	BEAKER B	1900–1800
	Early II	BONNANNARO A1	1800–1650
	Early II – Middle IA	NUR. IA?/BONNANNARO A2	1650–1550?
	Middle IA	NUR. IA1 / SA TURRICULA	1550–1500
	Middle IB	NUR. IA2 / MONTI MANNU	1500–1400
	Middle II	NUR. IB / S.COSIMO	1400–1330
	Late I	NUR. IIA / MURU MANNU	1330–1270
	Late II	NUR. IIB / ANTIGORI	1270–1150
	Final I	NUR. IIIA / ORISTANO	1150–1000
	Final II	NUR. IIIB / BARUMINI	1000–850
Iron Age I	Geometric	NUR. IVA	850–730
	Orientalising	NUR. IVB / PHOENICIAN	730–580
	Archaic	NUR. IVC	580–510
Iron Age II	A	NUR. VA PUNIC	510–238
	B	NUR. VB ROMAN R.	238–1 BC
	C	NUR. VC? ROMAN I	1–476 AD

Tabella 25.1. Absolute Chronology in Sardinia

più chiaramente col progredire delle ricerche. Sono tipici di questo orizzonte l'anfora a collo cilindrico, la brocca a collo troncoconico, la ceramica chiara acroma, l'ornato a bande verticali accoppiate di linee o di rettangolini impressi con uno strumento a doppia punta, i recipienti grezzi da cucina con corona di fori sotto l'orlo, il peso trapezoidale, le ansette a gomito, la fuseruola bitroncoconica, il *rhyton* conico nel rituale funerario.

Potrebbe essere questo il tempo delle statue-menhir tipo Genn'e Corte e Sa Iddocca di Laconi (Atzeni 1988: 198–213) e delle figurine antropomorfe schematiche delle *domus de janas* tipo Branca-Moseddu, Sas Concas-Oniferi e della grotta della Cava (Contu 1965a; Lilliu 1988: 232) come parrebbero indicare, oltre le già citate espressioni culturali funerarie, sia il peso da telaio trapezoidale, pur non esclusivo di questa cultura, contrassegnato da scene di culto con oranti, altare e simboli astrali da Conca Illonis-Cabras (Atzeni 1992: 60), sia il pugnale a lama triangolare raffigurato nelle stesse statue-stele sarcidanesi. Quest'arma, infatti, è affine ai pugnali di culture e di contesti collocabili nel Medio, se non nel Tardo Calcolitico, come Remedello I, Spilamberto e Grotta del Castello di Vecchiano (Bagolini 1981; Grifoni Cremonesi 1985; Cocchi Genick & Grifoni Cremonesi 1988: Atzeni 1988a: 454; 1988b: 526); Cazzella & Moscoloni 1992). La Cultura di Abealzu

chiude certamente il ciclo vitale del tempio a rampa di Monte d'Accoddi (Contu 1992a; Tinè 1992).

Per il complesso dei materiali Abealzu si possono istituire confronti con le *facies* italiane di Rinaldone I (Rittatore Von Willer & Fedele 1978), Spilamberto (Bagolini 1986), Conca d'Oro I, contesti di Sant'Isidoro e Uditore T2–T3 (cfr. Tusa 1983: figg. 14, 17, 22), Malpasso e Piano Quartara (Bernabò Brea 1988), Alba nel cuneese (Gambari & Venturino Gambari 1985–86) e di quella lombarda caratterizzata dalla *White Ware* (tipo Monte Covolo: Barfield *et al.* 1975–76), oltre che con la cultura franco-elvetica di Horgen (Petrequin 1988: 222). Significativi riscontri si colgono anche nell'Elladico Antico II in cui compaiono forme vascolari affini a Tzepi, oltre che tombe a tumulo circolare con rifascio ad anello, con camera e breve corridoio a Vrana-Maratona T.II–III (Schachermeyer 1976: 198, tav. 26; 248, tav. 67). Questi ultimi monumenti elladici richiamano alcuni circoli di Pranu Muttedu di Goni e di Masoni 'e Perdu (Atzeni 1988b: 527,2; fig. 5.2).

Per la collocazione cronologica di Abealzu vanno tenute in considerazione sia le datazioni intorno 2580 ± 100 al 2370 a.C. di S. Antonio di Buccino, relative alla fase antica di Gaudo (Holloway 1973; Cazzella & Moscoloni 1992: 514), e del 2490 a.C. circa di Rinaldone, sia gli altri riscontri cronologici di Remedello, Corano, Grotta dei Sassi e di Terrina IV, che conducono verso la metà del III Millennio (2600–2400 a.C. ca.) (Cazzella & Moscoloni 1992: 389). Con la stessa banda cronologica sono in linea gli stili di Malpasso (Tiné 1965: 215) e Piano Quartara, considerate le analogie con i complessi dell'EH II–III (Cavalier 1960–61).[1]

Per quanto detto, la data del 2480 ± 50 a.C. del campione Q–3030 di Filiestru (Trump 1983a) si addice non già alla cultura di Monte Claro, ma all'orizzonte di Abealzu per il quale si propone un *iter* compreso tra il 2600 e il 2400 a.C. La cultura di Monte Claro, pressochè assente a M. d'Accoddi (Contu 1992a; Tinè 1990), avvia un nuovo processo sia nell'ambito del megalitismo sacro, documentato a Biriai (Castaldi 1980) e a Monte Baranta (Moravetti 1981), sia nel campo dell'ipogeismo funerario con i sepolcri a pozzetto e celle a forno (Lilliu 1988; Atzeni 1967), sia infine nella sfera religiosa, connotata da un aniconismo (Biriai) che si radicherà nelle espressioni ideologiche e artistiche sarde sino alla soglia della I Età del Ferro.

Principalmente, sono le caratteristiche delle ceramiche che inducono a proporre uno sviluppo della cultura di Monte Claro in sincronia con gli stili di M. Lazzo (Weiss & Desneiges 1971; Weiss & de Lanfranchi 1976: 441), Ferrière tardo e Fontbouisse iniziale (Guilaine & Roudil 1976: 271–276; Guilaine 1988), Peu Richard II (Roussot Larroque 1976: 344), Gigantija (Evans 1961: 159, fig. 28), Vila Nova de Sao Pedro (Harrison 1974: 99), Baden, che però è riportato al 2600–2400 a.C. (Buchvaldech *et al.* 1988: 113–115), oltre che con i contesti di Piscina di Torre Spaccata (Bietti Sestieri 1988), della fase intermedia della *facies* toscana di Vecchiano (Cocchi Genick & Grifoni Cremonesi 1988: 343–345) e dello strato 10 di Romita di Asciano (Peroni 1962–63) che offre un appiglio cronologico indiretto molto importante per M. Claro: 2298 ± 115 a.C.

Problematico è invece da considerarsi l'avvicinamento di M. Claro a Piano Conte poichè l'aspetto eoliano, nonostante l'uso di scanalature in qualche forma fittile, appare ancora impregnato di radici lagozziane (Tusa 1983: 247) e quindi sarebbe in linea con i primi vettori della ceramica a scanalature risalenti al Calcolitico antico (Bernabò Brea 1980) cui pure viene ricondotto lo stile di Vollein (Mezzena 1981; 1982: 198–200, figg. 4–7; Burroni & Mezzena 1988).

Per contro, deviando dai percorsi tracciati da Bernabò Brea (1960: 104; 1988: 493) e in attesa di chiare sequenze stratigrafiche, propendo a credere in uno sviluppo almeno parzialmente sincronico di Monte Claro con Naro-Partanna. Questa ipotesi non può prescindere da una rilettura del quadro culturale siciliano tra il Calcolitico Finale e il Bronzo Medio che induce a collocare la *facies* di Naro-Partanna nel Calcolitico Recente, anteriormente e poi in sincronia con l'aspetto del Vaso Campaniforme, anzichè nel Bronzo Antico. Questa ipotesi si pone in parziale sintonia con un'altra già proposta da D. Amoroso nel 1984 (cfr. Bernabò Brea 1988: 493, n. 443).[2]

In rapporto diretto con Sant'Ippolito, lo stile dipinto di Naro-Partanna (Bernabò Brea 1960: 112) non solo conosce gli ipogei con pozzo e cellette a forno ma, come Monte Claro, propone contenitori fittili provvisti di anse a nastro straordinariamente sviluppate e ornati con temi geometrici, specie a reticolo, avvolgenti tutta la superficie in spartiti verticali e orizzontali.

Le più diffuse strutture sepolcrali di Monte Claro mostrano un pozzetto verticale con una o due celle ellittiche (Lilliu 1988: 137), analoghe agli ipogei pugliesi di Cellino S. Marco (Grifoni Cremonesi 1978: tav. XXXVII) e soprattutto siciliani dell'Uditore (Tusa 1983:fig. 2.9). Poichè questi ultimi sono pertinenti al Medio-Calcolitico (*facies* di Laterza e Malpasso), si potrebbe pensare o a una derivazione degli ipogei Monte Claro da precedenti prototipi sardi di Abealzu, che però non conosciamo, oppure al passaggio degli ipogei a pozzetto in Sardegna, verosimilmente dalla Sicilia, nel Calcolitico Tardo, quando si diffusero gli orizzonti di Sant'Ippolito e di Naro-Partanna.

La datazione della cultura maltese con ceramiche a scanalature e solcature di Gigantija al 2400 a.C. (Trump 1980) offre, forse, il limite più antico per Monte Claro; invece, le datazioni al C14 di Fontbouisse e di Peu Richard II fissano il confine più recente intorno al 2100 a.C. Prudenzialmente si potrebbe pensare a un attardamento della *facies* Monte Claro sino al 2000 a.C., dato che il numero considerevole degli stanziamenti indurrebbe a ipotizzare un lungo periodo di vita, ma va tenuto presente che il Campaniforme "internazionale" che in Sardegna si mostra in sovrapposizione stratigrafica ed è quindi successivo al Monte Claro, nella penisola italiana è datato al C14 intorno al 2100–2050 a.C. In particolare la cronologia del 2150 ± 100 a.C. è riferita a uno strato di Fosso Conicchio che contiene, tra l'altro, un ibrido vaso tetrapode campaniforme con labbro a tesa ornato a solcature, rapportabile a Monte Claro, più che a Fontbouisse (Vigliardi 1980, fig.7; Cazzella & Moscoloni 1992: 585). Pertanto occorre dedurne che la cultura di Monte Claro cessi il suo arco vitale intorno al 2150–2100 a.C., verosimilmente lasciando tra i suoi retaggi il vaso polipode che, tramite la Toscana, può essere pervenuto all'area centroeuropea. In conclusione, per la *facies* calcolitica di Monte Claro si può proporre un ciclo vitale compreso all'incirca tra il 2400 e il 2100 a.C.

Come già anticipato, nelle sequenze stratigrafiche sarde di strutture funerarie quali Padru Jossu (Ugas 1982: 19–25), Santu Pedru (Contu 1964: tav.7) e Su Crucifissu Mannu (Ferrarese Ceruti 1972–74: 118–123; 173–175), materiali della *facies* del Vaso Campaniforme appaiono in sovrapposizione netta e distinta rispetto ai manufatti Monte Claro, implicando la piena autonomia dell'aspetto sardo del Campaniforme "internazionale" nei confronti del Monte Claro (Ugas 1982), mentre appare possibile una parziale contemporaneità di quest'ultimo con la fase *corded ware* campaniforme.

Se per l'inizio delle manifestazioni del Campaniforme A (stile mediterraneo) nell'isola è plausibile la data intorno al 2100, *l'iter* del suo sviluppo non deve essere stato eccessivamente breve. Infatti, nonostante l'assenza quasi totale di dati sugli insediamenti, si può ipotizzare un arco di tempo che arrivi a toccare il 1800, poichè anche in Sardegna il Campaniforme appare in aspetti differenziati che, nell'ambito di un articolato sviluppo interno, precedono e introducono il Bronzo Antico.

Tra il Campaniforme A e il Campaniforme B inornato di Padru Jossu (Ugas 1982; Ferrarese Ceruti 1981), può ben inserirsi la *facies* intermedia Sulcitana o di Locci Santus caratterizzata da ceramiche con decoro a pannelli e ansa a gomito (Atzeni 1975; Ferrarese Ceruti 1988: fig. 8; Fadda 1988a; Contu in stampa; Atzeni in stampa). Nell'aspetto di Locci Santus si intravvedono affinità non solo con Asciano (Peroni 1989: fig. 4) e con la *facies* poladiana arcaica di stampo ancora "campaniforme" (cfr. Barich 1971; Peroni 1989: 60–61), ma anche con contesti di aree prossime all'Isola come quelli di Tanaccia della Brisighella (Farolfi 1976), di Calanchi (Cesari 1994: 40–41) e di altre località peninsulari (cfr. Sarti & Vigliardi 1988: 378–387; Peroni 1989). Né possono essere sottovalutate le analogie con un momento tardo di Castelluccio la cui ceramica, sebbene dipinta, conosce i riquadri inquartati e soprattutto il motivo, non comune, del triangolo con pendaglio a *w* (Bernabò Brea 1978: 106, fig. G,7), come il vasellame dello stile sulcitano del Campaniforme sardo (Atzeni 1987, fig. 9,10; Ferrarese Ceruti 1981: LXI,95) e come la ceramica di Polada I (es. Radmilli 1978, tav. XLIV:23). Al pendaglio a *w* va attribuito lo stesso significato simbolico dei pendagli a spirali e delle "perline ad *ailettes*", che si riscontrano frequentemente nei contesti e nelle stele della cultura campaniforme, ma anche di momenti più antichi (Buchvaldech *et al.* 1988: fig. 1; Burroni & Mezzena 1988: fig. 8).

Finora non esiste alcun riscontro cronometrico assoluto dei depositi in strato della cultura del Vaso Campaniforme in Sardegna. È però possibile che a questa *facies* appartengano tanto il campione di Noeddos-Mara datato al 2040 ± 50 a.C. quanto i pezzi in ossidiana di Palattu-Birori e di Fruscos-Paulilatino, risalenti rispettivamente al 1973 ± 125 e al 1904 ± 105 a.C.

Per risalire alla cronologia del Campaniforme isolano non possono essere tralasciate le datazioni di due contesti con manufatti del Vaso Campaniforme di siti extrainsulari che mostrano di aver avuto contatti, diretti o mediati, con la Sardegna quali Monte Covolo nel bresciano, che fuori contesto ha restituito anche ossidiana di Monte Arci (Barfield *et al.* 1975–76) e Calanchi in Corsica (Cesari 1994: 41).

Lo strato di Monte Covolo con bicchiere decorato in stile marittimo come quelli della fase A del Campaniforme sardo, viene datato al 2060 ± 40 a.C. Più recente appare il deposito di Calanchi, riferito al 1910 ± 150 a.C., che ha restituito un frammento fittile affine per l'ornato non solo a materiali romagnoli di Tanaccia di Brisighella (Farolfi 1976) e Piano della Querciola (Sarti & Martini 1988: 594; Sarti & Vigliardi 1988: 380, fig. 209), ma anche a manufatti della *facies* campaniforme recente o sulcitana (Atzeni 1995: 180, fig. 30,2–6. Potremmo definire Campaniforme A2 la *facies* sulcitana per differenziarla dall'aspetto sardo del Campaniforme internazionale, a sua volta distinguibile con la denominazione di Campaniforme A1.

Per quanto detto, è verosimile che nell'Isola le *facies* del Campaniforme con vasi decorati abbiano abbracciato un periodo compreso all'incirca tra il 2100–2050 e il 1950–1900 a.C.

Nell'ipogeo di Padru Jossu i vasi inornati del Campaniforme B occupano la posizione più alta del deposito tombale, dove ci saremmo aspettati strati intermedi con ceramica ornata sulcitana. Forme tipiche del Campaniforme B sono la tazza tipo Cadimarco (di cui però non va esclusa una sua origine già nel Campaniforme A1 essendo stata trovata dispersa in frammenti), il tripode a conca profonda e il bicchiere ansato. Gli innumerevoli elementi di collana in conchiglia sottintendono una componente veicolare molto forte di genti costiere mediterranee, mentre i bottoni e i pendenti in osso e in avorio presuppongono la circolazione di prodotti d'origine pastorale. Le lesine romboidali in rame denunciano l'avvio di relazioni con le aree centro-europee attraverso il Midi francese (Guilaine 1972: 60).

La *facies* del Campaniforme B si configura come un complesso chiaramente transizionale tra il Campaniforme A e la *facies* Bonnanaro del sito eponimo e dunque tra il Calcolitico Finale e il Bronzo Antico. Le maggiori affinità si colgono nella già citata *facies* siciliana di Rodì-Tindari-Vallelunga (Bernabò Brea 1960; Tusa 1983: 353–360), oltre che in un momento di Polada I (Peroni 1971; Barich 1971; Peroni 1989), caratterizzato da ceramica inornata, di tradizione tipologica campaniforme, appena successivo alla *facies* di Asciano.

Orientativamente si propone per il Campaniforme B, che segna l'avvio del Bronzo Antico in Sardegna, un *excursus* cronologico compreso tra il 1950–1900 e il 1850–1800 a.C.

La stratigrafia della "Tomba dei Guerrieri" di Sant'Iroxi-Decimoputzu (Ugas 1990: 86–87; 98–111) ha posto l'esigenza di una ripartizione interna nell'ambito della cultura di Bonnanaro A. Infatti alla *facies* caratterizzata dal tripode carenato con alti piedi trapezoidali e ansa a gomito semplice o appena sopraelevato, propria dell'ipogeo eponimo di Corona Moltana, segue un complesso caratterizzato dalle più antiche spade sarde e da ollette a collo spesso svasato, provviste di quattro anse a gomito sopraelevato o ad anello. I due momenti sono stati distinti rispettivamente in Bonnanaro A1 e Bonnanaro A2.

Il Bonnanaro A1 corrisponde alle *facies* culturali di Polada I, del Protoappenninico A e di Capo Graziano I. Finora sono pochissimi i riscontri cronometrici. Il contesto funerario in grotta di Sisaia (Ferrarese Ceruti & Germanà 1978), che ha restituito vasellame assegnabile al Bonnanaro A1, propone la data del 1850 ± 100 a.C.; questa è compatibile con l'arco cronologico del 1800–1600 a.C., già proposto per la cultura di Bonnannaro, ma può aprire anche uno spiraglio per un suo rialzo.

Altre due datazioni sono assegnabili problematicamente alla cultura di Bonnanaro A. La prima, del 1855 ± 40 a.C., teoricamente riferibile anche al Campaniforme B, è pertinente a uno strato della grotta di Filiestru privo di manufatti che si inserisce nella sequenza tra il Monte Claro e il Nuragico (Lilliu 1988: 20; Trump 1983). La seconda del 1740 ± 60 a.C., relativa a un campione della grotta Acqua Cadda-Nuxis (Lilliu 1988: 19), proviene da un deposito non omogeneo comprendente non solo materiali della cultura di Monte Claro, cui in un primo momento fu riferita la datazione radiometrica, ma anche delle *facies* Bonnanaro A e B.

L'aspetto Bonnanaro A2 di Sant'Iroxi funge da raccordo tra il Bronzo Antico e il Bronzo Medio e, pur essendo probabile che possa stare sul gradino iniziale della scala nuragica, non vi è stato inserito poichè finora non compare in chiari contesti stratigrafici sicuramente pertinenti ad edifici nuragici. Certo è che nel complesso di S. Iroxi le più antiche spade sarde fanno la loro apparizione insieme a forme ceramiche come l'olletta globoide a collo svasato a due o quattro anse impostate sul ventre, che accompagnano l'evolversi di tutta la civiltà nuragica. Per converso, scompare simultaneamente il vaso tripode che caratterizza tutto l'Eneolitico e il Bronzo Antico mentre l'ansa a gomito, pur persistendo, tende a svilupparsi in un profilo asciforme. Infine va considerato che uno dei pugnali di S. Iroxi è tipologicamente affine ad un'arma reperita a Sa Turricula (Ugas 1990: 107) e dunque i due aspetti di S. Iroxi e di Sa Turricula dovrebbero essere contigui e in rapporto di successione diretta, come per altro sembrano proporre anche le affinità dei loro contesti abitativi.

La comparsa delle spade in bronzo arsenicale marca in modo inequivocabile l'avvio di una nuova temperie sociale e culturale che pare coincidere non solo sul piano umorale, ma anche cronologico, con due ben noti fenomeni culturali: il Protoappenninico B e la Civiltà micenea (Peroni 1983). E' un clima che, qualche decennio prima o dopo il 1600 a.C., prelude o dà l'avvio alle innumerevoli poderose opere di fortificazione costruite a difesa e a controllo ad un tempo dei territori e delle comunità, protonuraghi prima e nuraghi poi, che connotano gran parte dell'Età del Bronzo isolana (Ugas 1990: 129–135).

Contesti esemplificativi del Bonnanaro A2, oltre Sant'Iroxi, sono: Fanne Massa, *domus* IV e Sa Rocca Tunda o Saline (Ferrarese Ceruti & Germanà 1978; Ferrarese Ceruti 1989: 68–69, tavv. 28–30). A questo momento potrebbe essere attribuita l'edificazione dei sepolcri ad *allée*, quali Li Lolghi, Coddu Vecchiu e Monte de S'Ape (Castaldi 1968: 8ss.; 1969: 2ss.; Lilliu 1988: 318), oltre che Sos Ozzastros (Lilliu 1988: fig. 126,1), poi ristrutturati come tombe di giganti, e infine forse M. Gonella (Atzeni 1975: 44,10–11; Lilliu 1988: 162, fig. 43,51). Infine è documentato il riuso degli ipogei funerari nei citati siti di S. Iroxi, Fanne Massa e Sa Rocca Tunda.

Le tracce insediative si limitano purtroppo ai soli resti di superficie individuati in particolare a Santu Srebestianu-San Sperate (Ugas 1990: 203, tav. II) e a M. Conella (Sebis 1986; 1994: 101, tav. II), dove però è documentata anche una fase successiva con ceramica a cordoni.

Per la *facies* Bonnanaro A2 si prospetta, sia pure in modo orientativo, un *excursus* cronologico tra il 1650 e il 1550 a.C. poichè ad esso indirizza il complesso delle relazioni con le regioni extrainsulari: Sicilia occidentale, aspetto di Contrada Pergola (Naro-Partanna), *allée* e ceramiche inornate con anse a gomito asciforme (Tusa 1983: 355s., fig. 58); Eolie, ceramica di Capo Graziano I finale (Bernabò Brea 1985: 140–141); Italia Settentrionale: ceramiche di Polada I finale e dell'area tosco-laziale (Ceccanti 1980: 337–339); manufatti della *facies* di Montemerano, di transizione al Bronzo Medio iniziale (Peroni 1971; Negroni Catacchio 1981: 104–109, tav. 19); daghe e spade dell'Italia Settentrionale tipo San Martino-Udine (Peroni 1971: fig. 8.2) e Roncoferraro-Mantova (Bianco Peroni 1970: tav. 2–3, 16; tav. 3:17); prime spade di El Argar (Almagro Gorbea 1972; Ugas 1990 e in stampa b), oggetto di controverse proposte di seriazioni e datazioni (Ayala Juan 1991; Lo Schiavo 1991).[3]

La civiltà nuragica

Le facies culturali

Confermando il quadro della Civiltà nuragica tracciato da Giovanni Lilliu (1988), pienamente condiviso nelle linee generali (Ugas 1992), una nuova analisi delle compagini culturali e delle associazioni tra i manufatti mobili e le strutture edilizie mi induce ora a prospettare una nuova seriazione interna dei periodi nuragici. Conseguente è la formulazione di una più dettagliata proposta cronologica e terminologica che vuole essere un punto d'orientamento in una problematica *in fieri* (Tab. 25.2).

Nell'ambito del Bronzo Medio I è stato enucleato l'orizzonte culturale caratterizzato dalla ceramica decorata a nervature plastiche, bozze e coppelle, documentata nel protonuraghe Monti Mannu di Serrenti (Ugas 1992). La nuova *facies*, che ora viene denominata di Monti Mannu, occupa una posizione intermedia tra la facies di Sa Turricula, connotata da una più rada ed elementare decorazione a cordoni verticali e propria del sito eponimo di Sa Turricula (Ferrarese Ceruti 1981), e la *facies* del Bronzo Medio II o di San Cosimo, con ceramica a decoro "metopale" (Ugas 1981).

Nella sequenza delle fasi nuragiche della Sardegna centro-meridionale, dopo la *facies* di San Cosimo trova collocazione, agli inizi del Bronzo Recente, l'aspetto culturale che trae la denominazione dall'insediamento nuragico di Muru Mannu (Santoni 1985). Connotato dalla ceramica liscia, spesso nero-lustrata, e da pochi tegami ornati a pettine, questo orizzonte, nello stesso sito di Muru Mannu (Bernardini 1989) e, presumiamo, a Nuraxi Arrubiu (Lo Schiavo & Vagnetti 1993), è vincolato sul piano cronologico alle ceramiche d'importazione del Myc. III A2:1 finale.

L'assegnazione del contesto di Muru Mannu al Bronzo Recente, anzichè come sinora prospettato al Bronzo Medio, discende dal fatto che le forme vascolari del sito tharrense preludono a quelle in pasta grigio-ardesia e non comprendono più le olle a tesa interna e la relativa decorazione metopale.[4] Con questa nuova posizione culturale e cronologica del complesso di Muru Mannu assumono ben altro significato le ceramiche d'importazione micenea da considerarsi in piena contestualità coi materiali nuragici in quanto questi ultimi sono l'espressione di un unico momento culturale.

Così allo stato attuale delle ricerche, salvo un eventuale rialzamento cronologico della ceramica micenea di Muru Mannu, non esiste alcun dato oggettivo che induca a collocare i classici nuraghi turriti nella prima metà del XIV secolo: finora infatti la ceramica metopale, attribuibile per l'appunto al pieno XIV secolo, non è mai stata rinvenuta in chiari strati di frequentazione pertinenti a tali strutture.[5]

L'aspetto della ceramica grigio-ardesia viene così ad occupare la seconda parte del Bronzo Recente. Ad esso

PERIODO NURAGICO I (PROTONURAGICO O DEI NURAGHI A CORRIDOI)
Facies Bonnannaro B o Bonnannaro II o Subbonnannaro
(Bronzo Medio: 1600/1550 – 1330 a.C.)
IA. (BM 1: XVI-XV sec. a.C.)
   A1. Facies di Sa Turricula (BM 1A: 1600/1550 – 1500)
   A2. Facies di Monti Mannu o della Ceramica nervature (BM 1B: 1500–1400 a.C.)
IB. Facies di San Cosimo o della Ceramica metopale (BM 2: 1400–1300 a.C)

PERIODO NURAGICO II (NURAGICO CLASSICO I O DEI NURAGHI TURRITI)
(Bronzo Recente: 1330–1150 a.C.)
IIA. Facies di Muru Mannu o della Ceramica lustrata (BR 1: 1330–1270 a.C.).
IIB. Facies di Antigori o della Ceramica grigio-ardesia (BR 2: 1270–1150 a.C)

PERIODO NURAGICO III (NURAGICO CLASSICO II O NURAGICO FINALE)
(Bronzo Finale: 1150–850 a.C.)
IIIA. Facies di Oristano (BF1: 1150–1000 a.C. circa)
IIIB. Facies di Barumini (BF2: 1000–900/850 a.C.)

PERIODO NURAGICO IV (PERIODO DEI NURAGHI-TEMPLI)
(I Età del Ferro: IX-VI sec. a.C.)
IVA. Facies del Geometrico (900/850–730 a.C.)
IVB. Facies Orientalizzante (730–600 a.C.)
   1. Orientalizzante I o antico (730–670 a.C.)
   2. Orientalizzante II o medio ed evoluto (670–600 a.C)
IVC. Facies Arcaica (600–510 a.C)

PERIODO NURAGICO V (PERIODO NURAGICO BARBARICINO)
(II Età del Ferro: sec. V a.C.- sec. I d.C.)
VA. Facies I barbaricina (510–238 a.C)
VB. Facies II barbaricina (238 a.C.–sec. I a.C.)
VC. Facies barbaricina (sec. I a.C.–sec. V d.C)

Tabella 25.2: Periodi, Fasi e Facies della Civiltà nuragica

---

ben si addice la titolatura di *facies* di Antigori, dal nuraghe in cui il vasellame-grigio ardesia è stato documentato in associazione a manufatti del Myc. III B dalla compianta prof.ssa Maria Luisa Ferrarese Ceruti (1983).

Durante il Bronzo Recente la Sardegna settentrionale pare interessata da una seriazione parallela in parte simile; ad analoghi complessi a ceramica liscia lustrata e con (pochi?) tegami decorati, sembrano succedere contesti con tegami frequentemente ornati a pettine, coevi di quelli meridionali a ceramica grigio-ardesia.

Anche i materiali del Bronzo Finale indirizzano al riconoscimento di due distinti aspetti. A un momento iniziale di quest'età vanno riferiti i contesti tipo Madonna del Rimedio di Oristano, strato II (Santoni & Sebis 1985) e Fondo Camedda strato II (Sebis 1987); essi appaiono in linea di discendenza diretta con la *facies* a ceramica grigio-ardesia di cui conservano diverse proprietà. Appartengono invece a una fase più tarda i contesti tipo Barumini (Su Nuraxi), strato sottostante la capanna 135 (Lilliu 1955), e tipo capanna R di S'Urbale (Fadda 1987), nei quali si afferma la ceramica punzonata e l'ansa a gomito rovescio; essi palesano oramai il superamento totale delle caratterisiche proprie della *facies* di Antigori.

Si ritiene che per i due aspetti del Bronzo Finale possa essere appropriata la titolatura di *facies* di Oristano, per il momento più antico, e di *facies* di Barumini per il momento più recente.

Qui appresso si propone, necessariamente in breve sintesi, e con tanti punti interrogativi, il profilo delle singole *facies* che compongono il sistema culturale nuragico mediante specifiche schede di riferimento.

Periodo Nuragico I
(Protonuragico o dei Nuraghi a corridoi)
Facies *Bonnanaro B (Bonnanaro II o Subbonnanaro)*
(Bronzo Medio: 1600/1550–1330 a.C)

IA. Facies Bonnannaro B1 (Bronzo Medio I: XVI–XV sec. a.C.)

SCHEDA 1

IA1. *Facies di Sa Turricula* (BM 1A: 1600/1550–1500 a.C.)

Complessi tipici: Sa Turricula-Muros (Ferrarese Ceruti-Germanà 1978; Ferrarese Ceruti 1981); S. Vittoria di Nuraxinieddu (Sebis 1992: 137, Tav.II,b); Fruscos-Paulilatino (Manca Demurtas & Demurtas 1984); Oridda (Castaldi 1968; 1975).

Manufatti: ceramica ornata a nervature semplici e a bozze; anse a gomito asciforme; pugnale tipo sa Turricula (Ferrarese Ceruti Germanà 1978); daga tipo Siniscola? (Lo Schiavo 1978: 85–87; Ugas 1990: 223).

Monumenti: inizialmente protonuraghi a pianta semplice lineare e corridoio passante, a taglio tronco-conico poco aggettante tipo Fruscos-Paulilatino, Tusari-Bortigali Fase I, Funtan'e Suei-Norbello (Lilliu 1982: 5,4–6, 8; Contu 1985: 59, c–d,f,h–i; Manca Demurtas & Demurtas 1984: 177–184, figg. 9–13; 1992: fig. 4; Moravetti 1992: figg. 7–9); successivamente primi protonuraghi a pianta semplice e corridoio chiuso tipo Peppe Gallu-Uri, Cunculu-Scano, Crastu A e S'Umboe di Ghilarza, Tusari Fase II (Lilliu 1988: figg. 49,1; 47,2; Manca Demurtas & Demurtas 1984: figg. 16–17; 5.8,1); all'inizio del periodo, se non già nel Bonnanaro A2, tombe di giganti con stele centinata, ortostati e camera a corridoio di sezione rettangolare tipo Goronna (Lilliu 1948), Li Lolghi (Castaldi 1969: 2ss.), Monte de S'Ape (Castaldi 1968: 7–25, fig. 26) e Thomes (Moravetti 1980: 83, tavv. XXIIs.); tombe di giganti ipogeiche in muratura con stele centinata, tipo Oridda (Castaldi 1975: 41–43, 60–68).

Insediamenti: capanne ellittiche in muratura (a copertura lignea?)

di Sa Turricula (Ferrarese Ceruti-Germanà 1978); area insediativa attorno al Nuraghe Chessedu? (Ferrarese Ceruti 1981: LXXI,c).

Relazioni extrainsulari: *talajots* balearici con corridoio passante tipo Ses Paisses, Rafal Roig e S. Monica (Lilliu 1982: fig. 6,2,4,6); *talajots* con corridoio chiuso tipo Frontadones de Baix-Mercadal (Lilliu 1988: fig. 49:2); *torri* corse a corridoio aperto tipo Torre (Lilliu & Shubart 1967: 19–20; fig. 5,c) e a corridoio chiuso tipo Balestra (Lilliu & Schubart 1967: fig. 5,a); corridoio a taglio tronco-conico di fortificazioni egee come Ajia Irini di Keos (Davis 1986: tavv. 39–40a); ceramica del Protoappenninico B (Lo Porto 1963: 317ss.; 1964; Peroni 1983: 217–227; Damiani *et al.* 1984: 1–38, figg. 1–9); ceramica di Capo Graziano II (Bernabò Brea & Cavalier 1980: 691ss.).

SCHEDA 2

IA2. Facies di Monti Mannu o della ceramica a nervature (BM 1B: 1500–1400 a.C)

Complessi: Monti Mannu-Serrenti (Ugas 1992: tav. IV); Su Molinu, Vano *Bs* (Ugas 1987: figg. 5.2-6); Bau Mendula (Santoni 1992: figg. 5–8).

Manufatti: ceramica a nervature; orli dei vasi spesso appiattiti a tesa; anse ad anello insellato; triade betilica delle stele centinate di Furrighesos e Campu Lontanu (Contu 1978: 19–21; figg.3–4,16, tavv. II–IV; Lilliu 1977: tavv. I–XIX; Tanda 1984; Lilliu 1988: fig. 85); spada corta a lama piatta e margini affilati tipo Su Molinu (Ugas 1987: fig. 5.6).

Monumenti: protonuraghi semplici con camera singola a pianta oblunga tipo Fronte Mola-Thiesi (Lilliu 1988: 47,13; Contu 1985: 67, fig. s., tavv. 98–99) e più tardi protonuraghi complessi con camere a volta troncoconica (naviforme), corridoi voltati a gradini rovesci, tipo Friarosu (Manca Demurtas & Demurtas 1984: fig. 15), Bruncu Madugui fase I (Badaṣ 1992: 36, tav. IV); successivamente protonuraghi con cellette subovali a ingresso fuori asse, provviste di volta gradonata proto-ogivale tipo Su Molinu Fase I (Ugas 1987: figg. 5.7,Va–Vc–ci9; ipogei con prospetto a stele centinata tipo Campu Lontanu (Contu 1978: 47, fig. 14, tav. III; Lilliu 1988); tombe di giganti con camera a taglio tronco-ogivale in muratura e stele centinata tipo Aiodda (Atzeni 1980) tempio bicellulare absidato tipo Malchittu (?) (Ferrarese Ceruti 1962: 5–27).

Insediamenti: capanne ellittiche in muratura tipo Bau Mendula-Villaurbana (Santoni 1992: 127–128, fig. 5:1); capanne oblunghe tipo S. Cristina-Paulilatino e Grutt'i Acqua-Sant'Antioco (?) (Lilliu 1980: 313–314).

Relazioni extrainsulari: tombe a camera oblunga a taglio tronco-ogivale tipo Thorikos I e IV (Mussche *et al.* 1984); tomba a *tholos* tronco-conica di San Vito ai Normanni (Lo Porto 1964: 101–142); prime *navetas* baleariche (Rosselló Bordoy 1992: 421–442; Veny 1992: 443–472); triade betilica in rilievo su brocche e *cantharoi* eoliani (Bernabò Brea 1985: 68,72, tav. VII,1,3); ceramiche del Protoappenninico B dell'Italia meridionale e delle regioni medio-tirreniche e ceramiche di contesti peninsulari settentrionali, tipo Bor-Cisano-Isolone, con decorazione plastica a bozze, scanalature e grosse cuppelle, e vasi con anse a gomito con appendice asciforme (Peroni 1989: 42–56, figg.7–10).

SCHEDA 3

IB. Facies di San Cosimo o della ceramica metopale (Bronzo Medio II: 1400–1330 a.C.)

Complessi: S. Cosimo (Ugas 1981: 7–12, figg. 1–6; 1982b), Palattu-Birori (Moravetti 1984: 69–94); Bruncu Madugui (Badas 1992: tav. IV), fase 2; Montigu Mannu (Sebis 1992: 135–139, tav. III; 1995: 103, tav. VIII); S. Maria Su Claru (Sebis 1995: tavv. VI–VII).

Manufatti: ceramica a decoro plastico e impresso in schemi metopali; olla biconica a tesa interna; olla a labbro ingrossato triangolare appiattito; collanine con perline globulari in vetro blu; *segmented beads*, rosette e dischetti in pasta verde-acqua tipo S. Cosimo (Ugas 1982c: tav. LXVIII); daghe in bronzo (?), con codolo a uncino tipo Is Lapideddas (Ugas, in stampa b); betili tipo Tamuli (Lilliu 1977; Contu 1978).

Monumenti: all'inizio del periodo, se non già alla fine del periodo precedente, protonuraghi evoluti con grandi camere oblunghe a volta tronco-ogivale tipo Su Molinu, Fase II, vano *e* (Ugas 1987: figg. 5.1-4; 1989–1990: 551–553: figg. 1–2); tombe di giganti con volta a taglio tronco-ogivale ed emiciclo frontale in muratura con stele tipo Tamuli (Contu 1978: 6) o senza stele tipo San Cosimo (Ugas 1981) e Palattu (Moravetti 1984); alla fine del periodo primi bastioni turriti con camere circolari e corridoi a *tholos* ogivale (?).

Insediamenti: Montigu Mannu-Massama (Sebis 1992: 135–139, tav. III; 1995: 103, tav. VIII); Antigori, strato sotto l'ambiente *q* (Ferrarese Ceruti 1987: 88); Domu Beccia-Uras (Ferrarese Ceruti & Lo Schiavo 1991–92: 132).

Relazioni extrainsulari: ceramica impressa e incisa in schemi metopali del Torreano (Atzeni 1966a: tav. X; Weiss 1992: 370–371), datata a Sant'Agata 1340 ± 80 a.C., e meso-appenninnica (Puglisi 1959; Peroni 1967; Fugazzola Delpino 1976; Peroni 1989); ceramiche impresse e incise a schemi metopali e forme architettoniche delle tombe a *tholos* delle culture di Thapsos e Milazzese (Ugas 1992a, cfr. Bernabò Brea 1960: 119–164; Tusa 1983: 389–442; Tomasello 1986: 93–104); camere delle tombe a *tholos* del Myc. III A2 (Ugas 1987); perline in vetro blu e *faïence* del Mediterraneo orientale (Egitto, Egeo, Ellade) (Ugas 1982b); testine in avorio di guerriero da ambiti micenei o minoici (Ferrarese Ceruti *et al.* 1987).

Periodo Nuragico II
(Nuragico Classico o dei Nuraghi Turriti)
(Bronzo Recente: 1330–1150 a.C.)

SCHEDA 4

IIA. Facies di Muru Mannu o della ceramica nero-lustrata (BR1: 1330–1270 a.C.)

Complessi: contesti arcaici centro-meridionali in parte già riferiti al Bronzo Medio, con rari tegami ornati a pettine, tipo Muru Mannu-Cabras (Santoni 1985), Madonna del Rimedio-Oristano, fase I (Santoni & Sebis 1985: tavv. III–IV; Sebis 1995) e Piscu-Suelli cap.1, strato VII (Santoni 1992a: tavv. IV–V); contesti settentrionali con limitata ceramica a pettine tipo Albucciu di Arzachena (Ferrarese Ceruti 1962a) e Don Michele-di Ploaghe (Fadda 1979: tav. IV).

Manufatti: ceramica inornata, lustrata a engobbio nero dei complessi citati; tegami con ornato a pettine (Lilliu 1982); olla a labbro triangolare a sviluppo tendenzialmente ellittico; dischetti e rosette in *faïence* tipo Perd'Accuzzai (Cocco & Usai 1992: 187–191).

Monumenti: monotorri e bastioni turriti con camera a volta conica tipo Don Michele di Ploaghe (Fadda 1979), Marfudi (Lilliu 1982: 77), Piscu (Santoni 1987), Nuraghe Arrubiu (Lo Schiavo & Sanges 1994); Su Nuraxi-Barumini fase I (Lilliu & Zucca 1984); tombe di giganti a taglio ogivale tipo Perd'Accuzzai (Cocco & Usai 1992); templi a pozzo a massi poligonali tipo S.Anastasia di Sardara? (Taramelli 1918).

Insediamenti: capanne circolari tipo Muru Mannu.

Relazioni extrainsulari: ambienti elladici o minoici sia per la ceramica d'importazione del Myc. III A2 finale di Muru Mannu (Bernardini 1989: 285–90) e di Nuraxi Arrubiu (Lo Schiavo 1990: 43–45; Lo Schiavo & Vagnetti 1993: 121–146), sia per la testina eburnea di guerriero da Mitza Purdia? (Sanna 1984; Ferrarese Ceruti *et al.* 1987); mediazione di Lipari per le perle in *faïence*?

SCHEDA 5

IIB. *Facies* di Antigori o della ceramica grigio-ardesia nel Centro-Sud; facies della ceramica a pettine evoluta (tipo La Prisciona) nel Settentrione (BR2: Metà XIII–metà XII sec. a.C.)

Complessi: contesti evoluti a ceramica grigio-ardesia della Sardegna centro-meridionale tipo Antigori, torre *f* strato 8 (Ferrarese Ceruti 1983: fig. 6,a), Is Argiddas-Samassi sacca 12 (Ugas 1989), M. Zara, str. 32 S (Ugas 1992), Cuccuru Arrius fase I (Sebis 1987), Cuccuru Nuraxi (Atzeni 1987a), Su Molinu vano F1 strato 4 (Ugas 1987: 81–82, fig. 5.15–16), Madonna del Rimedio, Fase II (Santoni & Sebis 1985: tav. II); contesti evoluti con tegami decorati a pettine della Sardegna settentrionale tipo Santu Antine (Bafico & Rossi 1988).

Manufatti: nel Centro-Sud: ciotole a calotta a labbro interno, conche a labbro ingrossato e anforette in ceramica grigio-ardesia; conche e olle in ceramica gialla; anfore a collo e olle a labbro ingrossato con anse a sviluppo ellittico nastriforme (Ugas 1989; Sebis 1995); pugnale in bronzo tipo Corti Beccia (Ugas 1982a: 41, tav. XXVII.82); nel Centro-Nord: tegami frequentemente ornati a pettine, anfore a collo e olle a labbro ingrossato triangolare con anse a profilo ellittico nastriforme tipo La Prisciona, trincea *a*, strati 4–5 (Contu 1966: figg. 13–18), Chessedu, Logomache, Pizzinnu e San Pietro-Torpè (Lilliu 1988: 72–78).

Monumenti: bastioni turriti terrazzati con coronamento di mensole, in opera subsquadrata o in *ashlar masonry* come su Nuraxi-Barumini fase II, piani superiori delle torri laterali (Lilliu & Zucca 1988: 39, fig.22), nuraghi Losa e S. Antine (Contu 1985; Lilliu 1988); tombe di giganti a emiciclo con camera a taglio ogivale tipo Is Concas-Quartucciu (Atzeni 1966: fig. 5, tavv. VIII–X) per i quali però non va esclusa la pertinenza ancora al Nuragico IIA; primi templi a pozzo e prime tombe di giganti a conci isodomi e a cornici a dentelli tipo Biristeddi (Lilliu 1988; Moravetti 1985).

Insediamenti: capanne circolari con nicchie tipo 1–2 di Monte Zara (Ugas 1992).

Relazioni extrainsulari: ceramica d'importazione del Myc. IIIB, Myc. III C1 e Minoico III B (Ferrarese Ceruti 1981b; Ferrarese Ceruti & Vagnetti 1982; Ugas 1992); contesti subappenninici; ollette con anse ellittiche dell'orizzonte recente della *facies* di Peschiera-Bovolone assegnato al BR (Peroni 1989: 70, fig. 18); ceramica grigio-ardesia e anfore a collo della Sardegna meridionale rinvenute a Kommós sulle coste della Creta sud-occidentale (Watrous 1989; Watrous, in questo volume); corridoi a taglio ogivale delle mura di Tirinto e di Hattushas (Ugas 1987); porte trilitiche e apparato in *ashlar masonry* della cinta di Micene (Ugas 1987: 89–93); tempio a pozzo di Gjiarlo in Tracia (Mitova Dzonova 1992: 587–595, tavv. 1–3,); corridoio gradonato a taglio ogivale della fonte Perseia di Micene (Ugas 1987: 89; fonte termale in *aslar masonry* di San Calogero-Lipari (Bernabò Brea & Cavalier 1990; Belli 1990); strutture termali egee con *tholos* conica (Belli 1992); *tholoi* sepolcrali micenee tipo Tesoro d'Atreo in *ashlar masonry*; *tholoi* ipogeiche del Bronzo Recente siciliano (Tomasello 1986).

Periodo Nuragico III o Nuragico Finale
(Bronzo Finale: 1150–900/850 a.C.)

SCHEDA 6

III A. *Facies* di Oristano (BF1: 1150–1000 a.C. circa)

Complessi: Madonna del Rimedio di Oristano, fase II (Santoni-Sebis 1986: 97–101); Cuccuru Arrius, area tempio Fase II (Sebis 1987: tav. II); Sianeddu-Cabras (Ugas 1995); Su Molinu-Villanovafranca vano F3 strati 4–5 rimestati (Ugas 1987); Su Fraigu-San Sperate T.6 (Ugas 1993: 103–115); Antigori, torre *f* strato non omogeneo 7 (Ferrarese Ceruti 1983).

Manufatti: ceramica inornata grigia e nerastra; olle a labbro ingrossato e anfore a collo con anse ad anello semplice.

Monumenti: templi a conci isodomi tipo Cuccuru Is Arrius (Sebis 1987) e Santa Cristina-Paulilatino (Lilliu 1988); tombe di giganti a dentelli nel centro-Nord (Lilliu 1982; Moravetti 1985) tombe semipogeiche in muratura absidate, senza esedra, tipo Su Fraigu, T6 (Ugas 1993: 103–104).

Insediamenti: edifici a moduli quadrangolari con muri di mattoni di fango tipo Monte Zara strutt. 6–7, 12, 19/23 (Ugas 1992); capanne circolari raccordate tipo Bruncu Madugui (Lilliu 1982: fig. 113).

Relazioni extrainsulari: Peloponneso, Creta e Cipro per la ceramica dipinta d'importazione e d'imitazione micenea di Antigori (Ferrarese Ceruti 1987) e Su Molinu (Ugas 1987); Peloponneso e Creta, con intermediazione di Lipari? (cfr. Bernabò Brea 1960: 126–133, fig. 24, tav. 55), per il sigillo a cilindro e le perline in *faïence* tipo su Fraigu (Ugas 1993).

SCHEDA 7

IIIB. *Facies* di Barumini (BF2: 1000–900/850 a.C.)

Complessi: Su Nuraxi-Barumini, area 135 (Lilliu 1955; 1982: fig. 120); S'Urbale-Teti, capanna R (Fadda 1985; 1987).

Manufatti: ceramica prevalentemente inornata. Olle e anfore a collo con ansa a gomito rovescio. Comparsa dell'ornato a punzone; spade a traforo e asce ad occhiello tipo M. Sa Idda (Lilliu 1988; Lo Schiavo 1981).

Monumenti: Su Nuraxi-Barumini, rifascio del bastione quadrilobato (Lilliu 1955; 1982).

Sepolture: tombe di giganti a conci isodomi?

Insediamenti: villaggi di Su Nuraxi-Barumini e di S'Urbale con capanne circolari a copertura straminea; M. Zara, case a più ambienti quadrangolari con muri di mattoni di fango e coperture lignee a spioventi (Ugas 1992).

Relazioni extrainsulari: ceramiche nuragiche a Lipari in contesti dell'Ausonio II (Contu 1978; Ferrarese Ceruti 1987); rapporti con la regione iberica di Huelva, Cipro e Fenicia (Lo Schiavo 1981; 1987a; Lilliu 1988).

Periodo Nuragico IV
(Periodo dei Nuraghi-Templi)
(I Età del Ferro: IX–VI Sec. a.C.)

Cessa l'edificazione dei nuraghi; in parte, distrutti?, vengono abbandonati. Molte fortezze sono trasformate in templi e santuari. Le comunità sono rette da aristocrazie. Sulle coste nascono i primi stanziamenti fenici. Nel vicino Tirreno sorgono dapprima le colonie euboico-cicladiche e poi greco-orientali, che insieme agli Etruschi e ai Cartaginesi, interferiscono sulle vicende politiche e culturali dell'isola. Il periodo comprende tre *aspetti*: Geometrico, Orientalizzante, *facies* arcaica.

SCHEDA 8

IV A. *Aspetto Geometrico* **(900/850–730 a.C)**

Complessi: Su Nuraxi-Barumini (Lilliu 1955; 1988) e Genna Maria-Villanovaforru, isolati a corte (Badas 1987: 133–138; tavv. VII); S. Anastasia-Sardara cap. 5 (Ugas & Usai 1987).

Manufatti: ceramica indigena d'impasto a decoro geometrico inciso e impresso tipo Su Nuraxi cap.135 (Lilliu 1955: 457) e Genna Maria (Badas 1987; Atzeni et al. 1988); bronzi figurati dello stile aulico, pugnali ad elsa gammata, spade ad antenne (Lilliu 1966; 1988); monili in ambra, oro, argento, cristallo di rocca e pasta vitrea, tipo Su Benatzu-Santadi (Lilliu 1974); Seddas Sos Carros (Lo Schiavo 1981; 1981a); Antas (Ugas & Lucia 1987); Su Molinu (Ugas 1989–90).

Monumenti: utilizzo dei templi a pozzo con atrio a timpano, come Su Tempiesu-Orune? (Fadda 1988; Fadda & Lo Schiavo 1992); nuraghi trasformati in templi come Su Molinu (Ugas 1987; 1990), S'Aneri-Lasplassas (E. Usai 1987) e Nurdole (Fadda & Madau 1991); sale del consiglio circolari con panchina e nicchie quali Su Nuraxi, Cap. 80 (Lilliu 1955), Palmavera (Moravetti 1977), S. Anastasia (Ugas & Usai 1987).

Sepolture: tombe monosome a pozzetto, tipo Antas (Ugas & Lucia 1987) e M. Prama (Lilliu 1977; Tronchetti 1978); tombe in tafoni (Ferrarese Ceruti 1968).

Insediamenti: case complesse a corte centrale tipo Su Nuraxi (Lilliu 1982; 1988) e Genna Maria (Badas 1987); insediamenti fenici sulle coste (Sulci) (Bernardini 1981–82; 1993).

Relazioni extrainsulari: Cartagine (Køllund in questi Atti); centri costieri fenici in Sardegna (Barreca 1986); città fenicie d'Occidente e d'Oriente? e colonie euboico-cicladiche per la ceramica dipinta d'importazione fenicia ed euboico-cicladica (Bernardini 1981–82; 1993); area etrusco-laziale per le ceramiche d'impasto a decoro geometrico (Contu 1966) e per i bronzi figurati nuragici (Bartoloni & Delpino 1975; Lilliu 1988); area tirrenica meridionale (Pontecagnano) per bottoni e altri manufatti nuragici in bronzo (Lo Schiavo 1994: 61–82); Sicilia occidentale per le affinità della ceramica geometrica elima (cfr. Bernabò Brea 1960; Fatta 1983).

IV B. Aspetto Orientalizzante (730–600 a.C.)

SCHEDA 9

IV B1. *Orientalizzante antico* **(730–670 a.C.)**

Complessi: Sant'Anastasia, pozzo "votivo" (Taramelli 1918); M. Olladiri vetta (Ugas 1986); Sant'Imbenia (Bafico 1986).

Manufatti: ceramica d'impasto con decoro a falsa cordicella, con segni alfabetici e figurata, ceramica dipinta d'imitazione euboico-cicladica (Ugas 1986; 1995); bronzi figurati; contenitori bronzei.

Monumenti: edificio quadrangolare di S. Brai-Furtei (Ugas 1985); uso del "pozzo votivo" di S. Anastasia (Taramelli 1918).

Relazioni extrainsulari: ceramica d'importazione fenicia ed euboico-cicladica (Bernardini 1981–82; Bernardini & Tore 1987); bronzi figurati, bacili, tripodi e torceri in bronzo di imitazione fenicio-cipriota (Lilliu 1974; Tore 1986; Barreca 1986; Lo Schiavo et al. 1985; Ugas & Usai 1987; Lilliu 1988).

SCHEDA 10

IV B2. *Orientalizzante medio ed evoluto* **(670–600 a.C.)**

Complessi: S. Brai (Ugas 1985); M. Leonaxi (Ugas & Zucca 1984); Piscu di Suelli (Santoni 1984; 1992a); Sant'Imbenia (Bafico 1986).

Manufatti: ceramica sub-geometrica d'impasto a decoro metopale inciso e impresso, ceramica d'impasto e tornita sub-geometrica dipinta (Ugas & Zucca 1984; Ugas 1985); bronzi figurati e navicelle in stile "orientalizzante" (Lilliu 1966); pesetti da bilancia litici e in bronzo (Ugas 1985).

Monumenti: strutture di aree ed edifici sacri che impiegano conci a decoro geometrico tipo Nurdole (Fadda & Madau 1991: figg. 2–4) o dipinti tipo Cuccuru Nuraxi, strato 3? (Atzeni 1987a: 286, tav. II).

Insediamenti: capanne con zoccolo in muratura e mattoni di fango: S. Brai, M. Leonaxi-Villagreca, Tuppedili-Villanovafranca, Cuccuru Nuraxi-Settimo S.P. (Ugas & Zucca 1984), Sant'Imbenia (Bafico 1986), Piscu (Santoni 1992a).

Relazioni extrainsulari: ceramica d'importazione fenicia, greca ed etrusca (Nicosia 1981; Ugas & Zucca 1984; Ugas 1985); bronzi e altri manufatti nuragici esportati nelle regioni medio-tirreniche (Lilliu 1966; 1988).

SCHEDA 11

IV C. *Facies* **arcaica (600–510 a.C.)**

Complessi: San Sperate, M. Leonaxi, M. Olladiri, Tuppedili (Ugas 1982c; Ugas & Zucca 1984).

Manufatti: ceramica tornita dipinta a bande.

Monumenti: ?

Insediamenti: abitati con edifici a pianta rettangolare e mattoni di fango: S. Sperate (Ugas 1993).

Relazioni extrainsulari: ceramiche d'importazione greco-orientale, fenicia ed etrusca (Tore 1978; Ugas & Zucca 1984); bronzi sardi in Etruria e in particolare nell'emporio greco-orientale di Gravisca (Lilliu 1971).

Periodo Nuragico V
(Periodo Nuragico Barbaricino o della Resistenza)
(II Età del Ferro: V Sec. a.C. – I Sec. d.C ?)

SCHEDA 12

V A. *Facies* **delle zone interne coeva all'occupazione cartaginese della Sardegna (510–238 a.C.)**

V B. *Facies* **delle zone interne coeva all'occupazione romana. (238 a.C.–I sec. a.C.)**

Mancano pressochè totalmente le indagini stratigrafiche relative agli insediamenti di questo periodo e si possiedono scarsissimi dati sulla cultura materiale indigena delle aree autonome nei tempi della presenza punica e romana nell'isola.

Sul problema dell'autonomia culturale e della resistenza delle popolazioni indigene ai Cartaginesi prima e ai Romani poi: Meloni 1975; Lilliu 1988; Rowland 1992; Webster & Webster in questo volume.

Le sequenze stratigrafiche nuragiche e la cronologia relativa

Oramai si ha un quadro già abbastanza nitido della posizione cronologica relativa delle diverse *facies* culturali nuragiche. Il rapporto, almeno binario, di precedenza o di successione cronologica di ciascuna di esse risulta documentato, ma con diverse lacune, dalle sequenze stratigrafiche, qui considerate a partire dal Bronzo Antico, come si evince dalla Tab. 25.3.

La sequenza Bonnanaro A1-Bonnanaro A2 è documentata a Sant'Iroxi-Decimoputzu, mentre non è stato ancora osservato il binomio stratigrafico Bonnanaro

Località	BA		BM			BR		BF	F1				F2	
	A1	A2	1A	1B	2	1	2	1	1	G	O	A	P	R
S. Iroxi	*	*												
Noeddos	*?	*?		*?										
Turricula			*											
M. Mannu S.				*										
Trobas				*?	*									
Su Molinu				*	?	*?	*	*	*	*	*	*	*	*
B. Madugui				*	*									
Duos Nuraghes				*?			*?							
Muru Mannu						*								
Rimedio						*	?	*						
Piscu						*	*		*	*	*	*		
M. Zara							*	*	*	*				
Albucciu							*	?	*	*				
Antigori							*	*	*	*	*			
Nuraxi B.									*	*	*	*		
S. Anastasia									*	*	*	*	*	*

BA = Bronzo Antico; BM = Bronzo Medio; BR = Bronzo Recente; BF = Bronzo Finale; F = Età del Ferro; G = fase geometrica; O = periodo Orientalizzante; A = Fase Arcaica; P = periodo dell'occupazione punica; R = periodo dell'occupazione romana.

Tabella 25.3. Sequenze stratigrafiche: Età del Bronzo-I Ferro

A2-Bonnanaro B1. Occorre considerare, però, che a Sa Turricula gli strati più profondi sembrano correlarsi bene col Bonnanaro A2 per la presenza ancora decisamente limitata di ceramiche a nervature.

Non si hanno riscontri neppure riguardo al trapasso dalla *facies* di Sa Turricula a quella di Monti Mannu, ma è probabile che in qualche complesso, come nel Brunku Madugui di Gesturi, i materiali appartenessero in origine a due orizzonti stratigraficamente separati: uno con ceramica a esclusivo decoro in rilievo; l'altro con vasellame ornato in stile metopale e, sebbene in misura ridotta, ancora a nervature. Anche nel caso del protonuraghe Trobas-Lunamatrona (Lilliu 1988) è possibile che i materiali degli strati più antichi documentassero una *facies* del Bronzo Medio anteriore a quella caratterizzata dalla ceramica metopale.

Gli strati del vano F3 di Su Molinu (Ugas 1987: fig. 5.25) attestano una sequenza dal Bonnanaro B2 al Bronzo Recente, poichè documentano materiali inquadrabili negli orizzonti M. Mannu-S. Cosimo (?) (strati 9–10) in sovrapposizione a ceramiche arcaiche dell'orizzonte grigio-ardesia (strato 8) avvicinabili ai fittili di Muru Mannu.

Meglio individuata è, invece, la transizione dal Bronzo Recente al Bronzo Finale, nelle sequenze Muru Mannu/Oristano e Antigori/Barumini nei siti di: Villanovafranca, Su Molinu, vano F3; Cuccuru S'Arriu, area del tempio a pozzo (Sebis 1987); nuraghe Albucciu-Arzachena (Ferrarese Ceruti 1962a); Monte Zara, strutt. 32 (Ugas 1990); Madonna del Rimedio (Santoni & Sebis 1985); nuraghe Antigori, torre *f* (Ferrarese Ceruti 1983; Ferrarese Ceruti & Lo Schiavo 1991–92) e sul nuraghe Piscu di Suelli (Santoni 1992).

Dal Bronzo Finale alla fase "geometrica" del Ferro, la successione diretta è attestata nel vano 135 di Su Nuraxi-Barumini (Lilliu 1955; 1982)), a S. Anastasia (Ugas, scavi inediti nel sett. C) e nell'area prossima al Nuraghe Piscu (Santoni 1992).

La sequenza dal momento "geometrico" a quello "Orientalizzante" è nota a Su Molinu, vano *e* (Ugas 1990), Piscu (Santoni 1992), S. Imbenia (Bafico 1986) e Santu Brai (Ugas & Zucca 1984), mentre, per quanto concerne la transizione dall'"Orientalizzante" alla fase "arcaica", essa è stata individuata stratigraficamente a Su Molinu vano *e* (Ugas & Paderi 1989; Ugas 1990) e nell'insediamento del Piscu (Santoni 1992).

Infine la posizione in strato dei più antichi contesti punici sopra i livelli di fase "arcaica" è palese sia a San Sperate, Via Giardini (Ugas 1984; Ugas & Zucca 1984) che negli insediamenti di Bangius e S. Brai di Furtei (Ugas & Zucca 1984).

Le datazioni al C14 e la cronologia assoluta delle facies e dei monumenti nuragici

Nel prendere in esame le date radiometriche della cultura nuragica (C14 non calibrato-half life 5730 ± 40), tratte dai lavori di E. Contu 1980; 1992: 18), G. Lilliu (1988: 20), R. Tykot (1994), il mio primo pensiero è stato quello di ripartirle in gruppi per periodi, sulla base della pertinenza alle singole *facies* culturali.

N.	Comune	Località	edificio	Data ^{14}C a.C.	campione
1	Birori	Palattu	tomba giganti	1973 ± 126	ossidiana
2	Paulilatino	Fruscos	protonuraghe	1904 ± 104	ossidiana
3	Gesturi	B. Madugui	protonuraghe	1875 ± 250	sughero
4	Birori	Palattu	tomba giganti	1588 ± 200	ossidiana
5	Muros	Turricula	capanna	1555 ± 50	carboni
6	Mara	Filiestru	grotta liv. B	1457 ± 40	carboni
7	Birori	Palattu	tomba giganti	1334 ± 175	ossidiana
8	Mogorella	Friarosu	protonuraghe	1268 ± 105	ossidiana
9	Sennori	Oridda	tomba giganti	1257 ± 50	carboni
10	Arzachena	Malchittu	tempio	920 ± 70	carboni
11	Uri	Peppe G.	protonuraghe	VI–IV sec.	carboni

Tabella 25.4. Dati del Nuragico I (BM I–II)

Il primo gruppo di datazioni riguarda i contesti di materiali e i monumenti attribuiti o attribuibili al Bronzo Medio I e II, dunque al Nuragico I (Tab. 25.4).

Mentre gli studiosi hanno proposto per la I Fase nuragica (o periodo protonuragico) un arco di tempo limitato a circa trecento anni, sia che venga riportato al Bronzo Antico (1800–1500 a.C.) (Lilliu 1982; 1988) sia che la si riconduca al Bronzo Medio (1600–1300) (Ugas 1990; 1992), diversamente le cronologie al C14, pur escludendo i dati di Malchittu e Peppe Gallu, indizierebbero un periodo compreso tra il 1973 e il 1257 a.C. della durata di oltre 700 anni, che diventano 940 prendendo in considerazione anche gli estremi 2099–1159 dell'intero arco di oscillazione. Pertanto i risultati radiometrici riguardanti i periodi in cui si diffondono i protonuraghi coprirebbero non solo entrambi i periodi del Bronzo Antico e del Bronzo Medio, ma sfonderebbero in alto la soglia dell'Eneolitico Finale (Cultura del Vaso campaniforme) e in basso la soglia del Bronzo Recente. Ciò senza tener conto delle datazioni non calibrate che amplierebbero ancor più il ventaglio cronologico, facendo retrocedere verso tempi addirittura del primo calcolitico le prime costruzioni protonuragiche.

Che le cose però stiano diversamente lo indica il fatto che nessuna tomba di giganti né alcun protonuraghe ha restituito ceramiche del Bronzo Antico o della cultura del Vaso Campaniforme. Teoricamente questo presupposto fondamentale potrebbe essere messo in discussione per i protonuraghi dato che finora sono relativamente pochi quelli indagati con scavi stratigrafici, ma non per le tombe di giganti già sottoposte a interventi scientifici in numerose circostanze. Occorre tener presente, a questo punto, che la proposta di contemporaneità dei protonuraghi con i semplici sepolcri ad *allée* e non già con le "tombe di giganti" a stele, non pare finora confortata dagli studi comparati sulle forme e sulle tecniche edilizie.

Esaminiamo in dettaglio le cronologie dei protonuraghi e dei contesti che hanno restituito ceramiche del Bronzo Medio, cominciando dalla tomba di Palattu. Sia i materiali recuperati nell'esedra, in particolare la ceramica a decoro metopale, che la tipologia edilizia (Lilliu 1988: 331; Moravetti 1984) riportano il sepolcro di Birori al Bronzo Medio II. Allo stesso periodo rimanda la data del 1334 ± 75 a.C. di uno dei tre campioni in ossidiana, tutti, pare, in giacitura secondaria. A esso si avvicina anche il limite inferiore (1388) della data c14 del 1588 ± 200 a.C. Invece, il dato radiometrico del 1973 ± 120 a.C. si addice piuttosto a un pezzo ritoccato nei tempi della Cultura campaniforme e successivamente impiegato senza nuova lavorazione.

Anche per l'atipico campione in ossidiana sottoposto ad analisi radiometrica del Fruscos (Manca Demurtas & Demurtas 1984) si può pensare a un pezzo trasferito da un deposito o sito archeologico di più antica frequentazione (nel BA o ancora ai tempi della cultura del Vaso Campaniforme) e non più rilavorato. Il Fruscos appartiene al tipo di protonuraghe da reputarsi il più antico, quello caratterizzato dal corridoio passante, una soluzione architettonica già adottata nel grande emiciclo di Monte Baranta (Moravetti 1981: 281–288), eppure non vi è documentato alcun manufatto che possa avvalorare l'ipotesi di una datazione agli inizi del II millennio: tutti i materiali ivi rinvenuti, seppure in superficie, sono pertinenti alla *facies* di Sa Turricula del BMI (Ugas 1992) e dunque al XVI sec. a.C.

Come già si supponeva la ceramica metopale assegna il Bruncu Madugui al Bronzo Medio (Ugas 1981; 1992). Ora rimuovono ogni ulteriore dubbio al riguardo lo studio sul complesso dei materiali dell'edificio (Badas 1992: 32–76) e l'ipotesi che i suoi vani fossero coperti con una volta di pietra (Puddu 1984: 64; Contu 1992: 21), non molto diversa supponiamo da quella troncoconica del vano *e* di Su Molinu di Villanovafranca (Ugas 1990). Il rifacimento del protonuraghe gesturese ipotizzato da Ubaldo Badas, che richiama quello di Su Molinu (Ugas 1987), suggerisce due fasi differenziate di frequentazione: la prima potrebbe coincidere con la diffusione esclusiva della ceramica ornata a nervature; la seconda con l'apparizione del vasellame a decoro metopale a fianco di quella a nervature.

La datazione del Bruncu Madugui al 1875 ± 250 a.C. appare in ogni caso troppo alta pure nel suo limite inferiore del 1625, anche perchè riferita ad un protonuraghe che non è tra i più antichi in assoluto. Mi pare perciò debba essere riproponibile (nonostante il ripensamento dello studioso) la considerazione di E. Contu (1978: 50–52, 185, n. 101; 1983: 96, n. 30) sulle cellule già morte del sughero sottoposto a campionatura e dunque sulla necessità di ribassare la datazione dell'edificio.

Riguardo al riscontro cronologico di Sa Turricula del 1555 ± 50 a.C., non ci sono molte riserve, poichè il campione esaminato viene da un deposito ben localizzato stratigraficamente e ben inquadrato culturalmente dalla compianta M. L. Ferrarese Ceruti (1962). L'attendibilità della datazione al C14 si basa in questo caso sul concorso di varie concomitanze.

Se, come pare, lo strato B di Filiestru è pertinente alla *facies* di Sa Turricula (Trump 1983), esso è in piena coerenza col campione Q-3031 che ha fornito la data del 1457 ± 40 a.C., assai prossima a quella della capanna di Sa Turricula, e potrebbe essere riferito al BM 1B.

Restano da interpretare le datazioni al radiocarbonio del 1268 ± 105 a.C. del Friarosu e al 1257 ± 50 a.C. di Oridda. Decisamente in controtendenza rispetto alle altre in quanto molto basse per i tempi del BM. In attesa dello scavo, si potrebbe pensare che il protonuraghe di Mogorella, oltre che nel corso del BM, cui risalgono i materiali rinvenuti in prossimità (Manca Demurtas & Demurtas 1984: figg. 23–24), fosse frequentato anche durante il BR, ma poiché non vi sono documentati manufatti di questo periodo è più verosimile che il campione in ossidiana sia stato scheggiato incidentalmente in tempi successivi alle fasi di vita del protonuraghe. Il limite inferiore (1373 a.C.) della data radiometrica indizierebbe un momento di frequentazione finale del protonuraghe nel primo quarto del XIV sec.

Come è stato rimarcato di recente le strutture architettoniche del Friarosu (Manca Demurtas & Demurtas 1984: fig. 14–15) sono assai simili a quelle del Bruncu Madugui (Badas 1992). Presumibilmente essi sono anche coevi dato che i più antichi reperti di entrambi sono simili. È assai probabile che l'uno e l'altro siano stati edificati quando entrò in auge la ceramica a nervature, nel XV secolo. Se non è dovuta all'incompletezza delle indagini, l'assenza di ceramica metopale nel Friarosu, che indurrebbe a prospettare una maggiore antichità di questa fortezza rispetto al Bruncu Madugui, va spiegata con l'abbandono precoce del protonuraghe di Mogorella, prima che apparisse la ceramica metopale. L'evento forse si verificò per cause analoghe a quelle che resero necessario il restauro del Bruncu Madugui; quest'ultimo però non gli sopravvisse molto più a lungo. In ogni caso è assolutamente incoerente lo stacco cronologico proposto dalle datazioni assolute dei due edifici rispettivamente al 1875 ± 250 e al 1268 ± 105 a.C.

Neppure la datazione 1257 ± 50 a.C. del sepolcro di Oridda (Lilliu 1988; Castaldi 1975; 1975a) è in sintonia con i materiali fittili del BM e in particolare del BM IB presenti nell'esedra, i quali fanno pensare a una cronologia del XV sec. a.C., così come le caratteristiche della "arcaica" architettura megalitica inserita in una struttura ipogeica. Nel caso di Oridda tuttavia, poiché sono documentate frequentazioni sino all'età romana, sono pienamente giustificabili interferenze cronometriche di materiali successivi al BM.

Il riscontro cronologico del 920 ± 70 a.C. relativo a materiali del tempio di Malchittu sembra riferirsi a un momento di frequentazione dell'edificio nel corso del Bronzo Finale e non già ai tempi della sua costruzione, considerato il ritrovamento di ceramiche a nervature che riporterebbero il monumento al Bronzo Medio (Ferrarese Ceruti 1962; Lilliu 1988).

Appare dunque evidente che la stragrande maggioranza dei dati radiometrici concernenti strutture edilizie del Bronzo Medio sinora noti debbano essere presi con molta prudenza poiché i campioni analizzati solo raramente provengono da contesti puri o almeno ben definiti.

Prendiamo ora in considerazione le datazioni al C14 degli edifici che restituiscono manufatti del Bronzo Recente (1330–1150 a.C.).

Come già osservato, i contesti del BR, caratterizzati dalla ceramica tipo Muru Mannu, dal vasellame grigio-ardesia e dai tegami ornati a pettine, la cui cronologia è saldamente ancorata a quella della ceramica d'importazione micenea, sono oramai ben documentati nei nuraghi a *tholos* e nelle tombe di giganti con camera a sezione ogivale.

Per contro in nessun nuraghe classico nè in sepolcri del tipo Perd'Accuzzai e Is Concas-Quartucciu con camera di taglio ogivale è stata finora riscontrata, in posizione stratigrafica e contestuale ben definita, la ceramica metopale del XIV sec. a.C. Nell'area dei nuraghi a *tholos* essa è stata recuperata esclusivamente in ricerche di superficie, come nel caso di Uras-Domu Beccia, o in situazioni stratigrafiche non chiarite in rapporto alla fortezza (Santu Antine) o, infine come nel caso di Antigori vano *q*, nell'ambito del villaggio adiacente, più antico della fortezza. Perciò non esiste alcun riscontro oggettivo che consenta di riferire i nuraghi a *tholos* al BM II, nonostante spesso sia stato sostenuto diversamente (in ultimo: Ferrarese Ceruti & Lo Schiavo 1991–92) e pur non escludendosi sul piano teorico.

È assai probabile che i contesti tipo Muru Mannu della prima fase del Bronzo Recente, i quali anticipano i complessi a ceramica grigio-ardesia, abbiano iniziato il loro corso già nell'ultimo quarto del sec. XIV a.C. Se invece la cronologia di questa *facies* dovesse giungere sino alla prima metà del XIV sec. a.C., come suggerirebbero alcune date al C14 relative ai nuraghi Pizzinnu, Ortu Comidu, Su Nuraxi Barumini e Noeddos, allora vorrebbe dire che dovremmo rivedere anche la banda cronologica della *facies* a ceramica metopale. Ma questa è vincolata al XIV secolo dalla connessione con il mesoappenninico, il Milazzese e soprattutto, tramite loro, con il Miceneo III A2. Pertanto, allo stato attuale della ricerca archeologica, i nuraghi a *tholos* non possono essere attribuiti già alla prima metà del XIV secolo, nonostante che i parallelismi tra l'architettura micenea e quella nuragica indurrebbero a sostenere il contrario.

L'interpretazione delle datazioni al C14 relative ai

monumenti propri del Bronzo Recente e del Bronzo Finale, quali i nuraghi e le tombe di giganti connotati da camere e corridoi con taglio ogivale (Ugas 1981; 1992) è resa oltremodo difficile dal fatto che esse quasi mai sono riferite a contesti stratigrafici omogenei, non rimestati e pertinenti a strati di fondazione o di prima frequentazione degli edifici. Tentiamo, tuttavia, una loro valutazione prendendo in considerazione i dati della Tab. 25.5.

La data del 1470 ± 200 a.C. relativa al trave ligneo della torre centrale di Su Nuraxi ha un arco d'oscillazione così ampio (1670–1270 a.C.) che può essere interpretata in vari modi. Tuttavia dello stesso trave di ginepro in un primo momento fu operato un rilevamento cronologico più recente: 1270 ± 200 a.C. (Contu 1974: 147). Se anche questo dato fosse "tecnicamente" valido, ne consegue che la data del monumento risulterebbe compresa nell'arco di tempo compatibile per entrambi i rilevamenti, cioè tra il 1470–1270 a.C. e dunque tra il BM e il BR. Considerato però che il Su Nuraxi non ha restituito materiali più antichi del Bronzo Recente, la datazione più probabile sulla scorta del responso radiometrico è da supporre intorno al 1330–1270 a.C.

Più problematico è il risultato cronometrico del Pizzinnu; la data del 1441 ± 50 a.C. indica senza dubbi il Bronzo Medio (1491–1391 a.C). Anche in questo caso però, le ceramiche più antiche, quali i tegami ornati a pettine, appartengono al Bronzo Recente. Diventa perciò difficile giustificare una data così alta. L'ipotesi più probabile è che i carboni impiegati come campioni per le analisi provenissero da legni già vecchi di oltre un centinaio d'anni quando furono utilizzati nel nuraghe.

Problemi parzialmente analoghi pongono le datazioni del nuraghe monotorre Noeddos di Mara (Trump 1990). La data del 1365 ± 50 a.C. del livello di fondazione indicherebbe che la torre di Noeddos fu edificata tra il 1415 e il 1315 a.C., cioè in pieno Bronzo Medio o agli inizi del Bronzo Recente. La rilevazione cronometrica di un successivo deposito (senza ceramiche a pettine?) propone una arco tra il 1410 e il 1270 a.C. Non escludendo interferenze di materiali più antichi rispetto alla fondazione del nuraghe sull'esito del responso cronometrico, in un sito abitato sin dal calcolitico i dati al C14 sarebbero coerenti col segmento cronologico del 1330–1270 a.C., qualora i manufatti dei depositi inferiori del Noeddos, non esaminati otticamente, fossero pertinenti alla *facies* di Muru Mannu.

Il rilevamento cronometrico del 1220 ± 60 a.C. su materiali pertinenti al pavimento della torre S del Nuraghe Ortu Comidu (Balmuth 1986: 385) suggerirebbe gli inizi del XIII secolo come data per la fondazione del nuraghe sardarese. Infatti l'indagine di M.S. Balmuth non ha finora documentato materiali riferili al Bronzo Medio mentre compaiono materiali del Bronzo Recente (Balmuth 1986: 373, fig. 26, torre E, liv. inf.; 1987: 231; Phillips *et al.* 1987: tav. I.855.1). Diversamente, considerate le risultanze delle ricerche, è probabile che il pezzo atipico

N.	Comune	Località	Data ¹⁴C a.C.
1	Barumini	Su Nuraxi	1470 ± 200
2	Sardara	Ortu Comidu t.S	1460 ± 50
3	Posada	Pizzinnu	1441 ± 50
4	Mara	Noeddos	1365 ± 50
5	Mara	Noeddos	1335 ± 70
6	Sardara	Ortu Comidu t.S	1220 ± 60
7	Arzachena	Albucciu	1257 ± 250
8	Villanovaforru	Genna Maria	1210 ± 60
9	Villanovaforru	Genna Maria	1190 ± 60
10	Borore	Duos Nuraghes	1118 ± 90
11	Sardara	Ortu Comidu a.M	1130 ± 60
12	Sardara	Ortu Comidu a.N	1040 ± 260
13	Arzachena	Albucciu	970 ± 50
14	Borore	Duos Nuraghes	890 ± 80

Tabella 25.5. Date al 14c riferite a nuraghi classici (Nuragico II: Bronzo Recente)

in ossidiana, che ha fornito la data del 1460 ± 50 a.C., provenga da un vicino, più antico, insediamento e sia stato reimpiegato nel nuraghe senza essere stato ulteriormente lavorato. E' verosimile infatti che in età nuragica, a causa della scarsa quantità e delle ridotte dimensione dei pezzi impiegati, fosse più conveniente far uso di ossidiane presenti in superficie nei vicini siti di più antica frequentazione anzichè approvviggionarsi di materie prime dal Monte Arci. Quanto alle datazioni del 1110 ± 60 e del 1040 ± 260 a.C. relative ai settori M ed N dello stesso nuraghe complesso sardarese (Balmuth 1986: 385), è evidente che esse possano ben riguardare momenti di frequentazione del Bronzo Finale, senza escludere però nel primo caso anche tempi del BR e, nell'altro, della Prima Età del Ferro.

L'arco di tempo compreso tra il 1270 e il 1130 a.C., individuato dalle datazioni 1210 e 1190 ± 60 del nuraghe Genna Maria (Lilliu 1988: 20), suggerisce un momento di frequentazione dell'edificio nel corso del Bronzo Recente o agli inizi del Bronzo Finale più che il momento dell'edificazione. Tuttavia, in assenza di elementi di valutazione del contesto da cui i campioni sono stati prelevati, diventa difficile procedere oltre nell'interpretazione.

Lo strato 6 di una delle torri dell'Albucciu, immediatamente soprastante il piano pavimentale, offre la datazione del 1257 ± 250 a.C. (Ferrarese Ceruti 1962a; Contu: 1980: 18). Purtroppo il ventaglio cronologico 1454–956 a.C. ci dice solo che la prima fase di frequentazione, appena successiva alla costruzione dell'edificio, è compresa tra il BM e il BF. Poichè le ceramiche dello strato 6 appartengono a un momento iniziale del BR, la fondazione del nuraghe arcaico di Arzachena, forse sottoposto a diversi interventi di ristrutturazione, andrebbe fissata negli ultimi decenni del XIV o, al più tardi, agli inizi del XIII secolo a.C.

La data del 3110 ± 90 BP ricavata da campioni provenienti dalla torre A della fortezza di Duos Nuraghes, che ha sconcertato G. Webster (1988: 467) il quale pensava ad una cronologia intorno al 1800–2000 a.C., può ben essere coerente con un deposito archeologico contenente materiali del BF o tutt'al più del BR.

Tra le datazioni al C14 relative agli edifici inquadrabili nel Nuragico II sono state prese in considerazione anche alcune cronologie pertinenti a momenti di continuità nell'uso degli stessi nel corso del Bronzo Finale. Ciò prova che tali nuraghi conservavano la funzione primaria di fortezza anche durante il Bronzo Finale. I depositi di materiali finora documentati tenderebbero invece ad escludere la costruzione di nuraghi in questo periodo poichè non sembra siano stati riscontrati strati di fondazione assegnabili chiaramente al Bronzo Finale. Ma si tratta di valutazioni su un complesso di dati ancora limitati. Per contro in questo periodo è certa l'avvenuta ristrutturazione di alcune fortezze come Su Nuraxi di Barumini; in quest'ultimo (Lilliu & Zucca 1984) fu rifasciato il bastione quadrilobato e rifatto interamente il terrazzo.

Il dato relativo alla capanna A di Mandra 'e Sa Giua del 1072 ± 70 a.C. riporta a tempi del BF, ma non abbiamo chiare indicazioni sui materiali contestuali e sulle relazioni con l'edifico, per cui diventa difficile valutarne la congruità.

Le datazioni di Grotta Pirosu-Santadi del 820 ± 60 e 730 ± 60 a.C. (Lilliu 1974; Atzeni 1987: 54) indicano momenti della vita santuariale da correlare con gli inizi e la fine della Fase geometrica della I Età del Ferro, se non ormai con la fase antica dell'Orientalizzante. Purtroppo lo sconvolgimento degli strati non consente di risalire al contesto di riferimento che presumiamo sia quello del tripodino bronzeo, del pugnaletto ad elsa gammata, della lucerna a spalla ornata a cerchielli. L'assenza di lucernine fittili a barchetta con protome (tipo Su Molinu, Ugas 1989–90: 559, fig. 9), bronzi figurati e anfore piriformi tipo Sardara (Taramelli 1918), può forse indicare, qualora i dati cronometrici provenissero da campioni dello stesso contesto, che la cronologia dell'ultima fase di frequentazione della grotta va fissata tra il 790 e il 760 a.C.[5]

Note

1. La fossa di Terrina IV (Camps 1988: 82–85) è datata nello strato d3 di prima frequentazione al 2480 ± 140 a.C. Per la sua forma a conca essa richiama i fondi di capanne seminterrate dell'insediamento di Su Coddu, generalmente ricolmati con depositi di discariche di diverse età. Le datazioni anomale degli strati superiori e le differenti tipologie dei materiali fanno supporre che nell'insediamento corso siano presenti, oltre che materiali propri dello stile di Terrina IV, anche manufatti pertinenti a due *facies* culturali più antiche, risalenti al 3000 e al 2700–2600 circa, nonchè ad un aspetto più recente riportabile al 2300–2200. Nel loro insieme i materiali della fossa di Terrina sembrano proporre una sequenza di quattro fasi eneolitiche parallele e in sintonia, rispettivamente, con le *facies* sarde di Ozieri, Filigosa, Abealzu e M. Claro.
2. Credo sia utile esporre, sia pure in breve in una nota, le motivazioni che inducono ad attribuire l'aspetto Naro-Partanna della cultura di Castelluccio al Calcolitico Recente, anzichè al Bronzo Antico. In primo luogo va rilevato che i ritrovamenti di San Bartolo e di Torrebigini (Tusa 1983: 241, 353; Bernabò Brea 1988) portano a ritenere che, nella seriazione culturale della Sicilia, il Castelluccio dipinto occidentale preceda inizialmente la Cultura del Vaso Campaniforme e sia più tardi affiancata e quindi sostituita da quest'ultima nei tempi della *facies* di Moarda.
Soprattutto però va evidenziato che l'aspetto di Contrada Pergola, connotato a Salaparuta sia dall'*allée* (aggiunta a una più antica cella ipogeica) che dal vasellame inornato caratterizzato dall'ansa a gomito asciforme (Tusa 1983: figg. 58–59), non può essere considerato in rapporto diretto con i vasi dipinti dello stile di Naro-Partanna. Infatti i materiali di Contrada Pergola risentono del clima culturale di Polada I nel momento finale, e non già iniziale, del Bronzo Antico, mediato attraverso la *facies* culturale sarda, affine e coeva di Sant'Iroxi o Bonnanaro A2 (Ugas 1990). Essi evidenziano ulteriormente i rapporti tra le due isole, ben colti dal Bernabò Brea (1985), enunciati dalle analogie tra manufatti della *facies* Bonnanaro A e Capo Graziano I.
Il Bronzo Antico iniziale è palesemente rappresentato in Sicilia dal Castelluccio bruno (Tiné 1965: 277, tav. XXXI) e dal gruppo di Rodì-Tindari-Vallelunga (Bernabò Brea 1985: 127–135). Infatti tanto il Castelluccio bruno quanto la *facies* di Rodì-Tindari-Vallelunga, che nel contesto della T.21 di Rodì (Tusa 1983: 272, fig.3) propone forme fittili irrigidite di derivazione castellucciana accanto ad altre tipiche di un precoce Bronzo Antico, appaiono in logica, immediata continuità col Campaniforme tardo (con vasi decorati a pannelli) e in piena sintonia culturale e cronologica con le *facies* di Capo Graziano iniziale, Polada I, e soprattutto con il Campaniforme sardo inornato (o Campaniforme B di Padru Jossu) che avvia il Bronzo Antico in Sardegna.
Resta da definire a questo punto il problema relativo allo spazio di tempo che corrisponde al Protoappenninico B (metà XVI–XV sec. a.C). Al riguardo va detto che nella Sicilia occidentale l'intervallo compreso tra la *facies* di Contrada Pergola e la Cultura di Thapsos può essere colmato da una *facies* culturale che, come Capo Graziano II, sia interessata da importazioni comprese tra il Myc. I–II e il Myc. III A (Tusa 1983: 367) e che continui a mantenere le relazioni con l'Occidente tramite la Sardegna, ora caratterizzata dall'architettura dei protonuraghi (Periodo Nuragico I).
3. Per le spade argariche più antiche ora si propone una cronologia della fine del XVIII secolo, in base ad una datazione dell'insediamento di Almendricos e ad un attento esame della necropoli (Ayala Juan 1991: 129). In attesa di altre conferme cronometriche, tale data potrebbe forse indiziare la comparsa, nel Mediterraneo occidentale, delle daghe corte prima degli spadoni massicci. Tuttavia questo riscontro radiometrico non può essere utilizzato per far derivare le spade da fendente di Decimoputzu dall'ambiente argarico, poichè al momento le analogie consentono di ipotizzare soltanto, per le spade argariche, sarde e dell'area padana risalenti alla fine del BA o agli inizi del BM, una *koinè* stilistica e tecnologica occidentale, di cui ancora ci sfugge la genesi. Nè è una prova la ceramica dell'ipogeo di Montessu (Atzeni 1987, fig. 10) che sembra proporre forme di tipo argarico (Lo Schiavo 1991: 72) ma che va meglio inquadrata in ambiti medio-calcolitici di Abealzu.
4. Il frammento fittile di Muru Mannu ornato con una solcatura e impressioni, considerato pertinente alla ceramica in stile metopale (Santoni & Sebis 1985: 63–64, fig. 9.122), è diversamente ben interpretabile come un pezzo di tegame decorato a pettine sia sul piano tipologico, sia perché dal complesso nuragico di Muru Mannu, eccezionalmente omogeneo, provengono altri frammenti di tegami ornati a punteggiato (Acquaro 1980: 82–87, tav. XXVI).

5. Da allievo dedico questo lavoro ai professori Giovanni Lilliu, Ercole Contu ed Enrico Atzeni, *maistus mannus de scientzia e umanidadi*, affinchè perdonino le mie fughe dal sentiero maestro. Considero un'opera grandemente meritoria la promozione, da parte della Tufts University, di un simposio dedicato a un tema quale la sequenza cronologica degli aspetti culturali, così importante per il progresso della scienza archeologica in Sardegna. Sono particolarmente grato alla prof.ssa Miriam S. Balmuth e all'amico Robert Tykot per la loro meravigliosa accoglienza. Un pensiero di ringraziamento a Gabriella Lai per la consueta collaborazione al computer.

Bibliografia

Acquaro, E. 1980. Tharros VI. Lo scavo del 1979. *Rivista di Studi Fenici* 8.

Almagro Gorbea, A.M. 1972. La espada de Guadalajara y sus parallelos peninsulares. *Trabajos Prehistoria* 29.

Amoroso, D. 1984. *Recenti ricerche sui rapporti tra la Sicilia e il Vicino Oriente e il problema della genesi della cultura di S. Ippolito e Castelluccio*. Catania.

Atzeni, E. 1966. Il dolmen di "Sa Coveccada" di Mores e la tomba di giganti "Sa Dom'e S'Orku" di Quartucciu. *Studi Sardi* 20.

Atzeni, E. 1966a. L'abri sous roche D' du village préhistorique de Filitosa (Sollacaro-Corse). *Congrés préhistorique de France*, 169–192. Issoudun, Ajaccio.

Atzeni, E. 1967. Tombe a forno di Cultura M. Claro nella Via Basilicata di Cagliari. *Rivista di Scienze Preistoriche* 22.

Atzeni, E. 1975. Nuovi idoli della Sardegna prenuragica (nota preliminare). *Studi Sardi* 23: 3–51.

Atzeni, E. 1978. La Dea Madre nelle culture prenuragiche. *Studi Sardi* 24: 3–69.

Atzeni, E. 1979–80. Menhirs antropomorfi e statue-menhirs della Sardegna. *Annali Museo La Spezia* II.

Atzeni, E. 1981. Aspetti e sviluppi culturali del Neolitico e della prima età dei metalli in Sardegna. In *Ichnussa. La Sardegna dalle origini all'età classica*. Libri Scheiwiller, Milano.

Atzeni, E. 1985. Tombe eneolitiche del Cagliaritano. In *Studi in onore di Giovanni Lilliu*, 11–49. Cagliari.

Atzeni, E. 1987. La preistoria del Sulcis-Iglesiente. In *Iglesias. Storia e società*, 5–53. Cagliari.

Atzeni, E. 1987a. Il tempio a pozzo di Cuccuru Nuraxi-Settimo San Pietro-Cagliari (nota preliminare). In Ugas, G., Lai, G. & Lilliu, G. (eds.), *La Sardegna nel Mediterraneo tra il secondo e il primo millennio a.C., Atti del II Convegno di studi di Selargius 1986*. Cagliari.

Atzeni, E. 1988. La statuaria antropomorfa sarda. In *La statuaria antropomorfa in Europa dal Neolitico Antico alla romanizzazione*. Pontremoli, La Spezia.

Atzeni, E. 1988a. Megalitismo e Arte. In *L'Età del Rame in Europa*. Rassegna di Archeologia 7: 449–456.

Atzeni, E. 1988b. Tombe megalitiche di Laconi (Nuoro). In *L'Età del Rame in Europa*. Rassegna di Archeologia 7: 526–527.

Atzeni, E. 1989. L'Età prenuragica. Il Neolitico antico e medio. In *Il Museo Archeologico Nazionale di Cagliari*. Milano.

Atzeni, E. 1990. Le premesse. Il mondo prenuragico. In *Sardegna Preistorica*. Pizzi, Milano.

Atzeni, E. 1992. Reperti neolitici dall'Oristancse. In *Sardigna antiqua. Studi in onore di Piero Meloni in occasione del suo settantesimo compleanno*, 35–62. Della Torre, Cagliari.

Atzeni, E. 1995. La "Cultura del Vaso Campaniforme" nella necropoli di Locci Santus (S. Giovanni Suergiu). In Santoni, V. (a cura di), *Carbonia e il Sulcis. Archeologia e territorio*, 117–143. Editrice S'Alvure, Oristano.

Atzeni, E. 1994. La statuaria antropomorfa sarda. In *La statuaria antropomorfa in Europa dal Neolitico alla romanizzazione*. La Spezia.

Atzeni, E. in stampa. La Cultura del Vaso Campaniforme e la facies di Bonnanaro nel Bronzo antico Sardo. In *Atti Congresso L'antica Età del Bronzo in Italia*. Viareggio.

Atzeni, E., Badas, U., Comella, A. & Lilliu, C. Villanovaforru. In *L'Antiquarium arborense e i civici musei archeologici della Sardegna*, 181–98. Banco di Sardegna, Sassari.

Ayala Juan, M.M. 1991. *El Poblamiento argarico en Lorca. Estado de la question*. Compobell S.A., Murcia.

Badas, U. 1987. Genna Maria-Villanovaforru (Cagliari). I vani 10–18. Nuovi apporti allo studio delle abitazioni a corte centrale. In Ugas G., Lai G. & Lilliu G. (eds.), *La Sardegna nel Mediterraneo tra il secondo e il primo millennio a.C., Atti del II Convegno di studi di Selargius 1986*, 133–146. Cagliari.

Badas, U. 1992. Il nuraghe Bruncu Madugui di Gesturi: un riesame del monumento e del corredo ceramico. *Quaderni della Soprintendenza Archeologica di Cagliari e Oristano* 9: 31–76.

Bafico, S. 1986. Materiali di importazione del villaggio nuragico di S. Imbenia. In Ugas, G. & Lai, G. (eds.), *Società e cultura in Sardegna nei periodi orientalizzante ed arcaico. Rapporti tra Sardegna, Fenici, Etruschi e Greci, Atti del I Convegno di studi "Un millennio di relazioni fra la Sardegna e i Paesi del Mediterraneo", Selargius-Cagliari 1985*, 91–93. Cagliari.

Bafico, S. 1991. Greci e Fenici ad Alghero. *Archeo* 74: 18.

Bafico, S. & Rossi, G. 1988. Il nuraghe Santu Antine di Torralba. Scavi e materiali. In Moravetti, A. (ed.), *Il nuraghe Santu Antine nel Logudoro-Meilogu*, 61–188. Sassari.

Bafico, S. & Rossi, G. 1992. Una proposta di attribuzione cronologica per le ceramiche decorate dal cortile del nuraghe Santu Antine di Torralba (SS). In Ugas, G., Lai, G. & Lilliu, G. (eds.), *La Sardegna nel Mediterraneo tra il Bronzo Medio e il Bronzo Recente (XVII–XIII sec. a.C.), Atti del III Convegno di Studi di Selargius, 1987*, 41–53. Della Torre, Cagliari.

Bagolini, B. 1981. Il sepolcreto e gli insediamenti eneolitici di Spilamberto-S. Cesario nel quadro culturale medio-padano. In *Il Neolitico e l'Età del Rame. Ricerca a Spilamberto e S. Cesario 1977–1980*. Bologna.

Bagolini, B. 1987. Il Neolitico in Veneto, Trentino-Alto Adige e Friuli. In *Atti della XXVI Riunione Scientifica, "Il Neolitico in Italia," Firenze, 7–10 Novembre 1985*, 189–196. Istituto Italiano di Preistoria e Protostoria, Firenze.

Bailloud, G. 1974. *Le néolithique dans les Bassin Parisien*.

Balmuth, M.S. 1986. Sardara (Cagliari). Preliminary Report of excavations 1975–1978 of the Nuraghe Ortu Comidu. *Notizie degli Scavi* ser. 8, 37: 353–410.

Balmuth, M.S. 1987. Studio architettonico del nuraghe Ortu Comidu. In Ugas G., Lai G. & Lilliu G. (eds.), *La Sardegna nel Mediterraneo tra il secondo e il primo millennio a.C., Atti del II Convegno di studi di Selargius 1986*, Cagliari.

Barfield, L.H. 1972. Scavi di un insediamento neolitico e della Prima Età del Bronzo sul Monte Cavolo. *Annali Museo di Gavardo* 10.

Barfield, L.H., Biagi, P. & Borrello, A. 1975–76. Scavi nella stazione di M.Covolo (1972–73). *Annali Museo di Gavardo* 12.

Barich, E. 1971. Il complesso industriale della stazione Polada alla luce dei più recenti dati. *Bullettino di Paletnologia Italiana* 22, 60.

Barreca, F. 1986. *La civiltà fenicio-punica in Sardegna*. Sardegna Archeologica. Studi e Monumenti 3. Carlo Delfino, Sassari.

Bartoloni, G. & Delpino, F. 1975. Un tipo di orciolo a lamelle metalliche: considerazioni sulla prima fase villanoviana. *Studi Etruschi* 43.

Belli, P. 1990. Note strutturali sulla tholos di S. Calogero a Lipari. *Studi Micenei ed Egeo-anatolici* 28: 67–83.

Belli, P. 1992. Sardinian Sacred Wells and Lipari's thermal tholos. In Tykot, R.H. & Andrews, T.K. (eds.), *Sardinia in the Mediterranean: a footprint in the sea. Studies in Sardinian archaeology presented to Miriam S. Balmuth*. Monographs in Mediterranean Archaeology 3. Sheffield Academic Press, Sheffield.

Bernabò Brea, L. 1960. *La Sicilia prima dei Greci*. Milano.

Bernabò Brea, L. 1978. Eolie, Sicilia e Malta nell'Età del Bronzo. *Kokalos* 22–23.

Bernabò Brea, L. 1985. *Gli Eoli e l'inizio della Età del Bronzo nelle Isole Eolie e nell'Italia Meridionale. Archeologia e Leggende*. Napoli.

Bernabò Brea, L. 1988. L'Età del Rame nell'italia insulare: Sicilia e Isole Eolie. In *L'Età del Rame in Europa, Viareggio 15/18 ottobre 1987*. Rassegna di Archeologia 7: 469–506.

Bernabò Brea, L. & Cavalier, M. 1980. *Meligunís Lipara IV. L'Acropoli di Lipari nella Preistoria*. Palermo.

Bernabò Brea, L. & Cavalier, M. 1990. La tholos termale di S. Calogero nell'Isola di Lipari. *Studi Micenei ed Egeo-anatolici* 28.

Bernardini, P. 1981–82. Pithekoussoi-Sulci. *Annuali Facoltà di Lettere Filosofia di Perugia*, 11–20.

Bernardini, P. 1989. Tre nuovi documenti di importazione dalla collina di Muru Mannu. *Rivista di Scienze Preistoriche* 17.

Bernardini, P. 1993. La Sardegna e i Fenici. Appunti sulla colonizzazione. *Rivista di Studi Fenici* 21(1).

Bernardini, P. & Tore, G. 1987. Sui materiali del tempio a pozzo di Cuccuru Nuraxi di Settimo S. Pietro (Cagliari). In Ugas G., Lai G. & Lilliu G. (eds.), *La Sardegna nel Mediterraneo tra il secondo e il primo millennio a.C., Atti del II Convegno di studi di Selargius 1986*, Cagliari.

Bianco Peroni, V. 1970. Le spade dell'Italia Continentale. *Präistorische Bronzefunde* IV.1. München.

Bietti Sestieri, A.M. & Gianni, A. 1988. L'insediamento eneolitico di Piscina di Torre Spaccata (Roma). In *L'Età del Rame in Europa, Viareggio 15/18 ottobre 1987*. Rassegna di Archeologia 7.

Buchvaldech, M., Novotny, B. & Pleslova Stikova, E. 1988. The copper in Czechoslovakia. In *L'Età del Rame in Europa, Viareggio 15/18 ottobre 1987*. Rassegna di Archeologia 7.

Burroni, D. & Mezzena, F. 1988. Megalitismo e arte rupestre in Italia Settentrionale durante L'Eneolitico. In *L'Età del Rame in Europa, Viareggio 15/18 ottobre 1987*. Rassegna di Archeologia 7.

Camps, G. 1988. La Metallurgie. *Terrina et le Terrinien. Recherches sur le Chalcolithique de la Corse*. Ecole Française de Rome 109. Roma.

Cardini, L. 1970. Praia a Mare, Relazione degli scavi 1957–1970. *Bullettino di Paletnologia Italiana*.

Castaldi, E. 1968. Nuove osservazioni sulle tombe di giganti. *Bullettino di Paletnologia Italiana* 19.

Castaldi, E. 1969. Tombe di giganti nel Sassarese. *Origini* III.

Castaldi, E. 1972. La datazione con il C-14 della Grotta del Guano o Gonagosula (Oliena-Nuoro). Considerazioni sulla cultura di Ozieri. *Archivio per l'Antropologia e la Etnologia* 102: 233–275.

Castaldi, E. 1975. Ancora sulla «stele» delle tombe di giganti. *Bullettino di Paletnologia Italiana* 29: 82.

Castaldi, E. 1975a. *Domus nuragiche*. Roma.

Castaldi, E. 1980. Relazione preliminare sullo scavo della Grotta del Guano o Gonagosula (Oliena-Nuoro). *Atti della XXII Riunione Scientifica, 'Sardegna Centro-Settentrionale', 21–27 ottobre 1978*, 149–160. Istituto Italiano di Preistoria e Protostoria, Firenze.

Castaldi, E. 1981. Villaggio con Santuario a Biriai (Oliena, NU). *Rivista di Scienze Preistoriche* 36: 153–221.

Castaldi, E. 1992. Il Santuario di Biriai. In Tiné, S. & Traverso, A. (eds.), *Monte d'Accoddi. Dieci anni di nuovi scavi*, Genova.

Cavalier, M. 1960. La stazione preistorica della Contrada Diana. *Meligunís Lipara* I. Palermo.

Cazzella, A. & Moscoloni, M.1992. Neolitico ed Eneolitico. *Popoli e Civiltà dell'Italia Antica* 11.

Cazzella, A., Damiani, I., Di Gennaro, F., Pacciarelli, M., Saltini, A.C., Tusa ,S. & Valente, I. 1986. L'isola di Vivara. In Marazzi, M., Tusa, S. & Vagnetti, L. (eds.), *Traffici micenei nel Mediterraneo. Problemi storici e documentazione archeologica, Atti del Convegno di Palermo*, Taranto.

Ceccanti, M. 1980. L'evoluzione tipologica dell'ansa ad ascia in Sardegna. *Atti della XXII Riunione Scientifica, 'Sardegna Centro-Settentrionale', 21–27 ottobre 1978*. Istituto Italiano di Preistoria e Protostoria, Firenze.

Cesari, J. 1994. *Corse des origines*. Imprimerie National, Paris.

Cocchi Genick, D. & Grifoni Cremonesi, R. (a cura di). 1985. *L'età dei metalli nella Toscana Nord-Occidentale*. Pisa.

Cocchi Genick, D. & Grifoni Cremonesi, R. 1988. Le *facies* locali della Toscana. In *L'Eta del Rame in Europa, Viareggio 15/18 ottobre 1987*. Rassegna di Archeologia 7: 338–347.

Cocco, D. & Usai, L. 1988. Un monumento preistorico nel territorio di Cornus. In *Amsicora e il territorio di Cornus*. Taranto.

Cocco, D. & Usai, L. 1992. Tomba megalitica in località Perda 'e Accuzzai (Villa S. Pietro-Cagliari). Nota preliminare. In Ugas, G., Lai, G. & Lilliu, G. (eds.), *La Sardegna nel Mediterraneo tra il Bronzo Medio e il Bronzo Recente (XVII–XIII sec. a.C.), Atti del III Convegno di Studi di Selargius, 1987*, 187–199. Della Torre, Cagliari.

Contu, E. 1960. Nuraghe Pizzinnu. Notiziario Sardegna. *Rivista di Scienze Preistoriche* 15.

Contu, E. 1962. Tombe dipinte e scolpite della Sardegna e l'ipogeo di Hal Saflieni. *Rivista di Scienze Preistoriche* 2.

Contu, E. 1964. La Tomba dei vasi tetrapodi in località Santu Pedru (Alghero-Sassari). *Monumenti Antichi dei Lincei* 47(1).

Contu, E. 1965. Filigosa (Macomer). *Rivista di Scienze Preistoriche* 20.

Contu, E. 1965a. Nuovi petroglifi schematici della Sardegna. *Bullettino di Paletnologia Italiana* 74.

Contu, E. 1966. Considerazioni su un saggio di scavo al nuraghe «La Prisciona» di Arzachena. *Studi Sardi* 19.

Contu, E. 1969. La Sardegna prenuragica e nuragica. In *Sardegna nuragica*. Milano.

Contu, E. 1974. La Sardegna dell'Età Nuragica. *Populi e Civiltà dell'Italia Anticaf* III.

Contu, E. 1978. Il significato della stele nelle tombe di giganti. *Quaderni della Soprintendenza ai Beni Archeologici delle Provincie di Sassari e Nuoro* 8. Dessì, Sassari.

Contu, E. 1980. La Sardegna preistorica e protostorica: aspetti e problemi. *Atti della XXII Riunione Scientifica, 'Sardegna Centro-Settentrionale', 21–27 ottobre 1978*. Istituto Italiano di Preistoria e Protostoria, Firenze.

Contu, E. 1980a. Ceramica sarda di eta nuragica a Lipari. *Meligunís Lipara* IV: 827–836.

Contu, E. 1981. L'architettura nuragica. In *Ichnussa. La Sardegna dalle origini all'età classica*, 5–175. Scheiwiller, Milano.

Contu, E. 1984. Monte d'Accoddi-Sassari. Problematiche di studio e di ricerca di un singolare monumento preistorico. In Waldren, W.H., Chapman, R., Lewthwaite, J. & Kennard, R.-C. (eds.), *The Deya Conference of Prehistory: Early Settlement in the Western Mediterranean Islands and the Peripheral Areas.* BAR International Series 229. British Archaeological Reports, Oxford.

Contu, E. 1984a. Sassari, loc. Monte d'Accoddi. In Anati, E. (ed.), *I Sardi*. Milano.

Contu, E. 1985. Il nuraghe. In *Sardegna preistorica. Nuraghi a Milano*, 45–110. Pizzi, Milano.

Contu, E. 1988. Problematica ed inquadramento culturale. L'età del Rame in Sardegna. In *L'Età del Rame in Europa, Viareggio 15/18 ottobre 1987*. Rassegna di Archeologia 7.

Contu, E. 1992. L'inizio dell'Età Nuragica. In Ugas, G., Lai, G. & Lilliu, G. (eds.), *La Sardegna nel Mediterraneo tra il Bronzo Medio e il Bronzo Recente (XVII–XIII sec. a.C.), Atti del III Convegno di Studi di Selargius, 1987*, 13–40. Della Torre, Cagliari.

Contu, E. 1992a. Nuove anticipazioni sui dati stratigrafici di M. d'Accoddi. Scavi 1952-58. In Tiné, S. & Traverso, A. (eds.), *Monte d'Accoddi. Dieci anni di nuovi scavi*, 21–36. Genova.

Contu, E. in stampa. Problematica e inquadramento culturale. In *Atti Congresso "L'antica Età del Bronzo in Italia", Viareggio 1995*.

Cremonesi, R.G. 1976. *La Grotta dei Piccioni di Bolognano nel quadro delle culture dal Neolitico all'Età del Bronzo in Abruzzo*. Pisa.

Cremonesi, R.G. & Tozzi, F. 1987. Il Neolitico dell'Abruzzo. In *Atti della XXVI Riunione Scientifica, "Il Neolitico in Italia," Firenze, 7–10 Novembre 1985*, 189–196. Istituto Italiano di Preistoria e Protostoria, Firenze.

Damiani, I., Pacciarelli, A.C. & Saltini, C. 1984. Le facies archeologiche dell'isola di Vivara e alcuni problemi relativi al Protoappenninico B. In *Archeologia e storia antica* 6: 1–38.

Davis, J. 1986. Ayia Irini: Period V. In *Keos*. Philipp von Zabern, Mainz am Rhein.

Evans, J.D. 1961. *Segreti dell'antica Malta*. Saggiatore, Milano.

Evans, J.D. 1971. *The Prehistoric Antiquities of Maltese Islands a Survey*. Athlone Press, London.

Fadda, M. A. 1979. Il nuraghe Don Michele di Ploaghe. In *Contributi su Giovanni Spano*. Sassari.

Fadda, M.A. 1985. Il villaggio. In *Sardegna preistorica. Nuraghi a Milano*. Pizzi, Milano.

Fadda, M.A. 1987. Il villaggio nuragico di S'Urbale (Teti-NU). I materiali del vano F. In Ugas G., Lai G. & Lilliu G. (eds.), *La Sardegna nel Mediterraneo tra il secondo e il primo millennio a.C., Atti del II Convegno di studi di Selargius 1986*, 53–61. Cagliari.

Fadda, M.A. 1988. *La fonte sacra di Su Tempiesu*. Sardegna Archeologica. Guide e itinerari 8. Dessì, Sassari.

Fadda, M.A. 1988a. Lo strato eneolitico del Riparo di S. Basilio di Ollolai (Nuoro). In *L'Età del Rame in Europa, Viareggio 15/18 ottobre 1987*, 535. Rassegna di Archeologia 7.

Fadda, M.A. & Lo Schiavo F. 1992. *Su Tempiesu di Orune, fonte sacra nuragica*. Quaderni della Soprintendenza ai Beni Archeologici per le Provincie di Sassari e Nuoro 18. Dessì, Sassari.

Fadda, M.A. & Madau, M. 1991. Nurdole. Un tempio nuragico in Barbagia punto d'incontro nel Mediterraneo. *Rivista di Scienze Preistoriche* 19(1).

Farolfi G. 1976. La Tanaccia di Brisighella: problemi cronologici e culturali. *Origini* 10.

Fatta, V. 1983. *La ceramica geometrica di Sant'Angelo Muxaro*. Studi monografici 2. Palermo.

Fedele, B. 1987. I materiali vascolari provenienti dalla prima campagna di scavo nella Grotta di Cala Scizzo presso Torre a Mare (Bari). In *Atti della XXV Riunione Scientifica, "Preistoria e Protostoria nella Puglia centrale," Monopoli 1984*. Istituto Italiano di Preistoria e Prostoria, Firenze.

Ferrarese Ceruti, M.L. 1962. Un singolare monumento della Gallura. Il tempietto di Malchittu. *Archivio Storico Sardo* 19.

Ferrarese Ceruti, M.L. 1962a. Nota preliminare alla I e alla II campagna di scavo nel Nuraghe Albucciu. *Rivista di Scienze Preistoriche* 17.

Ferrarese Ceruti, M.L. 1968. Tombe in tafoni nella Gallura. *Bullettino di Paletnologia Italiana* 77.

Ferrarese Ceruti, M.L. 1972–74. La Tomba XVI di Su Crucifissu Mannu e la cultura di Bonnannaro. *Bullettino di Paletnologia Italiana* 81:113–218.

Ferrarese Ceruti, M.L. 1981. La cultura del Vaso Campaniforme. In *Ichnussa. La Sardegna dalle origini all'età classica*, 55–77. Scheiwiller, Milano.

Ferrarese Ceruti, M.L. 1981a. La cultura di Bonnanaro. In *Ichnussa. La Sardegna dalle origini all'età classica*. Scheiwiller, Milano.

Ferrarese Ceruti, M.L. 1981b. Documenti micenei nella Sardegna meridionale. In *Ichnussa. La Sardegna dalle origini all'età classica*, 605–612. Scheiwiller, Milano.

Ferrarese Ceruti, M.L. 1982. Sardegna. Nuraghe Antigori. *Atti del Convegno "Magna Grecia e mondo miceneo, Taranto 1981*. Napoli.

Ferrarese Ceruti, M.L. 1983. La Torre f del complesso nuragico di Antigori a Sarroch-Cagliari. Nota preliminare. In *Atti XXII Convegno di Studi sulla Magna Grecia, Taranto 1982*, Napoli.

Ferrarese Ceruti, M.L. 1987. Minoici, Micenei e Ciprioti in Sardegna alla luce delle più recenti scoperte. La ceramica micenea. In Balmuth, M.S. (ed.), *Studies in Sardinian Archaeology III: Nuragic Sardinia and the Mycenaean World*. BAR International Series 387. British Archaeological Reports, Oxford.

Ferrarese Ceruti, M.L. 1988. Il Campaniforme in Sardegna. L'età del Rame in Sardegna. In *L'Età del Rame in Europa, Viareggio 15/18 ottobre 1987*, 456–467. Rassegna di Archeologia 7.

Ferrarese Ceruti, M.L. & Germanà, F. 1978. *Sisaia. Una deposizione in grotta della cultura Bonnannaro*. Quaderni della Soprintendenza ai Beni Archeologici per le Provincie di Sassari e Nuoro 6. Dessì, Sassari.

Ferrarese Ceruti, M.L. & Lo Schiavo, F. 1991–92. Sardegna. In *Atti del Congresso di Viareggio 1989*. Rassegna di Archeologia 10.

Ferrarese Ceruti, M.L., Lo Schiavo, F. & Vagnetti, L. 1987. Minoici e Micenei in Sardegna alla luce delle più recenti scoperte. In Balmuth, M.S. (ed.), *Studies in Sardinian Archaeology III: Nuragic Sardinia and the Mycenaean World*. BAR International Series 387. British Archaeological Reports, Oxford.

Foschi, A. 1980. La Tomba I di Filigosa (Macomer). *Atti della XXII Riunione Scientifica, 'Sardegna Centro-Settentrionale', 21–27 ottobre 1978*. Istituto Italiano di Preistoria e Protostoria, Firenze.

Fugazzola Delpino, M. 1976. *Testimonianze di cultura appenninica nel Lazio*. Parenti, Firenze.

Gambari, F.M. & Venturino Gambari, M. 1985–86. La ceramica a fori passanti nel quadro dell'Eneolitico dell'Italia Nord-occidentale. *Sibrium* 18.

Gardiner, A. 1971. *La civiltà egizia*. Milano.

Geniola, A. 1987. Il Neolitico della Puglia Centrale. In *Atti della XXV Riunione Scientifica, "Preistoria e Protostoria nella Puglia centrale," Monopoli 1984*. Istituto Italiano di Preistoria e Prostoria, Firenze.

Geniola, A. 1987a. Stratigrafia comparata delle grotticelle cultuali di Santa Barbara (Polignano a Mare) e di Cala Colombo e Cala Scizzo (Torre a Mare-Bari). In *Atti della XXV Riunione Scientifica, "Preistoria e Protostoria nella Puglia centrale," Monopoli 1984*. Istituto Italiano di Preistoria e Protostoria, Firenze.

Grifoni Cremonesi, R. 1985. Nuovi dati sul Neolitico e sulla piana del Fucino. In Liverani, A. & Peroni, R. (eds.), *Studi in onore di Salvatore M. Puglisi*. Roma.

Grifoni Cremonesi, R. 1987. Il Neolitico della Toscana e dell'Umbria. In *Atti della XXVI Riunione Scientifica, "Il Neolitico in Italia," Firenze, 7–10 Novembre 1985*, 189–196. Istituto Italiano di Preistoria e Protostoria, Firenze.

Guerreschi, G. 1965. La Lagozza di Besnate e il Neolitico superiore padano. *R.C.A.*

Guilaine, J. 1972. L'Age du Bronze en Languedoc Occidental,

Roussillon, Ariège. *Memoires de la Société Préhistorique Française*. Paris.

Guilaine, J. 1988. Le Calcolithique en France du Sud. In *L'Età del Rame in Europa, Viareggio 15/18 ottobre 1987*, 212–219. Rassegna di Archeologia 7.

Guilaine, J. & Roudil, J. 1976. Les Civilisations néolithiques en Languedoc. *Préhistoire française* II. Paris.

Gullini, G. 1992. Monte d'Accoddi e l'architettura delle ziqqurat mesopotamiche. In Tiné, S. & Traverso, A. (eds.), *Monte d'Accoddi. Dieci anni di nuovi scavi*. Genova.

Harrison, R.S. 1974. Origins of the Bell Beaker Cultures. *Antiquity* 48.

Holloway, R. 1973. *Buccino. The Eneolithic necropolis of S. Antonio and other discoveries made in 1968 and 1969 by Brown University, with A Study of human remains from the necropolis*. Roma.

Joussaume, R. 1976. Les Civilisations dans le Centre-Ouest. *Préhistoire française* II. Paris.

Lilliu, G. 1944. Rapporti tra la Civilà nuragica e la Civiltà fenicio-punica in Sardegna. *Studi Etruschi* 19: 323–370.

Lilliu, G. 1948. Uno scavo ignorato del dott. Ferruccio Quintavalle nella tomba di giganti di Goronna a Paulilatino (Cagliari). *Studi Sardi* 8.

Lilliu, G. 1955. Il nuraghe di Barumini e la stratigrafia nuragica. *Studi Sardi* 12–13(1952–54): 90–469.

Lilliu, G. 1966. *Sculture della Sardegna nuragica*. Verona.

Lilliu, G. 1971. Navicella di bronzo protosarda da Gravisca. *Notizie degli Scavi*.

Lilliu, G. 1974. Tripode bronzeo di tradizione cipriota dalla Grotta Pirosu-Su Benatzu di Santadi (Cagliari). *Estudios dedicados al Profesor Dr. Luis Pericot*. Barcelona.

Lilliu, G. 1975. *La Civiltà dei Sardi dal Paleolitico all'età dei nuraghi*. ERI, Torino.

Lilliu, G. 1977. Dal betilo aniconico alla statuaria nuragica, *Studi Sardi* 25.

Lilliu, G. 1980. *La Civiltà dei Sardi dal Paleolitico all'età dei nuraghi*. II ed. ERI, Torino.

Lilliu, G. 1982. *La Civiltà nuragica*. Sardegna Archeologica. Studi e Monumenti 1. Carlo Delfino, Sassari.

Lilliu, G. 1988. *La civiltà dei Sardi dal Paleolitico all'età dei nuraghi*. III ed. ERI, Torino.

Lilliu, G. 1992. Miti e rituali nella Sardegna preistorica. In Tykot, R.H. & Andrews, T.K. (eds.), *Sardinia in the Mediterranean: a footprint in the sea. Studies in Sardinian archaeology presented to Miriam S. Balmuth*. Monographs in Mediterranean Archaeology 3. Sheffield Academic Press, Sheffield.

Lilliu, G. & Schubart, H. 1967. *Civiltà mediterranee*. Milano.

Lilliu, G. & Zucca, R. 1988. *Su Nuraxi di Barumini*. Sardegna Archeologica. Guide e itinerari 9. Dessì, Sassari.

Lollini, D.G. 1965. Il Neolitico delle Marche alla luce delle recenti scoperte. *Atti VI Congresso Scienze Preistoriche e Protostoriche*. Roma.

Lo Porto, F.G. 1963. Leporano (Taranto). La stazione preistorica di Porto. *Notizie degli Scavi*. 280–380.

Lo Porto, F.G. 1964. La tomba di S. Vito dei Normanni e il protoappenninico B in Puglia. *Bullettino di Paletnologia Italiana* 73: 109–142.

Lo Porto, F.G. 1972. La Tomba neolitica con idolo in pietra da Arnesano (Lecce). *Rivista di Scienze Preistoriche* 27.

Loria, R. & Trump, D.H. 1978. Le scoperte a "Sa Ucca de Su Tintirriolu" e il Neolitico Sardo. *Monumenti Antichi dei Lincei* II, 249. Roma.

Lo Schiavo, F. 1978. Armi e utensili da Siniscola. In *Sardegna Centro-Orientale*. Sassari.

Lo Schiavo, F. 1981. Economia e società nell'età dei nuraghi. In *Ichnussa. La Sardegna dalle origini all'età classica*, 255–347. Scheiwiller, Milano.

Lo Schiavo, F. 1981a. Ambra in Sardegna. *Studi in onore di Ferrante Rittatore Vonwiller*.

Lo Schiavo, F. 1986. La Preistoria. In *Il Museo Archeologico G.A. Sanna in Sassari*. Milano.

Lo Schiavo, F. 1989. Le origini della metallurgia e i problemi della metallurgia nella cultura di Ozieri. In Campus, L.D. (a cura di), *La cultura di Ozieri. Problematica e nuove acquisizioni*, 279–292. Il Torchietto, Ozieri.

Lo Schiavo, F. 1990. Sotto il Nuraghe Rosso. *Archeo* 59.

Lo Schiavo, F. 1991. Note a margine delle spade argariche trovate in Sardegna. *Quaderni della Soprintendenza Archeologica per le Provincie di Cagliari e Oristano* 8.

Lo Schiavo, F. 1994. Bronzi nuragici nelle tombe della Prima Età del Ferro di Pontecagnano. *La presenza etrusca nella Campania*. Firenze.

Lo Schiavo, F., Macnamara, E. & Vagnetti, L. 1985. Late Cypriot imports to Italy and their Influence on Local Bronzework. *Papers of the British School at Rome* 53: 1–71.

Lo Schiavo, F. & Sanges, M. 1994. *Il nuraghe Arrubiu di Orroli*. Sardegna Archeologica. Guide e itinerari 22. Dessì, Sassari.

Lo Schiavo, F. & Vagnetti, L. 1993. Alabastron miceneo dal Nuraghe Attentu di Orroli (Nuoro). *Atti della Accademia Nazionale dei Lincei: Rendiconti* 4: 121–148.

Manca Demurtas, L. & Demurtas, S. 1984. Observaciones sobre los protonuragues de Cerdeña. *Trabajos de prehistoria* 41:165–204.

Manca Demurtas, L. & Demurtas, S. 1992. Tipologie nuragiche: protonuraghi con corridoio passante. In Tykot, R.H. & Andrews, T.K. (eds.), *Sardinia in the Mediterranean: a footprint in the sea. Studies in Sardinian archaeology presented to Miriam S. Balmuth*, 176–184. Monographs in Mediterranean Archaeology 3. Sheffield Academic Press, Sheffield.

Meloni, P. 1975. *La Sardegna romana*. Sassari.

Mezzena, F. 1981. La Valle d'Aosta nella Preistoria e nella Protostoria. *Archeologia in Valle d'Aosta. Catalogo Mostra*. Aosta.

Mezzena, F. 1982. Ricerche preistoriche e protostoriche in Valle d'Aosta. Risultati e prospettive. *Atti Congresso Città d'Aosta 1975*. Bordighera.

Mitova Dzonova, D. 1992. Elementi architettonici protosardi nella Penisola Balcanica. In Ugas, G., Lai, G. & Lilliu, G. (eds.), *La Sardegna nel Mediterraneo tra il Bronzo Medio e il Bronzo Recente (XVII–XIII sec. a.C.), Atti del III Convegno di Studi di Selargius, 1987*, 587–596. Della Torre, Cagliari.

Moravetti, A. 1977. Nuove scoperte nel villaggio nuragico di Palmavera (Alghero-Sassari). *Rivista di Scienze Preistoriche* 32: 277–291.

Moravetti, A. 1981. Nota agli scavi nel complesso megalitico di M. Baranta (Olmedo, Sassari). *Rivista di Scienze Preistoriche* 36(1–2): 281–290.

Moravetti, A. 1984. La tomba di giganti di Palattu (Birori-Nuoro). *Nuovo Bullettino Archeologico Sardo* 1.

Moravetti, A. 1985. Le tombe e l'ideologia funeraria. In *Sardegna preistorica. Nuraghi a Milano*. Pizzi, Milano.

Moravetti, A. 1988. Architettura. In Moravetti, A. (ed.), *Il nuraghe di S. Antine nel Logudoro-Meilogu*. Sassari.

Moravetti, A. 1992. Sui protonuraghi del Marghine e della Planargia. In Tykot, R.H. & Andrews, T.K. (eds.), *Sardinia in the Mediterranean: a footprint in the sea. Studies in Sardinian archaeology presented to Miriam S. Balmuth*, 185–197. Monographs in Mediterranean Archaeology 3. Sheffield Academic Press, Sheffield.

Müller Karpe, H. 1974. *Handbuch der Vorgeschichte*.

Mussche, H.J. *et al.* 1984. Rapport preliminaire sur les 9, 10, 11 campagnes de fouilles. *Thorikos* 8(1972–1976).

Negroni Catacchio, N. 1981. La valle del fiume Fiora. Le testimonianze archeologiche. *Sorgenti della Nova*. CNR, Roma.

Nicosia, F. 1981. La Sardegna nel mondo classico. In *Ichnussa. La Sardegna dalle origini all'età classica*, 421–476. Scheiwiller, Milano.

Peroni, R. 1962-63. La Romita di Asciano (Pisa). Riparo sotto roccia utilizzato dall'età neolitica alla barbarica. *Bullettino di Paletnologia Italiana* 71.

Peroni, R. 1967. Per una revisione critica della stratigrafia di Luni sul Mignone e della sua interpretazione. *Atti I Convegno Protostoria*, 167ss. Orvieto.

Peroni, R. 1971. *L'Età del Bronzo nella Penisola Italiana*. Firenze.

Peroni, R. 1983. Presenze micenee e forme socio-economiche nell'Italia protostorica. In Vagnetti, L. (ed.), *Magna Grecia e mondo miceneo. XXII Convegno di Studi Magna Grecia, Taranto 1982*, 211–284. Napoli.

Peroni, R. 1989. Protostoria dell'Italia Continentale. *Popoli e Civiltà dell'Italia Antica* 9.

Petrequin, P. 1988. La France de l'Est. In *L'Età del Rame in Europa, Viareggio 15/18 ottobre 1987*. Rassegna di Archeologia 7: 220–225.

Phillips, P., Nicholson, P. & Patterson, H. 1987. La ceramica nuragica di Ortu Comidu. In Ugas G., Lai G. & Lilliu G. (eds.), *La Sardegna nel Mediterraneo tra il secondo e il primo millennio a.C., Atti del II Convegno di studi di Selargius 1986*, 225–288. Cagliari.

Puddu, G. 1984. Gesturi (Cagliari). Località «Brunku Madugui». *Territorio di Gesturi, Censimento archeologico*. Cagliari.

Puglisi, S.M. 1941-42. Villaggi sotto roccia e sepolcri megalitici della Gallura. *Bullettino di Paletnologia Italiana* 5-6: 123–141.

Radi, G. 1986-87. Scavo preliminare a Fonti di San Callisto (L'Aquila). *Rassegna di Archeologia* 6: 143–170.

Radmilli, A.M. 1978. Culture della Polada. In Radmilli, A.M. (ed.), *Guida della Preistoria Italiana*. Firenze.

Ridgway, D. 1984. *L'alba della Magna Grecia*. Milano.

Rittatore von Willer, F. & Fedele, F. 1978. Cultura di Rinaldone. In Radmilli, A.M. (ed.), *Guida della Preistoria Italiana*. Firenze.

Rosselló Bordoy, G. 1992. Mallorca en el Bronce Final (ss. XVI–XIII a.C.). In Ugas, G., Lai, G. & Lilliu, G. (eds.), *La Sardegna nel Mediterraneo tra il Bronzo Medio e il Bronzo Recente (XVII–XIII sec. a.C.), Atti del III Convegno di Studi di Selargius, 1987*, 421–442. Della Torre, Cagliari.

Roussot Larroque, J. 1976. Les civilisations néolithique en Aquitaine. In *La Préhistoire française* II. Paris.

Rowland, R.J. Jr. 1992. When did the Nuragic Period in Sardinia end? In *Sardinia antiqua. Studi in onore di Piero Meloni in occasione del suo settantesimo compleanno*, 167–175. Della Torre, Cagliari.

Sanna, R. 1984. Materiali nuragici. Località Mitza Purdia-Decimoputzu. *Villaspeciosa. Censimento archeologico del territorio*. Quartu Sant'Elena.

Santoni, V. 1982. Cabras-Cuccuru S'Arriu (nota preliminare di scavo 1978, 1979, 1980). *Rivista di Studi Fenici* 10(1): 103–127.

Santoni, V. 1985. Tharros. Il villaggio nuragico di Su Muru Mannu. *Rivista di Studi Fenici* 13(1).

Santoni, V. 1986. Il complesso nuragico "Madonna del Rimedio" (I depositi del Bronzo Medio II). *Nuovo Bullettino Archeologico Sardo*.

Santoni, V. 1989. L'Orientalizzante antico-medio della capanna 1 del Nuraghe Piscu di Suelli, Cagliari. *Quaderni della Soprintendenza Archeologica per le Provincie di Cagliari e Oristano* 6: 73–110.

Santoni, V. 1992. Il nuraghe Baumendula di Villaurbana-Oristano. Nota preliminare. In *Sardigna antiqua. Studi in onore di Piero Meloni in occasione del suo settantesimo compleanno*, 123–144. Della Torre, Cagliari.

Santoni, V. 1992a. Il nuraghe Piscu di Suelli: documenti e materiali. In Ugas, G., Lai, G. & Lilliu, G. (eds.), *La Sardegna nel Mediterraneo tra il Bronzo Medio e il Bronzo Recente (XVII–XIII sec. a.C.), Atti del III Convegno di Studi di Selargius, 1987*, 167–178. Della Torre, Cagliari.

Santoni, V. 1993. Il nuraghe Losa di Abbasanta. *Quaderni della Soprintendenza Archeologica per le Provincie di Cagliari e Oristano* 6, supplemento.

Santoni, V. & Sebis, S. 1984. Il complesso nuragico "La Madonna del Rimedio" (Oristano). *Nuovo Bullettino Archeologico Sardo* 1.

Sarti, L. & Martini, F. 1988. L'Eneolitico nel territorio fiorentino. In *L'Età del Rame in Europa, Viareggio 15/18 ottobre 1987*. Rassegna di Archeologia 7: 594–595.

Sarti, L. & Vigliardi, A. 1988. Il Vaso campaniforme nell'Italia Centrale. In *L'Età del Rame in Europa, Viareggio 15/18 ottobre 1987*. Rassegna di Archeologia 7: 378–388.

Schachermeyer, F. 1976. *Die Agäische Frühzeit. 1. Die Vormykenischen Perioden*. Wien.

Sebis, S. 1986. Il villaggio d'Età del Bronzo a Monte Gonella (Nuraxinieddu-OR). *Studi Sardi*. 17–30.

Sebis, S. 1987. Ricerche archeologiche nel Sinis Centro-meridonale. Nuove acquisizioni di età nuragica. In Ugas, G., Lai, G. & Lilliu, G. (eds.), *La Sardegna nel Mediterraneo tra il secondo e il primo millennio a.C., Atti del II Convegno di studi di Selargius 1986*, 107–116. Cagliari.

Sebis, S. 1992. Siti con ceramica "a pettine" del Campidano Maggiore e rapporti con la facies Bonnanaro B. In Ugas, G., Lai, G. & Lilliu, G. (eds.), *La Sardegna nel Mediterraneo tra il Bronzo Medio e il Bronzo Recente (XVII–XIII sec. a.C.), Atti del III Convegno di Studi di Selargius, 1987*, 135–144. Della Torre, Cagliari.

Sebis, S. 1995. La ceramica del Bronzo Medio (XVI–XIV sec. a.C.) e del Bronzo Recente (XIII–XII sec. a.C.) nell'Oristanese. In *La ceramica racconta la storia*. S'Alvure, Oristano.

Tanda, G. 1989. L'arte del Neolitico e dell'Età del Rame in Sardegna. Nuovi studi e recenti acquisizioni. *L'arte dal Paleolitico all'Età del Bronzo in Italia*. Atti della XXVIII riunione scientifica – L'arte in Italia dal paleolitico all'eta del bronzo, 479–493. Nuova Italia, Firenze.

Taramelli, A. 1910. Il nuraghe Lugherras presso Paulilatino. *Monumenti Antichi dei Lincei* 20.

Taramelli, A. 1918. Il tempio nuragico di Sant'Anastasia in Sardara (prov. di Cagliari). *Monumenti Antichi dei Lincei* 25.

Tinè, S. 1965. Gli scavi nella Grotta della Chiusazza. *Bullettino di Paletnologia Italiana* 16: 123–286.

Tinè, S. 1975. La Civiltà neolitica del Tavoliere. In *Civiltà preistoriche e protostoriche della Daunia. Atti del Colloquio "Preistoria e Protostoria della Daunia"*. Firenze.

Tinè, S. 1987. Considerazioni sul Neolitico della Puglia. In *Atti della XXVI Riunione Scientifica, "Il Neolitico in Italia," Firenze, 7–10 Novembre 1985*, 189–196. Istituto Italiano di Preistoria e Protostoria, Firenze.

Tinè, S.1992. Italia Meridionale, Sicilia e Malta tra il XVI e il XIII sec. a.C. In Ugas, G., Lai, G. & Lilliu, G. (eds.), *La Sardegna nel Mediterraneo tra il Bronzo Medio e il Bronzo Recente (XVII–XIII sec. a.C.), Atti del III Convegno di Studi di Selargius, 1987*, 305–329. Della Torre, Cagliari.

Tinè, S.1992a. La cronologia assoluta di M. d'Accoddi. In Tiné, S. & Traverso, A. (eds.), *Monte d'Accoddi. Dieci anni di nuovi scavi*, 115–117. Genova.

Tomasello, F. 1986. L'architettura funeraria in Sicilia tra la Media e la Tarda Età del Bronzo. In *Traffici micenei nel Mediterraneo, Atti Convegno di Palermo 1984*, 93–104. Taranto.

Tore, G. 1978. Note sulle importazioni in Sardegna in età arcaica. In *Les céramiques de la Grèce de l'Est et leur diffusion en Occident*. Paris-Naples.

Tore, G. 1986. Intorno a un «torciere» in bronzo di tipo cipriota da San Vero Milis (S'Uraki)-Oristano. In Ugas, G. & Lai, G. (eds.), *Società e cultura in Sardegna nei periodi orientalizzante ed arcaico. Rapporti tra Sardegna, Fenici, Etruschi e Greci, Atti del I Convegno di studi "Un millennio di relazioni fra la Sardegna e i Paesi del Mediterraneo", Selargius-Cagliari 1985,* Cagliari.

Traverso, A. & Tiné, S. 1992. *Monte d'Accoddi. Dieci anni di nuovi scavi.* Genova.

Treuil, R. 1983. *Le Néolithique et le Bronze Ancien égéens. Les problemes stratigraphiques et chronologiques, les tecniques, les hommes.* De Boccard, Paris.

Treuil, R. et al. 1989. *Les civilisations égéennes du Néolithique et de l'Age du Bronze.* Presse Univ. France, Paris.

Tronchetti, C. 1978. Monte Prama (Com. di Cabras-OR). *Studi Etruschi.*

Trump, D.H. 1967. *Skorba and the Prehistory of Malta.* London.

Trump, D. H. 1978. Contatti siculo-maltesi prima dell'Età del Bronzo. *Kokalos* 1976-77,I.

Trump, D. H. 1983. *La preistoria del Mediterraneo.* Mondadori, Milano.

Trump, D. H. 1983a. *La grotta di Filiestru a Bonuighinu (Mara-SS).* Quaderni della Soprintendenza ai Beni Archeologici per le Provincie di Sassari e Nuoro 13. Dessì, Sassari.

Trump, D.H. 1990. *Nuraghe Noeddos and the Bonu Ighinu Valley. Excavations and Survey in Sardinia.* Oxbow Books, Oxford.

Tusa, S. 1983. *La Sicilia nella preistoria.* Palermo.

Tykot, R.H. 1994. Radiocarbon dating and absolute chronology in Sardinia and Corsica. In Skeates, R. & Whitehouse, R. (eds.), *Radiocarbon Dating and Italian Prehistory,* 115–145. Archaeological Monographs of the British School at Rome 8 and Accordia Specialist Studies on Italy 3. London.

Tykot, R.H. & Andrews, T.K. (eds.). 1992. *Sardinia in the Mediterranean: A Footprint in the Sea. Studies in Sardinian Archaeology Presented to Miriam S. Balmuth.* Monographs in Mediterranean Archaeology 3. Sheffield Academic Press, Sheffield.

Ugas, G. 1981. La tomba megalitica di San Cosimo-Gonnosfanadiga: un monumento del Bronzo Medio (con la più antica attestazione micenea in Sardegna). Notizia preliminare. *Archeologia Sarda* 2: 7–30.

Ugas, G. 1982. Padru Jossu. Tomba ipogeica ed elementi di cultura materiale delle fasi Campaniforme A e B. *Ricerche archeologiche nel territorio di Sanluri, Mostra grafica e fotografica, Sanluri (CA):* 19–26.

Ugas, G. 1982a. Corti Beccia. Il nuraghe e i reperti. *Ricerche archeologiche nel territorio di Sanluri,* Mostra grafica e fotografica, Sanluri (CA).

Ugas, G. 1982b. La Sardegna. S. Cosimo di Gonnosfanadiga. *Magna Grecia e mondo Miceneo. Nuovi documenti, XXII Convegno di studi sulla Magna Grecia, Taranto 1982.* Napoli.

Ugas, G. 1982c. Influssi greco-orientali nei centri tardo-nuragici della Sardegna meridionale. *Parola del Passato* 299–307.

Ugas, G. 1985. I rapporti di scambio fra Etruschi e Sardi. Considerazioni alla luce delle nuove indagini a Santu Brai. *Atti II Congresso Internazionale Etrusco.* Firenze.

Ugas, G. 1986. La produzione materiale nuragica. Note sull'apporto etrusco e greco. In Ugas, G. & Lai, G. (eds.), *Società e cultura in Sardegna nei periodi orientalizzante ed arcaico. Rapporti tra Sardegna, Fenici, Etruschi e Greci, Atti del I Convegno di studi "Un millennio di relazioni fra la Sardegna e i Paesi del Mediterraneo", Selargius-Cagliari 1985,* 41–53. Cagliari.

Ugas, G. 1987. Un nuovo contributo per lo studio della tholos in Sardegna. La fortezza di Su Molinu di Villanovafranca-Cagliari. In Balmuth, M.S. (ed.), *Studies in Sardinian Archaeology III: Nuragic Sardinia and the Mycenaean World.* BAR International Series 387: 77–128. British Archaeological Reports, Oxford.

Ugas, G. 1989. L'età nuragica. Il Bronzo Medio e il Bronzo Recente. In *Il Museo Archeologico Nazionale di Cagliari,* 79–92. Banco di Sardegna, Sassari.

Ugas, G. 1989–90. Il sacello del vano e nella fortezza nuragica di Su Mulinu-Villanovafranca (CA). *Scienze dell'Antichità* 3–4. Università "La Sapienza", Roma.

Ugas, G. 1990. *La tomba dei guerrieri di Decimoputzu.* Norax 1. Della Torre, Cagliari.

Ugas, G. 1992. Note su alcuni contesti del Bronzo Medio e Recente della Sardegna Meridionale. Il caso dell'insediamento di Monte Zara-Monastir. In Ugas, G., Lai, G. & Lilliu, G. (eds.), *La Sardegna nel Mediterraneo tra il Bronzo Medio e il Bronzo Recente (XVII–XIII sec. a.C.), Atti del III Convegno di Studi di Selargius, 1987,* 201–227. Della Torre, Cagliari.

Ugas, G. 1992a. Considerazioni sullo sviluppo dell'architettura e della società nuragica. In Tykot, R.H. & Andrews, T.K. (eds.), *Sardinia in the Mediterranean: a footprint in the sea. Studies in Sardinian archaeology presented to Miriam S. Balmuth.* Monographs in Mediterranean Archaeology 3. Sheffield Academic Press, Sheffield.

Ugas, G. 1992b. Dibattito e Contributi. In Tiné, S. & Traverso, A. (eds.), *Monte d'Accoddi. Dieci anni di nuovi scavi,* Genova.

Ugas, G. 1993. *San Sperate dalle origini ai Baroni.* Della Torre, Cagliari.

Ugas, G. 1993a. La metallurgia del piombo, dell'argento e dell'oro nella Sardegna prenuragica. *L'uomo e le miniere in Sardegna.* Della Torre, Cagliari.

Ugas, G. 1995. La ceramica del Bronzo Finale e della tarda Età del Ferro. *La ceramica racconta la storia.* S'Alvure, Oristano.

Ugas, G. in stampa a. Relazioni tra la Sardegna e l'Egeo attraverso l'architettura e le fonti letterarie. *Atti II Convegno di micenologia, Roma, 1991.*

Ugas, G. in stampa b. L'ipogeo dei guerrieri di Decimoputzu e le prime spade sarde. In *Atti del Congresso "L'Antica Età del Bronzo in Italia", Viareggio 1995.*

Ugas, G. in stampa c. Strutture insediative seminterrate e ipogeismo nella Sardegna preistorica. In *Atti Congresso L'ipogeismo nel Mediterraneo. Origini, sviluppo, quadri culturali, Sassari-Oristano 1994.*

Ugas, G., Usai, L., Nuvoli, M.P., Lai, G. & Marras, M.G. 1989. Nuovi dati sull'insediamento di Su Coddu. In Campus, L.D. (a cura di), *La cultura di Ozieri. Problematiche e nuove acquisizioni.* Il Torchietto, Ozieri.

Ugas, G., Lai, G. & Usai, L. 1985. L'insediamento prenuragico di Su Coddu (Selargius-Cagliari). Notizia preliminare sulle campagne di scavo 1981–1984. *Nuovo Bullettino Archeologico Sardo* 2: 7–40.

Ugas, G & Lucia, P. 1987. Primi scavi nel sepolcreto nuragico di Antas. In Ugas G., Lai G. & Lilliu G. (eds.), *La Sardegna nel Mediterraneo tra il secondo e il primo millennio a.C., Atti del II Convegno di studi di Selargius 1986,* 255–270. Cagliari.

Ugas, G. & Paderi, M.C. 1989. Persistenze rituali e cultuali in età punica e romana. Il sacello nuragico del vano e della fortezza di Su Molinu-Villanovafranca (Cagliari). *L'Africa romana* 7: 475–486.

Ugas, G. & Usai, L. 1987. Nuovi scavi nel santuario nuragico di Sant'Anastasia di Sardara. In Ugas G., Lai G. & Lilliu G. (eds.), *La Sardegna nel Mediterraneo tra il secondo e il primo millennio a.C., Atti del II Convegno di studi di Selargius 1986,* 167–218. Cagliari.

Ugas, G. & Zucca, R. 1984. *Il commercio arcaico in Sardegna. Importazioni etrusche e greche (640–480 a.C.).* Cagliari.

Usai, E. 1987. Materiali dell'Età del Ferro in Marmilla. In Ugas G., Lai G. & Lilliu G. (eds.), *La Sardegna nel Mediterraneo tra il secondo e il primo millennio a.C., Atti del II Convegno di studi di Selargius 1986,* 243–254. Cagliari.

Usai, L. 1987. Il villaggio di età neolitica di Terramaini presso

Pirri (Cagliari). *Preistoria d'Italia alla luce delle nuove scoperte, Atti IV convegno P. P.* Pescia. 175–192.

Vandier, J. 1952. *Manuel d'archéologie égyptienne* I. Picard, Paris.

Veny, C. 1992. Las navetas de Menorca. In Ugas, G., Lai, G. & Lilliu, G. (eds.), *La Sardegna nel Mediterraneo tra il Bronzo Medio e il Bronzo Recente (XVII–XIII sec. a.C.), Atti del III Convegno di Studi di Selargius, 1987*, 443–472. Della Torre, Cagliari.

Vigliardi, A. 1980. Rapporti tra Sardegna e Toscana nell'Eneolitico finale-Primo Bronzo: la Grotta del Fontino nel Grossetano. *Atti della XXII Riunione Scientifica*, 247–288. Istituto Italiano di Preistoria e Protostoria, Firenze.

Watrous, V.L. 1989. A preliminary report on imported «Italian» wares from the Late Bronze Age site of Kommos on Crete. *Studi Micenei ed Egeo-anatolici* 27: 69–80.

Webster, G. 1988. Duos Nuraghes, Preliminary results of the first three seasons of excavation. *Journal of Field Archaeology* 15: 465–472.

Weiss, M.C. 1992. La Corse du Nord entre le XVI et le XIII siècle av. J.-C. In Ugas, G., Lai, G. & Lilliu, G. (eds.), *La Sardegna nel Mediterraneo tra il Bronzo Medio e il Bronzo Recente (XVII–XIII sec. a.C.), Atti del III Convegno di Studi di Selargius, 1987*, 367–378. Della Torre, Cagliari.

Weiss, M.C.-De Lanfranchi F. 1976. La civilisation néolithique en Corse. *La préhistoire française*, 432–442.

Weiss, M.C. & Desneiges, G. 1971. Le gisement de Monte Lazzo a Tiuccia (Corse). *Bulletin de la Société Préhistorique française* 68.

Zervos, C. 1956. *L'Art de la Crète néolithique et Minoenne*. Paris.

Zervos, C. 1957. *L'Art des Cyclades*. Paris.

26. Una fase Ozieri dell'Età del Rame nella tomba I di Janna Ventosa (Nuoro)

Alba Foschi Nieddu

Indicazioni sul sito e studi precedenti (Figg. 26.1–26.2)

La necropoli di Janna Ventosa, o di Maria Frunza o di Sas Birghines, tra cui si preferisce la prima denominazione dalla località in cui è sita la domus I con corridoio megalitico, l'unica delle cinque tombe che abbia restituito reperti, si apre a quota 470 m nei graniti paleozoici della montagna di Nuoro, il suggestivo monte Ortobene, ancora nel secolo scorso ricoperto da fitti boschi di lecci (Rovinetti 1957; Alberti & Peluffo 1972; Corda 1979). La necropoli, citata fin dal 1887 (Lovisato 1887), è stata oggetto nel 1981 di una catalogazione (*Architettura nuragica e prenuragica*) a cura del Comune di Nuoro e nel 1985 di una esplorazione archeologica, condotta dalla scrivente, per conto della Soprintendenza Archeologica per le provincie di Sassari e Nuoro (Foschi Nieddu 1985).

La domus I destava particolare interesse perché davanti al portello d'ingresso alle camere ipogeiche presentava

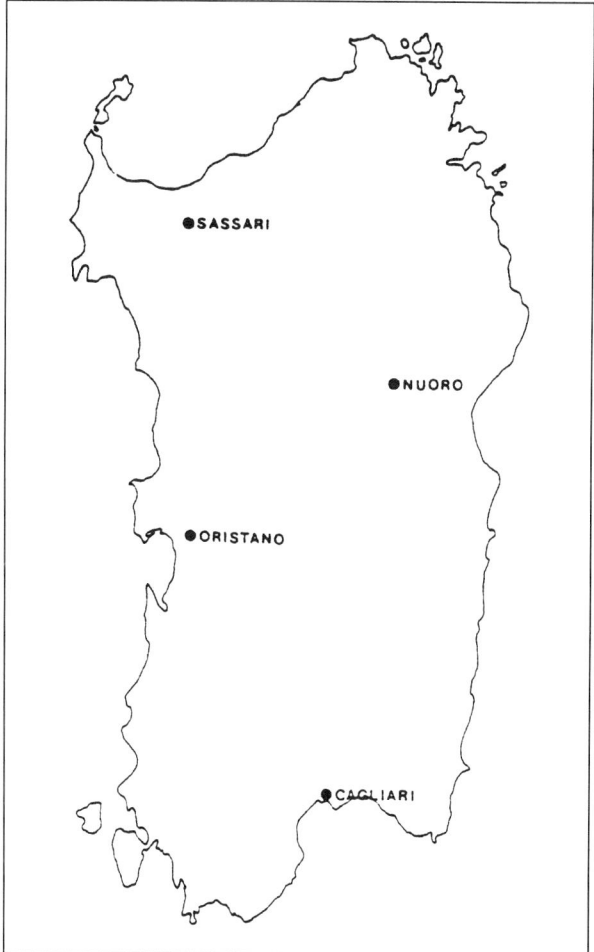

Fig. 26.1. Janna Ventosa (NU). Ubicazione.

Alba Foschi Nieddu, Soprintendenza ai Beni Archeologici per le Provincie di Sassari e Nuoro, Via Ballero 30, 08100 Nuoro, Sardegna, Italia

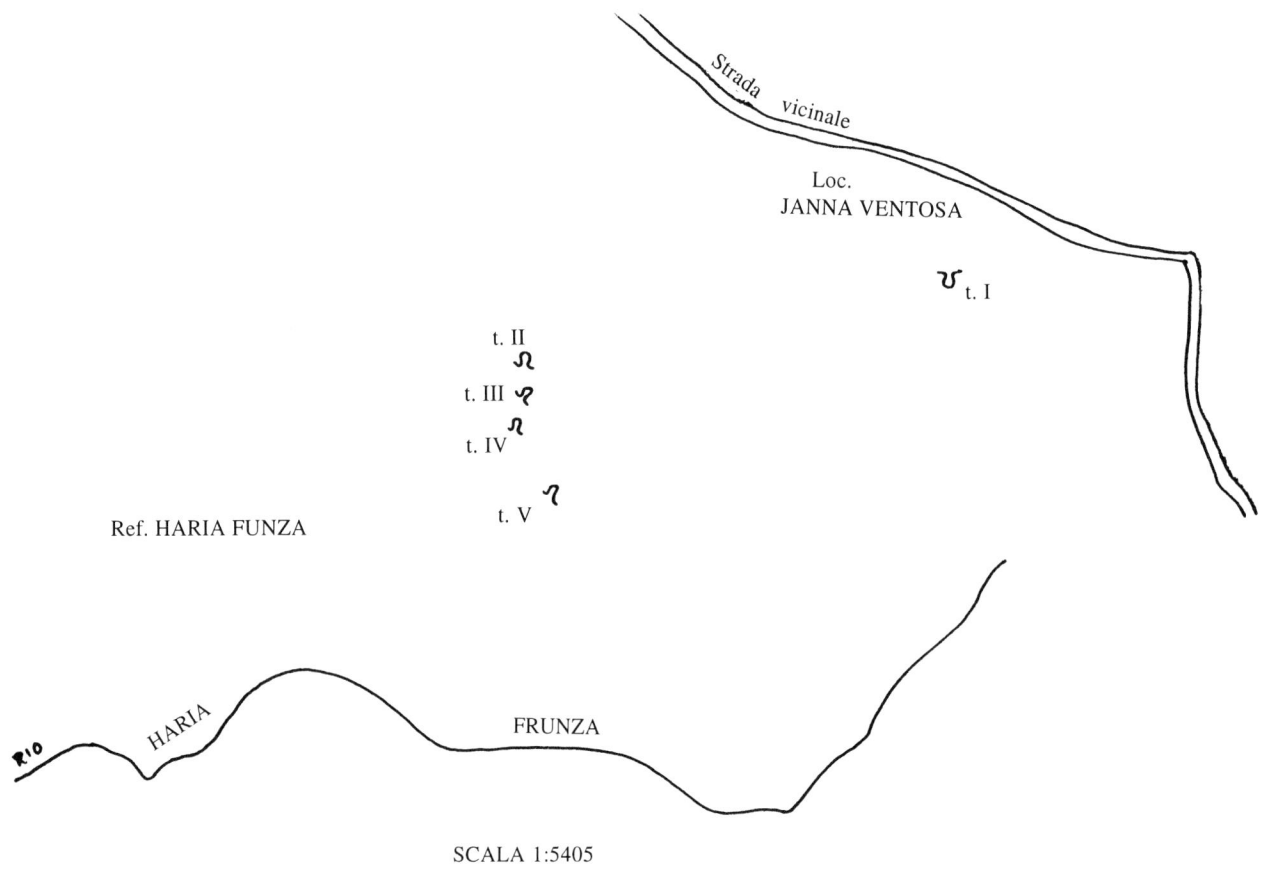

Fig. 26.2. Janna Ventosa (NU). Corografia.

un semicerchio di grosse pietre. Sfogliando il deposito di terra fu però evidente che il recinto era piuttosto recente, probabilmente un ricovero per il bestiame. Al di sotto venne rinvenuto un corridoio in filari di pietre sbozzate, lungo m 2,90 e largo m 2 con i muri spessi non più di 70 cm e alti al massimo 40 cm, in cui si trovarono sigillati reperti archeologici molto antichi, risalenti a una fase tarda della cultura di Ozieri. Per il repertorio originale, caratteristico e sufficientemente variato, Janna Ventosa potrebbe dare il nome a questa fase che, poiché sembra interessare, come meglio specificato più avanti, particolari siti distribuiti in tutta la Sardegna, è definibile anche come Ozieri megalitica.

Lo studio della cultura di Ozieri e del neolitico della Sardegna ha avuto un notevole incremento a partire dagli anni 80 finché si è giunti, nel 1989, alla pubblicazione del volume di sintesi sulla cultura di Ozieri, che si può considerare un punto fermo su cui basare i futuri studi e le future ricerche (Campus 1989). In quella occasione la scrivente fece un breve accenno agli elementi Ozieri venuti in luce nell'anticella e nel corridoio della tomba I di Janna Ventosa (Foschi Nieddu 1989), che in questa sede si presentano in modo più analitico.

Architettura (Figg. 26.3–26.7)

L'ipogeo con corridoio megalitico di Janna Ventosa si allinea ad altri monumenti consimili di tecnica mista (Demurtas *et al.* 1987). Non sembra il caso di ipotizzare la costruzione della tomba in due tempi, in quanto la tecnica megalitica è conosciuta e utilizzata in diversi siti Ozieri, come Monte d'Accoddi (Contu 1953; 1984; Tinè *et al.* 1989), i circoli della Gallura (Puglisi 1941–42), Pranu Mutteddu-Goni (Atzeni 1981: XL). Per il resto lo schema planimetrico della parte ipogeica è a T, un tipo che si riscontra quasi esclusivamente nel centro-nord della Sardegna e che è spesso associato a ricche decorazioni dipinte e a rilievo (Santoni 1978; Tanda & Mangold 1985).

Orientata a S-O, la tomba I ha l'anticella subrettangolare ad angoli smussati con una soglia d'ingresso costituita da una pietra trapezoidale, pareti lisciate a martellina, pavimento leggermente concavo, focolare rituale e fossetta ovale e, in asse, una grande cella irregolarmente rettangolare tripartita, con due larghi banconi laterali, alti 80 cm, e tracce di intonaco rosso. La tomba II è a tre celle, larghe rispettivamente al massimo m 2,70, 1,55 e 3,80 e alte m 1,70, 1,10 e 1,35, e presenta

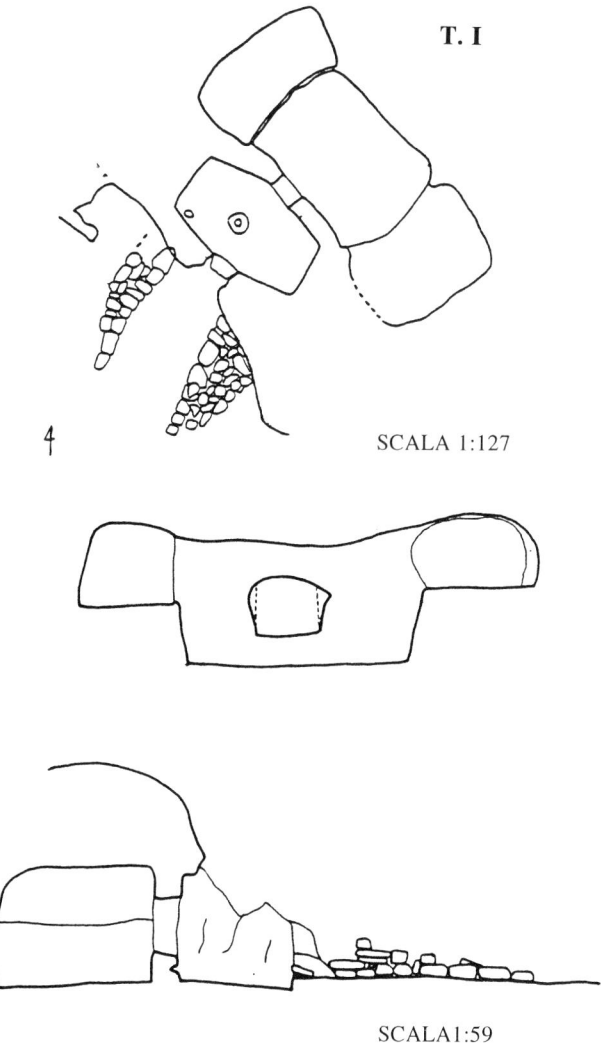

Fig. 26.3. Janna Ventosa (NU). Tomba I. Pianta e sezione.

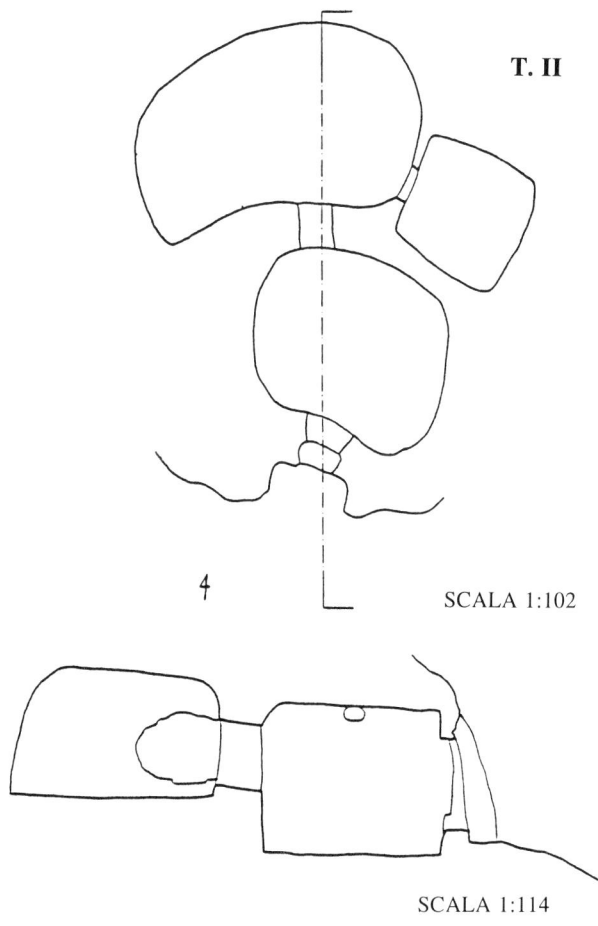

Fig. 26.4. Janna Ventosa (NU). Tomba II. Pianta e sezione.

una fossetta nella parete sud dell'anticella, appena sotto il soffitto. La III ha un impianto simile con due celle in asse e una perpendicolare, a piano rialzato di 30 cm; la larghezza massima delle camere è di m 1,65, 1,45 e 1,80 rispettivamente, le altezze 1,10, 1, 25 e 0,90. La tomba IV ha una scalinata di accesso con cinque gradini, di cui il terzo interrotto da una vaschetta, una camera d'ingresso larga m 4,90 x 3,20 e alta m 1,80 con un lettuccio funebre, dalle dimensioni di m 2 x 0,88 x 0,12 di altezza, fra la parete nord e un pilastro, e due cellette minori a pareti arrotondate. La tomba V ha due celle curvilinee, di m 1,90 x 2,10 x 1,55 di altezza e di m 2,50 x 1,55 x 1,05 di altezza rispettivamente, in asse, a cui si accede da un invito trapezoidale, scavato nel banco roccioso, cella conserva tracce di intonaco rosso.

Tutte le tombe rientrano nel repertorio, ricco e diversificato, delle strutture sepolcrali della cultura di Ozieri, sia per gli schemi planimetrici che per i particolari architettonici, ma presentano fossette sulle pareti, focolare rituale nell'anticella e tipologia degli ingressi che anticipano caratteristiche consimili dei più tardi ipogei Abealzu-Filigosa (Santoni 1978). Pur essendo scavate nel granito, non hanno la semplicità di impianto e la relativa angustia di altre domus del Nuorese (Fadda 1989).

Scavo 1985 (Fig. 26.8)

Mentre le altre quattro tombe sono state solo ripulite perché vuote, all'esterno della domus I, al di sotto di uno strato superficiale con pochi reperti moderni, romani e nuragici di 40 cm di spessore, si è rinvenuto uno stratarello più compatto di terreno completamente sterile di circa 14 cm. Asportato il livello sterile, fra alcune pietre sono stati trovati schiacciati diversi frammenti di due vasi decorati di tradizione Beaker, presentati di recente a un congresso a Viareggio (Foschi Nieddu 1995a).

Procedendo nell'esplorazione, è risultato evidente che le pietre appartenevano a uno dei due muretti di un corridoio in stretta connessione con la tomba ipogeica. Il terreno di riempimento è stato asportato in tre tagli di circa 10 cm, ma non ha mostrato variazioni: si trattava di un terriccio scuro, quasi nero, molto grasso. Fra il *dromos* subaereo e l'anticella si è trovata, come già osservato, una soglia in pietra lavorata; anche il pavimento del

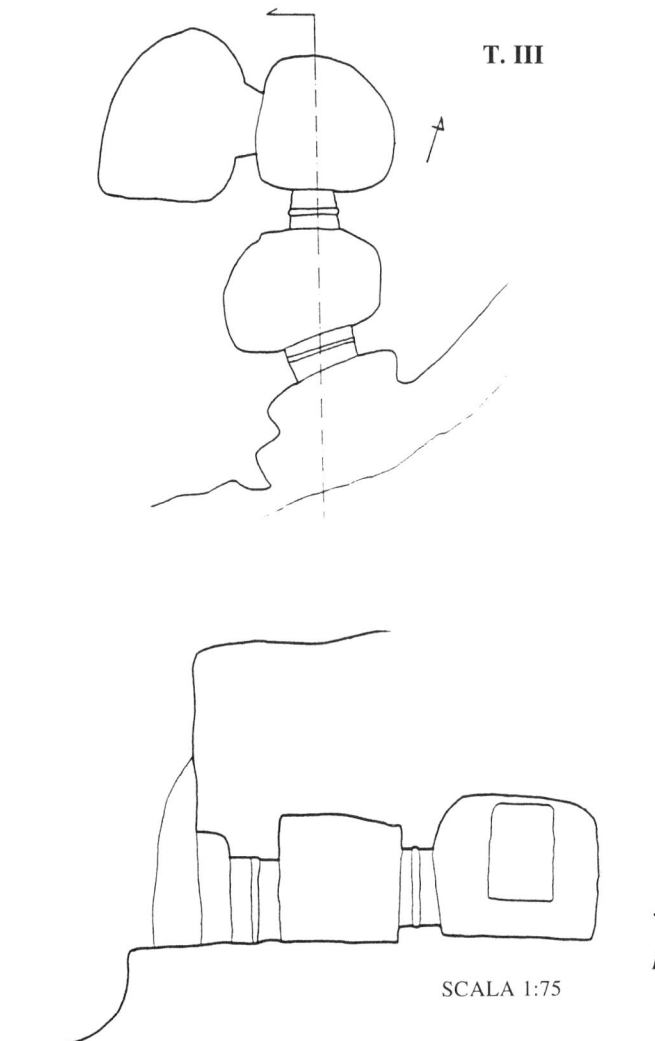

Fig. 26.5. Janna Ventosa (NU). Tomba III. Pianta e sezione.

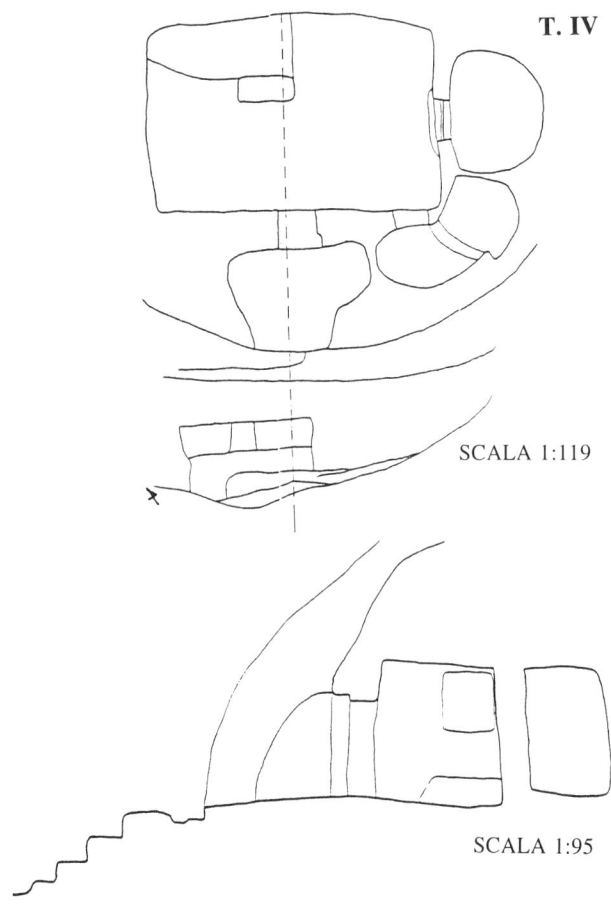

Fig. 26.6. Janna Ventosa (NU). Tomba IV. Pianta e sezione.

corridoio, come quello delle celle, è in roccia viva accuratamente lisciata.

Delle due camere interne, la maggiore era pressoché vuota metre l'anticella con il pavimento a una quota inferiore è risultata rialzata in epoca imprecisabile e, al di sotto delle pietre utilizzate per il passaggio, si sono messi in luce reperti ceramici e litici di cultura Ozieri, del tutto simili a quelli provenienti dal corridoio, oltre ad una daga in rame (Lo Schiavo 1989) e ad alcuni frammenti ceramici di tipologia Monte Claro. Piante e sezioni delle tombe sono di F.Tendas; la documentazione grafica è stata eseguita dalla scrivente; le foto da G. Pitzalis.

I materiali di cultura Ozieri (Figg. 26.9–26.16)

Sono stati contati novanta oggetti, fra ceramici e tipologia Ozieri. La ceramica, in larga percentuale decorata, è molto frammentaria; l'aspetto, l'impasto e il trattamento delle superfici sono indubbiamente assai diverse dai fittili dei contesti classici di S. Michele (Lilliu 1967), Sa Ucca de Su Tintirriolu (Loria & Trump 1978), Filiestru (Trump 1983) e San Gemiliano (Atzeni 1962). Le superfici sono in prevalenza brune, in tonalità dal rossiccio al grigiastro, spesso lisciate e lucidate e talle forme ricostruibili risultano aperte e semplici, prevalgono le ciotole emisferiche, le ciotole carenate, i vasi a cestello, i vasi globulari a collo distinto. I fittili sono decorati all'esterno, e alcuni anche all'interno con motivi incisi: a nastro tratteggiato, zigzag, festone e impressi a trattini, unghiate e punteggio. Sono meno frequenti gli ornati a dentelli lineari e a festone, mentre in un solo caso è attestato un cordone plastico orizzontale.

Una ciotola frammentaria e lacunosa, di particolare interesse, è riccamente decorata sotto l'orlo da un nastro orizzontale inciso, sul corpo da festoni dentellati e sul fondo arrotondato da riquadri risparmiati da tratteggi incisi. Le figurine umane incise sulle pareti interna ed esterna hanno tuniche rigatino, teste incappucciate (?) e agitano mani e piedi nudi.

Il tema della figura umana, abbastanza frequente nei reperti Ozieri (Loria 1971; Tanda 1990), è trattato in modo inusuale anche perché i cappucci e le mosse degli

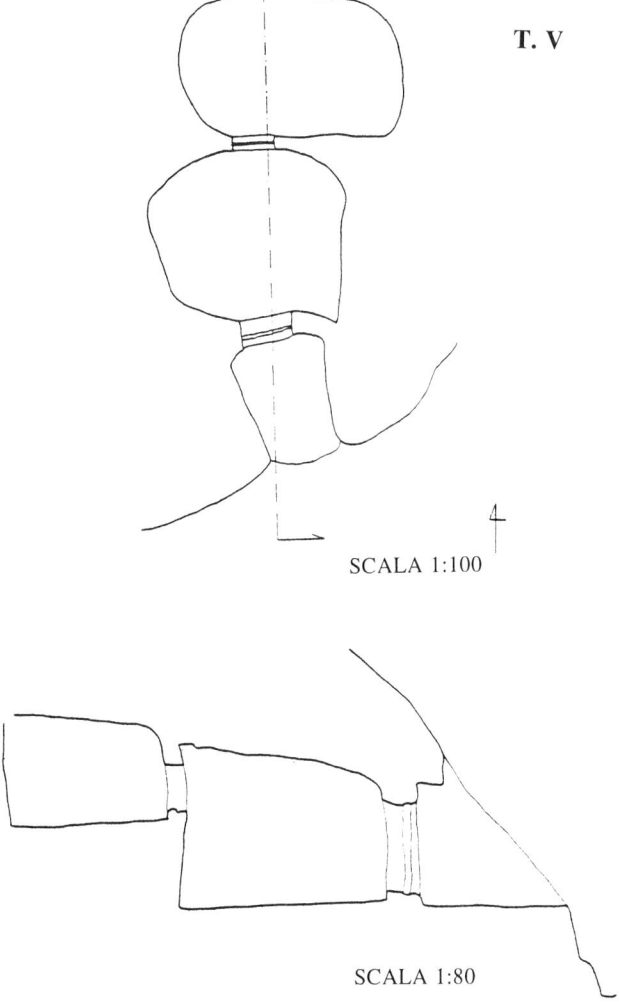

Fig. 26.7. Janna Ventosa (NU). Tomba V. Pianta e sezione.

individui sono indicativi di attività non quotidiane, legate alla sfera del rituale o della rappresentazione drammatica. Il miniaturismo che si riscontra, con poche eccezioni, nelle dimensioni dei vasi e negli ornati calligrafici appare molto distante dal gusto esuberante e barocco, delle ceramiche Ozieri finora note. Questo stile particolare di Janna Ventosa si può definire "rigido", in quanto dà un senso di minore libertà e articolazione rispetto allo stile classico.

Di fattura più grossolana, sono attestate anche tre anse acuminate, trovate in associazione ai reperti Ozieri (Foschi Nieddu 1995a), che hanno puntuali riscontri nella *domus de janas* dell'Ariete di Perfugas (Lo Schiavo 1982: 149). Circa venti manufatti litici provengono dal livello inferiore caratterizzato dalle ceramiche decorate tardo Ozieri; si tratta di punte, ogive, punte di freccia a ritocco bifacciale e codolo, lame e coltelli in selce e ossidiana, accettine in pietra verde e piccole macine a sezione pianoconvessa in granito, una delle quali impregnata di ocra rossa. La materia prima è scelta in base al tipo di selce utilizzata, se bionda o listata, e la lavorazione appare molto accurata. Il repertorio degli strumenti di Janna Ventosa ha numerosi riscontri in siti Ozieri (Lilliu 1980: 108–112) e Subozieri (Santoni 1992a; 1992b) e in quelli francesi Chassey e Saone-Rhone (Bocquet 1976).

Attribuzione culturale e cronologia

Come si è già accennato, la scrivente ritiene che la necropoli di JannaVentosa si situò in un momento di crisi della cultura Ozieri, dovuta all'incalzare dei nuovi tempi dell'età del Rame. La sua opinione, espressa di recente e pertanto non sa quanto condivisa, è che l'eneolitico

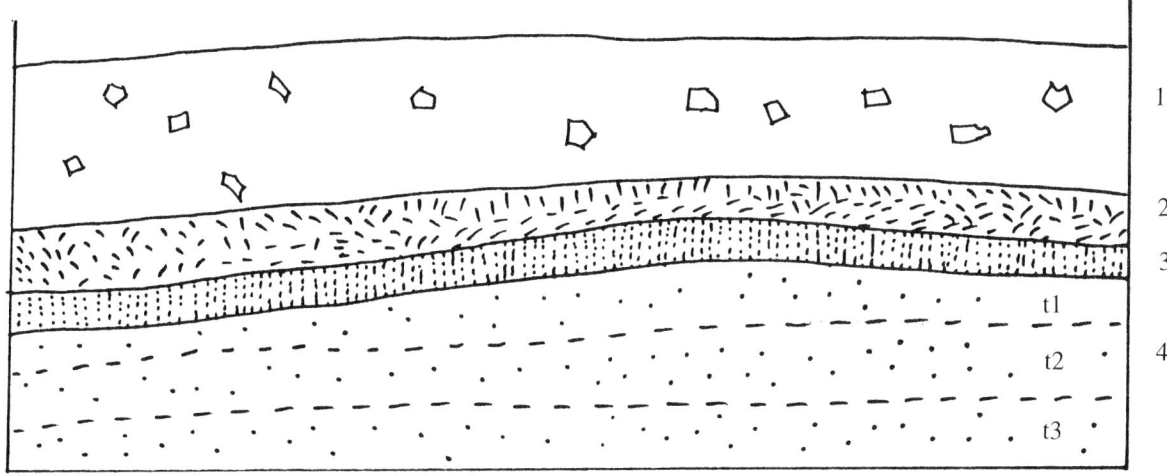

1. Reperti Nuragici e Romani
2. Sterile
3. Reperti del Bronzo Antico
4. Reperti Ozieri

40 cm

Fig. 26.8. Janna Ventosa (NU). Deposito stratificato nel dromos della tomba I.

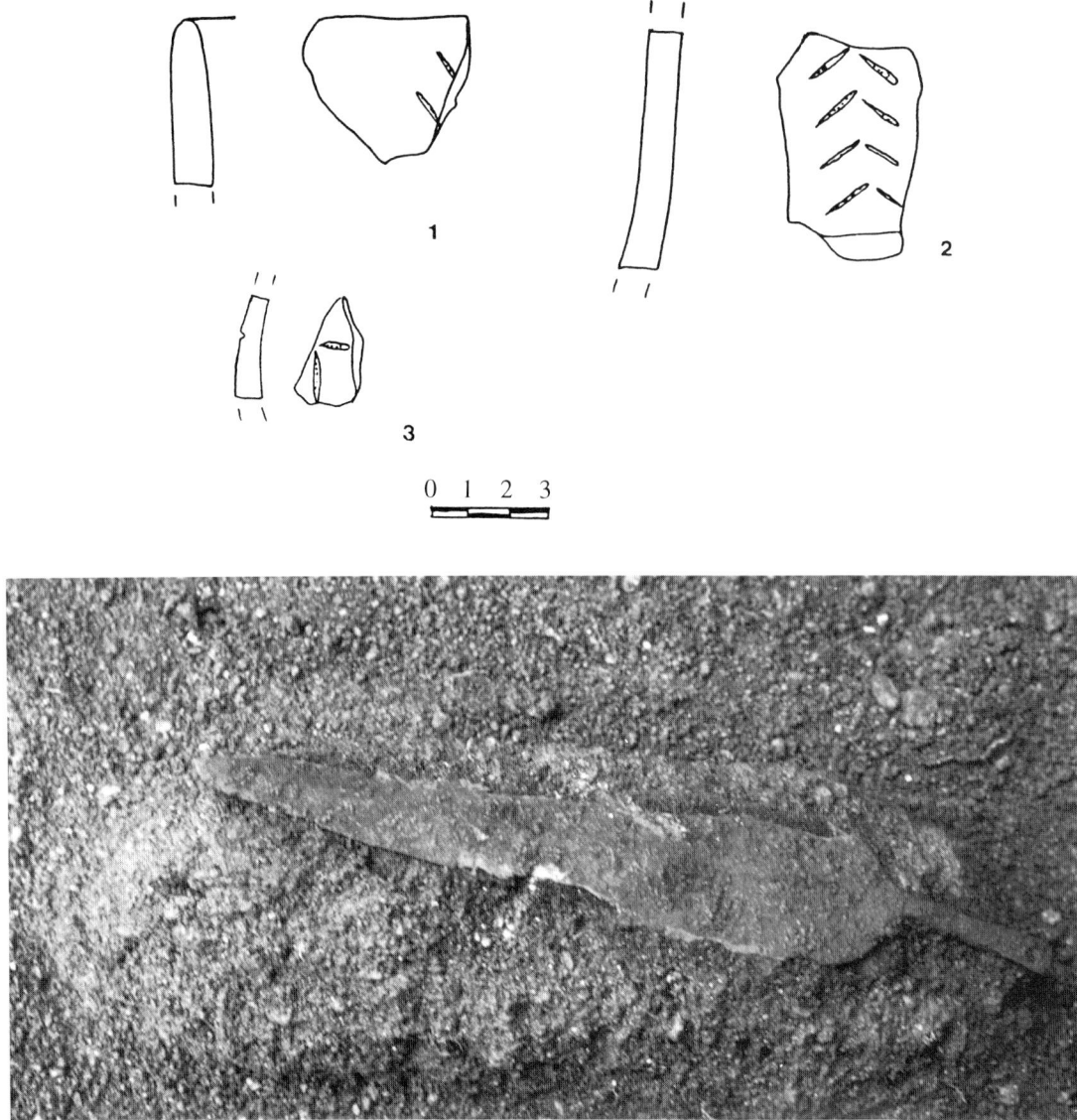

Fig. 26.9. Motivi decorative sulle ceramiche.

isolano sia di origine orientale, in quanto i portatori della cultura di Monte Claro con le tombe a forno, le armi di rame, le ceramiche scanalate, le case absidate e i santuari sembrano del tutto estranei alla tradizione dell'isola (Foschi Nieddu 1995b). A supporto di questa tesi, si sottolinea come i materiali Monte Claro nei siti stratificati subentrino quasi sempre a quelli Ozieri e di rado, e solo nel nord-ovest della Sardegna, ai reperti Abealzu-Filigosa (Contu 1964: 157; Moravetti 1990: 18).

Gli oggetti rinvenuti nella tomba I di Janna Ventosa, con le loro caratteristiche di miniaturismo e di irrigidimento dei motivi ornamentali, non sembrano prodotti locali contemporanei delle necropoli e abitati di Ozieri neolitica, ma i documenti significativi di una fase tarda, finale di questa importante cultura mediterranea. Di tali elementi si parla infatti anche per i materiali di Pranu Mutteddu-Goni (Cocco 1989) e per quelli di Perfugas (Lo Schiavo 1992), siti con evidenze megalitiche.

Altri studiosi hanno visto la necessità di articolare in fasi la cultura di Ozieri (Ferrarese Ceruti 1980; Tanda 1980); si ritiene che sia possibile enuclearne altre in aggiunta alle due già precisabili in base all'evidenza stratigrafica. Nel momento di passaggio all'età dei metalli, oltre alla tecnica metallurgica viene importato il megaliti grande diffusione, data l'elevata potenzialità del suolo sardo. Il megalitismo di Janna Ventosa non è certo quello dolmenico, fortemente intriso di significati religiosi e sacrali, probabilmente contemporaneo; ne sembra piuttosto un'eco in un ambiente non ancora influenzato dai nuovi rituali. I due grandi fenomeni del megalitismo e della metallurgia potrebbero essere coevi, ma il secondo

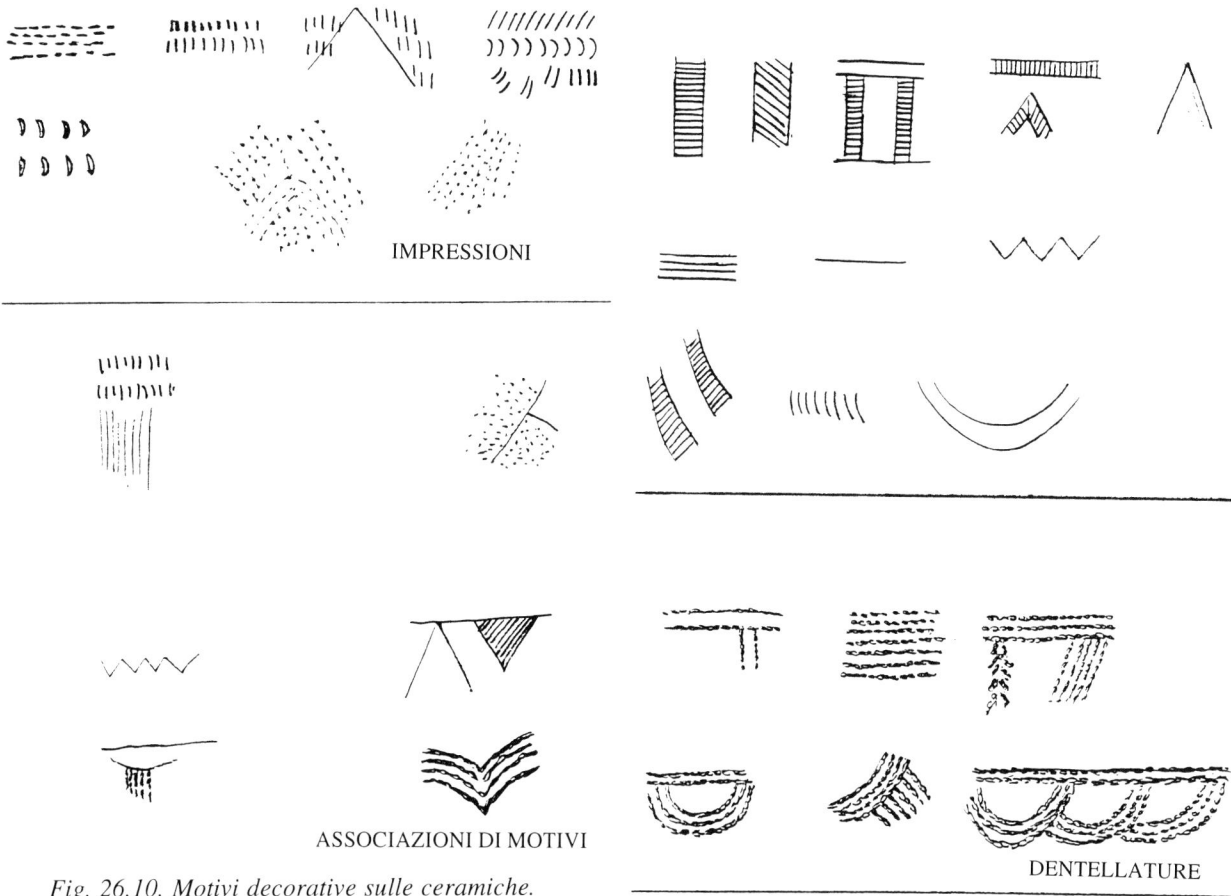

Fig. 26.10. Motivi decorative sulle ceramiche.

Fig. 26.11. Motivi decorative sulle ceramiche.

è considerato più indicativo di un cambiamento epocale (Lilliu 1986; Ugas 1990; 1993). L'aspetto Ozieri di Janna Ventosa dovrebbe pertanto appartenere all'eneolitico iniziale sardo, a cui si possono riferire anche le culture di Monte Claro (Contu 1988: 442), Subozieri e Abealzu-Filigosa. A parere della scrivente è infatti accettabile la definizione di Subozieri (Santoni 1992b), con cui si intende una *facies* a ceramiche dipinte in evidente linea di continuità con la cultura di Ozieri e con elementi di conoscenza della metallurgia, presente per lo più in siti meridionali, ma non quella di subneolitico.

Per quanto riguarda il problema della cronologia assoluta si è ancora nell'oscurità e le indicazioni da insediamenti che si presume siano coevi non appaiono convergenti (Contu 1982); soprattutto le datazioni al ^{14}C per la cultura di Monte Claro variano dal 2500 (Trump 1983; Contu 1988:442) al 1740 a.C. (Lilliu 1982). Fra gli studiosi non c'è accordo in quanto alcuni seguono le datazioni calibrate, altri quelle non calibrate e altri hanno numerose riserve nei riguardi del ^{14}C (cfr. Ehrich 1992).

Considerazioni finali

Dalla presenza degli elementi culturali Monte Claro soprastanti quelli della fase tarda di Ozieri si può dedurre che i gruppi umani a tradizione Ozieri furono costretti, nel migliore dei casi, ad abbandonare la zona di insediamento, certamente nei pressi della necropoli anche se non ancora identificata. Il maggiore sito di cultura Monte Claro finora rinvenuto, quello di Biriai-Oliena (Castaldi 1981; 1984), era molto vicino in linea d'aria e doveva costituire un serio pericolo. In questa fase epocale della Sardegna, di passaggio all'età dei metalli, due culture vennero in contatto ma non si integrarono. Le componenti indigene, presumibilmente rinforzate da gruppi accorsi dalle regioni tradizionalmente amiche della Spagna, Francia e Italia peninsulare, con le quali avevano consolidato rapporti commerciali e interrelazioni pacifiche ed a cui sembrano dovute almeno in parte le numerose innovazioni, dettero infatti origine alla cultura di Abealzu-Filigosa (Foschi Nieddu 1986; Basoli & Foschi Nieddu 1993).

Si presume in definitiva, da parte dei gruppi Ozieri, una scelta di indipendenza dovuta a molteplici fattori, ma significativa essenzialmente delle differenziazioni nel sistema di valori, usi, costumi, eredità rispetto ai gruppi Monte Claro. Il fenomeno della colonizzazione orientale si dovrebbe inserire nei processi di modificazione interni alle evolute culture egeo-anatoliche.

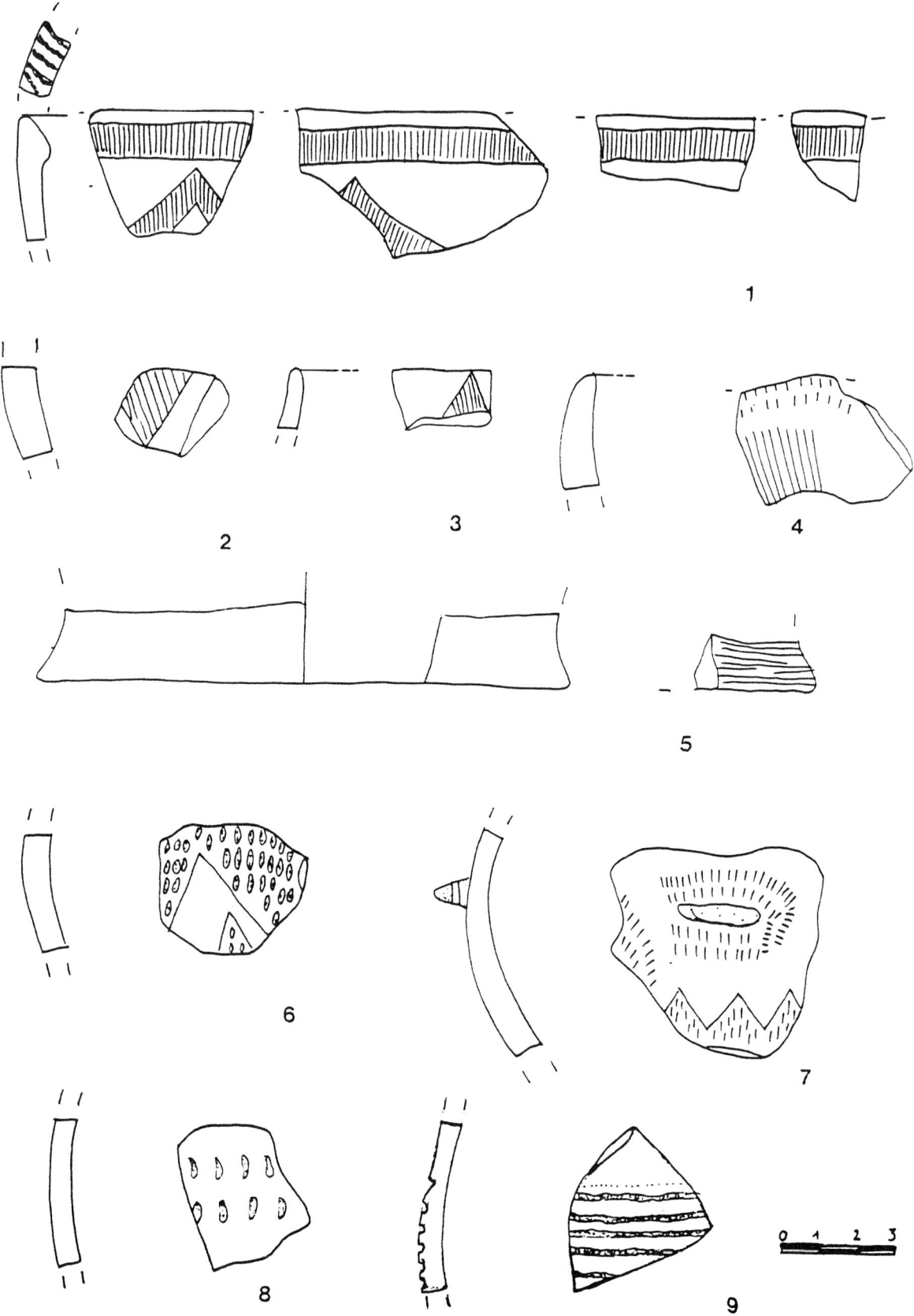

Fig. 26.12. Motivi decorative sulle ceramiche.

Fig. 26.13. Ciotola con figurazioni antropomorfe.

Bibliografia

Albertil, O. & Peluffo, S. 1972. *Il Nuorese cuore della Sardegna*. Cagliari.
Atzeni, E. 1962. I villaggi preistorici di San Gemiliano di Sestu e di Monte Olladiri di Monastir e le ceramiche della facies di Monte Claro. *Studi Sardi* 17: 3–216.
Atzeni, E. 1981. Aspetti e sviluppi culturali del neolitico e della prima età dei metalli in Sardegna. In *Ichnussa. La Sardegna dalle Origini all'età Classica*, XXI-LI. Libri Scheiwiller, Milano.
Basoli, P. & Foschi Nieddu, A. 1993. Alcune annotazioni riguardo ai rapporti tra la culture di Rinaldone e quella di Abealzu-Filigosa. In *La cultura di Rinaldone. Ricerche e scavi*, 69–74. Milano.
Bocquet, A. 1976. Les Civilisations néolithiques dans les Alpes. In *La Préhistoire Française*. T. II: 292–300. Paris.
Castaldi, E. 1981. Villaggio con santuario a Biriai (Oliena-Nuoro). *Rivista di Scienze Preistoriche* 36: 153–218.
Castaldi, E. 1984. L'architettura di Biriai (Oliena-Nuoro). *Rivista di Scienze Preistoriche* 39: 25–36.
Cocco, D. 1989. La cultura materiale. In Atzeni, E. & Cocco, D., Note sulla necropoli megalitica di Pranu Mutteddu-Goni. In Campus, L.D. (a cura di), *La cultura di Ozieri. Problematiche e nuove acquisizioni*, 201–216. Il Torchietto, Ozieri.
Contu, E. 1953. Costruzione megalitica in località Monte d'Accoddi (Sassari). *Rivista di Scienze Preistoriche* 8: 199–202.
Contu, E. 1964. La tomba dei Vasi Tetrapodi in località Santu Pedru Alghero-Sassari). *Monumenti Antichi dell'Accademia dei Lincei* 47: 2–201.
Contu, E. 1982. Alcuni problemi cronologici della preistoria sarda nel contesto mediterraneo. *Archivio Storico Sardo* 33: 91–102.
Contu, E. 1984. Monte d'Accoddi. Sassari. Problematiche di studio e di ricerca di un singolare monumento megalitico preistorico. In Waldren, W.H., Chapman, R.W., Lewthwaite, J.G. & Kennard, R.-C. (eds.), *The Deya Conference of Prehistory*, BAR International Series 229: 591–608.
Contu, E. 1988. Problematica ed inquadramento culturale. In Atzeni, E., Contu, E. & Ferrarese Ceruti, M.L., L'età del rame nell'Italia insulare: la Sardegna. *L'età del Rame in Europa, Viareggio 15-18 ottobre 1987*. Rassegna di Archeologia 7: 441–448.
Corda, E. 1979. *Una montagna chiamata Ortobene*. Sassari.
Demurtas, S., Manca Demurtas, L. & Sebis, S. 1987. Domus de janas di Su Tiriarzu a Paulilatino (Oristano). *Quaderni della Soprintendenza Archeologica per le Provincie di Cagliari e Oristano* 4(1): 35–47.
Ehrich, R.W. (ed.). 1992. *Cronologies in Old World Archaeology*. University of Chicago Press, Chicago.
Fadda, M.A. 1989. Aspetti della cultura di S.Michele nel territorio della Barbagia. In Campus, L.D. (a cura di), *La cultura di Ozieri. Problematiche e nuove acquisizioni*, 163–168. Il Torchietto, Ozieri.
Ferrarese Ceruti, M.L. 1980. Le domus de janas di Mariughia e Canudedda e il dolmen di Motorra. In *Dorgali. Documenti archeologici*, 57–65. Sassari.
Foschi Nieddu, A. 1985. La tomba di Janna Ventosa (Nuoro). In *10 Anni di attività nel territorio della provincia di Nuoro*, 35. Nuoro.
Foschi Nieddu, A. 1986. *La tomba di I di Filigosa (Macomer-Nuoro). Alcune considerazioni sulla cultura di Abealzu-Filigosa nel contesto eneolitico della Sardegna*. Coop Grafica Nuorese, Nuoro.
Foschi Nieddu, A. 1989. Documenti di cultura Ozieri provenienti dalla grotta di Sa Korona di Monte Majore-Thiesi e dalla In Manconi, F. (a cura di), *Le Miniere e i Minatori della Sardegna*, 7–18. Consiglio Regionale della Sardegna, Cagliari.
Foschi Nieddu, A. 1995a, b. I.c. corso di pubblicazione.
Loria, R. 1971. Figurette schematiche femminili nella ceramica eneolitica della Sardegna. *Rivista di Scienze Preistoriche* 26: 179–202.
Loria, R. & Trump, D.H. 1978. Le scoperte a Sa Ucca de Su Tintirriolu e il Neolitico sardo. *Monumenti Antichi dell'Accademia dei Lincei*. II Serie miscellanea. Roma.
Lo Schiavo, F. 1982. La domus dell'Ariete (Perfugas-Sassari). *Rivista di Scienze Preistoriche* 37: 135–180.
Lo Schiavo, F. 1989. Le origine della metallurgia e il problema della metallurgia nella cultura di Ozieri. In Campus, L.D. (a cura di), *La cultura di Ozieri. Problematiche e nuove acquisizioni*, 279–294. Il Torchietto, Ozieri.
Lovisato, D. 1887. Nota II ad una pagina di preistoria sarda. *Rendiconti dell'Accademia dei Lincei* 3: 85–86.

Fig. 26.14. *Figurazioni antropomorfe Ozieri (n. 13 da Monte Majore-Thiesi, scavi Foschi 1980; gli altri da Loria & Trump 1978; Atzeni 1981; Santoni 1989; Tanda 1990).*

27. Aegean Chronology Session: Introductory Remarks

Lucia Vagnetti

I would like to thank Miriam Balmuth and Robert Tykot for having included in the program a specific session on Aegean chronology. It is a matter of personal satisfaction, having devoted more than half of my scholarly work to the study of the relationships between the Aegean and the Central Mediterranean, to see that eminent scholars, working specifically on the Aegean and the Eastern Mediterranean, have accepted the invitation to bring us the most current views about the thorny problem of Aegean relative and absolute chronology as it relates to Sardinia. Aegean chronology of the Bronze Age is of crucial importance for the Central Mediterranean sequence which, thanks to imported and imitated material found in local contexts, can be related to the Eastern Mediterranean sequence. To this evidence one can now add the very important discovery of some Sardinian imports in the Cretan harbor town of Kommos (Watrous 1989; 1992: 163–168; this volume; Jones & Vagnetti 1991: 134). As a matter of fact this conference has firmly established that Sardinia is tightly linked to the pattern of Bronze Age long distance trade in the Mediterranean, but we must also remember that there are other regions of the area, such as Sicily and Southern Italy, that provide extremely important information, especially for their early links with the Aegean, going back to the beginning of the Mycenaean age (Vagnetti 1993a; 1996).

In order to facilitate the use of this volume of conference proceedings, a distribution map of Myceanean finds in Sardinia and a gazetteer of the sites pinpointed on the map, has been prepared by Licia Re and can be found in the following pages. The most recent and relevant bibliography is given for each site.

Cypriot evidence has been considered only in relation to pottery, leaving aside the vast and important issue of ox-hide ingots and other metalwork, already mentioned in a number of papers, but less chronology-sensitive than pottery (Lo Schiavo *et al.* 1985; Lo Schiavo *et al.* 1990; Gale 1987; Vagnetti & Lo Schiavo 1989).

I would only comment briefly on some of the most significant points emerging from the distribution map and the gazetteer:

First of all the distribution pattern: leaving aside Pozzomaggiore (no. 2) for the doubtful classification of the sherd found there, all the other sites are located along the coasts or not far from rivers. Actually the earliest finds, going back to LH IIIA (Wiener, this volume), come from inland sites like Nuraghe Arrubiu (no. 5), an outstanding monument in the Flumendosa valley, and Gonnosfanadiga (no. 7) and Mitza Purdia (no. 8) in the Sulcis-Iglesiente, one of the most important mining districts on the island. Such locations presuppose coastal landing sites – unfortunately yet unknown to us – and are indicative of the inland circulation of esteemed, exotic products. They vary from a Mycenaean alabastron from Nuraghe Arrubiu, to a glass-bead necklace from Gonnosfanadiga, to an ivory head of a warrior from Mitza Purdia, originally set on a wooden object. The presence of this object, belonging to a rare and very distinctive Mycenaean type, may perhaps be referred to as an esteemed gift, not devoid of symbolic value (Vagnetti 1996; *contra* Krzyszkowska 1991: 120). The peak of the imports, mostly pottery, can be assigned to LH IIIB, the main locations being the area of Orosei (no. 1) and Nuraghe Antigori (no. 11); evidence for LH IIIC imports is very limited. Several varieties of pottery have been identified using archaeological criteria (Ferrarese Ceruti *et al.* 1987) and in several cases archaeological attributions have been validated by physico-chemical analysis (Jones & Day 1987). Imports from mainland Greece, Crete and Cyprus are sure. Apart from the most usual types of pottery, sherds belonging to big pithoi imported from Crete and from Cyprus represent significant evidence of trade that can be linked to similar finds from the Ulu Burun and the Cape Iria shipwrecks (Bass 1986; 1991; Pulak 1988; Lolos 1991) and elsewhere;

Author's Address: Lucia Vagnetti, Consiglio Nazionale delle Ricerche, Istituto per gli studi Micenei ed Egeo-Anatolici, Via Giano della Bella 18, I-00162, Roma, Italia

the recent finds of sherds from similar pithoi of the Cypriot variety at Cannatello in southern Sicily offer a confirmation of the use of these cumbersome vessels in long-distance trade (Karageorghis 1993; Deorsola 1996).

However, the large majority of the painted pottery is not imported. Physico-chemical analysis confirmed the suspicion that painted pottery in Aegean style was produced in Sardinia. This class of pottery, whose decoration can be traced back to Mycenaean and Cretan prototypes, seems associated in the same layers with local Nuragic hand-made ware and with imported Aegean pottery. It does not seem to survive long after the end of the Aegean imports (Vagnetti & Jones 1988). The variety of imports found at Antigori make us think that this Nuragic complex or another coastal site in the vicinity might be considered as a sort of "international emporium", reflecting the characteristics of similar sites in the Near East, Cyprus and the Aegean, with very few parallels in Italy (Ferrarese Ceruti *et al.* 1987; Vagnetti 1993b).

Two more considerations are suggested by the distribution map: the first is the inner circulation of locally produced pottery of Mycenaean type, found sporadically at sites such as Barumini (no. 4) and Nuraghe Nastasi (no. 6). The second is the limited but meaningful evidence of Myceanean and/or Mycenaean-type pottery, recently emerged from sites that later became major Phoenician centres, such as Nora and its surroundings (no. 13) and Tharros (no. 3). This may add further fuel to the discussion of the role of Sardinia in the crucial transition between the Bronze and Iron Ages, when long distance trade fades and colonization is imminent.

References

Bass, G.F. 1986. A Bronze Age shipwreck at Ulu Burun (Kas): 1984 campaign. *American Journal of Archaeology* 90: 269–296.

Bass, G.F. 1991. Evidence of trade from Bronze Age shipwrecks. In Gale, N.H. (ed.), *Bronze Age Trade in the Mediterranean.* Studies In Mediterranean Archaeology 90: 69–82. Jonsered.

Deorsola, D. 1996. Il villaggio del Medio Bronzo di Cannatello presso Agrigento. In De Miro, E., Godart, L. & Sacconi, A. (eds.), *Atti e Memorie del Secondo Congresso Internazionale di Micenologia (Roma-Napoli 1991).* Incunabula Graeca 98(3): 1029–1038. Roma.

Ferrarese Ceruti, M.L., Vagnetti, L. & Lo Schiavo, F. 1987. Minoici, Micenei e Ciprioti in Sardegna alla luce delle più recenti scoperte. In Balmuth, M.S. (ed.), *Studies in Sardinian Archaeology III. Nuragic Sardinia and the Mycenaean World.* BAR International Series 387: 7–37. British Archaeological Reports, Oxford.

Gale, N.H. & Stos-Gale, Z.A., 1987. Oxhide ingots from Sardinia, Crete and Cyprus and the Bronze Age copper trade: new scientific evidence. In Balmuth, M.S. (ed.), *Studies in Sardinian Archaeology III. Nuragic Sardinia and the Mycenaean World.* BAR International Series 387: 135–178. British Archaeological Reports, Oxford.

Jones, R.E. & Day, P.M. 1987. Late Bronze Age Aegean and Cypriot-type pottery on Sardinia. Identification of imports and local imitations by physico-chemical analysis. In Balmuth, M.S. (ed.), *Studies in Sardinian Archaeology III. Nuragic Sardinia and the Mycenaean World.* BAR International Series 387: 257–269. British Archaeological Reports, Oxford.

Jones, R.E. & Vagnetti, L. 1991. Traders and craftsmen in the central Mediterranean: archaeological evidence and archaeometric research. In Gale, N.H. (ed.), *Bronze Age Trade in the Mediterranean.* Studies in Mediterranean Archaeology 90: 127–147. Jonsered.

Karageorghis, V. 1993. Le commerce chypriote avec l'Occident au Bronze Récent: quelque nouvelles découvertes. *Comptes Rendues de l'Academie des Inscriptions et de Belle Lettres*: 577–88.

Krzyszkowska, O.H. 1991. The Enkomi Warrior Head reconsidered. *Annual of the British School at Athens* 86: 105–120.

Lolos, Y., 1991. Ypovrichia Epiphaniaki erevna sto Navagio tis Ysteris Epochistou Chalkou sto Akrotirio Irion. *Enalia* III (1/2): 15–20.

Lo Schiavo, F., Macnamara, E. & Vagnetti, L. 1985. Late Cypriot imports to Italy and their influence on local bronzework. *Papers of the British School in Rome* 53: 1–70.

Lo Schiavo, F., Maddin, R., Merkel, J., Muhly, J.D. & Stech, T. 1990. *Analisi metallurgiche e statistiche sui lingotti di rame della Sardegna.* Quaderni della Soprintendenza ai Beni Archeologici per le Province di Sassari e Nuoro 17. Il Torchietto, Ozieri.

Pulak, C. 1988. The Bronze Age shipwreck at Ulu Burun, Turkey: 1985 campaign. *American Journal of Archaeology* 92: 1–37.

Vagnetti, L. 1993a. Mycenaean pottery in Italy. Fifty years of study. In Zerner, C.P., Zerner, F. & Winder, J. (eds.), *Wace and Blegen. Pottery as evidence for trade in the Aegean Bronze Age 1939–1989. Proceedings of the International Conference held at the American School of Classical Studies at Athens (December 1–3, 1989),* 143–154. Gieben, Amsterdam.

Vagnetti, L. 1993b. Aspetti della presenza micenea nel sud-est italiano. In *I Messapi. Atti del trentesimo Convegno di Studi sulla Magna Grecia (Taranto-Lecce 1990),* 363–382. Taranto.

Vagnetti, L. 1996. Espansione e diffusione dei Micenei. In Settis, S. (ed.), *I Greci. Storia, Cultura, Arte, Società* vol. 2.1: 133–172. Einaudi, Torino.

Vagnetti, L. & Jones, R.E. 1988. Towards the identification of local Mycenaean pottery in Italy. In French, E.B. & Wardle, K.A. (eds.), *Problems in Greek Prehistory. Papers presented at the Centenary Conference of the British School of Archaeology at Athens, (Manchester April 1986),* 335–348. Bristol Classical Press.

Vagnetti, L. & Lo Schiavo, F. 1989. Late Bronze Age long distance trade in the Mediterranean. The role of the Cypriots. In Peltenburg, E. (ed.), *Early Societies in Cyprus,* 217–243. Edinburgh University Press, Edinburgh.

Watrous, L.V. 1989. A preliminary report on imported "Italian" wares from the Late Bronze Age site of Kommos on Crete. *Studi Micenei ed Egeo Anatolici* 27: 69–79.

Watrous, L.V. 1992. *Kommos III. The Late Bronze Age Pottery.* Princeton University Press, Princeton.

28. A Catalog of Aegean Finds in Sardinia

Licia Re

1) Orosei – Orosei (Nuoro)
Top. Map: Orosei 195 III SE
Twelve Mycenaean sherds datable to LH IIIB, most of them imported (identified through typological comparations and archaeometric analysis), were delivered in 1976 to the Archaeological Service (Soprintendenza di Sassari e Nuoro). They probably come from a clandestine excavation carried out in the Orosei area in the northern part of Sardinia.
Lo Schiavo & Vagnetti 1980: 371–74; fig. I, 1–5; Vagnetti 1982: 186–187, tav. LXIX, 1–4; Jones 1986: 208; Jones & Day 1987: 257–270.

2) Pozzomaggiore (Sassari)
Top. Map: Pozzomaggiore 193 III SE
Contour elevation: 400 m
Distance from sea: 18 km
Found in a cave located between the Logudoro area and the Campeda plateau, not far from the town of Pozzomaggiore in the district of Sassari, a sherd, probably imported to Sardinia on the basis of archaeometric analysis, has been attributed to a LH IIIC vessel, although it may belong to later production of the Orientalizing period. It was found in a mixed deposit with some prehistoric pottery and later material.
Trump 1985: 185–199; Lo Schiavo & Vagnetti 1986: 199–203, figs. 2–3; Jones & Day 1987: 257–270.

3) Tharros – S. Giovanni di Sinis (Oristano)
Top. Map: Capo San Marco 216 I SE
Contour elevation: 10 m
Distance from sea: 0 km
The archaeological site of the ancient town of Tharros lies on a peninsula located on the northwestern edge of the gulf of Oristano. A sherd, found near the area of the Punic tophet (Bernardini 1989), seems Mycenaean, datable to LH IIIA2/B, while some alleged Mycenaean sherds published in the past belong to later production. This discovery, along with the presence of a great deal of Nuragic evidence on the promontory of Tharros, confirms that the site was already active in the Bronze Age.
Acquaro 1982: 37–51, tav. 26; Acquaro 1983: 49–89, tav. 18:1; Bernardini 1989: 285–290.

4) Su Nuraxi – Barumini (Cagliari)
Top. Map: Barumini 218 III SO
Contour elevation: 238 m
Distance from sea: 60 km
The Nuragic complex of Barumini, the best known monument of Nuragic Sardinia, lies on the fertile Marmilla area, in the central part of the Sarcidano. It is a quadrilobate nuraghe with outer walls surrounded by a Nuragic village. A Mycenaean sherd of local imitation (LH IIIC) was identified among the pottery from vano 17 (Lilliu excavation) and has been illustrated by Ferrarese Ceruti (1981).
Ferrarese Ceruti 1981: 611, fig. M 16–17; Vagnetti 1982: 212; 1987: 21, fig. 6:8.

5) Nuraghe Arrubiu – Orroli (Nuoro)
Top. Map: Lago di Mulargia 226 I NO
Contour elevation: 509 m
Distance from sea: 50 km
The Nuragic complex lies on the plateau of the Sarcidano, in the vicinity of the middle course of the Flumendosa river. It is the largest nuraghe excavated to date in Sardinia; a huge central tower (A) is surrounded by five towers (C-G) linked by walls enclosing a courtyard (B). The nuraghe was also strengthened with an outer wall consisting of seven towers and three courtyards. From layer 3 of the central courtyard (B), datable to the Late Bronze Age (*Bronzo Recente e Finale*), comes a LH IIIA2-(B?) angular alabastron (FS 94) attributed to the Peloponnese on the bases of typological comparisons and archaeometric analysis.

Lo Schiavo & Vagnetti 1993: 121–143, fig. 4, tav. II; Jones 1993: 144–145.

6) Nuraghe Nastasi – Tertenia (Nuoro)
Top. Map.: Tertenia 227 IV NE
Contour elevation: 60 m
Distance from sea: 2 km
Nuraghe Nastasi lies on a low hill in the eastern central part of Sardinia, in the vicinity of Tertenia. The excavation, carried out at different levels of the nuraghe, revealed no evidence of stratigraphy. A doubtful sherd with a painted band, possibly a local LH IIIC imitation, was found in the deepest level of the western tower along with Nuragic pottery, two fragments of an ox-hide ingot, and a fragment of a bronze figurine.
Basoli 1980: 429–440, fig. 2.

7) San Cosimo – Gonnosfanadiga (Cagliari)
Top. Map: Gonnosfanadiga 225 III NE
Contour elevation: 165 m
Distance from sea: 16 km
The giants' tomb of San Cosimo is located in the Iglesiente area of the southwestern part of Sardinia. During the excavation, together with Nuragic pottery, were found seventy faience and glass beads that seem, in part, to have typological similarity with Aegean examples (LH IIIA?).
Ugas 1981: 7–11; 1982: 180–185, tav. LXVIII,1–27.

8) Mitza Purdia – Decimoputzu (Cagliari)
Top. Map: Villaspeciosa 203 I NE
Contour elevation: 30 m
Distance from sea: 30 km
Remains of walls of a prehistoric building were found at Mitza Purdia, a site located on a wide alluvial plain between the Campidano area and the Iglesiente. It was destroyed by farming. During an archaeological survey in the area, together with a lot of local pottery (Middle and Late Bronze Age), was found a fragment of an ivory head of warrior wearing a boar's tusk helmet of Mycenaean manufacture datable to LHIIIA-B.
Sanna 1984: 19–41; Ferrarese Ceruti et al. 1987: 7–37, fig. 2.3:1–3; Krzyszkowska 1991.

9) Su Fraigu – San Sperate (Cagliari)
Contour elevation: 60 m
Distance from sea: 25 km
The site lies on the southern part of Sardinia, in the Campidano plain, close to Monte Zara- Monastir (n. 10). There is a considerable depth of archaeological deposit and occupation seems to have been continuous from the Chalcolithic period to the Middle Ages. From the excavation of a funerary hypogeum with apsidal plan, datable to the advanced part of the Late Bronze Age (*Bronzo Finale Iniziale*), come at least six necklaces consisting of round, cylindrical and globular beads of faïence and vitreous paste, and a very worn carved cylinder seal of green stone, probably of Near Eastern or Cypriot manufacture.
Ugas 1987: 118–119; 1993: 103–107, tav. LX, b-d.

10) Monte Zara – Monastir (Cagliari)
Contour elevation: 40 m
Distance from sea: 30 km
The site is located in the southern part of Sardinia, in the Campidano plain. The excavation revealed a Nuragic village and some graves datable from the Late Bronze Age (*Bronzo Recente e Finale*) through the first part of the Iron Age. Some sherds, probably local imitations of Mycenaean pottery (LH IIIB-C?), come from a circular dwelling (unit 34S).
Ugas 1987: 119–124; 1992: 201–227.

11) Nuraghe Antigori – Sarroch (Cagliari)
Top. Map: Villa d'Orrì 234 II NO
Contour elevation: 109 m
Distance from sea: 0.5 km
The Nuragic fortress lies on a hill in the western side of the gulf of Cagliari, in the southern part of Sardinia. A massive circuit wall with some circular towers encloses the top of the hill. Structures C, P, Q, N, datable to the Late Bronze Age (Bronzo Recente e Finale), yielded more than fifty Mycenaean sherds datable to LH IIIB and LH IIIC. Archaeological classification and archaeometric analysis have identified imports from the Peloponnese, Crete and Cyprus as well as local imitations in Mycenaean style.
Ferrarese Ceruti 1981: 605–612, tav. M3-14; 1982: 167–176, tavv. LXIII-LXV; 1983: 187–206, fig. 8 nn. 2–9; 1985: 249; 1986: 183–193, figs. 4, 7–8; Ferrarese Ceruti et al. 1987: 7–37; fig. 2.4; Jones & Day 1987: 257–270.

12) Domu s'Orku – Sarroch (Cagliari)
Top. Map: Pula 234 III SO
Contour elevation: 107 m
Distance from sea: 2 km
The Nuragic complex is located on the western side of the gulf of Cagliari, on a hill in the vicinity of Sarroch, 2 km southeast from Nuraghe Antigori (n. 11). The nuraghe consists of two towers linked by a central courtyard (*a tancato*). A few sherds, imported from the Peloponnese and Crete, were identified through archaeometric analysis; there are also some sherds of local Sardinian imitations (LH IIIC).
Ferrarese Ceruti 1982: 177–79, tav. LXIV, 10–12.; Vagnetti 1983: 7–13; Jones & Day 1987: 257–70.

13) Nora – Pula (Cagliari)
Contour elevation: 10 m
Distance from sea: 0 km
During the excavation of the northeastern sector (*ambiente 4*) of a Roman building (*macellum*) at the site of the ancient town of Nora, located on a peninsula along the

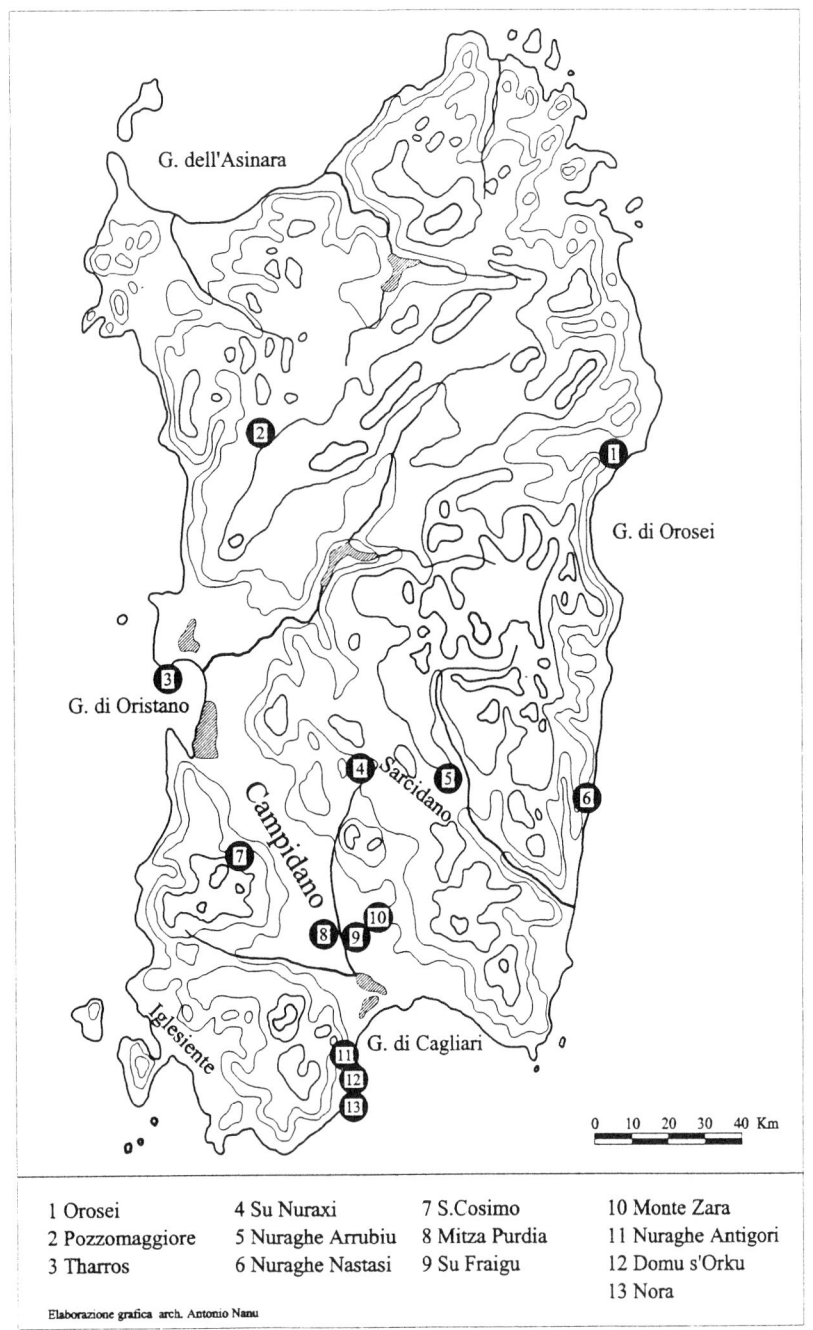

Figure 28.1. Findspots of Aegean Material in Sardinia.

western coast of the Gulf of Cagliari, a Mycenaean sherd was found, out of context, probably of local imitation, datable to LH IIIC. At least two other unpublished fragments of Mycenaean pottery are reported from a survey carried out in the area between Nora and Sarroch.
Rossignoli *et al.* 1994: 224–237.

References

Acquaro, E. *et al.* 1982. Tharros VIII. *Lo scavo del 1981. Rivista di Studi Fenici* 10(1): 37–51.

Acquaro, E. *et al.* 1983. Tharros IX. *Lo scavo del 1982. Rivista di Studi Fenici* 11(1): 49–89.

Basoli, P. 1980. L'architettura e i materiali del nuraghe Nastasi di Tertenia (NU). *Atti della XXII Riunione Scientifica dell'Istituto Italiano di Preistoria e Protostoria*, 429–440. Istituto Italiano di Preistoria e Protostoria, Firenze.

Bernardini, P. 1989. Tre nuovi documenti di importazione dalla collina di Muru Mannu. *Rivista di Studi Fenici* 17(1): 285–290.

Ferrarese Ceruti, M.L. 1981. Documenti micenei nella Sardegna meridionale. In *Ichnussa*, 605–612. Credito Italiano, Milano.

Ferrarese Ceruti, M.L. 1982. Il complesso Nuragico di Antigori (Sarroch, Cagliari). In Vagnetti, L. (ed.), *Magna Grecia e Mondo Miceneo. Nuovi Documenti*, 167–176. Istituto per la

Storia e l'Archeologia della Magna Grecia, Taranto.

Ferrarese Ceruti, M.L. 1982. Nuraghe Domu s'Orku (Sarroch, Cagliari). In Vagnetti, L. (ed.), *Magna Grecia e Mondo Miceneo. Nuovi Documenti*, 177–179. Istituto per la Storia e l'Archeologia della Magna Grecia, Taranto.

Ferrarese Ceruti, M.L. 1983. Antigori: la torre F del complesso nuragico di Antigori (Sarroch- Cagliari). Nota preliminare. In Vagnetti, L. (ed.), *Magna Grecia e Mondo Miceneo. Atti del XXII Convegno*, 187–206. Istituto per la Storia e l'Archeologia della Magna Grecia, Taranto.

Ferrarese Ceruti, M.L. 1985. In *Sardegna preistorica. Nuraghi a Milano*. Electa, Milano.

Ferrarese Ceruti, M. L. 1986. I vani c, p, q, del complesso nuragico di Antigori (Sarroch-Cagliari). In Marazzi, M., Tusa, S. & Vagnetti, L. (eds.), *Traffici Micenei nel Mediterraneo*, 183–193. Istituto per la Storia e l'Archeologia della Magna Grecia, Taranto.

Ferrarese Ceruti, M.L., Vagnetti, L. & Lo Schiavo, F. 1987. Minoici, micenei e ciprioti in Sardegna alla luce delle più recenti scoperte. In Balmuth, M.S. (ed.), *Studies in Sardinian Archaeology III. Nuragic Sardinia and the Mycenaean World*. BAR International Series 387: 7–37. British Archaeological Reports, Oxford.

Jones, R.E. 1993. Chemical analysis of ceramic samples from nuraghe Arrubiu di Orroli (NU). *Rendiconti Accademia dei Lincei* serie 9,4: 144–145.

Jones, R.E. & Day, P. 1987. Aegean Type Pottery on Sardinia: identifications of imports and local imitations by chemical analysis. In Balmuth, M.S. (ed.), *Studies in Sardinian Archaeology III: Nuragic Sardinia and the Mycenaean World*. BAR International Series 387: 257- 270. British Archaeological Reports, Oxford.

Lo Schiavo, F. & Vagnetti, L. 1986. Frammento di un vaso miceneo (?) da Pozzomaggiore (SS). In Marazzi, M., Tusa, S. & Vagnetti, L. (eds.), *Traffici Micenei nel Mediterraneo*, 199–203. Istituto per la Storia e l'Archeologia della Magna Grecia, Taranto.

Lo Schiavo, F. & Vagnetti, L. 1993. Alabastron miceneo dal nuraghe Arrubiu di Orroli (NU). *Rendiconti Accademia dei Lincei* serie 9,4: 121–148.

Rossignoli, C., Lachin, M.T. & Bullo, S. 1994. Nora III. Lo scavo. Area D (macellum). *Quaderni della Soprintendenza Archeologica per le Provincie di Cagliari e Oristano* 11: 225–237.

Sanna, R. 1984. *Villaspeciosa. Censimento archeologico del territorio*. Cagliari.

Trump, D.H. 1985. Bonu Ighinu site and setting. In Malone, C. & Stoddart, S. '(eds.), *Papers in Italian Archaeology IV: The Cambridge Conference*. BAR International Series 243: 185–199. British Archaeological Reports, Oxford.

Ugas, G. 1981. La tomba dei giganti di San Cosimo di Gonnosfanadiga (Cagliari): un documento del BM con la più antica attestazione micenea in Sardegna. *Archeologia Sarda*: 7–11.

Ugas, G. 1982. S. Cosimo (Gonnosfanadiga, Cagliari). In Vagnetti, L. (ed.), *Magna Grecia e Mondo Miceneo. Nuovi documenti*, 180–187. Istituto per la Storia e l'Archeologia della Magna Grecia, Taranto.

Ugas, G. 1987. Indagini ed intervento dopo lo scavo lungo la SS 131 tra il Km. 15 e il Km. 32. Breve notizia. *Quaderni della Soprintendenza Archeologica per le Provincie di Cagliari e Oristano* 4(1): 117–128.

Ugas, G. 1992. Note su alcuni contesti del Bronzo Medio e Recente della Sardegna meridionale. Il caso dell'insediamento di Monte Zara B Monastir. In *La Sardegna nel Mediterraneo tra il Bronzo Medio e il Bronzo Recente (XVI-XIII sec. a.C.). Atti del III Convegno di Studi "Un Millennio di relazioni tra la Sardegna e i paesi del Mediterraneo, Selargius 1987*, 201–227. Edizioni della Torre, Cagliari.

Ugas, G. 1993. *San Sperate dalle origini ai baroni*. Edizioni della Torre, Cagliari.

29. The Chronology of the Aegean Late Bronze Age: Unanswered Questions

Philip P. Betancourt

Introduction

Chronological problems have been debated since the beginning of archaeological studies because they are essential to any analysis of the interrelation between different areas. The Aegean, situated in an intermediate position between the civilizations of Egypt and Western Asia on the one hand and of the Central and Western Mediterranean and Europe on the other hand, occupies an important position in any discussion of Mediterranean chronology. Its absolute dates are still debated.[1]

For the beginning of the Late Bronze Age in the Aegean, two main views and several variations on those views exist today. The "late chronology" holds that Late Minoan I and Late Helladic I began about 1600–1580 BC. It is best discussed in the fine publication by Peter Warren and Vronwy Hankey, *Aegean Bronze Age Chronology* (1989). The "early chronology" suggests that the same periods must begin about a century earlier, ca. 1700–1675 BC.

The two chronologies differ because of different interpretations of the Aegean imports in Egypt and Western Asia as well as eastern imports in the Aegean, and in the fact that the "late chronology" rejects three types of scientific evidence: radiocarbon dates suggesting an early date for the eruption of Thera, frost rings presumably caused by a volcanic eruption of Thera in 1627 BC, and the identification of a sulfate deposit in the Greenland ice sheet most recently dated to 1623 BC as related to volcanic emission from the eruption of Thera. The "early chronology" accepts the scientific evidence, and it also suggests alternate conclusions from the archaeological dating.

Radiocarbon Dating

The largest group of radiocarbon dates for the Aegean comes from carbon buried at the time of the eruption of the volcano of Thera in LM IA. The dates are from a time near or at the end of the period. After calibration, they have been used to suggest a date in the second half of the 17th century BC, with different precise mid-points depending on the type of statistical analysis employed (Betancourt 1987; Betancourt & Michael 1987). However, the Akrotiri samples, like other samples from the Aegean, have unexplained problems. They have a larger time spread than one should expect statistically, and they have yielded erratic results whose nature is not yet fully understood (see the discussions by Manning 1990 and in this volume).

Frost Rings

The issue with the frost rings is based on the recognition that tree rings formed in 1627 BC demonstrate an extremely severe winter with climate disruptions continuing into successive years (LaMarche & Hirschboeck 1984, with the correction from the published date of 1626 explained in Kuniholm 1990: 15; Baillie 1990). The tree rings have been recognized both in Californian bristlecone pine and in Irish oak, suggesting a world-wide disruption in the northern hemisphere. Such records in tree rings can be associated with volcanic eruptions that emit enough volcanic materials to affect the climate for a period of a year or more. That the eruption of Thera expelled a considerable volume of ash has been obvious for some time. The latest confirmation of the extent of the ash fall is the discovery of its deposition (up to 12 cm thick) in lakes in western Turkey hundreds of kilometers from Thera (Sullivan 1990). The climate event recorded in the tree rings of 1627–1626 is the only such event for the next several centuries, so it is the only candidate for the recording of the eruption of Thera. If this data does not record Thera, then the volcano must not have affected the climate significantly.

Ice Sheets in Greenland

An additional piece of evidence comes from the measurement of sulfate content in ice cores in Greenland. These cores are drilled through the permanent ice sheet, and they record the annual deposition of snow fall, so that they have a continuous yearly record from the present to the first recorded deposition. The most recent core records annual depositions from ca. 7000 BC to the present (Zielinski *et al.* 1994). The amount of sulfate in the snowfall is related to the emission of sulfur by volcanoes, and recorded eruptions can be noted in the ice record. The core records a volcanic event emitting substantial sulfur in 1623 BC, with no comparable event in the following century and a half.

Synchronisms with Egypt and Western Asia

In addition to these scientific methods for measuring chronology, one can base absolute dating on the historical dates recorded for Egypt by using the pattern of imports from other regions into Egypt and of Egyptian exports to its neighbors. For imports into Egypt (the most numerous of the synchronisms), the methodology is that the latest Aegean object in a context from a certain period provides a *terminus ante quem* for the Aegean object. Problems with specific points leading to different conclusions include disputes in the dating of the Egyptian context, or the date of the Aegean object, or in the original Egyptian dates on which the whole chronology is based.

For any discussion of the current state of scholarship on the absolute dates of the Aegean, the following points are worth emphasizing:

1. The internal correlations within the Aegean are generally accepted except that some overlapping may exist at the beginning and end of periods. The nomenclature is not the same for Minoan Crete and Helladic Greece. Late Minoan IA (LM IA) is equivalent to Late Helladic I (LH I), and Late Minoan IB (LM IB) is generally contemporary with Late Helladic IIA (LH IIA). Late Minoan II (LM II) equates with Late Helladic IIB (LH IIB). From this point on, the nomenclature is the same (LM IIIA:1 is contemporary with LH IIIA:1, etc.).
2. The pottery sequence in the Aegean is well understood. No disputes exist on the general sequence of styles, the ways that they overlap, and their successive nature. Present scholarship is now moving to a refinement of the sequence and a recognition of regional and local characteristics, the definition of workshops, and other details that do not materially affect the basic problems of correlations with Egypt and Western Asia.
3. General agreement exists on the absolute dates for Aegean chronology for the period from LM IIIA:2 until the end of the Late Bronze Age. Many synchronisms exist (Warren & Hankey 1989: 146–69), and the radiocarbon dates are in perfect agreement with them (Betancourt & Lawn 1984).
4. Absolute dates for the period near the beginning of the Aegean Late Bronze Age are less perfectly known, and it is here that disputes exist. Disagreement between specialists is caused by the ambiguous nature of the correlations that survive. Most of the correlations are so imprecise that they could accommodate either an early or a late chronology for the beginning of LM IA/LH I.

The following archaeological discoveries are important for dating the early years of the Late Bronze Age:

Late Minoan I

1. Minoan Wall Paintings in the East. Wall paintings in Aegean style have now been discovered at the Hyksos capital of Avaris in Egypt (Bietak *et al.* 1994), at Tel Kabri in northern Israel (Niemeier 1990), and at Alalakh in Syria (Woolley 1955; Niemeier 1991). Absolute dates for the sites in question are still under discussion, but they are clearly before the beginning of the 18th Dynasty in Egypt. It is also obvious that the paintings reflect a mature stage of the Aegean painting style, not its beginnings. So far the most often cited Aegean parallels are with LM IA for the Palestinian and Syrian paintings and LM IB for the Egyptian ones, but precisely where the paintings lie in Aegean terms is by no means certain.
2. Pottery and Other Imports and Exports. All the LM I parallels are imprecise. Palestinian MB II stone vessels and a transport amphora come from Akrotiri on Thera (Niemeier 1990), showing that the period of these objects was already in existence, but the absolute dates for MB II are still disputed. A reused Egyptian squat alabastron found in Shaft Grave V at Mycenae, regarded by Cline as 18th Dynasty (Cline 1994: no. 597), might instead come from the Second Intermediate period as suggested by Phillips (1991: no. 455). In spite of considerable discussion on the LM IB/LH IIA pottery found in Egypt, not a single piece is sufficiently well dated to be useful for chronological purposes. Warren and Hankey mention several examples of LM IB/LH IIA vases which, although their date is not certain, might come from the reign of Tuthmosis III (including sherds from Tell Ta'anek, Kerma, and elsewhere, Warren & Hankey 1989: 138–44). Because LM II/LH IIB and LM IIIA:1/LH IIIA:1 were already in existence during the reign of Tuthmosis III (see below), it is probable that the LM IB/LH IIA vases from this reign were heirlooms, although they would be almost new.

One must remember that the LM IB pottery we have as intact vases in Crete is from the very end of the period, at its destruction. LM IB might end at about the time of the accession of Tuthmosis III, as in the early chronology presented here, or within the reign of this king, as suggested by Warren in this volume. The available correlations could permit either view.

Late Minoan II/LH IIB

One of the most often-cited synchronisms for Aegean-Egyptian connections is a vase from LH IIB from Kahun, from a tomb dated to the time of Tuthmosis III (Hankey & Tufnell 1973). It might demonstrate that LH IIB had already begun by the time of this ruler, but Warren and Hankey (1989: 145) have pointed out that questions exist on the Egyptian dating.

Late Minoan IIIA:1/LH IIIA:1

A jar of Egyptian alabaster (travertine) inscribed with the name of Tuthmosis III comes from a Minoan tomb of LM IIIA:1 date from Katsambas, near Knossos (Alexiou 1967: pl. 10). The tomb's date is a *terminus ante quem* for some period within the reign of Tuthmosis III, but this supports either chronology.

An Egyptian or Nubian copy of an Aegean squat alabastron found at Aniba comes from the time of Tuthmosis III (Kemp & Merrillees 1980: 242–4; Weinstein 1983). It has been regarded by this writer as a copy of Minoan work from LM IIIA:1 (Betancourt 1987: 46). In spite of attempts to suggest it is LM I, the absolutely earliest it can be is LM II/LH IIB because that is when the shape was invented (Mountjoy 1986: 40–1; fig. 43, no. 2). Since the piece is a copy rather than an actual Aegean object, its date in Aegean terms has been questioned, and not everyone has agreed with the LM II-IIIA:1 date proposed by this writer (see Warren 1987: 207–8, where the vase is dated to LM IB/LH IIA on incorrect parallels).

A scarab of Amenhotep III comes from a Tomb at the Sellopoulo cemetery near Knossos. Its contents are from LM IIIA:1 (plus a Mycenaean LH IIIA:1 import), and the plain vases are consistent with the date of the painted ones (Warren & Hankey 1989: 148). The find indicates that the reign of Amenhotep III had begun by the time of the tomb. This context is important because it is the earliest really precise correlation linking Egypt with both Minoan and Mycenaean pottery styles. It is a firm piece of evidence. From this point, most Aegean specialists agree on the absolute dates to within a couple of decades.

Can LM IIIA:1 have lasted from the reign of Tuthmosis III until the time of Amenhotep III? One additional piece of evidence bearing on this problem is the representation of Aegeans in Egyptian tombs from the reign of Tuthmosis III. The paintings depict rows of men in Aegean dress carrying gifts for presentation in Egypt. The paintings in the Tomb of Rekh-Mi-Re are unique in that they have the costumes of the Aegeans re-painted to cover up the earlier Minoan abbreviated cod-pieces and replace them with kilts (Davies 1944: pls. 19–20). Although one might question the original dates of other parts of the paintings, suggesting that they could be based on earlier tomb paintings or even model books, the re-painted costumes must represent a contemporary detail from the period of this tomb. The kilts are important for chronology because they have designs that closely mirror Aegean pottery designs. The Mycenaean character of the designs on the kilts has been noted by Barber (1990: 336), but it has not been used for chronological purposes. Fig. 29.1 shows that the designs consist of bands of repeated motifs, with complex chevrons, diamonds, and arcs in the majority. Although a few of these designs begin in LM II (Popham *et al.* 1984: pl. 147, no. 1), their main period is LM IIIA. Examples of pottery from Kommos published by Watrous (1992) show that the variations are well within the usual repertoire of LM IIIA decoration in Crete (Fig. 29.2). It is likely that the tomb was painted no earlier than the end of LM II or the beginning of LM IIIA:1.

Discussion

These pieces of evidence suggest a chronology such as is shown in Fig. 29.3. A major point is the length of LM IB (and the contemporary LH IIA). This period was originally assigned a length of only 50 years by Evans (1921–35: IV, 881). Although it was not well represented in his excavations at Knossos, other sites have shown it is a substantial period with several architectural phases and an enormous volume of ceramics. Its total length is difficult to judge, but it must surely be well over a century. At Pseira, for example, it is represented by several building phases, and it is long enough to incorporate changes in architectural style. The large quantities of LM IB pottery and other objects suggest it is longer than LM IA.

The Relevance of Aegean Chronological Synchronisms to Sardinia and Other Parts of the Mediterranean and Europe

The problem for those dealing with Sardinia and elsewhere in the central and western Mediterranean or with northern or western Europe is that synchronisms usually exist only with the Aegean rather than with Egypt or western Asia. Two examples can illustrate the problems involved with choosing the wrong chronology as a comparison.

1. In 1968, Colin Renfrew wrote an excellent article entitled "Wessex without Mycenae." He pointed out that radiocarbon dates placed the Wessex culture of southern Britain with its faience beads and sophisticated weaponry in the 17th century BC, a date that the then current Aegean chronology regarded as much too early. His conclusion, implied in the title, called for either an independent invention in England of Egyptian faience and Cretan swords and daggers or a stylistic leap from Egypt and Crete over Mycenae to reach England first

Fig. 29.1. Aegeans from the Tomb of Rekh-mi-re at Thebes wearing kilts painted with linear decorations.

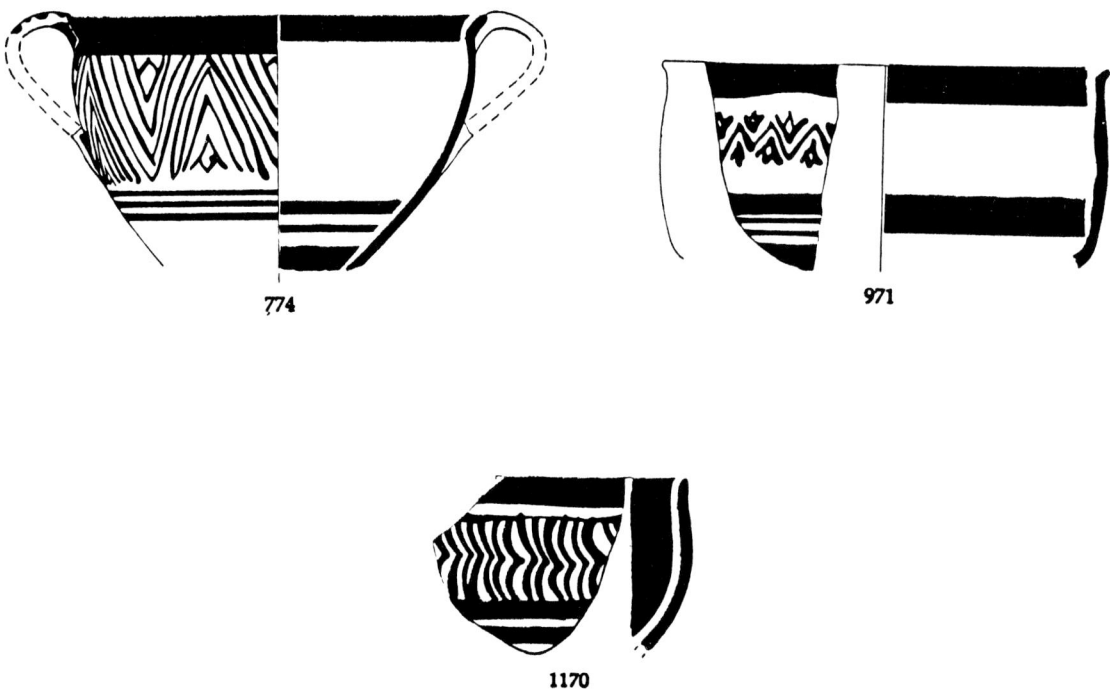

Fig. 29.2. Pottery from Kommos, Crete, from LM IIIA:1 illustrating designs like those on the kilts worn by Aegeans in the Tomb of Rekh-mi-re (after Watrous 1992).

```
Chronological Chart for the Early Chronology
LM IA              Eruption of Thera, ca. 1627 B.C.
  ca. 1620/1600 BC ────────────────────────────────
                   Beginning of New Kingdom, ca. 1550 B.C.
LM IB

  ca. 1490/1470 BC Accession of Tuthmosis III, ca. 1479 B.C.  ───
LM II
  ca. 1450/1430 BC ────────────────────────────────
LM IIIA:1
  ca. 1385/1365 BC ────────────────────────────────
LM IIIA:2
  ca. 1335/1305 BC ────────────────────────────────
```

Fig. 29.3. Chronological Chart for the "Early Chronology" of the Aegean.

and then a return to Greece (i.e., that Crete traded first with England and only later with nearby Greece). Neither suggestion is likely.

2. An alternative was chosen by Jan Bouzek in his book *The Aegean Anatolia and Europe: Cultural Interrelations in the Second Millennium B.C.* (1985). Describing in detail the many synchronisms between Mycenae and Europe in metallurgy, amber, faience, jewelry, and other items and then looking at their radiocarbon dates in Europe, he concluded about the dates: "they can very hardly, if at all, be made to fit into the picture based upon the archaeological evidence ... around the time of the Mycenae Shaft Graves" (Bouzek 1985: 19). As a result, he ignored radiocarbon for all of Europe.

The problem is that the discovery of the absolute dates is not as important as the question of the relative chronology. For historical conclusions, moving an event a hundred years forward or back in time is not as important at our present level of knowledge as understanding its relevance to other events from approximately the same time.

Radiocarbon dating operates the same way in the Central Mediterranean as it does in the Eastern Mediterranean. In comparison with the "late chronology" of the Aegean, radiocarbon dates always suggest an earlier trend. One cannot mix one's classes of evidence and date Mycenae and Crete based on the traditional chronology of Egyptian synchronisms and the rest of Europe based on the radiocarbon dates, and then draw meaningful conclusions. For parts of Europe and the Mediterranean that are themselves dated by radiocarbon, one must use the "high Aegean chronology" in order to understand the proper historical correlations.

Note

1. This paper is based on the one delivered at the Tufts Colloquium in March 1995. Since that time, much new bibliography has appeared.

References

Alexiou, St. 1967. Ὑστερομινωικοί τάφοι λιμένος Κνωσού (Κατσαμπά). Archaeological Society of Athens, Athens.

Baillie, M.G.L. 1990. Irish Tree Rings and an Event in 1628 BC. In Hardy, D.A. with Renfrew, A.C. (eds.), *Thera and the Aegean World III. Volume 3: Chronology*, 160–6. The Thera Foundation, London.

Barber, E.J.W. 1990. *Prehistoric Textiles*. Princeton University Press, Princeton.

Betancourt, P.P. 1987. Dating the Aegean Late Bronze Age with Radiocarbon. *Archaeometry* 29: 45–9.

Betancourt, P.P. & Lawn, B. 1984. The Cyclades and Radiocarbon Chronology. In MacGillivray, J.A. & Barber, R.L.N. (eds.), *The Prehistoric Cyclades*, 277–95. Department of Classical Archaeology, University of Edinburgh, Edinburgh.

Betancourt, P.P. & Michael, H.N. 1987. Dating the Aegean Late Bronze Age with Radiocarbon: Addendum. *Archaeometry* 29: 212–3.

Bietak, M., Dorner, J., Hein, I. & Jánosi, P. 1994. Neue Grabungsergebnisse aus Tell el-Dab'a und 'Ezbet Heimi im šstlichen Nildelta (1989–1991). *Ägypten und Levante* 4: 9–80.

Bouzek, J. 1985. *The Aegean, Anatolia and Europe: Cultural Interrelations in the Second Millennium B.C.* Göteborg.

Cline, E.H. 1994. *Sailing the Wine-Dark Sea*. BAR International Series 591. Tempus Reparatum, Archaeological and Historical Associates Limited, Oxford.

Davies, N. de G. 1944. *The Tomb of Rekh-Mi-Rê' at Thebes*. Reprinted 1973. Arno Press, New York.

Evans, A.J. 1921–35. *The Palace of Minos at Knossos*. MacMillan & Co., London.

Hankey, V. & Tufnell, O. 1973. The Tomb of Maket and its Mycenaean Import. *Annual of the British School at Athens* 68: 103–11.

Kemp, B. & Merrillees, R.S. 1980. *Minoan Pottery in Second Millennium Egypt*. Philipp von Zabern, Mainz.

Kuniholm, P.I. 1990. Overview and Assessment of the Evidence for the Date of the Eruption of Thera. In Hardy, D.A. with Renfrew, A.C. (eds.), *Thera and the Aegean World III. Vol 3: Chronology*, 13–18. The Thera Foundation, London.

LaMarche, V.C., Jr. & Hirschboeck, K.K. 1984. Frost Rings in Trees as Records of Major Volcanic Eruptions. *Nature* 307: 121–6.

Manning, S. 1990. The Eruption of Thera: Date and Implications. In Hardy, D.A. with Renfrew, A.C. (eds.), *Thera and the Aegean World III*, Volume III: 29–40. The Thera Foundation, London.

Mountjoy, P.A. 1986. *Mycenaean Decorated Pottery: A Guide to*

Identification. Paul Åströms Förlag, Göteborg.

Niemeier, W.-D. 1990. New Archaeological Evidence for a 17th Century Date of the 'Minoan Eruption' from Israel (Tel Kabri, Western Galilee). In Hardy, D.A. with Renfrew, A.C. (eds.), *Thera and the Aegean World III. Voume 3: Chronology*, 120–126. The Thera Foundation, London.

Niemeier, W.-D. 1991. Minoan Artisans Traveling Overseas: The Alalakh Frescoes and the Painted Plaster Floor at Tel Kabri (Western Galilee). In Laffineur, R. & Basch, L. (eds.), *Thalassa. L'Égée Préhistorique et la Mer*, 189–201. Histoire de l'art et archéologie de la Grèce antique, Liège.

Phillips, J. 1991. The Impact and Implications of the Egyptian and Egyptianizing Objects found in Bronze Age Crete ca. 3000-ca. 1100 B.C. Ph.D. Dissertation, University of Toronto.

Popham, M.R. with Betts, J.H. 1984. *The Minoan Unexplored Mansion at Knossos*. The British School of Archaeology at Athens supplementary vol. 17. Thames & Hudson, Oxford.

Renfrew, C. 1968. Wessex without Mycenae. *Annual of the British School at Athens* 63: 277–85.

Sullivan, D.G. 1990. Minoan Tephra in Lake Sediments in Western Turkey: Dating the Eruption and Assessing the Atmospheric Dispersal of the Ash. In Hardy, D.A. with Renfrew, A.C. (eds.), *Thera and the Aegean World III. Volume 3: Chronology*, 114–119. The Thera Foundation, London.

Warren, P.M. 1987. Absolute Dating of the Aegean Late Bronze Age. *Archaeometry* 29: 205–11.

Warren, P.M. & Hankey, V. 1989. *Aegean Bronze Age Chronology*. Bristol Classical Press, Bristol.

Watrous, L.V. 1992. *Kommos III. The Late Bronze Age Pottery*. Princeton University Press, Princeton..

Weinstein, J.A. 1983. Tomb SA 17 at Aniba and its 'Aegean' vase. In Betancourt, P.P., *Minoan Objects Excavated from Vasilike, Pseira, ... and Other Sites*, Appendix A. University Museum Press, Philadelphia.

Woolley, C.L. 1955. *Alalakh*. Oxford University Press, Oxford.

Zielinski, G.A., Mayewski, P.A., Meeker, L.D., Whitlow, S., Twickler, M.S., Morrison, M., Meese, D.A., Gow, A.J. & Alley, R.B. 1994. Record of Volcanism Since 7000 B.C. from the GISP2 Greenland Ice Core and Implications for the Volcano-Climate System. *Science* 264: 948–52.

30. Aegean and Sardinian Chronology: Radiocarbon, Calibration and Thera

Sturt W. Manning

Introduction

Aegean archaeologists have always tended to turn to the Near East to acquire, or test, or extrapolate, any chronological data. The diffusionism of V.G. Childe and his generation may be no more in discussions of the development of European civilisation (since Renfrew 1972; 1973), but in chronology it is very much alive and well (e.g. Warren & Hankey 1989; Manning 1996).The preoccupations of Aegean archaeologists still concern debates in Egyptology, Mesopotamian history and archaeology, finds of Aegean or Aegean-related objects and stylistic traits in the east Mediterranean, and so on. At present, the most talked about site in Aegean archaeology is not in the Aegean, but at Tell el-Dab‛a in the Nile delta of Egypt (Bietak 1996; Davies & Schofield 1995). Aegean archaeologists rarely look west. Everyone has long known of Aegean contacts with the west (e.g. Taylour 1958; Dickinson 1977: 104; Chapman 1985: fig. 3.2; Smith 1987; Vagnetti 1993; Dickinson 1994: 249), but these have only rarely been seen as associated with, or relevant to, Aegean chronology. Instead, they have been employed either by Italian (and western Mediterranean) archaeologists to supply some chronological framework to the local regional sequences (as summarized in e.g. Smith 1987: table 1; Chapman 1985: fig. 3.1; for details, see Peroni 1971; 1989; 1994; Peroni *et al.* 1994), and a tie to the "historical" chronologies of the east Mediterranean, or in discussions of Bronze Age trade and interaction (Bietti Sestieri 1988; Vagnetti 1993; Jones & Day 1987; Jones & Vagnetti 1991; Stos-Gale & Gale 1992).

However, the Conference at Tufts in March 1995 brought the welcome challenge to do the reverse, and for Aegean archaeology to look west. Furthermore, it is important to do so. There are many circular problems of evidence (as now famously highlighted by Leonard 1988), interpretation and chronology, and conflicts between approximate "historical" chronologies, versus archaeological synchronisms, versus science-based dating, when one considers the chronologies of the Aegean, east Mediterranean, and Near East. A new perspective would be welcome. It is also time to appreciate fully the logic first enunciated by Renfrew (1968). Egypt is no longer the only source of absolute chronology in Old World archaeology; there are now both independent high-precision radiocarbon chronologies, and dendrochronologies. Such alternative dating frameworks exist in the Aegean, Italy and Europe (see papers in *Acta Archaeologica* 67, 1996 by Guidi & Whitehouse, Rychner *et al.*, and Martinelli). Aegean chronology may thus inform Italian chronology, and also vice versa; both may test each other, and thus act as a test and counterbalance to "traditional" chronologies for the Aegean derived solely from the interpretation of cultural contacts between the Aegean and Egypt. Indeed, northern Italy (linked to Switzerland and southern Germany) offers an increasingly long and securely dated dendrochronological sequence, and related radiocarbon chronologies, which may soon be able to form the basis for a totally independent, accurate, and precise archaeological chronology (e.g. Cardarelli 1993: 368 with refs.; Barfield 1991; papers in *Acta Archaeologica* 67; Becker *et al.* 1989; Randsborg 1991; Fasani & Martinelli 1994; etc. I thank A. Vanzetti, L. Fasani & N. Martinelli for discussion and information.).

This brief paper cannot possibly seek to offer a comprehensive review on Aegean and Italian chronology; instead, it reviews one aspect of the chronological relationship between the Aegean and Sardinia in order to illustrate the beneficial mutual advantages to be gained from further, detailed, studies.

Sturt W. Manning, Department of Archaeology, University of Reading, PO Box 218, Whiteknights, Reading RG6 6AA, UK

Reverse Diffusionist Logic: Making the Most of Archaeology and ^{14}C

Tykot (1994: 128) argues that "the presence of Mycenaean artefacts in the Western Mediterranean ... makes it particularly possible for Sardinia, with its many findspots of Mycenaean pottery and oxhide ingots ... to make a contribution to Aegean chronology...". In other words, we can usefully reverse the conventional diffusionist logic. However, by itself, this does not necessarily escape the usual problems associated with studies based on artefact linkages: possible and unquantifiable timelags between manufacture, use, and then final deposition; possible and unquantifiable timelags in influence or imitation; broad-ranging conclusions from just a few data which may not be representative; etc., etc. Such issues of course exist. However, many years of relative chronological study appear to have established fairly secure "standard" material culture linkages between the Aegean and Italy. Thus Tykot's proposition is possible if absolute dates may be attached to Sardinian contexts.

In Sardinia, at present, the potential source of direct independent absolute chronology is radiocarbon dating (Tykot 1994). The relative sequences, and especially the correlations, are based first on those with Italy, and thence to imported Aegean objects or influences. The dates for imported Aegean objects in the central Mediterranean can either be contemporary with their Aegean context, or slightly later (depending on the time-lag in transport, use or imitation, and then deposition from the Aegean to Italy). The central Mediterranean evidence thus sets *termini ante quos* for the date of manufacture of the imports (as indeed do the Egyptian contexts with Aegean imports – although this logical fact is often rather overlooked). Therefore, an absolute date for an Italian context with, or linked to, a specific Aegean object or style, should be either contemporary with, or set a *terminus ante quem* for, the Aegean period. In other words, such evidence should set a *minimum* chronology. The evidence from the central Mediterranean in effect offers an independent test on existing ceramic and radiocarbon chronologies in the Aegean and the east Mediterranean.

For the purposes of this paper, let us consider the period in Sardinia relevant to the Late Bronze 1 period in the Aegean, as this time period is the subject of some chronological controversy in the Aegean. In Italy and Sardinia, we are conventionally referring to the EBA/MBA transition, with MBI (=Protoappennine B) equated with Late Helladic I (or the Shaft Graves at Mycenae in broad terms: in general, see Dietz 1991 for the LHI period, p. 301 for links to Italy). With older Aegean chronologies this led to a starting date c. 1600 BC or later (e.g. Ugas 1992); with newer Aegean chronologies, and especially the proposals to date the eruption of Thera c. 1628 BC, a revised date of c. 1700 BC is now often given (e.g. Cardarelli 1993: 368; Guidi 1993: 420–421). However, let us reverse the logic, and consider the direct and independent radiocarbon evidence provided from Sardinia, and see how this fits with Aegean chronology.

The initial problem is exactly which radiocarbon dates to employ, as Sardinian archaeologists have been redefining their periods for the early Nuragic phase. Dates for the structures have been based on the style of architecture, depending upon whether they were built as towers with vaults, or as lower buildings, or with relatively flat ceilings and chambers going off continuous corridors. The assumption first made was that the vaulted *nuraghi* were the earlier shape and the ones with corridors a later, degenerate type. It was because of excavation and the analysis of material found plus a single ^{14}C date that the building with corridors is now considered to be the earlier type of the two. The changing concepts of architectural development (Balmuth 1992: 677–678), now suggest that the style might even have been determined by geographical rather than temporal considerations (see Fadda, this volume). Whereas formerly it was standard to regard the early *nuraghi* ("corridor" and earliest vaulted *nuraghi*) as MBI (and so Protoappennine B and LHI-II) (Ugas 1992), instead Lilliu (1982) and Webster (1988; 1996: 18–19, 87) regard these as EBA to EBA-MBA (Bonnanaro B, or Nuragic I) – although in advocating "early" first *nuraghi* dates Webster appears to place over-reliance on a couple of very unsatisfactory "early" radiocarbon determinations with very large measurement errors. Nuragic II, which sees the appearance of the true vaulted *nuraghi* is now instead regarded as defining the start of MBA (Ugas 1992 instead sees this as MBII), and Nuragic II is linked to Protoappennine B (although, of course, some overlap of the corridor and vaulted types is apparent: Tykot 1994: 126 and refs.). Dates for the earliest vaulted nuraghi should therefore approximately correlate with LHI(-II) in Greece and the Aegean (combining Ugas 1992; Contu 1992; this volume; Lilliu 1982; Tykot 1994: 125–126).

LHI-II ceramics are known from several Italian sites (e.g. Vagnetti 1993: 145, fig. 2; Dickinson 1994: 249), and, as noted, they are correlated with the Italian Proto-appennine B culture and thence to the MBI period on Sardinia (Ugas 1992). Contu (this volume) argues that MBI lasts from the 16th century BC to the end of the 15th century BC; Ugas (1992) also sees a beginning for the MBA c. 1600 BC (although he favors a lower chronology); and Trump (1990) offers a date from the early 17th century BC. LHI, which is broadly comparable with Late Minoan IA (LMIA) in chronological terms (Warren & Hankey 1989: 96–97), should thus be more or less contemporary with the first phase of vaulted *nuraghi* on Sardinia.

Tykot (1994: 125–126, 131) collects a number of radiocarbon determinations relevant to the first phases of the Nuragic period on Sardinia (Nuragic I-II), ranging from Bonnanaro B to pre-comb-decorated (*a pettine*) ceramic contexts (Q-3031, R-963a, Gif-?, K-151, Q-3070, I-14,774, Gif-243, Gif-242, Q-3169, and P-2788): see Figures 30.1 and 30.2. The next issue is which high-precision radiocarbon calibration curve to employ to

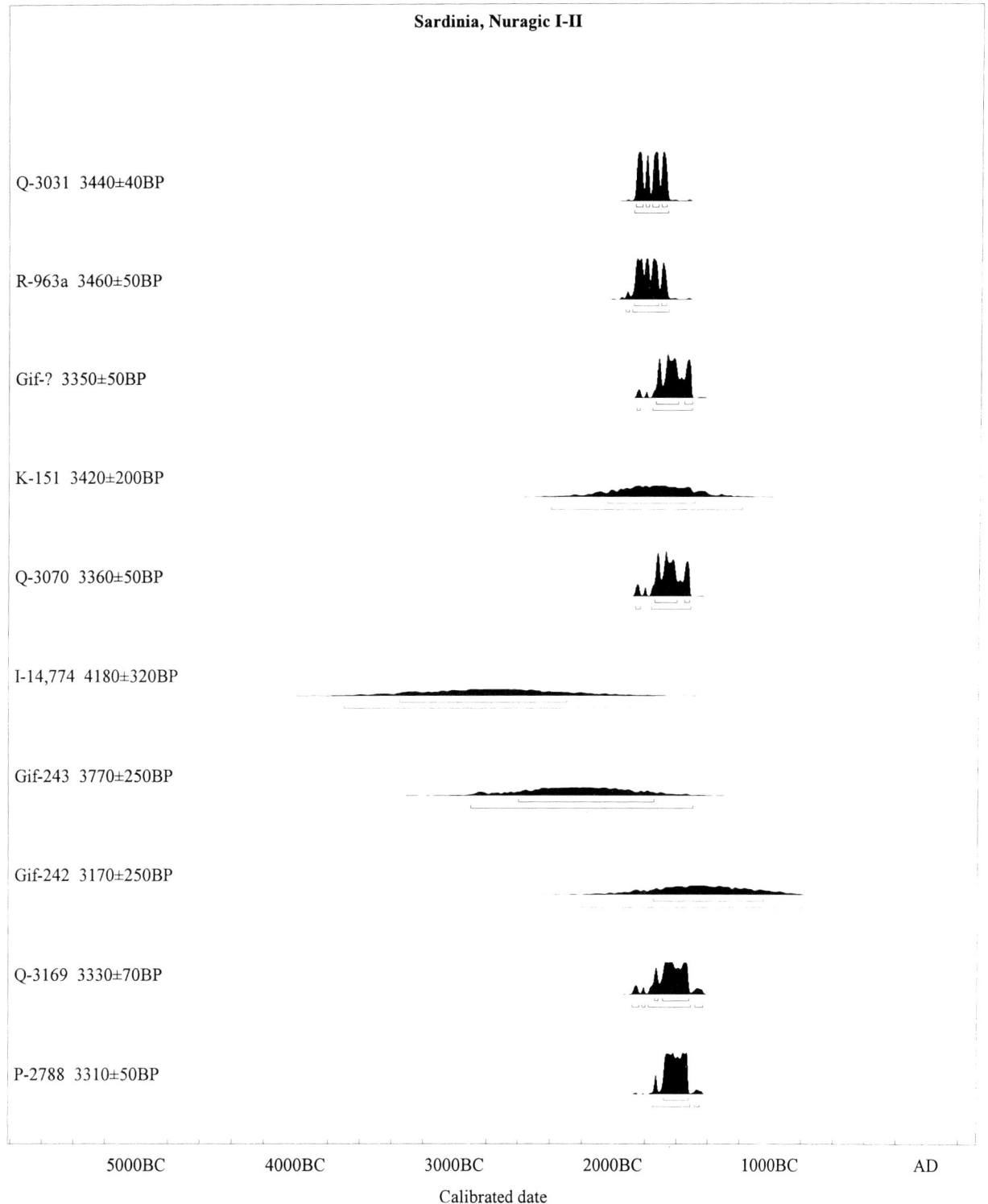

Fig. 30.1. Calibrated calendar age ranges for radiocarbon determinations from Nuragic I-II contexts from Tykot (1994). Calibrated probability distributions and 1 and 2 ranges (upper and lower marked intervals for each range respectively) from Ramsey (1995) employing Pearson et al. (1986).

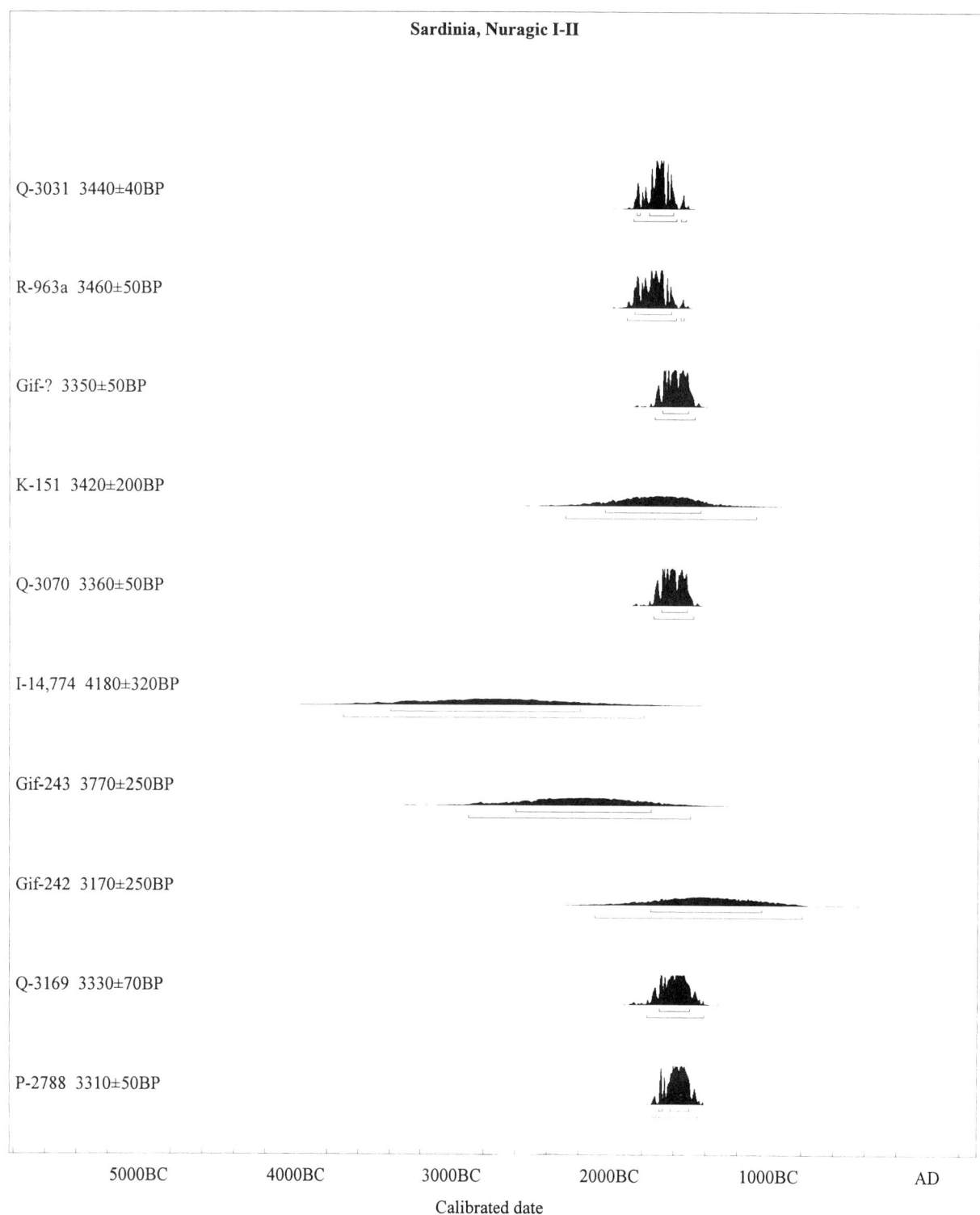

Fig. 30.2. Calibrated calendar age ranges for radiocarbon determinations from Nuragic I-II contexts from Tykot (1994). Calibrated probability distributions and 1 and 2 ranges (upper and lower marked intervals for each range respectively) from Ramsey (1995) employing Stuiver and Becker (1993).

calibrate these measurements into calendar years? At present there are two suitable choices for European samples (new, revised, high-precision calibration data will become available in 1998; this discussion here is based on the pre-1998 data). First, the 1986 Belfast bi-decadal dataset on Irish oak (Pearson *et al.* 1986; and *not* the 1993 "revision" of this data: see Kalin *et al.* 1995; McCormac *et al.* 1995; van der Plicht & McCormac 1995; van der Plicht *et al.* 1995; Damon 1995b; Bowman 1994: 839–841; F.G. McCormac, pers. comm.; M.G.L. Baillie, pers. comm.), and second, the 1993 Seattle decadal dataset based for this BC period on German oak (Stuiver & Becker 1993 – this replaces the previous 1986 dataset for the reasons stated in Stuiver & Becker 1993). These two datasets are similar, and preserve a broadly identical record of natural variations of radiocarbon levels in the atmosphere of the northern hemisphere over several thousand years. However, in precise details, there are small variations and differences between these two datasets – whether due to small systematic inter-laboratory offsets, or minor regional differences in radiocarbon levels, or other factors (work is in progress to try to resolve these issues). With relevance to the Sardinian data above, choice of the Belfast data offers slightly "earlier" date ranges, whereas choice of the Seattle data offers slightly "later" date ranges. I give results from both.

The combined calendar age calibrations of this set of 10 determinations at 2σ (95%) confidence using the OxCal 2.18 computer programme (Ramsey 1995, here and hereafter with the round ranges function "on") are: (i) with the 1986 Belfast bi-decadal calibration data (Pearson *et al.* 1986), 1745–1670 BC; and (ii) with the 1993 Seattle decadal calibration data (Stuiver & Becker 1993), 1740–1610 BC (Probability = 0.88), 1580–1550 BC (Probability = 0.12). However, the set has a very poor agreement statistic in either case, with I-14,774 in particular revealed as aberrant (*even with* its huge quoted measurement error), and it is thus not a consistent set of data. Webster (1988: 467) employs I-14,774 to argue for an initial use of Tower A at Duos Nuraghes c. 2000–1800 BC; however, reliance of this very poor quality measurement seems unwise, and its age may be clearly distinguished from the other "initial" Nuragic I-II radiocarbon determinations available – making it unlikely to offer a valid Nuragic I-II date. Instead, it is most probably revealed as an irrelevant, aberrant, datum. The other serious concern involves the fact that a number of the determinations have (very) large measurement errors (by modern standards), which render them seriously suspect (or, at best, of little utility); further, measurements carried out before the significant improvements in radiocarbon dating procedures and analysis in the early 1980s, and without proper pretreatment, must also be regarded as suspect. The set of data above looks decidedly unhealthy in these terms.

If one were rigorous, at least half the measurements should be deleted from analysis. However, whether by luck or good management, the various determinations are largely similar, even if of different quality. Thus, for example, if one ignores the date of laboratory measurement, and merely removes determinations with measurement errors of ±200 radiocarbon years, then the remaining six determinations (Q-3031, R-963a, Gif-?, Q-3070, Q-3169, P-2788) offer a set with an almost acceptable agreement statistic (R-963a is the only, minor, outlier) and combined calibrated calendar age ranges at 2σ confidence of: (i) with the 1986 Belfast bi-decadal calibration data (Pearson *et al.* 1986), 1750–1640 BC; and (ii) with the 1993 Seattle decadal calibration data (Stuiver & Becker 1993), 1740–1600 BC (Probability = 0.8), 1580–1550 BC (Probability = 0.2). This is not significantly different from our previous conclusion.

These calendar ranges should more or less correspond to, or offer *termini ante quos* for, the LHI period from the archaeological synchronisms. The results are notable for two reasons; first, they confirm the general Aegean chronology derived from archaeology, history and radiocarbon versus recent radical attempts to lower Mediterranean chronology (e.g. James *et al.* 1991; Rohl 1995); and second, the Sardinian dates offer approximate support for a chronology broadly consistent with the long, or "early", LBA chronology in the Aegean (see Betancourt 1987; Manning 1988; 1995: 30–31, 200–229; 1996; Kuniholm *et al.* 1996), with LHI underway by, or before, a date range from the mid-17th to mid-16th centuries BC. In particular, there is strong support for a 17th century BC start for the LHI period, and so the general case for a c. 1628 BC date for the eruption of Thera.

Relevance of the Selection of Calibration Curve

I noted above the issue of minor variations in published radiocarbon calibration data. At present, a definitive resolution to current debates (e.g. McCormac *et al.* 1995), is still pending. Nonetheless, a strong case has been made for the approximate validity of the 1986 formally recommended bi-decadal calibration curve of Pearson & Stuiver (1986) (Mook 1986) versus the (not internationally recommended) revised 1993 bi-decadal calibration curve of Pearson & Stuiver (1993) (see McCormac & van der Plicht 1995; van der Plicht *et al.* 1995; McCormac *et al.* 1995). For information, the calibration (OxCal 2.18) of the ten Nuragic I-II data shown in Figures 30.1 and 30.2 calibrated instead on the 1986 recommended Pearson & Stuiver (1986) curve is shown in Figure 30.3, and the combined calibration of the six data with measurement errors of ±250 radiocarbon years at 2σ confidence is 1750–1640 BC.

However, even here, the case is not straightforward, as the Seattle (Stuiver) component of the 1986 data has been shown to be incorrect, and in need of minor correction due to the recognition of a radon problem with the Seattle measurements (Stuiver & Becker 1993). It is

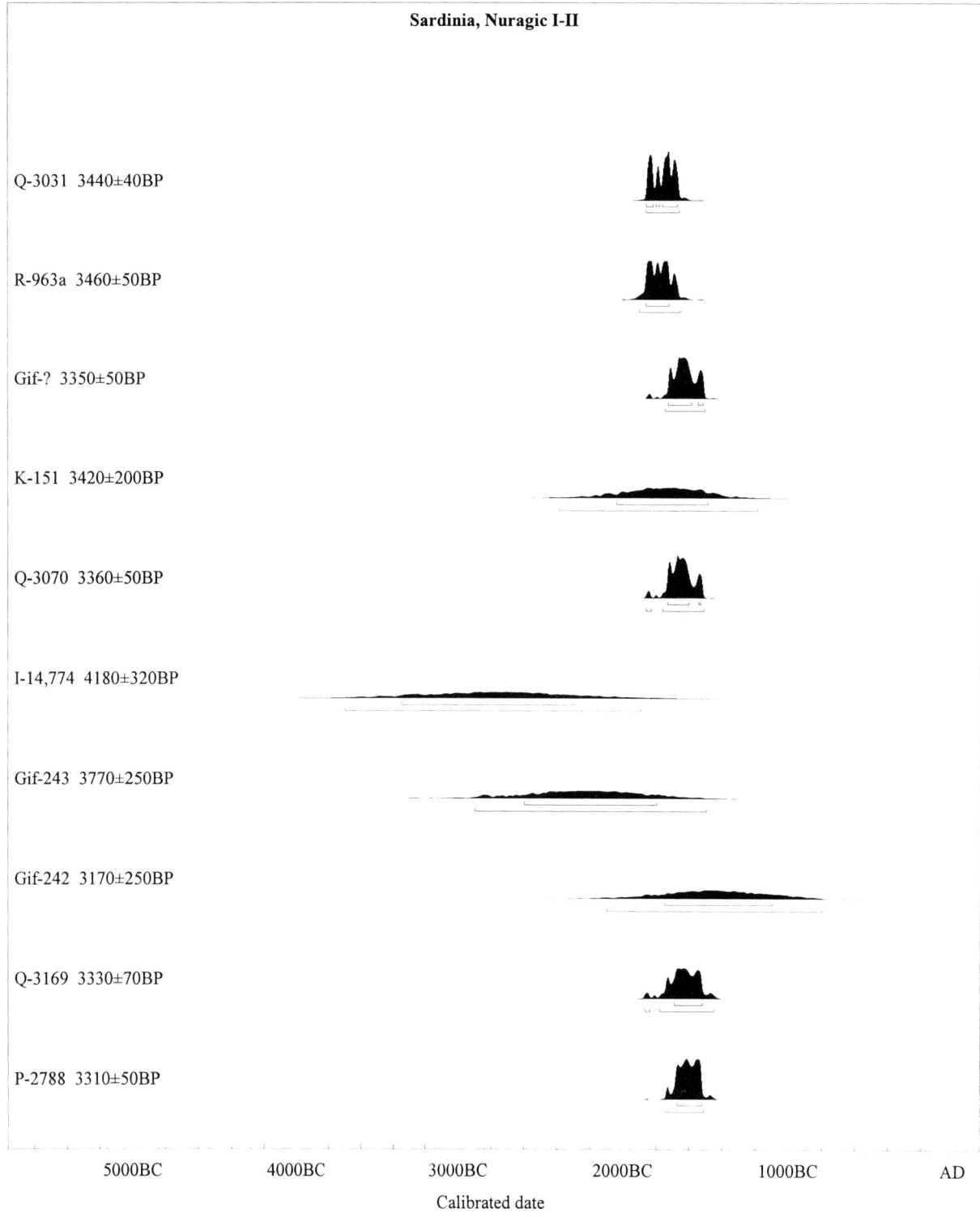

Fig. 30.3. Calibrated calendar age ranges for radiocarbon determinations from Nuragic I–II contexts from Tykot (1994). Calibrated probability distributions and 1 and 2 ranges (upper and lower marked intervals for each range respectively) from Ramsey (1995) employing Pearson & Stuiver (1986).

Thera ^{14}C Data	1σ (68.2%) confidence calibrated range(s) BC from OxCal 2.18 (Ramsey 1995)		
	P et al. 86	P&S86	S&B93
1. 3356±32BP	1740–1720 (P=0.19)	1740–1720 (P=0.11)	1690–1530 (P=1.0)
	1690–1620 (P=0.65)	1700–1610 (P=0.89)	
	1560–1530 (P=0.16)		
(weighted average of the Copenhagen data: Friedrich et al. 1990)			
2. 3338±17BP	1680–1620 (P=0.78)	1675–1620 (P=1.0)	1690–1650 (P=0.15)
	1560–1530 (P=0.22)	1620–1530 (P=0.85)	
(weighted average of the Oxford data: Housley et al. 1990)			

P et al. 86 = Pearson et al. 1986   S&B93 = Stuiver & Becker 1993
P&S86 = Pearson & Stuiver 1986

Table 30.1. Thera calibration by calibration dataset.

the unjustified "revision" of the Belfast 1986 dataset in Pearson & Qua (1993) that forms the problem with Pearson & Stuiver (1993). But, another issue is that whereas Pearson & Stuiver (1986) and Pearson & Stuiver (1993; generally see Stuiver & Pearson 1993; Stuiver & Pearson 1992) claimed a very close correlation of the Belfast and Seattle measurements on synchronous wood, the employment of what now stands as the "best", valid, data – Belfast 1986 and Seattle 1993 – means there is in fact a small and largely systematic offset between the two datasets, with Seattle obtaining slightly older radiocarbon ages than Belfast for dendrochronological samples of the same calendar age. This could be explained as inter-laboratory offset, or it could be a small regional difference in radiocarbon levels between Ireland (source of the Belfast data on Irish oak), and southern Germany (source of the Seattle data in the BC period on German oak) (possible differences in ^{14}C activity in wood from different locations was first raised by Damon et al. 1989; and was mentioned as a possible factor in minor inter-laboratory differences by, e.g., Stuiver & Pearson 1993: 1 (who, however, suggested 20 ^{14}C years relevance); Stuiver & Pearson 1992: 21; new work arguing for such regional differences has recently been reported by Jirikowic & Kalin 1993; McCormac et al. 1995; and Damon 1995a; 1995b), or a combination of these.

The question for Sardinia and the Aegean is which calibration curve (of those presently available) offers the most appropriate data for these regions. Here there is no clear guidance from published literature. The high-precision radiocarbon wiggle-matching (a technique developed to reconcile the non-linearity of the radiocarbon calibration curve) of medieval oak timbers from the Netherlands, and another study on medieval oak from Ireland, from measurements made at Groningen would support the Pearson & Stuiver (1986) data (van der Plicht et al. 1995; van der Plicht & McCormac 1995), or, more specifically, the Pearson et al. (1986) data (although, it should be noted that, given the true measurement and fit error on such a wiggle-match, the data reported *could be* consistent with either calibration dataset, although it clearly *favors* the 1986 one). Both are "European" studies, and it is likely that they should be relevant to Sardinia and the Aegean since there is no major difference in altitude, nor any *major* intervening oceanic input (i.e. the slightly different radiocarbon activities of the Pacific versus Atlantic Oceans are not relevant). On this basis, the 17th century BC date range offers a minimum date for Nuragic I-II. Furthermore, for the Aegean, the calibration of the extensive radiocarbon data from mature LMIA Akrotiri on Thera on the Belfast 1986, or Pearson & Stuiver (1986) curves strongly supports a 17th century BC date range: see Table 30.1.

However, one other set of data exist which offers different evidence. Kuniholm et al. (1996) published a set of 18 high-precision radiocarbon measurements on wood from Gordion in central Anatolia. Within the range of fit of the resultant wiggle-match, Kuniholm et al. (1996) observed a remarkable coincidence whereby two unusual growth anomalies 470 years apart in the Anatolian dendrochronology could be correlated with an identical pattern in the absolute Irish dendrochronology, and, generally, a unique anomaly could be correlated with a well-known event ca. 1628 BC in Irish, American, English and German dendrochronologies. An absolute date for the Anatolian dendrochronology was thus proposed. If this correlation of dendrochronological patterns is accepted, then, in reverse, we may compare the wiggle matched radiocarbon data to see which calibration curve offers the best fit with the hypothesized absolute dates. As published in Kuniholm et al. (1996), a wiggle-match against the 1993 decadal calibration data of Stuiver & Becker (1993) offered a match (the Chi-square fitting match: see Kuniholm et al. 1996: fig. 2 and table 1) a mere 13 years too old (alternatively, 11–19 years from Ramsey 1995). In contrast, a match against the data of either Pearson & Stuiver (1986) or Pearson et al. (1986) or Pearson & Stuiver (1993) offers a fit which is less close (even older): see Table 30.2. This might be held to favor the data of Stuiver & Becker (1993) as more relevant. Further, the measurements on German oak similar to those measured at Seattle by Stuiver at Pretoria (Vogel et al. 1993) offer data largely consistent with the data of Seattle, and stand in contrast to the slightly "different" data from Belfast on Irish wood, notably even at times when there is a maximum offset between the Irish and German data: see Figure 30.4. Along

Dendro Age*	Wiggle-Match range (1σ) from OxCal 2.18 (Ramsey 1995)			
	S&B93	P et al. 86	P&S86	P&S93

1. All 18 radiocarbon data, see Kuniholm et al. (1996:Table 1)

807BC	826–818BC	852–845BC	871–854BC	848–841BC
offset (from mid-point of range)	+15 years	+41.5 years	+56 years	+37.5 years

2. "Best" 14 radiocarbon data
(rings 1325, 1405, 1415 and 1435 excluded as potentially inconsistent to varying degrees)

807BC	829–821BC	858–850BC	870–856BC	853–842BC
offset (from mid-point of range)	+17.5 years	+47 years	+56 years	+40.5 years

*mid-point last dated decade; absolute age on the basis of analysis in Kuniholm et al. 1996

S&B93 = Stuiver & Becker 1993 P&S86 = Pearson & Stuiver 1986
P et al. 86 = Pearson et al. 1986 P&S93 = Pearson & Stuiver 1993

Table 30.2. Comparison of Gordion wiggle-match (Kuniholm et al. 1996) versus dendrochronological age by calibration dataset.

with an inter-laboratory comparison on identical German oak between the Heidelberg and Seattle laboratories which yielded an offset of <15 ^{14}C years (B. Kromer, pers. comm.), this suggests the approximate accuracy (and reproducibility: cf. Damon 1995b: 958) of the Seattle data on German wood (and so, if the Belfast data are equally solid, the apparent reality of the regional difference in ^{14}C activity proposed by McCormac et al. 1995).

The comparison of the wood from Gordion in central Anatolia would support the better relevance there of the calibration curve from German wood (and, certainly, between central Europe and Anatolia no significant oceanic or altitude difference can be offered; whereas, perhaps, Atlantic Ocean mechanisms relevant to Ireland (and The Netherlands) may be adduced to help explain a difference between wood from Ireland and continental southern Germany). If these central Anatolian data were held to be relevant also to Sardinia and the Aegean, then a 17th century BC minimum date for Nuragic I–II is still very likely (80%), but a date for Thera in the mid-16th century BC does become more likely, with the odds between a 17th century BC or a 16th century BC date range close to 50/50 based on the simple calibration of the various datasets available (see e.g. Manning 1995: 207, table 2, 210, table 3) – although, unfortunately, this dating largely rests on just two Seattle data for 1575 BC and 1565 BC which have much larger measurement errors than the rest of the Seattle measurements in this region of the calibration curve (Manning 1995: 201), just to complicate matters a little further! How can we decide? On current data we cannot reach a definitive conclusion. In each case, Groningen and Heidelberg, we do not know the systematic measurement history of the particular laboratories vis à vis each of the two laboratories which produced the standard radiocarbon calibration curves (Belfast, Seattle) as determined by intercomparison of measurements on identical wood (i.e. ruling out any possible regional difference). Groningen did re-measure Irish oak and achieved results very compatible with the 1986 data (van der Plicht & McCormac 1995). For Heidelberg, we do not have comparable data at present with respect to the Belfast laboratory and measurements on Irish oak – although, as noted, intercalibration studies between Heidelberg and Seattle on German oak would indicate close compatibility (B. Kromer, pers. comm.). This, however, leaves us none the wiser concerning which calibration dataset to employ for Sardinia or the Aegean. Data from the region itself is required.

Discussion

Radiocarbon evidence from Sardinia shows that dates on long-lived samples from Nuragic I–II contexts offer construction/use *termini post quos* in the 18th–17th centuries BC. A date for the cultural contexts by or before 1600 BC (17th century BC) is therefore likely. Given cultural linkages, this offers broad support to a 17th century BC date for the LHI period, and so general support for a 1628 BC date for the mature LMIA Thera eruption. Further precision depends on details of the radiocarbon calibration dataset employed. The radiocarbon evidence from Sardinia and the Aegean is consonant for consonant cultural phases – and therefore mutually reinforcing. If the Belfast 1986 dataset is shown to be appropriate, this provides further, stronger, support for the "early" Aegean LB1 chronology, and for a definite 17th century BC *terminus ante quem* for the early nuraghi. If the Seattle 1993 dataset is employed the situation remains similar in Sardinia, but the date for the Thera eruption becomes more ambiguous between later 17th century BC or mid-16th century BC ranges (without either further statistical manipulation of the data (cf., e.g., Manning 1995: 206–213; Manning et al. 1994: 225–226), or the incorporation of additional data sets from surrounding cultural periods (Middle Minoan III to Late Minoan II) which may constrain the single-case LMIA

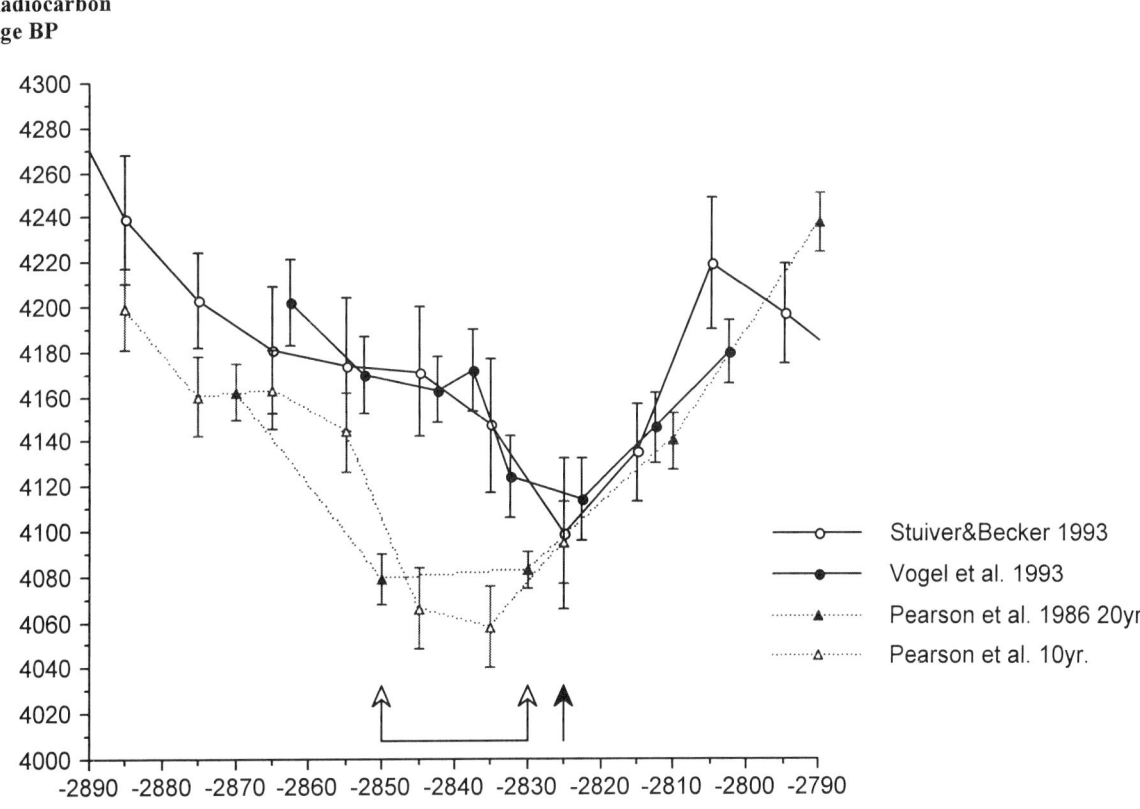

Fig. 30.4. Comparison at a time of maximum difference between German and Irish wood ^{14}C activity, 2890–2790 BC, of the 1993 decadal calibration curve from Seattle on German wood (Stuiver & Becker 1993) and the similar data obtained by Pretoria on similar German wood (Vogel et al. 1993) versus the significantly differing data from Belfast (1986 data: Pearson et al. 1986) both as bi-decadal and decadal measurements (decadal data from Pearson et al. 1986: 934, table 3B). The notable feature is that the major abscissa (downwards wiggle) in the later 29th century BC is 5–25 years earlier in the Belfast measurements/Irish wood (range marked by the hollow arrows) than in the Seattle and Pretoria data on German wood (solid arrow). Since the data on the German wood is replicated, and other studies (van der Plicht et al. 1995; van der Plicht & McCormac 1995) support the Belfast measurements on Irish wood, the likely conclusion must be that the difference is real.

ambiguity, and so suggest a most likely choice: Manning 1992: 249; Housley *et al.* n.d.).

References

Balmuth, M.S. 1992. Archaeology in Sardinia. *American Journal of Archaeology* 96(4): 663–697.

Barfield, L.H. 1991. Wessex with and without Mycenae: new evidence from Switzerland. *Antiquity* 65: 102–107.

Betancourt, P.P. 1987. Dating the Aegean Late Bronze Age with radiocarbon. *Archaeometry* 29: 45–49.

Bietak, M. 1996. *Avaris: the capital of the Hyksos*. British Museum Press, London.

Bietti Sestieri, A.M. 1988. The "Mycenaean connection" and its impact on the central Mediterranean societies. *Dialoghi di Archeologia* 6: 23–51.

Bowman, S. 1994. Using radiocarbon: an update. *Antiquity* 68: 838–843.

Cardarelli, A. 1993. Le età dei metalli nell'Italia settentrionale. In Guidi, A. & Piperno, M. (eds.), *Italia preistorica*, 366–419. Second edition. Editori Laterza, Roma.

Chapman, R.W. 1985. The later prehistory of western Mediterranean Europe. *Advances in World Archaeology* 4: 115–187.

Contu, E. 1992. L'inizio dell'età nuragica. In *La Sardegna nel Mediterraneo tra il Bronzo Medio e il Bronzo Recente (XVI-XIII Sec. a.C.). Atti del III Convegno di studi "Un millennio di relazioni fra la Sardegna e I Paesi del Mediterraneo," Selargius-Cagliari, 19–22 novembre 1987*, 13–40. Edizioni Della Torre, Cagliari.

Damon, P.E. 1995a. A note concerning "location-dependent differences in the ^{14}C content of wood" by McCormac *et al. Radiocarbon* 37: 829–830.

Damon, P.E. 1995b. Note concerning "intercomparison of high-precision ^{14}C measurements at the University of Arizona and the Queen's University of Belfast radiocarbon laboratories" by Kalin *et al.* (1995) and the regional effect. *Radiocarbon* 37: 955–959.

Damon, P.E., Cheng, S. & Linick, T.W. 1989. Fine and hyperfine structure in the spectrum of secular variations of the atmospheric ^{14}C. *Radiocarbon* 31: 704–18.

Davies, W.V. & Schofield, L. (eds.) 1995. *Egypt, the Aegean and the Levant: Interconnections in the second millennium BC*. British Museum Publications, London.

Dickinson, O.P.T.K. 1977. *The origins of Mycenaean civilisation*. Studies in Mediterranean Archaeology 49. Paul Åströms Förlag, Göteborg.

Dickinson, O.P.T.K. 1994. *The Aegean Bronze Age*. Cambridge University Press, Cambridge.

Dietz, S. 1991. *The Argolid at the Transition to the Mycenaean Age. Studies in the Chronology and Cultural Development in the Shaft Grave Period*. The National Museum of Denmark, Department of Near Eastern and Classical Antiquities, Copenhagen.

Fasani, L. & Martinelli, N. 1994. Problemi relativi alle palafitte italiane alla luce della ricerca dendrocronologica. In Skeates, R. & Whitehouse, R. (eds.), *Radiocarbon dating and Italian prehistory*, 39–44. Accordia Specialist Studies on Italy 3, Archaeological Monographs of the British School at Rome 8. The British School at Rome and Accordia Research Centre, University of London, London.

Friedrich, W.L., Wagner, P. & Tauber, H. 1990. Radiocarbon dated plant remains from the Akrotiri excavation on Santorini, Greece. In Hardy, D.A. with Renfrew, A.C. (eds.), *Thera and the Aegean world III. Volume 3: Chronology*, 188–196. The Thera Foundation, London.

Guidi, A. 1993. Le età dei metalli nell'Italia centrale e in Sardegna. In Guidi, A. & Piperno, M. (eds.), *Italia preistorica*, 420–470. Second edition. Editori Laterza, Roma.

Housley, R.A., Hedges, R.E.M., Law, I.A. & Bronk, C.R. 1990. Radiocarbon dating by AMS of the destruction of Akrotiri. In Hardy, D.A. with Renfrew, A.C. (eds.), *Thera and the Aegean world III. Volume 3: Chronology*, 207–215. The Thera Foundation, London.

Housley, R.A., Manning, S.W., Cadogan, G., Jones, R.E. & Hedges, R.E.M. n.d. Radiocarbon, calibration, and the chronology of the Late Minoan IB phase. *Journal of Archaeological Science*. In press.

James, P., Thorpe, I.J., Kokkinos, N., Morkot, R. & Frankish, J. 1991. *Centuries of Darkness*. Jonathan Cape, London.

Jirikowic, J.L. & Kalin, R.M. 1993. A possible ENSO indicator in the spatial variation of tree-ring radiocarbon. *Geophysical Research Letters* 20: 439–442.

Jones, R.E. & Day, P. 1987. Late Bronze Age Aegean and Cypriot type pottery on Sardinia: identification of imports and local imitations by physico-chemical analysis. In Balmuth, M.S. (ed.), *Studies in Sardinian Archaeology III. Nuragic Sardinia and the Mycenaean World*. BAR International Series 387: 257–269. British Archaeological Reports, Oxford.

Jones, R.E. & Vagnetti, L. 1991. Traders and craftsmen in the central Mediterranean. In Gale, N.H. (ed.), *Bronze Age Trade in the Mediterranean*. Studies in Mediterranean Archaeology 90: 125–145. Paul Åström, Göteborg.

Kalin, R.M., McCormac, F.G., Damon, P.E., Eastoe, C.J. & Long, A. 1995. Intercomparison of high-precision ^{14}C measurements at the University of Arizona and the Queen's University of Belfast radiocarbon laboratories. *Radiocarbon* 37: 33–38.

Kuniholm, P.I., Kromer, B., Manning, S.W., Newton, M., Latini, C.E. & Bruce, M.J. 1996. Anatolian tree-rings and the absolute chronology of the east Mediterranean 2220–718 BC. *Nature* 381: 780–783.

Leonard, A. 1988. Some problems inherent in Mycenaean/Syro-Palestinian synchronisms. In French, E.B. & Wardle, K.A. (eds.), *Problems in Greek prehistory. Papers presented at the centenary conference of the British School of Archaeology at Athens, Manchester April 1986*, 319–330. Bristol Classical Press, Bristol.

Lilliu, G. 1982. *La civiltà nuragica*. Carlo Delfino, Sassari.

McCormac, F.G., Baillie, M.G.L., Pilcher, J.R. & Kalin, R.M. 1995. Location-dependent differences in the ^{14}C content of wood. *Radiocarbon* 37: 395–407.

Manning, S.W. 1988. The Bronze Age eruption of Thera: absolute dating, Aegean chronology and Mediterranean cultural interrelations. *Journal of Mediterranean Archaeology* 1: 17–82.

Manning, S.W. 1992. Thera, sulphur, and climatic anomalies. *Oxford Journal of Archaeology* 11: 245–253.

Manning, S.W., De Mita, F.A. Jr., Monks, S.J. & Nakou, G. 1994. The Fatal Shore, the Long Years, and the Geographical Unconscious. Considerations of Iconography, Chronology and Trade in Response to Negbi's "The "Libyan Landscape" from Thera: A Review of Aegean Enterprises Overseas in the Late Minoan IA Period" (*JMA* 7.1). *Journal of Mediterranean Archaeology* 7: 219–235.

Manning, S.W. 1995. *The Absolute Chronology of the Aegean Early Bronze Age: archaeology, history and radiocarbon*. Monographs in Mediterranean Archaeology 1. Sheffield Academic Press, Sheffield.

Manning, S.W. 1996. Dating the Aegean Bronze Age: without, with, and beyond, radiocarbon. *Acta Archaeologica* 67: 15–37.

Mook, W.G. 1986. Business meeting. *Radiocarbon* 28: 799.

Pearson, G.W., Pilcher, J.R., Baillie, M.G.L., Corbet, D.M. & Qua, F. 1986. High-precision ^{14}C measurements of Irish oaks to show the natural ^{14}C variations from AD 1840–5210 BC. *Radiocarbon* 28: 911–934.

Pearson, G.W. & Qua, F. 1993. High-precision ^{14}C measurement of Irish oaks to show the natural ^{14}C variations from AD 1840–5210 BC: a correction. *Radiocarbon* 35: 105–124.

Pearson, G.W. & Stuiver, M. 1986. High-precision calibration of the radiocarbon time scale, 500–2500 BC. *Radiocarbon* 28: 839–862.

Pearson, G.W. & Stuiver, M. 1993. High-precision bidecadal calibration of the radiocarbon time scale, 500–2500 BC. *Radiocarbon* 35: 25–34.

Peroni, R. 1971. *L'Età del Bronzo nella penisola italiana. I. L'antica età del Bronzo*. L.S. Olschki, Florence.

Peroni, R. 1989. *Protostoria dell'Italia continentale. La penisola italiana nelle età del Bronzo e del Ferro*. Biblioteca di storia patria, Rome.

Peroni, R. 1994. *Introduzioni alla protostoria italiana*. Laterza, Rome.

Peroni, R., Trucco, et al. 1994. *Enotri e Micenei nella Sibaritide*. Magna Graecia 8. Istituto per la storia e l'archeologia della Magna Grecia, Taranto.

Ramsey, C.B. 1995. Radiocarbon calibration and analysis of stratigraphy: the OxCal program. *Radiocarbon* 37: 425–430.

Randsborg, K. 1991. Historical implications: chronological studies in European archaeology 2000–500 B.C. *Acta Archaeologica* 62: 89–108.

Renfrew, C. 1968. Wessex without Mycenae. *Annual of the British School at Athens* 63: 277–285.

Renfrew, C. 1972. *The emergence of civilization: the Cyclades and the Aegean in the third millennium BC*. Methuen, London.

Renfrew, C. 1973. *Before civilization: the radiocarbon revolution and prehistoric Europe*. Jonathan Cape, London.

Rohl, D.M. 1995. *A test of time. Volume One: the Bible – from myth to History*. Century, London.

Smith, T. 1987. *Mycenaean trade and interaction in the west central Mediterranean, 1600–1000 BC*. BAR International Series 371. British Archaeological Reports, Oxford.

Stos-Gale, Z.A. & Gale, N.H. 1992. New light on the provenience of the copper oxhide ingots found on Sardinia. In Tykot, R.H. & Andrews, T.K. (eds.), *Sardinia in the Mediterranean: a footprint in the sea. Studies in Sardinian archaeology presented to Miriam S. Balmuth*. Monographs in Mediterranean

Archaeology 3: 317–346. Sheffield Academic Press, Sheffield.
Stuiver, M. and Becker, B. 1993. High-precision decadal calibration of the radiocarbon time scale, AD 1950–6000 BC. *Radiocarbon* 35: 35–65.
Stuiver, M. & Pearson, G.W. 1992. Calibration of the radiocarbon time scale, 2500–5000 BC. In Taylor, R.E., Long, A. & Kra, R.S. (eds.), *Radiocarbon after four decades: an interdisciplinary perspective*, 19–33. Springer-Verlag, New York.
Stuiver, M. & Pearson, G.W. 1993. High-precision bidecadal calibration of the radiocarbon time scale, AD 1950–500 BC and 2500–6000 BC. *Radiocarbon* 35: 1–23.
Taylour, W.D. 1958. *Mycenaean pottery in Italy and adjacent areas*. Cambridge University Press, Cambridge.
Trump, D.H. 1990. *Nuraghe Noeddos and the Bonu Ighinu valley: excavation and survey in Sardinia*. Oxbow Books, Oxford.
Tykot, R.H. 1994. Radiocarbon dating and absolute chronology in Sardinia and Corsica. In Skeates, R. & Whitehouse, R. (eds.), *Radiocarbon dating and Italian prehistory*, 115–145. Accordia Specialist Studies on Italy 3, Archaeological Monographs of the British School at Rome 8. The British School at Rome, and Accordia Research Centre, University of London, London.
Ugas, G. 1992. Considerazioni sullo sviluppo dell'architettura e della società nuragica. In Tykot, R.H. & Andrews, T.K. (eds.), *Sardinia in the Mediterranean: a footprint in the sea. Studies in Sardinian archaeology presented to Miriam S. Balmuth*. Monographs in Mediterranean Archaeology 3: 221–234. Sheffield Academic Press, Sheffield.

Vagnetti, L. 1993. Mycenaean pottery in Italy: fifty years of study. In Zerner, C.P., Zerner, F. & Winder, J. (eds.), *Wace and Blegen. Pottery as evidence for trade in the Aegean Bronze Age 1939–1989. Proceedings of the International Conference held at the American School of Classical Studies at Athens (December 1–3, 1989)*, 143–154. J.C. Gieben, Amsterdam.
van der Plicht, J. & McCormac, F.G. 1995. A note on calibration curves. *Radiocarbon* 37: 963–964.
van der Plicht, J., Jansma, E. & Kars, H. 1995. The "Amsterdam Castle": a case study of wiggle-matching and the proper calibration curve. *Radiocarbon* 37: 965–968.
Vogel, J.C., Fuls, A., Visser, E. & Becker, B. 1993. Pretoria calibration curve for short-lived samples, 1930–3350 BC. *Radiocarbon* 35: 73–85
Warren, P. & Hankey, V. 1989. *Aegean Bronze Age chronology*. Bristol Classical Press, Bristol.
Webster, G.S. 1988. Duos Nuraghes: preliminary results of the first three seasons of excavation. *Journal of Field Archaeology* 15: 465–472.
Webster, G.S. 1996. *A Prehistory of Sardinia 2300–500 BC*. Monographs in Mediterranean Archaeology. Sheffield Academic Press, Sheffield.
Whitehouse, R. 1978. Italian prehistory, carbon 14 and the tree-ring calibration. In Blake, H.M., Potter, T.W. & Whitehouse, D.B. (eds.), *Papers in Italian Archaeology I: the Lancaster Seminar*. BAR Supplementary Series 41: 71–91. British Archaeological Reports, Oxford.

31. The Absolute Chronology of Late Helladic IIIA2

Malcolm H. Wiener

The contexts of LH IIIA2 pottery in Sardinia and other parts of the western Mediterranean constitute a fundamental point of reference for the absolute chronology of the area (see generally Vagnetti 1996).[1] The significance of datable pottery for chronology is magnified by the current lack of dendrochronological data and paucity of high-resolution radiocarbon evidence for the western Mediterranean (Tykot 1994).

The Late Helladic IIIA2 phase provides the most prominent and chronologically diagnostic deposits of all exported Aegean pottery. During the first part of what has been termed the "Mycenaean Century" covering pottery phases IIIA2 and IIIB1, but more correctly described as the "Mycenaean Century-and-a-Half" (see below), LH IIIA2 (imported and locally made) is found in large quantities in Rhodes and Kos (Mee 1982), at Anatolian coastal sites such as Miletus and the Müsgebi cemetery (Niemeier & Niemeier 1997), in Cyprus and the Levant (Hankey 1967; Åström 1972: 289–415; Leonard 1994; Koehl 1985: 142–146), and at Tell el Amarna in Egypt (Petrie 1894; Kemp 1979; 1980; 1981; Hankey 1995; Hankey & Aston 1995), where it forms the basic Aegean link to Egyptian absolute chronology as described below. Moreover, the determination of absolute dates for the IIIA2-IIIB transition provides a *terminus post quem* for LH/LM IIIB, the Aegean pottery most prevalent in the western Mediterranean and specifically in Sardinia where Nuraghe Antigori in particular produced significant amounts (Vagnetti 1996: 160).

The cemetery of Thapsos in Sicily produced significant quantities of LH IIIA2 (Orsi 1895; Bernabò Brea 1970; Voza 1972; 1973a; 1973b; 1976–77), as have other cemeteries in the Syracuse region. Small amounts come from Broglio di Trebisacce in Calabria and Milazzese on the Aeolian island of Panarea (Mountjoy 1993: 172–173; for an overview of Mycenaean imported pottery found in Italy see Vagnetti 1993). In addition to the standard stirrup jars, fine alabastra of a type (FS 94) most common in LH IIIA2, but which first appears in LH IIIA1 (e.g., Mycenae Chamber Tomb 520:14, to which E. French has kindly drawn my attention) and continues into IIIB1 (Vagnetti in Lo Schiavo & Vagnetti 1993), have been found at Thapsos and Floridia in Sicily, at Santa Sabina in Apulia, and at Nuraghe Arrubiu at Orroli in Sardinia, as well as along the Anatolian and Syrian coasts and in Cyprus (Lo Schiavo & Vagnetti 1993; see also Warren, this volume, and references therein).

Three factors affect the absolute dates assignable to imported Aegean pottery of a particular ceramic phase: (1) the length of time between creation and deposition in the archaeological record; (2) the extent of time over which the pottery type(s) in question were produced; and (3) the links between the ceramic phase and absolute dates derived from Egyptian historical chronology or scientific means.

1. The length of time between creation and deposition may be a particular problem in the case of Aegean pottery which, in the eastern Mediterranean at least, is often prized, retained and found in contexts significantly later than its creation. A jar filled with perfumed oil given to a bride at her wedding at the age of 15 and deposited in her grave at age 40 adds a quarter-century without even attaining the status of an heirloom. Six of ten stirrup jar sherds found in royal or high official tombs at Saqqara in 19th Dynasty contexts came from jars common a century earlier and reused, while stirrup jar styles had evolved (Hankey & Aston 1995: 78). Indeed, sherds of Mycenaean pottery smoothed at the edges and used as counters in a game have been found in Egypt in contexts centuries later than the time of their creation (Bourriau & Eriksson forthcoming). When large numbers of pots are found in a variety of discrete contexts at a site or at a number of sites of a common archaeological horizon, however, the risk that the context is significantly later than in its place of origin decreases.

Malcolm H. Wiener, Institute for Aegean Prehistory, 1270 Avenue of the Americas, New York, NY 10020–1795 USA

2. Consensus is lacking as to the chronological span of the production of Late Helladic and Late Minoan IIIA2 pottery. (Late Minoan IIIA2 may begin slightly later than LH IIIA2. Chania sherds described as LH IIIA2 were found in a deposit of LM IIIA1 pottery, but not all scholars have been willing to accept the description [Pålsson Hallager 1988: 180–181; comments by E. French in Pålsson Hallager 1988: 181]. It may be that LH/LM IIIA2 originates in the Peloponnese and that certain Late Minoan IIIA2 forms develop in imitation, perhaps with the intention of indicating the contents of the pots.) Warren & Hankey (1989: 88, 148–154), in their invaluable compendium on Aegean Bronze Age chronology, propose a duration of 20 to 40 years between 1370/60 and 1340/30 BC for LH/LM IIIA2, but note in a postscript that "recent discoveries of substantial LM IIIA2 levels in southern Crete, especially Haghia Triadha, may require this view to be modified" (214). Manning (1995: 217) suggests 1390/1370 BC to 1360/1325 BC. Mountjoy (1993: 3) gives 60 years (1360–1300 BC) in the text, but the accompanying Table (4) suggests 75 years (1375–1300 BC). Cline (1994: 7) allows only 20 twenty years (1360–1340 BC). In her massive survey of Late Minoan III pottery deposits in Crete, Kanta (1980) allows the whole of the fourteenth century (1400–1300 BC) for LM/LH IIIA2, as did Furumark in his basic study of Mycenaean pottery published in 1941. Wace (1957: 222) contended that IIIB as a whole covered a longer period of time than IIIA1 plus IIIA2, but on the basis of a definition of IIIB different from that now in use, including in IIIB, for example, the large store of pottery from Petsas' House at Mycenae which today is called IIIA2 (I am grateful to E. French for this observation). Most excavators working on the Greek mainland would regard LH IIIA2 as a longer period than LH IIIB1, which itself is regarded as covering two generations at least (Deger-Jalkotzy, pers. comm.). Popham (1990: 27–28 and pers. comm.), skeptical that LM IB, LM II or LM IIIA1 can last more than a generation each, is willing to accept three generations for LM IIIA2 based on comparative depth of deposits at various sites in Crete. Estimates as to the duration of the IIIA2 ceramic phase thus range between 20 and 100 years.

LH IIIA2 is a period of new settlements and of settlement expansion or rebuilding. The *Gazetteer* (Hope Simpson & Dickinson 1979: 385) refers to a "population explosion" during the Mycenaean "koine" of LH IIIA2-B. At Nichoria in Messenia near the southern coast of the Peloponnese three phases of LH IIIA2 ceramic development were observed in a stratified sequence in one area of the site (Shelmerdine 1992: 495). The large corpus of LH IIIA2 mainland pottery comes mostly from tombs. Settlement deposits are generally scarce on the mainland because of the lack of IIIA2 destructions (Mountjoy 1993: 71) during what may have been a "pax Mycenaeana", thus perhaps contributing to a tendency to underestimate the duration of the period. In Crete, successive levels of LM IIIA2 pottery deposits in the south-central area occur not only at Haghia Triadha, which experienced a major building program, but also at Kommos and Phaistos. In the east, Palaikastro has significant IIIA2 levels. At Knossos in north-central Crete the situation is less clear; after a massive destruction of the palace in the earlier part of IIIA2, the site may have been less intensively inhabited for a time. (Comparisons are further complicated by the fact that in the early excavation of Phaistos all whole pots, decorated and undecorated, were saved, but almost all sherds, decorated as well as undecorated, were discarded, whereas at Knossos all decorated pots and most sherds were kept, but undecorated pots as well as sherds were discarded.) In the Dodecanese on Rhodes the number of known settlements expanded from 6 in IIIA1 to 23 in IIIA2, encompassing the west and south of Rhodes as well as the previously settled northwest coast (Mee 1982: 83), and on the Anatolian coast the 24 tombs in use in IIIA2 in the cemetery of Müsgebi produced 80 percent of the pottery (Mee 1978: 137–142).

Unfortunately neither developments in style nor depth of deposits provide a reliable indicator of the chronological duration of a pottery style. Conservatism of style may be the rule for centuries, particularly when the shape and decoration of containers become a trademark for their contents; when vessels used in cult practices acquire a canonical form and decoration; and/or when the prestige of one center in setting cultural norms is paramount. Depth of deposit will be greatly affected by the number and type of destructions at a site. A severe earthquake followed by a rebuilding over the debris, for example, or abandonment and subsequent collapse of roofs rather than a thoroughgoing clean-up after a destruction, are likely to provide large ceramic deposits for future excavators.

Both conservatism of style and earthquake destruction may be relevant in IIIA2. The expanding export of perfumed oil in stirrup jars identified with their contents by shape and design may have discouraged stylistic change. In Crete, at least, earthquakes may have accounted for the depth of some IIIA2 deposits. For example, at Palaikastro the excavator believes a major earthquake at the close of IIIA2 or the beginning of IIIB may have ended significant occupation of the site (MacGillivray 1997: 196). In south-central Crete, either an earthquake or an abandonment that left pots *in situ* because of the sudden appearance of a hostile force early in IIIA2 could have been the cause of the superimposed LM IIIA2 levels at Kommos, in which case the depth of IIIA2 deposits there need not necessarily indicate a significant passage of time. (The frequency of earthquakes in south-central Crete is discussed by La Rosa (in Myers *et al.* 1992: 238–239).

These problems of interpretation notwithstanding, it would appear that even without the evidence for duration derived from absolute chronology discussed below, it would be prudent to allow at least two and perhaps three generations for LH/LM IIIA2.

3. The absolute chronology of LH/LM IIIA2 is based

on interconnections with Egyptian historical chronology and on a dendrochronological date near the close of the period. The absolute Egyptian dates used here follow the Egyptian "middle" chronology advocated by Kitchen (see, e.g., 1986; 1987; 1992; 1996; forthcoming), which the author believes is unlikely to vary from true dates by more than about a decade for the relevant horizon. Recent years have seen significant change and improvement in the foundations of Egyptian chronology. A synopsis of these changes and the current position is provided in the Addendum to this paper. The middle chronology places the accession of Amenhotep III circa 1390 BC, the accession of Akhenaten circa 1349 BC, and the move of the capital to Memphis ending the Amarna Age by the third year of Tutankhamen circa 1330 BC.

The beginning of IIIA2 is difficult to date on Egyptian evidence. Two LH IIIA2 vases found in a destruction at Qatna were attributed by Furumark to a first Hittite campaign in Syria during the lifetime of Amenhotep III (thus providing Furumark his date of 1400 BC for the beginning of IIIA2), but the stratigraphy at Qatna is badly confused. Redford thought that the Qatna destruction occurred during a second Syrian campaign in the reign of Akhenaten (evidence summarized in Warren & Hankey 1989: 148–149). Neither Hittite nor Syrian texts provide direct evidence of a destruction, as distinguished from a conquest of Qatna. From the Aegean standpoint, the absence of IIIA2 pottery in Tomb 4 of the Sellopoulo cemetery of Knossos, whose last burial was of a woman wearing a necklace with a faience scarab in excellent condition with a cartouche of Amenhotep III (Popham 1974: 216–217) and accompanied by an LM IIIA1 stirrup jar (Popham 1974: 209), has been taken to indicate that LM IIIA1 must have continued at least into the beginning of the reign of that pharaoh. Two earlier burials in the tomb, on a different alignment from the final burial, were accompanied by LM IIIA1 pottery plus one imported piece of LH IIIA1 pottery, but nothing of LM II. Of course, someone buried in a high-status tomb during the early part of the IIIA2 period could have been accompanied by a treasured, very fine large IIIA1 stirrup jar of the type found with the last burial, thus raising the possibility that IIIA2 could have begun before the accession of Amenhotep III. On the other hand, the fact that the cartouche appears to have been copied by someone relatively unfamiliar with Egyptian hieroglyphs (Manning 1995: 227), suggesting production outside Egypt, may indicate the passage of some time between the accession of Amenhotep III and the deposition in the tomb, thus implying a somewhat later date for the final burial in a Minoan tomb with no pottery later than LM IIIA1 and for the end of that phase. The possibility that LH IIIA2 begins slightly before LM IIIA2 may be relevant here. Other possible associations of Amenhotep III with IIIA1 are noted by Cline (1994: 7), but described as "less helpful for precise synchronisms", and by Warren & Hankey (1989: 142).

On balance, the evidence (including the evidence for interconnections between Egypt and the preceding Aegean periods discussed in Wiener forthcoming) suggests that LH IIIA2 and LM IIIA2 begin early in the reign of Amenhotep III circa 1390–1375 BC.

Establishing a terminal date for IIIA2 presents challenges of a different kind. Warren & Hankey date the end of LH/LM IIIA2 to the reign of Akhenaten or Tutankhamen. This judgment rests partly on evidence from Kamid El-Loz at the southern end of the Beq'a Valley in Lebanon, where eight Amarna-type tablets, one of them mentioning a name known from the Amarna correspondence, were found in a palace closely associated with a temple containing items both of LH IIIA2 and IIIB1 (Warren & Hankey 1989: 153, citing Hachmann 1978a; 1978b; 1980; 1982). E. French (pers. comm., 9 June 1997) also identifies at least one kylix from this deposit (KL 69:13 in Hachmann 1980: 88, pl. 26.2) as clearly LH IIIB1 in both shape and decoration. French believes the rhyton KL 72:333 with palm motif and the psi figurine KL 69:266, both identified as IIIB by Warren & Hankey, could equally well be IIIA2.

Assuming that (1) the temple was destroyed at the same time as the palace and that it did not receive a subsequent offering of an imported kylix and perhaps other vessels, and (2) the tablets were contemporaneous with and not later than the Amarna tablets and had not been retained as a record for a significant length of time before the destruction, then the contemporaneous existence of the kylix with tablets from the Amarna horizon would indeed suggest an early appearance of IIIB1, and hence a shortened IIIA2. It is worth noting, however, that at Amarna itself the tablet archive is believed to cover a span of about 30 years, from the 30th year of Amenhotep III (1360 BC on the middle chronology) to the first or second year of Tutankhamen (1332–1331 BC, middle chronology) (Moran 1992: xxxiv). The proposed 10–12 year Amenhotep III-Akhenaten co-regency noted in the Addendum would reduce the span by a corresponding number of years. Moreover, with regard to the name-bearing Kamid El-Loz tablet, if the name in question on the tablet is Biryawaza, mayor of Damascus, rather than Biridiya, mayor of Megiddo, and if the addressee of Amarna letter 7 is Akhenaten (Amenhotep IV) as proposed by Kühne (1973: 60, n. 292, cited in Moran 1992: 14, n. 1), then the 11 years prior to the 1349 accession of Akhenaten are not relevant with respect to the Amarna comparandum. Of course, correspondence continued between the Egyptian court and its officials or satraps in Syria after the transfer of the capital from Amarna to Memphis; thus the tablets could be post-Amarna in date of composition as well as destruction, but the associated Syro-Canaanite pottery does not appear to be post-Amarna (E. Oren, pers. comm.). Given the uncertainty as to the number of years the tablets would have been retained after receipt, the connection between the IIIB1 kylix from Kamid El-Loz and the Amarna period remains somewhat tenuous.

Warren and Hankey's main argument for beginning LH IIIB1 in the Amarna period rests on the evidence from Amarna itself, the site of one of the largest deposits of LH IIIA2 pottery found abroad. Here, among seven whole or restored pots and 1350 sherds of LH IIIA2, two sherds from stirrup jars are assigned to IIIB1 by Warren and Hankey. One of the sherds (NCL 725 + 742) is in London with the bulk of the collection and the other is in Bonn (295.15). Hankey remarks that the London joined fragment "stands out as different in fabric, shape and style from the run of IIIA2 pottery", and that the Bonn fragment's narrow neck and shoulder line suggest Furumark shape 171 or 173, which together with its lozenge pattern place it within the IIIB1 repertoire. Kaiser (1976: 82–96) noted that the decorative motif of the Bonn sherd is known in IIIA2, but not its location on the shoulder zone. Podzuweit (1994: 457–474) observed that what little comparanda exists for the Bonn sherd suggests a IIIB designation, but subject to the qualification that the dating of stirrup jars is particularly difficult due to the lack of adequate stratigraphic phasing in the Argolid itself (I am grateful to V. Hankey for these references). Neither sherd was illustrated or specifically mentioned by Petrie, but both are registered as found by Petrie at Amarna, presumably in the central rubbish dumps (Petrie 1894: 16–17; Warren & Hankey 1989: 149; Popham 1970: 84, n. 87), although Petrie also recorded nine sherds as coming from the palace and three from House 11; a few sherds from other areas have been discarded subsequently (V. Hankey, pers. comm.). Hankey further reports that the three Minoan pieces from the deposit, a cup and two coarse-ware pots, could span LM IIIA late to LM IIIB.

In asssessing whether IIIB1 pottery is already present at Amarna, it is important to understand that Furumark in his classification of Mycenaean pottery (1941; for Amarna, see II, 113) did not develop his typological criteria based on deposits in Greece and then categorize the Amarna deposit, but rather used what he regarded as the closed and datable Amarna deposit as published by Petrie to define LH IIIA2; accordingly, shapes and motifs (such as those of the sherds in question) not illustrated by Petrie were excluded from his characterization of IIIA2. Concerning the decorative motifs on the Amarna stirrup jars described by Warren and Hankey as IIIB1, E. French (pers. comm., 7 June 1996) comments as follows:

> Hankey has stated that two stirrup jars from Amarna (not known to Furumark), which she considers to be FS 173 and 182, may still be considered LH IIIB1. Mountjoy has suggested (pers. comm.) that Hankey 1995: 117, no. 8 (Warren & Hankey 1989: 150, fig. 9), University College London 725–742, is FS 166 and thus "fine for A2 even with belly dec!" (It could also be FS 178.) [P. Mountjoy observes (pers. comm.) that FS 178 does not usually have a decorated belly zone in IIIA2.] It is the lozenge pattern on Hankey 1995: 117, no. 6; Bonn 295.15, that at first glance makes this piece appear to be LH IIIB. In fact the pattern, though not common, starts in LH IIIA2 (French 1965). That the Amarna example comes early in the series is clear by contrast to the pot from Tell Aphek (Warren & Hankey 1989: 155, fig. 10). There is no justification for a reassessment of the whole group on the basis of this single piece. Accordingly, I see no archaeological reason to abandon the acceptance of the Amarna material as at least a homogeneous deposit, if not a closed one, of LH IIIA2. (I am most grateful to E. French for this assessment and for permission to quote it here, and to P. Mountjoy as well.)

Another example of what may be FS 182 comes from a closed context at Saqqara that must be at least one hundred years later than the main Amarna deposit, as noted by Hankey & Aston (1995: 77). Neither the deep bowl nor the Zygouries kylix, the canonical LH IIIB vessels that normally appear in LH IIIB1 deposits in quantity, are present in the Amarna deposit, but they were rarely exported and in addition the Amarna deposit consists largely of closed shapes.

Warren and Hankey discount M. Bell's (1985) belief that occupation of or visits to Amarna after its abandonment as the capital cast doubt on the chronologgical integrity of the deposit, arguing that the nature of subsequent occupation was not such as to make likely the importation of such vessels. LH III stirrup jars may be found in Egypt in "middle class" contexts, however, as the distribution of such jars at the workman's village of Deir El-Medina demonstrates (Bell 1982). As to the possibility that Mycenaean stirrup jars containing perfumed oil were exchanged for the faience amulets believed still produced at Amarna after the transfer of the capital (Petrie 1894: 43–44, discussed in Warren & Hankey 1989: 149, where the production is termed a glass factory) or that a IIIB1 jar was the property of one of the functionaries working at the factory or supervising the subsequent demolition of Amarna in the time of Horemheb, Hankey (letter of 24 September 1996) notes that it is unlikely that such a putative later import would have been discarded in the vicinity of the central city dumps, the presumed find spot of both the sherds in question.

At Saqqara, IIIA2 pots were recovered from the tomb of Aper-El, a vizier of Amenhotep III, in a context indicating a time of use between 1360 and 1342 BC on the middle chronology (Hankey & Aston 1995: 69). The tomb of Maya, the Treasurer of Tutankhamen, and his wife Merit (Martin 1981: 7–9), contained two pots described by Warren & Hankey (1989: 151–152) as undistinguished borderline specimens, difficult to classify as either IIIA2 or IIIB1. They come from a closed deposit with material including Horemheb Year 8, 1315 BC on the middle chronology.

Oren, summarizing the evidence from Levantine

settlement sites (as distinguished from less chronologically diagnostic tomb deposits), observes that at sites such as Lachish, Tell Abu-Hawam, Kamid El-Loz and Megiddo, where Aegean, Cypriote, Canaanite and Egyptian pottery or objects are all present, LH IIIB pottery does not appear before 19th Dynasty contexts (letter of 4 August 1997, for which I am most grateful. On the middle Egyptian chronology, the 19th Dynasty begins in 1295 BC).

An intriguing suggestion of another absolute chronological point of reference for the IIIA2-IIIB1 transition is provided by the evidence from the 1996 season of the current excavation of Miletus under the direction of W.-D. Niemeier. All or almost all of the pottery from the destruction following the "Second Building Period" of Bronze Age Miletus, a major Anatolian coastal site where imported and locally made pottery of Mycenaean shape, decoration and method of manufacture comprises about 98 percent of all vessels, is LH IIIA2. The two sherds that may be exceptions are fragments of kylikes with octopus decoration of a type that Furumark classified as transitional IIIA2 to IIIB1. The best-known comparanda come from multi-period tombs in Rhodes and Kos rather than from stratified deposits, thus making precise chronological placement difficult. Based on present evidence, the destruction seems to have occurred just at the end of IIIA2, when IIIB elements had perhaps already begun to appear (Niemeier & Niemeier 1997: 197; Niemeier 1998: 32–33 and pers. comm.).

If "Ahhiyawa" of the Hittite texts refers to the Achaean (Mycenaean) realm or to a part of it, and the site called "Millawanda" in the Hittite texts is Miletus, as most recently reaffirmed by Hawkins (1998), then a link to Egyptian historical chrononlogy exists. Niemeier has summarized the evidence as follows:

"According to The Annals of Mursili II (in the most plausible reading of A. Goetze 1933: 36ff., 253f.) followed by H.G. Güterbock (1983: 135) and T.G. Bryce (1989a; 1989b: 299) in the upheavals which followed Mursili's accession, Millawanda took sides with the king of Ahhiyawa. In response, Mursili sent forth his two generals, Gulla and Malaziti, who conquered the city. The relevant destruction at Miletus has already been connected with this attack (Mellink 1983: 139–140). Wilhelm & Boese (1989: 108, table on 117) date the accession of Mursili II 1322/21 or 1318/17. His third year would thus be 1319/18 or 1315/14 which fits rather well with the dendrochronological date of 1316 BC [but see below] for the Ulu Burun wreck. Wilhelm and Boese use Kitchen's Egyptian chronology dating the battle of Qadesh (in the 5th year of Ramses II's rule) to 1275/74 BC."

I am deeply grateful to W.-D. Niemeier for this communication and his permission to publish it here. Dendrochronological reanalysis of the Uluburun date subsequent to this communication has resulted in a later date as described below.

Finally, the Ulu Burun shipwreck (Bass 1986; 1987; Bass et al. 1984; Bass et al. 1989; Pulak 1988; 1989; 1990; 1991; 1992; 1996), to which Niemeier refers, provides both a complement of LH IIIA2 pottery and a dendrochronologically derived absolute date for the sinking of the ship off the coast of Anatolia at Uluburun, Turkey, of sometime after 1305 BC.

The Aegean pottery carried aboard the ship is presently being cleaned and mended, preparatory to study and publication by Rutter, who has kindly provided the preliminary analysis that follows (letter of 23 September 1996, for which I am most grateful; see also Pulak 1996). Twenty-three whole or partial LH (or LM) pots were recovered from the Uluburun wreck. Nine were large coarse-ware transport stirrup jars whose morphology over time has not been established and hence are not chronologically diagnostic. A second group consists of eight small fine-ware stirrup jars and a flask; all are to be placed in the later part of LH/LM IIIA2. A final group of five vases (which Rutter suggests may have been a drinking set) includes a beaked jug and a kylix that exhibit features typical of an earlier phase of LH IIIA2. Two other LH IIIA2 shapes, a teacup and a dipper, may also be early. The final pot, however, a round-mouthed jug (FS 120) whose decoration has not yet been determined because of heavy marine concretions masking the surface of the many sherds, could be either IIIA2 or IIIB. (Rutter's reference in Kuniholm et al. 1996: 782 to this jug as IIIB should be held in abeyance pending further study.) Thus all 13 of the presently diagnostic Aegean pots recovered from the Uluburun wreck are IIIA2. In summary, there is nothing from the Uluburun wreck thus far that need be later than IIIA2. The Cypriote pottery carried on board is LC IIC, and appears to be freshly made. Oren notes that a Canaanite biconical krater from the wreck appears to belong in the thirteenth century BC (letter of 4 August 1997).

The wreck also included a gold scarab with the cartouche of Nefertiti, showing signs of considerable wear. Some of the other jewelry found nearby was also badly worn. Weinstein (in Bass et al. 1989: 23) suggests that these objects were carried as scrap and represent a post-Amarna horizon.

The Uluburun wreck also contained the chronologically significant piece of cedarwood described below.

The dendrochronological absolute date for this assemblage is derived as follows. Calendar dates for the Anatolian "floating chronology" of 1,503 continuous years are anchored to fixed dendrochronological dates from long-lived trees with a continuous annual sequence by (1) historical, (2) radiocarbon and (3) dendrochronological means (Kuniholm et al. 1996), and the ring widths of a log carried aboard the Uluburn ship are matched to the Anatolian "floating chronology".

1) The Anatolian "floating chronology" includes wood

from the Midas Mound Tumulus and Tumulus B at Gordion and from a palace built late in the reign of Rusa II at Ayanis on the shore of Lake Van in Urartu that together provide a date determinable to within about ten years on historical grounds. The examination of a timber from a cedar sarcophagus in Gordion Tumulus B establishes a last-preserved ring at 627 BC in conditions that suggest very few rings are missing from the exterior (Kuniholm 1997). The date is thus very close to the date of c. 630 BC previously suggested by Kohler (1995: 15) on historical grounds. The 37 timbers initially examined from Ayanis, several of which retained their outer bark, give a final year of 651 BC (Kuniholm 1996). The site includes an inscribed monument reciting the accomplishments of Rusa II from the late years of his reign, which has been placed on historical grounds to c. 685 to 645 BC (Çilingiroğlu & Salvini, cited in Kuniholm 1996).

2) Radiocarbon data from many points in the Anatolian "floating chronology" provide dates that are consistent with the historically derived dates.

3) The continuous dendrochronological sequences in Ireland and Germany show major events occurring in 1629/28 BC and 1159 BC, 470–469 years apart. There is no dendrochronologically significant event indicated between these two dates. The floating Anatolian sequence for the relevant time frame as determined by the historical and radiocarbon analysis also displays two events 470–469 years apart. Accordingly, it appears highly likely that the "floating Anatolian chronology" can be anchored at 1629/28 and 1159 BC, and provide exact dates for the intervening years.

The Uluburun wreckage contained a badly-twisted piece of cedar, about six inches in diameter and over four feet long. G. Bass has suggested it was carried as dunnage or firewood (Bass 1997; see also Pulak 1996: 12 "...presumably fresh-cut firewood...").

The date of 1316 BC cited by Niemeier was given in preliminary reports as the year of the final observable ring of the timber by Kuniholm *et al.* (1996) and Pulak (1997: 4). The timber showed no evidence of trimming by human agency and hence was not believed to be missing many rings on its exterior.

The initial examination of the timber was necessarily undertaken while the timber was still wet. Subsequent careful drying over a three-year period has improved the readability of the timber. Reexamination and reanalysis performed by P.I. Kuniholm and L. Steele at the Laboratory for Aegean and Near Eastern Dendrochronology at Cornell University prior to final publication has altered the picture as follows.

1. An additional faint ring was discovered on a single radius 28 years before the final ring, and an additional 9 rings were discovered on a newly observable node on the reverse side of the timber. The final observable ring is accordingly now placed at 1305 BC.

2. The latest observable ring is preserved for eleven hundredths of one millimeter on the circumference, and is barely discernable microscopically (Kuniholm, pers. comm. of 1 September 1997, for which I am most grateful). There is no way of determining whether this latest observable trace of a ring represents the original exterior of the tree. Where 99.9 percent of a ring is no longer visible, as is the case here, the possibility exists that 100 percent of another ring or rings may be missing. Since there is no indication of removal of rings by human agency, any missing rings would have been dissolved through the action of sand and water during the course of 3300 years.

3. As Kuniholm (1997) has noted, "any dates from a sampling of only two timbers must be treated with caution, especially when the wood is cedar which can often have eccentric growth characteristics". (The other timber is not of direct chronological relevance). The timber in question is particularly twisted and gnarled, and thus is unable to provide a conclusive computer-generated statistical match with the Anatolian master Bronze Age-Iron Age chronology, although the match (by Student's t-score, Trend coefficient and D-score) which results in 1305 BC as the year of the last observable ring is superior to that for any other relevant year. The microscopic visual fit is convincing, however (Kuniholm & Steele, pers. comm.). Thus there is a high likelihood that the last observable ring represents the year 1305 BC.

A further question arises as to whether any years elapsed between the time the timber was cut and the time it was placed aboard ship. Deliberate seasoning of wood intended for use in major construction or shipbuilding to prevent subsequent splitting is well-attested anthropologically, but such seasoning would be meaningless in the case of a twisted trunk intended for use as dunnage or firewood.

The dendrochronological evidence cited thus indicates that the Uluburun ship sank at some point after 1305 BC. In brief summary, one may say that "the Uluburun ship sank around 1300 BC."

That the ship carried 13 pieces of LH IIIA2 pottery, but thus far no identifiable LH IIIB, is significant with respect to the absolute chronology of the LH IIIA2-IIIB transition. Bass (1997) believes that the Uluburun vessel was a Syro-Canaanite ship, in which case there is no reason why it necessarily would have carried the latest pottery style of the Argolid, but since IIIA2 is a period of frequent contact, a lag of much more than a decade seems unlikely given the amount of pottery in question.

Of course pottery forms and decoration change over a period of time, and the rate of change need not be continuous; rather a single potter or pot painter may introduce a new profile or motif which only becomes part of the general repertory after the passage of some years. In light of the evidence presented in this paper, the bulk of the IIIA2-IIIB1 transition occurred within the decades

1320–1300 BC (on the middle Egyptian chronology, which can vary by about a decade as described in the Addendum to this paper). While a few LH IIIB1 elements may precede the general repertoire, a destruction or abandonment level containing a group of standard IIIB1 vessels of several types, or sherds from such vessels, is unlikely to be earlier than 1320 BC, and a major deposit of LH IIIB1 pottery with IIIA2 present is unlikely to predate 1300 BC.

In summary, the production of LH IIIA2 pottery on current evidence spans a period of about 70 to 80 years from 1390/70 to 1320/00 BC. When found in secure contexts in the western Mediterranean, LH/LM IIIA2 pottery provides a point of reference for the absolute chronology of the region. The establishment of a date range for the termination of production in turn provides a *terminus post quem* for pottery of the succeeding IIIB phase.

Addendum

Egyptian absolute chronology is based on (a) our understanding and interpretation of Egyptian texts containing astronomical observations of Sirius and the moon; (b) king lists, sometimes compiled long after the fact; (c) synchronisms with dates derived from the astronomical observations and historical records from Babylonia, Assyria, Anatolia, and the Hebrew Bible; and most importantly (d) inscriptions from temples, tombs, stelae and rock faces (and, in some cases in the Third Intermediate Period, texts from mummy bandages) stating lengths of reigns, giving regnal years for events or celebrating jubilees of rulers, together with corroborating evidence from inscriptions dealing with the lives of relatives, court officials, priests and military officers.

Until ten years ago, any proposed Egyptian absolute chronology required the utilization of astronomy, king lists and inscriptions. Today, however, because of the progress made by a number of scholars, particularly Kitchen, with respect to the formidable chronological challenges of the Third Intermediate Period (Kitchen 1986; 1996; see also 1987; 1992; and forthcoming), the strongest case for a fixed Egyptian absolute chronology from the beginning of the New Kingdom relies only to a slight extent on astronomical observations, resting instead largely on Egyptian texts. (Kitchen has recently joined Helck and Luft in disavowing the readability and reliability of the astronomical data contained in a text known as Papyrus Ebers, thus removing the sole Sothic cycle astronomical anchor from Egyptian New Kingdom chronology). Potential lunar cycle dates for the accession of Ramesses II are available at 1304 BC, 1290 BC, 1279 BC and 1265 BC. The most recent study by Casperson (1988), reanalyzing the data provided by Parker (1950) in his seminal work on Egyptian astronomical dating, concludes that the nature of the information concerning a lunar sighting in the reign of Ramesses II suggests that 1279 BC is more likely than 1290 BC or 1304 BC as his accession date, thus supporting what has become known as the "middle chronology" whose principal advocate and expounder has been Kitchen.

The primary areas of uncertainty regarding Egyptian absolute historical dates after 1390 BC are found in the 21st and overlapping 22nd/23rd Dynasties of the Third Intermediate Period. The period between about 924 and 874 BC on the middle chronology covering the reigns of Osorkon I, Shoshenq II and Takeloth I of the 22nd Dynasty presents particular problems. During this span there is a gap in the records from the Serapeum on the life spans of successive sacred Apis bulls that provide vital chronological data for most of the Third Intermediate Period. Takeloth I, for example, is known principally from his appearance in the king list compiled long after by the priest Manetho, from items of his burial found in the tomb of Osorkon II (Dodson 1994: 89) and from a reference in the genealogy given on the Serapeum stele of the Memphite priest Pasenhor B, who provided a list of 14 ancestors ending in 3 pharaohs, one of whom was Takeloth I. Kitchen gives Takeloth I 14–15 years on the basis of Nile level texts "whose authors do not even deign to name a pharaoh" (Kitchen 1996: 121; forthcoming) but which are assignable (largely through a process of elimination) to the reign of Takeloth I. A 14–15 year duration for the reign of Takeloth I would also fit the proposed date of a campaign in Palestine by Shoshenq I depicted and described in Egyptian reliefs (Kitch 1992: 327; 1996: 72–76) and by inference in the Hebrew Bible (I Kings 14: 25–26; II Chronicles 12: 2–12) and in the form of a raid by "Shishak" on Jerusalem in the fifth year of Rehoboam, which Kitchen dates narrowly to 926/5 BC following calculations by Thiele (1951; 1965; 1983). Thiele's calculations depend (for reigns prior to the participation by Ahab in the battle of Qarqar dated to 853 BC in the Assyrian annals) on the application of Near Eastern/Egyptian dating methods to the biblical texts, and the rationalization of conflicting biblical accounts through a number of proposed co-regencies, some of which have not won general acceptance (Cryer 1995; Cogan 1985; 1992; Tadmor 1979; I am grateful to K. Kitchen for his observations concerning the important positive contribution of the work of Thiele). Thus a variation of perhaps as much as a decade in the absolute dates for the 22nd/23rd Dynasties from those stated in the middle chronology seems possible. The unsettled aspects of this period are illustrated by the fact that as recently as four years ago Dodson (1993: 58) was able to establish the existence of a previously unknown pharaoh, Shoshenq IV, to the satisfaction of Kitchen (1996: preface xxvi) and other Egyptologists. (The existence of Shoshenq IV is, however, generally regarded as affecting the relative length of the reigns of adjacent pharaohs rather than the duration of the dynasty.)

The 21st Dynasty presents a second major area of uncertainty. The documentation for the high priests and other officials from Thebes in the south of Egypt is extensive, but the records pertaining to the kings in the north is scanty. Scholarly controversy in recent years has centered in the middle years of the 21st Dynasty (Kitchen 1995: 24). A mummy bandage (now lost) was reported as giving a Year 49 for Amenemope, against a tradition preserved in the various later versions of the lost history of the third century BC Egyptian priest Manetho of only 9 years for Amenemope but 41 (or in another version 46) years for his predecessor Psusennes I. Kitchen (1995: 24–39) considers the two major possibiltiies to be (1) 26 years for Psusennes I and 52 years for Amenemope (total 78 years) or (2) 49 years for Psusennes I and 9 years for Amenemope (total 58 years), and after a careful and methodical analysis of the many uncertainties, states a preference for the second alternative. A major reason is that if the first alternative is adopted, the term of office of the high priest Menkheperre which appears to span both royal reigns lasts not less than 75 years (Kitchen 1995: 28, n. 117). Moreover, Menkheperre is apparently immersed in political struggles soon after his appointment to succeed his brother, thus making it unlikely that he became high priest much before the age of 20. (I am grateful to M. Bierbrier for this observation.) While earlier priests and supervisors of workers at Thebes are known to have lived into their eighties and in two cases into their nineties (see below), the chance of this occurring in any individual case is small. The areas of uncertainty respecting the 21st Dynasty may permit some modest raising or lowering of dates.

Apart from the uncertainties of the Third Intermediate Period, it is possible that a few years may be missing in the period around 1185 BC before, during or after the reign of Queen Twosret in the 19th Dynasty. A previous generation of scholars (Rowton 1948; Drioton & Vandier 1962; Wilson 1951) was prepared to accept the prospect of an interregnum of 20 years in light of the state of affairs depicted in the Papyrus Harris. This text, prepared by Ramesses IV to accompany the burial of his father Ramesses III and celebrate his achievements, including the restoration of order (and hence subject to the possibility of exaggeration), describes the situation preceding the accession of Ramesses III as follows:

"The land of Egypt was outcast. Every man was his own standard. *They had no one above them for many years* previously, at other times, and the land of Egypt was [under the control of] chiefs and local rulers. Each killed another, whether respected or beggar. *Another time of empty years came after it,* when 'Self-made,' a Syrian, was with them as chief, having put the entire land in his control before him. Each killed his neighbor and stole his things, and they treated the gods like the people, with no offerings made inside the temples". (Emphasis supplied. The "Syrian" of the Papyrus is presumably the Chancellor Bay, the power behind the throne in the reigns of Siptah and Twosret. I am much indebted to J. Allen for the translation.)

More recent scholarship (Horning 1964; Bierbrier 1975: 43), especially the work of Bierbrier, has argued for narrowing the possible interregnum to five years at most on the basis of the periods of office of viziers and viceroys, and of the established genealogies of four families, two families of priests at Thebes, and two families of overseers of workmen at Deir El-Medina. Genetically and occupationally favored, these families produced 33 long-lived individuals, 2 of whom probably lived into their nineties, 5 into their eighties, 11 into their seventies, and at least 15 into their sixties (Bierbrier 1975: 15). To extend the putative interregnum beyond five years would accordingly require, for example, that several more of the workman-supervisors from Deir El-Medina already known as septuagenarians become octogenarians (Bierbrier 1975: 43). Accordingly the "empty" years of Papyrus Harris are probably best understood as references to the "kingless" periods of the struggle between Amenmesse and Seti II (if they were rivals) and the Siptah-Twosret period when the real power was held by Bay (J. Allen, pers. comm.). A stele of Sethnacht carries a text which describes the contest for power and succession but makes no reference to empty years or an interregnum, confirming the impression that the absolute chronology for this period is well established (Drenkhahn 1980).

Finally, the 28/29 years given for the reign of Horemheb by the middle chronology may also be subject to a variation of some years in either direction. The last attested year, from a jar likely to belong to the burial of one of his wives, is 13; references to 59 years in an inscription of Mes and in the list of Manetho are thought to include the Amarna period, thus reflecting the *damnatio memoriae* of Akhenaten (Wente & van Siclen 1976: 231–232). Calculations based on references to the length of the 18th Dynasty and Near Eastern interconnections suggest 28/29 years as a likely, but not certain, duration of the reign.

While the remote possibility exists that there was at some point in the history of Egypt a period of chaos due to a struggle for control, war or plague that resulted in a number of years without any surviving record, a further constraint is provided by the correspondence of the certain pharaohs with various Near Eastern rulers, and in particular of the Amarna rulers with Kadashman-Enlil I and Burnaburiash II of Babylonia. Their absolute dates, derived from Babylonian/Assyrian chronologies and Babylonian astronomical observations, perhaps no more but no less reliable than Egyptian absolute dates, fit generally the dates proposed by the Egyptian middle chronology for the Amarna rulers. With regard to the Assyrian dates, there exists a period of uncertainty between the reigns of Tukulti-Ninurta I and Tiglath-Pileser I corresponding roughly with the period of uncertainty in Third Intermediate Period Egyptian dates. It is of course the case that similar unrecorded periods in two separate civilizations are less likely than an undocumented period in just one. (The effect of such hypothetical double periods without documentation would, of course, be to raise, but not to lower, dates.) Moreover, on the assumption that the campaign of Shoshenq I encompassed the raid of "Shishak" in the fifth year of Rehoboam, the date of 926/25 BC calculated by Thiele (1965: 56, table I; Kitchen 1966: 75, n. 371) for the raid is unlikely to be much more than a decade off the mark, setting a boundary to the margin of error for the 22nd/23rd Dynasties, one of the two periods of uncertainty noted above (Kitchen 1996: 75–76). Dates for the 21st Dynasty could also vary by a decade, and the putative corrections required could be either cumulative or offsetting. Accordingly, Egyptian New Kingdom dates might conceivably be raised by 11 years to an accession date for Ramesses II at 1290 BC, or might even be lowered, although a reduction by 14 years to fit the next appropriate lunar date for the accession of Ramesses II in 1265 BC presents problems in terms of Egyptian textual evidence, and would require the lowering of the standard Babylonian/Assyrian dates as well. Raising dates by 25 years (one full lunar cycle) for an accession of Ramesses II in 1304 BC would require some combination of a lengthening of the 21st and 22nd/23rd Dynasties and the reign of Horemheb as indicated, plus a Babylonian/Assyrian interregnum or time of unacknowledged and/or unrecorded rule during a period of confusion stemming from internal conflict, war, plague or famine, matched by an absence of administrative texts and seal impressions for the putative period, and is far less likely in light of the accumulated evidence.

Finally, a proposed co-regency of Amenhotep III and his son Akhenaten during the last 10–12 years of Amenhotep III's reign (as recently advocated by Johnson 1996) would shrink the Amarna period and lower absolute chronological dates correspondingly (unless met by a countervailing increase in accordance with one of the possibilities described above). While the issue is open at present, it appears the proposed co-regency has not been accepted by a majority of specialists in the Amarna Age.

Notwithstanding various intervals of uncertainty, it is thus highly unlikely (for these reasons and others set forth in detail by the author in a forthcoming work, *The Chronology of the Late Bronze Age from Egypt to the Aegean: Science, Texts, Interconnections*) that Egyptian absolute dates can vary greatly from the middle chronology. These dates are used in this text, subject to the caveat that they could be raised by up to 11 years with some, but not overwhelming, difficulty, might conceivably move down by 14 years, but with greater difficulty, and are unlikely to fall outside this range of uncertainty for dates subsequent to the beginning of the 14th century BC.

Note

1. This paper is dedicated to Vronwy Hankey, in fond and grateful rememberance. This paper benefited at every stage of its evolution from her interest, advice and assistance. Hankey's knowledge of Aegean pottery and of Egyptian, near Eastern and Aegean prehistory informed her critical contribution to the establishment of the chronology of the Late Bronze Age. Her unstinting support of colleagues and indomitable spirit will be long remembered.

Acknowledgments

I am extremely grateful to those colleagues whose personal communications and advice are cited herein; to P. Betancourt, P.I. Kuniholm, S. Manning and P. Warren for providing me with their contributions to this publication; to O.T.P.K. Dickinson, E. French, V. Hankey, K. Kitchen, P. Machinist, E. Oren, J. Rutter, L. Steele and J. Warner for reading the manuscript in its entirety and offering many helpful comments; and particularly to P.I. Kuniholm and L. Steele of the Laboratory for Aegean and Near Eastern Dendrochronology at Cornell University for immediately re-examining and reanalyzing the critical piece of wood from the Uluburun wreck and instantly communicating the results, and to P.I. Kuniholm for permission to communicate this important new information in this paper.

Bibliography

Åström, P. 1972. *The Swedish Cyprus Expedition: Vol. IV, Part 1C: The Late Cypriote Bronze Age Architecture and Pottery.* Lund.

Bass, G.F. 1986. A Bronze Age Shipwreck at Ulu Burun (Ka): 1984 Campaign. *American Journal of Archaeology* 90: 269–296.

Bass, G.F. 1987. Oldest Known Shipwreck Reveals Splendors of the Bronze Age. *National Geographic* 172.6: 692–733.

Bass, G.F. 1997. Sailing Between the Aegean and the Orient in the Second Millennium B.C. Paper presented at The Aegean and the Orient in the Second Millennium. 50th Anniversary Symposium, Cincinnati, 18–20 April 1997.

Bass, G.F., Frey, D.A. & Pulak, C. 1984. A Late Bronze Age Shipwreck at Ka , Turkey. *International Journal of Nautical Archaeology and Underwater Exploration* 13: 271–279.

Bass, G.F., Pulak, C., Collon, D. & Weinstein, J. 1989. The Bronze Age Shipwreck at Ulu Burun: 1986 Campaign. *American Journal of Archaeology* 93: 1–29.

Bell, M.R. 1982. Mycenaean pottery from Deir el Medina (1979–1980). *Annales du Service des Antiquités de l'Égypte* 68: 143–163.

Bell, M.R. 1985. Gurob Tomb 605 and Mycenaean Chronology. *Mélanges Gamal Eddin Mokhtar*, Volume I. Bibliothèque d'Étude 97: 61–86.

Bernabò Brea, L. 1970. Thapsos, primi indizi dell'Abitato dell'eta del bronzo. In *Adriatica praehistorica et antiqua. Zbornik radova posvecen Grgi Novaku*, 139–151. Zagreb.

Bierbrier, M.L. 1975. *The Late New Kingdom in Egypt (c. 1300–664 B.C.).* Warminster.

Bourriau, J.D. & Eriksson, K.O. forthcoming. A Late Mycenaean Sherd from an Early 18th Dynasty Context at Kom Rabi'a, Memphis. *Ancient Egypt, the Aegean and the Near East. Studies in Honor of Martha Rhoades Bell.*

Bryce, T.G. 1989a. The Nature of Mycenaean Involvement in Western Anatolia. *Historia* 38.

Bryce, T.G. 1989b. Ahhiyawans an Mycenaeans – an Anatolian Viewpoint. *Oxford Journal of Archaeology* 8.

Casperson, L.W. 1988. The Lunar Date of Ramesses II. *Journal of Near Eastern Studies* 47: 181–184.

Cline, E.H. 1994. *Sailing the Wine-Dark Sea: International Trade and the Late Bronze Age Aegean.* BAR International Series 591. Tempus Reparatum, Oxford.

Cogan, M. 1985. The Chronicler's Use of Chronology as Illuminated by Neo-Assyrian Royal Inscriptions. In Tigay, J.H. (ed.), *Empirical Models for Biblical Criticism*, 197–209. Philadelphia.

Cogan, M. 1992. Chronology: Hebrew Bible. In Freedman, D.N. (ed.), *The Anchor Bible Dictionary.* Volume 1: 1002–1011. New York.

Cryer, F.H. 1995. Chronology: Issues and Problems. In Sasson, J.M., Baines, J., Beckman, G. & Rubinson, K.S. (eds.), *Civilizations of the Ancient Near East*, Volume 2, 651–664. New York.

Dodson, A. 1993. A New King Shoshenq Confirmed? *Göttinger Miszellen* 137: 53–58.

Dodson, A. 1994. *The Canopic Equipment of the Kings of Egypt.* London and New York.

Drenkhahn, R. 1980. *Die Elephantine-Stele des Sethnacht und ihr historischer Hintergrund.* Ägyptologische Abhandlungen 36. Wiesbaden.

Drioton, E., & Vandier, J. 1962. *L'Egypte,* 4th Edition. Paris.

French, E. 1965. Late Helladic IIIA2 Pottery from Mycenae. *Annual of the British School at Athens* 60: 159–202.

Furumark, A. 1941. *The Chronology of Mycenaean Pottery.* Stockholm.

Goetze, A. 1933. Die Annalen des Mursilis. *MVAG* 38.

Güterbock, H.G. 1983. The Hittites and the Aegean World I: The Ahhiyawa Problem Reconsidered. *American Journal of Archaeology* 87.

Hachmann, R. 1978a. Rapport préliminaire sur les fouilles au Tell de Kamid El-Loz de 1969 à 1972, avec un appendice sur des découvertes epigraphiques, par G. Wilhelm. *Bulletin du Musée de Beyrouth* 30: 7–26.

Hachmann, R. 1978b. Rapport préliminaire sur les fouilles au Tell de Kamid El-Loz en 1973. *Bulletin du Musée de Beyrouth* 30: 27–42.

Hachmann, R. 1980. *Kamid El-Loz 1968–70.* Bonn.

Hachmann, R. 1982. *Kamid El-Loz 1971–74.* Bonn.

Hankey, V. 1967. Mycenaean Pottery in the Middle East: Notes on Finds Since 1951. *Annual of the British School at Athens* 62: 107–148.

Hankey, V. 1995. Stirrup Jars at El-Amarna. In Davies, W.V. & Schofield, L. (eds.), *Egypt, the Aegean and the Levant. Interconnections in the Second Millennium B.C.*, 116–124. London.

Hankey, V. & Aston, D. 1995. Mycenaean Pottery at Saqqara: Finds From Excavations by the Egypt Exploration Society of London and the Rijksmuseum van Oudheden, Leiden, 1975–1990. In Carter, J.B. & Morris, S.P. (eds.), *The Ages of Homer. A Tribute to Emily Townsend Vermeule*, 67–91. Austin, Texas.

Hawkins, D. 1998. University College London Mycenaean Seminar, 14 January.

Hope Simpson, R. & Dickinson, O.T.P.K. 1979. *A Gazetteer of Aegean Civilisation in the Bronze Age*, Vol. I: *The Mainland and Islands.* Studies in Mediterranean Archaeology 52. Göteborg.

Hornung, E. 1964. *Untersuchungen zur Chronologie und Geschichte des Neuen Reichs.* Wiesbaden.

Johnson, W.R. 1996. Amenhotep III and Amarna: Some New Considerations. *Egyptian Journal of Archaeology* 82: 65–82.

Kaiser, B. 1976. *Corpus Vasorum Antiquorum. Deutschland.* Munich.

Kanta, A. 1980. *The Late Minoan III Period in Crete: A Survey of Sites, Pottery and Their Distribution.* Studies in Mediterranean Archaeology 58. Gothenburg.

Kemp, B.J. 1979. Preliminary Report on the El-'Amarna Survey. *Journal of Egyptian Archaeology* 65: 5–12.

Kemp, B.J. 1980. Preliminary Report on the El-'Amarna Expedition, 1979. *Journal of Egyptian Archaeology* 66: 5–16.

Kemp, B.J. 1981. Preliminary Report on the El-'Amarna Expedition, 1980. *Journal of Egyptian Archaeology* 67: 5–20.

Kitchen, K.A. 1986. *The Third Intermediate Period in Egypt (1100–650 B.C.)*, 2nd Edition. Warminster.

Kitchen, K.A. 1987. The Basics of Egyptian Chronology in Relation to the Bronze Age. In Åström, P. (ed.), *High, Middle or Low? Acts of an International Colloquium on Absolute Chronology Held at the University of Gothenburg 20–22 August 1987*, Part 1, 37–55. Gothenburg.

Kitchen, K.A. 1992. History of Egypt (Chronology). In Freedman, D.N. (ed.), *The Anchor Bible Dictionary*, Volume 2, 322–331. New York.

Kitchen, K.A. 1996. *The Third Intermediate Period in Egypt (1100–650 B.C.)*, 2nd Edition with Supplement. Warminster.

Kitchen, K.A. forthcoming. The Historical Chronology of Ancient Egypt, A Current Assessment. In Randsborg, K. (ed.), *Acta Archaeologica*.

Koehl, R. 1985. *Sarepta III: The Imported Bronze and Iron Age Wares from Area II, X.* Beyrouth.

Kohler, E.L. 1995. *The Lesser Phrygian Tumuli. Part I: The Inhumations. The Gordion Excavations (1950–1973) Final Reports Volume II.* Philadelphia.

Kühne, C. 1973. *Die Chronologie der internationalen Korrespondenz von El-Amarna.* Alter Orient und Altes Testament. Veröffentlichungen zur Kultur und Geschichte des Alten Orients und des Alten Testaments. Neukirchen-Vluyn.

Kuniholm, P.I. 1996. *Aegean Dendrochronology Project: 1996 Annual Progress Report.* Laboratory for Aegean and Near Eastern Dendrochronolgy, Cornell University, Ithaca, New York.

Kuniholm, P.I. 1997. Aegean Dendrochronology Project: 1995–1996 Results. *XII Arkeometry Sonuçlari Toplantisi, 27–31 Mayis 1996*, 163–175. Ankara.

Kuniholm, P.I., Kromer, B., Manning, S.W., Newton, M., Latini, C.E. & Bruce, M.J. 1996. Anatolian Tree Rings and the Absolute Chronology of the Eastern Mediterranean, 2220–718 B.C. *Nature* 381: 780–783.

La Rosa, V. 1992. Phaistos. In Myers, J.W., Myers, E.E. & Cadogan, G. (eds.), *The Aerial Atlas of Ancient Crete*, 232–243. Berkeley and Los Angeles.

Leonard, A. 1994. *An Index to the Late Bronze Age Aegean Pottery from Syria-Palestine.* Studies in Mediterranean Archaeology 114. Jonsered.

Lo Schiavo, F. & Vagnetti, L. 1993. Alabastron Miceneo dal Nuraghe Arrubiu di Orroli (Nuoro). *Rendiconti della Accademia Nazionale dei Lincei*, Series 9, vol. IV, fasc. 1: 121–148.

MacGillivray, J.A. 1997. Late Minoan II and III Pottery and Chronology at Palaikastro: An Introduction. In Hallager, E. & Hallager, B.P. (eds.), *Late Minoan III Pottery Chronology and Terminology. Acts of a Meeting held at the Danish Institute at Athens, 12–14 August 1994*, 193–207. Athens.

Manning, S.W. 1995. *The Absolute Chronology of the Aegean Early Bronze Age: Archaeology, Radiocarbon and History.* Monographs in Mediterranean Archaeology 1. Sheffield Academic Press, Sheffield.

Mee, C. 1978. Aegean Trade and Settlement in Anatolia in the Second Millenium B.C. *Anatolian Studies* 28: 121–156.

Mee, C. 1982. *Rhodes in the Bronze Age. An Archaeological Survey.* Warminster.

Mellink, M.J. 1983. The Hittites and the Aegean World II:

Archaeological Comments on Ahhiyawa-Achaians in Western Anatolia. *American Journal of Archaeology* 87: 139–140.

Moran, W.L. 1992. *The Amarna Letters.* Baltimore and London.

Mountjoy, P. 1993. *Mycenaean Pottery: An Introduction.* Oxford.

Myers, J.W., Myers, E.E. & Cadogan, G. 1992. *The Aerial Atlas of Ancient Crete.* Berkeley and Los Angeles.

Niemeier, B. & Niemeier, W.-D. 1997. Milet 1994–1995. Projekt 'Minoisch-mykenisches bis protogeometrisches Milet': Zielsetzung und Grabungen auf dem Stadionhügel und am Athenatempel. *Archäologischer Anzeiger.*

Niemeier, W.-D. 1998. The Mycenaeans in Western Anatolia and the Problem of the Origin of the Sea Peoples. In Gitin, S., Mazar, A. & Stern, E. (eds.), *Mediterranean Peoples in Transition. Proceedings of the International Symposium in Jerusalem in Honor of T. Dothan, 3–7 April 1995.* Jerusalem.

Orsi, P. 1895. Thapsos. *Monumenti Antichi* 6: 85–150.

Pålsson Hallager, B. 1988. Mycenaean Pottery in the LM IIIA1 Deposits at Khania, Western Crete. In French, E.B. & Wardle, K.A. (eds.), *Problems in Greek Prehistory, Papers Presented at the Centenary Conference of the British School of Archaeology at Athens, Manchester, April 1986,* 173–181. Bristol.

Parker, R.A. 1950. *The Calendars of Ancient Egypt.* Studies in Ancient Oriental Civilization 26. Chicago.

Petrie, W.M.F. 1894. *Tell el Amarna.* London.

Podzuweit, C. 1994. Bemerkungen zur mykenischen Keramik von Tell el-Amarna. In Dobiat, C. & Vorlauf, D. (eds.), *Festschrift für Otto-Herman Frey zum 65 Geburstag,* 457–474. Marburg.

Popham, M.R. 1970. *The Destruction of the Palace at Knossos. Pottery of the Late Minoan IIIA Period.* Studies in Mediterranean Archaeology 12. Göteborg.

Popham, M.R. 1974. Sellopoulo Tombs 3 and 4, Two Late Minoan Graves Near Knossos. *Annual of the British School at Athens* 69: 195–257.

Popham, M.R. 1990. Pottery Styles and Chronology. In Hardy, D.A. & Renfrew, A.C. (eds.), *Thera and the Aegean World III.* Volume 3: *Chronology,* 27–28. The Thera Foundation, London.

Pulak, C. 1988. The Bronze Age Shipwreck at Ulu Burun, Turkey: 1985 Campaign. *American Journal of Archaeology* 92: 1–37.

Pulak, C. 1989. Ulu Burun: 1989 Excavation Campaign. *The Institute of Nautical Archaeology Newsletter* 16.4: 4–11.

Pulak, C. 1990. Ulu Burun: 1990 Excavation Campaign. *The Institute of Nautical Archaeology Newsletter* 17.4: 8–13.

Pulak, C. 1991. The Late Bronze Age Shipwreck at Ulu Burun, 1991 Field Season: 'Ingot Summer'. *The Institute of Nautical Archaeology Newsletter* 18.4: 4–10.

Pulak, C. 1992. The Shipwreck at Ulu Burun, Turkey: 1992 Excavation Campaign. *Institute of Nautical Archaeology Quarterly* 19.4: 4–11, 21.

Pulak, C. 1996. Dendrochronological Dating of the Uluburun Ship. *Institute of Nautical Archaeology Quarterly* 23.1: 12–13.

Pulak, C. 1997. The Uluburun Shipwreck. In Hohlfelder, R. & Swiny, S. (eds.), *Res Maritima 1994: Cyprus and the Eastern Mediterranean, Prehistory through the Roman Period.* BASOR Archaeological Reports 4. Atlanta.

Rowton, M.B. 1948. Manetho's Date for Ramesses II. *Journal of Egyptian Archaeology* 34: 62–63.

Rudolf, W. 1973. *Tiryns. Die Ergebnisse der Ausgrabungen des deutsches archaologisches Institut.* Athens.

Shelmerdine, C.W. 1992. Mycenaean Pottery from the Settlement, Part III: Late Helladic IIIA2-IIIB2 pottery. In McDonald, W.A. & Wilkie, N. (eds.), *Excavations at Nichoria II: The Bronze Age Occupation,* 495–517. Minneapolis.

Tadmor, H. 1979. The Chronology of the First Temple Period. A Presentation and Evaluation of the Sources. In Malamat, A. & Eph'al, I. (eds.), *The Age of the Monarchies: Political History.* Volume 4.1: 44–60. Jerusalem.

Thiele, E.R. 1951. *The Mysterious Numbers of the Hebrew Kings.* Chicago.

Thiele, E.R. 1965. *The Mysterious Numbers of the Hebrew Kings,* 2nd Edition. Grand Rapids, Michigan.

Thiele, E.R. 1983. *The Mysterious Numbers of the Hebrew Kings,* New Revised Edition. Grand Rapids, Michigan.

Tykot, R.H. 1994. Radiocarbon Dating and Absolute Chronology in Sardinia and Corsica. In Whitehouse, R. & Skeates, R. (eds.), *Radiocarbon Dating and Italian Prehistory,* 115–145. London.

Vagnetti, L. 1993. Mycenaean Pottery in Italy: Fifty Years of Study. In Zerner, C.P., Zerner, F. & Winder, J. (eds.), *Wace and Blegen. Pottery as evidence for trade in the Aegean Bronze Age 1939–1989. Proceedings of the International Conference held at the American School of Classical Studies at Athens (December 1–3, 1989),* 143–154. Amsterdam.

Vagnetti, L. 1996. Espansione e diffusione dei Micenei. In Settis, S. (ed.), *I Greci: Storia Cultura Arte Società . 2 Una storia greca. I. Formazione,* 133–172. Rome.

Voza, G. 1972. Thapsos. *Atti della XIV riunione scientifiche dell' Istituto italiano di preistoria e protostoria,* 175–205. Florence.

Voza, G. 1973a. Thapsos. *Atti della XV riunione scientifiche dell' Istituto italiano di preistoria e protostoria,* 133–157. Florence.

Voza, G. 1973b. *Archeologia della Sicilia sud-orientale* (Exhibition Catalog), 30–52.

Voza, G. 1976–77. *Kokalos* 22–23, Volume 1, Part 2: 562–568.

Wace, A.J.B. 1957. Mycenae 1939–1956, 1957. Part V. The Chronology of Late Helladic IIIB. *Annual of the British School at Athens* 52: 220–223.

Warren, P. & Hankey, V. 1989. *Aegean Bronze Age Chronology.* Bristol.

Wente, E.F. & van Siclen, C. 1976. A Chronology of the New Kingdom. In Johnson, J. & Wente, E.F. (eds.), *Studies in Honor of George H. Hughes.* Studies in Ancient Oriental Civilizations 34: 217–261. Chicago.

Wiener, M.H. forthcoming. *The Chronology of the Late Bronze Age from Egypt to the Aegean: Science, Texts, Interconnections.*

Wilhelm, G. & Boeses, J. 1989. Absolute Chronologie und die hethitische Geschichte des 15. und 14. jahrunderts v. Chr. In Åström, P. (ed.), *HIgh, Middle or Low. Part 1.*

Wilson, J.A. 1951. *The Burden of Ancient Egypt.* Chicago.

32. The Late Cypriot White Slip I-Ware as an Obstacle to the High Aegean Chronology[1]

Manfred Bietak

A distinct tree ring anomaly, observed in America, Ireland and northern/central Europe can be dated to 1628 BC. It had been claimed by several scholars that this anomaly must have been caused by the enormous eruption of the volcano of Thera, an event which happened some time before the end of LM IA. What was originally only a suggestion became a firm dogma of many colleagues, despite warnings and counter arguments in particular by Peter Warren. As this subject also became a matter of hot debate at the 1995 Tufts colloquium, this notice from the excavator is meant to inform the participants about the context of Late Cypriot White Slip I pottery in the stratigraphy of Tell el-Dabʿa/Eastern Nile Delta. A White Slip I bowl had been found in the old French excavations on Thera. In the meantime Robert Merrillees was able to locate a second White Slip I-bowl from Thera in the Cairo Museum which purchased this object decades ago. (Merrillees kindly informed me of his findings and showed me photographs of the object). There can be little doubt about the association of this ware with the pre-eruption level of Thera.

In 15 main strata, the excavations of the Austrian Archaeological Institute in Cairo have revealed remains of a town dated from the beginning of the 12th Dynasty until the middle of the 18th Dynasty, with a distinct break at the beginning of the 18th Dynasty (ca. 1530 BC). Of particular interest is the presence of Middle and Late Cypriot pottery within this stratigraphy which shows that Egypt was in constant contact with Cyprus from the late Middle Kingdom onwards. White Painted III-IV Ware was present in the strata G-E/1, White Painted V appeared in D/3 and had a floruit in D/2. White Painted VI- and Bichrome-Ware appeared in stratum D/2 and continued into stratum C of the early 18th Dynasty. Proto White Slip appeared only in stratum D/2 and one occurrence only in the early 18th Dynasty. White Slip I has so far appeared only in early 18th Dynasty stratigraphy and not before (Hein 1994a: 42f. 12d, pl. 13B; 1994b: no. 248).

Let us concentrate on the evidence of the Proto White Slip- and the White Slip I-Ware. Their appearance is not based on just a single sherd but on multiple evidence. We have four Proto White Slip occurrences in (late Hyksos period) stratum D/2 (Bietak 1991a: 312 f., Fig. 288/4) and another Proto White Slip from New Kingdom fill which contained, however, only Second Intermediate Period material. We have five White Slip I occurrences in contexts of the Early 18th Dynasty together with other Late Cypriot pottery as Bichrome-Ware, White Painted VI-Ware, Base Ring I-Ware and Red Slip Wheel Made-Ware. The numbers and the occurrences showed that this is no coincidence. It is important to correct here a previous statement of a White Slip I occurrence in stratum D/2 in area A/V in Tell el-Dabʿa (Bietak 1991b: fig. 13; 1995: 21, fig. 1). The site supervisor, Irmgard Hein, showed that the sherd in question is from a later pit, cutting into stratum D/2 (Hein, in press).

The early 18th Dynasty contexts are well dated by scarabs with royal names from Ahmose onwards (Jánosi 1994: 32f., pl. 7A), as well as typical early 18th Dynasty pottery which appears in Avaris only after its conquest at the time of the takeover of the 18th Dynasty. If the White Slip I-Ware had begun a century earlier (before 1628 BC) it would have appeared in much earlier strata at Tell el-Dabʿa from stratum E/2 onwards. But until stratum E/1 we have purely Middle Cypriot as White Painted Cross Line Style and White Painted Pendant Line Style imports (Maguire 1993: 115–120; 1994; 1995: 54–65; forthcoming). This spectrum of Middle and Late Cypriot wares strongly suggests that the eruption in Thera did not happen before the beginning of the New Kingdom. This argument is even more cogent than the presence of many lumps of pumice originating from the Theran eruption at five sites of the Early New Kingdom in an area of 2.5 sq. km at Tell el-Dabʿa (Jánosi 1994: 35, pl. 10B). After many

Manfred Bietak, Institut für Ägyptologie, Univ. Wien, Frankgasse 1, 11 Wien, Austria & Österreichisches Archäologisches Institut in Kairo, Zamalek, 6A, Sharia Ismail Mohamed, Cairo, Egypt

years of excavation, it can be seen that no pumice of this kind has ever appeared before the time of the New Kingdom.

In the meantime, attempts have been made to bridge the gap between the beginning of the New Kingdom and the so-called scientific date of the Theran eruption at 1628 BC by pushing back the beginning of the 18th Dynasty to the beginning of the 16th century BC and forgetting that the first occurrence of White Slip I in Egypt dates after the fall of Avaris (ca. 1530 BC) and not from the time of the accession of Ahmose.[2] This would add to the gap another 18–20 years. K.A. Kitchen, M. Bierbrier, J. Von Beckerath and others have shown by studies of regnal and the dense network of genealogical data of Ancient Egypt that it is hardly possible to push back the beginning of the 18th Dynasty beyond the middle of the 15th century BC even without using the Sothis date of Amenhotep I which became a matter of controversy: this Sothis date is considered as insecure by Helck (1983 43–49), and Luft (1986: 69–77), while the value of this Sothis date is defended by Von Beckerath (1987: 27–33). Also according to the calculations of von Beckerath, however, the 18th Dynasty starts at the middle of the 16th century BC.

Even if one were to use the unlikely high chronology with the beginning of the New Kingdom at ca. 1575 BC, and a conquest of Avaris at about 1560–1557 BC, one could not reach the time beyond 1628 BC. It is also not feasible that the two White Slip I bowls reached Thera in the year of the eruption. One should go back to 1650–1640 BC for its earliest production, and this is entirely incompatible with any form of Egyptian and Syro-Palestinian chronology.

Therefore I see little or no chance for the high Aegean chronology to last. No proof has been produced so far that the Theran eruption is responsible for the 1628 BC tree ring anomaly. One kind of proof would be the identification of the origin of particles of volcanic ash from dated Greenland ice deposits by scientific methods. Another kind would be to probe for volcanic ash in Egyptian stratigraphic deposits. Both possibilities will be exploited in the near future. With the evidence of the appearance of White Slip I-Ware at Tell el-Dabʿa from the early 18th Dynasty onwards, I doubt very much that samples from a deposit around 1628 BC would reveal the fingerprints of the volcano of Thera.

It will give me great pleasure to have the lines above read in 10 years!

Note

1. This extracolloquial note appears at the request of the author, whose work at Tell el-Dabʿa is invoked by the contributors to the Aegean section of this volume. A more detailed report on this subject with a publication of the relevant pottery will appear (Bietak & Hein 1999).

2. Ahmose' mummy shows a man of about 30 years of age. He reigned 5 years and came to the throne as a child under the tutelage of his mother ʿAhhotep. This was surely not the time to think of an uprising against the Hyksos. As the predecessor of Ahmose, Kamose, was still in charge under the last but one Hyksos Apophis, Avaris began to be besieged in the 11th year of the last Hyksos (Papyrus Rhind, verso) and Ahmose could have started this campaign only an uncertain time after 11 years of his own reign. Paleographic features of inscriptions on spear heads would suggest even more than 18 years of his reign (Franke 1988), and not from the time of the accession of Ahmose!

References

Bietak, M. 1991a. *Tell el Dabʿa V: ein Friedhofsbezirk der mittleren Bronzezeitkultur mit Totentempel und Siedlungsschichten, Band I.* Verlag der Österreichischen Akademie der Wissenschaften, Vienna.

Bietak, M. 1991b. Egypt and Canaan during the Middle Bronze Age. *Bulletin of the American Schools of Oriental Research* 281: 27–72.

Bietak, M. 1995. Connections Between Egypt and the Minoan World: New Results from Tell el-Dabʿa/Avaris. In Davies, W.V. & Schofield, L. (eds.), *Egypt, the Aegean and the Levant: Interconnections in the Second Millennium BC*, 19–28. British Museum, London.

Bietak, M. & Hein, I. 1999. Die White Slip-Ware in Tell el-Dabʿa (ein Hindernis für die höhe Chronologie). *Egypt and the Levant* 9. Forthcoming.

Franke, D. 1988. Zur Chronologie des Mittleren Reiches, Teil II. *Orientalia* 57: 145–174.

Hein, I. 1994a. Erste Beobachtungen zur Keramik aus ʿEzbet Helmi. *Egypt and the Levant* 4: 39–43.

Hein, I. 1994b. Entries no. 248, 252. In Bietak, M. & Hein, I. et al., *Pharaonen und Fremde, Catalogue of an exhibition of the Historisches Museum der Stadt Wien, September 7 – October 20, Vienna 1994*, 217, 258. Vienna.

Hein, I. in press. 'Ezbet Helmi-Tell el-Dabʿa: Chronological Aspects of Pottery'. In *Proceedings of the 7th International Congress of Egyptologists, Cambridge Sept. 1995*.

Helck, W. 1983. Schwachstellen der Chronologie-Diskussion. *Göttinger Miszellen* 67: 43–49.

Jánosi, P. 1994. Tell el-Dabʿa- ʿEzbet Helmi. Vorbericht über den Grabungsplatz H/I (1989–92). *Ägypten und Levante* 4: 20–38.

Luft, U. 1986. Noch einmal zum Ebers-Kalender. *Göttinger Miszellen* 9: 69–77.

Maguire, L.C. 1993. A Cautious Approach to the Middle Cypriot Bronze Age Chronology of Cyprus. *Ägypten und Levante* 3: 115–120.

Maguire, L.C. 1994. Die Verbreitung zyprischer Keramik in der Levante in der Zeiten Zwichenzeit. In Bietak, M. & Hein, I. et al., *Pharaonen und Fremde, Catalogue of an exhibition of the Historisches Museum der Stadt Wien, September 7 – October 20, Vienna 1994*, 216–217. Vienna.

Maguire, L.C. 1995. Tell el-Dabʿa, The Cypriot Connection. In Davies, W.V. & Schofield, L. (eds.), *Egypt, the Aegean and the Levant*, 54–65. British Museum, London.

Maguire, L.C. forthcoming. *The Circulation of Cypriot Pottery in the Middle Bronze Age*. (revised Ph.D. thesis, University of Edinburgh 1991).

Von Beckerath, J. 1987. Das Kalendarium des Papyrus Ebers im das Sothisdatum vom 9. Jahr Amenhopis I. *Studien altägyptischer Kultur* 14: 27–33.

33. Aegean Late Bronze 1–2 Absolute Chronology: Some New Contributions[1]

Peter Warren

To return, yet again, to the absolute chronology of the earlier part of the Aegean Late Bronze Age requires justification, especially in a context which has the chronology of early Sardinia as a major focus. The Sardinian justification is rapidly given. In a mere fifteen years our knowledge of Sardinian interconnections with the Aegean has been utterly transformed. Lord William Taylour in 1958 could not record a single Aegean sherd from the island. One good illustration of our growing knowledge of the complexity of the exchange networks is the Cypriote pithos, now known outside Cyprus from Ugarit, Ulu Burun (shipwreck), Iria (shipwreck), Kommos, Marsa Matruh, Agrigento and Sardinia (Vagnetti & Lo Schiavo 1989; Karageorghis 1993: 581, 583–587). Meanwhile existing chronological interconnections between central and southern Italy and the Aegean in the Bronze Age have recently been carefully reviewed by Cazzella (1994), as have those of individual sites, such as Filicudi and Broglio di Trebisacce, by Vagnetti (1991; Vagnetti & Panichelli 1994: 411–413). At the same time the Aegean chronological position, exciting enough in itself, is now open to further advance, possibly to solution.

Dendrochronology apart, precision in absolute dating depends much on the area of study. Following Robert Tykot's setting out of the Sardinian sequence based on radiocarbon dates (1994: especially 129) I am discussing the time corresponding to Early and Middle Nuragic I, or Final Capo Graziano in Aeolian terms, broadly 1600–1400 BC. Egyptologists work with greater precision. When one reads the title of a 1994 article, "The astronomical evidence for dating the end of the Middle Kingdom of ancient Egypt to the early second millennium: a reassessment" (Rose 1994), one is apprehensive that fundamentals may be at stake. When one then reads the very detailed arithmetical discussion to the effect that the Sothic rising under Sesostris III may be dated not to 1872 BC but to 1871 BC, or, that worse, it may not actually be possible to get closer than 1870 BC ± about six years, one smiles with relief. In the Aegean and, I suspect, in Sardinia too one can live with that degree of uncertainty.

To come then to the Aegean. It is convenient to begin by summarizing the position in 1989. That was the year of the third Thera International Congress. Volume 3 of *Thera and the Aegean World III* (Hardy & Renfrew 1990) is devoted entirely to chronology, relative and absolute, in relation to the LBA eruption of Thera; in that year too Vronwy Hankey and I published *Aegean Bronze Age Chronology*. By then (and since) two absolute chronologies were being argued for Aegean LB 1–2. One, primarily that of Philip Betancourt (1987; Betancourt & Weinstein 1976; Michael & Betancourt 1988) and Sturt Manning (1988; 1990a; 1990b; 1991; 1992; 1995: 200–216) each in their own series of papers and book, was based essentially on the calibrated radiocarbon dates from short-life samples from the volcanic destruction level at Akrotiri, at first with support from the proxy evidence that a Dye 3 ice-core acidity peak date of 1645 BC ± 20 and frost ring damage to bristlecone pines in the White Mountains of eastern California in 1628 BC might, one or both, be products of the Theran eruption. Betancourt's tentative chronology for the periods under discussion was, therefore (1987: 47, table 1):

Crete	Greece	Dates BC
LM I A	LH I	c. 1700–1610
LM I B	LH II A	c. 1610–1550
LM II	LH II B	c. 1550–1490

Manning (1988: especially 56, table 10) is even higher: LM I A 1725/1700–1630/20 BC, lowered more recently to 1675/1650–1600/1550 (1995: 217), LM I B 1630/20-(1570/40). For the eruption, which we have known since 1989 occurred in later LM I A, the "most probable date" according to Betancourt was 1619 BC within a 1 calibrated interval of 1639–1600 BC (Michael & Betancourt 1988:

Peter Warren, Department of Archaeology, University of Bristol, Bristol BS8 1TB, UK

173). He has since proposed 1628 BC (this volume, and pre-conference abstract).

This paper is not intended as an extended review of the radiocarbon evidence for dating Thera, nor of the relevance or irrelevance of the ice-core and frost ring data. The recent availability of a refined version of the high precision calibration curve (for this period Pearson & Stuiver 1993) and the adoption of archaeological wiggle matching and probabilistic calibration to produce calendar probability distributions (e.g. Manning 1992: 248, fig. 2 for Akrotiri short-life samples) still leaves us, and one suspects always will leave us, with a significant degree of ambiguity in respect of the Theran radiocarbon dates. Manning, who has produced the most detailed current arguments for the high/radiocarbon chronology of Thera and thus too for Aegean LB 1, ends by repeating, as have others, the 1989 outcome of the Oxford Theran date series from the volcanic destruction: "there is about a 70% chance of a 17th century BC date, and about a 30% chance of a mid-16th century BC date" (1991: 255). To this one must add the currently unresolved and serious general radiocarbon problem of interlaboratory variability (Scott *et al.* 1984; 1990a; 1990b), as well as the specific problem of older contaminants affecting the dates of the Theran samples (Olsen 1987; Manning 1990a: 36: "this problem leaves a large question mark over all the radiocarbon evidence"). We note simply that the dating of the Oxford Series II samples, from which the contaminants had been removed, favoured a 16th century BC calibrated date range (Housley *et al.* 1990, especially table 6 Series II; cf. Manning 1990a: 36).

While the Theran calibrated radiocarbon dates as such indicate a stronger probability for a late 17th century BC date for the eruption and for later LM I A, they offer no more than that probability. Add the other ^{14}C problems referred to, both general and those specific to Thera, add too the fact that the Myrtos Pyrgos LM I B short-life samples have calibrated dates older than some of the Theran LM I A samples and the present limits of radiocarbon dating for the Thera eruption are starkly revealed. While more short-life samples from a wider range of Aegean LB 1–2 sites may be helpful, with wiggle matching and calendar probability distributions, I believe the inherent nature of the calibration curve or, rather, the horizontal wiggle at this time to be such that the future for Aegean MBA-LBA chronology no longer lies with radiocarbon dating.

With regard to the possible application to the Theran eruption of ice core acidity peaks and frost-damaged tree ring dates, in particular the evidence of the latter for a widespread climatic event in 1628 BC, we recall first the original case made by LaMarche and Hirschboeck (1984) and the fact of relatively poor correlation between these two kinds of data in relation to known volcanic eruptions (Warren 1984). From the data recently presented by Zielinski *et al.* (1994) from the GISP 2 Greenland Summit ice core and those of LaMarche and Hirschboeck, covering years AD 508–1965, we may note that of 11 eruptions with a Volcanic Explosivity Index of 6 or higher (Thera is estimated at 6.9 [Dekker 1990: 451]) only 2 have acidity peaks coinciding with frost ring events, 5 appear only as acidity peaks, 2 only as frost ring events, while 2 appear in neither record. Thus only 4 out of these 11 high VEI eruptions appear as anomalies in the tree ring record. (I am grateful to Dr. Paul Buckland, University of Sheffield, for discussion. See Buckland *et al.* 1997).

We also note that at the Thera congress in 1989 the amount of sulphur discharge from the eruption was estimated to have been far below that required to account for the Dye 3 acidity peak (Pyle 1989; 1990; Sigurdsson *et al.* 1990). This caused Manning (1990b: 92) to write in 1990: "for the time being, the conclusion must be that it is not appropriate to date the Thera eruption from either of these two sources of evidence." He has since argued that petrologic estimates of sulphur emissions may underestimate the amount of sulphur actually produced by an eruption, since the anhydrite indicator of high sulphur content of the magma may not have survived (Manning 1992). A negative argument that Thera may actually have generated a very large amount of sulphur, but that the critical evidence for such an amount has since dissolved, does not seem as convincing as the positive arguments against such a scale. Moreover the determination at the 1989 congress of the existence of a large Theran caldera already before the Minoan eruption (Druitt & Francaviglia 1990; Heiken *et al.* 1990, with reference to their earlier work; Eriksen *et al.* 1990; see now also Forsyth 1996) has the effect of reducing the cubic quantity of magma once thought to have been displaced in the Minoan eruption to 25–31 km^3 and at the same time supporting the arguments of Pyle, Sigurdsson and their colleagues for the (reduced) scale of the eruption.

A further potential complication for the Theran eruption as the cause of the 1628 event is the recently made case for another significant eruption in the Aegean itself, namely on Giali (Liritzis *et al.* 1996), though the TL date ranges for this eruption, attributed to the second millennium, are much wider than the date range for the later LM IA eruption of Thera.

While the future for Aegean absolute dating from the natural sciences does not appear to lie with radiocarbon dating, it surely does lie with dendrochronology. The remarkable achievements of Peter Kuniholm and his laboratory at Cornell are not yet at the point of establishing an unbroken Aegean tree ring sequence back to and beyond the time period under discussion here. But they are not far off and the speed of their dendrosequence construction has been such that we may be confident they will achieve their target, an achievement all the greater in that it will have depended on smaller tree ring runs and on matching a more diverse range of trees than the Irish and German oaks. Of course there will remain the tricky matter of then matching to the master sequence future well stratified and well dated (in relative terms) wood samples from archaeological contexts. Then our problems will be solved.

In the meantime we must note two points relevant to the date of the Theran eruption from the recent paper of Kuniholm and his colleagues, publishing the results of Anatolian tree ring sequences in relation to eastern Mediterranean chronology (Kuniholm *et al.* 1996). The first point is that the major climatic event in 1628 BC known from frost damage causing restricted growth of trees in eastern California and Ireland is argued to be confirmed by a significant growth *increase* in trees at Porsuk, north-west of the Cilician Gates in southern Turkey, dated to 1641+76/-22 BC from decadal, wiggle-matched radiocarbon dates. It is suggested that the eruption of Thera, 840 km away to the west, is likely to have been responsible, as having caused unusually wet and cool conditions and thus "a sharp reduction in midsummer evapotranspiration", i.e. retaining moisture for tree growth. Whether this abrupt climatic change was caused by the Theran eruption remains to be established. We shall see from the second point that Thera is most unlikely to have been the cause. This point is Kuniholm's and his colleagues' statement that the Anatolian (calibrated) radiocarbon dated tree ring sequence supports "either a Low or lower Middle" Assyrian and Mesopotamian chronology (Kuniholm *et al.* 1996: 782). This is a major chronological observation, in my opinion the most significant outcome of the Cornell Laboratory's current work, since it gives a wholly independent means of assessing the long disputed question of whether the high, middle or low historical chronology for that region is correct. The importance of this for the Aegean will become clear below.

This brings us back to the historical chronology, that is to the cross-links established by datable Egyptian objects in stratified or homogeneous Aegean contexts and Aegean objects with good relative dating in datable Egyptian contexts, including in this the important evidence of LC I Cyprus. The Aegean chronology thus derived, the so-called historical chronology, is in approximate figures (Warren & Hankey 1989: 135–146 and 169 table 3.1):

MM III B-LM I A border	1600	
LM I A	1600/1580–1480±	LH I 1600–1510/1500
LM I B	1480±–1425	LH IIA 1510/1500–1440
LM II	1425–1390	LH IIB 1440–1390

The material available up to 1989 has been very extensively discussed (recently Betancourt 1987; 1990; Michael & Betancourt 1988; Warren 1987; 1988; 1990; Warren & Hankey 1989: 135–146; Manning 1988; 1995: 217–229; Muhly 1991; Eriksson 1992). One element of it merits a further comment. Betancourt in 1987 and 1988 dated the locally made and decorated imitation of an Aegean squat alabastron from tomb SA 17 at Aniba (tomb dated to the time of Tuthmosis III) to LM III A 1 (Betancourt 1987: 46–7; Michael & Betancourt 1988: 170), thus allowing an LM III A 1/Tuthmosis III correlation. At Thera in 1989 he appeared to leave the position more open: "If the vase is from LM III A 1...... if it is from LM I......" (1990: 21). He then concludes that the vase does "argue in favour of" an LM III A 1/Tuthmosis III correlation (1990: 22). My own view is that the alabastron is certainly earlier than LM III A 1 and is an imitation of LM I or LH II A work (Warren 1987: 207–208; 1988: 176–177) and that it joins other early XVIIIth Dynasty/Tuthmosis III correlations with Aegean ceramics. Betancourt's overall conclusion is that the quality of the archaeological evidence as a whole is insufficient on its own to demonstrate the validity of either a 'high' (LM I A 17th century BC) or 'low' (LM I A 16th century BC) chronology. My view is that the existing LM I A-B/LH I-II B archaeological correlations in Egypt (eleven, including the Aniba alabastron), though superior in quality to the current Aegean radiocarbon dating evidence, do nevertheless require further support in order to be fully convincing. The main thrust of these connexions is that LM I B belongs to the time of early and middle Tuthmosis III (1479–1425 BC for his 54 year reign), though an earlier beginning for the period is quite likely, as discussed below.

The present paper therefore considers seven new pieces of archaeological evidence and includes two others of the previous eleven. It may be helpful first to quote the relevant early New Kingdom regnal dates, taken from K.A. Kitchen's basic papers (1987; 1989), noting that his high (NB *high*) chronology is used for the first four kings.

AHMOSE	1550 – 1525
AMENOPHIS I	1525 – 1504
TUTHMOSIS I	1504 – 1492
TUTHMOSIS II	1492 – 1479
HATSHEPSUT	1479 – 1457
TUTHMOSIS III	1479 – 1425
AMENOPHIS II	1427 – 1401
TUTHMOSIS IV	1401 – 1391
AMENOPHIS III	1391 – 1353

1. A blue frit figurine of a monkey with a cartouche of Amenophis II was found in an LH III A (not III A 1, *pace* Manning 1988: 36) context at Tiryns (Cline 1991: 34–38). Such a find might therefore take LH III A into the time of that king (1427–1401 BC) and the sequence evidence of the historical chronology, as we shall see, presents no bar to an early LH III A link with Amenophis II. But there appear to be no other contacts of his with the Aegean other than a monkey figurine from Mycenae and Cline's balanced discussion concludes that the two figurines are more likely to have been recent heirlooms arriving soon afterwards during the period of prolific contact under Amenophis III.

2. Hartmut Matthäus has recently argued (1995) that a significant change is observable in the depiction of two metal types, amphoras and jugs, carried by Aegeans in the Tombs of the Nobles at Thebes. In the tomb of Menkheperreseneb (no. 86) these vases display for the

first time a distinct band across the shoulder or upper body. Matthäus argues that this reflects the masking band used to cover the two joining parts of metal vases also for the first time in LH II B (Dendra tomb 12) and then also in LM/LH III A 1 (Sellopoulo tomb 4, Dendra tomb 2). Chronologically this would suggest that LH II B (and LM II) began in the later part of Tuthmosis III's reign (Menkheperreseneb), confirming the evidence of the well known LH II B squat jar from the tomb of Maket at Kahun, again within Tuthmosis III (Warren & Hankey 1989: 145–146; Eriksson 1992: 33–35 [clear re-argument for coffin 9, with LH II B jar, as one of the latest burials]).

3. The tomb of Menkheperreseneb also contains a ceiling pattern of rows of concentric diamonds in blue separated by a horizontal zigzag line in red, together with a border of more diamonds and alternating upright and pendent concentric chevrons (Barber 1991: 347–348 and col. pl. 3, lower left). Barber suggests this pattern is taken from LM III A 1, where there are ceramic parallels (Popham 1984: pl. 171, 4). There may be a connexion, through the medium of textiles, though the pattern does look rather simple and capable of independent creation. Any connexion would be with late Tuthmosis III, the date of Menkheperreseneb's tomb (*pace* Barber *ibid*. Menkheperreseneb was not the son of Rhekmire).

4. A much stronger case for interconnection comes from a ceiling pattern in the tomb of Amenemhet (Thebes no. 82), from early in the reign of Tuthmosis III (Barber 1991: 339 table 15.1). Here a complex design in interlocking quatrefoils in red, blue, green, orange, white and black is remarkably close to the complex blue and red interlocking quatrefoil pattern of the dress of the lady or goddess on the great LM I B fresco from Haghia Triadha room 14 (Barber 1991: col. pls 2 and 3 top left). As Barber notes, it is very likely that the ceiling pattern is taken from a contemporary Aegean weaving. This provides a connexion between early Tuthmosis III, i.e. about 1480–1460 BC, and LM I B.

5. Thanks to brilliant investigations by Christine Lilyquist a very fine LM I B bridge-spouted jug with spiral and arcade pattern, closely comparable in design to that of the taller bridge-spouted jar from Ta' annek (Warren & Hankey 1989: 142 and figs. 6–7), can be shown to have formed part of the contents of the 'Schatzhaus' (royal tomb) at Kamid el-Loz in Lebanon; Lilyquist was able to show that a body sherd with handle, which remained to be excavated (Miron 1990: no. 670 and figs. 82–83), was that of a bridge-spouted jug on the international art market (Lilyquist 1994: 207–208, figs. 33–34 and pl. 16). Her broad date for the 'Schatzhaus' objects is 18th Dynasty, pre-Amenophis III (i.e. within 1550–1390 BC), though she draws attention to parallels from the tomb of Kenamun, who was a companion of Amenophis II (1427–1401 BC) and to the alabaster and serpentine vessels as 'Tuthmoside', meaning the time of Tuthmosis III or somewhat before (1994: 217–218).

6. At Kom Rabia, Memphis, a sherd (RAT 530.1301) from the collar neck of a vase, probably a bridge-spouted jug and likely to have been LM I A or B, on the basis of its horizontal band of irregular small solid dots, was reported to have been found in a stratified context of early 18th Dynasty date above Second Intermediate Period levels (Bourriau 1989; cf. Warren & Hankey 1989: 139; Eriksson 1992: 18–19). Forthcoming full publication of the sherd and its context by Bourriau and Eriksson, in the volume in memory of Martha Bell, will replace Bourriau's preliminary account (1989). A date at about the time of Tuthmosis I for example would fit the traditional or historical date for Late Minoan I A; if the vase, of which only the collar fragment has been found, were Late Minoan I B, such a context date would slightly raise the time by which LM I B had begun (Tuthmosis I 1504–1492 BC). Body fragments are in fact needed before assignment to LM I A or LM I B or to any other specific Aegean ceramic phase is possible. For LM I A examples of the decoration, on jug necks, see Marinatos (1972: pl. 66a; 1974: pl. 78b and col. pl. 10 lower right) and Marthari (1993: 45 and pl. 58 [amphora 5245 – band of dots on collar between two solid bands, with a band of white dots on the lower solid band]; 45 and pl. 57ß [amphora 3702 – band of small dots on the top of the shoulder just below the collar rib]). For the decoration in LM I B see the collar of a tall alabastron with Marine Style octopus (Zervos 1956: pl. 560; Mountjoy 1984: 162, 173–174 Kn 1, and pl. 14a).

7. Saqqara Teti pyramid tomb NE 1, its objects including an LH II A alabastron and a late LH II A cup, is usually dated to the time of early Tuthmosis III (Warren & Hankey 1989: 144 (with references) and pls. 15 B-D; 16). Current discussion among Egyptologists (I am grateful to J.H. Taylor and Kathryn Eriksson for information) may suggest a date earlier in the 18th Dynasty for Egyptian objects in the tomb (coffin, painted jar, scarab), possibly of the time of Tuthmosis I. A date for late LH II A (= LM I B in Cretan terms) around 1525–1492 BC (Amenophis I-Tuthmosis I) would slightly raise and offer firmer evidence than hitherto for the date of the LM I A-B transition. If LM I A ended in this period a date of 1628 BC for the only slightly earlier mature or later LM I A of the Thera destruction (a date based on radiocarbon and the proxy evidence of tree rings and ice cores – see above) would be impossible. On the other hand an end for LM I A within 1525–1492 BC fits closely with a date around 1520 BC proposed below for later LM I A and the Theran eruption.

8. Tell el-Dabʿa/Avaris. Recent discoveries on the 'Ezbet Helmi I site play a fundamental part in establishing the absolute chronology of Aegean LB 1, since they offer

a combination of stratified and dated evidence of exceptionally high quality (Jánosi 1994; 1995). A large rectangular building, whose mudbrick foundation platform survived for excavation, was erected by Ahmose, conqueror of Avaris after the fifteenth, possibly after the eighteenth year of his reign, *i.e.* (with accession in 1550 BC) after 1535 or 1532 BC (Bietak 1996a: 67–73, 81 [for the year dating of the conquest] and fig. 55; 1996b). It must be noted that Jánosi's important and detailed stratigraphical analyses and observations (1994; 1995) are not in any way invalidated by Bietak's subsequent dating of the great platform to Ahmose; his sequence stands, only his and Bietak's previous absolute (late Hyksos) date for the building being superseded. This was the building (or some part of it) decorated with Minoan wall paintings. Abandoned or destroyed at the end of Ahmose's reign, the building was succeeded by workmen's houses just to the east (Jánosi 1994: 32–35 [Stratum IV], fig. 9; 1995: fig. 1; Bietak 1996a: 72, fig. 57 and pls. 30 A-B, 34 A). Their contents included a remarkable 145 scarabs, cowroids, amulets and small plaques, of which no fewer than 18 bore king names, from Ahmose to Amenophis II (Jánosi 1994: 32–35 and pl. 7 A; Bietak 1996a: 72 and pl. 31 A). These scarabs, moreover, were stratified in a sequence corresponding to the known order of king names and reigns, that of Ahmose lying immediately above the 'garden level', those of Tuthmosis III and Amenophis II in the uppermost levels (Jánosi *ibid.*). There was no later disturbance of these levels, which thus yield a sequence from Ahmose to Amenophis II (1550–1401 BC). In these same levels of Stratum IV, chiefly in the deeper ones, was found a large number of lumps of pumice, up to fist size (Bietak 1992: 28; 1996a: 76, 78 and pl. 34 B; Jánosi 1994: 35 and pl. 10 B). The pumices occurred in no earlier stratum, nor in any overlying level (Jánosi *ibid.*). Within the stratigraphy of Stratum IV Jánosi's provisional conclusion, with the evidence of the dated scarab sequence, is to date the pumice to approximately the time of Tuthmosis I (1504–1492 BC) (Jánosi *ibid.*). The broader limits are in any case after ca. 1535 BC (conquest of Avaris) and before 1401 (death of Amenophis II), though we note the position in the deeper, i.e. earlier levels of the fill of the houses in Stratum IV.

Samples of the pumice have now been analysed by Professors A. Preisinger (Institut für Mineralogie und Kristallographie, Technische Universität Wien) and M. Bichler (Atominstitut der Österreichischen Universitäten Wien) and shown to be from the Theran eruption (Bichler *et al.* 1997; Bietak 1996a: 78). Pumice came not only from the Helmi I site, but also from Helmi II and III, there too in early New Kingdom contexts. It might be argued that the pieces could have been lying around on the adjacent shore for an unspecified length of time before their collection and use some years after c. 1535 BC. Given (1) their quantity, (2) their sudden appearance at the site in three distinct areas, and (3) their confinement to a single level, such an argument appears improbable. Contemporaneity of arrival and collection becomes even more likely when we note that pumice is now reported from a second Egyptian site, Tell Hebwa, 15 km. east of the Suez Canal (Bietak 1996a: 78), where it was found on top of the last Hyksos settlement level. We have then evidence for the Theran eruption, and thus too for late LM I A, after c. 1535 BC (probably after 1525 BC, death of Ahmose), but no later than about 1504–1492 BC (Tuthmosis I).

9. Cyprus. Kathryn Eriksson, in her detailed analysis and critique of Sturt Manning's high chronology paper of 1988, has emphasized that the relative chronology of Cyprus performs the vital function of linking the Aegean sequence to the Syro-Palestinian and Egyptian (Eriksson 1992). Her detailed restatement of LC I A associations with the Near East and Egypt shows the impossibility of dating LM I A/LC I A from 1725/ 1700 BC, which Sturt Manning originally proposed. The relative sequence and dating of el-Dabᶜa is decisive: while Stratum D/2 of the main site, i.e. the final Hyksos level, contained Proto White Slip (Bietak 1996a: 76), and earlier strata White Painted Wares and Bichrome Ware (Maguire 1995; Bietak 1996a: pl. 26 A-B), the full panoply of LC I wares characterizes the immediately following early XVIIIth Dynasty levels of Stratum IV of 'Ezbet Helmi (Hein 1994: 42, fig. 12d and pl. 13B; forthcoming; Maguire 1995: 55; Bietak 1996a: 70, 76; 1996b: 16 n.35), after c. 1535 BC. Thus not only is the early 18th Dynasty the context of WS I and other LC I wares, but their relative date is also confirmed by the contextual sequence at el-Dabᶜa being in full accord with the Cypriot sequence. To this precise evidence we need only add two points, the presence of the well known White Slip I (LC I A) bowl at Thera (Niemeier 1980: 72–74 and fig. 44; cf. Warren & Hankey 1989: 116, 140) and the fact, emphasized to me by Vassos Karageorghis, that WS I had a short *floruit*, to be followed by the long period of WS II. All this evidence anchors the final town at Thera to the time of the early 18th Dynasty (1550 BC onwards), even if LM I A/Late Cycladic I began not long before the end of the Hyksos Period.

Finally the chronological significance of the links of LC I is emphasized by the Anatolian tree ring evidence referred to above. At Alalakh White Slip I and Base Ring I appear first in level VI B and continue throughout level V, with WS II from V A, if not already VI B (Gates 1987: 63–64 and fig. 1) (thus confirming the evidence from Cyprus itself for WS I as a short phase). Level VI B is dated 1550–1525 BC (Gates 1987: 75–79), essentially on the Low historical chronology. This is the chronology independently supported by the Anatolian tree ring data.

Most of the new Aegean LB 1–2 cross-links with Egypt given in this paper, like the earlier ones, are individually open to some degree of uncertainty and cannot individually offer convincing precision. The context may not be as tightly datable as we could wish (the Kamid-el-Loz 'Schatzhaus' for example), an object may be only a fragment (Kom Rabia 530.1301), or a pattern connexion may not appear completely convincing (Menkheperreseneb ceiling and LM III A 1). Yet taken together and *in their sequence* (cf. Warren & Hankey 1989: 137–138) the eighteen pieces of evidence now available, seven here being added to the eleven discussed in 1989 in relation to Aegean LB 1–2, considerably reduce the degree of uncertainty and go far towards establishing the validity of Aegean absolute chronology derived from the historical chronology of Egypt. Salient points, summarizing the above discussion, are:

1. The unexpected and closely dated evidence of the Tel el-Dabᶜa pumice and White Slip I pottery provides powerful evidence for an eruption date and for late LM I A around 1520 BC. The Tell Hebwa pumice appears to confirm this precisely.
2. Saqqara Teti pyramid tomb NE 1 may offer a date for the LM I A/LM I B transition in the last quarter of the 16th century B.C. (c. 1525–1490 BC).
3. Kom Rabia may show that LM I B began before Tuthmosis III (1479–1425 BC), or confirm that LM I A did. The context date may be close in time to that of Saqqara Teti tomb NE 1.
4. Then a number of finds link LM I B/LH II A with Tuthmosis III (notably but not exclusively Gurob tomb 245 – LH II A alabastron; Sidmant/Sedment tomb 137 – LM I B alabastron; Amenemhet (Thebes no. 82) ceiling pattern – Haghia Triadha LM I B fresco; Ta'annek LB I level, possibly of the time of Tuthmosis III – Late Minoan I B bridge-spouted jar (cf. Eriksson 1992: 16 and n. 74 on increasing evidence that Syro-Palestinian LB I may not be clearly definable before Tuthmosis III, being preceded by a transitional MB IIC/LB I phase).
5. The LH II B squat jar from the tomb of Maket at Kahun and the LH II B metal vase types in the tomb of Menkheperreseneb (Thebes no. 86) show that LH II B was in existence in the later reign of Tuthmosis III, i.e. from about 1440 BC.
6. A case can be made, indeed Philip Betancourt has made it, that LM/LH III A 1 had also begun before the end of Tuthmosis III's reign. I do not think the Aniba alabastron can be made part of that case (see above), but if the chevron-edged ceiling pattern from Menkheperreseneb is thought to derive from LM III A 1 the well known alabaster jar with its cartouche of Tuthmosis III from Katsamba tomb B could be added as a contemporary cross-link. This would then require LH II B to be set in the middle period of Tuthmosis's long reign, say about 1460–1440 BC, because the preceding LM I B also has links with his time (see above), even if it began a little earlier. But the case for an LM III A 1 – Tuthmosis III link is not particularly strong and everyone, except perhaps Sturt Manning, is in any case agreed that LM/LH III A 1 is closely linked to Amenophis III (1391–1353 BC) through the Sellopoulo tomb 4 scarab and succeeding LM/LH III A 2 Amenophis III links.

I therefore commend an Aegean LB 1–2 absolute chronology derived from cross-links to Egypt, with LM I A (and LC I A) beginning in the late Hyksos/Second Intermediate Period, i.e. around or soon after 1580 BC, with the eruption of Thera around 1520 BC, the LM I A-B transition around the last quarter of the 16th century BC and the LM I B destruction of Crete within 1450–1425 BC. Against this stands *only* a 70% (at best) likelihood of Theran 17th century B.C. radiocarbon dates for the eruption, with their specific problems.

Addendum

The above paper presents arguments against the 1628 BC climatic event as having been caused by the Theran eruption, here dated *circa* 1520 BC on the evidence of many cross-links to the historical chronology of Egypt. It was therefore with no small interest that I received the following information, dated 16 April 1997, from Professor Gregory A. Zielinski in reply to an enquiry about what I had recently heard of the GISP 2 Summit ice-core:

1. Zielinski and his team had found tephra in the same layer as the 1623 ± 36 BC strong acidity peak in the core (Zielinski *et al.* 1994);
2. He considers that the 1623 BC signal is from the same eruption as the 1628 BC climatic event documented by the tree rings;
3. The tephra in the core does not match that of Thera (not even the Thera eruption samples he has himself run for confirmation). I am most grateful to Professor Zielinski for communicating this fundamental information to me ahead of publication. See now Zielinski & Germani 1998. Thus liberated from any attachment to 1628 BC we are now free to return to the case for the (long argued) late 16th century date for the late LM I A eruption, with all its historical consequences.

Note

1. Because there have been significant developments bearing on Aegean Late Bronze 1 chronology in the three years since the Tufts Conference it seemed to me not useful to submit a paper which was not up to date. I have therefore made revisions to reflect the current state of research. The paper is complementary to, has some overlap with and is able to take account of more recent work than was available for a paper given to the Verona Conference (April 1995), *Absolute Chronology. Archaeo-*

logical Europe 2500–500 B.C. The latter paper, Warren 1996, concentrates on radiocarbon dating for the Aegean Bronze Age.

References

Åström, P. (ed.). 1987. *High, Middle or Low? Acts of an International Symposium on Chronology held at the University of Gothenburg 20th-22nd August 1987. Part 1.* Studies in Mediterranean Archaeology and Literature Pocket-book 56. Paul Åströms Förlag, Göteborg.

Åström, P. (ed.). 1987. *High, Middle or Low? Acts of an International Symposium on Chronology held at the University of Gothenburg 20th-22nd August 1987. Part 2.* Studies in Mediterranean Archaeology and Literature Pocket-book 56. Paul Åströms Förlag, Göteborg.

Åström, P. (ed.). 1989. *High, Middle or Low? Acts of an International Symposium on Chronology held at the University of Gothenburg 20th-22nd August 1987. Part 3.* Studies in Mediterranean Archaeology and Literature Pocket-book 56. Paul Åströms Förlag, Göteborg.

Barber, E.J.W. 1991. *Prehistoric Textiles. The Development of Cloth in the Neolithic and Bronze Ages with Special Reference to the Aegean.* Princeton.

Betancourt, P.P. 1987. Dating the Aegean Late Bronze Age with radiocarbon. *Archaeometry* 29: 45–49.

Betancourt, P.P. 1990. High chronology or low chronology: the archaeological evidence. In Hardy, D.A. & Renfrew, A.C. (eds.), *Thera and the Aegean World III. Volume Three. Chronology*, 19–23. The Thera Foundation, London.

Betancourt, P.P.& Weinstein, G.A. 1976. Carbon-14 and the beginning of the Late Bronze Age in the Aegean. *American Journal of Archaeology* 80: 329–48.

Bietak, M. 1989. The Middle Bronze Age of the Levant – a new approach to relative and absolute chronology. In Åström, P. (ed.), *High, Middle or Low? Acts of an International Symposium on Chronology held at the University of Gothenburg 20th-22nd August 1987. Part 3*: 78–123. Studies in Mediterranean Archaeology and Literature Pocket-book 56. Paul Åströms Förlag, Göteborg.

Bietak, M. 1992. Minoan wall-paintings unearthed at ancient Avaris. *Egyptian Archaeology (Bulletin of the Egypt Exploration Society)* 2: 26–28.

Bietak, M. 1994. Die Wandmalereien aus Tell el-Dabʿa/ʿEzbet Helmi. Erste Eindrücke, *Ägypten und Levante/Egypt and the Levant* 4: 44–58.

Bietak, M. 1996a. *Avaris. The Capital of the Hyksos. Recent Excavations at Tell el-Dabʿa.* London.

Bietak, M. 1996b. Le début de la XVIIIᵉ dynastie et les Minoens à Avaris. *Bulletin de la Société française d'Égyptologie* 135 (Mars 1996): 5–29.

Bourriau, J. 1989. Aegean pottery from stratified contexts at Memphis, Kom Rabia. Paper to the Aegean Bronze Age Seminar, New York, 15 February 1989, and to the Department of Classical Archaeology, University Museum, Philadelphia, 16 February 1989 (with acknowledgment to Dr. J.Bourriau and the Egypt Exploration Society).

Cazzella, A. 1994. Cronologia radiocarbonica calibrata e cronologia 'storica' nell' Italia centro-meridionale durante l'età del Bronzo. In Skeates, R. & Whitehouse, R. (eds.), *Radiocarbon Dating and Italian Prehistory.* Accordia Specialist Studies on Italy 3, Archaeological Monographs of the British School at Rome 8: 73–83. London.

Cline, E. 1991. Monkey business in the Bronze Age Aegean: the Amenhotep II faience figurines at Mycenae and Tiryns. *Annual of the British School at Athens* 86: 29–42.

Dekker, R.W. 1990. How often does a Minoan eruption occur? In Hardy, D.A., Keller, J., Galanopoulos, V.P., Flemming, N.C. & Druitt, T.H. (eds.), *Thera and the Aegean World III. Volume 2: Earth Sciences*, 444–452. The Thera Foundation, London.

Druitt, T.H. & Francaviglia, V. 1990. An ancient caldera cliff line at Phira, and its significance for the topography and geology of pre-Minoan Santorini. In Hardy, D.A., Keller, J., Galanopoulos, V.P., Flemming, N.C. & Druitt, T.H. (eds.), *Thera and the Aegean World III. Volume 2: Earth Sciences*, 362–369. The Thera Foundation, London.

Eriksen, U., Friedrich, W.L., Buchardt, B., Tauber, H. & Thomsen, M.S. 1990. The Stronghyle caldera: geological, palaeontological and stable isotope evidence from radiocarbon dated stromatolites from Santorini. In Hardy, D.A., Keller, J., Galanopoulos, V.P., Flemming, N.C. & Druitt, T.H. (eds.), *Thera and the Aegean World III. Volume 2: Earth Sciences*, 139–50. The Thera Foundation, London.

Eriksson, K. 1992. Late Cypriot I and Thera: relative chronology in the eastern Mediterranean. *Acta Cypria* 2: 1–72.

Forsyth, P.Y. 1996. The pre-eruption shape of Thera: a new model. *The Ancient History Bulletin* 10: 1–10.

Gates, M-H. 1987. Alalakh and chronology again. In Åström, P. (ed.), *High, Middle or Low? Acts of an International Symposium on Chronology held at the University of Gothenburg 20th-22nd August 1987. Part 2*, 60–86. Studies in Mediterranean Archaeology and Literature Pocket-book 56. Paul Åströms Förlag, Göteborg.

Hardy, D.A. & Renfrew, A.C. (eds.). 1990. *Thera and the Aegean World III. Volume Three. Chronology.* The Thera Foundation, London.

Heiken, G., McCoy, F. & Sheridan, M. 1990. Palaeotopographic and palaeogeologic reconstruction of Minoan Thera. In Hardy, D.A., Keller, J., Galanopoulos, V.P., Flemming, N.C. & Druitt, T.H. (eds.), *Thera and the Aegean World III. Volume 2: Earth Sciences*, 370–376. The Thera Foundation, London.

Hein, I. 1994. Erste Beobachtungen zur Keramik aus ʿEzbet Helmi. *Ägypten und Levante/Egypt and the Levant* 4: 39–43.

Hein, I. forthcoming. ʿEzbet Helmi – Tell el-Dabʿa: chronological aspects of pottery. In *Proceedings of the 7th International Congress of Egyptologists, Cambridge, September 1995.*

Housley, R.A., Hedges, R.E.M., Law, I.A. & Bronk, C.R. 1990. Radiocarbon dating by AMS of the destruction of Akrotiri. In Hardy, D.A. & Renfrew, A.C. (eds.), *Thera and the Aegean World III. Volume 3: Chronology*, 207–15. The Thera Foundation, London.

Jánosi, P. 1994. Tell el-Dabʿa – ʿEzbet Helmi. Vorbericht über den Grabungsplatz H/I (1989–92), *Ägypten und Levante/Egypt and the Levant* 4, 20–38.

Jánosi, P. 1995. Die stratigraphische Position und Verteilung der minoischen Wandfragmente in den Grabungsplätzen H/I und H/IV von Tell el-Dabʿa. *Ägypten und Levante/Egypt and the Levant* 5: 63–71.

Karageorghis, V. 1993. Le commerce chypriote avec l'occident au Bronze récent: quelques nouvelles découvertes. *Académie des Inscriptions et Belles-Lettres. Comptes Rendus*, 577–88.

Kitchen, K.A. 1987. The basics of Egyptian chronology in relation to the Bronze Age. In Åström, P. (ed.), *High, Middle or Low? Acts of an International Symposium on Chronology held at the University of Gothenburg 20th-22nd August 1987. Part 1*, 37–55. Studies in Mediterranean Archaeology and Literature Pocket-book 56. Paul Åströms Förlag, Göteborg.

Kitchen, K.A. 1989. Supplementary notes on 'The basics of Egyptian chronology.' In Åström, P. (ed.), *High, Middle or Low? Acts of an International Symposium on Chronology held at the University of Gothenburg 20th-22nd August 1987. Part 3*, 152–159. Studies in Mediterranean Archaeology and Literature Pocket-book 56. Paul Åströms Förlag, Göteborg.

Kuniholm, P.I., Kromer, B., Manning, S.W., Newton, M., Latini,

C.E. & Bruce, M.J. 1996. Anatolian tree rings and the absolute chronology of the eastern Mediterranean, 220–718 BC. *Nature* 381: 780–783.

Lamarche, V.C. Jr. & Hirschboeck, K.K. 1984. Frost rings in trees as records of major volcanic eruptions. *Nature* 307: 121–126.

Lilyquist, C. 1994. Objects attributable to Kamid el-Loz and comments on the date of some objects in the 'Schatzhaus'. In Adler, W., *Kamid el-Loz. 11. Das 'Schatzhaus' im Palastbereich. Die Befunde des Königsgrabes.* Saarbrücker Beiträge zur Altertumskunde 47: 207–220. Bonn.

Liritzis, I., Michael, C. & Galloway, R.B. 1996. A significant Aegean volcanic eruption during the second millennium BC revealed by thermoluminescence dating. *Geoarchaeology* 11: 361–371.

Maguire, L.C. 1995. Tell el-Dab'a. The Cypriot connexion. In Davies, W.V. & Schofield, L. (eds.), *Egypt, the Aegean and the Levant. Interconnections in the Second Millennium BC,* 54–65. London.

Manning, S.W. 1988. The Bronze Age eruption of Thera: absolute dating, Aegean chronology and Mediterranean cultural inter-relations. *Journal of Mediterranean Archaeology* 1: 17–82.

Manning, S.W. 1990a. The eruption of Thera: date and implications. In Hardy, D.A. & Renfrew, A.C. (eds.), *Thera and the Aegean World III. Volume 3: Chronology,* 29–40. The Thera Foundation, London.

Manning, S.W. 1990b. The Thera eruption: the Third Congress and the problem of the date. *Archaeometry* 32: 91–100.

Manning, S.W. 1991. Response to J.D. Muhly on problems of chronology in the Aegean Late Bronze Age. *Journal of Mediterranean Archaeology* 4: 249–262.

Manning, S.W. 1992. Thera, sulphur and climatic anomalies. *Oxford Journal of Archaeology* 11: 245–253.

Manning, S.W. 1995. *The Absolute Chronology of the Aegean Early Bronze Age: Archaeology, Radiocarbon and History.* Monographs in Mediterranean Archaeology 1. Sheffield Academic Press, Sheffield.

Marinatos, S. 1972. *Excavations at Thera V (1971 Season).* Athens.

Marinatos, S. 1974. *Excavations at Thera VI (1972 Season).* Athens.

Marthari, M. 1993. *Akrwt»ri Q»raj: h kerameik» tou strèmatoj thj hfaisteiak»j katastrof»j.* Doctoral Dissertation, Athens.

Matthäus, H. 1995. Representations of Keftiu in Egyptian tombs and the absolute chronology of the Aegean Late Bronze Age. *Bulletin of the Institute of Classical Studies* 40: 177–86.

Michael, H.N. & Betancourt, P.P. 1988. The Theran eruption: II. Further arguments for an early date. *Archaeometry* 30: 169–175.

Miron, R. 1990. *Kamid el-Loz. 10. Das Schatzhaus im Palastbereich. Die Funde.* Saarbrücker Beiträge zur Altertumskunde 46. Bonn.

Mountjoy, P.A. 1984. The Marine Style pottery of LM I B/LH II A: towards a corpus. *Annual of the British School at Athens* 79: 161–219.

Muhly, J.D. 1991. Egypt, the Aegean and Late Bronze Age chronology in the eastern Mediterranean: a review article. *Journal of Mediterranean Archaeology* 4: 235–247.

Niemeier, W-D. 1980. Die Katastrophe von Thera und die spätminoische Chronologie. *Jahrbuch des Deutschen Archäologisches Instituts* 95: 1–76.

Olsson, I.U. 1987. Carbon-14 dating and the interpretation of the validity of some dates from the Bronze Age in the Aegean. In Åström, P. (ed.), *High, Middle or Low? Acts of an International Symposium on Chronology held at the University of Gothenburg 20th-22nd August 1987. Part 2,* 4–38. Studies in Mediterranean Archaeology and Literature Pocket-book 56. Paul Åströms Förlag, Göteborg.

Pearson, G.W. & Stuiver, M. 1993. High precision bidecadal calibration of the radiocarbon timescale, 500–2500 BC. *Radiocarbon* 35: 25–33.

Popham, M.R. 1984. *The Minoan Unexplored Mansion at Knossos.* British School at Athens Supplementary Volume 17. London.

Pyle, D.M. 1989. Ice-core acidity peaks, retarded tree growth and putative eruptions. *Archaeometry* 31: 88–91.

Pyle, D.M. 1990. The application of tree-ring and ice-core studies to the dating of the Minoan eruption. In Hardy, D.A. & Renfrew, A.C. (eds.), *Thera and the Aegean World III. Volume 3: Chronology,* 167–173. The Thera Foundation, London.

Rose, L.E. 1994. The astronomical evidence for dating the end of the Middle Kingdom of ancient Egypt to the early second millennium: a reassessment. *Journal of Near Eastern Studies* 53: 237–261.

Scott, E.M., Aitchison, T.C., Harkness, D.D., Cook, G.T. & Baxter, M.S. 1990a. An overview of all three stages of the international radiocarbon intercomparison. *Radiocarbon* 32: 309–319.

Scott, E.M., Baxter, M.S. & Aitchison, T.C. 1984. A comparison of the treatment of errors in radiocarbon dating calibration methods. *Journal of Archaeological Science* 11: 455–66.

Scott, E.M., Baxter, M.S., Harkness, D.D., Aitchison, T.C. & Cook, G.T. 1990b. Radiocarbon: present and future perspectives on quality assurance. *Antiquity* 64: 319–22.

Sigurdsson, H., Carey, S. & Devine, J.D. 1990. Assessment of mass, dynamics and environmental effects of the Minoan eruption of Santorini volcano. In Hardy, D.A., Keller, J., Galanopoulos, V.P., Flemming, N.C. & Druitt, T.H. (eds.), *Thera and the Aegean World III. Volume 2: Earth Sciences,* 100–112. The Thera Foundation, London.

Tykot, R.H. 1994. Radiocarbon dating and absolute chronology in Sardinia and Corsica. In Skeates, R. & Whitehouse, R. (eds.), *Radiocarbon Dating and Italian Prehistory.* Accordia Specialist Studies on Italy 3/Archaeological Monographs of the British School at Rome 8, 115–46. London.

Vagnetti, L. 1991. Appendice III. Le ceramiche egeo-micenei. In Bernabò Brea, L. & Cavalier, M. (eds.), *Meligunìs Lipára VI. Filicudi. Insediamenti dell'età del bronzo (Palermo),* 263–305.

Vagnetti, L. & Lo Schiavo, F. 1989. Late Bronze Age long distance trade in the Mediterranean: the role of Cyprus. In Peltenburg, E. (ed.), *Early Society in Cyprus,* 217–43. Edinburgh.

Vagnetti, L. & Panichelli, S. 1994. Ceramica egea importata e di produzione locale. In Peroni, R. & Trucco, F. (eds.), *Enotri e Micenei nella Sibaritide. I. Broglio di Trebisacce,* 373–413. Taranto.

Vermeule, E.D.T. & Wolsky, F.Z. 1990. *Toumba tou Skourou: a Bronze Age Potters' Quarter on Morphou Bay in Cyprus. The Harvard University-Museum of Fine Arts, Boston, Cyprus Expedition.* Cambridge, MA and London.

Warren, P.M. 1984. Absolute dating of the Bronze Age eruption of Thera (Santorini). *Nature* 308: 492–493.

Warren, P.M. 1987. Absolute dating of the Aegean Late Bronze Age. *Archaeometry* 29: 205–211.

Warren, P.M. 1988. The Thera eruption: continuing discussion of the dating. III. Further arguments against an early date. *Archaeometry* 30: 176–179, 181–182.

Warren, P.M. 1990. Summary of evidence for the absolute chronology of the early part of the Aegean Late Bronze Age derived from historical Egyptian sources. In Hardy, D.A. & Renfrew, A.C. (eds.), *Thera and the Aegean World III. Volume 3: Chronology,* 24–26. The Thera Foundation, London.

Warren, P.M. 1990–91. The Minoan civilization of Crete and the volcano of Thera. *Journal of the Ancient Chronology Forum* 4: 29–39.

Warren, P.M. 1996. The Aegean and the limits of radiocarbon dating. In Randsborg, K. (ed.), *Absolute Chronology. Archaeo-*

logical Europe 2500–500 BC. Acta Archaeologica 67 = *Acta Archaeologica Supplementa Vol. I*: 283–290.

Warren, P.M. & Hankey, V. 1989. *Aegean Bronze Age Chronology*. Bristol.

Zervos, C. 1956. *L'art de la Crète néolithique et minoenne*. Paris.

Zielinski, G.A. & Germani, M.S. 1998. New ice core evidence challenges a 1620s B.C. age for the Santorini (Minoan) eruption. *Journal of Archaeological Science* 25: 279–289.

Zielinski, G.A., Mayewski, P.A., Meeker, L.D., Whitlow, S., Twickler, M.S., Morrison, M., Meese, D.A., Gow, A.J., & Alley, R.B. 1994. Record of volcanism since 7000 BC from the GISP 2 Greenland ice core and implications for the volcano-climate system. *Science* 264: 948–952.

34. Round Table: Introduction[1]

Fulvia Lo Schiavo

Relations between Corsica and Sardinia have been a reality for many years and François de Lanfranchi stresses that one has to look at the two islands, especially the south of Corsica and the north of Sardinia, as if they constituted one territory, from the Pleistocene period of the "Sardinian-Corsican land-bridge" and the phases of population of the Holocene and the "pre-Neolithic." He cites such examples as the trade of obsidian and flint during the Neolithic, and the tombs with circular enclosures (*tombe a circolo*) and the affinities between the nuraghi and the "*torri-casteddu*" for the following period - Copper and Bronze Ages - of which an outstanding example is Presa Tusiu.

As far as Sicily is concerned, Sebastiano Tusa shows the most recent chronological pattern from 3000 to 600 BC for Sicily and the Aeolian islands, based on a collection and critical analysis of all the absolute dates of Sicilian pre- and protohistory. The Sicilian chronological and structural references in relation to Sardinia are still open to discussion, especially those concerning the introduction and development of small artificial cavities as tombs, for which there is still no correlation; the characteristics and diffusion of Beakers; and the introduction of the two islands into the earlier Mycenaean routes.

With respect to the Aeolian islands, a summary of a published article is included. Written in 1986 by the late, lamented Maria Luisa Ferrarese Ceruti treating Sardinian material on the island of Lipari, it remains valid and accurate, both in the definition of a precise typological aspect and in its classification in a set chronological period, which turns out to be later than that of Kommos and earlier than the Nuragic sherds found in Carthage.

Concerning the Iberian peninsula, Antonio Gilman warns us against chronological comparison that overlooks the notion of historical process. Undoubtedly, throughout prehistory, many similarities can be observed between Sardinia and the Iberian peninsula, such as the presence of Beakers, of rock-cut tombs, of the geometric motives and concentric circles on the figurines, etc., but these do not represent chronologically reliable evidence. The affinities between *motillas* and the Nuragic citadels at this point allow us only to assume a similar economic and social structure. After the 16th century BC, the Iberian peninsula and Sardinia are increasingly important protagonists of trade in the Mediterranean (and in the Atlantic). In historical periods, with the foundation of Phoenician colonies, the parallels are so consistent that they can be called "standard".

The relations of Cyprus with Sardinia are now widely acknowledged and so is the presence in the latter of Cypriot Late Bronze Age products. There is still controversy about how to interpret the oxhide ingots on the western island, renowned for its copper mines. The explanation, according to Vassos Karageorghis, is to be found both in the relations between Cyprus and the Levant in general and between the central and eastern Mediterranean - where the controversy concerning "Shardana" as a tribe of "Sea Peoples" has yet to be settled - and in a broader perspective on the trading of metals, especially iron.

In the case of Crete, L. Vance Watrous has acknowledged and published ever since the late 1980s evidence of Sardinian pottery in Kommos. This is one of the most important discoveries in this respect during the last ten years of Sardinian archaeology. The importance of the contribution is due to the presentation of results of chemical and petrographic analysis, which offer extraordinary support to typological classifications and stratigraphic data.

It is also on Crete that Lucia Vagnetti and Maria Luisa Ferrarese Ceruti had already reported the presence of a typically Nuragic askoid jug (*brocchetta askoide*) found in a tomb at Khaniale Tekke. This find analyzed with respect to 'ethnicity' (Peckham this volume) now acquires special importance when considering the latest

---

Fulvia Lo Schiavo, Soprintendente ai Beni Archeologici per le Provincie di Sassari e Nuoro, Piazza S. Agostino 2, Sassari 07100, Sardegna, Italia

discoveries in Carthage. It was precisely in Carthage, during the excavations directed by Hans Georg Niemeyer, that Magna Køllund found three fragments of two or three Nuragic askoid jugs (*brocchette askoidi*) of the same type, stratified in a secondary position in the oldest inhabited levels; naturally, this not only stresses the efficiency of Phoenician trade networks from the western colonies toward the East, but it also suggests the perspective of local participation in the trade, perhaps sailing along the same routes already opened in the Final Bronze Age.

For this reason another extra-colloquial contribution was added to these proceedings: Susanna Bafico (1991) about the finds from the nuragic village of Sant'Imbenia, which after the excavations of the last decade is increasingly obvious as an incredible Phoenician emporium open in the Porto Conte roadstead on the northwestern tip of Sardinia. Phoenician, Greek, and Nuragic material are now being studied and whose beginning one could set at least in the early eighth century, earlier than that of Sulcis where a Greek Geometric motif painted on a Phoenician pot has been interpreted as datable to the eighth century (Bernardini).

Some possibilities of the "Sea Peoples" were briefly discussed (Cross, Mazar). Like oxhide ingots, this is another controversial subject that involves Sardinia on which entire colloquia can be and are held.

References

Bafico, S., D'Oriano, R. & Lo Schiavo, F. 1995. Il villaggio nuragico di S. Imbenia ad Alghero (Sassari). Nota Preliminare. In *Atti del III Convegno Internazionale di Studi Fenici e Punici, Tunis 11–16 nov. 1991*, 1: 87–98. Tunis.

Ferrarese Ceruti, M.L. 1987. Considerazioni sulla ceramica nuragica a Lipari. In *La Sardegna nel Mediterraneo tra il Secondo e il Primo Millennio a.C., Atti del II Convegno di Studi "Un millennio di relazioni fra la Sardegna e i Paesi del Mediterraneo," Selargius-Cagliari 27–30 novembre 1986*, 431–442. Cagliari.

Ferrarese Ceruti, M.L. 1991. Creta e Sardegna in età postmicenea. Una nota. In *La transizione dal Miceneo all'alto arcaismo, Dal palazzo alla città, Atti del Convegno Internazionale Roma, 14–19 marzo 1988*, 587–589. Roma.

Vagnetti, L. 1989. A Sardinian askos from Crete. *Annual of the British School at Athens* 84: 355–360.

Note

1. The purpose of the Round table was to speak of Sardinian material identified off the island, and of extrainsular material found on Sardinia – Eds.

35. Remarks on the Presence of Nuragic Pottery on Lipari[1]

Maria Luisa Ferrarese Ceruti

An examination was made of all the pottery found on the Aeolian island of Lipari that is considered to be Sardinian, both that exhibited in museums, and that kept in storage. Since not all of the pottery attributed to Nuragic manufacture actually is, selected groups were studied both of pottery or single fragments unmistakably from ancient Sardinia. They must originally have belonged to about thirty pots.

Most striking was the total absence of incised concentric circles, *a cerchielli ad occhi di dado* which characterize one of the salient moments of Nuragic pottery.

Overall, the Nuragic pottery found at Lipari consists of a limited number of forms and types, the most common being for foodstuffs, large pots with elbow handles and those with corded rims, *le olle a gomito rovescio e quelle ad orlo a cordone*, and askoid jugs (*brocchette askoidi*), especially large ones. There is only a small number of other shapes such as bowls and oil-lamps. All this suggests that rather than being a trade in exotic products, valuable for their rarity and not for their aesthetic value, it was a trade in the contents of these pots.

Metal is probably what motivated exchange between the two areas.

The fact that small boats figure as themes in Nuragic votive bronzes and in pottery as well shows that Nuragic peoples might have been more inclined to sail in ancient times than in more recent or modern times.

It is important to find the original site or sites on Lipari at which Nuragic pottery was found. The history of Lipari's acropolis has preserved only a small section of a settlement that had certainly been larger. It is no longer possible therefore to determine more precisely the real extent of Sardinian presence on the small Sicilian island. The fact that more Nuragic pottery was found in and around the '*alpha*' area is probably due to a different use of that area, which is now difficult to assess.

Sardinian materials are found on Lipari only during Ausonian II, and particularly in the stratum of activity and of the fire. This limits exchanges between Sardinia and Aeolian islands and places it at the end of Ausonian II, rather than before. The trade with Lipari might have taken place slightly before the use of decoration of incised concentric circles, *a cerchielli ad occhi di dado*. This assertion is supported by the absence of this type of decoration and the presence, on the other hand, of ceramics typical of the geometric type, such as the askoid jugs with a beaked spout, *beccuccio versatoio*, the bowl decorated with slip, *a stralucido*, and small pottery boats.

It is still necessary to define the relationship, if there is one, between similar decorative motives on the pottery of S. Angelo Muxaro and on Sardinian *ceramica geometrica impressa*.

It is highly probable that most of the Nuragic pottery found in Lipari came from the south rather than the north of Sardinia. Since the clay and its inclusions have not been analyzed, however, only hypotheses can be made, and they need careful verification. Such analyses would have been very important for a better understanding of currents of trade involving Nuragic Sardinia.

Note

1. Adapted from M.L. Ferrarese Ceruti, 1987. La Sardegna nel Mediterraneo fra il secondo e il primo millennio. *Atti del II Convegno di Studi, "Un millennio di relazioni fra la Sardegna e i Paesi del mediterraneo," Selargius-Cagliari, 27–30 novembre, 1986*, 431–42. Cagliari.

Reference

Contu, E. 1980. Ceramica sarda di età nuragica a Lipari. In Bernabò Brea, L. & Cavalier, M., *Meligunìs-Lipàra IV*: 827–36. Palermo.

36. The Sardinian Pottery from the Late Bronze Age Site of Kommos in Crete: Description, Chemical and Petrographic Analyses, and Historical Context

L. Vance Watrous, Peter M. Day and Richard E. Jones

The archaeological site of Kommos is located on the southern coast of Crete, on a natural harbor. Excavation there over the last 20 years, under the direction of Joseph Shaw from the University of Toronto, has revealed a Bronze Age town built around a monumental harbor complex, containing a large open court, a covered stoa, shipsheds, a wing of storage magazines and a residential structure (J). Finds from the complex, including a potter's kiln, a metallurgical workshop, stone ships' anchors and the largest collection of imported pottery known from any site in the Aegean, leave little doubt that Kommos was the main Minoan port town on the southern coast of the island. Ceramic imports found on the site come from the Aegean islands, Mycenaean Greece, Anatolia, Cyprus, Syria, Palestine, and Egypt, as well as from Italy and Sardinia. The imported pottery from the 1976 – 1983 excavations has now been published in the volume, L.V. Watrous, *Kommos III. The Late Bronze Age Pottery*, Princeton University Press 1992.

Description

During the 1976 – 1983 excavations some fifty-five vases from the central Mediterranean area were uncovered at Kommos. The great majority of these vases are impasto ware. They are handmade, slipped and well burnished. In shape and fabric they are utterly unlike Minoan wares. Preliminary petrographic analysis of several examples by Peter Day at the Fitch Laboratory in Athens (see Chemical and Petrographic Analyses below) have shown that their composition is volcanic/igneous, which rules out a Cretan origin for them. The color of their clay is usually dark, with various varieties of black, brown, gray and even red. Inclusions are numerous and include sand, dark grit and mica. The range of these vases is not large. They include collared jars, *dolii*, bowls, an amphora, and a kantharos. At least 14 of the vases are collared jars: six are *dolii* and eleven are bowls. The types of collared jar, *dolio* and bowl from Kommos find their closest parallels in Sardinia, at sites such as Nuraghe Antigori and Domu s'Orku. One gray ware vase, perhaps a pedestalled bowl, may be from Subappenine Italy.

Most of these vases have been found in clear stratigraphic contexts, that is, in floor deposits from the settlement and the harbor complex. Because these central Mediterranean vases were found together with other Minoan and Mycenaean vessels they can be dated relatively closely. The principal purpose of this paper will be simply to present the main examples from Kommos in chronological order. Vases are listed by catalogue number in *Kommos III*; numbers preceeded by a "C" (*i.e.* C5463) are the original numbers assigned to the vases during excavation. Unless otherwise indicated, these vases are taken to be impasto ware.

Late Minoan IIIA1, CA. 1420 – 1380 BC

The earliest group of vases, which *may* be of Central Mediterranean origin (see now below), dates to the early 14th century BC These vases have a fabric close to but not identical to the later impasto pieces. Their fabric has the same range of inclusions but is slightly finer and not as well burnished as the later impasto vessels. Whether this difference is due to geographic or chronological reasons is uncertain. The shape of the following three examples is uncertain; their decoration, medallions in relief, is unique at Kommos.

Dish? 1966
Dish? 522
Dish? 813

Authors' Addresses: L. Vance Watrous, Classics Department, 712 Clemens Hall, State University of New York, Buffalo, New York 14260 USA; Peter M. Day, Department of Archaeology & Prehistory, University of Sheffield, Sheffield S10 2TN, UK; Richard E. Jones, Department of Archaeology, University of Glasgow, Glasgow G12 8QQ, Scotland, UK

Late Minoan IIIA2 – B, CA. 1360 – 1200 BC
Bowl 1761
Dolio 1542
Dolio 1452
Amphora 1752 This vase is not made of the usual impasto fabric found at Kommos. The fabric is quite gritty, with some white and micaeous inclusions.

Late Minoan IIIB2, CA. 1250 – 1225 BC
Collared Jar 1343
Collared jar 1377
Collared jar 1423
Bowl 1424
Pedestaled bowl(?) 1425. The clay of this vase is not the canonical impasto fabric found at Kommos; it is gray, very hard, and slightly gritty. The vase was slipped and burnished and was probably wheel-made.
Large collared jar 1426
Cup? 1561
Kantharos 1697
Jug 1971
Collared jar 1426
Dolio? 1699

Chemical and Petrographic Analyses

Twenty-four examples of Dark Burnished pottery – the suspected 'Impasto' – from Kommos were examined by petrographic analysis and atomic absorption spectrophotometry (AAS). The aim was to characterise the paste of the ceramic in mineralogical and elemental terms; to assess their homogeneity as a class and to suggest provenance. The data obtained were compared to a large number of samples from Crete, the Aegean and West Mediterranean. This contribution forms a summary presentation of the material. Full petrographic descriptions and analytical data will be published elsewhere.

Chemical Analysis by Atomic Absorption Spectrophotometry

A range of eleven elements was determined by the usual procedures at the Fitch Laboratory, British School at Athens (Liddy 1989). Visual examination of the data indicates significant variation in the major and minor elements but relative uniformity in the concentration of the two origin-sensitive elements, Cr and Ni. Three groupings are identified tentatively:

1. 1770 (C4470) and 814 (C5731). This is a very distinctive composition: high iron (>12% oxide), low calcium (<5% oxide) and low sodium.
2. 1561 (C731), C843, 1424 (C863), 1377 (C1147), 1037 (C1520), 1543 (C3311), 1429 (C5465). High calcium (8–12.2% oxide), low iron (2–5% oxide).
3. 1968 (C469), 1293 (C1699), 1296 (C1900), 1696 (C2137), 1338 (C2928), 1542 (C3310), 1307 (C4625), 522 (C4936), 1426 (C5348), 1427 (C5349), 1753 (C6694), 1740 (C6710), C8173. Low calcium (<8% oxide).

In the light of the comparative uniformity of the Cr and Ni data, it is possible that all the samples were the product of a single region. That region cannot be Central Crete owing to the discrepancy in composition (especially Cr and Ni) with the reference chemical data for Central Crete. Instead one or more sources in Italy provide close comparanda, notably Sardinia.

The distinctive features of high iron and low calcium and sodium contents in Group 1, for instance, which have not yet been encountered in pottery on the Italian mainland, are shared by some of the 'local' material (identified as Provincial Mycenaean and one possible example of wheel-made impasto) found at Antigori and analysed by Jones and Day (1987). The match, however, is imperfect in that these Antigori samples have a very high nickel content. The Fitch Laboratory's data bank has only two comparanda for Group 2 compositions: one piece from Alghero (F131) and one example of Local Grey Burnished Impasto from Antigori (69). As for Group 3, some examples of Impasto previously analysed from Orroli and Alghero, as well as some Local Mycenaean from Antigori, present similarities, but it must be emphasised that Group 3 compositions, lacking distinguishing features, are found in, for example, Latium (chemical data for Casale Nuovo near Rome).

Petrographic Analysis

Two main groups were distinguished in the petrographic analysis, which we shall refer to here as 2 and 3. The members of chemical Group 3 are, with one exception, all members of petrographic Fabric 3. This is characterised by porphyritic volcanic rocks with zoned plagioclase varying from andesites to rhyolites displaying devitrification. This fabric is completely incompatible with a Cretan source, and originates in geologically recent volcanic deposits. The only related pottery examined in the Aegean have been from Aegina, but the present samples can be easily distinguished from those. Aspects of the mineralogy of this group have been observed in pottery from Sardinia. Jones and Day (1987) and Phillips *et al.* (1986) reported a related petrographic fabric from Ortu Comidu in Sardinia. The combination of non-plastics found in these samples is indicative of an origin in the area of Italy and Sardinia.

The second major fabric contains fragments derived from acid igneous rock such as granite, devitrified porphyritic volcanic rocks in combination with foraminifera microfossils and fossil shell. Although clearly separable from Fabric 3, this fabric was created by the mix of a fossiliferous, calcareous deposits with plutonic and volcanic igneous rock fragments. The presence in some samples of this group of volcanic rock fragments show at least a broad relationship with Fabric 3 in terms of its probable provenance. The high calcite content – notably the shell and foraminifera – account for the high Ca reading in the AAS for Fabric 2.

The combination of granitic and such volcanic rocks with fossiliferous marls is compatible with an origin in Sardinia. Granite and the Miocene calc-alkaline volcanics are present in most of the east and especially the central parts if the island.

Fabric 1 comprises two samples, both of which contain biotite and white mica schist, phyllite, polycrystalline quartz, epidote, foraminifera microfossils, chert, occasional plagioclase and quartz. This fabric has its origin in an area of low grade metamorphism, for these an origin in the Aegean cannot be ruled out and further work is needed. 1966 (C4470) was identified as being different by chemistry.

Fabric 4 is represented by one sample, 814 (C5731), which contains polycrystalline quartz, chert and rare schist in a red fabric. This too is markedly different from Fabrics 2 and 3 and is not incompatible with an origin in the Aegean. This fabric is very similar to Fabric 1.

Comment

There is excellent agreement between petrography and chemistry on general groupings of the materials (see table). These confirm that the majority of samples (Petrographic groups 2 and 3) do not have their origin in Crete or the broader Aegean area, but are likely to have been imported from the West Central Mediterranean, probably Sardinia, where there is good fit with geology and petrographic and chemical reference groups (analyses of Day and Jones in Jones & Vagnetti 1991). They are clearly different but related clay mixes, and may represent two production centres on Sardinia.

Fabrics 1 and 4 contain material of quite different origin, which may indeed be from a geologically metamorphic area of the Aegean. It is worthy of note that these samples are earlier than the rest, coming as they do from LM IIIA1 contexts (Watrous 1989).

Summary of Results:

Sample	REJ Group	PMD Group
C469	3	3
C731	2	2
C848 ?	2	2
C863	2	2
C1147	2	2
C1520	2	2
C1699	3	3
C1900	3	3
C2137	3	3
C2928	3	3
C3310	3	3
C3311	2	2
C4470	1	1
C4625	3	3
C4936	3	1
C5348	3	3
C5349	3	3
C5464	-	3
C5465	2	2
C5731	1	4
C6673	-	3
C6694	3	3
C6710	3	3
C8173	3	3

Historical Context

These Central Mediterranean vases signal a major shift in the pattern of international trade at Kommos in the 14th and 13th century BC. During the 14th century BC the principal overseas trade contacts of Kommos were with Cyprus, Syria, Palestine and Egypt. Late in the 14th century ceramic imports from these sources begin to fall off, at the same time as vases from Chania (in West Crete), the southern Peloponnese and the Central Mediterranean increase. By the middle of the 13th century ceramic imports at Kommos are dominated by the latter group. The shift in trade, in other words, is from East to West.

The cause for the drop-off of Eastern pottery at Kommos is not hard to explain, for the same phenomenon is also apparent further east. Cypriote pottery practically ceases to be imported into Egypt after the Amarna period, probably because of the Hittite assumption of control of Syria. Cypriote ceramics imported into Palestine also fall off sharply during the 14th century, apparently because of unstable political conditions in the eastern Mediterranean. The rise in western ceramic imports at Kommos looks as if it is a response to the drop-off of Eastern imports there. Maritime traders at Kommos may have turned to the western Mediterranean when Eastern harbors were no longer available to them.

What was the nature of this trade with the West? The collared jars and *dolii* at Kommos are closed shapes which would make them good storage jars. Their companions, the impasto bowls, normally have a diameter slightly larger than that of the collared jars and *dolii*, which suggests that they may have come to Kommos as lids on these storage jars. Italian and Sardinian sites are well known for their caches of scrap-metal, which were at times stored in vases, as the example from the Lipari Islands. Thus it is possible that the jars and *dolii* came to Kommos as containers of scrap-metal. This suggestion is strengthened by the fact that metal-working was an important activity at Kommos during the LM III A2 – B period. Moreover, the vases have actually been found in metal-working areas on the site. It is therefore tempting to interpret these Central Mediterranean vases as indicators of a 14th and 13th century metals trade between Kommos and the Central Mediterranean, particularly with Sardinia.

References

Jones, R.E. & Day, P.M. 1987. Late Bronze Age Aegean and Cypriot-type Pottery in Sardinia – Identification of Imports and Local Imitations. In Balmuth, M.S. (ed.), *Nuragic Sardinia and the Mycenaean World*. BAR International Series 387: 257–70. British Archaeological Reports, Oxford.

Jones, R.E. & Vagnetti, L. 1991. Traders and craftsmen in the Central Mediterranean: archaeological evidence and archaeometric research. In Gale, N.H. (ed.), *Bronze Age Trade in the Mediterranean*. Studies in Mediterranean Archaeology 90: 127–147. Paul Åströms Forlag, Jonsered.

Liddy, D.J. 1989. A provenance study of decorated pottery from an Iron Age cemetery at Knossos, Crete. In Maniatis, Y. (ed.), *Archaeometry: Proceedings of the 25th International Archaeometry Symposium, Amsterdam*, 559–570. Elsevier.

Phillips, P., Nicholson P., & Patterson, H. 1987. La ceramica nuragica di 'Ortu Comidu.' In *Atti del II Convegno di studi "Un millennio di relazioni fra la Sardegne e i Paesi del Mediterraneo," Selargius-Cagliari, 27–30 novembre, 1986*, 225–32. Selargius.

Watrous, L.V. 1989. A preliminary report on imported 'Italian' wares from the Late Bronze Age site of Kommos on Crete. *Studi Micenei ed Egeo Anatolici* 27: 69–79.

37. Protocolonizzazione fenicia in Sardegna

Piero Bartoloni

In tempi molto recenti è stato ampio argomento di studio e si è anche discusso a lungo attorno a quel periodo particolarmente importante della cosiddetta diaspora fenicia verso l'Occidente mediterraneo (Bartoloni 1995: 245–59; Garbini 1995: 195–201), che si pone tra la fine del Secondo e gli inizi del Primo millennio a.C. L'arco di tempo considerato in questa sede riveste grande interesse poichè costituisce il perno per la storia dei Fenici in Occidente e rappresenta una svolta nei costumi e nelle attività non solo di questo popolo e, quindi, anche nei suoi modi di commercio, ma anche dalle popolazioni occidentali entrate in loro contatto e quindi da questo aperte alla storia.

La messe di scoperte archeologiche effettuata nell'ultimo decennio soprattutto nel Mediterraneo centro-occidentale ha consentito un notevole balzo in avanti degli studi e, per quanto riguarda la scuola italiana, in modo particolare di quelli afferenti alla civiltà fenicia e punica nella Sardegna. L'esegesi dei materiali, in comparazione con le fonti storiche e con quanto emerso nelle regioni anche più distanti del Mediterraneo, ha permesso di avanzare nuove proposte, sviluppatesi soprattutto negli ultimi anni (Aubet 1994: 145–72; Bondì 1979: 163–225; Moscati 1983: 1–7).

Un importante supporto è offerto dalla ceramica fenicia e in particolare di quella prodotta nella madre patria, della quale tuttavia ancora non si conoscono che pochi aspetti, legati alla casualità dei ritrovamenti (Seeden 1991: 39–87; Moscati 1993: 147–52; Bartoloni 1993: 153–56) e quindi dovuti talvolta a studi di materiali fuori contesto. È da poco più di dieci anni che il quadro delle conoscenze va ampliandosi, soprattutto grazie al compianto William Culican e a Patricia Maynor Bikai, ma senza dubbio anche ad opera di altri validi studiosi (Bikai 1978; 1987; Anderson 1988), quantunque sia ben lontano dall'essere del tutto chiaro e completo.

Come accennato, diversa è la situazione che riguarda lo stato degli studi della ceramica fenicia di Occidente, che deve la sua identità e la sua omogeneità ad un contesto sociale ed economico abbastanza unitario e non a una congerie di componenti etniche. Si fa riferimento in modo particolare agli esiti della ceramica fenicia orientale importata negli insediamenti della Penisola iberica meridionale e qui felicemente rielaborata dall'ambiente tartessico o irradiata verso i fondaci del Mediterraneo centrale in un itinerario a ritroso (Aubet 1989).

Tuttavia, ad un'analisi attenta delle pur scarse testimonianze si possono riconoscere ad iniziare dalla prima età del ferro quattro grandi correnti commerciali e culturali protese verso occidente provenienti dall'area siro-palestinese, definita talvolta 'levantina' (Buchner 1978: 130–37; Garbini 1978: 143–50; 1988: 235–42). La prima e più settentrionale, che chiameremo per convenzione 'aramea' o 'nord-siriana', sembra avere origine dai centri della costa nord-siriana, tra i quali ad esempio Al Mina, Ras Ibn Hani, Ras el Basit o il più meridionale Tell Sukas, tradizionali porti fluviali di Oriente (Bartoloni 1995: 248–49). Questa corrente risulta composta soprattutto da elementi nord-siriani e aramei, con alcuni fenici, e riceve probabile impulso dai sovrani damasceni (Garbini 1993b). La seconda, invece, che denomineremo in questo caso 'filistea', in pratica è contemporanea alla prima e sembra aver fatto perno soprattutto sui centri della Palestina a sud del Carmelo e, al pari della corrente 'nord-siriana', è entrata presto in contatto commerciale con il mondo greco (Garbini 1988: 235–42; 1993c: 220–21; Waldbaum 1994: 53–66). Come rilevato da Sandro Filippo Bondì, queste due prime correnti, assieme agli apporti etnici e culturali prima micenei e poi euboici e rodii, danno origine a quel filone, denominabile 'egeo', che domina i mercati del Levante e

---

Piero Bartoloni, Istituto per la Civiltà Fenicia e Punica – Consiglio Nazionale delle Ricerche; Istituto di Archeologia e Storia dell'Arte Antica dell'Università di Urbino, Via del Balestriere n. 2, 61029 Roma-Urbino, Italia

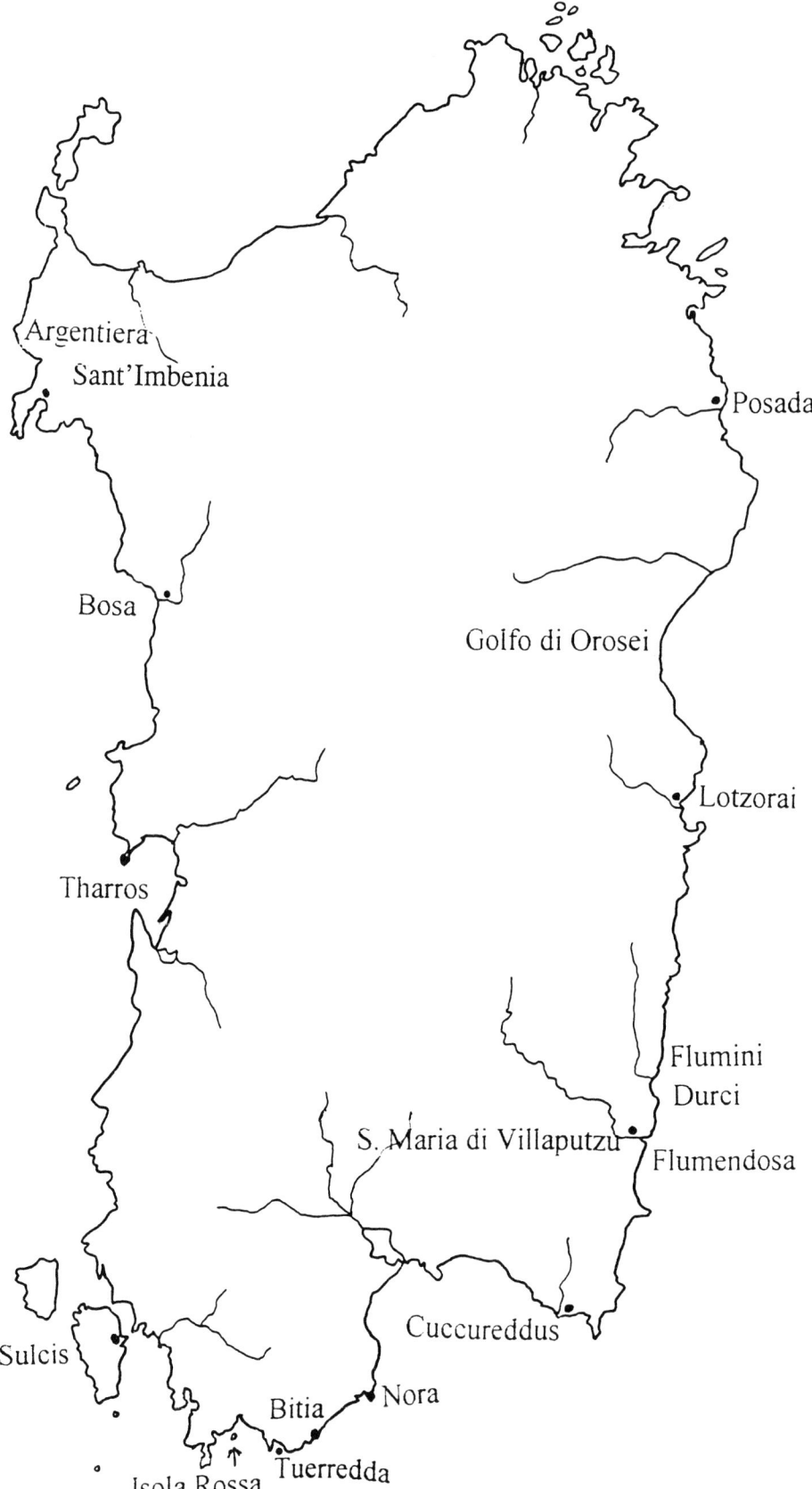

Fig. 37.1. Sardegna

dell'Occidente dal Tardo Bronzo fino alla metà dell'VIII sec. a.C. (Bondì 1987: 129–45, 436–40; 1988: 243–55).

Dalla Fenicia vera e propria hanno invece origine le ultime due correnti, una delle quali potremo chiamare convenzionalmente 'sidonia' unicamente per distinguerla dalla successiva. Si usa il termine di 'sidonia' con riferimento alla posizione egemonica che questa città ebbe verso la fine del Secondo Millennio a.C. Questa corrente dunque si distingue in modo particolare poiché appare attiva verso la fine del IX sec. a.C. ed è impinguata da una componente cipriota (Garbini 1980: 117–23, 133–34; Baurain 1988: 15–27; Bisi 1988: 29–41; Botto 1990).

L'ultima corrente, che denomineremo invece 'tiria' nasce probabilmente con il concorso di tutti i centri costieri del Libano, forse riuniti appunto sotto la supremazia tiria. E, come giustamente ha riaffermato Giovanni Garbini, è proprio il mondo greco che, definendoli tutti indistintamente Phoinikes, unificò in una sincronia fittizia le componenti di questi quattro gruppi vicino-orientali (Garbini 1993a: 184; 1993b).

Che vi sia un divario anche etnico tra i diversi gruppi appare ancor più manifesto, soprattutto per quanto riguarda quelli realmente fenici, se si considererà il diverso rituale funerario predominante nelle due comunità, che nel caso dei Fenicio-Ciprioti di Cartagine è quello dell'inumazione e, invece, per quanto riguarda la maggior parte dei Fenici di Occidente è l'incinerazione (Bartoloni 1981: 13–29).

Sostanziale è anche la differenza di approccio verso Occidente, poichè, nel caso delle prime due correnti, si tratta solo di attività connesse con imprese commerciali, mentre nel caso delle correnti più propriamente fenicie siamo ormai di fronte a veri e propri stanziamenti coloniali, che a questo punto sembrano differire minimamente dalle colonie di popolamento greche. Inoltre, l'ultima corrente, cioè quella denominata 'tiria', si sviluppa e si radica nelle colonie in due momenti diversi e ben distinguibili. Una prima ondata è composta da elementi facenti parte di imprese organizzate e quindi non necessariamente indigenti e si insedia palesemente, a seconda dei luoghi, tra il secondo terzo e la fine dell'VIII sec. a.C. La seconda ondata invece è una diretta conseguenza della politica assira nei confronti delle città situate lungo la costa del Levante e, composta in questo caso da elementi più eterogenei e di varia estrazione sociale, si stanzia nelle colonie nella seconda metà del VII sec. a.C. L'interesse di questi eventi è anche nel pur breve iato che divide i due momenti, iato che è quantificabile in poco meno di un cinquantennio e che sottintende un deterioramento dei primi insediamenti il quale risulta già evidente nel secondo quarto del VII sec. a.C. (Bondì 1995: 37–38).

Si noterà che, mentre le prime due correnti 'nord-siriana' e 'filistea' sono attive soprattutto tra il XII e il IX sec. a.C. e sembrano etnicamente più differenziate e composite, quella 'sidonia' non sembra consolidata fino alla fine del IX sec. a.C. Questa cronologia è valida solo per questa corrente, che vede anche la partecipazione cipriota e che in effetti si concretizza almeno apparentemente solo con la fondazione di Cartagine, nello scorcio del IX sec. a.C. Invece, per quanto riguarda la corrente definita 'tiria', la sua azione a prima vista diventa palese non prima del secondo terzo dell'VIII sec. a.C. Questa corrente, che forse è più omogenea etnicamente se non politicamente, appare stanziata soprattutto in Sardegna, in Sicilia e nella Penisola Iberica. Una presenza cipriota è comunque registrabile anche nei secoli precedenti il IX, come si evince dai dati non abbondanti ma significativi che sono stati raccolti lungo le coste italiane (Lo Schiavo et al. 1985: 1–71). La scarsità di reperti fittili e di converso l'abbondanza di bronzi, lavorati e non, ci suggeriscono forse che, almeno in questo periodo, questi materiali non furono necessariamente trasportati dai loro produttori, ma costituirono parte dei carichi di armatori nord-siriani o filistei.

Se si analizzano brevemente le testimonianze lasciate dalla prima corrente, si potrà osservare la presenza di una forte componente aramaica, che, unita a quella rodia e a quella euboica, si trasferisce nel mondo occidentale ed è visibile in modo palese fino a Pithekoussai (Ridgway 1983: 71, 76; Garbini 1993b: 184–88). A onor del vero anche in questa fase non manca una componente di marca propriamente fenicia, ma è del tutto minoritaria. Infatti, sempre nell'isola campana, i materiali veramente fenici sono decisamente in numero assai scarso, appartengono soprattutto all'orizzonte LGII e in buona parte alla classe della *red slip*, che, oltre al resto, può essere considerata un prodotto a diffusione internazionale (Buchner 1981: 268; Ridgway 1984: 149; Maas-Lindemann 1990: 169–77; Moscati 1992: 54–55) e quindi portato e utilizzato da una qualsiasi delle componenti. A questo punto occorre solo osservare come non sia un caso che anche nei centri costieri nord-siriani, quali ad esempio Al Mina, la ceramica di produzione realmente fenicia invece sia ben poco rappresentata (du Plat Taylor 1959: 79–86).

Queste correnti commerciali orientali sono desumibili tra l'altro attraverso l'esame dell'insediamento di Pithekoussai. Come è noto, il fondaco ebbe la sua stagione felice per circa un cinquantennio per poi declinare rapidamente in concomitanza con la fondazione di Cuma (Ridgway 1984: 134–35). Come già accennato, la storia del sito e i suoi materiali risultano un eccellente esempio della corrente commerciale proveniente dall'area nord-siriana.

L'insediamento di Pithekoussai rappresenta uno degli ultimi esempi ai quali partecipa la corrente nord-siriana, che sembra esaurirsi nel momento in cui l'elemento euboico passò dalla fase mercantile a quella coloniale. Quindi il centro pithekousano costituisce probabilmente l'ultimo insediamento a noi noto con vocazione commerciale a carattere 'misto' (Moscati 1988: 137) piuttosto che la prima colonia greca di popolamento in Italia, caratteristica questa che può essere rivendicata con maggior diritto da Cuma.

Che le rotte percorse fino ai primi decenni dell'VIII sec. a.C. fossero in parte diverse da quelle tracciate nella seconda metà del secolo e poi in quelli successivi è strato già adombrato più volte, ma le prove archeologiche ci derivano ormai da numerosi indizi che riguardano tutto l'Occidente e soprattutto la Sardegna, in qualità di meta finale o di luogo di transito verso Occidente. Per quanto riguarda la costa nord-africana a Occidente di Cartagine, rari sono i fondaci che alludono a insediamenti precoloniali e per di più spesso sono privi di sovrapposizioni di età arcaica (Moscati 1994: 67–69). Questa situazione sembra dimostrare differenze di approccio e diversità di intenti tra le correnti commerciali e di popolamento che toccarono la costa del Nord-Africa. Non si possono certo escludere anche i mutamenti delle condizioni geografiche, ma è assai probabile che il luogo che si prestava all'installazione di un fondaco non fosse adatto ad accogliere un impianto di tipo urbano. Ad una prima analisi si può forse intuire da parte degli elementi indigeni una certa resistenza agli insediamenti di popolamento, situazione alla quale sembrano alludere le vicende leggendarie legate alla fondazione di Cartagine, o forse si può arguire che una mancanza di risorse che abbia dirottato i primi insediamenti stabili.

La sovrapposizione degli insediamenti fenici ai fondaci precoloniali presuppone che questi ultimi fossero ubicati in bacini le cui risorse fossero sufficienti anche per i nuovi abitanti. I fondaci precoloniali che per i motivi più diversi non risposero a questi requisiti, quali ad esempio le mutate condizioni morfologiche della costa o le insufficienti risorse agricole, furono necessariamente abbandonati dopo un lasso di tempo più o meno breve. Si intende dunque che quella che potremo chiamare 'fenicizzazione', e che fu una sovrapposizione, avvenne quasi sempre ma che i luoghi non rispondenti ai requisiti richiesti furono abbandonati in tempi probabilmente diversi e comunque non necessariamente contemporanei. Si veda ad esempio il fondaco di Sant'Imbenia (Fig. 37.1), del quale si tratterà anche in seguito, il quale, se cronologicamente è attivo ancora in epoca coloniale, invece, per quanto riguarda l'aspetto culturale ed economico ha caratteristiche assolutamente precoloniali. Tra i requisiti indispensabili ad una colonizzazione infatti vi era non solo un buon porto, ma soprattutto un retroterra fertile e produttivo.

Non possono essere attribuiti solo all'azione di popolamento fenicia i numerosissimi insediamenti collocati lungo la costa portoghese (Tavares 1993: 7–12). Si tratta di centri tutti già ben attivi nella seconda metà dell'VIII sec. a.C. e del tutto speculari, sia geograficamente che culturalmente a quelli della costa andalusa. Se si può usare un'immagine figurata, questi due gruppi di insediamenti appaiono come le ali di un gabbiano, la cui testa è Cadice, tradizionalmente la più antica colonia 'fenicia' di Occidente e quindi capofila dell'impresa. Tra gli insediamenti portoghesi non mancano infatti anche testimonianze collocabili cronologicamente nella prima parte dell'VIII sec. a.C. In sostanza, appare quanto meno improbabile che tutti questi insediamenti disseminati lungo la pensola iberica siano da ascrivere unicamente allo sforzo colonizzatore fenicio e non siano invece il risultato di una sovrapposizione più o meno indolore.

Per quanto riguarda la Sardegna, si potrà osservare innanzi tutto che, dopo la metà dell'VIII sec. a.C., ben poco seguito ha la rotta 'micenea?' e poi 'levantina' che si dipanava lungo la costa orientale della Sardegna. Questo tracciato è stato posto in evidenza dai ben noti rinvenimenti micenei del Golfo di Orosei (Vagnetti 1982: 186–87; Gras 1985: 72–79; Lo Schiavo et al. 1985: 1–71) e attualmente da un'ancora orientale da sabbia rinvenuta alla foce del Riu Flumini Durci a nord della foce del Flumendosa (Ledda 1989: 352–54; Benoit 1961: 400–408).

Tra gli altri insediamenti presto abbandonati sono da citare il fondaco di Santa Maria di Villaputzu ubicato alla foce del Flumendosa e forse distrutto durante l'intervento cartaginese nell'isola (Bartoloni 1990: 165). Altri insediamenti di origine precoloniale sono probabilmente quello di Posada e quello di Lotzorai, la cui situazione geografica ricorda il paesaggio precoloniale, esemplificato dai centri di Bosa o di Rachgoun (Bartoloni 1990: 163–66) e che può essere accostato anche alla precedente (frequentazione 'micenea'?), come si è verificato nel caso dell'isola Rossa e l'isolotto di Tuerredda presso Teulada (Bartoloni 1991: 13). Quindi, tutti questi centri sono accostabili a quelli di Cuccureddus di Villasimius, di Nora, di Bitia, la cui origine è probabilmente precoloniale (Bartoloni 1990: 157–67). Un discorso a parte merita l'insediamento di Sulcis, che, se è certamente la prima e più antica base della corrente 'fenicia', per il momento non offre tracce anteriori al secondo terzo dell'VIII sec. a.C. (Bartoloni 1992: 202–203), nè, se vogliamo, ha il caratteristico 'aspetto' precoloniale.

Per quanto riguarda la costa occidentale della Sardegna, fino alla metà dell'VIII sec. a.C. questa era frequentata dalle navi orientali per tutta la sua lunghezza, come dimostrano ampiamente la stessa Tharros (Acquaro 1983: 69–70), il fondaco di Bosa e quello di Sant'Imbenia, che doveva la sua esistenza al ricchissimo bacino delle miniere dell'Argentiera (D'Oriano 1990: 138–40).

Dopo il periodo indicato, la maggior parte di questi insediamenti viene abbandonata o cade in una depressione economica che in alcuni casi ne fa perdere anche il ricordo. Se ciò è accaduto, non è certo da imputare alle popolazioni nuragiche collocate nei cantoni costieri, le quali sembrano avere eccellenti rapporti col mondo fenicio, poichè, dopo la metà dell'VIII sec. a.C., risultano in gran parte inurbate. È da attribuire invece a un mutamento degli interessi commerciali e ad un diverso approccio delle correnti cosiddette 'Sidonia' e 'Tiria' che si sovrapposero alle precedenti.

La prepotenza dorica e assira prima e poi, dopo cento

anni, la nascita e il repentino incombere di imperialismi affacciati sul mare, quali quello di Cartagine, metteranno fine al sogno di un Mediterraneo senza frontiere.

Bibliografia

Acquaro, E. 1983. Tharros IX. Lo scavo del 1982. *Rivista di Studi Fenici* 11: 69–70.

Anderson, W.P. 1988. *Sarepta* I. Beyrouth.

Aubet, M.E. 1989. *Tartessos. Arqueologia protohistorica del Bajo Guadalquivir*. Barcelona.

Aubet, M.E. 1994. *Tiro y las colonias fenicias de Occidente*. Barcelona: Grijalbo Mondadori.

Bartoloni, P. 1981. Contributo alla cronologia delle necropoli fenicie e puniche di Sardegna. *Rivista di Studi Fenici* 9 suppl.: 13–29.

Bartoloni, P. 1990. Aspetti precoloniali della colonizzazione fenicia in Occidente. *Rivista di Studi Fenici* 18: 157–67.

Bartoloni, P. 1991. Le più antiche rotte del Mediterraneo. *Civiltà del Mediterraneo* 2: 7–14.

Bartoloni, P. 1992. Ceramica fenicia da Sulcis. *Lixus. Actes du Colloque, Larache 1989*, 195–205. Roma.

Bartoloni, P. 1993. Considerazioni sul 'tofet' di Tiro. *Rivista di Studi Fenici* 21: 153–56.

Bartoloni, P. 1995. Le linee commerciali all'alba del primo millennio. *Atti del Convegno I Fenici: ieri oggi domani. Roma 1994*, 245–59. Roma: Accademia Nazionale dei Lincei.

Baurain, C. 1988. Le role de Chypre dans la fondation de Carthage. *Studia Phoenicia* 6: 15–27.

Benoit, F. 1961. Pièces de gréement et d'armement en plomb. *Actas de III Congreso Internacional de Arqueologia submarina*, 398–411. Barcelona.

Bikai, P.M. 1978. *The Pottery of Tyre*. Warminster.

Bisi, A.M. 1988. Chypre et les premiers temps de Carthage. *Studia Phoenicia* 6: 29–41.

Bondì, S.F. 1979. Penetrazione fenicio-punica e storia della civiltà punica in Sicilia. La problematica storica. *Storia della Sicilia* I: 163–225. Napoli-Palermo.

Bondì, S.F. 1987. La frequentazione precoloniale fenicia. *Storia dei Sardi e della Sardegna I. Dalle origini all'età bizantina*, 129–45, 436–40. Milano.

Bondì, S.F. 1988. Problemi della precolonizzazione fenicia nel Mediterraneo centro-occidentale. *Momenti precoloniali nel Mediterraneo antico*, 243–55. Roma.

Bondì, S.F. 1994. Le fondazioni fenicie d'Occidente: aspetti topografici e strutturali. *Atti del Convegno Nuove fondazioni nel Vicino Oriente Antico: realtà e ideologia Pisa 1991*, 357–68. Pisa: Giardini.

Bondì, S.F. 1995. Gli studi storici tra bilanci e prospettive. *Proceedings of the Convegno I Fenici: ieri oggi domani Roma 1994*, 37–38. Roma: Accademia Nazionale dei Lincei.

Botto, M. 1990. *Studi storici sulla Fenicia. L'VIII e il VII secolo a.C.* Pisa: Università degli Studi.

Briend, J. & Humbert, J.-B. 1980. *Tell Keisan*. Paris.

Buchner, G. 1978. Testimonianze epigrafiche semitiche dell'VIII secolo a.C. a Pithekoussai. *La parola del passato* 179: 130–37.

Buchner, G. 1981. Pithekoussai: alcuni aspetti particolari. *Annuario delle Scuola Archeologica di Atene* 61: 268.

Culican, W. 1982. The Repertoire of Phoenician Pottery. *Phönizier im Westen*, 45–82. Mainz.

D'Oriano, R. 1990. La Sardegna sulle rotte dell'Occidente, II - L'età storica (VIII-I sec. a.C.). *Atti del XXIX Convegno di Studi sulla Magna Grecia*. Taranto.

du Plat Taylor, J. 1959. The Cypriot and Syrian pottery from Al Mina, Syria. *Iraq* 21: 79–86.

Garbini, G. 1978. Un'iscrizione aramaica a Ischia. *La parola del passato* 179: 143–50.

Garbini, G. 1980. *I Fenici. Storia e religione*. Napoli.

Garbini, G. 1988. 'Popoli del mare', Tarsis e Filistei. *Momenti precoloniali nel Mediterraneo antico*, 235–42. Roma: C.N.R.

Garbini, G. 1993a. *Aramaica*, 184–88. Roma.

Garbini, G. 1993b. Fenici e Cartaginesi nel Tirreno. *Atti del XXXIII Convegno di Studi sulla Magna Grecia*. Taranto.

Garbini, G. 1993c. Tharros XVIII-XIX. Iscrizioni fenicie a Tharrros - II. *Rivista di Studi Fenici* 21: 220–21.

Garbini, G. 1995. I Fenici di ieri, di oggi, di domani. *Proceedings of the Convegno "I Fenici: ieri oggi domani" Roma 1994*, 195–201. Roma: Accademia Nazionale dei Lincei.

Gras, M. 1985. *Trafics tyrrhéniens archaïques*. Paris.

Ledda, R. 1989. *Censimento archeologico nel territorio del comune di Villaputzu*. Cagliari.

Lo Schiavo, F., Macnamara, E., & Vagnetti, L. 1985. Late Cypriot imports to Italy and their influence on local bronze work. *Papers of the British School at Rome* 53: 1–71.

Maass-Lindemann, G. 1990. Orientalische Importe vom Morro de Mezquitilla. *Madrider Mitteilungen* 31: 169–77.

Mazza, F. 1988. La "precolonizzazione" fenicia: problemi storici e questioni di metodo. *Momenti precoloniali nel Mediterraneo antico*, 191–203. Roma.

Moscati, S. 1983. Precolonizzazione greca e precolonizzazione fenicia. *Rivista di Studi Fenici* 11: 1–7.

Moscati, S. 1985. I Fenici e il mondo mediterraneo al tempo di Omero. *Rivista di Studi Fenici* 13: 179–87.

Moscati, S. 1988. Dimensione tirrenica. *Rivista di Studi Fenici* 16: 137.

Moscati, S. 1989. *Tra Tiro e Cadice*. Roma: II Università degli Studi di Roma.

Moscati, S. 1992. *Chi furono i Fenici*. Torino.

Moscati, S. 1993. Non è un tofet a Tiro. *Rivista di Studi Fenici* 21: 147–52.

Moscati, S. 1994. I Fenici sulla costa nord-africana. *Rivista di Studi Fenici* 22: 67–69.

Niemeyer, H.G. 1984. Die Phönizier und die Mittelmeerwelt im Zeitalter Homers. *Jahrbuch des Römisch-Germanischen Zentral Museum* 31: 1–94.

Ridgway, D. 1984. *L'alba della Magna Grecia*. Milano.

Ruiz Mata, D. et al. (redd.). 1993. *Os Fenícios no Território Português*. Estudios Orientais 4. Lisboa.

Seeden, H. 1991. A tophet in Tyre. *Berytus* 39: 39–87.

Tavares, A. 1993. Apresentação. Os Fenicios no território português. In Ruiz Mata, D. et al. (redd.), *Estudios Orientais* 4: 9–12.

Vagnetti, L. 1982. Teritorio di Orosei (?) (Nuoro). *Atti del XXXII Convegno di Studi sulla Magna Grecia*, 186–87. Taranto.

Waldbaum, J.C. 1994. Early Greek Contacts with the Southern Levant, ca. 1000–600 B. C.: The Eastern Perspective. *Bulletin of the American Schools of Oriental Research* 293: 53–66.

38. Phoenicians in Sardinia: Tyrians or Sidonians?

Brian Peckham

Introduction

The term "Phoenician" lacks specificity. It is distinguished from "Punic" and refers in a vague undifferentiated way to people and products from the Levant. This generality is conspicuous when compared to the precision available, for instance, on the origins of Greek and Cypriot merchants and wares. I would like to suggest that more precision (Bikai 1989: 206), if it were possible, might contribute to a better understanding of Sardinia's peculiar role in Mediterranean history.

The Phoenician City-States

Phoenicia was not a country, but a conglomerate of cities, or city-states, with diverse traditions and interests. The main cities were Tyre, Sidon, and Byblos. They could be distinguished from each other on the Levantine mainland by their character and political affiliations, and they moved through the Mediterranean at different times, by different routes, for different reasons or purposes, and with different friends and destinations.

The Tyrians were city-builders and settlers. In the Amarna letters (Moran 1992: 162, 233), Tyre is called a "Great City" (ālu rabītu). In letters to the king of Ugarit, the king of Tyre always refers to his capital as a "city" while the king of Sidon, by contrast, usually does not mention his capital, but instead speaks of his "land" (Arnaud 1992). The Sidonians, apparently, were not totally urbanized at home and were not settlers abroad. It seems, to gauge the evidence from Cyprus, Crete, Rhodes and Italy, that they were not city-builders or colonizers, but rather temple-builders in the places that they visited – such as Kition (Karageorghis 1981) and Kommos (Shaw 1989) – and that they would travel individually or as families to trade or ply their crafts, or as corporations organized, as in fourth century Athens (Baslez & Briquel-Chatonnet 1991), around the temples they founded.

Tyrians and Sidonians, whatever the ethnic or political or commercial relations between them, had distinct characteristics and a sense of their separate identities. An inscription from the mid-eighth century BC mentions the "King of the Sidonians" (Lipiński 1983) and a nearly contemporary, or perhaps slightly later, seal belongs to the "King of the Tyrians" (Bordreuil 1986: 298–305). Each city had its peculiar Gods. Byblos was the city of the "Lady of Byblos" (b`lt gbl) and of Adonis ('dn) (Bordreuil 1977). Sidon was devoted to Eshmun and Astarte (Xella 1993). Tyre was the city of Melqart, whose name signified 'King of the *City*', and who was worshipped as Milk`aštart, the God of the underworld city. Tyre was eclectic, notably in welcoming Egyptian Gods, and syncretistic, in its worship of composite and politically astute city-Gods (mlk`štrt, tnt`štrt, 'šmnmlqrt), but Sidon and Byblos were cosmologically oriented and conservative to the last. Each city also differed in its religious attitudes and practices, specifically in their attitude toward death: Byblians, in their memorials, claimed to have lived justly, hoped for a long life, and were preoccupied with their physical appearance in the tomb; Sidonians thought of death as undisturbed rest among their ancestors the Healers (rp'm), and they worshipped the genius of healing (šdrp'); the Tyrians erected stelae (mṣbt) to their dead (Peckham 1987).

Each city was also distinguished by its script, Byblos by its dialect. In each city there were onomastic preferences: Tyre included Egyptian divinities such as Horus and Osiris; Byblos went with names containing the elements 'El,' 'Baal,' 'King' and 'Life;' Sidonian names were formed from 'Eshmun' and 'Astarte,' from the name of the eponymous God d, from cosmic elements (e.g. šmš, the Sun), or sometimes were composed of verbal elements, or of nominal elements ending in 'aleph.

The Mainland Connections of Tyre, Sidon and Byblos

From the earliest documentation, Sidon is aligned with the coastal cities of Northern Syria, in particular with Arvad, and with kings of Cilicia (Que, the Danuna). In the Amarna letters, it tries to draw Byblos, dependent on Egypt, into its conspiracy with Amurru. In the Tale of Wen Amon it seems to be in commercial contact with the kings of Cilicia. Tyre, by contrast, was drawn in the other direction, to Egypt and Arabia. Byblos seems to have tagged along with the Sidonians in North Syria and throughout the Mediterranean (Peckham 1992).

It might be supposed that the Phoenician inscriptions from Zinjirli and Karatepe reflect early Sidonian involvement in these northern regions, and that it was from Sidonians in north Syria that the Aramaeans borrowed the alphabet, no later than the tenth century B.C., as the inscriptions from Tell Halaf (Dankwarth & Müller 1990) and Tell Fekherye (Naveh 1987) determine.

The Kilamuwa texts from Zinjirli (ca. 825 B.C.) illustrate the kind of presence that Sidonians exercised outside their own land. They intermarried with the indigeneous population but they did not colonize. They brought with them, besides their skills, their products and their trades, learning, literature and trained scribes. They transformed their adopted environment, but they left no distinctive, no "Phoenician" mark. Thus, Kilamuwa, the king of Zinjirli, was an Aramaean with a Luwian name. His brother and his father were also Aramaeans (Saul [š'l] and Haya [ḥy]), as were the earlier kings of the dynasty (gbr, bnh). His inscription is written in high relief, as were the later Aramaic inscriptions from the same region, and it is written in Aramaic script (Cross 1969). But the language of his inscription is elegant, literary Phoenician (O'Connor 1977); the great deeds which his inscription mentions are, in accordance with the populist principles of his Byblian and Sidonian mentors, kindness and generosity to his people; the dynastic Gods whom he invokes are local (b`lḥmn, "Lord of the Amanus") or warlike (b`lṣmd, "Lord of Retribution," rkb'l, "Charioteer of El") manifestations of the El and Baal of Byblos. He had no heir. The kings who followed him were Luwians who wrote in a hybrid dialect, essentially Aramaic, but a kind of archaizing patois, filled with reminiscences of the once familiar Phoenician pronunciation.

The Karatepe inscription, similarly, witnesses to Sidonian and Byblian interests in Cilicia. Ba'al is the principal God; establishment of peace, prosperity and right worship are central issues (Amadasi Guzzo 1984); the justice and wisdom of the "king" are crucial; words like "mighty" and "kindly" are characteristic; an interest in the land and its boundaries is a feature which it shares with later texts.

Sidonian interests in Cilicia are attested into the time of Esarhaddon when the king of Sidon, in alliance with the king of this region, Sanduarri, King of Kundi and Sizu, rebelled and was killed for his trouble. The broken and enigmatic inscription from Hassan-beyli, on the eastern slopes of the Amanus (Lemaire 1983), comes from the eastern border of Sanduarri's kingdom and may be ascribed to this king. Sidonian involvement with the Luwians also might be reflected, but in the opposite direction, by the ninth century inscription from Khalde, south of Beirut, inscribed with the Luwian name (ptty) read (gtty) by Bordreuil (1982: 191).

This North Syrian, or specifically Aramaean, attachment of the Sidonians may be attested by the Samian and Eretrian bronze blinkers from the mid-ninth century (Eph'al & Naveh 1989). The inscription is identical on both: "This was given in honor of our lord Hazael by `Umqi in the year that our lord crossed the river" (zy ntn hdr [not: hdd] lmr'n ḥz'l mn `mq bšnt `dh mr'n nhr). The people of `Umqi were not sailors, but their land was a gateway to the West, and their port was Al Mina, frequented by Euboeans and Sidonians (Boardman 1990). The bronzes, therefore, probably were not presented to Hazael of Damascus on his triumphal tour, but were given to the Sidonian merchants to be dedicated in his honor in the Heraion in Samos. The ivories in Syrian style, from the ninth century, some of which may have inspired the bronze blinkers, might be ascribed to Sidonian influence (cf. Winter 1976a; 1976b; 1989). But those in Phoenician style, from the eighth century, would be indicative of Tyrian workmanship and inspiration (Barnett 1982: 43–55). Further, it is possible that the ivories in South Syrian style (Winter 1981) – said to be from Hamath or Damascus – reflect involvement by the Byblians in the ivory trade.

The Tyrians, in connivance with their Assyrian suzerains, also had some dealings with North Syria. This is attested, for instance, by the late-ninth century Bir-Hadad inscription from Arpad with its dedication to Tyrian Melqart (Puech 1992), by the late-eighth century incantations from Arslan Tash invoking the entire Tyrian pantheon against the male and female demons of the area (Cross & Saley 1970; Cross 1974), and by ivories in Phoenician style belonging to the eighth century that were found in the Assyrian governor's palace at the same site (Barnett 1982: 48; Albenda 1988). The Tyrians, however, generally tended to move to the South. Tyrians, for instance, had professional ties to Judah and Jerusalem, as is attested by the Phoenician buildings at Ramat Rahel, while the Sidonians were connected by marriage with the Northern Kingdom of Israel. The Sidonians, besides, were anathema to the biblical writers, while the Tyrians were welcome mentors and allies. It is typical of the distinction between the cities, that Sidon should exert its influence through individual and family relationships, through the marriage of Jezebel with the king of Samaria, and that Tyre should be remembered by the biblical historian not only for its arts and crafts, but for its dispute about the *cities* it received in payment for building the temple of Solomon (Briquel-Chatonnet 1992).

It might be supposed that Tyrians settled in coastal

cities (such as, `Akko, Achzib, Tell Abu Hawam) and that it was Tyrians who alphabetized the Philistines. Phoenician inscriptions found in Palestine from Tell Jemmeh to Tell Qasile (Naveh 1985), a late Phoenician ostracon from 'Akko whose technical lexicon is Philistine (Dothan 1985), and Philistine names preserved in Assyrian sources, indicate that the Philistines had been West-Semitized, specifically "Tyrianized." That they participated in or at least profited from Tyrian long-distance trade may be indicated by "gold from Ophir" mentioned in an ostracon from Tell Qasile.

The earliest inscriptions which might be ascribed to the Tyrians are those from the South Arabian way station at Kuntillet `Ajrud in southern Judah (ninth century BC; Lemaire 1984), and an Egyptian writing board (ca. 800–775 BC; Zauzich & Röllig 1990) inscribed in Egyptian style by the Phoenician son of an Egyptian father: "Life and Prosperity! Cedar [writing] board of `Ayyalam [son of] Si`" (ḥy wtb / 'rz `ylm s`). Inscriptions from Sarepta (Pritchard 1978: 97–110; Masson 1982) were left by pilgrims from Cyprus (a Greek-Cypriot bilingual), Sidon (lšdrp', l'šmnytn), Byblos (l'dnn) and Tyre (a dedication to tnt`štrt). It is symptomatic of Tyre's Egyptian and North African interests that two Punic, specifically Carthaginian, inscriptions have been found in the vicinity of the city: the names, titles, script are Carthaginian; one stele was set up by an official visitor to Tyre whose ancestors in the fifth and sixth generation – his great great grandfather, and great great great grandfather – were city councillors (rb) in Carthage (Sader 1991–92).

Inscriptions from the necropolis in Tyre (Sader 1991; 1992) range from the mid-eighth to the mid-seventh centuries BC. There is a high percentage of women's graves, and their names (e.g. 'mtšmn, `štrtl't) are Tyrian and typically eclectic. Some of the men also have Tyrian names (e.g. 'lm, mlqrt'b), but there are also names of men and women invoking Tannit and Hamon (tntšb` and grḥmn), Gods who are familiar from the Carthaginian pantheon. The eighth century pottery (Seeden 1991) is typical of Tyre and its vicinity. There is pottery like it from Sidon, Sarepta and Khalde, but the most impressive array of parallels is from Southwest Cyprus (Amathus, Paleokastro) and Spain. The seventh century pottery, similarly, is local, but by this time most of the comparable material is found in Sicily, Sardinia and Spain.

Stages on the Journeys Westward

There is some slight evidence to suggest that Tyre, Sidon and Byblos took similar, yet divergent, routes to the West. In general, Sidon – along with Byblos – travelled two routes: up the Levantine coast to Bassit and Al Mina, along the coast of Cilicia to the Aegean, and ultimately to Euboea (a route followed in the opposite direction by Euboeans); or across to Cyprus, perhaps at about Kition, along the eastern and northern coast of Cyprus, and off to Crete. The Tyrians, on the contrary, at first concentrated on the southern and western sites (Amathus, Paphos, Palaeokastro, Ayia Irini), travelling from there to the Aegean or to Crete and Egypt; but later, when Sidon was destroyed and languished under Assyrian rule, established a brief settlement at Kition, and took over the ancient Sidonian routes. The Euboeans, to judge from the pottery remains, travelled the Sidonian route to North Syria, and the Tyrian route to Tyre and the coast of Palestine.

Al Mina was not a Sidonian settlement, but a North Syrian town where Aramaeans, Assyrians, Sidonians, Cypriots and Greeks convened (Boardman 1990). Bassit, just to the South, was a Greek foundation, which in the eighth century abounds in North Syrian, Cycladic, and Cypriot ware, but has only a few Sidonian burials (Courbin 1990). It was not a Phoenician colony, but a place where individual Phoenicians, or typically Sidonians, settled, with or without their families: a sixth century amphora is inscribed with the Byblian or Sidonian owner's name (Bordreuil 1982: 191–192), "Client-of-Baal" (lgrb`l). Further south at Amrit, in the sixth century, there was a temple with a lustral pool (Dunand & Saliby 1985), like the temple of Eshmun at Sidon where there was a pool fed by a spring called "Tender Care" (ydll) in recognition of its healing effect. There are inscriptions in Sidonian and Byblian script (Puech 1986), and dedications to the Sidonian God Shadrapa, as well as to the Byblian-Sidonian composite "Adonis-Eshmun" (l'dny l'šmn). In true Sidonian fashion, they did not establish colonies or even build settlements, but merely settled among the natives and built temples to their own Gods.

To judge from later epigraphic evidence, Byblians settled on the northern coast of Cyprus at Lapethos. The inscriptions are from the fourth and third centuries, and the evidence for Byblian influence is their use of the Byblian dialect, and a reference in the earliest of them to "the Gods of Byblos who are in Lapethos" (Greenfield 1987). But there is also an inscription from Pyrgi in Italy (Knoppers 1992), from the end of the sixth century, which alludes to the Byblian rituals of Adonis, and displays archaic elements of the Byblian dialect and traces of its local Cypriot development: these include the date formula, the demonstrative 'z, the pronominal suffix -w, the precative (lm's <*lym's), enclitic mem in a modal context (hkkbm 'l), and the preposition ('b). It follows from this understanding of the Pyrgi inscription that Byblian artisans from Cyprus were living in Italy or that they had travelled there for the construction and inauguration of the temple to Astarte by the Etruscan King of Caere.

Kition in Cyprus was not a Phoenician settlement until about the seventh century and then was settled by Tyrians: it was these who, along with the local Greek inhabitants, were known to Judean writers as Kittiyim (ktym) and who served as mercenaries in Judah at the end of the century (Dion 1992); Judeans, in turn, settled with them in Kition, where inscribed stelae from their fourth century cemetery have been discovered (Heltzer 1989). Before the seventh century, Kition was a Sidonian and Byblian port-of-call where, typically, they built a temple to Astarte, the Mistress of Byblos and the Goddess of Sidon, as well as a few residences or workshops for the individual Sidonians, or for the members of the mercantile corporation which had funded it. The temple itself had a courtyard with a rectangular pool (Karageorghis 1981) which, like those at Sidon or at Amrit in the sixth and fifth centuries, perhaps was used for lustral rites. The earliest inscription from this temple, from about 750 BC, alludes to a ritual in honor of Astarte and complementary rites of Adonis (Karageorghis 1976: 106). Her cult was firmly established, and a sixth century tariff from Kition (Healey 1974) lists the payments to those who joined in her solemn processions through the city.

The Sidonian inscriptions from Cyprus are as isolated as the individuals in whose memory they are inscribed. There is an early seventh century inscription from Chytroi (Kythrea), southeast of Lapethos and about 10 kms from the north coast of Cyprus (Masson & Sznycer 1972: 104–107). It is written on a ceramic sarcophagus, and has the same expressions and curse formulae that are found in the later inscriptions from Sidon. The earliest inscription from Cyprus (Puech 1979: 19–26) has similar formulae but, like the inscriptions from Zinjirli (Niehr 1994), mentions the rituals to be performed for the dead, in Zinjirli for the dead king, but in Cyprus for an individual. It is broken at the top and quite worn and the readings are often uncertain:

> "... [in the tomb where] he is resting, there is no surprise (mpt). But whoever might forget the peace offerings for the tomb which is over this illustrious person (gbr), may these Gods destroy that man by the hand of Baal and by the hand of a citizen ('dm) and by sudden calamity (šbr). Let fat not be burned for him forever. May Baal and citizen not accord that man a name, nor place peace offerings before him."

Both texts are funerary and belong to persons who lived and died in an alien land, among the indigenous people, not in a community of their own. The earliest distinguishes between the totality of the Gods and the God Baal who handles their affairs, and between the person of rank (gbr) who has died and the general population ('dm) among whom he lived, and may shed some light on the social situation of the itinerant Sidonian traders and craftsmen on the island at this time.

Among the early inscriptions which might be ascribed to Sidonian travellers in Cyprus and the Aegean, there is a late eighth century inscribed sherd from Salamis which, if it is not to be read "Ninety" (tš`m), may contain the monogram of someone called "Shema" (šm`) whose name is preceded by a symbol which resembles "T" (Sznycer 1980)). But the most interesting is the eleventh or early tenth century (ca. 1000 BC) inscription on a bronze bowl from Tekke. It is inscribed "The Cup of Shema, son of La'amon" (ks . šm` . bn l'mn). It has been interpreted as the work of a Phoenician craftsman who had taken up residence at Knossos (Coldstream 1982: 271), whose name is Phoenician, but whose father's name, while also Phoenician, possibly contains a reference to Cretan Minos, Egyptian Min, and so to be rendered "Minos-prevails" (Puech 1983: 374–391). The tomb where the bowl was found contained two burials and, if this interpretation of the name is correct, the inscription suggests that Shema was born to a Sidonian father who had adapted to Cretan ways, but still maintained Sidonian identity. Since the bowl on which the name is inscribed has a shallow hemispherical shape of Cypriot origin, it is also conceivable that, while the craftsman Shema was born at Knossos, his father's family was originally from Cyprus, rather than from the Sidonian mainland.

This tomb was separated by about fifty yards, and about one generation, from the tomb of a goldsmith who was buried with some of his treasures (Boardman 1967). This too is understood as the family tomb of a resident alien. However, his work resembles North Syrian products and is especially like that found at Tell Halaf, and he and his family were probably the offspring of Sidonians who had moved at some earlier time into North Syria. It was characteristic of the Sidonians to settle and assimilate: the oriental traditions of this goldsmith, who had married into a Cretan family, were maintained for some time by his children, but gradually were adapted to local styles and taste. It was in this same tomb, but with a later burial, that a Sardinian *askos* was buried with its Sardinian owner (Vagnetti 1989), or with a Sidonian traveller from Crete, one of the itinerant craftsmen who frequented the western island.

Sidonians survived and prospered in Cyprus, Crete and the Aegean, largely due to their association with the Euboeans. This lasted about a century (850–750 BC) during which the Euboeans travelled to North Syria, and the Sidonians travelled with them to the West, especially to Italy, where their ephemeral presence is marked by inscriptions which, not surprisingly, have North Syrian or Aramaic affiliations (Amadasi Guzzo 1987). There is an indecipherable eighth century graffito from Pithekoussai with two complete letters and traces of two others (McCarter 1975); an early sixth century graffito on a burial urn, possibly of Rhodian origin, which has been analyzed as Aramaic, is actually written in Phoenician script and has a North Syrian name (kpln) attested centuries earlier at Ugarit. The Praeneste bowl is inscribed with the name "May-Eshmun-be-propitious, son of the Thinker" ('šmny`d bn `št') where the father's name ("Thinker") is composed of a verbal root which is known only from Aramaic (`št = "think, consider") and an afformative 'aleph which is common in Sidonian and Byblian names (e.g. `bd', 'bh' bn mr', b`n'). The artist's name on the Pontecagnano bowl (d'Agostino & Garbini 1977) seems to be "Balaša', son of Ḥimilk" (blš' bn ḥmlk): the artist's name (blš') can be explained with reference to blš meaning "search, enquire," and would be the equivalent of the name "Saul," but his father's name "Ḥimilk" is more common in Tyre and Carthage, and the bowl with its name may be Tyrian rather than Sidonian. Similarly, the scarab from Francavilla Marittima (Amadasi Guzzo 1979), belonging to the Lyre Player Group and inscribed Padi (pdy), is from the late eighth century and probably should be considered Tyrian or proto-Carthaginian rather than Sidonian. As these names might illustrate, Sidonians were the first to travel the Mediterranean, but toward the end of the eighth century, when Sidonian hegemony and its Euboean connection dissipated, their place was taken by people from Tyre, true "Phoenicians," who had travelled to the West from Cyprus and laid the groundwork for the foundation of the western colonies.

Sidonians apparently had a predilection for Greeks. There are inscriptions at Delos, and an inscription of a mercantile group (mrzḥ) in Athens. Sidon acquired Dor and Joppa and the plain of Sharon, and almost immediately a Greek sanctuary was established at Dor. The fourth century king of Sidon ʿAbdʿaštart acquired a Greek name and was honored as a philhellene. And so, throughout their travels in the Mediterranean, Sidonians freely associated with Greeks: with Mycenaeans in the Late Bronze Age; and in the Iron Age with Euboeans, Athenians, and Cypriot Greeks.

In northwestern Sardinia these Sidonians left an inscription (at Bosa) and, in the handiwork of their Nuragic apprentices, figurines in a vaguely oriental but not quite Phoenician style. Off the coast of Sicily, travelling perhaps with Cypriots, they dropped a statue – in North Syrian style – of the smiting God, and at Nora, with these or other adventurers, they left an eleventh century Phoenician inscription (Cross 1986). From Tharros, or from Cyprus by a more direct route, they may have reached Spain by the end of the ninth century: a statuette of Astarte, in semi-Syrian style and from the latter part of the eighth century, was made by the two sons of a Sidonian craftsman whose family had settled in Spain, and was dedicated by them to the Syrian Astarte (ʿštrt ḥr) whom their father and grandfather had venerated at home (Amadasi Guzzo 1993).

The transition from Sidonian to Tyrian hegemony, or at least predominance, may be illustrated by a development in the style of unguent jars. On the island of Cos unguent flasks from the MG period (850–750 BC) were 'Syro-Phoenician' but soon became hellenized (Coldstream 1982: 268–269). During the same century on Rhodes there was one oriental shape that inspired countless local imitations. But soon after 750 new forms suddenly appear, much nearer to their oriental prototypes, and not hellenized. It was at this time, around 750 BC, when Assyria began to subjugate the Aramaean and Neo-Hittite states in North Syria and Anatolia, that Sidonian influence, the influence of North Syrian traditions and individual Sidonian artists, began to decline (Doumet-Serhal 1993–94). Suddenly, and thanks to the Assyrians,

their place was taken by "Phoenicians," the people from Tyre and its dependencies.

The Tyrians had not been waiting listlessly at home for the opportunity to travel and see the world. They had travelled to western Cyprus, Mycenaeans and Euboeans had met them and returned with them to Tyre, and had travelled with them to places where the Tyrians ventured on the coast of Palestine and inland. Their chief point of contact in Cyprus was Amathus, and it was there, or at nearby Limassol, that the earliest Tyrian inscription in Cyprus was found (Lipiński 1983). It attests that the Tyrians had founded a city on Cyprus, that it was named after the mother city ("New City" [qrtḥdšt]) and that it was a true colony, with a governor and with enduring political links to the founding city. It was from here that Tyrians went on to found similar cities, North African Carthage, eventually Carthage in Spain. One of these colonial Tyrians, when he sailed to Carthage, brought with him a Cypriot God, Pygmalion, a local Greek adaptation of a Tyrian original, whose name was simply transliterated into Tyrian characters (Krahmalkov 1981). In fact, it is particularly in this determination to found cities, and to maintain relations with the motherland, that the Tyrians differed from the Sidonians.

Sardinia and the Western Mediterranean

It can be supposed, therefore, that Phoenician colonies in Sardinia, and throughout the western Mediterranean, were Tyrian foundations. The critical questions, consequently, concern their place of origin (Tyre itself or some prior colony), their routes, the place of purchase of the wares which they brought with them either to keep, sell, exchange, distribute or bestow as gifts. It becomes important, therefore, to differentiate between the styles and products of Tyre, and those of its markets in Judah, or its settlements in Palestine; to distinguish Egyptian artifacts from locally made Egyptianizing items (as Hölbl [1986] does for Egyptian figurines found in Sardinia – some with exact parallels in Byblos – and scarabs whose parallels are from ʿAthlit, Tell Abu Hawam, Tell Keisan, Sidon, and Amrit); to be able to identify the distinctive products and styles of the Tyrian towns in Cyprus; and especially to distinguish between the mainland Tyrian works found in Carthage, the Cypriot influences, and the locally inspired Carthaginian products. On the analogy of Sidonian genius in distributing literacy, literature, artistic traditions and religious values, it would also be important to trace the development or decline of culture in the areas under special Tyrian influence. On the basis of Tyrian eclecticism, finally, it might be important to isolate and locate exactly, in time and in place, the various influences impinging on its composite works.

These Tyrian foundations may have followed on Sidonian intervention in Sardinia (as at Tharros), or they may have been preceded by mainland Tyrian exploration or specifically Cypriot commerce in the western Mediterranean (as at Nora). It is useful to distinguish Tyrian (mainland or colonial) from what is not, and to distinguish colonial intention from travel and commerce. A colony would seem to require at least: (1) the movement of a whole group or community, rather than individuals or a family, (2) the approval or encouragement of the founding city, (3) building of a walled or otherwise distinct settlement, (4) establishment of a system of government which did not derogate from the authority of the founding city, and (5) the maintenance of social, economic, political, religious and cultural ties with the motherland. The Tyrians founded colonies – on the mainland, in Cyprus, Sardinia, Spain, – where the Sidonians had been content to travel and trade and settle among the indigenous population.

The Nora inscription, from the mid-ninth century – despite recent confusion on the date (Amadasi Guzzo & Guzzo 1986) – is evidence that around 850–825 BC a ship, with its captain and crew, dropped anchor in Sardinia, on its way from Tarshish, under adverse conditions, and that their safe arrival prompted them to offer thanks to the Cypriot God PMY and set up a stele recording the events (Zuckerman 1991). The connection between Sardinia, Spain and Cyprus inferred from this inscription is interesting, but the other implications of the inscribed stele should not go unnoticed. First, it has to be observed that either the ship carried a scribe, like the ship lost at Ulu Burun, and a not unlikely feature of commercial travel, or there was a resident Phoenician scribe in Nora. Second, Nora was either a colony or settlement at this time, or it was a regular port of call for Tyrian, and specifically Cypro-Tyrian, ships, because otherwise there would be no point in setting up the stele. Since there is no evidence for Phoenician settlement in Nora at this time, it seems likely that Nora was a port of call on voyages between Cyprus and Spain and that the stele, the work of the captain or of a skilled and literate crew member, commemorated a particular voyage when the port provided safe haven in a storm. This tallies with the archaeological evidence from Nora and its vicinity: Mycenaean and Cypriot materials in a Nuragic settlement, some eighth century pottery from the sea, a Tyrian or "Phoenician" town at the end of the seventh century having ties (stelae with inset frames or "inquadramenti") with western Cyprus (in particular with Kourion and Palaepaphos), and with Achziv, a Tyrian settlement, on the mainland (Bondì 1978).

Sulcis apparently was a typical Tyrian colony, built on the remains of Sidonian interests in the West. The earliest pottery is Euboean, from Pithekoussai, from about the end of the eighth century, brought for their own use by Phoenicians on their way to settle (Moscati 1986). Trade with Ischia remained brisk as long as the Tyrians maintained the Levantine character of the site (Bartoloni 1987), and this Tyrian phase is marked by inscriptions in the old mainland hand (Barreca 1965: 55–57). Sulcis lost its eastern style and became a western colony, trading with Etruria, by the mid-seventh century.

Tharros was different and seems to have maintained links to its Sidonian past. The earliest phase is "pre-Phoenician", i.e. without any of the characteristics of Tyrian settlement. There are, for instance, Nuragic bronzes, a set of large round beads of rock crystal, with an exact parallel in Tomb 1 at Salamis, and a ninth century two-story Phoenician lamp (Barnett & Mendleson 1987: 39, 52). In later phases, there is still a residue of Sidonian or North Syrian inspiration, e.g. in pendant earrings, a pendant with a female bust in North Syrian style, "step altars" (altari a gradino), or thrones, which served as bases for statues or cult objects (Moscati 1987a). But starting in the early seventh century there is a clear connection with Carthage, not with the westernized or proto-Punic city, but between the Tyrians who had settled Tharros and those Tyrians from Cyprus who founded Carthage in North Africa (Moscati 1987b).

Conclusion

The indeterminate "Phoenicians" can be identified as Tyrians who settled the Mediterranean world and assumed many faces. It is important, therefore, to follow them, and to trace their products and their ideas to their various, concatenated points of origin.

Sidon was the heir of great cities such as Ugarit which had been destroyed at the end of the Late Bronze Age. The network of cultural and commercial relationships which had been established by this time between North Syria, Cilicia, Cyprus and the Mycenaean world survived the collapse of Late Bronze empires. It was repaired by Sidonians who not only had managed to escape the destruction, but probably were accessories to it, and most certainly had profited from it.

It is clear that the Aramaeans in North Syria had borrowed the alphabet from the Sidonians by early in the eleventh century: the script of the ninth century Aramaic inscription from Tell Fekherye was copied by a bilingual Assyrian scribe from tables of scripts prepared in the eleventh; this represented a deliberate attempt at archaizing, consistent with the archaic character of the Assyrian writing and with the scribe's reliance on ancient literary traditions, since the more advanced script of the tenth century inscription from nearby Tel Halaf illustrates the normal development of the script which was effected by constant use. It is also certain that the Sidonians brought their script, with the orthographic innovations which the Aramaeans introduced, to Crete and mainland Greece at least by the tenth century.

Sidonians went where those carrying Mycenaean goods had gone, perhaps with them as they went. Over the centuries they spread the network to mainland Greece, especially Euboea, and went with the Euboeans in their expeditions westward. The ancient network was extended even further when they touched Italy and Sardinia and Spain. It was in memory of them that pilgrims to Antas from Cagliari ('/hklry) and Sulcis (hslky) left dedications to their eponymous ancestor, "To the Lord, to Sid, mighty in his Paternity" (l'dn lṣd 'dr b'by, or Sardus Pater Ba'by).

Tyre did not flourish and achieve worldwide renown until the destruction of Sidon was complete (ca. 750–675 BC). It began by staying out of Sidon's way, sailing to parts of Cyprus which Sidonians did not frequent, and from there, or by land, to Arabia and Egypt and the shores of North Africa. Unlike the Sidonians, the Tyrians did not assimilate, but became eclectic, deliberate in maintaining their individuality and style, systematic in their adaptation or absorption of other peoples' beliefs and artistry. A part of this deliberation is manifested in their foundation of colonies, where they could live, still in spiritual and material contact with their motherland, without yielding to the indigenous population: it was this aloofness, for instance, that made them acceptable to the biblical historian who dreaded contamination by or assimilation with foreigners, while the Sidonians, who had the habit of intermarrying and assimilating, were simply anathema. In the end, if they lost their individuality – as at Carthage – it was less because they succumbed to the manner of foreigners, than because the local population changed, became impervious to their influence, and overwhelmed them with their numbers and their lack of sophistication.

Mainland Tyrian influence ceased with the siege and capture of the island city in the early sixth century. Ezekiel connects the fall of Tyre with the invasion of Egypt by the Babylonians, and describes these two events as if they were the end of the known world. From this time the Tyrian colonies ceased and became independent cities, totally isolated from their origins, and subject to the dominant powers of the time. In the East, Persia took over, and Tyre, Sidon, Byblos and Arvad became vassals of the Great King and purveyors of imperial tastes. In Cyprus, it was Greeks and Cypriots who ruled, except in Kition which maintained some semblance of the old order, and in a few towns where links to the Phoenician past still lingered. In the West, new nations arose, and it was Carthage that carried on the Cypro-Tyrian tradition. A few generations, two centuries at most, was Tyre's to transform the Mediterranean world.

References

Albenda, P. 1988. The Gateway and Portal Stone Reliefs from Arslan Tash. *Bulletin of the American Schools of Oriental Research* 271: 5–30.
Amadasi Guzzo, M.G. 1979. Note epigrafiche. *Vicino Oriente* 2: 3–8.
Amadasi Guzzo, M.G. 1984. Le roi qui fait vivre son peuple dans les inscriptions phéniciennes. *Die Welt des Orients* 15: 109–118.
Amadasi Guzzo, M.G. 1987. Fenici o Aramei in occidente nell' VIII sec. a. C.? *Studia Phoenicia* 5: 35–47.
Amadasi Guzzo, M.G. 1993. Astarte in Trono. In Heltzer, M., Segal, A.D. & Kaufman, D. (eds.), *Studies in the Archaeology and History of Ancient Israel in Honour of Moshe Dothan*, 163–180. Haifa University Press, Haifa.
Amadasi Guzzo, M.G. & Guzzo, P.G 1986. Di Nora, di Eracle gaditano e della più antica navigazione fenicia. *Aula Orientalis* 59–71.
Arnaud, D. 1992. Les ports de la 'Phénicie' à la fin de l'âge du bronze récent (xiv-xiii siècles) d'après les textes cunéiformes de Syrie. *Studi micenei ed egeo-anatolici* 30: 179–194.
Barnett, R.D. 1982. *Ancient Ivories in the Middle East and Adjacent Countries*. Qedem 14. Hebrew University, Jerusalem.
Barnett, R.D. & Mendleson, C. (eds.). 1987. *Tharros. A Catalogue of Material in the British Museum from Phoenician and Other Tombs at Tharros, Sardinia*. British Museum, London.
Barreca, F. 1965. Nuove iscrizioni feniche da Sulcis. *Oriens Antiquus* 4: 53–57, pls. I-II.
Bartoloni, P. 1987. Orrizonti commerciali sulcitani tra l'viii e il vii sec. a. C. *Rendiconti dell'Accademia Nazionale dei Lincei* 41: 219–226
Baslez, M. F. & Briquel-Chatonnet, F. 1991. Un exemple d'intégration phénicienne au monde grec: les Sidoniens au Pirée à la fin du IVe siècle. *Atti del II congresso internazionale di studi fenici e punici*, vol. I: 229–240. Consiglio Nazionale delle Ricerche, Roma.
Bernardini, P. 1991. Un insediamento fenicio a Sulci nella seconda metà dell'vii sec. a. C. *Atti del II Congresso internazionale di studi fenici e punici*, vol. II: 663–673. Consiglio Nazionale delle Ricerche, Roma.
Bikai, P.M. 1989. Cyprus and the Phoenicians. *Biblical Archaeologist* 52: 203–209.
Boardman, J. 1967. The Khaniale Tekke Tombs, II. *Annual of the British School at Athens* 62: 57–75.
Boardman, J. 1990. Al Mina and History. *Oxford Journal of Archaeology* 9: 169–190.
Bondì, S.F. 1978. Un tipo di inquadramento architettonico fenicio. *Atti del I convegno italiano sul vicino oriente antico*, 147–155, pls. VII-XII. Centro per le Antichità e la Storia dell'Arte del Vicino Oriente, Roma.
Bordreuil, P. 1977. Une inscription phénicienne champlevée des environs de Byblos. *Semitica* 27: 23–27, pl. 5.
Bordreuil, P. 1982. Epigraphes phéniciennes sur bronze, sur pierre et sur céramique. *Archéologie au Levant. Recueil à la mémoire de Roger Saidah,* 187–192. Maison de l'Orient, Lyon.
Bordreuil, P. 1986. Charges et fonctions en Syrie-Palestine d'après quelques sceaux ouest-sémitiques du second et du premier millénaire. *Académie des Inscriptions et Belles Lettres, Comptes Rendus* 290–308.
Briquel-Chatonnet, F. 1992. *Les relations entre les cités de la côte phénicienne et les royaumes d'Israël et de Juda*. Studia Phoenicia 12. Peeters, Leuven.
Coldstream, J.N. 1969. The Phoenicians of Ialysos. *Bulletin of the Institute of Classical Studies* 16: 1–6, pls. 1–3.
Coldstream, J.N. 1982. Greeks and Phoenicians in the Aegean. In Niemeyer, H.G. (ed.), *Phönizier im Western*. Madrider Beiträge 8: 261–275. Philipp von Zabern, Mainz.
Courbin, P. 1992. Bassit-Posidaion in the Early Iron Age. In Descoeudres, J.-P. (ed.), *Greek Colonists and Native Populations*. Proceedings of the First Australian Congress of Classical Archaeology, 503–509. Clarendon Press, Oxford.
Cross, F.M. 1969. Epigraphic Notes on the Amman Citadel Inscription. *Bulletin of the American Schools of Oriental Research* 193: 13–19.
Cross, F.M. & Saley, R.J. 1970. Phoenician Incantations on a Plaque of the Seventh Century B. C. from Arslan Tash in Upper Syria. *Bulletin of the American Schools of Oriental Research* 197: 42–49.
Cross, F.M. 1974. A Second Phoenician Incantation Text from Arslan Tash. *Catholic Biblical Quarterly* 36: 486–490.
Cross, F.M. 1986. Phoenicians in the West. The Early Epigraphic

Evidence. In Balmuth, M.S. (ed.), *Studies in Sardinian Archaeology, Vol. II: Sardinia in the Mediterranean*, 117–130. University of Michigan Press, Ann Arbor.

D'Agostino, B. & Garbini, G. 1977. La patera orientalizzante da Pontecagnano riesaminata. *Studi Etruschi* 45: 51–62.

Dankwarth, G. & Müller, Ch. 1990. Zur altaramäischen 'Altar'-Inschrift vom Tell Halaf. *Archiv für Orientforschung* 35: 73–78.

Dion, P.E. 1992. Les *ktym* de Tel Arad: Grecs ou Phéniciens? *Revue Biblique* 9: 70–97.

Dothan, M. 1985. A Phoenician Inscription from 'Akko. *Israel Exploration Journal* 5: 81–94, pl. 13.

Doumet-Serhal, C. 1993–94. La cruche à "arête sur le col": un fossile directeur de l'expansion phénicienne en Méditerranée aux 9ème et 8ème siècles avant J.-C. *Berytus* 41: 99–136.

Dunand, M. & Saliby, N. 1985. *Le temple d'Amrith dans la Pérée d'Aradus*. Librairie Orientaliste Paul Geuthner, Paris.

Eph'al, I. & Naveh, J. 1989. Hazael's Booty Inscriptions. *Israel Exploration Journal* 39: 192–200.

Greenfield, J.C. 1987. Larnax tes Lapethou revisited. In Lipiski, E. (ed.), *Phoenicia and the East Mediterranean in the First Millennium B. C.* Studia Phoenicia 5: 391–401. Peeters, Leuven.

Healey, J.P. 1974. The Kition Tariffs and the Phoenician Cursive Series. *Bulletin of the American Schools of Oriental Research* 216: 53–60.

Heltzer, M. 1989. Epigraphic Evidence Concerning a Jewish Settlement in Kition (Larnaca, Cyprus) in the Achaemenid Period (IV cent. B.C.E.). *Aula Orientalis* 7: 189–206.

Hölbl, G. 1986. *Ägyptisches Kulturgut im phönikischen und punischen Sardinien*. E. J. Brill, Leiden.

Karageorghis, V. 1976. *Kition. Mycenaean and Phoenician Discoveries in Cyprus*. Thames & Hudson, London.

Karageorghis, V. 1981. The Sacred Area of Kition. In Biran, A. (ed.), *Temples and High Places in Biblical Times*, 82–90, pls. 6–7. Hebrew Union College, Jerusalem.

Knoppers, G.N. 1992. 'The God in his Temple': The Phoenician Text from Pyrgi as a Funerary Inscription. *Journal of Near Eastern Studies* 51: 105–120.

Krahmalkov, C.R. 1981. The Foundation of Carthage, 814 B. C. The Douïmès Pendant Inscription. *Journal of Semitic Studies* 26: 177–191.

Lemaire, A. 1983. L'inscription phénicienne de Hassan-Beyli reconsiderée. *Rivista di Studi Fenici* 11: 9–19, pl. I.

Lemaire, A. 1984. Date et origine des inscriptions hébraïques et phéniciennes de Kuntillet 'Ajrud. *Studi epigrafici e linguistici* 1: 131–143.

Lipiski, E. 1983. La Carthage de Chypre. *Studia Phoenicia* 1: 209–234.

McCarter, P.K., Jr. 1975. A Phoenician Graffito from Pithekoussai. *American Journal of Archaeology* 79: 140–141.

Masson, O. 1982. Pèlerins chypriotes en Phénicie (Sarepta et Sidon). *Semitica* 32: 45–49.

Masson, O. & Sznycer, M. 1972. *Recherches sur les Phéniciens à Chypre*. Librairie Droz, Paris.

Moran, W.L. 1992. *The Amarna Letters*. The Johns Hopkins University Press, Baltimore.

Moscati, S. 1986. Fenici e Greci in Sardegna. *Rendiconti dell' Accademia Nazionale dei Lincei* 40: 265–271.

Moscati, S. 1987a. Due statue di Tell Halaf e i troni fenici. *Rendiconti dell'Accademia Nazionale dei Lincei* 41: 53–56, pls. I-II.

Moscati, S. 1987b. Découvertes phéniciennes à Tharros. *Académie des Inscriptions et Belles-Lettres, Comptes Rendus* 483–503.

Naveh, J. 1985. Writing and Scripts in Seventh-Century B.C.E. Philistia. The Evidence from Tell Jemmeh. *Israel Exploration Journal* 35: 8–21, pls. 1–4.

Naveh, J. 1987. Proto-Canaanite, Archaic Greek, and the Script of the Aramaic Text on the Tell Fakhariyah Statue. In Miller, P.D., Jr., Hanson, P.D. & McBride, S.D. (eds.), *Ancient Israelite Religion. Essays in Honor of Frank Moore Cross*, 101–113. Fortress Press, Philadelphia.

Niehr, H. 1994. Zum Totenkult der Könige von Sam'al im 9. und 8. Jr. v. Chr. *Studi epigrafici e linguistici* 11: 57–73.

O'Connor, M. 1977. The Rhetoric of the Kilamuwa Inscription. *Bulletin of the American Schools of Oriental Research* 226: 15–29.

Peckham, B. 1987. Phoenicia and the Religion of Israel: The Epigraphic Evidence. In Miller, P.D., Jr., Hanson, P.D., & McBride, S.D. (eds.), *Ancient Israelite Religion. Essays in Honor of Frank Moore Cross*, 79–99. Fortress Press, Philadelphia.

Peckham, B. 1992. Phoenicia, History of. *The Anchor Bible Dictionary*, vol. 5: 349–363. Doubleday, New York.

Pritchard, J.B. 1978. *Recovering Sarepta, a Phoenician City. Excavations at Sarafand, Lebanon, 1969–1974, by the University Museum of the University of Pennsylvania*. Princeton University Press, Princeton.

Puech, E. 1979. Remarques sur quelques inscriptions phéniciennes de Chypre. *Semitica* 29: 19–43.

Puech, E. 1983. Présence phénicienne dans les îles à la fin du IIe millénaire. A propos de deux coupes inscrites. *Revue Biblique* 90: 365–395.

Puech, E. 1986. Les inscriptions phéniciennes d'Amrit et les dieux guérisseurs du sanctuaire. *Syria* 53: 327–342.

Puech, E. 1992. La stèle de Bar-Hadad à Melqart et les rois d'Arpad. *Revue Biblique* 99: 311–334, pl. XV.

Sader, H. 1991. Phoenician Stelae from Tyre. *Berytus* 39: 101–126.

Sader, H. 1991–92. Nouvelle inscription punique découverte au Liban. *Semitica* 41/42: 107–116.

Sader, H. 1992. Phoenician Stelae from Tyre (continued). *Studi epigrafici e linguistici* 9: 53–79.

Seeden, H. 1991. A *Tophet* in Tyre? *Berytus* 39: 39–87.

Shaw, J.W. 1989. Phoenicians in Southern Crete. *American Journal of Archaeology* 93: 165–183.

Sznycer, M. 1980. Salamine de Chypre et les Phéniciens. In, *Salamine de Chypre: Histoire et Archéologie. Etat des Recherches*, 123–129. Conseil Nationale de Recherche Scientifique, Paris.

Vagnetti, L. 1989. A Sardinian Askos from Crete. *Annual of the British School at Athens* 84: 355–360, pl. 52.

Winter, I.J. 1976a. Phoenician and North Syrian Ivory Carving in Historical Context: Questions of Style and Distribution. *Iraq* 38: 1–22.

Winter, I.J. 1976b. Carved Ivory Furniture Panels from Nimrud: A Coherent Subgroup of the North Syrian Style. *Metropolitan Museum Journal* 11: 25–54.

Winter, I.J. 1981. Is there a South Syrian Style of Ivory Carving in the Early First Millennium B. C.? *Iraq* 43: 101–130.

Winter, I.J. 1989. North Syrian Ivories and Tell Halaf Reliefs. The Impact of Luxury Goods upon 'Major' Arts. In Leonard, A., Jr. & Williams, B.B. (eds.), *Essays in Ancient Civilization Presented to Helene J. Kantor*, 321–332, pls. 62–66. The Oriental Institute of the University of Chicago, Chicago.

Xella, P. 1993. Eschmun von Sidon. Der phönizische Asklepios. In Dietrich, M. & Loretz, O. (eds.), *Mesopotamica – Ugaritica – Biblica. Festschrift für Kurt Bergerhof*, 481–498. Neukirchener Verlag, Neukirchen.

Zauzich, K.-T. & Röllig, W. 1990. Eine ägyptische Schreibpalette in phönizischen Umgestaltung. *Orientalia* 59: 320–332, pl. XII.

Zuckerman, B. 1991. The Nora Puzzle. *Maarav* 7: 269–301.

39. Sardinian Pottery from Carthage

Magna Køllund

Introduction

Between 1986 and 1994 Prof. Hans Georg Niemeyer of the Archäologisches Institut, Universität Hamburg conducted five major campaigns of excavation in Carthage. During these campaigns at least three Sardinian ceramic fragments were found (Fig. 39.1) (two of the fragments are previously published in Køllund 1996).

The excavation area is situated in the Carthage-Dermech region on the eastern slopes of the Byrsa hill – more or less in the crossing of the Decumanus Maximus and the Cardo X of the Roman street system (Rakob 1989: fig. 5, A3). A preliminary report, which mainly concerns the early phases, has been published by Hans Georg Niemeyer and Roald Docter (1993) and another report concerning the later periods has just appeared (Niemeyer *et al.* 1995).

The excavators have defined nine major building phases spanning from Phase I in the second half of the 8th century BC to Phase IX in the first half of the 2nd century BC. Phase I to IV (Niemeyer & Docter 1993: figs. 2–3) are the most interesting in this connection and I shall therefore give a very brief outline of them.

Phase I is very poorly preserved, but the few traces of walls are the oldest known house-remains from Carthage so far. They have been dated to the second half of the 8th century BC.

In Phase II the whole area was restructured after a new plan and orientation, that lasted until the end of the Punic period. House 1, and other houses joining it wall to wall, were built on the site. This phase has two sub-phases 'A' and 'B', respectively dated to the late 8th and the beginning of the 7th century BC.

In Phase III, dated to the first half and the middle of the 7th century BC, House 1 was totally restructured – the exterior plan was preserved but all the inner walls

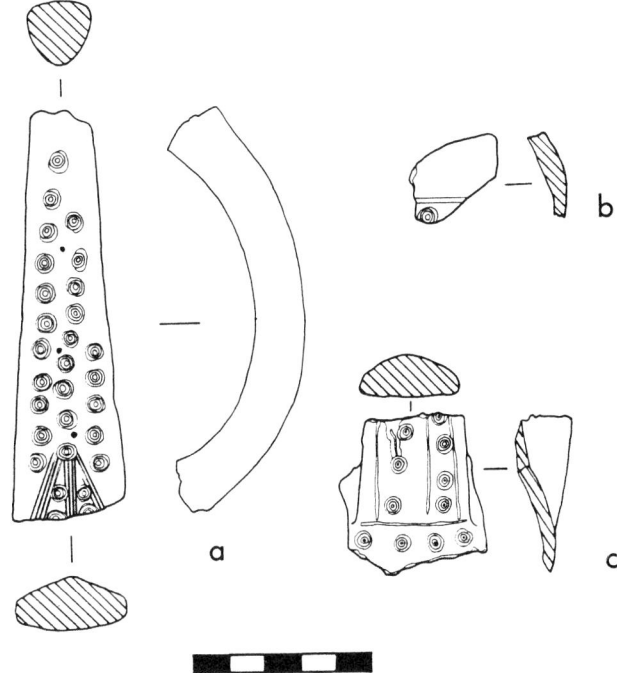

Fig. 39.1 Geometric Nuragic pottery from Carthage: a. Handle (KA 86/068/001); b. Body sherd (KA 91/434/080); c. Handle fragment (KA 93/543/200).

were rearranged after a new plan, and it is possible that the house had two floors.

In Phase IV, House 1 was expanded towards the East. The new building technique, *opus africanum*, was used for the first time and the roof of this house was definitely tiled. The house has two sub-phases: 'A' dated to the last quarter of the 7th century, and 'B' dated to the first half of the 6th century BC.

Magna Køllund, Institute of Archaeology and Ethnology, University of Copenhagen, Vandkunsten 5, DK-1467 Copenhagen K, Denmark

Because of the sloping of the landscape, each new phase inevitably meant an extra large amount of levelling, which definitely brought older material into younger layers. The dating of the different phases are therefore based on the chronology of the youngest imported pottery in the different layers.

Sardinian Finds in Carthage

Among the rich ceramic material found in the excavations were three fragments of Nuragic pottery with the very characteristic incised lines and stamped concentric circles of the Nuragic Geometric period (9th – 8th century BC). The three fragments (Fig. 39.1) – two handle fragments (one with part of wall) and one wall fragment – are all decorated and probably belong to at least two askoid jugs (Niemeyer & Docter 1993: 226–227; Køllund 1996: 211–212). The first handle (Fig. 39.1, a) was found in stratum IIIa1 – a levelling layer for Phase IV – together with material mainly belonging to the first half of the 7th century. The second handle (Fig. 39.1, c) was found in stratum IV, which has been dated to the last quarter of the 7th century, but the layer also contained older material. Finally the body fragment (Fig. 39.1, b) was found in a layer, which had been disturbed in Roman times. Taking into account the Sardinian date of these fragments (probably 9th-8th century BC) the contexts of all three fragments must be considered secondary. They probably all originally belonged to either Phase I or Phase IIA but were moved by one of the many levellings.

The three fragments are probably not the only Sardinian material from Carthage. As an example it can be mentioned that the thin-section of an amphora handle belonging to stratum IVb1 (first half of the 6th century BC) has found perfect matches in fragments found by the Riu Mannu survey in west central Sardinia conducted by the University of Leiden, Holland (Annis *et al.* 1994; van Dommelen 1997) and thus also should be considered of Sardinian origin. Furthermore R. Docter and K. Mansel are still working on the early pottery and trying to ascertain the places of origin of the different groups of handmade plain pottery, which accounts for a very large proportion of the pottery in the early phases of the settlement (Niemeyer & Docter 1993: 216–217, table 1–3); it is possible that some of these may stem from Sardinia.

The material from the Hamburg excavations in Carthage generally reflects a wide range of contacts in the early phases of the Phoenician city (Niemeyer & Docter 1983: 226–230, figs. 11–12, pl. 58; Docter & Niemeyer 1994). Besides the Sardinian material the excavations also show early contacts to: A) Pithekoussai – from the second half of the 8th century – Pithekoussan imitations of Late Geometric I to Middle Protocorinthian pottery (skyphoi, kotylai, oinochoai and juglets); B) Central Italy, transport amphorae – the so-called Zita-amphorae from the second half of the 8th century (most predominant in Phases I to IIIa); but also from layer IIIa1 and later: impasto (kantharos fragment with graffito), bucchero (skyphoi, kantharoi/kyathoi, a spiral amphora, and an oinochoe) (von Hase 1989: 330–332, n. 15), and Etrusco-Corinthian pottery (alabastron, aryballos); C) Greece: Cycladic-Geometric shallow bowl with encircling bands (layer IIa1); Late and Subgeometric Euboean skyphoi (layer IIa1-IIIa1) and Early Protocorinthian kotylai, skyphoi, jugs and kraters.

Other Evidence of Sardinian Pottery Found Outside of Sardinia (Fig. 39.2)

Seen from a Sardinian perspective the Nuragic pottery is the latest of a series of Nuragic pottery found outside Sardinia. We now have Late Bronze Age (13th century BC) finds from Kommos on Crete (Watrous, this volume), Final Bronze Age/Ausonian II (11th – first half of 9th century BC) Protogeometric finds from Lipari, (Ferrarese Ceruti 1987, abstracted in this volume) and Early Iron Age (9th – 8th century BC) finds from Etruria (Køllund 1996: 205), Sicily (Orsi 1912: 317, Sep. SE. 81, pl. IX no. 66.), Crete (Vagnetti 1989; Ferrarese Ceruti 1991) and Carthage. In the two early contexts – habitation layers in Kommos and Lipari – we have several different shapes including large storage jars. In the Early Iron Age the finds are all made up of one shape only – namely the askoid jug. Before the discoveries in Carthage all the Early Iron Age jugs had been found in tombs. In fact the find-circumstances in Carthage resembles those of Nuragic pottery found in the Phoenician colonies on Sardinia itself more than those of any other site outside Sardinia. As I have argued elsewhere (Køllund 1996) there are two plausible explanations for the jugs found outside Sardinia. The first is that they were traded for their contents – perhaps some kind of perfumed oil. The second and perhaps more intriguing is that they were the personal belongings of Nuragic people travelling abroad for instance brought along because they were needed in some kind of religious ritual. I still see both possibilities for Carthage.

Conclusion

To sum up: the evidence from Carthage does not give much exact chronological evidence for Sardinia, which was the main concern of this conference, but the presence of Sardinian Nuragic pottery in the earliest habitation layers of the Phoenician town of Carthage certainly gives an extra spark to the discussion of the amount of Nuragic presence in the Phoenician colonies in Sardinia and to the general discussion on the nature of the relationship between the Phoenicians – both in and outside Sardinia – and the Nuragic people of Sardinia.

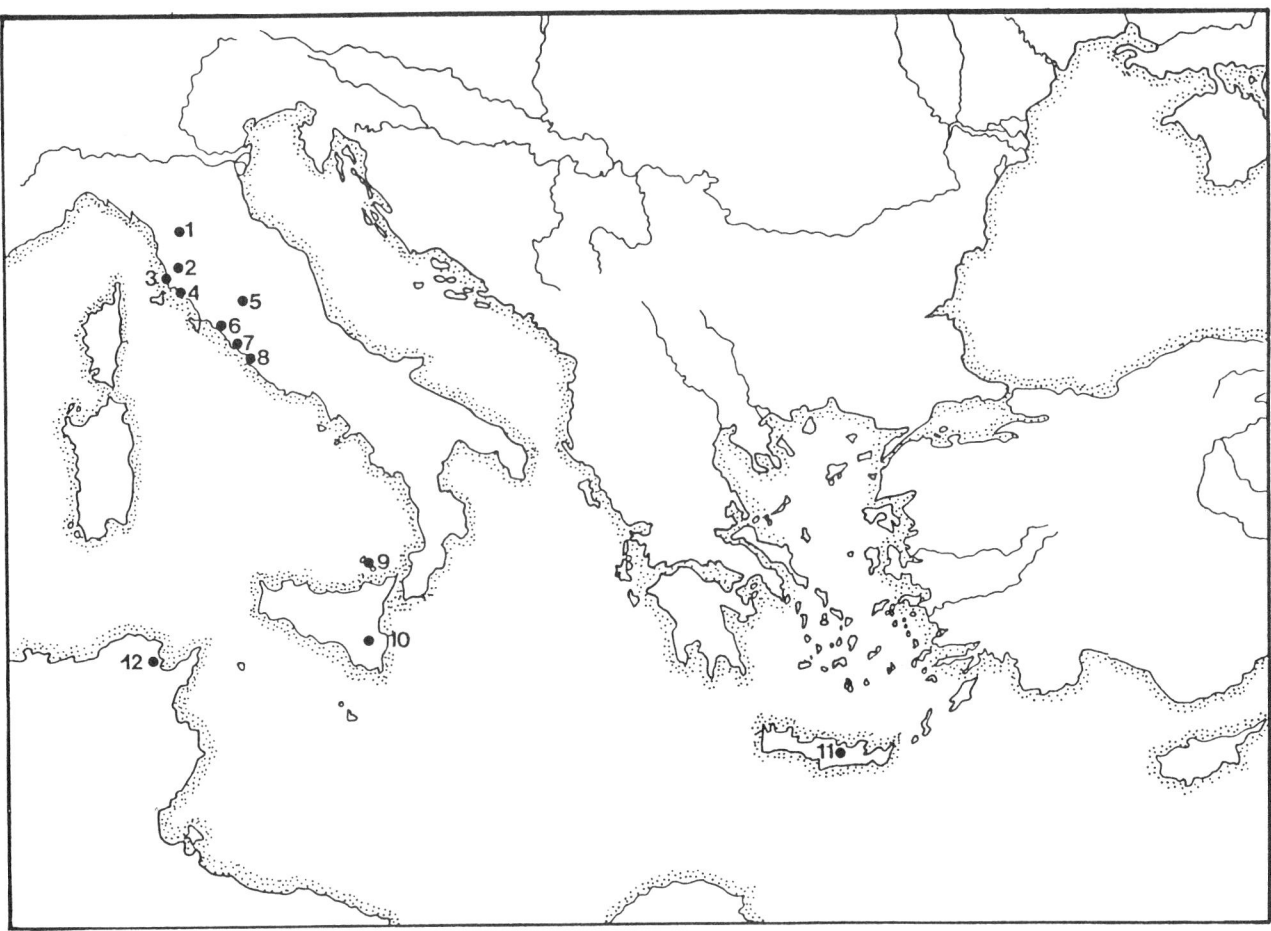

Fig. 39.2. Distribution of Nuragic pottery found outside of Sardinia: 1. Volterra; 2. Massa Marittima; 3. Populonia; 4. Vetulonia; 5. Bisenzio; 6. Vulci; 7. Tarquinia; 8. Cerveteri; 9. Lipari; 10. Pantalica; 11. Crete – Khaniale Tekke and Kommos; 12. Carthage.

Acknowledgments

My warmest thanks to Professor Hans Georg Niemeyer for giving me the opportunity and encouragement to study and publish the finds presented here. I also thank his assistant Dr. Roald Docter for his help (providing specific data and drawings) and kind suggestions.

Catalogue

Askoid jugs

1. Handle (KA 86/068/001) (Fig. 39.1, a)
   Provenance: Stratum IIIa1, House 2.
   Clay: hard 10YR 4/2, Clay (mgg1), lime (mff2), mica (mff2). Black burnished surface.
   Handmade with stamped and incised decoration.
   Decorated with stamped concentric circles and near the transition to the body three groups of lines radiating from a common concentric circle towards the body. Between the groups are concentric circles.
   Date of context: Stratum IIIa1 is a filling for a floor (stratum IV – 2a1), which the excavators preliminarily date to the last quarter of the 7th century BC. Most of the material in the layer probably belongs to the first half of the 7th century BC.
   References: von Hase 1989: 330 n. 15 (falsely called bucchero); Køllund 1996: fig. 5; Niemeyer & Docter 1993: 226–227.

2. Body sherd (KA 91/434/080) (Fig. 39.1, b)
   Provenance: layer disturbed in Roman times.
   Clay: hard, black, quartz (mmf1), mica (mff3). Black burnished surface. Handmade with stamped and incised decoration.
   Decorated with a stamped concentric circle and two horizontal incised lines.
   Date of context: The layer containing the sherd was disturbed in the Roman period.
   References: Køllund 1996: fig. 5; Niemeyer & Docter 1993: 226–227.

3. Handle fragment (KA 93/543/200) (Fig. 39.1, c)
   Provenance: Room U in House 3, Phase IV.
   Clay: hard black, Clay, lime, mica. Black burnished surface.
   Handmade with stamped and incised decoration.
   Lower part of handle at the point of juncture.
   The handle is decorated with three vertical lines going from the top of the fragment to a horizontal line at the transition to the body. The middle line is slightly off-centered to the right. Between the lines are vertical rows of concentric circles (3 to the left and 4 to the right). Below the vertical line is a vertical row of four concentric circles.
   Date of context: Phase IV is currently dated to the late 7th and early 6th centuries BC.

4. Amphora fragment (handle) KA 91/478/344

Provenance: IVb1, Room C-D, House 1.
Date of context: first half of the 6th century BC.

References

Annis, M.B., van Dommelen P., & van de Velde, P. 1994. *The Riu Mannu Survey Project in West Central Sardinia: A First Interim Report.* Newsletter, Department of Pottery Technology, Leiden University, 11/12 (1993-4): 31-44.

Docter, R.F. & Niemeyer, H.G. 1994. Pithekoussai: The Carthaginian Connection. On the archaeological evidence of Euboeo-Phoenician partnership in the 8th and 7th centuries BC. In *APOIKIA, Scritti in onore di Giorgio Buchner.* Annali del Istituto Universitario Orientale di Napoli, Archeologia e Storia Antica n.s. 1: 101-115.

Dommelen, P. van. 1997. Some reflections on urbanization in a colonial context: west central Sardinia in the 7th to 5th century BC. In H. Damgaard Andersen, H. Horsnæs & S. Houby-Nielsen (eds.), *Urbanization in the Mediterranean in the 9th to 6th centuries BC, Acts of the International Symposium in Copenhagen (May 1994).* Acta Hyperborea 7: 243-278.

Ferrarese Ceruti, M.L. 1987. Considerazioni sulla ceramica nuragica a Lipari. In *La Sardegna nel Mediterraneo tra il Secondo e il Primo Millennio a. C, Atti del II Convegno di Studi "Un millennio di relazioni fra la Sardegna e i Paesi del Mediterraneo" Selargius-Cagliari 27-30 novembre 1986,* 431-442. Cagliari.

Ferrarese Ceruti, M.L. 1991. Creta e Sardegna in età postmicenea. Una nota. In *La transizione dal Miceneo all'alto arcaismo. Dal palazzo alla città. Atti del Convegno Internazionale, Roma, 14-19 marzo 1988,* 587-591. Roma.

von Hase, F.-W. 1989. Der Etruskische Bucchero aus Karthago, Ein Beitrag zu den frühen Handelsbeziehungen im westlichen Mittelmeergebiet (7.-6. Jahrhundert v. Chr.), *Jahrbuch des Römisch-Germanischen Zentralmuseums Mainz* 36: 327-410.

Køllund, M. 1996. Sea and Sardinia. In Briese, C., Docter, R.F. & Mansel, K. (eds.), *Die Akten des Internationalen Kolloquiums "Interactions in the Iron Age: Phoenicians, Greeks and the Indigenous Peoples of the Western Mediterranean" in Amsterdam am 26. und 27. März 1992.* Hamburger Beiträge zur Archäologie 19/20(1992/93): 201-214. Phillipp von Zabern, Mainz.

Niemeyer, H.G. & Docter, R.F. 1993. Die Grabung unter dem Decumanus Maximus von Karthago. *Mitteilungen des Deutschen Archäologischen Instituts, Römische Abteilung* 100: 201-244.

Niemeyer, H.G., Docter, R.F. & Rindelaub, A. 1995. Zweiter vorbericht über die Grabung unter dem Decumanus Maximus von Karthago. *Mitteilungen des Deutschen Archäologischen Instituts, Römische Abteilung* 102: 475-502.

Orsi, P. 1912. La necropoli sicula di Pantalica e Dessueri. *Monumenti Antichi Reale Accademia dei Lincei* 21: 301-346.

Rakob, F. 1989. Karthago. Die frühe Siedlung. Neue Forschungen. *Mitteilungen des Deutschen Archäologischen Instituts, Römische Abteilung* 96: 155-208.

Vagnetti, L. 1989. A Sardinian Askos from Crete. *Annual of the British School at Athens* 84: 355-360.

40. The Nuraghe and Village of Sant'Imbenia, Alghero (Sassari)

Susanna Bafico

Although the nuraghe and village of Sant'Imbenia have been known since the beginning of this century, the site was practically invisible because it was covered by dense vegetation and a recent building. Located on the northwestern coast of Sardinia, near Alghero in the province of Sassari, it came to light by chance early in the 1980s and its importance, which is due to its location in an area rich in agricultural and mineral resources and endowed with many convenient places for approach, was quickly revealed.

Three phases of the site have been identified: a) the nuraghe, b) the nuragic village immediately surrounding the tower, and c) an extensive village on the surface, of a type composed of separate blocks (*isolati*).

a) The nuraghe, once it had been freed from the remains of the building recently placed over it, turned out to be of a complex type, with a curtain wall and two towers on the eastern side. Between the towers, there must have been an entryway.
b) The nuragic village, which arose as early as the Middle Bronze Age, was identified by trial trenches north of the bastion.
c) Like others of the same articulated type, the village composed of separate blocks included rooms for different use: among others, one had a central basin and benches along the wall, known as a "breadmaking room," and so forth.
d) the recurrent appearance of imported pottery, especially Phoenician but also Greek, documents the existence on the site of an *emporion*, of the Early Iron Age, with connections to the East Mediterranean and to Carthage on the coast of North Africa.

The excavation program has been regular to date, extending from 1982 to 1994 (Bafico 1986; 1990; 1991a; 1991b; Bafico *et al.* 1991; 1997). It was originally intended to define the extent of the site, and then to explore it. Currently, in view of the significance of the finds, a project is under way to cover the entire village in an attempt at conservation because it poses serious problems, being built of limestone and sandstone in a very windy area near the sea.

There has been collaboration with specialists in geomorphology, pedology, and paleozoology. Uncalibrated radiocarbon dates, ranging between 1000 and 2000 BC, are in the process of being evaluated.

This excavation has highlighted many problems, among which is the complex problem of the relationship between the Nuragic world of the Iron Age and the precolonial world of extrainsular areas. If, as it seems, the eastern merchants followed the routes opened by the Mycenaeans in their search for mineral resources, this site is about equidistant between the mines of Calabona, Argentiera, Canaglia, etc. and also presented a safe harbor on the searoute to Spain and perhaps even an alternative route west to Etruria.

The imported material includes, among other examples, a Phoenician amphora with painted metopal decoration reminiscent of Cintas Type B1, a Euboean *skyphos* with pendent semicircles, a Euboean *skyphos* with chevron decoration, and *kotylai* of subgeometric and protocorinthian periods. The local pottery associated with these seem sufficiently homogeneous with respect to clay and shape, but in some cases seem to have absorbed eastern influences such as the use of the fast wheel, the adoption of geometric impressed or incised decorations on characteristic Nuragic askoid jugs (*brochette askoidi*), and the imitation of the shape of exotic vessels.

Since the Euboean cup with pendent semicircles seems datable to the end of the 9th and beginning of the 8th century BC, the finds at Sant'Imbenia may represent a moment preceding the foundation of other Phoenician colonies on Sardinia; at Sulcis, now considered the first

Susanna Bafico, Soprintendenza ai Beni Archeologici per le Provincie di Sassari e Nuoro, Piazza S. Agostino 2, Sassari 07100, Sardegna, Italia

Phoenician site on the island, the imports found so far date back only to 750 BC.

Bibliografia

Bafico, S. 1986 Materiali di importazione del villaggio nuragico di S. Imbenia. In Ugas, G. & Lai, G. (eds.), *Società e cultura in Sardegna nei periodi orientalizzante ed arcaico. Rapporti tra Sardegna, Fenici, Etruschi e Greci, Atti del I Convegno di studi "Un millennio di relazioni fra la Sardegna e i Paesi del Mediterraneo", Selargius-Cagliari 1985*, 91–93. Cagliari.

Bafico, S. 1990. Alghero (Sassari). Località S. Imbenia. *Bollettino di Archeologico* 1–2 (gennaio-aprile): 264.

Bafico, S. 1991a. Alghero (Sassari). Località S. Imbenia. *Bollettino di Archeologia* 10 (luglio-agosto): 97–100.

Bafico, S. 1991b. Greci e Fenici ad Alghero. *Archeo* 74 (gennaio): 18.

Bafico, S., D'Oriano, R., & Lo Schiavo, F. 1995. Il villaggio nuragico di S. Imbenia ad Alghero (Sassari). Nota Preliminare. In *Atti del III Convegno Internazionale di Studi Fenici e Punici, Tunis 11–16 novembre 1991*, 1: 87–98. Tunis.

Bafico, S., Oggiano, I., Ridgway, D., Garbini, G. 1997. Fenici e indigeni a S. Imbenia (Alghero). In Bernardini, P., D'Oriano, R. & Spanu, P.G. (a cura di), *Phoinikes B Shrdn. I Fenici in Sardegna. Nuove acquisizioni*. Catalago della Mostra, luglio-decembre 1997, Oristano, Antiquarium Arborense, 44–53. La Memoria Storica, Oristano.

41. Bearing Greek Gifts: Euboean Pottery on Sardinia

Sarah P. Morris

The discovery of Euboean pottery on Sardinia is welcome, even unsurprising, to archaeologists specializing in the Late Bronze and Early Iron Ages in the eastern Mediterranean. Two maps illustrate how the western Mediterranean was the natural extension of what I believe (Morris 1992a: 117–210) was a Levantine-dominated quest for metals. The map tracing the imagined journey of the Ulu Burun ship (Bass 1987: 697–98) suggests a scenario for Bronze Age trade which includes Sardinia as a western findspot of Mycenaean pottery and a source of minerals. Newly discovered Mycenaean sherds in Spain (Martin de la Cruz 1990) have in fact been attributed to explorers who arrived via Sardinia (Podzuweit 1990). Later maps suggest the continuity of this network into the Iron Age, with the Phoenicians taking the role once held by Cyprus and Syria, and Euboean sherds the place of Mycenaean pottery (Liverani 1987: figs 7.1, 7.3). With these images in mind, I will address two aspects of the new discovery.

My first point involves the value of these sherds for dating local contexts and refining regional chronologies in Sardinia, currently in broader periods than the phases of Greek Geometric pottery. A chart compiled by Ian Morris (1987: 12, fig. 3) attempts to coordinate the many regional styles of Geometric Greece into a single timeframe; next, however, you will see from John Papadopoulos how complex its regional varieties are. For Sardinian purposes, the Euboean column is most critical, and pendent semi-circle skyphoi usually denote the Late and Sub-Protogeometric periods, especially the ninth century. But what are our sources for such absolute dates?

Let us remind ourselves that the absolute chronology of Greek Geometric pottery is shaky, at best, and heavily dependent on synchronisms with other cultures. Its fragility is under constant scrutiny: I continue to praise an unpublished Harvard dissertation by Diane (Daniella) Saltz on Geometric pottery in the Near East, for its vigorous attack on the nightmare of Greek, Cypriote, and Levantine findspots and dates (Saltz 1978). Her conclusions went largely unheeded and are now outdated by more recent discoveries and analyses (e.g. Forsberg 1995, typical of new studies unaware of Saltz's work), but one of her suggestions should have been heeded years ago: to raise the beginning of the (Attic) Protogeometric style. Other scholars, like Anita Yannai and Patricia Bikai, reached much the same conclusion from observing a consistent discrepancy between Greek and Near Eastern chronologies. The latest to argue for this elevation is Guenter Kopcke, from the evidence of a new Protogeometric krater from Moshe Kochavi's excavations at Tell Hadar in Israel (Kopcke, personal communication). Conventional Greek chronology would place this vessel well after 900 B.C., but its Near Eastern destruction (Hadar level IV), according to the excavators (but not all archaeologists working in Israel), cannot post-date 1000 B.C. If such discrepancies are heeded, Attic Protogeometric should be adjusted to begin well before 1100 B.C.; this would provide a welcome elimination of "Submycenaean," unfeasible as a phase or a style (despite recent attempts to legitimate and expand this phenomenon: Mountjoy 1987; Papadopoulos 1993). The point is that Greek pottery is too often used to date foreign contexts, as it is now expected to do for Sardinia, but it derives its own dates from Near Eastern destruction levels which can be blamed on any one of several historical events. What is needed is an intensive workshop by archaeologists struggling with Greek sherds in the western Mediterranean, Italy, Greece, Cyprus, Israel, Syria, and Lebanon to put their sherds on the table, so to speak, and agree on a workable system. This is what our Cypriote colleagues did with a ceramics workshop in Philadelphia (Barlow *et al.* 1992), and it's high time it happened for Greek Geometric pottery.

Sarah P. Morris, Department of Classics, University of California, Los Angeles, 405 Hilgard Avenue, Los Angeles, California 90024–1475 USA

My own chief concern, the legacy of my doctoral work on the seventh century, lies at the end of the Geometric time line, where it has long been problematic that Late Geometric is too short and too crowded. I suspect this is because the period has been artificially ended too early: the presence of Late Geometric sherds at sites like Hama, Tarsus and Samaria (destroyed by Sargon of Assyria) should not be overestimated (Francis & Vickers 1985; Forsberg 1995, etc.). The Geometric period lasted well into the seventh century, and its Subgeometric followers into the Archaic period. In ceramics I have studied from Naxos, a subgeometric style far outlasted short-lived Orientalizing fashions: kraters in both styles come from the same cemetery on Naxos, and cups from the cave of Zas on the same island perpetuate a Protogeometric design until as late as 500 B.C. (Morris 1997: fig. 3). Spreading the Late Geometric style over another half century, as some would advocate, would greatly dilute a population explosion of the Late eighth century (Snodgrass 1977: 10–16; 1980: 19–24, estimates from burials an annual growth rate over 4%, inconceivable under pre-modern conditions). Finally, what is the significance of Greek pottery in the west? In my opinion, the presence of Mycenaean sherds in places like Italy, Sicily, Sardinia, and Spain does not make the Mycenaeans active in the west: I believe that their ceramic products were carried there in Levantine ships, or craft like the Ulu Burun wreck, with an international crew. Likewise, finding Euboean pottery does not guarantee the presence of Euboeans, whether the site is Knossos, Al Mina, or Sulcis. The recent identification of Euboean sherds at Carthage (Vegas 1992) puts our models to the test: these are more likely to reflect the travels of Phoenicians between Ischia (Pithekussae) and North Africa than Euboeans themselves (see Køllund, this volume). We should resist referring to phantom "Euboeans" or Euboean colonization: this is the prevailing scenario for British colleagues at Lefkandi, Knossos, Ischia, and Al Mina, where I call Euboeans "more plausible as apprentices, then [not "than"!] partners in trade with...non-Greeks..."). Those who brought Euboean sherds to Sardinia may have gotten them from Lefkandi, and may well be the same Levantine merchants who brought Italian vases back to Crete. This paper ends with a plea to beware of non-Greeks bearing Euboean gifts: John Papadopoulos elaborates next.

References

Barlow, J., Bolger, B., & King, B. 1991. *Cypriot Ceramics: Reading the Prehistoric Record.* University Museum Monographs 74. Philadelphia.

Bass, G. 1987. Oldest Known Shipwreck Reveals Splendors of the Bronze Age. *National Geographic* 172(6): 693–733.

Forsberg, S. 1995. *Near Eastern destruction dating as sources for Greek and Near Eastern Iron Age chronology: archaeological and historical studies.The cases of Samaria (722 B.C.) and Tarsus (696 B.C.).* Uppsala.

Francis, E.D. & Vickers, M. 1985. Greek Geometric pottery at Hama and its implications for Near Eastern chronology. *Levant* 17: 131–138.

Liverani, M. 1987. The collapse of the Near Eastern regional system at the end of the Bronze Age: the case of Syria. In Rowlands, M., Larsen, M., & Kristiansen, K. (eds.), *Centre and Periphery in the Ancient World,* 66–73. Cambridge.

Martin de la Cruz, J.C. 1990. Die erste mykenische Keramik von der iberischen Halbinsel. *Prähistorische Zeitschrift* 65: 49–52.

Morris, I. 1987. *Burial and Society: the rise of the Greek city-state.* Cambridge.

Morris, S. 1992a. *Daidalos and the Origins of Greek Art.* Princeton.

Morris, S. 1992b. Greece beyond East and West: perspectives and prospects. Introduction to Kopcke, G., & Tokumaru, I. (eds), *Greece Between East and West: 10th-8th Centuries B.C.:* xiii-xvii. Mainz.

Morris, S. 1997. Greek and Near Eastern Art in the Age of Homer. In S. Langdon (ed.), *New Light on a Dark Age: Exploring the Culture of Geometric Greece,* 56–70. Columbia, Mo.

Mountjoy, P. with Hankey, V., 1988. LH IIIC vs. Submycenaean: The Kerameikos Pompeion Cemetery Revisited. *Jahrbuch des Deutschen Archäologischen Instituts* 103: 1–37.

Osborne, R. 1996. *Greece in the Making 1200–479 B.C.* London.

Papadopoulos, J.K. 1993. To Kill a Cemetery: The Athenian Kerameikos and the Early Iron Age in the Aegean. *Journal of Mediterranean Archaeology* 6: 175–206.

Podzuweit, C. 1990. Bemerkungen zur mykenischen Keramik von Llanete de los Moros, Montoro, Prov. Cordoba. *Prähistorische Zeitschrift* 65: 53–58.

Saltz, D. 1978. *Greek Geometric Pottery in the East: The Chronological Implication.* Ph.D. Thesis, Near Eastern Languages and Civilizations, Harvard University.

Snodgrass, A. 1977. *Archaeology and the Rise of the Greek State.* Inaugural Lecture, Laurence Professorship, University of Cambridge.

Snodgrass, A. 1980. *Archaic Greece: The Age of Experiment.* London.

Vegas, M. 1992. Carthage: La ville archaïque. Céramique d'importation de la période du Géométrique Récent. In *Lixus. Actes du Colloque organisé par l'Institut des sciences et de l'archéologie et du patrimoine de Rabat avec le concours de l'Ecole Française de Rome, Larache 8–11 novembre 1989*, Collection de l'Ecole Française de Rome, 181–189. E. de Boccard, Paris.

42. From Macedonia to Sardinia: Problems of Iron Age Aegean Chronology, and Assumptions of Greek Maritime Primacy

John K. Papadopoulos

Despite warnings to the contrary (e.g. Graham 1986; Papadopoulos 1996a), the illusion that *ceramics = history* is still very much alive in Aegean Late Bronze and Early Iron Age studies. The tenacity of fired terracotta and its ability to survive most archaeological contexts has given pottery an exaggerated importance. The problem, if it could be confined to the Aegean, might be manageable, but the presence of Greek pottery sherds, often in proportionately small quantities, in the coastal Levant and North Africa, Cyprus, Italy, Sicily, Sardinia and beyond, has given rise to two widely held notions, that are questioned in this paper. The first is the belief that Greek pottery is well dated and that the Aegean painted pottery sequence represents a chronological "yardstick" or even a "neatly labelled 'chest of drawers'" (Ridgway & Serra Ridgway 1992: 357, referring to Boardman 1990). The second is the idea of the primacy of Greek, particularly Euboean, maritime enterprise and colonial expansion in the Mediterranean, most recently argued in Boardman (1990), Lemos (1992) and Popham (1994). I have stated elsewhere that pottery alone can be a misleading and inadequate indicator of social realities, and that the vicissitudes of ceramic history should never be confused with social, political or economic developments (Papadopoulos 1996a: 158; cf. Papadopoulos 1993; 1997).

One purpose of this paper is to restate this view and to stress that Euboean pottery does not necessarily equal Euboean presence, nor does that pottery have to be carried by a Euboean. In so doing, this paper also attempts to address another imbalance, albeit from an Aegean perspective, by emphasizing the growing understanding that what really may have been Phoenician colonial or pre-colonial maritime enterprise in the Mediterranean has often been attributed to the Greeks. Hostility towards the Phoenicians is not just a symptom of 19th and 20th century scholarship, but is a feature that goes back to the earliest Greek alphabetic writing (Kopcke 1992; Winter 1995).

This paper echoes Sarah Morris's warning: Beware Greek Painted Pottery, ... and especially those phantom Greeks – or Euboeans – bearing it (cf. James *et al.* 1991: 56).

Sardinia is in a unique position to shed light on these problems, especially since Euboean pottery has been found at both Sant'Imbenia (Bafico 1991a; 1991b; Ridgway 1992: 29) and at Sulcis (Bartoloni *et al.* 1988; Bartoloni 1989; Davison 1992: 384; Ridgway 1994: 40). It is generally agreed that Sardinia was never Greek (Ridgway 1990: 72; Ridgway & Serra Ridgway 1992: 355; Davison 1984; 1986; 1992), despite the growing, though not substantial quantities of Mycenaean (Ferrarese Ceruti *et al.* 1987; Balmuth 1992: 215–217) and Aegean Early Iron Age (Ridgway 1992: 29; cf. Ridgway 1986) pottery and even despite attempts to establish a relationship between Mycenaean and Nuragic architecture, now demolished (Cavanagh & Laxton 1987; Ridgway & Serra Ridgway 1992: 355). Indeed, the Phoenician material at Sant'Imbenia, and actual Phoenician settlement at Sulcis can be read as compelling evidence, rather than as a ceramic hint, of Phoenician involvement. Phoenician carriers would also account for the growing quantities of Greek pottery at Carthage (Vegas 1992). [see Køllund this volume – eds.].

The problems with Aegean chronology of the later Bronze and Early Iron Age are many, and they are not only confined to the controversial challenges to the conventional absolute chronology proposed by James and his collaborators (James *et al.* 1991), as well as those of Francis and Vickers (Francis 1990; Francis & Vickers 1983; 1985; Vickers 1985; 1987; cf. Bowden 1991; and summary by Biers 1992: 82–85). Although a great deal of attention has been placed on determining the absolute chronology of the Aegean and Mediterranean in these periods, the relative sequences have been largely neglected, particularly from a methodological point of view, and it is often assumed that although absolute chronology is

---

John K. Papadopoulos, Antiquities Department, The J. Paul Getty Museum, P.O. Box 2112, Santa Monica, CA 90407–2112 USA
References to Pl. refer to the section of colour plates.

flexible and can be changed according to new evidence, the relative sequence is firmly established. Before embarking on any reassessment of the absolute chronology, it is the relative chronology that is in need of critical reappraisal.

The three most fundamental problems in Aegean Early Iron Age relative chronology are: (1) the notion of the rigidly linear development of style; (2) the method of allocating time to a given or discerned phase, even when there are no chronological "fixed-points" for anchoring the relative sequence; and (3) the strong regionality of style. The last does not only apply to pottery, but to all aspects of material culture (cf. Papadopoulos 1996b). There is no such thing as a pan-Hellenic or pan-Aegean style, and the process of cross-linking the various Aegean styles into a coherent and consistent weave is not straightforward.

In addition to providing a false sense of chronological comfort, the occurrence of Greek painted pottery outside the Aegean has, for too long, been taken as evidence of the impact of Greek traders, even colonists. Such a view overemphasizes the role of Greeks, especially Euboeans, while minimizing that of Phoenicians, Cypriots and others from the eastern Mediterranean. This not only highlights the inadequacy of current models, whether explicity stated or implied, in the way Aegean archaeologists perceive trade, colonisation and the movement of peoples, but also the whole question of recognizing ethnicity in the archaeological record (Papadopoulos 1997).

In order to illustrate this, and the fact that Aegean ceramic sequences are far from the 'neatly labelled chest of drawers' they have been characterized as, I would like to focus on the fragments of two pendent semi-circle skyphoi found recently in Macedonia (Figs. 42.1, 42.4, 42.5). This example attempts to show that while scholars working on a Late Bronze or Early Iron Age site in Italy, North Africa or Sardinia would welcome a painted Minoan or Mycenaean, Attic or Euboean, sherd to assist with dating, colleagues working in many parts of the Greek mainland, coastal Asia Minor, the northern Aegean, as well as the Aegean and Ionian islands would equally welcome the same sherd. Essentially, whether one is working in Sardinia, Magna Graecia, the greater western or eastern Mediterranean, or parts of the Aegean, the problems are very similar.

For Hellenocentricists the pendent semi-circle skyphos has been the harbinger of Greek, especially Euboean, maritime prowess and the incidence and distribution of this distinctive shape the backbone of Aegean merchantile, colonial and pre-colonial expansion. The pendent semi-circle skyphos has been the object of numerous studies (Skeat 1934; Desborough 1952: 180–194; Desborough in Popham *et al.* 1980: 28–29, 32, 37–38, 42–43, 297; Coldstream 1968: 148–157, 310–313; Descœudres & Kearsley 1983) and, most recently, a monograph (Kearsley 1989; reviewed by Popham & Lemos 1992). Despite such careful treatment, the shape remains a difficult one to date

Fig. 42.1. Torone T82–2. Pendent semi-circle skyphos. Preserved height: 0.118 m; Diameter (rim): 0.170 m.

Fig. 42.2. Torone T48–1. Krater. Height: 0.299 m; Diameter (base): 0.150 m; Diameter (rim): 0.355 m.

Fig. 42.3. Torone T102–1. Krater. Height: 0.265 m; Diameter (base): 0.136 m; Diameter (rim): 0.335–0.370m.

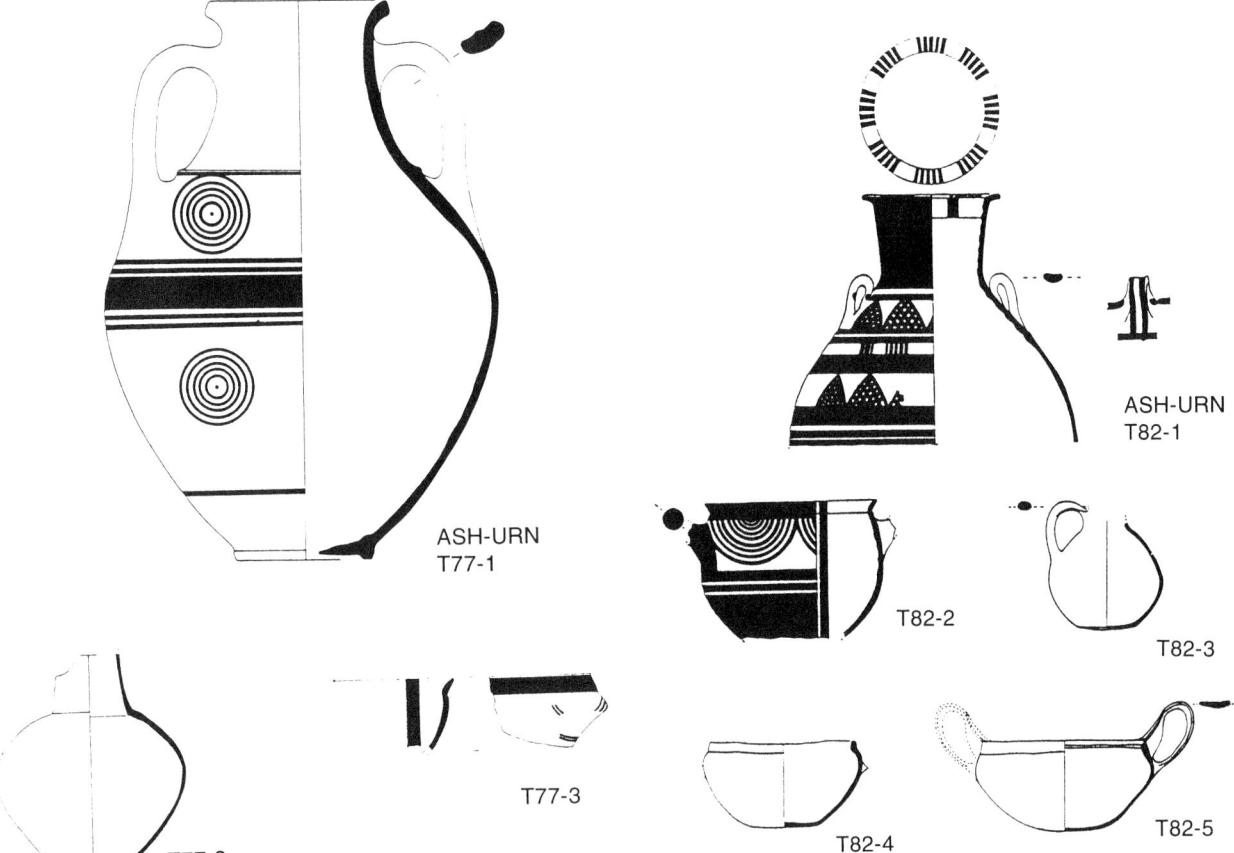

Fig. 42.4. Contents of Torone Tomb 77, including pendent semi-circle skyphos (T77–3). Scale 1:3.

Fig. 42.5. Contents of Torone Tomb 82, including pendent semi-circle skyphos (T82–2). Scale 1:3.

and the question of its origin is as problematic today as it was 50 years ago. The problems are well appreciated by Ridgway (1994: 37) who writes: "When I compare the discussion of their absolute chronology in Kearsley (1989: 126–132) with the comments by Popham & Lemos (1992), I feel rather like a traveller trying to plan a journey by consulting two different timetables: and, based as I am in the Far West, I am only too well aware that neither of them has been compiled with my specific needs in mind." Although working in coastal Chalkidike, in central Macedonia, I share Ridgway's lament.

There are two basic difficulties with the pendent semi-circle skyphos that still exercise Aegean pottery specialists. The first is the question of its origin. Desborough (1952: 180–94), for example, believed that the shape evolved somewhere in the north Cycladic region under the influence of the Attic Protogeometric skyphos. Others have argued that it was a direct derivative of the Mycenaean deep bowl, as suggested by Heurtley (1927: 49, 54; 1939: 106) and reasserted by Verdelis (1958: 55–6, 83–4). Be that as it may, a large proportion of Kearsley's Type 1 skyphoi, as well as the early Type 2, are found in Macedonia (cf. Skeat 1934; Andronikos 1969: 168–174). The latter is an area outside the assumed "home region" of the pendent semi-circle skyphos, which is loosely defined as the *koine*

comprising Thessaly, Euboea and the northern Cyclades. Of the five Type 1 skyphoi listed by Kearsley (1989: 84), one comes from Tenos, one from Delphi, one from Marmariane in inland Thessaly, and two from Macedonia (from Chauchitsa and Vergina). In addressing this question, Kearsley noted that the two areas where the very earliest pendent semi-circle skyphoi are found are Euboea and mainland Greece north of Euboea (Thessaly and Macedonia). She concludes that it was *probably* Euboea, and in particular Lefkandi, where the "initiative" occurred of modifying the old Mycenaean bowl shape and applying to it the new decoration (Kearsley 1989: 136; cf. Popham *et al.* 1980: 301); this scenario also assumes that it *diffused* from there to other regions. One important aspect that has never been seriously considered in this context is the possibility that the "initiative" for pendent semi-circles as a decorative scheme need not involve the skyphos or deep bowl, and that developments in north Greece need not follow those of Euboea. In order to highlight this, I publish here photographs and drawings of two kraters from Torone (Figs. 42.2, 42.3, 42.6, 42.7), one with pendent semi-circles, the other with pendent, upright and lateral semi-circles. Both kraters are locally produced and both are earlier than the skyphoi presented (for other kraters at Torone see Papadopoulos 1990); pendent semi-circles also

Fig. 42.6. Torone T48–1. Krater with pendent, upright and lateral semi-circles. Scale 1:3.

occur on a number of amphorai from Torone. When viewed from Macedonia, the primacy of Euboea in the case of the pendent semi-circle skyphos is a moot point (cf. Papadopoulos 1996a).

The other problem with the pendent semi-circle skyphos is that there are difficulties with Kearsley's presented typology, as Popham and Lemos (1992) have pointed out. Kearsley's typology (1989: 84–104) is based only on the shape of the skyphoi; by neglecting decoration *in relation* to shape, her "well-defined" types do not form groups that are related stylistically (Kearsley 1989: 105). The features of shape that Kearsley focuses on are the ratios of the diameter of the rim to the height, and the diameter of the base to the height; as well as the shape and height of the lip and the foot. Here, as in the eleven primary attributes Kearsley (1989: 116–117) lists for her numerical proximity analysis, complete skyphoi are required; fitting fragments into this typology is no easy matter. Moreover, her numerical proximity analysis, one of the purposes of which was to discover whether the clustering into types by purely visual classification would be confirmed by a more overtly defined numerical analysis, was based on 55 skyphoi, out of a total of 246 catalogued. The statistical validity of such a sample is open to considerable doubt (cf. Popham & Lemos 1992: 153). A more basic problem is that Kearsley's typology does not distinguish between regions. Locally-made Macedonian pendent semi-circle skyphoi are considered and clustered together with Euboean, Thessalian, Cycladic, and perhaps Cypriot versions of the shape. A more fruitful survey would have attempted to differentiate between pendent semi-circle skyphoi from various centres, as Descœudres did for the chevron skyphoi (Descœudres & Kearsley 1983: 11–29). Such a survey would illustrate that the type is less homogeneous in terms of shape, decoration, chronology and geographical distribution than is currently assumed. The result of all this is clear: not only is it difficult to place a newly-found pendent semi-circle skyphos, especially if it is fragmentary, within the existing typology, it is also difficult to date. Here the examples of the shape from Torone in Macedonia are worth discussing in more detail.

There were only two pendent semi-circle skyphoi from the Early Iron Age cemetery at Torone in Chalkidike in northern Greece, among the more than 500 objects deposited in tombs. The skyphoi, previously unpublished, pose a number of well-known problems and both are difficult to date with any precision. One is locally produced (T82–2), while the other (T77–3) is an import, probably from Euboea (this was verified chemically by R.E. Jones). Both skyphoi were found in cremation tombs that had been damaged by modern ploughing, which accounts for their fragmentary state, as well as that of the other vessels deposited in them. The ash-urn of Tomb 77 is a wheelmade neck-handled amphora of local manufacture, and the only other offering in the tomb is the small handmade jug with cut-away neck of a type common in northern Greece during the Bronze and Iron Ages (Fig. 42.4).

Similarly, the pottery deposited in Tomb 82 provided little chronological assistance in order to fix the date of T82–2 more precisely. The fragmentary ash-urn is a distinctive local type of amphora with belly and shoulder handles; the tomb also yielded three handmade pots, a jug and two kantharoi, which afford little chronological comfort (Fig. 42.5). Not surprisingly, the skyphoi constitute the most reasonably "datable" artefacts in their respective tombs. Since both skyphoi are fragmentary, fitting them into Kearsley's typology on the basis of the ratio of rim diameter / height / base diameter is not possible. Since decoration is not a primary element of this typology, we are left to consider the shape of rim. Despite its

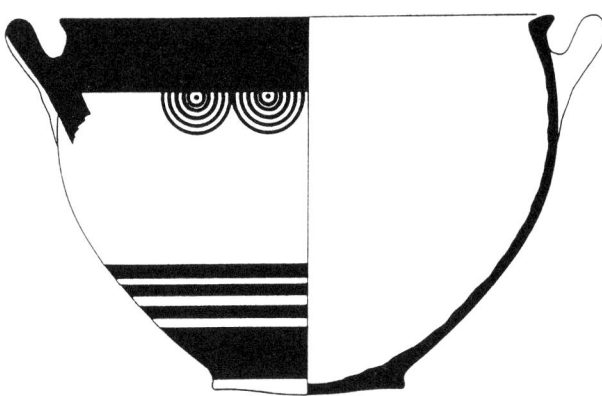

Fig. 42.7. Torone T102–1. Krater with pendent semi-circles. Scale 1:3.

fragmentary state and poorly preserved decoration, T77–3 is easier to place than T82–2. The lip is of medium height (approximately 1.5 cm) and is offset; it clearly does not belong to Type 1, which has a tall lip, which is not offset. The offset lips of Type 2 are similar to T77–3, but these have an average height of 1.8 cm. Kearsley's Type 3 skyphoi are virtually identical to those of her Type 2 except that the short lip never exceeds 1.4 cm. It seems reasonably clear that T77–3 cannot be of Types 4, 5 or 6. We are therefore left with a choice of Type 2 (average lip height 1.8 cm) or Type 3 (< 1.4 cm). Happily, having to guess between the two on the basis of a millimetre here or there is of little consequence, since Kearsley's Types 2 and 3 are both dated to the period "900–825/800 B.C." on the basis of the material from Lefkandi, while examples of Type 2 from Cyprus are dated 850–800 B.C. (Kearsley 1989: 128). Thus we have a conventional date for T77–3 anywhere in the 9th century; greater precision is not possible. If we wish to link this to the Attic sequence, it would cover, more or less, the phases of Early Geometric I and II and Middle Geometric I, though such a link is based on very little, if any, direct evidence and involves circular arguments.

Although comparatively well preserved, T82–2 poses a number of difficulties, which stem from the fact that it is locally produced; this highlights the problem of regionality in the Aegean. Unfortunately it is the only local skyphos of this type from Torone, and one would dearly like to know the form of its base. When compared to Euboean, Thessalian and Cycladic pendent semi-circle skyphoi, it is reasonably clear that Kearsley's Types 1, 4, 5 and 6 can be ruled out. The short lip (about 1.2 cm high) would suggest Type 3 rather than Type 2, but the vessel does display certain peculiarities, such as the two horizontal bands at the mid-point; this is a feature found on only one of the seven pendent semi-circle skyphoi from Vergina in Macedonia (Andronikos 1969: 169, fig. 23, pl. 50, no. P21), classified as Type 2(a) by Kearsley (1989: 68, 87, no. 233). The lip of the latter (1.8–1.6 cm) is considerably taller than that of T82–2. At present, on the basis of Kearsley's typology, the best that can be done is to assign T82–2 to Type 3, noting its idiosyncracies and the fact that it is different from T77–3, and to reach a tentative date, on the basis of the Lefkandi material, of 900–825/800 B.C. Given the problems already enumerated with the chronology of the pendent semi-circle skyphos, a 9th-century date is the best we can do for both skyphoi from Torone, that is if the conventional chronology is correct.

I wonder what conclusions would have been reached, in terms of both chronology and Aegean maritime expansion, had these two fragments been found in Sardinia or anywhere else in the Mediterranean outside the Aegean? Chronologically they would be just as difficult to date whether found in the Aegean, or in the western or eastern Mediterranean, except that a non-Aegean, particularly western, context could potentially provide non-Aegean associations which would help to date more accurately the Aegean product. The absolute dates for both Attic and Corinthian pottery, after all, rely totally on contexts outside Athens and Corinth. For many Aegean archaeologists, particularly those of pro-Euboean leanings, the discovery of these two skyphos fragments in Sardinia would be just one more piece of evidence for the mercantile and cultural pre-eminence of Euboea in this period, despite the fact that one of the skyphoi is clearly not Euboean, and not of an easily recognisable Aegean fabric. Ironically, one example of a pendent semi-circle skyphos recently found at Sant'Imbenia in 1990 is perhaps of Cypriot, rather than Euboean or Aegean origin (Bafico 1991a; Ridgway 1992: 29).

The present state of Greek contact with Sardinia down to the 4th century B.C. is well summarized by Ridgway and Serra Ridgway (1992) and Davison (1992; cf. 1984; 1986). Take away the Aegean pottery and there is very little Greek residue left. Sardinia, however, is only one part of a much larger Mediterranean story, and here I would concur with Ridgway's statement: "Not all the `First Western Greeks' were Greek, in fact; and much light remains to be shed on them by their neighbours in Sardinia — the one area of modern Italy that was never permeated directly or indirectly by Hellenism" (Ridgway 1990: 72). Even more recently, Ridgway (1995: 80–81), in reviewing the distribution map of the pendent semi-circle skyphoi, particularly in the west and the new evidence from Sant'Imbenia, turns around Coldstream's earlier statement of "Euboean merchants who also had Levantine contacts" (Coldstream 1977: 224), to read: "*Levantine* merchants (or prospectors? or miners?) who also had *Euboean* contacts."

Whether merchants, prospectors or miners, or whether Greeks or Levantines, the quest for Euboean versus Phoenician primacy in the Mediterranean (cf. Crielaard 1996) has obscured one important aspect in both the archaeology of Sardinia and that of Macedonia: the local populations (Papadopoulos 1997). Perhaps it is time to view Sardinia from the island's own perspective, and to apply the case of Sardinia and its Greek sherds to illuminate similar contexts around the Mediterranean.

Acknowledgments

I am grateful to Miriam Balmuth for her invitation for me to take part in the colloquium held at Tufts, and also for answering numerous questions about Sardinia and of Greek pottery found there. I am also grateful to her, to Robert Tykot and to many other friends for their hospitality while in Boston. This paper has benefitted greatly from discussions with many of the participants of the conference, too numerous to name here. Special thanks are, however, due to my wife, Sarah Morris, for reading drafts of this paper and for her customary astute remarks.

References

Andronikos, M. 1969. *Vergina I. To nekrotapheion ton tymvon*. Athens Archaeological Society, Athens.

Bafico, S. 1991a. Greci e fenici ad Alghero. *Archeo* 74 (Aprile): 18.

Bafico, S. 1991b. Alghero (Sassari). Località Santa Imbenia. Villagio nuragico. *Bollettino di Archeologia* 10: 97–100.

Balmuth, M.S. (ed.). 1986. *Studies in Sardinian Archaeology II: Sardinia in the Mediterranean*. The University of Michigan Press, Ann Arbor.

Balmuth, M.S. (ed.) 1987. *Studies in Sardinian Archaeology III. Nuragic Sardinia and the Mycenaean World*. BAR International Series 387. British Archaeological Reports, Oxford.

Balmuth, M.S. 1992. Phoenician Chronology in Sardinia: Prospecting, Trade and Settlement Before 900 B.C. In T. Hackens and G. Moucharte (eds.), *Studia Phoenicia. Travaux du Groupe de contact interuniversitaire d'études phéniciennes et puniques sous les auspices du Fonds National de la Recherche Scientifique. IX. Numismatique et histoire économique phéniciennes et puniques. Actes du Colloque tenu à Louvain-la-Neuve, 13– 16 Mai 1987*, 215–227. Publications d'histoire et d'archéologie de l'université catholique de Louvain, Louvain-la-Neuve.

Balmuth, M.S. & Rowland, R.J. Jr. (eds.). 1984. *Studies in Sardinian Archaeology*. The University of Michagan Press, Ann Arbor.

Bartoloni, P. 1989. Nuove testimonianze arcaiche da Sulcis. *Nuovo Bullettino Archeologico Sardo* 2: 167–92.

Bartoloni, P., Bernardini, P. & Tronchetti, C. 1988. S. Antioco: area del Cronicario (campagne di scavo 1983–86). *Rivista di Studi Fenici* 16: 73–119.

Biers, W.R. 1992. *Art, Artefacts, and Chronology in Classical Archaeology*. Routledge, London and New York.

Boardman, J. 1990. Al Mina and History. *Oxford Journal of Archaeology* 9: 169–190.

Bowden, H. 1991. The Chronology of Greek Painted Pottery: Some Observations. *Hephaistos* 10: 49–59.

Cavanagh, W.G. & Laxton, R.R. 1987. Notes on Building Techniques in Mycenaean Greece and Nuragic Sardinia. In Balmuth, M.S. (ed.), *Studies in Sardinian Archaeology III. Nuragic Sardinia and the Mycenaean World*. BAR International Series 387: 39–55. British Archaeological Reports, Oxford.

Coldstream, J.N. 1968. *Greek Geometric Pottery. A Survey of Ten Local Styles and Their Chronology*. Methuen, London.

Coldstream, J.N. 1977. *Geometric Greece*. Methuen, London.

Crielaard, J.P. 1996. How the West was Won: Euboeans vs. Phoenicians. In *Die Akten des Internationalen Kolloquiums 'Interactions in the Iron Age: Phoenicians, Greeks and the Indigenous Peoples of the Western Mediterranean' in Amsterdam am 26. und 27 März 1992*. Hamburger Beiträge zur Archäologie 19/20(1992–93): 235–260.

Davison, J.M. 1984. Greeks in Sardinia: The Confrontation of Archaeological Evidence and Literary Testimonia. In Balmuth, M.S. & Rowland, R.J. (eds.), *Studies in Sardinian Archaeology*, 67–82. The University of Michagan Press, Ann Arbor.

Davison, J.M. 1986. Greek Presence in Sardinia: Myth and Speculation. In Balmuth, M.S. (ed.), *Studies in Sardinian Archaeology II: Sardinia in the Mediterranean*, 187–200. The University of Michigan Press, Ann Arbor.

Davison, J.M. 1992. Greeks in Sardinia: Myth and Reality. In Tykot, R.H. & Andrews, T.K. (eds.), *Sardinia in the Mediterranean: A Footprint in the Sea. Studies in Sardinian Archaeology Presented to Miriam S. Balmuth*. Monographs in Mediterranean Archaeology 3: 384–393. Sheffield Academic Press, Sheffield.

Desborough, V.R.d'A. 1952. *Protogeometric Pottery*. Oxford University Press, Oxford.

Descœudres, J.-P. & Kearsley, R.A. 1983. Greek Pottery at Veii: Another Look. *Annual of the British School at Athens* 78: 9–53.

Ferrarese Ceruti, M.L., Vagnetti, L. & Lo Schiavo, F. 1987. Minoici, micenei e cipriotti in Sardegna nella seconda metà dell II millennio a.C. In Balmuth, M.S. (ed.), *Studies in Sardinian Archaeology III. Nuragic Sardinia and the Mycenaean World*. BAR International Series 387: 7–34. British Archaeological Reports, Oxford.

Francis, E.D. 1990. *Image and Idea in Fifth-Century Greece: Art and Literature After the Persian Wars*. Routledge, London.

Francis, E.D. & Vickers, M. 1983. "Signa priscae artis": Eretria and Siphnos. *Journal of Hellenic Studies* 83: 49–67.

Francis, E.D. & Vickers, M. 1985. Greek Geometric Pottery at Hama and its Implications for Near Eastern Chronology. *Levant* 17: 131–138.

Graham, A.J. 1986. The Historical Interpretation of Al Mina. *Dialogues d'Histoire Ancienne* 12: 51–59.

Heurtley, W.A. 1927. Early Iron Age Pottery from Macedonia. *Antiquaries Journal* 7: 44–59.

Heurtley, W.A. 1939. *Prehistoric Macedonia. An Archaeological Reconnaissance of Greek Macedonia (West of the Struma) in the Neolithic, Bronze and Early Iron Ages*. Cambridge University Press, Cambridge.

James, P., Thorpe, I.J., Kokkinos, N., Morkot, N. & Frankish, J. 1991. *Centuries of Darkness: A Challenge to the Conventional Chronology of Old World Archaeology*. Jonathan Cape, London & New York..

Kearsley, R.A. 1989. *The Pendent Semi-Circle Skyphos. A Study of Its Development and Chronology and an Examination of it as Evidence for Euboean Activity at Al Mina*. University of London, Bulletin of the Institute of Classical Studies Supplement 44. Institute of Classical Studies, London.

Kopcke, G. 1992. What Role for Phoenicians? In Kopcke, G. & Tokumaru, I. (eds.), *Greece Between East and West: 10th – 8th Centuries B.C. Papers of the Meeting at the Institute of Fine Arts, New York University, March 15th – 16th 1990*, 103–113. Verlag Philipp von Zabern, Mainz.

Lemos, I.S. 1992. Euboean Enterprise in the Eastern Mediterranean: Early Import at Lefkandi. *American Journal of Archaeology* 96: 338–339.

Papadopoulos, J.K. 1990. Protogeometric Birds from Torone. In J.-P. Descœudres (ed.), *EYMOYSIA. Ceramic and Iconographic Studies in Honour of Alexander Cambitoglou*. Mediterranean Archaeology Supplement 1: 13–24. Mediterranean Archaeology, Sydney.

Papadopoulos, J.K. 1993. To Kill a Cemetery: The Athenian Kerameikos and the Early Iron Age in the Aegean. *Journal of Mediterranean Archaeology* 6: 175–206.

Papadopoulos, J.K. 1996a. Euboians in Macedonia? A Closer Look. *Oxford Journal of Archaeology* 15: 151–181.

Papadopoulos, J.K. 1996b. Dark Age Greece. *Oxford Companion to Archaeology*, 253–255. Oxford University Press, Oxford.

Papadopoulos, J.K. 1997. Phantom Euboians. *Journal of Mediterranean Archaeology* 10: 191–206.

Popham, M.R. 1994. Precolonisation: Early Greek Contact with the East. In Tsetskhladze, G.R. & F. De Angelis (eds.), *The Archaeology of Greek Colonisation: Essays Dedicated to Sir John Boardman*, 11–34. Oxford Committee for Archaeology, Oxford.

Popham, M.R. & Lemos, I.S. 1992. Review of Kearsley 1989. *Gnomon* 64/2: 152–155.

Popham, M.R., Sackett, L.H. & Themelis, P.G. 1980. *Lefkandi I. The Iron Age*. British School at Athens Supplementary Volume 11. British School at Athens, Oxford.

Ridgway, D. 1986. Sardinia and the First Western Greeks. In Balmuth, M.S. (ed.), *Studies in Sardinian Archaeology II: Sardinia in the Mediterranean*, 173–185. The University of Michigan Press, Ann Arbor.

Ridgway, D. 1990. The First Western Greeks and Their Neighbours, 1935–1985. In Descœudres, J.-P. (ed.), *Greek Colonists and Native Populations. Proceedings of the First Australian Congress of Classical Archaeology held in honour of Emeritus Professor A.D. Trendall, Sydney 9–14 July 1985*, 61–72. Clarendon Press, Oxford.

Ridgway, D. 1992. *The First Western Greeks*. Cambridge University Press, Cambridge.

Ridgway, D. 1994. Phoenicians and Greeks in the West: A View from Pithekoussai. In Tsetskhladze, G.R. & F. De Angelis (eds.), *The Archaeology of Greek Colonisation: Essays Dedicated to Sir John Boardman*, 35–46. Oxford Committee for Archaeology, Oxford.

Ridgway, D. 1995. Archaeology in Sardinia and South Italy, 1989–1994. *Archaeological Reports* 1994–95: 75–96.

Ridgway, D. & Serra Ridgway, F.R. 1992. Sardinia and History. In Tykot, R.H. & Andrews, T.K. (eds.), *Sardinia in the Mediterranean: A Footprint in the Sea. Studies in Sardinian Archaeology Presented to Miriam S. Balmuth*. Monographs in Mediterranean Archaeology 3: 355–363. Sheffield Academic Press, Sheffield.

Skeat, T.C. 1934. *The Dorians in Archaeology*. Alexander Moring Ltd., London.

Tsetskhladze, G.R. & F. De Angelis. 1994. *The Archaeology of Greek Colonisation: Essays Dedicated to Sir John Boardman*. Oxford Committee for Archaeology, Oxford.

Tykot, R.H. & T.K. Andrews (eds.). 1992. *Sardinia in the Mediterranean: A Footprint in the Sea. Studies in Sardinian Archaeology Presented to Miriam S. Balmuth*. Monographs in Mediterranean Archaeology 3. Sheffield Academic Press, Sheffield.

Vegas, M. 1992. Carthage: la ville archaïque. Céramique d'importation de la période du Géométrique Récent. In *Lixus: Actes du colloque organisé par l'Institut des sciences de l'archeologie et du patrimoine de Rabat avec le concours de l'Ecole Française de Rome, Larache 8–11 novembre 1989*, Collection de l'Ecole Française de Rome, 181–189. E. de Boccard, Paris.

Verdelis, N.M. 1958. *O Protogeometrikos rhythmos tes Thessalias*. Athens Archaeological Society, Athens.

Vickers, M. 1985. Early Greek Coinage, A Reassessment. *Numismatic Chronicle* 145: 1–44.

Vickers, M. 1987. Dates, Methods and Icons. In Bérard, C. (ed.) *Actes du Colloque International "Images et société en Grèce ancienne: l'iconographie comme méthode d'analyse", 1984*, 19–25. Institut d'archéologie et d'histoire ancienne, Université de Lausanne, Lausanne.

Winter, I.J. 1995. Homer's Phoenicians: History, Ethnography, or Literary Trope? [A Perspective on Early Orientalism]. In Carter, J.B. & Morris, S.P. (eds.), *The Ages of Homer. A Tribute to Emily Townsend Vermeule*, 247–271. University of Texas Press, Austin.

43. Problemi di cronologia ceramica nella Sardegna romana

Carlo Tronchetti

Lo studio della ceramica romana di Sardegna non è mai stato particolarmente approfondito, nè in passato nè in tempi più recenti, dal momento che gli interessi preminenti degli studiosi si sono rivolti prevalentemente agli aspetti delle culture peculiari dell'isola. Queste sono particolarmente evidenti sopratutto durante la preistoria e la protostoria, ma, anche passando all'epoca storica, l'attenzione si è indirizzata in primo luogo alla civiltà fenicio-punica che in Sardegna trova una delle principali attestazioni sul territorio italiano. L'archeologia romana, invece, messa in secondo piano da queste emergenze rilevanti ed individuali sarde, è stata coltivata soltanto in misura ridotta e si è indirizzata verso classi di monumenti particolarmente significative, quali i sarcofagi (Pesce 1957), le sculture (Equini Schneider 1979; Saletti 1989), i mosaici (Angiolillo 1981), la decorazione architettonica (Nieddu 1992). Pochissimi, invece, e di non particolare rilevanza, i contributi dedicati alla ceramica romana, in prevalenza occasionati dall'edizione di ritrovamenti o collezioni od anche singole classi, ma di solito senza mai l'approfondimento dei complessi problemi che la situazione sarda presenta (Boninu 1971-72; Moravetti 1976; Paderi 1982; Tronchetti 1988; 1990).

Specificando che in questo studio ci si riferirà prevalentemente alla Sardegna centro-meridionale, dove lo scrivente opera, iniziamo a presentare tre delle più importanti problematiche da affrontare nello studio della ceramica romana in Sardegna. Queste sono così riassumibili: a) la *regionalizzazione* del territorio sardo; b) il problema delle produzioni locali: cronologia e centri di produzione; c) cronologia di arrivo e periodo di uso delle ceramiche importate.

Regionalizzazione

Il concetto di *regionalizzazione* è ben presente nella letteratura archeologica sarda fin dalla preistoria e, specificamente per la ceramica, esso trova riscontro in periodo punico (Bartoloni & Tronchetti 1981: 33–34; Bartoloni 1983 *passim*); possiamo constatare che tale fenomeno è verificabile anche in epoca romana. Se difatti prendiamo in esame diverse *facies* ceramiche coeve restituite da porzioni territoriali diverse, anche se adiacenti, possiamo rilevare agevolmente aspetti che si diversificano talora in modo netto.

Questo fatto, allo stato attuale degli studi, è particolarmente evidente in età imperiale, ma è più che verosimile che esso si sia verificato anche in epoca repubblicana quando, secondo il pensiero dello scrivente, la regionalizzazione delle produzioni ceramiche è la logica prosecuzione della precedente simile attitudine di epoca punica; sarà da attuare in futuro una indagine volta a valutare le possibili coincidenze e discordanze di queste partizioni territoriali nella lunga durata.

Alcuni casi emblematici potranno chiarire meglio questo concetto di *regionalizzazione*. La zona del Sarrabus (Fig. 43.1) è caratterizzata da un tipo di sepoltura ad incinerazione che utilizza, come contenitore, una sorta di urna realizzata in rozza terracotta (Pl. 47), talora lavorata a mano o al tornio lento, di forma grosso modo cilindrica o rastremata verso l'alto, con due piccole prese sub-rettangolari impostate sotto il bordo. L'arco cronologico attestato dai corredi corre dal periodo tardo-repubblicano sino almeno all'età medio-imperiale (seconda metà del II sec. d.C.) (Tronchetti 1980; Ventura 1990). Al di fuori di tale area questa forma non viene adottata e le incinerazioni adottano altri e diversi tipi di contenitori.

Parimenti esaminiamo una brocca in ceramica comune depurata caratteristica del III sec. d.C. (Pl. 48): brocca con base concava, corpo panciuto, schiacciato, collo cilindrico appena rigonfio, orletto ingrossato ed ansa dalla spalla al bordo o poco al di sotto; di solito

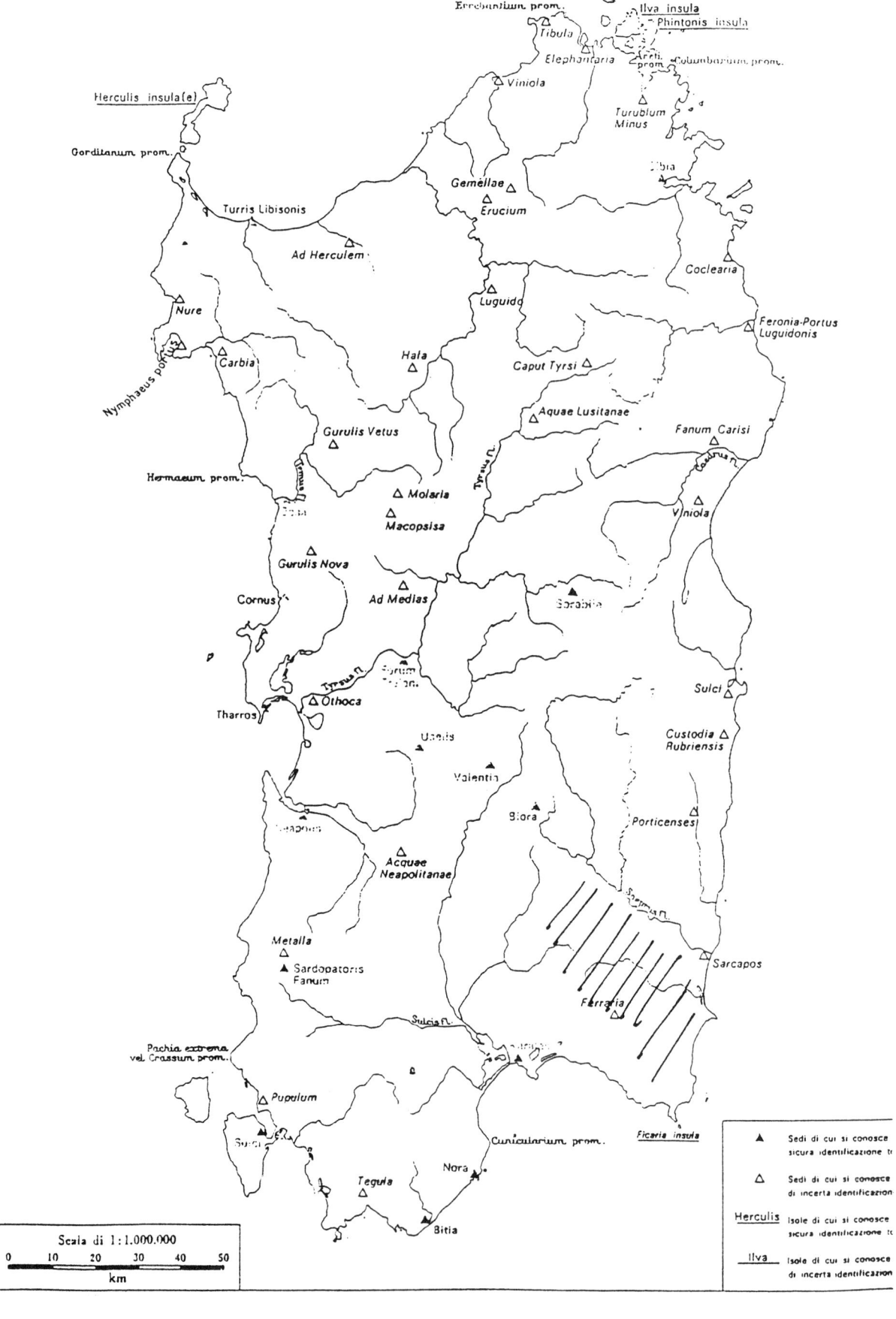

Fig. 43.1. Sardegna: zona del Sarrabus

la superficie, color ocra scuro, è notata da steccature verticali.

Cronologia	Contesti
post 150 d.C.	Sanluri t. 34
fine II – III sec. d.C.	Villasalto t. 5
post 222–235 d.C.	Barumini
post 231 d.C.	Vallermosa t. A
post 238–244 d.C.	Barumini
prima metà III sec. d.C.	Monserrato
post 293–295 d.C.	Vallermosa t.B

Analizzando la sua area di diffusione (Fig. 43.2) (che non coincide con la tabella sopra presentata, perchè comprende anche esemplari rinvenuti fuori contesto), vediamo che essa copre il basso Campidano, da Barumini in giù, con un buon numero di attestazioni e giunge con esemplari sporadici a Villasalto ad oriente e Sulci ad occidente, dove sono presenti due soli esemplari (Paderi 1982; Ventura 1990; Lilliu 1939: 370–373; Ortu 1993). Infatti a Sant'Antioco la forma caratteristica ed assolutamente maggioritaria di brocchetta del III sec. d.C. (Tronchetti 1990) è completamente diversa (Pl. 49): corpo piriforme allungato e superficie costantemente chiara quasi bianca; tale forma, peraltro, è sostanzialmente limitata a Sulci stessa.

Due aree adiacenti come il Sulcitano ed il Campidano restituiscono, così, nello stesso arco di tempo, due forme di brocchetta in ceramica comune prodotte localmente e comunemente adottate, assolutamente diverse.

Il fenomeno della regionalizzazione, come si può capire, pone seri ostacoli per l'attribuzione cronologica di corredi o contesti *poveri*, privi di materiali importati, dal momento che la maggior parte dei "fossili guida" locali validi per una zona non sono utilizzabili per le altre.

Produzioni locali

La seconda problematica concerne i centri di produzione di ceramiche fabbricate localmente e diffuse un pò in tutto il territorio isolano. L'individuazione di uno soltanto ovvero di diversi centri di produzione è assai importante per le implicazioni di carattere economico che sottointende. É ovvio che la diffusione a livello regionale di una ceramica prodotta in un unico centro presuppone un tipo di organizzazione commerciale e produttiva assolutamente diversa da quella che vede numerose piccole officine fabbricare il vasellame per una distribuzione limitata al solo ambito locale.

Una delle produzioni isolane senz'altro più diffuse, se non addirittura la più numerosa in senso assoluto, è quella della ceramica a vernice nera a pasta grigia. Prodotta da poco prima la metà del II sec. a.C. sino almeno a gran parte del I sec. d.C., essa si esplica in una ampia gamma di fogge, fra cui si possono agevolmente individuare le più importanti (Tronchetti 1987; 1988; 1988a).

Queste si trovano associate ad elementi datanti, sia in contesti di scavo che in tombe monosome. Esaminiamo le associazioni :

CERAMICA A VERNICE NERA A PASTA GRIGIA				
ASSOCIAZIONI	Forma 1 (F 2323)	Coppa 1/8 (F 2567)	Patere F 2276 e F 2277	Patera F 2286
asse di Q. Marcius Libo (2/4 II sec. a.C.)	X			
boccalino Mayet 2	X		X	
boccalino Mayet 24/ Marabini 15	X	X	X	X
coppetta Mayet 28/ Marabini 42	X			
coppetta Mayet 33 o 35	X			
lucerna Deneauve IV a	X			
coppa "imitazione sig. chiara" Hayes 8a		X		

Come si vede, la coppa Forma 1 (F 2323) (Fig. 43.3) appare essere già attestata nel II sec. a.C. (anche se la moneta è utilizzabile solo come *terminus post quem*) ed attraversa entrambi i secoli I a.C. e I d.C.: a Nora si trova associata con materiali della prima età flavia, mentre la coppa 1/8 (F 2567) sembra nascere più tardi ed essere caratteristica del I sec. d.C. Per le patere possiamo constatare che la F 2276 e la F 2277 (Fig. 43.4) contraddistinguono i contesti dei decenni finali del I sec. a.C. e quelli del I d.C., mentre la patera F 2286 (Fig. 43.5), di grandi dimensioni, con piede pesante e pareti spesse, è peculiare del I sec. d.C., con attestazioni nella sua parte avanzata. L'US 70/71 di Nora contiene un frammento di patera di questa forma assieme a ceramica africana da cucina; l'US è databile nell'ultimo quarto del I sec. d.C. Sempre a Nora l'US 68, datata dalla presenza di una scodella in sigillata africana di forma Atlante XVI,10 dopo la metà del II sec. d.C., mostra un frammento di orlo di grande patera pertinente alla forma F 2286 che dovremo in questo periodo considerare un residuo. Oltre a queste forme più diffuse e rappresentate esistono numerose altre fogge di coppette, pissidi, piatti, scodelle e patere che coprono sostanzialmente l'arco di tempo dei secoli I a.C. e I d.C., con maggiore concentrazione nel primo.

Di vasi a vernice nera a pasta grigia sono stati trovati scarti di fornace nei pressi di Masainas nel Sulcis. Nella vicinanze non esiste alcun sito importante, nè vie fluviali che avrebbero potuto consentire una commercializzazione lungo le coste, e neppure ci troviamo su grandi vie di comunicazione interna. Sembra, quindi, difficile ipotizzare che Masainas abbia potuto essere il solo ed unico centro produttore fornitore di tutta l'isola di questo vasellame.

La sua larghissima diffusione e la grande quantità di questi vasi attestata nei contesti dei secoli sopra indicati, unite ad una discreta varietà di pasta e vernice, pur nell'ambito di una tecnica sostanzialmente unitaria (nota peraltro in varie regioni mediterranee nello stesso arco temporale), portano a supporre numerose fabbriche

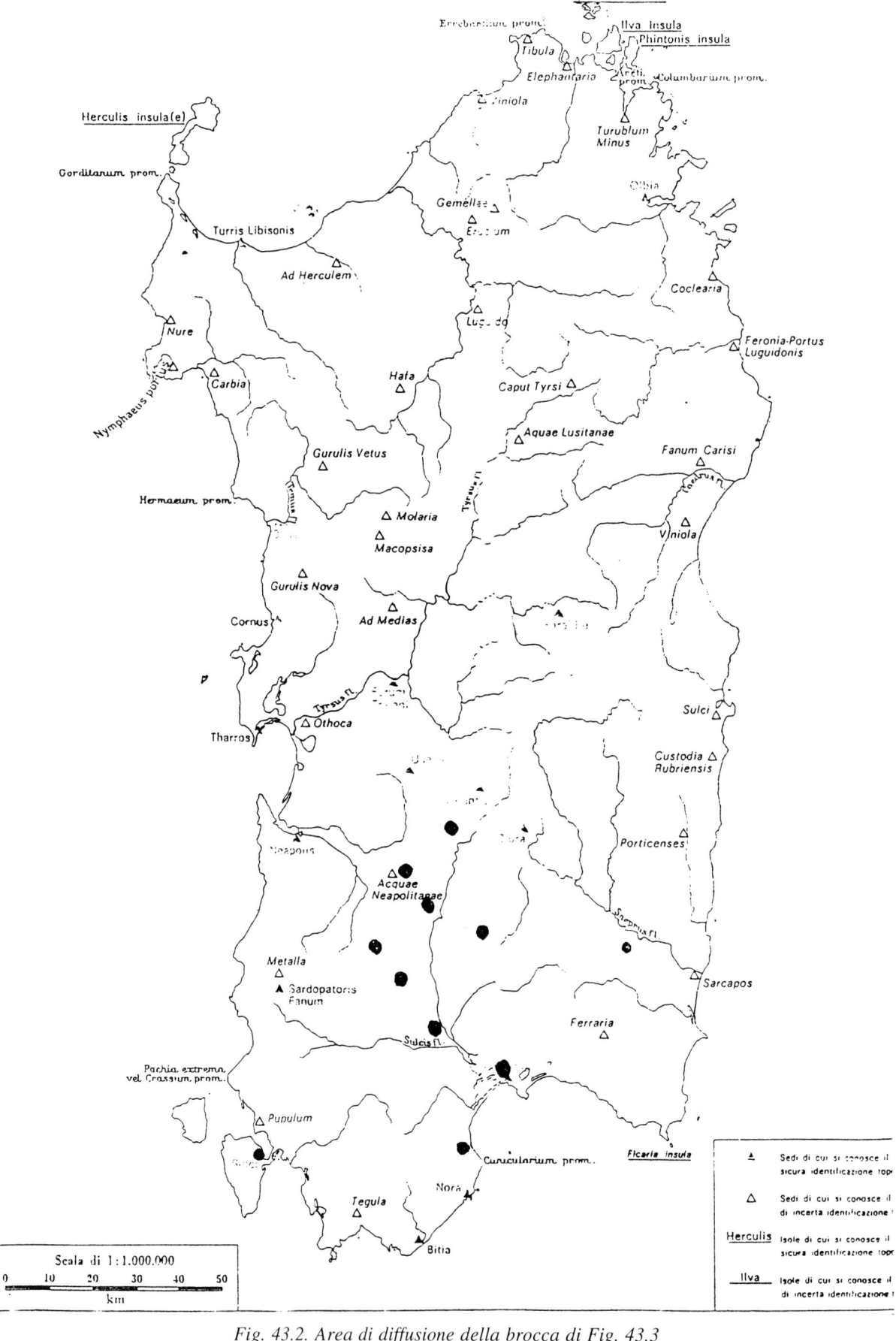

Fig. 43.2. Area di diffusione della brocca di Fig. 43.3

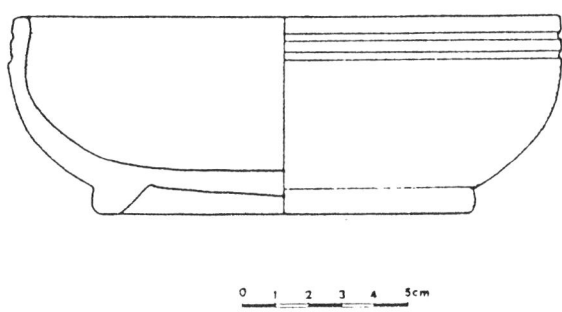

Fig. 43.3. Coppa F 2323 in ceramica a vernice nera a pasta grigia (fine II sec. a.C. – I sec. d.C.)

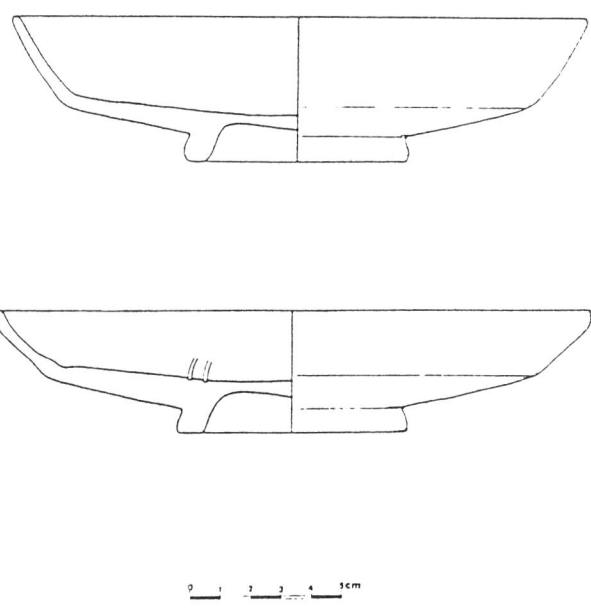

Fig. 43.4. Patere F 2277 in ceramica a vernice nera a pasta grigia (I sec. a.C. – I sec. d.C.)

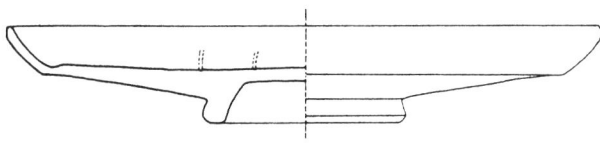

Fig. 43.5. Patera F 2286 in ceramica a vernice nera a pasta grigia (I sec. d.C.) (scala 1:3)

diversificate per esigenze locali, di maggiore o minore ampiezza, tutte ancora da individuare. Soltanto una diffusa analisi delle argille dei vasi potrà auspicabilmente offrirci soluzioni (o quantomeno indicazioni) in questo senso.

Scendendo nel pieno periodo imperiale troviamo altre attestazioni di produzioni locali ad ampia diffusione.

La ceramica definita "fiammata" dallo scrivente (Tronchetti 1990: 179) (Pl. 50), è fabbricata in argilla molto ben depurata, sempre assai chiara, che varia dal bianco al rosato all'ocra. La decorazione comune a tutte le forme è a larghe bande di colore bruno o rossiccio, con andamento orizzontale, ovvero ondulato in maniera più o meno marcata, oppure a "fiamme", cioè bande di piccole pennellate curve parallele. Spesso il bordo delle forme aperte e chiuse è notato da grandi punti di vernice.

Le forme si articolano in brocche di diverse fogge e dimensioni (piriformi, a spalla rialzata, con anse tri- o quadricostolate ecc.), anfore e bacili con motivi "a pizzicato" sotto il bordo, muniti di piede; di norma gli esemplari maggiori, che raggiungono talora il diametro di 40 cm, sono dotati di piccole anse a maniglia orizzontali aderenti il corpo.

La ceramica fiammata, pur apparendo concentrata prevalentemente nella parte meridionale della Sardegna si trova distribuita un pò in tutta l'isola. Questa classe è assai largamente diffusa da Sulci sino a Cagliari e nell'immediato entroterra, per una distanza di qualche decina di chilometri; giunge a Tharros ed è attestata anche a Porto Torres, sia pure in misura non rilevante (Villedieu 1984: 152, figg. 334–335; AA.VV. 1987: 88, tav. XXI, 8–9) (Fig. 43.6). La Villedieu propende, per i materiali turritani, per una cronologia entro il III sec. d.C.; i due frammenti ivi rinvenuti in contesti del V secolo appaiono essere dei residui. Al di fuori dell'isola, a mia conoscenza è solo il ritrovamento di due frammenti ad Ostia in contesti di II-III sec. d.C. (AA.VV. 1977: 54, tav. XXXIII, 239). La cronologia di questa ceramica, sulla base dei pochi contesti studiati sino ad oggi, corre dalla fine del II sino almeno a tutto il IV sec. d.C., con la possibilità di uno scivolamento ai primi decenni del successivo, come ci dimostra una brocca rinvenuta integra in una Unità Stratigrafica di abbandono di un vano del *macellum* di Nora in associazione ad un vassoio in sigillata africana D di forma Hayes 59 (= Atlante tav. XXXIII, 4), ma la cronologia precisa e l'evoluzione delle diverse forme sono ancora da determinare con esattezza.

In modo del tutto preliminare ed ipotetico ho proposto di individuare in Sulci il luogo di produzione di questa classe; tale ipotesi si basa sull'abbondanza e varietà di forme rispetto ad altri centri, e sopratutto per la consonanza dell'argilla con quella di altre produzioni locali sulcitane; un ulteriore indizio è la presenza di forme in ceramica fiammata che riprendono esattamente, sia pure in dimensione leggermente superiore, la foggia della brocchetta piriforme già citata sopra (Pl. 51). Anche la

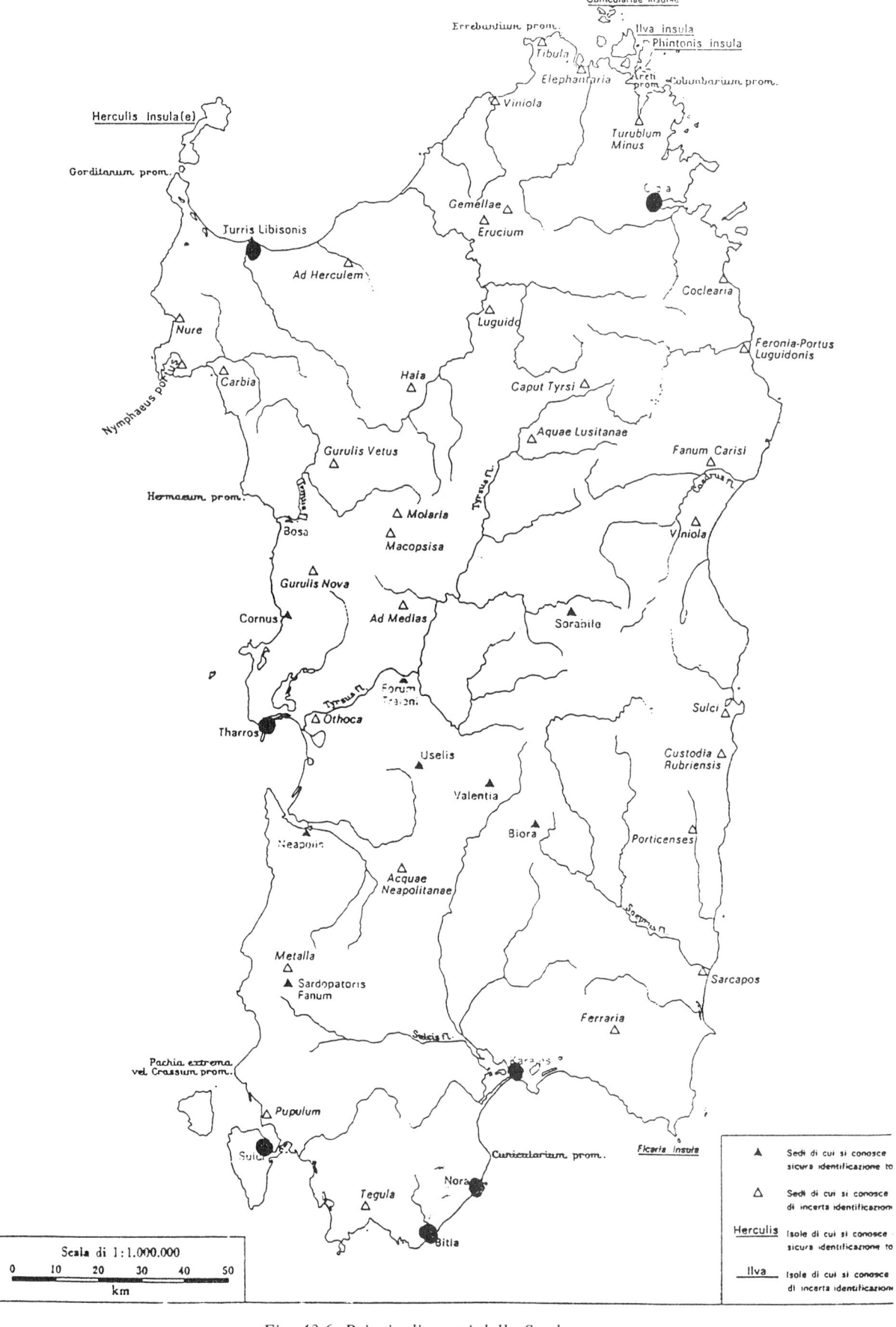

Fig. 43.6. Principali centri della Sardegna romana

concentrazione nella parte meridionale dell'isola potrebbe essere di conforto nel localizzare in quest'area il centro di produzione.

Sempre in periodo imperiale troviamo una forma prodotta localmente di boccalino a pareti sottili (Pinna 1981–85: 291) (Pl. 52) databile nella seconda metà del II sec. d.C., così caratterizzato come morfologia e associazioni: Boccalino a pareti sottili, corpo da globulare a ovoide, piede circolare, orletto estroflesso, ansa ad orecchia, corpo decorato con strie a rotella. Il corpo può avere la parete senza soluzione di continuità (tipo A) ovvero con risalto sotto il bordo (tipo B); in taluni casi il tipo B presenta delle strozzature sul corpo.

Cronologia	Associazioni
II/III sec. d.C.	Askos in sigillata africana Hayes 123
Seconda metà del II sec. d.C.	Coppa in sigillata africana Hayes 3c
Seconda metà del II sec. d.C.	Bottiglia in sigillata africana Hayes 160
Seconda metà del II sec. d.C.	Coppa in sigillata africana Hayes 16

Di questi boccalini è stato rinvenuto uno scarto di fornace nei vecchi scavi di Nora, senza che, purtroppo, sia stato conservato il ricordo del punto esatto di reperimento. Anche in questo caso, come per la vernice nera a pasta grigia, le diversità delle argille e della colorazione della superficie dei boccalini trovati in diverse parti dell'isola portano ad ipotizzare centri di produzione diversificati.

Appare chiaro, comunque, che tutte queste ipotesi sono destinate a rimanere solamente tali fino a che non si potranno effettuare le analisi delle argille dei reperti.

Cronologia delle ceramiche importate

Il terzo problema è quello della cronologia delle ceramiche importate. Si tratta di definire, quanto più esattamente possibile, il periodo in cui determinate classi iniziano a giungere in Sardegna e quando cessa il loro uso (che non sempre coincide con la fine della produzione).

Per l'età repubblicana non abbiamo dati consistenti. La Campana A si presenta prevalente durante il II sec. a.C. mentre quella B vera e propria è scarsamente rappresentata. Più abbondanti sono le produzioni B-oidi, di cui però non mi sentirei sicuro dell'assegnazione a fabbriche esterne all'isola, mentre è più probabile che si tratti di produzioni locali a pasta chiara che riprendono le forme dei vasi dell'Italia centrale ed etrusca.

Dallo scorcio del II sec. a.C. inizia la diffusione delle ceramiche locali a vernice nera a pasta grigia, di cui si è già parlato sopra, che aumentano la loro importanza nel corso del I sec. a.C. e proseguono in uso sino a ben oltre la metà del I sec. d.C.

Il vasellame a vernice nera importato si esaurisce immediatamente dopo la metà del I sec. a.C., rimanendo attestato come residuo in quantità minime; i vasi a vernice nera a pasta grigia locali sono il vasellame da mensa maggiormente diffuso, nei due secoli a cavallo dell'anno 0, non solo tra le ceramiche a vernice nera, ma in assoluto, prevalendo numericamente anche sulla sigillata italica.

Non abbiamo dati precisi sull'inizio di uso dei vasi a pareti sottili. Boccalini di forma Mayet 2 sono associati con coppe a vernice nera a pasta grigia di forma 1 databili, come si è visto, dallo scorcio del II sec. a.C. sino a parte del I sec. d.C.; la loro cronologia non dovrebbe comunque risalire più in alto dell'ultimo quarto del II sec. a.C. e può scendere nella prima metà del secolo successivo.

Anche per la sigillata italica e sud-gallica non abbiamo sinora contesti che ci offrano dati per la cronologia iniziale di presenza nell'isola. Possiamo rilevare, comunque, una sostanziale prevalenza di sigillata italica liscia, essendo quella decorata assai più rara, ma non sono in grado di precisare se si tratti di semplice incidenza percentuale derivata dalla diversità numerica delle produzioni. La sigillata sud-gallica ha generalmente una diffusione numericamente ampia e con buona presenza anche di vasi decorati e si trova in buona misura ancora in contesti del II sec. d.C., come ci mostra, ad esempio, la US 4340 di Nora (Fig. 43.7), databile a poco dopo il 150 d.C.:

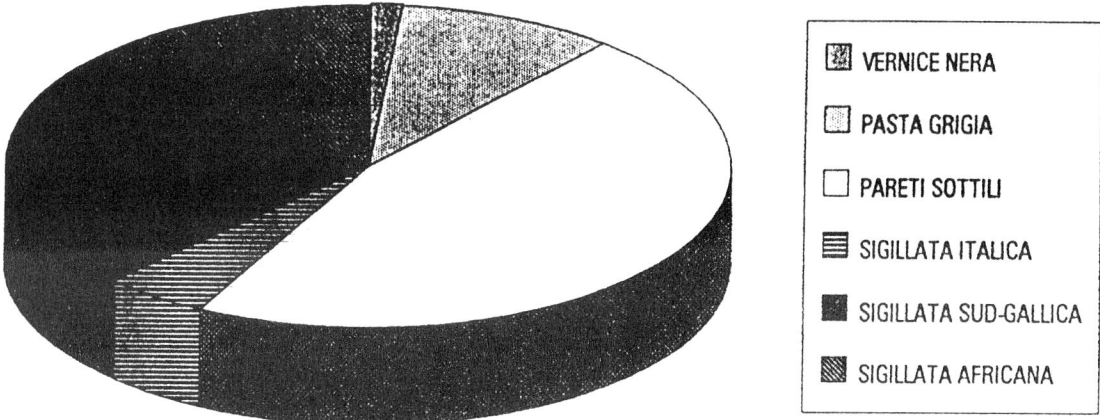

Fig. 43.7. Distribuzione delle ceramiche fini da mensa nella US 4340 di Nora (Pula-Cagliari)

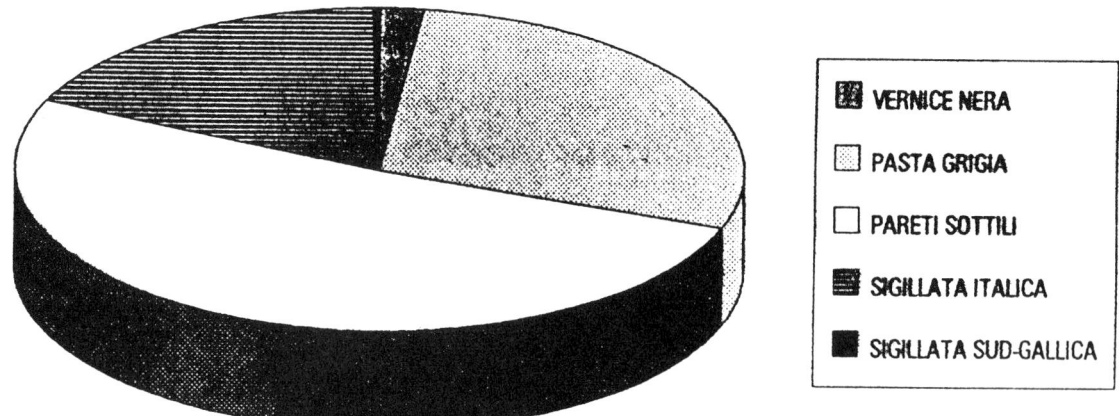

Fig. 43.8. Distribuzione delle ceramiche fini da mensa nella US 77 di Nora (Pula-Cagliari)

Sigillata africana	24	12,70%
Sigillata sud-gallica	47	24,90%
Sigillata italica	9	4,80%
Pareti sottili (importate e locali)	88	45,60%
Ceramica a vernice nera	3	1,60%
Ceramica a pasta grigia	18	9,50%

Le percentuali sono calcolate sul totale di 189 individui delle ceramiche fini da mensa e si vede agevolmente che la sigillata africana sta iniziando ad affermarsi, mentre è ancora ben attestato l'utilizzo della sud-gallica; l'italica e la pasta grigia sono ormai in fase di residui, ma ancora quest'ultima è in misura doppia della prima.

Un indizio per l'inizio della massiccia diffusione della sigillata sud-gallica in Sardegna può, forse, essere individuato esaminando due unità stratigrafiche grosso modo coeve di Nora e Sulci, la cui analisi è utile anche per quanto concerne la ceramica sigillata africana e la ceramica africana da cucina.

Lo scavo di Nora ha messo in luce una Unità Stratigrafica (US 77) databile in età flavia, verosimilmente nella sua parte iniziale, che offre i seguenti dati per le ceramiche fini da mensa (Fig. 43.8):

Pareti sottili (importate e locali)	617	51%
Sigillata italica	218	18%
Sigillata sud-gallica	3	0.25%
Ceramica a vernice nera	26	2.15%
Ceramica a pasta grigia	346	28.60%

Le percentuali sono calcolate sul totale degli individui delle ceramiche fini da mensa considerate, che assomma a 1.210.

Salta immediatamente all'occhio che la maggiore quantità di vasi è tenuta dalle pareti sottili. Ma occorre tener presente che la massima parte di questi frammenti è stato considerato come appartenente a questa classe solo in base alla sottigliezza della parete, senza che sia possibile identificare la forma; ove questa è riconoscibile si riconoscono in prevalenza boccalini a pareti striate a pettine (per la maggior parte di imitazione locale) e pochi esemplari di coppette importate a fronte di un vastissimo numero di orli pertinenti ad urnette o bicchieri prodotti in Sardegna che non rientrano nelle tipologie canoniche della classe.

Il discorso necessita di un approfondimento ben maggiore che coinvolge, fra l'altro, anche la definizione stessa di "pareti sottili" e che, allo stato attuale, non è possibile prendere in considerazione.

Per quello che ci riguarda si nota che i vasi in pasta grigia (Fig. 43.9) sono in numero ben superiore a quelli in sigillata italica (Fig. 43.10). Dal momento che siamo nel periodo finale di fabbricazione ed uso di quest'ultima, e quindi non possiamo considerarla un residuo, dovremo inferirne che anche la pasta grigia è in fase di piena fioritura. La sigillata sud-gallica è presente in misura minima.

In questa unità stratigrafica si riscontra la totale assenza di sigillata africana e di ceramica africana da cucina, ma la sua pertinenza ad epoca flavia ci è indicata senza ombra di dubbio da un orlo di anfora Tripolitana I (Fig. 43.10), attestata ad Ostia in contesti sin dall'epoca flavia.

L'Unità Stratigrafica 270 di Sant'Antioco (Tronchetti 1998a: 115–116), databile alla fine del I sec. d.C. ovvero ai primissimi decenni del secolo successivo, è una US di abbandono improvviso di ambienti di abitazione, composta dal disfacimento di mattoni crudi in cui si sono rinvenuti inglobati numerosi vasi integri o comunque ricostruibili dai frammenti rinvenuti in posto. Fra le ceramiche fini da mensa sono attestati vasi a pasta grigia, a pareti sottili ed in sigillata italica (Pl. 53); mancano la sigillata sud-gallica e quella africana. La maggior parte del vasellame rinvenuto è da cucina e fra esso non si rinviene ceramica di produzione africana, ma soltanto pentole e tegami di officine locali (Pl. 54, 55).

I dati dell'esame congiunto della US 77 di Nora e della US 270 di Sulci ci evidenziano due fatti importanti.

Il primo è la scarsissima presenza, direi addirittura

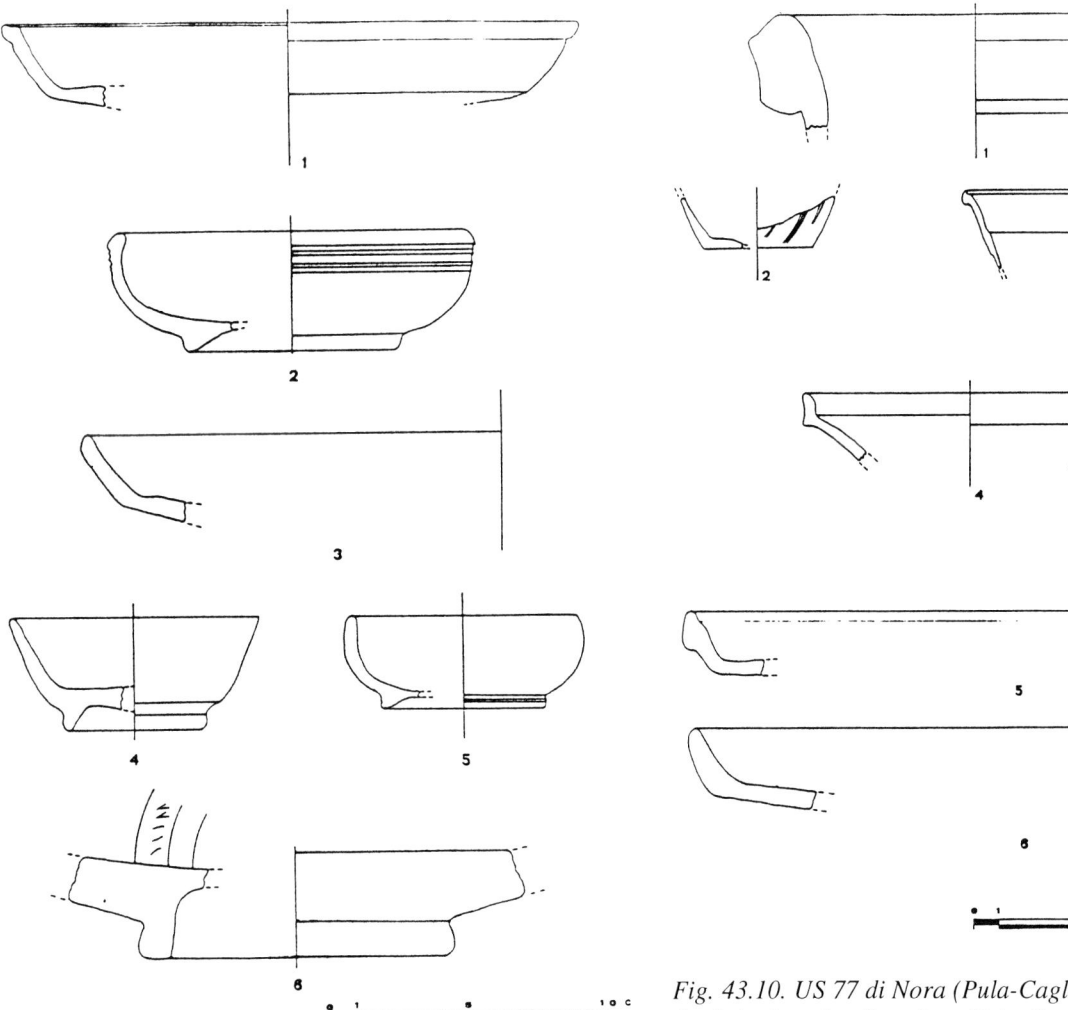

Fig. 43.9. *US 77 di Nora (Pula-Cagliari) (inizi dell'età flavia): ceramiche a vernice nera a pasta grigia*

Fig. 43.10. *US 77 di Nora (Pula-Cagliari) (inizi dell'età flavia): 1: orlo di anfora Tripolitana I; 2: fondo di boccalino a pareti sottili; 3-6: sigillata italica.*

episodica, della ceramica sud-gallica. Su questa base, e secondo quanto rilevato nelle US appartenenti al II sec. d.C., si potrebbe ipotizzare che la sua diffusione nella Sardegna meridionale avvenga sostanzialmente a partire dallo scorcio del I sec. d.C..

Il secondo elemento concerne la sigillata africana e la ceramica africana da cucina. Queste due classi sono assenti sia a Nora che a Sulci nelle US considerate e ciò può significarci che l'arrivo dei vasi africani non avviene sostanzialmente prima degli anni 80-90 del secolo, essendo coeva la diffusione della sigillata A e dell'africana da cucina; ciò contrasta con quanto è stato talvolta affermato, e cioè che la Sardegna ha recepito i prodotti africani in anticipo rispetto ad altre parti dell'impero, grazie alla sua posizione geografica.

Ciò ci viene confermato dai materiali provenienti dalla US 70/71 sempre di Nora, immediatamente posteriore nel tempo alla US 77, datandosi verosimilmente fra l'età flavia e quella traianea, in cui comincia ad apparire, sia pure in misura minima, l'africana da cucina assieme alla sigillata A.

Un confronto di alcune US di Nora in successione stratigrafica cronologica, anche se non fisica, ci aiuta a comprendere questo fenomeno (Figg. 43.11, 43.12).

Le US in esame sono la 77, databile agli inizi dell'età flavia, la 73, databile nella prima metà del II sec. d.C., la 4340, immediatamente successiva alla metà del II d.C. e la 4310 che si può collocare fra la metà e la fine dello stesso secolo.

Lasciando da parte i vasi a pareti sottili, dei cui problemi si è già fatto cenno sopra e che comunque in questo momento non interessano, possiamo costatare agevolmente la assoluta preminenza della ceramica a vernice nera a pasta grigia nelle US 77 e 73, largamente superiore alla sigillata italica ed assai più persistente, come si vede nella US 73, dove l'italica (in senso lato, comprendendo anche la tardo-italica) si riduce in modo notevole. Nella 73 iniziano ad apparire la sigillata sud-gallica e la sigillata africana, in misura pressoché identica.

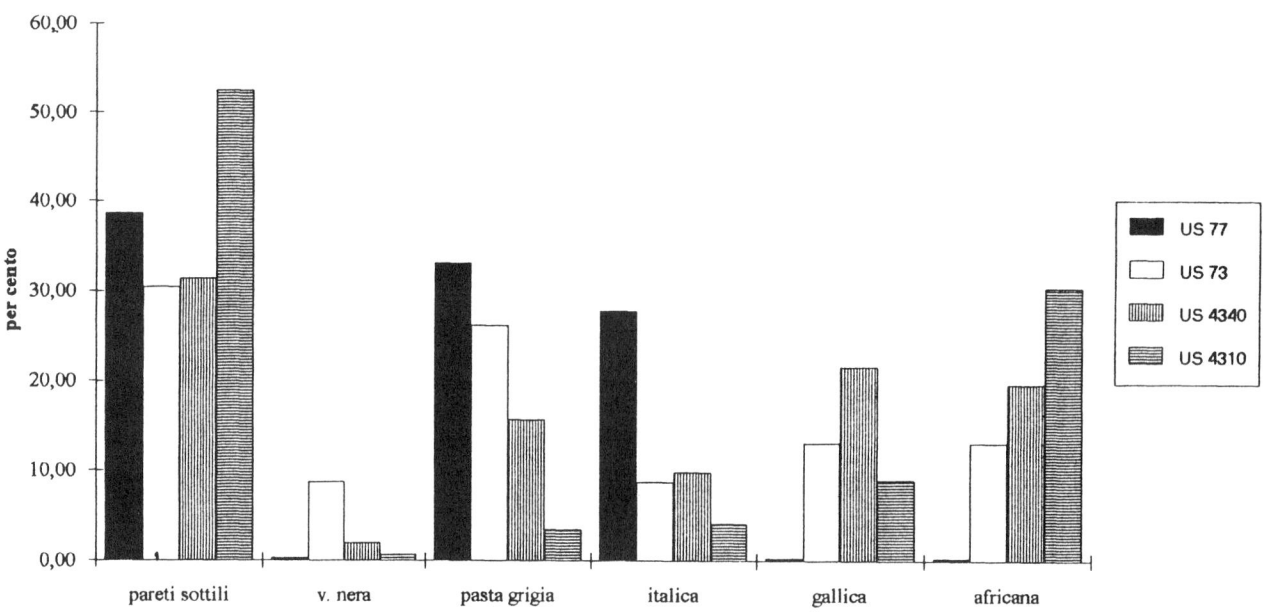

Fig. 43.11. Nora: distribuzione delle ceramiche fini da mensa calcolata sul numero minimo degli individui distinta per classi ceramiche.

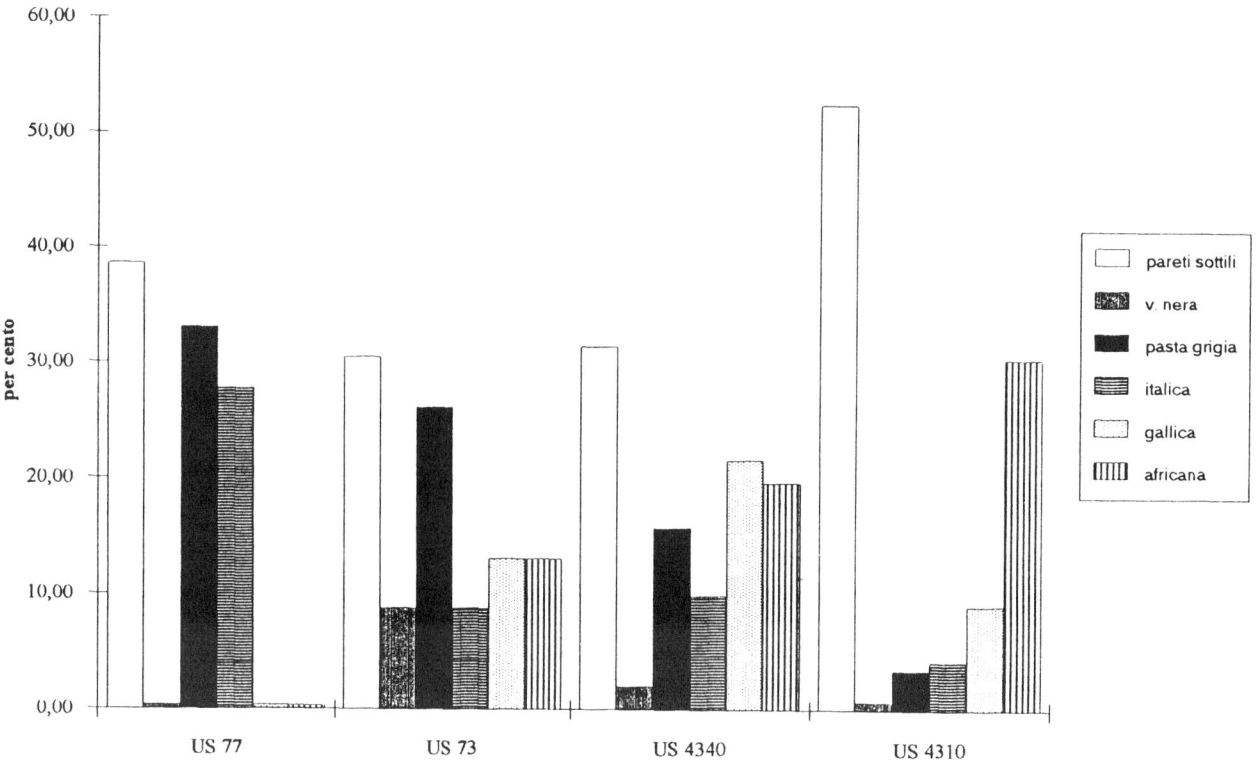

Fig. 43.12. Nora: distribuzione delle ceramiche fini da mensa calcolata sul numero minimo degli individui distinta per Unità Stratigrafiche.

Nella US 4340 la vernice nera a pasta grigia perde la sua prevalenza ed è soppiantata dalle sigillate sud-gallica ed africana, la prima in misura leggermente superiore alla seconda. Addentrandosi nella seconda metà del II sec. d.C. si percepisce chiaramente come la ceramica assolutamente dominante sia la sigillata africana, mentre le altre sono ormai solo residui.

La massima diffusione della sud-gallica sembrerebbe, dunque, collocarsi entro il II sec. d.C., sino a subito dopo la metà del secolo, e il pieno affermarsi della sigillata africana si avrebbe soltanto, grosso modo, fra il 150 ed il 200.

Naturalmente quanto detto va preso con beneficio di inventario e considerato solamente come una proposta di studio tutta ancora da verificare. I dati su cui mi sono basato sono estremamente parziali e limitati, sia come ampiezza di territorio esaminato, sia come quantità di dati. Non è detto che, ad esempio, a Cagliari, la situazione non possa essere diversa, con grosse quantità di sigillata africana presenti sin da livelli flavi.

Solo quando la base documentaria sarà più ampia, consistente e sopratutto omogenea (cioè quando saranno presi in esame molti contesti stratigraficamente affidabili, compiutamente esaminati e con dati statistici basati sul numero minimo degli individui, distribuiti quantomeno su tutta la parte meridionale costiera della Sardegna), sarà possibile raggiungere un certo grado di attendibilità delle nostre teorie che, è sempre opportuno ricordarlo, sono e saranno sempre soltanto *modelli interpretativi* del passato.

Bibliografia

AA.VV. 1977. *Ostia IV*. Studi Miscellanei 23. Roma.

AA.VV. 1987. *Turris Libisonis. La necropoli meridionale o di San Gavino. Intervento di scavo 1979–1980*. Quaderni della Soprintendenza ai Beni Culturali delle Provincie di Sassari e Nuoro 16. Dessì, Sassari.

Angiolillo, S. 1981. *Mosaici antichi in Italia. Sardinia*. Roma.

Atlante. 1981. *Enciclopedia dell'Arte Antica, Supplemento*. Atlante delle forme ceramiche I. Roma.

Bartoloni, P. 1983. *Studi sulla ceramica fenicia e punica di Sardegna*. Collezione di Studi Fenici 15. Roma.

Bartoloni, P. & Tronchetti, C. 1981. *La necropoli di Nora*. Collezione di Studi Fenici 12. Roma.

Boninu, A. 1971–72. Catalogo della "sigillata chiara africana" del Museo di Cagliari. *Studi Sardi* 1971–72: 293–358.

Equini Schneider, E. 1979. *Catalogo delle sculture romane del museo "G.A.Sanna" di Sassari e del Comune di Porto Torres*. Quaderni della Soprintendenza ai Beni Culturali delle Provincie di Sassari e Nuoro 7. Dessì, Sassari.

Lilliu, G. 1939. Barumini – Necropoli, pagi, ville rustiche romane. *Notizie degli Scavi* 370–380.

Moravetti, A. 1976. Necropoli romana in località S.Antonio – Ossi. In *Nuove testimonianze archeologiche della Sardegna centro-settentrionale*, 79–91. Sassari.

Nieddu, G. 1992. *La decorazione architettonica della Sardegna romana*. Oristano.

Ortu, A. 1993. Alcune sepolture della necropoli romana di Pau Cungiaus (Vallermosa-CA). *Quaderni della Soprintendenza Archeologica per le Provincie di Cagliari e Oristano* 10: 219–230.

Paderi, M.C. 1982. Bidd'e Cresia. Sepolture e corredi di età romana. In *Ricerche archeologiche nel territorio di Sanluri*, 67–80. Sanluri.

Pesce, G. 1957. *Sarcofagi romani in Sardegna*. Roma.

Pinna, M. 1981–85. La ceramica a pareti sottili del Museo di Cagliari. *Studi Sardi* 26: 239–302.

Saletti, C. 1989. La scultura di età romana in Sardegna: ritratti e statue iconiche. *Rivista di Archeologia* 13: 76–100.

Tronchetti, C. 1980. Tomba romana con una nuova forma in sigillata chiara A. In *Studi in onore di Nino Lamboglia*. Rivista di Studi Liguri 46: 236–240.

Tronchetti, C. 1987. Nora: la ceramica a vernice nera non attica. *Quaderni di Pula* 11–21.

Tronchetti, C. 1988. Bithia II: la ceramica a vernice nera a pasta grigia. *Quaderni della Soprintendenza Archeologica per le Provincie di Cagliari e Oristano* 5: 141–152.

Tronchetti, C. 1988a. Sant'Antioco: area del Cronicario (Campagne di scavo 1983–1986). La fase romana. *Rivista di Studi Fenici* 16: 111–119.

Tronchetti, C. 1990. La necropoli romana di Sulci – Scavi 1978: relazione preliminare. *Quaderni della Soprintendenza Archeologica per le Provincie di Cagliari e Oristano* 7: 173–192.

Ventura, M. 1990. La necropoli romana di "Cea Romana", agro di Villasalto-Cagliari. In *Le sepolture in Sardegna dal IV al VI secolo*, 37–65. Oristano.

Villedieu, F. 1984. *Turris Libisonis. Fouille d'un site romain tardif à Porto Torres, Sardaigne*. BAR International Series 224. British Archaeological Reports, Oxford.

44. The Chronological and Cultural Definition of Nuragic VII, AD 456–1015

Gary Webster and Maud Webster

Introduction[1]

Today, we know a good deal about the archaeological manifestations of the Nuragic culture of Sardinia. Credit for much of this must go to the efforts and brilliance of Giovanni Lilliu, best exemplified perhaps in his masterful work *La civiltà nuragica* published in 1982 (Lilliu 1982). As a major synthesis of the evidence, based in part on the findings from his own pioneering excavations at Su Nuraxi in Barumini, it remains the standard cultural-historical framework within which new findings are given a chronological and cultural context. Although the results of new field projects have done little to challenge the basic validity of Lilliu's scheme, the use of increasingly refined techniques of excavating and dating stratified deposits has led to revisions of the chronology. In this regard, one of the questions attracting discussion is whether the standard chronological divisions adequately accommodate the latest Nuragic manifestations. Rowland recently put the problem quite simply: "When did the Nuragic Period in Sardinia end?" (Rowland 1992: 165–175). The conventional answer is 238 BC, at the close of Nuragic V when, as an outcome of the First Punic War, Rome seized control of the island from Carthage.

Lilliu's widely accepted chronology divides the Nuragic sequence into five cultural phases, Nuragic I through V, spanning the entirety of the Sardinian Bronze and Iron Ages, a period of a little over 2000 years. It is during Nuragic V, in the context of Punic domination between ca. 500 BC and 238 BC, that Nuragic culture is thought to have been assimilated and disappeared from the archaeological record. Yet, Lilliu's more recent statements qualify the traditional wisdom concerning "Nuragico di Sopravvivenza": "It is evident that, in the mountains, the ancestral forms of life must have survived for a long time, penetrating largely into historical times. The Romanization of the indigenous peoples of the central island was---a matter of language and to a lesser degree of culture. Much less was it a matter of spirit" (Lilliu 1988: 480–481).

The implication, that traditional Nuragic culture may have been preserved among some native communities after 238 BC, has now been given considerable archaeological support. While assimilation and/or elimination of Nuragic populations appears to have been early and thorough in the more heavily colonized lowland-coastal zones, it is just as clear that many Nuragic settlements survived and even flourished at least into the Roman Imperial period. Over 530 of the ca. 7000 known nuraghi report evidence of Roman period native habitation. While they are found in all the island regions, sometimes quite near colonial sites, most come from the interior. This is not surprising: the Romans called this *Barbaria*, the "reserve" of the *civitates barbariae* who, as history records, resisted Roman rule well into Imperial times. There can be little doubt that these unpacified "barbarian tribes" are the social (and perhaps ethnic) correlates of Roman period Nuragic remains.

Still, there have as yet been few formal suggestions on how the existing Nuragic chronology should best be revised to account for these findings. Tykot has suggested extending Nuragic V to ca. 456 AD or when the Vandal invasion of the island effectively ended the period of Roman rule (Tykot 1994), but this seems less than satisfactory. There is the fear that collapsing the Punic and Roman periods under a single label may weaken the heuristic value of the scheme by obscuring potentially important temporal variations. There is a growing body of data suggesting that there were important differences between Nuragic cultural adaptations to Punic and Roman influence (G. Webster & Teglund 1992: 448–473). In light of this, we suggest preserving Nuragic V as chronologically Punic, and adding a Nuragic VI to accommodate native adaptations during the Roman period after 238 BC.

In this paper, we will address the question that inevitably

arises from the evidence just mentioned: did Nuragic culture survive into the post-Roman period? We are not the first to raise the issue, nor the first to conclude that there now exists sufficient evidence – both literary and archaeological – to suspect that some native communities preserved recognizably Nuragic lifeways during the period of Vandal and Byzantine domination. It has become evident that the implications of a growing number of reports from Nuragic sites bearing Medieval remains must be evaluated. At the same time, we recognize that the possibility of a Medieval Nuragic archaeology carries its own methodological and conceptual difficulties.

Nuragic Traditions and Acculturation

The question of late Nuragic survivals is also a question of acculturation. To what degree were traditional Nuragic features lost or modified due to contact with non-Nuragic cultural influences? The problem is both methodological and conceptual. How does one go about measuring acculturation? How does one decide at what point along the continuum of acculturative change Nuragic culture stopped being Nuragic and started becoming something else? Detecting acculturation archaeologically is difficult mainly because it is so often a gradual process. If history and ethnography have taught anything, it is that traditions die hard; modification through cultural contact may take centuries. The result for the archaeologist is that its material manifestations will rarely take the form of recognizable replacements of entire assemblages. More likely, it will amount to incremental changes in the proportion of non-traditional to traditional traits in the stratigraphic record. Determining cultural context is thus all-important. The archaeologist must try to determine where an assemblage falls along a cultural continuum from one demonstrating little or no acculturation to one demonstrating near cultural replacement or assimilation; in the present case from one with but a few non-Nuragic traits in an otherwise Nuragic context, to one with but a few Nuragic traits in an otherwise non-Nuragic context.

Unfortunately, Nuragic research has often neglected this, and instead harbored unrealistic assumptions about the nature of culture-change and hence expectations about how it should look archaeologically. It is too often assumed, for example, that Nuragic culture was completely replaced or radically altered by contact with colonial Punic, Roman and Byzantine cultures. This in turn has influenced the way cultural deposits are perceived and treated analytically. Colonial items recovered in otherwise Nuragic contexts are often considered intrusive rather than potentially diagnostic of an acculturative environment. Similarly, Nuragic items in otherwise colonial contexts have been taken as evidence for stratigraphic contamination from earlier Nuragic strata rather than evidence of Nuragic survivals in later non-Nuragic contexts. Regrettably, such assumptions have sometimes led to the scrapping of entire culture-bearing deposits thought to be disturbed. Stratigraphic mixing from natural and human agencies is undoubtedly a reality with which we must deal. It is also true that many Nuragic sites have been "contaminated" by cultural remnants from visitations having little to do with cultural continuity. Still, only with careful regard for the latest cultural strata can one hope to distinguish these from important evidence of cultural transition. Clearly, we must revise the way we view cultural stratification in Sardinia and re-evaluate assumptions about culture-change which have been cast in terms of culturally "pure" periods and resulting expectations of culturally "pure" strata. Acculturation being gradual and history being one of transitions rather than replacements, cultural overlaps and mixed strata will be the archaeological norm: we must devise ways to document these.

The Question of Ethnicity

In anthropology, questions of cultural survival are often framed in terms of the effects of acculturation on ethnicity (Barth 1968[1958]: 324–331). But archaeologists have found it difficult to detect ethnic groups, and much of the difficulty seems to stem from the complexity of the concept of ethnicity itself. Dragadze defines the ethnic group or *ethnos* as "a firm aggregate of people, historically established on a given territory, possessing in common relatively stable peculiarities of language and culture, and also recognizing their unity and expressing this in a self-appointed name (*ethnomen*)" (Renfrew & Bahn 1991: 169). Thus, attempts to recognize ethnicity archaeologically have tended to focus on the material manifestations of "boundary behavior" among ethnic groups and the means by which ethnic groups symbolize membership to and identity with that group – what Bartel calls the "overt signals of identity with *ethnos*" (Bartel 1989: 177–185). But here, problems abound for the archaeologist. It is not clear whether the cognitive features of ethnicity always correlate with material features. So cultural boundaries, even if detected archaeologically, may not imply ethnic boundaries, nor cultural continuity always ethnic unity (Gillin & Raimy 1940: 380; Spiro 1955: 1240–1252; Hodder 1982).

At the present, little can be said with certainty about the role of ethnicity in Nuragic acculturation, nor even whether Nuragic culture at any time constituted a single *ethnos*. There is little evidence for or against a common Nuragic language, since the pre-colonial natives were apparently illiterate. Similar darkness shrouds the question of a common *ethnomen*. The "tribal" names of Roman period *Civitates Barbariae* and Medieval *Barbaricini* found in the documentary sources could, in fact, imply the presence of a number of Nuragic ethnic groups. Alternatively, one might view traditional iconographic similarities as symbolizing a common island-wide ethnic identity. One example would be those portraying possibly "national" cults of the *Dio Toro* and *Dea Madre*; another may be the Nuraghe-form itself, the symbol of commonly felt security and social membership, of military strength and strong leadership depicted, as it occurs in edifices, votive bronzes, ritual *stelae*, and bronze buttons (G. Webster 1996: 189-190).

In addition to material-trait approaches, some researchers have turned to studies of human skeletal material in hopes of defining ethnic boundaries. These rest on the hypothesis that since ethnic groups tend to be endogamous, ethnic boundaries should be visible in the genetic clustering of skeletal traits. Although such studies have yet to be carried out on Sardinian burials, they may one day provide insights on the relationship between Nuragic ethnicity and material culture. In addition, because history and ethnology are rich with examples of violations of endogamy rules, the approach may have important implications for examining the role of marriage exchanges in acculturation. Inter-ethnic marriages were no doubt common between natives and colonists in the island from antiquity, although their extent and effects have been little studied.

For the present, we remain ignorant of the relationship between the analyst's definition of Nuragic culture and the native's definition of Nuragic *ethnos* or *ethnoi*. Even if established, it is likely that certain emic dimensions of acculturation will always elude us. For example, it will always be hard, if not impossible, to document the survival of Nuragic ethnicity unless manifested in some artifactual or symbolic way. Thus, the hypothetical "closet" Nur will remain undetectable. For the same reasons, the antithesis – the "closet" Greek (the native living a Nuragic lifestyle but identifying with Byzantine culture) will also remain archaeologically invisible. For the time being, we must rest on a rather cruder logic: if they lived as Nur and died as Nur, they probably were Nur.

If we are less than certain about Nuragic ethnic identity, we can be quite certain that during the periods in question, Sardinia was ethnically complex – a mosaic of entities both foreign and indigenous. Centuries of immigration meant that numerous lines of ancestry were present, if not always demonstrable. Some families may have traced genealogies to ancient Punic and Roman, or less deeply to Byzantine Greek or Arab roots. Some of these in turn may have preserved a sense of common heritage as ethnic enclaves. But given the centuries involved, we can be sure that many, if not most, islanders probably found their ancestral trees "hopelessly" mixed. Their ancient ethnic origins having long dissolved into amorphous memories, leaving instead only the common identification with place and recent past. They may simply have called themselves Sards and no longer identified with their exotic origins but with the island itself or, more likely, with one of its regions and with a common island culture neither Punic, Roman, nor Byzantine Greek – but Sardinian. Many of these, too, no doubt traced ancestry to even more ancient, Nuragic cultures. However, as has occurred in similar colonial settings elsewhere, it is unlikely that any majority of Sardinians in the Middle Ages identified closely with surviving native cultures. Yet it is here, in the diversity of Medieval Sardinia, that we should search for Nuragic survivals.

Historical Background[2]

Sardinia came under Vandal dominion, as a province of Africa, between AD 456 and 468: the sources do not allow for a more specific date. There is little evidence to suggest that any substantial change of administration came about during the eight decades or so of Vandal rule. Vandal religious programs did have some effect, however. The Vandal kings were fervid Christians and, most often, Aryans. Conflicts of faith were pursued energetically, and dissenters punished with death or exile. Orthodox Christians were exiled to Sardinia in unknown numbers during the reigns of Genseric (-477), Hunneric (477–484) and Thrasamund (496–523). Thus, the Vandals actually spread a creed which they were trying to suppress. Exiles were generally well received in Cagliari, where a non-Aryan Christian community already was established. Notably, two popes came from Sardinia during this time: Hilarius and Symmachus – the latter declaring himself a converted pagan. An additional 3000 North-Africans also arrived in Sardinia during Genseric's reign. It appears likely that they settled in the Barbagia-Gerrei.

The last Vandal king, Gelimer (530–533) was defeated in the Byzantine war and lost Sardinia. In AD 534, the Byzantine administration came into vigour through the orders of the emperor Justinian. In addition to an island governor in Cagliari, Sardinia (still an African province), a *dux*, responsible for military undertakings, was also installed, most likely at Fordongianus – Byzantine Chrysopolis. In the 6th century, there was an Ostrogoth incursion, and in the beginning of the 7th century, a Longobardian. These proved minor threats when compared to that of the Arabs, which grew stronger after Arabs had taken Carthage in AD 698. Indeed, the Franks, who had interests in Corsica, allied themselves with the Sards against the Arabs. But in AD 753, a violent attack on Sardinia led the Sards to accept an agreement to pay taxes not only to Byzantium but also to the Arabs. This, in turn, led the Byzantines to keep some distance from Sardinia, although remaining nominally in rule until AD 1015.

The island economy was rather unstable during these centuries. While the authors of the classical period repeatedly described Sardinia as rich and fertile, there is no such mention for the Byzantine period. This may be in part due to the unevenness of the sources, but probably also to a real decline in productivity after the fall of Rome and with it at least a partial decline of the agricultural systems maintained for export to that city. In Sardinia, the large proprietors were the Church, the monasteries, private landowners, and farmer-collectivities. The tax-burden was generally considered excessive, and was heavy enough to render farmers insolvent, occasionally bringing about widespread tax-evasion. In addition to agricultural endeavors, salt- and metal-extraction continued to some extent.

The settlement pattern of Medieval Sardinia is still only partially understood. It would seem that most cities of Punic and Roman foundation continued until the 8th century, and some survived longer still. Nora and Tharros suffered considerably from the Vandal takeover and declined steadily thereafter – although Tharros retained its bishopric for some time. Both towns were abandoned by the 11th century. The inhabitants of Tharros seem to have withdrawn inland, and may have constituted part of the founding nucleus of the new settlement of Oristano. Sant'Antioco (Punic-Roman Sulci), also a see, was sacked by Arabs in AD 705 and subsequently abandoned. Turris Libisonis/Porto Torres, likewise a bishopric, survived the enemy incursions rather better, but was nevertheless gradually abandoned around the end of this period and its inhabitants withdrew from the coast – perhaps contributing to the budding settlement of Sassari. There can be no doubt that piracy played a part in the reduction of the coastal settlements as well.

There were sees also at Cagliari, Cornus (= Senafer, see Zucca 1986), Olbia (Phausania) and Fordongianus. A notable exception to the otherwise bleak impression of urban reduction, Fordongianus increased in importance, as indicated also by its new name Chrysopolis (see Conti 1984). Now a center both of military and ecclesiastical authority, it also possessed a local patron saint in the martyr Luxorius, and it probably retained its traditional roles as market- and recreation center.

A glance at the distribution of places named for Byzantine Greek saints shows that they penetrated into the interior, but dating is problematic in this regard. The known Christian sites more securely dated to this period, however, show some tendency to cluster around the old urban areas of western Sardinia: the greater Turritano, the Cagliaritano and the Sinis areas. This holds true in particular for the 30 or so extant churches dating to this period and the 10 or so later churches thought to have foundations of this period; the more notable exceptions being of course Olbia and Fordongianus. Most Christian tombs and cemeteries have so far been found near the churches, or in the same general areas. Of the 20 or so rock-cut chapels, mostly reused prehistoric *domus de janas*, only four fall outside the western part of today's Sassari Province. If these preliminary distribution data are at all representative, it seems that while Christianity was indeed spreading in Sardinia, the conversion process was both slow and uneven, and much of the island remained pagan at least through the 6th or 7th century.

Little is known of interior settlement patterns, but it would seem probable that the countryside was dotted with smallish agricultural and agro-pastoral/polycultural hamlets, largely relying on local subsistence production.

Epigraphy does seem to evince some small-scale exchange of commodities as well.

Investments in public works appear to have been minimized during Byzantine times. There is, for example, only one road in Sardinia known to be a Byzantine construction – the "Via Grecisca" between the Turritano/ Algherese and the Logudoro. The Roman bridges, Ezzu in Ittireddu and Romano in Alghero, were apparently repaired in Byzantine days, evincing reuse of existing facilities with some minimum of maintenance – an economizing strategy no doubt employed also with regards to roads and other amenities. It is not impossible that the "Via Grecisca" was built to meet military needs, as were the fortresses of Medusa in Samugheo and Castro in Oschiri – two of the few known fortifications of the early Middle Ages.

As mentioned above, the ethnic composition of Sardinia was by this time rather complex. The major immigrant groups: Semitic (Phoenician, Punic, and to a lesser degree Jewish), Roman/Latin, North-African and Byzantine Greek (and perhaps the possible minor ones, ancient Greek and Iberian and Medieval Vandal and Arabic) were most concentrated in the western part of the island. Linguistically, it seems that Greek remained within the administrative sphere, and left very few traces in the popular dialects. Outside this sphere, Latin would instead have been the main spoken language. Most people were, however, illiterate.

As Byzantine dominion slackened and Arab presence was accentuated, Sardinia began sliding into a state of semi-autonomy, a political climate in which the Sardinian *giudicati* had their roots. In AD 1015, the Arabs made a final attempt to conquer Sardinia, and despite its limited success, the attack put an end to Byzantine rule in the island.

Documentary Evidence for a Nuragic VII

Written sources which can confidently be said to refer to native or Nuragic survivals are fewer for the Medieval period than for the Roman. However, those concerning the interior peoples called *Barbaricini* are promising. The term derives from the Roman name for the mountainous region, *Barbaria*, named for the "barbarian" characteristics of its inhabitants. Although it is possible that the term *Barbaricini* in the Middle Ages may have meant nothing more than "peoples of the *Barbaria*", it is also very possible that it still retained its "barbarian" connotation, that the region was still named after its inhabitants and hence that these refer to traditional natives: perhaps survivals.

What is clear, however, is that whomever the term referred to, measures were taken on the part of the Byzantine government to control them, at least through the 6th century. The *dux*, installed by Justinian as a magistrate responsible for military undertakings, had his base at the foot of the interior mountains, probably at

Fordongianus. Apart from an imperial mobile army, Justinian created special frontier troops of soldier-farmers, settled on strategic spots on the island to control internal affairs (*Codex Justinianus* 1,27; 2,3; Bellieni 1973: 152). Procopius wrote that Fordongianus itself was fortified (Procopius, *De Aedif* 6,7), and what may be a Byzantine incision has been found on Ponte Allai nearby (Caprara 1986: 270). Justinian's caution proved well-founded: only four years after the Byzantine takeover, there was an uprising in which the North African exiles settled in southern Barbagia apparently raided the Campidano plains (Procopius, *De Bello Vandalico* 2,13). The focused concern with internal threats may in fact have eased the way for the Ostrogoth invasion of the 6th century. Boscolo has argued that the efforts made against the *barbaricini* caused the Byzantines to leave the coasts largely unguarded, thus enabling the enemy to raid (Procopius, *De Bello Gothico* 4,24; Boscolo 1978: 34).

Statements on the economic conditions of the time are few, especially for the interior. But an inscription from the reign of the emperor Mauritius and found at Donori presents a municipal register tariff concerning taxes due on products brought in to Cagliari. The fees are for consumer-products and payable mainly in kind. The products listed are grain (transported by pack-animals or small boats), palms, sheep (taxed per 20 animals), legumes (measured in baskets), wine (?), and birds (taxed per 30 animals) (Pani Ermini and Marinone 1981: no. 77). It is uncertain whether these products were for direct market sale or longer distance trade, or both. However, given the date (582–602), the provenience (Donori, between Cagliari and the *Barbaria*) and the inscription's municipal nature, Guillou has argued that the tariff probably concerned transactions with the *barbaricini* as a consequence of the peace established by the *dux* (see below) (Guillou 1987–88: 361–362).

Literature on the spread of Christianity in Sardinia holds promising information regarding possible survivals. Christianity took hold in the cities in the late Roman period, and by the end of the 5th century there were several bishoprics in the island. But the conversion of the general population proceeded slowly. By the end of the 6th century, the issue became a major concern to pope, Gregorius Magnus. A series of papal letters directed to the bishop of Cagliari and referring to farmers on church-owned land near that city and perhaps the other sees, suggests that classical pagan practices still survived in the areas where Punic and Roman cults had previously flourished (Greg. Ep. 23,3; 26,3 in Tola 1984). But other papal documents refer to the *barbaricini* and suggest pagan cults of another kind. These seem to be of a "naturalistic" type, perhaps of Nuragic origin.

Paganism in the interior, no doubt coupled with the threat of occasional raiding from there, made the *barbaricini* a great concern to the authorities – as they had been for centuries. The emperor Mauritius ordered the Sardinian *dux* Zabardas to wage war on them until they were pacified and also ready to convert. In AD 594, pope Gregorius wrote to Zabardas to congratulate him on the victory over the *barbaricini* (Greg. Ep. 25,3 in Tola 1984). He also wrote to a chief of the *barbaricini*, referred to as Hospito: "Since none of your people (*gente*) is a Christian, I know that in this you are better than all your people since you are a Christian---While all the *barbaricini* live like beasts without reason, not knowing the true God, worshipping trees and stones, you show how much you are superior to them in that you worship the true God. But the faith that you have received must also be accompanied by good acts and words---you must bring to Christ all those that you can, have them baptized and teach them to choose the eternal life" (Greg. Ep. 27,3 in Tola 1984). Another letter from Gregorius, written to the bishop of Cagliari in 594, relates to the pagans of the Gallura and the see at Olbia (Phausania) (Guillou 1987–88: 378; cf. Pani Ermini and Guintella 1989: 67–69), which had been left vacant: "Since we have come to know that because of the lack of priests some remain pagan and, living like wild beasts, they know not of the cult of God, we demand of Your brotherhood to hurry and consecrate a bishop, according to the former tradition" (Greg. Ep. 29,3 in Tola 1984).

Some letters tell of the conversion methods used. These involved preaching and baptizing, and sometimes quite secular methods such as fines and imprisonment (see below). Procopius described the practices used in North African provinces which were probably much the same as those in Sardinia: Byzantine officials offered local chiefs benefits like precious attire and money in return for his services to the Empire, mainly keeping peace in his region and converting his people to Christianity (Guillou 1987–88: 341–342). It may well have been an agreement of this kind that the Sardinian chief Hospito came to with the *dux* Zabardas – but conversion remained a dubious accomplishment. In the following year of AD 595, Gregorius wrote to the Empress Constantina asking her to confer with her husband, the emperor Mauritius, about a problem. The pope had now been informed of a "sacrilegious thing: those that sacrifice to the idols pay a sum to the official in order to obtain his permission. Of some, who had already been baptized and had ceased to sacrifice to the idols, the above-mentioned official of the island still exacts, after baptism, the sum that they previously had the habit of giving him to sacrifice to the idols" (Greg. Ep. 33,4 in Tola 1984). It is unclear which Sardinians are concerned here, but it is evident that the Church had difficulties uprooting their pagan cults. The next extant letter on the subject, written with increased severity, was dispatched to the bishop of Cagliari in AD 599. The pope stated that if preaching was not enough, then corporeal punishment must be applied: "if they are slaves, we want you to punish them with blows and torments capable of bringing them to correct themselves; if they are free men, they shall be brought to repentance by a severe prison term" (Greg. Ep. 67,7 in Tola 1984). Again, the referents are unspecified, but the mention of slaves is interesting. From a letter of

AD 599 by Gregorius to his rector at Sant'Antioco, we learn that the Church and the *barbaricini* were involved in a slave-market. The rector was informed that a notary had been sent from Rome to Sardinia "to buy *barbaricini* slaves for use in the parish. And your experience should therefore be of help to him in every way and with eagerness and energy so that he may buy them, at a good price, and he should purchase such that can be useful in the service of the parish" (Greg. Ep. 18,9 in Tola 1984). In AD 600, there is something of a report on the state of the conversion process, as the pope wrote to the island governor Spesindeus: "I am informed that many barbarians from the province of Sardinia, by the grace of God, hurry with devotion toward the Christian faith" and then he added that he wished Spesindeus to take active part and "eagerly collaborate with our brother Victor to convert them and baptize them" (Greg. Ep. 17,9 in Tola 1984). Since Victor was the new bishop of Olbia (Greg. Ep. 8,7; 1,17 and 1,9 in Tola 1984), and the only bishop named here, we may conclude both that the see had been filled on the pope's earlier request, and that the pope felt the pagan resistance in the Gallura to be heavier than elsewhere in the island.

It is clear that early Christianity in the island retained some pagan elements. From later evidence, it appears that the new religion was practiced with emphasis on healing, a feature which had very ancient roots (Boscolo 1978: 99–107). Still today in Sardinia, Christian holidays are observed with strong pagan colouring (Lilliu 1988: 261, 567; Bottoglioni 1922: 40–44; Boscolo 1978: 99–107; see also Lanternari 1955: 64–95; Turchi 1992: 4–9; Lilliu 1988: 258–260, 566–569). The persistence of paganism is no doubt to be found in the sheer habit and familiarity of the traditional cults, and even in the facilities used by early Christian establishments. Christian celebrations were often connected to ritual sites, like the large sanctuary of Santa Vittoria di Serri. In AD 601, Gregorius wrote a letter to a bishop in Britain on this very subject. As a general *credo*, it is probably relevant for Sardinia as well. Here, the pope stated that the pagan shrines should not be destroyed, but instead Christianized and reused: "One should provide sanctified water, sprinkle it in the temples, build altars, deposit relics of saints there, for if these temples are well built, they should absolutely be transformed from demonic worship to the worship of the true God so that they may free their hearts from wrongs and while they come to know and worship the true God assemble more naturally in the places to which they had been accustomed. And since they usually slaughter many cattle when they sacrifice to the demons, some of the custom should be transferred also from here so that, on the days of the dedications and nativities of the holy martyrs whose relics are deposited there, they build tents from tree-branches around the churches which are transformed from temples and celebrate the holidays with pious feasts and no longer sacrifice the animals to the devil" (Greg. Ep. 11,56, *Corpus Christianorum Series Latina* CXLA: 961). Similar feasts are still celebrated in Sardinia today.

Following Pope Gregorius' death in AD 604, there is no further extant documentation of the conversion process in Sardinia. It may be an indication of its continued faltering pace that another 400 years passed before another bishopric was installed in the interior, at Suelli (Motzo 1924: 57–82).

Archaeological Evidence for a Nuragic VII

As yet, we have nothing for the Medieval period as extensive as Rowland's typological inventory of Roman age nuraghi (Rowland 1988: 740–874).' Several reasons can account for this. The first, already noted, is the legacy from a general neglect of those latest cultural strata which could bear evidence of post-Roman occupation. A second relates to the practical difficulties in dating late occupations in the absence of chronologically diagnostic artifacts. Native ceramics do not yet provide securely datable historical types, and very few sites are routinely dated by "independent" means like obsidian hydration and radiocarbon determinations. As a result, the recognition and dating of late colonial period native occupations are closely dependent on the dating of any exotic ceramics and metal work that happens to be present. Given these methodological difficulties, it is probably safe to assume that the current number of known post-Roman (Nuragic VII) native sites is but a small sample of the number yet to be discovered. Still, a review of even the more recent field reports indicates that late survivals did exist in several island regions. In this regard, it is noted that in at least one region (discussed below) the lower Tirso River area, surveys have revealed not only a strikingly high degree of Roman – Medieval-period continuity at settlements, but furthermore that late Roman pottery like African Red Slip ware (*terra sigillata chiara africana D*) was imported into some nuraghi as late as the 6th century. One implication from this is clear: the inventories of the ca. 530 known Roman-period nuraghi, most of which are dated on early reports of "Roman pottery", may include a number of early Medieval occupations with late variants of African Red Slip ware.

At the moment, the best evidence for post-Roman survivals comes from two types of sites: settlements with Medieval use, and ritual sites with Medieval use. The former are far more common and include both traditional residences with continuous or later reuse for similar purposes and residential sites with later non-residential (usually ritual) use. The latter are rarer and include some mortuary sites and sanctuaries. One additional category of sites which has not yet been studied with reference to the question of native acculturation is the still hypothetical Medieval site (context) with traditional elements or artifacts. But here, we treat only sites (contexts) with Medieval remains.

Medieval sites are presently reported from a dozen or so island areas. As one might anticipate from the known distribution of Roman age nuraghi, few are in the heavily colonized lowland-coastal areas but come mainly from the interior of the Barbagia. It is more surprising, perhaps, that these are reported not only from the mountainous reaches of Monte Acuto, Goceano, Gallura and the Nuorese, but also from the middle uplands of Trexenta, Marmilla, the Lower Tirso, Barigadu, the Marghine, the Middle Tirso, and the Sassarese. In fact, their distribution reveals an interesting correlation: Medieval nuraghi appear to follow the main arteries of the Roman road system, especially the road from Caralis to Turris Libisonis and its main branch to Olbia (Belli 1988: 339). Since it is assumed that much of this network continued in use in the Middle Ages, the relationship has potential importance for questions of acculturation. However, we cannot be certain whether the distribution is a reflection of the original pattern or an artifact of the still small sample of Medieval nuraghi.

In the Marmilla, the large complex of Genna Maria in Villanovaforru was used as a shrine for pagan cults of Punic-Roman origin from the 4th century BC to the 7th century AD. The ritual use of the interior and adjoining courtyard of this trilobate edifice followed several centuries after its abandonment as a residential and political center during the early Iron Age. Diagnostic artifacts included votive offerings of coins, a *terra sigillata* lamp of *Anselmino X* form, and glass vases (C. Lilliu 1988: 109). Another large nuraghe, Su Mulinu in nearby Villanovafranca, may have seen similar Medieval utilization of its antemural tower F from late Punic times (Ugas 1987: 77, 81). The prolongation of pre-Christian cults at both sites well into the period of Byzantine rule is even more notable given their close proximity to the Christian site of Baressa (Rowland 1978: 33). These late pagan cult survivals at nuraghi contrast the evidence for more rapid acculturation at Su Nuraxi in Barumini less than 10 kms north. Su Nuraxi and its dependent communities were abandoned during the Imperial period and part of the local population no doubt absorbed into nearby *latifundia*. Soon after, the location was Christianized as evinced by the appearance of a paleo-Christian church in Vicus Bangius made by rebuilding Roman period baths, probably in the 5th century (Lilliu & Zucca 1988: 24-25).

To the southeast, in the Trexenta, Nuraghe Su Nuraxi in Siurgus Donigala was used for a Byzantine collective burial. Similar Nuraghe-tombs of the 7th and 8th centuries are recorded at Nuraghe Candala-Sorradile, Sa Jacca-Busachi and Zinnuri-Bauladu and may represent a common VII pattern of using nuraghi as sepulcres following periods of habitation (Santoni *et al.* 1987: 83-86; Dyson & Rowland 1988: 133).

Especially important for the question of late survivals are the findings of surveys conducted by Dyson and Rowland in the lower Tirso valley around Bauladu, Paulilatino and Fordongianus. Here, based on the dating of ceramics collected from over 120 sites, an unexpectedly high degree of continuity was documented not only from precolonial to colonial periods but also into the later Imperial and post-Roman periods. Nuraghi used in the 4th to 6th centuries contained materials along with many imports including African Red Slip ware at more than one quarter of the sites visited. Many sites had more typical Medieval pottery as well. Although little can be said about the nature of these early Medieval nuraghi, frequent finds of rooftiles and plain ceramics along with the imports suggest that most supported some kind of habitation (Dyson & Rowland 1989: 157-185).

Further north in the adjacent areas of Barigadu, Middle Tirso and Marghine, a number of sites have yielded evidence of Medieval use. A program of survey and excavations by Santoni in the communes of Busachi, Ardauli, Tadasuni, Bidoni, Sorradile and Aidomaggiore (parts of these areas are now under Lake Omodeo) has documented Medieval reuse of at least four of the 22 sites investigated. One of these, Nuraghe Candala in Sorradile, offers detailed information from excavations (Santoni *et al.* 1987: 67-115). Within the main ground floor chamber, the earliest occupational phase dated to the 12th-8th centuries BC (with possible precursors) and contained exclusively native materials. A second phase of use during the late Imperial-early Medieval period seems to represent the reoccupation of the structure as a habitation after a hiatus of some 1200 years. The pottery repertory – some 240 specimens- is domestic in nature, comprising mainly plain, coarse tempered, often poorly fired and roughly smoothed wares in dark brown to black pastes along with some finer tempered, lighter (yellows to light browns) wares. With the probable exception of a single painted, wheelmade vessel with ring-base, all the pottery seems to be local. Closed forms predominate and both handmade (*impasto*) and vessels turned on a slow wheel (*tornita*) are represented. Interestingly, the repertory is remarkably similar to that found at the proto-nuraghe Sa Jacca in nearby Busachi. At both sites were found handmade *tegami* with horizontal tongue handles, low hemispherical bowls made on a wheel, handmade cylindrical cups, small wheelmade *olle* with trunco-conical necks, and larger jars, some wheelmade with distinctive quadrangular rim-sections, or with vertical "waisted" neck, and large handmade vessels with vertical ribbon handles. A few large *olle* were also decorated: a large vessel with extroverted lip has a raised ridge on the rim and a band *a pettine strisciato* on the shoulder; another, with belly-body has vertical incisions by the shoulder. Many are widespread Medieval forms. In addition, several sherds of recognizably traditional pottery were recovered from the Medieval occupational stratum at Candala: a bolstered mouth jar, and two hemispherical cups. Although Santoni dated these to the Late Bronze Age and deemed them intrusive from an underlying stratum, their Medieval stratigraphic context may be secure and one should not abandon the possibility that they represent late survivals of traditional forms.

A third phase of use of Nuraghe Candala is represented

by burials dating to the late 7th and early 8th centuries, found in the upper third of the "guard's niche". The small tomb with elliptical plan (without extant bones) is believed to have held the remains and personal belongings of two separate burials of a male and a female. Objects thought to be related to the male – possibly a freedman and a warrior according to the excavators – include a one-piece iron dagger with affinities in 7–8th century tombs at Tissi, Borutta, Cheremule, Laerru and Sant'Andrea Frius, and a bronze blade of uncertain affiliation. The iron *bandoliera* buckle is known also from funerary contexts of 7th century date at San Saturnino-Bultei and Sa Conca-Oniferi. The bronze buckle with perforated plaque may be a variety of a well known 7th century Byzantine Corinthian type and is also widespread in island sites including Nuragic ones: Su Nuraxi-Siurgus Donigala, Santa Vittoria-Serri, and possibly Toscono-Borore (Guido 1987: 128). The incised letter CHI seems to leave little doubt of the Christian and apothropaic character of the object, if not the burial, and similar *graffiti* find numerous analogies in Christian mortuary contexts in Sardinia and Italy. The vitrified paste beads and stone necklace beads, presumably with the female burial, include both types common to 7th century burials on the island and could be Sardinian as well as Italian peninsular types (possibly imported). The two *brocchette* and obsidian fragments are interpreted as pagan offerings. One piriform wheelmade jar finds parallels in paleo-Christian tombs in the island at Nurachi and Cornus, and on the peninsula; and a second decorated *a pettine* is a type known from a collective tomb in Cheremule. The obsidian may be votive in nature, as in the excavators' words "prophylactical amulets with an apotropaic character" (Santoni *et al.* 1987: 108–109). In sum, Nuraghi Candala and Sa Jacca along with several other sites appear to document periods of both habitational and mortuary use during the early Medieval period. It is important to note in addition, that such possible VII sites did not exist in social isolation. At least seven non-Nuragic historical sites are inventoried in Sorradile and Bidoni (Santoni *et al.* 1987) – some or all of which were probably in communication with the settlements.

Continuing north into the Marghine region, evidence for Medieval sites comes from Abbassanta, Dualchi, Borore and Macomer. At the large complex of Losa in Abbassanta, Taramelli's excavations revealed evidence both of late Roman-early Medieval period use in finds of 5–6th century lamps, and later use. Probably from the later phase, perhaps 7–8th century, came large storage jars, some with diagnostic stamped decorations. Within a prehistoric hut, there were funerary deposits also, probably Christian (Taramelli 1916: 248–250; Pani Ermini & Marinone 1981: 206, 240, 284). This settlement was very near Roman *Ad Medias* on the main Caralis-Turris Libisonis road.

Also near this major route were the nuraghi of Borore. Excavations at five of these (Toscono, Urpes, Serbine, San Sergio and Duos Nuraghes) by the Penn State Sardinia Program have revealed Medieval remains. Nuraghe Toscono appears to have been visited only very sporadically in the centuries following a rather substantial occupation in the 4th century. Finds include only two coins (Vandal and Byzantine, 5–6th century) and a bronze buckle, probably Vandal (Guido 1987: 127–28). By contrast, Nuraghe Urpes, a quadrilobate structure, has evidence of two small settlements, one in the 5–7th centuries and a second in the 8–10th centuries. These comprised some structural remains, just to the northwest of the nuraghe, of what may have been several small houses with clay floors, floor hearths and tiled roofs. Much pottery and some stone artifacts were associated. If the series of 43 obsidian hydration dates are reliable, the site was resettled about 500 years after the last Roman (Republican period) occupation. Of the dated obsidian flakes, 25 date from the 5th to 10th centuries (Michels 1987: 125). These, along with simple chert flakes, suggest a late retention of ancient lithic industries at Urpes (and the other Borore sites). This phenomenon has been recognized elsewhere in Europe, and Runnels has suggested that stone and obsidian flakes were used as bits in threshing sledges or *tribuli* (Runnels 1982: 363–373). Bones from butchered cows, swine, sheep/goats and fowl (probably poultry) suggest a traditional agro-pastoral farmstead economy at Urpes (Webster 1987: 69–92). The pottery repertory was quite complex, including late Roman plain wares along with both locally produced utilitarian and probably imported glazed Medieval wares (Webster *et al.* 1987: 45–68). Glazed wares (*ceramica invetriata*) were produced in comparable vessel forms on the peninsula during the late Imperial-early Medieval centuries (Lusuardi & Sannazaro 1985: 31–45). These were widely imported and/or copied and diffused in the island including into some sites by no later than the 9th century (Morgan 1942: 40). Although the repertory from Urpes has not yet received detailed analysis, it can be noted that few are decorated, save some of the glazed vessels which have incisions or painted lines. Vessel forms are probably similar to those at Candala although many are distinctive by their often partially glazed and/or slipped surface treatments. In addition, two spindle whorls were found at Urpes, suggesting textile working. Also, in contrast to Candala, the majority of pottery finds are from traditional wares, mainly *impasto* bowls with smooth surfaces in a range of paste colors from black to red. Ongoing excavations at Duos Nuraghes are revealing a long history of settlement from the Bronze Age through late Byzantine times. Overlying a Roman Imperial period habitation, the upper levels in the village and both nuraghi contained Medieval common and glazed wares along with Roman Included Ware and *terra sigillata* as well as *impasto*. As at Urpes, obsidian use is reflected in 15 of 144 flakes with dates ranging between the 5th and 11th centuries. Advanced degrees of plow disturbance in the village have eradicated any Medieval structures that may once have existed, but high concentrations of organic matter in Medieval strata in both towers hint to their use as barns or silos (Webster 1988: 465–472; Teglund & Webster 1993). A briefer test was conducted at Nuraghe San Sergio in the very center of Borore. Within deposits disturbed by later historical construction, a similar repertory of glazed and plain Medieval, late Roman and pottery was recovered. Seven of 19 obsidian flakes gave dates from the 7th to 9th centuries (Webster 1985: 14–18). Tests were also conducted in the interior of the proto/composite nuraghe Serbine located about five kms northeast of Borore. Although obsidian dates from here did not run beyond the 4th century, the upper stratum did contain an assemblage of late Roman, Medieval and ceramics comparable to those from Urpes, San Sergio and Duos. In addition, late glazed wares and roof tiles are common on the ground surrounding the site. What appear to be masonry additions to the exterior of the nuraghe, perhaps open animal pens and small covered barns, may date to Medieval times (Webster 1991: 22–25).

Not far to the northeast of Borore, in Dualchi, recent excavations at the multi-occupation site of Sa Corte by Sanna are revealing Roman and Medieval use of a village lacking nuraghi. From the walled habitation area came Roman common and imported wares, some associated with a Roman *cappuccina* burial, while Medieval pottery included some possibly Iberian imports. Although stratification was poor, some of the "*ceramica d'impasto di fattura a mano*" could be of Medieval date (Sanna 1990: 265–66).

To the northwest, on the southern edge of the Campeda above Macomer, sits Nuraghe Santa Barbara. Work here by Moravetti has revealed evidence of reuse of the structure in Roman times, possibly as a pagan shrine, and later visits beginning in the 6th century. In the second floor chamber of this quadrilobate nuraghe was found Medieval jewelry, a bronze ring and *fibula*, and a similar repertory came from outside the ground floor entrance. Also recovered in the interior courtyard were fragments of large jars with stamped decorations on the outside and below the rim (rounds filled with an X) like those at Bau Nuraxi-Triei, Losa-Abbassanta and elsewhere dating to the 6–8th centuries (Moravetti 1986: 49–113).

Further north, the number of reports of Medieval sites declines. A notable exception may be the large nuraghe of Santu Antine in the Meilogu near Torralba. As is well known, this trilobate nuraghe with adjacent huts supported settlements from the Bronze Age well into colonial times. Roman remains are quite abundant and include imported and locally copied Roman fine and common wares from most of the structures including the central works, as well as a Roman-style building complex with rectangular plan (see Moravetti 1988). The site seems to have been what we have termed a "nuraghe-villa" inhabited perhaps by Romanized native elite (see Webster & Teglund 1992). Most analyzed materials date before the 5th century, but there are later finds. These include several sherds of African Red Slip Ware from Tower B dated to the 6th century, and from Hut 5 a lamp probably in locally imitated *terra sigillata chiara* of similar date (Manca di Mores 1988: 278–280). Other sherds include three from a closed, wheelmade, and stamp-decorated vessel with Longobardian affinities, and another with incised decorations, probably a local imitation inspired by painted Byzantine wares of the 11–12th century (Caprara 1988: 431–432).

From the Sassarese still further north, reports are ambiguous. Nuraghe Don Michele in Ploaghe reported finds of along with Roman and Medieval remains, but with few details (Maetzke 1961: 652–654). Surveys in Codrongianus found a tomb *a tafoni* with Medieval materials near the church of Saccargia, and a small cave near Mascatellu contained bones and materials dated to the 4–6th century, but it is unclear whether or not these constitute paleo-Christian shrines (Manconi 1991: 120–123).

For additional evidence of possible Medieval native sites, one must turn east and inland to the foot of the mountains. In the Monte Acuto area, at Pattada, Basoli is excavating an extraordinary site with multiple settlements (Basoli 1991: 138–141). The site comprises two or three rectangular stone structures (15 X 5m and 10 X 4m) near nuraghe Lerno. These contained ceramics, lithics and metal dating from late Neolithic to Medieval times including materials recognized as Ozieri, Monte Claro, Iron Age, Roman and Byzantine. Not far away, in Ozieri, the complex of Sa Mandra 'e Sa Giua (better known for its wealth of Late Bronze-Iron Age bronzes) is also yielding later materials. Recent work by Basoli near one of the lateral towers turned up fragments of storage jars with diagnostic stamped decorations (concentric rounds, circles, rounds with an X and with reticulates and triangles and rounds filled with lines) as at Santa Barbara and the other nuraghi already noted and dating to the 7–8th century. According to the excavator, these "document in this locality a continuity of settlement from the Nuragic and Roman period to the Middle Ages" (Basoli 1989 [1986]: 41). There are also hints of late, possibly native activities in Ittireddu near the complex nuraghe Funtana at Monte Zuighe where Bronze to Roman Age materials are well documented (Galli 1991). Here, Galli reports finds of a bronze ring with five-point-star decoration datable to the 6–7th century and, of similar date, fragments of two large storage jars with the familiar stamped decorations. Like Sa Mandra 'e Sa Giua, any native settlements that may have survived here would have been near more typically Medieval edifices including the churches of Sant'Elena and Santa Croce (Caprara 1988: 408–412).

To the north in the Gallura, but a few nuraghi report Medieval remains. One is the composite nuraghe Majori in Tempio. Excavations by Ruju document intermittent settlement during the middle and late Bronze Age, with reuse during the Roman period, and again in early Medieval times (Ruju 1986: 9–18). The Medieval pottery, fire blackened from use and probably locally produced, included collared jars with decorations *a pettine strisciato ondulato*. It was noted by Ruju that comparable pottery came from two probably native sites nearby: Lu Muracciu-Padulo, a Medieval settlement next to a nuraghe, and Zighina-Tempio on the surface. Also worth noting is a curious site excavated by Solinas at Monte Sajacciu in Palau. To the original Bronze Age "Giants' Tomb" complex (with dentillated frieze and exedra with a circular hut) were later added two large stone structures with rectangular plans – one measuring 11 X 4m. Both of these, as well as the hut, contained Medieval materials (Solinas 1991: 91–92).

Turning south into the remote mountain fastness of the Nuorese and Barbagia, one might expect the number of reported late survivals to increase markedly. The fact that they do not must be attributed not to a cultural paradox but an archaeological one: the methodological difficulties in detecting the least acculturated communities. The situation may be changing, however, especially in the Nuorese where finds of handmade, poorly fired pottery that was once thought to be prehistoric is turning out to be Medieval on closer examination (Rowland 1992b: 157; Caprara 1980). A synthesis of these materials revealed the existence of a recognized class of crude, handmade, often undecorated pottery – many obviously local (native?) copies of established 6–8th century Longobard-inspired types. They are widely distributed in the mountain regions, within nuraghi as at Bau Nuraxi-Triei, Orgomonte-Orani, Monte Nule-Orani and Mannu-Dorgali; in some rock-cut tombs as at Marras-Dorgali, and in other localities. At some sites, an entire domestic repertory is represented, including loom-weights and a range of vessels: jars and large bowls often with quadrangular or triangular rim sections, while some of the funerary inclusions may be imported. In both contexts, decorative techniques, some common in other island localities (see above), included stamps and more rarely grooves *a pettine strisciato* about the upper vessel body and mouth, concentric circles or single circles embossed with a punch placed without precise syntax; rosette-stamps with four or more radial ridges, or ovoid with a median ridge and five transversals; grooves placed as bands or at angles; and combed impressions of wide quadrated dents in zig-zags; and plastic appliques in the shape of ears or tridents (Manunza 1989: 46–50).

In closing this preliminary review of the archaeological evidence, brief note can be made also of a potentially large category of prehistoric native sites which bear evidence of later reuse for non-traditional purposes but not necessarily denoting survivals. One is the sanctuary of Santa Vittoria in Serri which was a major civico-ritual center during the the Iron Age (Zucca 1988: 19–20, 34–38). The site bears witness to Roman period presence, possibly military in nature. In later Byzantine times, similar activities may be indicated by finds of a number of bronze buckles, military types found in other parts of the island in and other contexts. This pagan sanctuary seems to have become a Christian one at least by the 11th century (but quite possibly earlier) evinced by the appearance of a chapel built over part of the nuraghe. The well-temple, sacked in Roman days, was later used for Byzantine burials. Some graves had iron crosses and military-type buckles of the 6–7th century. A major question – not yet answerable – is whether the latest remains at Santa Vittoria represent Byzantine soldiers (or Christianized natives serving perhaps as mercenaries) in the historically documented Byzantine offensives against the *barbaricini*.

Assessment

It must be admitted that the evidence for assessing the probability that culture survived into the Medieval period in Sardinia is uneven and difficult to interpret. Literary references to the native situation during the critical period, although tantalizingly suggestive, are frustratingly sketchy and are likely to remain so. The archaeological record – of greater potential importance to the question – is similarly fraught with problems. As discussed in section I, this is due in part to uncertainties about the representation of the sample of reported Medieval finds from contexts, and in part to difficulties of interpretation brought about by the inherent complexity of related concepts like tradition, acculturation and ethnicity. Still, and notwithstanding these real (but, it is hoped, temporary) difficulties, there would appear to be sufficient evidence of adaptations at least in some parts of the island during the periods of Vandal and Byzantine domination. The picture emerging of what might be justifiably termed Nuragic VII is, however, quite skeletal.

Archaeologically, several categories of deposits have been identified as potentially significant. Most promising among these are surely the sites of traditional settlements – nuraghi and other habitations – with Medieval remains suggesting continuity from earlier periods or later reuse. The nature of these deposits varies considerably, and it is clear that caution must be observed when interpreting them as evidence for survivals.

Among such sites, a first distinction can be made between those with habitational evidence and those in which the reuse was for non-traditional purposes, like burial. The former sub-category, of Medieval habitations, is certainly stronger evidence for the survival of traditions than the latter. But even among these, there are important differences which make interpretation tricky. Post-Roman remains at some settlements, like Santa Barbara, Toscono, Santu Antine and Monte Zuighe, appear to reflect no more than mere visitations to the ancient Nuraghe-villages, perhaps by shepherds or itinerant traders who took refuge in and around their walls and occasionally left traces of lost or broken personal belongings. It is likely that many nuraghi saw little more than this kind of intermittent frequentation from earliest colonial times, as many still do today. These sites would seem to lend little to the concept of late survivals.

At the same time, many other residential sites do seem to bear evidence of extended, if not permanent, settlement during the early Middle Ages and these make a far stronger case for a Nuragic VII. The most promising examples, discussed above, are currently nuraghi Candala, Sa Jacca, Losa, Duos Nuraghes, San Sergio, Urpes, Serbine, Sa Mandra 'e Sa Giua, Majori (and perhaps others in the Gallura, Nuorese and Barbagia). These are all notable not only by the presence of a great quantity of Medieval remains, but also by the wide variety of both local and imported materials which together constitute basically domestic assemblages. At a few sites there are also remnants of structural and other features including hearths, flooring, and roofing indicative of more permanent settlement. It is from deposits like these that one may begin to sketch the nature of VII settlements. At some, like Urpes and perhaps Duos Nuraghes, Serbine, Lu Muracciu and Sa Mandra 'e Sa Giua, the actual habitation structures, perhaps largely perishable wattle-and-daub walled, tile roofed houses, flanked the nuraghe while the tower was used rather as a barn or storage magazine – a layout not uncommon in rural farmsteads even today. At others, like Candala, Sa Jacca, Majori, perhaps Losa and those in the mountains of Triei, Orani and Dorgali mentioned above, the nuraghe itself was the center of habitation while additional structures may or may not have been present. Both types may have precursors among the earlier Roman period *nuraghe-villae*.

Variation is also evident in the duration and continuity of habitation. At some sites, the Medieval settlement simply continued from earlier Roman periods as was apparently the case at some nuraghi in the lower Tirso valley and perhaps at Losa, Duos Nuraghes, San Sergio, Serbine, and Majori. At others however, in the lower Tirso and elsewhere, like Urpes, Sa Mandra 'e Sa Giua and Candala, Medieval settlement commenced after long periods of abandonment. The question of settlement continuity versus reoccupation has been little studied in Sardinia, but Dyson's and Rowland's statement referring to the Fordongianus area provides food for thought: "Given the abundant evidence for later Roman occupation at the sites, the possibility of late imperial, early Medieval reoccupation has to be considered. This would be the refugee phenomenon, a situation where highland sites abandoned during the period of *pax Romana* were reoccupied when the Roman system collapsed" (Dyson & Rowland 1989: 174).

Of the economic and social dimensions of these late communities little can be said. As in earlier periods, agropastoralism no doubt supplied the bulk of subsistence. But if the frequent finds of imported and/or locally copied Late Roman and Byzantine items, especially pottery, are any clue, then trade must have been brisk among at least the less remote settlements. Given that many Medieval nuraghi were near non-native settlements (even large centers) it is likely that local and regional markets played an important part in integrating native and non-native household economies. Such interactions were, of course, also mechanisms of acculturation which affected more than subsistence and it is in the VII assemblages that one sees the results. Domestic assemblages like those from Candala, Urpes and Sa Mandra 'e Sa Giua are notable by their mixture of traditional and non-traditional artifact types. Crude *impasto* vessels are found alongside finer wheeled forms; locally made traditional wares are found with imported or copied decorated types popular in 6th-8th century Lombardia and Lazio and later with imported or copied painted and glazed wares. Even the decorative techniques and motifs most widely adopted by communities from common types – stamped circles, ridges, combed punctates and striates – harked back to more ancient designs of the Late Bronze and Iron Ages, some now incorporating the newer Christian iconography.

Little is known of the geo-political and ethnic parameters of Nuragic VII. But, as Rowland recently concluded, "Who was living in the countless villages around nuraghi throughout the Roman period and who was still worshipping wood and stone idols in the late 6th century A. D. if not (Latin speaking) Nuragic folk?" (Rowland 1992: 175). Who indeed, but the archaeological equivalents of the unpacified *barbaricini* who, under chiefs like Hospito, opposed Byzantine rule, resisted Christianization, and provided urban parishes with barbarian slaves?

Ideological acculturation is evinced especially in the ritual sites. This diverse class of deposits is both important and problematical. At Nuraghi Genna Maria and Su Mulinu, for example, the evidence of Medieval shrines for Punic-Roman cults is difficult to interpret. It will require more detailed reports on the extent of Medieval finds before it will be possible to distinguish Nuragic VII communities retaining classical cult practices, from Medieval survivals of Roman and Roman-Sard communities. In either case, perhaps they represent the very instances of idolatry that so annoyed Pope Gregorius in the 6th century. Mortuary sites are equally problematic. The few traditional burial contexts reporting Medieval materials, like those in Codrongianus and Palau, may represent late Nuragic rites. But on the whole, we are still ignorant about where and how most Sards of the Medieval period were buried, especially before the 8th century. Perhaps they were interred along with their non-countrymen in the relatively common Christian cemeteries like that adjacent to the nuraghe-village of Sant'Imbenia in Alghero (Rovina 1989: 25–27; Rovina & Lissia 1989: 29–38). A closer examination of these and other early Medieval Christian burials for identifiable elements might prove rewarding.

It is significant that several Nuraghi of Medieval use, some with early occupation like Candala, Sa Jacca and Su Nuraxi di Siurgius Donigala have subsequent 7–8th century burials. Although Christian influences are unmistakable, the placement of burials within those very edifices which represent perhaps the purest attribute of traditional culture, is telling. At the Candala burial, for example, offerings of small water jars (*brocchette*) and obsidian flakes within the otherwise Byzantine funerary assemblage, seem to imply an attempt to retain links with a remote pagan past; with those traditions no longer sustained in lifestyle but only in memory. Perhaps it is just this sort of fundamental transformation in the cultural taxonomy, where material-architectural structures of secular history become sacred monuments of myth and lore, that marks the end of traditional culture.

When did the Nuragic period end in Sardinia? No single date can suffice for the whole island. The point along the acculturative continuum at which recognizable native communities became something else no doubt varied greatly from place to place. One might agree with Rowland that native settlements still survived in many areas of the interior at least through the 6th century. After that time, their numbers must have declined rapidly, and few such communities would have remained in the 10th. Perhaps a date of A.D. 1015, which marks the Arab invasion and the end of Byzantine rule, is a convenient date for the close of VII and the final end of the Nuragic period in Sardinia (Fig. 44.1).

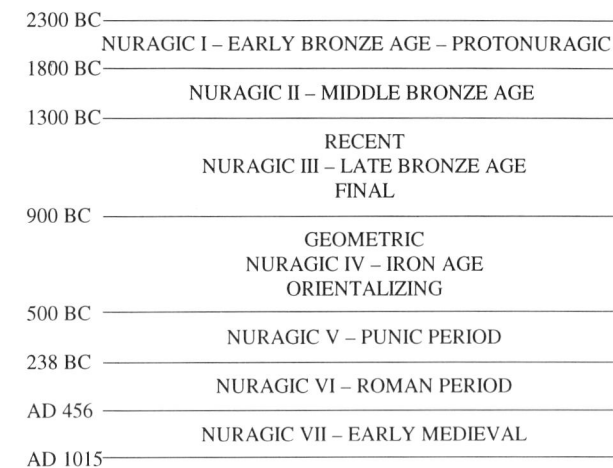

Fig. 44.1. *Proposed extension of Nuragic chronology.*

Notes

1. Translations are by Maud Webster, and in the case of Pope Gregory's correspondence with the assistance of Dr. Marianne Wifstrand Schiebe.
2. Many of the primary written sources for the periods in question are compiled in Tola (1984[1861]), while a catalog of relevant artifacts can be found in Pani Ermini & Marinone (1981). Some of the more crucial secondary and interpretive sources are Pani Ermini (1987–88); Boscolo (1978) and Guillou (1987–88). M. Webster (1997) provides a synthesis of all relevant literary and epigraphical sources in English.

References

Bartel, B. 1989. Acculturation and ethnicity in Roman Moesia Superior. In Champion, T.C. (ed.), *Centre and Periphery: Comparative Studies in Archaeology,* 177–185. Unwin Hyman, London.

Barth, F. 1968(1958). Ecological relations of ethnic groups in Swat, North Pakistan. In Cohen, Y. (ed.), *Man in Adaptation,* 324–331. Aldine, Chicago.

Basoli, P. 1989. Ozieri. Loc. San Nicola, Nuraghe Sa Mandra 'e Sa Giua. In *Il suburbio delle città in Sardegna: Persistenze e trasformazioni. Mediterraneo tardoantico e medievale.* Scavi e ricerche 7: 41. Scorpione Editrice, Taranto.

Basoli, P. 1991. Pattada (Sassari). Nuraghe Lerno – Campagna di Scavo. *Bollettino di Archeologia* 10: 138–141.

Belli, E. 1988. La viabilità Romana nel Logudoro-Meilogu. In Moravetti, A. (ed.), *Il Nuraghe S. Antine nel Logudoro-Meilogu,* 339, fig. 1. Carlo Delfino, Sassari.

Bellieni, C. 1973. *La Sardegna e i Sardi nella civiltà dell'Alto Medioevo 1.*

Boscolo, A. 1978. *La Sardegna bizantina e alto-giudicale.* Chiarella, Sassari.

Bottiglioni, G. 1922. *Vita Sarda.*

Caprara, R. 1980. Documenti archeologici Medievali. In *Dorgali: Documenti Archeologici,* 247- 268. Chiarella, Sassari.

Caprara, R. 1986. Le chiese rupestri medievali della Sardegna. *Nuovo Bullettino Archeologico Sardo* 3: 251–278.

Caprara, R. 1988. L'eta altomedievale nel territorio del Logudoro-Meilogu. In Moravetti, A. (ed.), *Il nuraghe S. Antine nel Logudoro-Meilogu,* 397–441. Carlo Delfino, Sassari.

Conti, P. 1984. Parma e Fordongianus. *Archivio Storico Prov. Parmensi* 36: 447–457.

Dyson, S. & Rowland, R.J. Jr. 1988. Survey Archaeology in the territory of Bauladu. Preliminary Notice. *Quaderni della Soprintendenza Archeologica per le provincie di Cagliari e Oristano* 5: 129–139.

Dyson, S. & Rowland, R.J. Jr. 1989. The University of Maryland-Wesleyan Survey in Sardinia. *Quaderni della Soprintendenza Archeologica per le provincie di Cagliari e Oristano* 6: 157-185.

Dyson, S. & Rowland, R.J. Jr. 1992. Survey and Settlement Reconstruction in West-Central Sardinia. *American Journal of Archaeology* 96: 203–224.

Galli, F. 1991. *Ittireddu: Il museo e il territorio.* Sardegna Archeologica: Guide e Itinerari 14. Carlo Delfino, Sassari.

Gillin, J. & Raimy, V. 1940. Acculturation and personality. *American Sociological Review* 5: 371–380.

Guido, F. 1987. Bronze Coins and Materials found in Toscono. In Michels, J. & Webster, G. (eds.), *Studies in Nuragic Archaeology: Village Excavations at Nuraghe Urpes and Nuraghe Toscono in West-Central Sardinia.* BAR International Series 373: 127–128. British Archaeological Reports, Oxford.

Guillou, A. 1987–88. La lunga età bizantina; La diffusione della cultura bizantina. *Storia dei Sardi e della Sardegna* 1: 329–371; 373–423.

Hodder, I. 1982. *Symbols in Action: Ethnoarchaeological Studies of Material Culture.* Cambridge University Press, Cambridge.

Lanternari, V. 1955. La politica culturale della Chiesa nelle campagne: la festa di San Giovanni. *Società* 5: 64–95.

Lilliu, C. 1988. Un culto di età punico-romana al nuraghe Genna Maria di Villanovaforru. *Quaderni della Soprintendenza Archeologica per le provincie di Cagliari e Oristano* 5: 109–127.

Lilliu, G. 1982. *La civiltà nuragica.* Studi e Monumenti 1. Carlo Delfino, Sassari.

Lilliu, G. 1988. *La civiltà dei Sardi dal paleolitico all'età dei nuraghi.* Nuova ERI, Torino.